Principles of Accounting

Second Edition

Principles of Accounting

Second Edition

PAUL H. WALGENBACH
The University of Wisconsin

NORMAN E. DITTRICH
The University of Tennessee

ERNEST I. HANSON
The University of Wisconsin

HARCOURT BRACE JOVANOVICH, INC.
New York   San Diego   Chicago   San Francisco   Atlanta
London   Sydney   Toronto

Printed in the United States of America
Library of Congress Catalog Card Number: 79-64365
ISBN: 0-15-571336-1

Illustrations by Evanelle Towne.

Photo on page 219 courtesy of Burroughs Corporation; photos on pages 222 and 224 courtesy of International Business Machines Corporation.

PREFACE

In the first edition of *Principles of Accounting*, our goal was to provide a comprehensive first course in accounting with an approach that was appropriate for students planning a career in the field as well as students seeking a general understanding of accounting. This approach featured a balance of conceptual and procedural material, simple language, straightforward exhibits, interesting problem material, and carefully organized study aids and ancillary materials.

In this Second Edition, we have attempted to enhance this approach by changing the order of certain topics, breaking down the more involved concepts and procedures into smaller, more manageable steps, and introducing business situation problems. We believe that the Second Edition will be even more flexible and teachable than the first edition.

Innovations in this edition and successful features carried over from the first edition include the following:

■ Demonstration Problems for Review are new to this edition. Comprehensive problems that illustrate the main principles, procedures, and computations explained in key chapters, Demonstration Problems are designed to reinforce understanding of the chapter and prepare students for the end-of-chapter problem material. Solutions immediately follow the demonstration problems.

■ Business Decision Problems have been added to each chapter of the Second Edition. Each Business Decision Problem presents an unstructured situation requiring students to apply concepts to a realistic business situation.

■ Thoroughly up-to-date discussions of FASB pronouncements, APB Opinions, and selected S.E.C. reporting requirements have been incorporated in the Second Edition, including the major provisions of *FASB Statement No. 33* on inflation accounting.

■ Approximately 60 percent of the boxed inserts (enrichment pieces) are new to this edition. These enrichment pieces are not only topical and interesting, but they give students greater insight into accounting concepts. New boxed inserts treat minicomputers, bad checks, retail markups, treasury stock acquisitions, corporate takeovers, inflation, factories in space, the role of CPAs in management advisory services, and productivity, innovation, and profit.

■ More single-topic exercises have been included in this edition. Designed for classroom use, these exercises enable the instructor to cover most of the salient points of each chapter in a single lecture.

■ Alternate problems, most of which parallel a basic problem given at the end of each chapter, are provided for all the main concepts of each chapter. Thus, the instructor may alternate problems from term to term, or if desired, may assign additional problems of a particular type in a given term.

■ Simple examples and exhibits are used throughout the book to illustrate important concepts, and, where possible, the dollar amounts are in round figures. Color is used instructively to highlight important definitions and procedures.

■ As in the previous edition, Key Points to Remember are provided at the end of each chapter to aid students in reviewing the material.

■ An extensive glossary of accounting terminology appears at the back of the book. This location makes it easy for students to locate the definition for any particular term or concept at any point in their study of the material.

■ A Checklist of Key Figures is included at the back of the text. Total and summary figures are provided so that students can check their work without having all the solution given.

HIGHLIGHTS OF CHANGES AND ADDITIONS IN THE SECOND EDITION

In this edition, an introduction to accounting principles in the first chapter of the book serves as a frame of reference for students during their study of the early chapters. The material on automated data processing in Chapter 6 has been updated and expanded. Because of the increased importance of leases, an introduction to this subject is given in Chapter 10. Material on inflation accounting from Chapter 17 of the first edition has been updated, condensed, and incorporated into Chapter 16. This chapter now has a complete exposition of inflation accounting, including examples of current-value accounting. Chapter 17, "Statement of Changes in Financial Position: Analysis of Funds and Cash Flows" (formerly Chapter 19) has been completely rewritten to make this difficult material more accessible to students; in particular, an innovative worksheet has been introduced to simplify the material. Chapter 18, "Analysis of Financial Statements," has been rewritten, with new and forthright examples, to clarify the concepts presented in the chapter.

Chapter 19, "Consolidated Financial Statements," has been totally rewritten so that each major concept is treated clearly and individually. Wholly owned subsidiaries are treated before majority-held subsidiaries, the consolidated income statement has been simplified, and a basic treatment of "pooling of interests" has been moved to the end of the chapter. A worksheet approach has been used to convey each basic idea of consolidated statements.

The sequence of cost and managerial accounting chapters—the previous edition's Chapters 23 through 28—has been expanded by one chapter in the Second Edition and moved to Chapters 21 through 27. The sequence has been extensively revised to include more basic material on accounts and procedures unique to manufacturing firms (Chapter 21), providing students with a better background for their study of job order and process cost accounting.

Other changes in the Second Edition are positioning partnership accounting before corporation accounting and moving "Income Taxes and Their Effect on Business Decisions" to the end of the book; instructors may cover or omit the latter material, depending on the time available or the thrust of the course. The chapter on income taxes has been substantially revised to reflect major tax legislation for the time between the first edition and the present.

PROGRAM OF SUPPLEMENTARY AIDS

TEST ITEM FILE A class-tested test-item file (test bank), totally new to the Second Edition, is part of the instructional package. This booklet provides 30 multiple-choice and 10 other objective questions for each chapter of the book—more than 1,100 questions in all.

STUDY GUIDE Prepared by Imogene Posey of the University of Tennessee, the *Study Guide* provides a comprehensive chapter review, a Check Your Knowledge section, and a set of exercises for each chapter and Appendixes A and B. Answers to questions and solutions to exercises appear at the end of each chapter of the study guide.

PRACTICE SETS Four practice sets, keyed to the chapters in the book, cover the central concepts and procedures of accounting. Both Practice Set A and Alternate Set A with Business Papers deal with a single proprietorship. Practice Set B deals with a corporation. Practice Set C covers a job order cost accounting system. All the practice sets provide printed forms, with headings, names, and much of the preliminary data provided to eliminate busywork and to permit the students to concentrate on concepts and procedures. The new practice sets were prepared by Rosanne Mohr, of the University of Wisconsin.

WORKING PAPERS Two sets of working papers are provided for the problems at the end of the chapters, including the alternate problems. All are identified by problem number and name. When appropriate, given problem data have been entered to save time for the students.

SOLUTIONS MANUAL The *Solutions Manual* describes all the problem material and offers probable difficulty and estimated time for solution of each problem. Answers are given for all the questions, exercises, and problems at the end of each chapter.

ACHIEVEMENT TESTS Sixteen achievement tests—14 two-chapter tests suitable for 50-minute class periods, and two comprehensive tests, each covering 14 chapters of material, are available on spirit masters to adopters of the book. A key to the achievement tests is also furnished.

TRANSPARENCIES Transparencies of the problem solutions given in the *Solutions Manual* are available on request to departments adopting the textbook.

ACKNOWLEDGMENTS

We are indebted to many people for the success of the first edition of *Principles of Accounting* and for their contributions to the Second Edition. We are particularly grateful to Joe Goetz, Northern Arizona University; Robert E. Lamden, California State University, Fullerton; and Roy S. Matthews, Lewis University, who reviewed the text in detail. We also gratefully acknowledge the constructive comments and assistance of James B. Bower, University of Wisconsin; Richard L. Townsend, University of Tennessee; Richard W. Jones, Lamar University; Loren E. Long, Elgin Community College; Ernest J. Whitaker, North Seattle Community College; and Roger D. Hillyard, Southern Utah State College. Our thanks also go to editors Steven A. Dowling, Karen Bierstedt, and Jack Thomas of Harcourt Brace Jovanovich, Inc. for their patient assistance throughout the revision process, and to Geri Davis, who designed the book.

We wish to acknowledge the assistance of a number of users of the first edition who responded to detailed questionnaires relating to the Second Edition while it was in the planning stages: Gerry Axel, Nassau Community College; Sonia Brecha, Wright State University; George M. Brooker, Dean Junior College; Cody Bryan, Western Washington University; John Burns, Genesee Community College; Mel Choate, North Seattle Community College; Carolyn Conn, Stephen F. Austin State University; Pauline Corn, Virginia Polytechnic Institute; Devin F. Dahline, Hibbing Community College; John A. Dettmann, University of Minnesota; Walter Doehring, Genesee Community College; Phillip S. Doherty, Dean Junior College; Paul Doran, Jefferson State Junior College; Milton Fink, University of Alaska; Dick Gilman, University of Hartford; John Gilmore, Rutgers University; R. Glassberg, Kean College of New Jersey; John Goering, University of Cincinnati; Orville Goulet, De Paul University; Dick Hauser, Northern Arizona University; Arthur Hirschfield, Bronx City College; Thomas Holowaty, St. Vincent College; Ira Houghton, Washington Technical College; Rita Huff, Sam Houston University; Raymon Juenke, Wright State University; Stanley Kaiz, Rutgers University; William Kamenoff, Community College of Baltimore; Robert Landry, Massasoit Community College; Shirley Larson, Blue Mountain Community College; Robert Lewis, Kishwaukee Community College; Bruce Lindsey, Genesee Community College; Raymond Luoma, East Tennessee State University; Calvin Mercer, East Tennessee State University; William Newman, Jefferson State Junior College; Marcia Niles, University of Montana; Bryan O'Neil, Castleton

State College; James Quinn, University of Tennessee; E. Louis Raverta, Western New England College; Richard Romanowski, Parkersburg Community College; C. Ruthford, North Seattle Community College; Peggy Self, Stephen F. Austin State University; Sue Siferd, Wright State University; James Skidmore, Grand Rapids Junior College; Daniel R. Strang, State University of New York at Geneseo; Daniel R. Strong, Keuka College; John Talbot, Wright State University; Joseph Techavichitr, Columbia College; Philip Tucker, Bronx City College; Ed Wiener, Kingsborough Community College; Arnold M. Wright, California State University, Fullerton; and John D. Wright, University of Wisconsin.

PAUL H. WALGENBACH
NORMAN E. DITTRICH
ERNEST I. HANSON

CONTENTS

7   INTERNAL CONTROL: CASH CONTROLS   241

8   TRADE ACCOUNTS AND NOTES   279

9   INVENTORIES   313

16 ACCOUNTING PRINCIPLES; ACCOUNTING FOR INFLATION   547

17 STATEMENT OF CHANGES IN FINANCIAL POSITION: ANALYSIS OF FUNDS AND CASH FLOWS   585

18 ANALYSIS AND INTERPRETATION OF FINANCIAL STATEMENTS   627

19 CONSOLIDATED FINANCIAL STATEMENTS   667

20 ACCOUNTING FOR BUSINESS SEGMENTS: DEPARTMENTS AND BRANCHES   703

21 ACCOUNTING FOR MANUFACTURING OPERATIONS   735

Principles of Accounting

Second Edition

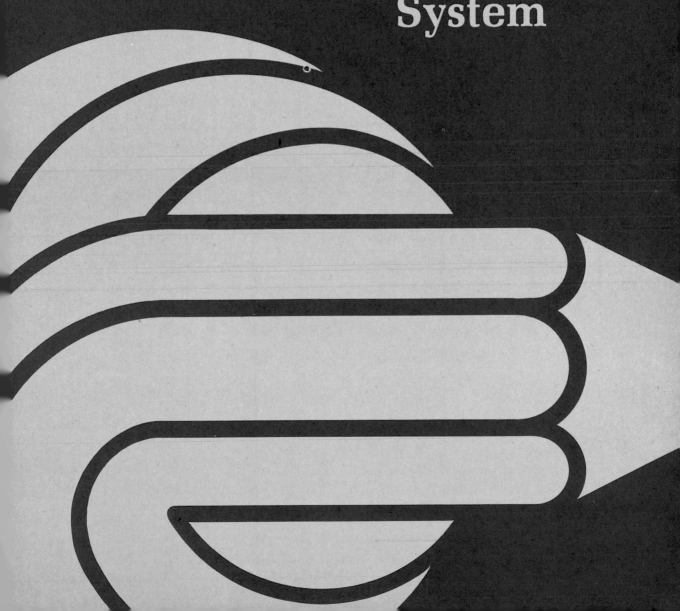

1
Accounting:
An Information
System

Ours is the Age of the Machine.
Also, it is the Age of Accounts.
A little literacy in accounting has become a prime necessity.

PAUL A. SAMUELSON

Modern accounting is widely recognized as a basic component of business management. Accounting is the means by which managers are informed of the financial status and progress of their companies, thus contributing to the continuing processes of planning, control of operations, and decision making. Accounting provides a method of systematically recording and evaluating business activities. This is, perhaps, the most fundamental reason for business managers and business students to familiarize themselves with the accounting discipline.

A large portion of the information that a business manager requires is derived from accounting data. The ability to analyze and use these data helps managers accomplish their objectives. Through your study of accounting, you will discover the types of business activities that can be accounted for usefully, the methods used to collect accounting data, and the implications of the resulting information. Furthermore—and often just as important—you will become aware of the limitations of accounting reports.

ACCOUNTING AS AN INFORMATION SYSTEM

Virtually all profit-seeking organizations and most nonprofit organizations maintain extensive accounting records. One reason is that these records are often required by law. A more basic reason is that, even in a very small organization, a manager is confronted with a multitude of complex variables. Not even the most brilliant manager can be sufficiently informed just by observing daily operations. Instead, he or she must depend on the accounting process to convert business transactions into useful statistical data that can be abstracted and summarized in accounting reports. In every sense, this process is essential to the coordinated and rational management of most organizations—regardless of their size. Thus, accounting is an *information system* necessitated by the great complexity of modern business.

In today's society, many persons and agencies outside of management are involved in the economic life of an organization. These persons frequently require financial data. For example, stockholders must have financial information in order to measure management's performance and to evaluate their own holdings. Potential investors need financial data in order to compare prospective investments. Creditors must consider the financial strength of an organization before permitting it to borrow funds. Also, labor unions, financial analysts, and economists often expect a considerable amount of reliable financial data. Finally, many laws require that extensive financial information be reported to the various levels of government. As an information system, the accounting process serves persons both inside and outside an organization.

THE ACCOUNTING PROCESS

Accounting can be defined as the process of (1) recording, (2) classifying, and (3) reporting and interpreting the financial data of an organization. Once an accounting system has been designed and installed, recording and classifying data may become somewhat routine and repetitive. While it is important for accountants to have a sound knowledge of this phase of the accounting process, it is often a relatively minor part of their total responsibility. Accountants direct most of their attention to the reporting and interpretation of the meaningful implications of the data.

Except in smaller businesses, much routine accounting work has become highly mechanized and automatic. Thus, many persons not acquainted with current accounting trends think that the profession is becoming progressively narrower. Quite the contrary is true. The emergence of mechanized and electronic data processing has freed accountants from the routine aspects of recording and classifying data, enabling them to concentrate more on the analytical and interpretive aspects of the accounting function. But these are the areas most affected by the new demands for accounting information. Indeed, the number of licensed accountants in the United States grew from a few hundred in 1900 to about 40,000 in the early 1950s when computers first appeared on the business scene. There are now approximately 180,000 accountants in this country, about half of them added during the past fifteen years—more than the number added during the profession's first fifty years. The demand for better educated and more experienced accountants will undoubtedly continue to rise in the future.

Whether the accounting records for a given organization should be maintained manually, mechanically, or electronically will depend on several things, such as the size of the organization, the amount of data to be processed, the amount of information required, and the need for prompt access to stored data. At one extreme, the modest accounting requirements of a small organization would not justify the cost of an electronic computer, while on the other hand, a manually maintained accounting system would not fill the extensive requirements of a large organization.

Regardless of the method used, however, the underlying accounting concepts are essentially the same. Because a manually maintained system is most easily handled in the classroom and in problem situations, this is the type we will use throughout this book. Where appropriate, however, we include comments relating to mechanized and electronic systems.

THE REPORTING PROCESS

The reporting process, comprising four main channels of information flow, is graphically represented in Exhibit 1–1.

Channel (1): Managerial Data and Reports

A major function of accounting is to provide management with the data needed for decision making and for efficient operation of the firm. Although management people routinely receive the financial reports, tax returns, and special reports prepared for outsiders, they also require various other information, such as the unit cost of a product, estimates of the profit earned from a specific sales campaign, cost comparisons of alternative courses of action, and long-range budgets.

EXHIBIT 1–1
Typical Flows of Accounting Information

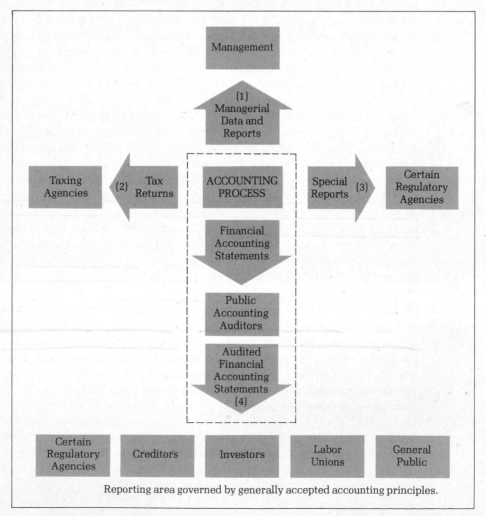

Reporting area governed by generally accepted accounting principles.

Because of the strategic nature of some of this information, it may be available only to the firm's high-level management. The process of generating and analyzing such data is often referred to as **managerial accounting.** Emphasis on this area of accounting has increased in recent years as a result of the implementation of computers and sophisticated quantitative tools.

Channel (2): Tax Returns

Most businesses are required to file many kinds of tax returns—for example, federal, state, and municipal income taxes, excise taxes, and payroll taxes. The preparation of these returns is governed by the rulings and special reporting requirements of the taxing agencies involved. Proper compliance is generally a matter of law and can be quite complicated. Consequently, many firms, especially when preparing income tax returns, retain certified public accountants or attorneys specializing in taxation.

Channel (3): Special Reports

Some companies, by the nature of their activities, are required to report periodically to certain regulatory agencies. For example, commercial trucking companies must report to the Interstate Commerce Commission, and most public utility companies must report to a public utility commission. The regulatory agency may use the reported information to establish the rates to be charged (as in the trucking industry) or the rate of income to be earned (as in the case of public utilities). Although these reports are based primarily on accounting data, often they must be prepared in accordance with additional conditions, rules, and definitions. Some agencies, such as stock exchanges and the Securities and Exchange Commission, do require reports prepared in accordance with the generally accepted accounting principles that we shall discuss later. We have therefore shown certain regulatory agencies in both channels (3) and (4) of Exhibit 1-1.

Channel (4): Financial Accounting Statements

One of the most important functions of the accounting process is to accumulate and report accounting information that shows an organization's financial position and the results of its operations. Many businesses publish such financial statements at least annually. The subdivision of the accounting process that produces these general-purpose reports is referred to as **financial accounting.** Financial accounting is essentially retrospective, because it deals primarily with historical information, or events that have already happened. Its focus is on income determination and financial position as an aggregate financial picture of an enterprise.

Although financial accounting data are primarily historical, they are also useful for planning and control. Indeed, a considerable amount of planning must be based on what has happened in the recent past. In addition, historical financial information is inherently a control mechanism, since it can be used to measure the success of past planning. We should also emphasize that, although financial accounting is primarily historical, it is not merely a process of "filling in the numbers." As you study further, you will discover that determining the financial position and profitability of an enterprise is an exceedingly complex job that requires professional judgment.

Financial accounting statements are the main source of information for parties—other than governmental agencies—outside the business firm. Because these

ACCOUNTING PREDATES WRITING

Archaeologists generally agree that writing first appeared in Mesopotamia around 3100 B.C. in the form of an elaborate system of symbols that were probably used for keeping temple records. But where did the ancients get the idea for their epochal invention? A University of Texas archaeologist may have at last provided the answer. Denise Schmandt–Besserat has found evidence that writing evolved from a much older record-keeping system that is still used in the Middle East. If her theory is correct, it pushes the roots of writing back at least 5,000 years.

Schmandt–Besserat, 43, a French-born assistant professor of art and an expert on the ancient uses of clay, bases her theory on studies started in 1969. For decades archaeologists had been puzzled by the great numbers of small, geometric clay tokens—some as old as 10,000 years—discovered in digs from Egypt to the Indus Valley. Several experts had speculated that these tokens were toys or pieces from a still undiscovered prehistoric game. In 1966 Pierre Amiet, curator of Near Eastern art at the Louvre, suggested that the tokens were an ancient recording system. Schmandt–Besserat agrees. After comparing the tokens with samples of early writing discovered in Warka, a community in Mesopotamia (modern Iraq), she concluded that they were part of a sophisticated system of record keeping that eventually evolved into writing. Said she: "This is not writing at 8000 B.C., but a totally different process of written communication."

The process, Schmandt–Besserat believes, evolved in four stages. In the first, which ran from about 8500 B.C.—the date of the oldest tokens found—to around 3500 B.C., the small (up to 5 cm., or 2 in., in diameter) cones, disks, spheres and pellets represented such commodities as sheep, jugs of oil, bread or clothing and were used by merchants and others in the Middle East to keep records. In the second stage, merchants shipping goods from one place to another began enclosing tokens in sealed clay balls known as *bullae*, which were broken open upon delivery so the shipment could be checked against the invoice; the *bullae*, in effect, were the first bills of lading. The third stage, which followed closely, began when merchants realized that cargoes could be checked without breaking open the *bullae* if each of the tokens to be enclosed in the ball was first impressed on the wet clay surface. That would leave a record on the outside of the envelope as well as inside.

Once this stage was reached, the fourth step came quickly. Realizing that impressing their shapes on the *bullae* made enclosing the tokens

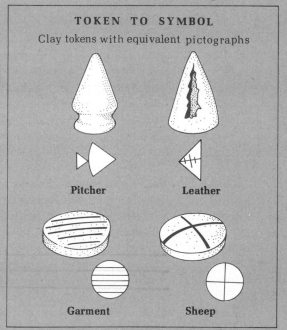

TOKEN TO SYMBOL

Clay tokens with equivalent pictographs

Pitcher   **Leather**

Garment   **Sheep**

unnecessary, people abandoned the counters and began keeping their records directly on clay tablets. The efficiency of that technique was immediately obvious, says Schmandt–Besserat, and could explain not only how written record keeping evolved but also why writing spread so rapidly along the trade routes and quickly took hold throughout the civilized world of that day. But even the development of writing did not lead to the disappearance of the tokens. The written word, after all, helps only those who can read. Today, in some parts of the Middle East, illiterate herdsmen still use tokens to keep a tally of their flocks.

reports will often be used to evaluate management, their objectivity could be subject to question. To establish the validity of their financial statements, most firms have them audited by independent public accountants. The independent auditor examines the statements and suggests any changes that may be warranted. He or she then expresses a professional opinion that the financial statements are fairly stated "in accordance with generally accepted accounting principles" or indicates any reservations about the statements. Usually, outside parties have greater faith in financial statements that have been audited. Both the role of the professional public accountant and the nature of "generally accepted accounting principles" are complex. Therefore, each is treated separately in later sections of this chapter.

ACCOUNTING PRINCIPLES AND PRACTICE

To be useful, financial accounting information must be assembled and reported objectively. Those who must rely on such information have a right to be assured that the data are free from bias and inconsistency—whether deliberate or not. For this reason, financial accounting relies on certain standards or guides that have proved useful over the years in imparting economic data. These standards are called **generally accepted accounting principles.** Because accounting is more an art than a science, these principles are not immutable laws like those in the physical sciences. Instead, they are _guides to action_ and may change over time. Sometimes specific principles must be altered or new principles must be formulated to fit changed economic circumstances or changes in business practices.

Because accounting principles are based on a combination of theory and practice, there has always been, and probably always will be, some controversy about their propriety. A number of organizations exist that are concerned with the formulation of accounting principles. The most prominent among these is the Financial Accounting Standards Board (FASB). The FASB, organized in 1973, is a nongovernmental body whose pronouncements have the force of dictating authoritative rules for the general practice of financial accounting. Before the creation of the FASB, the Accounting Principles Board (APB) of the American Institute of Certified Public Accountants (AICPA) fulfilled the function of formulating accounting principles. If the _attest function (auditing and independent reporting)_ of the independent certified public accountant is to be meaningful, the business enterprises of this country must generally observe substantially comparable accounting principles.

Various regulatory bodies, such as the Securities and Exchange Commission and the Internal Revenue Service, also prescribe rules to be used in financial accounting. Because these rules often touch upon accounting principles and may conflict with the rules and practices specified by other agencies, compromises sometimes have to be made in financial reporting. This has been especially true when the rules of a regulatory body have conflicted with those considered "generally accepted" by accounting practitioners.

Often, income determined by tax regulations differs from that determined by generally accepted accounting principles. When rules or methods prescribed by the Internal Revenue Service for the determination of taxable income conflict with those acceptable for business reporting, an enterprise may keep more than one set of records to satisfy both reporting requirements. Sometimes uninformed people think that this practice is illegal or unethical; actually, there is nothing sinister or illegal about keeping separate records to fulfill separate needs, as long as all the records are subject to examination by the appropriate parties.

As Exhibit 1-1 indicates, generally accepted accounting principles are primarily relevant to financial accounting. In managerial accounting, the main objective is to assist management in making decisions and in operating effectively, and in such cases it is frequently useful to depart from concepts utilized in financial accounting. On many occasions, financial accounting data must be reassembled or altered to be most useful in solving internal business problems.

FIELDS OF ACCOUNTING ACTIVITY

Accountants perform many diverse services and are engaged in various types of employment. The three major fields of accounting activity are private accounting, public accounting, and governmental accounting. Because each of these may comprise many aspects of accounting activity, it is possible to give only a broad description for each type of accounting employment.

Private Accounting

More accountants are employed in private accounting than in any other field. Private employers of accountants include manufacturers, wholesalers, retailers, and service firms. Depending on the size and complexity of the business, the private accountant's duties may vary from routine reporting to the design and implementation of electronic accounting systems. The major objective of the private accountant, however, is to assist management in planning and controlling the firm's operations. In many large business firms, the head of the accounting department is called the **controller** and is a key executive who works closely with other management personnel.

Frequently, a large company will have an **internal auditing** staff, operating under the controller or another high-ranking management officer. Internal auditing is an appraisal activity conducted within the business firm to determine if management's financial and operating controls are effective and are being properly utilized. An internal auditor investigates policies and procedures designed to safeguard assets, promote operational efficiency, and provide reliable information and reports to management.

Public Accounting

The field of public accounting is composed of firms that render independent, expert reports on financial statements of business enterprises. Public accounting firms also perform a wide variety of accounting and managerial services, acting as consultants to their clients. Most accountants in a public accounting firm are certified public accountants (CPAs), holding certificates from the particular states in which they work.[1] These certificates attest to the fact that the CPA has passed a

[1]Most states still allow certain accountants who are not "certified" to practice public accounting.

rigorous examination and has met the requirements for education and experience set by the state to assure high standards of performance. The CPA profession, like the older professions of law and medicine, has a comprehensive code of ethics—a set of rules of professional conduct—that governs the behavior of its practitioners in the performance of their work.

The professional responsibility of the certified public accountant is unique. While the attorney and the physician are responsible only to their clients and patients, the certified public accountant may be professionally responsible to "third parties" who rely on the financial statements the CPA has audited. This is true even though the "third party" in no way contributes to the fee paid for the audit and has no contractual relationship whatsoever with the accountant.

Governmental Accounting

A large number of accountants are employed by federal, state, and local governmental agencies. The services performed by these accountants parallel those of private and public accountants and may cover the entire spectrum of financial and managerial accounting. For example, the General Accounting Office of the federal government and the Department of Audit in the various state governments engage in auditing activities similar to those of public accountants. Audits may be conducted not only of governmental agencies but of private firms doing business with a governmental unit. Accounting personnel of the Internal Revenue Service and the corresponding state agencies conduct accounting investigations of firms and individuals in connection with their tax liabilities. Among the many other governmental agencies and regulatory bodies that employ accountants are the Securities and Exchange Commission, the Department of Defense, the Federal Power Commission, the Interstate Commerce Commission, and state utility commissions and agencies.

BASIC FINANCIAL REPORTS

As we mentioned earlier, one of the major functions of accounting is to provide periodic reports to management, owners, and outsiders. The two principal reports resulting from the process of financial accounting are the balance sheet and the income statement. Although the form of these financial statements may vary among different business firms or other economic units, their basic purpose is the same. The **balance sheet** is designed to portray the financial position of the organization at a particular point in time. The **income statement** is designed to portray the operating results for a period of time. These financial statements are prepared at least yearly, but quarterly or monthly reports are also customary.

Another basic statement, called the **Statement of Changes in Financial Position,** is generally required in reporting to outsiders. This statement will be discussed in Chapter 17.

Although the balance sheet and income statement are the end result of the process of financial accounting, we shall introduce them in simplified form here, early in our study. Having some knowledge of the ultimate objective of financial accounting will help you understand the various steps in the accounting process.

THE BALANCE SHEET

The balance sheet, sometimes called the **statement of financial position** is a listing of a firm's assets, liabilities, and owners' equity on a given date (these terms are explained below). Exhibit 1–2 is a balance sheet prepared for Perfection Printers, a single-owner business, showing its financial position at December 31, 19XX.

The proper heading of a balance sheet consists of (1) the name of the organization, (2) the title of the statement, and (3) the date for which the statement was prepared.

Notice that the body of the statement contains three major sections: assets, liabilities, and owner's equity. This presentation allows the reader to tell at a glance that the resources of this firm total $52,000 and that these assets are being financed by two sources: $12,000 by the creditors (liabilities) and $40,000 by the owner (owner's equity). Occasionally, the right-hand portion of this statement is called *Equities*, with subdivisions called *Creditors' Equity* and *Owners' Equity*. The total assets always equal the sum of the creditors' and owners' equities. This balancing is sometimes described as the **accounting equation**—an equation that dictates that all of the listed resources are attributed to claims of creditors and owners. Conversely, the claims of both creditors and owners must be balanced by total listed resources. These relationships can be diagrammed as follows:

Technical terms:	**Assets**	=	**Liabilities**	+ **Owners' Equity**
Basic meanings:	Business resources	=	Outsiders' claims	+ Owners' claims
Amounts (Exhibit 1–2):	$52,000	=	$12,000	+ $40,000

Let us now briefly explain each of the three elements in the accounting equation.

Assets

Assets are the economic resources of the business that can usefully be expressed in monetary terms. Assets may take many forms. Some, such as land, buildings, and equipment, may have readily identifiable physical characteristics. Others may simply represent claims for payment or services, such as amounts due from customers (accounts receivable) or prepayments for future services (for example, prepaid insurance). As a convenience to the reader of the balance sheet, the assets are usually listed in an established order, with the most liquid assets (cash, receivables, supplies, and so on) preceding the more permanent assets (equipment, building, land).

Assets are usually recorded at their acquisition price, or cost. The recorded costs of assets may be reduced for a variety of reasons. Supplies are used up, and assets such as equipment and building depreciate. For example, in Exhibit 1–2, the equipment of Perfection Printers, originally costing $30,000, has been reduced

EXHIBIT 1-2

Perfection Printers
Balance Sheet
December 31, 19XX

Assets			Liabilities		
Cash		$ 2,000	Accounts Payable	$ 1,000	
Accounts			Mortgage Payable	11,000	
Receivable		1,500	Total Liabilities		$12,000
Supplies on Hand		2,500			
Equipment	$30,000				
Less: Accumulated					
Depreciation	8,000	22,000	**Owner's Equity**		
Building	$25,000		George Taylor,		
Less: Accumulated			Capital		40,000
Depreciation	5,000	20,000	Total Liabilities		
Land		4,000	and Owner's		
Total Assets		$52,000	Equity		$52,000

by $8,000 depreciation over the years, and the building originally costing $25,000 has been reduced by $5,000 accumulated depreciation. We shall introduce the concept of depreciation later in this chapter and discuss it fully in Chapter 10.

Accounting principles do not permit upward valuation of assets, simply because it is often difficult or impossible to determine the *actual value* of an asset at regular intervals in a completely *objective* way. Assume, for example, that ten years ago a firm purchased some real estate for $20,000. Today the property may well be worth considerably more, at least in "current" dollars. Although it may be helpful to assign a more current dollar value to the real estate, it would be difficult to accomplish unless the property were offered for sale. Most business firms do not plan to sell their long-term operating assets, but to use them. Therefore, the accounting convention of reflecting assets in financial statements at acquisition cost has persisted, although criticism is frequently leveled at this practice.

Liabilities

Liabilities, or creditors' equity, are the obligations, or debts, that the firm must pay in money or services at some time in the future. They therefore represent creditors' claims on the firm's assets. Liabilities are listed on the balance sheet in the order that they will come due. Short-term liabilities, such as notes payable given for money borrowed for relatively short periods, accounts payable to creditors, and salaries owed employees, are usually shown first. Below the short-term liabilities, the long-term debt is presented. Mortgages and bonds payable are examples of long-term debts that will normally not be repaid in full for several years.

Although most liabilities are payable in cash, some may involve the performance of services. A magazine publisher, for example, may receive advance payments for three- or five-year subscriptions. These constitute a liability that the publishing company will reduce periodically by supplying the publication during the subscription period. Should the publisher be unable to fulfill this commitment, the unexpired portion of the subscription amount must be refunded.

Owners' Equity   The owners' equity in the resources, or assets, of the firm is shown below the liabilities. The owners' interest is equal to the **net assets** of the business, which is defined as the difference between the assets and the liabilities. Thus, owners' equity is a *residual claim*—a claim to the assets remaining after the debt to creditors has been discharged. Formerly, the term "net worth" was frequently used to describe owners' equity. This expression is no longer considered good terminology, because it conveys an impression of value, and as we have seen, the value, or current worth, of assets may not be portrayed in the balance sheet. We also often employ the term **capital** to describe the owners' interest in a firm. (This practice is derived from legal usage of the term.) Sometimes in economic literature the assets of a business are referred to as the firm's "capital." This use of the term is avoided in accounting literature.

The owner's equity in Perfection Printers amounts to $40,000. It consists of the amounts invested in the organization and the net earnings of the organization that have not been withdrawn by the owner.

FORMS OF BUSINESS ORGANIZATION

The principal forms of business organization are the sole proprietorship, the partnership, and the corporation. Although sole proprietorships, or single-owner businesses, are probably the most numerous, the corporate form of business is the most important in our economy. The partnership form is often used when two or more sole proprietorships are merged into one business. For many years, professional people such as physicians, attorneys, and public accountants operated as partnerships because their codes of ethics or state laws prohibited incorporation. Most states now permit a special type of incorporation or association, and professional organizations have changed their codes of ethics to accommodate this change. Most professional firms, however, still operate as partnerships. For large-scale operations, there are many advantages to the corporate form of organization. These will be discussed in Chapter 13.

The principal differences in the balance sheets for the three types of business organizations just described appear in the owners' equity section. State corporation laws require that corporations segregate, in their balance sheets, the owners' investment (the amount paid for their stock) and any accumulated earnings. Because there are no comparable legal restrictions on sole proprietorships and partnerships, these types of businesses do not have to distinguish between amounts invested by owners and undistributed earnings.

The following illustrations demonstrate the variations in the balance sheet presentation of owners' equity for the three forms of business organization. In Chapters 12–15 we will consider in more detail the distinctive features of corporation and partnership accounting.

CASE I: SOLE PROPRIETORSHIP   George Taylor originally invested $25,000 in a printing business. Subsequent earnings left in the business amounted to $15,000. The owner's equity section of the firm's balance sheet would appear as follows:

Owner's Equity

George Taylor, Capital $40,000

CASE II: PARTNERSHIP   George Taylor, Robert Williams, and John Young invested $10,000, $8,000, and $7,000, respectively, in a printing business. Each partner's share of subsequent earnings not withdrawn from the business was $5,000. The owners' equity section of this firm's balance sheet would appear as follows:

Owners' Equity

George Taylor, Capital	$15,000
Robert Williams, Capital	13,000
John Young, Capital	12,000
Total Owners' Equity	$40,000

CASE III: CORPORATION   George Taylor, Robert Williams, and John Young began a corporation, investing $10,000, $8,000, and $7,000, respectively, and receiving shares of stock for those amounts. Subsequent earnings not distributed, identified as retained earnings, amounted to $15,000. The owners' equity section of this firm's balance sheet would appear as follows:

Owners' Equity

Capital Stock	$25,000
Retained Earnings	15,000
	$40,000

The owners may, from time to time, withdraw money or property from the business for personal use or to engage in other business activities. Such withdrawals reduce both the assets and the owners' equity of the business. In sole proprietorships and partnerships, withdrawals are made quite informally at the owners' discretion; in corporations, withdrawals must be accomplished more formally. The board of directors, elected by the stockholders, must meet and "declare a dividend" before a distribution can be made to the stockholders. Declaration of dividends reduces the retained earnings portion of the owners' equity of the corporation and creates a liability called Dividends Payable. Payment of the dividend eliminates the liability and reduces assets (usually cash).

UNDERLYING ACCOUNTING CONCEPTS

Certain fundamental concepts provide a framework for recording and reporting business transactions. These concepts have been developed over time to provide general guides to making financial reports as objective and as useful as possible. Although various terms, such as **principle, standard, assumption,** and **convention,** are often used to describe such guides, a distinction among these terms is not essential to an understanding of the guides. At this point, a brief discussion of certain of these guides may be helpful in understanding the structure of the accounting process. A more thorough discussion is given in Chapter 16.

The Accounting Entity

Any business enterprise—whether a sole proprietorship, a partnership, or a corporation—is an individual accounting unit separate and distinct from the other economic activities and the personal affairs of the owners. Thus, in Case I of our previous example, if George Taylor, the sole proprietor, owned other businesses or participated in other economic ventures, these activities would be accounted for separately and would not affect the accounting for the sole-proprietorship printing business. A separate set of accounting records would be maintained and a separate set of financial statements would be prepared for each enterprise. Similarly, the three partners in Case II and the three stockholders in Case III might have other business interests, but none of these activities would become mingled in accounting for the partnership or corporation.

Historical Cost

In our previous discussion, we mentioned that assets are recorded and subsequently reported at their acquisition price, or **historical cost.** Although other measurements, such as appraised values or market prices, might be used for reporting in subsquent periods, accountants have long recognized that historical cost is probably the most objective and verifiable basis for reporting assets. As you will learn, reported asset costs are often *reduced* over time to reflect expiration, and in some cases, they may be reduced to market values; upward revaluations, however, are not permitted in conventional financial statements. As we explain later, certain reported *supplemental* information departs from the cost principle.

Objectivity

Because accounting data are most useful when they are objective and verifiable, the recording of transactions should be based on actual invoices, physical counts, and other relatively bias-free evidence whenever possible. Undocumented opinions of management or others do not provide a good basis for accounting determinations. Even when a certain amount of subjectivity cannot be avoided—as in estimating the useful lives of plant assets, collectibility of accounts receivable, or possible liability for product warranties—it is important that such estimates be supported by some sort of objective analysis.

Going Concern

The "going concern" concept is based on the presumption that a business firm will continue indefinitely and will not be sold or liquidated. This assumption permits the accountant to carry certain incurred costs such as plant assets and supplies into future periods and, as you will learn, to reflect them as costs of operation when items are used in operations. The concept also supports the cost principle, because it assumes that such assets will be *used* in operating the business rather than sold; hence, it is considered rational to use cost, rather than market price or liquidation value, as the basis for measurement.

The Measuring Unit

Accounting transactions and their results appearing in financial statements are expressed in terms of a monetary unit (the dollar in the United States). Unfortunately, the U.S. dollar (as well as the currency of other countries) is not a *stable* unit of measure. The worldwide inflation of the past several years has caused all currencies to decline sharply in purchasing power. As a result, use of the cost principle has had a distorting effect on the financial statements of business firms, because the amounts appearing in the statements are expressed in dollars of different vintages. Over the years, there have been many proposals to adjust the amounts in financial statements by the use of price indexes, or to substitute some current value such as replacement cost or appraisal value. At present, conventional financial statements prepared in this country are still unadjusted, cost-based statements. For the past few years, however, the Securities and Exchange Commission has required many firms to reveal the replacement cost of certain items in **supplementary disclosures.** In addition, in 1979, the Financial Accounting Standards Board issued a proposal requiring certain large publicly held firms to make supplementary disclosures concerning the effects of inflation on their operations. A more detailed discussion of the problem will be given in Chapter 16.

EFFECT OF TRANSACTIONS ON THE BALANCE SHEET

Earlier, we observed that the balance sheet of a business indicates the firm's financial position at a particular point in time. We emphasized that the total assets should always equal the sum of the creditors' and owners' equities. If a balance sheet were prepared after each business transaction was completed, this equality of assets and equities would always hold true. Obviously, no one would care to do this, since the statements are required only periodically. It is useful, however, to keep in mind that although each transaction changes the complexion of the balance sheet, equality of assets and equities is always maintained.

Transactions Not Affecting Owners' Equity

Certain transactions may change the character and amounts of assets, liabilities, or both, but have no effect on owners' equity. For example, if Mr. Taylor of Perfection Printers (see Exhibit 1–2) purchases additional equipment for $1,000 in cash, the asset Equipment will increase by $1,000 but the asset Cash will decrease by $1,000. Obviously, this transaction results only in a shift in assets on the balance sheet. In the same way, collection of Accounts Receivable results only in a shift of assets. Collection of $500 of Accounts Receivable would result in a decrease in this asset and an increase in Cash of $500.

If the $1,000 worth of equipment had been purchased on credit rather than for cash, the result would have been a $1,000 increase in Equipment and an equal increase in the liability Accounts Payable. On the other hand, payment of liabilities reduces both assets and liabilities. If Taylor paid $500 to his creditors, both Cash and Accounts Payable would decrease by $500.

Transactions Affecting Owners' Equity

Four types of transactions change the amount of owners' equity:

	Effect on Owners' Equity
(1) Owner contributions	Increase
(2) Owner withdrawals	Decrease
(3) Revenue	Increase
(4) Expense	Decrease

When an owner contributes cash or other assets to a business firm, the firm's balance sheet shows an increase in assets and an increase in owners' equity. Conversely, when an owner withdraws assets from the firm, both assets and owners' equity decrease. The primary goal of any business, however, is to increase the owners' equity by earning profits, or **net income**. The net income of a firm is determined by subtracting *expenses incurred* from *revenue earned*. Owners' equity is increased by revenue and decreased by expenses. Let us examine the nature of revenue and expenses.

Revenue

A business firm earns **revenue** by providing goods or services for its customers. The revenue earned is measured by the *assets received* in exchange, usually in the form of cash or an account receivable. It is important to recognize that *revenue is earned and reflected in the accounting process at the time that goods or services are provided*. Receipt of cash by a business does not necessarily indicate that revenue has been earned. It is true that in a cash sale revenue is earned at the same time as cash is received. Revenue is also reflected, however, when services are rendered *on credit;* assets are increased when Accounts Receivable is increased. Subsequent collection of an account does not increase revenue—it merely results in a shift in assets from Accounts Receivable to Cash. Neither is revenue earned when a business borrows money or when the owners contribute assets. Such increases in assets are not earned, because the business firm has provided no goods or services.

Expenses

Expenses are costs incurred by the firm in the process of earning revenue. Generally, expenses are measured by the costs of *assets consumed or services used* during an accounting period. Depreciation on equipment, rent, employees' salaries, costs of heat, light, and other utilities are examples of expenses incurred in producing revenue.

Because expenses are deducted from revenue to determine net income, the accounting process must relate expense in a period to the revenue of that same period. For example, January rent—no matter when it is paid—should be related to January revenue in determining net income for that month. If an annual rent of $6,000 is prepaid on January 1, only $\frac{1}{12}$ of the $6,000, or $500, is considered expense for January. At the end of January, the remaining prepayment of $5,500 constitutes an asset (called Prepaid Rent) to be apportioned over the remaining 11 months. Other examples of assets that are used up over a period of time in this way are Prepaid Insurance and Prepaid Advertising.

Cash expenditures made to acquire assets do not represent expenses and have no effect on owners' equity. Cash expenditures made to pay liabilities, such as the payment of an account payable, also do not represent expenses and have no effect on owners' equity. Similarly, owners' withdrawals, although they reduce owners' equity, do not represent expenses. Expenses are directly related to the earning of revenue. They are determined by measuring the amount of assets or services consumed (or expired) during an accounting period.

Accrual Basis   The foregoing concepts of revenue and expense apply to firms that employ an accrual basis accounting system. In accrual accounting, expense incurred is matched with related revenue earned to determine a meaningful net income figure for a particular time period. As we mentioned earlier, the revenue and expenses for determining net income do not depend on when cash is actually received or expended.

Certain businesses, principally service enterprises (such as law, architecture, or hairdressing), often use a cash basis mode of accounting. In contrast to accrual basis accounting, the cash basis system does recognize revenues when money is received and expenses when money is paid. Cash basis accounting is used primarily because it can provide certain income tax benefits and because it is simple. Cash basis financial statements, however, may distort the portrayal of financial position and operating results of a business. Consequently, most business firms use the accrual basis of accounting.

TRANSACTIONS AND THE BALANCE SHEET: AN ILLUSTRATION

Now that we have described the basic concepts underlying the preparation of financial statements, let us illustrate their application with an example.

A. B. Cole, a resident physician in a local hospital, decided to enter private practice on December 1 of the current year and established a proprietorship called the Cole Clinic. The transactions for the first month of operations are analyzed below. A balance sheet is presented after each transaction so that the effect of the transaction on the balance sheet may be examined.[2]

(1) Dec. 1. Dr. Cole invested $30,000 of his personal funds in the clinic. This first business transaction results in an increase in the asset Cash and an increase in Cole's equity (Capital) on the clinic's balance sheet.

---

[2]Note that the totals in the various financial statements shown in this chapter have been double-ruled. Accountants do this principally to signify that all necessary calculations have been performed and to emphasize final amounts for the benefit of readers. We shall also employ double rulings in various other accounting records and forms illustrated in this text for these reasons and also to separate certain recorded data by time periods.

Balance Sheet

Assets		Liabilities	
Cash	$30,000	(none)	
		Owner's Equity	
	_____	Cole, Capital	$30,000
		Total Liabilities and	
Total Assets	$30,000	Owner's Equity	$30,000

(2) Dec. 1. The doctor paid $600 rent for clinic office space for December. This expenditure is an expense for the month of December. Since formal financial statements will be prepared at the end of the month, the $600 will be a cost incurred for services received during the month. The effect is to reduce assets (Cash) and owner's equity (Cole, Capital) by $600.

Balance Sheet

Assets		Liabilities	
Cash	$29,400	(none)	
		Owner's Equity	
	_____	Cole, Capital	$29,400
		Total Liabilities and	
Total Assets	$29,400	Owner's Equity	$29,400

(3) Dec. 1. Dr. Cole purchased medical equipment for $20,000 cash. Buying equipment for cash reduces the cash balance and results in the appearance of another asset for an equivalent amount. This transaction is merely the conversion of one asset to another.

Balance Sheet

Assets		Liabilities	
Cash	$ 9,400	(none)	
Equipment	20,000		
		Owner's Equity	
	_____	Cole, Capital	$29,400
		Total Liabilities and	
Total Assets	$29,400	Owner's Equity	$29,400

(4) Dec. 5. Dr. Cole purchased $800 worth of supplies on account (that is, he charged them). This transaction increases assets (Supplies on Hand) by $800 and results in a liability (Accounts Payable) of $800. Although assets are increased, there is no change in owner's equity. Instead, a liability appears on the balance sheet. Because we cannot anticipate the amount of supplies

that will be *used* (become expense) in December, the entire $800 is classified as an asset. Later, when the amount of supplies used is determined, an expense will be reflected—see item (11).

Balance Sheet

Assets		Liabilities	
Cash	$ 9,400	Accounts Payable	$ 800
Supplies on Hand	800		
Equipment	20,000	**Owner's Equity**	
		Cole, Capital	29,400
		Total Liabilities and	
Total Assets	$30,200	Owner's Equity	$30,200

(5) Dec. 15. Patients were billed $2,600 for services performed during the first half of December. As medical services are rendered, the asset Accounts Receivable is generated and owner's equity is increased. Note that the firm has earned revenue amounting to $2,600 by providing services, and that revenue increases assets and owner capital when earned—even though payment may not be received until a later period.

Balance Sheet

Assets		Liabilities	
Cash	$ 9,400	Accounts Payable	$ 800
Accounts Receivable	2,600		
Supplies on Hand	800	**Owner's Equity**	
Equipment	20,000	Cole, Capital	32,000
		Total Liabilities and	
Total Assets	$32,800	Owner's Equity	$32,800

(6) Dec. 20. Dr. Cole paid $400 on account for supplies purchased December 5 (4). Paying $400 of the $800 owed for supplies reduces both Cash and Accounts Payable. Both assets and liabilities are therefore reduced. This payment is *not* an expense. It is the partial settlement of a previously recorded obligation; no new supplies were received.

Balance Sheet

Assets		Liabilities	
Cash	$ 9,000	Accounts Payable	$ 400
Accounts Receivable	2,600		
Supplies on Hand	800	**Owner's Equity**	
Equipment	20,000	Cole, Capital	32,000
		Total Liabilities and	
Total Assets	$32,400	Owner's Equity	$32,400

(7) Dec. 31. Nurse's salary for December was paid, $900. This amount is an expense for December, decreasing both assets and owner's equity, because the amount represents services used during the period. Cash and Cole, Capital both are reduced by $900.

Balance Sheet

Assets		Liabilities	
Cash	$ 8,100	Accounts Payable	$ 400
Accounts Receivable	2,600		
Supplies on Hand	800	**Owner's Equity**	
Equipment	20,000	Cole, Capital	31,100
		Total Liabilities and	
Total Assets	$31,500	Owner's Equity	$31,500

(8) Dec. 31. Dr. Cole received $1,600 on account from patients billed December 15. This increases Cash and decreases Accounts Receivable—merely a shift in assets. Note that the revenue, resulting in an increase in owner's equity, had already been reflected when billings were made on December 15.

Balance Sheet

Assets		Liabilities	
Cash	$ 9,700	Accounts Payable	$ 400
Accounts Receivable	1,000		
Supplies on Hand	800	**Owner's Equity**	
Equipment	20,000	Cole, Capital	31,100
		Total Liabilities and	
Total Assets	$31,500	Owner's Equity	$31,500

(9) Dec. 31. Patients were billed $2,500 for services performed during the last half of December. This transaction is the same as that explained in (5). There is a $2,500 increase in both Accounts Receivable and Cole, Capital.

Balance Sheet

Assets		Liabilities	
Cash	$ 9,700	Accounts Payable	$ 400
Accounts Receivable	3,500		
Supplies on Hand	800	**Owner's Equity**	
Equipment	20,000	Cole, Capital	33,600
		Total Liabilities and	
Total Assets	$34,000	Owner's Equity	$34,000

(10) Dec. 31. Dr. Cole withdrew $1,200 cash for personal use. This withdrawal

reduces Cash and owner's equity by $1,200. Note that the effect of this transaction is the reverse of the very first transaction in which Cole invested funds in the clinic.

Balance Sheet

Assets		Liabilities	
Cash	$ 8,500	Accounts Payable	$ 400
Accounts Receivable	3,500		
Supplies on Hand	800	**Owner's Equity**	
Equipment	20,000	Cole, Capital	32,400
		Total Liabilities and	
Total Assets	$32,800	Owner's Equity	$32,800

(11) Dec. 31. Dr. Cole counted supplies and found $300 worth on hand, indicating that $500 worth of supplies were used in December. When supplies were purchased December 5 (4), their entire cost, $800, was reflected as an asset. At the end of the period, the remaining supplies are counted and the amount is subtracted from Supplies on Hand. The difference is the amount used, or expense, for the period. The result is a decrease in the asset Supplies on Hand and a decrease in Cole, Capital.

Balance Sheet

Assets		Liabilities	
Cash	$ 8,500	Accounts Payable	$ 400
Accounts Receivable	3,500		
Supplies on Hand	300	**Owner's Equity**	
Equipment	20,000	Cole, Capital	31,900
		Total Liabilities and	
Total Assets	$32,300	Owner's Equity	$32,300

We can view transaction (11) as a summary of a number of internal transactions for Cole Clinic. Actually, supplies are being used (and therefore, expense incurred) throughout the period. It is more convenient, however, to reflect this expense at the end of the period, after counting the remaining supplies on hand. Therefore, this item can be regarded as an **adjustment** of the supplies on hand and owner's capital at the end of the period. Most enterprises make a number of such adjustments at the end of an accounting period. Transactions (12) and (13) explained below introduce two additional common adjustments, and we will discuss others throughout the text.

(12) Dec. 31. Dr. Cole estimated that the office utilities (heat, electricity, and telephone) used but not yet paid for would amount to $140. Because the amount of utilities used during December should be shown as expense in this

month, it is necessary to estimate them. This amount should be reflected by increasing liabilities (Accounts Payable) and decreasing owner's equity (Cole, Capital) by $140.

Balance Sheet

Assets		Liabilities	
Cash	$ 8,500	Accounts Payable	$ 540
Accounts Receivable	3,500		
Supplies on Hand	300	**Owner's Equity**	
Equipment	20,000	Cole, Capital	31,760
		Total Liabilities and	
Total Assets	$32,300	Owner's Equity	$32,300

(13) Dec. 31. Dr. Cole estimated one month's depreciation on equipment to be $180. Depreciable assets such as Cole's medical equipment are used up with the passage of time. Therefore, each accounting period in which these assets are used to earn revenues should reflect as expense a portion of the cost of such assets. The amount is obtained by dividing the estimated life of the assets into their total cost. Both the asset Equipment and Cole, Capital are reduced by this amount. Notice, however, that Equipment is not reduced directly on the balance sheet. As shown in Exhibit 1–2, we indicate the amount of reduction in cost of this asset in Accumulated Depreciation. This procedure gives the reader of the balance sheet an idea of the original cost of these assets and the amount that has been *written off* over time. We shall explore this process further in Chapter 10.

Balance Sheet

Assets			Liabilities	
Cash		$ 8,500	Accounts Payable	$ 540
Accounts Receivable		3,500		
Supplies on Hand		300	**Owner's Equity**	
Equipment	20,000		Cole, Capital	31,580
Less: Accumulated				
Depreciation	180	19,820	Total Liabilities and	
Total Assets		$32,120	Owner's Equity	$32,120

Exhibit 1–3 summarizes the foregoing activities and shows their effect on the balance sheet equation. The final results are, of course, identical with those given on the balance sheet prepared after transaction (13). This December 31 balance

EXHIBIT 1-3
Summary of December Activities and
Their Effect on Balance Sheet Equation

			Assets					= Liabilities +	Owner's Equity
Transactions	Cash	+ Accounts Receivable	+ Supplies on Hand	+ Equipment	− Accumulated Depreciation	=	Accounts Payable	+	A. B. Cole, Capital
(1)	+ $30,000								+ $30,000
(2)	− 600								− 600
(3)	− 20,000			+ $20,000					
(4)			+ $800				+ $800		
(5)		+ $2,600							+ 2,600
(6)	− 400						− 400		
(7)	− 900								− 900
(8)	+ 1,600	− 1,600							
(9)		+ 2,500							+ 2,500
(10)	− 1,200								− 1,200
(11)			− 500						− 500
(12)							+ 140		− 140
(13)					+ $180				− 180
	$ 8,500 +	$3,500 +	$300 +	$20,000 −	$180	=	$540 +		$31,580

$32,120 = $32,120

sheet is the only one that the Cole Clinic would actually prepare, since it is the end of the accounting period.

As a result of the clinic's December activities, Dr. Cole increased his capital from his original investment of $30,000 to $31,580—an increase of $1,580. Had Dr. Cole not withdrawn $1,200 for personal use, the increase would have been $2,780. This latter amount represents the net income, or net earnings, for December.

THE INCOME STATEMENT

Although it is important to know the amount of net income, it is equally important to know how it was earned. To show the results of operations for a period, an **income statement** is prepared, which lists the revenues and expenses. When total revenues exceed total expenses the resulting amount is net income; when expenses exceed revenues, the resulting amount is a net loss. To prepare a December income statement for the Cole Clinic, we must identify the revenues and expenses by analyzing the changes in owner's equity for the period. The changes in Dr. Cole's capital, taken from Exhibit 1–3, are shown below, with an explanation of each change:

(1) Capital contribution	+	$30,000
(2) Rent expense	−	600
✳ (5) Billings to patients	+	2,600
(7) Salary expense (nurse)	−	900
✳ (9) Billings to patients	+	2,500
(10) Withdrawal by Cole	−	1,200
(11) Supplies expense	−	500
(12) Utilities expense	−	140
(13) Depreciation expense	−	180
Ending Capital Balance		$31,580

From this list of transactions, we see that revenue, or fees earned, amounts to $5,100—the sum of the billings to patients of $2,600 and $2,500 in (5) and (9). The expenses are derived from transactions (2) and (7) for rent and salary and the calculations made by Cole in (11), (12), and (13) to reflect the amounts of supplies used, utilities consumed, and depreciation expense incurred. Items (1) and (10), representing contributions and withdrawals by Cole, are ignored in preparing the income statement.

The formal income statement for the month of December, which would be prepared to accompany the December 31 balance sheet, appears in Exhibit 1–4.

EXHIBIT 1–4

Cole Clinic
Income Statement
For the Month of December, 19XX

Revenue		
Fees Earned		$5,100
Expenses		
Rent Expense	$600	
Salary Expense	900	
Supplies Expense	500	
Utilities Expense	140	
Depreciation Expense	180	
Total Expenses		2,320
Net Income for December		$2,780

RELATIONSHIP OF
BALANCE SHEET AND INCOME STATEMENT

We have seen that the balance sheet and the income statement complement each other. The income statement summarizes the operating results for the accounting period, and these results are reflected in the owners' equity on the balance sheet. For yearly statements, the complementary relationship might be shown graphically as follows:

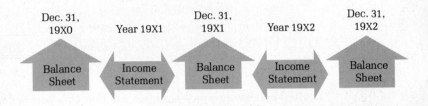

STATEMENT OF OWNERS' EQUITY

Frequently at the end of an accounting period, a statement of owners' equity is prepared to accompany the balance sheet and income statement. This is simply a summary of the changes in the owners' capital balance during the period. Exhibit 1–5 shows this type of statement for the Cole Clinic. Note that the ending balance on this statement agrees with the owner's capital balance on the balance sheet at December 31, 19XX.

EXHIBIT 1–5

Cole Clinic
Statement of Owner's Equity
For the Month of December, 19XX

Balance, December 1, 19XX	$ -0-
Add: Contributions	30,000
Net Income for December	2,780
	$32,780
Less: Withdrawals in December	1,200
Balance, December 31, 19XX	$31,580

This statement further demonstrates the relationship between the income statement and the balance sheet. The net income (or net loss) for a period is an input into the statement of owners' equity, while the ending owners' equity balance on the statement is an input into the balance sheet at the end of the period. When financial statements are prepared, the sequence suggested by this relationship is customarily followed; that is, the income statement is prepared first, then the statement of owners' equity (when such a statement is prepared to accompany the income statement and balance sheet), and then the balance sheet.

DEMONSTRATION PROBLEM FOR REVIEW

L. D. Ford operates a single proprietorship known as Ford Appliance Repairs. On January 1 of the current year, the assets and liabilities of the business were: Cash, $2,000; Accounts Receivable, $400; Supplies, $500; Equipment, $5,000; and Accounts Payable, $800. The business transactions for January were as follows:

(1) Paid $200 on Accounts Payable.
(2) Received $500 for repair work performed for cash customers.
(3) Received $150 on account from customers.
(4) Purchased $125 worth of supplies on account.
(5) Paid rent for January, $170.
(6) Billed customers for repair work performed on account, $1,200.
(7) Purchased equipment for $2,000, giving $500 cash and a non-interest-bearing note payable for $1,500.
(8) Paid wages expense of part-time employee, $420.
(9) Paid utilities expense, $75.
(10) Withdrew $200 cash for personal use of Mr. Ford.
(11) Estimated depreciation on equipment for the month, $80.
(12) Counted supplies on hand at the end of January, $525.

REQUIRED

(a) From the data in the first paragraph, prepare a balance sheet for Ford Appliance Repairs as of January 1 of the current year. Use the horizontal form illustrated in Exhibit 1–3 and place the amounts on the first line of the form.
(b) Following the form of Exhibit 1–3, show the effects of transactions (1) through (12) on the beginning balance sheet, and total the columns to prove that total assets equal liabilities plus owner's equity at January 31.
(c) Prepare an income statement for January.

SOLUTION TO DEMONSTRATION PROBLEM

assets — *Lia* — *OE*

		Cash +	Accounts Receivable +	Supplies on Hand +	Equipment −	Accumulated Depreciation =	Notes Payable +	Accounts Payable +	Ford, Capital
(a)		$2,000 +	$ 400 +	$500 +	$5,000	=		$800 +	$7,100
(b)	(1) −	200					−	200	
	(2) +	500							+ 500
	(3) +	150 −	150						
	(4)			+ 125				+ 125	
	(5) −	170							− 170
	(6) +		1,200						+ 1,200
	(7) −	500			+ 2,000		+ $1,500		
	(8) −	420							− 420
	(9) −	75							− 75
	(10) −	200							− 200
	(11)					+ $80			− 80
	(12)			− 100					− 100
		$1,085 +	$1,450 +	$525 +	$7,000 −	$80 =	$1,500 +	$725 +	$7,755

$9,980

$9,980

(c)

Ford Appliance Repairs
Income Statement
For the month of January, 19XX

Revenue		
Fees Earned		$1,700
Expenses		
Rent Expense	$170	
Wages Expense	420	
Utilities Expense	75	
Depreciation Expense	80	
Supplies Expense	100	
Total Expenses		845
Net Income for January		$ 855

KEY POINTS TO REMEMBER

(1) Although a balance sheet and an income statement are usually prepared at the same time, <u>a balance sheet presents financial position *at a point in time,*</u> while the <u>income statement presents operating results for a *period of time.*</u>

(2) The accounting equation, Assets = Liabilities + Owners' Equity, represents the basic structure of the balance sheet and holds true after each business transaction.

(3) In determining net income (revenue minus expenses) on the *accrual* basis, revenue is recognized *when earned* rather than when cash is collected, and expenses are recognized when goods and services are *used* rather than when they are paid for.

(4) Owners' equity can be increased by contributions from owners and by revenue. It can be decreased by withdrawals and expenses. Only revenue and expenses are used in determining net income.

(5) Certain fundamental concepts underlying the accounting process are:
Accounting entity. Each business venture is a separate unit, accounted for separately.

Historical cost. Assets are reported at acquisition price and are not adjusted upward.

Objectivity. Where possible, recording of transactions should be supported by verifiable evidence.

Going concern. The assumption is made in accounting that a business will continue indefinitely.

Measuring unit. Conventional accounting statements are not adjusted for changes in the value of the dollar.

QUESTIONS

1-1 Distinguish between financial and managerial accounting.

1-2 Name some outside groups that may be interested in the financial data of a company and state their particular interests.

1-3 What factors are important in determining a firm's need for electronic data processing?

1-4 Since financial accounting data are primarily historical, in what way are they useful for control purposes?

1-5 What are "generally accepted accounting principles," and by whom are they established?

1-6 Why do business firms frequently keep more than one set of records on certain aspects of their financial activities?

1-7 How do the functions of private accountants and public accountants differ?

1-8 What is the purpose of a balance sheet? an income statement?

1-9 Define assets, liabilities, and owners' equity.

1-10 Explain how the presentation of the owners' equity in the balance sheet of a corporation differs from that of a single proprietorship.

1-11 State the effect on a corporation's balance sheet of:
(a) the declaration of a dividend.
(b) the payment of a dividend.

1-12 What is meant by "the accounting entity"?

1-13 Explain the concepts of historical cost, objectivity, and "going concern." How are they related?

1-14 When the owners of a business withdraw cash, do the withdrawals appear as expenses on the income statement? Explain.

1-15 If the owner's capital on a particular balance sheet is $30,000, can it be said, without seeing the rest of this financial statement, that the owner should be able to withdraw $30,000 in cash from the business? Justify your answer.

1-16 How do the accrual basis and the cash basis of accounting differ?

1-17 Describe a transaction that would:
(a) increase one asset but not change the amount of total assets.
(b) decrease an asset and a liability.
(c) decrease an asset and decrease owners' equity.
(d) increase an asset and a liability.

1-18 Indicate whether each of the following would increase, decrease, or have no effect on owners' equity:
(a) Purchased supplies for cash.
(b) Withdrew supplies for personal use.
(c) Paid salaries.
(d) Purchased equipment.
(e) Invested cash in business.
(f) Rendered service for customers, on account.
(g) Rendered service for customers, for cash.

1-19 On December 31 of the current year, the Wilson Company had $500,000 in total assets and owed $200,000 to creditors. If the capital stock of this corporation amounted to $250,000, what amount of retained earnings should appear on a balance sheet prepared on December 31?

1-20 During 19XX, the owners' equity of the Gordon Sports Shop increased from $60,000 to $72,000 even though the owners withdrew $15,000 for personal use. What was the net income (or loss) during 19XX if capital contributions were $5,000?

22,000

1-21 A business had total liabilities of $40,000 at the beginning of the year and $30,000 at year-end. At year-end, net assets were $70,000 and total assets were $10,000 greater than at the beginning of the year. If capital contributed exceeded capital withdrawn by $5,000, what was the net income for the year?

EXERCISES

1-22 Following the example shown in (a) below, indicate the effects of the listed transactions on the assets, liabilities, and owner's equity of the balance sheet of Ray Benson, attorney, a sole proprietorship.

(a) Purchased, for cash, a typewriter for use in office.
   ANSWER: Increase: ASSETS (Office Equipment)
              Decrease: ASSETS (Cash)
(b) Rendered service and billed customer.
(c) Paid rent for month.
(d) Rendered service and collected cash immediately from customer.
(e) Received amount due from customer in (b) above.
(f) Purchased, on account, supplies estimated to last two years.
(g) Paid salaries of employees for month.
(h) Paid for supplies purchased in (f) above.
(i) Withdrew cash for personal use.

1-23 At the beginning of the current year, Wesley's Masonry had the following balance sheet:

Assets			Liabilities	
Cash		$ 8,500	Accounts Payable	$ 1,000
Equipment	$1,600			
Less: Accumulated			**Owner's Equity**	
Depreciation	100	1,500	J. Wesley, Capital	14,000
Truck	$6,000			
Less: Accumulated				
Depreciation	1,000	5,000		
			Total Liabilities and	
Total Assets		$15,000	Owner's Equity	$15,000

(a) At the end of the current year, Wesley had the following assets and liabilities: Cash, $15,000; Supplies on Hand, $600; Equipment, $1,600; Accumulated Depreciation—Equipment, $200; Truck, $6,000; Accumulated Depreciation—Truck, $2,000; Accounts Payable, $500. Prepare a balance sheet for Wesley's Masonry at the end of the current year.
(b) Assuming that Wesley did not invest any money in the business during the year, but withdrew $12,000 for personal use, what was the net income or net loss for the current year?
(c) Assuming that Wesley invested an additional $3,000 early in the year, but withdrew $12,000 before the end of the year, what was the net income or net loss for the current year?

1-24 The balance sheet of G. Burke, architect, at the beginning of an accounting period is given in equation form below, followed by nine transactions whose effects on the equation are shown.

(a) For each numbered item, describe the transaction that occurred. Of all the transactions affecting G. Burke, Capital, only transaction (9) had no effect on net income for the period.
(b) What is the amount of net income for the period?

	Cash	+	Accounts Receivable	+	Supplies on Hand	+	Equipment	−	Accumulated Depreciation	=	Accounts Payable	+	G. Burke, Capital
Balance	5,000	+	8,000	+	600	+	15,000	−	3,000	=	5,600	+	20,000
(1)	− 600					+	600						
(2)	+ 6,000	−	6,000										
(3)				+	200						+	200		
(4)		+	4,000										+	4,000
(5)	− 2,000										−	2,000		
(6)				−	400								−	400
(7)								+	1,500				−	1,500
(8)	+ 800												+	800
(9)	− 600												−	600
	8,600	+	6,000	+	400	+	15,600	−	4,500	=	3,800	+	22,300

26,100 =   26,100

1-25 The following income statement and balance sheet information are available for Carlton Cleaners at the end of the current month:

Supplies on Hand	+ $4,000	Cash	+ $ 3,000
Equipment	+ 9,600	Accounts Payable	− 4,000
Accumulated Depreciation	− 600	Salaries Expense	− 6,000
Supplies Expense	− 800	Cleaning Service Revenue	+ 9,000
Depreciation Expense—Equipment	− 200	L. Carlton, Capital (at beginning of month)	+ 10,500

(a) Without preparing a formal income statement, calculate the net income or net loss for the month.

(b) If L. Carlton made no additional investment during the month, but withdrew $500, what is the amount of her capital at the end of the month?

1-26 For the four unrelated situations below, compute the unknown amounts indicated by the letters appearing in each column.

	A	B	C	D
Beginning:				
Assets	$4,000	$6,000	$15,000	$ (d)
Liabilities	1,800	2,000	4,500	7,000
	2,200	4,000	10,500	(?)
Ending:				
Assets	5,000	8,500	18,000	24,000
Liabilities	1,800	(b)	6,600	4,000
	3,200	(?)	11,408	20,000
During year:				
Capital Contributed	600	1,200	(c)	3,000
Revenue	(a)	4,300	6,500	16,000
Capital Withdrawn	400	500	1,600	1,000
Expenses	2,800	3,000	4,700	12,500

1-27 The following information is shown in the records of Duluth Printing Corporation at the end of the current year and last year.

	December 31, This Year	December 31, Last Year
Accounts Receivable	$ 48,000	$ 35,000
Accounts Payable	15,000	8,000
Cash	?	12,000
Equipment	140,000	140,000
Accumulated Depreciation—Equipment	20,000	15,000
Retained Earnings	35,000	?
Supplies on Hand	8,000	5,000
Capital Stock	150,000	150,000

(a) Prepare a balance sheet at December 31 of each year.
(b) If the company declared and paid $4,000 in dividends during this year, what was the amount of this year's net income?

PROBLEMS

1-28 Bennett's Key and Lock Service is a sole proprietorship owned and operated by R. D. Bennett. On January 1 of the current year the assets and liabilities of the business were: Cash, $1,600; Accounts Receivable, $800; Supplies on Hand, $1,200; Equipment, $5,000; Accumulated Depreciation, $400; and Accounts Payable, $1,100. The business transactions during January are as follows:

✳ (1) Paid rent for January, $300.
   (2) Received $450 on account from customers.
   (3) Paid $600 on accounts payable.
— (4) Received $500 for work performed for cash customers.
   (5) Purchased $600 worth of supplies on account.
— (6) Billed various state and other agencies for consulting on security systems and for key and lock service, $3,850.
   (7) Purchased equipment for $2,500, giving $500 in cash and a note payable for $2,000.
   (8) Withdrew $200 cash for personal use of R. D. Bennett.
✳ (9) Paid wages expense, $700.
✗(10) Paid utilities expense, $100.
✗ (11) Estimated depreciation expense on equipment for the month, $70.
✗ (12) Counted supplies on hand at the end of January, $800.

REQUIRED
(a) From the data in the first paragraph, prepare a balance sheet equation for Bennett's Key and Lock Service as of January 1 of the current year. Use the horizontal form illustrated in Exhibit 1–3 and place the amounts on the first line of the form.
(b) Following the form of Exhibit 1–3, show the effects of transactions (1) through (12) on the beginning balance sheet amounts, and total the columns to prove that total assets equal liabilities plus owner's equity at January 31.
(c) Prepare an income statement for January.

(d) Using the form of Exhibit 1–5, prepare a statement showing changes in owner's equity for January.

1–29 An analysis (similar to Exhibit 1–3) of the transactions of the Conrad Employment Service for the month of May appears below. Line (1) summarizes Conrad's balance sheet data on May 1; lines (2) through (11) represent the business transactions for May.

	Cash	+	Accounts Receivable	+	Supplies on Hand	+	Prepaid Insurance	+	Equipment	−	Accumulated Depreciation	=	Accounts Payable	+	Conrad, Capital
(1)	$1,200	+	$1,600	+	$780	+	$120	+	$15,000	−	$3,000	=	$500	+	$15,200
(2)				+	300								+	300		
(3) +	900	−	900													
(4)		+	1,700												+	1,700
(5) +	1,100														+	1,100
(6) −	300							+	700				+	400		
(7) −	800														−	800
(8)						−	20								−	20
(9) −	150														−	150
(10)				−	480										−	480
(11)										+	100				−	100

REQUIRED

(a) Prove that assets equal liabilities plus owner's equity at May 1.

(b) Describe the apparent transaction indicated by each line. [For example, line (2): Purchased $300 of supplies on account.] If you believe that any line could reasonably represent more than one type of transaction, describe each type of transaction.

1–30 The following information is available at December 31 of the current year for Golfer's Haven, a miniature golf course and driving range owned and operated by Herb Macy, a sole proprietor.

Land	$18,000	Accounts Receivable	$ 3,800
Building (less accumulated		Cash	4,500
depreciation)	40,000	Salaries Expense	58,000
Supplies Expense	4,000	Accounts Payable	6,800
Supplies on Hand	1,700	Depreciation Expense—	
Taxes Expense	2,500	Building	1,200
Salaries Payable	3,200	Depreciation Expense—	
Equipment (less accumulated		Equipment	900
depreciation)	12,000	Herb Macy, Capital (at the	
Utilities Expense	3,200	beginning of the year)	53,800
Fees Revenue	90,000		

Macy made no additional investments in the business during the year but withdrew $4,000 for personal use.

REQUIRED

(a) Prepare an income statement for the current year.

(b) Prepare a statement of owner's equity for the current year.

(c) Prepare a balance sheet at December 31 of the current year.

1-31 James Landry began the Landry Packaging Service last year in rented quarters. Late this year, the firm purchased its own facilities. Balance sheet information at the end of the last two years follows.

	December 31, This Year	December 31, Last Year
Prepaid Insurance	$ 300	$ 600
Accounts Receivable	2,100	1,300
Accounts Payable	2,800	2,500
Cash	3,200	2,400
Land	10,000	—
Equipment	40,000	32,000
Accumulated Depreciation—Equipment	6,000	4,000
Mortgage Payable	45,000	—
Building	48,000	—
Supplies on Hand	1,800	1,200
James Landry, Capital	?	?

REQUIRED

(a) Prepare balance sheets for December 31 of each year. Notice that there is no accumulated depreciation on the building, which was acquired near the end of this year.

(b) Landry contributed $5,000 to the business early this year but withdrew $8,000 in December of this year. Calculate the net income for the year.

1-32 On April 1 of the current year, Jill Bryant purchased Madison Delivery Service, a firm providing mailing and delivery service for film dealers, drug houses, computer centers, and various small businesses. The assets acquired were: delivery equipment, $40,000; land, $7,000; building, $50,000; office equipment, $10,000; and supplies, $3,000. To make the purchase and to provide $20,000 cash for initial operations, Jill Bryant invested $80,000 of her own funds and borrowed $50,000 from her father, giving him a non-interest-bearing note payable. The following transactions occurred during April:

(1) Paid $900 for a one-year insurance premium for delivery equipment.
(2) Billed customers $12,500 for delivery services rendered.
(3) Purchased $1,200 of supplies on account.
(4) Collected $8,700 from customers on account.
(5) Paid $4,500 in wages to drivers and dispatcher.
(6) Paid $850 for gas, oil, and repairs (delivery expense).
(7) At the end of April, the following estimates were made: prepaid insurance, $825; supplies on hand, $2,800; estimated utilities expense, $250; monthly depreciation—on building, $150, on delivery equipment, $600, on office equipment, $80.

REQUIRED

(a) From the information given in the first paragraph, prepare a balance sheet equation for Madison Delivery Service at April 1. Use the horizontal form illustrated in Exhibit 1-3 and place the balance sheet amounts at April 1 on the first line of the form. Column headings should include: Cash, Accounts Receivable, Supplies on Hand, Prepaid Insurance, Delivery Equipment, Accumulated Depreciation—Delivery Equipment, Office Equipment, Accumulated Depreciation—Office Equipment, Building, Accumulated Depreciation—Building, Land, Notes Payable, Accounts Payable, and J. Bryant, Capital.

(b) Following the form of Exhibit 1-3, show the effects of the April transactions on the balance sheet amounts, and total all columns to prove that assets equal liabilities plus owner's equity.

(c) Prepare an income statement for April.

1-33 On January 1 of the current year, a group of recent college graduates formed the Entre-Nous Catering Company by selling $50,000 capital stock for cash. The group then purchased kitchen equipment for $25,000 from one of the stockholders, paying $15,000 in cash and giving a $10,000 non-interest-bearing note due in two months. Next, the firm leased two delivery vans from a local dealer to provide delivery service. The remaining transactions for the first month of operations are given below:

(1) Paid leasing cost of delivery vans for January, $540.
(2) Paid insurance premium for six months, $420.
(3) Purchased supplies on account, $3,600.
(4) Paid rent for January, $350.
(5) Received $3,000 cash for catering services.
(6) Paid $260 for advertising.
(7) Billed various firms for catering services, $7,200.
(8) Paid wages expense, $2,100.
(9) Received $3,200 on account from customers.
(10) Paid fuel bill, $130.
(11) Declared and paid a dividend, $1,000.
(12) Estimated depreciation on equipment for January, $120.
(13) Estimated supplies on hand at January 31, $1,200.
(14) Estimated utilities expense for January, $150.
(15) Estimated insurance expense for January, $70.

REQUIRED

(a) From the data in the first paragraph, prepare a balance sheet equation for Entre-Nous Catering Company at the beginning of January. Use the horizontal form illustrated in Exhibit 1-3 and place the amounts on the first line of the form. The column headings should be as follows: Cash, Accounts Receivable, Prepaid Insurance, Supplies on Hand, Equipment, Accumulated Depreciation, Notes Payable, Accounts Payable, Capital Stock, Retained Earnings.

(b) Following the form of Exhibit 1-3, show the effects of transactions (1) through (15) on the beginning balance sheet amounts, and total the columns to prove that total assets equal liabilities plus owners' equity (Capital Stock plus Retained Earnings) at January 31. (Remember that changes in owners' equity resulting from revenues and expenses are reflected in Retained Earnings in a corporation.)

(c) Prepare an income statement for January.

(d) Prepare a balance sheet at January 31.

ALTERNATE PROBLEMS

1-28A D. R. Richards operates a concrete flatwork firm, Construction Service, as a sole proprietorship. On January 1 of the current year, the assets and liabilities of the business were: Cash, $2,800; Accounts Receivable, $1,200; Supplies on

Hand, $1,500; Equipment, $7,000; and Accounts Payable, $900. The business transactions for January were as follows:

(1) Received $800 for work performed for cash customers.
(2) Paid $500 on Accounts Payable.
(3) Paid rent for January, $500.
(4) Received $700 on account from customers.
(5) Purchased $400 worth of supplies on account.
(6) Billed customers for work performed on account, $3,750.
(7) Purchased equipment for $1,200, giving $700 cash and a note payable for $500.
(8) Withdrew $400 cash for personal use of D. R. Richards.
(9) Paid wages expense, $1,450.
(10) Paid utilities expense, $230.
(11) Estimated depreciation on equipment for the month, $50.
(12) Counted supplies on hand at the end of January, $900.

REQUIRED

(a) From the data in the first paragraph, prepare a balance sheet equation for Construction Service as of January 1 of the current year. Use the horizontal form illustrated in Exhibit 1–3 and place the amounts on the first line of the form.
(b) Following the form of Exhibit 1–3, show the effects of transactions (1) through (12) on the beginning balance sheet amounts, and total the columns to prove that total assets equal liabilities plus owner's equity at January 31.
(c) Prepare an income statement for January.
(d) Prepare a statement showing changes in owner's equity for January, using the form illustrated in Exhibit 1–5.

1–29A Appearing below is an analysis (similar to Exhibit 1–3) of the transactions of the Bond Upholstery Service for the month of June. Line (1) summarizes Bond's balance sheet data on June 1; lines (2) through (12) represent the business transactions for June.

	Cash	+	Accounts Receivable	+	Supplies on Hand	+	Prepaid Insurance	+	Equipment	−	Accumulated Depreciation	=	Accounts Payable	+	Notes Payable	+	Bond, Capital
(1)	$ 600	+	$1,200	+	$2,000	+	$360	+	$8,000			=	$400	+	$2,000	+	$9,760
(2)				+	500								+	500				
(3) +	1,500																+	1,500
(4) −	1,000												−	1,000				
(5) −	500							+	800				+	300				
(6) +	800	−	800															
(7)		+	900												+	900		
(8)						−	20								−	20		
(9) −	500														−	500		
(10)													+	80			−	80
(11)				−	450										−	450		
(12)										−	100				+	100		

REQUIRED

(a) Prove that assets equal liabilities plus owner's equity at June 1.
(b) Describe the apparent transaction indicated by each line. [For example, line (2): Purchased $500 of supplies on account.] If you believe that any line

could reasonably represent more than one type of transaction, describe each type of transaction.

1–31A The records of Burns Plumbing Contractors show the information listed below for 19X1 and 19X2. Late in December of 19X2, the organization moved from rented quarters and purchased its own office.

	December 31, 19X2	December 31, 19X1
Notes Payable	$ 8,000	$10,500
Accounts Payable	4,000	1,500
Land	8,000	—
Cash	2,500	1,800
Equipment	55,000	50,000
Building	24,000	—
Accounts Receivable	9,000	6,000
Mortgage Payable	20,000	—
Supplies on Hand	1,500	3,200
R. Burns, Capital	?	?

REQUIRED
(a) Prepare balance sheets as of December 31 of each year.
(b) R. Burns contributed $4,000 to the business early in 19X2. In November of 19X2, Burns withdrew $12,000 from the firm. Calculate the net income for the year.

1–33A At the beginning of the current year, a group of automotive mechanics organized a corporation called the Auto Diagnostic Center by selling capital stock for $50,000 cash. The group then purchased $40,000 worth of equipment, consisting of electronic analyzing equipment and tools, by paying $30,000 cash and giving a non-interest-bearing note payable for the balance. The remaining transactions for the first six months of the current year are given below:
(1) Purchased supplies on account, $3,000.
(2) Paid rent for the six-month period, $4,800.
(3) Paid insurance expense for the six-month period, $720.
(4) Received $4,000 cash for diagnostic work.
(5) Paid $1,200 for repairs and maintenance.
(6) Billed various firms for diagnostic work, $26,000.
(7) Paid wages expense, $8,400.
(8) Received $18,000 on account from customers.
(9) Paid utilities expense for five months, $600.
(10) Declared and paid a dividend, $1,500.
(11) Estimated depreciation expense on equipment for six months, $200.
(12) Estimated supplies used for six months, $700.
(13) Estimated utilities expense for June, $120.

REQUIRED
(a) From the data in the first paragraph, prepare a balance sheet equation for Auto Diagnostic Center at the beginning of the period. Use the horizontal form illustrated in Exhibit 1–3 and place the amounts on the first line of the form. The column headings should be as follows: Cash, Accounts Receivable, Supplies on Hand, Equipment, Accumulated Depreciation, Notes Payable, Accounts Payable, Capital Stock, Retained Earnings.

(b) Following the form of Exhibit 1-3, show the effects of transactions (1) through (13) on the beginning balance sheet amounts, and total the columns to prove that total assets equal liabilities plus owners' equity (Capital Stock plus Retained Earnings) at June 30. (Recall that changes in owners' equity resulting from revenues and expenses are reflected in Retained Earnings in a corporation.)

(c) Prepare an income statement for the six months ended June 30.

(d) Prepare a balance sheet at June 30.

BUSINESS DECISION PROBLEM

Jeff Waters, a friend of yours, is negotiating for the purchase of a sanitation firm called Gillette Pest Control Service. Waters has been employed by a national pest control service and knows the technical side of the business, but he knows little about accounting. He is therefore asking for your assistance. The sole owner of the firm, W. Gillette, has provided Jeff with income statements for the past three years, which show an average net income of $24,000 per year. The latest balance sheet shows total assets of $75,000 and liabilities of $25,000. Included among the assets are a number of vans listed at $25,000 after accumulated depreciation and pest and weed control equipment listed at $35,000 after accumulated depreciation. Waters brings the following matters to your attention:

(1) Gillette is asking $60,000 for the firm. He has pointed out to Waters that, because the firm has been earning 48% on the owner's investment, the price should be higher than the net assets on the balance sheet.

(2) Waters has noticed no salary for Gillette on the income statements, even though he worked half-time in the business. Gillette explained that, because he had other income, he withdrew only $5,000 each year from the firm for personal use. Waters expects to hire a full-time manager for the firm at an annual salary of $18,000 if he decides to purchase the firm.

(3) Waters wonders whether the vans and the pest control equipment are really "worth" $60,000, the net amount shown on the balance sheet.

(4) Waters has seen Gillette's tax returns for the past three years. Because they report a lower income for the firm than the amounts shown in the financial statements, he is skeptical about the accounting principles used in preparing the financial statements.

REQUIRED

(a) How did Gillette arrive at the 48% return given in (1)? If Waters accepted Gillette's average income figure of $24,000, what would Waters's percentage return be, assuming that net income remained at the same level and that the firm was purchased for $60,000?

(b) Should Gillette's withdrawals have had any effect on the net income reported in the financial statements? What will Waters's return be if he takes into consideration the $18,000 salary he plans to pay for a full-time manager?

(c) What explanation would you give Waters with respect to the value of the vans and pest control equipment?

(d) Could there be legitimate reasons for the difference between net income shown in the financial statements and net income reported on the tax returns, as mentioned in item (4)? What might they be? How might Waters obtain additional assurance about the propriety of the financial statements?

**2
The
Double-Entry
Accounting
System**

The format for analyzing and recording transactions illustrated in Chapter 1 was useful in conveying a basic understanding of how transactions affect financial statements. This approach would not be effective, however, in meeting management's needs for financial information on a timely basis. The transactions of most business firms are numerous and complex, affecting many different items appearing on the financial statements. Therefore, a formal system of classification and recording is required so that data may be gathered for day-to-day management requirements and timely accounting reports. In this chapter, we will examine the classification and recording system commonly called double-entry accounting. At the same time, we will expand on several of the basic ideas introduced in Chapter 1.

CATEGORIES OF DATA NEEDED

We know from Chapter 1 that the balance sheet and the income statement forms are as shown in Exhibit 2-1. Exhibit 2-1 indicates that to prepare both the balance sheet and the income statement we need five categories of information from the accounting system: **assets, liabilities, owners' equity, revenues,** and **expenses.** The first three relate to the balance sheet and the last two relate to the income statement.

In Chapter 1 we analyzed the effect of transactions on the balance sheet equation by starting with the three major categories: assets, liabilities, and owners' equity. When we used the basic accounting equation (assets = liabilities + owners' equity) we noted that owners' equity *included* increases from revenue and decreases from expenses. Specifically, we observed that the owners' equity at the balance sheet date consisted of (1) beginning balance, (2) net capital contributions (additional contributions less withdrawals), and (3) net income for the period (revenues less expenses). In preparing an income statement, we had to analyze changes in owners' equity to obtain the necessary revenue and expense data.

EXHIBIT 2-1
The Basic Financial Statements

ABC Company Balance Sheet December 31, 19XX				ABC Company Income Statement For Month of December, 19XX	
(List of assets)	$ XX XX XX XX	(List of liabilities)	$ XX XX	Revenues	$XXX
		Total Liabilities	$ XX	Less Expenses:	$XX XX XX XX
		Owners' Equity	XX	Total Expenses	XX
Total Assets	$XXX	Total Liabilities and Owners' Equity	$XXX	Net Income	$ XX

Since in a typical business, most transactions relate to revenue and expense, it is more efficient to keep track of revenue and expense as a separate part of owners' equity. It is useful to employ an expanded form of the accounting equation, as follows:[1]

ASSETS = LIABILITIES + ———————————OWNERS' EQUITY———————————

$$\left[\text{Beginning Capital} + \text{Contributions} - \text{Withdrawals}\right] + \left[\text{Revenue} - \text{Expense}\right]$$

(capital stock)   (dividends)

[1] In a corporation, beginning capital consists of both capital stock and retained earnings. Contributions would equal additional capital stock sold, whereas withdrawals would be the amount of dividends declared during the period.

If we had used this expanded equation in summarizing the December transactions of the Cole Clinic (see Exhibit 1-3, page 23), the changes in the owner's
equity column would have been shown in three columns, as follows:

	A. B. Cole, Capital + Contributions − Withdrawals	+	Revenue	−	Expense
(1) Capital contribution	+$30,000				
(2) Rent expense					−$ 600
(5) Billings to patients			+$2,600		
(7) Salary expense (nurse)					− 900
(8) Billings to patients			+ 2,500		
(10) Withdrawal by Cole	− 1,200				
(11) Supplies expense					− 500
(12) Utilities expense					− 140
(13) Depreciation expense					− 180
	$28,800	+	$5,100	−	$2,320

$31,580

Observe that the column totals in the above illustration, when added together, amount to $31,580, exactly the amount of the ending owner's equity shown
in Exhibit 1-3. Segregating revenue and expense amounts, however, permits us to
prepare an income statement without first having to analyze all changes in the
owner's capital for the period. The desirability of doing this is apparent even in a
situation as simple as our Cole Clinic example. In more complex business situations, where there are many sources of revenue and possibly hundreds of different types of expenses, separate recording of revenue and expenses is imperative.

So far, our discussion of transaction analysis has been conceptual; we have
tried to convey an understanding of how transactions affect the financial statements. Obviously, the type of transaction recording we have illustrated would be
entirely inadequate for even relatively simple businesses, since even they will
usually have a substantial number of transactions involving a variety of data to be
reported in financial statements. In practice, the necessary data are accumulated
in a set of records called *accounts*.

THE ACCOUNT

The basic component of the formal accounting system is the **account,** which is an
individual record of increases and decreases in specific assets, liabilities, owner
capital, revenues, and expenses. The Cash account for the Cole Clinic might
appear as shown in Exhibit 2-2.

The amounts in the Cole Clinic Cash account consist of the additions and deductions in the cash column of Exhibit 1-3. In the Cash account, the increases have been placed on the left side and the decreases on the right side. A formal system of placement for increases and decreases in various accounts is explained later in this chapter. In our example, there was no beginning amount (balance), because December was the first month of business. If there had been a beginning amount, it would have appeared with the increases, above the entry for $30,000.

The form illustrated in Exhibit 2-2, called a "two-column" account form, is often used in a manually maintained recordkeeping system. Another popular

INVENTION OF ACCOUNTING

Historical facts about "inventions" are sometimes particularly difficult to ascertain since the person who popularizes a procedure (or develops the significant "breakthrough") gets credit for the developments or creations which are attributable to a long line of predecessors.

In the case of double-entry bookkeeping we do not know exactly how the process originated. In all probability the process resulted from a series of developments based on the need for keeping records of financial transactions. If in fact there was an originator of the "breakthrough" concept, his identity is a mystery. . . .

In general, the so-called ledgers which have been preserved in Italy, France, and Germany from the period 1300-1400 illustrate further the primitive beginnings of bookkeeping. The development of systematic bookkeeping becomes evident, however, when accounts were required to be submitted to others and not solely for the private information of the trader or merely as a reporting of detached notes to be produced for a settlement between creditors. Thus the development of banks and partnerships, as well as the increased volume of transactions, gave rise to ideas for an orderly method of bookkeeping.

Double-entry is specifically identified in the accounts of the *massari* (stewards) in their accounting to the local authority in 1340. The date when they began these procedures cannot be determined since the earlier books were destroyed, but it is clearly evident that the stewards' books of 1278, which have been preserved, were not kept in double-entry.

Other double-entry records were found of a merchant in Prato, Italy, beginning in 1390, and of a bank in Genoa (1408) which apparently were begun some years earlier. The double-entry books (with dates beginning in 1406) preserved in Venice, are of particular interest, however, because of the care and neatness with which they were kept and especially because they became identified as the "Method of Venice."

Based on this historical development, Paciolo in 1494 states, in the first chapter of his *Summa de Arithmetica Geometria Proportioni et Proportionalita,* that . . . "The system employed in Venice will be adopted here, for it is certainly recommended above all others." (See the translation in *Paciolo on Accounting* by R. Gene Brown and Kenneth S. Johnston [1963].) Apparently all authorities agree, however, that Paciolo's is the first printed treatise on bookkeeping.

From Charles W. Lamden, "Luca Paciolo and the Invention of Accounting," *World,* Peat, Marwick, Mitchell & Co., Winter 1974, pp. 12–15.

form, called a "running balance," or "three-column" account, is illustrated later in this chapter. Most account forms are designed to facilitate recording the following information:

(1) The account title and number.
(2) Amounts reflecting increases and decreases.
(3) Cross references to other accounting records.
(4) Dates and descriptive notations.

Each account will have a short account title that describes the data being recorded in that account. Some common account titles are Cash, Accounts Receivable, Notes Payable, Professional Fees, and Rent Expense. In manually maintained records, increases and decreases are recorded in ruled columns under headings that indicate the meaning of the amounts appearing there. These amounts are referred to as **entries.** In other words, making an entry in an account consists of recording an amount in a particular place to represent either an increase or a decrease in the account. The normal balance of any account is simply the excess of increases over decreases that have been recorded to date. In our illustration, we have indicated this balance, $8,500, on the left side of the account beside the last entry for an increase. This is the difference between the sum of the increases, $31,600, and the sum of the decreases, $23,100, both of which have been written in pencil to provide temporary totals. Finally, most accounts contain space for presentation of other types of information—for example, the date of any entry, possibly some memoranda explaining a particular entry, and a posting reference column (indicated by Post. Ref.). The posting reference column is used for noting the records from which entries into this account may have been taken. This practice will be explained more fully in the next chapter.

EXHIBIT 2–2
Cash Account for Cole Clinic

Cash   Account No._____

Date	Description	Post. Ref.	Amount	Date	Description	Post. Ref.	Amount
19XX				19XX			
Dec. 1			30,000	Dec. 1			600
31	*8,500*		1,600	1			20,000
			31,600	20			400
				31			900
				31			1,200
							23,100

The account is an extremely simple record and can be summarized in terms of four money elements:

(1) Beginning balance.
(2) Additions.
(3) Deductions.
(4) Ending balance.

Obviously, if any three elements are known, the fourth can easily be computed. Normally, after transactions have been recorded, only the ending balance needs to be computed. Accountants, however, are sometimes confronted with situations in which available data are incomplete and reconstruction of accounts is necessary. Let us demonstrate the analysis to be used with the following example:

	A	B	C	D
Beginning balance	$10	$70	$ 40	$ (?)
Additions	40	30	(?)	100
Deductions	20	(?)	160	120
Ending balance	(?)	10	0	40

In A above, the ending balance must be $20 greater than the beginning balance, because the additions exceed the deductions by $20. Hence, the ending balance is $30. In B, the account balance decreased by $60, so the deductions must exceed the additions by $60. Therefore, total deductions are $90. Show that the unknown variable in C is $120 and in D is $60.

A simplified form often used to represent the account in accounting textbooks and in the classroom is referred to as the **T account** (because it resembles the letter T). This is merely a skeleton version of the account illustrated for actual recordkeeping. A T-account form with the December changes in Cash entered for the Cole Clinic follows.

Cash

(1)	30,000	(2)	600
(8)	1,600	(3)	20,000
	31,600	(6)	400
		(7)	900
		(10)	1.200
			23,100

Because dates and other related data are usually omitted in T accounts, it is customary to "key" the entries with a number or a letter to identify the transaction or entry. This permits a systematic review of the entries in the event that an error has been made. It also enables anyone to review a set of such accounts and match related entries. The numbers in this example are the ones used to identify the December transactions for Cole Clinic in our Chapter 1 example.

The printed account form in Exhibit 2-2 is appropriate for classifying accounting data in manual types of recordkeeping. In accounting systems employing computers, the account form may not be obvious because the actual data might be stored on media such as punched cards or magnetic tapes. Every accounting system, however, whether manual or automated, must provide for the retrieval and printing out of the types of information shown in the manual form.

THE SYSTEM OF DEBITS AND CREDITS

One basic characteristic of all account forms is that entries recording increases and decreases are separated. In some accounts, such as the Cash account illustrated in Exhibit 2-2, increases are recorded on the left-hand side of the account and decreases on the right-hand side; in other accounts the reverse is true. The method used in different types of accounts is a matter of convention—a simple set of rules is followed. The remainder of this chapter is devoted to the discussion and illustration of such rules.

The terms **debit** and **credit** are used to describe the left-hand and the right-hand sides of an account, as shown below.

(Any type of account)

Debit	**Credit**
Always the left side	Always the right side

Regardless of what is being recorded in an account, an entry made on the left-hand side is considered a debit to the account, while an entry recorded on the right-hand side is described as a credit to the account. Sometimes the abbreviations dr. and cr. are used.

The terms *debit* and *credit* are not synonymous with the words *increase* and *decrease*. The system of debits and credits related to increases and decreases in each of the five categories of accounts—assets, liabilities, owners' equity, revenue, and expenses—is shown in Exhibit 2-3.

The system of debits and credits illustrated here is the standard method followed by persons keeping records on the double-entry system (so-called because at least two entries, a debit and a credit, are made for each transaction). The system of rules is analogous to a set of traffic rules whereby everyone (at least everyone in this country) agrees to drive on the right-hand side of the road. Obviously, the system would work if we reversed everything; the important point is that we all follow the same rules.

EXHIBIT 2–3
Pattern of Increases and Decreases, Debits and Credits, and Normal Balances

Five Major Categories of Accounts

	Assets		Liabilities		Owners' Equity		Revenues		Expenses	
	Debit	Credit	Debit	Credit	Debit	Credit	Debit	Credit	Debit	Credit
(1) Always true										
(2) Increases	+			+		+		+	+	
(3) Decreases		−	−		−		−			−
(4) Normal balance	★			★		★		★	★	

Observe the following relationships in Exhibit 2–3:

(1) Debits always refer to the left side of any account, and credits refer to the right side.

(2) Increases in asset and expense accounts are debit entries, while increases in liability, owners' equity, and revenue accounts are credit entries.

(3) Decreases are logically recorded on the side opposite increases.

(4) The normal balance of any account is on the side on which increases are recorded—asset and expense accounts normally have debit balances, while the other three groups normally have credit balances. This result occurs because increases in an account are customarily greater than or equal to decreases.

Note that the pattern for assets is opposite that for liabilities and owners' equity. Also observe that the pattern for revenue is the same as for owners' equity. This is to be expected, because revenue increases owners' equity. Following the same logic, the pattern for expenses should be opposite that of owners' equity, because expenses reduce owners' equity.

THE RUNNING BALANCE ACCOUNT

In manually maintained accounting records, the "running balance," or "three-column," form of ledger account is often used rather than the symmetrical two-column form that was illustrated in Exhibit 2–2. The Cash account for Cole Clinic in running balance form is shown in Exhibit 2–4. Notice that the account contains all the information shown in the two-column account but also provides a balance after each transaction.

The major advantage of this type of account over the two-column account is that the account balance for any date during the period can be easily perceived. Use of the running balance account also avoids the monthly ruling of accounts, which is customarily done when the two-column account is used. A slight disadvantage is that one must be careful to note whether the balance of the account is a normal balance or not. If an account balance is abnormal, it should be placed in parentheses. For example, if we overdrew our bank balance, the balance of the cash account would be abnormal (a credit balance).

We shall employ the running balance account in our formal illustrations throughout the succeeding chapters. To assist you in the earlier chapters, we have placed an asterisk (*) in the column of the account that designates its normal balance. In other illustrations in which detail is not needed and concepts are emphasized, we will use T accounts.

ILLUSTRATION OF DEBIT AND CREDIT ANALYSIS

The following illustration of debit and credit analysis uses the transactions given in Chapter 1 for the first month's operations of the Cole Clinic. Each transaction is stated, analyzed, and followed by an illustration of the appropriate debit and

EXHIBIT 2–4
Cash Account for Cole Clinic

Cash   Account No. _____

Date		Explanation	Post. Ref.	Debit*	Credit	Balance
19XX						
Dec.	1			30,000		30,000
	1				600	29,400
	1				20,000	9,400
	20				400	9,000
	31				900	8,100
	31			1,600		9,700
	31				1,200	8,500

credit entries in the various accounts, using T accounts for simplicity. We have numbered each transaction for reference. In the transaction analysis and the resulting debits and credits, each entry resulting from a particular transaction is parenthetically keyed to the transaction number.

TRANSACTION (1):   On December 1, Dr. Cole deposited $30,000 of his personal funds in a special checking account for Cole Clinic.

   Analysis: This is the first transaction of Cole Clinic. The owner's initial contribution of capital increases both the assets and the equities of Cole Clinic. Specifically, the asset Cash is increased by $30,000, and the owner's equity account, A. B. Cole, Capital, is increased by the same amount. The entries are:

   Debit Cash $30,000   **Credit** A. B. Cole, Capital $30,000

The related T accounts would appear as follows:

(assets)   *Q, E)*

Cash		A. B. Cole, Capital	
(1) 30,000			(1) 30,000

TRANSACTION (2):   On December 1, a $600 check was written to pay December's rent for office space.

   Analysis: The cost of using the office is a December operating expense. When financial statements are prepared at the end of December, the month's rent will appear on the income statement as an expense. Thus, the result of the transaction is to reduce Cash and increase Rent Expense. The entries are:

   Debit Rent Expense $600   **Credit** Cash $600

The related accounts would appear as follows:

(assets)   *(Expense)*

Cash		Rent Expense	
(1) 30,000	(2) 600	(2) 600	

TRANSACTION (3): On December 1, Dr. Cole purchased medical equipment for the clinic for $20,000 cash.

Analysis: This transaction represents the conversion of one asset to another, resulting in an increase in the asset Equipment and a decrease in the asset Cash. The entries are:

Debit Equipment $20,000   **Credit** Cash $20,000

The related accounts would appear as follows:

			(assets)				(assets)	
		Cash					Equipment	
(1)	30,000	(2)	600		(3)	20,000		
		(3)	20,000					

TRANSACTION (4):   On December 5, $800 worth of medical supplies were purchased on account.

Analysis: Dr. Cole purchased the medical supplies he needed on credit terms rather than for cash. This transaction increases both the asset Supplies on Hand and the liability Accounts Payable. At the end of the month, supplies will be counted to determine the amount used during the month. The asset will then be reduced and the related expense increased [see transaction (11)]. Whenever any business firm pays for services in advance, the amount is customarily recorded as an asset. As portions of such services are consumed, the asset is reduced and entries are made in expense accounts to reflect the amount used. A familiar example is the prepayment of insurance. If the premium on a 12-month policy is paid in advance, the asset account Prepaid Insurance is debited for the premium. At the end of each month, the expired portion (1/12 of the original premium) is deducted from the asset account and recorded as Insurance Expense. Other examples, such as prepaid advertising and prepaid rent, are also common in business. The entries to record the purchase of supplies are:

Debit Supplies on Hand $800   **Credit** Accounts Payable $800

The related accounts would appear as follows:

	(asset)				(Liability)	
	Supplies on Hand				Accounts Payable	
(4)	800				(4)	800

TRANSACTION (5):   On December 15, Dr. Cole billed his patients for $2,600 for services performed during the first half of December.

Analysis: As is customary, Dr. Cole received no cash at the time he performed his services. Instead, his patients agreed to pay the amounts to be billed them at a later date. Thus, by performing services on account, Dr. Cole increased the asset Accounts Receivable and increased revenue in the form of Professional Fees. The entries are:

Debit Accounts Receivable $2,600   *Credit* Professional Fees $2,600

The related accounts would appear as follows:

Accounts Receivable		Professional Fees	
(5) 2,600			(5) 2,600

TRANSACTION (6): On December 20, Dr. Cole mailed a $400 check to the supplier from whom he purchased medical supplies on December 5. This was partial payment of the account.

Analysis: Dr. Cole's check reduced by $400 the supplier's claim against the assets of Cole Clinic. This transaction involves a decrease in assets and a decrease in a liability; the effect is to reduce Cash and Accounts Payable. The entries are:

Debit Accounts Payable $400   **Credit** Cash $400

The related accounts would appear as follows:

Cash			Accounts Payable		
(1) 30,000	(2) 600		(6) 400	(4) 800	
	(3) 20,000				
	(6) 400				

TRANSACTION (7): On December 31, Dr. Cole paid the salary of $900 to the nurse he hired to assist him in his office.

Analysis: The services received from the nurse during the month represent an expense that will be shown on the income statement prepared at the end of December. Therefore, this transaction is recorded as an increase in expense (Salaries Expense) and a decrease in the asset Cash. The entries are:

Debit Salaries Expense $900   **Credit** Cash $900

The related accounts would appear as follows:

	Cash					Salaries Expense	
(1)	30,000	(2)	600		(7)	900	
		(3)	20,000				
		(6)	400				
		(7)	900				

TRANSACTION (8):   On December 31, Dr. Cole received $1,600 from patients in response to the bills sent out on December 15.

   Analysis: Receipt of this sum represents the collection of claims against patients, not new revenues. Recall that the related revenues were recorded in transaction (5), when the claims against patients were recognized as the asset Accounts Receivable. The essence of this transaction is to change one asset form (Accounts Receivable) into another asset form (Cash). Cash is increased and Accounts Receivable is decreased. The entries are:

   Debit Cash $1,600   **Credit** Accounts Receivable $1,600

The related accounts would appear as follows:

	Cash					Accounts Receivable	
(1)	30,000	(2)	600		(5)	2,600	(8)	1,600
(8)	1,600	(3)	20,000				
		(6)	400				
		(7)	900				

TRANSACTION (9):   On December 31, Dr. Cole billed his patients $2,500 for professional services rendered during the last half of December.

   Analysis: The transaction is similar to transaction (5). The result is an increase in the asset Accounts Receivable and an increase in revenue in the form of Professional Fees. The entries are:

   Debit Accounts Receivable $2,500   **Credit** Professional Fees $2,500

The related accounts would appear as follows:

	Accounts Receivable					Professional Fees	
(5)	2,600	(8)	1,600			(5)	2,600
(9)	2,500					(9)	2,500

TRANSACTION (10): On December 31, Dr. Cole withdrew $1,200 from the Clinic for his personal use.

Analysis: Dr. Cole has withdrawn this amount for his personal living expenses. The effect is to reduce the asset Cash and to decrease Dr. Cole's equity in the assets of the Cole Clinic.

Although the reduction in owner's equity may be entered as a debit directly to the A. B. Cole, Capital account, Dr. Cole prefers to have a separate account show all his withdrawals. The use of a separate account, called the **drawing** account, makes it easy for a proprietor to determine quickly the total amounts withdrawn during a period, without having to analyze the capital account. Drawing accounts (sometimes called *personal* accounts) are commonly used in sole proprietorships and partnerships. The account, A. B. Cole, Drawing, is called a **contra** account because its balance represents a reduction, or offset, to its related account, A. B. Cole, Capital. Debiting the drawing account to reflect the reduction in owner's equity has the same effect as debiting the owner's capital account. At the end of the period, after the net income has been added to the credit balance in the owner's capital account, the debit balance in the drawing account is deducted to arrive at the ending amount of owner's capital. Thus, the entries for Cole's withdrawal are:

Debit A. B. Cole, Drawing $1,200   **Credit** Cash $1,200

The related accounts would appear as follows:

Cash				A. B. Cole, Drawing	
(1)	30,000	(2)	600	(10)	1,200
(8)	1,600	(3)	20,000		
		(6)	400		
		(7)	900		
		(10)	1,200		

TRANSACTION (11): On December 31, Dr. Cole counted the supplies and found that an amount costing $300 was on hand.

Analysis: In transaction (4), supplies costing $800 were purchased and recorded as an asset. Since supplies on hand now amount to only $300, apparently the $500 difference represents the supplies used during December. As we explained in the analysis of transaction (4), supplies *used* are an expense of December. Thus, an entry should be made to reduce Supplies on Hand by $500 and increase Supplies Expense by $500. The entries are:

Debit Supplies Expense $500   **Credit** Supplies on Hand $500

The related accounts would appear as follows:

Supplies on Hand				Supplies Expense	
(4)	800	(11)	500	(11)	500

TRANSACTION (12): On December 31, Dr. Cole estimated that he would be billed $140 in January for utility services received in December.

Analysis: Because the $140 utilities services were used in December, they must be reflected as expense in this month. Likewise, a liability for the services has accrued, which must be reflected in the balance sheet prepared at the end of the period, inasmuch as payment will not be made until the utility bill is received in January. The entries are:

Debit Utilities Expense $140   **Credit** Accounts Payable $140

The related accounts would appear as follows:

Utilities Expense			Accounts Payable		
(12)	140		(6)	400	(4) 800
					(12) 140

TRANSACTION (13): On December 31, Dr. Cole estimated that the depreciation on his medical equipment for December amounted to $180.

Analysis: Through its use, Dr. Cole's medical equipment helps him earn professional fees. Since the equipment has a limited life, its cost becomes an operating expense over its useful life. In a sense, the medical equipment is being partially used up each month. The effect of this is to reduce the asset Equipment and increase the expense Depreciation. Although the reduction in the amount of the asset may be recorded by crediting the Equipment account directly, it is better to record the reduction in a contra account called **Accumulated Depreciation.** As we explained in Chapter 1, the reason for this procedure is that when a balance sheet is later prepared, the asset Equipment can be shown at its original cost with the accumulated amount of depreciation deducted separately. Readers of the balance sheet are thus informed of the aggregate size of the original investment in fixed assets, together with the total amount subsequently "written off" to depreciation. The entries for the Cole Clinic are:

Debit Depreciation Expense $180   **Credit** Accumulated Depreciation $180

The related accounts would appear as follows:

Accumulated Depreciation		Depreciation Expense	
(13)	180	(13)	180

After the foregoing transactions have been entered properly, the account balances can be determined. The accounts of the Cole Clinic are shown in Exhibit 2–5 (see pp. 56–57), together with the financial statements prepared from the balances of these accounts. Observe the following:

(1) Accounts accumulate data, especially revenue and expense accounts, which provide data for the income statement.

(2) Keying transactions permits tracing any entry to both its originating transaction and its related change in some other account.

(3) Dr. Cole's equity of $31,580 at the end of December can be shown to result from:

(a) His original capital contribution	$30,000
(b) Plus his earnings for December	2,780
	$32,780
(c) Minus his withdrawals	1,200
Ending balance in balance sheet	$31,580

(4) Using the two contra accounts (Accumulated Depreciation and A. B. Cole, Drawing) does not change the net amount of equipment or owner's equity shown on the financial statements.

The December activities of the Cole Clinic that we have just analyzed included both transactions with individuals, for which documents such as bills or checks are usually available, and activities that are sometimes described as **internal** transactions. For example, items (11), (12), and (13), reflecting supplies used, utilities expense, and depreciation expense, are internal in the sense that they represent adjustments to accounts not initiated by documents. In Chapter 3 you will learn that entries for adjustments are usually made at a particular point and are a significant part of the accounting process.

EXHIBIT 2-5

The Accounts and Financial Statements of Cole Clinic

debit / credit

Assets	=	Liabilities	+	Owner's Equity
(+)	(−)		(−)	(+)		

Cash

(1)	30,000	(2)	600
(8)	1,600	(3)	20,000
		(6)	400
		(7)	900
		(10)	1,200
Bal.	8,500		

Accounts Receivable

(5)	2,600	(8)	1,600
(9)	2,500		
Bal.	3,500		

Supplies on Hand

(4)	800	(11)	500
Bal.	300		

Equipment

(3)	20,000	

Accumulated Depreciation

	(13)	180

Accounts Payable

(6)	400	(4)	800
		(12)	140
		Bal.	540

A. B. Cole, Capital *(Initial Earnings)*

(−)	(1)	30,000 (+)

A. B. Cole, Drawing *(Withdrawals)*

(10)	1,200

Professional Fees *(Revenue)*

(−)	(5)	2,600 (+)
	(9)	2,500
	Bal.	5,100

Rent Expense *(Expense)*

(2)	600 (+)

Salaries Expense

(7)	900

Supplies Expense

(11)	500

Utilities Expense

(12)	140

Depreciation Expense

(13)	180

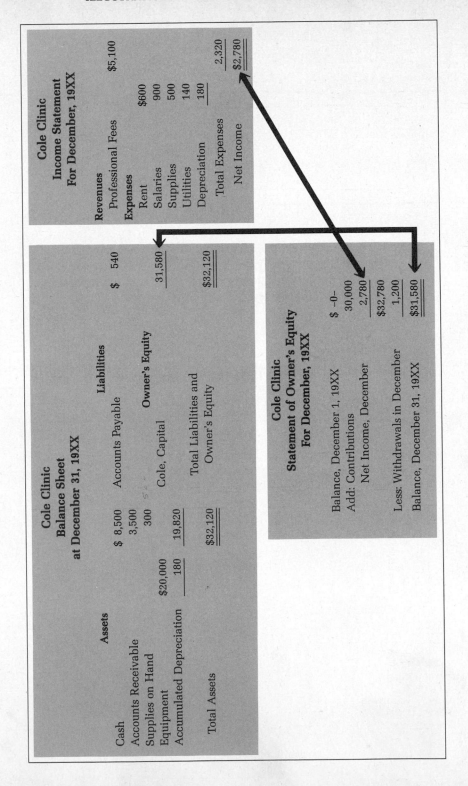

Cole Clinic
Income Statement
For December, 19XX

Revenues		
Professional Fees		$5,100
Expenses		
Rent	$600	
Salaries	900	
Supplies	500	
Utilities	140	
Depreciation	180	
Total Expenses		2,320
Net Income		$2,780

Cole Clinic
Balance Sheet
at December 31, 19XX

Assets

Cash		$ 8,500
Accounts Receivable		3,500
Supplies on Hand		300
Equipment	$20,000	
Accumulated Depreciation	180	19,820
Total Assets		$32,120

Liabilities

Accounts Payable	$ 540

Owner's Equity

Cole, Capital	31,580
Total Liabilities and Owner's Equity	$32,120

Cole Clinic
Statement of Owner's Equity
For December, 19XX

Balance, December 1, 19XX		$ -0-
Add: Contributions		30,000
Net Income, December		2,780
		$32,780
Less: Withdrawals in December		1,200
Balance, December 31, 19XX		$31,580

THE GENERAL LEDGER AND THE TRIAL BALANCE

The **general ledger** is the grouping or binding of the accounts that are used to prepare financial statements for a business. The 14 accounts that we used in our example for the Cole Clinic would each constitute a page in the general ledger, which is usually maintained in a binder so that, when necessary, accounts may be added or removed. Usually, the accounts are grouped by category in the following order: (1) assets, (2) liabilities, (3) owners' equity, (4) revenues, and (5) expenses.

The **trial balance** is a list of the account titles in the ledger with their respective debit or credit balances. It is prepared at the close of an accounting period after transactions have been recorded. Exhibit 2-6 illustrates a trial balance for the Cole Clinic at the end of December.

The two main reasons for preparing a trial balance are:

(1) To serve as an interim mechanical check to determine if the debits and credits in the general ledger are equal.

EXHIBIT 2-6

Cole Clinic
Trial Balance
December 31, 19XX

	Balances	
	Debit	Credit
Cash	$ 8,500	
Accounts Receivable	3,500	
Supplies on Hand	300	
Equipment	20,000	
Accumulated Depreciation		$ 180
Accounts Payable		540
A. B. Cole, Capital		30,000
A. B. Cole, Drawing	1,200	
Professional Fees		5,100
Rent Expense	600	
Salaries Expense	900	
Supplies Expense	500	
Utilities Expense	140	
Depreciation Expense	180	
Totals	$35,820	$35,820

(2) To show all general ledger account balances on one concise record. This is often convenient when preparing financial statements.

Note that a trial balance should be dated; the trial balance of the Cole Clinic was taken at December 31, 19XX.

ERRORS IN TRANSACTION ANALYSIS

It is always reassuring, of course, when a trial balance does balance. Even when a trial balance is in balance, however, there still may be errors in the accounting records. A balanced trial balance simply proves that, *as recorded,* the debits equal the credits. Among those errors that may not be detected by taking a trial balance are the following:

(1) Failing to record or enter a particular transaction.

(2) Entering a transaction more than once.

(3) Entering one or more amounts in the wrong accounts.

(4) Making a compensating error that exactly offsets the effect of another error.

Several types of errors will cause a trial balance to be out of balance. If only one of these is present, it may be identified and located by one of the approaches suggested below. If several errors exist, however, often the only way to find them is to retrace each entry, check the arithmetic performed in balancing the accounts, and make certain that no error has occurred in transcribing amounts or in adding the trial balance. If it is necessary to search for errors, one should systematically follow certain procedures so that all steps are retraced only once and no steps are overlooked.

When there is a mistake in a trial balance, the first step is to determine the amount by which the total debits and credits disagree. Certain characteristics of this amount may provide a clue to identifying the type of error and finding where it was made.

DEBITS AND CREDITS INTERCHANGED   When a debit is entered as a credit (or vice versa), the trial balance totals will differ by twice the amount involved. For example, if the credits exceed the debits by $246, one should look for a $123 debit that has been treated as a credit. Note that with this type of error, the amount of the discrepancy in the trial balance totals is divisible by two. If this is not the case, either another type of error or a number of errors are involved.

ARITHMETIC ERRORS   Single arithmetic errors frequently cause a trial balance totals to differ by amounts such as $1,000, $100, $1, and so on. Multiple arithmetic errors may either combine or offset and result in discrepancies such as $990 (errors of $1,000 and $10 offsetting) and $101 (errors of $100 and $1 combining).

✱ TRANSPOSITION OF NUMBERS Transposing numbers is simply reversing their order. For example, transposing the first two digits in $360 would result in $630. This type of error usually occurs when amounts are transcribed from one record to another. The resulting discrepancy is easily identified because it is always divisible by 9 ($630 − $360 = $270, and $270/9 = $30). Therefore, if total debits exceeded total credits by $270, one would suspect a transposition error.

(÷9)

✱ AMOUNTS OMITTED An amount can be omitted if one enters only part of an entry, fails to include an entry when balancing an account, or leaves out an account balance in a trial balance. The resulting discrepancy is equal in amount to the omitted item. Of course, the omission of a debit amount will cause an excess of credits by that amount, and vice versa.

KEY POINTS TO REMEMBER

(1) In recording changes in owners' equity, the primary reason for segregating revenue and expense items is to facilitate preparation of the income statement.

(2) The rules of debit and credit are:
   (a) The left side of an account is always the debit side; the right side is always the credit side.
   (b) Increases in assets and expenses are debit entries; increases in liabilities, owners' equity, and revenues are credit entries.
   (c) The normal balance of any account appears on the side for recording increases.

(3) In transaction analysis:
   (a) Each business transaction should be analyzed into equal debits and credits.
   (b) All business transactions are analyzed using one or more of the five basic account categories: (1) assets, (2) liabilities, (3) owners' equity, (4) revenues, and (5) expenses.

QUESTIONS

2-1 Why is it useful to record revenues and expenses separately from the owner's capital account?

2-2 Name the five categories of information needed to prepare the balance sheet and the income statement. Which categories are identified with the balance sheet? Which are identified with the income statement?

2-3 What information is recorded in an account?

2-4 Identify the following as asset, liability, owner's equity, revenue, or expense accounts and indicate whether a debit entry or a credit entry is required to increase the balance of the account:

Professional Fees	Adams, Capital
Accounts Receivable	Depreciation Expense
Accounts Payable	Supplies on Hand

2-5 Indicate the normal balance (whether debit or credit) of each account in Question 2-4.

2-6 Justify the use of the contra account Accumulated Depreciation when recording depreciation.

2-7 What is the justification for using a separate owner's drawing account?

2-8 "During the year the total owner's equity of Avon Florist increased from $33,000 to $45,000. Therefore, the annual earnings must have been $12,000." Is this statement necessarily true? Explain.

2-9 Explain why purchases of supplies are usually charged to an asset account rather than to an expense account.

2-10 Describe three distinct types of errors that may be present even when a trial balance is in balance.

2-11 "A trial balance is a list showing all account titles in the general ledger and the total of debits and credits in each account." Do you agree with this statement? Why or why not?

2-12 Discuss the types of errors that may be present in each of the following independent sets of trial balance totals:

	Trial Balance Totals	
Trial Balance	**Debits**	**Credits**
A	$76,150	$77,150
B	54,780	55,050
C	36,224	36,335
D	65,668	67,392
E	41,269	41,929

2-13 The assistant bookkeeper of Ward Printers prepared a trial balance that had total debits of $94,200 and total credits of $98,280. Compute the correct trial balance totals by assuming that only the following errors were involved:
(1) Accounts Payable of $5,160 was listed as a debit.
(2) During the current period a $500 check for Salaries Expense was debited to Office Expense.
(3) Supplies on Hand of $3,600 had been omitted.
(4) Depreciation Expense of $3,600 was included twice as a credit.

EXERCISES

2-14 Make T accounts for the following accounts that appear in the general ledger of A. C. Buckley, a veterinarian: Cash; Accounts Receivable; Supplies on Hand;

Office Equipment; Accounts Payable; A. C. Buckley, Capital; A. C. Buckley, Drawing; Professional Fees; Salaries Expense; Rent Expense. Next, record the following transactions in the T accounts and key all entries with the number identifying the transaction. Finally, prove equality of debits and credits by preparing a trial balance.

✓ (1) Buckley opened a checking account on December 1 at the United Bank in the name of Animal Hospital and deposited $20,000.

✓ (2) Paid rent for December, $400.

✓ (3) Purchased office equipment on account, as follows: desks, $600; typewriters, $750; filing cabinets, $400; and chairs, $650.

✓ (4) Purchased supplies for cash, $300.

✓ (5) Billed clients for services rendered, $2,800.

✓ (6) Paid secretary's salary, $950.

✓ (7) Paid $800 on account for the equipment purchased in (3) above.

✓ (8) Collected $900 from clients previously billed for services.

✓ (9) Withdrew $1,000 for personal use.

2-15 In the five independent situations below, replace the question marks with the amounts that should appear.

	A	B	C	D	E
Owner's Equity:					
Beginning Balance	$16,000	$42,000	$28,000	$ (?)	$47,000
Capital Contributions	14,000	23,000	(?)	8,000	5,000
Net Income (loss)	(?)	16,000	10,000	(3,000)	(?)
Capital Withdrawals	12,000	(?)	4,000	5,000	6,000
Ending Balance	$22,000	$45,000	$39,000	$11,000	$45,000

2-16 Match each of the following transactions of R. James, Cleaners, with the appropriate letters, indicating the debits and credits to be made. The correct answer for transaction (1) is given.

	Answer
(1) The owner contributed cash to the business.	a, f
(2) Purchased equipment on account.	_____
(3) Received and immediately paid advertising bill.	_____
(4) Purchased supplies for cash.	_____
(5) Borrowed money from bank, giving a note payable.	_____
(6) Billed customers.	_____
(7) Made partial payment on account for equipment.	_____
(8) Paid salary of employee.	_____
(9) Collected amounts due from customers billed in (6) above.	_____

Effect of Transaction

(a) Debit an asset	(f) Credit owner's capital
(b) Credit an asset	(g) Debit revenue
(c) Debit a liability	(h) Credit revenue
(d) Credit a liability	(i) Debit expense
(e) Debit owner's capital	(j) Credit expense

2-17 The accounts below are from the ledger of a local attorney. For each letter given in the T accounts, describe the type of business transaction(s) or event(s) that would most probably be reflected by entries on that side of the account. For example, the answer to (a) is: The amounts of services performed for clients on account.

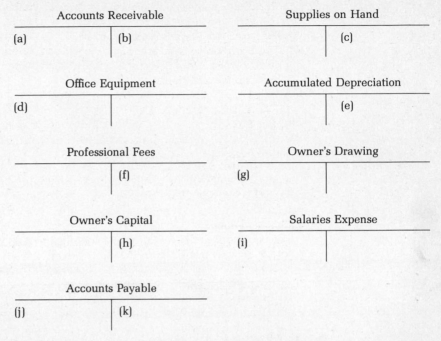

2-18 Using the data for each of the following five independent situations, compute the unknown amount required in each. The answer to situation (a) is given as an example.

Account	Beginning Balance	Ending Balance	Other Information
(a) Cash	$ 2,800	$ 4,650	Total cash disbursed, $6,200
(b) Accounts Receivable	3,000	2,800	Services on account, $4,000
(c) Supplies on Hand	650	290	Supplies used, $460 675 (?)
(d) Equipment (net of accumulated depreciation)	6,000	6,400	Equipment depreciation, $500
(e) Owner's Equity	18,000	17,900	Withdrawals, $9,300

Unknown Amounts Required:

(a) Total cash received $8,050

(b) Total amount received from credit customers   _____

(c) Supplies purchased during the period   _____

(d) Amount of equipment acquired   _____

(e) Capital contributions if net income was $2,700   _____

2–19 Indicate how each of the following errors would affect the trial balance totals. For each error, specify whether the debit or credit totals would be overstated, understated, or whether both totals would be unaffected.
  (1) The Accounts Receivable balance of $53,900 was listed in the trial balance as $59,300.
  (2) A $560 payment for Advertising Expense was debited to Office Expense during the accounting period.
  (3) The Accounts Payable balance of $33,200 was omitted from the trial balance.
  (4) The Depreciation Expense of $870 was listed in the trial balance as a credit.
  (5) The Owner's Drawing account, with a debit balance of $14,000 was listed as a credit in the trial balance.

PROBLEMS

2–20 James Sanchez opened a mailing service on May 1 of the current year. The following accounts will be needed to record his transactions for May: Cash; Accounts Receivable; Office Supplies on Hand; Prepaid Insurance; Office Furniture and Fixtures; Accumulated Depreciation; Notes Payable; Accounts Payable; J. Sanchez, Capital; J. Sanchez, Drawing; Fee Revenues; Rent Expense; Salaries Expense; Supplies Expense; Depreciation Expense; and Insurance Expense. The following transactions occurred in May:
  (1) Sanchez invested $10,000 in his business and opened a special checking account at the bank for the business.
  (2) Purchased office furniture and fixtures for $3,200; paid $1,200 in cash and gave a non-interest-bearing note payable for the balance.
  (3) Paid the premium for a one-year liability insurance policy, $360.
  (4) Purchased office supplies on account, $500.
  (5) Paid rent for May, $600.
  (6) Billed clients for professional services rendered, $3,700.
  (7) Paid $350 on account to stationers for the office supplies purchased in (4) above.
  (8) Collected $1,500 on account from clients billed in (6) above.
  (9) Paid salaries for May, $1,800.
  (10) Withdrew $300 for personal use.
  (11) Counted supplies on hand at May 31, $280.
  (12) Estimated depreciation for May on office furniture and fixtures, $40.
  (13) One month's insurance premium expired during May.

  REQUIRED
  (a) Record the above transactions in T accounts, and key entries with the numbers of the transactions.
  (b) Prepare a trial balance of the general ledger as of May 31.

2–21 The following account balances, in alphabetical order, are from the ledger of Bowen's Cleaning Shops at January 31, 19XX. The firm's accounting year began on January 1. All accounts had normal balances.

Accumulated Depreciation	$ 7,500
Accounts Payable	9,500

Accounts Receivable	$16,500
Bowen, Capital	40,000
Bowen, Drawing	2,400
Cash	4,600
Depreciation Expense	3,000
Equipment	38,000
Fee Revenue	60,000
Rent Expense	9,000
Salaries Expense	30,000
Supplies Expense	7,200
Supplies on Hand	3,500
Utilities Expense	2,800

REQUIRED

(a) Prepare a trial balance in good form from the given data.

(b) Prepare an income statement for the month of January.

(c) Prepare a balance sheet at January 31.

2-22 The following T accounts contain numbered entries for the May transactions of Nancy Bradshaw, a consulting engineer, who opened her offices on May 1 of the current year:

Cash				N. Bradshaw, Capital			
(1)	15,000	(2)	4,000			(1)	15,000
(9)	600	(4)	600				
		(6)	800				
		(8)	500				

Accounts Receivable				N. Bradshaw, Drawing			
(5)	2,400	(9)	600	(8)	500		

Supplies on Hand				Professional Fees			
(3)	1,200	(7)	450			(5)	2,400

Office Equipment				Rent Expense			
(2)	4,000			(4)	600		

Accounts Payable				Supplies Expense			
(6)	800	(3)	1,200	(7)	450		

REQUIRED

(a) Give a reasonable description of each of the nine numbered transactions entered in the above accounts. Example: (1) Nancy Bradshaw invested $15,000 of her personal funds in her consulting business.

(b) The following trial balance, taken for Bradshaw's firm on May 31, contains several errors. Itemize the errors and indicate the correct totals for the trial balance.

Nancy Bradshaw, Consultant
Trial Balance
May 31, 19XX

	Debit	Credit
Cash	$ 7,900	
Accounts Receivable	2,400	
Supplies on Hand	750	
Office Equipment	4,000	
Accounts Payable		$ 400
N. Bradshaw, Capital		15,000
N. Bradshaw, Drawing	500	500
Professional Fees		2,400
Rent Expense	600	
	$15,650	$18,300

2-23 Robert Hayes owns Pronto-Print, a fast copy service. On July 1 of the current year his ledger contained the following account balances:

Cash	$ 5,000	Accumulated Depreciation	$ 6,200
Accounts Receivable	1,800	Notes Payable	5,000
Prepaid Insurance	30	Accounts Payable	3,250
Supplies on Hand	3,600	Robert Hayes, Capital	23,980
Equipment	28,000		

The following transactions occurred in July:

(1) Paid rent for July, $650.
(2) Collected $800 on account from customers.
(3) Paid $1,000 installment due on the non-interest-bearing note payable of $5,000.
(4) Billed customers for duplicating and collating services rendered, $5,500.
(5) Rendered copy services for cash, $800.
(6) Purchased various supplies on account, $550.
(7) Paid $1,200 to creditors on account.
(8) Collected $2,300 on account from customers.
(9) Paid $150 to cab company for the delivery of copy work to commercial firms.
(10) Paid July salaries, $1,850.
(11) On July 31, renewed for one year insurance policies expiring on this date; annual premium of $360 was paid.
(12) Counted supplies inventory amounting to $2,150.
(13) Recorded depreciation for July, $300.

(14) Withdrew $500 for personal use.

(15) Recorded insurance expense for July.

REQUIRED

(a) Set up the appropriate T accounts, and enter the beginning balances. Also provide the following T accounts: Robert Hayes, Drawing; Service Revenue; Rent Expense; Salaries Expense; Delivery Expense; Supplies Expense; Insurance Expense; and Depreciation Expense. Record the listed transactions in the T accounts, and key entries with transaction numbers.

(b) Prepare a trial balance at July 31.

(c) Prepare an income statement for July.

(d) Prepare a statement of owner's equity for July.

(e) Prepare a balance sheet as of July 31.

2-24 Carol Roberts owns and operates Dentalab, serving more than fifty dentists in the city. Her trial balance at October 1 of the current year was as follows:

Dentalab
Trial Balance
October 1, 19XX

	Debit	Credit
Cash	$ 8,200	
Accounts Receivable	12,500	
Supplies on Hand	8,500	
Furniture and Equipment	32,000	
Accumulated Depreciation		$ 4,200
Notes Payable		6,000
Accounts Payable		9,000
Roberts, Capital		42,000
	$61,200	$61,200

During October the following transactions occurred:

(1)	Oct.	2	Paid October rent, $1,200.
(2)		4	Purchased equipment on account, $800.
(3)		7	Purchased supplies on account, $3,100.
(4)		8	Collected $6,500 from client dentists on account.
(5)		9	Paid $2,500 to creditors on account.
(6)		15	Billed client dentists for services, $14,800.
(7)		20	Collected $6,300 from client dentists in payment of their accounts.
(8)		25	Paid a $4,500 note payable due today. The note was payable to a relative of Carol Roberts and was non-interest bearing.
(9)		31	Paid salaries of technicians and assistants, $5,200.
(10)		31	Billed client dentists for services, $8,700.
(11)		31	Withdrew $600 for personal use.
		31	Estimated the following:
(12)			Utilities Expense for October, $150.
(13)			Depreciation Expense for October, $350.
(14)			Supplies on Hand, October 31, $6,200.

REQUIRED

(a) Set up T accounts for each item in the October 1 trial balance. Also, provide these additional accounts: Roberts, Drawing; Professional Fees; Rent Expense; Salaries Expense; Utilities Expense; Depreciation Expense; and Supplies Expense. Record the balances from the trial balance in the accounts.

(b) Record the October transactions in the accounts, and key entries with the numbers of the transactions.

(c) Take a trial balance at October 31.

(d) Calculate the net income for October.

(e) Prepare a balance sheet as of October 31.

2-25 The ABC Corporation operates two car wash facilities in the city. The balance sheet for the company at December 31, 19X0, is as follows:

ABC Corporation
Balance Sheet
December 31, 19X0

Assets			Liabilities and Stockholders' Equity		
Cash		$ 18,000	Accounts Payable		$ 7,400
Accounts Receivable		22,000	Notes Payable		15,000
Prepaid Insurance		2,400	Total Liabilities		$ 22,400
Supplies on Hand		8,000	Common Stock	$100,000	
Land		20,000	Retained Earnings	20,000	
Buildings	$45,000		Total Stockholders' Equity		120,000
Less: Accumulated Depreciation	3,000	42,000			
Equipment	$34,000				
Less: Accumulated Depreciation	4,000	30,000	Total Liabilities and		
Total Assets		$142,400	Stockholders' Equity		$142,400

During January, 19X1, the firm engaged in the following transactions:

(1) Rendered services as follows:
   Car washes for cash, $18,000
   Fleet car washes on account, $32,000
(2) Paid salaries of $12,000.
(3) Purchased supplies on account, $3,100.
(4) Paid non-interest-bearing note, $10,000.
(5) Collected $25,000 on account.
(6) Paid $4,200 on accounts payable.
(7) Paid $570 for advertising.
(8) Declared and paid a dividend to stockholders, $4,000.
(9) Recorded insurance expired in January, $200.
(10) Estimated January utilities expense, $3,800.
(11) Estimated January 31 supplies on hand, $5,200.
(12) Estimated January depreciation on buildings, $250.
(13) Estimated January depreciation on equipment, $320.

REQUIRED

(a) Set up T accounts for each item in the December 31, 19X0, balance sheet. Also, provide the following T accounts: Car Wash Revenue; Salaries Expense; Advertising Expense; Insurance Expense; Utilities Expense; Supplies Expense; Depreciation Expense—Buildings; and Depreciation Expense—Equipment. Record the balances from the December 31, 19X0, balance sheet. Next, record the listed transactions for January in the T accounts, and key entries with transaction numbers.

(b) Prepare a trial balance at January 31, 19X1.

(c) Prepare an income statement for January.

(d) Prepare a balance sheet at January 31, 19X1.

ALTERNATE PROBLEMS

2-20A Sandra Clark began her accounting practice on June 1 of the current year. The following accounts will be needed to record her transactions for June: Cash; Accounts Receivable; Office Supplies on Hand; Prepaid Insurance; Office Furniture and Fixtures; Accumulated Depreciation; Notes Payable; Accounts Payable; S. Clark, Capital; S. Clark, Drawing; Professional Fees; Rent Expense; Salaries Expense; Supplies Expense; Depreciation Expense; and Insurance Expense. The following transactions occurred in June:

(1) Clark invested $6,000 in her practice and opened a special checking account at the bank for the business.

(2) Purchased office furniture and fixtures for $3,500, paid $2,000 in cash and gave a non-interest-bearing note payable for the balance.

(3) Paid the premium for a one-year liability insurance policy, $480.

(4) Purchased office supplies on account, $280.

(5) Paid rent for June, $400.

(6) Billed clients for professional services rendered, $2,800.

(7) Paid $180 on account to stationers for the office supplies purchased in (4) above.

(8) Collected $900 on account from clients billed in (6) above.

(9) Paid salaries for June, $1,100.

(10) Withdrew $400 for personal use.

(11) Counted supplies on hand at June 30, $150.

(12) Estimated depreciation for June on office furniture and fixtures, $60.

(13) One month's insurance premium expired during June.

REQUIRED

(a) Record the above transactions in T accounts, and key entries with the numbers of the transactions.

(b) Prepare a trial balance of the general ledger as of June 30.

2–21A The following account balances were taken (out of order) from the ledger of J. Arkin, Travel Service at January 31, 19XX. The firm's accounting year began on January 1. All accounts had normal balances.

Prepaid Insurance	$ 550
Insurance Expense	50
Supplies on Hand	2,350
Depreciation Expense	250
Common Stock	28,200
Cash	12,800
Accounts Payable	3,000
Accumulated Depreciation	1,700
Rent Expense	1,500
Supplies Expense	600
Utilities Expense	300
Equipment	20,000
Fee Revenue	20,500
Accounts Receivable	6,500
Salaries Expense	10,200
Retained Earnings	1,700

REQUIRED
(a) Prepare a trial balance in good form from the given data.
(b) Prepare an income statement for the month of January.
(c) Prepare a balance sheet at January 31.

2–22A The following T accounts contain numbered entries for the May transactions of Cliff Evans, an attorney, who opened his offices on May 1 of the current year:

Cash					Cliff Evans, Capital		
(1)	7,000	(2)	3,000			(1)	7,000
(10)	1,200	(4)	600				
		(6)	360				
		(8)	500				
		(9)	400				

Accounts Receivable					Cliff Evans, Drawing	
(5)	1,850	(10)	1,200		(8)	500

Prepaid Insurance					Professional Fees		
(6)	360	(11)	30			(5)	1,850

Supplies on Hand					Rent Expense	
(3)	600	(7)	100		(4)	600

Office Equipment		Insurance Expense	
(2) 3,000		(11) 30	

Accounts Payable		Supplies Expense	
(9) 400	(3) 600	(7) 100	

REQUIRED

(a) Give a reasonable description of each of the eleven numbered transactions entered in the above accounts. Example: (1) Cliff Evans invested $7,000 of his personal funds in his law firm.

(b) The following trial balance, taken for Evans's firm on May 31, contains several errors. Itemize the errors, and indicate the correct totals for the trial balance.

Cliff Evans, Attorney
Trial Balance
May 31, 19XX

	Debit	Credit
Cash	$3,430	
Accounts Receivable	850	
Supplies on Hand	600	
Office Equipment	3,000	
Accounts Payable		$ 200
C. Evans, Capital		7,000
C. Evans, Drawing		500
Professional Fees		1,850
Rent Expense	600	
Insurance Expense	30	
Supplies Expense	100	
	$8,610	$9,550

2–23A Ann Parker owns and operates the Elite Catering Service, which specializes in weddings, banquets, and church affairs. On June 1 of the current year, the firm's ledger contains the following account balances:

Cash	$5,000	Delivery Equipment	$ 4,500
Accounts Receivable	1,200	Accumulated Depreciation—	
Prepaid Insurance	30	Delivery Equipment	500
Supplies on Hand	3,500	Notes Payable	1,500
Catering Equipment	5,700	Accounts Payable	1,800
Accumulated Depreciation—		A. Parker, Capital	15,500
Catering Equipment	630		

The following transactions occurred in June:
(1) Paid rent for June, $450.
(2) Collected $800 on account from customers.
(3) Paid $750 installment due on the non-interest-bearing note payable of
$1,500.
(4) Billed customers for catering services rendered, $3,000.
(5) Rendered catering services for cash, $420.
(6) Purchased various supplies on account, $700.
(7) Paid $650 to creditors on account.
(8) Collected $2,400 on account from customers.
(9) Paid $120 for fuel expense.
(10) Paid June salaries, $900.
(11) On June 30, renewed for one year insurance policies expiring on this date;
annual premium of $360 was paid.
(12) Counted supplies inventory amounting to $1,200.
(13) Recorded depreciation on catering equipment for June, $50.
(14) Recorded depreciation on delivery equipment for June, $90.
(15) Withdrew $500 for personal use.
(16) Recorded insurance expense for June.

REQUIRED
(a) Set up the appropriate T accounts and enter the beginning balances. Also
provide the following T accounts: A. Parker, Drawing; Service Revenue;
Rent Expense; Salaries Expense; Fuel Expense; Supplies Expense; Insurance Expense; Depreciation Expense—Catering Equipment; and Depreciation Expense—Delivery Equipment. Record the listed transactions in the
T accounts, and key entries with transaction numbers.
(b) Prepare a trial balance at June 30.
(c) Prepare an income statement for June.
(d) Prepare a statement of owner's equity for June.
(e) Prepare a balance sheet as of June 30.

2–25A On December 1 of the current year, a group of individuals formed a corporation, Rollerdrome, Inc., to purchase and operate a skating rink. The December
transactions are summarized below:
(1) Dec. 1 Sold $120,000 capital stock for cash.
(2)   2 Purchased a skating facility that included the following: equipment, $9,000; building, $60,000; land, $8,000. The purchase was
made by giving $40,000 cash and a long-term mortgage note pay-
able for the balance.
(3)   5 Paid $960 for a one-year insurance policy.
(4)   6 Paid $220 for advertising.
(5)   9 Purchased supplies on account, $580.
(6)   21 Total admission receipts for the first full week of operation (the
rink opened December 14) were $3,200.
(7)   24 Paid $200 on accounts payable.
(8)   31 Total admission receipts for December 22 through 31 were
$6,180.
(9)   31 Received $650 concession revenue from Canteen Sales, Inc. as
commission on concession sales.
(10)   31 Paid wages for month, $2,400.

(11)	31	Estimated the month's utilities expense, $450.
(12)	31	Estimated depreciation on building, $120.
(13)	31	Estimated depreciation on equipment, $90.
(14)	31	Estimated supplies on hand, $280.
(15)	31	Recorded one month's insurance expense. (See December 5 transaction.)

REQUIRED

(a) Set up the following T accounts: Cash, Prepaid Insurance, Supplies on Hand, Equipment, Accumulated Depreciation—Equipment, Building, Accumulated Depreciation—Building, Land, Accounts Payable, Mortgage Payable, Capital Stock, Admission Fees, Concession Revenue, Wages Expense, Advertising Expense, Supplies Expense, Insurance Expense, Utilities Expense, Depreciation Expense—Equipment, Depreciation Expense—Building. Record the listed transactions in the T accounts, and key entries with transaction numbers.

(b) Prepare a trial balance at December 31.

(c) Prepare an income statement for December.

(d) Prepare a balance sheet as of December 31.

BUSINESS DECISION PROBLEM

R. F. Matthews is a masonry contractor who specializes in remodeling work. He began business in January of the current year, but has not yet arranged for a formal set of records. Mrs. Matthews has prepared cash receipts and disbursements statements for each of the first three months of the year, but Mr. Matthews has become uneasy about relying on them. He asks you to prepare a "proper" set of financial statements for the month of March.

By reviewing the bank statements, check stubs, invoice files, and other data, you derive a set of balance sheets at March 1 and March 31. These are shown below, followed by a statement of cash receipts and disbursements for March.

Matthews Concrete and Masonry
Balance Sheets

Assets	March 31, 19XX	March 1, 19XX
Cash	$ 3,500	$ 2,100
Accounts Receivable	2,800	3,200
Supplies on Hand	1,000	1,200
Equipment	28,000	24,000
Accumulated Depreciation (credit)	(2,000)	(1,800)
	$33,300	$28,700
Liabilities and Owner's Equity		
Salaries Payable	$ 1,500	$ 1,200
Utilities Payable	200	-0-
R. F. Matthews, Capital	31,600	27,500
	$33,300	$28,700

Matthews Concrete and Masonry
Statement of Cash Receipts and Disbursements
March, 19XX

Cash Receipts

Received on account from customers	$ 7,700
Contributed by R. F. Matthews	3,000
Total cash receipts	$10,700

Cash Disbursements

Paid for supplies purchased	$1,400	
Purchase of equipment	4,000	
Payment of salaries	2,200	
Paid for March rent	300	
Miscellaneous expense	400	
Cash withdrawn by R. F. Matthews	1,000	
Total cash disbursements		9,300
Net increase in cash balance		$1,400

REQUIRED

(a) From the above information, prepare an income statement on the accrual basis for the month of March. To obtain the data needed, you may wish to reconstruct the accounts, using T accounts.

(b) Illustrate the apparent correctness of your net income amount by preparing a statement of owner's equity for March.

3
The
Accounting
Cycle

Ah, but my Computations, People say,
Reduced the Year to better Reckoning?

EDWARD FITZGERALD

The double-entry accounting system provides a basic framework for the analysis of business transactions. Now we wish to go into greater detail about the accounting procedures used to account for the operations of a business during a specific time period. The accounting procedures of most businesses involve certain basic steps that are accomplished in a given order. This sequence of procedures is known as the *accounting cycle.*

STEPS IN THE ACCOUNTING CYCLE

The **accounting cycle** can be divided into the following steps:

(1) Analyze transactions from source documents.

(2) Record in journals.

(3) Post to general ledger accounts.

(4) Adjust the general ledger accounts.

(5) Prepare financial statements.

(6) Close temporary accounts.

The steps in the accounting cycle enable the accountant to combine and summarize the net results of many business transactions into two relatively concise reports showing the financial position and the results of operations for a specific period of time. Even a medium-sized business has many thousands of transactions evidenced by one or more source documents (Step 1); these transactions are recorded and summarized (Step 2) in possibly only five or six journals. Next, data from these journals might be posted (Step 3) to one general ledger having, say, 100 accounts. After certain adjustments are made (Step 4), these accounts provide the balances necessary to prepare the two basic financial statements (Step 5). Much of the analytical usefulness of the accounting process is a result of this ability to condense and summarize business data.

The various steps in the accounting cycle do not occur with equal frequency. Usually, analyzing, journalizing, and posting (Steps 1–3) take place during each operating period, whereas accounts are adjusted and statements are prepared only when management requires financial statements—usually at monthly or quarterly intervals, but at least annually. Temporary accounts are customarily closed (Step 6) only at the end of the accounting year.

Business firms whose accounting year ends on December 31 are said to be on a **calendar-year** basis. Many firms prefer to have their accounting year coincide with their "natural" business year; thus the year ends when business is slow and inventory quantities are small and easier to count. At this time, end-of-year accounting procedures are most efficiently accomplished. For example, most department stores choose a year ending on the last day of January or February, when their inventories are depleted from the normally heavy holiday sales and from post-holiday clearance sales. An accounting year ending with a month other than December is called a **fiscal year.**

Frequency of Accounting Cycle Steps
Required for Quarterly Financial Statements

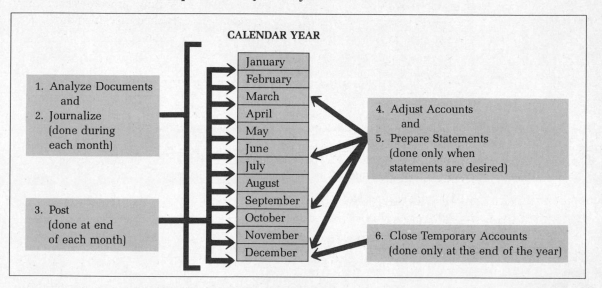

This diagram illustrates the timing of steps in the accounting cycle during a calendar year for a business that prepares quarterly financial statements.

In the remainder of this chapter and in Chapter 4, we shall explain the various steps in the accounting cycle. As an example, we use the first month's transactions of the Monroe TV Service, a repair business begun by Carl Monroe on December 1 of the current year.

SOURCE DOCUMENTS

Step 1: Analyze Transactions from Source Documents

Source documents are usually printed or written forms that are generated when the firm engages in business transactions. Even brief source documents usually specify the dollar amounts involved, the date of the transaction, and possibly the party dealing with the firm. Some examples of source documents are (1) a sales invoice received in evidence of a purchase of supplies on account, (2) a bank check indicating payment of an obligation, (3) a deposit slip showing the amount of funds turned over to the bank, (4) a cash receipt in evidence of funds received from a customer, and (5) a cash register tape listing a day's over-the-counter sales to customers.

Exhibit 3–1 lists the December transactions of the Monroe TV Service, to-

EXHIBIT 3–1

December Transactions
Monroe TV Service

Number	Date	Brief Description	Related Source Documents
(1)	Dec. 1	Carl Monroe deposited $20,000 in the firm's bank account.	Bank deposit slip
(2)	1	Paid December rent, $400.	Bank check
(3)	2	Purchased truck for $7,200 cash.	Bank check, invoice
(4)	2	Purchased test equipment for $3,000; paid $2,000 down; remainder to be paid in 60 days.	Seller's invoice, bank check
(5)	2	Signed two service contracts to perform:	Contract, dealer's check
		(a) Service work for a local TV dealer for four months, December through March, at $200 per month. Received $800 in advance.	
		(b) Service work for a local hotel at rate of $6 per hour. Settlement to be made whenever 50 hours of service has been rendered.	Contract, periodic bills
(6)	3	Purchased supplies and parts on account, $600.	Seller's invoice
(7)	7	Performed TV service for various customers during first week of December and received $550 in cash.	Duplicates of customer receipt forms
(8)	14	Billed various agencies and customers for TV service rendered on account, $750.	Bills to customers
(9)	14	Paid wages of assistant for first two weeks of December, $420.	Bank check
(10)	14	Performed TV service for various customers during second week of December and received $480 in cash.	Duplicates of customer receipt forms
(11)	17	Paid advertising bill, $50.	Invoice, bank check
(12)	19	Received $500 on account from customers.	Customers' checks
(13)	21	Performed TV service for various customers during third week of December and received $320 in cash.	Duplicates of customer receipt forms
(14)	28	Paid truck expenses (gas and oil), $170.	Invoice, bank check
(15)	28	Billed various agencies and customers for TV service rendered on account, $2,400.	Bills to customers
(16)	28	Paid wages of assistant for second two weeks of December, $420.	Bank check
(17)	28	Withdrew $600 for personal use.	Bank check
(18)	28	Performed TV service during fourth week in December and received $200 in cash.	Duplicates of customer receipt forms.

No Posting Req'd (handwritten note next to transaction 5b)

gether with their related source documents. Ordinarily, source documents or business papers such as those listed with the transactions in Exhibit 3-1 will alert the bookkeeper to the need for an entry in the records. Usually the bookkeeper is able to analyze the transaction by examining the documents to determine the appropriate accounts to be debited and credited. For example, in transaction (2), a scrutiny of the check stub from the rent payment would reveal the need for debiting Rent Expense and crediting Cash. In transaction (4) the seller's invoice or bill of sale would probably indicate both the cost of the equipment and the down payment. The check stub would further corroborate the amount paid, so that the bookkeeper would debit Test Equipment for $3,000, credit Cash for $2,000, and credit Accounts Payable for $1,000, the amount still owing.

Some transactions can be analyzed only by making further inquiry or by referring to previously received documents and the accounting records themselves. For example, let us consider the two contracts signed by Carl Monroe on December 2 (transaction 5). The mere signing of the contracts would not require bookkeeping entries, since the contracts are just agreements to provide services. In transaction (5a), however, Monroe TV Service received $800 in advance. This would require a debit to Cash and a credit to Unearned Service Fees; in this case, the Unearned Service Fees of $800 represents an obligation (liability) to provide services for four months. At the end of each of these months, an entry must be made to reduce the obligation and to reflect an appropriate amount in the revenue account Service Fees. To ensure the proper entry, the bookkeeper can refer to the terms of the contract or review the entry made when the advance was received.

As a result of transaction (5b) it would be necessary to record an account receivable from the hotel and to credit the revenue account Service Fees at the end of each accounting period. To do this, the bookkeeper might wish to check the terms of the contract to calculate the amounts of such entries. The periodic entries required to properly reflect the services rendered under these two contracts fall into the category of _adjusting entries;_ we describe these under Step 4 of the accounting cycle and show that such entries frequently require reference to previous accounting records.

JOURNALS

Step 2: Record in Journals

For simplicity, the entries we used in Chapter 2 were made directly into the general ledger accounts. This method would not prove feasible in reality, however, for even a modest-sized business. For instance, suppose an owner wished to investigate a $1,000 credit in the Cash account. If entries were actually recorded directly in the general ledger, it could be difficult to determine the purpose of the $1,000 expenditure. The owner might be forced to search through the entire general ledger to discover the offsetting debit of $1,000. Consequently, accounting records include a set of **journals,** or **records of original entry**, which show the total effect of a business transaction in one location.

Journals are tabular records in which business transactions are analyzed in terms of debits and credits and recorded in chronological order before they are entered in the general ledger. An accounting journal may be one of a group of special journals or it may be a general journal. A special journal is designed to record a specific type of frequently occurring business transaction. For example, a business with 100 employees who are paid every two weeks would probably find it desirable to use a special journal for payrolls. Because there would normally be two paydays in a month, there would be at least 200 payroll transactions to record. Other types of transactions that are often kept in special journals are cash receipts, cash disbursements, merchandise sales, and merchandise purchases.

In contrast to the special journals, the general journal is a relatively simple record in which any type of business transaction may be recorded. Transactions that do not occur often enough to warrant entry in a special journal are recorded in the general journal. All businesses, even those using many special journals, have a general journal. In this chapter, we shall illustrate only the use of a general journal; in Chapter 6 we will introduce the use of special journals.

Exhibit 3–2 shows the first four transactions from Exhibit 3–1 as they would appear after being recorded in Monroe's general journal. The procedure for recording entries in the general journal is as follows:

(1) Indicate the year, month, and date of the entry. Usually the year and month are rewritten only at the top of each page of the journal or at the point where they change.

(2) Enter titles of the accounts to be affected in the description column. Accounts to receive debits are entered close to the left-hand margin and are traditionally recorded first. Accounts to receive credits are then recorded with an indentation.

(3) Place the appropriate money amounts in the left-hand (debit) and right-hand (credit) money columns.

(4) Write an explanation of the transaction below the account titles. The explanation should be as brief as possible consistent with disclosure of all the information necessary to understand the transaction being recorded.

Most journal entries are based on information appearing on a source document resulting from a transaction between the business and an outside party. Each transaction entered in the journal should be stated in terms of equal debits and credits. The account titles cited in the description column should correspond to those used for the related general ledger accounts. To separate clearly the various entries, a line is left blank between entries. We explain the use of the column headed "Post. Ref." (posting reference) later, in Step 3 of the accounting cycle.

COMPOUND JOURNAL ENTRIES   Whenever a journal entry involves more than just two accounts, it is called a **compound** journal entry. The last journal entry in Exhibit 3–2 is an example of a compound journal entry involving three accounts. The debit of $3,000 to Test Equipment is offset by credits of $2,000 to Cash and $1,000 to Accounts Payable. Any number of accounts may appear in a compound entry, but regardless of how many accounts are used, the total of the debit amounts must always equal the total of the credit amounts.

CORRECTION OF JOURNAL ERRORS   Certain procedures should be followed when errors are found in journal entries. Because erasures completely remove the original recording, errors should not be erased. As you might imagine, the acceptance of erasures might conveniently allow someone to falsify accounting records; consequently, other procedures are used.

If an erroneous journal entry has not been transferred to the ledger, a single line is drawn through the erroneous amount or account title in the journal entry and the correction is entered on the same line just above the error. Often the person correcting the entry is required to place his or her initials near the correction. This facilitates any subsequent inquiry about the nature of or reason for the correction. Once an erroneous journal entry has been transferred to the ledger accounts, both records contain the error. The recommended procedures for correcting this situation are discussed under Step 3.

EXHIBIT 3–2
General Journal   Page 1

Date		Description	Post. Ref.	Debit	Credit
19XX Dec.	1	Cash Carl Monroe, Capital Opened the TV Service's bank account using personal funds.		20,000	20,000
	1	Rent Expense Cash Paid rent for December.		400	400
	2	Truck Cash Purchased pick-up truck for cash.		7,200	7,200

	2	Test Equipment
		    Cash Compound entry
		    Accounts Payable
		Purchased electronic test equipment for $3,000.
		Terms: $2,000 down, remainder due in 60 days.
				3,000	2,000
					1,000

POSTING

Step 3: Post
to Ledger
Accounts

After transactions have been journalized, the next step in the accounting cycle is to transcribe the debits and credits in each journal entry to the appropriate general ledger accounts. This transcribing process is called **posting** to the general ledger. Thus, data from a journal that stresses the total effect of particular transactions (such as the collection of accounts receivable) are transcribed to a ledger that stresses the total effect of many business transactions on particular business variables (such as cash, accounts receivable, and so on). This latter type of data is specifically needed for the preparation of financial statements.

POSTING REFERENCES   It is important to be able to trace any entry appearing in a ledger account back to the journal from which it was posted. Consequently, accounting records use a simple system of references. Both journals and accounts have posting reference columns. Entries in the posting reference columns of journals indicate the account to which the related debit or credit has been posted. Posting references appearing in ledger accounts identify the journal from which the related entry was posted.

To keep accounting records uncluttered, we make posting references simple and brief. For example, the posting reference of the general journal might be GJ or even simply J. Similarly, special journals such as Cash Receipts and Payroll might be indicated by posting references of CR and PR, respectively. Because both general and special journals usually involve many pages of entries, journal pages are numbered in sequence. Thus a posting reference of J9 appearing on the line with a $1,000 debit entry to the Cash account would mean that the ninth page of the general journal contains the entire entry in which the $1,000 debit to Cash appears. Because all entries should be posted from some journal, every entry appearing in a ledger account should have a related posting reference. Posting references appearing in journals are usually the numbers that have been assigned to the general ledger accounts.

CHART OF ACCOUNTS   In all but the very simplest accounting systems, a number is assigned to each general ledger account. Such a numbering system permits easy reference to accounts even though the account title may contain several words. Hence, the account Depreciation Expense—Test Equipment might be referred to simply as account No. 57.

To facilitate the analysis of transactions and the formulation of journal entries, a **chart of accounts** is usually prepared. The chart of accounts is a listing of the titles and numbers of all accounts found in the general ledger. The account titles should be grouped by, and in order of, the five major sections of the general ledger (assets, liabilities, owners' equity, revenue, expense). Exhibit 3-3 shows a chart of accounts for the Monroe TV Service, indicating the account numbers that will now be used.

EXHIBIT 3–3
Monroe TV Service
Chart of Accounts

Assets — 1X

11. Cash
12. Accounts Receivable
14. Supplies and Parts on Hand
16. Test Equipment
17. Accumulated Depreciation—Test Equipment
18. Truck
19. Accumulated Depreciation—Truck

Liabilities 2X

21. Accounts Payable
22. Utilities Payable
23. Wages Payable
24. Unearned Service Fees

Owner's Equity 3X

31. Carl Monroe, Capital
32. Carl Monroe, Drawing
33. Income Summary

Revenues — 4X

41. Service Fees

Expenses — 5X

51. Rent Expense
52. Wages Expense
53. Advertising Expense
54. Supplies and Parts Expense
55. Utilities Expense
56. Truck Expense
57. Depreciation Expense—
      Test Equipment
58. Depreciation Expense—
      Truck

The method of assigning account numbers usually involves a grouping technique so that all accounts in a major section of the general ledger start with the same digit. In the above example, all asset accounts begin with 1, liabilities with 2, and so on. Very involved accounting systems may use three- or four-digit account numbers and may even employ suffixes to designate various branches, departments, or divisions.

Exhibit 3–4 (page 84) diagrams the posting of Monroe TV Service's first transaction from the general journal to the ledger accounts. Each debit entry and each credit entry is posted as follows:

(1) The date (year, month, and day) is entered in the appropriate account. Note that this is the date of the journal entry—not necessarily the date of the actual posting. As was the case with journals, the year and month are restated only at the top of a new account page or at the point where they change.

(2) The amount is entered in the account as a debit or a credit, as indicated in the journal's money columns, and the new balance is calculated.

(3) The posting reference from the journal (both symbol and page number) is placed in the posting reference column of the ledger account.

(4) The account number is placed in the posting reference column of the journal.

· EXHIBIT 3–4
Diagrams of Posting to Ledger Accounts

General Journal   Page 1

Date		Description	Post. Ref.	Debit	Credit
19XX Dec.	1	Cash	11	20,000	
		Carl Monroe, Capital	31		20,000
		Opened the TV Service's bank account using personal funds.			

❶   **General Ledger** ❸   ❷   ❹
                                     Cash
                                                                      Account No. 11

Date		Description	Post. Ref.	Debit*	Credit	Balance
19XX Dec.	1		J1	20,000		20,000

General Journal   Page 1

Date		Description	Post. Ref.	Debit	Credit
19XX Dec.	1	Cash	11	20,000	
		Carl Monroe, Capital	31		20,000
		Opened the TV Service's bank account using personal funds.			

❶   **General Ledger**   ❸   ❷   ❹
                  Carl Monroe, Capital
                                                           Account No. 31

Date		Description	Post. Ref.	Debit	Credit*	Balance
19XX Dec.	1		J1		20,000	20,000

Regardless of the types of journals or the number of entries involved, the total debits posted should equal the total credits posted. Exhibit 3-5 (see pp. 86–91) is a comprehensive illustration of the journalizing and posting of the December transactions of the Monroe TV Service. You should review each transaction in the illustration for (1) the nature of the transaction, (2) the related journal entry, and (3) the subsequent postings. Bear in mind that the account numbers in the posting reference column of the journal are not entered when the journal entry is recorded; they are inserted after the entry has been posted.

TAKING A TRIAL BALANCE   After the entries in journals have been posted to the ledger accounts, the next step is to determine the balance of each account and take a trial balance of all the accounts. The trial balance of the Monroe TV Service at December 31 is shown in Exhibit 3-6 (page 91).

CORRECTING ERRONEOUS POSTINGS   Even the most carefully kept accounts will occasionally contain posting errors. If an error involves only the wrong amount being posted, it may be corrected by drawing a line through the incorrect amount, entering the correct amount above, and initialing the correction. When an amount has been posted to the wrong account, however, the correction should be made through journal entries. Let us assume that the Monroe TV Service purchased test equipment for $100 cash and that the bookkeeper erroneously debited the amount to Supplies and Parts on Hand instead of to the Test Equipment account. The most direct way of correcting the error is to make the following entry in the journal, transferring the debit to the correct account:

Test Equipment	100	
Supplies and Parts on Hand		100

To correct entry for purchase of test equipment.

An alternative method is to reverse the erroneous entry and to record the entry as it should have been made:

Cash	100	
Supplies and Parts on Hand		100

To reverse incorrect entry for purchase of test equipment.

Test Equipment	100	
Cash		100

To correctly record purchase of test equipment.

EXHIBIT 3–5
Journalizing and Posting for Monroe TV Service

General Journal

Page 1

Date		Description	Post. Ref.	Debit	Credit
19XX Dec.	1	Cash	11	20,000	
		Carl Monroe, Capital	31		20,000
		Opened the TV Service's bank account using personal funds.			
	1	Rent Expense	51	400	
		Cash	11		400
		Paid rent for December.			
	2	Truck	18	7,200	
		Cash	11		7,200
		Purchased pick-up truck for cash.			
	2	Test Equipment	16	3,000	
		Cash	11		2,000
		Accounts Payable	21		1,000
		Purchased electronic test equipment for $3,000. Terms: $2,000 down, remainder due in 60 days.			
	2	Cash	11	800	
		Unearned Service Fees	24		800
		Received advance on four-month contract at $200 per month.			
	3	Supplies and Parts on Hand	14	600	
		Accounts Payable	21		600
		Purchased supplies and parts on account; 60-day terms.			
	7	Cash	11	550	
		Service Fees	41		550
		Service for cash, Dec. 1–7.			
	14	Accounts Receivable	12	750	
		Service Fees	41		750
		Service rendered on account.			
	14	Wages Expense	52	420	
		Cash	11		420
		Paid wages for first two weeks of December.			

General Journal (continued)

Date		Description	Post. Ref.	Debit	Credit
19XX Dec.	14	Cash Service Fees Service for cash, Dec. 8–14.	11 41	480	480
	17	Advertising Expense Cash Paid *Daily News* for December advertising.	53 11	50	50
	19	Cash Accounts Receivable Received $500 on account from credit customers.	11 12	500	500
	21	Cash Service Fees Service for cash, December 15–21.	11 41	320	320
	28	Truck Expense Cash Gas and oil for December.	56 11	170	170
	28	Accounts Receivable Service Fees Services rendered on account.	12 41	2,400	2,400
	28	Wages Expense Cash Paid wages for second two weeks of December.	52 11	420	420
	28	Carl Monroe, Drawing Cash Withdrew $600 for personal use.	32 11	600	600
	28	Cash Service Fees Service for cash, December 22–28.	11 41	200	200

EXHIBIT 3–5 (continued)
General Ledger

Cash   Account No. 11

Date		Description	Post. Ref.	Debit*	Credit	Balance
19XX						
Dec.	1		J1	20,000		20,000
	1		J1		400	19,600
	2		J1		7,200	12,400
	2		J1		2,000	10,400
	2		J1	800		11,200
	7		J1	550		11,750
	14		J1		420	11,330
	14		J2	480		11,810
	17		J2		50	11,760
	19		J2	500		12,260
	21		J2	320		12,580
	28		J2		170	12,410
	28		J2		420	11,990
	28		J2		600	11,390
	28		J2	200		11,590

Accounts Receivable   Account No. 12

Date		Description	Post. Ref.	Debit*	Credit	Balance
19XX						
Dec.	14		J1	750		750
	19		J2		500	250
	28		J2	2,400		2,650

Supplies and Parts on Hand   Account No. 14

Date		Description	Post. Ref.	Debit*	Credit	Balance
19XX						
Dec.	3		J1	600		600

Test Equipment — Account No. 16

Date		Description	Post. Ref.	Debit*	Credit	Balance
19XX Dec.	2		J1	3,000		3,000

Truck — Account No. 18

Date		Description	Post. Ref.	Debit*	Credit	Balance
19XX Dec.	2		J1	7,200		7,200

Accounts Payable — Account No. 21

Date		Description	Post. Ref.	Debit	Credit*	Balance
19XX Dec.	2		J1		1,000	1,000
	3		J1		600	1,600

Unearned Service Fees — Account No. 24

Date		Description	Post. Ref.	Debit	Credit*	Balance
19XX Dec.	2		J1		800	800

Carl Monroe, Capital — Account No. 31

Date		Description	Post. Ref.	Debit	Credit*	Balance
19XX Dec.	1		J1		20,000	20,000

EXHIBIT 3–5 (continued)
Carl Monroe, Drawing

Account No. 32

Date		Description	Post. Ref.	Debit*	Credit	Balance
19XX Dec.	28		J2	600		600

Service Fees

Account No. 41

Date		Description	Post. Ref.	Debit	Credit*	Balance
19XX Dec.	7		J1		550	550
	14		J1		750	1,300
	14		J2		480	1,780
	21		J2		320	2,100
	28		J2		2,400	4,500
	28		J2		200	4,700

Rent Expense

Account No. 51

Date		Description	Post. Ref.	Debit*	Credit	Balance
19XX Dec.	1		J1	400		400

Wages Expense

Account No. 52

Date		Description	Post. Ref.	Debit*	Credit	Balance
19XX Dec.	14		J1	420		420
	28		J2	420		840

Advertising Expense   Account No. 53

Date		Description	Post. Ref.	Debit*	Credit	Balance
19XX Dec.	7		J2	50		50

Truck Expense   Account No. 56

Date		Description	Post. Ref.	Debit*	Credit	Balance
19XX Dec.	28		J2	170		170

*Throughout this chapter, the asterisk indicates the column that designates the normal balance.

EXHIBIT 3-6

Monroe TV Service
Trial Balance
December 31, 19XX

	Debit	Credit
Cash	$11,590	
Accounts Receivable	2,650	
Supplies and Parts on Hand	600	
Test Equipment	3,000	
Truck	7,200	
Accounts Payable		$ 1,600
Unearned Service Fees		800
Carl Monroe, Capital		20,000
Carl Monroe, Drawing	600	
Service Fees		4,700
Rent Expense	400	
Wages Expense	840	
Advertising Expense	50	
Truck Expense	170	
	$27,100	$27,100

ADJUSTMENTS

Step 4: Adjust
the Ledger
Accounts

It is important that accounts appearing in financial statements at the end of an accounting period be properly stated. Clearly, if the income statement is to portray a realistic net income figure based upon accrual accounting, all revenues *earned* during the period and all expenses *incurred* must be shown. It is therefore necessary to make a proper alignment of revenues and costs for the reporting period in question. This process of aligning costs and expenses with related revenue is the **matching** concept frequently referred to in accounting literature.

Many of the transactions reflected in the accounting records through the first three steps in the accounting cycle affect the net income of more than one period. Therefore, to achieve a proper matching of costs and expenses with revenue, one must often adjust the account balances at the end of each accounting period. The **adjusting** step of the accounting cycle occurs after the journals have been posted, but before financial statements are prepared.

There are four general types of adjustments to be made at the end of an accounting period:

(1) Aligning *recorded costs* with the appropriate accounting periods.

(2) Aligning *recorded revenue* with the appropriate accounting periods.

(3) Reflecting *unrecorded expenses* incurred during the accounting period.

(4) Reflecting *unrecorded revenue* earned during the accounting period.

ALIGNING RECORDED COSTS Many business outlays are made to benefit a number of accounting periods. Some common examples are purchases of buildings, equipment, and supplies, and payments of insurance premiums covering a period of years. Ordinarily, these outlays are debited to an asset account at the time of expenditure. Then, at the end of each accounting period, the estimated portion of the outlay that has expired during the period or that has benefited the period is transferred to an expense account. As an example, let us suppose that a company pays $360 for a three-year fire insurance premium at the beginning of the current year. The entry for the outlay would usually be recorded as a debit to Prepaid Insurance, an asset account, and as a credit to Cash. Since the expenditure was made to benefit a 36-month period, $\frac{1}{36}$, or $10, of the premium would expire each month. Therefore, at the end of each month an entry would be made to adjust the accounts, as follows:

Jan. 31	Insurance Expense	10	
	Prepaid Insurance		10

To record insurance expense for January.

Using the above adjustment, we would show the proper expense of $10 on the first month's income statement and the proper amount of the unexpired asset,

$350, on the balance sheet prepared at the end of the month. Similarly, for each succeeding month of the 36-month period, we would transfer $10 to the Insurance Expense account from Prepaid Insurance. At the end of the 36-month period, no balance would remain in the asset account. At this time the firm would probably renew its insurance coverage by another outlay to benefit subsequent periods.

Under most circumstances, we can discover where adjustments are needed by inspecting the monthly trial balance. By looking at the December 31 trial balance of the Monroe TV Service (Exhibit 3-6), we would find that adjustments are required to apportion the cost of supplies and parts between December and subsequent periods and to reflect depreciation on the company truck and test equipment.

Supplies and parts. During December, the Monroe TV Service purchased supplies and parts and recorded the outlay in an asset account, Supplies and Parts on Hand, as follows:

Dec. 3	Supplies and Parts on Hand	600	
	Accounts Payable		600

Purchased supplies and parts on account.

The firm would not find it convenient, however, to keep a daily count of parts and supplies used in service work. Instead, at the end of December, it would make a count of items still on hand. Suppose that the count shows $220 worth of supplies and parts on hand at the end of the month, indicating that $380 worth of supplies and parts have been used in service work during the month. Therefore, at the end of the period, an adjusting entry will be made to transfer this amount to an expense account, Supplies and Parts Expense, as follows:

Dec. 31	Supplies and Parts Expense	380	
	Supplies and Parts on Hand		380

To record expense of supplies and parts
used in December.

When this adjusting entry is posted, it will properly reflect the December expense for supplies and parts and will reduce the asset account Supplies and Parts on Hand to $220, the actual amount of the asset remaining at December 31. After the entry is posted, the related ledger accounts would appear as follows:

Supplies and Parts on Hand   Account No. 14

Date		Description	Post. Ref.	Debit*	Credit	Balance
19XX Dec.	3		J1	600		600
	31		J3		380	220

Supplies and Parts Expense   Account No. 54

Date		Description	Post. Ref.	Debit*	Credit	Balance
19XX Dec.	31		J3	380		380

Obviously, if financial statements were prepared without this adjustment, the December income statement would omit an important expense and would overstate the net income by $380. Similarly, the balance sheet would show an overstatement of $380 in assets, because the Supplies and Parts on Hand balance would remain at $600. As a result of overstating net income, owner's equity in the balance sheet would also be overstated by $380.

Depreciation. In Chapter 1 we saw that to apportion the cost of long-lived assets, such as buildings and equipment, we record the estimated depreciation. To obtain the yearly amount of depreciation expense, we must divide the cost of the asset by its estimated life in years. (This method of calculation is called straight-line depreciation. Other methods will be explored in Chapter 10.)

Let us assume that the truck purchased by Monroe TV Service for $7,200 has an estimated life of six years and that the $3,000 worth of test equipment is expected to last five years. The depreciation to be recorded on the truck is therefore $1,200 per year, or $100 per month. Similarly, the depreciation on the test equipment will be $600 per year, or $50 per month. At the end of December we would make the following adjusting entries:

Dec. 31	Depreciation Expense—Truck	100	
	Accumulated Depreciation—Truck		100
	To record December depreciation on truck.		
Dec. 31	Depreciation Expense—Test Equipment	50	
	Accumulated Depreciation— Test Equipment		50
	To record December depreciation on test equipment.		

When the above entries are posted, they will properly reflect the cost of using these fixed assets during the month of December so that the correct expense will appear in the December income statement. As you will recall from the discussion in Chapter 1, the credits to Accumulated Depreciation are subtracted in the balance sheet from the related long-term assets. The resulting balances (cost less accumulated depreciation) represent unexpired asset costs to be applied against future operating periods.

After the adjusting entries have been posted, the asset accounts, accumulated depreciation accounts, and depreciation expense accounts would appear as follows:

Truck   Account No. 18

Date		Description	Post. Ref.	Debit*	Credit	Balance
19XX Dec.	2		J1	7,200		7,200

Accumulated Depreciation—Truck   Account No. 19

Date		Description	Post. Ref.	Debit	Credit*	Balance
19XX Dec.	31		J3		100	100

Depreciation Expense—Truck   Account No. 58

Date		Description	Post. Ref.	Debit*	Credit	Balance
19XX Dec.	31		J3	100		100

Test Equipment   Account No. 16

Date		Description	Post. Ref.	Debit*	Credit	Balance
19XX Dec.	2		J1	3,000		3,000

Accumulated Depreciation—Test Equipment   Account No. 17

Date		Description	Post. Ref.	Debit	Credit*	Balance
19XX Dec.	31		J3		50	50

Depreciation Expense—Test Equipment   Account No. 57

Date		Description	Post. Ref.	Debit*	Credit	Balance
19XX Dec.	31		J3	50		50

If the firm failed to record the adjusting entries for depreciation, expenses would be omitted from the income statement. In the above situation, the result of such an omission would be an overstatement of net income by $150. Furthermore, assets and owner's equity would be overstated by the same amount on the balance sheet.

ALIGNING RECORDED REVENUE   Sometimes a business receives fees for services before service is rendered. Such transactions are ordinarily recorded by debiting cash and crediting a liability account. The liability account in this situation, sometimes referred to as a **deferred credit,** shows the obligation for performing future service. For example, a monthly magazine publisher receiving $36 for a three-year subscription would debit Cash and credit Unearned Subscription Revenue for $36. Each month that magazines are supplied to the subscriber, $\frac{1}{36}$ of the publisher's obligation is fulfilled. Therefore, the bookkeeper would transfer $1 from the liability account Unearned Subscription Revenue to a revenue account, Subscription Revenue, at the end of each month. Therefore, this procedure reflects revenue when service is performed rather than when it is paid for.

During December, the Monroe TV Service entered one transaction that requires an end-of-month adjustment to recorded revenue. On December 2, the firm signed a four-month contract to perform service for a local TV dealer at $200 per month, with the entire contract price of $800 received in advance. The entry made on December 2 was as follows:

| Dec. 2 | Cash | 800 | |
| | Unearned Service Fees | | 800 |

Advance received on four-month contract
at $200 per month.

On December 31, an adjusting entry would be made to transfer $200, the revenue earned in December, to Service Fees and reduce the liability Unearned Service Fees by the same amount:

| Dec. 31 | Unearned Service Fees | 200 | |
| | Service Fees | | 200 |

To record portion of advance earned
in December.

After this entry is posted, the liability account will show a balance of $600, the amount of future services still owing, and the Service Fees account will reflect the $200 earned in December:

Unearned Service Fees — Account No. 24

Date		Description	Post. Ref.	Debit	Credit*	Balance
19XX Dec.	2		J1		800	800
	31		J3	200		600

Service Fees — Account No. 41

Date		Description	Post. Ref.	Debit	Credit*	Balance
19XX Dec.	7		J1		550	550
	14		J1		750	1,300
	14		J2		480	1,780
	21		J2		320	2,100
	28		J2		2,400	4,500
	28		J2		200	4,700
	31		J3		200	4,900

A similar entry would be repeated at the end of each month of the contract period. As a result, each month, $200 in revenue would be included in Service Fees in the income statement and the liability account in the balance sheet would be reduced by $200.

Let us emphasize here that if the adjusting entries are ignored, the revenue is never reflected in any income statement and the liability remains on the balance sheet after the obligation has been discharged. Therefore, it is important to make these adjustments carefully.

REFLECTING UNRECORDED EXPENSES Often a business will use certain services before paying for them. An obligation to pay for such services as salaries, utilities, and taxes may build up, or accrue, over a period of time. Most businesses make adjusting entries for such **accrued expenses in** order to reflect the proper cost in the period when the benefit was received. The bookkeeper must realize that services received have not yet been reflected in the accounts and make appropriate adjustments. If source documents are not available, amounts may be estimated.

Accrued utilities. During December, the Monroe TV Service used telephone service and utility service for heat and light. Bills from the telephone and power companies will not arrive until January. Let us assume, however, that inquiries to the landlord and knowledge of local rates enable the firm to estimate that it received a total of $80 worth of service during the month. On December 31, an adjusting entry would be made as follows:

Dec. 31   Utilities Expense   80
                Utilities Payable   80

            To record estimated amount of December
            utilities expense.

This adjustment reflects both the cost of services received during the period bene-fited and the estimated amount owed for such services to be included on the balance sheet. If this adjustment were not made, net income would be overstated by $80 in the December income statement; on the balance sheet at December 31, liabilities would be understated and owner's equity overstated by $80.

Note that the credit in the adjusting entry above could have been made to Accounts Payable. Since the amount is estimated, however, many businesses would prefer to credit an account such as Utilities Payable.

After the bookkeeper posts the adjusting entry for estimated utilities expense, the expense and liability accounts would appear as follows:

Utilities Expense   Account No. 55

Date		Description	Post. Ref.	Debit*	Credit	Balance
19XX Dec.	31		J3	80		80

Utilities Payable   Account No. 22

Date		Description	Post. Ref.	Debit	Credit*	Balance
19XX Dec.	31		J3		80	80

Suppose that when the utility bill arrives in early January, it is for $84, indicating that the firm has underestimated the December expense by $4. Obviously $84 will be credited to Cash, since the full amount of the bill must be paid. But what would be debited to balance the $84 credit? One answer is to remove the liability, by debiting $80 to Utilities Payable, and debiting the remaining $4 to Utilities Expense for January. This has the effect of placing some of December's

ACCRUAL ACCOUNTING
AND THE YALE EXPRESS CASE

Perhaps the most famous court case dealing with accrual accounting was the so-called Yale Express Case, settled in the early 1970s.* Stockholders and creditors of the Yale Express System sued the officers, directors, underwriters, and independent auditors because the audited $1,140,000 net income for the year 1963 was eventually determined to be a $1,880,000 loss and because management-reported (unaudited) earnings for 1964 were clearly overstated.

In 1963, Yale Express, essentially a short-haul regional trucking firm, acquired Republic Carloading & Distributing Co. (a freight-forwarding company about twice the size of Yale). From the start, the combined companies had numerous operating and financial problems that contributed to the downfall of the combination. One of the most crucial problems was that Yale Express imposed its semicash (fast cutoff) accounting methods to the operations of both companies. Because Yale Express was an overnight trucker, most of its bills came in shortly after freight was trucked. Therefore, it was able to pick up most late-arriving bills within twenty days after its accounting year ended. Yale expected that (as in the past) freight costs not accrued at the end of the period would be counterbalanced by those not accrued at the beginning of the period. In fact, this system is fairly reasonable if volume of activity remains fairly constant from year to year. However, with the merger this situation did not exist.

The freight-handling bills of Republic often came in months after service was received from other truckers. Before the merger, Republic was on a full accrual basis, which means that it estimated unrecorded freight costs at the end of each year and accordingly debited these costs and credited an estimated liability account. After the combination, these costs were not fully accrued. It was subsequently discovered that freight costs surfacing in 1964 but incurred in 1963 (when the related revenue was recorded) were substantial enough to reduce the reported 1963 net income of over $1 million to an almost $2 million loss.

Evidence in the case suggested that the outside auditors were aware of the basic problem but failed to follow through in insisting upon reasonable year-end accruals of estimated costs. However, further evidence indicated that management withheld certain documentary evidence from the auditors that would have enabled them to estimate the necessary additional 1963 costs. Furthermore, the problems resulting from the merger of two separate sets of accounting systems and personnel and the implementation of a new automated system of accounting made the examination of the Yale Express System extremely difficult for the independent auditors.

*Details of this case [officially *Fischer* v. *Kletz*, 266 F. Supp. (S.D. N.Y. 1967)] are given in Richard J. Whalen, "The Big Skid at Yale Express," *Fortune*, November 1965, p. 144ff.

utilities expense in January. Such a small discrepancy as $4 is not material, however, and most persons would not be disturbed about the minor inaccuracy. Another method of handling the accrual in the subsequent period, involving *reversing entries*, will be explained in Chapter 4.

Accrued wages. Carl Monroe pays his assistant every two weeks at the rate of $210 for each six-day work week. During December, the assistant was paid $420 on December 14 and December 28. Let us assume that both these dates fell on Saturday and that Sunday is the assistant's day off. If financial statements are to be prepared at the close of business on Tuesday, December 31, the assistant will have worked two days (Monday and Tuesday) during December for which he will not be paid until January. Because the assistant's wages are $35 per day ($210 ÷ 6), additional wages expense of $70 should be reflected in the income statement for the month of December. The adjusting entry at the end of December would be as follows:

Dec. 31	Wages Expense	70	
	Wages Payable		70
	To record accrued wages for December 30 and 31.		

After posting, the Wages Expense and Wages Payable accounts would appear as follows:

Wages Expense   Account No. 52

Date		Description	Post. Ref.	Debit*	Credit	Balance
19XX Dec.	14		J1	420		420
	28		J2	420		840
	31		J3	70		910

Wages Payable   Account No. 23

Date		Description	Post. Ref.	Debit	Credit*	Balance
19XX Dec.	31		J3		70	70

This adjusting procedure enables the firm to reflect as expense of the period all wages *earned* by the assistant, rather than just the wages *paid* during the period. In addition, the balance sheet will show the liability for unpaid wages at the end of the period. Omitting such an adjustment would cause a $70 overstatement of net income in the December income statement, with a concurrent $70 overstatement of owner's equity and a $70 understatement of liabilities in the December 31 balance sheet.

When the assistant is paid on the next regular payday in January, the bookkeeper must make sure that the two days' pay accrued at the end of December is not again charged to expense. If we assume that $420 is paid to the assistant on Saturday, January 11, the following entry can be made:

Jan. 11	Wages Payable *(Liabilities)*	70	
	Wages Expense	350	
	Cash		420
	To record wages paid.		

This entry eliminates the liability recorded in the adjusting entry at the end of December, and debits January Wages Expense for only those wages earned by the assistant in January. Another method of avoiding dual charges, that of reversing entries, will be explained in Chapter 4.

REFLECTING UNRECORDED REVENUE   Sometimes a company provides services during a period that are neither billed nor paid for by the end of the period. Yet the value of these services represents revenue earned by the firm and should be reflected in the firm's income statement. Such accumulated revenue is often termed **accrued revenue.** For example, a firm may have loaned money on which interest has been earned by the end of the period. The amount of the interest should be reflected in the net income of the period in which it is earned.

In the case of Monroe TV Service, the service contract with the local hotel negotiated on December 2 could result in accrued revenue. The terms of the contract provided that Monroe TV Service would bill the hotel for work at $6 per hour whenever 50 hours of work had been completed. Suppose that by December 31, Monroe had performed 30 hours of work for the hotel. Unbilled revenue of $180 (30 × $6) has accrued during the month and should be reflected in the accounts by the following adjusting entry:

Dec. 31	Accounts Receivable	180	
	Service Fees		180
	To record unbilled revenue earned during December.		

The effect of this entry is to include in the December accounts the revenue that has been earned by performing service but has not yet been billed to the hotel. It also causes the amount owed by the hotel to be entered as a receivable on the balance sheet. After the entry is posted, the related accounts would appear as follows:

Accounts Receivable

Account No. 12

Date		Description	Post. Ref.	Debit*	Credit	Balance
19XX						
Dec.	14		J1	750		750
	19		J2		500	250
	28		J2	2,400		2,650
	31		J3	180		2,830

Service Fees

Account No. 41

Date		Description	Post. Ref.	Debit	Credit*	Balance
19XX						
Dec.	7		J1		550	550
	14		J1		750	1,300
	14		J2		480	1,780
	21		J2		320	2,100
	28		J2		2,400	4,500
	28		J2		200	4,700
	31		J3		200	4,900
	31		J3		180	5,080

Again, the bookkeeper must be careful when the regular 50-hour billing is made to the hotel in January. Let us assume that 50 hours of work has accumulated by January 14. Because the revenue from 30 hours of work ($180) was recorded in the December 31 adjusting entry, the billing made on January 14 contains only $120 (20 hours × $6) of revenue earned during January. The following entry could be made when the hotel is billed for $300 (50 hours × $6):

| Jan. 14 | Accounts Receivable | 120 | |
| | Service Fees | | 120 |

To record revenue earned during January; customer billed $300 for work performed in December and January.

As we mentioned earlier, an alternative way of handling this situation is discussed in Chapter 4.

If we did not make the adjustment for accrued revenue, the net income of Monroe TV Service for December would be understated by $180 and the January net income would be overstated by the same amount. On the December 31 balance sheet, assets and owner's equity would also be understated.

PREPAYMENTS RECORDED IN EXPENSE AND REVENUE ACCOUNTS

Expenditures made to benefit future periods and amounts received for services yet to be performed should be recorded initially in balance sheet accounts. When this is done, the adjusting procedure consists of transferring the expired portion of prepaid expenses to expense accounts and transferring the earned portion of prepaid revenue to revenue accounts. Essentially these are the procedures we have just described.

Occasionally, an outlay benefiting future periods may be debited to an expense account rather than to prepaid expense, or an amount received for future services may be credited to a revenue account rather than to unearned revenue. In such situations, the adjusting procedure consists of removing the unexpired or unearned portion of the recorded amount and transferring it to the appropriate balance sheet account. For example, suppose that a one-year insurance premium of $1,200 was initially debited to Insurance Expense. At the end of the first month after the outlay, the following adjusting entry is appropriate:

Prepaid Insurance (Assets)	1,100	
Insurance Expense (Expense)		1,100

To transfer unexpired insurance cost to asset account.

This entry sets up an asset of $1,100 and leaves $100 in the expense account.

Suppose also that the firm received six month's prepayment of rent totaling $1,200 from a tenant and credited the entire amount to Rental Income (a revenue account). After the first month has elapsed, the appropriate adjusting entry is:

Rental Income	1,000	
Unearned Rental Income		1,000

To transfer unearned rental income to liability account.

This adjustment records $1,000 as a liability and reflects $200 as the remaining balance in the revenue account.

KEY POINTS TO REMEMBER

(1) There are six major steps in the accounting cycle:

Steps	When Normally Done
1. Analyze transactions	Throughout every period
2. Record in journals	
3. Post to ledgers	At the end of each period
4. Adjust the accounts	When statements are required
5. Prepare statements	
6. Close temporary accounts	At the end of the year

(2) Accounting entries are initially recorded in a journal; the entries are in chronological order, and the journal shows the total effect of each transaction or adjustment.

(3) After journal entries are posted to the accounts, a trial balance is taken to make sure that the general ledger is in balance.

(4) Adjusting entries made to align revenue and expense with the appropriate periods consist of four types:
   1. Apportioning recorded costs to periods benefited.
   2. Apportioning recorded revenue to periods in which it is earned.
   3. Accruing unrecorded expenses.
   4. Accruing unrecorded revenue.

QUESTIONS

3–1 List in their proper order the steps in the accounting cycle.

3–2 Assuming that a business prepares quarterly financial statements, at what time(s) during the year is each step in the accounting cycle accomplished?

3–3 Explain the nature and purpose of a general journal.

3–4 What is the appropriate procedure for correcting an erroneous general journal entry (a) before it has been posted and (b) after it has been posted?

3–5 Explain the technique of posting references. What is the justification for their use?

3–6 Describe a chart of accounts, and give an example of a coding system for identifying different types of accounts.

3–7 Why is the adjusting step of the accounting cycle necessary?

3–8 At the beginning of January, Prepaid Insurance was debited with the cost of a one-year premium, $180. What adjusting entry should be made on January 31?

3-9 Referring to Question 3-8, suppose the bookkeeper had charged the entire $180 premium to Insurance Expense when it was paid on January 1. What adjusting entry should be made on January 31 before financial statements are prepared for the month?

3-10 At the beginning of January, the first month of the accounting year, the Supplies on Hand account had a debit balance of $200. During January, purchases of $300 worth of supplies were debited to the account. Although there were $100 worth of supplies on hand at the end of January, the necessary entry to adjust the account was omitted. What effect will the omission have on (a) the income statement for January and (b) the balance sheet prepared at January 31?

3-11 What four different types of adjustments are frequently necessary at the close of an accounting period? Give examples of each type.

3-12 *Sporting World*, a monthly magazine, received three-year subscriptions amounting to a total of $7,200 on January 1. (a) What entry should be made to record the receipt of the $7,200? (b) What entry should be made at the end of January before financial statements are prepared for the month?

3-13 The Elite Bakery pays an employee $250 in wages each Friday for the five-day work week ended on that day. The last Friday of January falls on January 26. What adjusting entry should be made on January 31? *(2 day)*

3-14 If the Elite Bakery in Question 3-13 fails to make the necessary adjusting entry on January 31, what effect will the omission have on (a) the income statement for January and (b) the balance sheet prepared at January 31?

3-15 Alan Ford earns interest amounting to $125 per month on some of his investments. He receives the interest every six months, on December 31 and June 30. What adjusting entry should he make on January 31?

EXERCISES

3-16 Creative Graphics, a firm providing art services for advertisers, has the following accounts in its ledger: Cash; Accounts Receivable; Supplies on Hand; Office Equipment; Accounts Payable; Ellen Coyle, Capital; Ellen Coyle, Drawing; Fees Earned; Rent Expense; Utilities Expense; and Salaries Expense. Record the following transactions for June in a two-column general journal:

June	1	Ellen Coyle invested $20,000 cash to begin the business.
	2	Paid rent for June, $500.
	3	Purchased office equipment on account, $6,000.
	6	Purchased art materials and other supplies for cash, $720.
	11	Billed clients for services, $2,400.
	17	Collected $1,250 from clients.
	19	Paid $3,200 on account to office equipment firm (see June 3, above).
	25	Ellen Coyle withdrew $650 for personal use.
	28	Paid utilities bill for June, $58.
	30	Paid salaries for June, $1,750.

3-17 Selected accounts of Redi-Rentals, a real-estate firm, are shown below as of January 31 of the current year before any adjusting entries have been made.

	Debit	Credit
Prepaid Insurance	$2,700	
Supplies on Hand	750	
Office Equipment	8,400	
Unearned Rental Fees		3,000
Salaries Expense	2,100	
Rental Fees Earned		12,000

Based on the following information, record in a general journal the necessary adjusting entries on January 31:
(a) Prepaid Insurance represents premiums for three years paid on January 1.
(b) Supplies of $450 were on hand January 31.
(c) Office equipment is expected to last 10 years.
(d) The firm collected six months' rent in advance on January 1 from a tenant renting space for $500 per month.
(e) Accrued salaries not recorded as of January 31 are $360.

3-18 For each of the following unrelated situations, prepare the necessary adjusting entry, in general journal form.
(a) Unrecorded depreciation expense on equipment is $600.
(b) The Supplies on Hand account has a balance of $425. A count of supplies at the end of the period shows that supplies worth $240 are on hand.
(c) On the date for preparing financial statements, it is estimated that utilities expense of $60 has been incurred for which no utility bill has yet been received.
(d) On the first day of the current month, rent for two months was paid and recorded as a $300 debit to Rent Expense and a $300 credit to Cash. Monthly statements are now being prepared.
(e) Four months ago, Ace Insurance Company sold a one-year policy to a customer and recorded the sale by debiting Cash for $480 and crediting Premium Revenues Earned for $480. No adjusting entries have been prepared during the four-month period. Annual statements are now being prepared.
(f) At the end of the accounting period, wages expense of $250 had been incurred but not paid.
(g) At the end of the accounting period, $120 of repair services had been rendered to customers who had not yet been sent bills.

3-19 The Acme Janitor Service offers its services on both a contract basis and an hourly basis. On January 1 of the current year, Acme collected $7,200 in advance on six-month contracts for work to be performed evenly during the next six months.
(a) Give the general journal entry to record the receipt of $7,200 for contract work.
(b) Give the adjusting entry to be made on January 31 for the contract work done during January.
(c) At January 31, a total of 40 hours of hourly rate janitor work was unbilled. The billing rate is $7.50 per hour. Give the adjusting entry needed on January 31.

3-20 Selected T accounts for the Weston Company are shown below as of January 31 of the current year; adjusting entries have already been posted. The firm operates on a calendar year.

Supplies on Hand	Supplies Expense
Jan. 31 Bal. 360	Jan. 31 Bal. 560

Prepaid Insurance	Insurance Expense
Jan. 31 Bal. 500	Jan. 31 Bal. 100 *X 12 months* = *$1200 for yr.*

Wages Payable	Wages Expense
Jan. 31 Bal. 750	Jan. 31 Bal. 4,500

(a) Assuming no balance existed in Wages Payable or Wages Expense on January 1, how much was paid in wages during January?

(b) The amount in the Insurance Expense account represents the adjustment made at January 31 for the January insurance expense. If the original premium was for one year, what was the amount of the premium and on what date did the insurance policy start?

(c) If the amount in Supplies Expense represents the January 31 adjustment for the supplies used in January, and $800 worth of supplies were purchased during January, what was the balance of Supplies on Hand on January 1?

3-21 The Appliance Repair Service shows the following account balances at the end of its first month of operations:

	Debit		Credit
Cash	$ 5,000	Accounts Payable	$ 3,500
Supplies on Hand	1,500	Owner's Capital	16,000
Equipment	15,000	Service Revenue	4,600
Wages Expense	2,100		
Utilities Expense	350		
Advertising Expense	150		
	$24,100		$24,100

The repair service's bookkeeper prepared an income statement for the period showing a net income of $2,000. He obtained this sum by deducting the $2,600 total of Wages Expense, Utilities Expense, and Advertising Expense from the Service Revenue of $4,600. However, he did not consider the following:

(1) Depreciation for the month should have been $240.
(2) Supplies on hand at the end of the month were $800.
(3) Accrued wages payable at the end of the month were $180.
(4) Unbilled service revenue at the end of the month was $450.

Using the preceding information, calculate the correct net income for the month.

PROBLEMS

3–22 James Riley opened the ABC Window Cleaning Service on April 1 of the current year. Transactions for April are as follows:

Apr. 1   Riley contributed $18,000 of his personal funds to begin the business.
     2   Purchased two used trucks for $7,000, paying $3,000 in cash, with the balance due in 60 days.
     2   Purchased ladders, scaffolding, and other equipment for cash, $800. (Classify this outlay as Equipment.)
     3   Paid three-year premium on liability insurance, $540.
     5   Purchased supplies on account, $450.
   12   Billed customers for service, $1,900.
   18   Collected $1,200 on account from customers.
   29   Paid bill for truck fuel used in April, $120.
   30   Paid April newspaper advertising, $50.
   30   Paid wages of assistants, $1,600.
   30   Billed customers for services, $1,450.

REQUIRED
(a) Record the above transactions in general journal form.
(b) Devise a chart of accounts for the firm and set up the general ledger. Be sure to allow for accounts that may be needed when adjusting entries are made at the close of accounting periods [see (e) below].
(c) Post journal entries to the ledger accounts.
(d) Take a trial balance.
(e) Make the journal entries to adjust the books for insurance expense, supplies expense, depreciation expense on trucks, and depreciation expense on equipment. Supplies on hand on April 30 amounted to $180. Depreciation for April was $120 on trucks and $30 on equipment. Post the adjusting entries.

3–23 George Travis started The Wheel Thing on March 1 of the current year to provide automotive wheel alignment and balancing at three locations in a metropolitan area. On March 31, the unadjusted balances of the firm's accounts are as follows:

The Wheel Thing
Trial Balance
March 31, 19XX

	Debit	Credit
Cash	$ 7,200	
Accounts Receivable	3,800	
Prepaid Rent	1,200	
Supplies on Hand	450	
Equipment	28,000	
Accounts Payable		$ 6,000
George Travis, Capital		30,000
George Travis, Drawing	1,200	
Service Revenue		13,400
Wages Expense	7,550	
	$49,400	$49,400

The following information is also available:

(1) The balance in Prepaid Rent was the amount paid on March 1 to cover the first three months' rent.

(2) Supplies on hand on March 31 amounted to $200.

(3) Depreciation on equipment for March was estimated at $225.

(4) Unpaid wages for March were $450 at the end of the month.

(5) Utility services used during March were estimated at $120. A bill is expected early in April.

REQUIRED

In general journal form, make the adjusting entries needed at March 31.

3-24 Lettershop, a mailing service, has just completed its first full year of operations on December 31 of the current year. The firm's ledger account balances before year-end adjustments are given below. No adjusting entries have been made to the accounts at any time during the year. Assume that all balances are normal.

Cash	$ 8,400	Jean Foster, Drawing	$ 1,200
Accounts Receivable	4,500	Mailing Fees Earned	45,000
Prepaid Advertising	480	Wages Expense	28,500
Equipment	9,500	Rent Expense	3,600
Accounts Payable	2,500	Utilities Expense	920
Jean Foster, Capital	12,000	Supplies Expense	2,400

An analysis of the firm's records reveals the following:

(1) The balance in Prepaid Advertising represents the amount paid for newspaper advertising for one year. The agreement, which calls for the same amount of space each month, covers the period from September 1 of the current year to August 31 next year.

(2) Depreciation on equipment is estimated at 10% per year ($950).

(3) Utilities expense does not include expense for December, estimated at $80. The bill will not be received until January of the next year.

(4) At year-end, employees have earned $500 in wages that will not be paid until January.

(5) All supplies purchased during the year were debited to Supplies Expense. Supplies on hand at year-end amounted to $300.

(6) Mailing services amounting to $3,000 were rendered to customers who have not yet been billed for the services.

(7) The firm's lease calls for rent of $300 per month payable on the first of each month, plus an amount equal to $\frac{1}{2}\%$ of annual mailing fees earned. The rental percentage is payable within 15 days after the end of the year.

REQUIRED

(a) Set up T accounts and enter the unadjusted balances shown above. Prove that debits and credits are equal by preparing a trial balance.

(b) Record adjusting entries in general journal form, and post these entries in the T accounts opened in (a) above. Add any additional accounts needed.

3-25 For the *unrelated* accounts given below, the present balances and the balances they should have after adjusting entries have been made and posted are indicated.

Account Title	Present Balance	Adjusted Balance
✓(1) Supplies on Hand	$300	$160
(2) Depreciation Expense—Delivery Truck	500	650
(3) Utilities Payable	—	75
(4) Insurance Expense	450	500
(5) Wages Payable	—	900
(6) Unearned Fees	—	420
(7) Accumulated Depreciation—Equipment	700	800
(8) Prepaid Rent	900	450
(9) Unearned Commissions Revenue	210	—
(10) Prepaid Advertising	—	400

REQUIRED

For each item listed, prepare a general journal entry (including an explanation) that would be *most probable* for each adjustment.

3-26 New Directions, a market research firm, had the following transactions in June, its first month of operations.

June 1 J. Conway invested $25,000 personal funds in the firm.
   1 The firm purchased the following from an office supply company: Office Equipment, $8,000; Supplies, $600. Terms called for a cash payment of $3,500, with the remainder due in 60 days. (Make a compound entry.)
   2 Paid rent for June, $400.
   3 Contracted for one-year's advertising from a local newspaper at $80 per month, paying four months' advertising in advance.
   5 Signed a six-month contract with an electronics firm to provide research consulting services at a rate of $1,200 per month. Two months' fees were received in advance.
   10 Billed various customers for services rendered, $2,400.
   14 Paid two-weeks' salaries (five-day week) to employees, $1,500.
   15 Paid travel expenses of J. Conway, $675.
   18 Paid post office for bulk mailing of survey research questionnaire, $260 (postage expense).
   22 Billed various customers for services rendered, $3,200.
   28 Paid two-weeks' salaries to employees, $1,500.
   30 Collected $3,000 for customers previously billed.
   30 Conway withdrew $450 for personal use.

REQUIRED

(a) Set up a ledger that includes the following accounts, using the account numbers shown: Cash (11); Accounts Receivable (12); Office Supplies on Hand

(14); Prepaid Advertising (15); Office Equipment (16); Accumulated Depreciation—Office Equipment (17); Accounts Payable (21); Salaries Payable (22); Unearned Fees (23); Conway, Capital (31); Conway, Drawing (32); Fees Earned (41); Salaries Expense (51); Advertising Expense (52); Supplies Expense (53); Rent Expense (54); Travel Expense (55); Depreciation Expense—Office Equipment (56); Postage Expense (57).

(b) Record June transactions in general journal form and post to the ledger accounts.

(c) Take a trial balance at June 30.

(d) Record adjusting journal entries in general journal form, and post to the ledger accounts. The following information is available on June 30:

Supplies on hand, $360
Accrued salaries, $600
Depreciation on office equipment for June, $75
Unbilled services rendered, $1,200

Also, make any necessary adjusting entries for advertising and for service fees indicated by the June transactions.

3–27 The following information relates to the December 31 adjustments for Sta-Dry, a firm providing waterproofing services for commercial and residential customers.

(1) The firm paid a $2,700 premium for a three-year insurance policy, coverage to begin October 1 of the current year. The entire amount of the premium was debited to Insurance Expense; no other entry concerning this premium has been recorded.

(2) Weekly wages for a five-day work week total $1,500 and are payable on Fridays. December 31 of the current year is a Tuesday.

(3) Sta-Dry received $1,400 during December for services to be performed during the following year. When received, this amount was credited to Fees Earned.

(4) During December, Sta-Dry provided $620 worth of services to clients who will not be billed until early in January.

(5) At December 31, the firm's Truck Expense account does not include $480 of unpaid fuel and repair bills.

(6) The Supplies on Hand account has a balance of $3,600 on December 31. However, the December purchases of supplies, totaling $700, were inadvertently debited to the Supplies Expense account, which now has a balance of $700. A count of supplies on December 31 indicates that $1,800 worth of supplies are still on hand.

(7) On December 1, Sta-Dry borrowed $6,000 from the bank, giving an interest-bearing note payable. Interest is not payable until the note is due near the end of January. However, the interest expense for December is $45. No entries have been made for the interest expense or interest payable.

REQUIRED

Prepare the necessary December 31 adjusting entries in general journal form.

ALTERNATE PROBLEMS

3-22A The Lin Painting Service began business on June 1 of the current year. Transactions for June were as follows:

June 1	Jim Lin, the proprietor, contributed $12,000 of his personal funds to begin business.
2	Purchased a used truck for $3,000; $2,000 was paid in cash, with the balance due in 60 days.
2	Purchased scaffolding and other equipment for $900 cash. (Classify this outlay as Equipment.)
3	Paid three-year premium on liability insurance, $432.
5	Purchased supplies on account, $450.
15	Billed customers for service, $1,700.
20	Collected $900 on account from customers.
29	Paid bill for truck fuel used in June, $70.
30	Paid for June newspaper advertising, $50.
30	Paid wages of assistant, $1,200.
30	Billed customers for service, $700.

REQUIRED
(a) Record the given transactions in a general journal.
(b) Devise a chart of accounts for the firm and set up the general ledger. Be sure to allow for accounts that may be needed when adjusting entries are made at the close of accounting periods [see (e) below].
(c) Post journal entries to the ledger accounts.
(d) Take a trial balance.
(e) Make the journal entries to adjust the books for insurance expense, supplies expense, depreciation expense on truck, and depreciation expense on equipment. Supplies on hand on June 30 were $225. Depreciation for June was $60 on the truck and $30 on equipment. Post entries.

3-23A Bond Carpet Cleaners ended its first month of operation on June 30 of the current year. The unadjusted account balances are listed below.

Bond Carpet Cleaners
Trial Balance
June 30, 19XX

	Debit	Credit
Cash	$1,200	
Accounts Receivable	900	
Prepaid Rent	400	
Supplies on Hand	160	
Equipment	4,000	
Accounts Payable		$ 600
Bond, Capital		4,260
Bond, Drawing	600	
Service Fees		3,500
Wages Expense	1,100	
	$8,360	$8,360

The following information is also available:
(1) The balance in Prepaid Rent was the amount paid to cover the first two months' rent.
(2) Supplies on hand at June 30 were $90.
(3) Depreciation for the month was estimated at $140.
(4) Wages expense incurred but unpaid at June 30 amounted to $220.
(5) Utility services used during June were estimated at $80. A bill is expected next month.

REQUIRED
In general journal form, make the adjusting entries needed at June 30.

3-24A Portraits, Inc., a commercial photography studio, has just completed its first year's operations, and annual financial statements are to be prepared. The ledger account balances prior to year-end adjustments are listed below. No adjusting entries have been made during the year. Assume that all balances are normal.

Cash	$2,200	Retained Earnings	$ –0–
Accounts Receivable	2,760	Photography Fees Earned	14,400
Prepaid Advertising	540	Wages Expense	3,800
Equipment	6,400	Rent Expense	2,520
Accounts Payable	830	Utilities Expense	910
Capital Stock	5,000	Supplies Expense	1,100

An analysis of related records discloses the following items:
(1) Photography services of $600 have been rendered, but customers have not yet been billed.
(2) Depreciation on equipment for the year is estimated to be $850.
(3) Utility expense for the last month of the year is estimated to be $90, but bills will not be received until next month.
(4) At year-end, a part-time helper had earned $70 in wages, to be paid on the 15th of next month.
(5) The lease calls for rent of $210 per month to be paid on the first of each month plus an annual amount equal to 2% of the annual photography fees earned. The rental percentage is to be paid within 30 days after the company's books are closed.
(6) The balance in Prepaid Advertising represents the amount paid to rent billboard space for one year. The rental agreement was entered into six months ago.
(7) All supplies purchased during the year were debited to Supplies Expense. At year-end, supplies on hand total $330.

REQUIRED
(a) Set up T accounts, and enter the unadjusted balances as shown above. Prove that debits and credits are equal by preparing a trial balance.
(b) Record adjusting entries in a general journal, and post these entries in the T accounts opened in (a) above. Add any additional accounts needed.

3–26A The Green Landscaping Service had the following transactions in July, its first
month of operations:

July 1 Bob Green contributed $7,000 of personal funds to the business.
   1 The firm purchased the following items for cash from a landscaping
      firm that was going out of business (make a compound entry): Truck,
      $2,500; Equipment, $900; Supplies, $600.
   2 Paid premium on a one-year liability insurance policy, $300.
   2 Entered into contract with local bank to provide lawn care for one
      year at a charge of $80 per month. Five months' charges were re-
      ceived in advance.
   7 Billed customers for services rendered, $450.
   12 Paid for July advertising in the *Chronicle*, $30.
   14 Paid two weeks' wages (five-day week) to helper, $250.
   17 Purchased supplies on account, $160.
   21 Billed customers for services rendered, $800.
   28 Paid two weeks' wages to helper, $250.
   30 Paid July bill for gas, oil, and repairs on truck, $60.
   30 Collected $720 from customers previously billed.
   31 Green withdrew $200 for personal use.

REQUIRED
(a) Set up a ledger that includes the following accounts, using the account
   numbers shown: Cash (11); Accounts Receivable (12); Supplies on Hand
   (14); Prepaid Insurance (15); Truck (16); Accumulated Depreciation—Truck
   (17); Equipment (18); Accumulated Depreciation—Equipment (19); Accounts Payable (21); Wages Payable (22); Unearned Service Fees (23);
   Green, Capital (31); Green, Drawing (32); Service Fees (41); Wages Expense
   (51); Advertising Expense (52); Supplies Expense (53); Insurance Expense
   (54); Truck Expense (55); Depreciation Expense—Truck (56); and Depreciation Expense—Equipment (57).
(b) Record July transactions in general journal form and post to the ledger
   accounts.
(c) Take a trial balance at July 31.
(d) Record adjusting journal entries in the general journal, and post to the
   ledger accounts. The following information is available on July 31:

      Supplies on hand, $170.
      Accrued wages, $60.
      Depreciation for July: Truck, $110; Equipment, $30.
      Unbilled services rendered, $90.

   Also, make any necessary adjusting entries for insurance and for service
   fees indicated by the July transactions.

3–27A The following information relates to December 31 adjustments for QuikPrint, a
printing company:
(1) Weekly salaries for a five-day week total $1,200 and are payable on Fri-
   days. December 31 of the current year is a Monday.
(2) QuikPrint received $600 during December for printing services to be per-
   formed during the following year. When received, this amount was credited to Printing Fees.

(3) During December, QuikPrint provided $300 of printing service; clients will be billed on January 2.

(4) All maintenance work on QuikPrint's equipment is handled by Zip Repair Company under an agreement whereby QuikPrint pays a fixed monthly charge of $120. QuikPrint paid three months' service charge in advance on December 1, debiting Prepaid Maintenance for $360.

(5) The firm paid a premium of $2,400 for a three-year insurance policy beginning on August 1 of the current year. The entire amount of the premium was debited to Insurance Expense; no other entry concerning this premium had been recorded.

(6) The Supplies on Hand account has a balance of $2,600 on December 31. However, the December purchases of supplies, totaling $450, were inadvertently debited to the Supplies Expense account, which now has a balance of $450. $1,130 worth of supplies were still on hand on December 31.

(7) QuikPrint purchased $2,500 worth of securities during the year and earned interest of $175 on these securities by December 31. No interest will be received until January. No entries have been made for the interest receivable or interest income.

REQUIRED
Prepare the required December 31 adjusting entries in general journal form.

BUSINESS DECISION PROBLEM

Engineering Research Associates, a firm started several years ago by Rodney Mann, offers testing services for structural systems, metal fatigue, and thermal and noise transmission. The balance sheet prepared by the firm's bookkeeper at the close of the current year is shown below:

Engineering Research Associates
Balance Sheet
December 31, 19XX

Assets			Liabilities		
Cash		$ 14,000	Accounts Payable	$28,000	
Accounts Receivable		34,000	Notes Payable—Bank	25,000	
Supplies on Hand		5,400	Total Liabilities		$ 53,000
Testing Equipment	$65,000				
Less: Accumulated Depreciation	18,000	47,000	**Owner's Equity**		
			R. Mann, Capital		47,400
Total Assets		$100,400	Total Liabilities and Owner's Equity		$100,400

Earlier in the year, Mann obtained a bank loan of $25,000 for the firm. One of the provisions of the loan is that at the end of the year the ratio of total liabilities to total owner's equity shall not exceed 1:1. Based on the above balance sheet, the ratio at the end of the current year is 1.12:1.

Mann is concerned about being in violation of the loan agreement and asks your assistance in reviewing the situation. His bookkeeper is quite inexperienced, and

Mann believes that the bookkeeper may have overlooked some items at year-end.

In discussions with Mann and the bookkeeper, you learn the following:

(1) On January 1, 19XX, the firm paid a $3,600 insurance premium for three years of coverage. The full amount was debited to Insurance Expense.

(2) Although depreciation on the testing equipment for 19XX was $1,500, it was not recorded.

(3) Interest on the bank loan has been paid through the end of the current yeat.

(4) The firm concluded a major consulting engagement in December, doing acoustical testing for the new city auditorium. The fee, amounting to $6,500, has not been billed or recorded in the accounts.

(5) On December 29, 19XX, the firm received a $500 advance payment from Steel Structures, Inc. for testing services to be rendered next year. This payment was credited to the Consulting Fees account.

(6) $5,100 worth of supplies were on hand on December 31. The bookkeeper filed the record of the count but made no entry in the accounts.

REQUIRED

What is the correct ratio of total liabilities to owner's equity at December 31, 19XX? Is Mann's firm in violation of the loan agreement? Prepare a schedule to support your computation of the correct total liabilities and owner's equity at December 31, 19XX.

4
The Accounting Cycle
Concluded

The first four major steps in the accounting cycle—analyzing and recording transactions, posting to accounts, then adjusting the accounts—are essential to the process of classifying financial data and, where necessary, aligning the data with appropriate time periods. The goal of these procedures is to prepare the data so that they can be summarized in a set of meaningful financial statements.

In this chapter, we shall explain the two remaining principal steps in the accounting cycle: preparation of financial statements and closing procedures. Our discussion is based on the December financial data given in Chapter 3 for the Monroe TV Service, a sole proprietorship.

PREPARING FINANCIAL STATEMENTS

Step 5: Prepare Financial Statements

Once the appropriate adjusting entries have been made and posted to the ledger accounts, an income statement and a balance sheet may be prepared directly from the account balances. In actual practice, however, many accountants find that drawing up a worksheet first facilitates the preparation of the statements. The basic structure of the worksheet is presented in Exhibit 4-1, which includes an explanation of the scheme being used. A completed worksheet for the Monroe TV Service appears in Exhibit 4-2. A careful study of these two illustrations shows the following advantages of the worksheet:

(1) The balances of all general ledger accounts are apparent because they appear in one location.

(2) The total effect of any adjustment, whether contemplated or actually made on the worksheet, can be readily determined.

(3) Once all the adjustments have been made, the adjusted account balances can be determined and separated into a group for the income statement and a group for the balance sheet, thus simplifying the preparation of these statements.

The worksheet is prepared in the order indicated by the circled numbers in Exhibit 4-1.

Refer to both illustrations when reading through the following procedures for preparing a worksheet.

(1) Heading. The worksheet heading should include (a) the name of the accounting entity involved, (b) the term "worksheet" to indicate the type of analysis performed, and (c) a date describing the time period covered. The worksheet includes both income statement data (for the period described) and balance sheet data (for the end of the period described).

The worksheet form we have illustrated has a description column and eight (money) amount columns. A set of debit and credit columns is provided for each of the four headings "Trial Balance," "Adjustments," "Income Statement," and "Balance Sheet."

(2) Unadjusted trial balance. The trial balance, taken in Step 3 of the accounting cycle, is entered in the description column and the first pair of money columns. Because this trial balance reflects the account balances before adjustment, it is often designated the **unadjusted trial balance.** Once the trial balance is placed on the worksheet and double ruled, it reflects the state of the general ledger.

(3) Adjustments. The adjustments recorded on the worksheet are identical with those recorded in general journal form in Step 4 of the accounting cycle (see

EXHIBIT 4–1
Basic Structure of Worksheet

①
(Heading for worksheet)

Description	Trial Balance		Adjustments		Income Statement		Balance Sheet	
	Debit	Credit	Debit	Credit	Debit	Credit	Debit	Credit
② (The unadjusted trial balance)			③ (Amounts of adjustments)		④ (Extension of adjusted account balances)			
(Titles of accounts not in unadjusted trial balance, added as needed)					(Income statement accounts)		(Balance sheet accounts)	
					⑤ (Balancing of columns for each statement)			

EXHIBIT 4–2
Monroe TV Service
Worksheet
For the Month Ended December 31, 19XX

Description	Trial Balance Debit	Trial Balance Credit	Adjustments Debit	Adjustments Credit	Income Statement Debit	Income Statement Credit	Balance Sheet Debit	Balance Sheet Credit
Cash	11,590						11,590	
Accounts Receivable	2,650		(g) 180				2,830	
Supplies and Parts on Hand	600			(a) 380			220	
Test Equipment	3,000						3,000	
Truck	7,200						7,200	
Accounts Payable		1,600						1,600
Unearned Service Fees		800	(d) 200					600
Carl Monroe, Capital		20,000						20,000
Carl Monroe, Drawing	600						600	
Service Fees		4,700		(d) 200 (g) 180		5,080		
Rent Expense	400				400			
Wages Expense	840		(f) 70		910			
Advertising Expense	50				50			
Truck Expense	170				170			
	27,100	27,100						
Supplies and Parts Expense			(a) 380		380			
Depreciation Expense—Truck			(b) 100		100			
Accumulated Depreciation—Truck				(b) 100				100
Depreciation Expense—Test Equipment			(c) 50		50			
Accumulated Depreciation—Test Equipment				(c) 50				50
Utilities Expense			(e) 80		80			
Utilities Payable				(e) 80				80
Wages Payable				(f) 70				70
			1,060	1,060	2,140	5,080	25,440	22,500
Net Income for December					2,940			2,940
					5,080	5,080	25,440	25,440

4–2. This procedure makes it easy to check the equality of debits and credits in each entry and to identify all the amounts related to a particular adjustment.

We repeat the adjusting journal entries made at the end of December for the Monroe TV Service and explain their placement on the worksheet (Exhibit 4–2).

(a) Supplies and Parts Expense *(Expense)*	380	
Supplies and Parts on Hand *(assets)*		380

Because $220 worth of supplies were found to be on hand at the end of December, it was necessary to reduce the asset Supplies and Parts on Hand from $600 to $220 and to record the difference, $380, as expense. Note that the expense account, Supplies and Parts Expense, does not appear in the unadjusted trial balance and must be added below the accounts already listed, to accommodate this adjusting entry.

(b) Depreciation Expense—Truck *(expense)*	100	
Accumulated Depreciation—Truck *(asset)*		100
(c) Depreciation Expense—Test Equipment *(Expense)*	50	
Accumulated Depreciation— *(asset)*		
Test Equipment		50

These entries were made to record the expiration of fixed asset costs for December. The entries to record depreciation expense and reduce the fixed asset accounts (via accumulated depreciation contra accounts) require accounts that do not appear in the unadjusted trial balance. Therefore, the four accounts in entries (b) and (c) must be listed in the description space below the accounts in the trial balance.

(d) Unearned Service Fees *(Liability)*	200	
Service Fees *(Revenue)*		200

This adjustment was made to reflect the portion of an $800 advance that was earned in December. The liability account Unearned Service Fees, originally credited for the $800 advance, was reduced by a debit for $200, and a corresponding credit was made to the revenue account Service Fees. Since both accounts appear in the unadjusted trial balance, this adjustment is reflected on the lines already provided for these accounts.

(e) Utilities Expense *(Expense)*	80	
Utilities Payable *(Liability)*		80
(f) Wages Expense *(Expense)*	70	
Wages Payable *(Liability)*		70

These adjusting entries were made to reflect expenses incurred in December but not paid until January. The utilities expense was the estimated cost of services consumed in December. Wages accrued were for the last two days in December. Because no utilities expense was paid in December, the expense account does not appear in the unadjusted trial balance. Both the expense account and the liability Utilities Payable must be added below the accounts already listed. Since wages were paid during December, Wages Expense appears in the trial balance, but Wages Payable must be added.

(g)	Accounts Receivable	180
	Service Fees	180

This entry was made to reflect unbilled service fees earned in December. Since both accounts appeared in the unadjusted trial balance, this adjustment is reflected on the lines already provided for these accounts.

(4) **Extension of adjusted balances.** After entering the adjusting entries on the worksheet, we total the adjustments columns to prove the equality of debits and credits. Then, we combine the amounts of the adjustments with any related amounts in the unadjusted trial balance and extend the amounts into the two remaining pairs of columns as follows:

Income Statement
(+) Expenses ──────────→ Debit column of income statement
(−) Revenues ──────────→ Credit column of income statement

Balance Sheet
(+) Assets and owner's drawing account ──────────→ Debit column of balance sheet
(−) Liabilities, owner's capital and contra assets, such as accumulated depreciation ──────────→ Credit column of balance sheet

Note that the position of the adjusted balances in the worksheet corresponds with the normal balances of the accounts. That is, expenses and assets are debits on the income statement and balance sheet, respectively; revenue is a credit on the income statement, while liabilities and owner's capital are credits on the balance sheet. The owner's drawing account is a debit on the balance sheet columns because it is a contra owner's equity account. The accumulated depreciation accounts are credits on the balance sheet because they are contra asset accounts. Once the proper extensions are made, the worksheet is complete except for the balancing of the four columns containing the adjusted balances.

(5) **Balancing the worksheet.** The first step in balancing is to add each of the income statement and balance sheet columns and record their respective totals on the same line as the totals of the adjustments columns. The difference between the total debits and total credits in the income statement columns will be the difference between total revenues and total expenses—that is, the net income

for the period. The net income should also be the amount by which the debit and credit columns for the balance sheet differ. This is true because the capital account balance, as extended, does not yet reflect the net income for the current period.

When revenues exceed expenses, the two pairs of statement columns can be balanced by adding the net income figure to both the debit column of the income statement and the credit column of the balance sheet. If expenses exceed revenues, we add the amount of net loss to the credit column of the income statement and to the debit column of the balance sheet. When we have determined the net income (or loss) and added it to the proper columns, we total and double rule the four columns. The worksheet is now complete and contains the account data necessary to prepare an income statement and a balance sheet. Note that Carl Monroe's equity at this point is indicated by three amounts appearing on the worksheet:

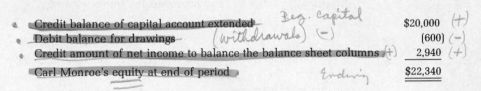

- • Credit balance of capital account extended   *Beg. capital* $20,000 *(+)*
- • Debit balance for drawings   *(withdrawals) (−)*   (600) *(−)*
- • Credit amount of net income to balance the balance sheet columns *(+)*   2,940 *(+)*

  Carl Monroe's equity at end of period   *Ending* $22,340

Exhibits 4–3 and 4–4 illustrate an income statement and a balance sheet for the Monroe TV Service, prepared from the worksheet.

EXHIBIT 4–3

Monroe TV Service
Income Statement
For the Month of December, 19XX

Revenues		
Service Fees		$5,080
Operating Expenses		
Rent Expense	$400	
Wages Expense	910	
Advertising Expense	50	
Truck Expense	170	
Supplies and Parts Expense	380	
Depreciation Expense—Truck	100	
Depreciation Expense—Test Equipment	50	
Utilities Expense	80	
Total Operating Expenses		2,140
Net Income for December		$2,940

EXHIBIT 4-4

Monroe TV Service
Balance Sheet
December 31, 19XX

Assets			Liabilities		
Cash		$11,590	Accounts Payable	$1,600	
Accounts Receivable		2,830	Utilities Payable	80	
Supplies and Parts on Hand		220	Wages Payable	70	
Test Equipment	$3,000		Unearned Service Fees	600	
Less: Accumulated Depreciation	50	2,950	Total Liabilities		$ 2,350
Truck	$7,200		**Owner's Equity**		
Less: Accumulated Depreciation	100	7,100	Carl Monroe, Capital		22,340
			Total Liabilities and		
Total Assets		$24,690	Owner's Equity		$24,690

A formal set of financial statements frequently includes a statement of owners' equity. This statement simply lists the beginning balance, additions, deductions, and ending balance of owners' equity for the accounting period. Exhibit 4-5 illustrates such a statement for the Monroe TV Service for the month of December.

When capital contributions have been made during the accounting period, we cannot determine from the worksheet alone the beginning balance of owners' capital and amounts of capital contributions during a period. Consequently, in preparing a statement of owner's equity, we must examine the owner's capital account in the general ledger.

EXHIBIT 4-5

Monroe TV Service
Statement of Owner's Equity
For the Month of December, 19XX

Carl Monroe, Capital—Dec. 1, 19XX		$ -0-
Add: Capital contributed in December	$20,000	
Net income for December	2,940	22,940
		$22,940
Less: Capital withdrawn in December		600
Carl Monroe, Capital—Dec. 31, 19XX		$22,340

RECORDING AND POSTING ADJUSTING ENTRIES Thus far in our example of end-of-period procedures, we have assumed that adjusting entries could be recorded and posted whenever financial statements are prepared. In practice, when monthly or quarterly statements are prepared, many accountants prefer to reflect adjustments only on a worksheet and do not record them in a journal or post them to the accounts.

At the close of the calendar or fiscal year, however, the necessary adjusting entries must be recorded in the general journal and posted to the ledger accounts

EXHIBIT 4–6
Adjusting Entries

General Journal

Page 3

Date		Description	Post. Ref.	Debit	Credit
19XX Dec.	31	Supplies and Parts Expense	54	380	
		Supplies and Parts on Hand	14		380
		To record expense of supplies and parts used in December.			
	31	Depreciation Expense—Truck	58	100	
		Accumulated Depreciation—Truck	19		100
		To record December depreciation.			
	31	Depreciation Expense—Test Equipment	57	50	
		Accumulated Depreciation—Test Equipment	17		50
		To record December depreciation.			
	31	Unearned Service Fees	24	200	
		Service Fees	41		200
		To record portion of advance earned in December.			
	31	Utilities Expense	55	80	
		Utilities Payable	22		80
		To record estimated amount of December utilities expense.			
	31	Wages Expense	52	70	
		Wages Payable	23		70
		To record accrued wages for Dec. 30–31.			
	31	Accounts Receivable	12	180	
		Service Fees	41		180
		To record unbilled revenue earned during December.			

in order to accomplish the proper closing procedures described below. Although the Monroe TV Service has been in business only for December, its accounting year ends on December 31. Therefore, the adjusting entries are entered in the records and closing procedures are followed. The adjusting entries appear in the general journal as shown in Exhibit 4–6.

These journal entries are posted to the ledger accounts of the Monroe TV Service shown in Exhibit 4–9 (pp. 130–35). The entries are identified by the parenthetical notation (adjusting).

CLOSING PROCEDURES

Step 6: Close Temporary Accounts

Revenue, expense, and drawing accounts are temporary accounts used to accumulate data related to a specific accounting year. These temporary accounts are maintained to facilitate preparation of the income statement and to provide additional information. At the end of each accounting year, the balances of these temporary accounts are transferred to the capital account (the Retained Earnings account for corporations). Hence, the balance of the owner's capital account will include on a cumulative basis the net result of all revenue, expense, and drawing transactions. This final phase in the accounting cycle is referred to as **closing procedures.**

An account is said to be "closed" when an entry is made that changes its balance to zero. Any account is closed by an entry that is equal in amount to the account's balance but opposite to the balance as a debit or credit. When an account is closed, it is said to be closed *to* the account that receives the offsetting debit or credit. Thus, the effect of a closing entry is simply to transfer the balance of one account to another account. In this manner, closing procedures transfer the balances of temporary accounts to the capital account.

Some type of summary account is traditionally used to close the temporary accounts. For our illustration, we shall use an account titled "Income Summary," although a variety of different titles are found in practice ("Revenue and Expense Summary," "Income and Expense Summary," "Profit and Loss Summary," and so on). The entries for opening and closing the Income Summary are quite simple and occur only during the closing procedures. The entries that close the temporary accounts are as follows:

(1) Debit each revenue account in an amount equal to its balance, and credit the Income Summary for the total revenue involved.

(2) Credit each expense account in an amount equal to its balance, and debit the Income Summary for the total expense involved.

After the temporary accounts have been closed, the balance of the Income Summary account is equal to the net income for the period—hence the title "Income Summary." The remaining closing steps are:

EXHIBIT 4-7
Closing Revenue and Expense Accounts
General Journal

Page 4

Date		Description	Post. Ref.	Debit	Credit
19XX					
Dec.	31	Service Fees	41	5,080	
		Income Summary	33		5,080
		To close the revenue account.			
	31	Income Summary	33	2,140	
		Rent Expense	51		400
		Wages Expense	52		910
		Advertising Expense	53		50
		Truck Expense	56		170
		Supplies and Parts Expense	54		380
		Depreciation Expense—Truck	58		100
		Depreciation Expense—Test Equipment	57		50
		Utilities Expense	55		80
		To close the expense accounts.			

Rent Expense

| 400 | 400 |

Supplies and Parts Expense

| 380 | 380 |

Wages Expense

| 910 | 910 |

Depreciation Expense—Truck

| 100 | 100 |

Advertising Expense

| 50 | 50 |

Depreciation Expense—Test Equipment

| 50 | 50 |

Truck Expense

| 170 | 170 |

Utilities Expense

| 80 | 80 |

Income Summary

| 2,140 | 5,080 |

Service Fees

| 5,080 | 5,080 |

(3) Debit the Income Summary for its balance, and credit the capital account (Retained Earnings for a corporation) for the same amount. In the case of a net loss, debit the capital account and credit the Income Summary.

(4) For noncorporate businesses, credit the drawing account in an amount equal to its balance and debit the capital account for the same amount.

In Exhibit 4–7, we illustrate the entries for closing the revenue and expense accounts to the Income Summary account of the Monroe TV Service as they would be recorded in the general journal. The effect of these two entries is shown on page 127 using T accounts.

At this point, the balance of the Income Summary is a credit equal to the net income of $2,940. The closing procedure is completed by closing the Income Summary and Carl Monroe, Drawing accounts to the Carl Monroe, Capital account. These two entries are recorded in the general journal as shown in Exhibit 4–8. The effect of these entries on the general ledger is also diagrammed.

It is probably most convenient to take the data necessary for formulating the closing entries from the worksheet, although the information can also be derived from the ledger. After the closing entries have been recorded and posted to the general ledger, all temporary accounts have zero balances and the capital account has a balance equal to the amount shown on the Monroe TV Service's balance sheet (see Exhibit 4–4). Finally, the closing entries for the Monroe TV Service are

EXHIBIT 4–8
Closing the Income
Summary and Drawing Accounts

General Journal
Page 4

Date		Description	Post. Ref.	Debit	Credit
19XX Dec.	31	Income Summary	33	2,940	
		Carl Monroe, Capital	31		2,940
		To close the Income Summary account.			
	31	Carl Monroe, Capital	31	600	
		Carl Monroe, Drawing	32		600
		To close the drawing account.			

Carl Monroe, Drawing		Carl Monroe, Capital		Income Summary	
600	600	600	20,000	2,140	5,080
			2,940	2,940	

posted to the firm's general ledger accounts. These entries are identified by the parenthetical notation (closing). Exhibit 4–9 illustrates the general ledger of the Monroe TV Service after all the closing procedures have been followed.

As explained in Chapter 3, the entries involving owners' equity would be different had Monroe TV Service been organized as a corporation. The $20,000 cash capital contribution would be recorded as a debit to Cash and a credit to Capital Stock. The $600 withdrawal of cash would be considered a cash dividend and would be recorded as a debit to Retained Earnings and a credit to Cash. As shown below, once the revenue and expense accounts have been closed to the Income Summary account, the closing procedures for a corporate firm are completed by closing the Income Summary account to Retained Earnings.

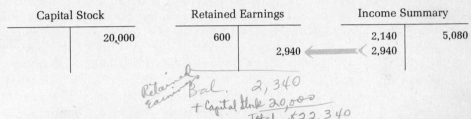

Capital Stock		Retained Earnings		Income Summary	
	20,000	600		2,140	5,080
			2,940 ⟵	2,940	

Retained Earnings Bal. 2,340
+ Capital Stock 20,000
Total $22,340

After closing entries are posted, the Retained Earnings account would reflect the $2,340 earned and retained in the business. Combined with the Capital Stock of $20,000, total owners' equity would be $22,340, the same as the amount shown for the proprietorship form of organization.

POST-CLOSING TRIAL BALANCE A post-closing trial balance is usually taken after the closing process. This procedure assures that an equality of debits and credits has been maintained throughout the adjusting and closing procedure. Obviously, since the temporary accounts have been closed, only balance sheet accounts appear in this trial balance. Exhibit 4–10 presents the post-closing trial balance for the Monroe TV Service.

REVERSING ENTRIES In our discussion of adjusting entries for accrued items in Chapter 3, we pointed out that certain precautions are necessary to avoid reflecting the same expense or revenue in two successive periods. We will now review the procedures followed in aligning the proper amount of wages expense incurred in December for the Monroe TV Service.

Reversing wages expense accrual. As you will recall from Chapter 3, the wages of Carl Monroe's assistant were $210 for each six-day work week ($35 per day) and the assistant was paid every other Saturday. We assumed that the two

EXHIBIT 4–9
Monroe TV Service
General Ledger

Assets

Cash

Account No. 11

Date		Explanation	Post. Ref.	Debit*	Credit	Balance
19XX						
Dec.	1		J1	20,000		20,000
	1		J1		400	19,600
	2		J1		7,200	12,400
	2		J1		2,000	10,400
	2		J1	800		11,200
	7		J1	550		11,750
	14		J1		420	11,330
	14		J2	480		11,810
	17		J2		50	11,760
	19		J2	500		12,260
	21		J2	320		12,580
	28		J2		170	12,410
	28		J2		420	11,990
	28		J2		600	11,390
	28		J2	200		11,590

Accounts Receivable

Account No. 12

Date		Explanation	Post. Ref.	Debit*	Credit	Balance
19XX						
Dec.	14		J1	750		750
	19		J2		500	250
	28		J2	2,400		2,650
	31	(adjusting)	J3	180		2,830

Supplies and Parts on Hand

Account No. 14

Date		Explanation	Post. Ref.	Debit*	Credit	Balance
19XX						
Dec.	3		J1	600		600
	31	(adjusting)	J3		380	220

Test Equipment — Account No. 16

(Assets)

Date		Explanation	Post. Ref.	Debit*	Credit	Balance
19XX Dec.	2		J1	3,000		3,000

Accumulated Depreciation—Test Equipment — Account No. 17

(Assets)

Date		Explanation	Post. Ref.	Debit	Credit*	Balance
19XX Dec.	31	(adjusting)	J3		50	50

Truck — Account No. 18

(Assets)

Date		Explanation	Post. Ref.	Debit*	Credit	Balance
19XX Dec.	2		J1	7,200		7,200

Accumulated Depreciation—Truck — Account No. 19

(Assets)

Date		Explanation	Post. Ref.	Debit	Credit*	Balance
19XX Dec.	31	(adjusting)			100	100

Accounts Payable — Account No. 21

(Liability)

Date		Explanation	Post. Ref.	Debit	Credit*	Balance
19XX Dec.	2		J1		1,000	1,000
	3		J1		600	1,600

EXHIBIT 4–9 (continued)

 Utilities Payable   Account No. 22

Date		Explanation	Post. Ref.	Debit	Credit*	Balance
19XX Dec.	31	(adjusting)	J3		80	80

 Wages Payable   Account No. 23

Date		Explanation	Post. Ref.	Debit	Credit*	Balance
19XX Dec.	31	(adjusting)	J3		70	70

 Unearned Service Fees   Account No. 24

Date		Explanation	Post. Ref.	Debit	Credit*	Balance
19XX Dec.	2		J1		800	800
	31	(adjusting)	J3	200		600

Carl Monroe, Capital   Account No. 31

Date		Explanation	Post. Ref.	Debit	Credit*	Balance
19XX Dec.	1		J1		20,000	20,000
	31	(closing)	J4		2,940	22,940
	31	(closing)	J4	600		22,340

Carl Monroe, Drawing *(O.E.)*   Account No. 32

Date		Explanation	Post. Ref.	Debit*	Credit	Balance
19XX Dec.	28		J2	600		600
	31	(closing)	J4		600	–0–

Income Summary *(O.E.)*   Account No. 33

Date		Explanation	Post. Ref.	Debit	Credit*	Balance
19XX Dec.	31	(closing)	J4		5,080	5,080
	31	(closing)	J4	2,140		2,940
	31	(closing)	J4	2,940		–0–

Service Fees *(Revenue)*   Account No. 41

Date		Explanation	Post. Ref.	Debit	Credit*	Balance
19XX Dec.	7		J1		550	550
	14		J1		750	1,300
	14		J2		480	1,780
	21		J2		320	2,100
	28		J2		2,400	4,500
	28		J2		200	4,700
	31	(adjusting)	J3		200	4,900
	31	(adjusting)	J3		180	5,080
	31	(closing)	J4	5,080		–0–

Rent Expense *(Expense)*   Account No. 51

Date		Explanation	Post. Ref.	Debit*	Credit	Balance
19XX Dec.	1		J1	400		400
	31	(closing)	J4		400	–0–

EXHIBIT 4–9 (continued)
Wages Expense   Account No. 52

Date		Explanation	Post. Ref.	Debit*	Credit	Balance
19XX						
Dec.	14		J1	420		420
	28		J2	420		840
	31	(adjusting)	J3	70		910
	31	(closing)	J4		910	–0–

Advertising Expense   Account No. 53

Date		Explanation	Post. Ref.	Debit*	Credit	Balance
19XX						
Dec.	17		J2	50		50
	31	(closing)	J4		50	–0–

Supplies and Parts Expense   Account No. 54

Date		Explanation	Post. Ref.	Debit*	Credit	Balance
19XX						
Dec.	31	(adjusting)	J3	380		380
	31	(closing)	J4		380	–0–

Utilities Expense   Account No. 55

Date		Explanation	Post. Ref.	Debit*	Credit	Balance
19XX						
Dec.	31	(adjusting)	J3	80		80
	31	(closing)	J4		80	–0–

Expenses

Truck Expense   Account No. 56

Date		Explanation	Post. Ref.	Debit*	Credit	Balance
19XX Dec.	28		J2	170		170
	31	(closing)	J4		170	–0–

Depreciation Expense—Test Equipment   Account No. 57

Date		Explanation	Post. Ref.	Debit*	Credit	Balance
19XX Dec.	31	(adjusting)	J3	50		50
	31	(closing)	J4		50	–0–

Depreciation Expense—Truck   Account No. 58

Date		Explanation	Post. Ref.	Debit*	Credit	Balance
19XX Dec.	31	(adjusting)	J3	100		100
	31	(closing)	J4		100	–0–

paydays in December fell on December 14 and 28. The calendar for the latter part of December and the first part of January appeared as follows:

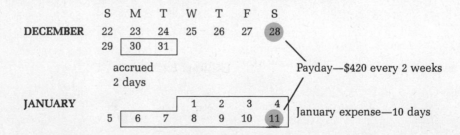

At the end of December $70 wages expense was accrued for December 30 and 31 in order to reflect the proper expense for December. We made the following adjusting entry:

Dec. 31   Wages Expense *(Expense)*   70
           Wages Payable *(Liability)*   70
           To record accrued wages
           for December 30 and 31.

After this adjusting entry was posted, the Wages Expense account had a debit balance of $910. This consisted of two debits of $420 made on December 14 and 28 and the $70 accrual on December 31. Along with other expenses, the Wages Expense account of $910 was closed to the Income Summary account on December 31. After the closing procedures, the Wages Expense account and the Wages Payable account appeared in the ledger (in T account form) as follows:

	Wages Expense *(Expense)*		
Dec. 14	420	Dec. 31 (closing)	910
28	420		
31 (adjusting)	70		
	910		910

EXHIBIT 4–10

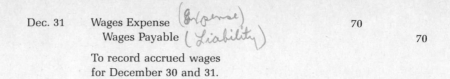

Monroe TV Service
Post-Closing Trial Balance
December 31, 19XX

	Debit	Credit
Cash *(assets)*	$11,590	
Accounts Receivable *(assets)*	2,830	
Supplies and Parts on Hand *(assets)*	220	
Test Equipment *(assets)*	3,000	
Accumulated Depreciation—Test Equipment *(asset)*		$ 50
Truck *(assets)*	7,200	
Accumulated Depreciation—Truck *(assets)*		100
Accounts Payable *(Lia)*		1,600
Utilities Payable "		80
Wages Payable "		70
Unearned Service Fees *Lia)*		600
Carl Monroe, Capital *(O.E.)*		22,340
	$24,840	$24,840

Wages Payable (*Liability*)

	Dec. 31 (adjusting)	70

Now, when the assistant receives his two-weeks' wages of $420 on January 11, only $350 of this amount should be reflected as expense for January, since only 10 days were worked in January. In recording the payment on January 11, the bookkeeper might debit Wages Expense for $350, debit the liability Wages Pay-

THE MYSTERIOUS DOUBLE REVERSING ENTRY

Most large firms find it necessary to estimate unrecorded revenue and expenses at the close of the accounting period so that revenue and expenses are properly reflected on an accrual basis. The amount of adjustments is often computed using statistical analysis or formula estimates because precise accruals would require analysis of a myriad of transactions. In the subsequent accounting period, the adjusting entries are *reversed* (as explained in this chapter) and transactions for the new period are recorded in the usual way, that is, as if they were transactions of the current period. Firms following this procedure normally find that it is either too difficult or too inefficient to analyze subsequent cash settlements by period affected, especially when automated data processing systems are employed.

In our anecdote in Chapter 3, we mentioned that the Yale Express System imposed its semi-cash basis on its acquired company, Republic Carloading and Distributing Company, and failed to accrue a large amount of freight costs at the end of the 1963 accounting year. However, using estimates, they *did* accrue a portion (approximately $790,000) of these costs, debiting 1963 expenses and crediting accounts payable.

In early 1964, the firm recorded the reversing entry *twice*. This procedure had the effect of understating costs (and payables) in the first quarter's statements for 1964 by approximately $790,000. It is impossible to tell from the evidence in the case whether the double reversal was inadvertent or intentional. The enlarged firm was, after all, in the process of merging two accounting departments and implementing a new computer system. However, in view of the fact that 1963 reported net income was close to $1.14 million, although the firm was later shown to have a loss of $1.88 million, the double reversal of an adjusting entry amounting to better than three-fourths of a million dollars makes it difficult to understand why the company or its auditors failed to detect this grossly material accounting error.

The double-reversal error that occurred in this case in no way invalidates the concept of reversing entries. Overstatement of net income and understatement of payables can occur if accruals are omitted or improperly recorded, or for that matter if transactions are omitted or improperly recorded. The lesson to be gained from this example of double reversal is that it is extremely important for a firm to exercise control over its accounting procedures and to obtain proper internal and external audits of its financial operations.

able for $70, and credit Cash for $420. This procedure, however, requires extreme vigilance in recording routine transactions on the part of the bookkeeper, who must keep in mind previously made accruals in order to record subsequent payments correctly. Many bookkeepers find this a nuisance and avoid the problem by reversing adjustments made for accruals. Reversing entries are made after all closing procedures have been completed, and they are dated the first day of the following period. For example, the reversing entry for the accrual of wages would be:

| Jan. 1 | Wages Payable | 70 | |
| | Wages Expense | | 70 |

To reverse accrual made Dec. 31.

The reversing entry reduces the liability Wages Payable to zero and results in a $70 abnormal credit balance in the Wages Expense account at the start of the new accounting period. On the next payday, however, the wage payment of $420 is recorded in the usual way, as follows:

| Jan. 11 | Wages Expense | 420 | |
| | Cash | | 420 |

Paid wages for two weeks ended Jan. 11.

After the reversing entry and the January 11 payment have been posted, the Wages Expense and Wages Payable accounts appear as follows:

Wages Expense

Dec. 14	420	Dec. 31 (closing)	910
28	420		
31 (adjusting)	70		
	910		910
Jan. 11	420	Jan. 1 (reversing)	70

Wages Payable

| Jan. 1 (reversing) | 70 | Dec. 31 (adjusting) | 70 |

Note that the above procedure removes the $70 Wages Payable that was properly accrued at December 31, enables the bookkeeper to record the first January payroll without specifically considering the amount of wages expense accrued at December 31, and reflects the proper wages expense, $350, in January.

Reversing other accruals. Reversing entries would also be employed for two other accruals made by Monroe TV Service: the $80 estimated utilities expense and the $180 unbilled service fees. The appropriate reversing entries to make for these two accruals, after the books are closed, are:

Jan. 1	Utilities Payable	80	
	Utilities Expense		80

To reverse accrual made Dec. 31.

Jan. 1	Service Fees	180	
	Accounts Receivable		180

To reverse accrual made Dec. 31.

These entries eliminate the accrued amounts from the liability and asset accounts and create an abnormal credit balance of $80 in Utilities Expense and an abnormal debit balance of $180 in Service Fees.

The credit balance in Utilities Expense will be eliminated when the bills for utilities are received and paid in January. Assuming bills amounting to $84 arrived and were paid on January 5, the entry would be:

Jan. 5	Utilities Expense	84	
	Cash		84

To record payment of December utilities.

After the entry for payment is posted, Utilities Expense will have a $4 debit balance to be absorbed in January. As we mentioned in Chapter 3, charging a small amount of one period's expense in another period must be tolerated when estimates are used.

The debit balance in Service Fees is eliminated when Monroe TV Service sends out its billing to the local hotel whenever 50 hours of work have been completed (per its contract with the hotel). This billing, made on January 14, is recorded as follows:

Jan. 14	Accounts Receivable	300	
	Service Fees		300

To record billing for 50 hours
of work at $6 per hour.

This entry leaves a credit balance of $120 in the Service Fees revenue account, the proper amount of revenue to be reflected for work performed in January (20 hours @ $6). The $300 debit to Accounts Receivable represents the amount of cash to be collected from the hotel.

The reversing procedure is needed only for adjusting entries that involve accrued expense and accrued revenue. Reversals are not required for adjustments involving prepayments of expense or unearned revenues. Accruals are always followed by subsequent payments or receipts, and the object of the reversing procedures is to ensure that entries for such subsequent payments or receipts do not erroneously cause expense or revenue for a previous period to be reflected in accounts for the current period.

Interim Financial Statements

We mentioned earlier that most companies prepare interim financial statements from worksheet data because they prefer to adjust the accounts in the general ledger only at the close of the year. When making adjusting entries on the worksheet, the bookkeeper must take into account the period for which the adjustments are to be made. Some adjustment amounts will accumulate, while others will not. For example, in writing off a one-year prepaid insurance premium of $1,200 paid on January 1 and debited to the asset account, the bookkeeper would debit Insurance Expense and credit Prepaid Insurance for $100 at January 31. The amount of the adjustment would be $200 at the end of February, $300 at the end of March, and so on. Similarly, the amount of the adjusting entry for depreciation will increase each month. On the other hand, an adjusting entry to accrue salaries at the end of any month will consist only of unpaid salaries at the date of adjustment, because salaries accrued at the end of each month are ordinarily paid during the ensuing month.

When the end-of-the-year worksheet is prepared, the adjusting data will pertain to the entire year. Therefore, the adjusting entries to be journalized and posted to the ledger accounts can be taken directly from this worksheet.

It is a simple matter to prepare income statements for portions of a year by merely subtracting data on earlier worksheets from those prepared later. For example, income statement data for the month of February can be obtained by subtracting the relevant data on the January 31 worksheet from the same data on the February 28 worksheet, since the latter worksheet would be cumulative. Similarly, income statement data for the second quarter of the year can be found by subtracting data on the March 31 worksheet from data on the June 30 worksheet, and so on.

KEY POINTS TO REMEMBER

(1) The worksheet is used to facilitate the preparation of financial statements.
(2) The trial balance is recorded directly on the worksheet; adjustments usually are made only on the worksheet when interim financial statements are being prepared.
(3) Adjusted balances, which are extended into the income statement and balance sheet columns of the worksheet, provide the data for formal financial statements.
(4) Adjusting and closing entries are recorded in the journal and ledger at the end of the accounting year.

(5) "Closing the books" consists of closing the revenue, expense, and other temporary accounts. Revenue and expense account balances are transferred to the Income Summary account. The balances of the Income Summary account and the owners' drawing accounts are closed to the owners' capital accounts. For corporations, the Income Summary account is closed to Retained Earnings.

(6) The method of reversing adjustments made for *accrued* items is an expedient to permit normal recording of subsequent payments or receipts. It is a safeguard against reflecting the same revenue or expense in successive periods.

QUESTIONS

4–1 Assume that at the close of the accounting year on December 31, all transactions have been posted, a trial balance has been prepared, and adjusting entries have been posted to the accounts. What two major steps of the accounting cycle are yet to be completed?

4–2 What are the advantages of preparing a worksheet?

4–3 When would adjusting entries be entered only on a worksheet and not in the accounts? Why?

4–4 Identify each of the eight amount columns of the worksheet and indicate in which columns the adjusted balances of the following accounts would appear:
- (a) Accounts Receivable
- (b) Accumulated Depreciation
- (c) Barker, Drawing
- (d) Wages Payable
- (e) Depreciation Expense
- (f) Rent Receivable
- (g) Prepaid Insurance
- (h) Service Fees
- (i) Capital Stock
- (j) Retained Earnings

4–5 Suppose the total adjusted revenue of a business is $90,000 and total adjusted expense is $75,000. (a) In which columns of a worksheet would the $15,000 difference appear when the worksheet is completed? (b) If total adjusted expenses amounted to $100,000, in which columns of the computed worksheet would the $10,000 difference appear?

4–6 What are some reasons why the totals of the balance sheet columns of the worksheet may differ from the total asset amount on the formal balance sheet?

4–7 When adjusted balances were extended on the worksheet, Unearned Fees of $700 was extended as a credit in the income statement columns and Accounts Receivable of $500 was extended as a debit in the income statement columns. All other extensions were properly made. (a) Would the worksheet balance? (b) How would these incorrect extensions affect the calculation of the net income shown on the worksheet?

4–8 Which groups of accounts are closed at the end of the accounting year? *nominal*

4–9 Why and how is the Income Summary account used in the closing procedure?

4–10 Which of the following accounts should not appear in the post-closing trial balance: Cash; Unearned Revenue; Jensen, Drawing; Depreciation Expense; Wages Payable; Supplies Expense; Retained Earnings?

4-11 A firm on a calendar-year basis prepares cumulative statements monthly, using a worksheet. Adjusting and closing entries are entered in journals and posted only on December 31. On January 1, the firm paid $720 for a three-year insurance policy. What worksheet adjustments for insurance are to be made on (a) January 31, (b) February 28, and (c) May 31?

4-12 A firm accrued wages of $500 on December 31. The next payday, January 3, the firm paid $5,000 in wages. The company does not make reversing entries. On January 3, the company debited Wages Expense and credited Cash for $5,000. How will this procedure affect January net income?

4-13 Since the firm in Question 4-12 did not make a reversing entry, what entry should have been made to record the January 3 payment of wages?

4-14 Assume that the firm in Question 4-12 did use reversing-entry procedures. What reversing entry should have been made on January 1? How should the January 3 payment have been recorded if a reversing entry had been made?

4-15 At the end of January, the following accounts had balances as shown in column (1). If correct adjusting entries had been made, the adjusted balances would be as shown in column (2). Assume that adjusting entries were not made. State the effect of such an omission on (a) January net income and (b) February net income.

	(1)	(2)
Supplies on Hand	$ 500	$ 180
Accounts Receivable	4,000	5,200
Unearned Service Fees	800	560
Wages Payable	–0–	450

EXERCISES

4-16 Assume that the last four columns of the worksheet are numbered as follows: (1) "Income Statement Debit," (2) "Income Statement Credit," (3) "Balance Sheet Debit," and (4) "Balance Sheet Credit." Indicate the number of the worksheet column in which the adjusted balances of the following accounts would appear:
(a) Accounts Receivable
(b) Depreciation Expense
(c) Advertising Expense
(d) Unearned Service Fees
(e) Utilities Payable
(f) Utilities Expense
(g) Travis, Capital
(h) Travis, Drawing
(i) Service Fees
(j) Accumulated Depreciation
(k) Capital Stock
(l) Retained Earnings

4-17 Nancy Ames has just completed a worksheet for January. Before she entered a net income or loss, the debit total of the balance sheet was $22,000 and the credit total of the income statement was $8,000. Give the grand totals of the income statement columns and the balance sheet columns after she entered (a) net income of $6,000; (b) net loss of $4,000.

4-18 On January 1, the credit balance of the John Simmons, Capital account was $18,000. On December 31 of the same year, the credit balance before closing entries was $25,000.The John Simmons, Drawing account had a debit balance of $4,200 on December 31. After revenue and expense accounts were closed, the Income Summary account had a debit balance of $1,800. Prepare a statement of owner's equity for the year.

4-19 The following selected accounts appeared in a firm's unadjusted trial balance at December 31, the end of the accounting year:

Prepaid Advertising	$ 480 (debit)	Unearned Service Fees	$ 2,800
Wages Expense	16,500 (debit)	Service Fees	36,000
Prepaid Insurance	520 (debit)	Rental Income	860

(a) Make the necessary adjusting entries in general journal form at December 31, assuming the following:
  (1) Prepaid advertising at December 31 is $350.
  (2) Unpaid wages earned by employees in December are $640.
  (3) Prepaid Insurance at December 31 is $430.
  (4) Unearned service fees at December 31 are $1,600.
  (5) Rental income of $230 owed by a tenant is not recorded at December 31.
(b) If the company consistently makes reversing entries, which of the adjustments in part (a) require reversing?
(c) Assume that the company does not make reversing entries. Give the early January entries to record payment of $1,150 in wages and receipt from a tenant of $230 rental income.

4-20 The income statement columns of a worksheet prepared December 31 contain only the following:

	Debit	Credit
Service Fees		$28,200
Rent Expense	$ 2,400	
Salaries Expense	18,300	
Supplies Expense	750	
Depreciation Expense	600	

Included among the accounts in the balance sheet columns of the worksheet are Dunn, Capital, $21,000 (credit) and Dunn, Drawing, $900 (debit). Prepare entries to close the accounts, including the owner's drawing account. After these entries are made, what is the balance of the Dunn, Capital account?

4-21 In the midst of closing procedures, the bookkeeper of Lambert Corporation became ill and was hospitalized. You have volunteered to complete the closing of the books, and you find that all revenue and expense accounts have zero balances and that the Income Summary account has a single debit entry for $81,350 and a single credit entry for $97,180. Apparently the only entry in Retained Earnings this year was a debit of $3,000 for dividends, which reduced the balance to $42,000. Capital Stock has a normal balance of $100,000 and shows no entries for the year. Give the journal entries to complete the closing procedures and calculate the balance of owners' equity.

PROBLEMS

4–22 The trial balance and adjustments columns of the worksheet for Eagle Roofing Service at December 31 of the current year are shown below.

	Trial Balance		Adjustments			
	Debit	Credit		Debit		Credit
Cash	3,720					
Accounts Receivable	6,150		(a)	800		
Supplies on Hand	1,800				(b)	550
Prepaid Insurance	480				(c)	240
Truck	8,600					
Accumulated Depreciation— Truck		600			(d)	700
Equipment	16,200					
Accumulated Depreciation— Equipment		1,700			(e)	850
Accounts Payable		1,200				
J. D. Eagle, Capital		14,750				
J. D. Eagle, Drawing	1,100					
Service Fees		46,100			(a)	800
Salaries Expense	23,900		(f)	1,100		
Rent Expense	1,800					
Advertising Expense	340					
Miscellaneous Expense	260					
	64,350	64,350				
Supplies Expense			(b)	550		
Insurance Expense			(c)	240		
Depreciation Expense— Truck			(d)	700		
Depreciation Expense— Equipment			(e)	850		
Salaries Payable					(f)	1,100
				4,240		4,240

REQUIRED

(a) Complete the worksheet.

(b) Prepare the necessary closing entries at December 31 in general journal form.

4–23 The July 31 trial balance of C. Cordell, who operates Rainy Lake Outfitters, a sole proprietorship renting equipment and supplies to canoeists and fishermen, is shown below.

Rainy Lake Outfitters
Trial Balance
July 31, 19XX

	Debit	Credit
Cash	$ 4,250	
Supplies on Hand	5,600	
Prepaid Insurance	2,400	
Equipment	86,500	
Accumulated Depreciation		$ 12,500
Accounts Payable		3,700
Unearned Rental Fees		2,450
C. Cordell, Capital		41,000
C. Cordell, Drawing	1,600	
Rental Fees Earned		75,650
Wages Expense	27,300	
Rent Expense	4,500	
Advertising Expense	2,730	
Miscellaneous Expense	420	
	$135,300	$135,300

The data in the trial balance are cumulative for the first three months of the firm's fiscal year, which begins May 1. No adjusting entries have been made in the accounts during the quarter. The following additional information is available:

(1) Supplies on hand at July 31 amount to $2,200.

(2) Insurance expense for the first quarter was $600.

(3) Depreciation for the first quarter was $2,100.

(4) The unearned rental fees consist of advance deposits received from customers when reservations are made. During the quarter, $1,750 of the unearned rental fees were earned.

(5) At July 31, unbilled revenue from rental services earned for outfitting several church groups during July amounted to $1,820.

(6) Accrued wages payable for equipment handlers and guides amounted to $850 at July 31.

REQUIRED

(a) Enter the trial balance in a worksheet and complete the worksheet using the adjustment data given above.

(b) Prepare an income statement for the first quarter and a balance sheet at July 31.

4-24 The following is a partially completed worksheet for the Atwood Upholstery Service.

Atwood Upholstery Service
Worksheet
December 31, 19XX

	Trial Balance Debit	Credit	Adjustments Debit	Credit	Income Statement Debit	Credit	Balance Sheet Debit	Credit
Cash	600						(r)600	
Accounts Receivable	(a)200		(d)300				500	
Prepaid Rent	180			(i)80			100	
Supplies on Hand	90			(j)50			40	
Equipment	3,000						(s)3000	
Accumulated Depreciation— Equipment		(b)200		60				260
Accounts Payable		100						100 (v)
R. Atwood, Capital		(c)2100						2100(w)
R. Atwood, Drawing	300						(t)300	
Service Fees		4,800		300		5100 (p)		
Wages Expense	2,500		140		(m)2640			
Utilities Expense	130		(e)30		160			
Rent Expense	200		(f)80		(n)280			
	7,200	7,200						
Supplies Expense			(g)50		50			
Depreciation Expense			(h)60		60			
Wages Payable				(k)140				(x)140
Utilities Payable				(l)30				30
Totals			660	660	3,190	(q)5100	4,540	(y)2630
Net Income = 1,910					1,910 (o)			(z)1,910
Totals					5,100	5,100	(u)4540	4,540

Rev 5100
Inc. Sum 5100

Capital 2100
With < 300
NI 1910
3,710

REQUIRED
Compute the missing amounts (indicated by the letters) and complete the worksheet (sufficient information is given). Assume all adjustments are usual and routine. The letters do not necessarily indicate the order in which the amounts should be derived.

4-25 Hike and Bike magazine has the following trial balance at December 31 of its current year of operation. Financial statements are prepared annually.

Hike and Bike
Trial Balance
December 31, 19XX

	Debit	Credit
Cash	$ 17,500	
Accounts Receivable	4,200	
Supplies on Hand	5,450	
Prepaid Insurance	840	
Office Equipment	24,200	
Accumulated Depreciation—Office Equipment		$ 1,900
Building	80,000	
Accumulated Depreciation—Building		2,000
Land	30,000	
Accounts Payable		1,400
Unearned Subscription Revenue		7,800
Capital Stock		100,000
Retained Earnings		32,500
Subscription Revenue		125,200
Advertising Revenue		21,600
Salaries Expense	76,150	
Printing and Mailing Expense	43,600	
Advertising Expense	8,120	
Utilities Expense	2,340	
	$292,400	$292,400

The following information for adjusting the accounts is available at December 31:
(1) Supplies on hand amount to $3,750.
(2) Prepaid insurance at December 31 is $420.
(3) Accrued salaries at December 31 are $3,100.
(4) $2,400 of the unearned subscription revenue shown in the trial balance was earned during the year.
(5) Advertising revenue earned during the period but unbilled at December 31 was $2,700.
(6) Depreciation on office equipment for the year was $1,800.
(7) Depreciation on the building for the year was $2,000.

REQUIRED
(a) Prepare an eight-column worksheet as of December 31. Set up any additional accounts needed.
(b) Prepare an income statement for the year and a balance sheet at December 31.
(c) Prepare closing entries in general journal form.

4-26 R. Ashton, attorney, opened her practice on December 1 of the current year. December transactions were as follows:

Dec. 1   R. Ashton invested $20,000 in the firm.
2   Paid rent for two months to Acme Realty, $500.
2   Paid $450 for various supplies.
3   Purchased furniture and fixtures for office on account, $5,000.
8   Paid $1,200 on account for furniture and fixtures purchased December 3.
13   Paid salary of assistant for two weeks, $900.
20   Performed legal services for cash, $2,800.
27   Paid salary of assistant for two weeks, $900.
30   Billed clients for legal work completed during the month, $1,400.
31   Ashton withdrew $1,200 from the business.

REQUIRED

(a) Open the following ledger accounts, using the account numbers shown: Cash (11); Accounts Receivable (12); Prepaid Rent (13); Supplies on Hand (14); Furniture and Fixtures (15); Accumulated Depreciation (16); Accounts Payable (21); Salary Payable (22); R. Ashton, Capital (31); R. Ashton, Drawing (32); Income Summary (33); Attorney's Fees (41); Supplies Expense (51); Salary Expense (52); Rent Expense (53); and Depreciation Expense (54).

(b) Journalize the December transactions, and post to the ledger.

(c) Prepare a trial balance directly on a worksheet, and complete the worksheet using the following information:
  (1) Supplies on hand at December 31 are $300.
  (2) Accrued salary payable at December 31 is $50.
  (3) Depreciation for December is $60.
  (4) Ashton has spent 20 hours on an involved tax fraud case during December. When completed in January her work will be billed at $40 per hour.
  (5) Prepaid rent at December 31 is $250.

(d) Prepare a December income statement and a December 31 balance sheet.

(e) Journalize and post adjusting and closing entries.

(f) Prepare a post-closing trial balance.

(g) Journalize and post the appropriate reversing entries.

4-27 Newport Engineering Services, Inc. prepares monthly income statements and balance sheets, but makes adjusting and closing entries in its accounts only at December 31 of each year. The firm's income statement for the three months ended March 31 of the current year and its trial balance at April 30 of the current year are given on page 149.

Newport Engineering Services, Inc.
Income Statement
For the three months ended March 31, 19XX

Revenue

Service Fees		$32,400

Expenses

Salaries Expense	$ 10,525	
Depreciation Expense—Equipment	2,550	
Rent Expense	1,430	
Advertising Expense	1,760	
Utilities Expense	635	
Supplies Expense	1,480	
Insurance Expense	240	
Total Expenses		18,620
Net Income for the Quarter		$13,780

Newport Engineering Services, Inc.
Trial Balance
April 30, 19XX

	Debit	Credit
Cash	$ 16,600	
Prepaid Insurance	720	
Supplies on Hand	5,100	
Equipment	88,000	
Accumulated Depreciation—Equipment		$ 5,100
Accounts Payable		3,200
Capital Stock		50,000
Retained Earnings		27,400
Service Fees		46,250
Salaries Expense	15,200	
Advertising Expense	3,500	
Rent Expense	1,900	
Utilities Expense	930	
	$131,950	$131,950

The following data for adjustments are available at April 30, 19XX:
(1) Prepaid insurance at April 30 was $400.
(2) Supplies on hand at April 30 were $3,000.
(3) Depreciation on equipment per month was $850.
(4) Accrued salaries at April 30 were $300.

REQUIRED
(a) Record the April 30 trial balance on an eight-column worksheet. Enter the necessary adjusting entries and complete the worksheet for the four months ended April 30, 19XX.
(b) Prepare an income statement for the four months ended April 30, 19XX.
(c) Prepare an income statement for the month of April, 19XX.

ALTERNATE PROBLEMS

4–22A Ward Cleaning Service will prepare financial statements on December 31 of the current year. The trial balance and adjustments columns of the worksheet for the firm at December 31 of the current year are shown below.

	Trial Balance		Adjustments		
	Debit	Credit	Debit		Credit
Cash	1,800				
Accounts Receivable	2,100				
Supplies on Hand	600			(a)	220
Prepaid Insurance	420			(b)	180
Equipment	10,100				
Accumulated Depreciation		900		(c)	650
Accounts Payable		1,600			
B. Ward, Capital		10,900			
B. Ward, Drawing	700				
Cleaning Fees		4,300			
Salaries Expense	1,400		(d)	170	
Rent Expense	350				
Miscellaneous Expense	230				
	17,700	17,700			
Insurance Expense			(b)	180	
Supplies Expense			(a)	220	
Depreciation Expense			(c)	650	
Salaries Payable				(d)	170
				1,220	1,220

REQUIRED
(a) Complete the worksheet.
(b) Prepare the closing entries at December 31 in general journal form.

4–23A The following trial balance was taken at March 31 of the current year:

Davis Travel Agency
Trial Balance
March 31, 19XX

	Debit	Credit
Cash	$ 1,900	
Supplies on Hand	400	
Prepaid Insurance	280	
Equipment	8,700	
Accumulated Depreciation		$ 940
Accounts Payable		530
Unearned Commissions		310
C. Davis, Capital		5,540
C. Davis, Drawing	2,100	
Commissions Earned		15,600
Salaries Expense	7,450	
Rent Expense	1,100	
Advertising Expense	820	
Utilities Expense	170	
	$22,920	$22,920

The data in the trial balance are cumulative for the first three months of the current year. No adjusting entries have been made in the accounts during this period. The following additional information is available:
(1) Depreciation for the first quarter is $150.
(2) Supplies on hand at March 31 cost $170.
(3) During the quarter, $160 of the unearned commissions were earned.
(4) Insurance expense for the quarter was $90.
(5) Accrued salaries payable were $330 at March 31.
(6) Unbilled commissions earned during the quarter were $520.

REQUIRED
(a) Enter the trial balance on a worksheet and complete the worksheet using the adjustment data given above.
(b) Prepare an income statement for the first quarter of the year and a balance sheet at March 31.

4-25A The trial balance shown below is for Dobbs Freight Service at December 31 of the current year.

	Debit	Credit
Cash	$ 2,300	
Accounts Receivable	1,750	
Supplies on Hand	460	
Prepaid Insurance	320	
Equipment	1,600	
Accumulated Depreciation—Equipment		$ 540
Trucks	18,900	
Accumulated Depreciation—Trucks		3,200
Accounts Payable		1,100
Notes Payable		2,000
S. Dobbs, Capital		6,870
S. Dobbs, Drawing	3,600	
Service Fees		46,500
Rent Expense	1,900	
Salaries and Wages Expense	28,400	
Utilities Expense	820	
Miscellaneous Expense	160	
	$60,210	$60,210

The following data for adjustments are also available at December 31:
(1) Supplies on hand amount to $170.
(2) Prepaid insurance is $120.
(3) Depreciation for the year is as follows: Equipment, $80; Trucks, $1,100.
(4) Accrued wages payable are $260.
(5) Accrued utilities payable are estimated to be $90.
(6) Dobbs has completed, but not yet billed, work amounting to $710.

REQUIRED
(a) Prepare an eight-column worksheet as of December 31. Set up any additional accounts needed.

(b) Prepare an income statement for the year and a balance sheet at December 31.

(c) Prepare closing entries in general journal form.

4–26A W. Stevens, tax consultant, began business on December 1 of the current year. December transactions were as follows:

Dec.	1	W. Stevens invested $9,000 in the business.
	2	Paid rent for two months to Acme Realty, $600.
	2	Paid $360 for various supplies.
	3	Purchased furniture and fixtures for office on account, $3,000.
	8	Paid $500 on account for furniture and fixtures purchased December 3.
	13	Paid wages of assistant for two weeks, $425.
	20	Performed consulting services for cash, $1,200.
	27	Paid wages of assistant for two weeks, $425.
	30	Billed customers for consulting work completed during the month, $2,700.
	31	Stevens withdrew $900 from the business.

REQUIRED

(a) Open the following ledger accounts, using the account numbers shown: Cash (11); Accounts Receivable (12); Prepaid Rent (13); Supplies on Hand (14); Furniture and Fixtures (15); Accumulated Depreciation (16); Accounts Payable (21); Wages Payable (22); W. Stevens, Capital (31); W. Stevens, Drawing (32); Income Summary (33); Consulting Fees (41); Supplies Expense (51); Wages Expense (52); Rent Expense (53); and Depreciation Expense (54).

(b) Journalize the December transactions, and post to the ledger.

(c) Prepare a trial balance directly on a worksheet, and complete the worksheet using the following information:

(1) Supplies on hand at December 31 are $80.

(2) Accrued wages payable at December 31 are $45.

(3) Depreciation for December is $25.

(4) Stevens has spent 20 hours on an involved tax fraud case during December. When completed in January his work will be billed at $20 per hour.

(5) Prepaid rent at December 31 is $300.

(d) Prepare a December income statement and a December 31 balance sheet.

(e) Journalize and post adjusting and closing entries.

(f) Prepare a post-closing trial balance.

(g) Journalize and post the appropriate reversing entries.

4–28A The last four columns of an eight-column worksheet prepared at December 31 of the current year for Hall, Inc. are reproduced on page 153.

| | Income Statement | | Balance Sheet | |
	Debit	Credit	Debit	Credit
Cash			4,100	
Accounts Receivable			6,020	
Prepaid Insurance			600	
Equipment			18,500	
Accumulated Depreciation				990
Accounts Payable				820
Capital Stock				12,000
Retained Earnings				6,330
Service Fees		17,900		
Miscellaneous Income		400		
Salaries Expense	7,100			
Rent Expense	1,500			
Insurance Expense	420			
Salaries Payable				300
Depreciation Expense	500			
	9,520	18,300	29,220	20,440
Net Income	8,780			8,780
	18,300	18,300	29,220	29,220

REQUIRED

From the given information, prepare closing entries in general journal form.

BUSINESS DECISION PROBLEM

As an alternative to a summer job paying $3 per hour between his junior and senior years in college, Bob Dixon accepted an opportunity to lease and operate the tennis court concession in a local city recreational complex that was open during June, July, and August. Although no accounting records were kept, Bob was careful to handle all funds related to the tennis concession through a special bank account opened for that purpose. An analysis of those deposit slips and check stubs for the three months is summarized below:

Receipts:

Dixon's investment of personal funds	$2,000
Rental of courts and equipment	5,190
Proceeds of loan from bank	2,000
Total receipts	$9,190

Disbursements:

Purchase of ball-throwing machines	$ 600
Supplies purchased	400
Utilities	360
Lease payments to city	1,200
Wages to part-time assistant	450
Liability insurance premiums	120
Partial repayment of bank loan and interest	540
Withdrawals of cash for personal expenses	1,950
Total disbursements	$5,620
Cash balance, August 31	$3,570

Bob confides in you, as a personal friend who happens to be studying accounting, that he is pleased with his apparent profit of $3,570 for the summer. Anxious to practice your newly acquired skills, you offer to review his records and prepare an income statement for the three months and a balance sheet at the end of August. In discussions with Bob, you learn that:

(1) Rental receipts include all revenues earned except for $180 due from a company that rented the entire set of courts for a weekend late in August.

(2) The ball-throwing machines can be sold as used equipment for one-half their original cost.

(3) Of the total supplies purchased, an amount originally costing $120 was on hand at August 31. Although half of the remaining supplies can be returned for a refund of 90% of their cost, the balance represents opened packages that cannot be returned and will deteriorate and become useless before the next tennis season. Bob estimates that each month during the summer, he took home for personal use supplies costing $20.

(4) The insurance premiums represent coverage for six months with no cancellation privilege.

(5) Repayment to the bank included the $40 of interest expense on the loan due through the end of August.

(6) All lease payments due the city were paid except for a final amount of $320.

(7) Bob estimated that the utility bill for August, when received, would be for $150.

REQUIRED

Prepare the financial statements for Bob. It is suggested that you formulate general journal entries summarizing the cash receipts and the cash disbursements and incorporating the additional data. After posting these to T accounts, you will be able to prepare the financial statements.

In further talks with Bob, you learn that the amount he contributed had been in a savings account earning 6% interest and that he worked an average of 60 hours in each of the 13 weeks the tennis concession was operated. What observations might you offer Bob regarding the financial success of the summer venture? What nonfinancial considerations are involved?

5
Merchandising Operations

Thus far in our discussion of the accounting cycle, we have used as examples firms providing services rather than those selling products. Revenue for small service enterprises such as the medical practice and the television service consisted of fees earned for the services performed. In these firms, net income is determined in a relatively simple way by deducting total expenses incurred from total fees earned during a period.

Revenue for firms that sell products consists of the total amount for which the products are sold. To determine net income for such firms, we deduct from the revenue (called *Sales*) for the period not only the operating expenses incurred, but also the costs of acquiring the products sold. In this chapter we shall discuss the procedures followed in accounting for the costs of acquiring and selling products.

THE NATURE OF MERCHANDISING OPERATIONS

The total business segment of society is often classified into three broad types of enterprises: (1) service, (2) manufacturing, and (3) merchandising. Commercial airlines, physicians, lawyers, other professionals, insurance companies, and banks are examples of service enterprises. We identify manufacturing enterprises by their basic operation of converting raw materials into finished products through the application of skilled labor and machine operations. Merchandising enterprises are characterized by the basic operation of buying and selling finished products, and including both wholesalers and retailers. Exhibit 5-1 illustrates the position of merchandising enterprises in the manufacturing and distribution process.

As you might surmise, the accounting records of a merchandising firm must accommodate many transactions for the purchase of products and payment of the related accounts. Moreover, one should be able to tell from the accounting reports whether the difference between the acquisition price and the sales price to customers is sufficient to cover the costs of storing, displaying, advertising, selling, delivering, and collecting for the merchandise. Finally, the accounting records must reflect not only cash sales but individual accounts receivable for a large number of customers.

EXHIBIT 5-1
The Manufacturing and Distribution Process

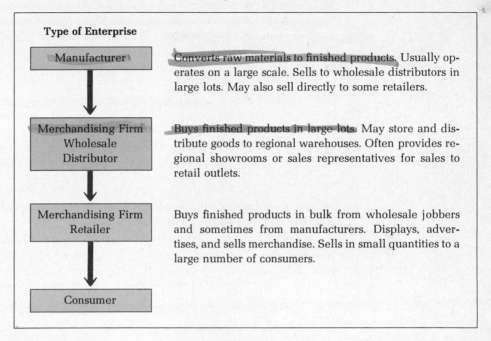

Type of Enterprise

Manufacturer
Converts raw materials to finished products. Usually operates on a large scale. Sells to wholesale distributors in large lots. May also sell directly to some retailers.

Merchandising Firm Wholesale Distributor
Buys finished products in large lots. May store and distribute goods to regional warehouses. Often provides regional showrooms or sales representatives for sales to retail outlets.

Merchandising Firm Retailer
Buys finished products in bulk from wholesale jobbers and sometimes from manufacturers. Displays, advertises, and sells merchandise. Sells in small quantities to a large number of consumers.

Consumer

INCOME STATEMENT FOR A MERCHANDISING FIRM

Exhibit 5-2 is an income statement for a merchandising firm, Madison Electronics Company. For simplicity, we have condensed the operating expenses into two

EXHIBIT 5-2

Madison Electronics Company
Income Statement
For the Year Ended December 31, 19XX

Sales		$160,000
Cost of Goods Sold		104,000
Gross Profit on Sales		$ 56,000
Operating Expenses:		
Selling Expenses	$32,000	
Administrative Expenses	16,000	
Total Operating Expenses		48,000
Net Income		$ 8,000

amounts: selling expenses and administrative expenses. (These classifications will be explained later in the chapter.)

When we compare the income statement of a merchandising firm with that of a service business, the major difference we find is that an amount for the cost of goods sold to customers is included. Ordinarily, this amount is deducted from the revenue figure, Sales, to arrive at an intermediate amount called gross profit on sales. The operating expenses are then deducted from the gross profit on sales to obtain the net income for the period.

In a merchandising firm, gross profit on sales (sometimes called gross margin) is highly significant to management. It is usually expressed as a percentage of sales. In our illustration, the gross profit is 35% of sales ($56,000/$160,000 = 0.35 = 35%). This means that after 65 cents is deducted from each sales dollar to cover the cost of goods sold, 35 cents of each sales dollar remains to cover operat-

MARKUPS

The reader may wonder about the general range in which markups fall. In 1969, E.B. Weiss wrote an article in *Advertising Age* in which he predicted that average markups in retailing were heading for 50% by the end of the 1970s. (Statistics are not currently available to confirm or deny this figure, but there is evidence that there has been a substantial increase.)

According to Weiss, mail order chains, variety store chains, and drug store chains were already using an average markup of 40% and higher. Food chains were using an average markup of 22% in 1969 and discount chains an average of 28 to 32%. As the reader can see, the average markup figure varies for different types of firms. The difference has two causes. First, there is a difference in the amount of competition between the types of retailing. For example, food chains are highly competitive, hence usually rely on a lower markup and higher volumes. The food business commonly employs advertised bargains, known as "loss leaders," which are sometimes sold below the cost to acquire the item. This type of practice tends to reduce the average markup in highly competitive retail business.

The second reason for difference in markups used by the particular type of business relates to additional services that are expected as part of normal business. For example, such things as providing carry-out services for customers, granting credit and "carrying customers," providing large numbers of clerks to help customers, and liberal return privileges all result in higher markups in a particular industry. Each of the services mentioned results in higher costs for the retail outlet. The cost may take the form of higher employee salaries if more clerks are employed to help customers or to carry out parcels. The cost may be in the form of higher bad debts expense if the firm grants credit. In any case, the costs will, where possible, be passed on to the consumer by using a higher markup.

At the time that Weiss wrote his comments, he suggested that in the future retailers might not have to include so many things in their markups since they were expected to press manufacturers for more assistance in the form of more allowances for returned goods, greater return to manufacturer privileges, and taking on more of the functions performed by retailers. These functions might include such things as advertising and backing credit granted to the retailer's customers. Each function that the manufacturer takes over from the retailer will tend to slow the increase in markup.

From John C. Lere, *Pricing Techniques for the Financial Executive* (New York: John Wiley & Sons, 1974) pp. 69–70. Reprinted by permission of John Wiley & Sons.

ing expenses and net profit. Sometimes the gross profit percentage is called average mark-up percentage on sales.

Management usually compares its current gross profit percentage with similar calculations for prior periods or with industry averages. Frequently, such comparisons alert management to a need to modify prices, purchasing policies, or merchandise control procedures. Industry averages are usually available from such sources as trade associations or credit reporting agencies that compile statistics for various industries.

Cost of Goods Sold

To calculate the cost of goods sold to customers, we must consider data from a number of special merchandise accounts. We shall discuss the treatment of such accounts in detail in later sections of this chapter. To provide a perspective, however, we show in condensed form in Exhibit 5-3 how cost of goods sold was calculated for the income statement of Exhibit 5-2.

We see from the illustration that at the beginning of the year, Madison Electronics had a supply of merchandise costing $19,000. During the year, the firm purchased additional merchandise with a net cost of $106,000. Adding these two amounts together gives us $125,000, the total cost of all goods that were available for sale to customers during the year. Since a count of the merchandise on hand at the end of the year revealed that merchandise costing $21,000 remained unsold, we must deduct this amount to arrive at the cost of goods sold to customers, which is $104,000.

STEPS IN A MERCHANDISE TRANSACTION

Whenever a transaction is initiated for the purchase or sale of merchandise, the buyer and the seller should agree on the price of the merchandise, the terms of payment, and which party is to bear the cost of transportation. Owners or managers of small merchandising firms may settle the terms of the transaction informally by telephone or by discussion with a sales representative of the supplier.

EXHIBIT 5-3
Computation of Cost of Goods Sold

Beginning Inventory, Jan. 1	$ 19,000
Add: Net Purchases	106,000
Cost of Goods Available for Sale	$125,000
Less: Ending Inventory, Dec. 31	21,000
Cost of Goods Sold	$104,000

Most large businesses, however, fill out a purchase order when ordering merchandise. A typical sequence of events for a large firm is as follows:

(1) A request for a purchase, called a purchase requisition, is initiated by the person in charge of merchandise stock records whenever certain items are needed or when quantities of certain merchandise fall below established re-order points. These requisitions may also be initiated by other authorized personnel, such as department heads. The requisition is forwarded to the purchasing department.

(2) The purchasing department then prepares a purchase order after consulting price lists, quotations, or suppliers' catalogs. The purchase order, addressed to the selected vendor, indicates the quantity, description, and price of the merchandise ordered. It may also indicate expected terms of payment and arrangements for transportation, including payment of freight costs.

(3) After receiving the purchase order, the seller, upon shipment, makes out an invoice, which is forwarded to the purchaser. The invoice, called a sales invoice by the seller and a purchase invoice by the buyer, defines the terms of the transaction. A sample invoice is shown in Exhibit 5–4.

(4) Upon receiving the shipment of merchandise, the purchaser's receiving department counts and inspects the items in the shipment and makes out a receiving report detailing the quantities received.

(5) Before approving the invoice for payment, either the purchasing department or the accounts payable department compares copies of the purchase order, invoice, and receiving report to determine that quantities, descriptions, and prices are in agreement.

Although all the above papers—purchase requisition, purchase order, receiving report, and invoice—are source documents, only the invoice provides the basis for an entry in the purchaser's accounting records. The other three documents are merely supporting documents. The purchaser makes no entries until the invoice is approved for payment. The seller enters the transaction in the records when the invoice is prepared, usually upon shipment of the merchandise.

TERMS OF TRANSACTIONS

Merchandise may be purchased and sold either on credit terms or for cash on delivery. Most merchandise transactions today are made "on account" rather than on cash (sometimes referred to as *net cash*) terms. When goods are sold on account, a period of time, called the credit period, is allowed for payment. The length of this time varies among business firms and may even vary within a firm, depending on the type of product. A typical credit period for wholesalers is 30 days. Payment is expected within 30 days of the invoice date, after which the purchaser is considered delinquent. The credit period is frequently described as the *net credit period,* or *net terms,* and the notation commonly used to designate this period is "n/" followed by the length of the period in days; for example, n/30 indicates that the credit period is 30 days.

Cash Discounts
To encourage earlier payment of bills, many firms designate a period that is shorter than the credit period as the discount period. Purchasers who remit payment during this period are entitled to deduct an amount, called a cash discount, from the total payment. In reality, this is a discount for prompt payment. The discount is designated by such notation as "2/10," which means that 2% may be deducted if payment is made within 10 days. For example, if an invoice for $800,

EXHIBIT 5–4
Invoice

MADISON ELECTRONICS COMPANY 1400 South Park St. Madison, Wisconsin 53705	FOR CUSTOMER'S USE ONLY

Customer's
Order No. & Date 1503
Requisition No.
Contract No.

Refer to
Invoice No. 12015
Invoice Date Nov. 20, 19XX
Vendor's Nos.

SOLD ABC Company
TO   120 Weston Street
      Kenosha, Wisconsin

FOR CUSTOMER'S USE ONLY

Register No.   Voucher No.

F.O.B. Checked

Terms Approved | Price Approved *L.N.A.*

Calculations Checked *R.S.D.*

Transportation

Freight Bill No.   Amount

Material Received

Date   Signature   Title

Satisfactory and Approved

Adjustments

Accounting Distribution

Audited | Final Approval

Shipped to
and
Destination Same
Date Shipped Nov. 20, 19XX   From Madison   Prepaid or Collect
Car Initials and No.
How Shipped and   F.O.B. Kenosha   Prepaid
Route
Terms 2/10, n/30

QUANTITY	DESCRIPTION	UNIT PRICE	AMOUNT
7	Model E Voicemaster Tape Recorders	$70	$490

dated November 10, carries terms of 2/10, n/30, the purchaser may deduct 2% from the invoice price if the bill is paid by November 20. In this case, the cash discount would be $16 (2% of $800), and the amount of the remittance would be $784. The full amount of the invoice, $800, would be expected if the purchaser paid between November 20 and December 10. After December 10, the amount would be overdue.

Most business firms find it important to maintain a good cash position so they can take advantage of discounts offered to them. For example, assume that a firm purchased $800 worth of merchandise on terms of 2/10, n/30. The firm has a choice of paying $784 within 10 days of the invoice date or the full amount before the end of another 20 days. Passing up the discount is essentially the same as paying 2% interest for the use of $800 for 20 days, and a flat 2% charge for 20 days is equivalent to a 36% annual interest rate (360 days/20 days $\times$ 2%). Clearly, the firm would be wiser to borrow from a bank at an annual interest rate of 10–12%, rather than lose a discount that amounts to a much higher rate.

Trade Discounts Certain business firms may furnish customers with price lists or catalogs showing suggested retail prices for their products. These firms, however, also include a schedule of discounts from the listed prices that enable a customer to determine the price to be paid. Such discounts are called trade discounts. Suppose that the Madison Electronics Company quoted a list price of $100 for Model E tape recorders, less discounts of 30% if purchased in lots of ten items or less and 40% if purchased in lots of more than ten. If the ABC Company ordered seven tape recorders, it would calculate its invoice cost as follows:

List Price ($100 $\times$ 7)	$700
Less 30%	210
Invoice Cost	$490

Trade discounts enable a supplier to vary prices between small and large purchasers and, by changing the discount schedule, to alter prices periodically without the inconvenience and expense of revising catalogs and price lists.

Trade discounts are simply a means of determining invoice prices and should not be confused with cash discounts. Trade discounts and list prices are not reflected in the accounts of either the purchaser or seller of merchandise. In the foregoing example, both the purchaser and the seller would record only the $490 invoice amount.

RECORDING MERCHANDISE SALES

After a vendor has processed a customer's purchase order and prepared the goods for shipment, a sales invoice is prepared in several copies. The original copy is usually sent to the customer; duplicate copies are retained by the seller. The duplicates may be distributed to the shipping department to support its shipping records; to the sales department so it can analyze sales by product, territory, or sales representatives; or to the accounting department so that the transaction will be recorded in the accounts.

Suppose the accounting department of Madison Electronics Company receives its copy of the invoice, dated November 20, for the sale of the tape recorders described in the previous section. The entry to record the sale (shown in general journal form) would be:

Nov. 20	Accounts Receivable	490	
	Sales		490

To record the sale of seven Model E tape
recorders to the ABC Company.
Terms 2/10, n/30.

The Sales account is the standard account that almost all manufacturing and merchandising companies use to record revenue transactions. It is the same type of account as the Professional Fees (revenue) account used by the Cole Clinic described in earlier chapters. This account is credited whenever credit or cash sales are made, and invariably it has a credit balance at the end of the accounting period. *Only sales of merchandise held for resale are recorded in the Sales account.* If a merchandising firm sold one of its delivery trucks, the credit would be made to the Delivery Equipment account, not the Sales account. At the end of the accounting period, the Sales account is closed to the Income Summary account in the same way that the Professional Fees account is closed. Sales is debited and the Income Summary account is credited for the accumulated credit balance in the Sales account.

As we mentioned earlier, the sales invoice is the document used to record credit sales. For cash sales, however, the procedure is different. If the volume of cash sales is large, as in a retail merchandising establishment, cash sales are recorded and accumulated on a cash register tape as they are made. At the end of each day, the amount of accumulated sales shown on the tape is recorded on a summary sheet or report. The totals on these reports are usually recorded in the Sales account each week. Shorter or longer recording intervals may be used, depending on management's reporting needs. In general journal form, the entry to record the week's cash sales of $3,200 would be:

Cash	3,200	
Sales		3,200

To record cash sales for week of Nov. 22–26.

In our description of the sales recording procedures, we have used general journal entries to illustrate the analysis of sales transactions. In practice, recording repetitive transactions of the same type in the general journal is somewhat primitive and inefficient. In Chapter 6 we will discuss a more efficient system of recording such transactions in special journals, along with a means of keeping records for individual customers.

RECORDING MERCHANDISE PURCHASES

When a business purchases merchandise for resale to customers, the amount is debited to the Purchases account. The credit is made to Accounts Payable or to Cash, depending on whether the purchase was on credit or cash terms. Assume that on November 23, the ABC Company received its shipment of tape recorders from the Madison Electronics Company, along with the vendor's invoice for $490. To record the credit purchase of the seven tape recorders, the ABC Company makes the following entry:[1]

Nov. 23	Purchases	490	
	Accounts Payable		490

To record the purchase of seven Model E
tape recorders from Madison Electronics
Company. Terms 2/10, n/30.

Only merchandise purchased for resale is recorded in the Purchases account. Acquisitions of such things as equipment, supplies, and investments are entered in the corresponding asset accounts rather than in Purchases.

The Purchases account normally has a debit balance at the end of the accounting period. The account is treated as an income statement account and, like the other temporary accounts, is closed at the end of the accounting year. Actually, the portion of goods purchased that remains unsold is moved to the asset account Inventory at the end of the period. Then the remainder becomes a part of Cost of Goods Sold. The closing of the Purchases account is explained in a later section of this chapter.

RETURNS AND ALLOWANCES

Sometimes a customer returns merchandise to the seller because of defects or damage in transit or because the wrong merchandise was shipped. Upon returning merchandise, the customer requests that the original amount billed be appropriately reduced. Similar requests are made when there has been an invoicing error. Upon receiving notification that the buyer has returned goods or has requested an allowance, the seller usually issues the customer a credit memorandum such as the one illustrated in Exhibit 5-5.

The credit memorandum (sometimes called credit memo) is a formal acknowledgement that the seller has agreed to a reduction of the amount owed by the customer. When the seller issues a credit memorandum, a duplicate copy is retained by the accounting department and serves as the basis for an entry crediting the customer's account. For example, suppose two of the seven tape recorders

[1]The *gross price* method of recording purchases is described here. Another method, called the *net price* method will be explained in Chapter 6.

EXHIBIT 5-5
Credit Memorandum

MADISON ELECTRONICS COMPANY **1400 South Park St.** **Madison, Wisconsin 53705**	CREDIT MEMORANDUM No. 23

TO: ABC Company

     120 Weston Street

     Kenosha, Wisconsin

Date Nov. 25, 19XX

We credit your account as follows:

Return of two Model E tape recorders,
our invoice No. 12015 . . . . $140.00

sold to the ABC Company were returned for credit. Upon issuing a credit memo to the ABC Company, the Madison Electronics Company would make the following entry:

Nov. 25   Sales Returns and Allowances   140

             Accounts Receivable   140

             To record the issuance of credit memo
             No. 23 for two Model E tape recorders
             returned by the ABC Company.

Upon receipt of the credit memo, the ABC Company would make the following entry:

Nov. 27   Accounts Payable   140

             Purchases Returns and Allowances   140

             To record receipt of credit memo No. 23
             for two Model E tape recorders returned to
             Madison Electronics Company.

    In the first entry above, the Madison Electronics Company could have debited the Sales account rather than Sales Returns and Allowances. If Sales were debited, however, the balance of the Sales account at the end of the accounting period would not reveal total sales made, but total sales less all returns and allowances. Most companies prefer to record sales returns and allowances in a separate contra account in order to determine whether the aggregate amount of such items is becoming too large. When the amount becomes abnormally large, an investigation should be made to determine the reason. Returns may be caused by defective products, faulty packing or shipping, or improper billing procedures. The additional handling of goods and the additional clerical work of making adjustments can be costly, and customers may be lost in the process.

For similar reasons, the purchaser ordinarily credits the Purchases Returns and Allowances account rather than the Purchases account when a credit memorandum is received. The separate accounting permits a company to determine whether its purchasing or requisitioning procedures should be reviewed. The company may discover, for instance, that not enough care is being exercised in filling out requisitions and purchase orders or in selecting reliable suppliers.

The Sales Returns and Allowances account invariably has a debit balance at the end of the accounting period. On the income statement for the period, the amount is shown as a deduction from the Sales amount. The Purchases Returns and Allowances account has a credit balance at the end of the accounting period, and the balance is subtracted from the Purchases amount on the income statement. Both the Sales Returns and Allowances and the Purchases Returns and Allowances accounts are closed at the end of the accounting year in a manner we shall explain shortly.

Many companies record all credit memos in the returns and allowances accounts. When the memos are issued as a result of mere clerical or arithmetical errors, however, it is better to record the adjustment in the Sales or Purchases accounts.

Buyers frequently request merchandise adjustments by letter. Some companies, however, may issue a standard form for such requests, called a debit memorandum. This form is similar to the credit memorandum illustrated in Exhibit 5-5.

When a merchandise adjustment is necessary because of the negligence of the transportation company, the seller notifies the transportation company of its liability and asks for an adjustment. If the claim is acknowledged, the seller makes an additional entry debiting an account receivable from the transportation company. The credit is made either to the Sales Returns and Allowances account or to a special account for Transportation Claims.

RECORDING RECEIPTS AND PAYMENTS

A set of merchandise transactions concludes when the seller receives the proper remittance from the purchaser and each makes the appropriate entries for the settlement of accounts. To illustrate, let us review the entries made thus far for the sale of the tape recorders made by Madison Electronics Company to the ABC Company.

Seller (Madison Electronics Company)				Buyer (ABC Company)			

To Record Sale

Nov. 20   Accounts Receivable   490

        Sales   490

To record the sale of seven Model E tape recorders to the ABC Company. Terms 2/10, n/30.

To Record Purchase

Nov. 23   Purchases   490

        Accounts Payable   490

To record the purchase of seven Model E tape recorders from Madison Electronics Company. Terms 2/10, n/30.

To Record Return of Merchandise

Nov. 25   Sales Returns and Allowances   140

        Accounts Receivable   140

To record the issuance of credit memo No. 23 for two Model E tape recorders returned by the ABC Company.

To Record Return of Merchandise

Nov. 27   Accounts Payable   140

        Purchases Returns and Allowances   140

To record the receipt of credit memo No. 23 for two Model E tape recorders returned to Madison Electronics Company.

After these transactions have been posted, the seller's Accounts Receivable account and the buyer's Accounts Payable account appear as follows:

	Seller (Madison Electronics Company)		Buyer (ABC Company)	
	Accounts Receivable		**Accounts Payable**	
19XX		19XX	19XX	19XX
Nov. 20 490		Nov. 25 140	Nov. 27 140	Nov. 23 490

If the ABC Company wishes to take advantage of the 2% discount allowed, its remittance must be made within ten days of the invoice date, November 20. Usually, the discount is granted if the remittance is at least postmarked on the last day of the discount period. The amount that the ABC Company should remit by November 30 is $343 ($350 balance owing, less 2% discount of $7). Note that the discount is calculated only on the cost of merchandise kept by the purchaser, not on the invoice price of the goods originally shipped. The entries to be made on the books of the seller and buyer are:

Seller (Madison Electronics Company)			Buyer (ABC Company)		

Dec. 2   Cash   343

    Sales Discounts   7

        Accounts Receivable   350

To record remittance in full of account.

Nov. 30   Accounts Payable   350

        Purchases Discounts   7

        Cash   343

To record payment of account.

After this entry is posted, the seller's Accounts Receivable and the purchaser's Accounts Payable appear as follows:

Seller
(Madison Electronics Company)

Accounts Receivable

19XX		19XX	
Nov. 20	490	Nov. 25	140
		Dec. 2	350

Buyer
(ABC Company)

Accounts Payable

19XX		19XX	
Nov. 27	140	Nov. 23	490
30	350		

Note that the discount taken in this transaction is not revealed in either the seller's Accounts Receivable account or the buyer's Accounts Payable account. Discounts are accumulated only in Sales Discounts on the seller's books and Purchases Discounts on the buyer's books.

The other accounts relevant to the set of transactions for the tape recorders are shown below in T-account form, after the appropriate postings have been made.

Seller
(Madison Electronics Company)

Sales

	19XX	
	Nov. 20	490

Buyer
(ABC Company)

Purchases

19XX		
Nov. 23	490	

Sales Returns and Allowances

19XX		
Nov. 25	140	

Purchases Returns and Allowances

	19XX	
	Nov. 27	140

Sales Discounts

19XX		
Dec. 2	7	

Purchases Discounts

	19XX	
	Nov. 30	7

From the illustration we have just considered, we can see that both the accounts Sales Returns and Allowances and Sales Discounts have debit balances, while the Sales account has a credit balance. This relationship will always hold true, and at the close of the accounting period the net sales for the period can be calculated by subtracting the sum of the Sales Returns and Allowances balance and the Sales Discounts balance from the Sales account. The revenue section of the income statement for the year will exhibit this calculation as shown on page 169 (amounts are taken from the income statement of Madison Electronics Company, Exhibit 5-2, page 157).

Revenue			
Sales			$163,500
Less: Sales Returns and Allowances		$ 500	
Sales Discounts		3,000	3,500
Net Sales			$160,000

Similarly, Purchases Returns and Allowances and Purchases Discounts will have credit balances at the close of the accounting period, just as they have after the set of transactions illustrated. On the income statement for the period, the sum of the balances of these accounts is deducted from the Purchases account balance. To arrive at net purchases, however, another amount, *Transportation In*, is usually added (see next section). Thus, the concept of net purchases is a net *delivered* cost. The calculation of net purchases for Madison Electronics Company for the year is shown on its income statement as follows:

Net Purchases			
Purchases			$104,600
Less: Purchases Returns and Allowances		$ 300	
Purchases Discounts		1,500	1,800
			$102,800
Add: Transportation In			3,200
Net Purchases			$106,000

The above calculation appears in the Cost of Goods Sold section of the income statement, which we shall examine more closely later in this chapter.

TRANSPORTATION ACCOUNTS

When merchandise is forwarded by a common carrier—a railroad, a trucking company, or an airline—the carrier prepares a freight bill in accordance with the instructions of the party making the transportation arrangements. (As mentioned earlier, such arrangements may be specified in the purchase order.) The freight bill designates which party is to bear the shipping costs and whether the shipment is to be made prepaid or collect.

Freight bills usually show whether the shipping terms are F.O.B. shipping point or F.O.B. destination (F.O.B. is an abbreviation for "free on board"). When the freight terms are F.O.B. shipping point, the purchaser has agreed to bear the shipping costs; when the terms are F.O.B. destination, the seller is to bear the shipping costs.

The shipping costs borne by a purchaser are debited to an account called Transportation In. The balance in this account is added to net purchases to arrive at the net delivered cost of purchases on the firm's income statement. Transportation costs incurred by a seller of merchandise are debited to an account called Transportation Out. This account, sometimes called Delivery Expense, is listed with expenses on the income statement. The primary reason for such treatment is that the seller ordinarily has a number of different types of expenses directly associated with selling merchandise. Such expenses as advertising, salespersons' salaries, and insurance are frequently grouped in the income statement under the caption "Selling Expenses"; including Transportation Out with this group is logical.

Usually, the party assuming the freight cost is directed to pay the carrier. Thus, goods are shipped "freight collect" when the terms are F.O.B. shipping point and "freight prepaid" when the terms are F.O.B. destination. Sometimes, as a matter of convenience, the firm not assuming the freight costs is directed to pay the carrier. When this situation occurs, the seller and buyer simply make the necessary adjustment in collecting or paying for the merchandise. To illustrate, let us assume that Madison Electronics Company sells $600 worth of merchandise on account to Chicago Supply Company on terms F.O.B. shipping point, 2/10, n/30, and shipping costs of $60 are prepaid by the seller. Madison Electronics Company adds the $60 freight charge to the invoice amount, billing Chicago Supply Company for $660. On its records, Chicago Supply Company reflects the freight cost as Transportation In.

In this situation, the buyer is not entitled to a discount on the amount of the freight. Thus, if Chicago Supply Company paid the invoice during the discount period, the amount to be remitted is calculated as follows:

Invoice amount ($600 plus $60 prepaid freight)	$660
Less: Discount (2% of $600)	12
Amount to be remitted	$648

On the other hand, if freight terms are F.O.B. destination but the buyer pays the shipping charges (freight collect), the buyer deducts the freight charges in remitting to the seller. The buyer, however, is entitled to a discount calculated on the invoice price of the merchandise. Thus, if $600 worth of merchandise is purchased and freight is $60, a 2% discount of $12 would be taken and the remittance would be $528 ($600 worth of merchandise less the $12 discount less the $60 shipping charge paid by the buyer).

THE INVENTORY ACCOUNT

The inventory of a merchandising firm consists of a stock of goods that are on hand waiting to be sold to customers. The dollar amount of this stock of goods is carried in an asset account called Merchandise Inventory, or simply Inventory. When a firm records acquisitions of merchandise during the period in a Purchases account, the firm is said to be on a periodic inventory basis.[2] This implies that the inventory account remains unchanged during the period. Before the

---

[2]Under the perpetual inventory system, described in Chapter 9, the Inventory account is adjusted throughout the accounting period for the cost of goods purchased and sold.

firm prepares financial statements at the close of the period, it must determine the amount of unsold goods to be reported in the statements. The amount of this asset is usually calculated by counting and pricing individual items in stock, multiplying unit costs by number of items, then adding all amounts to obtain an aggregate measure.

When the ending merchandise inventory is known, the bookkeeper adjusts the Inventory account to agree with the amount of unsold goods on hand. The adjustment is made through the Income Summary account and is frequently accomplished in two entries. The first entry removes the beginning (old) inventory balance, and the second entry records the ending (new) inventory balance. The adjusting entries for the Madison Electronics Company (see Exhibits 5–2 and 5–3) at the end of the year are:

(1)	Dec. 31	Income Summary	19,000	
		Inventory		19,000
		To transfer beginning inventory to Income Summary.		
(2)	31	Inventory	21,000	
		Income Summary		21,000
		To record ending inventory.		

WORKSHEET FOR A MERCHANDISING FIRM

We pointed out in Chapter 4 that it is customary at the close of an accounting period to prepare a worksheet to facilitate preparation of financial statements. The worksheet in Exhibit 5–6 was prepared after all transactions for the year were recorded and posted to the accounts of Madison Electronics Company.

The structure of a worksheet for a merchandising firm is the same as that used in Chapter 4 for a service firm; there are pairs of columns for the trial balance, adjustments, income statement, and balance sheet. Certain procedures for handling the merchandise accounts, however, must be carefully followed.

Inventory Adjustment in the Worksheet

In Exhibit 5–6, the inventory figure that appears in the unadjusted trial balance at the end of the year is the January 1 inventory. This amount is still in the account because additions and deductions have not been reflected during the year. The change in the inventory balance is indicated by placing the two adjusting entries for the inventories in the adjustments column of the worksheet. In making these adjusting entries, a line is added for Income Summary below the trial balance accounts.

After adjustments have been entered on the worksheet, cross-totaling the Inventory line results in extending the ending inventory of $21,000 into the balance sheet columns as a debit. This is logical, of course, because the inventory is an asset that will appear in the December 31 balance sheet. We extend the

EXHIBIT 5-6
Madison Electronics Company
Worksheet
For the Year Ended December 31, 19XX

	Trial Balance		Adjustments		Income Statement		Balance Sheet	
Cash	7,500						7,500	
Accounts Receivable	8,200						8,200	
Inventory	19,000		(2) 21,000	(1) 19,000			21,000	
Prepaid Insurance	360			(3) 120			240	
Supplies on Hand	700			(4) 240			460	
Delivery Equipment	12,000						12,000	
Accumulated Depreciation		2,400		(5) 1,200				3,600
Accounts Payable		7,300						7,300
J. Madison, Capital		32,500						32,500
J. Madison, Drawing	2,500						2,500	
Sales		163,500				163,500		
Sales Returns and Allowances	500				500			
Sales Discounts	3,000				3,000			
Purchases	104,600				104,600			
Purchases Returns and Allowances		300				300		
Purchases Discounts		1,500				1,500		
Transportation In	3,200				3,200			
Sales Salaries Expense	26,000		(6) 500		26,500			
Advertising Expense	1,500				1,500			
Delivery Expense	2,680				2,680			
Office Salaries Expense	9,200				9,200			
Rent Expense	5,400				5,400			
Utilities Expense	1,160				1,160			
	207,500	207,500						
Income Summary			(1) 19,000	(2) 21,000	19,000	21,000		
Insurance Expense			(3) 120		120			
Supplies Expense			(4) 240		240			
Depreciation Expense			(5) 1,200		1,200			
Salaries Payable				(6) 500				500
			42,060	42,060				
					178,300	186,300	51,900	43,900
Net Income					8,000			8,000
					186,300	186,300	51,900	51,900

amounts in the adjustments column on the Income Summary line into both income statement columns, with the beginning inventory of $19,000 as a debit and the ending inventory of $21,000 as a credit. Balances of the merchandise accounts, such as Purchases, Purchases Returns and Allowances, Purchases Discounts, and

Transportation In, are extended into the income statement columns of the worksheet, with the same debit and credit positions as they had in the trial balance. These items, together with the extended inventory amounts, constitute the cost of goods sold. In Exhibit 5-6, we have entered these amounts in color only to emphasize the manner in which the cost of goods sold is reflected in the income statement section of the worksheet. The result of combining these six items is a net debit of $104,000—the cost of goods sold. The details of this calculation appear in the formal income statement prepared from the worksheet (Exhibit 5-7, page 174). As a result of the inventory adjustments and the extensions of the merchandise accounts, all necessary elements for the computations are correctly positioned in the worksheet.

Other Adjustments in the Worksheet

In addition to the inventory adjustments, numbered (1) and (2) on page 171, the following adjusting journal entries were reflected on the worksheet:

(3)	Dec. 31	Insurance Expense	120	
		Prepaid Insurance		120

To charge one year's premium to expense. (Three-year premium, $360, paid Jan. 1.)

(4)	31	Supplies Expense	240	
		Supplies on Hand		240

To charge to expense the supplies used during year. (Inventory of supplies is $460 on Dec. 31.)

(5)	31	Depreciation Expense	1,200	
		Accumulated Depreciation		1,200

To charge to expense one year's depreciation on delivery equipment.

(6)	31	Sales Salaries Expense	500	
		Salaries Payable		500

To reflect the salaries earned by salespersons but not paid at Dec. 31.

In order to make adjusting entries (1) through (6), we had to add at the bottom of the worksheet certain accounts not included in the trial balance. In addition to the Income Summary, the accounts we added were Insurance Expense, Supplies Expense, Depreciation Expense, and Salaries Payable. After entering the adjustments, we extended the amounts in the trial balance (revised where necessary) to the appropriate income statement or balance sheet columns. Then, after making all extensions, we totaled the columns for the income statement and the balance sheet.

EXHIBIT 5–7

Madison Electronics Company
Income Statement
For the Year Ended December 31, 19XX

Revenue

Sales			$163,500
Less: Sales Returns and Allowances		$ 500	
Sales Discounts		3,000	3,500
Net Sales			$160,000

Cost of Goods Sold

Inventory, Jan. 1			$ 19,000
Add: Net Purchases			
Purchases		$104,600	
Less: Purchases Returns and Allowances	$ 300		
Purchases Discounts	1,500	1,800	
		$102,800	
Add: Transportation In		3,200	106,000
Cost of Goods Available for Sale			$125,000
Less: Inventory, Dec. 31			21,000
Cost of Goods Sold			104,000
Gross Profit on Sales			$ 56,000

Operating Expenses

Selling Expenses			
Sales Salaries Expense		$ 26,500	
Delivery Expense		2,680	
Advertising Expense		1,500	
Depreciation Expense		1,200	
Insurance Expense		120	
Total Selling Expenses		$ 32,000	
Administrative Expenses			
Rent Expense		$ 5,400	
Office Salaries Expense		9,200	
Utilities Expense		1,160	
Supplies Expense		240	
Total Administrative Expenses		16,000	
Total Operating Expenses			48,000
Net Income			$ 8,000

We made the final adjustment by inserting the necessary figure to balance the income statement and balance sheet columns. This amount was $8,000, the net income for the year. As we pointed out in Chapter 4, a net income is indicated whenever the income statement credits exceed the debits, while a net loss results when the debits exceed the credits.

FINANCIAL STATEMENTS OF A MERCHANDISING FIRM

Once the worksheet is completed, preparing the formal financial statements for the period is a simple matter. In Exhibits 5–7 and 5–8 we show the income statement for the year and the balance sheet at the end of the year; both were prepared from the worksheet in Exhibit 5–6. Note that these are *classified* financial statements, meaning that accounts are separated into various categories. The financial statements in previous illustrations did not need to be classified because only a few accounts were used. When a business has many accounts and transactions, however, classifying the items on the statements facilitates analysis and interpretation of the given data.

The Income Statement

The major categories of the income statement are revenue, cost of goods sold, and operating expenses. For a merchandising firm, the major revenue source is sales of goods to customers. In the revenue section, sales returns and allowances and sales discounts are deducted from the gross sales to yield net sales.

We stated earlier that the cost of goods sold is obtained by adding the beginning inventory and net purchases and deducting the ending inventory. To calculate net purchases, we deduct purchases returns, allowances, and discounts from the purchases amount and add transportation costs of purchased goods.

A business firm's *operating expenses* are those that relate to its primary function and appear with some regularity on the income statement. The operating expenses of a merchandising business are typically classified as selling or administrative expenses. Note that expenses resulting from sales efforts, such as salespersons' salaries, advertising, and delivery costs, are classified separately from expenses of rent, utilities, and other administrative costs. It is possible, of course, for certain types of expenses to appear under both categories. For example, the insurance in this example is apparently on merchandise or delivery equipment, because it appears as a selling expense. Insurance on a company-owned office building, on the other hand, would appear with the administrative expenses.

Some business items affecting the determination of a final net income amount may not relate to the primary operating activity of the business. Interest income and interest expense, for example, may be viewed as relating more to financing and investing activities than to merchandising efforts. For this reason, such items are often shown in a separate category called "Other Income and Expense" at the bottom of the income statement. Likewise, any extraordinary items (explained in Chapter 14), such as catastrophic loss from an earthquake, will be shown in a separate "Extraordinary Items" category before the final net income amount is figured. The firm in our example had no transactions or events to list in either of these categories on the income statement.

Because the income statement is divided into the major categories just discussed, and expenses are classified into selling and administrative expenses, the reader of the statement may pick out key figures at a glance. The first thing the reader might do is observe the net income figure, $8,000, and perhaps relate it (as a percentage) to the net sales figure, $160,000. This result, called return on sales, is 5% for Madison Electronics Company. Next, the reader might determine the gross margin percentage by performing the calculation

$$\frac{\$56,000 \text{ (gross profit)}}{\$160,000 \text{ (net sales)}} = 35\%$$

In a similar fashion, we can relate the total expenses, expense categories, or even individual expenses to net sales. In each case, the results might be compared with those of prior periods or industry averages to determine whether the company is making satisfactory progress. We consider a detailed treatment of such analysis in Chapter 18.

The Balance Sheet

The balance sheet for Madison Electronics Company at December 31 is shown in Exhibit 5–8. Note that the company's assets have been classified into *current assets* and *long-term assets.*

CURRENT ASSETS Current assets are cash and assets that will be converted into cash or used up during the normal operating cycle of the business or one year, whichever is longer. The *normal operating cycle* of a business is the average period required for merchandise to be bought and sold and the resulting accounts receivable to be collected. For many businesses, this period is a year or less, although certain industries, such as lumbering and distilling, may have an operating cycle of several years. Examples of current assets other than those shown in

EXHIBIT 5–8

Madison Electronics Company
Balance Sheet
December 31, 19XX

Assets			Liabilities and Owner's Equity		
Current Assets			**Current Liabilities**		
Cash	$ 7,500		Accounts Payable	$7,300	
Accounts Receivable	8,200		Salaries Payable	500	
Inventory	21,000		Total Current Liabilities		$ 7,800
Prepaid Insurance	240				
Supplies on Hand	460				
Total Current Assets		$37,400			
Long-term Assets			**Owner's Equity**		
Delivery Equipment	$12,000		J. Madison, Capital		38,000
Less: Accumulated Depreciation	3,600	8,400			
Total Assets		$45,800	Total Liabilities and Owner's Equity		$45,800

Exhibit 5–8 are notes receivable and marketable securities that are acquired as a temporary investment. Current assets are usually listed in the order of their "liquidity," or convertibility into cash.

Prepaid expenses such as rent, insurance, and supplies are normally consumed during the operating cycle rather than converted into cash. These items are included with current assets, however, because the prepayments make cash outlays for services unnecessary during the current period.

LONG-TERM ASSETS The classification long-term assets is used for noncurrent, relatively long-lived assets used in operating the business and includes such accounts as land, buildings, and equipment. Sometimes the balance sheet caption is Fixed Assets or Plant and Equipment. Although Madison Electronics had only one fixed asset, delivery equipment, many firms own their own land, buildings, machinery, and store fixtures. Depreciable assets are normally shown at their original cost, and the accumulated portion of the cost taken as depreciation to date is credited to a separate account.

OTHER ASSETS Assets not properly included as current assets or as long-term assets are shown last on the balance sheet under the caption "Other Assets." Some examples might be (1) funds not available for current operations because they are restricted to special uses, such as future building programs or debt retirement; (2) land not currently used in operations but held for future expansion; and (3) intangible assets, such as patents, trademarks, and franchises. When large amounts are involved, any of the foregoing items may appear in a separate category on the balance sheet.

CURRENT LIABILITIES The term current liabilities is applied to those amounts due within the normal operating cycle or one year, whichever is longer. Examples of current liabilities are accounts payable, accrued wages and salaries payable, income or property taxes payable, and short-term notes payable. Any amounts a firm has received from customers but has not yet earned as revenue are also customarily included in this category, for example, customers' deposits on future purchases and magazine subscriptions covering future periods.

LONG-TERM DEBT After current liabilities, the balance sheet lists all long-term debts—amounts that are not due for a relatively long time, typically more than one year. Long-term notes, mortgages, and bonds payable are a few examples. Madison Electronics Company had no long-term debts when its balance sheet was compiled (Exhibit 5–8).

Once again we see that such classifications as current assets and current liabilities are useful in analyzing financial statements. Consider the data in Exhibit 5–8; the difference between the current assets and current liabilities ($37,400 − $7,800 = $29,600), called working capital, is a significant figure, because it represents the net current capital with which the company conducts its operations. Insufficient working capital may prevent a firm from meeting its debts on time. Sometimes, when a company borrows using long-term notes or bonds, the lender requires the borrower to maintain a stipulated amount of working capital. Also, one may calculate various ratios involving current assets, current liabilities, working capital, and other balance sheet and income statement data, in order to evaluate the progress and financial health of a firm. We shall discuss these relationships in Chapter 18, "Analysis and Interpretation of Financial Statements."

OWNERS' EQUITY   The owners' interest in the assets of the firm is portrayed in the owners' equity section of the balance sheet. In Exhibit 5-8, the capital balance of J. Madison at December 31 is determined as follows (data from Exhibit 5-6):

J. Madison, Capital, Jan. 1	$32,500
Add: Net Income for the Year	8,000
	$40,500
Less: Withdrawals for the Year	2,500
J. Madison, Capital, Dec. 31	$38,000

ADJUSTING AND CLOSING ENTRIES

As we explained in Chapter 4, a company often will prepare monthly or quarterly financial statements directly from worksheets and not record adjusting and closing entries in the general ledger until the end of the year. Let us examine the end-of-year procedures for Madison Electronics Company.

Adjusting Entries

After financial statements have been prepared from the worksheet, the adjusting entries shown on the worksheet are recorded in the general journal and posted to the accounts. These entries were given in general journal form on pages 171 and 173 and will not be repeated here.

Closing Entries

As a result of the adjusting process, the Income Summary account has received a debit for the beginning inventory and a credit for the ending inventory. When the other accounts appearing in the income statement are closed to the Income Summary, the latter account balance is the net income or net loss for the period. This balance is finally closed to the appropriate owners' equity account. In our example, the balance is transferred to the J. Madison, Capital account.

The closing entries follow the adjusting entries in the general journal. The simplest procedure to clear the balances of the temporary capital accounts is as follows:

(1) Close all income statement accounts with *credit* balances by reducing them to zero, and credit the total to the Income Summary.

(2) Close all income statement accounts with *debit* balances by reducing them to zero, and debit the total to the Income Summary.

(3) Transfer the balance of the Income Summary to the owner's capital account (or to retained earnings in a corporation).

(4) Transfer any balance in the owner's drawing account to the owner's capital account.

Closing entries for Madison Electronics Company are given below:

Dec. 31	Sales	163,500	
	Purchases Returns and Allowances	300	
	Purchases Discounts	1,500	
	Income Summary		165,300
	To close temporary accounts with credit balances.		
31	Income Summary	159,300	
	Sales Returns and Allowances		500
	Sales Discounts		3,000
	Purchases		104,600
	Transportation In		3,200
	Sales Salaries		26,500
	Advertising Expense		1,500
	Delivery Expense		2,680
	Office Salaries		9,200
	Rent Expense		5,400
	Utilities Expense		1,160
	Insurance Expense		120
	Supplies Expense		240
	Depreciation Expense		1,200
	To close temporary accounts with debit balances.		

| 31 | Income Summary | 8,000 | |
| | J. Madison, Capital | | 8,000 |

To close the Income Summary account
and transfer net income to the owner's
capital account.

| 31 | J. Madison, Capital | 2,500 | |
| | J. Madison, Drawing | | 2,500 |

To close the drawing account to the owner's
capital account.

After the adjusting and closing entries have been recorded and posted, the Income Summary and J. Madison, Capital accounts will appear as shown below. Although we have labeled the entries in this example for illustrative purposes, they would ordinarily not be labeled in the actual accounts.

Income Summary

Beginning Inventory (adjusting)	19,000	Ending Inventory (adjusting)	21,000
Purchases, Expenses, and other		Sales and other Credits (closing)	165,300
Debits (closing)	159,300		
Net Income (closing)	8,000		
	186,300		186,300

J. Madison, Capital

Withdrawals (closing)	2,500	Beginning Balance	32,500
Ending Balance	38,000	Net Income (closing)	8,000
	40,500		40,500
		Ending Balance	38,000

POST-CLOSING TRIAL BALANCE   As we explained in Chapter 4, another trial balance of the ledger accounts is customarily taken after the books have been closed to be certain that the ledger is in balance and ready for recording transactions in the next period. A post-closing trial balance for Madison Electronics Company on December 31 is shown in Exhibit 5–9.

EXHIBIT 5–9

Madison Electronics Company
Post-Closing Trial Balance
December 31, 19XX

	Debit	Credit
Cash	$ 7,500	
Accounts Receivable	8,200	
Inventory	21,000	
Prepaid Insurance	240	
Supplies on Hand	460	
Delivery Equipment	12,000	
Accumulated Depreciation		$ 3,600
Accounts Payable		7,300
Salaries Payable		500
J. Madison, Capital		38,000
	$49,400	$49,400

REVERSING ENTRIES   If Madison Electronics Company employs reversing entries in its accounting system (see Chapter 4), only one reversing entry would be needed on January 1. The only accrual made by the firm at the end of December was for salespersons' salaries; therefore, the entry to reverse this accrual on January 1 would be:

Jan. 1	Salaries Payable	400	
	Sales Salaries Expense		400

To reverse accrual of salespersons' salaries
made on Dec. 31.

DEMONSTRATION PROBLEM FOR REVIEW

Sportcraft, Inc., a wholesaler of sporting goods, had the following trial balance at December 31 of the current year:

Sportcraft, Inc.
Trial Balance
December 31, 19XX

	Debit	Credit
Cash	$ 6,200	
Accounts Receivable	28,000	
Inventory, Jan. 1	45,000	
Office Supplies on Hand	800	
Prepaid Insurance	2,100	
Land	34,000	
Building	82,000	
Accumulated Depreciation—Building		$ 16,000
Office Equipment	21,300	
Accumulated Depreciation—Office Equipment		5,300
Accounts Payable		19,000
Capital Stock		100,000
Retained Earnings		51,200
Sales		252,000
Sales Discounts	3,500	
Purchases	151,000	
Purchases Returns and Allowances		2,400
Transportation In	8,200	
Sales Salaries Expense	27,600	
Transportation Out	7,800	
Advertising Expense	6,100	
Office Salaries Expense	22,300	
	$445,900	$445,900

Information for end-of-year adjusting entries is as follows:
(1) Inventory, December 31, $43,500.
(2) Office Supplies on Hand, December 31, $250.
(3) Prepaid Insurance, December 31, $1,500.
(4) Depreciation for the year: Building, $2,000; Office Equipment, $2,400.
(5) Salaries payable at December 31: Sales Salaries, $300; Office Salaries, $200.

REQUIRED
(a) Prepare an eight-column worksheet for the year.
(b) Prepare a classified income statement for the year. 75% of the insurance expense and depreciation expense on building is treated as selling expense; 25% is treated as administrative expense.
(c) Prepare a classified balance sheet at December 31.
(d) Prepare adjusting entries in general journal form.

(e) Prepare closing entries in general journal form.

(f) Show in T account form how the Income Summary and Retained Earnings accounts would appear after posting the closing entries.

SOLUTION TO DEMONSTRATION PROBLEM

(a)

Sportcraft, Inc.
Worksheet
For the Year Ended December 31, 19XX

	Trial Balance Debit	Trial Balance Credit	Adjustments Debit	Adjustments Credit	Income Statement Debit	Income Statement Credit	Balance Sheet Debit	Balance Sheet Credit
Cash	6,200						6,200	
Accounts Receivable	28,000						28,000	
Inventory, January 1	45,000		(1b) 43,500	(1a) 45,000			43,500	
Office Supplies on Hand	800			(2) 550			250	
Prepaid Insurance	2,100			(3) 600			1,500	
Land	34,000						34,000	
Building	82,000						82,000	
Accumulated Depreciation—Building		16,000		(4) 2,000				18,000
Office Equipment	21,300						21,300	
Accumulated Depreciation—Office Equip.		5,300		(4) 2,400				7,700
Accounts Payable		19,000						19,000
Capital Stock		100,000						100,000
Retained Earnings		51,200						51,200
Sales		252,000				252,000		
Sales Discounts	3,500				3,500			
Purchases	151,000				151,000			
Purchases Returns and Allowances		2,400				2,400		
Transportation In	8,200				8,200			
Sales Salaries Expense	27,600		(5) 300		27,900			
Transportation Out	7,800				7,800			
Advertising Expense	6,100				6,100			
Office Salaries Expense	22,300		(5) 200		22,500			
	445,900	445,900						
Income Summary			(1a) 45,000	(1b) 43,500	45,000	43,500		
Office Supplies Expense			(2) 550		550			
Insurance Expense			(3) 600		600			
Depreciation Expense—Building			(4) 2,000		2,000			
Depreciation Expense—Office Equip.			(4) 2,400		2,400			
Salaries Payable				(5) 500				500
			94,550	94,550	277,550	297,900	216,750	196,400
Net Income					20,350			20,350
					297,900	297,900	216,750	216,750

(b)

Sportcraft, Inc.
Income Statement
For the Year Ended December 31, 19XX

Revenue
 Sales $252,000
  Less: Sales Discounts   3,500
   Net Sales $248,500

Cost of Goods Sold
 Inventory, Jan. 1 $ 45,000
 Add: Net Purchases
  Purchases $151,000
  Less: Purchases Returns and Allowances   2,400
                                                  $148,600
   Add: Transportation In   8,200   156,800
 Cost of Goods Available for Sale $201,800
 Less: Inventory, Dec. 31   43,500
 Cost of Goods Sold   158,300
 Gross Profit on Sales $ 90,200

Operating Expenses
 Selling Expenses
  Sales Salaries Expense $ 27,900
  Transportation Out   7,800
  Advertising Expense   6,100
  Insurance Expense   450
  Depreciation Expense—Building   1,500
   Total Selling Expenses $ 43,750

 Administrative Expenses
  Office Salaries Expense $ 22,500
  Office Supplies Expense   550
  Insurance Expense   150
  Depreciation—Building   500
  Depreciation—Office Equipment   2,400
   Total Administrative Expenses   26,100
    Total Operating Expenses   69,850
Net Income $ 20,350

(c)

Sportcraft, Inc.
Balance Sheet
December 31, 19XX

Current Assets

Cash	$ 6,200	
Accounts Receivable	28,000	
Inventory	43,500	
Office Supplies on Hand	250	
Prepaid Insurance	1,500	
Total Current Assets		$ 79,450

Long-term Assets

Land		$ 34,000	
Building	$82,000		
Less: Accumulated Depreciation	18,000	64,000	
Office Equipment	$21,300		
Less: Accumulated Depreciation	7,700	13,600	
Total Long-term Assets			111,600
Total Assets			$191,050

Liabilities and Stockholders' Equity

Current Liabilities

Accounts Payable	$ 19,000	
Salaries Payable	500	
Total Current Liabilities		$ 19,500

Stockholders' Equity

Capital Stock	$100,000	
Retained Earnings	71,550	
Total Stockholders' Equity		171,550
Total Liabilities and Stockholders' Equity		$191,050

(d) Adjusting Entries.

Dec. 31	Income Summary	45,000	
	Inventory		45,000
	To transfer beginning inventory to Income Summary.		
31	Inventory	43,500	
	Income Summary		43,500
	To record ending inventory.		

| Dec. 31 | Office Supplies Expense | 550 | |
| | Office Supplies on Hand | | 550 |

To reflect as expense supplies used during the year.

| 31 | Insurance Expense | 600 | |
| | Prepaid Insurance | | 600 |

To reflect as expense insurance expired during the year.

31	Depreciation Expense—Building	2,000	
	Depreciation Expense—Office Equipment	2,400	
	Accumulated Depreciation—Building		2,000
	Accumulated Depreciation—		
	Office Equipment		2,400

To record depreciation on building and office equipment.

31	Sales Salaries Expense	300	
	Office Salaries Expense	200	
	Salaries Payable		500

To reflect salaries earned by employees but unpaid at Dec. 31.

(e) Closing Entries.

19XX

Dec. 31	Sales	252,000	
	Purchases Returns and Allowances	2,400	
	Income Summary		254,400

To close temporary accounts with credit balances

31	Income Summary	232,550	
	Sales Discounts		3,500
	Purchases		151,000
	Transportation In		8,200
	Sales Salaries Expense		27,900
	Transportation Out		7,800
	Advertising Expense		6,100
	Office Salaries Expense		22,500
	Office Supplies Expense		550
	Insurance Expense		600
	Depreciation Expense—Building		2,000
	Depreciation Expense—		
	Office Equipment		2,400

To close temporary accounts with debit balances.

| Dec. 31 | Income Summary | 20,350 | |
| | Retained Earnings | | 20,350 |

To close the Income Summary account and transfer the net income to Retained Earnings.

(f)

Income Summary

Dec. 31		45,000	Dec. 31		43,500
31		232,550	31		254,400
31 (Net Income)		20,350			
		297,900			297,900

Retained Earnings

| | | | Dec. 31 (Balance) | | 51,200 |
| | | | 31 (Net Income) | | 20,350 |

KEY POINTS TO REMEMBER

(1) Purchase and sales invoices are the basic documents initiating entries for merchandise transactions.

(2) Cash discounts (for prompt payment during the discount period) are normally reflected in financial records, while trade discounts are not. Cash discounts are calculated on the billed price of merchandise retained in a purchase or sale—not on amounts representing returns and allowances or transportation costs.

(3) The terms "prepaid" and "collect" designate the party expected to remit to the freight company. The party who is to bear transportation costs is designated by the terms "F.O.B. destination" (seller) and "F.O.B. shipping point" (buyer).

(4) A major difference between the statements of service and merchandising firms is the inclusion of Cost of Goods Sold in the income statement of merchandising firms. Cost of Goods Sold is deducted from net sales to obtain gross profit. Expenses are then deducted from gross profit to arrive at net income.

(5) Under a periodic inventory system, a firm determines its inventory only at the end of a period and adjusts its records through the Income Summary account.

(6) In closing procedures for a merchandising firm, income statement accounts with credit balances are closed first to the Income Summary. Next, income statement accounts with debit balances are closed. Finally, the Income Summary balance, representing net income or net loss, is closed to the Owner's Capital account, and the balance in the Owner's Drawing account is likewise closed.

QUESTIONS

5-1 What is the most significant difference between the income statement of a service firm and that of a merchandising firm?

5-2 What is meant by "gross profit on sales," and of what significance is this item to management?

5-3 Explain the nature, purpose, and key information appearing on each of the following forms:
(a) Purchase requisition.
(b) Purchase order.
(c) Sales invoice.
(d) Receiving report.
(e) Credit memorandum.

5-4 Differentiate between (a) credit period and discount period; (b) cash discounts and trade discounts.

5-5 For the accounts titled Sales Returns and Allowances and Purchases Returns and Allowances, indicate (a) the justification for their use; (b) their normal balances (debit or credit) and position in the financial statements.

5-6 Explain the appropriate treatment of the accounts Transportation In and Transportation Out in the income statement.

5-7 Who (buyer or seller) would *bear* the freight cost and who would *remit* to the freight company under each of the following selling terms?
(a) F.O.B. shipping point, freight collect.
(b) F.O.B. destination, freight prepaid.
(c) F.O.B. shipping point, freight prepaid.
(d) F.O.B. destination, freight collect.

5-8 On April 2, High Company purchased $600 worth of merchandise from Lowe Company, F.O.B. shipping point, freight collect, terms 2/10, n/30. On April 4, High Company returned $50 of the goods for credit. On April 5, High paid $30 freight on the shipment. High is paying its account with Lowe Company on April 11. How much should High remit?

5-9 How much would be remitted in Question 5-8 if the terms were F.O.B. destination rather than F.O.B. shipping point?

5-10 The gross purchases made during the accounting period by a wholesale firm were $80,000 and Transportation In was $2,500. If the firm returned goods amounting to $3,000 and took $1,000 in purchase discounts during the period, what was the net purchases cost for the period?

5-11 When an unadjusted trial balance of the general ledger is taken for a merchandising firm on a periodic inventory basis, will the beginning inventory or the ending inventory appear in the trial balance? Explain.

5-12 The beginning inventory for a merchandising firm was $41,000 and the ending inventory is $35,000. What entries are needed at the end of the accounting period to adjust the inventory account?

5-13 A portion of a worksheet for a merchandising firm is shown below. Identify the columns, A, B, C, or D, into which the balance of any of the listed accounts should be extended.

	Income Statement		Balance Sheet	
	Debit	Credit	Debit	Credit
	(A)	(B)	(C)	(D)
Inventory			X	
Sales		X		
Sales Returns and Allowances	X			
Purchases	X			
Purchases Returns and Allowances		X		
Purchases Discounts		X		
Transportation In	X			
Income Summary	X	X		
Salaries Payable				X

5-14 Define (a) current assets, (b) current liabilities, and (c) working capital. Why is working capital a significant figure?

5-15 The Hopper Company had net sales of $350,000, cost of goods sold of $238,000, and net income of $21,000. Compute (a) its gross margin percentage and (b) its return on sales.

EXERCISES

5-16 On April 1, Curtis Company sold merchandise with a list price of $1,200. For each of the sales terms below, determine (a) the amount to be recorded as a sale and (b) the proper amount of cash to be received.

	Applicable Trade Discount (%)	Credit Terms	Date Paid
(1)	30	2/10,n/30	April 8
(2)	40	1/10, n/30	April 15
(3)	—	2/10, n/30	April 11
(4)	20	1/15, n/30	April 14
(5)	40	n/30	April 28

5-17 For each of the following purchases of Wilson Company, assume that credit terms are 2/10, n/30 and that any credit memorandum was issued and known before payment was made by Wilson Company.

	Amount of Sale	Shipping Terms	Prepaid Freight (by seller)	Credit Memorandum
(1)	$ 800	F.O.B. shipping point	$ 50	$ 80
(2)	1,500	F.O.B. destination	120	100
(3)	1,000	F.O.B. shipping point	—	200
(4)	3,000	F.O.B. shipping point	150	—

In each case, determine (a) the appropriate cash discount available and (b) the cash to be remitted if the payment is made within the discount period.

5-18 On June 8, Acme Company sold merchandise listing for $600 to Ward Company on terms of 2/10, n/30. On June 12, $150 worth of the merchandise was returned because the color was not as specified. On June 18, Acme Company received a check for the amount due.

   Record, in general journal form, the entries made by Acme Company for the above transactions.

5-19 On March 10, Ford Company purchased $2,000 worth of merchandise from Cable Company on terms of 1/10, n/30, F.O.B. shipping point. On March 12, Ford paid $50 freight on the shipment. On March 15, Ford returned $200 worth of the merchandise for credit. Final payment was made to Cable on March 19.
   (a) Give the entries, in general journal form, that Ford should make on March 12, March 15, and March 19.
   (b) Give the entries that Ford should have made on these three dates if the terms had been F.O.B. destination.

5-20 Following are selected transactions of Westgate, Inc.

   April 20   Sold and shipped on account to Eaton Stores merchandise listing for $800, terms 2/10, n/30.
        27   Received a debit memorandum for $50 (and the related merchandise) from Eaton Stores covering part of the goods sold April 20 that were defective.
        29   Received from Eaton Stores a check for full settlement of the April 20 transaction.

   Record, in general journal entry form, the above transactions as they would appear on the books of (a) Westgate, Inc. and (b) Eaton Stores.

5-21 The diagram below contains portions of five unrelated income statements, each with certain data omitted. Fill in the lettered blanks with the appropriate amounts.

	(1)	(2)	(3)	(4)	(5)
Net Sales	$75,000	$ (d)	$80,000	$60,000	$140,000
Beginning Inventory	15,000	25,000	(g)	18,000	(m)
Net Purchases	45,000	(e)	60,000	30,000	90,000
Cost of Goods					
Available for Sale	(a)	(f)	80,000	(j)	(n)
Ending Inventory	10,000	15,000	(h)	(k)	20,000
Cost of Goods Sold	(b)	80,000	(i)	(l)	(o)
Gross Profit	(c)	30,000	25,000	22,000	45,000

5-22 The operating figures for a company for four consecutive periods are given below.

	Period (1)	(2)	(3)	(4)
Beginning Inventory	$25,000	$20,000	$15,000	$23,000
Net Purchases	45,000	55,000	50,000	45,000
Cost of Goods Available for Sale	$70,000	$75,000	$65,000	$68,000
Ending Inventory	20,000	15,000	23,000	16,000
Cost of Goods Sold	$50,000	$60,000	$42,000	$52,000

Assuming that the following errors were made, compute the correct Cost of Goods Sold for each period:

Period	Error in Ending Inventory
1	Overstated $2,000
2	Understated $3,000
3	Overstated $1,000

5-23 A portion of the December 31 worksheet for Davis Distributors, a corporation, is shown below. For simplicity, all operating expenses have been combined.

	Income Statement Debit	Credit	Balance Sheet Debit	Credit
Retained earnings				$128,000
Sales		$500,000		
Sales Returns and Allowances	$ 1,500			
Sales Discounts	4,500			
Purchases	330,000			
Purchases Returns and Allowances		3,400		
Purchases Discounts		6,600		
Transportation In	8,000			
Operating Expenses	126,000			
Income Summary	64,000	59,000		

Using the given information, prepare the general journal entries to close the books.

PROBLEMS

5-24 The following transactions occurred between the Pioneer Company and United Stores, Inc. during March of the current year.

Mar. 8 Pioneer sold $2,700 worth of merchandise to United Stores on terms 2/10, n/30, F.O.B. shipping point. Freight charges of $80 were paid by Pioneer and added to the amount of the invoice for the merchandise.

12 United Stores notified Pioneer of a $300 error in pricing the merchandise shipped on March 8. Pioneer issued a credit memorandum for this amount.

17 Pioneer received payment in full for the net amount due from the March 8 sale.

20 Pioneer received a debit memorandum from United Stores for goods returned that had been billed originally to United Stores at $120. Pioneer issued a check.

REQUIRED

Record the above transactions in general journal form as they would appear on (a) the books of Pioneer Company and (b) the books of United Stores, Inc.

5-25 Kirby Corporation, which began business on August 1 of the current year, sells on terms of 2/10, n/30, F.O.B. shipping point. Credit terms and freight terms for its purchases vary with the supplier. Selected transactions for the month of August are given below. Unless noted, all transactions are on account and involve merchandise held for resale.

Aug. 1 Purchased merchandise from Olympia, Inc., $900; terms 2/10, n/30, F.O.B. shipping point, freight collect.

4 Purchased merchandise from Victor Company, $1,500, terms 2/10, n/30, F.O.B. destination. Freight charges of $60 were prepaid by Victor Company.

5 Paid freight on shipment from Olympia, Inc., $40.

7 Sold merchandise to Sherwood Corporation, $800.

7 Paid freight on shipment to Sherwood Corporation, $55, and billed Sherwood for the charges.

9 Returned $80 worth of the merchandise purchased August 1 from Olympia, Inc., because it was defective.

9 Issued a credit memorandum to Sherwood Corporation for $100 worth of merchandise returned by Sherwood.

10 Paid Olympia, Inc. the amount due.

14 Purchased from Gaylord, Inc. goods with a list price of $1,600. Kirby Corporation was entitled to a 25% trade discount; terms were 1/10, n/30, F.O.B. shipping point, freight collect.

15 Paid freight on shipment from Gaylord, Inc., $70.

17 Received the amount due from Sherwood Corporation.

18 Sold merchandise to Pearson, Inc., $1,800.

19 Paid Victor Company for the net amount due on its invoice of August 4.

20 Paid freight of $85 for August 18 shipment to Pearson, Inc.

20 Received a credit memorandum of $80 from Gaylord, Inc. as an adjustment of the price charged for merchandise purchased on August 14.

24 Paid Gaylord, Inc. the amount due.

28 Received the amount due from Pearson, Inc.

REQUIRED

Record the transactions for Kirby Corporation in general journal form.

5-26 The unadjusted trial balance of Tappen Distributors on December 31 of the current year is shown below:

Tappen Distributors
Trial Balance
December 31, 19XX

	Debit	Credit
Cash	$ 5,200	
Accounts Receivable	38,500	
Inventory, Jan. 1	67,000	
Prepaid Insurance	1,600	
Supplies on Hand	1,200	
Delivery Equipment	35,000	
Accumulated Depreciation		$ 4,500
Accounts Payable		32,800
Tappen, Capital		52,000
Tappen, Drawing	11,000	
Sales		418,000
Sales Returns and Allowances	3,700	
Sales Discounts	6,300	
Purchases	258,000	
Purchases Returns and Allowances		600
Purchases Discounts		3,100
Transportation In	5,400	
Salaries and Wages Expense	52,000	
Rent Expense	18,000	
Gas, Oil, and Repairs Expense	7,200	
Utilities Expense	900	
	$511,000	$511,000

The following adjusting data are available at December 31:

(1) Inventory, December 31, $70,000.

(2) Prepaid Insurance at December 31 is $750.

(3) Supplies on Hand at December 31 amounted to $540.

(4) Depreciation on the delivery equipment is 20% per year.

(5) At December 31 the company owed its employees $400.

(6) At December 31 there was an unrecorded utility bill for $50.

REQUIRED

Prepare an eight-column worksheet for the Tappen Company for the year 19XX.

5-27 The following selected information is available for the Neptune Wholesale Company for March of the current year.

Purchases	$42,000
Sales	77,500
Transportation In	900
Purchases Discounts	700
Beginning Inventory, Mar. 1	30,000
Ending Inventory, Mar. 31	18,200
Purchases Returns and Allowances	600
Sales Returns and Allowances	1,500
Transportation Out	310
Rent Expense	750
Sales Salaries Expense	6,400
Sales Discounts	1,600
Depreciation Expense—Office Equipment	60
Office Supplies Expense	180
Office Salaries Expense	5,800
Advertising Expense	1,110
Insurance Expense	140

REQUIRED

(a) Prepare the March income statement for Neptune Wholesale Company.
(b) Calculate the ratio of gross profit to net sales and express as a percentage.
(c) Calculate the ratio of net income to net sales and express as a percentage.

5-28 Plateau Trading Company, whose accounting year ends on December 31, had the following normal balances in its general ledger at December 31 of the current year:

Cash	$ 5,200	Sales	$280,000
Accounts Receivable	14,000	Sales Returns and	
Inventory	48,000	Allowances	3,100
Prepaid Insurance	2,400	Sales Discounts	2,900
Office Supplies on Hand	1,800	Purchases	190,000
Furniture and Fixtures	12,500	Purchases Returns and	
Accumulated Depreciation—		Allowances	2,600
Furniture and Fixtures	2,500	Purchases Discounts	3,600
Delivery Equipment	38,000	Transportation In	4,800
Accumulated Depreciation—		Sales Salaries Expense	38,000
Delivery Equipment	8,000	Delivery Expense	6,200
Accounts Payable	21,300	Advertising Expense	2,400
Notes Payable (Long-term)	18,000	Rent Expense	7,500
R. Plateau, Capital	70,000	Office Salaries Expense	24,000
R. Plateau, Drawing	4,000	Utilities Expense	1,200

Rent expense and utilities expense are classified as administrative expenses. During the year, the accounting department prepared monthly statements using worksheets, but no adjusting entries were made in the journals and ledgers. Data for the year-end adjustments are as follows:

(1) Inventory, December 31	$34,500 = 13,500
(2) Prepaid Insurance, December 31 (70% of insurance expense is classified as selling expense, while 30% is classified as administrative expense)	400
(3) Office Supplies on Hand, December 31	1,250
(4) Depreciation Expense for the year, Furniture and Fixtures (an administrative expense)	900
(5) Depreciation Expense for the year, Delivery Equipment	4,500
(6) Sales Salaries Payable, December 31	400
(7) Office Salaries Payable, December 31	300

(handwritten annotations: Inc, Deb/Adm St., Cred 200 - Bal.)

REQUIRED

(a) Prepare a worksheet for the year ended December 31.
(b) Prepare a classified income statement for the year.
(c) Prepare a classified balance sheet at December 31.
(d) Record the necessary adjusting entries in a general journal.
(e) Record the closing entries in a general journal.
(f) Record any necessary reversing entries in a general journal.

5-29 Linda Miller, the treasurer of Cabincraft, Inc., was on her way to a local bank to negotiate a loan when she realized that the income statement for the current year was missing from her papers. She had a balance sheet at December 31, however, and, after searching through her papers, was able to locate an unadjusted trial balance taken at December 31. She arrives at your office shortly before her appointment at the bank and asks your assistance in preparing an income statement for the year. The available data at December 31 are given below:

	Unadjusted Trial Balance Debit	Credit	Balance Sheet Data
Cash	$ 14,000		$ 14,000
Accounts Receivable	21,000		21,000
Inventory	32,000		28,000
Office Supplies on Hand	450		300
Prepaid Insurance	750		500
Delivery Equipment	43,000		43,000
Accumulated Depreciation		$ 4,500	(6,000)
			$100,800
Accounts Payable		21,000	$ 21,000
Salaries Payable			600
Capital Stock		40,000	40,000
Retained Earnings		8,000	39,200
Sales		128,000	
Purchases	72,000		
Rent Expense	1,500		
Salaries Expense	12,500		
Advertising Expense	1,500		
Delivery Expense	2,800		
	$201,500	$201,500	$100,800

REQUIRED
Use the given data to prepare the year's income statement for Cabincraft, Inc. for Linda Miller.

5-30 The first four columns of a worksheet prepared for the Allendale Shop are as follows:

Allendale Shop
Worksheet
For the Year Ended December 31, 19XX

	Trial Balance		Adjustments	
	Debit	Credit	Debit	Credit
Cash	$ 5,000			
Inventory	32,000		$28,000	$32,000
Prepaid Insurance	600			
Equipment	25,000			
Accumulated Depreciation		$ 4,000		800
Accounts Payable		8,000		
A. Dale, Capital		38,000		
A. Dale, Drawing	3,000			
Sales		90,000		
Purchases	48,000			
Transportation In	400			
Rent Expense	2,000			
Salaries Expense	24,000		500	
	$140,000	$140,000		
Income Summary			32,000	28,000
Depreciation Expense			800	
Salaries Payable				500
			$61,300	$61,300

In completing the worksheet, Mr. Dale made the following errors:
(1) The amount for inventory extended as a debit in the balance sheet columns was $32,000.
(2) The adjustment for expired insurance was omitted; premiums amounting to $400 had expired during the year.
(3) The $3,000 balance of Dale's drawing account was extended as a debit in the income statement columns.
(4) The credit to Salaries Payable was extended as a credit in the income statement columns.
(5) The balance for Accumulated Depreciation extended as a credit in the balance sheet columns was $3,200.

REQUIRED
(a) Which of the errors would cause the worksheet not to balance?
(b) Without completing the worksheet, calculate the correct net income for the year. Assume that Mr. Dale made no other errors and that his worksheet totals, before adding any net income or net loss, were:

	Debit	**Credit**
Income Statement	$110,700	$118,500
Balance Sheet	62,600	49,200

ALTERNATE PROBLEMS

5–24A Nevin Distributing Company had the following transactions with Lander Stores, Inc.

Nov. 10   Nevin sold and shipped $2,000 worth of merchandise to Lander Stores on terms of 2/10, n/30, F.O.B. shipping point. Freight charges of $150 were paid in cash by Nevin and added to the amount of the invoice for the merchandise.

14   Upon notification from Lander Stores, Inc., Nevin issued a credit memo for $200 as an adjustment of the price originally charged for merchandise sold on November 10.

19   Nevin received payment in full for the net amount due on the November 10 sale.

24   Nevin received a debit memo from Lander Stores, Inc. for goods returned that had originally been billed to Lander at $90. A check was issued by Nevin to honor the debit memo.

REQUIRED
Record the above transactions in general journal form as they would appear (a) on the books of Nevin Distributing Company and (b) on the books of Lander Stores, Inc.

5–25A The Burton Company was established on July 1 of the current year. Its sales terms are 2/10, n/30, F.O.B. destination. Credit terms for its purchases vary with the supplier. Selected transactions for the first month of operations are given below. Unless noted, all transactions are on account and involve merchandise held for resale.

July 1   Purchases from Fowler, Inc., $500; terms 1/10, n/30, F.O.B. shipping point, freight collect.

2   Purchases from Starr Company, $1,000; terms 2/10, n/30, F.O.B. destination. Freight charges of $80 were prepaid by Starr.

3   Paid freight on shipment from Fowler, $30.

5   Sales to Hale, Inc., $700.

5   Paid freight on shipment to Hale, Inc., $50.

8   Returned $60 worth of the goods purchased July 1 from Fowler, Inc. because some goods were damaged.

9   Issued credit memorandum to Hale, Inc. for $70 worth of merchandise returned.

10   Paid Fowler, Inc. the amount due.

10   Purchased goods from Ward Company with a list price of $800, but Burton was entitled to a 20% trade discount; terms 2/10, n/30, F.O.B. destination, freight collect.

11   Paid freight on shipment from Ward Company, $45.

15   Received the amount due from Hale, Inc.

15   Sales to Acker Corporation, $1,200.

16   Mailed a check to Starr Company for the net amount due on its invoice of July 2.

17   Received a debit memorandum from Acker Corporation stating that it had paid freight of $65 on July 15 shipment.

18   Received a credit memorandum of $40 from Ward Company as an adjustment of the prices charged for the merchandise purchased on July 10.

19   Paid Ward Company the amount due.

25   Received the amount due from Acker Corporation.

REQUIRED

Record the transactions for Burton Company in general journal form.

5–26A The unadjusted trial balance of Lion Corporation on December 31 of the current year is shown below:

Lion Corporation
Trial Balance
December 31, 19XX

	Debit	Credit
Cash	$ 2,400	
Accounts Receivable	2,100	
Merchandise Inventory, Jan. 1	11,000	
Prepaid Insurance	200	
Supplies on Hand	400	
Furniture and Fixtures	2,000	
Accumulated Depreciation—Furniture and Fixtures		$ 400
Delivery Equipment	4,000	
Accumulated Depreciation—Delivery Equipment		1,000
Accounts Payable		4,000
Capital Stock		9,000
Retained Earnings		3,700
Sales		64,000
Sales Returns and Allowances	300	
Sales Discounts	1,300	
Purchases	45,000	
Purchases Returns and Allowances		400
Purchases Discounts		900
Transportation In	1,100	
Salaries Expense	12,000	
Rent Expense	1,500	
Delivery Expense	100	
	$83,400	$83,400

The following adjusting data are available at December 31:
(1) Inventory, December 31, $8,000.
(2) Prepaid Insurance at December 31 is $100.
(3) Supplies on Hand at December 31 amounted to $250.
(4) Depreciation on the delivery equipment is 25% per year.
(5) Depreciation on the furniture and fixtures is 10% per year.
(6) At December 31 there were accrued salaries of $600.

REQUIRED
Prepare an eight-column worksheet for Lion Corporation for the year 19XX.

5-27A The following selected information is available for the Viking Trading Company for February of the current year.

Purchases	$33,000
Sales	62,500
Transporation In	500
Purchases Discounts	400
Beginning Inventory, Feb. 1	10,200
Ending Inventory, Feb. 28	6,000
Purchases Returns and Allowances	700
Sales Returns and Allowances	800
Transportation Out	1,200
Rent Expense	3,000
Salaries Expense	5,800
Sales Discounts	1,700
Depreciation Expense	2,000

REQUIRED
(a) Prepare a February income statement for Viking Trading Company.
(b) Calculate the ratio of gross profit to net sales and express as a percentage.
(c) Calculate the ratio of net profit to net sales as a percentage.

5-28A Gemrock Distributors, whose accounting year ends on December 31, had the following balances in its ledger at December 31 of the current year:

Cash	$12,400	Sales	$305,000
Accounts Receivable	29,000	Sales Returns and	
Inventory	45,000	Allowances	1,100
Prepaid Insurance	2,100	Sales Discounts	2,900
Office Supplies on Hand	1,400	Purchases	192,000
Furniture and Fixtures	17,000	Purchases Returns and	
Accumulated Depreciation—		Allowances	800
Furniture and Fixtures	5,100	Purchases Discounts	3,600
Delivery Equipment	20,000	Transportation In	4,000
Accumulated Depreciation—		Sales Salaries Expense	29,200
Delivery Equipment	8,000	Delivery Expense	7,800
Accounts Payable	10,500	Advertising Expense	11,500
Notes Payable (long-term)	50,000	Rent Expense	12,200
O. Gemrock, Capital	35,300	Office Salaries Expense	15,000
O. Gemrock, Drawing	12,000	Utilities Expense	3,700

Rent expense and utilities expense are classified as administrative expenses. During the year, the accounting department prepared monthly statements using worksheets, but no adjusting entries were made in the journals and ledgers. Data for the year-end adjustments are as follows:

(1) Inventory, December 31	$61,600
(2) Prepaid Insurance, December 31 (Insurance Expense is classified as a selling cost)	900
(3) Office Supplies on Hand, December 31	600
(4) Depreciation Expense for year, Furniture and Fixtures (an administrative expense)	1,700
(5) Depreciation Expense for year, Delivery Equipment	4,000
(6) Sales Salaries Payable, December 31	900
(7) Office Salaries Payable, December 31	500

REQUIRED
(a) Prepare a worksheet for the year ended December 31.
(b) Prepare a classified income statement.
(c) Prepare a classified balance sheet.
(d) Make the necessary adjusting entries in a general journal.
(e) Make the closing entries in a general journal.
(f) Make any necessary reversing entries in a general journal.

BUSINESS DECISION PROBLEM

This year's income statement for Cardinal Wholesalers is given below in condensed form.

Sales	$336,000
Cost of Goods Sold	240,000
Gross Profit	$ 96,000
Operating Expenses	65,760
Net Income	$ 30,240

Cardinal allows its customers a trade discount of 30% of list price. To arrive at the list price, Cardinal adds a mark-up of 100% to its cost.

The president asks you to evaluate a proposal she has received from the sales manager to improve Cardinal's return on sales. The memo from the sales manager states, "I suggest we permit our customers a trade discount of 35% rather than 30%. My estimates show that with the higher trade discount, we will sell 20% more units next year than this year. We can achieve this increased volume with only a 10% increase in operating expenses."

REQUIRED
(a) Compute this year's Cardinal's return on sales.
(b) Compute what Cardinal's return on sales will be if the sales manager's proposal is accepted and his projections are correct. Support this computation with an income statement showing the effect of the sales manager's proposal.
(c) What is your recommendation with respect to the sales manager's proposal?

6
Data Processing: Manual and Automated Systems

TAKING IT EASY
When the day of complete
Automation comes,
We'll put up our feet
and twiddle our thumbs

But far from serene,
We'll say it's just middling,
And want a machine
To take over the twiddling.

RICHARD ARMOUR*

In the preceding chapters we limited our discussion of the processing of accounting transactions to recording in a general journal and posting to a general ledger. Such a system is satisfactory for introducing basic accounting procedures; however, there are two major reasons why this method would be inadequate for a business having even a moderate number of transactions. First, recording all transactions in the general journal would seriously curtail the number of transactions that could be processed in a day, simply because only one person at a time could make entries. Second, transactions recorded in a general journal must be posted individually, resulting in a great deal of posting labor. Therefore, even small and moderate-sized firms prefer to employ certain *special journals* to make their systems flexible and to reduce the amount of posting required. The use of special journals is one of the new features we consider in this chapter.

Our previous illustrations were simplified in that they contained a single Accounts Receivable account and a single Accounts Payable account. Because most business firms must keep accounts with individual customers and creditors, it would become quite burdensome to work with a general ledger containing a large number of customer and creditor accounts. Therefore, firms often use *control accounts* in the general ledger and keep separate *subsidiary ledgers* to record accounts of individual customers and creditors.

Finally, in large businesses, the sheer volume of transactions and the need for fast processing and retrieval of information call for more automatic processing systems. Hence, in the last section of this chapter, we introduce the principal types of mechanical and electronic equipment used in such systems.

CONTROL ACCOUNTS AND SUBSIDIARY LEDGERS

In Chapter 3 we entered all the charges to and payments from customers of Monroe TV Service in a single general ledger account. The following T account illustrates what was done:

*From *Nights with Armour*, by Richard Armour. Copyright 1958 by Richard Armour. Used with permission of McGraw-Hill Book Company.

Accounts Receivable

Dec. 14	750	Dec. 19	500
28	2,400		

Monroe cannot bill or mail statements to customers, answer inquiries about individual customer balances, or make any collection efforts if he has only a single record showing his total claims against customers. He needs to know each customer's name and address, the dates of transactions, amounts charged for services, and amounts received on account for each account receivable.

We could solve this problem by maintaining in the general ledger an individual Account Receivable for each customer. The trial balance of such a general ledger might appear as follows:

	Trial Balance	
	Debit	**Credit**
Cash	$ 4,210	
Accounts Receivable—Customer A	50	
Accounts Receivable—Customer B	100	
Accounts Receivable—Customer C	200	
Accounts Receivable—Customer D	300	
(All other assets)	8,400	
(All liabilities)		$ 2,400
(Owner's Equity)		9,400
Sales		2,700
(All expenses)	1,240	
	$14,500	$14,500

We can easily see the limitations of this approach. The general ledger becomes unreasonably large when hundreds of customers' accounts are involved. When there are thousands of customers, it becomes absolutely unworkable. An alternative is to use one control account titled Accounts Receivable in the general ledger and maintain individual customer accounts in a subsidiary ledger. Under this approach, the general ledger is kept to a more manageable size and there is a detailed record of transactions with individual customers.

The accounts receivable subsidiary ledger, like the general ledger, may be simply a group of accounts in a binder, or it may be a file card arrangement. In either case, the order is usually alphabetical by customer name. Exhibit 6–1 shows a typical form that might be used in the accounts receivable subsidiary ledger. When the three-column form is used, abnormal balances should be enclosed in parentheses or shown in red. The information one chooses to place at the top of the account varies with the needs of the business and the type of customer. Often, such information concerns the granting of credit.

EXHIBIT 6–1
Customer Account Form—Subsidiary Ledger

Name_____

Address_____   Phone_____

Employed at_____   Position_____

Special terms_____   Maximum
credit $_____

Date		Remarks	Debits	Credits	Balance

In the following diagram, we show the relationships between the Accounts Receivable control account in the general ledger and the accounts receivable subsidiary ledger.

Subsidiary Ledger

	General Ledger Trial Balance	
	Debit	Credit
Cash	$ 4,210	
Accounts Receivable	650	
(All other assets)	8,400	
(All liabilities)		$ 2,400
Owner's Equity		9,400
Sales		2,700
(All expenses)	1,240	
	$14,500	$14,500

Customer A: 50   Customer B: 100

Customer C: 200   Customer D: 300

Accounts Receivable (control account): 650

Because the total of all the balances in the accounts receivable subsidiary ledger must equal the balance in the Accounts Receivable control account in the general ledger, it follows that for every amount posted to the Accounts Receivable control account, an equal amount must be posted to one or more of the customers' accounts in the accounts receivable subsidiary ledger. We shall consider the specific posting procedures to be followed later in this chapter.

The control account–subsidiary ledger technique can be used to yield a detailed breakdown of many general ledger accounts, not just Accounts Receivable. Subsidiary ledgers are often used for Accounts Payable, Inventory, Buildings, and Equipment.

SPECIAL JOURNALS

Journals specifically designed in a tabular fashion to accommodate the recording of one type of transaction are called special journals. Most firms use, in addition to a general journal, at least the following special journals:

Special Journal	Specific Transactions to be Recorded
Sales journal	Sales on credit terms
Cash receipts journal	Receipt of cash
Invoice register (purchases journal)	Purchase of merchandise and other items on credit terms
Cash disbursements journal	Payment of cash

Cash sales are usually recorded in the cash receipts journal rather than the sales journal because cash can be better controlled when *all* routine cash receipts are recorded in one journal. Similarly, increased control over cash disbursements is obtained by recording purchases of merchandise for cash in the cash disbursements journal rather than in the purchases journal.

Advantages of Special Journals

A major advantage of special journals is that their use permits a division of labor. When special journals are used, the recording step in the accounting cycle can be divided among several persons, each of whom is responsible for particular types of transactions. Persons making entries in special journals do not have to be highly skilled or have a thorough knowledge of the entire accounting system.

Another advantage of special journals is that their use often reduces recording time. Because all special journal transactions are of a given type, routine explanations of each entry are unnecessary. Also, because special column headings are used, account titles need not be repeated as would be necessary in the general journal.

Probably the most significant advantage of using special rather than general journals is the time saved in posting from the journals to the ledgers. When a general journal is used, each entry must be posted separately to the general ledger. The tabular arrangement of special journals, however, often permits all entries to a given account to be added and posted as a single aggregate posting. For instance, if we entered a thousand sales transactions in a general journal, we would have to make a thousand separate credit postings to the Sales account. If we use a sales journal, however, the amounts of the thousand sales will appear in one money column. Thus, it is easy to obtain a total and post it as one credit to the Sales account. The sales journal has saved us the time necessary for 999 postings to the Sales account. Clearly, the more transactions that are involved, the greater the savings in posting time.

The advantages of special journals will be apparent in the examples we use on the following pages.

SALES JOURNAL

Exhibit 6-2, the sales journal of the Excel Company, lists all credit sales for the month of June. The information for each sale comes from a copy of the related sales invoice. Note that the tabular form of the journal is specifically designed to record sales on account.

If, as is often the case, the same credit terms are extended to all customers, there is no need to describe them in the sales journal. We assume that this is the case in our illustration. When credit terms vary from customer to customer, a column can be added in the sales journal to explain the terms of each particular sale.

As we might expect, the posting of any journal must result in equal debits and credits being posted to the general ledger. Also, for any posting to a control account in the general ledger, the same total amount must be posted to one or more related subsidiary ledger accounts. Exhibit 6-3 illustrates how the posting objectives are accomplished for the sales journal.

Usually, as entries in the sales journal are recorded throughout each month, they are posted to the accounts receivable subsidiary ledger. A customer's account then reflects a transaction within a day or two of its occurrence. Consequently, the credit office can check the balance of a customer's account at times other than a billing date. Daily postings to the accounts receivable subsidiary ledger also allow for cycle billings (for example, billing customers whose names begin with different letters at different times of the month). The advantage of cycle billings is that statements of account can be mailed throughout the month rather than in one large group at the end of the month.

A check mark is placed in the posting reference column of the sales journal to indicate that the amount has been posted to the customer's account. At the end of the month, when all sales have been recorded and the sales journal has been

EXHIBIT 6-2
Sales Journal   Page 1

Date		Invoice No.	Account	Post. Ref.	Amount
19XX					
June	1	101	J. Abarr	✔	$ 200
	5	102	D. Becker	✔	100
	12	103	C. Center	✔	1,000
	22	104	R. Douglas	✔	400
	29	105	M. Esser	✔	300
	30	106	N. Ford	✔	500
				12/40	$2,500

EXHIBIT 6-3
Posting the Sales Journal

Sales Journal		Page 1
Account	**Post. Ref.**	**Amount**
J. Abarr	✔	$ 200
D. Becker	✔	100
C. Center	✔	1,000
R. Douglas	✔	400
M. Esser	✔	300
N. Ford	✔	500
	12/40	$2,500

Accounts Receivable Subsidiary Ledger

J. Abarr

200

D. Becker

100

C. Center

1,000

R. Douglas

400

M. Esser

300

N. Ford

500

General Ledger

Accounts Receivable (12)	Sales (40)
2,500	2,500

totaled and ruled, the total sales figure is posted as a debit to the Accounts Receivable control account in the general ledger and as a credit to the Sales account. Note the double posting reference at the bottom of the posting reference column in the illustration; this indicates that Accounts Receivable is account No. 12 in the ledger and Sales is account No. 40. Posting of the sales journal is now complete.

Sales journals may be expanded to accommodate additional information. For example, columns could be included for sales by department or by product, so that a breakdown of sales is available to management. Columns may also be provided for sales tax information, where necessary.

CASH RECEIPTS JOURNAL

Assume that during the month of June the Excel Company engaged in certain transactions involving cash receipts, and that these transactions were recorded in the cash receipts journal illustrated in Exhibit 6–4. This is a special journal designed to simplify the handling of frequently occurring cash receipts transactions. Because cash sales and collections from credit customers occur most often, there are special columns for recording debits to Cash and to Sales Discounts and credits to Sales and Accounts Receivable. In addition, the columns on the right-hand side of the journal can be used for debits and credits to any other account.

We can analyze the recording procedure used for each entry in the cash receipts journal. Note that each transaction results in equal debits and credits.

June 1   The owner, H. Smith, makes an additional capital investment of $5,000 cash. The $5,000 debit to cash is offset by a $5,000 credit to Smith, Capital. This is recorded in the Other Accounts section of the cash receipts journal.

        8   Received $196 from J. Abarr in payment of a June 1 purchase of $200 less the 2% cash discount taken. The entry involves debiting Cash for $196, debiting Sales Discounts $4, and crediting Accounts Receivable $200.

     10   Received $3,000 as proceeds of a bank loan. The $3,000 debit to cash is offset by a $3,000 credit to Notes Payable in the Other Accounts section.

 15,30   Cash sales totaling $2,000 and $2,500 are recorded. The debits to Cash are offset by equal credits to Sales. In actual practice, cash sales would probably be recorded daily rather than semimonthly (the practice assumed here is for simplicity).

     21   Received $490 from C. Center. Center paid his account by remitting the $490 and signing a note for the balance of $500. Because the partial payment was made within 10 days, it qualified for the 2% discount amounting to $10. Thus, the entry includes debits to Cash for $490, Sales Discounts for $10, and Notes Receivable for $500, all of which are offset by the $1,000 credit to Accounts Receivable.

     29   Received $294 from R. Douglas, which pays his account in full because on June 25 he returned $100 worth of his $400 purchase made on June 22. The sales return would be recorded in the general journal; consequently, no indication of the return appears here. Note that the cash discount is granted only on the amount of the sale not returned. The debits to Cash for $294 and to Sales Discounts for $6 are offset by the credit to Accounts Receivable of $300.

EXHIBIT 6-4
Cash Receipts Journal

Page 1

Date		Explanation	Cash Debit	Sales Discounts Debit	Accounts Receivable Post. Ref.	Accounts Receivable Credit	Sales Credit	Other Accounts Account	Other Accounts Post. Ref.	Other Accounts Debit	Other Accounts Credit
19XX											
June	1	Investment by owner, H. Smith	$ 5,000					Smith, Capital	(31)		$5,000
	8	J. Abarr	196	$ 4	✔	$ 200					
	10	Federal Bank loan	3,000					Notes Payable	(23)		3,000
	15	Cash sales, June 1–15	2,000				$2,000				
	21	C. Center	490	10	✔	1,000		Notes Receivable	(15)	$500	
	29	R. Douglas	294	6	✔	300					
	30	Cash sales, June 16–30	2,500				2,500				
			$13,480	$20		$1,500	$4,500			$500	$8,000
			(10)	(42)		(12)	(40)			(X)	(X)

The cash receipts journal is totaled after the month's entries have been recorded. If each transaction has been properly entered in terms of equal debits and credits and the columns are correctly totaled, the column totals should contain equal aggregate debits and credits, as shown below.

	Debit	Credit
Cash	$13,480	
Sales Discounts	20	
Other Accounts (debit)	500	
Accounts Receivable		$ 1,500
Sales		4,500
Other Accounts (credit)		8,000
Totals	$14,000	$14,000

This procedure is often referred to as balancing the journal. The journal is now ready for posting to the ledgers.

Posting the Cash Receipts Journal

When posting any journal, we must be sure that the general ledger receives equal debits and credits and the subsidiary ledgers receive postings of the same type (debits or credits) equal in amount to any posting to a related control account in the general ledger.

The cash receipts journal has special columns for specific accounts and one set of columns for all other accounts. A three-part pattern is followed in posting such a special journal, in which each part is applicable to certain columns.

Posting Pattern	✓	✓ Examples and Explanation
(1) Only column totals are posted.		Cash, Sales Discounts, and Sales. Because no subsidiary ledgers are involved, only the column totals are posted at the end of the month.
(2) Both column details and totals are posted.		Accounts Receivable. The column total is posted at month's end to the Accounts Receivable control account in the general ledger. The detail amounts in the column are posted daily to the various customers' accounts in the accounts receivable subsidiary ledger.
(3) Only column details are posted.		Other Accounts debit and credit columns. The totals of these columns are usually the sum of various amounts related to several accounts. Consequently, they cannot be properly posted to any single account. These columns have been totaled only to prove that the journal balances. Thus, the only amounts to be posted are the detail figures in the columns.

Using the above pattern, we can post Excel Company's June cash receipts journal to the general ledger as follows:

	Debit	Credit
Cash	$13,480	
Sales Discounts	20	
Notes Receivable	500	
Accounts Receivable		$1,500
Sales		4,500
Smith, Capital		5,000
Notes Payable		3,000

If we look at Exhibit 6–4 again, we note that the posting references in the cash receipts journal indicate that (1) the above amounts were posted to general ledger accounts as indicated by their respective account numbers in parentheses, (2) the individual amounts in the Accounts Receivable column were posted to the subsidiary ledger as indicated by the check (✔) in the posting reference column, and (3) the totals of the Other Accounts columns were *not* posted, as indicated by the cross (X) rather than any account number.

Exhibit 6–5 shows how the Accounts Receivable control account and the accounts receivable subsidiary ledger would appear after both the sales journal and the cash receipts journal have been posted.

EXHIBIT 6–5
The Accounts Receivable Control Account
and Subsidiary Ledger after Posting

Accounts Receivable   Account No. 12

Date			Post. Ref.	Debit	Credit	Balance
19XX						
June	25	Sales Returns—R. Douglas	J1		100	100 cr.
	30		S1	2,500		2,400
	30		CR1		1,500	900

J. Abarr
123 47th Street, Madison, Wis.

Date		Post. Ref.	Debit	Credit	Balance
19XX					
June	1	S1	200		200
	8	CR1		200	—

D. Becker
456 48th Street, Madison, Wis.

Date		Post. Ref.	Debit	Credit	Balance
19XX					
June	5	S1	100		100

C. Center
789 Fir Avenue, Madison, Wis.

Date		Post. Ref.	Debit	Credit	Balance
19XX					
June	12	S1	1,000		1,000
	21	CR1		1,000	—

R. Douglas
2020 Rand Street, Madison, Wis.

Date			Post. Ref.	Debit	Credit	Balance
19XX						
June	22		S1	400		400
	25	Return	J1		100	300
	29		CR1		300	—

M. Esser
1920 Elm, Madison, Wis.

Date		Post. Ref.	Debit	Credit	Balance
19XX					
June	30	S1	300		300

N. Ford
2230 Maple, Madison, Wis.

Date		Post. Ref.	Debit	Credit	Balance
19XX					
June	30	S1	500		500

A schedule of the account balances in a subsidiary ledger is usually prepared at the end of each accounting period, to verify that the subsidiary ledger agrees with the related control account. The schedule of Accounts Receivable that follows indicates that the subsidiary ledger is in agreement with its control account in the general ledger.

Excel Company
Schedule of Accounts Receivable
June 30, 19XX

D. Becker	$100
M. Esser	300
N. Ford	500
Total	$900

INVOICE REGISTER (PURCHASES JOURNAL)

To record purchases of merchandise on account, we can use a single-column journal similar to the sales journal considered earlier. (See the illustration on page 231.) Then we would post each entry in the journal to the individual creditor's account in the subsidiary accounts payable ledger. At the end of the month, we would post the total of the amount column to the general ledger as a debit to the Purchases account and a credit to the Accounts Payable control account.

Most business, however, prefer to keep a multicolumn journal in which to record all acquisitions on account, including such items as supplies and equipment as well as merchandise. Although this journal may be called a **purchases journal,** it is usually called an **invoice register.** Exhibit 6–6 is an illustration of an invoice register.

In the illustration, there are special columns for debits to Purchases, Office Supplies on Hand, and Store Supplies on Hand as well as for credits to Accounts Payable. A general column is also provided for debits to accounts for which no special column is available.

Posting the Invoice Register

Throughout the month, the amounts in the Accounts Payable column are posted daily to the accounts payable subsidiary ledger. A check mark is placed in the posting reference column to indicate that this has been done. At the end of the month, the columns of the register are totaled and the totals are cross-totaled to prove the column totals. A proof for the invoice register is shown below:

	Debit	Credit
Purchases	$4,000	
Office Supplies on Hand	500	
Store Supplies on Hand	200	
Other Debits	1,200	
Accounts Payable		$5,900
	$5,900	$5,900

EXHIBIT 6-6
Invoice Register (Purchases Journal)

Page 1

Date		Account Credited	Post. Ref.	Accounts Payable Credit	Purchases Debit	Office Supplies on Hand Debit	Store Supplies on Hand Debit	Other Debits		
								Account	Post. Ref.	Amount
19XX June	3	Able, Inc.	✓	$ 700	$ 700					
	11	Barr Company	✓	1,900	1,900					
	23	Stix Supply Company	✓	1,200				Office Equipment	19	$1,200
	27	Ward Company	✓	1,400	1,400					
	29	Echo Distributors	✓	400		$400				
	30	Holt, Inc.	✓	300		100	$200			
				$5,900	$4,000	$500	$200			$1,200
				(21)	(50)	(16)	(17)			

The totals are then posted to the general ledger accounts indicated by the column headings. Items in the Other Debits column are posted individually; the total of this column is not posted. Exhibit 6-7 (page 214) illustrates the posting pattern. Some companies control all expenditures through the use of a *voucher system* and use a special journal called the *voucher register* to record all amounts for which expenditures must be made. We describe this system in Chapter 7.

CASH DISBURSEMENTS JOURNAL

In Exhibit 6-8 (page 215) we show the June cash disbursements journal for the Excel Company as it would appear after the related transactions have been recorded and the journal balanced and posted. Note that there are special columns for credits to Cash, credits to Purchases Discounts, and debits to Accounts Payable, because ordinarily these accounts will have the most entries. Also observe that, as it was in the cash receipts journal, the Other Accounts section of this journal is available for recording either debits or credits to any other accounts.

Below we describe each disbursement by Excel Company during June. You should trace each transaction to the cash disbursements journal.

June 2   Check No. 101 for $2,800 was cashed at the local bank to provide the cash needed for the May payroll.

3   Check No. 102 for $600 was sent to the landlord to pay the building rent for June.

12   Check No. 103 for $686 paid the account with Able, Inc. A cash discount of 2% was taken.

June 15 Check No. 104 for $500 was a one-half down payment on equipment purchased. A note was given for the balance of $500.

      19 Check No. 105 for $1,881 was sent to Barr Company to settle the account. A discount of 1% was taken.

      28 Check No. 106 for $150 was used to pay for merchandise purchased locally for cash.

      30 Check No. 107 for $120 paid the annual premium on the building fire insurance policy.

EXHIBIT 6-7
Posting the Invoice Register

Invoice Register   Page 1

Account Credited	Post. Ref.	Accounts Payable Credit	Purchases Debit	Office Supplies on Hand Debit	Store Supplies on Hand Debit	Other Debits		
						Account	Post. Ref.	Amount
Able	✔	$ 700	$ 700					
Barr	✔	1,900	1,900					
Stix	✔	1,200				Office Equipment	19	$1,200
Ward	✔	1,400	1,400					
Echo	✔	400		$400				
Holt	✔	300		100	$200			
		$5,900	$4,000	$500	$200			$1,200
		(21)	(50)	(16)	(17)			(X)

Accounts Payable Subsidiary Ledger

Able			Holt	
	700			300

Barr			Stix	
	1,900			1,200

Echo			Ward	
	400			1,400

General Ledger

Purchases	(50)
4,000	

Office Supplies on Hand	(16)
500	

Store Supplies on Hand	(17)
200	

Accounts Payable	(21)
	5,900

Office Equipment	(19)
1,200	

EXHIBIT 6-8
Cash Disbursements Journal

Page 1

Date	Ck. No.	Explanation	Cash Credit	Purchases Discounts Credit	Accounts Payable Post. Ref.	Accounts Payable Debit	Other Accounts Account	Other Accounts Post. Ref.	Other Accounts Debit	Other Accounts Credit
19XX June										
2	101	Paid employees	$2,800				Wages Payable	57	$2,800	
3	102	Paid June rent	600				Rent Expense	56	600	
12	103	Able, Inc.	686	$14	✓	$ 700				
15	104	Purchased equipment	500				Equipment	18	1,000	
							Notes Payable	23		500
19	105	Barr Company	1,881	19	✓	1,900				
28	106	Purchased merchandise	150				Purchases	50	150	
30	107	Insurance policy	120				Prepaid Insurance	14	120	
			$6,737	$33		$2,600			$4,670	$500
			[10]	[52]		[21]			[X]	[X]

Again we emphasize that each transaction must be analyzed and recorded in terms of equal debits and credits. When all transactions have been recorded and the journal correctly totaled, we can prove the balance of the column totals as follows:

	Debit	Credit
Accounts Payable	$2,600	
Other Accounts (debit)	4,670	
Cash		$6,737
Purchases Discounts		33
Other Accounts (credit)		500
	$7,270	$7,270

The journal is now ready to post to the ledgers.

Posting the Cash Disbursements Journal

The same posting objectives and techniques that we used in posting the cash receipts journal are applicable here. Equal debits and credits must be posted to the general ledger. The end-of-the-month posting to the general ledger can be summarized as follows:

	Debit	Credit
Accounts Payable	$2,600	
Wages Payable	2,800	
Rent Expense	600	
Equipment	1,000	
Purchases	150	
Prepaid Insurance	120	
Cash		$6,737
Purchases Discounts		33
Notes Payable		500

The details of the Accounts Payable columns are posted to the accounts payable subsidiary ledger during the month, and this is indicated by the appropriate check marks. As in the case of the cash receipts journal, crosses indicate that the Other Accounts column totals have not been posted.

After both the purchases journal and the cash disbursements journal have been posted, the Accounts Payable control account appears as follows:

Accounts Payable   Account No. 21

Date			Post. Ref.	Debit	Credit	Balance
19XX						
June	30		IR1		5,900	5,900
	30		CD1	2,600		3,300

Excel Company
Schedule of Accounts Payable
June 30, 19XX

Echo Distributors	$ 400
Holt, Inc.	300
Stix Supply Company	1,200
Ward Company	1,400
	$3,300

NET PRICE METHOD OF RECORDING PURCHASES

Some firms anticipate the cash discounts they will take on merchandise purchases and initially record such purchases net of cash discounts in the invoice register (or purchases journal). These firms do not, therefore, require a column for purchases discounts in their cash disbursements journals. If Excel Company followed the net price method, the purchase from Able, Inc. on June 3 would be recorded in the purchases journal (Exhibit 6–6) at $686; the purchase from Barr Company on June 11 would be recorded at $1,881, and so on. If these amounts are paid during the discount period, the debits to Accounts Payable and credits to Cash in the cash disbursements book are the same (net) amount, and no purchase discounts are ever recorded.

If, however, a firm delays payment beyond the discount period, the amount of the discount not taken is debited to an account called Discounts Lost. For example, suppose that Excel Company followed the net price method but failed to pay Able, Inc. during the discount period. The remittance would therefore be $700, $14 more than the Accounts Payable entry. When the payment is recorded in the cash disbursements journal, Accounts Payable is debited for $686, Discounts Lost is debited (in the Other Accounts column) for $14, and Cash is credited for $700.

The Discounts Lost account balance should normally be classified as an operating expense in the income statement. An alternative treatment adds Discounts Lost to Cost of Goods Sold in the income statement (an addition to Purchases cost).

The principal advantage of the net purchases method is that it focuses attention on discounts not taken, so that management can seek corrective action when the aggregate amount of lost discounts becomes significant.

USE OF THE GENERAL JOURNAL

When special journals are used, transactions that cannot be recorded appropriately in a special journal are recorded in the general journal. Examples include certain transactions involving notes receivable and notes payable, dispositions of

EXHIBIT 6-9
General Journal

Page 1

Date		Description	Post. Ref.	Debit	Credit
19XX July	2	Sales Returns and Allowances	41	100	
		Accounts Receivable—R. Douglas	12/✓		100
		R. Douglas returned $100 merchandise for credit.			
	5	Accounts Payable—Ward Company	21/✓	70	
		Purchases Returns and Allowances	51		70
		Returned $70 merchandise to Ward Company for credit.			

fixed assets, write-offs of uncollectible accounts, and merchandise returns. A special posting pattern is followed for posting to subsidiary ledgers. For example, purchases returns and allowances and sales returns and allowances are treated as shown in Exhibit 6-9. Note that whenever a posting is to be made to the Accounts Receivable control account or the Accounts Payable control account from the general journal, a posting must also be made to the related subsidiary ledger account. The latter posting is indicated by a check (✓) in the posting reference column.

AUTOMATED DATA PROCESSING

You are already familiar with the manner in which processing functions are accomplished in a manual recordkeeping system. Source documents are prepared and entered manually; classification and sorting are accomplished through a method of columnar arrangements such as journals and ledgers; computations are often done manually; and storage is achieved by manual filing. Storage is in the form of ledger accounts, subsidiary ledgers, and various files. Retrieval and summarization are entirely manual. Now we wish to examine the points in the accounting process at which machines can be used to save labor.

Machine-Assisted Manual Processing

The first way to speed processing and reduce workloads in manual processing is to introduce key-driven equipment, such as adding machines, calculators, and bookkeeping machines. Some of these devices afford only limited data storage during arithmetical calculations, so that practically all storage, retrieval, and summarization of data must still be performed manually. Certain bookkeeping machines, however, have auxiliary equipment, such as punched card and paper tape output, that allows data to be stored for further processing. In fact, some modern bookkeeping machines are compatible with electronic data processing, as we shall explain later in this chapter.

Bookkeeping machines reduce recordkeeping labor by making it possible to prepare several records at the same time. For example, a customer's ledger sheet, monthly statement, and the sales journal can be inserted into the machine together. When the keyboard operator enters a charge sale, the machine journalizes, posts, and prepares the statement all at the same time. Similarly, in recording remittances, the operator can process the customer's ledger sheet, statement, and the cash receipts journal together. Comparable routines that accomplish several recordkeeping tasks at the same time are available for handling cash disbursements and payrolls. Many current bookkeeping machines are essentially **minicomputers** programmed to perform automatically many of the basic logic and arithmetic functions involved in the processing of data. One type of accounting minicomputer is shown in Exhibit 6–10.

EXHIBIT 6–10
Bookkeeping Machine—Burroughs L9000 Accounting Computer

Punched-Card Systems

Punched-card systems might well be called semiautomatic systems. Many of the basic processing functions are performed automatically, but human intervention is needed both between and during various processing stages. Source documents

THE RISE OF MINICOMPUTERS

Sales of minicomputers have burgeoned during the past few years, mainly because they are relatively inexpensive and easy to use. In 1977, an estimated 200,000 of the small computers were in use, and by 1980, annual sales are expected to total about 115,000 units.[1]

With the rapid proliferation of the minis, however, there has been a concurrent increase in computer fraud. Ease of minicomputer operation by nonspecialists, from vice-presidents to secretaries, is creating an environment conducive to embezzlement and other types of fraud.

The risk of computer fraud is alarming to law-enforcement agencies and, particularly, to accounting firms, which have been targets for lawsuits in recent years by stockholders in corporate fraud cases. Indeed, the Securities and Exchange Commission has been urging accounting firms to detect and report fraud, despite the fact that, for many years, the profession has denied responsibility for fraud detection in audits whenever the fraud was not material in the financial statements or was not readily detectable by the application of generally accepted auditing standards.

A few of the many fraud cases that have surfaced recently are described below:[2]

• A salesman at a small West Coast manufacturing firm convinced a secretary to make a small change in the computer program. The program was originally designed to reject orders below a set minimum price. The change permitted lower than competitive prices, enabling the salesman to earn large commissions; these sales resulted in a $75,000 loss to the firm.

• A young accountant in a California hospital transferred small amounts (less than $4 per person) from the federal withholding accounts of other employees to his own account. He was able to obtain a huge refund of taxes after the end of the year. An investigation was triggered when an employee summed his deductions for the year and discovered a discrepancy between the total and the amount shown on his W-2 forms.

• A young accountant at an aerospace firm paid himself an extra $1,000 a month by adding "ghosts" to the payroll and cashing the payroll checks for the fictitious employees. The fraud was discovered by a company official who became curious about unfamiliar names appearing on a batch of cancelled checks.

The fraud, of course, is not the fault of the minicomputers themselves, which have added immeasurably to the data processing capabilities of small and medium-sized firms. The problem is that most of these firms have paid little attention to internal control measures. (The basic ideas of internal control are discussed in Chapter 7.) Often, minicomputers are scattered throughout a firm, spreading security resources over a wide area. By contrast, single data processing centers in large firms are easier to control; program changes are monitored, and control is ordinarily exercised over programing, computer operations, and tape files. Furthermore, only a small number of professionals are involved in data processing activities. It appears that, in the future, accountants and other affected parties will have to pay particular attention to control measures in small and medium-sized firms using minicomputers.

[1]1977 projections of International Data Corporation, Waltham, Massachusetts.
[2]Reported in the *Wall Street Journal*, October 4, 1977.

are prepared manually or by typewriter, although in some applications the punched card may also serve as a source document. Source documents are converted into machine-readable form (punched cards) by people operating keypunch machines. Ordinarily, the columns of a punched card are divided into *fields* of information so that the card can be used as a classification device. For example, we could design a sales card with fields for such information as customer number and name, location, salesperson number, product number, quantity, price, and invoice amount. We could then sort the cards by field and generate reports showing sales for any time period by product, territory, salesperson, or customer. The cards can also be used to update customers' master card files, which serve as an accounts receivable subsidiary ledger.

To merge or match cards in the routines we have just described, sorting and collating machines are used. Tabulating machines (sometimes called *accounting machines*) are equipped to make calculations and to output printed summary reports. In punched-card systems, storage is in the form of both the punched cards themselves and printouts from tabulating equipment.

Although the punched-card system has helped to reduce clerical labor, it has several limitations compared with electronic computer systems. Its logic capabilities are extremely limited and it cannot make decisions during processing. Another drawback is that any exceptions to routine processing must be handled manually. Finally, the mechanical nature of the equipment limits its speed compared with electronic equipment. Today, computers have supplanted most punched-card equipment in large businesses. Punched cards themselves, however, are sometimes used with computer processing, as input media and for data storage.

Electronic Data Processing

An electronic data processing (EDP) system can handle many of the basic record-keeping functions at incredible speeds. For example, some equipment can perform millions of arithmetic computations per second. Moreover, much of the processing is continuous; because of the logic, or decision-making, capabilities of the computer, human intervention is minimized. Detailed planning and complex programming, however, are required initially to prepare for each phase of information processing.

An electronic data processing system contains the following elements:

(1) A central processing unit (CPU), often called the computer, which performs arithmetic, logic, storage of data while processing, and control.

(2) Associated peripheral equipment, including data-preparation, input, and output devices.

(3) Personnel and programs to provide instructions for the computer.

(4) Procedures to coordinate the preparation and processing of data and the reporting of results.

The computer and associated equipment are often referred to as the hardware of the system, while the programs, written procedures, and other documentation for the system are called software. An example of the equipment for one data processing system is shown in Exhibit 6–11.

Exhibit 6–12 is a diagram of a typical system's hardware components, which are designed to perform the following functions: input, processing, storage, and output.

INPUT.   Input devices transmit the instructions to the computer and the data on which the various steps will be carried out. The major input media are punched cards, magnetic tape, magnetic characters, disks, and terminals. The devices used to transmit data include card readers, tape and disk drives, character recognition devices, and terminal keyboards.

In some cases, source document data are converted into machine-readable media by such data preparation devices as *keypunch* machines, *key-to-tape* devices, and *key-to-disk* devices. In other cases, certain source documents can be read directly. For example, in commercial banks, bank checks and deposit tickets with magnetic ink characters are processed directly by magnetic character readers. Data input by terminals is effected by a keyboard device, such as the one depicted in Exhibit 6–13. Terminal input, which is very slow compared with other input devices, is not designed to transmit large amounts of data. The use of terminals is expanding, however, because they permit direct interaction with the computer. Most terminals have a visual screen or printing capability for output. Thus, computer files can be interrogated and print out answers in a short period of time. Terminals have been used for years in airline reservation systems and in

EXHIBIT 6–11
An Electronic System—IBM 3033 Processor for System/370

savings departments of commercial banks to update depositors' accounts. In recent years, they have been employed by large retail department stores to record sales transactions. At the time of sale, salesclerks key into the accounting system such information as product number, quantity, selling price, and customer number; in this way, they directly update customers' accounts, sales records, and inventory records. When computer records are updated at the time transactions occur, the processing is often referred to as real time processing.

PROCESSING AND STORAGE. In an EDP system, practically all of the manipulative functions of recordkeeping—classifying, matching, calculating, and so on—are performed automatically by the central processing unit. These functions are directed by stored instructions called a program. The control unit interprets the instructions and directs the various processing operations. If fairly standardized programs are required, they may be obtained from equipment vendors. In other cases, special programs are written by programmers, who usually proceed by first working out a flowchart that shows the specific operations and decisions to be made by the computer and the sequence in which they should occur. The programmer then prepares the instructions in a special programming language, and the program is eventually stored in the computer to be called into use when needed.

EXHIBIT 6–12
Hardware Components of a Data Processing System

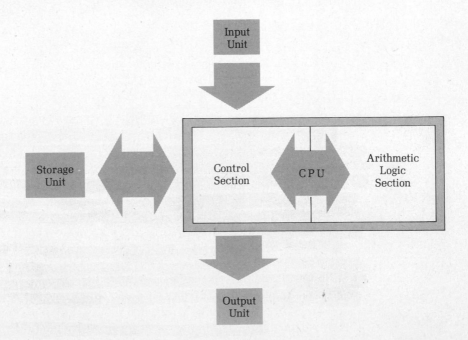

EXHIBIT 6–13
Terminal—IBM 3276 Control Unit Display Station

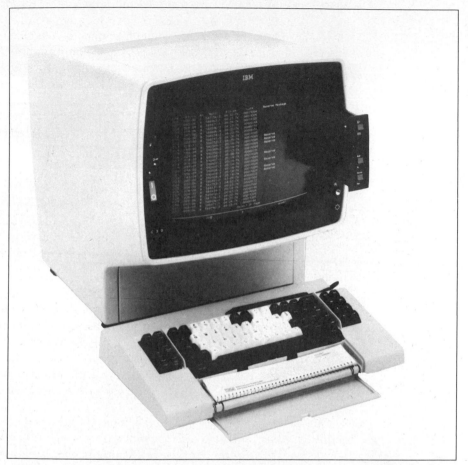

All computers have temporary storage facilities that are used during processing. Permanent storage of files (such as accounts receivable master files) may be external, on media such as magnetic tapes or punched cards, when the storage capabilities of the system are limited. This is called off-line storage, and these files must be processed periodically with current transaction files in order to "update" the master files. When storage capacity within the system is adequate (most often, core or disk storage), direct access to master files is possible; in this case, storage is on-line.

When storage is off-line, transactions data are usually accumulated for a period of time and processed in batches at specified intervals. Batch processing is useful when immediate processing of transactions is not required for information needs. Data must be organized (sequenced) in a particular order, however, because all master files must be read when they are processed with a current batch of transactions. This type of processing is called sequential processing.

Interactive processing is possible with on-line storage. Here, master file information is available at random, and sequencing is not necessary. Transactions can be processed immediately, in any order, without batching.

OUTPUT. Output devices provide either immediately usable information or results that can be stored for further processing and analysis. Terminals, because they perform both input and output, are important in providing immediately usable information. Printers, though less immediate, also provide useful output information that can be analyzed and interpreted. Output often is in the form of magnetic tapes or disks when further processing is contemplated. Punched cards, because they create a storage problem and slow down processing, are falling into disuse as an output medium.

Evolution of Computer Processing

When computers first became available in the 1950s, they were so massive and costly that only large corporations used them for processing data. Over the years, advancing technology has resulted in a reduction in both the size and cost of computer hardware. Today, even small- and medium-sized firms employ some form of computer processing. Some have purchased or leased minicomputers. These are designed for small- and medium-scale processing and can be operated by personnel with minimum training (see boxed insert, page 220). Other small firms may use service bureaus. For a fee, a service bureau takes input from its customers, processes the data, and returns the results. The user is relieved of the burden of hardware ownership, but must tolerate a reduction in timeliness of results. Some firms have avoided the problem of computer ownership and operation by using a time-sharing service. A time-sharing company owns and operates a large central computer and sells computer time to a number of firms. Usually the customers access the computers through terminals, which, in many cases, may be far from the computer.

The various systems of automated data processing can be quite detailed and complex, and an elaborate discussion of such systems is beyond the scope of this book. We hope, however, that the brief introduction in these pages will help you appreciate some of the basic concepts.

KEY POINTS TO REMEMBER

(1) A single *control* account for accounts receivable and another for accounts payable are used in the general ledger, while individual customer and creditor accounts are kept in separate *subsidiary* ledgers (often on file cards).

(2) When the journals have been posted at the end of the accounting period, balances in the subsidiary ledgers are totaled. The totals should agree with control account balances.

(3) The use of special journals for credit sales and purchases (sales journal and purchases journal, or invoice register) and for cash transactions (cash receipts journal and cash disbursements journal) has the following advantages: (a) It

permits a division of labor and often requires fewer skilled recordkeepers; (b) it reduces the labor required to enter transactions; and (c) it requires fewer postings.

(4) Only sales of *merchandise on account* are recorded in the sales journal. Cash sales are recorded in the cash receipts journal.

(5) Purchases of *any items on account* are recorded in the invoice register (purchases journal). Acquisitions of any items for cash are recorded in the cash disbursements journal.

(6) Transactions that cannot be appropriately recorded in a special journal are recorded in the general journal.

(7) When master files (such as customer records) in an EDP system are stored off-line (outside the system) transactions are batched and processed *sequentially* to update records at specific time intervals.

(8) When master files are stored on-line (within the system) they can be updated at random without batching. This type of processing is sometimes called an **interactive** system.

QUESTIONS

6-1 What is a control account? What is a subsidiary ledger?

6-2 Criticize the following statement: "Any time a debit entry is made to a control account, one or more credit entries of the same aggregate total must be posted to the related subsidiary ledger."

6-3 What are the benefits of using special journals compared with using only a general journal?

6-4 Explain why transactions should be posted to the subsidiary ledgers more frequently than to the general ledger.

6-5 How would you prove that a special journal "balances"?

6-6 Identify the type of transaction that would be entered in:
(a) A sales journal.   (b) A (single-column) purchases journal.
(c) An invoice register.   (d) A cash receipts journal.
(e) A cash disbursements journal.

6-7 A sale made on account to George Yates for $300 was recorded in a single-column sales journal on April 7. On April 9, Yates returned $50 worth of merchandise for credit. Where should the entry for the sales return be recorded on the books of the seller? What entry would be made and how would it be posted?

6-8 A $70 purchase of merchandise on account from L. Ford was properly recorded in the invoice register, but was posted as $90 to Ford's subsidiary ledger account. How might this error be discovered?

6-9 Indicate how the following errors might be discovered:
(a) The total of the Accounts Payable column of the invoice register was added incorrectly and overstated by $40.
(b) The total of the single-column sales journal was added incorrectly and understated by $60.

6-10 Describe how the "net price" method of recording purchases on account differs from the "gross price" method.

6-11 James Vance keeps an invoice register and employs the net method of recording purchases of merchandise. Assume that he makes a $600 purchase from Mead Company, terms 2/10, n/30. Which columns of the journal would be used to record the purchase and what are the debits and credits to be made?

6-12 Suppose that, in Question 6-11, Vance was unable to pay within the discount period and made his remittance 20 days after the date of purchase. State the amounts involved, and describe how the payment would be recorded in a multi-column cash disbursements journal.

6-13 How are time and effort saved when a bookkeeping machine is used instead of manual processing?

6-14 What are the limitations of punched-card accounting systems compared with electronic processing of data?

6-15 What are the major elements in an EDP system?

6-16 What is meant by "hardware" in an EDP system? What is meant by "software"?

6-17 What is meant by "real time" processing in a computer processing system?

6-18 Distinguish between *sequential processing* and *interactive processing* in EDP systems.

EXERCISES

6-19 Listed below are headings for the columns into which dollar amounts are entered for four special journals and a general journal. (For the sales journal, the accounts to which the single column relates are shown.) For each column heading, show, in the space provided, where the amounts in that column should be posted. Use the appropriate letter (or letters) from the following key.

Key
(a) Column total posted to general ledger
(b) Column detail posted to subsidiary ledger
(c) Column detail posted to general ledger

The correct answer for the first item is given.

Sales Journal
(1) Accounts Receivable	a, b
(2) Sales	a

Invoice Register
(3) Accounts Payable	a, b
(4) Purchases	
(5) Office Supplies on Hand	
(6) Store Supplies on Hand	
(7) Other Debits	

Cash Receipts Journal
(8) Cash _____
(9) Sales Discounts _____
(10) Accounts Receivable _____
(11) Sales _____
(12) Other Accounts—Debit _____
(13) Other Accounts—Credit _____

Cash Disbursements Journal
(14) Cash _____
(15) Purchases Discounts _____
(16) Accounts Payable _____
(17) Other Accounts—Debit _____
(18) Other Accounts—Credit _____

General Journal
(19) Debit column _____
(20) Credit column _____

6-20 Gordon Suppliers uses the four special journals illustrated in this chapter and a general journal. In which journal(s) would each of the following kinds of transactions be recorded?
(a) Owner's cash investment in business. *cash receipts*
(b) Sale of merchandise for cash. *cash*
(c) Sale of merchandise on account.
(d) Return of merchandise sold on account.
(e) Withdrawal of cash by owner.
(f) Withdrawal of merchandise by owner for personal use.
(g) Collections from customers on account.
(h) Purchase of merchandise for cash.
(i) Purchase of merchandise on account.
(j) Return of merchandise purchased on account.
(k) Purchase of office supplies on account.
(l) Purchase of equipment for cash and a note payable.

6-21 John Stanley is a wholesaler of office supplies, candy products, and commercial cleaning supplies. He prefers to have his income statement show Sales, Cost of Goods Sold, and Gross Profit amounts for each of his three product lines. He is able to take periodic inventories separately for each of these three departments. How would you design multicolumn sales and purchases journals to provide the information Mr. Stanley wants?

6-22 In recording transactions and posting from various journals, the bookkeeper made the following errors. In each case, state how the error might be discovered or whether discovery is unlikely.
(a) In the single-column sales journal, the total for the month was underfooted (underadded) by $300.
(b) The total of the purchases column of the multicolumn invoice (purchase) register, correctly footed as $9,350, was posted to the Purchases account as $9,530.

(c) In the single-column sales journal, a sale to J. Travis was correctly recorded at $790, but posted to Ramsey's account as $970.

(d) A remittance of $500 from L. Ames was correctly recorded in the cash receipts journal, but the amount was inadvertently posted to the account of L. Adams in the customers' ledger.

(e) A $240 payment to a creditor, M. Shaw, was recorded in the cash disbursements journal as $140.

6–23 Record, in general journal form, the following transactions of the Artway Company (a) under the net price method of recording purchases; (b) under the gross price method.

Dec. 3   Purchased merchandise on account from Martin, Inc. for $500, terms 2/10, n/30.

4   Purchased merchandise on account from Cable Company for $600, terms 2/10, n/30.

11   Paid Martin, Inc. the amount due for purchase of Dec. 3.

21   Paid Cable Company the amount due for purchase of Dec. 4

6–24 Describe how the following transactions would be recorded, indicating the journals to be used, the columns of each journal involved, and the way in which postings are to be accomplished. Assume the four special journals illustrated in the chapter are available, together with a general journal.

(a) Purchased equipment for $1,800, giving $800 cash and a note payable for $1,000.

(b) Returned to a creditor merchandise that had been purchased on account for $230.

(c) Owner contributed $900 in cash and $4,500 in delivery equipment to the business.

(d) The business sold the delivery equipment in (c) for $4,500.

(e) Sent check for $40 to a customer, T. Baker, who had overpaid his account by this amount.

(f) Paid $90 freight to Redball Express Company on sale to a customer, R. James. However, terms were F.O.B. shipping point, and customer was obligated to pay freight.

PROBLEMS

Note: In the following problems, the journal forms to be used should correspond to those illustrated in the chapter.

6–25 The Lancer Company makes all sales on terms of 2/10, n/30. Transactions for May involving sales, related returns and allowances, and cash receipts are shown below.

May 1   Sold merchandise on account to Benton, Inc. for $700. Invoice No. 901.

2   Collected $300 from Jenson, Inc., on account.

3   Sold merchandise to R. Jackson for cash, $70.

4   Issued credit memorandum to Benton, Inc. for return of $100 worth of merchandise purchased May 1.

May 7 Sold merchandise on account to Acecraft Company for $850. Invoice No. 902.

8 Received remittance from Benton, Inc. for the amount owed, less 2% discount.

11 Sold merchandise for cash to R. Mayberry, $90.

16 Sold merchandise to L. Jones, receiving a note receivable for $600. Invoice No. 903.

21 Collected a non-interest-bearing note receivable from R. Wayne, $800.

22 Sold merchandise on account to Boyd Company, $600. Invoice No. 904.

25 The owner, R. Lancer, contributed $2,000 cash to the business.

28 Acecraft Company paid for merchandise sold to it on May 7.

29 Issued credit memorandum to Boyd Company for $60 worth of merchandise sold to it on May 22.

30 Sold merchandise on account to Horizons, Inc. for $650. Invoice No. 905.

REQUIRED

(a) Record the given transactions in a single-column sales journal, a general journal, and a cash receipts journal.

(b) Open the following general ledger accounts and insert balances, where given: Cash (11) $1,000; Notes Receivable (15) $800; Accounts Receivable (16) $300; Lancer, Capital (31) $3,500; Sales (41); Sales Returns and Allowances (42); Sales Discounts (43). Also open a subsidiary ledger with the following customer accounts: Acecraft Co.; Benton, Inc.; Horizons, Inc.; Boyd Co.; and Jenson, Inc. Jenson's account had a balance of $300; the other accounts had no beginning balances.

(c) Post all necessary amounts to the general and subsidiary ledger accounts.

(d) Prove that the Accounts Receivable control account agrees with the subsidiary ledger.

6-26 Blackhawk Company had the following transactions involving purchases, purchases returns and allowances, and cash payments during the month of August. Blackhawk uses the gross price method to record purchases.

Aug. 1 Purchased merchandise on account from Ward Company for $800, terms 2/10, n/30, F.O.B. shipping point.

2 Paid Northern Freight bill for August 1 purchase, $60. Check No. 100.

5 Paid Melrose, Inc. $300 on account. Check No. 101.

8 Purchased store supplies on account from Tenner Supply Company, $200, terms n/30.

9 The owner, J. Blackhawk, withdrew $200 cash from the business. Check No. 102.

11 Paid Ward Company for purchase of August 1. Check No. 103.

12 Returned $30 worth of the store supplies purchased from Tenner Supply Company on August 8.

15 Purchased store supplies for cash from Varden Wholesalers, $80. Check No. 104.

17 Purchased merchandise on account from Britt, Inc. for $450, terms 1/10, n/30.

18 Paid Tenner Supply Company in full of account. Check No. 105.

19 Returned $70 worth of merchandise to Britt, Inc. for credit.

22 Paid Britt, Inc. for August 17 purchase. Check No. 106.

Aug. 24   Purchased office supplies on account from Melrose, Inc., $50, terms n/30.

      26   Purchased delivery equipment from Black, Inc. for $4,000, giving $500 cash and a note payable for $3,500. Check No. 107.

      29   Purchased office equipment from Melrose, Inc., $200, on account, terms n/30.

      31   Purchased merchandise on account from Ward Company for $500, terms 2/10, n/30, F.O.B. shipping point.

REQUIRED

(a) Record the above transactions in an invoice register (purchases journal), a cash disbursements journal, and a general journal.

(b) Open the following general ledger accounts and insert balances, where given: Cash (11) $4,000; Office Supplies on Hand (15) $350; Store Supplies on Hand (16) $80; Delivery Equipment (17) $6,000; Office Equipment (18) $900; Notes Payable (21); Accounts Payable (22) $300; Blackhawk, Drawing (32); Purchases (51); Purchases Returns and Allowances (52); Purchases Discounts (53); and Transportation In (54). Also open a subsidiary ledger with the following creditor accounts: Britt, Inc.; Melrose, Inc., $300; Tenner Supply Company; and Ward Company. Only the Melrose account had a beginning balance.

(c) Post all necessary amounts to the general and subsidiary ledger accounts.

(d) Prove that the Accounts Payable control account agrees with the subsidiary creditors' ledger.

6-27   Lauro Company began business on April 1. The purchases and sales made on account during April have been recorded in the sales and purchases journals below. Purchases are recorded using the gross price method.

Sales Journal   Page 1

Date		Customer	Terms	Post. Ref.	Amount
19XX					
Apr.	5	Sims, Inc.	2/10, n/30		$300
	10	James Wholesalers	2/10, n/30		600
	18	Webster, Inc.	2/10, n/30		500
	21	James Wholesalers	2/10, n/30		400
	28	R. Watson	2/10, n/30		900

Purchases Journal   Page 1

Date		Creditor	Terms	Post. Ref.	Amount
19XX					
Apr.	2	Owens Company	2/15, n/30		$1,200
	4	Little Corp.	n/30		800
	12	Peters, Inc.	2/10, n/30		500
	22	Owens Company	2/15, n/30		600
	29	Parker, Inc.	1/10, n/30		200

The April transactions to be recorded in the cash receipts and cash disbursements journals are:

Apr. 1 Lauro invested $8,000 cash and $5,000 office equipment in the firm, a sole proprietorship. (Use two lines for entry.)
      2 Paid rent for April, $800. Check No. 101.
      5 Received $200 rental income for space sublet to Robert's Hair Stylists.
      7 Purchased office supplies for cash, $450. Check No. 102.
     14 Paid Owens Company for April 2 purchase. Check No. 103.
     15 Received $294 from Sims, Inc. in payment of account.
     18 Received $588 from James Wholesalers in payment of account.
     21 Paid Peters, Inc. for April 12 purchase. Check No. 104.
     30 Paid salary of office clerk, $700. Check No. 105.

REQUIRED
(a) Record the given April transactions in cash receipts and cash disbursements journals.
(b) Total and balance the cash receipts and cash disbursements journals.

6-28 Gilman Distributors, which sells on terms of 2/10, n/30, had the following transactions during October, the first month of the current fiscal year.

Oct. 1 Paid October rent, $200. Check No. 200.
      2 Paid Frank, Inc. $343 for merchandise purchased September 28. Check No. 201. A 2% discount was taken.
      3 Issued checks of $90 to pay Blake Company and $60 to pay Downs Suppliers, both creditors. No discount was taken on these amounts. Checks No. 202 and No. 203.
      7 Sold merchandise on account to Devon, Inc. for $250. Invoice No. 470.
      8 Received checks in payment of accounts as follows: Devon, Inc., $147; Rivers Company, $50; Young Company, $98. Discounts had been taken by Devon, Inc. and Young Company.
      9 Sold merchandise on account to Rivers Company, $200. Invoice No. 471.
     10 Issued check for freight to Acme Freight, Inc. on Rivers shipment, $70. Terms were F.O.B. destination. Check No. 204.
     11 Issued credit memorandum to Rivers Company for merchandise returned, $40.
     14 Purchased merchandise on account from Blake Company, $400, terms 1/10, n/60.
     15 Issued check for freight to Ace Transport on purchase from Blake Company, $80. Terms were F.O.B. shipping point. Check No. 205.
     15 Paid office salaries, $600. Checks No. 206 and No. 207 for $300 each for W. Ames and K. Austin.
     16 Received a check in payment of account from Curtis Company, $350.
     17 Received a check from Devon, Inc. for $245 in payment of October 7 shipment.
     18 Purchased store supplies, $50, equipment, $200, and office supplies, $30, on account from Downs Suppliers, terms n/30.
     21 Paid Blake Company $396 for purchase of October 14. Check No. 208.

Oct. 22 Paid $30 for miscellaneous expense. Check No. 209.

  24 Issued check to R. Gilman for $350, a personal withdrawal. Check No. 210.

  28 Purchased merchandise on account from Frank, Inc., $300, terms 2/15, n/60.

  29 Returned $40 worth of merchandise to Frank, Inc. for credit.

  30 Sold merchandise on account to Young Company, $500. Invoice No. 472.

  31 Sold merchandise for cash to J. Briggs, $80.

  31 Collected $100 miscellaneous income from Fargo Advertising for use of billboard space.

REQUIRED

(a) Open the following general ledger accounts, and enter the indicated balances as of October 1. Number the accounts as shown.

Cash (11)	$ 2,700	Sales Discounts (43)
Accounts Receivable (12)	650	Miscellaneous Income (44)
Inventory (14)	7,000	Purchases (51)
Store Supplies on Hand (15)	200	Purchases Returns
Office Supplies on Hand (16)	50	and Allowances (52)
Equipment (17)	10,000	Purchases Discounts (53)
Accumulated Depreciation (18)	(2,500)	Transportation In (54)
Accounts Payable (21)	(500)	Rent Expense (61)
R. Gilman, Capital (31)	(17,600)	Salaries Expense (62)
R. Gilman, Drawing (32)		Transportation Out (63)
Sales (41)		Miscellaneous Expense (64)
Sales Returns and Allowances (42)		

(b) Open the following accounts in the subsidiary ledgers and enter the balances given at October 1:

Customers		Creditors	
Curtis Company	$350	Blake Company	$ 90
Devon, Inc.	150	Downs Suppliers	60
Rivers Company	50	Frank, Inc.	350
Young Company	100		
	$650		$500

(c) Record the transactions for October in the four special journals (sales, invoice register, cash receipts, and cash disbursements) and in the general journal. Gilman uses the gross price method to record purchases.

(d) Using the forms prepared in (a) and (b) above, post all necessary amounts to the general ledger and subsidiary ledgers from the journals. Postings should be made to the subsidiary ledgers throughout the month.

(e) Prepare a trial balance of the general ledger.

(f) Prepare a schedule of accounts receivable and a schedule of accounts payable to prove control account balances.

6-29 The post-closing trial balance at December 31 of last year for Brown Distributors is given below:

Brown Distributors
Post-closing Trial Balance
December 31, 19XX

	Debit	Credit
Cash	$ 3,700	
Accounts Receivable	14,200	
Inventory	38,600	
Office Supplies on Hand	280	
Store Supplies on Hand	160	
Office Equipment	6,000	
Accumulated Depreciation		$ 1,400
Accounts Payable		18,900
L. Brown, Capital		42,640
	$62,940	$62,940

At the end of January, 19X1, the totals of the firm's special journals, before being posted, are as follows:

Sales Journal	$37,500

Invoice Register:

Accounts Payable	$29,450
Purchases	27,300
Office Supplies on Hand	400
Store Supplies on Hand	250

Other Accounts:

Office Equipment (Dr.)	1,500

Cash Receipts Journal:

Cash	$44,100
Sales Discounts	460
Accounts Receivable	25,360
Sales	13,200

Other Accounts:

Brown, Capital (Cr.)	6,000

Cash Disbursements Journal:

Cash	$29,500
Purchases Discounts	320
Accounts Payable	26,370

Other Accounts:

Rent Expense (Dr.)	1,500
Advertising Expense (Dr.)	350
Salaries Expense (Dr.)	1,600

REQUIRED

Prepare an unadjusted trial balance for Brown Distributors at January 31. *Note:* A convenient method is to use a six-column worksheet, placing the post-closing trial balance in the first two columns and listing the other account titles needed for the temporary accounts below. The next two columns are used to record the debits and credits from the special journals, while the last two columns are used for the unadjusted trial balance at January 31.

ALTERNATE PROBLEMS

6–25A The Busby Company makes all sales on terms of 2/10, n/30. Transactions for June involving sales, related returns and allowances, and cash receipts are shown below.

June 3 Sold merchandise on account to Carney, Inc. for $400. Invoice No. 701.

4 Collected $600 from J. Solard on account.

5 Sold merchandise to D. Crown for cash, $50.

6 Issued credit memorandum to Carney, Inc. for return of $100 worth of merchandise purchased June 3.

9 Sold merchandise on account to Beaman Company for $750. Invoice No. 702.

10 Received remittance from Carney, Inc. for the amount owed, less 2% discount.

13 Sold merchandise for cash to C. Thorsen, $70.

16 Sold merchandise to W. Slater, receiving a note receivable for $600. Invoice No. 703.

20 Collected a non-interest-bearing note receivable from P. Hannon, $800.

23 Sold merchandise on account to Peters Company, $600. Invoice No. 704.

25 The owner, J. Busby, contributed $2,000 cash to the business.

26 Beaman Company paid for merchandise sold to it on June 9.

27 Issued credit memorandum to Peters Company for $90 worth of merchandise sold to it on June 23.

30 Sold merchandise on account to Geiger, Inc. for $450. Invoice No. 705.

REQUIRED
(a) Record the given transactions in a single-column sales journal, a general journal, and a cash receipts journal.
(b) Open the following general ledger accounts and insert balances, where given: Cash (11) $1,500; Notes Receivable (15) $800; Accounts Receivable (16) $600; Busby, Capital (31) $4,500; Sales (41); Sales Returns and Allowances (42); Sales Discounts (43). Also open a subsidiary ledger with the following customer accounts: Beaman Co.; Carney, Inc.; Geiger, Inc.; Peters Co.; and J. Solard. J. Solard's account had a balance of $600; the other accounts had no beginning balances.
(c) Post all necessary amounts to the general ledger and subsidiary ledger accounts.
(d) Prove that the Accounts Receivable control account agrees with the subsidiary ledger.

6–26A Ridge Company had the following transactions involving purchases, purchases returns and allowances, and cash payments during the month of May. Ridge uses the gross price method to record purchases.

May 2 Purchased merchandise on account from Wagner Company for $500, terms 2/10, n/30, F.O.B. shipping point.

       3 Paid freight bill to Kwik Trucking Company for May 2 purchase, $40. Check No. 400.

       7 Paid Elder, Inc. $100 on account. Check No. 401.

       9 Purchased store supplies on account from Martin Supply Company, $300, terms n/30.

    10 The owner, E. Ridge, withdrew $200 cash from the business. Check No. 402.

    11 Paid Wagner Company amount due for purchase of May 2. Check No. 403.

    14 Returned $40 worth of the store supplies purchased from Martin Supply Company on May 9.

    16 Purchased store supplies for cash from Davis Wholesalers, $100. Check No. 404.

    17 Purchased merchandise on account from Abbott, Inc. for $600, terms 2/10, n/30.

    18 Paid Martin Supply Company in full of account. Check No. 405.

    21 Returned $50 worth of merchandise to Abbott, Inc. for credit.

    23 Paid Abbott, Inc. for May 17 purchase, Check No. 406.

    24 Purchased office supplies on account from Elder, Inc., $70, terms n/30.

    26 Purchased delivery equipment from Green, Inc. for $5,000, giving $1,500 cash and a note payable for $3,500. Check No. 407.

    29 Purchased office equipment from Elder, Inc., $400, on account, terms n/30.

    31 Purchased merchandise on account from Wagner Company for $500, terms 2/10, n/30, F.O.B. shipping point.

REQUIRED

(a) Record the above transactions in an invoice register (purchases journal), a cash disbursements journal, and a general journal.

(b) Open the following general ledger accounts and insert balances, where given: Cash (11) $5,000; Office Supplies on Hand (15) $350; Store Supplies on Hand (16) $150; Delivery Equipment (17) $4,000; Office Equipment (18) $700; Notes Payable (21); Accounts Payable (22) $100; Ridge, Drawing (32); Purchases (51); Purchases Returns and Allowances (52); Purchases Discounts (53); and Transportation In (54). Also open a subsidiary ledger with the following creditor accounts: Abbott, Inc.; Elder, Inc., $100; Martin Supply Company; and Wagner Company. Only the Elder account had a beginning balance.

(c) Post all necessary amounts to the general ledger and subsidiary ledger accounts.

(d) Prove that the Accounts Payable control account agrees with the subsidiary creditors' ledger.

6-27A Hatch Company began business on November 1. The purchases and sales made on account during November have been recorded in the sales and purchases journals below. Purchases are recorded using the gross price method. All sales are made on terms of 2/10, n/30.

Sales Journal   Page 1

Date		Invoice No.	Customer	Post. Ref.	Amount
19XX					
Nov.	5	201	Jones, Inc.		$300
	10	202	Osburn and Sons		800
	18	203	Nichols, Inc.		500
	21	204	Osburn and Sons		600
	28	205	B. Landon		400

Purchases Journal   Page 1

Date		Creditor	Terms	Post. Ref.	Amount
19XX					
Nov.	2	Ryan Company	2/15, n/30		$1,200
	4	Potter Corp.	n/30		600
	12	Grant, Inc.	2/10, n/30		700
	22	Ryan Company	2/15, n/30		500
	29	Wilcox, Inc.	1/10, n/30		300

The November transactions to be recorded in the cash receipts and cash disbursements journals are:

Nov. 1 T. Hatch invested $5,000 in cash and $4,000 in office equipment in the firm, a sole proprietorship. (Use two lines for entry.)

2 Paid rent for November, $500. Check No. 101.

4 Received $90 rental income for space sublet to Jill's Book Corner.

8 Purchased office supplies for cash, $320. Check No. 102.

14 Paid Ryan Company for Nov. 2 purchase. Check No. 103.

15 Received $294 from Jones, Inc. in payment of account.

18 Received $784 from Osburn and Sons in payment of account.

21 Paid Grant, Inc. for Nov. 12 purchase. Check No. 104.

30 Paid salary of office clerk, $750. Check No. 105.

REQUIRED

(a) Record the given November transactions in cash receipts and cash disbursements journals.

(b) Total and balance the cash receipts and cash disbursements journals.

6–28A Winter Distributors, which sells on terms of 2/10, n/30, had the following transactions during July, the first month of the current fiscal year.

July 1 Paid July rent, $600. Check No. 200.

2 Paid Riley, Inc. $343 for merchandise purchased June 28. Check No. 201.

3 Issued checks of $150 to pay Cullen Company and $100 to pay Hogan Suppliers, both creditors. No discount was taken on these amounts. Checks No. 202 and No. 203.

7 Sold merchandise on account to Golden, Inc. for $400. Invoice No. 470.

8 Received checks in payment of accounts as follows: Golden, Inc., $196; Post Company, $240; Statz Company, $49. Discounts had been taken by Golden, Inc. and Statz Company.

9 Sold merchandise on account to Post Company, $210. Invoice No. 471.

10 Issued check for freight to Fast Freight, Inc. on Post Shipment, $70. Terms were F.O.B. destination. Check No. 204.

11 Issued credit memorandum to Post Company for merchandise returned, $40.

14 Purchased merchandise on account from Cullen Company, $300, terms 1/10, n/60.

15 Issued check for freight to Boyd Transport on purchase from Cullen Company, $50. Terms were F.O.B. shipping point. Check No. 205.

15 Paid office salaries, $700. Checks No. 206 and No. 207 for $350 each.

16 Received a check in payment of account from Archer Company, $360.

17 Received a check from Golden, Inc. for $392 in payment of July 7 shipment.

18 Purchased store supplies, $100, equipment, $180, and office supplies, $40 on account from Hogan Suppliers, terms n/30.

21 Paid Cullen Company $297 for purchase of July 14. Check No. 208.

22 Paid $30 for miscellaneous expense. Check No. 209.

24 Issued check to S. Winter for $300, a personal withdrawal. Check No. 210.

28 Purchased merchandise on account from Riley, Inc., $320, terms 2/15, n/60.

29 Returned $50 worth of merchandise to Riley, Inc. for credit.

30 Sold merchandise on account to Statz Company, $550. Invoice No. 472.

31 Sold merchandise for cash to T. Howell, $90.

31 Collected $125 miscellaneous income from Look Advertising for use of billboard space.

REQUIRED

(a) Open the following general ledger accounts, and enter the indicated balances as of July 1. Number the accounts as shown.

Cash (11)	$ 2,100	Sales Discounts (43)
Accounts Receivable (12)	850	Miscellaneous Income (44)
Inventory (14)	7,000	Purchases (51)
Store Supplies on Hand (15)	300	Purchases Returns
Office Supplies on Hand (16)	150	and Allowances (52)
Equipment (17)	12,000	Purchases Discounts (53)
Accumulated Depreciation (18)	(3,400)	Transportation In (54)
Accounts Payable (21)	(600)	Rent Expense (61)
S. Winter, Capital (31)	(18,400)	Salaries Expense (62)
S. Winter, Drawing (32)		Transportation Out (63)
Sales (41)		Miscellaneous Expense (64)
Sales Returns and Allowances (42)		

(b) Open the following accounts in the subsidiary ledgers and enter the balances given at July 1:

Customers		**Creditors**	
Archer Company	$360	Cullen Company	$150
Golden, Inc.	200	Hogan Suppliers	100
Post Company	240	Riley, Inc.	350
Statz Company	50		
	$850		$600

(c) Record the transactions for July in the four special journals (sales, invoice register, cash receipts, and cash disbursements) and in the general journal. Winter uses the gross price method to record purchases.

(d) Using the forms prepared in (a) and (b) above, post all necessary amounts to the general ledger and subsidiary ledgers from the journals. Postings should be made to the subsidiary ledgers throughout the month.

(e) Prepare a trial balance of the general ledger.

(f) Prepare a schedule of accounts receivable and a schedule of accounts payable to prove control account balances.

BUSINESS DECISION PROBLEM

Floor-to-Ceiling sells carpeting, lighting fixtures, and wall paneling. Most sales are on account; however, there are some cash sales over the counter for do-it-yourself customers. J. Stewart, the owner, seeks your assistance in setting up a system of special journals for Floor-to-Ceiling. Stewart wants the income statement to show sales, cost of goods sold, and gross profit for each of the firm's three departments. (Inventory of merchandise for each of the three departments will be taken separately.) Besides merchandise, the most frequent purchases on account of goods and services are for installation supplies. Stewart informs you that most cash disbursements are for payment on account to suppliers, for freight on purchases (almost all purchases are made on terms of F.O.B. shipping point), and for advertising. All spot advertising in local newspapers and television is paid when bills are received—no accounts payable are kept for the local newspaper or television company. Employees are paid monthly.

REQUIRED

Assume that you are designing the special journals for Floor-to-Ceiling. List the column headings (from left to right) that you would provide in the (a) sales journal, (b) invoice register, (c) cash receipts journal, and (d) cash disbursements journal.

7
Internal Control: Cash Controls

Most bankers dwell in marble halls,
Which they get to dwell in because they encourage
deposits and discourage withdralls.

OGDEN NASH*

Most people would agree that accounting is the most important part of any management information system. To be useful in assisting management in planning and controlling operations, the accounting system should be dependable and efficient and provide a measure of security for the firm's resouces. A system with these attributes is said to provide an adequate measure of *internal control.*

The elements of control are important to all aspects of a firm's operations, but they are particularly critical in establishing methods of handling and accounting for monetary assets. We shall therefore consider first the general features that are desirable in an accounting control system and then examine certain procedures that are especially important in accounting for and controlling cash transactions. The latter include bank reconciliations, petty cash procedures, and the voucher system.

THE NATURE OF INTERNAL CONTROL

Internal control has been defined as:

> the plan of organization and all of the coordinate methods and measures adopted within a business to safeguard its assets, check accuracy and reliability of its accounting data, promote operational efficiency, and encourage adherence to prescribed managerial policies.[1]

Sometimes the organization, planning, and procedures for safeguarding assets and the reliability of financial records are known as *accounting controls.* The procedures and methods concerned mainly with operational efficiency and managerial policies are called *administrative controls.* These include such controls as statistical analyses, time-and-motion studies, performance reports, and quality controls.

*From *Verses from 1929* by Ogden Nash, by permission of Little, Brown and Co. and Curtis Brown, Ltd. Copyright 1935 by Ogden Nash. Originally appeared in The New Yorker.

[1] *Auditing Standards and Procedures,* American Institute of Certified Public Accountants, New York, 1963, p. 27. Further clarified and explained in *Statement on Auditing Standards,* 1973, p. 15 et seq.

Accountants should be conversant with both accounting controls and administrative controls. Indeed, many controls within these two categories are interrelated. Naturally, an accountant is more directly concerned with accounting controls such as those we shall now discuss.

FEATURES OF AN ACCOUNTING CONTROL SYSTEM

The requirements for good internal accounting control are the following:

(1) Competent personnel.
(2) Assignment of responsibility.
(3) Division of work.
(4) Separation of accountability from custodianship.
(5) Adequate records and equipment.
(6) Rotation of personnel.
(7) Internal auditing.
(8) Physical protection of assets.

Competent Personnel

Employees should be carefully selected and their talents used intelligently in the operation of the accounting information system. Each individual should thoroughly understand his or her function and its relationship to other functions in the system. Above all, an employee must realize the importance of following the procedures prescribed by management and should be in sympathy with the system. An otherwise well-formulated system of internal control can be destroyed by lack of confidence or cooperation.

Assignment of Responsibility

The plan of organization should fix responsibility for the functions to be performed and confer the authority necessary to carry them out. Responsibility and authority for a given function should not be shared, because this often results in duplication of effort and may result in jobs going undone if each individual thinks that the other is performing the assignment. When one person has the responsibility for a function, praise or blame can be clearly assigned for specific results. Thus, if a department foreman in a plant is held responsible for staying within budgeted amounts for labor costs, he should be given the authority to assign personnel to jobs, control overtime, and so on.

Division of Work

Division of work is one of the most important facets of a good system of controls. The duties of individuals should be defined so that no single individual has complete control over a sequence of related transactions. That is, the person who authorizes a purchase order should not also be the one who confirms receipt of the merchandise or authorizes payment for the merchandise. Likewise, neither the person handling bank deposits nor the person keeping the cash books should be permitted to receive bank statements or make bank reconciliations. Improper segregation of duties increases the possibility of fraud, carelessness, and unreliable recordkeeping, while proper division of duties permits the work of one person or group to act as a check on work performed by another person or group. For example, when purchase orders and receiving reports are processed by different individuals, a third person can compare the order, receiving report, and vendor's invoice before approving payment. This practice reduces the likelihood of errors from carelessness as well as the possibility of fictitious purchases or fraudulent conversion of goods.

Work division is valuable not only in preventing errors and fraud, but in providing the advantages of specialization—better performance and easier training of employees.

Separation of Accountability and Custodianship

Employees who are responsible for keeping records of a firm's assets should not have custody of the assets nor access to them. Separating the custody of assets from the maintenance of records is another safeguard against fraud. An employee should not have the opportunity to convert assets for personal use and cover up the conversion by falsifying the records. In most cases in which custody of assets is adequately separated from recordkeeping, collusion among employees is necessary to perpetrate fraud. If collusion does exist, embezzlement can go undetected for a long time.

The separation feature should be incorporated in the system for the protection of all assets, but it is especially important in the handling of cash and negotiable items. For example, cash remittances from customers should be listed by personnel who have no access to accounting records. These listings can then be forwarded to the accounts receivable department for posting to customer accounts in the subsidiary ledger, while the remittances themselves are sent to the cashier for deposit. A duplicate listing of remittances should also be given to the person in charge of the cash receipts journal. This method provides several cross-checks, because bank deposits must agree with amounts recorded in the cash receipts journal, and the Accounts Receivable control account must agree with subsidiary ledger totals. Finally, the bank should send its statement to someone other than the cashier or those keeping the records, so that an independent bank reconciliation can be made.

Adequate Records and Equipment

Adequate records are important not only in accounting for a company's resources but in providing accurate and reliable information to management. One of the most important features in a satisfactory recordkeeping system is a comprehensive chart of accounts designed to classify information in a manner best suited to management's needs. Control accounts and subsidiary records should be used when appropriate. In this way, work can be subdivided, and cross-checks may be made when the two types of accounts are reconciled. Some of the principal areas in which control and subsidiary accounts can be used are accounts and notes receivable, payables, fixed assets, and such major expense classifications as manufacturing expense, selling expense, and administrative expense.

The paper forms used with the accounting records should be designed to promote accuracy and efficiency. If possible, individual forms should be prenumbered so that the sequence of forms used can be accounted for. Moreover, prenumbering helps a firm trace its transactions and reduces the possibility of failing to record a transaction. For example, suppose a firm issues prenumbered sales slips for each sale. A check of the numbering sequence would disclose any diversion of the proceeds of a sale accomplished by destruction of the sales slip. Likewise, accounting for the sequence of prenumbered checks is useful in detecting whether unrecorded checks have been issued for unauthorized purchases.

Various types of equipment can be used with the recordkeeping system to provide helpful controls. The cash registers used in retail operations, for example, have several important control features—a bell signals that the register has been opened, and a receipt allows the customer to check the transaction. Furthermore, most cash registers have a locked-in tape that accumulates and classifies transactions that have been registered. A responsible employee controlling the key can reconcile amounts shown on the tape with daily cash counts. Some registers contain separate cash drawers so that several clerks can handle the same cash register and each be accountable for his or her own operation. Another device that protects cash is the autographic register. This piece of equipment, used in over-the-counter sales, produces a locked-in copy of a sales invoice when the original is prepared. Check protectors, which perforate checks with indelible ink, are another example of a protective device for cash transactions. It is almost impossible to alter checks written with such a machine without the change being obvious.

Bookkeeping machines, punched-card equipment, and electronic data processing equipment all permit certain procedural controls or have built-in controls to reduce the possibility of errors and unauthorized actions. Most equipment of this type provides for printed forms, producing records more error-free and legible than those resulting from a manual system. In addition, the automatic features of such equipment reduce the incidence of error.

Rotation of Personnel

Some companies rotate the positions of certain operating personnel. For example, accounts receivable clerks, each responsible for a certain alphabetical segment of the accounts, might be rotated periodically to other segments. This procedure sometimes discloses errors and irregularities caused by carelessness or dishonesty. A similar measure, requiring employees to take vacations, sometimes helps to reveal lapses, carelessness, and dishonesty on the part of employees. Misappropriations of funds, especially in financial institutions such as banks, have often been discovered during an employee's absence, when the perpetrator was no longer in a position to control or manipulate records.

Internal Auditing

Another important feature of the internal control systems of large companies is the internal audit function. The internal auditing department independently appraises the firm's financial and operational activities. In addition to reviewing activities for errors and irregularities, the internal audit staff attempts to determine whether prescribed policies and procedures are being followed and attempts to uncover situations causing waste and inefficiency. Internal auditing is a *staff*, or advisory, function that consists of reviewing activities and making recommendations through reports to management. To be effective, the internal audit staff must be independent of operating (line) functions and should report to a high-ranking executive or to the firm's board of directors.

Physical Protection of Assets

Frequently, management will initiate a number of physical controls to protect company property. Although some of these controls may not be closely related to the accounting system, they are almost invariably discussed in the context of internal control.

It is important that a business be adequately insured against losses from fire, outside theft, and similar events. In addition to insuring its physical assets, a company should obtain fidelity insurance; employees having access to cash, securities, and other easily diverted assets should be bonded. For a fee, a bonding company guarantees to make good any loss from theft or embezzlement by the bonded person, up to some specified maximum amount. The bonding company investigates employees to be bonded, and anyone with a record of questionable integrity is not likely to qualify.

Only minimal amounts of cash or negotiable assets should be kept on the company premises, and these should be stored in a vault. It is best to lock up inventory stocks in enclosed areas and to maintain strict controls over issuances and physical counts of inventory. Security personnel are often engaged to protect inventories and other physical property. A company may avail itself of outside protection services as a safeguard against burglary and arson and might post gate-keepers at plant entrances and exits to provide surveillance of employees and others entering and leaving the plant.

CASH AND CASH CONTROLS

In accounting, the term **cash** means paper money, coins, checks, money orders, and bank deposits—all items that are acceptable for deposit in a bank. IOUs, postdated checks (checks dated in the future), and uncollected customers' checks returned by the bank stamped "NSF" (not sufficient funds) are not considered cash but are normally classified as **receivables.** Notes sent to the bank for collection remain classified as **notes receivable** until notification of collection is received from the bank.

Cash in the Balance Sheet

Various ledger accounts are used to record cash transactions; some common examples are Cash on Hand, Petty Cash, and Cash in Bank. The Cash on Hand account reflects cash receipts not yet deposited in the bank, while Petty Cash represents a fund used for small disbursements. Cash in Bank usually refers to demand deposits in a checking account.

When a business firm has several checking accounts, a separate ledger account should be maintained for each account rather than one overall Cash in Bank account. Although a balance sheet prepared for management may show all individual cash accounts, a balance sheet prepared for outsiders normally shows the combined balances of all cash accounts under a single heading, *Cash.* Management is interested in the detail because it must establish policies on balances to be maintained in various bank accounts and balances on hand. Most outsiders, on the other hand, are interested only in the aggregate cash balance and its relationship to other items on the financial statements.

Cash amounts subject to use or withdrawal without restriction are current assets and are normally shown first in the balance sheet listing of assets. Cash under the control of a trustee, such as sinking fund cash, and amounts in foreign banks subject to exchange restrictions are shown in a noncurrent section of the balance sheet.

Cash Control Procedures

It is essential to control the handling and recording of cash because it is so susceptible to misappropriation. An adequate system of internal control over cash would include the following features:

(1) Cash is handled separately from the recording of cash transactions.

(2) The work and responsibilities of cash handling and recording are divided in such a way that errors are readily disclosed and the possibility of irregularities is reduced.

(3) All cash receipts are deposited intact in the bank each day.

(4) All major disbursements are made by check, and an imprest (fixed amount) fund is used for petty cash disbursements.

In our earlier discussion of internal control, we described and explained the desirability of the first two of these features. Observing the last two—depositing all receipts intact daily at the bank and making all disbursements by check—permits a company to establish a double record of cash transactions. One record is generated by the firm's recordkeeping procedures, and another is furnished by the bank. Comparing the two records and accounting for any differences provides control. This important procedure is called *reconciling the bank statement with the book record of cash transactions* or, simply, making a *bank reconciliation*.

The Bank Account

When a firm opens a checking account at a bank, the members of the firm who are authorized to draw checks sign signature cards that are placed on file at the bank. Occasionally, bank employees may check the signatures on these cards against the signatures on the checks.

The bank submits monthly statements to the depositor showing the beginning cash balance, all additions and deductions for the month, and the ending cash balance. In addition, the bank returns the paid checks for the month, together with "advice" slips indicating other charges and credits made to the account. The bank may also send copies of such advice slips individually during the month to the depositor.

In Exhibit 7–1 we show a relatively simple bank statement. Most bank statements list checks paid and other debits in the left-hand section, deposits and other credits in the middle section, and cumulative balances in the right-hand section.

EXHIBIT 7-1

First National Bank · Madison

☐ EAST WASHINGTON – CAPITOL SQUARE

1st

STATEMENT OF ACCOUNT

G. A. Shaw Company
101 Beltline Highway
Madison, Wisconsin

ACCOUNT NUMBER

313111386

DATE OF STATEMENT: December 31, 19XX

Checks			Deposits	Date	Balance
				11-30-19XX	5,640.30
			300.00 ᴠ	12-1	5,940.30
125.00 ᴟ			750.00 ✓	12-2	6,565.30
56.25 ᴟ				12-3	6,509.05
107.15 ✓	35.40RT		560.80 ✓	12-7	6,927.30
441.21 ✓				12-8	6,486.09
135.00 ᴟ			480.25 ✓	12-10	6,831.34
27.14 ✓				12-11	6,804.20
			525.00 ✓	12-14	7,329.20
315.37 ✓				12-15	7,013.83
76.40 ✓			270.25 ✓	12-17	7,207.68
275.00 ✓				12-18	6,932.68
450.00 ✓	325.60 ✓	65.70 ✓	640.20 ✓	12-21	6,731.58
240.50 ✓				12-23	6,491.08
.50DM			200.00	12-26	
			475.00 ✓	12-26	7,165.58
482.43 ✓	260.00 ✓			12-28	6,423.15
370.11 ✓			440.00 ✓	12-30	6,493.04
122.50 ✓	5.00SC			12-31	6,365.54

Item Codes:	EC—Error Correction	SC—Service Charge
	LS—List of Checks	OD—Overdraft
	DM—Debit Memo	RT—Returned Item

Code letters identify charges and credits not related to paying checks or making deposits. A legend usually appears at the bottom of the statement explaining the code letters. Although such codes are not standardized from bank to bank, those normally used are easy to understand. As we mentioned before, the depositor also receives an advice slip from the bank explaining nonroutine entries.

In the statement illustrated in Exhibit 7–1, the codes used are as follows:

EC —Error correction. Identifies transcription, arithmetic, and similar errors and corrections made by the bank.

LS —List of checks. Identifies the total of a batch of checks too numerous to list separately on the statement. An adding machine tape listing the individual check amounts usually accompanies each batch of checks listed.

DM—Debit memo. Identifies collection charges, repayment of bank loans, and other special charges made by the bank against the depositor's account.

SC —Service charge. Identifies the amount charged by the bank for servicing the account. The amount is normally based on the average balance maintained and the number of items processed during the month. Service charges are usually made on small accounts that are not otherwise profitable for the bank to handle.

THE HIGH COST OF PAPERHANGING

Paperhanging' is a euphemism for passing bad checks. So many people do it that it accounts for millions of dollars lost annually.

In many sections of the country, paperhanging has become a profitable crime because it is so easy to accomplish and because both the victims and the courts are indifferent. It is a silent, nonviolent crime. Practically everyone cashes checks, and it is easy to slip from a legitimate check to a bad check. Federal Reserve Bank statistics indicate that nine out of every ten dollars spent in the United States is by way of checks. An accomplished paperhanger can steal more money with a pen than a gun, passing bogus paper amounting to several thousand dollars a day in retail stores. Although practically all retailers cash personal checks, supermarkets are the most vulnerable. Large supermarkets may cash as many as 10,000 checks a month, or roughly, 300 checks a day.

Losses on bad checks keep rising because many merchants prefer to add the costs of bad checks to their prices rather than take the time to report and prosecute offenders. Often the amount of the bad check is less than the cost of pursuing the offender, and a decision is made to include the cost as a part of doing business. An expert with the Los Angeles Police Department estimated that four out of five criminal check violations in the Los Angeles area are not reported.* In addition, the light sentences given to those who are reported and convicted provide little deterrent.

The 12th Federal Reserve District, which includes eight states, reported that one of every 114 checks processed in 1973 was returned "dishonored." The figure became one in 96 in 1974 and one in 91 in 1975.

To stem the tide of bad checks, some states are investigating proposals for statewide identification systems that would enable law enforcement authorities to keep track of paperhangers. In addition, some large banks are designing security systems for chain stores and supermarkets whereby consumers insert plastic cards into terminals along with their checks. The cardholder presses certain buttons to indicate the type of check to be cashed, whether personal, third party, or cash only checks. The information is transmitted to a computer center where it is scanned, and approval is indicated if funds are available to cover the check. The identification cards are designed for particular stores within the area served by the bank providing the service.

*Reported in a United Press International release, *Wisconsin State Journal*, September 3, 1979.

OD —Overdraft. Indicates a negative, or credit, balance in the account.

RT —Returned item. Indicates defective items such as postdated checks or checks without proper endorsement received from customers and deposited. Sometimes not sufficient funds (NSF) checks charged back to the account are identified with these letters in the statement. NSF checks may also be identified with the letters DM (debit memo), explained earlier.

The Bank Reconciliation

Almost invariably, the ending balance on the bank statement differs from the balance in the company's Cash in Bank account. Some reasons for differences are:

(1) Outstanding checks—checks written and deducted in arriving at the book balance, but not yet presented to the bank for payment.

(2) Deposits not yet credited by the bank—deposits made near the end of the month, processed by the bank after the monthly statement has been prepared. They will appear on next month's statement.

(3) Charges made by the bank but not yet reflected on the depositor's books—for example, service and collection charges, NSF checks, repayments of the depositor's bank loans.

(4) Credits made by the bank but not yet reflected on the depositor's books—collections of notes and drafts for the depositor by the bank.

(5) Accounting errors made either by the depositor or by the bank.

The bank reconciliation consists of a schedule to account for any of the above differences between the bank statement balance and the book balance. Although one could reconcile either of these figures to the other, it is more convenient to reconcile both figures to an **adjusted balance,** which is the cash balance that will appear on the balance sheet. This is the amount that could be withdrawn after all outstanding items have cleared. A convenient reconciliation form is illustrated below.

Balance per bank statement		$XXX	Balance per books		$XXX
Add: Deposits not yet credited by bank		XXX	Add: Items credited by bank, not yet entered on books (i.e., notes collected)		XXX
		$XXX			$XXX
Less: Outstanding checks: (list)	$XXX XXX XXX	XXX	Less: Items charged by bank, not yet entered on books (i.e., service and collection charges, NSF checks)		XXX
Adjusted balance		$XXX	Adjusted balance		$XXX

These final amounts should agree

After the reconciliation is prepared, the adjusted balance per bank statement and the adjusted book balance should agree. If these amounts do not agree, one should look carefully for reconciling items omitted from the schedule or for possible errors in recordkeeping. The bank reconciliation is made not only to bring to light transactions that must be recorded, but to detect errors or irregularities.

BANK RECONCILIATION PROCEDURE Assume that a December 31 bank reconciliation is to be prepared for the G. A. Shaw Company, whose bank statement is illustrated in Exhibit 7–1. In Exhibits 7–2 and 7–3, we show the company's December cash receipts and cash disbursements journals in abbreviated form. Cash receipts journals often have a column for bank deposits, as shown in Exhibit 7–2.

After the cash journals have been posted, the Cash in Bank account of the Shaw Company appears as follows:

Cash in Bank (First National Bank) Account No. 11

19XX						
Nov.	30	Balance				5,624.05
Dec.	31		CR	4,366.50		9,990.55
	31		CD		4,700.77	5,289.78

EXHIBIT 7–2
G. A. Shaw Company
(Partial) Cash Receipts Journal
December, 19XX

Date		Explanation	Cash Receipts	Bank Deposits
19XX				
Dec.	1	Jensen Brothers	$ 350.00	
	2	Cash sales	400.00	$ 750.00 ✔
	4	Denton Company	410.80	
	7	Jewel and Son	150.00	560.80 ✔
	8	Benson Company (note)	300.00	
	10	Cash sales	180.25	480.25 ✔
	14	Taylor Brothers	525.00	525.00 ✔
	17	Cash sales	270.25	270.25 ✔
	18	Johnson Company	250.15	
	21	Bates Company	390.05	640.20 ✔
	26	Jordan Brothers	475.00	475.00 ✔
	30	Cash sales	440.00	440.00 ✔
	31	Johnson Company	225.00	225.00
			$4,366.50	$4,366.50

EXHIBIT 7–3
G. A. Shaw Company
(Partial) Cash Disbursements Journal
December, 19XX

Date		Explanation	Check No.	Cash Payments
19XX				
Dec.	1	Jordan Company	156	$ 441.21 ✓
	2	Edson Brothers	157	107.15 ✓
	4	Rapid Transit, Transportation in	158	27.14 ✓
	7	Acme Realty, December rent	159	275.00 ✓
	8	Stanton Company	160	315.37 ✓
	10	Horder, Inc. Office supplies	161	76.40 ✓
	14	A. L. Smith Company	162	325.60 ✓
	17	J. B. Adams, Office salary	163	450.00 ✓
	17	O. L. Holmes, Office salary	164	240.50 ✓
	18	Abbot Van Lines, Transportation in	165	65.70 ✓
	21	Millston, Inc.	166	482.43 ✓
	21	Odana Corporation	167	301.66
	22	R. W. Knight, Cash purchase	168	149.50
	26	W. A. Sutton	169	260.00 ✓
	29	Border and Son, Cash purchase	170	122.50 ✓
	30	R. L. Olson	171	370.11 ✓
	31	J. B. Adams, Office salary	172	450.00
	31	O. L. Holmes, Office salary	173	240.50
				$4,700.77

The procedures for reconciling the December 31 bank statement balance of $6,365.54 with the $5,289.78 balance on the company's books are:

(1) Arrange in numerical sequence the paid checks that have been returned by the bank. (When checks are received from the bank, they are usually in the sequence in which they appear on the bank statement.)

(2) Trace outstanding items on the previous (November) bank reconciliation to this period's statement. Let us assume that the November reconciliation for the Shaw Company is as shown in Exhibit 7–4. The items identified with the ∨ mark, which were outstanding at the end of November, were all processed in December; these amounts are identified by the same mark (∨) on the bank statement in Exhibit 7–1. Any checks that have still not cleared in December should appear again on the December reconciliation.

(3) Compare the record of deposits in the cash receipts journal (Exhibit 7–2) with the list of deposits on the bank statement. A check mark (✓) has been placed next to the amounts that appear in both records. Note that the $225.00 deposit

EXHIBIT 7–4
G. A. Shaw Company
Bank Reconciliation
November 30, 19XX

Balance per bank statement		$5,640.30	Balance per books	$5,629.05
Add: Deposit not credited				
by bank		300.00 ⋁		
		$5,940.30		
Deduct: Outstanding checks:			Deduct: Bank service charge	5.00
No. 149	$125.00 ⋁			
No. 154	56.25 ⋁			
No. 155	135.00 ⋁	316.25		
Adjusted balance		$5,624.05	Adjusted balance	$5,624.05

made on December 31 does not appear on the bank statement. Enter this item in the December bank reconciliation as a deposit not yet credited by the bank.

(4) Compare the record of checks written from the cash disbursements journal (Exhibit 7–3) with the checks paid by the bank and returned with the bank statement. A check mark (✔) has been placed next to the amounts that appear in both records. Since checks numbered 167, 168, 172, and 173 have not cleared the bank, enter them in the December bank reconciliation as outstanding checks.

(5) Scan the bank statement for charges and credits not yet reflected in the company's records. Note that the statement contains a charge of $35.40 for a returned item, a debit memo of $0.50 and a service charge of $5.00. Also, a credit for $200.00 appears in the deposits column on December 26. Bank advices reveal the nature of these items. In this case, they indicate that an NSF check for $35.40 was charged against the company's account, that a $200.00 note receivable was collected on the company's behalf for which a $0.50 collection charge was made, and that a $5.00 service charge was made for the month. Enter these items also in the December bank reconciliation.

After the above procedures have been completed, the bank reconciliation appears as shown in Exhibit 7–5 (page 254).

Before financial statements are prepared for the period ended December 31, adjusting entries should be made to bring the cash account balance into agreement with the correct cash balance shown on the reconciliation. The entries for the Shaw Company would reflect the collection of the note receivable and the related collection expense, reclassification of the NSF check as an account receivable, and the bank service charge for the month:

EXHIBIT 7–5
G. A. Shaw Company
Bank Reconciliation
December 31, 19XX

Balance per bank statement		$6,365.54	Balance per books			$5,289.78
Add: Deposits not credited			Add: Collection of note	$200.00		
by bank		225.00	Deduct: Collection charge	.50		199.50
		$6,590.54				$5,489.28
Deduct: Outstanding checks:						
No. 167	$301.66					
No. 168	149.50					
No. 172	450.00		Deduct: NSF check	$35.40		
No. 173	240.50	1,141.66	Bank service charge	5.00		40.40
Adjusted balance		$5,448.88	Adjusted balance			$5,448.88

Cash	199.50	
Miscellaneous Expense	.50	
Notes Receivable		200.00

To record note collected by bank,
less service charge.

Accounts Receivable	35.40	
Cash		35.40

To reclassify NSF check as an account
receivable.

Miscellaneous Expense	5.00	
Cash		5.00

To record service charge for December.

THE PETTY CASH FUND

Most business firms find it inconvenient and expensive to write checks for small expenditures. Therefore, when small amounts of cash are needed to pay for such items as postage, delivery service, and purchases of supplies and notions, these expenditures are most conveniently handled by establishing a **petty cash fund.**

    The size of the petty cash fund depends on the number and the amounts of minor expenditures. Of course, it is unwise to have a large amount of cash on hand because of the risk of theft or misuse. Yet, the need for too frequent replenishment can be a nuisance. Many firms maintain funds that will last three or four weeks. The size of expenditures that may be made from the fund is also usually limited.

Although the use of a petty cash fund technically violates the control maxim of making all expenditures by check, control can be maintained by handling the fund on an *imprest* basis and by following certain well-established procedures. In accounting, an imprest fund is one of fixed amount.

Although expenditures from an imprest petty cash fund are made in currency and coin, the fund is established by writing a check against the general bank account. Replenishments are also accomplished by issuing checks—after reviewing expenditures. Therefore, in the final analysis, all expenditures are actually controlled by check.

Establishing the Fund

Assume that the Shaw Company has decided to establish a petty cash fund of $100. It draws a check payable to Cash and exchanges it at the bank for currency and coin in denominations that are convenient for small expenditures. The entry reflecting establishment of the fund is made in the cash disbursements journal. In general journal form, the entry is:

Petty Cash	100	
Cash in Bank		100

To establish imprest petty cash fund.

Whenever disbursements are made from the fund, the person in charge should place a prenumbered petty cash receipt in the petty cash box as evidence of the disbursement. Thus, at any time, the total cash on hand plus the amounts on the receipts should equal $100. Each receipt should give the date, amount, and nature of the expenditure and should be signed by the recipient of the cash. Such documents as cash register tapes and copies of invoices should be attached to the receipts.

Replenishing the Fund

When the fund must be replenished, a check is drawn to Cash in an amount that will bring the cash value of the fund back to $100. Expenditures from the fund are analyzed according to expense or other account category for the purpose of the book entry. For example, assume that the Shaw Company's fund has been drawn down to $28 and that analysis of the $72 in receipts reveals the following expenditures: Office Expense, $40; Transportation In, $27; and Postage Expense, $5. The bookkeeper makes the following entry in the cash payments journal (shown in general journal form):

Office Expense	40	
Transportation In	27	
Postage Expense	5	
Cash in Bank		72

To replenish petty cash fund.

The cashier of the fund cashes the replenishment check at the bank and places the cash in the petty cash box.

Once the imprest amount is found to be adequate, no further entries are made to the Petty Cash account itself. Notice that replenishment results in an entry to the Cash in Bank account. Only when the prescribed amount of the imprest fund is judged unsatisfactory will entries be made to the Petty Cash account, increasing or decreasing the amount of the fund.

One person in the firm's office should be made solely responsible for custody of the fund and expenditures made from it. The replenishment checks, however, should be written by another authorized person, after review of the petty cash receipts and the expense distribution. Furthermore, this person should stamp, perforate, or otherwise mutilate the supporting receipts and documents to prevent them from being used again. Firms desiring additional control over petty cash may keep a formal record of disbursements and replenishments called a *petty cash journal*. This record may be simply a memorandum of petty cash transactions, or it may be used for posting the entries for replenishment.

Cash Short and Over

Errors sometimes occur in making change from cash funds, resulting in less or more cash than can be accounted for. Usually, such shortages or overages are not material in amount. An account called **Cash Short and Over** is commonly used to record these discrepancies; shortages are debited to the account, and overages are credited. For example, suppose a $100 petty cash fund contains $80 in receipts for office expense and only $16 in currency and coins. The entry to replenish the fund and to record the $4 shortage would be:

Office Expense	80	
Cash Short and Over	4	
Cash in Bank		84

To replenish petty cash fund
and record shortage.

If the fund had contained $24 in cash together with the $80 in expense receipts, the $4 overage would be credited to the Cash Short and Over account. The credit to Cash in Bank for replenishment would be $76.

The Cash Short and Over account may also be used to record cash short or over from sales when cash register tape totals do not agree with the count of cash receipts. Some retail stores provide a column for Cash Short and Over in their cash receipts journals to record discrepancies, which may occur often. Large discrepancies, particularly recurring shortages, should always be investigated to determine what corrective steps should be taken.

If the Cash Short and Over account has a debit balance at the close of an accounting period, it is classified as Miscellaneous Expense on the income statement. A credit balance can be classified as Other Income.

THE VOUCHER SYSTEM

Many companies employ a method of controlling expenditures that is known as the **voucher system.** When a company acquires merchandise or other assets and services, it is concerned with assuring that

(1) The acquisitions are properly authorized.

 (2) The items received are as ordered.

(3) The liability recorded is valid and correctly computed.

(4) Payment is properly made, with discounts taken when possible.

The voucher system consists of authorization forms, records, and procedures designed to meet the above criteria. Under this system, a written authorization form, called a **voucher,** is initiated for every disbursement the firm makes. Before the designated responsible official approves the voucher for payment, several verification steps must be performed by different employees. These include the following:

(1) Comparison of purchase order, invoice, and receiving report for agreement of quantities, prices, type of goods, and credit terms.

(2) Verification of extensions and footings (additions) on invoice.

(3) Approval of account distribution (items to be debited).

Usually, each step in the verification process is listed on the face of the voucher along with space for the signature or initials of the various employees responsible for accomplishing the procedures. A voucher form is illustrated in Exhibit 7-6 (page 258). The original copies of the purchase order, invoice, and receiving report (if the item is merchandise) should be attached to the voucher. The voucher is then recorded in a book of original entry called the **voucher register.**

The Voucher Register

When a voucher system is used, the voucher register replaces the purchases journal (or invoice register) we discussed in Chapter 6. The voucher register provides columns for all items—merchandise, other assets, and services—for which payment must be made. Because all such items are recorded in the voucher register whether the transaction is for cash or on account, the voucher register also substitutes for part of the cash payments book illustrated in Chapter 6. Exhibit 7-7 (page 259) shows one form of a simple voucher register.

Vouchers are entered in the voucher register in sequence. They should be prenumbered, of course, so they can be accounted for and referred to easily. All entries result in a credit to Vouchers Payable, an account that serves as the accounts payable control account for the company. The register has columns for those expense and asset accounts most frequently debited, such as Purchases, Transportation In, Supplies on Hand, and Delivery Expense. Debits to accounts

EXHIBIT 7-6
Voucher Form

MONROE CHEMICALS, INC.
□ ROCK ISLAND, ILLINOIS

Voucher No. _121_
Date _12/1/XX_

PAY TO Olson Company

257 Arrowwood Drive

St. Louis, Missouri 63108

Front (Inside)

Date of Invoice	11/30/XX	Invoice Amount	$	350	00
Invoice Number	1457	Discount		7	00
		Net Amount	$	343	00

Verification:

Extensions and footings _w.c.s._
Credit terms _L.m._
Prices per purchase order _L.m._
Quantities per receiving report _ej_
Distribution to accounts _RW_

Approved _R.L Cassiday_

Back (Outside after folding)

| ACCOUNT DISTRIBUTION | | Date 12/1/XX   Voucher No. 121 |
| | | Date Due   12/9/XX |

Account Debited	Amount		Payee Olson Company
Purchases	350	00	257 Arrowwood Drive
Transportation in			St. Louis, Missouri 63108
Delivery expense			
Office supplies			Invoice Amount 350	00
Repairs expense			Discount 7	00
Sundry items:			Net Amount 343	00

			PAYMENT
Credit Vouchers Payable	350	00	Date 12/9/XX
			Check No. 528
			Amount 343.00

for which columns are not provided are made in the Other Accounts section. Although it is not often used, a credit column is also included in this section. The credit column may be used for adjustments to vouchers and for recording purchases returns and allowances.

After vouchers have been entered in the voucher register, they are filed in an

EXHIBIT 7-7
Voucher Register
December, 19XX

Voucher No.	Date	Name	Date Paid	Check No.	Vouchers Payable Credit	Purchases Debit	Transportation In Debit	Office Supplies on Hand Debit	Delivery Expense Debit	Other Accounts Account	Other Accounts Post. Ref.	Other Accounts Debit	Other Accounts Credit
121	12-1	Olson Company	12-9	528	$ 350	$ 350							
122	12-3	Tempo Freight	12-5	527	30		$ 30						
123	12-5	Horder, Inc.	12-15	531	120			$120					
.	.	.											
.	.	.											
.	.	.											
146	12-21	Jones Company	12-31	539	1,200					Office Equipment	15	$1,200	
147	12-27	Green Company			250	250							
148	12-30	Dee Delivery			25				$ 25				
					$18,500	$12,200	$850	$460	$320			$4,670	
					(32)	(55)	(56)	(16)	(68)			(X)	

unpaid vouchers file in the order of required date of payment. In this way, discounts will not be missed and the company's credit standing will not be impaired. When a voucher is processed, the due date is usually written on the face of the voucher for filing convenience.

On the due date, the voucher is removed from the unpaid file and forwarded to the firm's disbursing officer for final approval of payment. After signing the voucher, the disbursing officer has a check drawn and mailed to the payee. The check number and payment date are entered on the voucher, which is then returned to the accounting department. To safeguard against irregularities, the voucher should not be handled again by those who prepared it, and the underlying documents should be cancelled or perforated under the control of the disbursing officer before the voucher is returned to the accounting department.

After a voucher is paid, the check number and payment date are entered in the appropriate columns of the voucher register. The total unpaid ("open") vouchers at any time may be determined by adding the items in the vouchers payable column for which there is no entry in the date paid and check number columns. This total should, of course, agree with the total of vouchers in the unpaid file and, at the end of the month, with the amount in the Vouchers Payable account.

After these procedures have been followed, the payment is recorded in a book of original entry called the _check register_. Finally, the vouchers are filed in numerical sequence in a "paid" vouchers file.

The Check Register

In a voucher system, the **check register** is used in place of a cash disbursements journal. Because debits are made to asset, expense, and other accounts in the voucher register, only a few columns are required in the check register. As we see in Exhibit 7–8, these consist of a debit column for vouchers payable and credit

EXHIBIT 7–8
Check Register
December, 19XX

Check No.	Date	Payee	Voucher No.	Vouchers Payable Debit	Purchases Discounts Credit	Cash in Bank Credit
525	12–2	Able Corporation	120	$ 250		$ 250
526	12–4	Smith Company	119	500	$ 10	490
527	12–5	Tempo Freight	122	30		30
528	12–9	Olson Company	121	350	7	343
.						
.						
.						
539	12–31	Jones Company	146	1,200		1,200
				$16,700	$120	$16,580
				(32)	(57)	(11)

columns for purchases discounts and cash in bank. In addition, the check register has columns for the check number, date, and number of the voucher being paid.

The check register is a company's chronological record of all check payments. Since checks entered in the check register are also in numerical sequence, this record provides a convenient reference for payments when either the date or check number are known.

Under the voucher system we have just described, discounts may cause the amount of the check to differ from the gross amount of the voucher. For example, the entries for recording and paying the liability to the Olson Company for merchandise (voucher No. 121, dated December 1; see Exhibit 7–6) are summarized below in general journal form:

Voucher Register			Check Register		
Dec. 1	Purchases	350	Dec. 9	Vouchers Payable	350
	Vouchers Payable	350		Purchases Discounts	7
				Cash in Bank	343

Because both the gross and the net amount of the liability are indicated on the voucher, no difficulty should be created by this system. Some companies, however, anticipate taking all discounts and prepare vouchers at the net amount. When this procedure is followed, only two "money" columns are needed in the check register—one for a debit to Vouchers Payable and one for a credit to Cash in Bank. If, by chance, the company misses a discount, an adjustment must be made in the voucher (or the original voucher must be cancelled and a new one prepared). The bookkeeper must also make an entry in the general journal to record Discounts Lost. (We explained the "net of discount" procedure and the Discounts Lost account in Chapter 6.) An alternative solution for handling lost discounts when the net method of vouchering is used to provide a Discounts Lost column in the check register.

Recording Purchases Returns and Allowances

Several methods of processing purchases returns and allowances may be used under a voucher system. Perhaps the most formal method is to cancel the original voucher and issue a new one for the lower amount. Consider the following example.

Suppose that voucher No. 147 for $250 was prepared for a purchase of merchandise from the Green Company, and it was recorded in the voucher register on December 27. Assume that merchandise costing $50 was returned for credit, and a credit memo was received on December 30. The original voucher (No. 147, for $250) is cancelled and a reference made on it to a new voucher for $200. Furthermore, a note about the new voucher (No. 149) is made in the date paid column of the voucher register beside the entry for the original voucher. In recording the new voucher, the bookkeeper credits $200 in the vouchers payable column. In the Other Accounts section of the voucher register, Vouchers Payable is debited for $250 and Purchases Returns is credited for $50. The net effect of these recording procedures is a debit of $250 to Purchases, a credit of $200 to Vouchers Payable, and a credit of $50 to Purchases Returns (see Exhibit 7–9).

EXHIBIT 7–9
Voucher Register
December, 19XX

Voucher No.	Date	Name	Date Paid	Check No.	Vouchers Payable Credit	Purchases··· Debit	Other Accounts		
							Account	Debit	Credit
147 · · ·	12–27	Green Company	Cancelled, see #149		$250	$250 ···			
149	12–30	Green Company			200		Vouchers Payable Purchases Returns	$250	$50

Another way of handling the return is to reduce the original voucher by $50 and make the only correcting entry in the general journal; the bookkeeper debits Vouchers Payable and credits Purchases Returns for $50. One disadvantage of this method is that the correction does not appear in the voucher register and therefore might cause problems for persons compiling lists of unpaid vouchers from the register.

Recording Partial Payments

When installment or other partial payments are to be made on invoices, a separate voucher should be prepared for the amount of each check to be issued. If a single voucher has been prepared for an invoice and the firm later decides to pay in installments, the original voucher should be cancelled and new vouchers prepared. The issuance of new vouchers and the cancellation of the original voucher can be recorded in the same way that purchases returns are recorded.

INTERNAL CONTROL IN OTHER AREAS

While it is vitally important to establish effective controls over the handling of and accounting for cash, control should also be provided for other activities of the firm. As in the case of cash, most controls are designed to separate the authorization of a transaction, accounting for the transaction, and the custody of any related assets. For example, the purchase and sale of securities normally require authorization by a company's board of directors, and officers who have access to the securities should not have access to the accounting records. Other personnel should record security transactions and keep a record of security certificates by certificate number and amount.

Similarly, in the case of inventories, stores clerks handling inventory items should not have access to inventory records and should be separated from receiving departments and the processing of accounts payable. Similar controls should be exercised over receivables, long-term assets, payroll transactions, and every other facet of business activity.

The subject of internal control is quite complex. Both external and internal auditors devote a great deal of attention to internal control in analyzing an accounting system and preparing audits.

DEMONSTRATION PROBLEM FOR REVIEW

At December 31 of the current year, the cash account in Banning Company's ledger had a debit balance of $15,534.28. The bank statement at December 31 showed a balance of $16,426.40. In reconciling the two amounts, you discover the following:

(1) Bank deposits made by Banning on December 31 amounting to $1,845.20 do not appear on the bank statement.

(2) A non-interest-bearing note receivable for $1,500, left with the bank for collection, was collected by the bank near the end of December. The bank credited the proceeds, less a $5 collection charge, on the bank statement. Banning Company has not recorded the collection.

(3) Accompanying the bank statement is a debit memorandum indicating that the check of Edward Atwood for $350 was charged against Banning's bank account on December 30 because of insufficient funds.

(4) Check No. 586, written for advertising expense of $896.10, was recorded as $986.10 in Banning Company's cash disbursements journal.

(5) A comparison of the paid checks returned by the bank with the cash disbursements journal revealed that the following checks are still outstanding at December 31:

No. 561	$245.60	No. 591	$130.00
No. 585	380.00	No. 592	220.50
No. 588	415.30	No. 593	180.92

(6) The bank mistakenly charged Banning Company's account for check printing costs of $32.50, which should have been charged to the Bruning Company.

(7) The bank charged Banning Company's account $37.50 for rental of a safety deposit box. No entry has been made in Banning's records for this expense.

REQUIRED

(a) Prepare a bank reconciliation at December 31.

(b) Prepare any necessary adjusting entries at December 31.

SOLUTION TO DEMONSTRATION PROBLEM

(a)

Banning Company
Bank Reconciliation
December 31, 19XX

Balance per bank statement	$16,426.40	Balance per books		$15,534.28
Add: Deposits not credited		Add: Collection		
by bank	1,845.20	of note	$1,500.00	
Error by bank (Check		Less: Collec-		
printing charge of		tion		
Bruning Co.)	32.50	charge	5.00	1,495.00
		Error in		
		recording		
		check No.		
		586		90.00
	$18,304.10			$17,119.28
Less: Outstanding Checks		Less:		
No. 561	$245.60	NSF check	$350.00	
No. 585	380.00	Charge for		
No. 588	415.30	safety deposit		
No. 591	130.00	box	37.50	387.50
No. 592	220.50			
No. 593	180.92	1,572.32		
Adjusted		Adjusted		
Balance		$16,731.78	Balance	$16,731.78

(b)

Dec. 31	Cash		1,495.00	
	Miscellaneous Expense		5.00	
	Notes Receivable			1,500.00

To record collection of note by bank, less collection charge.

31	Cash		90.00	
	Advertising Expense			90.00

To correct error in recording advertising expense.

31	Accounts Receivable		350.00	
	Cash			350.00

To reclassify NSF check as accounts receivable.

31	Miscellaneous Expense		37.50	
	Cash			37.50

To record rental expense of safety deposit box.

KEY POINTS TO REMEMBER

(1) *Internal control* consists of the measures designed to safeguard a firm's assets, check accuracy and reliability of accounting data, promote operational efficiency, and encourage adherence to managerial policies. *Accounting controls* are related to the protection of assets and the reliability of accounting data; *administrative controls* deal mainly with efficiency and management's policies.

(2) An important cash control consists of depositing all receipts intact at the bank and making all cash disbursements by check. This procedure provides a double record of cash—the firm's record and the bank's record.

(3) Neither the book balance nor the bank statement balance of cash usually represents the cash balance to be shown on the balance sheet. Both are reconciled to a third figure, the adjusted balance—which appears on the balance sheet and is the amount that could be withdrawn after all outstanding items have cleared.

(4) Petty Cash is debited when an imprest fund for small expenditures is established or increased. When the fund is replenished, the individual accounts for which expenditures have been made are debited.

(5) When a voucher system is used to control cash disbursements, a written authorization (voucher) is prepared for each disbursement. The voucher is supported by both the related underlying documents (purchase order, receiving report, and invoice) and a verification procedure to be followed by employees.

(6) After preparation, vouchers are entered in a voucher register, which takes the place of an invoice register (or purchases journal). The typical entry is a credit to Vouchers Payable and a debit to an asset, liability, or expense account.

(7) Payments of vouchers are recorded in a check register, which takes the place of a cash disbursements journal. The typical entry is a debit to Vouchers Payable, with credits to Purchases Discounts and to Cash.

QUESTIONS

7-1 Define *internal control*. Name several specific features of a good system of internal control.

7-2 What is the difference between internal accounting controls and administrative controls?

7-3 Why is work division an important feature of good internal accounting control?

7-4 What internal control procedures are especially important in handling cash transactions?

7-5 Indicate whether the following statements relating to internal control systems are true or false:

(a) The principle of separating accountability and physical custodianship means that the accounts receivable bookkeeper should not be permitted to make bank deposits.

(b) Where possible, the general ledger bookkeeper should also be required to keep subsidiary records.

(c) Rotation of personnel in recordkeeping duties violates the rule that responsibility should not be shared.

(d) It is difficult to guard against defalcations and irregularities involving collusion among employees, even with careful attention to good internal control procedures.

(e) Internal auditing departments eliminate the need for audits by independent public accountants.

7-6 An acquaintance of yours who owns a medium-sized business asks you why she should be concerned with a system of internal control for the firm, since all officers and employees who have access to cash and liquid assets are bonded. How would you respond to this question?

7-7 What is the purpose of a bank reconciliation?

7-8 In preparing a bank reconciliation, what procedures should you follow to determine (a) deposits not recorded in the bank statement and (b) outstanding checks?

7-9 Indicate whether the following items in a bank reconciliation should be (a) added to the bank statement balance, (b) deducted from the bank statement balance, (c) added to the ledger account balance, (d) deducted from the ledger account balance:

(1) Bank service charge.

(2) NSF check.

(3) Deposit in transit.

(4) Outstanding check.

(5) Bank error charging company's account with check of another company.

(6) Difference of $180 in amount of check written for $758 but recorded in check register for $578.

7-10 Which of the items listed in Question 7-9 require an adjusting entry on the company's books?

7-11 What is meant by an "imprest petty cash fund"? How is such a fund established and replenished? Describe the accounting entries involved.

7-12 In preparing to replenish the $100 petty cash fund, the cashier discovers that the fund contains $90 in petty cash vouchers for office expense and $7 in currency and coins. (a) What should be the amount of the replenishment check? (b) How should the $3 discrepancy be recorded?

7-13 On December 31 of the current year, the $200 petty cash fund contained $30 in currency and coins. Vouchers and receipts totaling $170 represented office expense items of $140 and postage of $30. If the fund is not replenished until January 5 of next year, what effect will this have on the current year's financial statements? on next year's financial statements?

7-14 What is the purpose of a voucher system?

7-15 Which of the special journals studied earlier is replaced by the voucher register? the check register?

7-16 When a voucher is approved for the purchase of merchandise, what documents should support the approval?

EXERCISES

7-17 The following three situations occurred in the Travis Corporation:
  (a) The purchasing agent used a regular written purchase order to order building materials for the company. Later, she instructed the building supply company by telephone to deliver the materials to her home and to charge the Travis Corporation's account.
  (b) A vendor was paid twice for the same shipment. One payment was made upon receipt of the invoice and a second payment upon receipt of the monthly statement, which showed the amount of the open invoice but not the remittance, which arrived too late to appear on the statement.
  (c) The cashier pocketed cash received over the counter from certain customers paying their accounts. He then wrote off the receivables as uncollectible.
  For each situation, indicate the violations, if any, of good internal control procedures and describe the steps you would take to safeguard the system against this type of occurrence.

7-18 In each of the following unrelated cases, how does the stated procedure help to strengthen internal control?
  (a) The clerks of the Emporium Department Store are instructed to give each customer a cash register receipt along with the proper change.
  (b) The ticket-taker of the Cinema II theater is instructed to tear each admission ticket in half and give each patron a stub.
  (c) The Gourmet Restaurant provides each waitress with prenumbered customers' checks. The waitresses are instructed not to make alterations or corrections on the checks, but to void spoiled checks and issue new ones. Voided checks must be given to the manager at the end of the day.

7-19 Record the following activities of Perfecto Corporation in general journal form:

Apr. 1 Established a petty cash fund of $300 by writing a check on the First National Bank. Perfecto does not employ a voucher system.

      17 Replenished the petty cash fund by writing a check on the First National Bank. The fund contains the following:

Currency and coins	$ 25.00
Bills and receipts:	
Delivery Expense	80.00
Advertising Expense	140.00
Office Expense	55.00
	$300.00

      30 Replenished the petty cash fund and increased it to $350 by writing a check on the First National Bank. The fund contains:

Currency and coins	$ 33.00
Bills and receipts:	
Transportation In	175.00
Delivery Expense	50.00
Office Expense	42.00
	$300.00

7-20 Use the following information to prepare a bank reconciliation for the Dawson Company at June 30 of the current year.
(1) Balance per cash account, June 30, $9,475.30.
(2) Balance per bank statement, June 30, $11,520.50.
(3) Deposits not reflected on bank statement, $760.00.
(4) Outstanding checks, June 30, $2,975.20.
(5) Service charge on bank statement, not recorded in books, $10.
(6) Error by bank—check of Denton Company charged on Dawson Company's bank statement, $250.
(7) Check for advertising expense, $670, incorrectly recorded in books as $760.

7-21 The Grant Company uses a voucher system and had the following transactions during October:

Oct. 1 Recorded voucher No. 10–1 payable to North Realty for October rent, $700.

5 Recorded voucher No. 10–2 payable to Benson Company for $600 worth of merchandise, terms 2/10, n/30.

6 Issued check No. 621 in payment of voucher No. 10–1.

8 Purchased $1,500 worth of office equipment from Badger Company to be paid in installments of $900 and $600. Vouchers No. 10–3 and No. 10–4 were recorded for these installments.

14 Issued check No. 622 in payment of voucher No. 10–2.

15 Recorded voucher No. 10–5 for $360 premium on three-year insurance policy, payable to Prairie Insurance Company.

16 Issued check No. 623 to pay voucher No. 10–5.

21 Recorded voucher No. 10–6 for $900 worth of merchandise purchased from Rice Supply, terms 2/10, n/30.

24 Recorded voucher No. 10–7, amounting to $60 payable to Rapid Freight Company, for freight on shipment from Rice Supply (F.O.B. shipping point).

25 Issued check No. 624 for $900 to Badger Company (voucher No. 10–3).

26 Returned $100 worth of merchandise purchased from Rice Supply on October 21. Cancelled the old voucher and issued voucher No. 10–8 for correct amount.

28 Issued check No. 625 to pay voucher No. 10–7.

Indicate the book(s) of original entry in which each of the foregoing transactions would be recorded, and make the necessary entries in general journal form.

PROBLEMS

 7-22 The Western Branch of Sports Distributors, Inc. handles a significant amount of credit sales as well as over-the-counter and C.O.D. (cash on delivery) sales. The branch does its own billings and collects receivables from credit customers. At the end of each day, the cashier summarizes the over-the-counter cash sales and the amounts received from the delivery service for C.O.D. sales and sends the total to the bookkeeper for recording. Only one copy of sales tickets for these cash sales is prepared, and the cashier stamps them "paid" when cash is received from over-the-counter customers or from the delivery service. The cashier then files the sales ticket.

Mail remittances from credit customers are opened in the mailroom. Mailroom personnel make one copy of a list of remittances, which they forward, together with the customers' checks, to the bookkeeper. The bookkeeper verifies the cash discounts (credit sales are 2/10, n/30), records the remittances, then sends the checks to the cashier. The cashier makes up the daily deposits for the bank, including both cash sales and remittances received on account. At the end of the month, the cashier receives the bank statement and makes the bank reconciliation.

REQUIRED
(a) List the irregularities that might occur with the described system.
(b) Suggest improvements in the system of internal control.

7-23 Each of the lettered paragraphs (a)–(c) briefly describes an independent situation involving some aspect of internal control.

Answer the numbered questions following each paragraph.
(a) As the office manager of a small business, R. L. Grey opens all incoming mail, makes bank deposits, and keeps both the general ledger and the customers' ledger. Two assistants write up the cash, purchases, and sales journals and also prepare the customers' monthly statements.
  (1) If Mr. Grey pocketed Customer A's $50 remittance in full of account and made no effort to conceal his defalcation in the books, how would the misappropriation probably be discovered?
  (2) What routine accounting procedure would tend to disclose Grey's $50 defalcation in (1) even if he destroyed Customer A's subsidiary ledger card?
  (3) What circumstances might disclose Grey's $50 defalcation if he marked Customer A's account "paid in full" and set up a $50 account for fictitious Customer B with a fictitious address?
  (4) In (3) above, why might Mr. Grey be anxious to pick up and open the mail each morning?
  (5) In (3) above, why would Mr. Grey find it convenient to have the authority to write off accounts considered uncollectible?
(b) An employee of an ice cream parlor has purposely obscured (from customers) the window of the cash register with several display posters of national charitable organizations, such as the Red Cross. She has established a procedure of failing to register an average of three 50¢ ice cream sales each hour of her eight-hour shift, which she works seven days a week. She appears to ring up the sale and is able to make change when offered something other than the exact amount of the sale. The employee keeps track of and pockets cash in the amount of unrecorded sales.
  (1) How could the employee appear to be—but actually not be—ringing up the sale and be able to make change when needed?

(2) How much money is misappropriated each working day? Each month (assume 30-day months)? In a year (assume 360 days)?

(3) The annual amount misappropriated represents a 5% return on what amount of invested capital?

(c) A certain fast-food chain uses cash registers with locked-in counters, tapes, and so on. A prominently displayed sign tells customers that their purchase is free whenever their sales slip appears with a red star on it.

(1) How might the red star procedure be viewed as a sales promotion device?

(2) How might the red star procedure be viewed as an internal control device?

7-24 On July 31, the Cash in Bank account of the Wilson Company had a balance of $9,340.70. On that date, the bank statement indicated a balance of $12,920.15. Comparison of returned checks and bank advices revealed the following:

(1) Deposits in transit July 31 amounted to $920.00.

(2) Outstanding checks July 31 totaled $2,977.45.

(3) The bank erroneously charged a $600 check of the Walton Company against the Wilson bank account.

(4) A service charge made by the bank, not yet recorded on the books, was $4.

(5) Wilson borrowed $3,000 from the bank on a 9% six-month note but neglected to record it. The bank statement shows the $3,000 borrowed as a deposit.

(6) Included with the returned checks is a memo indicating that the check of J. Carter for $784 had been returned NSF. Carter, a customer, had sent the check to pay an account of $800 less 2% discount.

(7) Wilson Company had made an error in recording a payment for repairs as $675, the check was for $765.

REQUIRED

(a) Prepare a bank reconciliation for Wilson Company at July 31.

(b) Prepare, in general journal form, the entry or entries necessary to bring the Cash account into agreement with the adjusted balance on the bank reconciliation.

7-25 Syron, Inc. established an imprest petty cash fund on May 1 of the current year. The following transactions took place during May.

May 1 Wrote check against United Bank account to establish the petty cash fund, $150.

     12 Replenished the fund by check against the United Bank account for $143.50. The following bills and receipts were on hand:

Freight on C.O.D. purchase of merchandise	$ 28.75
Postage	90.00
Repairs to dictaphone equipment	18.75
Stationery and small office supplies	6.00
	$143.50

25 Replenished the fund and decided to increase it to $200. A check was written against the United Bank account. On this date, the fund contained $7.50 in currency and coins. Bills and receipts on hand were for postage, $22; office expense, $68.50; and charitable contributions, $50.

REQUIRED

Record the May petty cash transactions for Syron, Inc. in general journal form.

7-26 The bank reconciliation made by Westport, Inc. on March 31 of the current year showed a deposit in transit of $560 and two outstanding checks, No. 707 for $225 and No. 803 for $355. The adjusted balance per books on March 31 was $9,150. The following bank statement is available for the month of April:

Bank Statement

To: Westport, Inc. Fairbanks, Alaska			April 30, 19XX FAIRBANKS NATIONAL BANK	
Date	**Charges**		**Deposits**	**Balance**
Apr. 1	Balance			$ 9,170
1			$560	9,730
2	$355		640	10,015
5	425	330	620	9,880
8	210		270	9,940
13	190		410	10,160
17	355		150	9,955
19	235	250NSF		9,470
25	326		390	9,534
30	10SC		280	9,804

A list of deposits made and checks written during April, taken from the cash receipts journal and cash disbursements journal, respectively, is shown below:

	Deposits		Checks Written	
Apr. 1	$ 640	No. 807	$ 425	
4	620	808	330	
7	270	809	210	
12	410	810	190	
16	150	811	376	
24	390	812	235	
29	280	813	90	
30	330	814	355	
	$3,090	815	362	
		816	178	
			$2,751	

The Cash in Bank account balance on April 30 was $9,489. In reviewing checks returned by the bank, the bookkeeper discovered that check No. 811, written for $326, was recorded in the cash disbursements journal as $376. The check was for delivery expense. The NSF check for $250 was that of a customer, R. Benson, deposited in April.

REQUIRED
(a) Prepare a bank reconciliation for Westport, Inc. at April 30.
(b) Prepare the necessary journal entries to adjust the Cash in Bank account balance.

7-27 Oakwell, Inc. controls its disbursements through a voucher system. The following transactions occurred during July of the current year.

July 1 Recorded voucher No. 7–1 payable to Towne Realty for July rent, $475.
2 Recorded voucher No. 7–2 payable to Acme Supply, Inc. for $625 worth of merchandise purchased, terms 2/10, n/30.
3 Issued check No. 802 in payment of voucher No. 7–1.
5 Recorded voucher No. 7–3 payable to United Sales, Inc. for $360 worth of office supplies, terms n/30.
7 Recorded voucher No. 7–4 payable to Western Freight Company for transportation in on merchandise purchased, $60 (F.O.B. shipping point).
10 Issued check No. 803 in payment of voucher No. 7–2, less discount.
12 Issued check No. 804 in payment of voucher No. 7–3.
15 Recorded voucher No. 7–5 payable to Lord, Inc. for equipment, $2,500, terms 2/20, n/60. (Make voucher for net amount.)
18 Issued check No. 805 in payment of voucher No. 7–4.
22 Recorded voucher No. 7–6 payable to Mills, Inc. for merchandise purchased, $540, terms 2/10, n/30.
26 Recorded voucher No. 7–7 payable to Iowa Gas and Light Company for utilities expense, $130.
26 Issued check No. 806 in payment of voucher No. 7–7.
28 Received credit memo for $40 from Mills, Inc. for merchandise returned to it. Cancelled original voucher (No. 7–6) and issued voucher No. 7–8.
28 Issued check No. 807 in payment of voucher No. 7–5.
30 Recorded voucher No. 7–9 payable to Ward, Inc. for merchandise purchased, $750, terms 2/10, n/30.

REQUIRED
(a) Record Oakwell's transactions in a voucher register and a check register.
(b) Total the voucher register and the check register amount columns, and post the appropriate amounts to the following accounts:

No. 101	Cash in Bank	No. 803	Purchases Discounts
No. 107	Office Supplies on Hand	No. 804	Purchases Returns
No. 205	Equipment	No. 805	Transportation In
No. 401	Vouchers Payable	No. 836	Rent Expense
No. 801	Purchases	No. 839	Utilities Expense

(c) List the unpaid vouchers, and compare the total with the balance of the Vouchers Payable account.

7–28 The Cascade Company, which employs a voucher system, had the following transactions during May:

May 1 Recorded voucher No. 5–1 payable to R. Nelson for $500 in merchandise, terms 2/10, n/30.

  2 Recorded voucher No. 5–2 payable to Walton Rentals for May rent, $450.

  3 Issued check No. 803 in payment of voucher No. 5–2.

  9 Recorded voucher No. 5–3 payable to Whalen Express, Inc. for transportation in, $45 (F.O.B. shipping point).

  10 Issued check No. 804 in payment of voucher No. 5–1.

  11 Issued check No. 805 in payment of voucher No. 5–3.

  15 Recorded voucher No. 5–4 payable to Bailey Company for $700 worth of merchandise, terms n/30.

  20 Received credit memo from Bailey Company for $300 worth of merchandise purchased from them, recorded on voucher No. 5–4. Cancelled voucher No. 5–4 and issued voucher No. 5–5 for $400.

REQUIRED
Prepare, in columnar form, a voucher register and check register, and record the transactions for the Cascade Company.

ALTERNATE PROBLEMS

7–22A The Carter Company has three clerical employees who must perform the following functions:
(1) Maintain general ledger.
(2) Maintain accounts payable ledger.
(3) Maintain accounts receivable ledger.
(4) Prepare checks for signature.
(5) Maintain disbursements journal.
(6) Issue credits on returns and allowances.
(7) Reconcile the bank account.
(8) Handle and deposit cash receipts.
The office manager of the Carter Company wishes to assign the above functions to the three employees in the manner that achieves the highest degree of internal control.

REQUIRED
Distribute the functions among the employees in a manner compatible with good internal control.

7–24A On May 31, the Cash in Bank account of the Walden Company had a balance of $7,402.78. On that date, the bank statement indicated a balance of $8,143.65. Comparison of returned checks and bank advices revealed the following:

(1) Deposits in transit May 31 were $2,612.

(2) Outstanding checks May 31 were $1,140.37.

(3) The bank erroneously charged a $750 check of the Warden Company against the Walden bank account.

(4) Service charges made by the bank, not yet recorded on the books, were $15.

(5) Walden borrowed $3,000 from the bank on a 9% six-month note but neglected to record it. The bank statement shows the $3,000 borrowed as a deposit.

(6) Included with the returned checks is a memo indicating that the check of L. Jensen for $882 had been returned NSF. Jensen, a customer, had sent the check to pay an account of $900 less 2% discount.

(7) Walden Company had made an error in recording a payment for repairs as $955; the check was for $95.50.

REQUIRED

(a) Prepare a bank reconciliation for Walden Company at May 31.

(b) Prepare, in general journal form, the entry or entries necessary to bring the Cash in Bank account into agreement with the adjusted balance on the bank reconciliation.

7–25A Baker, Inc. established an imprest petty cash fund on May 1 of the current year. The following transactions took place during the month of May.

May   1   Wrote check against American Bank account to establish the petty cash fund, $75.

   12   Replenished the fund by check against the American Bank account for $65.55. The following bills and receipts were on hand:

Freight on C.O.D. purchase of merchandise	$19.75
Postage	20.00
Repairs to typewriters	15.00
Stationery and small office supplies	10.80
	$65.55

   25   Replenished the fund and decided to increase it to $100. A check was written against the American Bank account. On this date, the fund contained $2.50 in currency and coins. Bills and receipts on hand were for postage, $24; office expense, $22.50; and charitable contributions, $20.

REQUIRED

Record the May petty cash transactions for Baker, Inc. in general journal form.

7-26A The bank reconciliation made by Corbett, Inc. on August 31 of the current year showed a deposit in transit of $520 and two outstanding checks, No. 507 for $240 and No. 603 for $160. The adjusted balance per books on August 31 was $6,870.

The following bank statement is available for the month of September:

Bank Statement

TO: Corbett, Inc.   September 30, 19XX
    St. Louis, Mo.   UNITED BANK

Date	Charges		Deposits	Balance
Sept. 1	Balance			$6,750
1			$520	7,270
2	$160		270	7,380
5	426	305	550	7,199
8	160		340	7,379
13	185		480	7,674
17	342		190	7,522
19	248	190NSF		7,084
25	386		315	7,013
30	10SC		265	7,268

A list of deposits made and checks written during September, taken from the cash receipts journal and cash disbursements journal, respectively, is shown below:

Deposits			Checks Written		
Sept. 1	$	270	No. 607	$	426
4		550	608		305
7		340	609		160
12		480	610		185
16		190	611		486
24		315	612		248
29		265	613		124
30		335	614		342
		$2,745	615		253
			616		125
					$2,654

The ledger account balance for Cash in Bank on September 30 was $6,961. In reviewing checks returned by the bank, the bookkeeper discovered that check

No. 611, written for $386, was recorded in the cash disbursements journal as $486. The check was for repairs expense. The NSF check for $190 which Corbett deposited on September 16, was that of a customer, D. Boone.

REQUIRED
(a) Prepare a bank reconciliation for Corbett, Inc. at September 30.
(b) Prepare the necessary journal entries to adjust the Cash in Bank account balance.

7-27A Heritage, Inc. controls its disbursements through a voucher system. The following transactions occurred during May of the current year.

May 1 Recorded voucher No. 5-1 payable to Ready Rentals for May rent, $600.
     2 Recorded voucher No. 5-2 payable to Ace Supply, Inc. for $700 worth of merchandise purchased, terms 2/10, n/30.
     3 Issued check No. 902 in payment of voucher No. 5-1.
     5 Recorded voucher No. 5-3 payable to Oregon Sales, Inc. for $520 worth of office supplies, terms n/30.
     7 Recorded voucher No. 5-4 payable to Southern Freight Company for transportation in on merchandise purchased, $60 (F.O.B. shipping point).
    10 Issued check No. 903 in payment of voucher No. 5-2, less discount.
    12 Issued check No. 904 in payment of voucher No. 5-3.
    15 Recorded voucher No. 5-5 payable to Bates, Inc. for equipment, $2,000, terms 2/20, n/60. (Make voucher for net amount.)
    18 Issued check No. 905 in payment of voucher No. 5-4.
    22 Recorded voucher No. 5-6 payable to King, Inc. for merchandise purchased, $740, terms 2/10, n/30.
    26 Recorded voucher No. 5-7 payable to Tower Gas and Light Company for utilities expense, $145.
    26 Issued check No. 906 in payment of voucher No. 5-7.
    28 Received credit memo for $40 from King, Inc. for merchandise returned to it. Cancelled original voucher (No. 5-6) and issued voucher No. 5-8.
    28 Issued check No. 907 in payment of voucher No. 5-5.
    30 Recorded voucher No. 5-9 payable to Reed, Inc. for merchandise purchased, $620, terms 2/10, n/30.

REQUIRED
(a) Record Heritage's transactions in a voucher register and check register.
(b) Total the voucher register and the check register amount columns, and post the appropriate amounts to the following accounts:

No. 101	Cash in Bank	No. 803	Purchases Discounts
No. 107	Office Supplies on Hand	No. 804	Purchases Returns
No. 205	Equipment	No. 805	Transportation In
No. 401	Vouchers Payable	No. 836	Rent Expense
No. 801	Purchases	No. 839	Utilities Expense

(c) List the unpaid vouchers, and compare the total with the balance of the Vouchers Payable account.

BUSINESS DECISION PROBLEM

On December 15 of the current year, Bill Fischer, a friend of yours who owns the Pioneer Electrical Company, asks you to investigate the cash-handling activities in his firm. He is concerned about the possibility that an employee might be abstracting funds. "I have no proof," he says, "but I'm fairly certain that undeposited receipts on November 30 amounted to more than $5,000, although the November 30 bank reconciliation prepared by the cashier shows only $4,794.41. Also," he continues, "I notice that the bank reconciliation for November doesn't show several checks that have been outstanding for a long time. The cashier told me that these checks needn't appear on the reconciliation because he had notified the bank to stop payment on them and he had made the necessary adjustment on the books. Does that sound reasonable to you?"

At your request, Fischer shows you the following November 30 bank reconciliation prepared by the cashier:

Bank Reconciliation
November 30, 19XX

Balance per bank statement		$16,550.00	Balance per books			$21,011.62
Add: Deposits in transit		4,794.41				
Deduct:		$21,344.41	Deduct:			
Outstanding checks:			Bank service charge	$ 10		
			Unrecorded credit	100	110.00	
No. 4351	$290.71					
No. 4353	116.80					
No. 4354	135.28	442.79				
Adjusted balance		$20,901.62	Adjusted balance			$20,901.62

You discover that the $100 unrecorded bank credit represents a note collected by the bank on behalf of Pioneer; it appears in the deposits column of the November bank statement. Your investigation also reveals that the previous (October 31) bank reconciliation showed three checks that had been outstanding more than ten months: No. 2432 for $126, No. 2458 for $140, and No. 2512 for $253.50. You also discover that no entries were ever made on the books to add these items back into the Cash account. You confirm that the checks shown on the cashier's November 30 bank reconciliation were outstanding on that date.

To confirm the amount of undeposited receipts at November 30, you request a bank statement from the bank for the period December 1–12 (called a "cut-off" bank statement). This indeed shows a deposit on December 1 of $4,794.41. You discover, however, that a check payable to the cashier for $350 cleared the bank on December 2; it has never been recorded on the books, and there is no support for the disbursement.

REQUIRED
(a) Calculate the amount of funds abstracted by the cashier.
(b) Describe how the cashier concealed the abstraction.
(c) What sort of entry or entries should be made when it is decided that checks that have been outstanding for a long time should no longer be carried as outstanding in the bank reconciliation?
(d) What suggestions would you make to Mr. Fischer about procedures for control over cash?

8

Trade
Accounts
and
Notes

Our cash receipts have really slowed
So much, it's unbelievable!
It seems the dollars that we're owed
Are now Accounts Deceivable.

Business practice today is governed by credit. Indeed, it would be difficult to imagine how the vast daily sales of goods and services could be made without it. In recent years there has been an immense expansion in the use of credit, particularly in the retail field. Millions of consumers possess and regularly use several credit cards.

The growth of credit has created a need for more elaborate and sophisticated systems for processing transactions and gathering credit information. However, the basic accounting problems of keeping track of amounts owed to and due from others have remained essentially the same.

TRADE RECEIVABLES AND PAYABLES

The terms *trade-receivable* and *trade payable* usually refer to receivables and payables arising in the regular course of the company's transactions with customers and suppliers. Payments normally are to be made within 30 to 60 days. Thus, when merchandise is sold on account, the amount of the sale is debited to the appropriate customer's account in the subsidiary accounts receivable ledger; this amount is also debited to the Accounts Receivable control account when credit sales are posted periodically to it. The subsidiary record and the control account should reflect only trade accounts. If an advance is made to an employee or officer of the company, it should not be included here, nor should advances to affiliated companies, such as subsidiaries, be included. Such receivables should be recorded in separate accounts. In many instances such receivables are not current, and as a result, these items are often seen in the balance sheet under a noncurrent heading, such as Other Assets. Advances to subsidiary companies are frequently semipermanent, and they are found in the balance sheet under the Investments caption.

Likewise, trade accounts payable consist only of open amounts owing for the purchase of merchandise or materials or for the acquisition of services from outsiders. Amounts that a firm owes for salaries and wages and for various types of taxes, sundry accruals, and so on are recorded in separate current liability accounts.

*Reprinted by permission of *The Wall Street Journal*, © Dow Jones & Company, Inc. 1977. All Rights Reserved.

The principal reason for separating trade accounts from other receivables and payables is to facilitate analyses by both management and outsiders. As you will learn in Chapter 18, certain techniques employed in studying a company's current accounts depend upon such separation.

Occasionally, individual accounts within the accounts receivable or accounts payable subsidiary ledgers may show abnormal balances. A customer may have overpaid an account, made an advance for goods not yet shipped, or returned goods already paid for. If the amount is substantial, any resulting credit balance in a customer's account should be reclassified as a current liability when a balance sheet is prepared. On the other hand, if the firm itself makes advances on purchases or overpays accounts, the resulting debit balances in accounts payable are reclassified as current assets in the balance sheet.

INSTALLMENT ACCOUNTS

Many business concerns, such as mail-order houses and appliance dealers, do much of their business on the installment basis. Typically, a customer of such a firm signs an installment contract agreeing to a down payment plus installment payments of a fixed amount over a period of time such as 24 or 36 months. Normally, the total price of the merchandise sold includes an interest charge, and the contract provides that the seller may repossess merchandise if the installment payments are not made. If the installment contract conforms to normal trade practices and terms of the firm, the installment receivable should then be classified as a current asset.

LOSSES FROM UNCOLLECTIBLE ACCOUNTS

Few firms that extend credit to customers are immune to credit losses. Indeed, most companies anticipate them. As one might expect, the magnitude of such losses is often directly related to the firm's credit policy. Sometimes a company will deliberately liberalize its credit policy in order to obtain increased sales, fully anticipating that credit losses will increase.

Most large companies have credit departments to administer management's established credit policies. Credit personnel may set credit limits, conduct investigations of credit ratings, and follow up on unpaid accounts. They may also decide, after following established collection procedures, when a debt must be deemed uncollectible.

Credit losses are regarded as operating expenses of the business and are debited to an appropriately titled account such as *Uncollectible Accounts Expense.* Other account titles frequently used are *Loss from Uncollectible Accounts, Loss from Doubtful Accounts,* or *Bad Debts Expense.* Normally, the expense is classified as a selling expense on the income statement, although some companies may include it with administrative expenses.

CREDIT: SCORING AND CHECKING

Persons applying for credit for the first time—seeking a bank credit card, a charge account with a retail store, or a loan—are increasingly being evaluated by a "credit scoring system." Montgomery Ward & Company and Sears, Roebuck & Co., for example, use credit scoring systems.

Credit scoring is a system that assigns numeric values (points) to characteristics of an individual applying for credit. The total number of points must reach a certain minimum level for the individual to be granted credit. Income level, age, occupation, number of years in current job, and whether or not a home is owned are some of the characteristics that may be included in a credit scoring system.

The specific characteristics used may vary greatly among companies. The selection of characteristics, and the points assigned to them, are based on a statistical analysis of a company's past credit experience. After selecting a sample of credit applicants, a large number of the sample group's characteristics are analyzed to determine which ones most clearly distinguish the good credit risks from the bad risks. The few characteristics (usually from eight to twelve) that do the best job of separating the good risks from the bad risks are then included as questions on the company's credit application form.

There are several advantages to credit scoring.[1] The system permits an objective determination of the risk involved in extending credit to someone with a particular point score. Reliance on a credit manager's subjective judgment is therefore reduced. Sears, Roebuck & Co. confirmed the validity of this advantage. Sears kept track of the credit records of applicants approved by Sears' credit managers after the scoring system had shown no credit should be extended; 95% of the cases proved hard or impossible to collect.[2]

Credit scoring reduces the time, and therefore the cost, of processing credit applications. With credit scoring, it is also easier to implement a change in credit-granting policy. The minimum acceptable point score may be changed to incorporate a more restrictive or more lenient credit policy. Further, the objective nature of a credit scoring system provides a more defensible basis, legally, for denying credit than do systems relying on subjective judgments. The consistent treatment of applicants under credit scoring may also help companies in their compliance with the Equal Credit Opportunity Act, which requires a written explanation to credit applicants who are turned down.

The analytical capabilities of computers make credit scoring systems possible. Computers are also prominent in new systems for checking credit—point-of-sale credit verification.[3] Under one system handling about 160 stores, for example, a customer's Visa or Master Charge card is passed through a magnetic-stripe reader near the checkout counter. In a few seconds, a central computer, tied into Visa and Master Charge files around the world, checks to be sure the customer has not exceeded his or her credit limit, has been on time with payments, and that the card has not been reported lost or stolen.

A chain of department stores has installed a less elaborate point-of-sale credit check. The system is restricted to the company's own credit cards and uses electronic cash registers. Depending on the status of a customer's account, the cash register either authorizes or refuses to authorize the use of the customer's credit card.

The speed and accuracy of these point-of-sale verification systems help hold down credit card losses and portend their more widespread use.

[1]Gilbert A. Churchill, Jr., John R. Nevin, and R. Richard Watson, "The Role of Credit Scoring in the Loan Decision," The Credit World, March, 1977, pp. 6–10.
[2]Jeremy Main, "A New Way to Score with Lenders," Money, February, 1977, p. 74.
[3]Margaret Yao, "It's Easier to Charge, Harder to Cheat, Thanks to New Ways of Verifying Credit," The Wall Street Journal, January 10, 1979, p. 40.

Timing of Recognition

There are two methods for recognizing losses from uncollectible accounts. One is called the direct write-off method. The other method, which is preferable, is called the allowance method.

THE DIRECT WRITE-OFF METHOD. Under the direct write-off method, uncollectible accounts are charged to expense in the period when they are discovered to be uncollectible. Suppose that merchandise billed at $125 was sold in December of last year to J.B. Stone and that, after repeated attempts at collection, the credit department has decided on July 15 of the current year that the amount will never be collected. The following entry would be made to record the loss:

| July 15 | Uncollectible Accounts Expense | 125 | |
| | Accounts Receivable—J.B. Stone | | 125 |

To write off J.B. Stone's account.

The effect of this entry would be to charge the loss to the current year's expenses and to reduce the asset Accounts Receivable by $125. Also, J.B. Stone's subsidiary ledger account would no longer have a balance.

The major shortcoming of the direct write-off method is that credit losses are not matched with related sales. In the example above, the revenue from the sale to J.B. Stone would be reflected in the income statement of last year, but the loss would appear in the current year's income statement. The use of the direct write-off method also has the effect of consistently overstating Accounts Receivable on the balance sheet. Since currently acceptable accounting principles prescribe that receivables be shown at amounts expected to be collected, most accountants disapprove of the direct write-off method.

This method would be obviously inappropriate in certain situations. Suppose a firm liberalized its credit policy in one year, realizing a large increase in sales revenue. Much of the related uncollectible accounts expense would not appear on the income statement until the next year, because collection efforts and follow-up procedures often extend over long periods of time. Most accountants and credit people believe that the credit loss occurs at the time of sale and therefore should be reflected in the same period.

THE ALLOWANCE METHOD. Most businesses determine net income by employing the matching concept whenever possible. Therefore, they prefer to estimate the amount of uncollectible accounts expense that will eventually result from a period's sales in order to more realistically reflect the expense during the same period. This procedure not only matches credit losses with related revenue, but results in an estimated realizable amount for accounts receivable in the balance sheet at the end of the period. The estimate is introduced into the accounts by means of an adjusting entry.

Let us assume that a firm has accounts receivable of $100,000 at the end of its first business year and estimates that $4,000 of these accounts will be uncollectible. The following adjusting entry would be made:

Dec. 31   Uncollectible Accounts Expense   4,000
               Allowance for Uncollectible Accounts   4,000
         To record uncollectible accounts expense.

Note that in the adjusting entry, the credit is made to an account called *Allowance for Uncollectible Accounts* rather than to Accounts Receivable. This is done for two reasons. First, when the adjusting entry is made, a firm cannot tell which accounts in the subsidiary accounts receivable ledger will prove to be uncollectible. If the Accounts Receivable control account were credited and no entries were made in the subsidiary ledger, the two records would no longer agree in total. Second, because the amount involved is an estimate, it is preferable not to reduce directly Accounts Receivable.

The Allowance for Uncollectible Accounts is a *contra* asset account and will normally have a credit balance. To present the expected realizable amount of Accounts Receivable, the Allowance for Uncollectible Accounts is shown as a deduction from Accounts Receivable in the balance sheet as follows:

Current Assets		
Cash		$XXXXX
Accounts Receivable	$100,000	
Less: Allowance for Uncollectible Accounts	4,000	96,000
Inventory		XXXXX
Other Current Assets		XXXXX
Total Current Assets		$XXXXX

Writing Off Specific Accounts

The credit manager or other company official normally authorizes writing off a specific account. When the accounting department is notified of the action, it makes the following type of entry:

Jan. 5   Allowance for Uncollectible Accounts   250
               Accounts Receivable—James Baker   250
         To write off James Baker's account.

The credit in the above entry would be made to James Baker's account in the subsidiary accounts receivable ledger as well as to the Accounts Receivable control account; therefore, the entry does not alter agreement between the two records.

Note that the entry to write off an account has no effect on net income or on total assets. The expense was reflected, by means of the adjusting entry, in the period when the related revenue was recorded. Furthermore, because the Allowance for Uncollectible Accounts is deducted from Accounts Receivable in the balance sheet, the *net* realizable amount of Accounts Receivable is not changed by the write-off. After Baker's account has been written off, the Accounts Receivable and Allowance for Uncollectible Accounts ledger pages appear as follows:

Accounts Receivable — Account No. 12

Jan.						
	1	Balance				100,000
	5	Write-off, James Baker account			250	99,750

Allowance for Uncollectible Accounts — Account No. 13

Jan.						
	1	Balance				4,000
	5	Write-off, James Baker account		250		3,750

In the above accounts, the net realizable amount of accounts receivable on January 1 was $96,000 ($100,000 less $4,000 allowance). After the write-off on January 5, the net realizable amount of accounts receivable was still $96,000 ($99,750 less $3,750 allowance). Thus, the write-off of an account has no effect on the net asset balance.

Estimating Credit Losses

Estimates of credit losses are generally based on past experience, with consideration given to forecasts of sales activity, economic conditions, and planned changes in credit policy. The most commonly used calculations are related either to credit sales for the period or to the amount of accounts receivable at the close of the period.

ESTIMATES RELATED TO SALES Through experience, many companies can determine the approximate percentage of credit sales that will eventually prove to be uncollectible. At the end of an accounting period, the amount of the adjusting entry is determined by multiplying the credit sales by this percentage. Suppose that credit sales for a period amount to $200,000 and that past experience indicates a loss of $1\frac{1}{2}\%$. The adjusting entry to provide for expected losses would be:

Dec. 31	Uncollectible Accounts Expense	3,000	
	Allowance for Uncollectible Accounts		3,000

To record uncollectible accounts expense.

Because the periodic provisions for uncollectibles under this procedure are estimates related to sales, the allowance account should be reviewed regularly to be certain that its balance is reasonable. Should the balance in the allowance account become too large or too small, the percentage used for the periodic estimates of uncollectibles should be revised accordingly.

When a company estimates its credit losses from sales figures, it customarily uses credit sales only. In some cases, however, a percentage of credit and cash sales may be taken together. This procedure may prove satisfactory as long as the proportions of the two types of sales remain relatively constant over time. Whether sales discounts or sales returns and allowances should be deducted before applying a percentage to sales figures depends on how the percentage was developed; in the exercises and problems of this text, we will indicate when gross or net sales are to be used.

ESTIMATES RELATED TO ACCOUNTS RECEIVABLE   A company's experience may show that at the end of a period a certain percentage of Accounts Receivable is likely to prove uncollectible. The credit balance in the allowance account should be equal to this amount. Therefore, the company may simply derive the adjustment for uncollectibles as the amount needed to create the desired credit balance in the allowance account.

Suppose that a particular company estimates uncollectibles as 5% of Accounts Receivable and that the Accounts Receivable balance at the end of an accounting period is $50,000. Therefore, the credit balance desired in the allowance account is $2,500. If the allowance account already has a residual credit balance of $400, the amount of the adjustment will be $2,100. The corresponding entry would be a debit to Uncollectible Accounts Expense and a credit to Allowance for Uncollectible Accounts for $2,100.

Instead of using a fixed percentage of the aggregate customers' balances, some companies determine the amount needed in the allowance account after analyzing the age structure of the account balances. In order to do this, they prepare an **aging schedule** similar to the one in Exhibit 8–1. An aging schedule is simply an analysis of customers' balances that shows how long they have remained unpaid. Let us assume that the firm whose aging schedule appears in Exhibit 8–1 sells on net terms of 30 days. Alton's account is current, which means that the $320 billing is within the last 30 days. Baker's account is in the 0–30 days past due category, which means that the account is from 31 to 60 days old. Wall's balance consists of a $50 billing made from 91 to 150 days ago and a $100 billing made from 151 days to seven months ago, and so on.

EXHIBIT 8–1
Aging Schedule of Customer Balances, December 31, 19XX

Customer	Account Balance	Current	Past Due 0–30 Days	Past Due 31–60 Days	Past Due 61–120 Days	Past Due 121 Days – 6 Mo.	Past Due Over 6 Mo.
Alton, J.	$ 320	$ 320	$	$	$	$	$
Baker, C.	250		250				
•							
•							
•							
Wall, M.	150				50	100	
Zorn, W.	210			210			
	$50,000	$42,000	$4,000	$2,000	$1,000	$800	$200

Companies may analyze their bad accounts experience with the aged balances over time and develop percentages of each strata that they think are likely to prove uncollectible. At the end of each period, such percentages will be applied to the totals of each age group to determine the balance required in the allowance account. Suppose, in our example, that these percentages are as shown below. Applying the percentages to the totals in our aging schedule, we calculate an allowance requirement of $1,560.

	Amount	Percent Doubtful	Allowance Required
Current	$42,000	2	$ 840
0–30 days past due	4,000	3	120
31–60 days past due	2,000	5	100
61–120 days past due	1,000	20	200
121 days–6 months past due	800	25	200
Over 6 months past due	200	50	100
Total Allowance Required			$1,560

Again, if the allowance account had a residual credit balance of $400, the adjustment would be for $1,160. The entry would be:

Dec. 31	Uncollectible Accounts Expense	1,160	
	Allowance for Uncollectible Accounts		1,160

To record uncollectible accounts expense.

The adjustment brings the credit balance in the allowance account to the required amount—$1,560.

Recoveries of Accounts Written Off

Occasionally, accounts written off against the Allowance for Uncollectible Accounts later prove to be wholly or partly collectible. In such situations, it is preferable to first reinstate the customer's account for the amount recovered before recording the collection, so that a record of the payment will appear in the customer's account. This can be accomplished by reversing, to the extent of the recovery, the entry made for the write-off and then recording the receipt in the usual manner. For example, assume that a company using the allowance method wrote off the $250 account of James Baker on January 5 but received payment in full on April 20. The following entries (including write-off) illustrate the procedure.

To write off the account:

Jan. 5	Allowance for Uncollectible Accounts	250	
	Accounts Receivable—James Baker		250

To reinstate the account:

| Apr. 20 | Accounts Receivable—James Baker | 250 | |
| | Allowance for Uncollectible Accounts | | 250 |

To record remittance:

| Apr. 20 | Cash | 250 | |
| | Accounts Receivable—James Baker | | 250 |

These last two entries may be made even if the recovery occurs in a year other than the year of write-off.

A business employing the direct write-off method that recovered a written-off account during the year of write-off would simply reverse, to the extent of the recovery, the entry made to write off the account and record the remittance in the usual manner. Recoveries made in years after the write-off would normally require two entries also. One entry reinstates the customer's account balance, with the credit made to an income statement account titled Recoveries of Accounts Written Off. The second entry records the remittance in the usual manner.

CREDIT CARD FEES

Many retailing businesses have their credit sales handled through credit cards such as Visa and Master Charge cards issued by banks. The bank incurs the costs of processing and collecting the amounts charged on its credit cards and absorbs any losses from uncollectible accounts. In exchange for these services, the bank charges the retail firm a fee, usually ranging from $\frac{1}{2}$ to 5 percent of the amount of the credit sale. The retailer makes the credit card sale and deposits the charge slip with the bank. The bank credits the retailer's bank account for the amount of the sale less the credit card fee. Thus, the retailer records the transaction by debiting cash (for the amount of the sale less the fee), debiting a credit card fee expense account (for the amount of the fee), and crediting sales.

Credit sales may also be made to customers who use nonbank credit cards, such as American Express and Diners' Club cards. For these sales, the retailer sends the charge slips to the credit card company, then receives a check from that company for the sales amount less the credit card fee. Thus, the retailer records these sales by establishing a receivable from the credit card company (for the amount of the sale less the fee), debiting a credit card fee expense account (for the amount of the fee), and crediting sales. The receivable is credited when the check is received from the credit card company.

NOTES RECEIVABLE AND PAYABLE

Promissory notes are often used in merchandise and property transactions, particularly when the credit period is longer than the typical 30 or 60 days for open accounts. Although promissory notes are used more frequently in sales of equipment and real property, a note is sometimes exchanged for merchandise. Occasionally, a note is substituted for an open account when an extension of the usual credit period is granted. In addition, promissory notes are normally executed when loans are obtained from banks and other parties.

A promissory note is a written promise to pay a certain sum of money on demand or at a fixed and determinable future time. The note is signed by the maker, and it is made payable to the order of either a specific payee or to the bearer. The note may be *non-interest bearing* or it may be *interest bearing* at an annual rate specified on the note. An interest-bearing promissory note is illustrated in Exhibit 8–2.

A note held from a debtor is called a *note receivable* by the holder and a *note payable* by the debtor. A note is usually regarded as a stronger claim against a debtor than an open account because the terms of payment are specified in writing. Although open accounts can be sold (factored), it is much easier to convert a note to cash by discounting it at a bank. (We treat the discounting of notes in a later section of this chapter.)

Interest on Notes

Interest on notes is commonly paid at the maturity date of the obligation, except in certain discounting transactions. Interest incurred is debited to an Interest Expense account, while interest earned is credited to an Interest Income account.

EXHIBIT 8–2
A Promissory Note

$2,000.00	Madison, Wisconsin	May 3, 19XX

Sixty days _____ after date _____ I _____ promise to pay to

the order of _____ Robert Ward _____

Two Thousand and no/100————————————————————dollars

for value received with interest at __6%__

payable at American Exchange Bank

James Stone

When business firms make distinctions in their income statements between operating and other items of income and expense, interest expense and interest income are shown under the heading "Other Income and Expense."

INTEREST CALCULATION   The formula for determining simple interest is:

$$\text{Principal} \times \text{Rate} \times \text{Time} = \text{Interest}$$

Unless otherwise specified, we shall assume that interest rates on notes are for a year. For example, interest on a one-year note for $2,000 at 6% would be calculated as follows:

$$\$2,000 \times \frac{6}{100} \times 1 = \$120$$

When the note is for a certain number of months, the time is usually expressed in twelfths of a year. Thus, the interest on a six-month note for $2,000 at 6% would be calculated as follows:

$$\$2,000 \times \frac{6}{100} \times \frac{6}{12} = \$60$$

When the duration of a note is given in days, it is customary to express the time period as a fraction of a year; therefore, the number of days' duration is the numerator and 360 is the denominator. (It is general business practice to use 360 days here, although federal agencies and certain lenders may use 365 days.) Interest on a 60-day note for $2,000 at 6% would be calculated as follows:

$$\$2,000 \times \frac{6}{100} \times \frac{60}{360} = \$20$$

Note that the interest on this 60-day, 6% note is 1% of the principal amount ($60/360 \times 6\% = 1\%$). Some people prefer to approach interest calculations on notes by first calculating the interest at 6% for 60 days and then adjusting the calculation for variations in interest and time. For example, suppose a 72-day note for $3,000 carried interest at 9%. We may perform the calculation in the following manner:

$30	Interest for 60 days at 6%	$(0.01 \times \$3,000)$
6	Interest for **12** days at 6%	$(\frac{1}{5}$ of $30)
$36	Interest for 72 days at 6%	(total of first two lines)
18	Interest for 72 days at **3%**	$(\frac{1}{2}$ of $36)
$54	Interest for 72 days at 9%	

This method of calculation saves time in certain situations; often, many of the calculations can be performed mentally. For example, when interest is 9%, one merely adds $\frac{1}{2}$ of the 6% amount; when 4%, one subtracts $\frac{1}{3}$ of the 6% amount. If the duration of the note is 70 days, add $\frac{1}{6}$ of the 60-day amount; for 72 days, add $\frac{1}{5}$, and so on. When the calculations involve unusual fractions, however, this so-called shortcut method is not particularly useful.

DETERMINING MATURITY DATE   When the duration of a note is expressed in days, it is common practice to count the exact days in each calendar month to determine the maturity date. For example, a 90-day note dated July 21 would have an October 19 maturity date, which we determine as follows:

10 days in July (remainder of month—31 days minus 21 days)
31 days in August
30 days in September
<u>19</u> days in October (number of days required to total 90)
<u>90</u>

If the duration of a note is expressed in months, the maturity date is found simply by counting the months from the date of issue. Thus, a two-month note dated January 31 would mature on March 31, a three-month note of the same date would mature on April 30 (the last day of the month), and a four-month note would mature on May 31.

RECORDING NOTES AND INTEREST   When a note is received or given to settle an open trade account, an entry is made to reflect the note receivable or payable and to reduce the balance of the related account receivable or payable. For example, suppose Acme Company had sold $4,000 of merchandise to Baker Company. Also suppose that on October 1, after the regular credit period had elapsed, Baker Company gave Acme Company a 60-day, 9% note for $4,000. The following entries would be made by each of the parties:

Acme Company

Oct. 1	Notes Receivable	4,000	
	Accounts Receivable—Baker		4,000

Received 60-day, 9% note in payment of account.

Baker Company

Oct. 1	Accounts Payable—Acme	4,000	
	Notes Payable		4,000

Gave 60-day, 9% note in payment of account.

If Baker Company pays the note on the maturity date, November 30, the following entries would be made by the parties involved:

Acme Company

Nov. 30	Cash	4,060	
	Interest Income		60
	Notes Receivable		4,000

Collected Baker Company note.

Baker Company

Nov. 30	Notes Payable	4,000	
	Interest Expense	60	
	Cash		4,060

Paid note to Acme Company.

We can see from the above that the interest for 60 days at 9% is reflected by the respective parties at the maturity date of the note. This would be true even if the maker defaulted on the note. If Baker Company did not pay the note when due, the debit of $4,060 on Acme's books would be made to Accounts Receivable rather than to Cash. When a note receivable is dishonored at maturity, the combined principal and interest are converted to an open account. This procedure leaves only current, unmatured notes in the Notes Receivable account.

Discounting Notes

Occasionally, a business may prefer not to wait until the maturity date of a note receivable to obtain cash from a customer transaction. Instead, it will endorse the note over to a bank, "discounting" the note and receiving an amount equal to the maturity value of the note less the discount charged by the bank. By endorsing the note (unless it is endorsed "without recourse"), the business agrees to pay the note at the maturity date if the maker fails to pay it. Consequently, the note is a **contingent liability** of the endorser (that is, the liability is contingent on the failure of the maker to pay). While the note is outstanding, the contingent liability must be revealed in the balance sheet of the endorser, as we shall see below.

DISCOUNTING NON-INTEREST-BEARING NOTES RECEIVABLE Assume that the $4,000, 60-day note received on October 1 by Acme Company from Baker Company was non-interest bearing. Suppose that Acme Company decided to discount the note at the bank on October 31 and that the bank's discount rate is 9%.

The bank discount calculation is always based on the maturity value of the note and the number of days that the bank must hold the note. Because the note in our example is non-interest bearing, the maturity value is the same as the face value, $4,000. The bank will hold the note for 30 days—October 31 to November 30. (In calculating the discount period, ignore the discount date and count the maturity date as a full day.) The following illustration shows how to calculate the proceeds.

$$\text{Maturity Value} \times \text{Discount Rate} \times \text{Discount Period} = \text{Discount}$$
$$\$4,000 \quad\quad \times \quad 9\% \quad\quad \times \quad\quad \tfrac{30}{360} \quad\quad = \quad \$30$$

$$\text{Maturity Value} - \text{Discount} = \text{Proceeds}$$
$$\$4,000 \quad - \quad \$30 \quad = \quad \$3,970$$

To record the discounting transaction, Acme Company would make the following entry:

Oct. 31	Cash	3,970	
	Interest Expense	30	
	Notes Receivable Discounted		4,000

Discounted Baker's non-interest-bearing note.

The Notes Receivable Discounted account credited in the above entry is a contra account that is subtracted from the Notes Receivable account in the balance sheet. Only the notes still held by the company are added to the current assets total. This procedure, however, reveals the company's contingent liability for discounted notes. An example of the presentation used can be seen in Exhibit 8–3 (see page 300). Some firms do not exhibit the Notes Receivable Discounted account in the balance sheet; instead, they show the notes still held, with a footnote to this item in the balance sheet indicating the contingent liability.

DISCOUNTING INTEREST-BEARING NOTES RECEIVABLE   We use the same procedure—calculating discount on the maturity value of the note for the length of the discount period—for interest-bearing notes. In this case, however, maturity value includes interest for the full term of the note. The discount computation and calculation of proceeds for a $4,000, 60-day, 9% note dated October 1 and discounted at 9% on October 31 by Acme Company is as follows:

$$\text{Maturity Value} \times \text{Discount Rate} \times \text{Discount Period} = \text{Discount}$$
$$\$4,060 \qquad \times \qquad 9\% \qquad \times \qquad \tfrac{30}{360} \qquad = \$30.45$$

$$\text{Maturity Value} - \text{Discount} = \text{Proceeds}$$
$$\$4,060 \quad - \quad \$30.45 \ = \$4,029.55$$

Acme Company would record the discounting transaction as follows:

Oct. 31	Cash	4,029.55	
	Interest Income		29.55
	Notes Receivable Discounted		4,000.00

Discounted Baker's 60-day, 9% note at 9%.

Note that although Acme Company and the bank each hold the note 30 days, the bank exacts an additional amount of interest. The extra $0.45 is the interest for 30 days on $60 at the 9% bank discount rate. The bank considers the transaction a loan of $4,060, the amount that must be repaid at the end of the term of the note.

Normally, a firm discounting a customer's interest-bearing note at the bank earns interest income, as shown in our illustration. It may be possible, however, that the proceeds from discounting will be less than the note's face value. This can occur when the duration of the firm's holding period is fairly short and the bank's discount rate exceeds the interest rate on the note.

Suppose that Acme Company discounts the $4,000 note after holding it only 6 days, and the discount rate is 11%. The discount would be $4,060 $\times$ 11% $\times \frac{54}{360}$ = $66.99. Subtracting this amount from the $4,060 maturity value yields proceeds of $3,993.01. In this case Acme Company would record the $6.99 difference between face value and proceeds as interest expense:

Oct. 7	Cash	3,993.01	
	Interest Expense	6.99	
	Notes Receivable Discounted		4,000

Discounted 60-day, 9% note at 11%.

DISCOUNTED NOTES RECEIVABLE PAID   When the maker of a discounted note receivable pays the note at maturity, the discounting party (endorser) may then remove the note receivable amount and the contingent liability contra amount in Notes Receivable Discounted from its accounts. For example, in the illustrations in which Acme Company discounted Baker Company's $4,000 note, the following entry would be made by Acme Company when Baker Company paid the note on November 30:

Nov. 30	Notes Receivable Discounted	4,000	
	Notes Receivable		4,000

To remove contingent liability on discounted note.

Because these amounts were offsetting items in the company's accounts, this entry has no effect on the aggregate assets of the company.

DISCOUNTED NOTES RECEIVABLE DISHONORED   When the maker of a note receivable fails to pay it (dishonors it) at maturity, the bank will notify the endorsing party and charge the full amount owed, including interest, to the bank account of the endorser. In addition, the bank may also charge a small fee called a *protest fee*. Suppose that the $4,000, 60-day, 9% note of Baker Company, which Acme discounted on October 31, was dishonored by Baker Company at maturity. Assume also that the bank notified Acme Company on November 30 that the maturity value of the note, $4,060, plus a $5 protest fee was being charged against Acme Company's bank account.

In this situation, Acme Company would make two entries. First, since dishonor of the note discharged it and converted a contingent liability to a real liability, the company would remove the amount of the note and the contra amount from its accounts just as it would do if the note were honored:

Nov. 30	Notes Receivable Discounted	4,000	
	Notes Receivable		4,000

To remove contingent liability—note dishonored.

The second entry would be to record paying the maturity value of the note plus the protest fee and to charge the entire amount to Accounts Receivable— Baker Company:

Nov. 30	Accounts Receivable—Baker Company	4,065	
	Cash		4,065
	Paid Baker Company note and $5 protest fee.		

Acme Company would then endeavor to collect the $4,065 from Baker Company. If Acme failed in its efforts, it would write off the account as uncollectible, using the procedures described earlier in this chapter.

DISCOUNTING NOTES PAYABLE   When a business borrows from a bank by giving its own note, the bank often deducts the interest in advance. With this type of transaction, a business is said to be "discounting its own note." Suppose that Acme Company discounts at 9% its own $8,000, 60-day note, dated December 16, at the bank. The calculation of discount and proceeds follows the pattern used for discounting notes receivable:

$$\text{Maturity Value} \times \text{Interest Rate} \times \text{Discount Period} = \text{Discount (Interest)}$$
$$\$8,000 \qquad \times \qquad 9\% \qquad \times \qquad \tfrac{60}{360} \qquad = \qquad \$120$$

$$\text{Maturity Value} - \text{Discount (Interest)} = \text{Proceeds}$$
$$\$8,000 \qquad - \qquad \$120 \qquad = \$7,880$$

The entry to record this transaction would be:

Dec. 16	Cash	7,880	
	Discount on Notes Payable	120	
	Notes Payable		8,000
	Discounted our 60-day note at 9%.		

Note that we have charged the $120 to Discount on Notes Payable. This account is a *contra* account whose balance is subtracted from the Notes Payable amount on the balance sheet. As the time period for the note elapses, the discount is reduced and charged to Interest Expense. Thus, at December 31, after 15 days have elapsed, $30 would be charged to Interest Expense and credited to Discount on Notes Payable. A complete discussion of the adjustment procedure is offered in the next section.

Because the proceeds under this type of note are less than the maturity value of the note, the *effective interest rate* for the loan is greater than the stated interest rate. The effective interest rate may be calculated by the formula:

$$\text{Effective Interest Rate} = \frac{\text{Maturity Value of Note} \times \text{Stated Interest Rate}}{\text{Cash Proceeds from Note}}$$

For the above note, the effective interest rate is computed as:

$$\frac{\$8,000 \times 9\%}{\$7,880} = 9.14\%$$

Adjusting Entries for Interest

When the term of an interest-bearing note extends beyond the end of an accounting period, adjusting entries are usually necessary to reflect interest in the proper period. In cases where material amounts are involved, end-of-period adjustments are normally made to accrue interest income on notes receivable and interest expense on notes payable. Often, entries are also necessary to record interest expense on a company's own notes that have been discounted.

ACCRUED INTEREST   Assume that Acme Company received a $12,000, 60-day, 10% note from Cable Company on December 16 of the current year. By the close of the accounting period on December 31, Acme Company would have earned 15 days' interest, or $50, on the note, and Cable Company would have incurred an equal amount of interest expense. The adjusting entries to be made by each company on December 31 are shown below:

Acme Company

Dec. 31	Interest Receivable	50	
	Interest Income		50

To accrue interest income on Cable Company note.

Cable Company

Dec. 31	Interest Expense	50	
	Interest Payable		50

To accrue interest expense on note to Acme Company.

As a result of its adjusting entry, Acme Company would report the interest earned during the month of December in its income statement for the current year and would show the interest receivable at December 31 among the current assets in its balance sheet. Likewise, Cable Company would report the interest expense incurred during December in its income statement for the current year and the interest payable as a current liability in its December 31 balance sheet.

In Chapter 4 we mentioned that some accountants prefer to make reversing entries for all accrual adjustments, after the books have been closed and statements have been prepared. If Acme Company followed this practice, the reversing entry (debit Interest Income and credit Interest Receivable for $50) on January 1 would eliminate the Interest Receivable balance and reflect a debit balance of $50 in the Interest Income account (which had no balance after closing). Collection of the note and interest on the maturity date, February 14, would be recorded in the usual manner:

Feb. 14	Cash	12,200	
	Interest Income		200
	Notes Receivable		12,000

Collected Cable Company note and
interest.

After this collection entry had been posted to the accounts, the Interest Income
account would show a net credit balance of $150—the proper amount of income
on the note earned during the new year. The Interest Income account would
appear as follows:

Interest Income

| Jan. | 1 | Reversing entry | 50 | | (50) |
| Feb. | 14 | Collection of interest | | 200 | 150 |

Alternatively, if Acme Company had not reversed the accrual adjustment
on January 1, the entry to record the collection of principal and interest would
have been:

Feb. 14	Cash	12,200	
	Interest Receivable		50
	Interest Income		150
	Notes Receivable		12,000

Collected Cable Company note and
interest.

When accrual adjustments are not reversed, we must analyze the subsequent
related cash transaction as we did in the above entry. Although this procedure
accomplishes the same result with fewer entries, it requires that the accountant be
more circumspect in recording transactions during the period after adjustment.

Obviously, our remarks also apply to accrued interest on notes payable. For
example, if Cable Company reversed its accruals, the entry for payment of the
note and interest on February 14 would be:

Feb. 14	Notes Payable	12,000	
	Interest Expense	200	
	Cash		12,200

Paid note and interest to Acme Company.

If Cable Company did not follow the practice of reversing accruals, the entry
at maturity date would be:

Feb. 14	Notes Payable	12,000	
	Interest Payable	50	
	Interest Expense	150	
	Cash		12,200

Paid note and interest to Acme Company.

DISCOUNT ON NOTES PAYABLE   When a firm discounts its own note payable at the bank, the interest (discount) is deducted immediately from the note's face value to obtain the proceeds, as we pointed out earlier. In our earlier example, Acme Company's note payable for $8,000 was discounted for 60 days at 9% at the American Exchange Bank on December 16. The entries made by each of the parties are given below:

Acme Company

Dec. 16	Cash	7,880	
	Discount on Notes Payable	120	
	Notes Payable		8,000

Discounted our 60-day note at 9%.

American Exchange Bank

Dec. 16	Notes Receivable	8,000	
	Discount on Notes Receivable		120
	Cash		7,880

Discounted Acme Company's 60-day note at 9%.

At the close of the accounting period on December 31, 15 of the 60 days have elapsed, so that one-fourth, or $30, of the discount should be recognized as interest. The parties involved would make the following adjusting entries on December 31:

Acme Company

| Dec. 31 | Interest Expense | 30 | |
| | Discount on Notes Payable | | 30 |

To record interest expense on our discounted note.

American Exchange Bank

| Dec. 31 | Discount on Notes Receivable | 30 | |
| | Interest Income | | 30 |

To record interest income on Acme Company note.

In the balance sheet prepared December 31, Acme Company would show the remaining $90 Discount on Notes Payable as a *contra-liability* account, subtracted from the related notes payable. In its December 31 balance sheet, the American Exchange Bank would show Discount on Notes Receivable as a *contra-asset* account, subtracted from Notes Receivable.

When the note is paid on February 14, the parties involved would make the following entries:

Acme Company

Feb. 14	Notes Payable	8,000	
	Interest Expense	90	
	Discount on Notes Payable		90
	Cash		8,000

Payment of discounted note at maturity.

American Exchange Bank

Feb. 14	Cash	8,000	
	Discount on Notes Receivable	90	
	Interest Income		90
	Notes Receivable		8,000

Receipt of payment at maturity on Acme
Company note.

The use of contra accounts, such as Discount on Notes Payable and Discount on Notes Receivable, and the balance sheet treatment described in the foregoing paragraphs are in accordance with current accounting principles.[1] For many years, accountants treated the discount as a prepayment of interest. The borrower included prepaid interest as a current asset on its balance sheet, and the lender placed unearned interest among its liabilities. Such practices are no longer considered correct, because a prepayment would actually reduce the amount borrowed and make the effective interest rate higher. Discount on notes payable is still regarded as a prepayment by the Internal Revenue Service, however. For tax purposes, a cash basis taxpayer can deduct—as interest—the difference between the face value and the proceeds of a note in the period when the note is discounted.

Notes and Interest in Financial Statements

A business will show short-term trade notes receivable as current assets in the balance sheet; because they can normally be converted to cash fairly easily, these notes usually are placed above trade accounts receivable. As with accounts receivable, it is best to separate notes from officers and employees and notes representing advances to affiliated companies from trade notes receivable. If such notes are not truly short-term in character, they should be classified under a heading other than current assets. Interest receivable is normally shown with notes receivable.

Sometimes companies with a large volume of notes receivable find it necessary to provide for possible losses on notes. Frequently, the provision for credit losses is extended to cover losses on notes as well as on open accounts. In such cases, the Allowance for Uncollectible Accounts is deducted from the sum of Accounts Receivable and Notes Receivable in the balance sheet.

[1]*Opinions of the Accounting Principles Board*, No. 21, "Interest on Receivables and Payables," American Institute of Certified Public Accountants, New York, 1971.

Trade notes payable and notes payable to banks are usually shown separately in the current liabilities section of the balance sheet. Interest Payable is normally shown with Notes Payable—often as an addition, as presented in Exhibit 8–3. Discount on Notes Payable is deducted from the related notes payable amount. The order in which current payables appear is less important than the sequence of current assets; however, Notes Payable customarily precedes Accounts Payable.

A current section of a balance sheet is shown in Exhibit 8–3 to illustrate the presentation of items discussed in this chapter.

Because they are financial rather than operating items, we often separate Interest Expense and Interest Income from operating items in the income statement. As we see in Exhibit 8–4, they frequently appear under the classification *Other Income and Expense*. This type of presentation permits readers to make intercompany comparisons of operating results that are not influenced by financing patterns of the companies involved (such comparisons are explained more fully in Chapter 18).

EXHIBIT 8–3

Huron Company
Partial Balance Sheet
December 31, 19XX

Current Assets		
Cash		$ 2,000
Notes Receivable—Trade	$30,000	
Less: Notes Receivable Discounted	6,000	
	$24,000	
Interest Receivable	300	24,300
Accounts Receivable—Trade	$50,000	
Less: Allowance for Uncollectible Accounts	1,500	48,500
Inventory		75,000
Prepaid Expenses		200
Total Current Assets		$150,000
Current Liabilities		
Notes Payable—Banks	$ 8,000	
Less: Discount on Notes Payable	60	$ 7,940
Notes Payable—Trade	$20,000	
Interest Payable	400	20,400
Accounts Payable—Trade		30,000
Other Accrued Liabilities		11,660
Total Current Liabilities		$ 70,000

EXHIBIT 8-4

Huron Company
Partial Income Statement
For the Year 19XX

Sales		$200,000
Cost of Goods Sold		140,000
Gross Profit		$ 60,000
Operating Expenses:		
•		•
•		•
•		•
Total Operating Expenses		40,000
Net Operating Income		$ 20,000
Other Income and Expense:		
Interest Income	$1,400	
Interest Expense	800	600
Net Income		$ 20,600

KEY POINTS TO REMEMBER

Accounts Receivable

(1) When a debt is considered uncollectible, the *direct write-off* method of recording credit losses results in a debit to Uncollectible Accounts Expense and a credit to Accounts Receivable.

(2) The *allowance* method of recording credit losses can be summarized as follows:

(a) To provide for losses: Estimate them in advance; then debit Uncollectible Accounts Expense and credit Allowance for Uncollectible Accounts. The amount of the entry may be either a percentage of the period's credit sales or an amount necessary to bring the Allowance account to a desired balance that is based on an analysis of the receivables.

(b) To write off accounts: When accounts are considered uncollectible, debit Allowance for Uncollectible Accounts and credit Accounts Receivable.

Notes Receivable and Payable

(1) Discount is calculated on the maturity value of a note for the time period it is to be held by the bank. Proceeds of a note are obtained by subtracting the discount from the maturity value.

(2) To record the discounting of a customer's note, Cash is debited for the proceeds, and a credit is made to Notes Receivable Discounted, a contra account

to Notes Receivable, in order to reflect the contingent liability of the endorser. If proceeds exceed face value, the difference is credited to Interest Income. If proceeds are less than face value, the difference is debited to Interest Expense. When a firm discounts its *own* note, Notes Payable is credited.

(3) At maturity of a discounted customer's note, Notes Receivable Discounted is debited and Notes Receivable is credited, whether the note is honored or not. When a customer dishonors the note, the maturity value plus protest fees are charged to the customer's account.

(4) When a firm discounts its own note, Discount on Notes Payable is debited for the difference between face value and proceeds. This contra-liability account is deducted from the related notes payable on the balance sheet. As the term of the note expires, the discount is reduced by charges to Interest Expense by means of adjusting entries.

QUESTIONS

8-1 What events might result in credit balances in customers' accounts and in debit balances in creditors' accounts? How are such items classified in the balance sheet?

8-2 A mail-order firm regularly makes a large proportion of its sales on the installment basis, requiring a 20% down payment and monthly payments over a period of 6 to 24 months, depending on the type of item sold. Where should the installment receivables be classified in the balance sheet of this mail-order firm?

8-3 How do the "direct write-off" and "allowance" methods of handling credit losses differ with respect to the timing of expense recognition?

8-4 When a firm provides for credit losses under the allowance method, why is the Allowance for Uncollectible Accounts credited rather than Accounts Receivable?

8-5 Describe the two most commonly used methods of estimating the provision for uncollectible accounts expense when the allowance method is employed.

8-6 The Weber Company computes its estimate of uncollectibles by aging its accounts and applying percentages to various strata of the aged accounts. This year, it calculated a total of $1,200 in possible losses. On December 31, the Accounts Receivable balance is $80,000 and the Allowance for Uncollectible Accounts has a credit balance of $400 before adjustment. Give the adjusting entry to provide for credit losses. What would be the net amount of Accounts Receivable added into the current assets?

8-7 In May of last year, Beal, Inc. sold $200 worth of merchandise to Taylor Company. In November of last year, Beal, Inc. wrote off Taylor's account. In March of this year Taylor Company paid the account in full. Give the entries to be made by Beal, Inc. for the write-off and the recovery, assuming that Beal, Inc. uses (a) the direct write-off method, and (b) the allowance method of handling credit losses.

8-8 Shield Company sold a $1,000 stereo system to a customer who used a Visa bank credit card to charge the sale. Shield Company's bank charges a credit card fee of 4% of sales. What entry should Shield Company make to record the sale?

8-9 Frisk, Inc. received a 60-day, 8% note for $6,000 on September 10 of this year.
(a) What is the maturity date of the note?
(b) What is the maturity value of the note?
(c) If Frisk, Inc. discounted the note at 9% at the bank on September 25, what would be the proceeds of the note?

8-10 On October 15 of this year, Kevin Warner discounted at the bank his own 120-day note for $5,400 at 10%.
(a) What is the maturity date of the note?
(b) What is the maturity value of the note?
(c) What are the proceeds of the note?

8-11 Why is a discounted customer's note a contingent liability of the endorser?

8-12 The maturity value of a $4,000 customer's note discounted by Hodge Company is $4,040. The customer dishonored the note, and the bank charged the $4,040 plus a $5 protest fee to Hodge's bank account. What entries should Hodge make to record these events?

8-13 Nesbit Company received a 120-day, 8% note for $15,000 on December 1. What adjusting entry is needed to accrue interest on December 31?

8-14 On December 11, Alison Corey discounted her own 60-day note for $2,000 at the bank at 9% and charged the discount to Discount on Notes Payable. What adjusting entry is necessary on December 31?

8-15 Allen Howe gave a creditor a 60-day, 9% note for $7,200 on December 11. What adjusting entry should Howe make on December 31?

EXERCISES

8-16 Nikel Company uses the allowance method of handling credit losses; it estimates losses at 1% of credit sales, which were $400,000 during the current year. On December 31 of the current year, the Accounts Receivable balance was $90,000 and the Allowance for Uncollectible Accounts had a credit balance of $500.
(a) Give the adjusting entry to record credit losses for the current year.
(b) Show how Accounts Receivable and the Allowance for Uncollectible Accounts would appear in the December 31 balance sheet.

8-17 Petty, Inc. analyzed its Accounts Receivable balances at December 31 and arrived at the aged balances listed below. The percentages of each age group that have proven uncollectible in the past are shown next to the aged balances.

Age	Loss (%)	Balance
Current	1	$ 70,000
30–60 days past due	2	20,000
61–120 days past due	8	5,000
121 days–6 months past due	15	6,000
Over 6 months past due	30	4,000
		$105,000

The company handles credit losses with the allowance method. The credit balance of the Allowance for Uncollectible Accounts is $600 on December 31 before any adjustments.

(a) Prepare the adjusting entry for estimated credit losses on December 31.

(b) Give the entry to write off the account of Lisa Wood in April of the following year, $500.

8–18 On March 10 of this year, Hooper Company determined that a $350 account receivable from Randy Dunham would not be collectible and wrote off the account. On November 18 of this year, Hooper received a $350 payment on the account from Dunham.

(a) Assume Hooper uses the allowance method of handling credit losses. Give the entries to record the write-off and the subsequent recovery of Dunham's account.

(b) Assume Hooper uses the direct write-off method of handling credit losses. Give the entries to record the write-off and the subsequent recovery of Dunham's account.

(c) Assume the payment from Dunham was received on February 5 of next year rather than November 18 of this year. Give the entries to record the write-off and subsequent recovery of Dunham's account under the allowance method.

(d) Assume the payment from Dunham was received on February 5 of next year rather than November 18 of this year. Give the entries to record the write-off and subsequent recovery of Dunham's account under the direct write-off method.

8–19 For each of the following notes, determine the maturity date and compute the interest, using the 60-day, 6% method.

Date of Note	Principal	Interest Rate (%)	Term
(a) May 6	$4,750	6	60 days
(b) June 25	3,000	8	90 days
(c) July 17	1,600	9	75 days
(d) September 8	4,400	9	120 days
(e) October 1	9,000	12	42 days

8–20 Record the following transactions on the books of both Manhart Company and Cain, Inc.:

Oct.   1   Cain, Inc. gave Manhart Company an $8,000, 90-day, 8% note in payment of account.

     31   Manhart Company discounted the note at the bank at a 10% discount rate.

Dec. 30   On the maturity date of the note, Cain, Inc. paid the amount due.

8–21 Suppose that, in Exercise 8–20, Cain, Inc. dishonored its note and the bank notified Manhart Company that it had charged the maturity value plus a $5 protest fee to Manhart Company's bank account. What entries should Manhart Company make on the maturity date?

8–22 On October 12, Samson Company discounted its own $4,500, 120-day note at the bank at 8%.

(a) What is the maturity date of the note?

(b) What are the proceeds of the note?

(c) What amount of interest expense should be recorded as an adjustment at December 31?

(d) What will be the balance in the Discount on Notes Payable account at December 31?

(e) What is the effective interest rate on the note?

8-23 The following note transactions occurred on the dates indicated for the Golden Company during the current year.

Nov. 16   Golden received a 90-day, 8% note for $7,500 from North Company.

Dec.   6   Golden discounted its own 90-day, $4,000 note at the bank at 9%, charging the discount to Discount on Notes Payable.

      19   Golden gave Sloan, Inc. a $3,000, 8%, 60-day note in payment of account.

Give the general journal entries necessary to adjust the interest accounts at December 31.

8-24 Compute the interest accrued on each of the following notes receivable held by Arrow, Inc. on December 31, 19X6:

Maker	Date of Note	Principal	Interest Rate (%)	Term
Gaines	11/21/X6	$3,600	10	120 days
Black	12/13/X6	6,000	9	90 days
Carnes	12/16/X6	1,500	8	60 days

PROBLEMS

8-25 The Laker Company, which has been in business for three years, makes all sales on account and does not offer cash discounts. The firm's credit sales, collections from customers, and write-offs of uncollectible accounts for the three-year period are summarized below:

Year	Sales	Collections	Accounts Written Off
1	$250,000	$243,000	$1,500
2	370,000	365,000	2,700
3	410,000	402,000	3,000

REQUIRED

(a) If Laker Company had been following the *direct write-off* method of recognizing credit losses during the three years, what amount of Accounts Receivable would appear on the firm's balance sheet at the end of the third year? What total amount of uncollectible accounts expense would have appeared on the firm's income statement during the three-year period?

(b) If Laker Company had been on an *allowance* method of recognizing credit losses and had been providing for such losses at the rate of 1% of sales, what amounts of Accounts Receivable and Allowance for Uncollectible Accounts would appear on the firm's balance sheet at the end of the third year? What total amount of uncollectible accounts expense would have appeared on the firm's income statement during the three-year period?

(c) Comment on the use of the 1% rate to provide for losses in (b).

8-26 At the beginning of the current year, Overton, Inc. had the following accounts on its books:

Accounts Receivable	$50,000 (debit)
Allowance for Uncollectible Accounts	$ 1,400 (credit)

During this year, credit sales were $100,000 and collections on account were $105,000. The following transactions, among others, occurred during the year:

Feb. 17   Wrote off the account of R. Badger, $200.

May 28   Wrote off the account of T. Evans, $400.

Oct. 13   T. Evans paid $120 in final settlement of the account written off on May 28. He is in bankruptcy proceedings. This amount is not included in the $105,000 collections.

Dec. 15   Wrote off the account of B. Tract, $500.

     31   Recorded, in an adjusting entry, the provision for uncollectible accounts at $\frac{3}{4}$% of credit sales for the year.

REQUIRED

(a) Prepare entries in general journal form to record the credit sales, the collections on account, and the transactions shown for the various dates above.

(b) Show how Accounts Receivable and the Allowance for Uncollectible Accounts would appear in the balance sheet at December 31.

8-27 At December 31 of the current year, the Viking Company had a balance of $90,000 in its Accounts Receivable account and a credit balance of $800 in the Allowance for Uncollectible Accounts. The Accounts Receivable subsidiary balances consisted of $94,000 in debit balances and $4,000 in credit balances. The company has aged its accounts as follows:

Current	$76,000
0–60 days past due	9,000
61–180 days past due	6,000
over 6 months past due	3,000
	$94,000

In the past, the company has experienced losses as follows: 1% of current balances, 5% of balances 0–60 days past due, 15% of balances 61–180 days past due, and 25% of balances over six months past due. The company bases its provision for credit losses on the aging analysis.

REQUIRED

(a) Prepare the adjusting journal entry to record the provision for credit losses for the year.

(b) Show how Accounts Receivable (including the credit balances) and Allowance for Uncollectible Accounts would appear in the December 31 balance sheet.

8-28 The Spartan Company had the following transactions for the years 19X1 and 19X2:

19X1

April 18   Discounted its own $10,000, 120-day note at the bank at 9%.

Aug. 16   Paid the bank the amount due from the loan of April 18.

Nov. 1   Discounted its own $6,000, 90-day note at the bank at 10%.

Dec. 31   Made the appropriate adjusting entry for interest expense.

19X2

Jan. 30   Paid the bank the amount due from the loan of November 1.

REQUIRED

(a) Record the above transactions and adjustment in general journal form.

(b) Compute the effective interest rate on the loan of:
   (1) April 18.
   (2) November 1.

8-29 The Bigg Company had the following transactions during the current year:

Mar. 3   Received a $4,800, 45-day, 9% note from C. Davis in payment of account.

24   Wrote off the $200 account of V. Lake, a customer, against the Allowance for Uncollectible Accounts.

Apr. 17   C. Davis paid note in full.

Oct. 10   Gave a $5,400, 60-day, 8% note to J. Riggans in payment of account.

18   V. Lake paid account that had been written off on March 24.

Dec. 4   Discounted its own $10,000, 90-day note at the bank at 10%.

9   Paid principal and interest due on note to J. Riggans.

16   Received a $6,000, 60-day, 8% note from P. Kolb on account.

REQUIRED

(a) Record the above transactions in general journal form.

(b) Make any necessary adjusting entries for interest at December 31.

8-30 Cherokee, Inc. began business on January 1 of the current year. Certain of its transactions for the current year are given below.

May 1   Borrowed $25,000 from the bank on a six-month, 9% note, interest to be paid at maturity.

June 13   Received a $4,000, 60-day, 9% note on account from Jean Nance.

28   Discounted Nance's note at the bank at 10%.

Aug. 12   Jean Nance paid her note, with interest, to the bank.

Sept. 1   Received an $8,000, 90-day, $7\frac{1}{2}$% note from Bruce Handy on account.

19   Discounted Handy's note at the bank at 10%.

Nov. 1   Paid May 1 note and interest due bank.

21   Discounted its own $7,000, 120-day note at the bank at 9%.

30   The bank notified Cherokee, Inc. that Bruce Handy's note was dishonored. Maturity value of the note plus a $6 protest fee was charged against Cherokee's checking account at the bank.

Dec. 8 Wrote off the account of Handy as uncollectible. Cherokee, Inc. uses the allowance method of providing for credit losses.

16 Received a $12,000, 90-day, 8% note from Perry Jarr on account.

31 Recorded its expected credit losses for the year by an adjusting entry. Write-offs of accounts during this first year have created a debit balance in the Allowance for Uncollectible Accounts of $8,500. Analysis of aged receivables indicates that the desired balance of the allowance account is $1,100.

31 Made the appropriate adjusting entries for interest.

REQUIRED

Record the foregoing transactions and adjustments in general journal form.

 8-31 At December 31, 1980, Landcraft Company held a note receivable and a note payable. At December 31, 1981, Landcraft again held one note receivable and one note payable. The notes are described below.

	Dated	Principal	Interest Rate (%)	Term
December 31, 1980				
Note Receivable	11/25/80	$4,000	$10\frac{1}{2}$	90 days
Note Payable	12/16/80	8,400	10	30 days
December 31, 1981				
Note Receivable	12/11/81	3,000	12	60 days
Note Payable	12/7/81	6,000	$11\frac{1}{2}$	120 days

REQUIRED

(a) Assume that the appropriate adjusting entries were made at December 31, 1980, but that no reversing or adjusting entries were made in 1981. Give the journal entries to record payment of the notes that were outstanding December 31, 1980.

(b) Assume that the appropriate adjusting entries were made at December 31, 1980. However, no reversing or adjusting entries were made in 1981, and the bookkeeper neglected to consider the related interest receivable and interest payable when the notes were paid in 1981. Make the necessary adjusting entries for interest at December 31, 1981.

ALTERNATE PROBLEMS

8-26A At January 1 of the current year, Thoroseal, Inc. had the following accounts on its books:

Accounts Receivable	$75,000 (debit)
Allowance for Uncollectible Accounts	$ 1,800 (credit)

During this year, credit sales were $175,000 and collections on account were $165,000. The following transactions, among others, occurred during the year:

Jan. 11 Wrote off the account of R. Brent, $700.

Apr. 29 Wrote off the account of F. Logan, $600.

Nov. 15 F. Logan paid debt of $600, written off April 29. This amount is not included in the $165,000 collections.

Dec. 5 Wrote off the account of D. Nelson, $800.

31 Recorded, in an adjusting entry, the provision for uncollectible accounts at 1% of credit sales for the year.

REQUIRED

(a) Prepare entries in general journal form to record the credit sales, the collections on account, and the transactions shown for the various dates above.

(b) Show how Accounts Receivable and the Allowance for Uncollectible Accounts would appear in the balance sheet at December 31.

8-27A At December 31 of the current year, the Aquarius Company had a balance of $70,000 in its Accounts Receivable account and a credit balance of $400 in the Allowance for Uncollectible Accounts. The Accounts Receivable subsidiary balances consisted of $72,500 in debit balances and $2,500 in credit balances. The company has aged its accounts as follows:

Current	$60,000
0–60 days past due	7,000
61–180 days past due	4,000
over 6 months past due	1,500
	$72,500

In the past, the company has experienced losses as follows: 1% of current balances, 4% of balances 0–60 days past due, 10% of balances 61–180 days past due, and 30% of balances more than six months past due. The company bases its provision for credit losses on the aging analysis.

REQUIRED

(a) Prepare the adjusting journal entry to record the provision for credit losses for the year.

(b) Show how Accounts Receivable (including the credit balances) and Allowance for Uncollectible Accounts would appear in the December 31 balance sheet.

8-28A The Lyon Corporation had the following transactions for the years 19X3 and 19X4:

19X3

Feb. 6 Sold $1,800 worth of merchandise to B. Cleary and received a $1,800, 45-day, 8% note.

21 Discounted the note of B. Cleary at the bank at 10%.

Mar. 23 Cleary paid the bank the amount due on the note of February 6.

Dec. 11 Received a $2,000, 60-day, 9% note from J. Jackson in settlement of an open account.

31 Made the appropriate adjusting entry for interest income.

19X4

Jan. 1 Reversed the December 31 adjustment for interest income.

Feb. 9 Received payment from Jackson on the note of December 11.

REQUIRED

(a) Record the above transactions, adjustment, and reversal in general journal form.

(b) Assume Lyon Corporation does not make reversing entries. Give the entry to record the receipt of the note payment from Jackson on February 9, 19X4.

8–29A The Cheyenne Company had the following transactions during the current year:

July 15 Received a $3,600, 90-day, 7% note from R. Owens in payment of account.

Sept. 5 Wrote off the $400 account of B. Judd, a customer, against the Allowance for Uncollectible Accounts.

Oct. 3 Gave a $4,800, 60-day, 8% note to M. Lockwood in payment of account.

13 R. Owens paid note in full.

21 B. Judd paid account that had been written off on September 5.

Dec. 1 Discounted its own $9,000, 90-day note at the bank at 8%.

2 Paid principal and interest due on note to M. Lockwood.

19 Received a $3,000, 60-day, 7% note from E. Hull on account.

REQUIRED

(a) Record the above transactions in general journal form.

(b) Make any necessary adjusting entries for interest at December 31.

8–30A Century, Inc. began business on January 1 of the current year. Several of its transactions for the current year are given below:

Mar. 1 Borrowed $15,000 from the bank on a five-month, 8% note, interest to be paid at maturity.

May 2 Received a $12,000, 60-day, 6% note on account from John Andrews.

14 Discounted Andrews' note at the bank at 8%.

July 1 John Andrews paid his note, with interest, to the bank.

1 Received a $4,800, 60-day, $7\frac{1}{2}$% note from Linda Miller on account.

21 Discounted Miller's note at the bank at 7%.

Aug. 1 Paid March 1 note and interest due bank.

30 The bank notified Century, Inc. that Linda Miller's note was dishonored. Maturity value of the note plus a $5 protest fee was charged against Century's checking account at the bank.

Dec. 1 Discounted its own $3,000, 120-day note at bank at 8%.

9 Wrote off the account of Miller as uncollectible. Century, Inc. is on the allowance method of providing for credit losses.

11 Received an $8,000, 90-day, 9% note from Len Wood on account.

31 Recorded its expected credit losses for the year by an adjusting entry. The Allowance for Uncollectible Accounts has a debit balance of $5,100 as a result of write-offs of accounts during this first year.

Analysis of aged receivables indicates that the desired balance of the allowance account is $2,000.

Dec. 31 Made the appropriate adjusting entries for interest.

REQUIRED
Record the foregoing transactions and adjustments in general journal form.

BUSINESS DECISION PROBLEM

The latest income statement of Sunshine Wholesale Company is shown below. For several years, Alton Fromm, president of the firm, has been dissatisfied with his firm's rate of growth. He believes that if Sunshine's sales promotion and credit policies were liberalized, gross sales could be increased substantially. Specifically, Fromm is fairly confident that gross sales could be increased by 30% if the firm adopted the following plan:
(1) Make certain changes in the firm's schedule of trade discounts. This would reduce somewhat the average selling price of merchandise, but it would increase sales volume.
(2) Extend credit to an additional number of less "select" customers.

Sunshine Wholesale Company
Income Statement
For the Year Ended December 31, 19XX

Sales	$500,000	
Less: Sales Discounts	10,000	
Net Sales	$490,000	100%
Cost of Goods Sold	318,500	65
Gross Profit on Sales	$171,500	35%
Selling Expenses (excluding uncollectible accounts expense)	$122,500	25%
Uncollectible Accounts Expense	5,000	1
Administrative Expenses	25,000	5
Total Expenses	$152,500	31%
Net Income	$ 19,000	4%

An analyst for Sunshine has reviewed Fromm's proposal to increase gross sales by 30% for its likely impact on other income statement items. His comments are as follows:

Sales Discounts—The firm has been selling to selected retailers on terms of 3/15, n/30, with about two-thirds of total sales subject to the discount. Even with an increased number of customers, two-thirds of total sales are still expected to be subject to the discount.

Cost of Goods Sold—The slight decline in average selling prices of merchandise will cause cost of goods sold to increase, as a percentage of net sales, from 65% to $66\frac{2}{3}\%$.

Selling Expenses—Excluding uncollectible accounts expense, selling expenses are expected to remain at 25% of net sales.

Uncollectible Accounts Expense—Uncollectible accounts expense has been about 1% of gross sales for several years. The proposed liberalization of credit policies will cause this expense to increase to 2% of gross sales.

Administrative Expenses—These expenses of $25,000 are expected to remain constant even if gross sales increase.

REQUIRED

Prepare an income statement based on Fromm's proposal and the analyst's comments; based on your results, decide whether the firm should adopt Fromm's proposal.

9
Inventories

Virtually all firms find it necessary to invest in and carry inventories of a wide variety of items that they either use in their operations or sell to customers. Although most firms maintain inventories such as office and operating supplies, we are most interested in inventories of merchandise that is to be sold. To a great extent, the concepts, problems, and solution techniques we consider are applicable to all inventories regardless of their particular size or special purpose.

In earlier chapters we introduced the special source documents, business transactions, and accounting techniques related to routine inventory transactions. Now our objective is to build on those earlier chapters by briefly considering the basic notions of inventories, examining and illustrating the problems of inventory determination, and comparing the consequences for periodic income determination of various inventory pricing methods.

REVIEW OF BASIC CONCEPTS

Before discussing new material, let us review some of the pertinent concepts that were studied earlier.

We defined merchandise inventory as all merchandise owned by the company and held for resale to customers in the ordinary course of business. Inventories are classified as current assets, because they typically will be sold within a year, or during a firm's normal operating cycle if it should be longer than a year. For retailing firms, inventories are often the largest or most valuable current asset.

When we speak of inventory costs, we mean all costs necessary to acquire the merchandise and bring it to the site of sale. Inventory costs include the purchase price, plus any transportation or freight in, less purchase returns or allowances and purchase discounts.

The cost of goods sold is the net acquisition cost of the goods sold to customers in generating the sales revenues of the operating period. The following is a typical example of the computation of the cost of goods sold:

Beginning Inventory			$10,000
Add: Net Purchases			
Purchases		$31,000	
Less: Purchases Returns and Allowances	$2,100		
Purchases Discounts	400	2,500	
		$28,500	
Add: Transportation In		500	
Net Purchases			29,000
Cost of Goods Available for Sale			$39,000
Less: Ending Inventory			9,000
Cost of Goods Sold			$30,000

THE NEED FOR INVENTORIES

Most well-managed companies find it necessary and desirable to maintain large, varied inventories. Your personal experience as a consumer probably confirms the favorable buyer reaction to the availability of a wide assortment of colors, sizes, qualities, and types of the goods for which you shop. The prevailing affluence of our society and the related buyer habits, now considered customary, have probably made large, varied inventories an operating necessity for most retail firms.

Other business factors can justify the existence of relatively large inventories. Clearly, the only way a firm can sell more in a period than it can purchase or produce is by having beginning inventories. Beginning inventories are particularly important to seasonal industries or markets. The availability of attractive quantity discounts may justify a firm's buying in excess of its current sales requirements and therefore creating additional inventories. Strategic purchase situations offer still another reason for carrying inventories. Many firms—especially those that sell in seasonal markets—buy in excess of their needs when supply prices are favorable. They store the goods for a period of time and can then maintain sales during a period of unfavorable supply prices.

While progressive firms will take into account customer preferences and competitors' merchandising patterns as well as favorable market situations in determining inventory size and balance, they must also consider the costs of carrying large inventories. Often, savings obtained by purchasing in large quantities or under favorable market conditions may be more than offset by increased carrying costs. When large inventories are carried, storage and handling costs can mount. In addition, the firm may become vulnerable to losses from inventory deterioration and obsolescence. Finally, inventories tie up working capital that might be used more profitably elsewhere.

EXHIBIT 9–1
Relationship of Inventory Measurements to Reported Income

Assumed Data	Amount (in Thousands of Dollars)			
	A	B	C	D
Sales	$25	$25	$25	$25
Beginning inventory	3	3	3	3
Purchases	20	20	20	20
Goods available for sale	$23	$23	$23	$23
Ending inventory	4	5	6	7
Cost of goods sold	$19	$18	$17	$16
Reported Income	$ 6	$ 7	$ 8	$ 9

INCOME DETERMINATION
AND INVENTORY MEASUREMENT

Proper income determination depends on the appropriate measurement of all assets; the higher the asset amounts, the higher the income that will be reported. Because inventories are often relatively large and their size fluctuates, accounting correctly for inventories is important if net income is to be determined properly. Other things being equal, **changing the dollar amount of ending inventory changes net income dollar for dollar** (ignoring any income tax effects), as Exhibit 9–1 illustrates. Note that sales, beginning inventory, and purchases are identical in all four cases. As ending inventory increases by a given amount—$1,000 from A to B, $2,000 from B to D, for example—cost of goods sold decreases and income increases by the same amount.

Because of the role that inventory measurement plays in the determination of reported income, the accountant must be concerned with its problems, which we consider in the remainder of this chapter.

INVENTORY MEASUREMENT

The dollar amount of an inventory depends on two variables—quantity and price. We usually express inventories as the aggregate dollar value (quantity × price) of the goods on hand at a specific time. "Taking" an inventory consists of (1) counting the items involved, (2) pricing each item, and (3) summing the amounts. Exhibit 9–2 illustrates these three steps.

Inventory counts can be extremely complicated and expensive. Even moderate-sized firms may have thousands of items, hundreds of types, sizes, and

EXHIBIT 9-2
The Three Steps of Taking an Inventory

(1) Physical count		(2) Pricing	(3) Summation
Merchandise Item	Unit Count	Unit Price	Extension
A	3	$6	$18
B	4	7	28
C	5	8	40
			$86

qualities, purchased at a variety of unit prices and located in dozens of ware-houses, stores, branches, and departments. Proper planning and coordination are imperative if all items are to be counted, counted only once, and properly priced. Although some firms "close" for inventory-taking, many continue operations dur-ing the count and must, of course, know if sales during the inventory period were from counted or uncounted merchandise.

Another problem in inventory counts is deciding what goods should be counted. Often the proper inventory will not be simply "all merchandise on site." By definition, the inventory should include—and be limited to—those goods owned by the firm and *held* for resale. Thus, items that the firm has purchased but has not received (often called "goods in transit") should be included in the inventory count. As we indicated in Chapter 5, legal ownership depends on where title to the goods resides. A firm purchasing merchandise on terms of F.O.B. shipping point acquires title to the goods before it physically receives them.

Merchandise that has been sold to customers does not belong in the inven-tory count, even if it has not been removed from the store or warehouse. It is no longer owned by the firm nor held for resale. To include in the inventory count merchandise for which a sales transaction has been recorded overstates the in-ventory and therefore causes the firm's net income, assets, and owners' equity to be reported incorrectly. Similarly, goods held for resale that are on consignment from another firm are not included in the inventory count, because the goods are not owned by the firm holding them.

We see, therefore, that although a firm's ownership of merchandise often is indicated by the physical presence of goods, at times a firm can own goods that it has not yet received and not own goods that it still possesses.

INVENTORY PRICING METHODS

In general, inventories are priced at their cost. Inventory pricing is quite simple when acquisition prices remain constant. When prices for like items change dur-ing the accounting period, however, it is not always apparent which price should

be used to measure the ending inventory. Consequently, when cost prices fluctuate, one must either keep track of all costs for specific goods or else make simplifying assumptions about which goods have been sold and which goods are on
hand. The need for such assumptions has led to the several methods of inventory
pricing now in common use that we illustrate in this section. We illustrate a rising
price pattern because it is the most prevalent in our economy.

Two terms, "goods flow" and "cost flow," are useful in considering the problems of pricing inventories under fluctuating prices. We shall use goods flow to
describe the actual physical movement of goods in the operations of the firm.
Goods flow is a result of physical events. Cost flow is the real or *assumed* association of unit costs with goods either sold or on hand. We will discover that the
assumed cost flow does not always reflect the actual goods flow. Furthermore, the
use of an assumed cost flow that does *not* reflect the real goods flow is permitted
by generally accepted accounting principles. There is nothing illicit about this
practice; in fact, there are often compelling reasons for adopting it.

We shall introduce four generally acceptable methods of pricing inventories:
(1) specific identification, (2) weighted average, (3) first-in, first-out, and (4) last-in,
first-out. Again, the four methods illustrated are all based on historical costs. In
this section we shall concentrate primarily on the computational technique of
each method. A comparative evaluation is presented in the following section.

In order to more easily compare the four inventory methods, we shall illustrate all four with identical data. In each case, goods available for sale during the
period are as follows:

Beginning inventory	6 units @ $10 =	$ 60
Purchases:	10 units @ 11 =	110
	10 units @ 13 =	130
	4 units @ 15 =	60
Totals	30 units	$360

Thus, in each illustration:

(1) Beginning inventory is priced at $60.
(2) Three purchases are made during the period, as listed above.
(3) Goods available for sale during the period amount to 30 units at a total
cost of $360.

In each case, 22 units are sold during the period, leaving an ending inventory
of 8 units. The four inventory methods differ in the way in which they assign costs
to the units sold or to those remaining in inventory.

By assigning costs we are simply dividing the cost of the goods available for
sale between cost of goods sold and ending inventory. Therefore, we can compute
costs by:

(1) Pricing out *either* the cost of goods sold or the ending inventory.
(2) Subtracting the amount determined in step (1) from goods available for sale.
(3) Assigning the residual to the element not priced in (1).

It will usually be advantageous to price out the ending inventory (and assign the residual amount to cost of goods sold), because the ending inventory will involve fewer units than will cost of goods sold. One drawback to this shortcut approach is that certain types of errors are not as apparent because the residual is sort of a "plug figure." To make the following illustrations as clear as possible, we assign costs to both cost of goods sold and ending inventory.

Specific Identification

The specific identification method involves (1) keeping track of the purchase price of each specific unit, (2) knowing which specific units were sold, and (3) pricing the ending inventory at the actual prices of the specific units not sold. As you can easily imagine, this approach is not practical for merchandise having large unit volumes and a small unit price. Many accounting students think that specific identification comes close to being the "precise" way of evaluating inventory because the actual unit costs are attached to a given inventory. We shall see, however, that there is compelling justification for other inventory pricing methods.

Assume that the eight unsold units consist of two units from the beginning inventory, one unit from each of the first two purchases, and all four of the last units purchased. The costs to be assigned to the ending inventory and cost of goods sold are as shown in Exhibit 9–3.

Note that the full 30 units and the full $360 cost of the goods available have been accounted for as either ending inventory or cost of goods sold.

EXHIBIT 9–3
Specific Identification Inventory Pricing

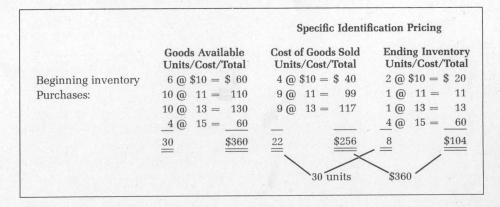

	Goods Available Units/Cost/Total	Specific Identification Pricing	
		Cost of Goods Sold Units/Cost/Total	Ending Inventory Units/Cost/Total
Beginning inventory	6 @ $10 = $ 60	4 @ $10 = $ 40	2 @ $10 = $ 20
Purchases:	10 @ 11 = 110	9 @ 11 = 99	1 @ 11 = 11
	10 @ 13 = 130	9 @ 13 = 117	1 @ 13 = 13
	4 @ 15 = 60		4 @ 15 = 60
	30 $360	22 $256	8 $104

30 units $360

EXHIBIT 9–4
Weighted Average Inventory Pricing

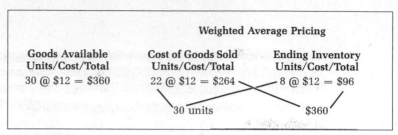

	Weighted Average Pricing	
Goods Available Units/Cost/Total	Cost of Goods Sold Units/Cost/Total	Ending Inventory Units/Cost/Total
30 @ $12 = $360	22 @ $12 = $264	8 @ $12 = $96
	30 units	$360

Weighted Average
The weighted average method spreads the total dollar cost of the goods available equally among all units. In our illustration, this is $360/30 or $12 per unit. Exhibit 9–4 diagrams the assignment of costs.

Note again that both the units and costs associated with goods available are fully accounted for.

Observe that it would be incorrect to use a *simple* average of the prices. The average price paid is ($10 + $11 + $13 + $15)/4 = $12.25; this fails to take into account the different numbers of units available at the various prices. The simple average yields the same figure as the weighted average only when the same number of units were purchased at each price.

First-In, First-Out (FIFO)
First-in, first-out (FIFO) pricing assumes that the oldest goods on hand (or earliest purchased) are sold first. Thus, ending inventories are always made up of the most recent purchases. Under FIFO, the only time that goods in the beginning inventory can also be in the ending inventory is when the number of units sold is less than the number of units in the beginning inventory. A FIFO approach would result in the cost allocations shown in Exhibit 9–5.

EXHIBIT 9–5
First-In, First-Out Inventory Pricing

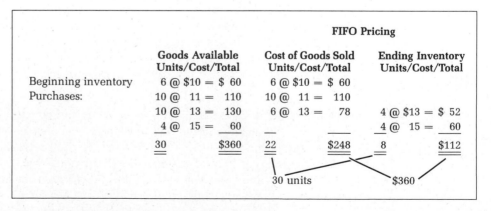

	Goods Available Units/Cost/Total	Cost of Goods Sold Units/Cost/Total	Ending Inventory Units/Cost/Total
Beginning inventory	6 @ $10 = $ 60	6 @ $10 = $ 60	
Purchases:	10 @ 11 = 110	10 @ 11 = 110	
	10 @ 13 = 130	6 @ 13 = 78	4 @ $13 = $ 52
	4 @ 15 = 60		4 @ 15 = 60
	30 $360	22 $248	8 $112
		30 units	$360

EXHIBIT 9–6
Last-In, First-Out Inventory Pricing

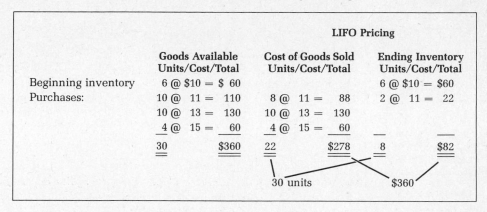

	Goods Available Units/Cost/Total	Cost of Goods Sold Units/Cost/Total	Ending Inventory Units/Cost/Total
Beginning inventory	6 @ $10 = $ 60		6 @ $10 = $60
Purchases:	10 @ 11 = 110	8 @ 11 = 88	2 @ 11 = 22
	10 @ 13 = 130	10 @ 13 = 130	
	4 @ 15 = 60	4 @ 15 = 60	
	30 $360	22 $278	8 $82

30 units $360

This method assumes the first 22 units acquired are sold and the last eight units are still on hand. Note the continued full consideration of the units and costs associated with goods available for sale.

Last-In,
First-Out (LIFO)

The **last-in, first-out (LIFO)** approach uses the frequently artificial assumption that the most recent purchases are sold first. Thus, unless sales exceed purchases, the beginning inventory remains on hand as part of the ending inventory. Exhibit 9–6 shows how this method works.

COMPARATIVE ANALYSIS
OF INVENTORY PRICING METHODS

Our objective in this section is to explore the effects of and reasons for using the various inventory pricing techniques just illustrated.

Variations in
Income Patterns

For comparative purposes, let us assume that the 22 units in the above illustration were sold for $20 each. Exhibit 9–7 shows the differences between gross profit figures resulting from each of the inventory pricing techniques. Remember that these differences in reported income do not arise from any difference in the physical flows but simply result from assumptions made about the flow of costs. Net income will also reflect the differences if operating expenses are equal in each case.

Assumed
Cost Flows

The specific identification approach to inventory most naturally fits operations that involve somewhat differentiated products of a relatively high unit value. New automobiles and construction equipment are good examples of merchandise that would justify the cost of maintaining the price of each inventory unit and specifically identifying each sale. Specific identification is not feasible where products are of a low unit value and involve large volumes.

EXHIBIT 9–7
Differential Gross Margins on Sales Based on
Various Inventory Pricing Methods

| | Inventory Pricing Techniques | | | |
	Sp. Id.	Average	FIFO	LIFO
Sales (22 units @ $20)	$440	$440	$440	$440
Beginning inventory	60	60	60	60
Total purchases	300	300	300	300
Goods available	$360	$360	$360	$360
Less: Ending inventories				
(See earlier computations)	104	96	112	82
Cost of goods sold	$256	$264	$248	$278
Gross profit on sales	$184	$176	$192	$162
Increased gross profit				
compared to LIFO	$22	$14	$30	

Specific identification offers a limited potential for income manipulation. To the degree that like units of inventory are available at various cost figures, one can maximize reported income by "choosing" to sell the unit with the lowest cost. Income could be minimized by choosing to sell the unit with the highest cost.

The weighted average approach to inventory measurement is best suited to operations that involve a large volume of undifferentiated goods stored in common areas. Liquid fuels, grains, and other commodities are good examples. The weighted average cost represents to some degree all the various costs experienced in accumulating the goods currently on hand. Consequently, weighted average costs typically fall between the extreme cost figures that can result from other methods.

Most companies—especially those with perishable or style-affected goods—as a matter of good business attempt to sell the oldest merchandise first. This is especially true of companies dealing in foods, certain chemicals, or drugs. In these cases, FIFO most nearly matches the flow of costs to the probable flow of goods.

Finding an example of business operations in which LIFO represents the natural flow of goods is more difficult. Purchases of coal or a similar commodity may all be dumped onto the same pile from an overhead trestle, and sales may be taken from the top of the pile by a crane. If beginning inventories have been maintained or increased, we must conclude that the firm still has its original purchases in inventory. In this case, LIFO represents the actual flow of goods. Although it does not do so for most businesses, it has been estimated that more than 50% of major businesses use LIFO to price some of their inventories. We shall explore the reasons for this choice later in this chapter.

In summary:

(1) Specific identification, in a physical sense, best presents actual cost of goods sold.

(2) Weighted average can be associated with certain types of business operations where like goods are commingled.

(3) FIFO probably represents most accurately the actual flow of goods for most firms.

(4) Although LIFO presents the least plausible flow of goods for most businesses, it is used by many major firms.

MATCHING OF COSTS AND REVENUES   Because the use of FIFO and LIFO can result in extreme differences in times of changing prices (see Exhibit 9-7), let us examine the effects of using these two methods.

Consider the data below, taken from our earlier computations, which show that FIFO matches the older costs against current revenues and LIFO matches the most recent costs against current revenues. Under FIFO, therefore, the ending inventory is measured at relatively recent prices, whereas under LIFO, the ending inventory amount reflects older prices.

	Units/Cost/Total
Beginning inventory	6 @ $10 = $ 60
Purchases:	10 @ 11 = 110
	10 @ 13 = 130
	4 @ 15 = 60

FIFO	**LIFO**
Cost of goods sold: $248 (oldest 22 units)	Cost of goods sold: $278 (latest 22 units)
Ending inventory: $112 (latest 8 units)	Ending inventory: $82 (oldest 8 units)

Most accountants agree that when prices are rising, FIFO tends to overstate income, because older and lower unit costs are included in cost of goods sold and matched against current sales prices. In other words, in our example, some of the units sold are charged to cost of goods sold at unit costs of $10, $11, and $13. If our latest purchases are indicative of current acquisition prices, then the units sold must be replaced by units costing $15 (or more if prices continue to rise). Thus one can argue that when prices rise, LIFO better matches current costs against current revenues, because the most recent purchases are reflected as cost of goods sold.

It is true, however, that while LIFO associates the current, more significant, unit prices with cost of goods sold, it consequently prices the ending inventory at the older, less realistic unit prices. Because of this, the LIFO inventory figure on the balance sheet often becomes quite meaningless in terms of current cost prices. As we noted earlier, when inventory quantities are maintained or increased, the LIFO method prevents the older prices from appearing in the cost of goods sold. No doubt, some firms still carry LIFO inventories at unit prices that prevailed more than 25 years ago.

We can use a highly simplified example to illustrate how one can at least reduce the undesirable effects of "phantom profits" that result from the use of FIFO in times of rising prices. The same computations will show a related tax advantage of using LIFO during such periods.

Assume that a firm has an opening inventory of five units costing $500 each. The firm sells five units for $750 each and replaces its inventory by purchasing five units just after their price has been raised from $500 to $625 per unit. All transactions are for cash and, for simplicity, it is also assumed that operating expenses are zero and the applicable income tax rate is 50%. Exhibit 9–8 shows how FIFO produces an element of phantom profit that is avoided under LIFO and also shows the tax benefit of LIFO when purchase prices are rising.

Note that under FIFO, even though $625 of after-tax net income is reported, the amount of cash from sales is only enough to replace the inventory sold and pay the income tax on the $1,250 of pretax income. Thus, the net income of $625 is not realized in cash that can be declared as dividends or reinvested in the business and is considered *phantom profit*. One can easily imagine how the phantom profit element could cause problems in the manager's planning of dividend policy and the use of net income as a source of capital investments.

When prices rise, LIFO's tax benefit is simple and obvious. Under LIFO, inventories are measured at older (lower) prices. This causes cost of goods sold to increase and net income (and therefore income taxes payable) to decrease. Use of LIFO in times of *falling* prices, however, can have quite the opposite tax consequence.

EXHIBIT 9–8
FIFO-LIFO Comparison: Phantom Profit Effect and Tax Benefit

	FIFO		LIFO	
	Income Statement	Cash In (Out)	Income Statement	Cash In (Out)
Sales (5 @ $750)	$3,750	$3,750	$3,750	$3,750
Cost of goods sold:				
Beginning inventories (5 @ $500)	$2,500		$2,500	
Purchases (5 @ $625)	3,125	(3,125)	3,125	(3,125)
Goods available (10 units)	$5,625		$5,625	
Ending inventory:				
5 @ FIFO	3,125			
5 @ LIFO			2,500	
Cost of goods sold	$2,500		$3,125	
Pretax income	$1,250		$ 625	
Income tax at 50%	625	(625)	312	(312)
Net after-tax income	$ 625		$ 313	
Net cash proceeds		$ 0		$ 313

Disclosure

A firm's financial statements should disclose the methods used in pricing inventories. This is often done in footnotes to the financial statements or parenthetically within the appropriate section of the statements.

LIFO DISCLOSURES

The footnotes to financial statements generally contain additional information about the accounting for a company's inventories. A few examples of these disclosures are presented below.

During the 1970s, a number of companies switched to the LIFO method, primarily to reduce their phantom (inventory) profits during inflation and to generate greater cash flows due to smaller income tax liabilities. The change usually had a significant impact on net income and the inventory amount in the balance sheet. Here is how Ford Motor Company described its change in 1976:

In 1976, the Company changed its method of accounting from First-In, First-Out (FIFO) to Last-In, First-Out (LIFO) for most of its U.S. inventories. The cost of the remaining inventories is determined substantially on a FIFO basis. Under LIFO, the cost of goods sold is based on the most recent prices for raw material and other inventory items. The change reflects earnings more realistically by matching current costs with current revenues.

The change to LIFO reduced net income in 1976 by $81 million or 86¢ a share. . . . If the FIFO method of inventory accounting had been used by the Company, inventories at December 31, 1976 would have been $166 million higher than reported.[1]

One of the risks of using LIFO during inflationary periods is that, in any given year, the amount of inventory on hand may be reduced, resulting in unusually low costs (incurred in prior years) being charged to cost of goods sold. In 1977, for example, Exxon Corporation's net income was increased by approximately $110 million as a result of a reduction in its LIFO inventory quantities during the year. Celanese Corporation had a similar event occur in 1977 and described it as follows:

The LIFO method of valuation was adopted for substantially all North American inventories beginning in 1974. During 1977, there was a reduction in some inventories carried at LIFO costs that were lower than 1977 costs. This resulted in an increase in net income of $1 million or 7¢ per share. The comparable amounts for both 1975 and 1976 were $3 million or 23¢ per share.[2]

LIFO inventory amounts may be considerably less than inventory amounts computed under FIFO. Companies may disclose the difference in their footnotes, as illustrated by Johnson & Johnson's footnote in its January 1, 1978 annual report:

The following inventory amounts have been valued using the methods noted:

	1977	1976
LIFO method	$169,008,000	$137,299,000
FIFO method	333,532,000	318,871,000
Total	$502,540,000	$456,170,000

If all inventories were valued on the FIFO basis, total inventories would have been $568,909,000 and $506,945,000 at January 1, 1978 and January 2, 1977, respectively.[3]

[1]Ford Motor Company, *Annual Report*, 1976, p. 34.
[2]Celanese Corporation, *Annual Report*, 1977, p. 45.
[3]Johnson & Johnson, *Annual Report*, 1978, p. 32.

DEPARTURES FROM COST

Inventories are generally measured at cost. They may be reduced below cost, however, if there is evidence that the utility of inventory has fallen below cost. Such *inventory write-downs* may occur when (1) merchandise must be sold at reduced prices because it is damaged or otherwise not in normal salable condition, or (2) the cost of replacing items in the ending inventory has declined below their recorded cost.

Net Realizable Value

Damaged, physically deteriorated, or obsolete merchandise should be measured and reported at **net realizable value** when this value is less than cost. Net realizable value is the estimated selling price less the expected costs of disposal. For example, assume that an inventory item cost $300, but, because it is damaged, can be sold for only $200. Related selling costs are estimated at $20. We should write down the item to $180 ($200 estimated selling price less $20 estimated disposal cost) and reflect a $120 loss for this period.

Lower of Cost or Market

The **lower of cost or market (LCM) rule** provides for the recognition of a loss from a price decline on new inventory items. The rule causes the loss to be reported in the period when the price decline occurs, rather than during a subsequent period of sale. Market is defined as the current replacement cost of the merchandise. If applicable, the LCM rule simply measures inventory at the lower (replacement) market figure. Consequently, reported income is decreased by the amount that the ending inventory has been written down. When the ending inventory becomes part of the cost of goods sold in a future period of lower selling prices, the fact that the carrying value has been reduced in the period of price decline helps maintain normal profit margins in the period of sale.

To illustrate, assume an inventory item with a cost of $80 has been selling for $100 during the year, yielding a gross profit of 20% of sales. At year-end, the replacement cost of the good has dropped to $60, a 25% decline, and a proportionate reduction in the selling price to $75 is expected. In this case, the inventory would be written down to the replacement cost of $60, reducing net income by the $20 loss this period. When the good is sold in a subsequent period for $75, a normal gross profit of 20% of sales will be reported ($75 − $60 = $15 gross profit).

Because of the scale and complexity of modern markets, not all declines in replacement prices are followed by proportionate declines in selling prices. In these cases, the application of the LCM rule is modified as follows:

(1) If selling price is not expected to drop, inventory may be carried at cost even though it exceeds replacement cost. Using the above example, assume the selling price is expected to stay at $100 even though the replacement cost drops to $60. In this case, there is no need to write down the inventory.

(2) If selling price is expected to decline—but less than proportionately to the decline in replacement cost—inventory need be written down only to the extent necessary to maintain a normal gross profit in the period of sale. Referring again to the above example, assume the selling price is expected to drop from $100 to $90 when the replacement cost declines to $60. In this case, inventory would be written down to $72, an amount that maintains a 20% gross profit when the good is sold ($90 − $72 = $18 gross profit).

One may apply the LCM rule to (1) each item in the inventory, or (2) the totals of major classes or categories of inventory, or (3) the total inventory. The following simple illustration shows the application of two of these alternatives and indicates that the inventory amount obtained depends on how the rule is applied.

| Inventory Item | Quantity | Unit Price | | Inventory Amounts | | |
		Cost	Market	Cost	Market	LCM (by Item)
A	4	$4	$3	$16	$12	$12
B	3	6	7	18	21	18
				$34	$33	$30

If we applied LCM to the total inventory, our result would be $33. Applied by item, however, we find the LCM amount to be $30. Although the item by item procedure is most commonly used, either way is acceptable. The method selected should be used consistently. One can find inventory market values in such sources as current price catalogs, purchase contracts with suppliers, and other forms of price quotations.

ESTIMATING INVENTORIES

There are several good reasons for estimating inventories. Because it may be impractical to take physical inventory counts when interim financial statements are prepared, an estimate will be sufficient. The adequacy of inventory insurance coverage may be determined on the basis of an inventory estimate. Finally, an estimate may be necessary to determine the loss from merchandise destroyed by fire. Therefore, it will be useful for us to examine some methods for estimating inventories.

Gross Profit Method

Suppose that over the past three years a company's gross profit averaged 30% of net sales. Assume also that the net sales for the interim period are $80,000, the inventory at the beginning of the period was $20,000, and net purchases for the period are $50,000. Exhibit 9–9 (page 328) shows the analysis that can be made to estimate the ending inventory.

This type of analysis, sometimes called the **gross profit method** of estimating inventories, is merely a rearrangement of the cost of goods sold section of the income statement. For the gross profit method to be valid, the gross profit percentage must be representative of the merchandising activities leading up to the time when the inventory is estimated.

EXHIBIT 9–9
Gross Profit Method of Estimating Inventory

Beginning inventory		$20,000
Net purchases		50,000
Cost of goods available for sale		$70,000
Net sales	$80,000	
Estimated gross profit (30%)	24,000	
Estimated cost of goods sold		56,000
Estimated ending inventory		$14,000

Retail Inventory Method

The second approach to estimating inventories is widely used by retail businesses, such as department stores, that are likely to keep periodic inventory records. Such firms typically mark each item of merchandise with the retail price and record purchases at both cost and retail price. A firm can estimate its ending inventory at *retail* price merely by subtracting sales from the retail price of merchandise available for sale. To determine the inventory *cost*, the firm will apply a cost-to-retail price percentage. This percentage is the ratio of cost to retail price of merchandise available. In Exhibit 9–10 this ratio is 70%, which, when applied to the $30,000 retail value of the inventory, yields a cost amount of $21,000.

The cost-to-retail ratio can also be used to compute the cost of an actual physical inventory taken at retail prices. Thus, the firm saves the considerable effort and expense of determining individual cost prices for each item of the inventory. Suppose, for example, that the sales clerks counted their stock and

EXHIBIT 9–10
Retail Inventory Estimation Method

	Cost	Selling Price
Beginning inventory	$14,000	$ 21,000
Net purchases	70,000	99,000
Total merchandise available	$84,000	$120,000
Cost-to-retail percentage: $\frac{\$84,000}{\$120,000} = 70\%$		
Deduct: Sales during period		90,000
Estimated ending inventory at retail prices		$ 30,000
Applicable cost percentage		0.70
Estimated ending inventory at cost		$ 21,000

determined that the ending inventory had an aggregate retail value of $40,000. If the store management knew that its cost-to-retail price ratio was 70%, it could easily obtain the estimated cost of the inventory, $28,000, that is needed to prepare financial statements.

The accuracy of the retail inventory method depends on the assumption that the ending inventory contains the same proportion of goods at the various mark-up percentages as did the original group of merchandise available for sale. To the extent that the mix of mark-up percentages does not remain constant, the accuracy of the estimate is impaired.

THE EFFECT OF INVENTORY ERRORS

In order to determine the effect of inventory errors on income determination, one must consider the method for calculating cost of goods sold. To see why this is necessary, look at Exhibit 9-11, where we assume an error was made overstating the ending inventory of Period 1 by $1,000.

Because the ending inventory in Period 1 is overstated by $1,000, the cost of goods sold is understated by $1,000, and thus reported income is overstated by that amount. Because the ending inventory in Period 1 is also the beginning inventory in Period 2, the reported income for both periods will be misstated unless the error is corrected. Note, however, that the error in Period 2 causes a misstatement of reported income that is equal in amount ($1,000) to the error in Period 1 but opposite in direction (an understatement); thus the errors in the two periods offset each other.

EXHIBIT 9-11
Effect of Inventory Error on Two Operating Periods

		(Amounts in Thousands)			
	Period 1		Period 2		
	Correct	Erroneous	Erroneous	Correct	
Sales	$80	$80	$100	$100	
Beginning inventory	$20	$20	$14	$13	
Net purchases	50	50	66	66	
Goods available	70	70	80	79	
Ending inventory	13	14	10	10	
Cost of goods sold	57	56	70	69	
Gross profit	$23	$24	$ 30	$ 31	
Overstatement (or under-statement) of net income	$1		($1)		

Therefore, uncorrected errors in ending inventories affect income determination for two periods. Overstating or understating ending inventory overstates or understates income, respectively. Regardless of the direction of the error, if it is not corrected, it will cause an offsetting error of like amount in the second period.

PERPETUAL INVENTORY PROCEDURES

Thus far in our discussion, we have assumed that all inventory situations involve a *periodic system*. Remember that this system (1) records acquisitions of merchandise as debits to a Purchases account, (2) makes no entry at the time of sale for the cost of goods sold, and (3) only periodically (hence its name) brings the Inventory account up to date by means of one or more adjusting entries. The periodic system is most suitable for businesses that have many sales transactions of relatively small unit product costs—for example, small retail grocery, drug, variety, or department stores.

Other types of business firms, notably those with fewer sales transactions but relatively high unit product costs, may use a *perpetual inventory system*. The perpetual inventory system, also descriptively named, provides for the Inventory account to be "perpetually," or continually (as opposed to periodically), maintained. Perpetual updating of the Inventory account requires (1) that at the time of purchase, merchandise acquisitions be recorded as debits to the Inventory account and (2) that at the time of sale, the cost of goods sold be determined and recorded by a debit to the Cost of Goods Sold account and a credit to the Inventory account. With a perpetual inventory system, Cost of Goods Sold is an actual account in the general ledger rather than merely a category on the income statement as it is with a periodic inventory system.

**Perpetual
Inventory
Entries**

When a firm employs perpetual inventory procedures, the Inventory account shows the amount of inventory on hand at the end of the period—assuming that there has been no theft, spoilage, or error. However, even if there is little chance or suspicion of inventory discrepancy, most companies make a physical inventory count at least once a year. At that time, an adjustment is made for any inaccuracies discovered.

The following entries demonstrate the recording procedures to be followed under the perpetual inventory system, contrasted with the periodic system.

Journal Entries

Periodic Inventory System		Perpetual Inventory System	

(1) Purchased $1,200 worth of merchandise on account; terms 2/10, n/30.

Purchases	1,200		Inventory	1,200	
Accounts Payable		1,200	Accounts Payable		1,200

(2) Returned $200 merchandise to vendors.

Accounts Payable	200		Accounts Payable	200	
Purchases Returns and Allowances		200	Inventory		200

(3) Paid for merchandise (discount taken).

Accounts Payable	1,000		Accounts Payable	1,000	
Purchases Discounts		20	Inventory		20
Cash		980	Cash		980

(4) Sold goods, costing $500, for $800.

Accounts Receivable	800		Accounts Receivable	800	
Sales		800	Sales		800
			Cost of Goods Sold	500	
			Inventory		500

(5) Counted inventory at end of period, $19,800. The balance in the Inventory account under the periodic inventory system is $25,000 (the beginning inventory). The balance in the Inventory account under the perpetual system is $20,000.

(Adjusting entries for inventory)

Income Summary	25,000		Loss on Inventory Shrinkage	200	
Inventory		25,000	Inventory		200
Inventory	19,800				
Income Summary		19,800			

Note that under a perpetual system the Inventory account is increased by purchases and decreased by the cost of goods sold, purchases returns and allowances, and discounts. Therefore, at the end of the period the only adjustment needed is to bring the Inventory account balance into agreement with the amount of the physical inventory. Because we assumed the physical inventory of goods on hand amounted to $19,800, while the Inventory account had a balance of $20,000, it was necessary to charge the difference, $200, to Loss on Inventory Shrinkage in reducing the Inventory account balance to $19,800.

Perpetual Inventory Records

Perpetual inventory records may be maintained by a manual system or by an electronic data processing system. Regardless of its sophistication, the record should provide the data shown on the form in Exhibit 9–12 (page 332).

We see from the illustration that perpetual inventory records must provide for both the inflow and outflow of merchandise as well as disclose the quantities and prices of items at any time. Although these records are continually maintained, their accuracy should be verified at least once each year by actual physical counts of merchandise.

EXHIBIT 9–12
Inventory Record Form

INVENTORY CONTROL

Part No. __1342__

Description __Flexible shaft (⅜")__   Maximum __15__

Prime Supplier __Ball Machinery Company__   Reorder Level __5__

Location __Small Parts Warehouse (Bin 32)__   Reorder Quantity __10__

Date	Received			Sold			Balance		
	Units	Cost/Unit	Total	Units	Cost/Unit	Total	Units	Cost/Unit	Total
19XX									
Jan. 1	Balance Fwd.						4	$30	$120
4	10	32	$320				{ 4	30	
							{ 10	32	440
7				4	$30	$120			
				4	32	128			
							6	32	192

Inspection of the record form in Exhibit 9–12 reveals that the inventory is being kept on the first-in, first-out basis. The sale of eight units on January 7 comprises the four units on hand at the beginning of the period at $30 each and four of the 10 units bought at $32 each on January 4. Perpetual inventories may also be kept on the last-in, first-out basis or on a weighted average cost basis. A detailed discussion of such systems is usually presented in more advanced accounting courses.

When a perpetual inventory system is used, a subsidiary record similar to Exhibit 9–12 is maintained for all the items in the inventory. At the close of the accounting period, the balances on all the subsidiary records are added, and their total dollar amount should agree with the amount in the Inventory account, which serves as a control account.

DEMONSTRATION PROBLEM FOR REVIEW

Mackey, Inc. began operations on April 1 of the current year. Sales revenue for April totaled $90,000. The company uses the periodic inventory system. Its beginning inventory was $4,000, consisting of 2,000 units at a cost of $2.00 per unit. A summary of purchases during April appears below.

April	8	5,000 units @ $2.50 =	$12,500
	19	10,000 @ 3.00 =	30,000
	29	6,000 @ 3.50 =	21,000
		Total	$63,500

At the end of April, 7,000 units were on hand.

REQUIRED

(a) How much gross profit on sales would Mackey, Inc. report for the month of April under (1) first-in, first-out inventory pricing, and (2) last-in, first-out inventory pricing?

(b) What would have been Mackey's gross profit on sales for April under (1) first-in, first-out, and (2) last-in, first-out if the purchase of goods on April 29 had been postponed until May?

(c) What would have been Mackey's gross profit on sales for April under (1) first-in, first-out, and (2) last-in, first-out if the purchase of goods on April 29 had been 9,000 units instead of 6,000 units?

(d) Based on your answers to parts (a), (b), and (c), what conclusion can you draw about the impact of the timing or amount of end-of-period purchases on the gross profit on sales computed under the (1) first-in, first-out, and (2) last-in, first-out methods of inventory pricing?

SOLUTION TO DEMONSTRATION PROBLEM

	FIFO	LIFO
Sales	$90,000	$90,000
Cost of Goods Sold:		
Beginning Inventory	$ 4,000	$ 4,000
Add: Purchases	63,500	63,500
Cost of Goods Available for Sale	$67,500	$67,500
Less: Ending Inventory		
FIFO: 6,000 × $3.50 = $21,000		
1,000 × $3.00 = 3,000	24,000	
LIFO: 2,000 × $2.00 = $ 4,000		
5,000 × $2.50 = 12,500		16,500
Cost of Goods Sold	$43,500	$51,000
Gross Profit on Sales	$46,500	$39,000

(b) If the purchase of 6,000 units on April 29 was postponed until May, then the inventory at April 30 would have been 1,000 units and purchases for April would have totaled $42,500 ($12,500 on April 8 + $30,000 on April 19). The gross profit on sales would then be computed as follows:

	FIFO	LIFO
Sales	$90,000	$90,000
Cost of Goods Sold:		
Beginning Inventory	$ 4,000	$ 4,000
Add: Purchases	42,500	42,500
Cost of Goods Available for Sale	$46,500	$46,500
Less: Ending Inventory		
FIFO: 1,000 × $3.00	3,000	
LIFO: 1,000 × $2.00		2,000
Cost of Goods Sold	$43,500	$44,500
Gross Profit on Sales	$46,500	$45,500

(c) If 9,000 units were purchased on April 29, then the inventory on April 30 would have been 10,000 units and purchases for April would have totaled $74,000 ($12,500 on April 8 + $30,000 on April 19 + $31,500 on April 29). The gross profit on sales would then be computed as follows:

	FIFO	LIFO
Sales	$90,000	$90,000
Cost of Goods Sold:		
Beginning Inventory	$ 4,000	$ 4,000
Add: Purchases	74,000	74,000
Cost of Goods Available for Sale	$78,000	$78,000
Less: Ending Inventory		
FIFO: 9,000 × $3.50 = $31,500		
1,000 × $3.00 = 3,000	34,500	
LIFO: 2,000 × $2.00 = $ 4,000		
5,000 × $2.50 = 12,500		
3,000 × $3.00 = 9,000		25,500
Cost of Goods Sold	$43,500	$52,500
Gross Profit on Sales	$46,500	$37,500

(d) Gross profit on sales under the FIFO method is the same in all three cases. The gross profit is unaffected by changes in the amount or timing of end-of-period purchases.

    Gross profit on sales under the LIFO method is different in each case. Gross profit is affected by changes in the amount or timing of end-of-period purchases, because—under the periodic LIFO method—the costs of the most recent goods purchased are the first costs charged to cost of goods sold expense.

KEY POINTS TO REMEMBER

(1) Inventories vary whenever sales and acquisitions of merchandise are not equal.

(2) To calculate cost of goods sold, it is necessary to add any inventory decrease to net purchases or deduct any inventory increase.

(3) Other things being equal, changing the dollar amount of ending inventory changes reported income by a like amount.

(4) Taking inventory consists of three stages: (a) counting, (b) pricing, and (c) summation.

(5) An inventory amount can be calculated by using any of the following methods: specific identification; weighted average; first-in, first-out (FIFO); last-in, first-out (LIFO).

(6) Reported income can be influenced by the choice of inventory pricing methods.

(7) When prices are rising, LIFO results in lower reported income than FIFO does and thus may provide a related tax benefit.

(8) Inventories can be estimated by the gross profit or retail inventory methods, both of which entail representative cost-to-sales price percentages.

(9) A perpetual inventory system (a) does not use a Purchases account, (b) records cost of goods sold at the time of sale, and (c) continually updates the balance in the Inventory account.

(10) Uncorrected ending inventory measurement errors cause the reported income of two periods to be misstated. The errors are equal in amount but opposite in direction and are therefore offsetting.

QUESTIONS

9-1 List six factors (or cost categories) typically included in the cost of goods sold computation under a periodic inventory system and indicate whether the amount of each normally tends to increase or decrease the cost of goods sold figure.

9-2 Define "merchandise inventory" and identify the costs that should be included as inventory costs.

9-3 Under a periodic inventory system, why is reported income affected "dollar-for-dollar" by any change in the dollar amount of ending inventory?

9-4 For a physical inventory count, explain (a) the three steps involved, (b) why firms maintaining perpetual inventory records still take physical counts, and (c) what merchandise should be included.

9-5 What is meant by "goods flow" and "cost flow"?

9-6 Briefly describe each of the following approaches to inventory pricing: (a) specific identification; (b) weighted average; (c) first-in, first-out; (d) last-in, first-out.

9-7 Describe an appropriate operating situation for each of the four approaches to inventory pricing methods listed in Question 9-6.

9-8 Why do stable purchase prices reduce the significance of one's choice of inventory pricing methods?

9-9 Briefly explain the nature of "phantom profits" during periods of rising merchandise purchase prices.

9-10 If prices have been rising, which inventory pricing method—weighted average; first-in, first-out; or last-in, first-out—will yield (a) the lowest inventory amount? (b) the lowest net income? (c) the largest inventory amount? (d) the largest net income?

9-11 Identify two situations in which merchandise may be inventoried at an amount less than cost.

9-12 At year-end, Bill's Appliance Shop has a refrigerator on hand that has been used as a demonstration model. The refrigerator cost $250 and, when new, sells for $420. In its present condition, the refrigerator will be sold for $200. Related selling costs are estimated at $10. At what amount should the refrigerator be carried in inventory?

9-13 During periods when prices are consistently rising, why would firms adopt last-in, first-out inventory pricing?

9-14 Discuss the effect on reported income of applying the lower of cost or market rule.

9-15 Under what circumstances might firms want to estimate the dollar amount of their inventories rather than actually count them?

9-16 Contrast the accounting procedures for periodic and perpetual inventory systems.

9-17 Biket Company made an error in its 19X1 inventory count and as a result overstated the 19X1 ending inventory by $6,000. Assuming the error was not discovered, what was the effect on net income for 19X1? for 19X2?

9-18 "Goods available for sale must equal ending inventory plus cost of goods sold." Is this statement true or false?

EXERCISES

9-19 Hailey Stores, Inc. uses the periodic inventory system. Its accounting records include the following balances:

Accounts Payable (all for merchandise)	$ 5,700
Delivery Expense	2,400
Inventory	12,600
Purchases	54,000
Purchases Discounts	2,700
Purchases Returns and Allowances	1,300
Sales	93,000
Sales Discounts	900
Sales Returns and Allowances	1,500
Transportation In	2,000

(a) Assuming that the ending inventory is determined by physical count to be $17,700, compute the cost of goods sold.

(b) In what ways would the above accounts differ if the firm were using a perpetual inventory system?

9-20 The following information is for the Dodge Company for the month of May. Dodge sells just one product.

	Units	Unit Cost
Beginning inventory	30	$10
Purchases: May 11	90	11
18	60	12
23	20	14

During May, 150 units were sold, leaving an ending inventory of 50 units. Compute the cost of goods sold and the ending inventory (assume periodic inventory procedures) using (a) first-in, first-out; (b) last-in, first-out; (c) weighted average.

9-21 A firm has gathered the following inventory data at the end of a period:

Commodity	Units on Hand	Unit Cost	Market Price to Replace
A	300	$ 1.70	$ 1.50
B	200	7.00	8.00
C	800	2.25	2.00
D	20	14.00	14.50

Determine the ending inventory amount by applying the lower of cost or market rule to (a) the total inventory and (b) each item of the inventory.

9-22 Over the past several years the Ellis Company's gross profit has averaged 45% of net sales. During the first six months of the current year, net sales are $300,000 and net purchases total $160,000. Inventory at the beginning of the period was $35,000. The company prepares interim financial statements every quarter. Use the gross profit method to determine the estimated cost of the inventory at the end of the current six-month period.

9-23 Rann Company uses the periodic inventory system and has these records for the month of July.

	Units	Unit Cost
Beginning inventory	45	$24
Purchases: July 6	50	23
15	25	20
28	30	17

There were 35 units in inventory at the end of July. Compute the cost of goods sold and the ending inventory using each of the following methods: (a) first-in, first out; (b) weighted average; (c) last-in, first-out.

9-24 Nolten Company's inventory on April 1 had a cost of $42,000 and a retail value of $70,000. During April, Nolten's net purchases of merchandise cost $88,000 and had a net retail value of $130,000. Net sales for April totaled $170,000.

(a) Compute the estimated cost of the inventory at April 30 using the retail inventory method.

(b) What key assumptions underlie the validity of this estimate of inventory cost?

9-25 The December 31, 19XX, inventory of Benway Company was determined to be $70,000. In arriving at this amount, the following items were considered:

(1) Excluded from the inventory count were goods costing $4,000 owned by

Benway Company that were on consignment to the Roth Company.

(2) Included in the inventory count were goods in transit at December 31 to Benway Company from Krill, Inc. The goods, costing $7,000, were shipped F.O.B. shipping point and arrived on January 3.

(3) Included in the inventory count were goods sitting on Benway Company's shipping dock on December 31. These goods, costing $3,500, were sold to Achin, Inc. on December 31 and were awaiting pickup by an Achin truck. They were picked up on January 2.

Compute the correct inventory amount for Benway Company at December 31, 19XX.

9-26 The following information is available for Merritt Company during four consecutive operating periods:

| | Amounts by Period | | | |
	1	2	3	4
Beginning inventory	$15,000	$19,000	$18,000	$22,000
Net purchases	60,000	51,000	40,000	43,000
Cost of goods available	75,000	70,000	58,000	65,000
Ending inventory	19,000	18,000	22,000	16,000
Cost of goods sold	$56,000	$52,000	$36,000	$49,000

Assuming that the company made the errors below, compute the revised cost of goods sold figure for each period.

Period	Error in Ending Inventory	
1	Understated	$2,000
2	Overstated	3,000
3	Understated	5,000

9-27 Present journal entries to record the given transactions if (a) a periodic inventory system is used and (b) a perpetual inventory system is used.

(1) Merchandise is purchased for $1,800; terms 1/10, n/30.

(2) Goods originally costing $300 (in the preceding transaction) are returned to the seller before payment is made.

(3) The remainder of the purchase in (1) is paid for and the related discount is taken.

(4) Goods originally costing $1,000 are sold on account for $1,600.

(5) The inventory account is adjusted at the end of the period. Assume that the beginning balance in this account was $500 and that a physical inventory at the end of the period shows $950 of goods on hand.

PROBLEMS

9-28 Loper Sales, Inc. had a beginning inventory for July comprising 1,600 units that had cost $40 per unit. A summary of purchases and sales during July follows.

	Unit Cost	Units Purchased	Units Sold
July 3			400
8	$45	1,400	
13			2,000
19	51	800	
23	54	600	
28			1,200

REQUIRED

(a) Assuming a periodic inventory system is used, calculate the amount of the ending inventory under each of the following pricing methods: first-in, first-out; last-in, first-out; weighted average.

(b) Which inventory pricing method would you choose:
(1) to reflect what is probably the physical flow of goods?
(2) to minimize income tax for the period?
(3) to report the largest amount of income for the period?
Justify your answers.

(c) Answer this part independently of part (a). Assume that perpetual inventory records are maintained on a first-in, first-out basis and that a physical count of the inventory at the end of July disclosed only 794 units on hand. How might this discrepancy be explained? What would be the nature of an accounting entry to properly reflect this fact?

9-29 Examine the data below for the month of April for Amling, Inc., which prices inventory on the last-in, first-out basis and uses the periodic inventory system. *(once a yr)*

Beginning inventory: 5,000 units @ $4 each

Purchases		Sales	
Apr. 5	10,000 @ $5	Apr. 8	7,000 @ $ 8
12	30,000 @ 6	16	25,000 @ 9
21	20,000 @ 7	22	25,000 @ 10
30	10,000 @ 8	27	5,000 @ 11

62,000

REQUIRED

(a) How much gross profit on sales would Amling, Inc. report for the month of April?

(b) By what amount would Amling's reported gross profit for April change if the final purchase of merchandise had been postponed for several days?

(c) What would be the difference in Amling's reported gross profit if the final purchase had been for 20,000 units instead of 10,000 units?

(d) If Amling priced inventory on the first-in, first-out method, what would be the answers to parts (a), (b), and (c)?

9-30 Following is a summary of the inventory amounts of the Foley Company at the end of each of its first three years of operations, assuming various inventory pricing procedures.

End of Year	First-In, First-Out	Last-In, First-Out	Weighted Average
1	$2,600	$2,300	$2,450
2	4,000	3,600	3,900
3	3,600	3,400	3,550

REQUIRED

Answer each of the following questions, providing supporting computations or other reasoning.

(a) For year 1, by how much could reported income be changed simply by choosing among the three inventory pricing methods?

(b) For year 2, which inventory pricing method would result in the *highest* reported income?

(c) For year 3, which inventory pricing method would result in the *lowest* reported income?

(d) For year 3, by how much and in what direction would reported income differ under first-in, first-out compared with weighted average?

(e) Which inventory pricing method would result in the *highest* reported income for the *three years combined*?

9-31 The Pierce Company had the following inventory at December 31, 19X1:

		Unit Price	
	Quantity	Cost	Market
Desks			
Model 9001	100	$180	$170
Model 9002	40	200	210
Model 9003	30	240	255
Cabinets			
Model 7001	300	50	54
Model 7002	80	70	65
Model 7003	60	100	110

REQUIRED

(a) Determine the ending inventory amount by applying the lower of cost or market rule to:
   (1) each item of the inventory.
   (2) each major category of the inventory.
   (3) the total inventory.

(b) Which of the LCM procedures from (a) will result in the lowest net income for the year 19X1? Explain.

9-32 Sales clerks for Grand Company, a retail concern, took a physical inventory at retail prices at the end of the current year and determined that the total retail value of the ending inventory was $95,000. The following information for the year is available:

	Cost	Selling Price
Beginning inventory	$ 54,000	$ 80,000
Net purchases	243,000	370,000
Sales		352,000

Management estimates its inventory loss from theft and other causes by comparing its physical ending inventory at retail prices with an estimated ending inventory at retail prices (determined by subtracting sales from goods available for sale at selling prices) and reducing this difference to cost by applying the proper cost ratio.

REQUIRED

(a) Compute the estimated cost of the ending inventory using the retail inventory method. This is the inventory amount that will appear in the balance sheet, and the calculation should be based on the physical inventory taken at retail prices.

(b) Compute the estimated inventory loss for the year from theft and other causes.

9-33 Selected operating data for Salem Sales Company, a franchised distributor for a high-quality snow-blower, are as follows.

Beginning inventory	300 units @ $160 each	
Purchases	500	@ 160
	200	@ 180
Sales	700	@ 340
Operating expenses	$54,000	

Salem uses the periodic inventory system priced at first-in, first-out. Assume all sales, purchases, operating expenses, and taxes are paid in cash and that a 50% income tax rate is applicable.

REQUIRED

(a) What is Salem's net income after taxes for the period?

(b) What is the net amount of cash generated by the period's activity?

(c) Why are the amounts in (a) and (b) different? How would you explain this to a stockholder who expected a cash dividend equal to one-half of the reported after-tax income?

(d) What would be your answers to (a) and (b) if the firm were to price its ending inventory on the last-in, first-out basis?

(e) Briefly explain the nature of any "phantom profit" on inventory in (a). Also explain the nature of any tax advantage of last-in, first-out inventory pricing in (d).

(f) Contrast the inventory carrying values under (a) and (d). Which is more meaningful? Why?

(g) Contrast the reported income under (a) and (d). Which is more meaningful? Why?

9-34 Assume that Meyer's Appliance Shop had an ending inventory balance of $6,000 at the close of the last period. The following sales and purchase transactions are for the current period.

(1) Purchased merchandise on account for $2,700; terms 2/10, n/30.

(2) Returned part of the above merchandise that had an original gross purchase price of $200.

(3) Paid for the balance of the purchase in time to receive the purchase discount.

(4) Sold goods costing $6,600 for $12,000. Cash of $6,800 was received, with the balance due on account.

REQUIRED

(a) Record the above transactions assuming that (1) a periodic inventory system is used and (2) a perpetual inventory system is used. Assume also that accounts payable are initially recorded at the full invoice price.

(b) Suppose that a physical inventory at the end of the current period shows inventory of $1,780 to be on hand. Present the entries (if any) required under each inventory system to adjust the inventory account.

(c) Which system would best disclose any possible inventory loss in the income statement? Why?

ALTERNATE PROBLEMS

9-28A Lambert Company's beginning inventory for June consisted of 3,000 units at a cost of $5 each. Purchases and sales during June were as follows:

	Purchases		Units Sold
	Units	Unit Cost	
June 5			1,000
11	2,000	$5.50	
16			3,000
20	5,000	6.20	
28			4,000

REQUIRED

(a) Assuming a periodic system, calculate the cost of the ending inventory under each of the following pricing methods: first-in, first-out; last-in, first-out; weighted average.

(b) Which inventory pricing method would you choose:
(1) to reflect what is probably the physical flow of goods?
(2) to minimize income tax for the period?
(3) to report the largest amount of income for the period?
Justify your answers.

(c) Answer this part independently of part (a). Assume that perpetual inventory records are maintained on a first-in, first-out basis and that a physical count of the inventory at June 30 disclosed only 1,950 units on hand. How might this discrepancy be explained? What would be the nature of an accounting entry to properly reflect this fact?

9-29A Examine the data below for the month of October for Mellow, Inc., which prices inventory on the last-in, first-out basis and uses the periodic inventory system.

Beginning inventory: 8,000 units @ $3.00 each

Purchases		Sales	
Oct. 3	16,000 @ $3.50	Oct. 4	18,000 @ $5.00
10	40,000 @ 4.00	12	36,000 @ 5.50
19	20,000 @ 4.50	20	14,000 @ 6.00
24	14,000 @ 5.00	26	20,000 @ 6.50
31	26,000 @ 6.00	30	4,000 @ 6.50

REQUIRED

(a) How much gross profit on sales would Mellow, Inc. report for the month of October?

(b) By what amount would Mellow's reported gross profit for October change if the final purchase of merchandise had been postponed for several days?

(c) What would be the difference in Mellow's reported gross profit if the final purchase had been 50,000 units instead of 26,000 units?

(d) If Mellow priced inventory on the first-in, first-out method, what would be the answers to parts (a), (b), and (c)?

9–31A The Kallis Company had the following inventory at December 31, 19X7:

| | | Unit Price | |
	Quantity	Cost	Market
Fans			
Model X1	400	$10	$11
Model X2	100	14	13
Model X3	200	25	22
Heaters			
Model B7	150	30	28
Model B8	90	20	21
Model B9	250	18	20

REQUIRED

(a) Determine the ending inventory amount by applying the lower of cost or market rule to:
(1) each item of the inventory.
(2) each major category of the inventory.
(3) the total inventory.

(b) Which of the LCM procedures from (a) will result in the lowest net income for the year 19X7? Explain.

9–32A Sales clerks for Disher Company, a retail concern, took a physical inventory at retail prices at the end of the current year and determined that the total retail value of the ending inventory was $80,000. The following information for the year is available:

	Cost	Selling Price
Beginning inventory	$ 49,500	$ 75,000
Net purchases	190,500	245,000
Sales		238,000

Management estimates its inventory loss from theft and other causes by comparing its physical ending inventory at retail prices with an estimated ending inventory at retail prices (determined by subtracting sales from goods available for sale at selling prices) and reducing this difference to cost by applying the proper cost ratio.

REQUIRED

(a) Compute the estimated cost of the ending inventory using the retail inventory method. This is the inventory amount that will appear in the balance sheet, and the calculation should be based on the physical inventory taken at retail prices.

(b) Compute the estimated inventory loss for the year from theft and other causes.

9–34A Assume that Carey's Radio Shop had an ending inventory balance of $5,000 at the close of the last period. The following sales and purchase transactions are for the current period.

(1) Purchased merchandise on account for $3,600; terms 1/10, n/30.
(2) Returned part of the above merchandise that had an original gross purchase price of $300.

(3) Paid for the balance of the purchase in time to receive the purchase discount.

(4) Sold goods costing $5,500 for $9,000. Cash of $4,600 was received, with the balance due on account.

REQUIRED

(a) Record the above transactions assuming that (1) a periodic inventory system is used and (2) a perpetual inventory system is used. Assume also that accounts payable are initially recorded at the full invoice price.

(b) Suppose that a physical inventory at the end of the current period shows inventory of $2,720 to be on hand. Present the entries (if any) required under each inventory system to adjust the inventory account.

(c) Which system would best disclose any possible inventory loss in the income statement? Why?

BUSINESS DECISION PROBLEM

Patt Company's entire inventory and many of its accounting records were destroyed by fire early in the morning of May 1, 19X5. Patt filed an inventory loss claim of $150,000 with Dependable Insurance Company. Dependable has hired you to evaluate the reasonableness of Patt's claim. You and the head bookkeeper of Patt have gathered the following information from various sources:

(1) The January 1, 19X5, inventory figure of $70,000 was found on a copy of a personal property tax declaration filed with the local municipality.

(2) From a statistical summary filed with a trade association, the sales and cost of goods sold for the preceding three years were determined to be:

	19X2	19X3	19X4
Net sales	$620,000	$840,000	$940,000
Cost of goods sold	403,000	544,320	612,680

(3) Patt buys an estimated 85% of its merchandise from three wholesale suppliers. According to the records of these three suppliers, Patt's purchases for the first four months of 19X5 were as follows:

Supplier	Purchases
Jackson Corporation	$ 80,000
Nevin Company	101,000
Voss, Inc.	57,000

(4) Patt's sales average 10% cash and the balance on credit. Adding machine tapes totaling the accounts receivable subsidiary ledger were found dated December 31, 19X4, and April 30, 19X5. These tapes showed $36,000 and $32,000, respectively. An analysis of bank deposit slips indicates that the amounts deposited in the bank as collections from credit customers were: $90,000 for January, $97,000 for February, $85,000 for March, and $92,000 for April of 19X5.

REQUIRED

Based on the preceding data, use the gross profit method to estimate the ending inventory of Patt Company destroyed by fire. Is the amount of Patt's loss claim reasonable?

10
Long-term
Assets

In this chapter we shall discuss the accounting problems related to the acquisition, use, and disposal of business assets that are typically held for many accounting periods. Such assets are classified as **long-term assets** in the balance sheet, but are often described by the terms **fixed assets, long-lived assets,** and **noncurrent assets.** Sometimes, financial statements include such subcategories as long-term investments;[1] property, plant, and equipment; and intangible assets. *Plant assets* is often used interchangeably with property, plant, and equipment.

The carrying values of long-term assets are normally based on historical costs, and any gains and most losses from holding such assets are recognized only when the assets are sold. As with other business assets, the costs related to the use of long-term assets must be properly calculated and matched against the revenues the assets help generate, so that periodic net income may be correctly determined. Each period's expired portion of the original outlay for an asset is an important part of these costs. Depending on the type of asset involved, this amount is called *depreciation, depletion,* or *amortization.* All of these terms have the same meaning in accounting—"a periodic charging to expense."

OVERVIEW OF RELATED PROBLEMS

Long-term assets usually are characterized by high economic values, many accounting periods, and a wide range of forms. Because these special aspects of their nature in turn create special accounting problems, an overall classification scheme is helpful in studying them. In Exhibit 10-1 we show the three major asset forms—**constructed assets, natural assets,** and **intangible assets.** Different terms are used to denote periodic write-off to expense for the three forms of assets. Note that site land (simply a place on which to operate) usually is considered as having an indefinite useful life and therefore does not require any periodic write-off to expense.

---

[1]We treat long-term investment accounting in Chapter 15, where the accounting procedures of investors and long-term borrowers are considered together.

EXHIBIT 10–1
Classification of Long-term Assets and Related Write-Off

Asset Forms	Examples	Terms for Periodic Write-Off to Expense
Constructed	Buildings, equipment, tools, furniture, fixtures, and vehicles	Depreciation
Natural	Oil, timber, and mineral deposits Land for site use	Depletion (No periodic write-off; considered to have an indefinite life.)
Intangible	Patents, copyrights, leaseholds, franchises, trademarks, and goodwill	Amortization

We shall consider the problems associated with the various asset forms in the order shown in Exhibit 10–2. This exhibit is a graphic presentation of the typical accounting problems created by long-term assets in relation to the life cycle of an asset.

Measurement problems associated with long-term assets include identifying the types and amounts of expenditures that make up the original recorded cost of the particular asset. During the use period, expenditures for simple maintenance (expense) must be properly differentiated from other expenditures that increase the capacity or extend the life of the asset (to be added to asset costs). During the use period, it is also important to charge the appropriate amounts against yearly revenues to reflect the consumption of limited-life assets. This involves estimating the useful life of the asset and its probable net salvage value at time of disposal. Upon disposal of the asset, the adjusted accounting cost of the asset must be compared with the net proceeds from disposal in order to determine any related gain or loss.

We shall discover that many of the problems are quite difficult, that no ultimate solution apparently exists, and that often the accounting methods used are more expedient and convenient than precise and scientific.

ORIGINAL MEASUREMENT OF ASSETS

Long-term assets are originally recorded at their cost. These measures are often referred to as "historical costs" because they provide the basis for accounting for the assets in subsequent periods. No attempt is made to reflect subsequent changes in market values. The general rule for determining cost is:

EXHIBIT 10–2
Typical Problem Areas
of Long-Term Asset Accounting

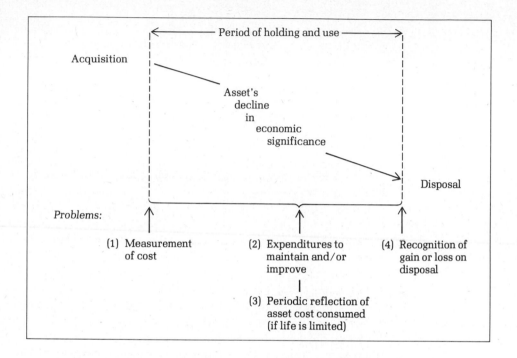

The initial cost of a long-term asset is equal to the cash and/or the cash equivalent of that which is given up in order to acquire the asset *and* to prepare it for use.

According to this rule, initial cost includes the asset's (1) "implied cash price" and (2) its "costs of preparation for use."

A corollary to this rule provides that, to be considered as part of the asset's cost, the expenditures to acquire and prepare the asset for use must be reasonable and necessary. Accountants do not capitalize (charge to an asset account) expenditures that are wasteful or inefficient. Costs of waste and inefficiency are expensed when incurred. For example, suppose equipment is damaged while it is being installed or a firm's receiving dock is damaged while equipment is being unloaded. Expenditures made to repair these damages are not part of the cost of the equipment; they are instead charged to expense.

**Cash and
Noncash
Purchases**

Very often, the historical cost of the asset will be simply the amount of cash paid when the asset is acquired and readied for use. Consider, for example, that the following expenditures are made to obtain a certain piece of equipment:

Purchase price factors:		
Gross invoice price	$10,000	
Less: Cash discount (1/10, n/30)	(100)	
Sales tax	400	$10,300
Related expenditures:		
Freight charges	$ 200	
Installation costs	500	
Testing of installed machine	300	1,000
Cost of equipment		$11,300

The total equipment cost is $11,300, consisting of a cash purchase price of $10,300 and "preparation for use" costs of $1,000. Because the sales tax is a necessary component of the purchase price, it should not be charged to a tax expense account. Similarly, the costs of freight, installation, and testing are expenditures necessary in order to get the asset in condition and location for use. These costs are included as part of the initial cost of the equipment.

Even if an asset's purchase price is not immediately paid in cash, we determine the cash equivalent purchase price at the date of acquisition and record that amount in the asset account. Suppose we purchased the above equipment on a financing plan requiring a $1,210 cash down payment and a non-interest-bearing note for $10,000 due in one year. The implied cash price remains $10,300, even though the financing plan is used. The difference between the $10,300 and the $11,210 total disbursement under the financing plan ($1,210 down payment plus $10,000 payment on note) represents the interest cost associated with the financing plan. The entry to record the purchase of the asset under the financing plan would be:

Equipment	10,300	
Discount on Notes Payable	910	
Cash		1,210
Notes Payable		10,000

To record purchase of equipment.

Of course, the expenditures for freight, installation, and testing will still be debited to the Equipment account when they are incurred.

**Related
Expenditures**

A purchase of land often raises some interesting questions about related expenditures. Suppose a firm seeking a site for its new office building retained a local real estate broker at a fee of $2,000 to locate an appropriate parcel. The property eventually chosen had an old residence on it, which was to be razed. The terms of the sale included a payment of $40,000 to the seller, with the buyer paying off an existing mortgage of $10,000 and $300 of accrued interest. In addition, the buyer agreed to pay accrued real estate taxes of $800. Other related expenditures included legal fees of $400 and a title insurance premium of $500. A bid was received and accepted from a local salvage company to raze the old residence, level the lot, keep all the materials, and pay the firm $200. If we apply the general asset measurement rule, we should compute the initial cost of the land as follows:

Payment to the seller	$40,000
Commission for finding property	2,000
Payment of mortgage and interest due at time of sale	10,300
Payment of property taxes owed by seller	800
Legal fees	400
Title insurance premium	500
	$54,000
Less: Net recovery from razing	(200)
Cost of land parcel	$53,800

Again, it would be erroneous to charge various expense accounts for the taxes, insurance, legal fees, and interest. All these expenditures should be capitalized as part of the land, because they were necessary for its acquisition and preparation for use.

Package Purchases

Sometimes several types of assets may be purchased concurrently as a package. For example, assume that a company purchased a small branch freight terminal including land, a building, and some loading equipment for a total price of $90,000. For accounting purposes, the total purchase price should be divided among the three asset forms because (1) they will be carried and reported in different accounts, (2) only the building and equipment are subject to depreciation, and (3) the equipment would no doubt have an estimated useful life different from the building.

The price of package purchases is most commonly allocated on the basis of relative market or appraisal values. We assume estimated market values to illustrate this approach.

Asset	Estimated Market Value	Percent of Total	Allocation of Purchase Price	Estimated Useful Life
Land	$ 40,000	40	$36,000	Indefinite
Building	50,000	50	45,000	30 years
Equipment	10,000	10	9,000	8 years
Totals	$100,000	100	$90,000	

In actual practice, the firm may obtain realistic market values from a knowledgeable employee, a professional appraiser, or from assessed values appearing on related property tax bills.

Nonroutine Acquisitions

Not all asset acquisitions involve specific amounts of money. Often nonmonetary assets are traded for other nonmonetary assets, in which case the implied cash price is not as readily apparent. Generally accepted accounting principles normally provide that the transaction price be considered as the market value of either the asset given up or the asset received, whichever is more objectively determinable. General-purpose property and equipment (standard office or factory equipment) and widely traded securities usually have more objectively determinable market values than do highly specialized buildings or equipment and securities that are new or seldom traded. These are just some examples of the many instances in which the accountant must exercise professional judgment.

An exception to this guideline occurs when a nonmonetary productive asset is exchanged for a similar asset. We consider this exception later in the chapter in our discussion of disposals involving trade-ins.

THE NATURE OF DEPRECIATION

With the exception of site land, the use of long-term assets to generate revenues tends to consume their economic potential. At some point of reduced potential, usually before they are totally worthless, these assets are disposed of and possibly replaced. We can diagram the typical pattern of long-term-asset utilization (indicated in Exhibit 10–2) as follows:

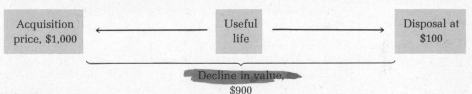

The asset is acquired for $1,000, used for several accounting periods, and then sold for $100. The $900 decline in value is, in every sense of the word, an expense of generating the revenues that were realized during the periods that the asset was used. Therefore, if income determination is to be meaningful, $900 of expense must be allocated to these periods and matched against the revenues. Failure to do so would overstate income for these periods.

Note that this process means estimating an asset's useful life and salvage value as well as properly determining its acquisition cost. Useful life refers to the expected period of economic usefulness to the current entity—the period from date of acquisition to expected date of disposal. Salvage value is the expected net recovery (sales proceeds less disposal costs) when the asset is sold or removed from service.

Because the useful life of an asset typically involves at least several accounting periods, the $900 in our example must be divided in some way. If we assume a five-year useful life, and each period is to receive equal amounts, then $900/5 = $180 would be shown as the periodic amount of depreciation for the asset. The basic entry to record each period's depreciation expense is:

Depreciation Expense	180	
Accumulated Depreciation—Equipment		180

To record depreciation expense for the year.

Like other expense accounts, Depreciation Expense is deducted from revenues in determining net income and is closed at year-end to the Income Summary account. The offsetting credit is posted to the contra account, Accumulated Depreciation, which is deducted from the related asset account on the balance sheet to compute the book value, or carrying value, of the asset. In this manner, the original cost of an asset is maintained in the asset account and the cumulative balance of depreciation taken is carried in the contra account as long as the asset is in service. When an asset is disposed of, the related cost and accumulated depreciation are removed from the accounts.

For our simple illustration, the table below shows the balances and progression of certain amounts and accounts during the asset's five-period life.

			End-of-Period Balance	
Period	Balance of Asset Account	Periodic Depreciation Expense	Accumulated Depreciation Account	Asset's Book Value
1	$1,000	$180	$180	$820
2	1,000	180	360	640
3	1,000	180	540	460
4	1,000	180	720	280
5	1,000	180	900	100
	Total depreciation	$900		

Observe that (1) the asset account continues to show the original cost of the asset, (2) each period reflects $180 of depreciation expense, (3) the Accumulated Depreciation account balance is cumulative and shows the portion of the original cost that has been taken as depreciation to date, and (4) the asset's book value is the original cost less total accumulated depreciation to date. Thus the book value decreases to the estimated salvage value as the asset is depreciated during its useful life.

The book value of the asset is shown on the balance sheet by deducting the Accumulated Depreciation account (normally a credit balance) from the asset account (normally a debit balance) in this manner:

Equipment (original cost)	$1,000
Less: Accumulated Depreciation	900
Book value	$ 100

Later, we shall examine some widely used depreciation techniques that do not allocate depreciation equally to all periods of an asset's useful life.

Allocation Versus Valuation

Although the idea is theoretically appealing, accountants do not specifically base depreciation on the changes in market value or the measured wear of assets—primarily because a reliable, objective, and practical source for such data rarely exists. Rather, depreciation accounting attempts to allocate in a rational and systematic manner the difference between acquisition price and estimated salvage value over the *estimated* useful life of the asset. Thus, depreciation accounting techniques are convenient expedients for measuring asset expirations and, in a sense, are not precise. As tentative as they are, depreciation estimates and allocations clearly provide better income determination than would result from completely expensing the asset at either the date of acquisition or the date of disposal.

Several factors are naturally related to the periodic allocation of depreciation. Depreciation can be caused by wear from use, natural deterioration through interaction of the elements, and technical obsolescence. Each factor tends to reduce the value of the asset. To some extent, maintenance (lubrication, adjustments, parts replacements, and cleaning) may partially arrest or offset wear and deterioration. Quite logically, then, when useful life and salvage values are estimated, a given level of maintenance is assumed. Therefore, the cost of using long-term assets tends to be the sum of periodic maintenance expenditures plus some measure of the depreciation that occurs despite the maintenance performed. As we would expect, maintenance expense tends to increase toward the latter stages of most assets' lives.

How to allocate depreciation expense is just one facet of the overall problem of matching revenues and expenses. The most defensible reason for choosing one allocation pattern as opposed to another is that one pattern may better portray economic reality than another. In any specific instance, it would be only coincidence if the adjusted carrying value of a particular asset were exactly equal at any time to its "market value." On the other hand, the general pattern of an asset's carrying value may be closely related to its decline in market value.

COMPUTATIONS OF PERIODIC DEPRECIATION

We will now illustrate four widely used methods of computing periodic depreciation. For each illustration, we assume that the asset costs $1,000 and has an estimated useful life of five years. The salvage value at the end of the five-year period is estimated at $100. The computations we present illustrate different ways to *allocate* the amount to be depreciated among each of the five accounting periods in the asset's life.

Straight-line Allocation

Straight-line depreciation is probably the simplest to compute. An equal amount of depreciation expense is allocated to each full period of the asset's useful life. Using straight-line depreciation,

$$\text{Annual Depreciation} = \frac{\text{Original Cost} - \text{Salvage Value}}{\text{Years of Useful Life}}$$

which in our example is

27,000 - 3,000   24,000
                                                                                 4

$$\frac{\$1,000 - \$100}{5 \text{ years}} = \$180/\text{year}$$

For periods of less than one year, straight-line depreciation amounts are simply proportions of the annual amount. If the asset had been acquired on April 1, depreciation for the period ended December 31 would be 9/12 × $180 = $135. Assets acquired or disposed of during the first half of any month are usually treated as if the acquisition or disposal occurred on the first of the month. When either event occurs during the last half of any month, it is assumed to have occurred on the first of the following month.

Straight-line allocation is best suited to assets whose periodic usage is relatively uniform and whose obsolescence factor is low. Examples include pipelines, storage tanks, fencing, and surface paving. These types of assets can be expected to provide approximately equal utility during all periods of their useful lives.

Units of Production

The units-of-production method allocates depreciation in proportion to the degree the asset is used for production. First, the depreciation per unit of production is computed by dividing the total expected depreciation (in our example, $900) by the estimated units-of-production capacity that has been projected for the asset. Thus,

$$\text{Depreciation per Unit} = \frac{\text{Original Cost} - \text{Salvage Value}}{\text{Estimated Total Units of Production}}$$

Units-of-production capacity may represent miles driven, tons hauled, or number of cuttings, drillings, or stampings of parts. Assume that our example is a drilling tool that will drill an estimated 45,000 parts during its useful life. The depreciation per unit of production is

$$\frac{\$1,000 - \$100}{45,000 \text{ parts}} = \$0.02 \text{ per part}$$

The periodic depreciation expense is found by multiplying the depreciation per unit of production by the number of units produced during the period. If 8,000 units were produced during the first year, then 8,000 × $0.02 = $160 is the year's depreciation expense. If 12,000 parts were drilled the next year, that year's depreciation expense would be 12,000 × $0.02 = $240.

The units-of-production approach is particularly appropriate when wear is the major cause of depreciation and the amount of use varies from period to period. Of course, if use is uniformly spread over the asset's life, the same allocation of depreciation would result from either the straight-line or units-of-production method. The units-of-production method may necessitate some extra recordkeeping in order to express the periodic use in terms of production capacity. However, this data may already be tabulated as part of a periodic production report.

Sum of the Years' Digits

The sum-of-the-year's-digits (SYD) method accelerates depreciation expense so that the amounts recognized in the earlier periods of an asset's useful life are greater than those recognized in the later periods. The SYD is found by estimating an asset's useful life in years, then assigning consecutive numbers to each year, and totaling these numbers. For N years,

$$SYD = 1 + 2 + 3 + \cdots + N$$

In our example, with an asset life of 5 years, the SYD would be $1 + 2 + 3 + 4 + 5 = 15$.

Determining the SYD factor by simple addition can be somewhat laborious for long-lived assets. For these assets, the formula $N(N + 1)/2$, where $N =$ the number of periods in the asset's useful life, can be applied to derive the SYD. In our example, we have

$$\frac{5(5 + 1)}{2} = \frac{30}{2} = 15$$

The yearly depreciation is then calculated by multiplying the total depreciable amount for the life of the asset by a fraction whose numerator is the remaining useful life and whose denominator is the SYD. Thus, the formula for yearly depreciation is

$$\text{Annual Depreciation} = (\text{Original Cost} - \text{Salvage Value}) \times \frac{\text{Remaining Useful Life}}{\text{SYD}}$$

The calculations for our example are shown below:

Years in Useful Life	Fraction of Total Depreciation Taken Each Year		Original Cost Less Salvage Value		Annual Depreciation Allocation
1	$\frac{5}{15}$	$\times$	$900	=	$300
2	$\frac{4}{15}$	$\times$	900	=	240
3	$\frac{3}{15}$	$\times$	900	=	180
4	$\frac{2}{15}$	$\times$	900	=	120
5	$\frac{1}{15}$	$\times$	900	=	60
SYD 15				Total	$900

When the acquisition of an asset does not coincide with the beginning of the fiscal period, the annual depreciation amounts are allocated proportionately to the appropriate fiscal periods. For example, assume we purchased the asset on April 1. Depreciation for the period ended December 31 would be $9/12 \times \$300 = \$225$. For the next fiscal year, a full year's depreciation would be calculated as $(3/12 \times \$300) + (9/12 \times \$240) = \$255$.

As an accelerated depreciation method, the SYD approach is most appropriate for those situations in which the asset is judged to render greater utility during its earlier life and less in its later life. An accelerated pattern of depreciation is suitable for assets with either a high technological obsolescense factor in the early life phase or a high maintenance factor in the late life phase. In addition, there are some related tax strategies, which we will explain shortly.

Double Declining Balance

Another accelerated depreciation method is the double declining-balance method, which derives its name from the fact that a *constant percentage* factor is determined and applied each year to the *declining balance* of the asset's book value.

Accelerated depreciation has been allowed for federal income tax purposes for many years. The IRS Code specifies that an accelerated rate up to *twice* the straight-line rate is permissible for new assets. Because of its prevalence, all of our examples will assume that declining-balance depreciation is to be computed at twice the straight-line rate.

The **straight-line rate** is simply the number of years in the asset's useful life divided into 100%. In our example, this would be $100\%/5 = 20\%$. Double the straight-line rate is then 40%. In equation form,

$$\text{Double Declining-Balance Rate} = \frac{100\%}{\text{Years of Useful Life}} \times 2$$

The simple rule for determining the annual double declining-balance depreciation expense is to *multiply the asset's book value at the beginning of the period by the constant rate (or percentage)*. Remember that an asset's book value at any time is its original cost less its accumulated depreciation to date. The book value of a depreciable asset *declines* as it is depreciated. The important thing to remember about double declining-balance depreciation is that the percentage depreciation rate remains constant—it is the book value, to which the percentage is applied, that declines. Salvage value is not considered in the calculations, except that depreciation stops when the asset's book value equals its estimated salvage value.

Applying the general rule for double declining-balance depreciation to our example, we obtain the accelerated depreciation pattern shown in the following table (amounts to nearest dollar).

Period of Useful Life	Original Cost	Beginning Accumulated Depreciation	Beginning Book Value	Twice Straight-line Percentage	Amount of Depreciation Expense
1	$1,000	$ 0	$1,000	40	$400
2	1,000	400	600	40	240
3	1,000	640	360	40	144
4	1,000	784	216	40	86
5	1,000	870	130		30

Total depreciation taken $900

Observe that in the fifth year depreciation expense is only $30, the amount needed to reduce the asset's book value to the estimated salvage value of $100. Assets are not to be depreciated below their salvage values. If no salvage value has been estimated, the double declining-balance technique automatically provides for some salvage value. When a fraction (40%, or 4/10) is applied to the undepreciated balance, the entire original cost can never be depreciated; though it may be small, some balance will always remain.

If an asset is purchased during the fiscal period, a pro-rata allocation of the first year's depreciation is necessary. If we assume the above asset was acquired on April 1, depreciation for the period ended December 31 would be 9/12 × (40% × $1,000) = $300. In subsequent periods the usual procedure is followed. The next year, for example, depreciation would be 40% × ($1,000 − $300) = $280.

Because double declining-balance depreciation is also an accelerated depreciation method, it is appropriate in the same situations as the SYD method.

FINANCIAL ADVANTAGES OF ACCELERATED DEPRECIATION

Certain financial advantages can be derived from using one of the accelerated depreciation methods as opposed to the straight-line method for income tax reporting purposes. In a sense, accelerated depreciation provides an interest-free loan to the taxpayer, because the accelerated methods allow the taxpayer to pay less tax in the earlier phase of the asset's life and more in the later phase. Therefore, during the intervening time, the taxpayer has use of an amount of funds equal to the postponed income tax payments.

In Exhibit 10-3, we illustrate the computations and reasoning involved in selecting an accelerated depreciation method over a straight-line method. The amount and timing of taxes due under straight-line depreciation are compared with the taxes due under the SYD method (depreciation figures are taken from earlier computations). Note that the total depreciation taken and the total dollar tax paid are the same under both methods, but the postponement of some tax payments creates an "interest-free loan" benefit. As shown in Exhibit 10-3, a tax payment of $60 is postponed the first year and $30 the second year. Part of this is

EXHIBIT 10–3
Interest-free Loan Effect of Accelerated Depreciation
Compared with Straight-line Depreciation

| | \multicolumn{6}{c}{Amounts by Years} |
	1	2	3	4	5	Total
Straight-line depreciation	$180	$180	$180	$ 180	$ 180	$900
SYD depreciation	300	240	180	120	60	900
Change in depreciation leads to decrease (increase) in taxable income	$120	$ 60	$ 0	$ (60)	$(120)	$ 0
Decreased (or increased) income tax (50% rate assumed)	$ 60	$ 30	$ 0	$ (30)	$ (60)	$ 0
Net cumulative tax postponement at year-end	$ 60	$ 90	$ 90	$ 60	$ 0	

repaid in year 4 and the balance in year 5. During the intervening time, however, these funds are available to the taxpayer.

Our example uses small amounts for simplicity. To realize the significance of this tax option, imagine that our illustrative figures are in millions of dollars.

REVISION OF DEPRECIATION

We have stressed that depreciation allocations are based on estimates of both useful lives and salvage values. Circumstances change, however, and it may become apparent that the original estimates were too high or too low. The net effect of erroneous estimates is to misstate depreciation expense in one or more periods. This, in turn, misstates reported net income, the asset's book value, and owners' equity.

In the past, revisions of depreciation expense were quite involved because efforts were made to restate earlier years' accounts to reflect the corrected amounts of depreciation. Currently accepted practice is simpler in that it attempts only to reflect the depreciation revision in the period of change and in any subsequent periods. This is accomplished by allocating the revised undepreciated balance of the asset over the revised remaining useful life. To illustrate this correction procedure, we shall use the data from our previous illustrations in which an asset costing $1,000 has a five-year life with an estimated salvage value of $100.

If, based on the original estimates, depreciation has been recorded at $180 for each of the first three years, the accumulated depreciation would be 3 × $180 = $540. Now suppose that just before the recording of the fourth year's depreciation, circumstances indicate that the asset's life will be six years instead of five and that its salvage value at the end of the sixth year should be $40. The revised depreciation expense to be taken during the revised remaining useful life is computed as follows:

Original asset cost	$1,000
Revised salvage value	40
Revised total depreciation	$ 960
Depreciation already recorded (3 years @ $180)	540
Revised remaining depreciation	$ 420

Revised remaining useful life	3 years

Revised periodic depreciation expense for fourth, fifth, and sixth years	$420/3 = $140/year

This revision method does not correct the overstatement of recorded depreciation and related misstatement of other accounts in the first three years. Instead, it offsets the earlier overstatements with an equal amount of understatement during the later years. The justification for this approach is that (1) such errors are often immaterial, (2) errors of overstatement are often offset by errors of understatement in the same accounting period, and (3) depreciation is a relatively imprecise estimate anyway. Recording the revision of depreciation in the above manner also complies with the recommendations of Accounting Principles Board *Opinion No. 9* and *Opinion No. 20*.

MAINTENANCE AND BETTERMENTS

We stated earlier that some level of maintenance is assumed when estimating useful lives and salvage values. Ordinarily, periodic upkeep (such as lubrication, cleaning, replacement of minor parts) is considered to maintain an asset's capacity, and the costs for this are charged to expense as they are incurred.

In contrast to routine or periodic maintenance, expenditures may be made for what are often termed extraordinary repairs or betterments. In these cases, the expenditures increase the capacity or extend the useful life of the asset or both. Examples of betterments include the major overhaul or rebuilding of machinery, replacement of airplane engines with others of substantially greater power, and adding accessories such as refrigeration equipment, special loading devices, or winches to trucks. To the extent that betterments increase capacity or extend useful life, the related costs should not be currently expensed, but should be accounted for in a way that better matches revenue and expense.

Proper matching requires that the cost of the betterment be allocated to the periods benefited. Therefore, betterments are charged to the asset account or to the related accumulated depreciation account. Note that debiting *either* account has the effect of increasing the asset's book value. In cases where capacity is increased and useful life remains constant, the betterment should be charged to the asset account and the subsequent periodic depreciation expense should be increased by a proportionate amount. This treatment is equivalent to depreciating the betterment over the related asset's remaining useful life. When the betterment simply extends the useful life, it is more appropriate to charge the related accumulated depreciation account. Subsequent depreciation entries should be for amounts that will lead to the revised salvage value at the end of the revised (extended) useful life.

CONTROL OF PLANT ASSETS

Firms with a large number of plant assets normally maintain some formal records and follow systematic inventory procedures so that specific persons can be held accountable for the assets' use and protection. Many firms assign a specific serial number to identify each significant asset. This is usually done by small decals, stampings, or etchings that are not easily removed or altered.

Coupled with the identification procedures will be a formal record of the assets called a **plant ledger** or an **equipment ledger.** This record is often a subsidiary ledger to the various plant asset accounts. The ledger may be maintained by a manual system or by an electronic data processing system. Regardless of the record's form, the following basic data are usually incorporated:

> Description
> Manufacturer's identification or model number
> Firm's assigned serial number and accounting classification
> Date purchased
> Assigned physical location
> Person accountable
> Original cost
> Major modifications and repairs
> Depreciation method and data
> Disposition data (date, price, remarks)

This record requires that any purchase, transfer, or disposition of property be formally noted. Also, a company should periodically verify its equipment ledger by a physical count of the items involved.

DISPOSAL OF PLANT ASSETS

Firms normally dispose of their plant assets once they are no longer efficient or useful. Generally, the asset still has some book value and some sales value in the used market.

Most asset disposals involve the following related factors:

(1) Assets are often sold before the last day of the accounting period. Consequently, there must be a special entry to record depreciation on the asset up to the date of the sale.

(2) Asset disposals are actually conversions of used assets into cash. Therefore, the disposal entry must remove from the accounts all balances related to the asset account and the accumulated depreciation (or amortization) related to the asset sold.

(3) Assets are most often sold for amounts either greater or less than their book values. Hence, gains or losses are incurred. Net proceeds in excess of book values are gains on disposal. Book values in excess of net proceeds are losses on disposal.

Let us review the basic data we shall use to illustrate two asset disposal situations:

Equipment's original cost	$1,000
Estimated salvage value after five years	100
Annual straight-line depreciation	180
(Unless stated otherwise, assume that depreciation	
to the date of sale has been recorded.)	

SOLD FOR LESS THAN BOOK VALUE   Assume the asset is sold for $30 at the end of the fifth year. The correct entry is:

Cash	30	
Loss on Sale of Plant Assets	70	
Accumulated Depreciation	900	
Equipment		1,000

To record sale of equipment for $30.

The loss is the book value of $100 minus the net proceeds of $30. The cash receipt is recorded, and both accounts related to the asset (the asset account and the contra account) are removed from the books.

SOLD FOR MORE THAN BOOK VALUE   Assume the asset is sold for $230 midway through the fifth year. Depreciation was last recorded at the end of the fourth year. The related entries are:

Depreciation Expense	90	
Accumulated Depreciation		90

To record depreciation expense for one-half year.

Cash	230	
Accumulated Depreciation	810	
Equipment		1,000
Gain on Sale of Plant Assets		40

To record sale of equipment for $230.

Note that recording depreciation to the date of sale adds $90 to the accumulated depreciation account; we have $(4 \times \$180) + \$90 = \$810$. To properly reflect the sale, this entire amount of accumulated depreciation must be removed from the books. The gain is the net proceeds of $230 minus the asset's book value of $190.

If the asset is sold for an amount exactly equal to its book value, no gain or loss is involved. Should the asset be abandoned (discarded) before the end of its expected useful life, a loss equal to its book value will be recorded.

Disposal Involving Trade-in

Sometimes, rather than selling assets outright, firms trade them in for new ones. The allowance for a trade-in is applied against the sale price of the new equipment, and the buyer is thus obligated to pay the seller only the difference.

When a nonmonetary productive asset is disposed of by exchanging it for a similar asset, the guidelines for analyzing the transaction differ from those that apply when an asset is sold outright. The Accounting Principles Board has concluded that an exchange of similar productive assets is not the culmination of an earnings process, and consequently no gain should be recognized on such an exchange.[2] Instead, the asset acquired is recorded at an amount equal to the sum of the book value of the asset traded in plus any cash expended in the exchange.

Assume that the equipment used in the earlier illustration (cost, $1,000) was traded in after three years (accumulated depreciation, $540) on new equipment that cost $1,400. A trade-in allowance of $600 was given. The entry to record the exchange of assets and the related payment would be:

Equipment (new)	1,260	
Accumulated Depreciation	540	
Equipment (old)		1,000
Cash		800

To record trade of equipment.

Note that this treatment is a departure from the general rule that newly acquired assets are recorded at their implied cash cost. The new equipment has a cash price of $1,400, but it is recorded at $1,260. Essentially, its book value has been reduced by the $140 gain that is not recognized in the exchange.

If an exchange of similar productive assets indicates that a loss has occurred, the loss is recognized. If in the preceding exchange the company was given a trade-in allowance of $400 (rather than $600), the entry to record the exchange would be:

Equipment (new)	1,400	
Loss on Trade-in	60	
Accumulated Depreciation	540	
Equipment (old)		1,000
Cash		1,000

To record trade of equipment.

[2]Opinions of the Accounting Principles Board, No. 29, "Accounting for Nonmonetary Transactions," American Institute of Certified Public Accountants, New York, 1973.

Trade-in and
Tax Regulations

The Internal Revenue Code specifies that any gains or losses on trade-in transactions involving similar assets are not to be reported in the year of exchange. With reference to gains, the treatment parallels the analysis discussed above. Losses, however, are to be treated as adjustments of the carrying value of the new asset. The above trade-in illustration resulting in a loss would be recorded as follows under the income tax guidelines:

Equipment (new) ($1,400 plus $60 loss)	1,460	
Accumulated Depreciation	540	
Equipment (old)		1,000
Cash		1,000

To record trade of equipment.

This treatment does not recognize the loss in the year of exchange, but increases the depreciation available in future years. Generally accepted accounting principles require that significant losses on trade-ins be recognized rather than deferred. Some firms, however, follow the income tax method when losses are immaterial, in order to avoid keeping a separate record for income tax purposes.

MEASUREMENT AND AMORTIZATION
OF NATURAL RESOURCES

Natural resources include such items as timber, petroleum, natural gas, coal, and other mineral deposits mined by the extractive industries. These assets are initially accounted for at their cost. When known deposits are purchased, the initial measurement is quite simple. When the natural resource is discovered after extensive exploration, however, determination of its initial cost is more difficult. Because not all exploration activities are successful, one must determine which activities were necessary to discover the resource. Expenditures for these activities are capitalized as the cost of the resource, and the remaining amounts are expensed.

The term **depletion** refers to the allocation of the cost of natural resources to the units extracted from the ground. Accounting for depletion of natural resources is comparable to units-of-production depreciation for constructed fixed assets. The average acquisition cost of each unit of natural resource is identified; then periodic depletion is recognized in proportion to that part of the total resource extracted in a period. For each period,

$$\text{Periodic Depletion} = \frac{\text{Cost of Natural Resource}}{\text{Total Estimated Units of Resource}} \times \text{Units Extracted in Current Period}$$

For example, assume that a company acquired for $600,000 a parcel of land whose only commercial value was its access to a soft coal mine estimated to contain 800,000 tons of extractable coal. We would calculate the depletion per ton as

$$\frac{\$600,000}{800,000 \text{ tons}} = \$0.75 \text{ per ton}$$

If, during the first period, 60,000 tons were extracted, that period's depletion charge would be $60,000 \times \$0.75 = \$45,000$. We would make the following entry:

| Depletion of Coal Deposit | 45,000 | |
| Accumulated Depletion | | 45,000 |

To record depletion of coal deposit.

In the balance sheet, accumulated depletion is a contra account deducted from the cost of the natural resource. This treatment is similar to the handling of accumulated depreciation accounts. The disposition of the periodic depletion charge depends on whether the extracted units are sold or are on hand at the end of the period. If the units are sold, the depletion amount is deducted in the income statement as part of the cost of the resource sold. Units on hand at year-end, however, constitute inventory items, so the depletion charge is carried in the balance sheet as part of the inventory cost. In addition to the depletion charge, the costs of extracting and processing the natural resource are part of the inventory cost.

The extraction of many natural resources requires the construction of "on-site" equipment such as drilling and pumping devices, roads, trackage, and conveyor systems. These are often in remote places and may be abandoned when the natural resource is exhausted. If the useful life of these assets will expire before the resources are exhausted, then ordinary depreciation techniques are appropriate. When the reverse is true (natural resources are exhausted and the asset is abandoned before the end of its physical life), depreciation should be based on the length of the extraction period. Alternatively, it would be appropriate to employ the units-of-production depreciation approach based on the estimated total resource to be extracted.

For example, assume coal mining equipment was acquired at a cost of $105,000 in the example above. The equipment is estimated to have a $5,000 salvage value after the coal is mined. Depreciation for the first year would be

$$\frac{\$105,000 - \$5,000}{800,000 \text{ tons}} \times 60,000 \text{ Tons Extracted} = \$7,500$$

Many companies in the extractive industries—especially oil- and gas-producing companies—have large discovered and proved reserve fields that are held for future operations. Most often these reserves are carried at historical cost figures that may represent only a small fraction of their current values. In such cases, supplemental disclosures in the financial statements may be made about the current values of the proved reserves.

MEASUREMENT AND AMORTIZATION OF INTANGIBLE ASSETS

The term **intangible asset** is not used with precision in accounting literature. Certain physically intangible assets such as investments and receivables are typically not considered intangible assets. Rather, by convention, only certain assets such as patents, trademarks, franchises, and goodwill are included in the intangible category. Because they lack physical substance, the existence and the useful life of intangible assets are often quite nebulous, and therefore the accounting procedures for them are somewhat arbitrary.

Examples of Intangible Assets

A **patent** is an exclusive privilege, granted by the federal government for a period of 17 years, for the right to use a specific process or to make a specific product. Patent laws were originated to encourage inventors by protecting them from unfair imitators who might usurp the invention for commercial gain. Just what is a patentable idea has become quite complex in the modern realm of technical knowledge. Consequently, long periods of patent "searching" and, frequently, successful defense of infringement suits may be necessary before the validity of a patent and some resulting commercial value become definite. Even though patents have a legal life of 17 years, technology or consumer tastes may make their economic life much shorter. Because of their tentative value, patents should probably be accounted for quite conservatively. When patents are purchased some time after having been granted, the buyer enjoys the privilege at most for only the remaining legal life.

Copyrights protect the owner against the unauthorized reproduction of a specific written work or a work of art. A copyright lasts for the life of the author plus 50 years. When valuable copyrights are purchased, the sums can be substantial, and proper measurement and amortization are necessary for valid income determination. But even with the related legal fees, the cost of most copyrights is seldom sufficiently material to present accounting problems.

Franchises most often involve exclusive rights to operate or sell a specific brand of products in a given geographical area. Although many franchises are agreements between two private firms, various governmental units award franchises for public utility operations within their legal jurisdictions. Franchises may or may not entail payment and may be for definite or indefinite periods of time.

Trademarks represent the exclusive and continuing right to use certain terms, names, or symbols, usually to identify a brand or family of products. An original trademark can be registered at nominal cost, so few accounting problems exist. On the other hand, the purchase of well-known, and thus valuable, trademarks may involve substantial amounts of funds.

Expenditures incurred in launching a business (usually a corporation) are called **organization costs.** These may include attorney's fees, fees paid to the state, and other costs related to preparation for operations. Most firms amortize these costs over a five- to ten-year period, although, strictly speaking, the expenditures benefit the firm throughout its operating life. Reinforcing this practice is the fact that income tax guidelines permit the amortization of organization costs for tax purposes over a period of not less than five years.

Goodwill is the value derived from a firm's ability to earn more than a normal rate of return on its physical assets. The existence and measurement of goodwill is complex, because it can stem from any factor that tends to make income rates high relative to investment. Examples of such factors include exceptional customer relations, advantageous location, operating efficiency, superior personnel relations, favorable financial sources, and even monopolistic position. Because measuring goodwill is difficult, a firm may record it in the accounts only when the amount paid to acquire a firm exceeds the recognized value of the other assets involved. To determine the amount of goodwill often requires complex negotiations, but the agreed-on amount is almost always based on the anticipated above-normal earnings.

HUMAN RESOURCES AS A LONG-TERM ASSET

The current resources of most firms are depicted on their balance sheets with a fair degree of fidelity. Long-term assets, on the other hand, usually are not. Quite apart from the limitations of cost (or depreciated cost) measurement and the changing value of the dollar, there is the question of *omitted* resources. One example is the *developed* goodwill of a firm. As pointed out in this chapter, only *acquired* goodwill can be reflected in the balance sheet. Another example is the human assets of a firm. A generation ago, Sir Matthew Webster Jenkinson wrote:

Though your balance-sheet's a model of what
    balance-sheets should be,
Typed and ruled with great precision in a type that
    all can see;
Though the grouping of the assets is commendable
    and clear,
And the details which are given more than usually
    appear;
Though investments have been valued at the sales
    price of the day,

And the auditor's certificate shows everything
    O.K.;
One asset is omitted—and its worth I want to
    know,
The asset is the value of the men who run the
    show.[1]

Values ascribed to the management and working force of a firm have always been regarded as an *expense* of the firm (through salaries and payroll costs). Until recently, little attention has been given to the idea that human resources are an asset that might be measured and reported in some way to both those within the business firm and outsiders. In recent years a number of accountants have been researching the problems of reporting the values of human resources.[2]

[1]From Archibald Bowman, "Reporting on the Corporate Investment," *The Journal of Accountancy*, May 1938, p. 399.
[2]For more information on human resources accounting, see Eric Flamholtz, *Human Resources Accounting* (Encino and Belmont, California: Dickenson Publishing Company, Inc., 1974).

Measurement of Intangible Assets

Intangible assets acquired by a firm from outside entities should initially be recorded in the accounts at their cost. Similarly, some intangible assets created internally by a firm are measured at their cost. For example, the costs incurred to form a business are charged to Organization Costs and the costs to secure a trademark, such as attorney's fees, registration fees, and design costs, are charged to the Trademarks account.

The accounting for other expenditures related to intangible assets varies, depending on the type of expenditure and the nature of the intangible asset. *Research and development costs* are not capitalized as a part of any intangible asset, because accounting guidelines require that these expenditures be expensed when incurred.[3] Thus, many significant costs incurred by a firm in developing a patentable product or process will not be capitalized. Legal costs associated with patent work may be capitalized, however. The costs of developing, maintaining, or restoring an intangible asset are also expensed when incurred, provided that the asset is not specifically identifiable, has an indeterminate life, or is inherent in the business as a whole—such as goodwill. As a result of these procedures, some companies may have important intangible assets that are carried at a nominal amount or may even fail to appear on the firm's financial statements.

Amortization of Intangibles

The amortization of an intangible asset is the periodic write-off to expense of the asset's cost over the term of its expected useful life. Because salvage values are ordinarily not involved, amortization typically entails: (1) determining the asset's cost, (2) estimating the time period over which it contributes revenues, and (3) allocating the cost in equal amounts to each accounting period involved. In 1970, the Accounting Principles Board modified this general rule by specifying in its *Opinion No. 17* that the period of amortization for intangibles should not exceed 40 years. The result of this limitation is that all intangibles are treated as if they have a limited life—even though some, such as trademarks, may legally have indefinite lives.

The basic entry for amortizing intangible assets parallels that for recording periodic depreciation, except, of course, that different account titles are involved. For example, assume that the periodic amortization for a patent originally costing $51,000 was determined to be $3,000. The proper entry would be:

Patent Amortization Expense	3,000	
Accumulated Amortization—Patents		3,000
To record patent amortization.		

---

[3]*Statement of Financial Accounting Standards No. 2,* "Accounting for Research and Development Costs," Financial Accounting Standards Board, Stamford, Conn., 1974.

The expense would be deducted from revenues, and Accumulated Amortization—Patents would be a contra account deducted from the related asset account on the balance sheet as follows:

Intangible Assets

Patents (original cost)	$51,000
Less: Accumulated amortization	3,000
Book value of patents	$48,000

The asset account is frequently credited directly (no contra account being used). In such cases, the amortization would be as follows:

Patent Amortization Expense	3,000	
Patents		3,000

To record patent amortization.

When no contra account is used, the asset account reflects the asset's book value, and the balance sheet presentation would be:

Patents (cost less amortization to date) $48,000

Intangible assets originally deemed to have specific useful lives should be reviewed periodically to determine if their value or their economic lives have decreased. If so, immediate write-off or some plan of periodic amortization at an increased rate is appropriate.

LEASES

A firm may rent property for a specified period of time under a contract called a **lease.** The company acquiring the right to use the property is known as the **lessee**; the owner of the property is the **lessor.** The rights transferred to the lessee are called a **leasehold.** Examples of leased assets are land, buildings, trucks, factory machinery, office equipment, and automobiles. A lessee's accounting treatment depends on whether a lease is an operating lease or a capital lease.

Operating Lease

The typical rental agreement illustrates an **operating lease**—the lessee pays for the use of an asset for a limited period of time, while the lessor retains the usual risks and rewards of owning the property. For these leases, the lessee usually charges each lease payment to rent expense. Sometimes leases extending over long periods of time require advance payments from the lessee. The lessee debits these payments to a **leasehold account,** then allocates the amount to rent expense over the period covered by the advance payment. For example, if an advance payment is made for the final year's rent on a 10-year lease, the amount will be carried in the leasehold account until the 10th year. It would then be allocated to rent expense in the final year of the lease.

Expenditures made by a lessee to alter or improve property leased under an operating lease are called **leasehold improvements.** For example, a company may construct a building on leased land or make improvements to a leased building. The improvements or alterations become part of the leased property and revert to the lessor at the end of the lease. Thus, the cost of leasehold improvements should be amortized over the life of the lease or the life of the improvements, whichever is shorter. Practice varies as to the classification of leasehold improvements—some businesses classify them as intangible assets, while others include them in the property, plant, and equipment section of the balance sheet.

Capital Lease

A **capital lease** transfers to the lessee substantially all of the benefits and risks related to the ownership of the property. A lease meeting one or more of the following criteria is a capital lease:[4]

(1) The lease transfers ownership of the property to the lessee by the end of the lease term.

(2) The lease contains a bargain purchase option.

(3) The lease term is at least 75% of the estimated economic life of the leased property.

(4) The present value of the lease payments[5] is at least 90% of the fair value of the leased property.

The economic effect of a capital lease is very similar to that of an installment purchase. As such, the lessee accounts for a capital lease by recording the leased property as an asset and establishing a liability for the lease obligation. The present value of the future lease payments determines the dollar amount of the entry. The leased property is then depreciated over the period it will benefit the lessee. Part of each lease payment made by the lessee will be charged to interest expense and the remainder will reduce the lease obligation.

The basic differences between operating and capital leases have been identified. There are many complexities in accounting for capital leases. Similar complexities face lessors because they may treat some leases as sales or financing transactions rather than typical rental agreements. These areas are beyond the scope of this text; they are covered in intermediate accounting texts.

---

[4]*Statement of Financial Accounting Standards No. 13,* "Accounting for Leases," Financial Accounting Standards Board, Stamford, Conn., 1976.

[5]Present values are discussed in Appendix A to Chapter 15.

EXHIBIT 10–4
Long-term Assets Section of a Balance Sheet

Long-term Assets (in Thousands of Dollars)	Original Cost	Accumulated Depreciation	Book Value
Plant assets:			
Fixtures	$ 90	$ 20	$ 70
Equipment	1,400	300	1,100
Buildings	4,600	1,200	3,400
Land	800	—	800
Total plant assets	$6,890	$1,520	$5,370
Intangible assets (less amortization to date):			
Patents			$ 200
Goodwill			500
Organization costs			100
Total intangible assets			$ 800
Total long-term assets			$6,170

BALANCE SHEET PRESENTATION OF LONG-TERM ASSETS

On the balance sheet, long-term assets usually are presented below the sections for current assets and investments. Exhibit 10–4 shows how the long-term assets section of a balance sheet may appear. Frequently, on highly summarized financial statements, long-term assets are all shown at their book value.

KEY POINTS TO REMEMBER

(1) Long-term assets are carried at historical cost less depreciation, if applicable.

(2) The historical cost of an asset is its implied cash price plus those expenditures necessary to prepare it for use.

(3) The cost (less salvage value) of a limited-life asset is periodically charged to expense over its useful life as follows:

Constructed assets: Depreciation
Natural assets: Depletion
Intangible assets: Amortization

(4) Ordinary maintenance is a current expense; betterments should be capitalized or charged to the related asset's accumulated depreciation account.

(5) The most commonly used depreciation methods are straight-line, units of production, sum of the years' digits, and double declining balance.

(6) Revisions of depreciation are normally accomplished by recalculating depreciation charges for current and subsequent periods.

(7) Gains and losses on sale or abandonment of assets are determined by comparing their book values to their net proceeds. Gains are not recognized on exchanges of similar productive assets, although losses are recognized on such exchanges.

(8) Intangible assets are amortized over the shorter of the economic life or the legal life (if any), with a maximum amortization period of 40 years.

QUESTIONS

10-1 List three major types of long-term assets, present examples of each, and indicate to what degree, if any, each is subject to periodic write-off.

10-2 Describe the typical sequence of transactions and related problem areas associated with long-term assets.

10-3 State the general rule for deriving the original measurement of long-term assets.

10-4 Explain why the recognition of depreciation expense is necessary to properly match revenue and expense.

10-5 How is the use of the contra account Accumulated Depreciation justified when recording depreciation?

10-6 "One cannot properly estimate the useful life of an asset without first considering the level of maintenance to be employed." Do you agree? Why or why not?

10-7 How can one justify the use of accelerated depreciation?

10-8 Briefly describe an operational situation that would lend itself most naturally to each of the following depreciation methods: (a) straight-line, (b) units of production, (c) sum-of-the-years'-digits or double declining-balance.

10-9 Explain the benefit of recording accelerated depreciation for income tax purposes even though the total depreciation taken is no more than would be taken if straight-line depreciation were used.

10-10 How would you handle a revision of depreciation charges due to a change in an asset's estimated useful life or salvage value? Which periods—past, present, or future—are affected by the revision?

10-11 What is the difference between expenditures for maintenance and those for betterments?

10-12 What factors determine the gain or loss on the disposition of depreciable assets?

10-13 Why is computing the depletion of natural resources similar to computations related to units-of-production depreciation?

10-14 Why does economic life take precedence over physical or legal life in the amortization or depreciation of assets?

10-15 List and briefly explain the nature of six different types of intangible assets.

10-16 Briefly state the general rules for (a) measurement and (b) amortization of intangible assets.

10-17 What is the difference between an operating lease and a capital lease?

EXERCISES

10-18 The following data relate to the purchase of a machine to be used by a firm in the manufacture of its product:

Invoice price	$16,000
Applicable sales tax	800
Purchase discount taken	320
Freight paid	400
Cost of insurance coverage on machine while in transit	50
Installation costs	1,000
Testing and adjusting costs	100
Repair of damages to machine caused by another of firm's employees	270

Compute the amount at which the machine should be originally carried in the accounts of the firm.

10-19 Kasten Company purchased a small established plant from one of its suppliers. The purchase price, totaling $500,000, included the land, a building, and factory machinery. The property tax bill for the plant showed the following assessed valuations for the items included:

Property Class	Assessed Values
Land	$142,000
Building	248,500
Machinery	319,500
	$710,000

Using the assessed valuations on the property tax bill as a guide, allocate the total purchase price of the plant to the various related accounts in the Kasten Company's records.

10-20 A delivery truck costing $6,000 is expected to have a 10% salvage value at the end of its useful life of four years or 120,000 miles.

(a) Assume the truck was purchased on January 2, 19X1. Compute the depreciation expense for the year 19X1 using each of the following depreciation methods: (1) straight-line, (2) sum-of-the-years'-digits, (3) double declining-balance, and (4) units-of-production (assume the truck was driven 42,000 miles in 19X1).

(b) Assume the truck was purchased on May 1, 19X1. Compute the depreciation expense for the year 19X2 using each of the following depreciation methods: (1) straight-line, (2) sum-of-the-years'-digits, (3) double declining-balance, and (4) units-of-production (assume the truck was driven 20,000 miles in 19X2).

(c) Present the general journal entry to record the sale of the truck for $700 cash at the end of its useful life.

10-21 At the end of last year, the balance sheet of Lindsay, Inc. shows a building with a cost of $550,000 and accumulated depreciation of $325,000. The company uses the straight-line method to depreciate the building. When acquired, the building's useful life was estimated at 40 years and its salvage value at $50,000. Early in January of the current year, Lindsay made structural improvements to the building costing $200,000. Although the capacity of the building was unchanged, it is estimated that the improvements will extend the useful life of the building to 50 years, rather than the 40 years originally estimated. The salvage value remains at $50,000.

(a) By the end of last year, how many years had the company depreciated the building?

(b) Present the general journal entry to record the cost of the structural improvements.

(c) Present the general journal entry to record the building's depreciation expense for the current year.

10-22 On January 2, 19X0, Royce, Inc. purchased new equipment for $35,000. The equipment was expected to have a $3,000 salvage value at the end of its estimated 8-year useful life. Straight-line depreciation has been recorded. While reviewing the accounts in anticipation of adjusting them for the 19X3 annual financial statements, Royce decided that the useful life of the equipment should be extended by 2 years and the salvage value decreased to $2,000.

(a) Present a general journal entry to record depreciation expense on the equipment for the year 19X3.

(b) What is the book value of the equipment at the end of 19X3 (that is, after recording the depreciation expense for 19X3)?

10-23 Redding Company has a used executive charter plane that originally cost $150,000. Depreciation on the plane has been recorded for five years on the straight-line method, with an assumed salvage value of $30,000 at the end of its estimated 8-year useful life. The last depreciation entry was made at the end of the fifth year. Four months into the sixth year, Redding has decided to dispose of the plane.

Present journal entries to record:
(a) Depreciation expense to the date of sale.
(b) Sale of the plane for cash at its book value.
(c) Sale of the plane for $75,000 cash.
(d) Sale of the plane for $60,000 cash.
(e) Trade-in of the plane on a new aircraft costing $200,000. (The trade-in allowance received is $62,000 with the balance paid in cash.)

10-24 Ella Copper Company recently acquired a parcel of land estimated to contain 500,000 tons of commercial grade copper ore. Ella paid $2,500,000 for the land, then acquired extraction equipment at a cost of $700,000. Although the equipment will be worthless when the ore is depleted, it is estimated that the land can be sold for $350,000 after reclamation efforts are made costing $150,000.

(a) Compute the proper depletion charge for a period during which 50,000 tons of ore are extracted and sold.

(b) Compute the proper depreciation expense on the extraction equipment, using the units-of-production method, for a period during which 50,000 tons of ore are extracted and sold.

10–25 For each of the following unrelated situations, calculate the annual amortization expense and present a general journal entry to properly record the expense.

(a) A two-year-old patent was purchased for $270,000. The patent will probably be commercially exploitable for another nine years.

(b) Certain sales counter fixtures, costing $60,000, were constructed and permanently installed in a building leased from another firm. The physical life of the counters was estimated to be 25 years. At the time of their installation, the operating lease had 12 years to run and contained no provision for the removal of the fixtures.

(c) A trademark is carried at a cost of $36,000, which represents the out-of-court settlement paid to another firm in exchange for an agreement to refrain from using or claiming the trademark or one similar to it. The trademark should have an indefinite life.

(d) A patent was acquired on a device designed by a production worker. Although the cost of the patent to date consisted of $10,000 in legal fees and an award to the worker of $5,300, the patent is thought to be commercially valuable during its entire legal life and to be currently worth approximately $255,000.

PROBLEMS

10–26 The items below represent expenditures (or receipts) related to the construction of a new home office for Behm Insurance Company.

Cost of land site on which was located an old apartment building appraised at $25,000	$ 150,000
Legal fees of the purchaser	700
Title insurance premiums on property	1,200
Pay-off of mortgage and related interest assumed by the purchaser	7,000
Delinquent property taxes assumed by the purchaser	2,300
Cost of razing the old apartment building	10,000
Proceeds from sale of salvaged materials	(1,800)
Grading and drainage on land site	8,000
Architect's fees on new building	30,000
Payment to building contractor	2,000,000
Payment of medical bills of employee accidentally injured while inspecting construction of building	600
Special assessment for paving of city sidewalks (paid to city)	14,000
Proceeds from condemnation action by the city for small strip of land to widen the street	(12,000)
Cost of "open house" party to celebrate opening of new building	2,500

REQUIRED

From the given data, compute the carrying value of the land and that of the building in the accounts of Behm Insurance Company.

10–27 On January 2, Reed, Inc. purchased a stamping machine to be used in the fabrication of a part for one of its key products. The machine cost $27,000 and was estimated to have a useful life of 4 years or 60,000 stampings, after which it could be sold for $3,000.

REQUIRED

Compute the depreciation expense for each year of the machine's useful life under each of the following depreciation methods:

(a) Straight-line.

(b) Sum-of-the-years'-digits.

(c) Double declining-balance.

(d) Units-of-production. (Assume annual production in stampings of 18,000, 20,000, 10,000, and 12,000.)

10–28 During the first few days of 19X6, the Wilcox Company began business and entered into the following transactions.

(1) Paid $7,000 in attorney's fees and other costs related to the organization of the company.

(2) Purchased a parcel of land with an old building on it for $90,000. The building was torn down at a net cash cost of $10,000.

(3) Erected a prefabricated, modular shell building on the site in three days at a cost of $170,000. The building has an estimated useful life of 15 years and an estimated salvage value of $5,000.

(4) Purchased an existing patent on a special production process for $54,000. The legal protection afforded the patent has 12 more years to run.

(5) Purchased and installed some used equipment to enable the company to begin operations. The purchase price plus installation costs totaled $67,000. The company expects to replace the equipment after 6 years. Its residual value is estimated to be $4,000.

(6) Entered into a 5-year operating lease for additional office space. Paid the last month's rent of $600 in advance.

REQUIRED

(a) Prepare general journal entries to record the above transactions.

(b) Prepare the general journal entries needed at December 31, 19X6 to record the proper amounts of depreciation and amortization expense for the year. Sum-of-the-years'-digits depreciation is used for the equipment, while straight-line depreciation is used for the building. Organization costs are amortized over 5 years.

10–29 Lite Mining Company has just purchased a site containing an estimated 900,000 tons of coal. The following expenditures were made by Lite before starting operations:

Cost of land survey	$ 2,000
Purchase price of the property	650,000
Legal fees to acquire title and secure the proper zoning for operations	8,000
Construction of on-site conveyance and loading facilities	210,000

After all the coal has been extracted, Lite expects to sell the property for $70,000 and certain parts of the conveyance and loading facilities for $30,000. Lite estimates that before selling the property it will have to spend $40,000 on the property to meet government safety and environmental standards concerning abandoned mines.

REQUIRED

(a) Compute the total depletion charge for a period during which 100,000 tons of coal are extracted from the mine.
(b) Compute the amount of depreciation on the conveyance and loading facilities during the period when 100,000 tons of coal are extracted. Use the units-of-production depreciation method.
(c) Compute the cost of a 15,000-ton inventory of coal at the end of a period for which all extraction and processing costs except depletion and depreciation of conveyance and loading facilities average $3.00 per ton.

10–30 Certain of the transactions of the Bridge Company during 19X6 are given below:

Jan. 2   Finished a major overhaul of a machine that was acquired for $8,500 on January 2, 19X1, and was estimated to have a useful life of 8 years and a salvage value of $500. The overhaul, which cost $900, is expected to extend the machine's useful life 2 years beyond the original useful life estimate. No change in residual value is expected. The machine is depreciated on a straight-line basis.
Apr. 1   Entered into a 7-year operating lease for additional warehouse space. Paid the last month's rent of $400 when the lease was signed.
June 30   Discarded office equipment and realized no salvage value. A salvage value of $100, after a 6-year useful life, had been estimated when the equipment was acquired for $1,900 on July 1, 19X0. Depreciation expense, under the straight-line method, was last recorded on December 31, 19X5.
July 1   Purchased equipment in exchange for a $2,000 non-interest-bearing note due in one year. The cash price of the equipment was $1,852. The equipment has an estimated useful life of 4 years and a salvage value of $200. The equipment is depreciated by the double declining-balance method.
Oct. 1   Constructed storage bins at a cost of $2,275 in the warehouse space leased April 1. The physical life of the storage bins is estimated to be 15 years. The lease contains no provision for the removal of the bins; the lessor will take control of the bins at the end of the lease. The storage bins are amortized by the straight-line method.

REQUIRED

(a) Prepare general journal entries to record the above transactions.
(b) Prepare the December 31, 19X6 general journal entries needed to record the proper amounts of depreciation and amortization expense for assets acquired during the year.

10–31 On March 1, 19X4, Walsh, Inc. purchased a new delivery truck. Costs associated with the transaction were as follows:

Base price	$ 8,200
Special accessories	1,400
Sales tax	500
License fee for 19X4	200
	$10,300

The truck will be used for 4 years, will be depreciated on a straight-line basis, and has an estimated salvage value of $1,700.

REQUIRED
Prepare journal entries for each of the following transactions:
(a) The truck was purchased for cash.
(b) Depreciation on the truck was recorded for 19X4.
(c) On July 1, 19X5, a $900 air conditioning unit was added to the truck. Although the truck's estimated useful life was not affected, its estimated salvage value was increased by $100.
(d) On September 1, 19X5, the truck was tuned and given a safety inspection at a cost of $200. Neither the estimated useful life nor the estimated salvage value was affected.
(e) Depreciation on the truck was recorded for 19X5.
(f) Depreciation on the truck was recorded for 19X6.
(g) On January 2, 19X7, the truck received a $600 major overhaul. The overhaul should extend the truck's useful life by one year, at which time the revised salvage value should be $1,300.
(h) Depreciation on the truck was recorded for 19X7.
(i) On May 1, 19X8, the truck was sold for $2,500.

ALTERNATE PROBLEMS

10–26A The items below represent expenditures (or receipts) related to the construction of a new home office for Gaines Investment Company.

Cost of land site on which was located an old apartment building appraised at $30,000	$ 200,000
Legal fees, including fee for title search	1,000
Pay-off of mortgage and related interest assumed by the purchaser	5,500
Delinquent property taxes assumed by the purchaser	2,000
Cost of razing the old apartment building	8,400
Proceeds from sale of salvaged materials	(1,500)
Grading and drainage on land site	9,000
Cost of basement excavation (contracted for separately)	7,500
Architect's fees on new building	40,000
Payment to building contractor—original contract price	1,600,000

Cost of changes during construction to make building more energy efficient	16,000
Cost of replacing windows broken by vandals	1,100
Out-of-court settlement for mud slide onto adjacent property	4,000
Special assessment for paving of city sidewalks (paid to city)	15,000
Proceeds from condemnation action by the city for small strip of land to widen the street	(8,000)

REQUIRED

From the given data, compute the carrying value of the land and that of the building in the accounts of Gaines Investment Company.

10-27A On April 1, 19X1, Morgan Company purchased a cutting machine to be used in the fabrication of a part for one of its key products. The machine cost $100,000 and was estimated to have a useful life of 5 years or 150,000 cuttings, after which it could be sold for $8,500.

REQUIRED

Compute the depreciation expense for each of the years 19X1 through 19X6 under each of the following depreciation methods:
(a) Straight-line.
(b) Sum-of-the-years'-digits.
(c) Double declining-balance.
(d) Units-of-production. (Assume annual production in cuttings as follows: 19X1, 15,000; 19X2, 22,500; 19X3, 30,000; 19X4, 37,500; 19X5, 37,500; 19X6, 7,500.)

10-28A During the first few days of 19X5, the Carlene Company opened and entered into the following transactions.
(1) Paid $3,000 for attorney's fees and other costs related to the organization of the company.
(2) Purchased a parcel of land with a building on it for $180,000. The building will be used in operations. Its useful life is estimated to be 20 years, with a residual value of $8,000. The assessed valuations for property tax purposes show land at $56,000 and the building at $84,000.
(3) Acquired an exclusive franchise for 10 years to handle a line of high-quality merchandise. The payment for the franchise was $45,000.
(4) Purchased store equipment, paying in cash the invoice price (including 5% sales tax) of $21,000. The estimated useful life of the equipment is 7 years, and the salvage value is $1,250.
(5) Paid $250 freight on the store equipment purchased.
(6) Paid $300 to repair damages to floor caused when the store equipment was accidently dropped as it was moved into place.

REQUIRED

(a) Prepare general journal entries to record the above transactions.
(b) Prepare the December 31, 19X5 general journal entries needed to record the proper amounts of depreciation and amortization expense for the year.

Sum-of-the-years'-digits depreciation is used for the equipment, while straight-line depreciation is used for the building. Organization costs are amortized over 5 years.

10-29A Pitz Gravel, Inc. has just purchased a site containing an estimated 1,200,000 tons of high-grade aggregate rock. The following expenditures were made by Pitz before starting production:

Purchase price of property	$300,000
Legal fees to acquire title and secure the proper zoning for operations	4,000
Removal of overburden and grading for drainage	56,000
Construction of on-site crushing, washing, and loading facilities	110,000

Once the rock deposits are no longer commercially valuable, the land will be worthless and Pitz will abandon the site. Local laws require that the quarry be drained and partially refilled, at an estimated cost of $60,000. Certain parts of the on-site crushing, washing, and loading facilities are estimated to have a salvage value of $14,000 at the time operations are to be terminated.

REQUIRED

(a) Compute the total depletion charge for a period during which 80,000 tons of rock are extracted from the quarry.

(b) Compute the amount of depreciation on the crushing, washing, and loading facilities during the period when 80,000 tons of rock are extracted. Use the units-of-production depreciation method.

(c) Compute the cost of a 9,000-ton inventory of rock at the end of a period for which all extraction and processing costs except depletion and depreciation of crushing, washing, and loading facilities average $0.47 per ton.

10-31A Flame Corporation had the following transactions and entries related to its local delivery trucks.

19X1

Jan. 5   Purchased for $8,200 cash a new Ford truck estimated to have a useful life of three years and a salvage value of $1,000.

Feb. 20   Installed a new set of rear view mirrors at a cost of $30.

June 9   Paid $90 for an engine tune-up, wheel balancing, and a periodic lubrication.

Aug. 2   Paid a repair bill of $150 for the uninsured portion of damages to the truck caused by Flame's own driver.

Dec. 1   Installed a set of parts bins in the truck at a cost of $300. This expenditure was not expected to increase the salvage value of the truck.

Dec. 31   Recorded annual depreciation on the truck.

19X2

May 5   A decision was made to trade in the Ford truck for a larger Dodge truck costing $9,560. A $5,500 trade-in allowance was received, with the difference to be paid in cash. The new truck was expected to have a salvage value of $1,500 at the end of its useful life of 5 years.

Dec. 31   Recorded depreciation on the Dodge truck for the year.

Flame's depreciation policies include (1) straight-line depreciation, (2) recording depreciation to the nearest whole month, (3) expensing all capital expenditures of $50 or less, and (4) following generally accepted accounting principles in recording exchanges of similar assets.

REQUIRED
Present general journal entries to record the activities listed above. Identify each entry by the date shown.

BUSINESS DECISION PROBLEM

You are the accountant for Easton Company, which is planning to acquire equipment to eliminate pollutants from one of its plants. Since the plant is scheduled to be phased out of operations over the next 4 years, its annual production (and generation of pollutants) will decrease each year over the four-year period. The pollution-control equipment will be technically obsolete at the end of this four-year period. It will cost $300,000, and its salvage value is estimated at $34,000.

REQUIRED
(a) For its financial reporting, do you recommend that Easton use the straight-line depreciation method or an accelerated depreciation method (either sum of the years' digits or double declining balance) for the pollution-control equipment? Explain.
(b) Prepare a schedule showing the annual depreciation for each of the 4 years under (1) the straight-line method, (2) the sum-of-the-years'-digits method, and (3) the double declining-balance method.
(c) Which of these depreciation methods should Easton use for income tax reporting purposes? Explain. Assume the income tax rate will be 50% over the next four-year period. To support your answer, prepare schedules showing the cumulative income tax postponement at the end of each of the next 4 years as a result of using the depreciation method you select compared with the other two methods. (Prepare two schedules, each comparing the method you select with one of the other two methods. See Exhibit 10–3.)

11
Current Liabilities
and Payroll Accounting

Liabilities, one of the three elements in the accounting equation, represent, in general, the obligations of a firm to nonowners. Total liabilities are divided into two subcategories—current liabilities and long-term liabilities. In this chapter, we focus on current liabilities, and because several liabilities are associated with a firm's payroll, we will examine payroll accounting procedures and requirements in some depth.

THE NATURE OF LIABILITIES

Liabilities are present obligations resulting from past transactions that require the firm to pay money, provide goods, or perform services in the future. The existence of a past transaction is an important element in the definition of liabilities. For example, a purchase commitment is actually an agreement between a buyer and a seller to enter into a *future* transaction. The performance of the seller that will create the obligation on the part of the buyer is, at this point, a future transaction; hence, a purchase commitment is not considered a liability. Another example is a long-term salary contract with an executive. At the time the agreement is signed, each party is committed to perform in the future—the executive is committed to render services and the company is committed to pay for those services. No liability is recorded for the company at the time the contract is signed, because at this point the executive has not yet rendered any services.

Although they involve quite definite future cash payments, the foregoing examples are not reportable as liabilities because they are related to future transactions. It is appropriate, however, to disclose both significant purchase commitments and executive compensation commitments in footnotes to the balance sheet.

In general, items shown as liabilities are often not legally due and payable on the balance sheet date. For example, the routine accrual of wage expense incurred but not paid during the period results in a credit balance account titled Wages Payable. In most cases, accrued wages are not legally due until several days after the balance sheet date. In the case of other accrued expenses, such as property taxes and executive bonuses, payment may not be legally due until months after the balance sheet date. Most obvious, of course, are bonds payable, which, although shown as liabilities, may not be actually payable for several decades. These items are all reported as liabilities, however, because they are obligations resulting from past transactions that will be settled as the business continues to operate.

The determination of liabilities is basic to properly accounting for a firm's operations. For example, if a liability is omitted, then either an asset or an expense has been omitted also. If expense is involved, then income and owners' equity are misstated as well. Thus, one or both financial statements can be erroneous if liabilities are not reported correctly.

Most liabilities are satisfied by the eventual remittance of cash. Some may require the furnishing of goods—for instance, a publisher obligated to provide issues of a magazine to customers who have subscribed in advance. Other liabilities may be obligations to provide services. Examples of this type are product warranties and maintenance contracts that may accompany the sale of a new appliance or automobile.

Definition of Current Liabilities

For many years, current liabilities were considered those obligations that were to be paid during the coming year—a simple and quite useful rule. The rule was subsequently changed to make it more flexible and broader in scope. The present version designates current liabilities as all obligations that will require within the coming year or the operating cycle, whichever is longer, (1) the use of existing current assets or (2) the creation of other current liabilities. We may contrast the two versions of the rule by noting, for example, that a one-year note payable that was to be satisfied by the issuance of another short-term note would be a current liability only under the later version of the rule. Also, the newer version has significant effects on firms in those industries (for example, distilling and lumber) whose typical operating cycle is longer than one year.

Obligations that do not meet these guidelines are classified as long-term liabilities. Two examples are mortgage notes payable and bonds payable, which we examine in Chapter 15.

Measurement of Current Liabilities

Generally speaking, current liabilities should be measured and shown in the balance sheet at the money amount necessary to satisfy the obligation. Of course, when future provision of services or goods is involved, the related dollar amount can only be an estimate of the costs involved. The liability for product warranties, for example, may have to be estimated. If the face amount of a note payable contains an identifiable element of interest, the interest is subtracted from the face amount when presenting the liability in the balance sheet. An example of this latter point is the situation in which a company discounts its own note at the bank. The Discount on Notes Payable arising from this transaction is classified as a contra account to the Notes Payable account.

EXAMPLES OF CURRENT LIABILITIES

In this section, we review many of the more common types of current liabilities. Although not exhaustive, the concepts conveyed here should enable you to look deeper into the accounting problems and techniques involved.

Trade Accounts and Notes Payable

In a balance sheet listing of current liabilities, amounts due to short-term creditors on open accounts or notes payable are commonly shown first. Most of the accounting procedures for reflecting accounts and notes payable in the records are fairly routine and have been discussed in previous chapters. One should be careful, however, that transactions occurring shortly before and after the end of the accounting period are properly accounted for. At the end of the period, recently received items included in inventory must be reflected in the records as accounts payable, if unpaid for, and as purchases of the period. Likewise, items that the company owns and for which a payable has been recorded must be included in inventory whether or not the items have been received. In other words, a proper "cut-off" of purchases, payables, and inventory is necessary for valid income determination and presentation of financial position.

Dividends Payable

Ordinary dividends are distributions of corporate earnings to stockholders. We discuss many of the accounting problems related to dividends in Chapter 14. Because the timing and amounts of dividends are determined solely at the discretion of the corporate board of directors, dividends do not accrue as does interest expense. Instead, dividends are shown as liabilities only upon formal declaration. Once formally declared, however, they become binding obligations of the corporation. Because they are almost always paid within several weeks of the time they are declared, dividends are current liabilities.

Portions of Long-term Debt

The repayment of many long-term obligations is scheduled as a series of installments over several years. To properly report liabilities involving installments, one should show the principal amount of the installments due within one year (or the operating cycle, if longer) as a current liability.

Sales and Excise Taxes

As we all know, many products and services are subject to sales and excise taxes. The laws governing these taxes usually require the retail (or selling) firm to collect the tax at the time of sale and to remit the collections periodically to the appropriate taxing agency. Assume that a particular product selling for $1,000 is subject to a 4% state sales tax and a 10% federal excise tax. No tax should be applied to another tax. Rather, each tax should be figured on the basic sales price only. We could record the above sale as follows:

Accounts Receivable (or Cash)	1,140	
Sales		1,000
Sales Tax Payable		40
Excise Tax Payable		100

To record sales and related taxes.

TO ERR IS HUMAN

Will they take the money and run? That's a natural question anyone who has accidentally mailed about $7.8 million too much to some 78,000 strangers would ask. Manufacturers Hanover Trust Co., one of the nation's largest banks, did just that about six months ago. The bank was supposed to send a quarterly common stock dividend of $32\frac{1}{2}$ cents a share to stockholders of American Home Products Corp. Accidentally, though, the bank added an extra five cents a share.

After discovering the blooper, horrified bank executives rushed out thousands of Mailgrams and letters to American Home Products stockholders, pleading for understanding—and the excess money.

The story has a happy ending. A bank official said in an interview that the bank has recovered "about 98.5%" of the money. Concerning the rest, about $117,000, the official said: "We expect to recover some of that as well."

The bank, however, is somewhat less open about how much it cost to recover the money, how the slip-up occurred, who did it and what happened to that unfortunate person. "All we want to say is that it was human error," a spokesman said cautiously. "All the safeguard mechanisms, all the checks and balances were in place. But the procedures weren't properly followed." Asked if anyone was punished, he said "no one was fired" but declined to comment further.

Bank officials and financial experts agree that one reason for Manufacturers Hanover's success in retrieving such a high percentage of the money is that most of American Home Products stock is held by large institutions, many of whom do business with the bank. "Seems to me this either shows that an awful lot of people are honest or an awful lot of people are afraid of Manufacturers Hanover, or both," said one investment counselor.

A random survey of some American Home Products stockholders indicates other possible reasons. "We're all in the same boat," said an official of a large mutual fund organization. "If Manny Hanny (Manufacturers Hanover) makes the error today, we could make it tomorrow." He added that "this kind of thing could happen to anyone, including us, so we were glad to cooperate."

Others indicated they felt they were legally obligated to refund the money. "There isn't any doubt in my mind that Manny Hanny could collect it from us in the courts if they had to," another mutual fund executive said. "Our attorneys said this fell under the heading of 'unjust enrichment.'"

A spokesman for T. Rowe Price Associates Inc., a large Baltimore-based investment counseling firm and mutual fund sponsor, said: "Obviously it was money we weren't entitled to. We returned the money because we felt it was morally the right thing to do. For us to even consider keeping it would be unthinkable. We like to take advantage of investment opportunities but not in this way."

This attitude was echoed by some individuals as well. "It would be the same as if the bank makes a mistake and puts $1 million in your account, right?" said John J. Gilbert, who attends numerous corporate annual meetings as an advocate of shareholder democracy. Mr. Gilbert, who said his sister owns some American Home Products stock, added that it would be unthinkable to profit from such a mistake.

Nevertheless, Mr. Gilbert's brother, Lewis, has said he plans to ask the bank a few questions about the matter at its next annual meeting.

The bank won't comment on the cost of the collection process except to say the amount "isn't material." A spokesman wouldn't even say how many letters and Mailgrams were necessary.

Asked what changes the bank has made in its procedures to insure against a repeat blooper, he replied: "What has been done is the procedures have been reviewed and then reemphasized to all the staff involved. The systems and all the built-in safeguards were working. What happened was a human error."

Recording this transaction as a $1,140 sale would be incorrect, because this would overstate revenues and possibly lead to the omission of the liabilities for the taxes collected. Periodically, a tax reporting form is filled out and the period's tax collections remitted with it. At that time, the tax liability accounts are debited and a credit is made to Cash.

As an expedient, some firms record sales at the gross amount including taxes collected. Then, to convert this type of revenue figure to actual sales, the transaction total of $1,140 must be divided by 1.14 to yield $1,000 as the basic sales price and $140 as the total tax.

Estimated or Accrued Liabilities

Estimated or accrued liabilities are often referred to as **accrued expenses.** Generally they originate as the credits offsetting a series of debit entries to various expense accounts that are necessary for matching periodic revenues and expenses. Examples are the accrual of incurred (but unpaid) product warranty expense, various taxes, and vacation pay.

PRODUCT WARRANTIES Many firms guarantee their products for a period of time after the sale. Proper matching of revenues and expenses requires that the estimated costs of providing these warranties be recognized as an expense of the period of sale rather than of a later period when the warranty costs may actually be paid.

Let us suppose that a firm sells a product for $300 per unit and this price includes a 30-day warranty against defects. Past experience indicates that 3% of the units will prove defective and that the average cost of repair is $40 per defective unit. Furthermore, during a particular month, product sales were $240,000, and 13 of the units sold in this month were found to be defective and were repaired during the month. Using this information, we calculate the accrued liability for product warranties at the end of the month as follows:

Number of units sold ($240,000/$300)	800
Rate of defective units	× 0.03
Total units expected to fail	24
Deduct: Units failed in month of sale	13
Units expected to fail in the remainder of the warranty period	11
Average repair cost per unit	× $ 40
Estimated liability for product warranty provision at end of period	$440

This accrued liability would be recorded by the following entry at the end of the period of sale.

Product Warranty Expense	440	
Estimated Liability for Product Warranty		440

To record estimated warranty expense.

In the future period when a unit fails, the subsequent repair costs will be recorded by debiting the accrued liability, Estimated Liability for Product Warranty, and crediting Cash, Supplies, and so forth.

PROPERTY TAXES   Property taxes are a primary source of revenue for city and county governments. The property taxes paid by business firms are, to some extent, the price for the many governmental services from which the firms benefit. Thus, property taxes are considered an operating expense that applies pro rata to each operating period.

Although procedures vary widely, most often property taxes are assessed annually. A typical sequence involves:

(1) Determination of the tax rate by relating the total revenue needed to the total value of property being taxed.

(2) Assessment of specific amounts of taxes against specific property parcels—at this time the taxes usually become liens against the property.

(3) Payment of taxes, usually in one or two installments.

Taxes may be assessed and paid after or before the tax year to which they relate. For example, if property taxes are not assessed until the taxing agency is into the fiscal year to which the taxes relate, firms must accrue an estimated amount of property tax expense (and the related liability) until their actual tax liability is known. To illustrate, assume Willetts Company ends its accounting year on December 31 and is located in a city whose fiscal year runs from July 1 to June 30. City taxes are assessed on October 1 (for the fiscal year starting the preceding July 1) and are to be paid by November 15. Willetts Company estimates in July that its property taxes for the next year will be $18,000. At the end of July, August, and September, the following entry would be made to reflect the estimated property taxes for the month ($18,000/12 = $1,500):

Property Tax Expense	1,500	
Estimated Property Taxes Payable		1,500

To record estimated property tax expense.

On October 1, Willetts Company receives a $19,008 property tax bill from the city. Willetts' estimate for the period July through September turns out to have been too low by $252 ($19,008/12 = $1,584; $1,584 − $1,500 = $84; $84 × 3 months = $252). The $252 difference may be handled as an increase in the property taxes for October. The entry to record the October taxes would then be:

Property Tax Expense ($1,584 + $252)	1,836	
Estimated Property Taxes Payable		1,836

To record estimated property tax expense.

The Estimated Property Taxes Payable account has a balance of $6,336 after the October entry. The entry on November 15 to record the payment in full of the property taxes would be:

Estimated Property Taxes Payable	6,336	
Prepaid Property Taxes	12,672	
Cash		19,008

To record payment of property taxes.

The balance in the Prepaid Property Taxes account would be amortized to Property Tax Expense over the months November through June—$1,584 each month.

In contrast with the preceding illustration, if property taxes are assessed and paid before the taxing agency's fiscal year begins, the entire tax payment is initially charged to Prepaid Property Taxes. No estimates are necessary; the prepayment is simply amortized over the year to which the taxes apply.

INCOME TAXES   The federal government, most states, and some municipalities levy income taxes against corporations, individuals, estates, and trusts. Sole proprietorships and partnerships are not taxable entities—their owners include income derived from these businesses on their personal tax returns. In the United States, income is generally reported annually on one or more income tax forms, and taxpayers compute (or assess themselves) the amount of tax due. The tax due is determined in accordance with generally accepted accounting principles, which are often modified by the various tax laws, rulings of the taxing agencies, and many applicable court decisions. Because administration of tax laws is quite complex and many honest differences exist in their interpretation, the final tax liability for certain firms may not be settled until several years after a given year is ended. Thus, to a degree, the liability for income taxes is often an estimated obligation for some period of time.

Because corporations are separable taxable entities, ordinarily a legal obligation for income taxes is incurred whenever corporate income is earned. Therefore, corporate financial statements should be routinely adjusted for income tax liabilities. This adjustment is often recorded as follows:

Income Tax Expense	XXX	
Income Tax Payable		XXX

To record estimated income tax.

Income Tax Expense may be included among the operating expenses in the income statement. An alternative presentation, designed to highlight the impact of income taxes, derives an intermediate figure in the income statement labeled "income before income taxes." All expenses except income taxes are subtracted from revenue to derive this figure. Income taxes are then the last item subtracted in the income statement. Income taxes are discussed more fully in Chapter 28.

VACATION PAY Most employees now enjoy annual vacation privileges—typically, at least two weeks off with regular pay. This means that an employee earns 52 weeks of pay during the 50 weeks he or she actually works each year. Therefore, vacation is given at the rate of 4% (for example, 2 weeks vacation/50 weeks worked) of the basic salary per period.

Depending on the particular agreement, some employees may earn and have due them each payroll period some fraction of their annual vacation. Other contracts may require a full year's employment before any vacation is given. In the latter case, the proportion of employees eventually earning annual vacations depends on the employee turnover rate.

Assume that a firm provides an annual two-week vacation for employees who have worked 50 weeks and that the employee turnover rate indicates that 80% of the staff will, in fact, receive vacation. The proper accrual of vacation benefits expense for a $10,000 payroll would be

$$\$10,000 \times 0.04 \times 0.8 = \$320$$

The appropriate journal entry would be

Vacation Benefit Expense	320	
Estimated Liability for Vacation Benefits		320

To record estimated vacation benefits.

At the time the vacation benefits are paid, the amount would be recorded as follows:

Estimated Liability for Vacation Benefits	XXX	
Cash		XXX

To record payment of vacation benefits.

This treatment would reflect the annual vacation expense in the appropriate periods and recognize throughout the year the accrued liability for vacation benefits.

CONTINGENT LIABILITIES

A contingent liability is an obligation that *may* develop out of an existing situation. Whether or not the obligation develops depends on the occurrence of a future event.

If it is probable that the future event will occur and the amount of the liability can be reasonably estimated, the liability should be recorded in the accounts.[1]

[1]*Statement of Financial Accounting Standards No. 5, Accounting for Contingencies,* Financial Accounting Standards Board, Stamford, Conn., 1975.

The estimated liability for product warranty discussed earlier in the chapter is an example of this situation. Our analysis assumed that customers were likely to make claims under warranties relating to goods that had been sold and that a reasonable estimate of the amount of warranty obligation could be made.

When the future event is not likely to occur or the amount of the liability cannot be reasonably estimated, contingent liabilities are not recorded in the accounts as liabilities. They should, when significant, be disclosed in the financial statements. Usually this is done in a parenthetical note in the body of the statements or as a footnote to the balance sheet. Some common examples of contingent liabilities are given below.

Notes receivable discounted. As explained in Chapter 8, firms that discount (sell to others) notes receivable with recourse are contingently liable for their payment should the original maker fail to honor the note. We noted previously that sometimes this contingent liability is disclosed in the balance sheet by presenting Notes Receivable Discounted as a contra account to Notes Receivable.

Credit guarantees. To accommodate important but less financially secure suppliers or customers, a firm may guarantee the other company's debt by cosigning a note. Until the original debtor satisfies the obligation, the cosigning firm is contingently liable for the debt.

Lawsuits. In the course of its operations, a firm may become the defendant in a lawsuit involving potential damage awards. Lawsuits are often pending for several years. During this time the firm should disclose in its financial statements the nature of the suit and any potential liability.

Additional income tax assessments. Earlier in this chapter, we explained that many aspects of the law and rulings relating to income taxes are subject to a significant degree of interpretation. Consequently, as a practical matter, many firms are not certain of their final income tax liability for a given tax period until the related return has been audited or until the applicable statute of limitations becomes effective. The federal statute of limitations for income taxes is three years. In cases of fraud or failure to file returns, there is no statute of limitations. Proposed assessments for additional taxes often are contested in court for extended periods. During this time the taxpaying firm is contingently liable for the proposed additional tax.

PAYROLL ACCOUNTING

Wages and salaries represent a major element in the cost structure of most businesses. Indeed, for some service businesses, the compensation paid to employees may be the largest single expense incurred. As we examine the procedures and requirements associated with accounting for salaries and wages, we shall also see that several different current liabilities are related to a company's payroll expense.

IMPACT OF LEGISLATION ON PAYROLL PROCEDURES

Payroll accounting procedures are influenced significantly by legislation enacted by the federal and state governments. These laws affect payroll accounting because they levy taxes based on payroll amounts, establish remittance and reporting requirements for employers, and set up certain minimum standards for wages and hours.

Levy of Taxes

FEDERAL INSURANCE CONTRIBUTIONS ACT   In the mid-1930s, the federal government enacted a national social security program designed to provide workers with a continuing source of income during retirement. The program has been expanded several times since then, one example being the 1965 enactment of the Medicare program for hospital and medical insurance protection to persons 65 years of age and older. Today, in addition to health insurance benefits for eligible people, social security represents a broad program that provides monthly payments to workers and their dependents when a worker retires, becomes disabled, or dies.

Monthly benefit payments and hospital insurance protection under Medicare are financed by taxes levied on employees, their employers, and self-employed people. Approximately 9 out of 10 employed persons in the United States are currently earning social security protection through this process. Medical insurance under Medicare is financed by premiums paid by persons enrolling for this protection and by amounts from the general revenues of the federal government. Because our focus in this chapter is on payroll accounting, we will consider in more detail the financing provided by a tax on employees and their employers.

The Federal Insurance Contributions Act (FICA) establishes the tax levied on *both* employee and employer. The following schedule indicates, at the time of this writing, the planned tax rates through the year 1984:

Calendar Year	FICA Rate
1979–1980	6.13%
1981	6.65
1982–1984	6.70

The FICA tax applies to wages paid to employees during a calendar year, up to a certain amount per employee. For example, in 1979 the tax was applied to the first $22,900 of an employee's wages. With a 6.13% rate, the maximum tax on any one employee in a year would be 6.13% × $22,900 = $1,403.77. Social security legislation provides for automatic increases in the amount of earnings subject to the FICA tax as wage levels increase in the future.

The employee's tax is deducted from each paycheck by the employer. The tax levied on the employer is the same as that assessed the employee. With a rate of 6.13%, the employer's total tax for a year would equal 0.0613 times the total wages subject to FICA tax paid to employees during the year.

The schedule of FICA tax rates may be changed by future legislation. For this reason, and for ease of calculation, we shall use a 6% rate in our illustrations and problems.

FEDERAL UNEMPLOYMENT TAX ACT　The Federal Unemployment Tax Act (FUTA) is also a part of the federal social security program. The states and the national Social Security Administration work together in a joint federal–state unemployment insurance program. The function of FUTA is to raise funds to help finance the administration of the system of unemployment compensation programs operated by the states. Generally, funds collected under this act are not paid out as unemployment compensation benefits, but are used to pay administrative costs at the federal and state levels. In times of high unemployment, however, the federal government may appropriate funds from its general revenues to provide extended unemployment benefits.

FUTA generates funds by a payroll tax levied *only* on the employer. The law established the rate at 3.4% of the first $6,000 paid to each employee, but the employer is entitled to a credit against this tax for unemployment taxes paid to the state. The maximum credit allowed is 2.7% of the first $6,000 of each employee's wages. Because states have typically set their basic unemployment tax rates at the level of this maximum credit, the effective FUTA rate on the employer will generally be 0.7% (3.4% − 2.7%) of the first $6,000 paid to each employee.

STATE UNEMPLOYMENT COMPENSATION TAXES　Benefit payments to individuals to compensate them for wages lost during unemployment are handled through unemployment compensation programs administered by each state. Generally, a worker who becomes unemployed through no fault of his or her own, is able to work, and is available for work will be eligible for unemployment benefits. The duration and amount of benefits are typically related to the worker's length of employment and average wage during a previous base period.

The funds to finance unemployment benefits are generated in most states by a payroll tax levied exclusively on *employers*. In a few states, the employee must also contribute. Owing to the credit allowed against the FUTA tax, states usually establish their unemployment tax rate for new employers at 2.7% of the first $6,000 of wages paid each employee. But because one objective of an unemployment compensation program is to reward employers with records of steady employment, the rate may be varied over time according to an experience rating. Employers with a favorable record of stable employment may pay less than the basic rate, while employers with an unfavorable, irregular employment record may pay more than the basic rate. An employer with a favorable experience rating who pays less than the basic rate is still entitled to the maximum 2.7% credit against the federal unemployment tax.

In calculating FICA, FUTA, and state unemployment taxes, it is important to remember that they are levied on certain maximum amounts of payroll. As employers progress through a calendar year, they must be alert to the fact that a greater amount of wages each pay period may no longer be subject to one or more of these taxes. The following schedule indicates the possible divergence that may arise between the total payroll for a period and the payroll subject to the FICA and unemployment taxes.

Total payroll	$205,000
Wages subject to FICA tax (In 1979, for example, this excludes any wages in excess of $22,900 per employee.)	$176,000
Wages subject to FUTA and state unemployment taxes (Excludes any wages in excess of $6,000 per employee.)	$ 59,000

FEDERAL INCOME TAX WITHHOLDING   Employers are required to withhold federal income taxes from wages and salaries paid to employees. Current withholding of income taxes facilitates the government's collection of the tax and also eliminates the possible burden on the employee of having to pay a tax on income after the income has been used for other purposes.

The amount of income tax withheld from each employee is based on the amount of the employee's wage or salary, the employee's marital status, and the number of withholding allowances to which the employee is entitled. When first employed, each employee reports his or her marital status, social security number, and number of withholding allowances to the employer on an *Employee's Withholding Allowance Certificate*, also known as *Form W-4*. Employees file new W-4s if there are subsequent changes in withholding allowances or marital status. Employees are entitled to each of the withholding allowances for which they qualify. These include one for the employee, one for his or her spouse, and one for each dependent. Additional allowances may be claimed if the employee is (1) 65 or older, or (2) blind, or if the employee's spouse is (3) 65 or older, or (4) blind. Also, an employee may claim one or more additional allowances based on expected excessive itemized deductions on the employee's annual income tax return.

EXHIBIT 11–1
Wage-Bracket Table

WEEKLY Payroll Period—Employee MARRIED												
And the wages are—		And the number of withholding allowances claimed is—										
At least	But less than	0	1	2	3	4	5	6	7	8	9	10 or more
		The amount of income tax to be withheld shall be—										
$300	$310	$47.50	$43.00	$39.00	$34.90	$30.90	$26.90	$23.40	$19.90	$16.50	$13.00	$10.00
310	320	49.90	45.30	41.10	37.00	33.00	28.90	25.20	21.70	18.30	14.80	11.50
320	330	52.30	47.70	43.20	39.10	35.10	31.00	27.00	23.50	20.10	16.60	13.20
330	340	54.70	50.10	45.50	41.20	37.20	33.10	29.10	25.30	21.90	18.40	15.00
340	350	57.10	52.50	47.90	43.30	39.30	35.20	31.20	27.20	23.70	20.20	16.80
350	360	59.50	54.90	50.30	45.70	41.40	37.30	33.30	29.30	25.50	22.00	18.60

EXHIBIT 11–2
Incidence of Taxes Related to Payroll Amounts

Tax	Employer	Employee
Federal Insurance Contributions Act	X	X
Federal Unemployment Tax Act	X	
State Unemployment Compensation Taxes	X	In a very few states
Federal Income Tax Withholding		X
State Income Tax Withholding		X

Employers usually use wage-bracket tables prepared by the government to determine the amount of federal income taxes to withhold from each employee. These tables indicate the amounts to withhold at different wage levels, for different numbers of withholding allowances. Exhibit 11–1 (page 393) illustrates a few lines from a 1979 wage-bracket table.

Alternatively, employers may follow a procedure called the percentage method, which is especially useful when there are no wage-bracket tables pertaining to the length of the particular payroll period in question. Both the wage-bracket tables and the percentage method incorporate a graduated system of withholding. That is, the rates of withholding increase as the earnings subject to withholding increase.

STATE INCOME TAX WITHHOLDING Most states now have an income tax that is also withheld by employers. Payroll procedures for withholding state income taxes are similar to those for withholding federal income taxes.

INCIDENCE OF PAYROLL TAXES Taxes related to payroll amounts may be levied on the employee, the employer, or both. Exhibit 11–2 summarizes the incidence of the various payroll taxes we have just discussed.

Employee versus Independent Contractor

Salaries and wages paid to employees provide the basis for withholding taxes from employees and levying payroll taxes on the employer. Independent contractors are not subject to withholding and must therefore be distinguished from employees. In general, an *employee* performs services subject to the supervision and control of another party known as the employer. Other variables that establish the existence of an employer–employee relationship are (1) the employer firm has the power to discharge the individual worker, (2) the employer firm sets the hours of work for the individual worker, and (3) the employer firm furnishes a place to work. An *independent contractor*, on the other hand, may also perform services for a business firm, but that firm does not have the legal right to direct and control the methods used by this person. Independent contractors are in business for themselves; examples are certified public accountants, lawyers, and physicians.

The earnings of employees who are paid on an hourly or piecework basis are often defined as *wages*. A *salary* is defined as the compensation of an employee whose pay is stated on a monthly or annual basis. In practice, however, the distinction between these terms becomes blurred and they are used more or less synonymously. Amounts paid to independent contractors are identified as *fees*. For example, the expense account Audit Fees may be charged for the amounts paid to a certified public accountant for audit work, and Legal Fees may be charged for payments to a lawyer for legal work.

Remittance and Reporting Requirements

The legislation levying various taxes on payroll amounts also specifies the procedures for remitting these taxes to the government and establishes the reports an employer must file. A sound system of payroll accounting ensures that these payments are made and reports are filed on time.

FICA TAXES AND FEDERAL INCOME TAXES WITHHELD   Employer remittance and reporting requirements are the same for both employer's and employees' FICA taxes and federal income taxes withheld, since these taxes are combined for payment and reporting purposes. The specific remittance requirements vary depending on the combined dollar amount of the taxes. Exhibit 11–3 details these remittance guidelines.

EXHIBIT 11–3
Remittance Requirements for FICA Taxes and Federal Income Taxes Withheld

Dollar Amount of FICA Taxes and Federal Income Taxes Withheld	Remittance Requirements
1. Undeposited amount is $2,000 or more at the 7th, 15th, 22nd, or end of month.	Deposit taxes in a Federal Reserve bank or authorized commercial bank within three banking days after the 7th, 15th, 22nd, or end of month, whichever date applies to the particular case.
2. Undeposited amount is $200 or more and less than $2,000 at the end of the first or second month in a calendar quarter.	Deposit taxes in a Federal Reserve bank or authorized commerical bank within 15 days of the end of the first or second month, whichever applies to the particular case.
3. Undeposited amount is $200 or more and less than $2,000 at the end of a calendar quarter.	Deposit taxes in a Federal Reserve bank or authorized commerical bank by close of next month.
4. Undeposited amount is less than $200 at the end of a calendar quarter.	Remit taxes directly to Internal Revenue Service along with employer's quarterly tax return or deposit taxes in Federal Reserve bank or authorized commercial bank.

Each quarter, employers file an Employer's Quarterly Federal Tax Return, Form 941, with the Internal Revenue Service. On this form the employer schedules a record of its liability for FICA taxes and withheld income taxes throughout the quarter and reports its deposits of these taxes.

By January 31, an employer must give each employee two copies of *Form W-2, Wage and Tax Statement,* which specifies the total wages paid to the employee, the federal income taxes withheld, the wages subject to FICA tax, and the FICA tax withheld for the preceding calendar year. The worker attaches one copy of Form W-2 to his or her federal income tax return. The employer also sends a copy of each employee's Form W-2 to the Social Security Administration, which, in turn, provides the Internal Revenue Service with the income tax data that it needs from these forms.

FEDERAL UNEMPLOYMENT INSURANCE TAXES   The amount due on federal unemployment insurance taxes must be reviewed quarterly. If at the end of any of the first three quarters of a year, the undeposited taxes exceed $100, a deposit must be made with a Federal Reserve bank or authorized commercial bank during the first month after the quarter. If the amount due is $100 or less, no deposit is necessary. By January 31, each employer must file a Form 940, Employer's Annual Federal Unemployment Tax Return, for the preceding year. If the annual tax reported on Form 940, less deposits made, exceeds $100, the entire amount due must be deposited by January 31. If this amount is $100 or less, it may be either deposited or remitted along with Form 940.

STATE UNEMPLOYMENT COMPENSATION TAXES   There is some variation among states in the filing and payment requirements for unemployment compensation taxes. Often, however, employers are required to file reports quarterly, with tax payments accompanying the report. Some states require payments to be made more frequently, sometimes monthly, if the taxes owed by an employer exceed a preestablished level.

Wages and Hours

FAIR LABOR STANDARDS ACT   The Fair Labor Standards Act establishes minimum wage, overtime pay, and equal pay standards for employees covered by the act and sets recordkeeping requirements for their employers. The act's coverage has been amended several times since its passage in 1938. Its provisions now extend, with certain exemptions, to employees directly or indirectly engaged in interstate commerce and to domestic service workers. Executive, administrative, and professional employees are exempt from the minimum wage and overtime provisions of the act.

At the time of this writing, for example, the minimum wage that an employee must receive in 1979 is $2.90 an hour. Of course, employers and employees may agree to higher wages. Employers often operate under contracts negotiated with their employees' unions that provide more favorable terms to employees than the standards provided by the Fair Labor Standards Act.

The law provides that a covered employee must be paid an amount equal to at least $1\frac{1}{2}$ times the employee's regular rate of pay for every hour beyond 40 that the employee works in a week. Following are some examples of overtime pay computations under this standard; the examples differ by the basic method of compensating the employee.

(1) Jody Green receives $5.10 an hour as her regular rate of pay. This week she worked 44 hours. Her overtime rate of pay is $7.65 ($5.10 + $2.55) per hour. Her gross earnings this week are $234.60, computed as 40 hours $\times$ $5.10/hour + 4 hours $\times$ $7.65/hour.

(2) Jack Tyler is paid on a piece rate basis. His earnings this week, before any overtime compensation, were $206.40 for 43 hours of work. For overtime pay computations, his regular hourly rate of pay is determined by dividing his weekly earnings on a piece rate basis by the number of hours worked in that week, or $206.40/43 = $4.80. For each hour worked over 40 in the week, Jack Tyler is entitled to an overtime premium of $2.40 ($\frac{1}{2}$ of $4.80). His total earnings this week are thus $206.40 + $7.20 (3 hours $\times$ $2.40) = $213.60.

The act permits an alternative way to compensate piece rate workers for overtime, if agreed upon in advance of the work. This is to pay $1\frac{1}{2}$ times the piece rate for each piece produced during overtime hours.

(3) Bill Jantz receives a salary of $240 for a 40-hour workweek. The current week he worked 46 hours. Bill's regular rate of pay per hour is computed as $6.00 ($240/40); his overtime rate of pay is $6.00 $\times$ $1\frac{1}{2}$, or $9.00 per hour. Bill's gross earnings for the current 46-hour week are thus $240 + 6 $\times$ $9.00, or $294.

Again we should note that employees may negotiate overtime rates of pay in excess of the minimum standard illustrated in the preceding discussion. A union contract, for example, may require double the regular rate of pay for hours worked on Sundays and holidays.

Under the Fair Labor Standards Act, employers may not discriminate on the basis of sex in the rates paid to men and women employees performing equal work on jobs demanding equal skill, effort, and responsibility and having similar working conditions. The equal pay provisions also provide that when illegal pay differentials exist employers must eliminate them by a means other than reduction of employee pay rates. The law does permit wage differentials between men and women when the differential is due to a job-related factor other than sex, such as a difference based on a bona fide seniority system or a merit system.

Employers are required under the law to maintain a record detailing certain information about each employee's wage and hours, such as the hour and day the employee's workweek begins, the regular hourly rate of pay, the total overtime pay for any week in which more than 40 hours are worked, the deductions from and additions to wages, and the employee's total wages paid each period. The law does not prescribe any particular form for these records. The payroll records maintained in a typical payroll accounting system will contain much of this information, since it is also needed to comply with other laws and regulations.

OTHER PAYROLL DEDUCTIONS

In additon to FICA taxes, federal income taxes, and perhaps state and local income taxes, other items may be deducted from an employee's gross earnings in arriving at the net "take-home" pay for the period. Each additional deduction must be authorized by the employee; often this will be done individually, although in some instances the union contract provides the authorization needed by the employer. Examples of these items are payments for:

(1) Union dues.
(2) Premiums on life, accident, hospital, surgical care, or major medical insurance.
(3) Installment loan from employees' credit union.
(4) Advance from employer.
(5) U.S. savings bonds.
(6) Contributions to charitable organizations.
(7) Retirement plan.

NET PAY COMPUTATION FOR INDIVIDUAL EMPLOYEE

To illustrate the computation of an individual employee's net pay for a payroll period, let us assume Donald Bork's regular salary is $320.00 for a 40-hour workweek. He is married and claims three withholding allowances on Form W-4. During the current week he worked 42 hours. He has authorized his employer to deduct $3.00 a week from his earnings for group hospital insurance and $2.00 a week as a contribution to the United Way Charity. Prior to the current week, he has gross earnings for the year of $1,328. The applicable FICA tax rate is 6%. The amount to be paid to Donald Bork is shown in the following summary:

Gross earnings		$344.00
Deductions:		
FICA tax (@ 6%)	$20.64	
Federal income tax withheld	43.30	
Group hospital insurance	3.00	
United Way Charity contribution	2.00	
Total deductions		68.94
Net earnings		$275.06

An explanation of these amounts follows:

(1) Gross earnings—Bork's regular hourly pay rate is $320 ÷ 40 hours, or $8.00. His overtime rate of pay is $1\frac{1}{2}$ × $8.00, or $12.00 per hour. Because Bork

worked 2 hours overtime, his overtime pay is $2 \times \$12.00 = \$24.00$. His gross pay is his regular salary plus his overtime pay, $\$320.00 + \$24.00 = \$344.00$.

(2) FICA tax—Bork's gross earnings to date for the year ($\$1,672$) have not yet exceeded the maximum to which the FICA tax is applicable. Therefore, the FICA tax on Bork is $6\% \times \$344.00 = \$20.64$.

(3) Federal income tax withheld—We assume the wage-bracket table of Exhibit 11–1 applies to the current year. From this table we see that the income tax to be withheld from a married employee with three withholding allowances earning wages of at least $340 but less than $350 per week is $43.30.

(4) Group hospital insurance and charitable contribution—Bork has specifically authorized his employer to make these deductions.

PAYROLL RECORDS

The precise nature of an enterprise's payroll records and procedures depends to a great extent on the size of the work force and the degree to which the record-keeping is automated. In some form, however, two records are basic to most payroll systems: the payroll register and individual employee earnings records.

The Payroll Register

The *payroll register* is a detailed listing, prepared each pay period, of the company's complete payroll. Each employee's earnings and deductions for the period are contained in the payroll register. Exhibit 11–4 (page 400) illustrates a payroll register typical of those prepared by a firm with a small number of employees. The pay period covered by this payroll register is one week.

In Exhibit 11–4, the column immediately after the name of the employee shows the total hours worked by that employee during the week. Data on the hours worked are taken from time cards or similar documents maintained for each employee. In this illustration, each employee is paid a regular salary for a 40-hour workweek. The regular salary is shown in the first column of the earnings section of the register. Overtime pay is computed at $1\frac{1}{2}$ times the regular hourly rate (regular weekly salary $\div$ 40) and presented in the next column. The employees' gross earnings are presented in the final column in the earnings section.

The 6% FICA tax is deducted from each employee's gross earnings. The payroll illustrated is early in the calendar year (week ended February 4), so no employee's earnings have yet gone beyond the maximum amount of wages subject to the FICA tax. As discussed earlier, the federal income tax withheld is based on an employee's earnings, marital status, and number of withholding allowances. In Exhibit 11–4, for example, David Plank's relatively high federal income tax withheld is due to the fact that he is single and claims only one withholding allowance. The deductions for hospital insurance, contributions to

EXHIBIT 11-4
Payroll Register
Week Ended February 4, 19X1

Employee	Total Hours	Earnings			Deductions					Payment		Distribution	
		Regular	Overtime	Gross	FICA Tax	Federal Income Tax	Hospital Insurance	Other (see key)	Total Deductions	Net Earnings	Check No.	Office Salaries	Sales Salaries
Donald Bork	42	320.00	24.00	344.00	20.64	43.30	3.00	(A) 2.00	68.94	275.06	566	344.00	
Jane Latt	40	210.00		210.00	12.60	24.50	2.50	(B) 5.00	44.60	165.40	567		210.00
Raul Lopez	44	200.00	30.00	230.00	13.80	17.70	3.00		34.50	195.50	568		230.00
David Plank	40	300.00		300.00	18.00	55.10	2.00	(B) 5.00	80.10	219.90	569		300.00
Myra Smiken	44	280.00	42.00	322.00	19.32	47.70	3.00		70.02	251.98	570		322.00
Fred Wells	40	180.00		180.00	10.80	15.60	2.50	(A) 1.50	30.40	149.60	571	180.00	
Beth White	40	200.00		200.00	12.00	19.20	2.50		33.70	166.30	572	200.00	
Totals		1,690.00	96.00	1,786.00	107.16	223.10	18.50	13.50	362.26	1,423.74		724.00	1,062.00

Key: A—United Way Charity
B—U.S. Savings Bonds

charity, and purchases of U.S. savings bonds are specifically authorized by each employee affected by the deductions. The variance in the hospital insurance premium deducted is due to differences in the number of persons covered by the plan.

An employee's gross earnings less total deductions is the amount of pay the employee receives for the pay period. These net earnings are shown in the payment section of the payroll register, along with the number of the check issued by the company in payment of the wages.

In the last two columns of the payroll register, the gross earnings are distributed between the office salaries and sales salaries categories. This division permits the total salaries for the period to be recorded in the proper expense accounts.

Recording the Payroll and Related Taxes

Some businesses use the payroll register as a special journal; in these cases the pertinent information in the payroll register is posted directly to the general ledger. Often, however, the payroll register serves as the basis for an entry in the general journal that is then posted to the general ledger. The journal entry to record the weekly payroll shown in Exhibit 11–4 would be:

Office Salaries Expense	724.00	
Sales Salaries Expense	1,062.00	
FICA Tax Payable		107.16
Federal Income Tax Withholding Payable		223.10
Hospital Insurance Premiums Payable		18.50
United Way Contributions Payable		3.50
U.S. Savings Bond Deductions Payable		10.00
Payroll Payable		1,423.74

To record payroll for week ended
February 4.

The employer company may, at the time of recording each payroll, also record its payroll tax liabilities. None of the year-to-date gross earnings for the employees in Exhibit 11–4 has exceeded the maximum limits for either the FICA or unemployment taxes. The entry to record the employer's taxes for the week's payroll follows:

Payroll Tax Expense	167.88	
FICA Tax Payable (6% × $1,786)		107.16
Federal Unemployment Tax Payable		
(0.7% × $1,786)		12.50
State Unemployment Tax Payable		
(2.7% × $1,786)		48.22

To record payroll tax expense for week
ended February 4.

**Payment of
the Liabilities**

The various liabilities established in the entries recording the payroll and the employer's payroll taxes are settled by the employer making payments to the appropriate parties. The issuance of the payroll checks to the employees results in the following entry:

Payroll Payable	1,423.74	
Cash		1,423.74

To pay net payroll for week ended
February 4.

The FICA taxes, federal income taxes withheld, and federal unemployment insurance taxes would be remitted to a depository bank in accordance with the remittance requirements discussed earlier. The state unemployment compensation taxes would be remitted to the appropriate state agency, according to the state requirements. The hospital insurance premiums would be sent to the company providing the coverage, the United Way contributions would be paid to that charitable organization, and the deductions for the purchase of U.S. savings bonds would be remitted to the financial institution handling the acquisition of the bonds. If any, or all, of these liabilities remain unpaid when financial statements are prepared, they are classified as current liabilities in the balance sheet.

**Accrual of
Employer
Payroll Taxes**

Employer payroll taxes are based on employees' salaries and wages. If a company makes an adjusting entry at the end of an accounting period to accrue wages and salaries, then the related employer payroll taxes should also be recorded as part of the year-end adjustments. Payroll taxes are properly an expense of the period during which the related salaries and wages were earned by the employees, although the employer becomes *legally* obligated for these taxes in the period the salaries and wages are actually paid. This circumstance, coupled with an amount of payroll taxes that may be immaterial, leads to an alternative procedure followed by some companies: They do not accrue year-end payroll taxes, but record the total amount of payroll taxes in the year the payroll is paid.

**Individual
Employee
Earnings
Record**

Employers maintain an *individual earnings record* for each employee. This record contains much of the information needed to permit the employer to comply with the various taxation and reporting requirements established by law. Exhibit 11-5 illustrates an individual earnings record, that of employee Donald Bork for the first five weeks of 19X1.

The individual earnings record contains the details on earnings and deductions shown earlier in the payroll register. In addition, the last column, headed "cumulative gross earnings," enables the employer to know when an employee's earnings for the year have exceeded the maximum amounts to which the FICA and unemployment taxes are applied.

EXHIBIT 11-5

Individual Employee Earnings Record

Employee's Name ___Donald Bork___ Social Security No. ___719-23-4866___ Employee No. ___6___

Address ___510 Many Lane___ Male ___X___ Single ___ Weekly Pay Rate ___$320.00___

___Archer, Florida 32600___ Female ___ Married ___X___ Hourly Equivalent ___$8.00___

Date of Birth ___May 6, 1946___ Withholding Allowances ___3___

Position ___Clerk-Analyst___ Date of Employment ___June 1, 19X0___

Date Employment Ended ___

19X1 Period Ended	Total Hours	Earnings			Deductions					Payment		Cumulative Gross Earnings
		Regular	Overtime	Gross	FICA Tax	Federal Income Tax	Hospital Insurance	Other: A—United Way B—Savings Bonds	Total Deductions	Net Earnings	Check No.	
Jan. 7	40	320.00		320.00	19.20	39.10	3.00	A 2.00	63.30	256.70	412	320.00
Jan. 14	44	320.00	48.00	368.00	22.08	48.10	3.00	A 2.00	75.18	292.82	447	688.00
Jan. 21	40	320.00		320.00	19.20	39.10	3.00	A 2.00	63.30	256.70	480	1,008.00
Jan. 28	40	320.00		320.00	19.20	39.10	3.00	A 2.00	63.30	256.70	525	1,328.00
Feb. 4	42	320.00	24.00	344.00	20.64	43.30	3.00	A 2.00	68.94	275.06	566	1,672.00

Employers prepare Form W-2, the required Wage and Tax Statement sent to every employee each year, from the individual employee earnings records. Although Form W-2 is sent out only once and covers an entire year, employers typically provide employees with an earnings statement each pay period, detailing the earnings and deductions for that period. These earnings statements may be a detachable portion of the employee's paycheck or may be enclosed as a separate document with the paycheck.

PAYMENT TO EMPLOYEES

A company with a small number of employees may pay them with checks drawn on the firm's regular bank account. With a large number of employees, it is usually more practical to establish a separate bank account to pay the payroll.

Payroll Bank Account

When a company uses a separate payroll bank account, each pay period it draws a check on its regular bank account in an amount equal to the total net earnings of the employees. This check is deposited in the payroll bank account. Individual payroll checks are then drawn on this account and delivered to the employees. The issuance of the payroll checks reduces to zero the book balance in the payroll bank account.

One advantage of maintaining a separate payroll bank account is that it readily permits a division of work between the preparation and issuance of regular company checks and payroll checks. A related advantage is that it simplifies the monthly reconciliation of the regular bank account. The large number of payroll checks, many of which may be outstanding at month-end, are not run through the regular bank account. Of course, the payroll bank account also needs to be reconciled, but, typically, the only reconciling item for this bank account will be payroll checks outstanding.

Payment in Cash

Sometimes employees are paid in currency and coin rather than by check. This may happen, for example, if the employees work in a location where it may not be convenient for them to deposit or cash checks. The company will prepare and cash one of its own checks for the payroll amount. Each employee's pay is put into a pay envelope and delivered to the employee. As a feature of internal control, and to have evidence of the payment made, an employee should sign a receipt for the payroll envelope. Often the outside of the envelope contains an itemization of the employee's gross earnings and deductions for the period.

KEY POINTS TO REMEMBER

(1) Liabilities are present obligations resulting from past transactions to pay money, provide goods, or perform services in the future.

(2) Current liabilities are those that must be satisfied within the coming year or the operating cycle, whichever is longer. To meet these obligations, a firm will have to use existing current assets or create other current liabilities.

(3) Failure to properly accrue liabilities will cause a misstatement of financial position and reported income.

(4) A contingent liability is an obligation that depends on the occurrence of a future event. A contingent liability is recorded in the accounts if the future event is likely to occur and if the amount of the liability can be reasonably estimated.

(5) Payroll accounting is influenced significantly by several legislative acts. Payroll transactions involve a series of withholdings from the employee's wages and a series of payroll taxes levied against the employer.

(6) A payroll register lists information on the gross earnings and deductions of all employees for each payroll period. Individual employee earnings records contain information on gross earnings and deductions for each employee for all payroll periods during the year.

QUESTIONS

11–1 For accounting purposes, how are liabilities defined?

11–2 Present a general rule for measuring current liabilities on the balance sheet.

11–3 Define "current liabilities."

11–4 "Because they are a matter of governmental discretion, property taxes should be recognized as expense in the period in which the assessment becomes a lien against the property involved." Comment on this statement.

11–5 Define "contingent liabilities." List three examples of contingent liabilities. When should contingent liabilities be recorded in the accounts?

11–6 Upon whom is the FICA tax levied? What does the FICA tax finance?

11–7 Upon whom are the federal and state unemployment insurance taxes levied? What do these taxes finance?

11–8 What is the purpose of an employee filing a Form W-4, Employee's Withholding Allowance Certificate, with his or her employer?

11–9 What is the difference between an employee and an independent contractor?

11–10 What does Form W-2, Wage and Tax Statement, report? Who receives copies of this form?

11-11 James Anderson is employed at $3.50 per hour. Under the Fair Labor Standards Act, how many hours in a week must he work before he is entitled to overtime pay? What is the minimum overtime rate of pay he must receive?

11-12 List at least five examples of items that may be deducted from an employee's gross earnings other than FICA taxes and federal income taxes withheld.

11-13 What is a payroll register? How does it differ from an individual employee earnings record?

11-14 If an accrual of earned but unpaid wages is made at the end of a year, should employer payroll taxes on these wages be accrued at the same time? Explain.

11-15 List two advantages of maintaining a special payroll bank account for the payment of a net payroll.

EXERCISES

11-16 For each of the following situations, indicate how much should be shown as a liability on the balance sheet of Brooks, Inc. at December 31, 19X2.
(a) Brooks has trade accounts payable of $40,000 for merchandise included in the ending inventory for 19X2.
(b) Brooks has agreed to purchase a $9,000 delivery truck in January, 19X3.
(c) During November and December of 19X2, Brooks sold products to a firm and guaranteed these products against product failure for 90 days. It is estimated that the costs of honoring this provision during 19X3 will be $700.
(d) On December 15, 19X2, Brooks declared a cash dividend of $23,000 payable on January 15, 19X3, to stockholders of record on December 31, 19X2.
(e) Brooks provides a profit-sharing bonus for its executives equal to 6% of the reported before-tax income for the current year. The estimated income (as defined above) for 19X2 is $180,000.

11-17 MacInnes Company has just billed a customer for $492.80, an amount that includes an excise tax of 7% and a state sales tax of 5%.
(a) What is the amount of revenue to be recorded?
(b) Present a general journal entry to record the transaction on the books of MacInnes Company.

11-18 Valley, Inc.'s current vacation policy for its production workers provides four weeks paid vacation at the end of a full year's employment. An analysis of employee turnover rates in this group indicates that approximately 8% of the employees will terminate employment before they are with the company a full year and consequently will forfeit their vacation benefit.
(a) Compute the proper provision for estimated vacation benefits for a four-week period in which the total pay earned by the employee group was $105,000.
(b) Present a general journal entry that would properly recognize the above vacation benefits.

11-19 Bracket Company sells a commercial food mixer that carries a 60-day unconditional warranty against product failure. Based on a reliable statistical analysis,

Bracket knows that between the time of sale and the lapse of the product warranty, 2% of the units sold will fail and require repair at an average cost of $35 per unit. The following data reflect Bracket's recent experience.

	October	November	December
Units sold	9,000	8,000	12,000
Known units of product failure from sales of:			
October	40	100	40
November		25	90
December			60

Calculate and prepare a general journal entry to properly record the estimated liability for product warranties at December 31. Assume that warranty costs of known failures have already been reflected in the records.

11-20 Tom Stock is an employee subject to the Fair Labor Standards Act. His regular rate of pay is $7.00 an hour, and he worked 46 hours in the current week. He is paid overtime at $1\frac{1}{2}$ times his regular rate of pay. His gross earnings prior to the current week were $8,900. He is married and claims five withholding allowances on Form W-4. No deductions other than FICA and federal income taxes are subtracted from his paycheck. Compute the following amounts related to his current week's wages:
(a) Regular earnings.
(b) Overtime earnings.
(c) FICA taxes (assume 6% rate).
(d) Federal income tax withheld (use wage-bracket table in Exhibit 11-1).
(e) Net earnings.

11-21 Pilgrim Company's August payroll register shows total gross earnings of $156,000. Of this amount, $11,000 is not subject to FICA taxes and $148,000 is above the maximum amount subject to federal and state unemployment taxes. Pilgrim Company has a favorable employment record, so its state unemployment tax rate is 2%. It is subject to a 6% FICA tax and a 0.7% federal unemployment tax. Prepare the general journal entry to record Pilgrim Company's payroll tax expense for August.

11-22 Karen Lydol is an employee subject to the Fair Labor Standards Act. She is paid on a piece rate basis. Her earnings for the current week, before any overtime compensation, were $299.20 for 44 hours of work. For each hour worked over 40 in a week, she receives an overtime premium of half her regular hourly rate of pay based on the total hours worked in that week. Her gross earnings prior to the current week were $7,500. She is married and claims one withholding allowance on Form W-4. No deductions other than FICA and federal income taxes are subtracted from her paycheck. Compute the following amounts related to her current week's wages:
(a) Regular hourly pay rate.
(b) Gross earnings.
(c) FICA taxes (assume 6% rate).
(d) Federal income tax withheld (use wage-bracket table in Exhibit 11-1).
(e) Net earnings.

PROBLEMS

11-23 The headquarters building of Moss Company, a firm that prepares monthly financial statements and ends its accounting year on December 31, is located in the city of Rockton. City taxes are assessed on September 1 of each year, are to be paid by October 15, and relate to the city's fiscal year ending the next June 30 (10 months after assessment). For the city tax year 19X5–X6, Moss paid $55,000 in property taxes on its headquarters building.

REQUIRED
(a) What amount of property tax expense should be accrued on the financial statements for July, 19X6, if property taxes for the city's year 19X6–X7 are estimated to be 8% higher than the preceding year?
(b) Assume that the 19X6–X7 tax bill received on September 1, 19X6, was for $61,200 and that the estimate in part (a) had continued to be used through August. What is the proper monthly property tax expense for September, 19X6, if the deficiencies in the monthly property tax estimates through August are handled as an increase in the property tax expense for September, 19X6?
(c) What effect does the payment of the tax bill on October 15, 19X6, have on the amount of property tax expense recognized for the month of October?

11-24 Dell Corporation had the following payroll for the month of February, 19X1:

Officers' salaries	$20,000
Sales salaries	75,000
Income taxes withheld	19,500
FICA taxes withheld	5,700
Hospital insurance premiums deducted	900
United Way contributions deducted	500
Salaries (included above) subject to unemployment taxes	85,000

REQUIRED
Present general journal entries to record:
(a) Accrual of the payroll.
(b) Payment of the net payroll.
(c) Accrual of employer's payroll taxes. (Assume that the FICA tax matches the amount withheld, the federal unemployment tax is 0.7%, and the state unemployment tax is 2.7%.)
(d) Payment of all liabilities related to the above payroll. (Assume they are all settled at the same time.)

11-25 Mountain Corporation initially records its sales at amounts that include any related excise and sales taxes. During June, 19XX, Mountain recorded total sales of $131,670. An analysis of June sales indicated the following:
(1) Three-tenths of sales were subject to both an 8% excise tax and a 3% sales tax.
(2) Four-tenths of sales were subject only to the sales tax.
(3) The balance of sales were for labor charges and were not subject to either excise tax or sales tax.

REQUIRED

Calculate the amount of sales revenue for June, 19XX, and the related liabilities for excise and sales taxes.

11-26 The following data are taken from McCarthy Wholesale Company's monthly payroll for June, 19X5:

Administrative salaries	$18,000
Sales salaries	29,000
Custodial salaries	3,000
Total payroll	$50,000
Wages subject to FICA tax	$42,000
Wages subject to FUTA and state unemployment taxes	$ 7,000
Income taxes withheld from all salaries	$ 9,300

Assume that (1) FICA taxes are 6% each for the employee and the employer, and (2) the company is subject to a 2% state unemployment tax (due to a favorable experience rating) and a 0.7% federal unemployment tax on the first $6,000 paid to each employee.

REQUIRED

Record, in general journal form:

(a) Accrual of the payroll.

(b) Payment of the net payroll.

(c) Accrual of the employer's payroll taxes.

(d) Payment of the payroll-related liabilities from above. (Assume they are all settled at the same time.)

11-27 The Barker Company employs five persons, one of whom receives a $500 salary for a 40-hour week; the other four are paid an hourly rate. All employees receive overtime pay at $1\frac{1}{2}$ times their regular pay rate. Data relating to the payroll for the week ended March 31 are given below:

Employee	Hours Worked	Pay Rate	Gross Earnings to End of Prior Week
Ann Austin	48	$8.00 per hour	$4,128
Karl Chen	40	$500 per week	6,000
Pam Hatt	44	$6.00 per hour	3,060
Henry Post	40	$6.00 per hour	2,970
John Shea	40	$8.00 per hour	3,960

Additional Data:

(1) Karl Chen's salary is charged to office salaries; the gross earnings of the other employees are charged to sales salaries.

(2) The FICA tax is 6% of the first $22,900 of salaries and wages.

(3) The federal unemployment tax is 0.7%, and the state unemployment tax is 2.7% of the first $6,000 of salaries and wages.

(4) Each employee has a $3.60 per week deduction for group medical insurance.

(5) Assume the federal income tax withheld the last week in March is:

Austin	$70.40
Chen	74.00
Hatt	46.80
Post	26.40
Shea	39.10

REQUIRED

(a) Prepare the payroll register for the week ended March 31, using the following column headings:

Employee	Earnings			Deductions				Net Earnings
	Regular	Overtime	Gross	FICA Tax	Federal Income Tax	Medical Insurance	Total	

(b) Prepare the general journal entry to record:
   (1) The week's payroll.
   (2) The employer's payroll taxes for the week.
   (3) The payment of the net payroll.
(c) Barker Company remits the group medical insurance premiums to the Guardian Insurance Company monthly. Total premiums withheld in March were $90. Prepare the general journal entry to record the monthly remittance of these premiums.
(d) The balances in the FICA Tax Payable and Federal Income Tax Withholding Payable accounts—after posting the entries from (b) above—on March 31 are $1,050 and $1,260, respectively. Prepare the general journal entry to record the monthly remittance of these taxes to an authorized commercial bank.
(e) Barker Company's total federal unemployment tax for the quarter ended March 31 is $149.59—after posting the entries from (b) above. Barker Company deposits the taxes quarterly in an authorized commercial bank. Prepare the general journal entry to record this remittance.
(f) The total state unemployment tax for the quarter ended March 31 is $576.99—after posting the entries from (b) above. Prepare the general journal entry to record the quarterly remittance of this tax.

ALTERNATE PROBLEMS

11-23A Schone Company, a firm that prepares monthly financial statements and ends its accounting year on December 31, owns a plant in the city of Monroe. City taxes are assessed on March 1 of each year, are to be paid by May 1, and relate to the city's fiscal year ending the next June 30 (4 months after assessment). For the city tax year 19X1–X2, Schone paid $30,000 in property taxes on its factory plant.

REQUIRED

(a) What amount of property tax expense should be accrued on the financial statements for July, 19X2, if property taxes for the city's year 19X2–X3 are estimated to be 9% higher than the preceding year?

(b) Assume that the 19X2–X3 tax bill received on March 1, 19X3, was for $33,300 and that the estimate in part (a) had continued to be used through February. What is the proper monthly property tax expense for March, 19X3, if the deficiencies in the monthly property tax estimates through February are handled as an increase in the property tax expense for March, 19X3?

(c) What effect does the payment of the tax bill on May 1, 19X3, have on the amount of property tax expense recognized for the month of May?

11-24A Matthews, Inc. had the following payroll for the month of March, 19X8:

Officers' salaries	$18,000
Sales salaries	52,000
Income taxes withheld	14,600
FICA taxes withheld	4,200
Hospital insurance deductions	1,200
Salaries (included above) subject to unemployment taxes	62,000

REQUIRED

Present general journal entries to record:

(a) Accrual of the payroll.

(b) Payment of the net payroll.

(c) Accrual of employer's payroll taxes (assume that the FICA tax matches the amount withheld, the federal unemployment tax is 0.7%, and the state unemployment tax is 2.7%).

(d) Payment of all liabilities related to the above payroll. (Assume they are all settled at the same time.)

11-25A Dunham Corporation initially records its sales at amounts that include any related excise and sales taxes. During May, 19XX, Dunham recorded total sales of $195,300. An analysis of May sales indicated the following:

(1) Four-tenths of sales were subject to both a 10% excise tax and a 5% sales tax.

(2) One-half of sales were subject only to the sales tax.

(3) The balance of sales were for labor charges and were not subject to either excise tax or sales tax.

REQUIRED

Calculate the amount of sales revenue for May, 19XX, and the related liabilities for excise and sales taxes.

11–26A The following data are taken from Frisch Lumber Company's monthly payroll for March, 19X4.

Administrative salaries	$ 9,000
Sales salaries	16,000
Custodial salaries	2,000
Total payroll	$27,000
Wages subject to FICA tax	$27,000
Wages subject to FUTA and state unemployment taxes	$17,000
Income taxes withheld from all salaries	$ 5,200

Assume that (1) FICA taxes are 6% each for the employee and the employer and (2) the company is subject to a 2.7% state unemployment tax and a 0.7% federal unemployment tax on the first $6,000 paid to each employee.

REQUIRED

Record, in general journal form:
(a) Accrual of the payroll.
(b) Payment of the net payroll.
(c) Accrual of the employer's payroll taxes.
(d) Payment of the payroll-related liabilities from above. (Assume they are all settled at the same time.)

11–27A The Linville Company employs five persons, one of whom receives a $450 salary for a 40-hour week; the other four are paid an hourly rate. All employees receive overtime pay at $1\frac{1}{2}$ times their regular pay rate. Data relating to the payroll for the week ended June 30 are given below:

Employee	Hours Worked	Pay Rate	Gross Earnings to End of Prior Week
Ruth Beal	44	$5.50 per hour	$ 5,830
Mary Fern	40	$450 per week	11,250
Tom Hay	44	$6.20 per hour	6,386
Will Penn	44	$6.20 per hour	6,293
Brad Tate	40	$5.50 per hour	5,500

Additional Data:
(1) Mary Fern's salary is charged to office salaries; the gross earnings of the other employees are charged to sales salaries.
(2) The FICA tax is 6% of the first $22,900 of salaries and wages.
(3) The federal unemployment tax is 0.7%, and the state unemployment tax is 2.7% of the first $6,000 of salaries and wages.
(4) Each employee has a $3.00 per week deduction for group medical insurance.
(5) Assume the federal income tax withheld the last week in June is:

Beal	$41.60
Fern	81.60
Hay	34.80
Penn	30.70
Tate	33.80

REQUIRED

(a) Prepare the payroll register for the week ended June 30, using the following column headings:

Employee	Earnings			Deductions				Net Earnings
	Regular	Overtime	Gross	FICA Tax	Federal Income Tax	Medical Insurance	Total	

(b) Prepare the general journal entry to record:
   (1) The week's payroll.
   (2) The employer's payroll taxes for the week.
   (3) The payment of the net payroll.
(c) Linville Company remits the group medical insurance premiums to the Solid Insurance Company monthly. Total premiums withheld in June were $75. Prepare the general journal entry to record the monthly remittance of these premiums.
(d) The balances in the FICA Tax Payable and Federal Income Tax Withholding Payable accounts—after posting the entries from (b) above—on June 30 are $890 and $1,104, respectively. Prepare the general journal entry to record the monthly remittance of these taxes to an authorized commercial bank.
(e) Linville Company's total federal unemployment tax for the quarter ended June 30 is $79.39—after posting the entries from (b) above. Although a deposit is not required (since the balance is under $100), Linville Company does deposit the taxes quarterly in an authorized commercial bank. Prepare the general journal entry to record this remittance.
(f) The total state unemployment tax for the quarter ended June 30 is $306.21—after posting the entries from (b) above. Prepare the general journal entry to record the quarterly remittance of this tax.

BUSINESS DECISION PROBLEM

Nelson Enterprises manages office buildings in several Midwestern cities. The firm has always maintained its own janitorial staff for all buildings managed. In Central City, where it manages 10 buildings, the firm maintains a staff of 40 people, with a total annual payroll of $470,000. Of this staff, only two supervisors earn more than $22,900 per year; each receives $26,000 annually. All of the staff earn more than $6,000 per year. The annual nonpayroll costs of the janitorial service are:

Supplies	$40,000
Depreciation on Equipment	30,000
Insurance	20,000
Miscellaneous	5,000
	$95,000

Nelson pays a 6% FICA tax on its payroll and is subject to a 3.0% state unemployment tax. Its federal unemployment compensation tax rate is 0.7%. The firm also pays a part of the health insurance costs for its employees, averaging $42 per employee.

The firm has had a high turnover of employees and has experienced difficulty in keeping tenants happy with the janitorial service. The president, Jane Nelson, has been approached by a commercial janitorial service chain, Cleaning Unlimited, which has submitted a bid of $590,000 annually to provide janitorial service for the 10 buildings in Central City. This firm is noted for efficiency and satisfactory service. Nelson estimates that if an outside firm were hired, $5,000 would be saved annually in bookkeeping costs and costs of contracting with other commercial firms for summer vacation substitutes for regular help. These costs are not included in the above list of nonpayroll costs.

REQUIRED

Prepare an analysis of costs for Nelson to help her decide whether to accept the bid of Cleaning Unlimited. Assume the FICA tax applies to the first $22,900 paid to each employee and the unemployment taxes apply to the first $6,000 paid to each employee.

12
Partnership
Accounting

We are the two halves of a pair of scissors, when apart,
Perksniff, but together we are something.

CHARLES DICKENS

The essence of the partnership form of business organization is captured by the proverb, "Two heads are better than one." A **partnership** is a voluntary association of two or more persons for the purpose of conducting a business for profit. The Uniform Partnership Act is the basic law governing the formation and operation of partnerships in many states. A partnership is easily formed—all it takes is that the parties agree to be in partnership. The ease of formation makes partnership an attractive form of organization for a business that requires more capital than a single proprietor can provide or for persons wanting to combine specialized talents. Professional people, such as physicians, attorneys, and public accountants, as well as many small business concerns, often operate as partnerships.

Although, generally, partnership agreements may be oral, it is sound business practice to put agreements in writing to avoid misunderstandings. A written partnership agreement constitutes the **articles of co-partnership.** The articles of co-partnership should detail the important provisions of the partnership arrangement, including the name and location of the partnership, the nature and duration of the business, the duties of partners, the capital contribution of each partner, the procedure for sharing profits and losses, permitted withdrawals of assets, the manner of keeping the books, the procedure for withdrawals of partners, and the procedure for dissolving and winding up the business.

CHARACTERISTICS OF A PARTNERSHIP

While a partnership is an accounting entity, it is not a legal entity separate from its owners. Ease of formation is only one of several characteristics relating to this aspect of partnerships.

Mutual Agency

Mutual agency means that every partner becomes an agent for the firm, with the authority to enter contracts binding to the partnership. This authority applies to all acts typical of a partner engaging in the usual activities of such a firm. Although the partners may agree to limit the authority of one or more partners to act on customary matters, a partner acting in contravention of a restriction may still contractually bind the partnership if the other party to the contract is unaware of the limitation. The partnership would not be bound, however, if the other party knew of the restriction.

416

THE BIG EIGHT

There are approximately 23,500 CPA firms in the United States. Over 16,000 of these operate as sole proprietorships; the rest are organized primarily as partnerships. Approximately 6,700 firms have fewer than 10 partners, another 400 firms have from 10 to 50 partners, and 35 firms have more than 50 partners.[1] Of these 35 large firms, the eight largest are referred to as the Big Eight.

The Big Eight firms are Arthur Andersen & Company; Arthur Young & Company; Coopers & Lybrand; Deloitte Haskins & Sells; Ernst & Whinney; Peat, Marwick, Mitchell & Company; Price Waterhouse & Company; and Touche Ross & Company. These firms each have several hundred partners and maintain offices in various countries throughout the world. They provide services to a wide spectrum of clients, but clearly the vast majority of large corporations in the United States use one of the Big Eight as their independent auditor. It has been estimated that better than 95 percent of the companies listed on the New York Stock Exchange are clients of Big Eight firms.[2]

An audit of a large, multinational corporation is a complex and costly undertaking. The Big Eight firm auditing General Electric Company in 1976, for example, used 429 auditors working out of 38 different offices around the world. The same firm used 400 auditors from 63 different offices to audit Singer Company.[3] The fees for these types of audits run into hundreds of thousands, or even millions, of dollars.

One technique used by Big Eight firms to better serve (and attract) clients is the development of expertise in the accounting and regulatory requirements of particular industries. Firms may establish specialities in a number of industries—one firm, for example, has set up specialist activities for thirty different industries and services. Another firm has created speciality units for the geothermal industry and state-financed housing. Continuing this practice has caused certain firms to become identified with specific industries. Some examples are: Arthur Andersen & Company—utilities; Arthur Young & Company—textiles and banks; Coopers & Lybrand—mining and utilities; Deloitte Haskins & Sells—brokerage houses; Ernst & Whinney and Peat, Marwick, Mitchell & Company—banks and insurance companies; Price Waterhouse & Company—oil and steel; and Touche Ross & Company—retailing.[4]

Approximately 70 percent of the total revenues of the Big Eight, on average, are derived from their auditing services. Opportunities to provide these services (for Big Eight and other CPA firms) are sometimes created by government legislation. The Securities Act of 1933 and the Securities Exchange Act of 1934, for instance, had a significant impact by requiring publicly owned companies to submit audited financial statements and other information to the Securities and Exchange Commission. More recently, the Employment Retirement Income Security Act of 1974 required audited financial statements for pension plans approved by the Internal Revenue Service (nearly one million plans).[5] In another example, municipalities receiving at least $25,000 in federal funds under the federal revenue-sharing program (over 11,000 municipalities) must have an independent financial audit.[6]

In addition to auditing services, CPA firms also offer tax and management advisory services. Expertise in the areas of tax planning and return preparation has become a valuable resource to businesses because of the complexity of tax laws. Big Eight firms average about 18 percent of their total revenues from tax services.

Management advisory services cover a wide range of consulting activities and provide the remaining revenues for Big Eight firms, an average of about 12 percent of the total amount. All of the firms offer financial management services, such as the design and implementation of financial information systems, inventory control systems, and computer forecasting models. Other services offered vary from firm to firm, but may include executive recruitment, feasibility studies, plant layout analysis, and marketing analysis.

In the late 1970s, the average annual earnings for partners of Big Eight firms was probably between $90,000 and $100,000. Of course, for a single firm it may have been higher. In 1977, for example, the average compensation for the 418 U.S. partners of one firm was $144,000.[7]

[1]Lawrence Minard and Brian McGlynn, "The U.S.' Newest Glamour Job," *Forbes*, September 1, 1977, p. 33.
[2]Steven Anreder, "Profit or Loss?" *Barron's*, March 12, 1979, p. 18.
[3]Minard and McGlynn, pp. 35–36.
[4]Peter W. Bernstein, "Competition Comes to Accounting," *Fortune*, July 17, 1978, p. 92.
[5]Minard and McGlynn, p. 36.
[6]Bernstein, p. 94.
[7]Bernstein, p. 91.

Unlimited Liability

Each partner in a **general partnership** is individually liable for the obligations of the firm regardless of the amount of personal investment. Thus, creditors of a general partnership unable to pay its debts may obtain payment from the personal assets of individual partners. In addition to at least one general partner, a **limited partnership** has one or more limited partners. The liability of a limited partner is restricted to his or her capital investment. A limited partner who becomes active in the control of the firm, however, takes on the unlimited liability status of a general partner, as provided by the Uniform Limited Partnership Act.

Limited Life

Because a partnership is a voluntary association of persons, many events may cause its dissolution. These include the expiration of the agreed-on term of partnership; the accomplishment of the business objective; the admission of a new partner; the withdrawal, death, or bankruptcy of an existing partner; and the issuance of a court decree because of a partner's insanity, incapacity, or misconduct. Even though a change in membership dissolves a partnership, business continuity is often unaffected. A new partnership is formed to carry on without interruption the operations of the former partnership.

Co-ownership of Property

Assets contributed by partners become partnership property jointly owned by all partners. Individual partners no longer separately own the specific resources invested in the firm. Unless there is an agreement to the contrary, each partner has an equal right to possess firm property for partnership purposes.

Nontaxable Entity

Although a partnership must file an information return for federal income tax purposes, the organization itself is not a taxable entity. The information return shows the distributive shares of the partnership's net income that the partners themselves include on their individual tax returns. The individual members must pay income taxes on their respective shares of partnership earnings whether or not these amounts have been withdrawn from the firm.

ADVANTAGES AND DISADVANTAGES OF A PARTNERSHIP

In contrast with a corporation, a partnership is easier and less expensive to organize and is subject to less government regulation and fewer reporting requirements. Certain corporate actions require the approval of stockholders or directors; partners operate with fewer constraints on their actions. Businesses of modest size or of planned short duration may find these features advantageous. The same may be true for new businesses hesitant to incur the cost of incorporation until their ventures prove successful.

Disadvantages of the partnership form of organization are mutual agency, unlimited liability, and limited life. The first two in particular underscore the importance of taking great care in the selection of partners and are no doubt partially responsible for the rule that no person may be admitted to a partnership without the consent of all existing partners. Because a corporation offers limited liability to investors, it is better able than a partnership to raise large amounts of capital.

The impact of taxes varies from one circumstance to the next. A partnership is a nontaxable entity; a corporation is a taxable entity. Partners' earnings are taxable whether distributed or not; corporate income is taxable a second time, but only when distributed as dividends. The tax rate on individuals in high tax brackets exceeds the corporate tax rate. To determine which form of organization is the most advantageous for tax purposes requires careful analysis of existing tax laws in the context of the tax status of the persons going into business.

CAPITAL, DRAWING, AND LOAN ACCOUNTS

Accounting for partnerships is similar in most respects to accounting for sole proprietorships. Each partner has a capital account and a drawing account that serve the same functions as the related accounts for a sole proprietor. A partner's capital account is credited for his or her investments, and each individual drawing account is debited to reflect assets withdrawn from the partnership. At the end of each accounting period, the balances in the drawing accounts are closed to the related capital accounts.

Occasionally a partner may aid the partnership by advancing it amounts beyond the intended permanent investment. These advances should be credited to the partner's loan account and classified among the liabilities, separate and distinct from liabilities to outsiders. By the same token, if a partner withdraws money with the intention of repaying, the debit should go to the partner's advance (or loan receivable) account and be classified separately among the receivables of the partnership.

The formation of partnerships, the division of profits and losses, the admission and retirement of partners, and the liquidation of partnerships represent areas of particular interest in accounting for these entities. We shall focus on these issues in the remainder of the chapter.

FORMATION OF A PARTNERSHIP

The books of a partnership are opened with an entry reflecting the net contribution of each partner to the firm. Asset accounts are debited for assets invested in the partnership, liability accounts are credited for any liabilities assumed by the partnership, and a separate capital account is credited for the amount of each partner's net investment (assets minus liabilities).

Assume that Earl Ames, who has been in business for himself, and John Baker decide to form a partnership. Ames invests $8,000 cash, office equipment with a current fair value of $25,000, and office supplies worth $2,000. The partnership agrees to assume a $5,000 balance on a note issued by Ames when he acquired the equipment. Baker invests $10,000 cash. The opening entries on the books of the partnership, to record the investments of Ames and Baker, would be:

Cash	8,000	
Office Equipment	25,000	
Office Supplies on Hand	2,000	
Notes Payable		5,000
Ames, Capital		30,000

To record Ames' investment in partnership.

Cash	10,000	
Baker, Capital		10,000

To record Baker's investment in partnership.

    Assets invested in the partnership should be recorded at their current fair values. These assets (less any liabilities assumed by the partnership) determine the opening capital balances for each partner. If the assets are not recorded initially at their fair values, inequities will develop among the partners in terms of their respective capital balances.

    For example, assume the office equipment invested by Ames was recorded incorrectly at $22,000 (its book value from his proprietorship records). If the partnership immediately sold the equipment for its current fair value of $25,000, the resulting $3,000 gain, upon closing, would increase the capital balances of both Ames and Baker. This is not equitable. The $3,000 "gain" was not the result of any value added to the asset by the operations of the partnership. Baker should not be credited with any part of this amount. A similar inequity develops if the equipment is used in operations rather than sold. Owing to a lower total depreciation over the life of the equipment, income would be $3,000 greater over the same time period. To avoid such inequities, the office equipment should be recorded initially at $25,000. Because they are so important, the values assigned to assets invested in a partnership should be agreeable to all partners.

DIVISION OF PARTNERSHIP PROFITS AND LOSSES

In the absence of a profit and loss sharing agreement, partnership profits and losses are divided equally. If the partners do not wish to share profits equally, they must specify, preferably in a formal written agreement, the manner in which profit and loss distributions are to be made. Such arrangements may specify a fixed ratio (such as $\frac{2}{3}$ to $\frac{1}{3}$, 60% to 40%, 5:3:2) or a sharing formula of some kind. The formula may be based on the relative financial participation of the partners, the services performed by the partners, or both. Any arrangement can be made, and losses may be shared differently from profits. If an agreement specifies the manner of sharing profits but is silent on the sharing of losses, losses will be divided in the same fashion as profits. In the following sections, we discuss several of the more common arrangements.

Capital Ratios   When the services performed or skills provided by the various partners are not relevant to an equitable sharing arrangement, it may be appropriate to divide profits and losses according to the partners' relative investments in the firm. Assume that the Ames and Baker partnership had a profit of $18,000 for the year and that the partners' capital balances before any profit distribution at the end of the year were as follows:

Ames, Capital		Baker, Capital	
19XX		19XX	
Jan. 1	30,000	Jan. 1	10,000
		July 1	10,000

The $18,000 profit might be divided according to the beginning capital investment ratio or the average capital investment ratio for the year.

BEGINNING CAPITAL RATIO   At the beginning of the year, the total capital investment in the firm was $40,000, consisting of $30,000 for Ames and $10,000 for Baker. If they shared according to the ratio of beginning capital balances, the distribution of profit would be 3 to 1, or $13,500 for Ames and $4,500 for Baker, computed as follows:

	Beginning Capital	Percent of Total	Division of Profit
Ames	$30,000	75%	$13,500
Baker	10,000	25	4,500
	$40,000	100%	$18,000

The following entry would be made to distribute the balance in the Income Summary account:

Income Summary	18,000	
Ames, Capital		13,500
Baker, Capital		4,500

To close the Income Summary account.

AVERAGE CAPITAL RATIO   Because the investments of partners may change during the year, the partners may decide that a more equitable division of profits would result from using *average* capital balances rather than beginning capital balances. Under this scheme, investment balances are *weighted* by multiplying the amount of the investment by the portion of the year that these funds were invested. Because Baker invested an additional $10,000 in the middle of the year, his average capital would be based on a $10,000 investment for the first six months and a $20,000 investment for the last six months. The computation might be made as follows:

		Dollars × Months		Average Investment
Ames				
$30,000 × 12 months		$360,000	÷ 12	$30,000
Baker				
$10,000 × 6 months	$ 60,000			
$20,000 × 6 months	120,000	180,000	÷ 12	15,000
		$540,000		$45,000

Profit Distribution

$$\text{Ames} \quad \frac{\$30,000}{\$45,000} \times \$18,000 = \$12,000$$

$$\text{Baker} \quad \frac{\$15,000}{\$45,000} \times \$18,000 = 6,000$$

$$\$18,000$$

The entry to close the Income Summary Account would credit Ames, Capital with $12,000 and Baker, Capital with $6,000.

Salaries and Interest

A sharing agreement may provide for variations in the personal services contributed by partners and their relative investments. *Salary allowances* provide for differences in personal services; *allowances for interest on capital balances* provide for differences in the financial participation of partners.

The terms "salary allowances" and "allowances for interest" are used here only to describe the process of dividing net income among partners. These terms should not be confused with any salary expense and interest expense appearing in the firm's records. Furthermore, they should not be confused with any cash withdrawals the partners may make. For example, the partnership agreement may provide that partners may make withdrawals equal to their salary allowances. These withdrawals would be debited to the partners' respective drawing accounts. Each partner's drawing account is eventually closed to that partner's capital account. The cash withdrawals in no way affect the division of net income among partners—the division of net income is governed by the sharing agreement.

SALARY ALLOWANCE   Suppose that Ames and Baker render different degrees of personal services and therefore specify an allowance for salaries in their sharing agreement. They agree to salary allowances of $6,000 for Ames and $4,000 for Baker, with the remainder of net income to be divided equally. The division of the $18,000 net income would be as follows:

	Ames	Baker	
Earnings to be divided			$18,000
Salary allowances:			
Ames	$ 6,000		
Baker		$4,000	10,000
Remainder			$ 8,000
Remainder ($8,000) divided equally	4,000	4,000	
Partners' shares	$10,000	$8,000	

The $18,000 balance in the Income Summary account would be closed with an entry crediting Ames, Capital for $10,000 and Baker, Capital for $8,000.

SALARY AND INTEREST ALLOWANCES   Next, assume that Ames and Baker wish to acknowledge the differences in their financial involvement as well as their personal services. They have the following sharing agreement: salaries of $6,000 to Ames and $4,000 to Baker; 8% interest on *average* capital balances; and the remainder to be divided equally. In an earlier computation, we found that average investments for Ames and Baker were $30,000 and $15,000, respectively. The net income of $18,000 would therefore be divided as follows:

	Ames	Baker	
Earnings to be divided			$18,000
Salary allowances:			
Ames	$ 6,000		
Baker		$4,000	10,000
			$ 8,000
Allowance for interest on average capital:			
Ames ($30,000 × 0.08)	2,400		
Baker ($15,000 × 0.08)		1,200	3,600
Remainder			$ 4,400
Remainder ($4,400) divided equally	2,200	2,200	
Partners' shares	$10,600	$7,400	

The entry closing the $18,000 net income in the Income Summary account would show a credit of $10,600 to Ames, Capital and a credit of $7,400 to Baker, Capital.

If Ames and Baker had withdrawn cash equal to their salary allowances, their drawing accounts at the end of the year would show debit balances of $6,000 and $4,000, respectively. The entry to close the drawing accounts would be:

Ames, Capital	6,000	
Baker, Capital	4,000	
Ames, Drawing		6,000
Baker, Drawing		4,000

To close the partners' drawing accounts.

ALLOWANCES EXCEED EARNINGS   Unless a special provision is included in the sharing agreement, the same allocation procedures would be followed in the event of a loss or earnings insufficient to cover allowances for salary and interest. For example, assume that net income for the year had been only $8,000. After salary and interest allowances were allocated, there would be a *sharing agreement loss* of $5,600, which would be divided equally between the partners to fulfill their agreement. The computations are shown below:

	Ames	Baker	
Earnings to be divided			$ 8,000
Salary allowances	$6,000	$4,000	
Interest allowances	2,400	1,200	
Total salary and interest	$8,400	$5,200	13,600
Remainder (sharing agreement loss)			($ 5,600)
Remainder divided equally	(2,800)	(2,800)	
Partners' shares	$5,600	$2,400	

The entry closing the $8,000 net income in the Income Summary account would credit Ames, Capital with $5,600 and Baker, Capital with $2,400.

PARTNERSHIP FINANCIAL STATEMENTS

A few unique features of partnership financial statements arise because a partnership consists of co-owners. The partnership income statement may show, at the bottom, how the net income is divided among the partners. In the owners' equity section of the balance sheet, there will be a capital account for each partner. The statement of partners' (or owners') capital must portray the changes in the capital balances of each partner, as shown in Exhibit 12–1.

EXHIBIT 12–1

Ames and Baker
Statement of Partners' Capital
For the Year 19XX

	Ames	Baker	Total
Capital Balances, January 1, 19XX	$30,000	$10,000	$40,000
Add: Additional Contributions		10,000	10,000
Net Income for 19XX	10,600	7,400	18,000
Totals	$40,600	$27,400	$68,000
Less: Withdrawals	6,000	4,000	10,000
Capital Balances, December 31, 19XX	$34,600	$23,400	$58,000

ADMISSION OF A PARTNER

New partners may be admitted to a partnership either by purchasing an interest from present members or by investing in the firm. When a person buys an interest from one or more of the present partners, the assets of the firm are not affected. Payment is made personally to the member or members from whom the interest is obtained, and there is merely a transfer among capital accounts. When an investment is made in the firm, however, total assets are increased by the amount contributed.

Economic circumstances usually dictate the mode of entry of a new partner. A firm with sufficient capital may seek the skills and services of a particular new partner. Or, present partners may wish to liquidate a part of their interests and scale down their individual investments. In these situations, the firm may be motivated to sell an interest in the present partnership. On the other hand, if additional capital is needed, adding a partner who will contribute assets may be a proper solution.

For the benefit of the existing partners, the net assets of the present partnership should reflect their current fair values at the time a new partner is admitted. This may require a revaluation of certain assets. The resultant gain or loss would be apportioned to the present partners in their profit and loss sharing ratio. If the net assets do not reflect their fair values, the new partner may share in gains and losses that developed before admission to the firm. In the following examples of new partner admissions, we assume that the recorded book values of the assets of the present partnership do not require restatement.

Purchase of an Interest

Suppose that Ames and Baker have capital balances of $30,000 and $10,000, respectively, and that Ames sells one-half of his interest to Sue Carter. For Carter to become a partner, both Ames and Baker must consent to the sale. The entry to record Carter's admission would be:

Ames, Capital	15,000	
Carter, Capital		15,000

To record admission of Carter.

The actual cash amount paid to Ames is not relevant in recording Carter's admission; it is entirely a personal matter between the two persons. Whether an interest is purchased from one partner or several, a transfer of capital is made only for the amounts of the interests purchased without regard to the payment made. Suppose that Carter purchased a one-fourth interest in the firm by obtaining one-fourth of each partner's present share. One-fourth interest would amount to $10,000 (one-fourth of $40,000 present capital). The entry for the admission of Carter would then be:

Ames, Capital	7,500	
Baker, Capital	2,500	
Carter, Capital		10,000

To record admission of Carter.

Clearly, if an incoming partner contributes assets to the firm, total capital will increase. If the present partners believe that their current capital balances are realistically stated, the simplest arrangement is to have the new partner contribute assets equal to the desired proportionate interest in the total capital of the new firm. In our example, present capital is $40,000, with balances of $30,000 for Ames and $10,000 for Baker. Carter wants to contribute enough cash to obtain one-third interest in the new firm. It follows that the present partners' capital of $40,000 represents two-thirds of the new firm's capital; therefore, Carter should contribute $20,000. The entry for admission would be:

Cash	20,000	
Carter, Capital		20,000

To record admission of Carter.

BONUS TO PRESENT PARTNERS If a partnership interest is especially attractive because of a superior earnings record or the promise of exceptional future earnings, the present partners may require that an additional amount be paid by the new partner as a "bonus" for admission. Suppose that Ames and Baker required a payment of $35,000 for a one-third interest in the new firm. The total capital of the new firm would then be $75,000, of which a one-third interest would be $25,000, as shown below:

Ames, Capital	$30,000
Baker, Capital	10,000
Present Capital	$40,000
Contribution of Carter	35,000
Capital of New Firm	$75,000
One-third Interest	$25,000

The $10,000 difference between Carter's payment of $35,000 and her interest of $25,000 is a bonus to the former partners, to be divided according to their profit and loss sharing ratio. If the agreement provided for equal sharing, then the entry to admit Carter would be:

Cash	35,000	
Ames, Capital		5,000
Baker, Capital		5,000
Carter, Capital		25,000

To record admission of Carter.

BONUS TO NEW PARTNER A firm anxious to add a new partner with ready cash or with unique skills, management potential, or other desirable characteristics may award the new partner a larger interest than would be warranted by the contribution made. Because the capital of the new partner will be greater than his or her asset contribution, the present partners must make up the difference (bonus to new partner) by reducing their capital balances. Assume that Carter is to receive a one-third interest by contributing only $14,000 to the new firm. This will increase the capital of the new firm to $54,000 ($40,000 + $14,000), of which a one-third interest is $18,000, as shown below:

Ames, Capital	$30,000
Baker, Capital	10,000
Present Capital	$40,000
Contribution of Carter	14,000
Capital of New Firm	$54,000
One-third Interest	$18,000

The $4,000 difference between Carter's $14,000 contribution and her interest of $18,000 is a bonus to Carter. Ames and Baker will have their capital balances reduced accordingly, with amounts based on the profit and loss sharing ratio. If there is equal sharing, the entry to admit Carter as a partner in the firm will be:

Cash	14,000	
Ames, Capital	2,000	
Baker, Capital	2,000	
Carter, Capital		18,000

To record admission of Carter.

RECORDING GOODWILL OF PRESENT FIRM When a new partner is admitted to a firm with a superior earnings record, the existing partners may feel that their capital balances do not portray the actual value of their interest in the firm because no goodwill has been recorded. In lieu of requiring a bonus from the new partner, they may decide to negotiate with the incoming partner to establish the goodwill of the present firm. Suppose that Carter is willing to pay $35,000 for a one-third interest in the Ames and Baker firm, which currently has $40,000 in owner capital. The partners might reason that Carter's offer implies a value of $105,000 ($35,000 × 3) for the new firm. The goodwill of the firm might be established as follows:

Valuation of New Firm ($35,000 × 3)		$105,000
Tangible Capital:		
Ames, Capital	$30,000	
Baker, Capital	10,000	
Contribution of Carter	35,000	75,000
Goodwill Indicated for Former Firm		$ 30,000

In the entry to record the admission of Carter, the goodwill increment would be shared by the present partners in the profit and loss sharing ratio (assume equal sharing) as follows:

Cash	35,000	
Goodwill	30,000	
Ames, Capital		15,000
Baker, Capital		15,000
Carter, Capital		35,000

To record admission of Carter.

Although this method of admission establishes goodwill by a transaction with an "outsider," many people view it with skepticism. A single offer for a partnership interest is not necessarily indicative of the net value of the firm. Certainly, a sustained record of exceptional earnings would be needed as conclusive evidence of the existence of goodwill. Because many organizations with exceptional performance records have not recorded goodwill, and because of its transitory and intangible nature, knowledgeable readers of financial statements often eliminate goodwill from assets and owner capital when they encounter it in a balance sheet. The above method of allowing goodwill to former partners is, therefore, rarely encountered in partnership admissions.

ACCORDING GOODWILL TO NEW PARTNER   A goodwill allowance may be accorded to an incoming partner who brings to the firm a successful business or professional practice. Suppose that Carter has a business with net tangible assets valued at $16,000. Ames and Baker may decide to allow her $4,000 for the goodwill of her firm when they allot her a one-third interest in the new partnership. The total capital of the new firm would be $60,000, consisting of $40,000 capital of the present firm and $20,000 to be credited to Carter's capital account. The entry for Carter's admission would be:

Goodwill	4,000	
Other Assets (identified)	16,000	
Carter, Capital		20,000

To record admission of Carter.

The reservations cited above about recording goodwill of the present firm apply in this case also.

RETIREMENT OF A PARTNER

Upon retiring, a partner may (1) sell his or her interest to an outsider, (2) sell that interest to one or more of the remaining partners, or (3) receive payment for the interest from partnership funds.

If a retiring partner sells to an outsider (with approval of the firm), the procedure for recording the sale is similar to that illustrated earlier for the purchase of an interest. Suppose that retiring partner Baker sells his $10,000 interest to Stan Dodge, who desires to join the firm. The entry to record Dodge's admission and Baker's departure, regardless of the amount of Dodge's actual payment to Baker, would be:

Baker, Capital	10,000	
Dodge, Capital		10,000

To record Dodge's purchase
of Baker's interest.

This transaction is a personal one between Baker and Dodge. Likewise, if Baker sold his interest to remaining partners Ames and Carter, there would merely be a transfer of Baker's interest to their capital accounts, regardless of the payment made. Suppose that Baker sold equal portions of his interest to the remaining partners. The entry would be:

Baker, Capital	10,000	
Ames, Capital		5,000
Carter, Capital		5,000

To record sale of Baker's interest
to Ames and Carter.

If the retiring partner receives funds from the partnership for his or her interest, any difference between the amount of this interest and the sum paid will affect the capital balances of the remaining partners. For example, assume that the capital balances of Ames, Baker, and Carter are $35,000, $15,000, and $25,000, respectively, at the time that Baker is to retire, and that $20,000 is to be paid by the firm for Baker's interest. The $5,000 bonus for Baker would be divided by the other partners according to their profit and loss sharing ratio (assumed here to be equal). The entry would be:

Ames, Capital	2,500	
Carter, Capital	2,500	
Baker, Capital	15,000	
Cash		20,000

To record Baker's withdrawal
from the partnership.

The negotiations for a partner's retirement may be an occasion for revising partners' capital balances. Because of such factors as appreciation of assets or an exceptional performance record, the capital balances may not provide a realistic basis for determining the value of partnership interests. In such situations, the partners may decide to adjust tangible assets to current values or to record a goodwill amount based on the price negotiated for the retiring partner's interest. These increments would be shared by all partners in their sharing ratio, after which the retiring partner would be paid the new balance in his or her capital account.

For example, if the firm's tangible assets are fairly valued, the $20,000 to be paid for Baker's $15,000 interest implies a goodwill amount of $15,000 (partners share profits and losses equally, so the $5,000 excess to be paid Baker represents one-third of the total goodwill). The entry to record the goodwill would be:

Goodwill	15,000	
Ames, Capital		5,000
Baker, Capital		5,000
Carter, Capital		5,000

To record goodwill
upon Baker's retirement.

Baker's retirement would then be recorded by the following entry:

Baker, Capital	20,000	
Cash		20,000

To record Baker's withdrawal
from the partnership.

LIQUIDATION OF A PARTNERSHIP

The situations that arise during partnership liquidations can be quite complex. Because they are treated comprehensively in advanced accounting texts, we shall provide only a basic approach to liquidations in this section. When a business partnership is discontinued, the assets are sold, liabilities are paid, and the remaining cash is distributed to the partners. Essentially, gains and losses realized in selling assets are carried to the partners' capital accounts (in the established profit and loss sharing ratio), and each partner eventually receives the balance remaining in his or her capital account.

As the basis for our illustrations, let us assume that Ames, Baker, and Carter share profits and losses in the ratio of 40%, 40%, and 20%, respectively, and that before liquidation their balance sheet appears as follows:

Cash	$ 15,000	Liabilities	$ 40,000
Other Assets	100,000	Ames, Capital	35,000
		Baker, Capital	15,000
		Carter, Capital	25,000
	$115,000		$115,000

Capital Balances Exceed Losses

If the Other Assets in the balance sheet in our example were sold for $80,000, the firm would sustain a loss of $20,000. Because the partners share the loss, their capital balances are reduced by the following amounts: Ames, $8,000; Baker, $8,000; and Carter, $4,000. The appropriate entry at this time might be made as follows:

Cash	80,000	
Ames, Capital	8,000	
Baker, Capital	8,000	
Carter, Capital	4,000	
Other Assets		100,000

To record sale of Other Assets.

After this entry has been recorded, the firm's balance sheet would appear as follows:

Cash	$95,000		Liabilities	$40,000
			Ames, Capital	27,000
			Baker, Capital	7,000
			Carter, Capital	21,000
	$95,000			$95,000

Finally, the entries to pay the liabilities and distribute the remaining cash to the partners would be:

Liabilities	40,000	
Cash		40,000

To record payment of liabilities.

Ames, Capital	27,000	
Baker, Capital	7,000	
Carter, Capital	21,000	
Cash		55,000

To record cash distribution to partners.

Observe, in the foregoing procedure, that *only gains* and *losses* on liquidation are shared in the profit and loss sharing ratio—not the residual cash. Remaining funds are distributed to partners *in the amounts of their capital balances* after all gains and losses have been shared.

Losses Exceed Partner's Capital

When there are liquidation losses, a partner's share of losses may exceed his or her capital balance. If this occurs, that partner will be expected to contribute cash to the partnership to offset the capital account debit balance. For example, suppose that in our illustration the $100,000 of Other Assets were sold for only

$60,000. The $40,000 loss would be distributed in the 40:40:20 sharing ratio as follows: Ames, $16,000; Baker, $16,000; and Carter, $8,000. After the sale of the assets and payment of liabilities were recorded, the following account balances would be left:

Cash	$35,000	Ames, Capital	$19,000
		Baker, Capital	
		(Debit)	(1,000)
		Carter, Capital	17,000
	$35,000		$35,000

If Baker pays the firm $1,000 to make up his deficit, the resulting $36,000 cash balance is the amount that can be distributed to Ames ($19,000) and Carter ($17,000). If Baker cannot make the contribution, the $1,000 is treated as a loss, to be distributed to Ames and Carter in the ratio in which they share profits and losses. Because the ratio of their respective shares is 40:20, we see that Ames will sustain 40/60, or two-thirds, of the $1,000 loss and Carter, 20/60, or one-third. The entry to redistribute Baker's debit balance will be:

Ames, Capital	667	
Carter, Capital	333	
Baker, Capital		1,000

To record distribution of Baker's deficit to Ames and Carter.

The $35,000 cash will then be paid to Ames and Carter in the amounts of their final capital balances:

Ames, Capital	18,333	
Carter, Capital	16,667	
Cash		35,000

To record cash distribution to partners.

Sometimes there may be doubt whether a partner with a capital account deficit will be able to make up the deficit. At the same time, the other partners may be anxious to distribute whatever cash is available after creditors have been paid. In our illustration, if Ames and Carter had doubts about receiving $1,000 from Baker, cash might be distributed as shown in the last entry: $18,333 to Ames and $16,667 to Carter. This would leave sufficient amounts in their capital accounts—$667 for Ames and $333 for Carter—to absorb a $1,000 loss in the sharing ratio if Baker defaults on payment. If he does contribute the amount needed, the other partners will be paid the balances of their capital accounts.

DEMONSTRATION PROBLEM FOR REVIEW

Baer and Petty have been partners for several years, operating The Clean Sweepers—a chimney cleaning business. The business has had its ups and downs, but overall it has been quite successful. In recognition of Baer's administrative responsibilities, the profit and loss sharing agreement allows Baer a salary of $5,000, with the remainder shared equally.

On January 1, 19X1, Baer and Petty had capital balances of $14,000 and $9,000, respectively. During 19X1, Baer withdrew $4,000 cash from the partnership. Net income for 19X1 was $11,000. On December 31, 19X1, the partnership had the following assets and liabilities: Cash, $4,000; Other Assets, $29,000; and Accounts Payable, $3,000.

Baer and Petty agree to liquidate the partnership on January 1, 19X2. On that date, the Other Assets are sold for $35,000, creditors are paid, and the remaining cash is distributed to Baer and Petty.

REQUIRED
(a) Prepare a schedule showing how the $11,000 net income for 19X1 should be divided between Baer and Petty.
(b) Prepare a statement of partners' capital for the year 19X1.
(c) Prepare a balance sheet at December 31, 19X1.
(d) Give the journal entries on January 1, 19X2, to record the sale of the Other Assets, the payment of liabilities, and the distribution of cash to the partners.

SOLUTION TO DEMONSTRATION PROBLEM
(a)

	Baer	Petty	
Earnings to be divided			$11,000
Salary allowance	$5,000		5,000
Remainder			$ 6,000
Remainder divided equally	3,000	$3,000	
Partners' shares	$8,000	$3,000	

(b)

The Clean Sweepers
Statement of Partners' Capital
For the Year 19X1

	Baer	Petty	Total
Capital Balances, January 1, 19X1	$14,000	$ 9,000	$23,000
Add: Net Income for 19X1	8,000	3,000	11,000
Totals	$22,000	$12,000	$34,000
Less: Withdrawals	4,000		4,000
Capital Balances, December 31, 19X1	$18,000	$12,000	$30,000

(c)

The Clean Sweepers
Balance Sheet
December 31, 19X1

Assets			Liabilities		
Cash	$ 4,000		Accounts Payable		$ 3,000
Other Assets	29,000				
			Owners' Equity		
			Baer, Capital	$18,000	
			Petty, Capital	12,000	30,000
			Total Liabilities and		
Total Assets	$33,000		Owners' Equity		$33,000

(d)

19X2				
Jan. 1	Cash		35,000	
	Other Assets			29,000
	Baer, Capital			3,000
	Petty, Capital			3,000

To record sale of Other Assets.

Jan. 1	Accounts Payable		3,000	
	Cash			3,000

To record payment of liabilities.

Jan. 1	Baer, Capital		21,000	
	Petty, Capital		15,000	
	Cash			36,000

To record cash distribution to partners.

KEY POINTS TO REMEMBER

(1) A partnership is a voluntary association of persons who agree to become joint owners of a business. Each general partner is an agent for the partnership, has unlimited liability for partnership obligations, and co-owns firm property with all partners. A partnership is a nontaxable entity and may be dissolved by any membership change or by court decree.

(2) Assets invested in a partnership should be recorded initially at their current fair values. This precludes future inequities in partners' capital balances resulting from the use of these assets.

(3) Partnership profits and losses are divided among partners according to the sharing agreement. If there is no sharing agreement, profits and losses are divided equally.

(4) New partners may be admitted to a partnership either by purchasing an interest or by investing asets. Because the purchase of an interest is a personal transaction between the incoming partner and one or more present partners, there is no change in the assets of the firm. Admission of a partner through an investment increases the assets of the partnership.

(5) A retiring partner may sell his or her interest to an outsider or to one or more of the remaining partners, or receive payment for the interest from partnership funds.

(6) The liquidation of a partnership involves conversion of assets to cash, payment of creditors, and distribution of any remaining cash to partners. The final distribution to partners is based on their capital balances.

QUESTIONS

12-1 What is meant by mutual agency? by unlimited liability?

12-2 A corporation is said to have continuity of existence, whereas a partnership is characterized by a limited life. Name several events that may cause the dissolution of a partnership.

12-3 Sayers understands that a partnership is a nontaxable entity and believes that if he does not withdraw any assets from the firm this year he will not have any taxable income from his partnership activities. Is Sayers correct in his belief? Why or why not?

12-4 Boone invests in his partnership a machine that originally cost him $12,000. At the time of the investment, it is carried on his personal records at a book value of $8,000. Its current market value is $9,000. At what amount should the partnership record the machine? Why?

12-5 What factors should persons going into partnership consider in arriving at a procedure for sharing profits and losses?

12-6 If a partnership agreement is silent on the sharing of profits and losses, how will profits and losses be divided? What if the agreement indicates the method of sharing profits, but states nothing about the sharing of losses?

12-7 What are salary allowances? What is the difference between a salary allowance and salary expense?

12-8 In what ways do the financial statements of a partnership differ from those of a sole proprietorship? What is the purpose of a statement of partners' capital?

12-9 Distinguish between the admission of a partner to a partnership by the purchase of an interest and by investment in the firm.

12-10 Why do many accountants hesitate to allow goodwill to present partners when recording the admission of a new partner?

12-11 Falk and Brogan, who share profits and losses equally, admit Pitman as a new partner. Pitman contributes $30,000 for a one-fourth interest in the firm. The entry to admit Pitman shows a bonus of $4,000 each to Falk and Brogan. What is the total capital of the new partnership?

12-12 When a partner retires, are the assets and capital of the partnership reduced? Explain.

12-13 When a partnership liquidates, how do accountants handle the gains and losses realized in the selling of assets?

12-14 In a partnership liquidation, the residual cash is distributed to partners in the amounts of their capital balances just prior to the distribution. Why is this the proper distribution procedure?

12-15 Assume that during liquidation a debit balance arises in a partner's capital account and the partner is unable to contribute any more assets to the partnership. What disposition is made of the debit balance in the capital account?

EXERCISES

12-16 Cochran and Long agree to form a partnership on May 1. Cochran contributes $40,000 cash and Long contributes the following items from a separate business:

> Marketable securities—cost of $8,000; current fair value of $11,000.
> Equipment—cost of $30,000; accumulated depreciation of $12,000; current fair value of $20,000.
> Land—cost of $15,000; current fair value of $23,000.
> Note payable (secured by equipment)—$8,000, to be assumed by partnership.

Give the opening entries of the partnership, in general journal form, to record the investments of Cochran and Long.

12-17 Kallis and Ellis are partners whose profit and loss sharing agreement gives salary allowances of $15,000 to Kallis and $10,000 to Ellis, with the remainder divided equally.
(a) Net income for the year is $57,000. Give the general journal entry to distribute the $57,000 income to Kallis and Ellis.
(b) Assume there was a $9,000 net loss for the year. Give the general journal entry to distribute the $9,000 loss to Kallis and Ellis.

12-18 Use the following data to prepare a statement of partners' capital for the year 19XX for Dean and Park, partners who share profits and losses in the ratio of 60% to Dean and 40% to Park.

Dean, Capital—January 1, 19XX	$81,000
Park, Capital—January 1, 19XX	55,000
Dean, Drawing	20,000
Park, Drawing	14,000
Additional investments by Dean	9,000
Net income for 19XX	60,000

12-19 Elson and Reilly are partners with capital balances of $50,000 and $30,000, respectively. They share profits and losses in the ratio of 70% to Elson and 30% to Reilly. Mann is admitted to a one-fourth interest in the firm upon the investment of $35,000 cash on May 4.

(a) Give the general journal entry to record the admission of Mann, assuming a bonus is to be allowed Elson and Reilly.

(b) Give the general journal entry to record the admission of Mann, assuming goodwill of the present firm is established.

12-20 Austin, Bloom, and Carey are partners sharing profits and losses in the ratio 5:3:2, respectively. Their capital balances are Austin, $40,000; Bloom, $32,000; and Carey, $26,000. Austin decides to retire from the firm and is paid $48,000 from partnership funds. Austin retires on June 30.

(a) Give the general journal entry to record the retirement of Austin, assuming that Bloom and Carey are to absorb the bonus paid Austin.

(b) Give the general journal entries to record the retirement of Austin, assuming the partners decide to record a goodwill amount based on the price to be paid Austin.

12-21 Just before liquidation, the balance sheet of Day and Weldon, who share profits and losses equally, appeared as follows:

Cash	$ 3,000	Liabilities	$ 5,000
Other Assets	18,000	Day, Capital	10,000
		Weldon, Capital	6,000
	$21,000		$21,000

(a) If all the Other Assets are sold for $12,000, what amounts will be paid to Day and Weldon as the final cash distribution?

(b) If all the Other Assets are sold for $22,000, what amounts will be paid to Day and Weldon as the final cash distribution?

(c) If Day receives $9,000 and Weldon receives $5,000 as the final (and only) cash distribution, what amount was received from the sale of the Other Assets?

12-22 Dugan, Nair, Pierce, and Rhodes are liquidating their partnership. All assets have been converted to cash, and all liabilities have been paid. At this point the capital accounts show the following: Dugan, $7,000 credit balance; Nair, $4,000 credit balance; Pierce, $6,000 debit balance; Rhodes, $8,000 credit balance. Profits and losses are shared equally.

(a) How much cash is available to distribute to partners?

(b) If there is doubt concerning Pierce's ability to make up the $6,000 deficit, how should the available cash be distributed?

PROBLEMS

12-23 Hunt and Mellon agreed to form a partnership and invested $50,000 and $30,000, respectively. During its first year the partnership earned a net income of $8,000.

REQUIRED
(a) Give the entry to close the Income Summary account and distribute the $8,000 net income under each of the following independent assumptions.
    (1) The partnership agreement is silent on the sharing of profits and losses.
    (2) Profits and losses are to be shared in the ratio of beginning capital investments.
    (3) Profits and losses are to be shared by allowing 8% interest on beginning capital investments, with the remainder divided equally.
(b) Assume the partnership had a $4,000 loss in its first year. Give the entry to close the Income Summary account and distribute the $4,000 loss under each of the foregoing assumptions.

12-24 The capital accounts and the Income Summary account of the MacNeil, Trevino, and Hawk partnership appear below. None of the partners withdrew capital during the year.

MacNeil, Capital				Trevino, Capital		
	19XX				19XX	
	Jan. 1	8,000			Jan. 1	10,000
	July 1	4,000			Oct. 1	20,000

Hawk, Capital				Income Summary		
	19XX				19XX	
	Jan. 1	5,000			Dec. 31	18,000

REQUIRED
(a) Give the entry to distribute the $18,000 net income if MacNeil, Trevino, and Hawk share profits and losses:
    (1) Equally.
    (2) In the ratio 4:3:2, respectively.
    (3) In the ratio of *average* capital balances for the year.
    (4) Under an agreement allowing $7,000 salary to Hawk, 10% interest on *beginning* investments, and the remainder shared equally.
(b) Assume that the net income was $8,400 rather than $18,000. Give the entry to distribute the $8,400 earnings if the agreement allows $7,000 salary to Hawk, 10% interest on beginning investments, and the remainder to be shared equally.

12-25 Daley and North are partners with capital balances of $33,000 and $18,000, respectively. Profits and losses are shared equally.

REQUIRED
Give the entries to record the admission of a new partner, Boone, under each of the following separate circumstances.
(a) Boone purchases one-half of North's interest, paying North $10,000 personally.
(b) Boone invests sufficient funds to receive exactly a one-fourth interest in the new partnership. (No bonuses or goodwill are to be recorded.)
(c) Boone invests $19,000 for a one-fifth interest, with any bonus distributed to the capital accounts of Daley and North.
(d) Boone invests $13,000 for a one-fourth interest, with any bonus credited to Boone's capital account.
(e) Boone invests $30,000 for a one-third interest. Goodwill is to be allowed the present partners and recorded in the accounts.
(f) Boone is to obtain a one-fourth interest in the new firm by contributing a business with a net asset value of $15,000. Goodwill is to be allowed Boone for the business and is to be recorded on the books.

12-26 Starr, Dahl, and Valdez are partners with capital balances of $70,000, $45,000, and $50,000, respectively. Profits and losses are shared equally. Valdez wishes to retire from the firm.

REQUIRED
Record the entries for Valdez's retirement in each of the following separate circumstances.
(a) Valdez's interest is sold to Bailey, a new partner, for $62,000.
(b) One-half of Valdez's interest is sold to each of the remaining partners for $31,000 apiece.
(c) Valdez receives $60,000 of partnership funds for his interest. No goodwill is to be recorded, and the remaining partners are to absorb the bonus paid Valdez.
(d) The partners agree that Valdez's $50,000 interest is worth $58,000. They decide to record goodwill on the books since the firm's tangible assets are fairly valued. Valdez is paid from partnership funds.

12-27 Gill and Capp formed a partnership on January 1, 19X1, with capital investments of $10,000 and $16,000, respectively. The profit and loss sharing agreement allowed Gill a salary of $6,000, with the remainder divided equally. During the year Capp made withdrawals of $3,000; no other investments or withdrawals were made in 19X1. The partnership incurred a net loss of $8,000 in 19X1.

On January 1, 19X2, Logan was admitted to the partnership. Logan purchased one-third of Gill's interest and paid $4,000 directly to Gill. Gill, Capp, and Logan agreed to share profits and losses in the ratio 3:5:2, respectively. The partnership earned a net income of $10,000 in 19X2.

On January 1, 19X3, Capp withdrew from the partnership. Capp received $12,000 of partnership funds for her interest. Gill and Logan absorbed the bonus paid Capp.

REQUIRED

(a) Give the entry at December 31, 19X1, to close the Income Summary account and distribute the $8,000 loss for 19X1.

(b) Compute the capital balances of Gill and Capp at December 31, 19X1.

(c) Give the entry to record the admission of Logan on January 1, 19X2.

(d) Give the entry at December 31, 19X2, to close the Income Summary account and distribute the $10,000 income for 19X2.

(e) Compute the capital balances of Gill, Capp, and Logan at December 31, 19X2.

(f) Give the entry to record the withdrawal of Capp on January 1, 19X3.

12-28 Allen and Foley formed a partnership in 19X1, agreeing to share profits and losses equally. On December 31, 19X1, their capital balances were Allen, $20,000; Foley, $14,000.

On January 1, 19X2, Poe was admitted to a one-fourth interest in the firm by investing $14,000 cash. Poe's admission was recorded by according bonuses to Allen and Foley. The profit and loss sharing agreement of the new partnership allowed salaries of $5,000 to Allen and $7,000 to Poe, with the remainder divided in the ratio 3:3:2 among Allen, Foley, and Poe, respectively.

Net income for 19X2 was $36,000. Allen and Poe withdrew cash during the year equal to their salary allowances. Immediately after the net income had been closed to the partners' capital accounts, Poe retired from the firm. Poe received $22,000 of partnership funds for his interest, and the remaining partners absorbed the bonus paid Poe.

REQUIRED

Prepare a statement of partners' capital for the year 19X2.

12-29 Fox, Glenn, and Hale are partners who share profits and losses in the ratio of 5:3:2, respectively. Their partnership is about to be liquidated. Prior to liquidation, the firm's balance sheet appears as follows:

Cash	$ 5,000	Accounts Payable	$18,000
Other Assets	90,000	Fox, Capital	15,000
		Glenn, Capital	23,000
		Hale, Capital	39,000
	$95,000		$95,000

REQUIRED

(a) Assuming that Other Assets are sold for $80,000, give the entries to record the sale of the Other Assets, pay liabilities, and distribute the remaining cash to the partners.

(b) Assuming that Other Assets are sold for $50,000, give the entries to record the sale of the Other Assets, pay liabilities, apportion any partner's deficit among the other partners (assuming any such deficit will not be made up by the partner involved), and distribute the remaining cash to the appropriate partners.

12-30 Ryan, Todd, and Lane are partners who share profits and losses in the ratio 3:2:1, respectively. They decide to liquidate the partnership. Prior to liquidation, the firm's balance sheet appears as follows:

Cash	$ 3,000	Accounts Payable	$ 5,000
Other Assets	64,000	Ryan, Capital	32,000
		Todd, Capital	18,000
		Lane, Capital	12,000
	$67,000		$67,000

REQUIRED

(a) Assuming that Other Assets are sold for $52,000, give the entries to record the sale of the Other Assets, pay liabilities, and distribute the remaining cash to the partners.

(b) Assuming that Other Assets are sold for $70,000, give the entries to record the sale of the Other Assets, pay liabilities, and distribute the remaining cash to the partners.

ALTERNATE PROBLEMS

12-24A The capital accounts and the Income Summary account of the Field, Mahoney, and Sack partnership appear below. None of the partners withdrew capital during the year.

Field, Capital			Mahoney, Capital		
	19XX			19XX	
	Jan. 1	18,000		Jan. 1	36,000
	July 1	12,000		Sept. 1	36,000

Sack, Capital			Income Summary		
	19XX			19XX	
	Jan. 1	8,000		Dec. 31	42,000

REQUIRED

(a) Give the entry to distribute the $42,000 net income if Field, Mahoney, and Sack share profits and losses:

(1) Equally.

(2) In the ratio 5:3:2, respectively.

(3) In the ratio of *average* capital balances for the year.

(4) Under an agreement allowing $5,000 salary to Sack, 8% interest on *beginning* investments, and the remainder shared equally.

(b) Assume that the net income was $7,500 rather than $42,000. Give the entry to distribute the $7,500 earnings if the agreement allows $5,000 salary to Sack, 8% interest on beginning investments, and the remainder to be shared equally.

12-25A Bates and Reed are partners with capital balances of $45,000 and $27,000, respectively. Profits and losses are shared equally.

REQUIRED
Give the entries to record the admission of a new partner, Lemon, in each of the following separate circumstances.
(a) Lemon purchases one-third of Reed's interest, personally paying Reed $12,000.
(b) Lemon invests sufficient funds to receive exactly a one-fifth interest in the new partnership. (No bonuses or goodwill are to be recorded.)
(c) Lemon invests $32,000 for a one-fourth interest, with any bonus distributed to the capital accounts of Bates and Reed.
(d) Lemon invests $24,000 for a one-third interest, with any bonus credited to Lemon's capital account.
(e) Lemon invests $25,000 for a one-fourth interest. Goodwill is to be allowed the present partners and recorded in the accounts.
(f) Lemon is to obtain a one-third interest in the new firm by contributing a business with a net asset value of $29,000. Goodwill is to be allowed Lemon for the business and is to be recorded on the books.

12-26A Tanner, May and Garman are partners with capital balances of $25,000, $20,000, and $15,000, respectively. Profits and losses are shared equally. Garman wishes to retire from the firm.

REQUIRED
Record the entries for Garman's retirement under each of the following separate assumptions.
(a) Garman's interest is sold to Wyatt, a new partner, for $18,000.
(b) One-half of Garman's interest is sold to each of the remaining partners for $9,000 apiece.
(c) Garman receives $17,000 of partnership funds for her interest. No goodwill is to be recorded, and the remaining partners are to absorb the bonus paid Garman.
(d) It is agreed among the partners that Garman's $15,000 interest is worth $19,000. They decide to record goodwill on the books because the firm's tangible assets are fairly valued. Garman is paid from partnership funds.

12-28A Bell and Page formed a partnership in 19X5, agreeing to share profits and losses equally. On December 31, 19X5, their capital balances were Bell, $28,000; Page, $22,000.

On January 1, 19X6, Kane was admitted to the partnership by purchasing one-half of Page's interest, personally paying Page $15,000 for this interest. The profit and loss sharing agreement of the new partnership allowed Page a salary of $6,000, with the remainder divided in the ratio 4:3:2 among Bell, Page, and Kane, respectively.

Net income for 19X6 was $33,000. Page withdrew $5,000 cash from the partnership during the year. Immediately after the net income had been closed to the partners' capital accounts, Bell retired from the firm. Bell sold equal portions of his interest to Page and Kane. Page and Kane each personally paid Bell $25,000 for their share of Bell's interest.

REQUIRED

Prepare a statement of partners' capital for the year 19X6.

12-29A King, Duran, and Fitch are partners who share profits and losses in the ratio of 4:3:3, respectively. Their partnership is about to be liquidated. Before liquidation, the firm's balance sheet appears as follows:

Cash	$ 4,000	Accounts Payable	$15,000
Other Assets	76,000	King, Capital	11,000
		Duran, Capital	30,000
		Fitch, Capital	24,000
	$80,000		$80,000

REQUIRED

(a) Assuming that Other Assets are sold for $61,000, give the entries to record the sale of the Other Assets, pay liabilities, and distribute the remaining cash to the partners.

(b) Assuming that Other Assets are sold for $46,000, give the entries to record the sale of the Other Assets, pay liabilities, apportion any partner's deficit among the other partners (assuming any such deficit will not be made up by the partner involved), and distribute the remaining cash to the appropriate partners.

BUSINESS DECISION PROBLEM

Hall and Ivy were in business for several years, sharing profits and losses equally. Because of Ivy's poor health, they agreed to liquidate the partnership. Hall managed the liquidation because Ivy was in the hospital. Just before liquidation, the partnership balance sheet contained the following information:

Cash	$ 10,000	Liabilities	$ 20,000
Other Assets	110,000	Hall, Capital	45,000
		Ivy, Capital	55,000
	$120,000		$120,000

Hall (1) sold the other assets at the best prices obtainable, (2) paid off all the creditors, and (3) divided the remaining cash between Ivy and himself equally, according to their profit and loss sharing ratio.

Ivy received a note from Hall that read "Good news—sold other assets for $130,000. Have $60,000 check waiting for you. Get well soon." Because he will not be released from the hospital for several days, Ivy asks you to review Hall's liquidation and cash distribution procedures.

REQUIRED
Do you approve of the liquidation and cash distribution procedures followed by Hall? Explain. If you believe Hall erred, what amount of final cash settlement should Ivy receive?

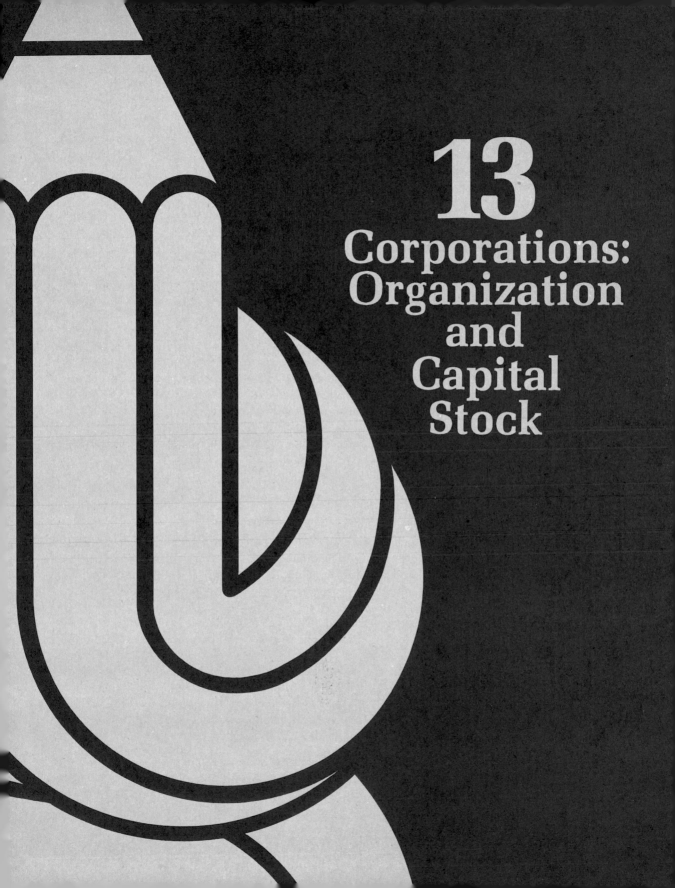

13
Corporations: Organization and Capital Stock

It has been truly said that a corporation has no conscience; but a corporation of conscientious men is a corporation *with* a conscience.

HENRY DAVID THOREAU

"It was once said that the sun never set on the British Empire. Today the sun does set on the British Empire, but not on the scores of corporate empires ..."[1] Without a doubt, the modern corporation dominates the national and international economic landscape. In the United States, corporations generate well over three-fourths of the combined business receipts of corporations, partnerships and proprietorships, even though fewer than one of every five businesses is organized as a corporation. The corporate form of organization is used for a wide variety of business efforts—from the large, multinational corporation with more than a million owners operating in countries all over the world to the small, family-owned business in a single community.

In this and the next two chapters, we shall consider various aspects of accounting for the corporation. In this chapter, we shall emphasize the organization of the corporation and the accounting procedures for its capital stock transactions.

NATURE AND FORMATION OF A CORPORATION

A corporation is a legal entity—an artificial legal "person"—created on the approval of the appropriate governmental authority. The right to conduct business as a corporation is a privilege granted by the state in which the corporation is formed. All states have laws specifying the requirements for creating a corporation. In some instances, such as the formation of a national bank, the federal government must approve the creation of a corporation.

To form a corporation, the incorporators (often at least three are required) must apply for a charter. The incorporators prepare and file the **articles of incorporation,** which delineate the basic structure of the corporation, including the purposes for which it is formed, the amount of capital stock to be authorized, and the number of shares into which the stock is to be divided. If the incorporators meet the requirements of the law, the government issues a charter or certificate of incorporation. After the charter has been granted, an organization meeting is held by the incorporators (or, in some states, by the subscribers to the

[1]Lester R. Brown, "How Big Are the Multinationals?" *The Saturday Evening Post*, March 1974.

corporation's capital stock) to accomplish such things as the election of the first board of directors and the adoption of the corporation's bylaws.

Because assets are essential to corporate operations, the corporation issues **certificates of capital stock** to obtain the necessary funds. As owners of the corporation, **stockholders,** or **shareholders,** are entitled to a voice in the control and management of the company. Stockholders whose shares represent voting stock are entitled to vote at the annual meeting and to participate in the election of the board of directors. The board of directors is responsible for the overall management of the corporation. Normally, the board selects such corporate officers as a president, one or more vice-presidents, a controller, a treasurer, and a secretary. The officers implement the policies of the board of directors and actively manage the day-to-day affairs of the corporation.

Creating a corporation is more costly than organizing a proprietorship or partnership. The expenditures incurred to organize a corporation are charged to Organization Costs, an intangible asset account. These costs include attorney's fees, fees paid to the state, and costs of promoting the enterprise. As we discussed in Chapter 10, organization costs typically are amortized over a period of five to ten years.

CHARACTERISTICS OF CORPORATIONS

Separate Legal Entity

When a business receives its corporate charter, it is empowered to carry on business affairs apart from its owners. The corporation, as a legal entity, may acquire assets, incur debt, enter into contracts, sue, and be sued—all in its own name. The owners, or stockholders, of the corporation receive stock certificates as evidence of their ownership interests; the stockholders, however, are separate and distinct from the corporation. This is in contrast to proprietorships and partnerships, which are not legal entities apart from their owners. Proprietorships and partnerships are accounting entities, but because they are not legal entities, their owners can be held responsible, separately and collectively, for unsatisfied obligations of the business.

Limited Liability

The liability of shareholders with respect to company affairs is usually limited to their equity in the corporation. Because of this limited liability, state laws restrict distributions to shareholders. Most of these laws have fairly elaborate provisions that define the various forms of owners' equity and describe distribution conditions. To protect creditors, the state places rigid controls on the distribution of contributed capital. Distributions of retained earnings (undistributed profits) are not legal unless the board of directors formally declares a dividend. Because of the legal delineation of owner capital available for distribution, it is important to maintain careful distinctions in the accounts to identify the different subdivisions of stockholder equity.

Transferability of Ownership

Shares in a corporation may be routinely transferred without affecting the operations of the company. The corporation does not recognize such transfers of ownership except to note them in the stockholders' records (ledger). Although corporations must have stockholders' records in order to notify shareholders of meetings and to pay dividends, no accounting recognition is given to the individual or aggregate price for which transfers are made.

Continuity of Existence

Because routine transfers of ownership do not affect a corporation's affairs, the corporation is said to have **continuity of existence.** In this respect, a corporation is completely different from a partnership. In a partnership, any change in ownership technically results in discontinuance of the old partnership and formation of a new one (even though many large professional service partnerships follow procedures that provide for continuity with changes in ownership).

In a partnership, the individual partners' capital accounts indicate their relative interests in the business. The owners' equity section of a corporate balance sheet does not present individual stockholder accounts. A shareholder, however, can easily compute his or her interest in the corporation by calculating the proportion of the total shares outstanding that his or her shares represent. For example, if there is only one class of stock outstanding, and it totals 1,000 shares, an individual owning 200 shares would have a 20% interest in the corporation's total stockholders' equity, which includes all contributed capital and retained earnings. The dollar amount of this interest, however, would be a "book" amount, rarely coinciding with the market value. A stockholder who wished to liquidate his or her investment would have to sell it to a buyer at a bargained price or, if the stock is traded on a stock exchange, at the quoted market price.

Capital-Raising Capability

The limited liability of stockholders and the ease with which shares of stock may be transferred from one investor to another are attractive features to potential stockholders. They enhance the ability of the corporation to raise large amounts of capital by issuing shares of stock. Both large and small investors may acquire ownership interests in a corporation. Thus, a wide spectrum of potential investors exists when a corporation seeks additional capital. Corporations with thousands of stockholders are not at all uncommon. The ability to accumulate and use tremendous amounts of capital makes the corporation the dominant form of business organization in the U.S. economy.

Taxation

As legal entities, corporations are subject to federal income taxes on their earnings, whether distributed or not. In addition, shareholders receiving the earnings as dividends must pay income taxes on such dividend income. In many small corporations in which the shareholders themselves manage the business affairs, large salaries may reduce the earnings to a point where the "double taxation" feature is not onerous. The firm may have to justify the reasonableness of such salaries to the Internal Revenue Service. Under certain circumstances, a corporation with fifteen shareholders or fewer may elect to be treated as a partnership for tax purposes. Although partnerships must submit "information" tax returns, an income tax is not imposed on their earnings. Instead, the partners must report their respective shares of partnership earnings on their individual income tax returns.

Usually, corporations are subject to state income taxes in the states in which they are incorporated or are doing business, and they may be subject also to real estate, personal property, and franchise taxes.

Regulation and Supervision

Corporations are subject to greater degrees of regulation and supervision than are proprietorships and partnerships. Each state has the right to regulate the corporations it charters. State statutes place certain limitations on the powers a corporation may exercise, identify reports that must be filed, and set forth the rights and liabilities of stockholders. If stock is to be issued to the general public, the corporation must comply with the provisions of laws governing the sale of corporate securities. Furthermore, corporations whose stock is listed and traded on organized security exchanges, such as the New York Stock Exchange, are subject to the various reporting and disclosure requirements of these exchanges.

OWNERS' EQUITY AND ORGANIZATIONAL FORMS

In the area of owners' equity, differences arise between accounting for a corporation and accounting for a sole proprietorship or partnership. In a sole proprietorship, only one account, the owner's capital account, is needed to reflect increases from capital contributions and net earnings as well as decreases from withdrawals and net losses. In practice, as illustrated in Chapter 2, many sole proprietors prefer to keep a separate drawing account to record cash withdrawals and withdrawals, at cost, of other business assets. This separate record is kept only for convenience, however; no subdivision of the owner's capital account is required either by law or by accounting principles.

A similar situation exists in most partnerships, in which capital and drawing accounts for each partner are customary. A partnership is simply an association of two or more persons who agree to become joint owners of a business. Because more than one individual is involved in the business, a written agreement should govern the financial participation and business responsibilities of the partners. But there is no legal or accounting requirement that a distinction be maintained between contributed capital and undistributed earnings.

A corporation, on the other hand, is subject to certain legal restrictions imposed by the government approving its creation. These restrictions focus on the distinction between contributed capital and retained earnings and make accounting for the owners' equity somewhat more complex for corporations than for other types of business organizations. In all honesty, we must observe that much of the accounting for corporate owners' equity is actually a polyglot mixture of legal prescription and accounting convention. The detailed reporting of stockholders' equity transactions, however, provides analytical information that is useful on occasion.

TYPES OF STOCK

The amounts and kinds of stock that a corporation may issue are enumerated in the company's charter. Provision may be made for several classes of stock, thereby permitting the company to raise capital from different types of investors. The charter specifies the maximum number of shares of each class stock that may be issued. This is the corporation's **authorized stock.** If a corporation wishes to issue more shares than its authorized number, it must first amend the charter. Shares that have been sold and issued to stockholders constitute the **issued stock** of the corporation. Some of this stock may be repurchased by the corporation. Shares actually held by stockholders are called **outstanding stock,** while those reacquired by the corporation are **treasury stock.** We shall discuss treasury stock later in the chapter.

Common Stock

When only one class of stock is issued, it is called **common stock.** Common shareholders compose the basic ownership class. They have rights to vote, to share in earnings, to participate in additional issues of stock, and—in the case of liquidation—to share in assets after prior claims on the corporation have been settled. We shall now consider further each of these rights.

As the owners of a corporation, the common shareholders elect the board of directors and vote on other matters requiring the approval of owners. Common shareholders are entitled to one vote for each share of stock they own. Owners who do not attend the annual stockholders' meetings may vote by proxy (and in large corporations this may be the case for most stockholders).

A common stockholder has the right to a proportionate share of the earnings of the corporation that are distributed as dividends. All earnings belong to the corporation, however, until the board of directors formally declares a dividend.

Each shareholder of a corporation has the right to maintain his or her proportionate interest in the corporation; this is called a **preemptive right.** If the company decides to issue additional shares of stock, present stockholders of that type of stock are given the first opportunity to acquire, on a pro rata basis, the new shares. In certain situations, management may request shareholders to waive their preemptive rights. For example, the corporation may wish to issue additional stock to acquire another company.

When a corporation dissolves, it converts its assets to a form suitable for distribution, usually cash, which it then distributes to parties having claims on the corporate assets. Any assets remaining after all claims have been satisfied belong to the residual ownership interest in the corporation—the common stockholders. These owners are entitled to receive the final distribution of the balance of the assets.

A company may occasionally use **classified common stock;** that is, it may issue more than one class of common stock. When two classes of common stock are issued, they are identified as Class A and Class B. The two classes usually differ in either their respective dividend rights or their respective voting powers. Usually, classified common stock is issued when the organizers of the corporation wish to acquire funds from the general public while retaining voting control. To illustrate, let us assume 10,000 shares of Class A stock are issued to the public at $40 per share, while 20,000 shares of Class B stock are issued to the organizers at $5 per share. If each shareholder receives one vote per share of stock, then the Class B stockholders have twice as many votes as the Class A stockholders. Yet the total investment of Class B stockholders is significantly less than that of the Class A stockholders. To offset the difference in the voting power per dollar of investment, the Class A stockholders may have better dividend rights, such as being entitled to dividends in early years while the Class B stockholders may not receive dividends until a certain level of earning power is reached.

Preferred Stock

Preferred stock is a class of stock with various characteristics that distinguish it from common stock. To determine the features of a particular issue, one must examine the stock contract. The majority of preferred issues, however, have certain typical features, which we discuss below.

DIVIDEND FEATURES When the board of directors declares a distribution of earnings, preferred stockholders are entitled to receive a certain annual amount of dividends before the common stockholders receive any distribution. The amount is usually specified in the preferred stock contract as a percentage of the face value (called par value) of the stock or in dollars per share if the stock does not have a par value. (Par value and no-par value stock are discussed later in this chapter.) Thus, if the preferred stock has a $100 par value and the dividend rate is 6%, the preferred shareholders will receive $6 per share in dividends. The amount is owed to the shareholders only if declared, however.

Preferred dividends are usually **cumulative.** This means that regular dividends to preferred stockholders omitted in past years must be paid in addition to the current year's dividend before any distribution can be made to the common shareholders. For example, a dividend may be omitted in an unprofitable year. If the $6 dividend on the preferred stock mentioned above were one year in arrears and a dividend was declared in the current year, preferred shareholders would be entitled to receive $12 per share before common shareholders received anything. If a preferred stock is noncumulative, dividends omitted in any year do not carry forward. Because investors normally consider the noncumulative feature unattractive, noncumulative preferred stock is rarely issued.

Dividends in arrears (that is, omitted in past years) on cumulative preferred stock are not an accounting liability and do not appear in the liability section of the balance sheet. They do not become an obligation of the corporation until the board of directors formally declares such dividends to be payable. Any arrearages are typically disclosed to investors through a footnote to the balance sheet.

Ordinarily, preferred stockholders receive a fixed amount, and they do not participate further in distributions made by the corporation. In rare circumstances, however, the stock contract may make the preferred a **participating** stock. To illustrate the participating feature, let us assume that a company had outstanding 1,000 shares of $100 par value, 6% *fully participating* preferred stock and 2,000 shares of $100 par value common stock. Assume also that the company declared total dividends of $27,000. The distribution would be made as follows:

	Preferred	Common	Total
Outstanding Stock (total par value)	$100,000	$200,000	$300,000
Regular dividend (6%) and matching rate to common (6%)	$ 6,000	$ 12,000	$ 18,000
$9,000 remainder ($27,000 less $18,000) divided to give each class the same rate: $9,000/$300,000 = 3%	3,000	6,000	9,000
Total distribution	$ 9,000	$ 18,000	$ 27,000
Rate of distribution	9%	9%	

Note that, after the preferred stock is accorded its regular 6% dividend, a like rate of 6%, amounting to $12,000, is allocated to the common stock. The remaining $9,000 to be distributed is then apportioned so both classes of stock receive the same *rate* of distribution. This rate can be determined by dividing the remainder to be distributed by the total stock of both classes ($300,000). It is important to note that the preferred stock does not begin to participate until the common stock is accorded an amount corresponding to the rate of the regular preferred dividend.

Preferred stock may also be *partially* participating. For example, suppose that the preferred shares were participating to 8%. They would then be entitled to only an additional 2% over their regular 6% dividend, and any remaining amount would be accorded the common shares.

In a participation scheme, any arrearage on the preferred stock must first be awarded to the preferred shareholders. Thus, had there been one year's arrearage on the fully participating stock in the foregoing example, $12,000 would have been allocated to the preferred stock, and then the normal 6%, or $12,000, to the common stock. Of the remaining $3,000, $1,000 would be assigned to the preferred stock and $2,000 to the common stock.

VOTING RIGHTS   Although preferred shareholders do not ordinarily have the right to vote in the election of directors, this right can be accorded by contract. Some state statutes require that all stock issued by a corporation be given voting rights. Sometimes, a preferred stock contract confers full or partial voting rights under certain conditions—as when dividends have not been paid for a specified period of time.

OTHER FEATURES   Preferred stock contracts may contain a variety of features that make them resemble the common stock equity at one end of a spectrum or a debt obligation at the other end. The stock may, for example, be **convertible** into common stock at some specified rate. This feature often causes the market price of the preferred to move with that of the common. When the price of the common stock rises, the value of the conversion feature is enhanced. Preferred stock may also be convertible into long-term debt securities (bonds). Furthermore, when a corporation is liquidated, preferred shareholders normally have a liquidation preference, that is, a prior claim to assets after creditor claims are satisfied.

Preferred stock may be **callable,** in which case the stock can be redeemed by the corporation after a length of time and at a price specified in the contract. The call feature makes such a security similar to a bond, which frequently is callable or has a limited life. Most preferred stocks are callable, with the call or redemption price set slightly above the original issuance price.

To be successful in selling its preferred stock, a corporation often must cater to current market vogues. Features are added or omitted, depending on market conditions and the desires of the investor group the corporation wishes to attract. Management must balance market requirements with its own goals. Sometimes compromises are necessary, and management may issue securities that it hopes to change over time, perhaps through conversion or refinancing, in order to arrive at the financial plan it desires.

Preferred stocks appeal to investors who want a steady rate of return that is normally somewhat higher than that on bonds. These investors often feel that preferred stock entails less risk than common stock, although the common will pay off more if the company does well.

From both the legal and the accounting standpoint, all types of preferred stock, whatever their features, are regarded as stockholders' equity. Dividends are regarded as distributions of earnings and, unlike interest on bonds, are not shown as expenses on the income statement. Also, because of the legal classification of preferred stock as stockholders' equity, dividends are not deductible by the company as an expense for income tax purposes, whereas interest on debt can be deducted as an expense.

PAR AND NO-PAR VALUE STOCK

The corporate charter may specify a face value, called **par value,** for each share of stock of any class. Although this face value may relate to the initial price of the stock, it is often arbitrary and has no connotation of value once operations begin. Par value may have legal implications, however, because it invariably is used to determine the *legal capital* of the business. State statutes normally define this term and impose restrictions on the distribution of legal capital. For this reason, accountants carefully segregate the par value amount of stock transactions and record this amount in an appropriate capital stock account.

Because investors may confuse par value with realistic values, many states have permitted the use of **no-par** stock since the early 1900s. Most states, however, permit the company's directors to set a **stated value** on the shares (and some insist that they do so). Again, this figure is arbitrary, but, in contrast to par value, the stated value is not printed on the stock certificates. From an accounting standpoint, stated value amounts are treated in a fashion similar to those of par value.

The amount in excess of par value paid to a corporation for its stock is often referred to as **premium,** while the excess of par over the amount paid may be called **discount.** In some states, persons purchasing stock for less than par value may have a liability for the discount should creditor claims remain unsatisfied in

CORPORATIONS: ORGANIZATION AND CAPITAL STOCK

the event of the company's liquidation. Stocks are rarely sold at a discount, however—in certain states this practice is even forbidden. When no-par stock with a stated value is sold, the price paid invariably exceeds the stated value. In accounting, the difference is called *excess of amount paid over stated value;* the terms "premium" and "discount" are not used with no-par stock.

To record differences between amounts paid for shares and par value, the accountant uses appropriately descriptive accounts. When an amount greater than par value is received, one may use the account Paid-in Capital in Excess of Par Value or simply Premium on Stock. The account Excess of Par Value over Amount Paid, or simply Discount on Stock, can be used when a discount is involved. For no-par stock with a stated value, accounts would have titles such as Paid-in Capital in Excess of Stated Value.

To illustrate how the stockholders' equity accounts present the amounts paid in for stock, let us assume that, in its first year of business, a corporation had the following transactions:

(1) Sold 1,000 shares of $100 par value, 7% preferred stock at $105 per share.

(2) Sold 1,000 shares of $100 par value, 6% preferred stock at $98 per share.

(3) Sold 5,000 shares of no-par common stock at $30 per share. Stated value assigned to the shares is $20 per share.

(4) The company earned $50,000 during the year. After it paid dividends of $7,000 on the 7% preferred stock, $6,000 on the 6% preferred stock, and $10,000 to the common shareholders, the company had $27,000 in retained earnings.

The stockholders' equity section of the company's December 31 balance sheet appears in Exhibit 13–1.

EXHIBIT 13–1
Stockholders' Equity

Paid-in Capital:		
7% Preferred Stock, $100 Par Value, 1,000 shares authorized, issued, and outstanding	$100,000	
Paid-in Capital in Excess of Par Value	5,000	$105,000
6% Preferred Stock, $100 Par Value, 1,000 shares authorized, issued, and outstanding	$100,000	
Excess of Par Value over Amount Paid	(2,000)	98,000
No-Par Common Stock, Stated Value $20, 10,000 shares authorized; 5,000 shares issued and outstanding	$100,000	
Paid-in Capital in Excess of Stated Value	50,000	150,000
Total Paid-in Capital		$353,000
Retained Earnings		27,000
Total Stockholders' Equity		$380,000

In the illustration, we assume that all authorized amounts of both classes of preferred stock and half of the 10,000 shares of common stock authorized have been issued. Note that both the premium on the 7% preferred stock and the excess received over stated value of the no-par common stock are added to the par and stated values, respectively, and the total amounts paid in for these two classes of stock are extended. On the other hand, the $2,000 discount on the 6% preferred stock is deducted from par value to show the amount paid for this class. All the accounts in the illustration would have credit balances in the general ledger, except for the account Excess of Par Value over Amount Paid on the 6% preferred stock, which would have a $2,000 debit balance.

Corporate owners' equity accounts are presented in a variety of ways in published reports. One popular format groups the par and stated values of the three classes of stock together under the heading Capital Stock, with a total of $300,000 in our example. Then the remainder of the paid-in capital items are placed under a heading such as Paid-in Capital. That is, the paid-in amounts in excess of par and stated value less the excess of par value over amount paid on the 6% preferred stock are shown for a total of $53,000. This type of presentation is not as clear as the one in Exhibit 13-1, because the capital stock of a firm is really a part of total paid-in capital.

STOCK ISSUANCES FOR CASH

In issuing its stock, a corporation may use the services of an investment banker. Investment bankers specialize in marketing securities to investors. The investment banker may **underwrite** the stock issue, in which case the banker buys the stock from the corporation and resells it to investors. The corporation thus does not risk being unable to sell its stock. The underwriter bears this risk in return for the profits generated by selling the stock to investors at a price higher than that paid the corporation. An investment banker who is unwilling to underwrite a stock issue may handle it on a *best efforts* basis. In this case, the investment banker agrees to sell as many shares as possible at a set price, but the corporation bears the risk of unsold stock.

The stock issues given in Exhibit 13-1, which were all for cash, would have been entered in the corporation's books by means of the following entries:

(1) Sale of 1,000 shares of $100 par value, 7% preferred stock at $105 per share.

Cash	105,000	
7% Preferred Stock		100,000
Paid-in Capital in Excess of Par Value		5,000

(2) Sale of 1,000 shares of $100 par value, 6% preferred stock at $98 per share.

Cash	98,000	
Excess of Par Value over Amount Paid	2,000	
6% Preferred Stock		100,000

(3) Sale of 5,000 shares of no-par common stock, stated value $20, at $30 per share.

Cash	150,000	
Common Stock		100,000
Paid-in Capital in Excess of Stated Value		50,000

As these entries show, the capital stock account is always credited with the par value of shares, or if the stock is no-par, with its stated value, if any. Cash received is debited, and any difference is placed in an appropriately named account. The $5,000 premium on the 7% preferred stock may be credited to an account called Premium on Preferred Stock, if desired. Similarly, the $2,000 discount on the 6% preferred stock may be debited to an account called Discount on Preferred Stock. The account titles we have used in the illustration, however, are most common in modern reporting.

When no-par stock has a stated value, as in entry (3), the stated value of the total shares issued is credited to the capital stock account and any additional amount received is credited to an account called Paid-in Capital in Excess of Stated Value. Although this amount is treated similarly to a stock premium, it should not be regarded as a premium—the stated value is arbitrarily set by the board of directors. If there is no stated value for no-par stock, the entire proceeds should be credited to the capital stock account. In entry (3), if the common stock had no stated value, the entire amount of $150,000 would have been credited to the Common Stock account.

STOCK SUBSCRIPTIONS

Sometimes a corporation will sell stock directly to investors rather than through an investment banker. The corporation may obtain signatures of prospective purchasers on *subscription contracts* prior to issuing shares. Frequently, such contracts provide for payment in installments. When subscriptions are obtained, the corporation debits a receivable account, Stock Subscriptions Receivable. Instead of crediting the regular stock account (Common Stock), the firm credits a temporary paid-in capital account called Common Stock Subscribed. The use of a temporary account signifies that the shares have not yet been paid for or issued. Until the shares are paid for, the account is shown separately in the stockholders' equity section of the balance sheet. Stock Subscriptions Receivable appears with the current assets. After all payments have been received and the stock is issued, the corporation debits the temporary account, Common Stock Subscribed, and credits the regular account, Common Stock.

To illustrate the accounting entries for stock subscription transactions, let us assume that 500 shares of $100 par value common stock were sold on subscription for $120 a share, to be paid in installments of $40 and $80. The entries would be:

To record receipt of subscriptions:

Stock Subscriptions Receivable—Common	60,000	
Common Stock Subscribed		50,000
Paid-in Capital in Excess of Par Value		10,000

Received subscriptions for 500 shares
at $120 per share.

To record collection of first installment:

Cash	20,000	
Stock Subscriptions Receivable— Common		20,000

Collected first installment of $40 per share.

To record collection of final installment and issuance of shares:

Cash	40,000	
Stock Subscriptions Receivable— Common		40,000

Collected final installment of $80 per share.

Common Stock Subscribed	50,000	
Common Stock		50,000

To record issuance of 500 shares.

STOCK ISSUANCES FOR ASSETS OTHER THAN CASH

Whenever stock is sold for property other than cash, the accountant must be careful in deciding the amount to be recorded. It should not be assumed that the par or stated value of the shares issued automatically sets a value for the property. In the early years of corporations in this country, such an assumption was frequently made and often resulted in the recording and reporting of excessive property valuations.

The property acquired should be recorded at its fair value or the fair value of the stock issued, whichever is more clearly determinable. If the stock is being actively traded on a securities exchange, the market price of the stock issued for property may indicate an appropriate value. Thus, if the current market price is $140 per share and 500 shares are issued for a parcel of land, this land may be valued, in the absence of other price indicators, at $70,000. An effort should be made, however, to determine a fair value for the property. Certainly, all aspects of the transaction should be carefully scrutinized to ascertain that the number of shares issued was objectively determined. Obviously, if no market value for the stock is available, one must rely on an independently determined value for the property.

Let us suppose the stock issued for the land is $100 par value common stock and its market value is the best indicator of the property's fair value. The entry to record the transaction would be:

Land	70,000	
Common Stock		50,000
Paid-in Capital in Excess of Par Value		20,000

To record issuance of 500 shares of
common stock for land valued at $70,000.

TREASURY STOCK

When a corporation reacquires its own outstanding shares for a purpose other than retiring them, the reacquired shares are called **treasury stock.** Treasury stock may be purchased for a variety of reasons, including to reissue them to officers and employees in profit-sharing schemes or stock-option plans. Whatever the purpose, the corporation is in reality reducing owner capital for a period of time. Consequently, treasury stock should not be regarded as an asset. The shares do not carry voting privileges nor are cash dividends paid on them. (In some states, stock dividends may be paid on treasury stock, however. Stock dividends are discussed in Chapter 14.) It would obviously be an anomaly to say that the corporation owned part of itself; likewise, it would be deceptive to have the corporation report dividend income paid to itself.

The most common procedure for recording treasury stock is to enter it at cost, debiting a Treasury Stock account. The aggregate cost is reported in the balance sheet as a deduction from the total stockholders' equity. Suppose a corporation had outstanding 2,000 shares of $100 par value common stock and then repurchased 100 shares at a price of $120 per share. The entry for the repurchase would be:

Treasury Stock	12,000	
Cash		12,000

To record purchase of 100 shares of
treasury stock at $120 per share.

The corporation may accept any price for the reissue of treasury stock. However, any additional capital obtained from reissuing such shares at more than cost is not regarded as earnings and is not added to retained earnings. Transactions in treasury shares are not operational transactions. Furthermore, any amounts paid by subsequent purchasers are really paid-in capital from the standpoint of the corporation as an entity. Therefore, increases in capital from reissue of treasury shares are credited to a paid-in capital account with a title such as Paid-in Capital from Treasury Stock. Should decreases occur upon reissue of treasury stock, they

TREASURY STOCK ACQUISITIONS

One of a variety of reasons may motivate a company to buy back its own stock.

Many firms regularly acquire their own stock so it is available for reissue to employees and owners. The stock may be reissued to executives under stock option plans or grants of stock appreciation rights, which are part of the executives' total compensation package. Or a corporation that provides a stock purchase plan for all its employees may need shares of stock to meet the demands of the plan. Further, additional stock may be needed for reissuance to owners should a corporation declare a stock dividend or split its stock (see Chapter 14).

Shares may be purchased because the company considers the stock to be a good buy. Treasury stock purchases surge when companies believe their shares are undervalued. During 1979, for example, stock prices were depressed and shares of many companies were trading at prices close to or below their book values. Stock buyback activity was high that year.

In 1979, Sears, Roebuck and Co. even borrowed money to finance the purchase of 10 million of its own shares. Sears reasoned that it was cheaper to pay interest on the money than to pay dividends on the stock. Sears was paying a dividend of $1.28 per share annually on stock that was selling below book value for $20 per share. Borrowing money at 11% thus cost Sears $2.20 interest to buy each share. Interest is tax-deductible, however, so the cost after taxes (using a 50% tax rate) was $1.10 per share. The saving per share was 18 cents ($1.28 less $1.10); on 10 million shares, the savings totaled $1,800,000 annually.[1]

Earnings per share is a key indicator of company performance to investors and financial analysts. Purchasing its own shares improves a company's earnings per share figure by reducing the number of outstanding shares. Treasury stock may be acquired, therefore, to offset the dilutive effect on earnings per share of stock issuances for stock dividends and stock option plans. A company facing an economic downturn may also acquire shares to lessen the decline in its earnings per share.

Sometimes a company with excess cash will acquire its own stock when the economic outlook is judged uncertain or negative. In this circumstance, the company may view its own stock as the safest investment, particularly if it is undervalued. Investing the cash in riskier ventures, such as a new product line, will await a more favorable economic forecast.

Mailing costs may be reduced by treasury stock purchases. Shareholders are mailed interim reports, annual reports, proxy statements, dividend payments, and other materials. The fewer the stockholders, the lower the mailing costs. As a result, some companies direct their buyback efforts toward holders of small numbers of shares.

A company that fears it may be a target for a takeover may try to discourage potential takeover companies through treasury stock purchases. The stock purchases use up excess cash (large cash balances may attract a takeover company) or, if financed by borrowed funds, make the balance sheet less attractive to potential buyers by increasing the amount of debt. Stock buybacks also give dissatisfied stockholders the opportunity to sell their stock to the company at a favorable price before a potential takeover company can make an offer for the stock.

In some instances, stock buybacks may be used as an alternative to cash dividends. One company, for example, declares no dividends but, instead, periodically offers to buy back stock, either for cash or in exchange for debt securities. The stockholder receives cash or debt securities and, because fewer shares are left outstanding after the buyback, may not even experience a decline in his or her percentage ownership in the company.

[1]Margaret Yao, "Many Firms Buy Back Their Own Stock, Sometimes at Prices Below the Book Value," *The Wall Street Journal*, May 3, 1979.

are offset against previously recorded paid-in capital from treasury stock transactions or, if that is not possible, against retained earnings.

Let us assume that half of the treasury stock reacquired, 50 shares, is resold by the corporation at $130 per share. The entry to record the reissue would be:

Cash	6,500	
Treasury Stock		6,000
Paid-in Capital from Treasury Stock		500

To record sale of 50 shares of treasury
stock at $130 per share.

Observe that the treasury stock is credited at the cost price of $120 per share, a basis consistent with the original debit to the account. The excess over cost is credited to Paid-in Capital from Treasury Stock. If a balance sheet were prepared after this transaction, the stockholders' equity section would appear as shown below (assuming retained earnings of $40,000).

Stockholders' Equity

Paid-in Capital:	
Common Stock, $100 Par Value, authorized and issued 2,000 shares, 50 shares in treasury, 1,950 shares outstanding	$200,000
Paid-in Capital from Treasury Stock	500
Retained Earnings	40,000
	$240,500
Less: Treasury Stock (50 shares) at Cost	6,000
Total Stockholders' Equity	$234,500

Note that the par value of all *issued* stock, $200,000, is shown as the common stock, although 50 shares are no longer outstanding. The total cost of the 50 shares, however, is later deducted from the total stockholders' equity.

In the above owners' equity situation, it appears that the corporation has $40,000 retained earnings unfettered by any legal restrictions, and that the entire amount might be distributed as dividends to shareholders if the corporation's cash position permits. In some states, however, the corporation must restrict (reduce) the retained earnings available for declaration of dividends by the cost of any treasury stock held. If this were required of the corporation in our illustration, only $34,000 in retained earnings would be available for dividends, and the reason would be disclosed in the stockholders' equity section. Methods of disclosing retained earnings restrictions are discussed in Chapter 14. The rationale for such statutory restriction is that a corporation that reduces its paid-in capital by repurchase of shares must protect creditors by "buffering" the reduced capital with its retained earnings in an amount equal to resources expended.

DONATED CAPITAL

Occasionally, a shareholder may donate shares to the corporation. Perhaps the donor received the shares for a process or patent and now wishes the corporation to raise additional capital to promote and market it. Because treasury shares represent stock that has already been issued once, they can be reissued at any price. Thus, the corporation may find it easier to market these shares than to sell unissued shares. This is especially true if there has been lack of interest in the venture and the unissued shares could be sold only at a discount. (As we mentioned earlier, a liability may attach to discounted shares in some states, while other states do not permit issuance at a discount.)

The reacquisition of treasury shares by donation, whatever the reason, is usually not entered in the records—except for a memorandum entry—at the time of reacquisition. When such shares are subsequently sold, the amount received is credited to Donated Capital, a form of paid-in capital. To illustrate, suppose a stockholder donates 100 shares of common stock to a corporation, which then resells the shares at $125 per share. The entries for these transactions would be:

To record receipt of donated treasury shares:

(Memorandum) Received 100 shares of donated common stock.

To record sale of donated treasury shares:

Cash	12,500	
Donated Capital		12,500

The Donated Capital account may also be credited for the amount of any other property donated to the corporation, assuming that a value can be determined objectively. For example, some corporations have been given land sites by communities wanting to attract industry. If fair values can be established by appraisal or by study of prices for similar local property, the amount may be recorded. In any event, amounts acquired through donation should never be credited to Retained Earnings, because this account is used solely for accumulating earnings obtained through operations.

Assume that a city donates a plant site to a corporation. An independent appraiser values the land at $26,000, and the board of directors accepts this as an appropriate valuation for the asset. The entry made by the corporation would be:

Land	26,000	
Donated Capital		26,000

To record receipt of donated land, valued at $26,000.

REDEMPTION OF PREFERRED STOCK

Corporations often retain the right to redeem their outstanding preferred stock by paying the preferred stockholders the par value of the stock plus a premium. For example, assume that a company had originally issued 1,000 shares of $100 par value preferred stock at a price of $105 per share. After such issue, the stockholders' equity would include the following accounts:

Preferred Stock, $100 Par Value,	
1,000 shares issued and outstanding	100,000
Paid-in Capital in Excess of Par Value	5,000

Suppose that half of the preferred shares, or 500 shares, are then redeemed at a price of $102 per share. When the redemption is recorded, the amounts in the above accounts related to the 500 shares redeemed must be eliminated. In other words, half of the preferred stock ($50,000) and half of the original premium ($2,500) must be removed from the accounts. Because the shares were redeemed for $3 less per share than the $105 issue price, a $1,500 premium is realized on redemption. This **redemption premium** is a form of paid-in capital. The entry to record the redemption is as follows:

Preferred Stock	50,000	
Paid-in Capital in Excess of Par Value	2,500	
Redemption Premium on Preferred Stock		1,500
Cash		51,000

To record redemption of 500 shares
of preferred stock at $102 per share.

Whenever preferred stock is redeemed at a price higher than the issue price, the excess would be debited to Retained Earnings, inasmuch as it represents a distribution of earnings to stockholders. If the redemption price in the above situation had been $106 per share, the appropriate entry would have been:

Preferred Stock	50,000	
Paid-in Capital in Excess of Par Value	2,500	
Retained Earnings	500	
Cash		53,000

To record redemption of 500 shares of
preferred stock at $106 per share.

BOOK VALUE PER SHARE

A measure often calculated for a class of stock, particularly common stock, is its **book value per share.** Book value per share is the dollar amount of net assets represented by one share of stock and is computed by dividing the amount of stockholders' equity associated with a class of stock by the number of outstanding shares in that class. The computation uses stockholders' equity, because a corporation's net assets (assets less liabilities) equals its stockholders' equity. The measure is based on amounts recorded in the books and presented in the balance sheet—hence the term book value per share.

For example, note the following stockholders' equity section of a balance sheet:

Stockholders' Equity

Paid-in Capital:	
Common Stock, $50 Par Value, 5,000 shares authorized, issued, and outstanding	$250,000
Paid-in Capital in Excess of Par Value	100,000
Retained Earnings	80,000
Total Stockholders' Equity	$430,000

Because this corporation has only one class of stock, the book value per share of common stock is the total stockholders' equity divided by the shares of common stock outstanding, that is, $430,000/5,000 = $86. Note that the divisor is shares outstanding. Shares of unissued common stock or treasury stock would not be included in the divisor.

To compute book values per share when there is more than one class of stock outstanding, the portion of stockholders' equity attributable to each class of stock must be determined. Preferred stocks are assigned the amounts their owners would receive if the corporation liquidated—that is, the liquidation preference of preferred stock plus any dividend arrearages on cumulative stock. The common shares receive the remainder of the stockholders' equity. For example, note the stockholders' equity section that follows:

Stockholders' Equity

Paid-in Capital:	
7% Preferred Stock, $100 Par Value, 1,000 shares authorized, issued, and outstanding	$100,000
Paid-in Capital in Excess of Par Value—Preferred Stock	5,000
No-Par Common Stock, Stated Value $40, 3,000 shares authorized, issued, and outstanding	120,000
Paid-in Capital in Excess of Stated Value—Common Stock	6,000
Retained Earnings	73,000
Total Stockholders' Equity	$304,000

If the stated liquidation preference is $103 per share for the preferred stock (and no dividends in arrears), then this is also the book value per share for the preferred stock. The computation for the common stock appears below.

Total Stockholders' Equity	$304,000
Deduct: Equity Applicable to Preferred Stock	103,000
Equity Allocated to Common Stock	$201,000
Shares of Common Stock Outstanding	3,000
Book Value per Share of Common Stock ($201,000/3,000)	$67

The book value per share of common stock may be used in many ways. Management may include the book value per share, and any changes in it for the year, in the annual report to stockholders. Two corporations negotiating a merger through an exchange of stock may find their respective book values per share to be one of several factors influencing the final exchange ratio. Or an individual may acquire an option to buy stock in the future, with the purchase price related in some way to the future book value of the stock.

MARKET VALUE AND LIQUIDATION VALUE

The book value of common stock should be distinguished from its market value and its liquidation value. The **market value per share** is the current price at which the stock may be bought or sold. This price reflects such things as the earnings potential of the company, dividends, book values, capital structure, and general economic conditions. Because book value is only one of several variables influencing market price (and usually not the most significant one at that), market values and book values rarely coincide.

The **liquidation value per share** of common stock is the amount that would be received if the corporation liquidated. The amounts recorded in the books are not intended to portray liquidation proceeds, so there is also no correlation between liquidation values and book values of common stocks. Liquidation values may not be easy to determine, but corporate managements need to be alert to the relationship between the market value and the approximate liquidation value of their common stock. A corporation whose liquidation value exceeds its market value may be the object of a "raid." A raider will acquire control of a corporation (by buying stock at market values) and then liquidate the business (at liquidation values), keeping the difference as a gain.

KEY POINTS TO REMEMBER

(1) A corporation is a separate legal entity chartered by the state or, in some cases, by the federal government.

(2) The liability of corporate shareholders is usually limited to their ownership investment, while claims against partners and sole proprietors may extend to their personal resources.

(3) Unlike proprietorships and partnerships, corporations must report paid-in equity capital separately from accumulated earnings, called retained earnings. Distributions to shareholders are limited by the amount of retained earnings and other capital specified by state law.

(4) Common stock represents the basic ownership class of stock for a corporation. Preferred stocks may differ from common stock in any of several characteristics. Typically, preferred stocks have some type of dividend preference and a prior claim to assets in liquidation.

(5) In financial statements, the par values or stated values of different forms of stock (preferred, common) are shown separately, as is any excess or deficiency received for the shares. These differences are called premium and discount, respectively, for par value stock. For no-par stock with a stated value, an appropriate title (for example, paid-in capital in excess of stated value) describes the difference.

(6) Other important sources of paid-in capital are capital from treasury stock transactions and donated capital. Treasury stock represents repurchased shares of the firm's own stock. It is commonly recorded at cost and shown as a deduction from total stockholders' equity in the balance sheet.

(7) The book value per share of common stock indicates the net assets, based on recorded amounts, associated with a share of common stock. Common stock book values are not the same as market values or liquidation values.

QUESTIONS

13-1 Explain the meaning of each of the following terms and, where appropriate, how they interrelate: articles of incorporation; corporate charter; board of directors; corporate officers; organization costs.

13-2 What is meant by the limited liability of a shareholder? Does this characteristic enhance or reduce the ability of a corporation to raise capital?

13-3 Contrast the federal income taxation of corporations with that of sole proprietorships and partnerships. Which of the three types of organizations must file a federal income tax return?

13-4 What is meant by the preemptive right of a shareholder?

13-5 What are the basic differences between preferred stock and common stock? What are the typical features of preferred stock?

13-6 What features make preferred stock similar to debt? similar to common stock?

13-7 What is meant by dividend arrearage on preferred stock? If dividends are one year in arrears on $200,000 of 8% preferred stock and dividends are declared this year, what amount of total dividends must be paid to preferred shareholders before anything can be distributed to common shareholders?

13-8 What is meant by participating preferred stock?

13-9 Distinguish between authorized stock and issued stock. Why might the number of shares issued be greater than the number of shares outstanding?

13-10 Distinguish between premium and discount on stock. Where do such amounts appear in the balance sheet?

13-11 What is meant by no-par stock? How is stated value, if any, of no-par stock determined?

13-12 A company acquired property with a fair market value of $60,000 in exchange for 500 shares of $80 par value common stock. At what amount should the property be recorded in the accounts?

13-13 Define treasury stock. Why would a corporation acquire treasury stock? How is treasury stock shown in the balance sheet?

13-14 If a corporation purchases 500 shares of its own common stock at $20 per share and resells it at $30 per share, where would the $5,000 increase in capital appear in the financial statements? Why is no gain reported?

13-15 A corporation has a total stockholders' equity of $234,000, and one class of $100 par value common stock. The company has issued 2,000 shares and currently holds 200 shares as treasury stock. What is the book value per share?

EXERCISES

13-16 On June 1, the Haven Company issued 4,000 shares of $50 par value preferred stock at $58 per share and 5,000 shares of no-par common stock at $30 per share. The common stock had no stated value. All issuances were made for cash.
(a) Give the general journal entries to record the issuances.
(b) Give the entry for the issuance of the common stock, assuming it had a stated value of $25 per share.

13-17 The Unger Company had 3,000 shares outstanding of $100 par value, 7% preferred stock and 20,000 shares of $20 par value common stock. The company declared cash dividends amounting to $77,000.
(a) If there was no arrearage on the preferred stock, how much in total dividends, and in dividends per share, would be paid to each class of stock?
(b) If there was one year's dividend arrearage on the preferred stock, how much in total dividends, and in dividends per share, would be paid to each class of stock?
(c) Assume that there is no arrearage on the preferred stock, but that it is fully participating. How much in total dividends, and in dividends per share, would be paid to each class of stock?

13-18 The Tomkin Company issued 20,000 shares of $40 par value common stock at $43 per share and 5,000 shares of $50 par value, 7% preferred stock at $48 per share. The company then repurchased 1,000 shares of common stock at $49 per share.

(a) Give the entries, in general journal form, to record the stock issuances and the repurchase of the common shares.

(b) Assume that Tomkin Company resold 600 shares of the treasury stock at $51 per share. Give the entry, in general journal form, to record the resale of this treasury stock.

13-19 The King Company has 3,000 shares outstanding of 6%, $100 par value preferred stock that were originally issued at par. The company redeemed all of the stock at $103 per share.

(a) Prepare the general journal entry to record the redemption of the stock.

(b) Assume that the original issue price was $104 per share; prepare the entry to record the redemption.

13-20 On May 1 of the current year, the Lahey Company received subscriptions for 3,000 shares of $20 par value common stock at a price of $22 per share, to be paid as follows: 40% with subscription, 30% on June 15, and 30% on July 1. All payments were received on schedule. Give the journal entries to be made on May 1, June 15, and July 1.

13-21 Sun Company has 5,000 shares of $10 par value common stock outstanding. Prepare the general journal entries (if required) to record the following transactions:

Aug. 12   The community in which the Sun Company will be building a new plant donated the land site to the company. The appraised value of the land is $25,000.

Oct.   7   Shareholders donated 500 shares back to the corporation.

Oct. 22   The company sold the donated shares for $40 cash per share.

13-22 The stockholders' equity section of the Slagle Company appears as follows:

Paid-in Capital:		
7% Cumulative Preferred Stock, $50 Par		
Value, 3,000 shares authorized, issued,		
and outstanding	$150,000	
Paid-in Capital in Excess of Par Value	9,000	$159,000
No-Par Common Stock, Stated Value $20, 8,000		
shares authorized, issued, and outstanding	$160,000	
Paid-in Capital in Excess of Stated Value	80,000	240,000
Paid-in Capital from Treasury Stock		19,000
Total Paid-in Capital		$418,000
Retained Earnings		50,000
Total Stockholders' Equity		$468,000

The preferred stock has a liquidation preference of $52 per share, and there are no dividends in arrears. Compute the book value per share of the common stock.

PROBLEMS

13-23 The Becker Corporation was organized on April 1 of the current year with an authorization of 5,000 shares of 6%, $40 par value preferred stock and 50,000 shares of $20 par value common stock. During April, the following transactions affecting stockholders' equity occurred:

Apr. 1 Issued 3,000 shares of preferred stock for $42 per share and 20,000 shares of common stock at $23 per share. Cash was received for the shares.

   3 Issued 500 shares of common stock to attorneys and promoters in exchange for their services in organizing the corporation (organization costs). The services were valued at $11,000.

   8 Issued 600 shares of preferred stock for equipment of J. Tripp. The fair market value of the equipment was determined to be $27,000.

   17 Holders of 1,000 shares of common stock donated their shares back to the Becker Corporation.

   20 The donated shares received on April 17 were sold for cash at par value.

   30 An entry was made to close the $15,000 net income for April from the Income Summary account to Retained Earnings.

REQUIRED

(a) Prepare entries, in general journal form, to record the foregoing transactions.

(b) Prepare the stockholders' equity section of the balance sheet at April 30.

13-24 The Meadow Corporation has outstanding 4,000 shares of $50 par value, 6%, fully participating, cumulative preferred stock and 30,000 shares of $20 par value common stock. The company has declared cash dividends of $84,000.

REQUIRED

(a) Calculate the total dividends and the dividends per share to be paid to each class of stock.

(b) Assuming that there is one year's dividend arrearage on the preferred stock, calculate the total dividends and the dividends per share to be paid to each class of stock.

(c) Assuming that the 6% preferred stock is participating only to 7½% (and no dividend arrearages), calculate the total dividends and the dividends per share to be paid to each class of stock.

(d) Assuming that the 6% preferred stock is nonparticipating (and no dividend arrearages), calculate the total dividends and the dividends per share to be paid to each class of stock.

13-25 The stockholders' equity of the Locket Corporation at January 1 of the current year appears below:

7% Preferred Stock, $50 Par Value, 6,000 shares authorized, 5,000 shares issued and outstanding	$250,000
Paid-in Capital in Excess of Par Value—Preferred Stock	35,000
Common Stock, $25 Par Value, 50,000 shares authorized, 30,000 shares issued and outstanding	750,000
Retained Earnings	260,000

During the current year, the following transactions occurred:

Jan. 10 The company issued 5,000 shares of common stock at $28 per share. Cash was received for the shares.

23 The company repurchased 3,000 shares of common stock for the treasury at $29 per share.

Mar. 2 Shareholders donated 1,000 shares of common stock back to the corporation.

14 The company sold half of the treasury shares acquired Jan. 23 for $30 per share.

14 The company sold the donated shares at $30 per share.

July 15 The company redeemed 1,000 shares of preferred stock at the redemption price of $52 per share. All shares of preferred stock had previously been issued at $57 per share.

Sept. 15 The company received subscriptions to 3,000 shares of common stock at $34 per share. One-third of the subscription price was received in cash.

Nov. 15 The balance due on the stock subscriptions of Sept. 15 was received in cash, and the stock certificates were issued.

Dec. 31 An entry was made to close the net income of $49,000 from the Income Summary account to Retained Earnings.

REQUIRED

(a) Set up T accounts for the stockholders' equity accounts at the beginning of the year, and enter January 1 balances.
(b) Prepare entries, in general journal form, to record the foregoing transactions, and post to T accounts (set up any additional T accounts needed).
(c) Prepare the stockholders' equity section of the balance sheet at December 31.
(d) Assume the preferred stock has a liquidation preference per share of $52. There are no dividends in arrears. Compute the book value per share of common stock at December 31.

13-26 The Faer Company has the following stockholders' equity section in its balance sheet:

Paid-in Capital:

8% Preferred Stock, $50 Par Value, 2,000 shares authorized, issued, and outstanding	$100,000	
Paid-in Capital in Excess of Par Value—Preferred	8,000	
Common Stock, $10 Par Value, 40,000 shares authorized, 15,000 shares issued and outstanding	150,000	
Paid-in Capital in Excess of Par Value—Common	20,000	
Paid-in Capital from Treasury Stock	8,000	$286,000
Retained Earnings		75,000
Total Stockholders' Equity		$361,000

REQUIRED

For each of the following independent cases, compute the book value per share for the preferred stock and the common stock.

(a) The preferred stock is noncumulative and nonparticipating and has a liquidation preference per share of $53.

(b) The preferred stock is cumulative and nonparticipating and has a liquidation preference per share equal to par value plus dividends in arrears. There are no dividends in arrears.

(c) The preferred stock is cumulative and nonparticipating and has a liquidation preference per share of $54 plus dividends in arrears. Dividends are two years in arrears.

13-27 Comparative stockholders' equity sections from two successive years' balance sheets of Stram, Inc. are as follows:

	Dec. 31, 19X2	Dec. 31, 19X1
Paid-in Capital:		
8% Preferred Stock, $50 Par Value; authorized 10,000 shares, issued and outstanding, 19X1: 10,000 shares; 19X2: 8,000 shares	$ 400,000	$ 500,000
In Excess of Par Value—Preferred Stock	64,000	80,000
Common Stock, No-Par Value, Stated Value $20, authorized 30,000 shares, outstanding, 19X1: 16,000 shares; 19X2; 24,000 shares	480,000	320,000
In Excess of Stated Value—Common Stock	72,000	40,000
Redemption Premium on Preferred Stock	6,000	
From Treasury Stock	12,000	
Donated Capital	46,000	
Retained Earnings	175,000	130,000
		$1,070,000
Less: Treasury Stock (3,000 shares common) at Cost		63,000
Total Stockholders' Equity	$1,255,000	$1,007,000

No dividends were declared or paid during 19X2. The company received a donated parcel of land from the city in 19X2.

REQUIRED

(a) What was the redemption price per share of preferred stock?
(b) For what price per share was the treasury stock sold?
(c) Prepare the general journal entries for the transactions affecting stockholders' equity that evidently occurred during 19X2.

13-28 The stockholders' equity section of the Burns Corporation's balance sheet at January 1 of the current year is shown on the next page:

6% Preferred Stock, $100 Par Value, 3,000 shares authorized, 2,000 shares issued and outstanding	$ 200,000
Paid-in Capital in Excess of Par Value—Preferred Stock	20,000
Common Stock, $50 Par Value, 30,000 shares authorized, 12,000 shares issued and outstanding	600,000
Paid-in Capital in Excess of Par Value—Common Stock	48,000
Retained Earnings	250,000
Total Stockholders' Equity	$1,118,000

The following transactions, among others, occurred during the year.

Jan. 12 All the preferred stock was redeemed at a price of $106 per share and retired.

20 Subscriptions were received for the sale of 1,000 shares of common stock at a price of $62 per share. Half of the subscription price was received in cash.

Feb. 9 The remainder of payment for the shares subscribed on January 20 was received in cash, and the stock certificates were issued.

Apr. 14 The company received, as a gift from the city, a plant site with a valuation of $43,000.

June 1 The corporation acquired equipment with a fair market value of $130,000 in exchange for 2,000 shares of common stock.

Sept. 1 1,200 shares of common stock were reacquired for cash at a price of $60 per share.

Oct. 12 600 treasury shares were resold at $61 per share.

Nov. 30 Subscriptions were received for the sale of 3,000 shares of common stock at a price of $57 per share. One-third of the subscription price was received in cash.

Dec. 28 Half of the remaining treasury shares were resold at $56 per share.

31 The Income Summary account, with net earnings of $90,000, was closed to Retained Earnings.

REQUIRED
(a) Set up T accounts for all stockholders' equity accounts needed. Enter the balances as of January 1 of the current year.
(b) Prepare entries in general journal form for the given transactions, and post them to the T accounts (set up any additional T accounts needed).
(c) Prepare the stockholders' equity section of the balance sheet at December 31 of the current year.

13-29 Appearing below in T accounts are keyed entries representing seven transactions involving the stockholders' equity of Diamond, Inc.

Cash				Preferred Stock, $40 Par			
(1)	37,600	(4)	2,100	(7)	1,600	(1)	32,000
(2)	50,000	(7)	1,760				
(5)	2,280						
(6)	1,350						

Paid-in Capital in Excess of Par Value—Preferred Stock	
(7) 280	(1) 5,600

Common Stock, $10 Par	
	(2) 50,000

Treasury Stock	
(3) (Received 100 shares of donated common)	(6) 1,260
(4) (50 shares of common) 2,100	

Paid-in Capital from Treasury Stock	
	(6) 90

Donated Capital	
	(5) 2,280

Redemption Premium on Preferred Stock	
	(7) 120

REQUIRED

Using this information, give detailed descriptions, including number of shares and price per share, for each of the seven indicated transactions. Assume transaction (5) involves 60 shares.

ALTERNATE PROBLEMS

13–23A The Minor Corporation was organized on July 1 of the current year with an authorization of 10,000 shares of 7%, $50 par value preferred stock and 10,000 shares of $100 par value common stock. During July, the following transactions affecting stockholders' equity occurred:

July 1   Issued 5,000 shares of preferred stock for $54 per share and 6,000 shares of common stock at par value. Cash was received for the shares.

      5   The local municipality donated a vacant building to the corporation as an inducement to organize and operate the business in the community. The fair value of the building was determined to be $150,000.

     12   Issued 900 shares of common stock for equipment of E. Hart. The fair market value of the equipment was determined to be $92,000.

     15   Holders of 500 shares of common stock donated their shares back to the Minor Corporation.

     23   The donated shares received on July 15 were sold for cash at $102 per share.

     31   An entry was made to close the $29,000 net income for July from the Income Summary account to Retained Earnings.

REQUIRED

(a) Prepare entries, in general journal form, to record the foregoing transactions.

(b) Prepare the stockholders' equity section of the balance sheet at July 31.

13-24A The Cohoe Corporation has outstanding 5,000 shares of $100 par value, 5% fully participating, cumulative preferred stock and 50,000 shares of $30 par value common stock. The company has declared cash dividends of $140,000.

REQUIRED

(a) Calculate the total dividends and the dividends per share to be paid to each class of stock.

(b) Assuming that there is one year's dividend arrearage on the preferred stock, calculate the total dividends and the dividends per share to be paid to each class of stock.

(c) Assuming that the 5% preferred stock is participating only to 6% (and no dividend arrearages), calculate the total dividends and the dividends per share to be paid to each class of stock.

(d) Assuming that the 5% preferred stock is nonparticipating (and no dividend arrearages), calculate the total dividends and the dividends per share to be paid to each class of stock.

13-25A The stockholders' equity of the Baxter Corporation at January 1 of the current year appears below.

Common Stock, $40 Par Value, 30,000 shares authorized, 15,000 shares issued and outstanding	$600,000
Paid-in Capital in Excess of Par Value—Common Stock	45,000
Retained Earnings	340,000

During the current year, the following transactions occurred:

Jan. 5   The company issued 6,000 shares of common stock at $43 per share. Cash was received for the shares.

   18   The company repurchased 1,000 shares of common stock for the treasury at $41 per share.

Mar. 10   Shareholders donated 500 shares back to the corporation.

   12   The company sold half of the treasury shares acquired Jan. 18 for $43 per share.

   12   The company sold the donated shares at $43 per share.

July 17   The company sold half of the remaining treasury stock for $39 per share.

Sept. 20   The company received subscriptions to 2,000 shares of common stock at $44 per share. One-fourth of the subscription price was received in cash.

Nov. 25   The balance due on the stock subscription of Sept. 20 was received in cash, and the stock certificates were issued.

Dec. 31   An entry was made to close the net income of $45,000 from the Income Summary account to Retained Earnings.

REQUIRED

(a) Set up T accounts for the stockholders' equity accounts at the beginning of the year, and enter January 1 balances.

(b) Prepare entries, in general journal form, to record the foregoing transactions, and post to T accounts (set up any additional T accounts needed).

(c) Prepare the stockholders' equity section of the balance sheet at December 31.

(d) Compute the book value per share of common stock at December 31.

13–28A The stockholders' equity section of the Baker Corporation's balance sheet at January 1 of the current year is shown below.

7% Preferred Stock, $50 Par Value, 5,000 shares authorized, 3,000 shares issued and outstanding	$150,000
Paid-in Capital in Excess of Par Value—Preferred Stock	13,500
Common Stock, $30 Par Value, 50,000 shares authorized, 20,000 shares issued and outstanding	600,000
Paid-in Capital in Excess of Par Value—Common Stock	50,000
Retained Earnings	180,000
Total Stockholders' Equity	$993,500

The following transactions, among others, occurred during the year:

Jan.   8   All the preferred stock was redeemed at $60 per share and retired.

25   Subscriptions were received for the sale of 5,000 shares of common stock at a price of $35 per share. Half of the subscription price was received in cash.

Feb. 15   The remainder of payment for the shares subscribed on January 25 was received in cash, and the stock certificates were issued.

Apr. 20   The company received, as a gift from the city, a plant site with a valuation of $55,000.

June 10   The corporation acquired equipment with a fair market value of $190,000 in exchange for 5,000 shares of common stock.

Sept. 3   1,500 shares of common stock were reacquired for cash at a price of $36 per share.

Oct. 15   600 treasury shares were resold at $38 per share.

Nov. 20   Subscriptions were received for the sale of 2,000 shares of common stock at a price of $39 per share. One-third of the subscription price was received in cash.

Dec. 23   Half of the remaining treasury shares were resold at $35 per share.

31   The Income Summary account, with net earnings of $110,000, was closed to Retained Earnings.

REQUIRED

(a) Set up T accounts for all stockholders' equity accounts needed. Enter the balances as of January 1 of the current year.

(b) Prepare entries in general journal form for the given transactions, and post them to the T accounts (set up any additional T accounts needed).

(c) Prepare the stockholders' equity section of the balance sheet at December 31 of the current year.

BUSINESS DECISION PROBLEM

Bob Hammond has been operating a very successful hardware store, Hammond Hardware, as a sole proprietorship. He feels that for the continued growth and success of his business he must increase its scale of operations, which will require additional working capital. He also wishes to relocate his store from its rented quarters to a new shopping area in town. After exploring several opportunities that would result in large personal debts, Bob decides instead to incorporate his business, taking in as stockholders Dr. Holt, who will invest cash, and Mr. Bond, a real estate developer who owns a suitable vacant building in the desired shopping area.

As an initial step, Bob and his attorney secure a corporate charter for General Hardware, Inc., authorizing it to issue 20,000 shares of $20 par value common stock. Other details of the agreement are set forth below.

(1) On June 1 of the current year, the date of incorporation, the post-closing trial balance of Hammond Hardware is as follows:

Cash	$ 2,800	
Accounts Receivable	14,700	
Allowance for Uncollectible Accounts		$ 500
Merchandise Inventory	57,000	
Store Equipment	20,000	
Accumulated Depreciation—Store Equipment		4,000
Accounts Payable		9,300
Note Payable (due two years hence)		20,000
Bob Hammond, Capital		60,700
	$94,500	$94,500

(2) After a detailed review of the accounts of Hammond Hardware, it is agreed that:
  (a) The allowance for uncollectible accounts should be increased by $500.
  (b) Because of damaged and shopworn goods, the merchandise inventory should be written down by $2,000.
  (c) The store equipment has a fair market value of $20,000 and will be recorded in the corporate accounts at that amount.
  (d) The new corporation is to assume at face value the recorded liabilities of the proprietorship.
  Bob Hammond has agreed to accept shares in the new corporation at par value in exchange for his adjusted equity in the assets of the proprietorship. He will purchase for cash at par value any additional shares necessary to bring his total holdings to the next even 100 shares.

(3) The total value of Mr. Bond's building and land is agreed to be $75,600, one-fifth of which is associated with the land. Mr. Bond has agreed to accept stock at an issue price of $21 per share for his land and building.

(4) As an effort to stimulate local business, the Business Development Commission of the local city government has agreed to deed to the corporation, for a token fee of $1,000, a small strip of land that will provide better delivery access to the rear of Mr. Bond's building. The fair value of the parcel is considered to be $5,000.

(5) Dr. Holt has agreed to purchase for cash 2,500 shares at $21 per share. He will subscribe to an additional 1,000 shares at $22 per share, paying 20% of the issue

price upon subscription and the balance in two equal installments, 90 and 180 days later.

(6) Legal and accounting costs of $2,000 associated with acquiring the corporate charter and issuing the stock are to be paid from corporate funds.

REQUIRED

(a) As Mr. Hammond's accountant, you are retained to prepare a balance sheet for the new corporation reflecting the shares that are to be issued to each stockholder, the stock subscription received, the parcel of land received from the city, and payment of legal and accounting costs. (*Hint:* You may wish to prepare a worksheet with headings as follows:

Accounts	Hammond Hardware Trial Balance		Adjustments and Organizational Transactions		General Hardware, Inc. Trial Balance	
	Dr.	Cr.	Dr.	Cr.	Dr.	Cr.

Properly combining and extending the amounts in the first two pairs of columns will provide amounts for the trial balance of General Hardware, Inc. When recording the Hammond Hardware trial balance, leave extra lines for the several transactions that will affect the cash, owner's capital, and capital stock accounts. Also, for purposes of review, you may wish to key your adjustments and transactions to the letters and numbers used in the problem data.)

(b) In contrast to what they contributed to the corporation, what specifically do Bob Hammond and Mr. Bond "own" after the incorporation?

(c) From Bob Hammond's point of view, what are the advantages and disadvantages of incorporating the hardware business?

14

Corporations:
Earnings
Disclosure,
Dividends,
and Retained
Earnings

Profits play a significant role in the organization and functioning of economic activity in the United States. A corporation's profitability is of utmost interest both to its owners and to potential investors. For this reason, earnings data are usually considered the most important financial information presented by corporate entities. Earnings data encompass not only the net income or loss for the period, but any prior period adjustments and earnings-per-share amounts.

The balance of the Retained Earnings account represents the stockholders' equity arising from the corporation's retention of assets generated from profit-directed activities. At the end of an accounting period, the Retained Earnings account is credited with the net income of the corporation (when the Income Summary account is closed to it) or debited if there is a net loss for the period. A debit balance in the account resulting from accumulated losses is called a **deficit.** In certain instances, Retained Earnings is charged or credited directly for corrections of errors made in past periods; these items then are not presented in the income statement.

The board of directors may decide, based on the income performance of the corporation, that assets should be distributed to the stockholders, in which case they declare a **dividend.** The board of directors may also decide that some of the assets resulting from profitable operations should be retained by the corporation for an identifiable purpose, such as expansion of operations or as a buffer for possible losses. They may then appropriate or restrict retained earnings.

Because of the importance of income data, accountants have developed several guidelines for their disclosure. In this chapter, we shall discuss the procedures for reporting earnings data and accounting for dividends and appropriations of retained earnings.

INCOME STATEMENT SECTIONS

Accountants believe that the usefulness of the income statement is enhanced if certain types of transactions and events are reported in separate sections. For this reason, information about extraordinary items, discontinued operations, and effects of changes in accounting principles are segregated and disclosed separately in an income statement. Segregating these categories of information from the results of ordinary, continuing operations should make it easier for users of financial statements to estimate the future earnings performance of the company.

The creation of several sections in the income statement, however, complicates the reporting of income tax expense. Items affecting the overall amount of income tax expense may appear in more than one section. If this is the case, then accountants allocate the income tax expense among those sections of the statement in which the items affecting the tax expense appear.

We will now examine these areas in more detail.

EXTRAORDINARY ITEMS

Extraordinary items are transactions and events that are *unusual in nature* and *occur infrequently*.[1] An item that is unusual in nature is highly abnormal and significantly different from the ordinary and typical activities of the firm. To decide which of a firm's activities are ordinary and typical, one must consider not only such things as the type of operations, lines of business, and operating policies, but also the environment in which the firm operates. The operating environment includes the characteristics of the industry, the geographic location of the firm's facilities, and the type of government regulation imposed. A transaction or event is considered to occur infrequently if there is no reasonable expectation that it will recur in the foreseeable future.

The two criteria, unusual nature and infrequent occurrence, considerably restrict the events and transactions that qualify as extraordinary items. For example, suppose a tobacco grower suffers crop loss from flood damage and floods are normally experienced every few years in this area. The history of flood damage creates a reasonable expectation that there will be another flood in the foreseeable future. The loss, therefore, does not meet the criteria for an extraordinary item. Now consider a different tobacco grower, who suffers flood damage to his crop for the first time because a dam has broken. The dam is repaired and there is no reasonable expectation that it will fail in the foreseeable future. The flood loss in this circumstance is an extraordinary loss.

Other events that may generate extraordinary losses are earthquakes, expropriation of property, and prohibitions under newly enacted laws (such as a government ban on a product currently being marketed). An extraordinary gain may result from a nonrecurring sale of an asset never used in operations. Assume a manufacturing company acquired land several years ago for future use, but then changed its plans and held the land for appreciation. If this is the only land the company owns and it does not intend to speculate in land in the foreseeable future, then any gain from the sale of the land would be considered extraordinary.

[1] *Opinions of the Accounting Principles Board, No. 30,* "Reporting the Results of Operations— Reporting the Effects of Disposal of a Segment of a Business, and Extraordinary, Unusual and Infrequently Occurring Events and Transactions," American Institute of Certified Public Accountants, New York, 1973.

The Financial Accounting Standards Board decreed one exception to these criteria defining extraordinary items. Gains and losses incurred when a company extinguishes its own debt shall be aggregated and, if material, must be classified as an extraordinary item.[2] An example of a debt extinguishment loss is presented in Chapter 15.

UNUSUAL OR NONRECURRING ITEMS

Events and transactions that are unusual *or* nonrecurring, but not both, are not extraordinary items. The Accounting Principles Board, in its *Opinion No. 30*, noted several examples of gains and losses that should be classified as other than extraordinary either because they are typical in nature or because they may be expected to recur as a result of continuing business activities. Examples of such items are gains and losses from (a) the write-down or write-off of receivables, inventories, and intangible assets; (b) the exchange or translation of foreign currencies; (c) the sale or abandonment of property, plant, or equipment used in the business; (d) the effects of a strike; and (e) the adjustments of long-term contract accruals. Unusual or infrequently occurring items of a material amount should be reported as a separate component of income before extraordinary items.

Exhibit 14-1 is an income statement for a corporation with an extraordinary item and an unusual, but recurring, item. During 19XX, the West Corporation, a manufacturing concern, sold a block of common stock of Z Company, a publicly traded company, at a gain of $80,000. The shares of stock were the only security investment the company had ever owned, and it does not intend to acquire other stocks in the foreseeable future. We shall assume that the normal tax rate is 40% but that the gain from the sale of stock is taxed at 25%. During the same year, the company incurred a loss of $45,000 because of a strike at one of its plants. The strike was not part of the company's ordinary and typical activities, but West Corporation has a history of labor difficulties. Note that the loss resulting from the strike is disclosed as a component of income before the extraordinary item while the gain from the sale of stock is disclosed in a separate section for extraordinary items.

TAX ALLOCATION WITHIN A PERIOD

Note that the extraordinary gain in Exhibit 14-1 is shown net of applicable income taxes. The total income tax expense of $70,000 has been allocated to two parts of the income statement: $50,000 is deducted in deriving income before

[2]Unless the gains or losses result from cash purchases of debt made to satisfy sinking-fund requirements. See *Statement of Financial Accounting Standards No. 4*, "Reporting Gains and Losses from Extinguishment of Debt," Financial Accounting Standards Board, Stamford, Conn., 1975.

EXHIBIT 14–1

West Corporation
Income Statement
For the Year 19XX

Sales		$700,000
Cost of Goods Sold		360,000
Gross Profit on Sales		$340,000
Less: Selling Expenses	$90,000	
Administrative Expenses	80,000	
Loss from Plant Strike	45,000	215,000
Income before Taxes and Extraordinary Item		$125,000
Less: Income Taxes		50,000
Income before Extraordinary Item		$ 75,000
Extraordinary Item:		
Gain from Sale of Z Company Stock	$80,000	
Less: Income Taxes	20,000	60,000
Net Income		$135,000

extraordinary items, and $20,000 is deducted in the extraordinary items section. This process, known as **tax allocation within a period,** causes the tax effect of an extraordinary item to be reported in the same section of the income statement as the item itself. By the same token, the income taxes deducted in the section reporting income before extraordinary items relate only to the revenues and expenses disclosed in that section. Thus, tax allocation within a period permits the portrayal of normal relationships within the income statement between income taxes and the items affecting their calculation.

A tax reduction due to an extraordinary loss would be deducted from the loss in the extraordinary items section. Suppose that instead of the $80,000 gain, the West Corporation incurred an extraordinary flood loss of $30,000, which reduced income subject to a 40% tax rate. The lower portion of the company's income statement, after tax allocation, would appear as follows:

Income before Taxes and Extraordinary Item		$125,000
Less: Income Taxes		50,000
Income before Extraordinary Item		$ 75,000
Extraordinary Item:		
Flood Loss	$30,000	
Less: Tax Reduction from Flood Loss	12,000	18,000
Net Income		$ 57,000

An alternative way of reporting the tax effects of extraordinary items is to disclose them parenthetically. Using this procedure, the extraordinary gain would be shown as:

Gain from Sale of Z Company Stock
(net of $20,000 of income taxes) $60,000

The extraordinary loss would be reported as follows:

Flood Loss (net of $12,000 reduction
of income taxes) $18,000

DISCONTINUED OPERATIONS

When a company sells, abandons, or otherwise disposes of a segment of its operations, a **discontinued operations** section of the income statement is established to report information about the discontinued segment. The discontinued operations section presents two categories of information:

(1) The income or loss from the operations of the segment for the portion of the year before its discontinuance.
(2) The gain or loss from the disposal of the segment.

The section is placed after information about the ordinary, continuing operations and before any extraordinary items.

A **segment of a business** is a unit, such as a department or a division, whose activities constitute a separate major line of business or a particular class of customer. The assets and operating results of the segment must be clearly distinguishable from the rest of the company. For example, a furniture manufacturing division of a diversified manufacturing company is a segment of the business.

To illustrate the reporting of discontinued operations, assume that on July 1 of the current year, North Corporation sold its Division Y. From January 1 through June 30, Division Y had operated at a loss, net of taxes, of $15,000 ($25,000 operating loss less a $10,000 reduction in income taxes caused by the operating loss). The loss, net of taxes, from the sale of the division was $42,000 ($70,000 loss on the sale less a $28,000 reduction in income taxes caused by the loss). Exhibit 14–2 is a comprehensive illustration portraying the income statement for North Corporation, including the information about Division Y in the discontinued operations section. Note that when there is a section on discontinued operations, the difference between the ordinary revenues and expenses is labeled "income from continuing operations."

EXHIBIT 14–2

North Corporation
Income Statement
For the Year 19XX

Sales		$1,900,000
Expenses:		
Cost of Goods Sold	$1,100,000	
Selling Expenses	200,000	
Administrative Expenses	180,000	
Interest Expense	20,000	
Income Taxes	160,000	
Total Expenses		1,660,000
Income from Continuing Operations		$ 240,000
Discontinued Operations:		
Loss from Operations of Discontinued		
Division Y (net of $10,000 reduction		
of income taxes)	$ 15,000	
Loss on Disposal of Division Y (net of		
$28,000 reduction of income taxes)	42,000	57,000
Income before Extraordinary Item and		
Cumulative Effect of a Change in		
Accounting Principle		$ 183,000
Extraordinary Item:		
Earthquake Loss (net of $16,000 reduction		
of income taxes)		(24,000)
Cumulative Effect on Prior Years of Changing		
to a Different Depreciation Method		13,000
Net Income		$ 172,000

CHANGES IN ACCOUNTING PRINCIPLES

Occasionally a company may find it necessary to change an accounting principle, that is, to switch from one generally accepted principle to another. A change in inventory pricing methods, such as from FIFO to weighted average, or a change in depreciation methods, such as from double declining-balance to straight-line, are examples. Because the comparability of financial data through time is enhanced by the consistent use of accounting principles, a company should change principles only when it can demonstrate that the new principle is preferable.

Almost all changes in accounting principles introduce a new item into the income statement—**the cumulative effect of a change in principle.** This item represents the total difference in the cumulative income for all prior years had the new principle been used in those years. It is equal to the difference between (a) the retained earnings at the beginning of the year and (b) what the retained earnings would have been at the beginning of the year if the new principle had been used in all years in which the previous principle was followed for the items in question. The cumulative effect is disclosed between the extraordinary items section and the net income figure.

To illustrate the reporting of the cumulative effect of a change in principle, assume the North Corporation in Exhibit 14–2 also changed the method it used to depreciate plant equipment in 19XX, switching from an accelerated method to the straight-line method. Cumulative income for years prior to 19XX would have been $13,000 greater if the straight-line method had been used to depreciate the plant equipment in those years. The following journal entry would be made to record the change in principle:

Accumulated Depreciation—Plant Equipment	13,000	
Cumulative Effect on Prior Years' Income		13,000

To record change in depreciation methods
on plant equipment.

Exhibit 14–2 shows how this change in an accounting principle is treated in North Corporation's income statement.

In addition to reporting the cumulative effect, the company should, in a note to the financial statements, justify the change and disclose the effect of the change on income of the current year exclusive of the cumulative adjustment. The effect of the change on earnings per share should also be reported.

Annual financial reports often include financial statements for prior periods for comparative purposes. These prior period statements do not have to be revised to reflect the new principle adopted this period. For each period reported upon, however, the income before extraordinary items, net income, and the related earnings-per-share amounts are recomputed as if the new principle had been in effect in that period, and these figures are also disclosed on the income statement.

The above disclosure requirements are an accommodation to two conflicting positions on the appropriate method of disclosing a change in accounting principle. One position stressed the possible dilution of public confidence in financial statements if previously reported statements were revised to reflect a new principle—hence the inclusion of a cumulative effect on prior years' income in the current year's income statement with no revision of prior period statements. The other position emphasized the importance of consistency in the use of accounting principles to allow comparative analysis of data—hence the disclosure of selected, significant pieces of information, recomputed using the new principle, for all periods presented in the financial statements.

For a few changes in principle, the financial statements must be revised, using the new principle, for all prior periods presented in the report. When this is done, the current year's income statement does not include an adjustment for a cumulative effect. Two types of changes requiring such disclosure are a change from LIFO to any other method of inventory pricing and a change in the method of accounting for long-term construction contracts.

SINGLE-STEP AND MULTIPLE-STEP INCOME STATEMENTS

Refer once again to Exhibit 14–2 (page 483), which illustrates a **single-step income statement.** In a single-step statement, the ordinary, continuing income of the business is derived in one step—by subtracting total expenses from total revenues. In Exhibit 14–2, all the expenses, totaling $1,660,000, are combined and then subtracted from the total revenues of $1,900,000. The single-step statement is a reporting format popular with businesses.

Exhibit 14–1 (page 481) is an example of a **multiple-step income statement.** In a multiple-step statement, one or more intermediate amounts are derived before the ordinary, continuing income is reported. In Exhibit 14–1, "gross profit on sales" and "income before taxes and extraordinary item" are two intermediate amounts presented before the "income before extraordinary item" figure. Both the multiple-step and the single-step reporting formats are acceptable procedures.

PRIOR PERIOD ADJUSTMENTS

Essentially, items qualifying as **prior period adjustments** are the corrections of errors made in financial statements of prior periods.[3] Errors may occur as a result of mathematical mistakes, oversights, incorrect applications of accounting principles, or improper analyses of existing facts at the time the financial statements are prepared.

Prior period adjustments are not included in the current year's income statement. Instead, corrections of material errors of past periods are charged or credited directly to Retained Earnings and are reported as adjustments to the beginning balance of Retained Earnings in the retained earnings statement. For example, in 19X2, a company discovered several mathematical errors in the computation of its December 31, 19X1, inventory. Inventory was understated by $11,000, a material amount for this company. The entry to correct the error would be:

---

[3]*Statement of Financial Accounting Standards No. 16,* "Prior Period Adjustments," Financial Accounting Standards Board, Stamford, Conn., 1977.

Inventory	11,000	
Retained Earnings		11,000

To correct inventory error of prior period.

The retained earnings statement in Exhibit 14–3 (page 497) illustrates the reporting of this prior period adjustment.

Of course, an error occurring in the current period does not require a prior period adjustment. The correction of current period errors was discussed in Chapter 3. As noted there, if a journal entry has been posted to the wrong account, the most direct way to correct the error is to make a new journal entry, transferring the amount to the proper account. If an error involves the right accounts but the wrong amounts, it may be corrected by drawing a line through the wrong amounts, entering the correct amounts above, and initialing the correction. Because these corrections are made in the same period as the errors, the financial statements will reflect the correct data.

CHANGES IN ACCOUNTING ESTIMATES

Estimates play an integral part in accounting. In preparing periodic financial statements, one must estimate the effect of transactions continuing into the future. For example, uncollectible accounts, useful lives of fixed and intangible assets, salvage values of fixed assets, and product warranty costs must be estimated. As a normal consequence of making such estimates, new information, changed conditions, or more experience may require previous estimates to be revised.

The effect of a change in an estimate should be reflected in the income statements of current and future periods, to the extent appropriate in each case. No part of the effect may be treated as a prior period adjustment and bypass the income statement.

The impact of some changes in estimates is included, in total, in the current year's income statement. A revision of an estimated liability booked in prior periods is one example. Assume that a company has underestimated its liability for product warranty carried into the current year by $900, because of unanticipated cost increases. The estimated liability is revised as follows:

Product Warranty Expense	900	
Estimated Liability for Product Warranty		900

To record estimated warranty expense.

An estimate revision may affect both the period of change and future periods. If so, the effect of the revision should be accounted for over the current and future periods. The revision of depreciation discussed on page 358 illustrates this type of change.

The Accounting Principles Board concluded in its *Opinion No. 20,* "Accounting Changes," that the restatement of amounts reported in financial statements of prior periods is an inappropriate way to account for changes in estimates. Presumably, the previous estimates were the best possible, given the information then available. Thus, the reporting of the estimates for those periods should not be changed.

EARNINGS PER SHARE

A financial statistic of great interest to corporation shareholders and potential investors is the earnings per share of common stock. Consequently, earnings-per-share data are widely disseminated, reaching interested persons through such channels as annual stockholder reports, financial newspapers, and financial statistical services. Because this financial information is so important, the Accounting Principles Board concluded that earnings-per-share data should be disclosed on the face of the income statement.[4]

In determining the presentation of earnings-per-share data, the Accounting Principles Board distinguished between corporations with *simple capital structures* and those with *complex capital structures.* A **simple capital structure** contains no securities that, if exercised or converted, would reduce (dilute) earnings per share of common stock. Convertible debt, convertible preferred stock, stock options, and stock warrants are examples of potentially dilutive securities, because if they are exercised or converted, the number of outstanding shares of common stock increases. A **complex capital structure** contains one or more potentially dilutive securities. Corporations with simple capital structures make a single presentation of earnings per share, while corporations with complex capital structures make a dual presentation.

Simple Capital Structure

For corporations with simple capital structures, earnings per share are calculated by dividing net income by a weighted average of the shares of common stock outstanding during the year. If preferred stock also is outstanding, its dividend requirements are subtracted from net income (to derive earnings available to common stockholders) as the first step in the calculation.

Suppose that the Owens Corporation has a net income of $39,000 for 19XX. On January 1, 19XX, 10,000 shares of common stock were outstanding. An additional 6,000 shares were issued on July 1. The company has no preferred stock. The weighted average shares of common stock outstanding during the year is computed as follows:

[4]*Opinions of the Accounting Principles Board,* No. 15, "Earnings Per Share," American Institute of Certified Public Accountants, New York, 1969.

Shares		Months Outstanding		Share Months
10,000	×	6	=	60,000
16,000	×	6	=	96,000
		12		156,000

$$\text{Weighted Average of Common Shares Outstanding} = \frac{156,000}{12} = 13,000$$

$$\text{Earnings per Share} = \frac{\text{Net Income}}{\text{Weighted Average of Common Shares Outstanding}}$$

$$= \frac{\$39,000}{13,000} = \$3.00$$

Complex Capital Structure

The dual presentation for corporations with complex capital structures consists of *primary earnings-per-share* and *fully diluted earnings-per-share* data. The computation of **primary earnings per share** considers the common stock outstanding during the year plus any potentially dilutive securities that are equivalent to common stock. (The Accounting Principles Board has established criteria for determining when a potentially dilutive security is a common stock equivalent.) The calculation of **fully diluted earnings per share** is based on the *assumption* that all dilutive securities are converted into common stock. The difference between the two per-share amounts shows the maximum dilution in earnings per share possible from any outstanding dilutive securities that are not the equivalent of common stock.

To illustrate the computation of primary and fully diluted earnings per share, let us suppose the Bodeen Company had a net income of $90,000 for the current year. All year the company had 40,000 shares of common stock and 5,000 shares of convertible preferred stock outstanding. The annual dividend on the convertible preferred stock is $0.80 per share, and each share is convertible into one share of common stock. The convertible preferred stock is a potentially dilutive security; we will assume it does not meet the criteria of the Accounting Principles Board for a common stock equivalent.

Primary Earnings per Share:

Net Income	$90,000
Deduct: Preferred Stock Dividend Requirement (5,000 shares × $0.80)	4,000
Earnings Available to Common Stockholders	$86,000
Weighted Average of Common Shares Outstanding	40,000

$$\text{Primary Earnings per Share} = \frac{\$86,000}{40,000} = \$2.15$$

Fully Diluted Earnings per Share:*

Net Income (under the assumption of preferred stock conversion, there is no deduction for a preferred stock dividend requirement) $90,000

Weighted Average of Common Shares Outstanding (40,000 shares of common stock + 5,000 shares from assumed conversion of preferred stock)   45,000

Fully Diluted Earnings per Share $= \dfrac{\$90,000}{45,000} = \$2.00$

*Assumes all preferred stock was converted into common stock at the beginning of the year.

Additional Per-Share Disclosures

The form in which earnings-per-share data are disclosed should correspond with the nature of the income statement content. Thus, if a firm has reported extraordinary gains or losses, an earnings-per-share amount should be disclosed for income before extraordinary items as well as for net income. It may also be desirable to disclose the effect of each extraordinary item. Similar disclosures should be made if the income statement contains an adjustment for the cumulative effect of a change in accounting principle. The following hypothetical data from a comparative income statement for a company with 10,000 shares of outstanding common stock illustrates the proper disclosure:

	19X2	19X1
Income before Extraordinary Items	$50,000	$60,000
Extraordinary Gain (net of tax)	18,000	
Net Income	$68,000	$60,000
Earnings per Share of Common Stock:		
Income before Extraordinary Items	$5.00	$6.00
Extraordinary Gain (net of tax)	1.80	
Net Income	$6.80	$6.00

This form of disclosure precludes drawing misleading inferences from comparative earnings-per-share data. Note that although the earnings per share for net income show an increase from 19X1 to 19X2, the data for 19X2 are shown to be influenced by an extraordinary (and thus unusual and nonrecurring) gain. A per-share comparison of income before extraordinary items shows an actual decrease from 19X1 to 19X2.

The variety of potentially dilutive securities and of events that affect outstanding common stock can make the computations of earnings per share quite complex. The analysis required for such computations is left for advanced courses.

DIVIDENDS

A corporation can distribute dividends to shareholders only after its board of directors has formally declared a distribution. Dividends are usually paid in cash, but may take the form of property or additional shares of stock in the firm. Legally, declared dividends become an obligation of the firm, and an entry to record the dividends payable is made on the **declaration date.** Although cash and property dividends payable are carried as liabilities, stock dividends to be distributed are shown in the stockholders' equity section of the balance sheet. At the time of declaration, a **record date** is established as well as a **payment date.** For example, on April 25 (declaration date), the board of directors might declare a dividend payable June 1 (payment date) to those who owned stock on May 15 (record date). Stockholders owning stock on the record date receive the dividend even if they dispose of their shares before the payment date. Therefore, the shares sold between the record date and payment date are sold **ex-dividend** (without right to the dividend).

Most dividend declarations reduce the balance of Retained Earnings; under certain conditions, however, state laws may permit distributions from paid-in capital. Whenever such dividends are distributed, shareholders should be informed of their source, because, in a sense, these dividends are a "return of capital" rather than a distribution of earnings.

Cash Dividends

The majority of dividends distributed by corporations are paid in cash. Although companies may pay such dividends annually, many large firms pay quarterly dividends. In addition, some companies may occasionally pay an "extra" dividend at the close of the year. Usually, this is done when the company wishes to increase the total annual distribution without departing from a standard quarterly amount that was established by custom or announced in advance.

In declaring cash dividends, a company must have both an appropriate amount of retained earnings and the necessary amount of cash. Too often, uninformed investors believe that a large Retained Earnings balance automatically permits generous dividend distributions. A company, however, may have been very successful in accumulating earnings and at the same time not be in a sufficiently liquid condition to pay large dividends. Many companies, especially new firms in the so-called growth industries, use retained earnings for expansion and may pay out only a small portion, or perhaps none, of their earnings.

When a company's directors declare a cash dividend, an entry is made in the records debiting Retained Earnings and crediting Dividends Payable, a current liability account. Assume, for example, that a company has outstanding 1,000 shares of $100 par value, 6% preferred stock and 3,000 shares of $50 par value common stock. If the company declares the regular $6 dividend on the preferred stock and a $4-per-share dividend on the common stock, $18,000 is required to make the dividend payments. The following entry would be made at the declaration date:

Retained Earnings	18,000	
Dividends Payable—Preferred Stock		6,000
Dividends Payable—Common Stock		12,000

To record declaration of $6 dividend
on preferred stock and $4 dividend on
common stock.

Until cash dividends are paid, they are carried as a current liability on the balance sheet. On the payment date, the following entry would be made in the cash disbursements journal:

Dividends Payable—Preferred Stock	6,000	
Dividends Payable—Common Stock	12,000	
Cash		18,000

To record payment of dividends on
preferred and common stocks.

Some companies, especially those paying quarterly dividends, debit an account called Dividends at the time of declaration. Until closing, this account is classified as a contra account to Retained Earnings. At the end of each year, the Dividends account is closed by a debit to Retained Earnings.

Stock Dividends   Companies frequently distribute shares of their own stock as dividends to shareholders in lieu of, or in addition to, cash dividends. There are a number of possible reasons for issuing **stock dividends.** One is to enable the company to continue a regular dividend at a time when it does not wish to deplete its working capital by paying a cash dividend. Distribution of a stock dividend may also signify management's desire to "plough back" earnings. The result of the distribution is to transfer a portion of retained earnings to the paid-in capital accounts. The so-called permanent capital is thereby increased although no new assets are acquired. Young and growing companies often issue stock dividends, inasmuch as earnings are needed to acquire new facilities and to expand. The use of stock dividends is by no means confined to such companies, however.

Although there are a number of forms of stock dividends, the most usual are those in which common shares are distributed to common shareholders. We will limit our discussion to this type of distribution.

For small stock dividends—additional shares issued are fewer than 20% to 25% of the number previously outstanding—the AICPA recommends transferring an amount equal to the market value of the shares issued from Retained Earnings to Paid-in Capital. In some respects, the issuance of new shares in the form of a dividend can be viewed as a transaction that avoids the test of the marketplace. If the shareholders received cash and immediately purchased additional shares of the firm's stock, the purchases would be made at market value. Thus, the number of shares to be issued in exchange for a given amount of retained earnings should be related to the market value of the shares.

To illustrate the entries reflecting a declaration of a stock dividend, assume that the stockholders' equity of a company appeared as follows before declaration of a 10% stock dividend:

Common Stock, $50 Par Value, 2,000 shares issued and outstanding	$100,000
Paid-in Capital in Excess of Par Value	5,000
Retained Earnings	80,000
Total Stockholders' Equity	$185,000

Since there are 2,000 shares outstanding, declaration of a 10% stock dividend requires the issuance of an additional 200 shares. Let us assume that the shares are selling at a market price of $70 per share. The amount to be transferred from Retained Earnings is $14,000, of which $10,000 (par value of the shares) is credited to the account Stock Dividend to Be Issued. The premium of $20 per share, or $4,000, is credited to Paid-in Capital in Excess of Par Value.

Retained Earnings	14,000	
Stock Dividend to Be Issued		10,000
Paid-in Capital in Excess of Par Value		4,000

To record declaration of 10% stock
dividend on common shares.

When the stock is distributed, the following entry is made:

Stock Dividend to Be Issued	10,000	
Common Stock		10,000

To record issuance of stock dividend
on common shares.

After the stock dividend is distributed, the stockholders' equity appears as follows:

Common Stock, $50 Par Value, 2,200 shares issued and outstanding	$110,000
Paid-in Capital in Excess of Par Value	9,000
Retained Earnings	66,000
Total Stockholders' Equity	$185,000

If a balance sheet is prepared between the date that a stock dividend is declared and the date it is distributed, the account Stock Dividend to Be Issued is shown as a separate item and is added to the account Common Stock.

The relative position of a common shareholder is not altered by the receipt of a common stock dividend. If a 10% stock dividend is distributed, all shareholders will increase their proportionate holdings by 10%, while at the same time the total stock outstanding is increased in the same proportion. Therefore, no income is realized by the shareholders. If the stock dividend distributed is not large in relation to the outstanding shares, however, there may be little or no change in the market value of the stock. If the market value does not decrease, and the company continues the same cash dividends per share, shareholders have benefited by the distribution.

When the number of shares issued as a stock dividend is large enough to reduce materially the per-share market value, the shareholders may not perceive the same benefits as they do for small stock dividends. The transaction is analogous to a stock split, whereby a company increases the number of outstanding shares and proportionately reduces the par or stated value of its stock. For this reason, the accounting analysis is different for large stock dividends (those in excess of 20% to 25%). The amount transferred from Retained Earnings to Paid-in Capital is the minimum required by law (that is, the legal capital). Usually this amount is the par or stated value of the stock.

In Chapter 13, we pointed out that cash dividends are not paid on treasury shares. Stock dividends, however, may be based on (1) all shares issued, including treasury stock, or (2) outstanding shares only. In the first case, the relative position of all shareholdings remains the same after the distribution. On the other hand, if stock dividends are distributed only on outstanding shares, the ratio of outstanding shares to total shares issued obviously increases.

STOCK SPLITS

Occasionally, a corporation will reduce the par or stated value of its common stock and issue additional shares to its stockholders. This type of transaction, called a **stock split,** is accomplished with no change in the balances of the stockholders' equity accounts—only a memorandum entry is made in the records to show the altered par or stated value of the stock. For example, if a company that has 1,000 shares outstanding of $100 par value common stock announced a 2 for 1 stock split, it would simply reduce the par value of its stock to $50 per share. Each shareholder would receive additional shares so that he or she would have twice the number of shares held before the split.

Note the difference between the accounting for a stock split, which requires a memorandum entry, and the accounting for a large stock dividend, which requires a transfer equal to the legal capital from Retained Earnings to Paid-in Capital. Under a stock split, the par or stated value of the stock is reduced, so the total par or stated value of shares outstanding is unchanged by the transaction. Under a stock dividend, no change occurs in the par or stated value per share, so an entry must be made to reflect the increased legal capital associated with the additional shares issued.

The major reason for a stock split is to reduce the market price of the stock. Some companies like their stock to sell within a certain price range. They may feel that higher prices narrow the breadth of their market, because investors often prefer to buy 100-share lots (purchases of fewer shares are odd-lot purchases and may be subject to higher brokers' fees) and, obviously, many small investors are not able to purchase high-priced stocks in 100-share lots. One textbook company, for example, has endeavored to keep the price of its common stock in the range of $20–$30. When the stock price increased to $36 per share, the company announced a 3 for 2 stock split, which lowered the price to $24 per share.

When shares are selling below the desired price, a *reverse split* can be accomplished by increasing the par value of the shares and reducing the number outstanding. Such transactions are encountered less frequently than stock splits.

IBM for All

IBM, the Wall Street glamour stock whose price once soared to a lofty $733 per share, is finally coming down to earth. Last week the $18 billion-a-year computer giant announced a 4-for-1 stock split effective next May.* That ought to bring the price of a single share down from about $284 last week to somewhere around $70—the lowest since 1932 and, for the first time in decades, within the reach of the average buyer. Says IBM Chairman and Chief Executive Frank T. Cary: "We want to make our stock more attractive to the small investor."

Why? IBM certainly does not need to raise any new money from investors; it has $5 billion in cash and securities, or more than the monetary reserves of most nations. Instead, its motives appear to be pride and politics. A rising stock price confers more prestige on corporate managers than one that is just high. Despite IBM's dazzling record of sales and profit gains, its stock, adjusted for past splits, sells for a bit less than it did ten years ago. Reason: institutional and pension fund managers hold about as many IBM shares as they care to, since they want to maintain balanced portfolios, and the stock has been too expensive for all but the richest individual investors; so demand for the

shares has declined. Politically, the more widely a company's stock is held, the more clout it has; A T & T's nearly 3 million shareholders, for example, constitute a powerful lobby. IBM could use support from more than the 579,384 shareholders it now has as it fights the Justice Department's attempt to split it up and moves into the heavily regulated field of satellite communications.

Still, the split represents a considerable shift in philosophy for a management that used to pride itself on having one of the highest-priced stocks around. Though IBM has declared six other splits in the past 20 years, they have been too modest (on the order of 5 for 4 or 3 for 2) to bring the price out of the stratosphere. But next year small investors are expected to seize the opportunity to buy in at Depression-era prices. As an extra inducement, IBM last week boosted dividends by $2.24 to an annual rate of $13.76 on the present stock or $3.44 on post-split shares. That means IBM shares will pay about the same yield—roughly 5%—as a bank savings account.

*The split was announced in December, 1978, to be effective in May, 1979.

APPROPRIATIONS OF RETAINED EARNINGS

Portions of the Retained Earnings balance are often restricted so that these amounts cannot be paid out as dividends. Often, the amounts so segregated are called **retained earnings appropriations.** The term *retained earnings reserves* may also be used to describe these restrictions.

In some instances, appropriations of retained earnings may be entirely *voluntary*—the board of directors may wish to restrict dividends in order to use corporate funds for a specific internal purpose. For example, the company may want to add to its plant or establish a buffer against possible adversity. By appropriating retained earnings, the directors inform the shareholders of the need to restrict dividend payments.

Other types of retained earnings appropriations may be *statutory* or *contractual.* In Chapter 13, we mentioned the example of a statutory appropriation in connection with treasury stock purchases—some states require retained earnings to be restricted in an amount equal to the cost of treasury stock purchased by the corporation.

A contractual appropriation sometimes results from agreements made when the company issues bonds or preferred stock. At one time, bond contracts commonly required the company to restrict retained earnings during the life of the contract in an amount equal to the debt. In most cases, a pro rata amount was set aside each year until the accumulated appropriation equaled the total amount of bonds outstanding, usually at the maturity date of the bonds. This type of arrangement is no longer common; contemporary bond contracts are more likely to dictate that the company maintain a specified working capital position to avoid restrictions on dividend payments.

Retained earnings may be appropriated by making an entry in the company's records. For example, assume that the board of directors has appropriated $60,000 for plant expansion. The following entry may be made:

Retained Earnings	60,000	
Retained Earnings Appropriated for Plant		
Expansion		60,000

To record retained earnings appropriation
for plant expansion.

The manner in which the appropriated amount is presented in the balance sheet is shown below:

Retained Earnings	
Appropriated for Plant Expansion	$ 60,000
Unappropriated	90,000
Total Retained Earnings	$150,000

Note that this company has total retained earnings of $150,000, of which only $90,000 is available for the declaration of dividends.

Certain points should be emphasized regarding the appropriation of retained earnings. First, segregating retained earnings for a particular objective accomplishes only one purpose: restriction of dividend amounts. The procedure does not assure that funds will be available for the avowed objective, because a company may have a large Retained Earnings balance without having an ample amount of liquid assets. When a company appropriates earnings for plant expansion, for example, management may also wish to *fund* the appropriation. This is accomplished by setting aside funds, as they become available, in a special asset account to permit eventual *spending* for plant expansion.

Second, expenditures are never charged against retained earnings appropriations. When the purpose is accomplished or the event transpires for which the appropriation was made, the restricted amount is returned, intact, to unappropriated retained earnings. For example, suppose that the company in our preceding illustration implemented its plans to expand, spending $55,000 for new facilities. After recording the purchase by debiting fixed assets and crediting cash for the amount spent, the company would reverse the entry made to appropriate retained earnings:

Retained Earnings Appropriated for Plant Expansion	60,000	
Retained Earnings		60,000

To return appropriation to Retained Earnings.

As an alternative to formally segregating retained earnings in the stockholders' equity section, a note to the balance sheet may be used to inform shareholders of restrictions on retained earnings. The note should indicate the nature and amount of the restrictions and the amount of retained earnings free from restrictions.

RETAINED EARNINGS STATEMENT

A **retained earnings statement** is an analysis of the retained earnings accounts (both appropriated and unappropriated) for the accounting period and is usually presented with the other corporate financial statements. The form of the statement is not standardized, and sometimes it is combined with the income statement. An example of a retained earnings statement is shown in Exhibit 14–3.

EXHIBIT 14–3

Holmes Corporation
Retained Earnings Statement
For the Year Ended December 31, 19X2

Appropriated:			
Appropriated for Plant Expansion, Balance, Jan. 1, 19X2		$40,000	
Appropriated in 19X2		10,000	$ 50,000
Unappropriated:			
Balance, Jan. 1, 19X2		$53,000	
Add: Correction of Prior Period Inventory Error		11,000	
Adjusted Balance, Jan. 1, 19X2		$64,000	
Add: Net Income		35,000	
		$99,000	
Less: Cash Dividends Declared	$15,000		
Appropriation for Plant Expansion (see above)	10,000	25,000	74,000
Total Retained Earnings, Dec. 31, 19X2			$124,000

KEY POINTS TO REMEMBER

(1) Special sections of the income statement are used to report:
   (a) Gains and losses from discontinued operations.
   (b) Extraordinary items, that is, items that are both unusual in nature and unlikely to recur.
   (c) The cumulative effects of most changes in accounting principles.

(2) Tax allocation within a period improves the reporting of income taxes by disclosing the tax effect and the items causing that effect in the same location in financial statements.

(3) Corrections of material errors made in previous periods are charged or credited directly to Retained Earnings.

(4) The effects of changes in accounting estimates are spread over the appropriate current and future periods.

(5) Corporations with complex capital structures present data on both primary earnings per share and fully diluted earnings per share. A single presentation of earnings per share is appropriate for corporations with a simple capital structure.

(6) Some of the major transactions related to retained earnings are:

  (a) Cash dividends, which reduce retained earnings and become a current liability when declared.

  (b) Stock dividends, which represent a transfer of retained earnings to the appropriate stock and paid-in capital accounts—at the market value of the shares for small stock dividends and at the legal minimum for large stock dividends.

  (c) Appropriations, which are actually segregations of retained earnings— the appropriated amount reduces the retained earnings available for dividends.

(7) Stock splits result in changes in the par or stated value of stock and affect the number of shares outstanding. No entries, except necessary memorandum notations, are made to record stock splits.

QUESTIONS

14-1 Define extraordinary items. How are extraordinary items shown in the income statement?

14-2 A manufacturing plant of the Task Corporation was destroyed by an earthquake. Earthquakes are rare in the region where the plant was located. Where should this loss be classified in the income statement?

14-3 A Florida citrus grower incurs material frost damage to crops. Frost damage typically is experienced every few years. How should the loss on the crops be shown in the income statement?

14-4 What is meant by tax allocation within a period? What is the purpose of this type of tax allocation?

14-5 Define a segment of a business. Why are gains and losses from a discontinued segment reported in a separate section of the income statement?

14-6 This year, the Sonic Company switched from the FIFO method of inventory pricing to the weighted average method. Cumulative income for previous years would have been $82,000 lower if the weighted average method had been used. (a) How should this $82,000 effect be shown in the income statement? (b) If a comparative income statement is presented in the annual report, is it necessary to revise last year's income statement using the weighted average method?

14-7 What is the difference between a single-step income statement and a multiple-step income statement?

14-8 The Beam Company discovered this year that a significant portion of its inventory was overlooked during inventory-taking at the end of last year. How should the correction of this error be disclosed in the financial statements?

14-9 Distinguish between an error and a change in an estimate. What are the differences between reporting corrections of errors and reporting changes in accounting estimates?

14-10 Distinguish between corporations with a simple capital structure and those with a complex capital structure. What does the type of capital structure imply regarding the presentation of earnings-per-share data?

14-11 The Hilo Company earned a net income of $56,000 in 19XX. The company, which has a simple capital structure, started the year with 8,000 shares of common stock outstanding and issued an additional 8,000 shares on April 1. What is Hilo Company's earnings per share for 19XX?

14-12 What assumption underlies the computation of fully diluted earnings per share? What is revealed by the difference between the amounts of primary earnings per share and fully diluted earnings per share?

14-13 What is a stock dividend? How does a common stock dividend paid to common shareholders affect their respective ownership interests?

14-14 Distinguish between a stock dividend and a stock split, by indicating (a) the effect of each on shareholders' individual interests, (b) the possible effect of each on the market price of stock, and (c) the entries necessary to record these events in the accounting records.

14-15 What is meant by an appropriation of retained earnings? Why and by whom are such appropriations made?

14-16 Where do the following accounts (and their balances) appear in the balance sheet?
(a) Dividends Payable—Common Stock
(b) Stock Dividend to Be Issued
(c) Retained Earnings Appropriated for Contingencies

EXERCISES

14-17 During the current year, Waxe Corporation incurred an extraordinary hurricane loss of $200,000 and sold a segment of its business at a gain of $90,000. Until it was sold, the segment had a current period operating loss of $120,000. The hurricane loss and the segment's operating loss both reduced income that was subject to a 40% tax rate. The gain from the sale of the segment was subject to a 40% tax rate. The company had income from continuing operations for the current year of $670,000. Prepare the lower part of the income statement, beginning with the $670,000 income from continuing operations. Follow tax allocation procedures.

14-18 Prepare entries in general journal form for the following three events of the current year for Rowen, Inc.:

Jan. 2 The company decided to change from the sum-of-the-years'-digits to the straight-line method of depreciating its equipment. Cumulative income for prior years would have been $31,000 higher under the straight-line method.

April 10 It was discovered that, because of a new employee's oversight, depreciation of $18,000 on an addition to the plant had been omitted last year. The amount is material.

Dec. 31   The company acquired a patent at a cost of $64,000 six years ago (including the current year) and estimated its useful life to be sixteen years. In reviewing accounts for the year-end adjustments, the company revised its estimate of the total useful life to thirteen years. (Record the current year's patent amortization under the straight-line method; the company does not use a contra account.)

14-19   The Klik Company began the year with a simple capital structure consisting of 4,000 shares of common stock outstanding. On April 1, 5,000 additional shares were issued, and another 1,000 shares were issued on October 1. The company had a net income for the year of $52,400.
(a) Compute the earnings per share of common stock.
(b) Assume that the company also had 2,000 shares of 6%, $80 par value preferred stock outstanding during the year. Compute the earnings per share of common stock.

14-20   During 19X8, the Rose Corporation had 12,000 shares of $40 par value common stock and 2,000 shares of 6%, $100 par value convertible preferred stock outstanding. The preferred stock is not a common stock equivalent. Each share of preferred stock may be converted into three shares of common stock. Rose Corporation's net income in 19X8 was $126,000.
(a) Compute the primary earnings per share for 19X8.
(b) Compute the fully diluted earnings per share for 19X8.

14-21   Stadium Corporation has 4,000 shares of $20 par value common stock outstanding and has a Retained Earnings balance of $80,000. The company declares a cash dividend of $3 per share and a 5% stock dividend. The market price of the stock at the declaration date is $35 per share.
(a) Give the entries in general journal form for (1) the declaration of dividends and (2) the payment (or issuance) of the dividends.
(b) Assume that the company had 200 shares of treasury stock when the dividends were declared and that state law provides for stock dividends (but not cash dividends) on treasury shares. Give the entries in general journal form for the declaration of dividends.

14-22   In each of the years 19X6 and 19X7, the Elm Company appropriated $50,000 of retained earnings for a future computer acquisition. In 19X8, the company acquired a computer for $97,000 cash. Prepare entries in general journal form to record the appropriation of retained earnings in 19X6 and 19X7, the purchase of the computer in 19X8, and the disposition of the balance in the appropriated retained earnings account after the purchase.

14-23   Use the following data to prepare the stockholders' equity section of the Swann Company balance sheet.

Unappropriated Retained Earnings	$230,000
Paid-in Capital in Excess of Par Value—Common Stock	35,000
Paid-in Capital in Excess of Par Value—Preferred Stock	15,000
Retained Earnings Appropriated—Treasury Stock Purchases	40,000
Preferred Stock, $50 Par Value, 7%, 3,000 shares outstanding	150,000
Common Stock, $40 Par Value, 10,000 shares issued	400,000
Treasury Stock (Common), 800 shares (at cost)	40,000
Retained Earnings Appropriated—Plant Expansion	120,000

PROBLEMS

14-24 The following information from the 19X1 operations of the Field Company is available from the accounting records:

Administrative Expenses	$ 73,000
Cost of Goods Sold	520,000
Sales	840,000
Flood Loss	45,000
Selling Expenses	92,000
Interest Expense	5,000
Loss from Operations of Discontinued Segment	35,000
Gain on Disposal of Discontinued Segment	10,000
Income Taxes:	
Amount applicable to ordinary operations	60,000
Reduction applicable to flood loss	18,000
Reduction applicable to loss from operations	
of discontinued segment	14,000
Amount applicable to gain on disposal of	
discontinued segment	4,000

The flood loss is an extraordinary item for the Field Company.

REQUIRED
(a) Prepare a multiple-step income statement for the Field Company.
(b) Prepare a single-step income statement for the Field Company.

14-25 The stockholders' equity of the Typo Corporation at January 1, 19X2, appears below.

Common Stock, $20 Par Value, 45,000 shares authorized,	
30,000 shares issued and outstanding	$600,000
Paid-in Capital in Excess of Par Value—Common Stock	120,000
Unappropriated Retained Earnings	215,000

During the current year, the following transactions occurred:

June 7   The board of directors authorized an appropriation of retained earnings of $60,000 for future land acquisition.

Dec. 10   The board of directors declared a cash dividend of $1.20 per share and a 5% stock dividend. Market value of the common stock was $26 per share.

31   An entry was made to close the net income of $117,000 from the Income Summary account to Retained Earnings.

REQUIRED
(a) Prepare entries, in general journal form, to record the foregoing transactions.
(b) Prepare a retained earnings statement for the year ended December 31, 19X2.

(c) The cash dividend was paid and the stock dividend was issued on January 17 of the following year. Give the entries, in general journal form, to be made on January 17.

(d) The board of directors dropped their plan to acquire land in the future and decided to eliminate the appropriation for future land acquisition. Make the necessary journal entry. (The action was taken on January 25.)

14-26 The Hilite Company began the year 19XX with 17,000 shares of common stock and 4,000 shares of convertible preferred stock outstanding. On February 1, an additional 4,000 shares of common stock were issued. On September 1, another 1,000 shares of common stock were issued. On November 1, 6,000 shares of common stock were reacquired for the treasury. The preferred stock has a $1.05 per-share dividend rate, and each share may be converted into one share of common. The preferred stock is not a common stock equivalent. Hilite Company had a net income of $85,200 in 19XX.

REQUIRED

(a) Compute primary earnings per share for 19XX.
(b) Compute fully diluted earnings per share for 19XX.
(c) If the preferred stock were not convertible, Hilite Company would have a simple capital structure. What would be its earnings per share for 19XX?

14-27 The stockholders' equity of the Mark Corporation at January 1, 19XX, appears below.

5% Preferred Stock, $40 Par Value, 6,000 shares authorized, 5,000 shares issued and outstanding	$200,000
Common Stock, $10 Par Value, 50,000 shares authorized, 30,000 shares issued and outstanding	300,000
Paid-in Capital in Excess of Par Value—Common Stock	90,000
Retained Earnings Appropriated for Plant Expansion	150,000
Unappropriated Retained Earnings	240,000
Total Stockholders' Equity	$980,000

The following transactions, among others, occurred during the year:

Jan. 10   It was discovered that a portion of inventory had been overlooked in computing the ending inventory at December 31 of the previous year. The inventory was understated by $16,000, a material amount.

June 18   A 6% stock dividend was declared on all issued shares of common stock. The market value of the stock (per share) was $20.

July 1   The stock dividend declared on June 18 was issued.

Aug. 25   A decision unfavorable to the Mark Corporation was rendered in a lawsuit in which the company had been involved for several years. The judgment against the company was for $60,000. No previous entry concerning the lawsuit had been made in the accounts. The unfavorable lawsuit decision is not an extraordinary item.

Sept. 8 The board of directors added $20,000 to the retained earnings appropriated for plant expansion.

Dec. 20 The annual cash dividend on the preferred stock and a cash dividend of $1.00 per share of common stock were declared, payable on January 20 to stockholders of record on December 28.

31 The Income Summary account, with net earnings of $120,000, was closed to Retained Earnings.

REQUIRED

(a) Prepare entries, in general journal form, to record the foregoing transactions.

(b) Prepare a retained earnings statement for the year ended December 31, 19XX.

14-28 The Rein Company presented the following earnings-per-share data:

Earnings per Share of Common Stock:	
Income before Extraordinary Items	$5.25
Extraordinary Gain (net of tax)	1.40
Net Income	$6.65

The company has a simple capital structure. It began the year with 14,000 shares of $20 par value common stock and 7,000 shares of 6%, $50 par value preferred stock outstanding. On September 1, 6,000 shares of common stock were issued.

REQUIRED

(a) What is the annual preferred stock dividend requirement?

(b) What was the net income for the current year for the Rein Company?

(c) What was the amount of the extraordinary gain, net of the tax effect? If the tax rate on the gain was 30%, what was the amount of the gain before the tax effect?

(d) If the tax rate on ordinary income is 40%, what amount of income tax expense was reported in the income before extraordinary items section of the income statement?

14-29 The stockholders' equity of the Drier Corporation at January 1, 19XX, is shown below.

7% Preferred Stock, $75 Par Value, 8,000 shares authorized, 4,000 shares issued and outstanding	$ 300,000
Paid-in Capital in Excess of Par Value—Preferred Stock	24,000
Common Stock, $50 Par Value, 20,000 shares authorized, 14,000 shares issued and outstanding	700,000
Paid-in Capital in Excess of Par Value—Common Stock	56,000
Unappropriated Retained Earnings	342,000
Total Stockholders' Equity	$1,422,000

The following transactions, among others, occurred during the year:

Jan. 25 Several mathematical errors were discovered in the computations of the ending inventory for the preceding year. In total, inventory had been understated by $10,000, a material amount.

May 1 The corporation announced a $2\frac{1}{2}$ for 1 stock split, reducing the par value of the common stock to $20 per share. The authorization was increased to 50,000 shares.

Sept. 1 2,500 shares of common stock were reacquired for cash at a price of $26 per share.

2 An appropriation was made of retained earnings equal to the cost of the treasury shares acquired September 1.

Dec. 5 A 6% stock dividend was declared on all issued shares of common stock, including treasury shares. The market value of the stock was $30 per share.

15 The stock dividend declared on December 5 was issued.

16 The annual cash dividend on the preferred stock and a cash dividend of $2 per common share were declared, payable on January 10 to stockholders of record on December 30.

30 Management decided to switch from the straight-line method of depreciation to the sum-of-the-years'-digits method on machinery and equipment. Cumulative income in prior years would have been $15,000 lower if the sum-of-the-years'-digits method had been used.

31 The annual patent amortization expense was recorded. In reviewing the accounts for year-end adjustments, management revised the estimated total useful life of the patent from seventeen years to eleven years. The patent had cost $119,000 when acquired at the beginning of last year. The company uses the straight-line method for amortization and does not use a contra account.

31 The Income Summary account, with net earnings of $180,000, was closed to Retained Earnings.

REQUIRED

(a) Prepare entries, in general journal form, to record the foregoing transactions.

(b) Prepare a retained earnings statement for the year ended December 31, 19XX.

(c) Prepare the stockholders' equity section of the balance sheet at December 31, 19XX.

ALTERNATE PROBLEMS

14-24A The following information from the 19X8 operations of the Maxim Company is available from the accounting records:

Loss from Expropriation of Property	$ 60,000
Administrative Expenses	95,000
Sales	960,000
Selling Expenses	115,000
Cost of Goods Sold	605,000
Cumulative Effect (Increase) on Prior Years' Income from Changing Depreciation Methods	19,000
Income Taxes:	
Amount applicable to ordinary operations	58,000
Reduction applicable to loss from expropriation of property	24,000
Retained Earnings, Jan. 1	410,000
Retained Earnings Appropriated for Plant Expansion (appropriated on Nov. 1)	80,000
Cash Dividends Declared	32,000

The loss from expropriation of property is an extraordinary item for the Maxim Company.

REQUIRED
(a) Prepare a single-step income statement for the Maxim Company.
(b) Prepare a retained earnings statement for the Maxim Company for the year ended December 31, 19X8.

14-25A The stockholders' equity of the Western Corporation at January 1, 19X9, appears below.

Common Stock, $10 Par Value, 30,000 shares authorized, 24,000 shares issued and outstanding	$240,000
Paid-in Capital in Excess of Par Value—Common Stock	72,000
Unappropriated Retained Earnings	170,000

During 19X9, the following transactions occurred:

May 12 Fearing a strike early next year, the board of directors authorized an appropriation of retained earnings of $45,000 for contingencies.

Dec. 5 The board of directors declared a cash dividend of $0.50 per share and a 10% stock dividend. Market value of the common stock was $14 per share on this date.

31 An entry was made to close the net income of $92,000 from the Income Summary account to Retained Earnings.

REQUIRED
(a) Prepare entries, in general journal form, to record the foregoing transactions.
(b) Prepare a retained earnings statement for the year ended December 31, 19X9.
(c) The cash dividend was paid and the stock dividend was issued on January 20 of the following year. Give the entries, in general journal form, to be made on January 20.

(d) The expected employee strike did not materialize, and the board of directors decided on January 22 to eliminate the appropriation for contingencies. Make the necessary journal entry.

14-26A The Radd Company began the year 19XX with 5,000 shares of common stock and 3,000 shares of convertible preferred stock outstanding. On May 1, an additional 2,000 shares of common stock were issued. On July 1, another 3,000 shares of common stock were issued. On September 1, 1,000 shares of common stock were reacquired for the treasury. The preferred stock has a $2.00 per-share dividend rate, and each share may be converted into two shares of common. The preferred stock is not a common stock equivalent. Radd Company had a net income of $93,825 in 19XX.

REQUIRED
(a) Compute primary earnings per share for 19XX.
(b) Compute fully diluted earnings per share for 19XX.
(c) If the preferred stock were not convertible, Radd Company would have a simple capital structure. What would be its earnings per share for 19XX?

14-27A The stockholders' equity of the Opan Corporation at January 1, 19XX, appears below.

6% Preferred Stock, $50 Par Value, 3,000 shares authorized, 2,000 shares issued and outstanding	$ 100,000
Common Stock, $70 Par Value, 20,000 shares authorized, 9,000 shares issued and outstanding	630,000
Paid-in Capital in Excess of Par Value—Common Stock	45,000
Retained Earnings Appropriated for Future Litigation	60,000
Unappropriated Retained Earnings	340,000
Total Stockholders' Equity	$1,175,000

The following transactions, among others, occurred during the year:

Jan. 22 It was discovered that a portion of inventory had been counted twice in computing the ending inventory at December 31 of the previous year. The inventory was overstated by $24,000, a material amount.

June 1 The corporation announced a 2 for 1 split of the common stock, reducing the par value of the stock to $35 per share. The authorized number of common shares was increased to 40,000 shares.

Aug. 10 A 10% stock dividend was declared on all issued shares of common stock. The market value of the stock (per share) was $40.

26 The board of directors added $20,000 to the retained earnings appropriated for possible future litigation.

Sept. 5 The stock dividend declared on August 10 was issued.

Dec. 5 The annual cash dividend on the preferred stock and a cash dividend of $1.25 per share of common stock were declared, payable on January 25 to stockholders of record on December 27.

Dec. 30   The board of directors appropriated $60,000 of retained earnings for general contingencies.

31   The Income Summary account, with net earnings of $135,000, was closed to Retained Earnings.

REQUIRED

(a) Prepare entries, in general journal form, to record the foregoing transactions.

(b) Prepare a retained earnings statement for the year ended December 31, 19XX.

BUSINESS DECISION PROBLEM

The stockholders' equity section of the Universal Corporation's comparative balance sheet at the end of 19X7 and 19X8, part of the financial data just reviewed at a stockholders' meeting, is presented below.

	December 31, 19X8	December 31, 19X7
Common Stock, $25 Par Value, 200,000 shares authorized; issued at December 31: 19X8, 144,000 shares; 19X7, 120,000 shares	$3,600,000	$3,000,000
Paid-in Capital in Excess of Par Value	1,290,000	450,000
Retained Earnings:		
Appropriated for Plant Expansion	700,000	600,000
Unappropriated	890,000	2,280,000
Total Stockholders' Equity	$6,480,000	$6,330,000

Among the items disclosed at the stockholders' meeting were the following: Net income after income taxes for 19X8 was $510,000; a 20% stock dividend was issued December 14, 19X8, when the market value per share was $60; the market value per share at December 31, 19X8, was $52; management plans to borrow $300,000 to help finance a new plant addition, which is expected to cost a total of $750,000; and the customary $3 per-share cash dividend has been revised to $2.50.

As part of their stockholders' goodwill program, management distributed during the stockholders' meeting a special form on which stockholders were asked to write any questions they might have concerning the firm's operations or finances. As assistant controller, you are handed a stack of the completed forms.

REQUIRED

Prepare and present brief but reasonably complete answers to the following questions:

(1) What did Universal do with the cash proceeds from the stock dividend issued in December?

(2) What was my book value per share at the end of 19X7 and 19X8?

(3) I owned 2,000 shares of Universal in 19X7 and have not sold any shares. How much more or less of the Corporation do I own at December 31, 19X8, and what happened to the market value of my interest in the Company?

(4) I heard someone say that stock dividends don't give me anything I didn't already have. Why did you issue one? Are you trying to fool us?

(5) Instead of a stock dividend, why didn't you declare a cash dividend and let us buy the new shares that were issued?

(6) Why are you cutting back on the dividends I will receive?

(7) If you have $700,000 put aside for the new plant addition, which will cost $750,000, why are you borrowing $300,000 instead of just the $50,000 needed?

15
Corporations: Long-term Liabilities and Investments

> **It saves a lot of trouble if, instead of having to earn money and save it, you can just go and borrow it.**
>
> WINSTON CHURCHILL

At various times in the course of business operations, particularly during phases of expansion, firms find it necessary to secure additional long-term funds. Often they choose long-term borrowing, rather than issuing additional capital stock, to avoid diluting the ownership interests or because the borrowed funds may have a lower net cost to the present stockholders.[1] The interest cost of long-term debt has identifiable limits, and the creditors do not receive an increased return on investment if profits grow. Furthermore, the borrowing firm may deduct interest payments on debt for tax purposes, whereas it may not deduct dividend distributions to owners.

Not all aspects of long-term debt are necessarily desirable for the borrowing company. In contrast with dividends on common stock, interest on debt represents a fixed periodic expenditure that the firm is contractually obligated to make. Fixed interest charges can become a financial burden when operations do not develop as favorably as expected. Long-term debt normally has a definite maturity date, so the firm must also provide for repayment of the obligation. Finally, a long-term borrowing agreement may restrict the financial policies of the company while the debt is outstanding.

LONG-TERM LIABILITIES

The two major types of long-term liabilities are mortgage notes and bonds. As accounting principles are the same for both, this chapter will focus on bonds, with only a brief description of mortgage notes.

Mortgage Notes   One way for a firm to borrow long-term funds is to issue a **mortgage note,** which is actually two related documents. The note is an agreement to repay the principal and to pay specified interest amounts on certain dates; the mortgage is a legal agreement that certain property of the borrower will be pledged as security for repayment of the note. Usually, a mortgage note is used when the borrowed funds all come from one lender. Sometimes a firm will find it more strategic or even necessary to borrow large amounts of funds from several smaller lenders. In these latter cases, it is more practical to issue bonds.

---

[1]The concept of investment leverage is explained in Chapter 18.

Bonds   **Bonds** are, in essence, notes payable. Their special characteristics are dictated by the specific objectives in a given borrowing situation. Because a complete discussion of the wide variety of bonds is beyond the scope of this text, only the more significant characteristics of bonds are described below.

Bonds are used most often in situations in which a borrower is to receive funds from a large number of lenders contributing various amounts. Consequently, bonds are usually drawn up to be negotiable. Because many parties are involved, it helps if the borrower selects a **trustee,** often a large bank, to represent the group of bondholders. As a third party to the transaction, the trustee may take security title to any pledged property and is likely to initiate any action necessitated by failure to meet the terms of the bond agreement.

If the borrower fails to meet the provisions of a bond agreement, the bondholders, represented by the trustee, may institute a variety of actions. Examples of less significant actions are enforcing agreements related to restrictions on the payment of dividends, prescribing minimum cash balances or financial operating ratios, placing restrictions on additional financing, and electing new members to the board of directors. The ultimate action, of course, is to bring foreclosure proceedings. The trustee may also maintain a record of current bond owners and may act as disbursing agent for the interest and principal payments.

CHARACTERISTICS OF BONDS   Bond agreements may be formulated to capitalize on certain lending situations, appeal to special investor groups, or provide special repayment patterns. Below we list some examples of common bond characteristics.

Secured bonds are those for which some specific property is pledged as security for meeting the terms of the bond agreement. The specific title of the bonds may indicate the type of property pledged—for example, real estate mortgage bonds (land and/or buildings), chattel mortgage bonds (machinery or equipment), and collateral trust bonds (negotiable securities). Some property may be subject to two or more mortgages. In such cases, the relative priority of each mortgage is denoted by its identification as a "first," "second," or even "third" mortgage.

Bonds that have no specific property pledged as security for their repayment are called **debenture bonds.** Holders of such bonds rely on the general credit reputation of the borrower. Because the lender's risk is usually greater than in the case of secured bonds, the sale of unsecured bonds may require that a higher rate of interest be offered.

The maturity dates of **serial bonds** are staggered over a series of years. For example, a serial bond issue of $15 million may provide for $1 million of the bonds to mature each year for 15 years. An advantage of serial bonds is that potential lenders can choose bonds with maturity dates that correspond with the length of investment they specifically desire.

The issuing corporation (or its trustee) maintains a record of the owners of **registered bonds.** At appropriate times, interest payments are mailed to the registered owners. Interest on **coupon bonds** is paid in a different manner. A coupon for interest payable to the bearer is attached to the bond for each interest period.

Whenever interest is due, the bondholder detaches a coupon and deposits it with his or her bank for collection.

Callable bonds contain provisions for the borrower to "call in" (retire) the bonds and pay them off after a stated date. Usually, an extra amount or premium must be paid to the holders of the called bonds. Callable bonds offer borrowers an additional flexibility that may be quite significant if funds become available at interest rates substantially lower than those being paid on the bonds. To some degree, borrowers can in effect "call" any of their bonds by buying them in the open market.

Convertible bonds grant the holder the right to convert them to capital stock at some specific exchange ratio. This provision permits an investor to enjoy the security of a creditor during a certain stage of a firm's life, with the option of becoming a stockholder if the firm should become sufficiently profitable.

RECORDING BOND ISSUES   Firms often authorize more bonds than they actually anticipate issuing at one time. Authorization of bonds usually includes (1) formal action by the board of directors, (2) application to and approval of some government agency, (3) retention of a trustee, and (4) all the attendant negotiations and legalities. For secured bonds, the total value of the bonds authorized is typically some fraction of the value of the property to be pledged. The difference between the dollar amount of the bonds issued and the value of the pledged property represents a margin of safety to bondholders.

Because individual bond issues may have widely varying characteristics, separate accounts with reasonably descriptive titles should be used for each bond issue. When the bonds are authorized, an account is opened in the general ledger, and a memorandum entry may be made in the account stating the total amount of bonds authorized.

The **face value** of a bond is the amount of principal to be repaid at the maturity date. Interest on bonds is usually paid semiannually, with the payments six months apart (such as January 1 and July 1). The annual rate of interest payable on a bond is stated in the bond agreement and is often referred to as the "coupon" or "nominal" rate of interest. Thus, the amount of interest paid semiannually on such bonds would be the face value multiplied by half the nominal rate of interest. If financial statements are prepared between interest payment dates, the periodic interest expense and the related liability for interest payable should be accrued to the date of the statements.

To provide a simple illustration, we use informal account titles and an unrealistically short bond life. Assume that on January 1, Ross, Inc. issues at face value ten $10,000, 10% bonds that mature in four years with interest paid on June 30 and December 31. The entry to record the bond issue is:

Jan. 1	Cash	100,000	
	Bonds Payable		100,000
	To record issuance of bonds.		

Interest of \$5,000 (\$100,000 $\times$ 0.10 $\times$ $\frac{6}{12}$) will be paid on each of the eight payment dates (four years, semiannual payments). For example, the entry on June 30, the first interest payment date, would be:

June 30	Bond Interest Expense	5,000	
	Cash		5,000
	To record payment of semiannual interest on bonds payable.		

When the bonds mature, Ross, Inc. would record their retirement in the following manner:

(final year)

Dec. 31	Bonds Payable	100,000	
	Cash		100,000
	To record retirement of bonds.		

Issuance between interest dates. Not all bonds are sold on the exact day on which their interest begins to accumulate. For example, issuance may be delayed in anticipation of a more favorable bond market. Investors who buy bonds after the interest begins to accrue are expected to "buy" the accrued interest. Such bonds are said to be sold at some price "plus accrued interest." If Ross, Inc. had sold its bonds on April 1 instead of January 1, the entry would have been:

Apr. 1	Cash	102,500	
	Bonds Payable		100,000
	Bond Interest Payable		2,500
	To record bond issuance at face value plus three months' accrued interest.		

We see that the interest accrued on the bonds on April 1, the issue date, is \$2,500 (\$100,000 $\times$ 0.10 $\times$ $\frac{3}{12}$). On the first interest payment date, June 30, Ross, Inc. would make the following entry:

June 30	Bond Interest Payable	2,500	
	Bond Interest Expense	2,500	
	Cash		5,000
	To record payment of semiannual interest on bonds payable.		

This entry records interest expense at \$2,500, the appropriate amount for the three months the bonds have been outstanding. The other \$2,500 represents the return of the accrued interest collected from the bond purchasers on April 1.

Bonds issued at a discount. If the nominal rate of interest on the bonds to be issued is less than the current market rate of interest for the type and quality of the bonds, they can be sold only at a price less than their face value. In such cases, investors "discount" the bonds in order to earn the amount of interest reflected in the current money market. For example, assume that Ross, Inc.'s $100,000 issue of 10%, four-year bonds were sold on January 1 at 98 (meaning 98% of their face value), because the applicable market rate was in excess of their 10% nominal rate. The entry to record the issue of these bonds would be:

Jan. 1	Cash	98,000	
	Bond Discount	2,000	
	Bonds Payable		100,000

To record issuance of bonds at 98.

The $2,000 discount is not an immediate loss or expense to Ross, Inc. Rather, it represents an adjustment of interest expense over the entire life of the bonds. We can illustrate this by comparing the funds Ross, Inc. received with the funds it must pay to the bondholders. Regardless of their selling price, the bonds are an agreement to pay to the bondholders $140,000 ($100,000 principal plus eight semiannual interest payments of $5,000 each). Thus we have

Total funds paid to bondholders	$140,000
Total funds received from bond sale	98,000
Difference equals total interest paid	$ 42,000
Average expense per year ($42,000/4)	$ 10,500

Although Ross, Inc. will pay only two $5,000 interest payments, a total of $10,000, each year, its full annual interest expense on the bonds is in excess of that amount. To reflect the larger periodic interest expense, the bond discount is *amortized*. Amortization of bond discount means that periodically an amount is transferred from bond discount to interest expense.

Basically, there are two methods of amortization, the straight-line method and the effective interest method. Under the *straight-line method*, equal amounts are transferred from bond discount to interest expense for equal periods of time. For Ross, Inc., this amount would be $250 every six months ($2,000 total bond discount ÷ 8 semiannual interest periods). Some companies may amortize the discount annually rather than semiannually; the annual amortization for Ross, Inc. is $500. The *effective interest method*, which is more complex, reflects a constant rate of interest over the life of the bonds. The effective interest method is discussed and illustrated in Appendix A at the end of this chapter.

Assuming the straight-line method of amortization, the journal entries each year to record interest expense for Ross, Inc. are as follows. (We assume that the bond sale is already recorded as illustrated above and that the bonds were issued on the day they are dated.)

| June 30 | Bond Interest Expense | 5,000 | |
| | Cash | | 5,000 |

To record first semiannual interest payment.

| 30 | Bond Interest Expense | 250 | |
| | Bond Discount | | 250 |

To record semiannual amortization of bond discount.

| Dec. 31 | Bond Interest Expense | 5,000 | |
| | Cash | | 5,000 |

To record second semiannual interest payment.

| 31 | Bond Interest Expense | 250 | |
| | Bond Discount | | 250 |

To record semiannual amortization of bond discount.

We see that these entries result in four debits to the Bond Interest Expense account each year, reflecting a $10,500 annual interest expense. Amortizing the bond discount over the four-year life of the bonds at $250 every six months will leave a zero balance in the Bond Discount account at the maturity date of the bonds. The retirement of the bonds can then be recorded by debiting Bonds Payable and crediting Cash for $100,000, the amount of their face value.

Bonds issued at a premium. If the market rate of interest had been below the 10% offered by Ross, Inc.'s bonds, investors would have been willing to pay a premium for the bonds. Like a bond discount, a bond premium should be considered an adjustment of interest expense over the life of the bonds. We just saw that bond discount increases interest expense; now we shall see that bond premium reduces interest expense. The following entries illustrate the sale of Ross, Inc. bonds at 104 (104% of face value), the payments of interest, the amortization of bond premium, and the retirement of the bonds at maturity.

Jan. 1	Cash	104,000	
	Bonds Payable		100,000
	Bond Premium		4,000

To record sale of bonds at a premium.

| June 30 | Bond Interest Expense | 5,000 | |
| | Cash | | 5,000 |

To record first semiannual interest payment.

| June 30 | Bond Premium | 500 | |
| | Bond Interest Expense | | 500 |

To record semiannual amortization of bond premium.

| Dec. 31 | Bond Interest Expense | 5,000 | |
| | Cash | | 5,000 |

To record second semiannual interest payment.

| 31 | Bond Premium | 500 | |
| | Bond Interest Expense | | 500 |

To record semiannual amortization of bond premium.

(final year)

| Dec. 31 | Bonds Payable | 100,000 | |
| | Cash | | 100,000 |

To retire bonds at maturity.

The eight semiannual $500 amortization entries to the Bond Premium account will leave it with a zero balance at the time the bonds mature. We can verify the total annual interest expense of $9,000 reflected by the above entries as follows:

Total funds paid to bondholders	$140,000
Total funds received from bondholders	104,000
Difference equals total interest paid	$ 36,000
Average interest expense per year ($36,000/4)	$ 9,000

The related interest expense account would have a balance of $9,000 as shown in the following T account.

Bond Interest Expense

First semiannual interest payment	5,000	First semiannual amortization of bond premium	500
Second semiannual interest payment	5,000	Second semiannual amortization of bond premium	500

Year-end or interim adjustments. When a periodic interest payment date does not correspond with the end of a year, adjustment of the general ledger accounts should include an entry reflecting the amount of interest expense incurred but not paid and an entry reflecting a pro rata amortization of bond discount or bond premium for the portion of the year involved. Similar adjustments are appropriate when interim financial statements are prepared and the interim date does not correspond with an interest payment date.

For this illustration, let us assume the bonds issued by Ross, Inc. at 98 were issued on April 1 and had interest payment dates of April 1 and October 1. At December 31 of each year, the following entries would be made:

Dec. 31	Bond Interest Expense	2,500	
	Bond Interest Payable		2,500

To accrue interest expense for three months ($100,000 $\times$ 0.10 $\times$ $\frac{3}{12}$).

31	Bond Interest Expense	125	
	Bond Discount		125

To amortize bond discount for three months ($500 annual amortization $\div$ 4).

If the bonds were issued at a premium rather than at a discount, an entry would be made amortizing the bond premium for three months. The Bond Interest Payable account is classified as a current liability in the balance sheet.

BONDS PAYABLE ON THE BALANCE SHEET   In this section we use the data relating to Ross, Inc. bonds with interest payment dates of June 30 and December 31 and straight-line amortization. Exhibit 15–1 shows that regardless of whether bond premium or bond discount is involved, the book value of bonds progresses toward and equals their face value at the time of maturity.

EXHIBIT 15–1
Amortization Schedule

At End of Year	Ross, Inc. Bonds Sold at 104 (Premium) (Straight-Line Amortization) Balances Bonds Payable (Credit)	Bond Premium (Credit)	Book Value	Ross, Inc. Bonds Sold at 98 (Discount) (Straight-Line Amortization) Balances Bonds Payable (Credit)	Bond Discount (Debit)	Book Value
At issue	$100,000	$4,000	$104,000	$100,000	$2,000	$ 98,000
19X1	100,000	3,000	103,000	100,000	1,500	98,500
19X2	100,000	2,000	102,000	100,000	1,000	99,000
19X3	100,000	1,000	101,000	100,000	500	99,500
19X4	100,000	0	100,000	100,000	0	100,000

If we assume that Ross, Inc. issued bonds at the end of 19X0 corresponding to each of the examples above, at the end of the second year the firm's trial balance would include the following accounts:

	Debit	Credit
Bond Discount, Second Mortgage Series	$1,000	
Bonds Payable, 10%, 19X4, First Mortgage Series		$100,000
Bonds Payable, 10%, 19X4, Second Mortgage Series		100,000
Bond Premium, First Mortgage Series		2,000

The Bond Premium and Bond Discount accounts are classified properly as an addition to and as a deduction from, respectively, the face value of the bonds in the balance sheet. This is done as follows:

Long-term Liabilities:

Bonds Payable, 10%, 19X4, First Mortgage Series	$100,000	
Add: Unamortized Premium	2,000	$102,000
Bonds Payable, 10%, 19X4, Second Mortgage Series	$100,000	
Less: Unamortized Discount	1,000	99,000

Bonds payable maturing within the next year should be classified as a current liability. An exception to this classification guideline arises when a bond sinking fund, a noncurrent asset, will be used to retire the bonds. In that case, because a current asset will not be utilized to retire the bonds, the bonds payable may continue to be classified as long-term liabilities.

Retirement of Bonds before Maturity

Bonds are usually retired at their maturity dates with an entry debiting Bonds Payable and crediting Cash for the amount of the face value of the bonds. However, bonds may be retired before maturity—for example, to take advantage of more attractive financing terms.

In accounting for the retirement of bonds before maturity, the following factors should be considered:

(1) Amortization of any related premium or discount to the retirement date.
(2) Removal of both the bond liability account and any related Bond Premium or Bond Discount accounts.
(3) Recognition of any gain or loss on the retirement of the bonds.

For this example, assume that the Ross, Inc. bonds were issued at 104 and were called for retirement at 105 plus accrued interest on April 1 of their fourth and final year. From Exhibit 15–1, we see that the related account balances at the end of their third year would be:

Bonds Payable	$100,000
Bond Premium	1,000

Because it is assumed that interest is paid semiannually, on June 30 and December 31, and that financial statements are prepared annually, no premium amortization entry has been made since the end of the third year. Thus, the following entries properly reflect the retirement of the bonds on April 1:

Apr. 1	Bond Premium	250	
	Bond Interest Expense		250
	To amortize bond premium for three months ($1,000/4).		
1	Bonds Payable	100,000	
	Bond Premium	750	
	Bond Interest Expense	2,500	
	Loss on Bond Retirement	4,250	
	Cash		107,500
	To retire bonds at 105 plus interest and record the loss on retirement.		

The loss on retirement is the difference between the retirement amount ($105,000) and the book value of the bonds at retirement ($100,750). The amount of interest paid at retirement ($2,500) does not affect the gain or loss on retirement. The gain or loss, if material, should be classified as an extraordinary item on the income statement.

Conversion of Bonds

Few convertible bonds are redeemed for cash, since typically, at some point in time, these bonds are converted into common stock. Because, as noted earlier, the conversion feature is attractive to potential investors, a company may issue convertible bonds at a lower interest rate than it would pay in the absence of the conversion feature.

Another reason a company may issue convertible bonds is to reduce the dilutive effect on earnings per share that would result if common stock were issued. This is because when the convertible bonds are issued, the conversion price is higher than the current market price of the stock. For example, suppose a company wishes to acquire $100,000 of funds and could issue additional common stock at $20 per share. The company would need to issue 5,000 shares to obtain $100,000. Alternatively, the firm may issue $100,000 of convertible bonds and establish a conversion price of $25 per share. When the bonds are converted into stock in the future (and the company expects this to happen), the number of common shares issued will be 4,000 ($100,000/$25). The fewer number of common shares associated with the convertible bonds produces higher earnings per share than if common stock had been issued initially.

Convertible bonds include a call feature. When the market value of the stock to be received upon conversion is significantly higher than the call price on the bond, a company may force conversion by putting a call on the bonds. Of course, one of the risks of issuing convertible bonds is that the market price of the stock may not increase in the future. Bondholders may then decide it is not to their advantage to convert the bonds, and the company is unable to force conversion by exercising the call feature.

The entry to record a bond conversion transfers the book value of the bonds to the common stock accounts. For example, assume that the Ross, Inc. bonds were issued at 98 and were convertible into 2,000 shares of $40 par value common stock. All the bonds were converted into stock on January 1 of the third year. Exhibit 15–1 shows that the book value of the bonds at the end of the second year is $99,000. The entry to record the conversion would be:

Jan. 1	Bonds Payable	100,000	
	Bond Discount		1,000
	Common Stock		80,000
	Paid-in Capital in Excess of Par Value		19,000

To record conversion of bonds into 2,000 shares of $40 par value common stock.

BOND SINKING FUNDS

To provide additional security to bondholders, some bond agreements specify that the borrower is to make periodic cash deposits to a separate fund that will be used to retire the bonds. Such a fund is termed a **bond sinking fund.** The fund is often controlled by a trustee—usually a bank or a trust company. The trustee invests the cash deposited periodically in the sinking fund in income-producing securities. The objective is to accumulate investments and investment income sufficient to retire the bonds at the time of their maturity.

We now illustrate the typical transactions for a simple bond sinking fund managed by a trustee. Assume that Ross, Inc. establishes such a fund to retire its $100,000 bond issue, which matures in four years. Ross, Inc. agrees to make equal annual deposits to the sinking fund at the end of each of the four years.

PERIODIC DEPOSIT OF CASH TO THE FUND   The amount of the equal periodic contributions is determined by compound interest tables and assumes an average annual rate of net investment income. If the trustee estimates that the sinking fund securities will earn 8% annually, Ross, Inc.'s annual cash payment to the trustee will be $22,192. Earning 8% annually, the fund will grow to $100,000 after four years, as follows:

	Annual Cash Deposit	8% Annual Interest	Fund Balance at End of Year
Year 1	$22,192	—	$ 22,192
Year 2	22,192	$1,775	46,159
Year 3	22,192	3,693	72,044
Year 4	22,192	5,764	100,000

The entry to record the annual cash deposit is:

Bond Sinking Fund	22,192	
Cash		22,192

INCOME REPORTED ON SINKING FUND SECURITIES Each period the trustee reports on the earnings of the sinking fund securities, and Ross, Inc. records these earnings on its books. For example, if the fund earned $1,775 during the second year, Ross, Inc. would make the following journal entry:

Bond Sinking Fund	1,775	
Bond Sinking Fund Income		1,775

RETIREMENT OF BONDS Usually, the trustee sells the sinking fund securities and pays the bondholders with the proceeds. Ross, Inc. would then record the retirement of the bonds as follows:

Bonds Payable	100,000	
Bond Sinking Fund		100,000

Any deficit in the sinking fund needed to retire the bonds would require Ross, Inc. to make an additional cash payment. Any surplus would be transferred to the general cash account in closing out the sinking fund.

The Bond Sinking Fund is classified in the balance sheet as an investment. Bond Sinking Fund Income is reported under Other Income and Expense in the income statement.

INVESTMENTS

Corporate stocks and bonds may be acquired by a wide variety of investors, including individuals, partnerships, corporations, mutual funds, pension funds, foundations, and trusts. Our discussion will focus on investments in stocks and bonds made by corporations.

A firm issuing stocks or bonds may sell directly to investors, or the securities may be sold through an underwriter. Most investments, however, do not involve original issues. In the typical investment, one investor purchases from another investor who happens to be selling at that time. Stocks and bonds are bought and sold on organized exchanges, such as the New York Stock Exchange, and through a less formal channel known as the *over-the-counter market*. Both the buyer and the seller of a security normally use the services of a broker to acquire or dispose of their investments.

Temporary Investments

To employ seasonal excesses of cash, many firms make short-term investments in highly marketable securities. Furthermore, some firms invest in high quality bonds and stocks as a form of "back-up cash." Management may not intend to sell these investments in the near future, but they could be converted to cash, if needed, without interfering with the normal operations of the company. In both of these cases, the investments are accounted for and classified as temporary investments.

MEASUREMENT OF TEMPORARY INVESTMENTS   Temporary investments, whether in stocks or bonds, are recorded at cost (including any acquisition costs such as brokerage commissions) and should appear on the balance sheet just below Cash. Bond investments continue to be carried at historical cost unless their market value is substantially below cost and evidence indicates the decline in market value is not due to a temporary condition. If the latter situation exists, the investments are written down to market value.

Stock investments having a ready market are generally carried at the lower of cost or market value of the portfolio, determined at the balance sheet date. Thus, their carrying value may increase or decrease from period to period (but may never increase above cost), with the unrealized losses or recoveries of unrealized losses being included in the income statement.[2] For example, assume that a company has the following portfolio of temporary investments in marketable stocks at the end of its first year of operations:

Portfolio	Cost	Market Value
Stock A	$17,000	$15,000
Stock B	12,000	13,000
Stock C	14,000	11,000
Total	$43,000	$39,000

The stock investments will be shown at $39,000 on the balance sheet, with an unrealized loss of $4,000 reported in the current year's income statement. Now, suppose the market value of the portfolio at the end of the next year improves by $1,000 (so that it is now only $3,000 below total cost). The carrying value of the stock investments is then adjusted upward by $1,000, and the $1,000 recovery of the unrealized loss is reported in that year's income statement.

TEMPORARY INVESTMENTS IN BONDS   Let us assume that $10,000 of International Manufacturing 9% bonds are bought on May 1 at 97 plus accrued interest. The brokerage commission is $20. The bonds pay interest semiannually on January 1 and July 1. The accrued interest from January 1 to May 1 is $300 ($10,000 $\times$ 0.09 $\times$ $\frac{4}{12}$) and should be recorded separately in a Bond Interest Receivable account. The cost to be entered in the bond investment account is $9,720, including the brokerage commission. The following entry records the acquisition:

---

[2]Unrealized losses are losses on securities still owned by the firm. For details, see *Statement of Financial Accounting Standards No. 12, Accounting for Certain Marketable Securities*, Financial Accounting Standards Board, Stamford, Conn., 1975.

May 1	International Manufacturing Bonds	9,720	
	Bond Interest Receivable	300	
	Cash		10,020

To record purchase of bonds at 97 plus
commission of $20 plus four months'
accrued interest.

The entry to record the receipt of the semiannual interest payment on July 1 would be:

July 1	Cash	450	
	Bond Interest Receivable		300
	Bond Interest Income		150

To record receipt of semiannual interest on
International Manufacturing bonds.

The credit to interest income for $150 reflects the interest earned for the two months the bonds have been held. No amortization of bond discount (or bond premium where appropriate) is shown. The amortization is usually omitted because it would not be sufficiently material. Furthermore, often it is not expected that the bonds will be held to maturity.

Temporary investments are usually sold at a gain or loss. The gain or loss on the sale of bonds is computed by comparing the proceeds of the sale, net of any accrued interest received, to the carrying value of the investment. If the proceeds from the sale of the International Manufacturing bonds on September 1 were $9,800 plus accrued interest for two months, the following entry would be made:

Sept. 1	Cash	9,950	
	International Manufacturing Bonds		9,720
	Bond Interest Income		150
	Gain on Sale of Investments		80

To record sale of bond investment for
$9,800 plus interest of $150.

TEMPORARY INVESTMENTS IN STOCKS   As with bonds, the initial recording of a short-term investment in stock is based on the expenditures incurred to acquire the security. Suppose 100 shares of United Pride common stock are acquired on October 1 at a cost of $4,290, including commissions and taxes. The investment is recorded as follows:

| Oct. 1 | United Pride Stock | 4,290 | |
| | Cash | | 4,290 |

To record purchase of 100 shares of
common stock for $4,290.

Dividends do not accrue on shares of stock. A corporation has no legal obligation to pay a dividend until it is declared by the board of directors. A company holding stock may record the dividend after it has been declared by debiting Dividends Receivable and crediting Dividend Income, but ordinarily no entry is made until the dividend is received. If the United Pride board of directors declares a dividend of $1.00 per share, and assuming dividend income is recorded when received, the entry to record the receipt of the dividend would be:

Cash	100	
Dividend Income		100

To record receipt of $100 dividend on
investment in United Pride stock.

The receipt of a stock dividend (rather than a cash dividend) does not constitute income, and thus no formal journal entry is required. A memorandum of the number of shares received, however, should be recorded in the investment account. The recipient of the stock dividend now holds more stock without further investment, so the average cost of each share held has been reduced. If United Pride declares a 10% common stock dividend, the company holding 100 shares of United Pride would make the following notation upon receipt of 10 additional shares:

(Memorandum)   Received 10 shares of United Pride common stock
as stock dividend. Average cost per share of 110 shares held is now
$39.00 ($4,290/110).

A gain or loss on the sale of stock is computed in the same manner as on the sale of bonds—it is equal to the difference between the proceeds of the sale and the carrying value of the stock investment. Dividend income, interest income, and gains and losses on the sale of temporary investments are reported on the income statement under Other Income and Expense.

Long-term Investments

Both stocks and bonds may be acquired as long-term investments. Commonly, a firm makes such investments to provide financial assistance to, or to gain influence over, important supplier or customer firms. All long-term investments are initially recorded at cost and are presented on the balance sheet as noncurrent assets in a section just below current assets and above plant assets.

LONG-TERM INVESTMENTS IN BONDS   Because bonds acquired as a long-term investment may be held for extended periods, the related premium or discount is usually amortized to interest income. Let us consider a brief illustration. Assume that ten National Telephone $10,000, 8% bonds are purchased on one of their semiannual interest dates (January 1) 10 years prior to maturity. The bonds were purchased at 98 plus a $200 commission and therefore cost $98,200. Because the bonds will have a maturity value of $100,000 in 10 years, the bond discount is $1,800, which will be amortized (using the straight-line method) at the rate of $90 at the end of each of the 20 remaining semiannual interest periods ($1,800/ 20 = $90). The entry to record the purchase is:

Jan. 1	National Telephone Bonds	98,200	
	Cash		98,200

To record purchase of ten bonds at 98 on interest date plus commission of $200.

Note that although the bond discount is to be amortized, no Bond Discount account is established. The investment is initially recorded at cost, and the discount amortization entry is made directly to the asset account. For example, on the next interest date, the entries to record receipt of interest and amortization of discount are:

July 1	Cash	4,000	
	Bond Interest Income		4,000

To record receipt of semiannual interest on National Telephone bonds.

1	National Telephone Bonds	90	
	Bond Interest Income		90

To record semiannual amortization of discount on National Telephone bonds.

As in the case of Bonds Payable on the books of borrowers, the carrying value of the bonds will increase until they reach their maturity value on their maturity date.

When the purchase price of a bond exceeds its maturity value, the bond is still recorded at cost and the related premium amortization entry involves a debit to Bond Interest Income and a credit to the Investment account. Thus, the carrying value of bonds acquired at a premium progresses downward toward maturity value. Also, the net amount of interest income reported is less (by the amount of premium amortized) than the cash being received as interest income each period.

Bonds may be sold before they reach maturity. Assume that on January 1, five years after they were purchased, the National Telephone bonds were sold at $99\frac{1}{2}$ less a commission of $150. Discount amortization, over the ten semiannual interest periods during which the bonds were held, would have raised their carrying value to $99,100 ($98,200 + [10 × $90] = $99,100). Again, one figures the accounting gain by comparing the book value of the asset to the net proceeds from the sale. The sale is recorded as follows:

Jan. 1	Cash	99,350	
	National Telephone Bonds		99,100
	Gain on Sale of Investments		250

To record sale of bond investment at $99\frac{1}{2}$ less a commission of $150.

LONG-TERM INVESTMENTS IN STOCKS   Although all long-term investments in stock are first entered in the accounts at cost, the subsequent accounting procedures differ according to the circumstances. Basically, the accounting treatment employed depends on whether the ownership interest acquired is a controlling interest, an interest that permits the investor company to exercise significant influence over the company whose stock is held, or an interest that is neither controlling nor influential.

Noncontrolling and noninfluential interest. Investments amounting to less than 20% of the voting stock of a corporation are considered small enough to preclude the investor company from significantly influencing the policies of the company whose stock is acquired. These investments are initially recorded at cost, and cash dividends are recorded as income when received. These procedures are known as the **cost method** of accounting for such investments. For each balance sheet presentation, however, these investments are carried at the lower of cost or market value of the portfolio, determined at the balance sheet date.

BOND INVESTMENTS AND THEIR RATING

In general, bonds present less risk than stocks do: they do not fluctuate as much in price and, since they do pay a fixed interest, they always have some value as long as the company is able to pay that interest. Stocks can drop much faster and farther when a company encounters a few rough years during which it sustains losses and pays no dividends. Even when a company manages to survive a stormy period, its stock can shrink to a fraction of what it was at its height. But as long as the company remains solvent, it will continue to pay interest to its bondholders. Even if the company goes bankrupt, its bondholders have prior claim to its assets, ahead of its stockholders.

Any investor in bonds wishing to minimize his risk can limit his purchases to the bonds of the soundest major corporations, those which are most unlikely to go bankrupt or default on interest payments. You can be fairly sure that you are buying a quality bond by checking on its rating. Bonds are rated by four investment advisory companies: Standard & Poor's, Moody's, Fitch's, and Dun & Bradstreet. Standard & Poor's, for example, rates bonds as AAA, AA, A, BBB, and so on, down to D, which means "defaulted."

If you buy only bonds rated A or higher, your investment *should* be secure. But you can never have complete assurance. The Penn Central's bonds had a good rating even when the railroad company stood on the brink of bankruptcy. Even among experts there were apparently few who realized how serious the company's problems were.

Usually, however, a high rating for a bond means that you can feel relatively safe. If you buy a bond with a lower rating, your increased risk will usually buy you higher interest—which is fair enough. Why should you take on a greater risk with your money without getting a greater reward? . . .

When you pick stocks, you choose industries and companies that you like. When you pick bonds, you are making a judgment about interest rates; all bonds of comparable quality tend to rise and fall in unison.

From Everett B. Mattlin and the editors of Dreyfus Publications, *Understanding and Using the Language of Wall Street* (New York: Dreyfus Publications Ltd., 1973), pp. 148–49, 152.

Thus, like temporary stock investments, their carrying value may increase or decrease from period to period (but may never increase above cost). Unlike temporary stock investments, however, any unrealized losses or recoveries of unrealized losses are not shown in the income statement; instead, the net unrealized loss on the portfolio of long-term stock investments is reported separately as a contra owners' equity account in the balance sheet.[3]

Influential but noncontrolling interest. If a corporation owns 20% or more of the voting stock of another corporation, it is in a position to exert a significant influence on the operating or financial decisions of that company. However, if the voting stock owned is 50% or less of the total, the investment will not usually represent a controlling interest. Investments in the ownership range of 20% through 50% may therefore be considered as influential but noncontrolling interests. The **equity method** is appropriate for investments in this category.

Under the equity method, the investor company records as income or loss each period its proportionate share of the income or loss reported for that period by the company whose stock is held. For example, if Warner Company owns 30% of the voting stock of Rose Corporation and Rose Corporation reports earnings of $20,000 for the current year, Warner Company would make the following entry under the equity method:

Investment in Rose Corporation Stock	6,000	
Income from Investment in Rose		
Corporation		6,000

To record as income 30% of Rose Corporation's current year earnings of $20,000.

The investor company reports no income when cash dividends are received. As the preceding entry shows, when the investor company does record its share of the other corporation's income, the investment amount is also increased. The receipt of a dividend, then, is treated as a reduction of the investment balance. To illustrate, suppose the Rose Corporation declared and paid a $7,000 dividend for the current year. Warner Company's entry upon receipt of its share of the dividend is:

Cash	2,100	
Investment in Rose Corporation Stock		2,100

To record receipt of $2,100 dividend from Rose Corporation.

Controlling interest. A company holding more than 50% of the stock of another corporation owns a controlling interest. In some cases, such as by agreement

---

[3]See *Statement of Financial Accounting Standards No. 12, Accounting for Certain Marketable Securities*, Financial Accounting Standards Board, Stamford, Conn., 1975.

with other stockholders, control may exist with a lesser percentage of stock ownership. The financial data of the controlled corporations are usually consolidated with the data of the investor company in a consolidated financial statement. Either the cost or equity method may be used for investments in these controlled corporations; in either case, the application of consolidation procedures yields the same final result. The equity method should be used for controlling investments in corporations whose data will not be consolidated. This topic is examined in more detail in Chapter 19, which deals with consolidated financial statements.

CORPORATION BALANCE SHEET

Exhibit 15–2 is a comprehensive illustration of a corporation's balance sheet and contains many of the items discussed in this chapter and in Chapters 13 and 14.

EXHIBIT 15–2

Superior Corporation
Balance Sheet
December 31, 19XX

ASSETS

Current Assets

Cash		$ 20,000	
Short-term Investments (at lower of cost or market)		10,000	
Accounts Receivable	$65,000		
Less: Allowance for Uncollectible Accounts	5,000	60,000	
Inventories (at lower of cost or market)		120,000	
Prepaid Expenses		10,000	
Total Current Assets			$220,000

Investments

Sinking Fund for Bond Retirement			20,000

Plant Assets	Cost	Accumulated Depreciation	Book Value	
Machinery and Equipment	$170,000	$30,000	$140,000	
Buildings	100,000	20,000	80,000	
Land	30,000	—	30,000	
Total Plant Assets				250,000

Intangible Assets

Goodwill		$ 28,000	
Patents (less $6,000 accumulated amortization)		12,000	
Total Intangible Assets			40,000
Total Assets			$530,000

EXHIBIT 15–2 (continued)

Superior Corporation
Balance Sheet
December 31, 19XX (continued)

LIABILITIES

Current Liabilities

Accounts Payable	$ 45,000	
Income Taxes Payable	18,000	
Dividends Payable	15,000	
Accrued Payables	2,000	
Total Current Liabilities		$ 80,000

Long-term Liabilities

First Mortgage, 9% Bonds Payable (due 1990)	$100,000	
Premium on First Mortgage Bonds	6,000	106,000
Total Liabilities		$186,000

STOCKHOLDERS' EQUITY

Paid-in Capital

Common Stock, $100 Par Value, authorized and issued 2,000 shares, 50 shares in treasury	$200,000	
Paid-in Capital in Excess of Par Value	20,000	
Total Paid-in Capital		$220,000

Retained Earnings

Appropriated for Plant Expansion	$ 44,000	
Appropriated for Treasury Stock	6,000	
Unappropriated	80,000	
Total Retained Earnings		130,000
		$350,000
Less: Treasury Stock (50 shares) at Cost		6,000
Total Stockholders' Equity		$344,000
Total Liabilities and Stockholders' Equity		$530,000

KEY POINTS TO REMEMBER

(1) To sell bonds payable is to borrow money for which interest expense is incurred.

(2) The amount of bond discount or premium (a) is determined by the difference between the nominal interest rate on the bonds and the applicable market rate of interest, and (b) should be considered a long-term adjustment of interest expense.

(3) Bonds payable should be presented in the balance sheet at their face value plus any related premium or less any related discount.

(4) When convertible bonds are converted, the book value of the bonds is transferred to the common stock accounts.

(5) Investments in bonds are recorded at cost, and related interest income is accrued. Bond premium and discount are normally amortized on long-term investments, but omitted on short-term investments.

(6) Short-term investments in stock are normally carried at the lower of cost or market value of the portfolio. Unrealized losses or recoveries of unrealized losses are included in the income statement.

(7) Long-term investments in stock are carried as follows:

  (a) *Noninfluential and noncontrolling interest* (usually less than 20% of the voting stock): carried at the lower of cost or market value of the portfolio. The net unrealized loss is shown as a contra account in the owners' equity section of the balance sheet.

  (b) *Influential but noncontrolling interest* (usually 20% through 50% of voting stock): carried on the equity method.

  (c) *Controlling interest* (usually more than 50% of voting stock): if the statements of the controlled firm are consolidated with the investor's, either the equity method or the cost method can be used. Otherwise, the equity method is used.

QUESTIONS

15–1 Define the following terms:

(a) mortgage notes	(b) bonds payable
(c) trustee	(d) secured bonds
(e) serial bonds	(f) callable bonds
(g) convertible bonds	(h) face value
(i) nominal interest rate	(j) bond discount
(k) bond premium	(l) amortization of bond premium or discount

15–2 Explain how issuing bonds at a premium or discount "adjusts the nominal rate to the applicable market rate of interest."

15–3 A $1,000,000 issue of 10-year, 9% bonds was sold at 97 plus accrued interest two months after the bonds were dated. What is the net amount of cash to be received?

15–4 What generalization can be made, regardless of whether premium or discount is involved, about the change in the book value of bonds payable during the period in which they are outstanding?

15–5 How should bond premium and bond discount on bonds payable be presented in the balance sheet?

15–6 On May 31, 19X6, 7 months before maturity, the Rockton Company retired $10,000 of 9% bonds payable at 103 plus accrued interest. The book value of the bonds on May 31 was $9,800. Bond interest had last been paid on December 31, 19X5. What is the gain or loss on the retirement of the bonds?

15-7 Give reasons why a convertible bond may be attractive to both an investor and the issuing company. Why do corporations typically include a call feature in a convertible bond?

15-8 What is the purpose of a bond sinking fund? Where is the bond sinking fund classified in the balance sheet?

15-9 Why do corporations make temporary investments in securities? Where should temporary investments be classified in the balance sheet?

15-10 Why are premiums and discounts on short-term investments in bonds usually not amortized?

15-11 Interest on temporary bond investments is accrued, but dividends on stock investments are not accrued. Why?

15-12 What entry, if any, should be made when a corporation receives a stock dividend on a temporary stock investment? What entry should be made when a cash dividend is received on a temporary stock investment?

15-13 The Norse Company invested in bonds at a premium on a long-term basis. Should the bond premium be amortized? Where should the bond investment be classified in the balance sheet?

15-14 How are temporary stock investments and long-term stock investments of less than 20% of a corporation's voting stock reported in the balance sheet? Where are unrealized losses on the portfolio of temporary stock investments reported? Where is the net unrealized loss on the portfolio of noncontrolling and noninfluential long-term stock investments reported?

15-15 Describe the accounting procedures to be used for long-term stock investments when the stock held represents from 20% through 50% of the voting stock.

EXERCISES

15-16 On January 1, the Rollins Company issued $80,000 of 20-year, 9% convertible bonds at 101. Interest is payable semiannually on June 30 and December 31. Each $1,000 bond may be converted into 40 shares of $25 par value common stock. Present journal entries to reflect (a) the issuance of the bonds, (b) the payment of interest for the first six months, (c) the premium amortization for the first six months, and (d) the conversion of $40,000 face amount of bonds into stock exactly five years after the issuance of the bonds.

15-17 The Perk Company issued $300,000 of 10-year, 8% bonds at 99. The bonds were issued on March 1, 19X1, with interest payable semiannually on March 1 and September 1. Present journal entries to reflect (a) the issuance of the bonds, (b) the payment of interest for the first six months, (c) the discount amortization for the first six months, and (d) the retirement of the bonds at 102 plus accrued interest on July 1, 19X5.

15-18 The adjusted trial balance for the Carroll Corporation at the end of the current year contains the following accounts:

Bond Interest Payable	$ 23,500
9% Bonds Payable	300,000
10% Bonds Payable	200,000
Discount on 9% Bonds Payable	6,000
Premium on 10% Bonds Payable	4,000
Sinking Fund for Bond Retirement	90,000

Prepare the long-term liabilities section of the balance sheet. Indicate the proper balance sheet classification for accounts listed above that do not belong in the long-term liabilities section.

15-19 As a short-term investment, ten $1,000, 8% bonds were purchased at 97 three months after they were dated. Present journal entries to reflect (a) their purchase for cash, (b) the receipt of the first semiannual interest payment, and (c) the receipt of the second semiannual interest payment (assume bond discount is not amortized).

15-20 Present a journal entry to record the sale of the bonds described in Exercise 15–19 at 98 plus accrued interest exactly two years after their purchase.

15-21 As a long-term investment, six 10-year $1,000, 9% bonds were purchased at 105 on the first day of their first semiannual interest period. Present journal entries to record (a) their purchase for cash, (b) the receipt of the first two semiannual interest payments, (c) the two semiannual amortizations of bond premium for the first year, and (d) the sale of the bonds at 101 three years after they were purchased.

15-22 As a long-term investment, 1,200 shares of Snider Company common stock were acquired on March 10, 19X1, at a total cost of $60,720. The shares held represent 10% of the voting stock of the company. On December 28, 19X1, Snider Company declared a cash dividend of $1.00 per share. The dividend was received on January 15, 19X2. Present the necessary journal entries to reflect (a) the purchase of the stock, and (b) the receipt of the cash dividend. Dividend income is recorded when dividends are received.

15-23 Assume the 1,200 shares purchased in Exercise 15–22 represent 25% of the voting stock of Snider Company. Snider Company's 19X1 net income was $20,000. Using the equity method, present the journal entries to reflect (a) the purchase of the stock, (b) the proportionate share of Snider Company's 19X1 net income (dated December 31, 19X1), and (c) the receipt of the cash dividend.

PROBLEMS

15-24 On January 1, 19X3, Patch, Inc. sold at 96 a $600,000 issue of 10% bonds that mature in 10 years. Bond interest is payable on June 30 and December 31. Patch's accounting year ends on December 31.

REQUIRED
(a) Show all entries pertaining to the bonds for the year 19X3.

(b) Present the entries necessary to properly record the retirement of half of the bonds at 101 plus accrued interest on March 1, 19X6.

15-25 Hizer, Inc., which closes its books on December 31, is authorized to issue $800,000 of 9%, 12-year bonds dated April 1, 1980, with interest payments on October 1 and April 1.

REQUIRED

Present general journal entries to record the events listed below, assuming the bonds were (a) sold at $98\frac{1}{2}$ on April 1, 1980; (b) sold at $103\frac{1}{2}$ plus accrued interest on August 1, 1980.

(1) The bond issue.

(2) Payment of the first semiannual period's interest and amortization on that date of any related bond premium or discount (straight-line method).

(3) Accrual of bond interest expense and any related bond premium or discount amortization at December 31, 1980.

(4) Retirement of $200,000 of the bonds at 102 on April 1, 1986.

15-26 Rodon, Inc. issued $50,000 of bonds and is required by its bond agreement to maintain a bond sinking fund managed by a trustee. The following transactions relate to the fund at various times in its life.

(1) A periodic cash deposit of $3,450 is made to the fund.

(2) The trustee reports the sinking fund had earnings of $1,244 during the period.

(3) The trustee reports the sinking fund securities have been sold and the $50,000 of outstanding bonds have been retired. Just before this report, the Bond Sinking Fund account for Rodon, Inc. showed a balance of $50,000. The trustee also reports the sale of the securities generated an unexpected gain of $1,000, and a check for this amount accompanies the trustee's report (credit to Bond Sinking Fund Income).

REQUIRED

Present general journal entries for the above sinking fund transactions.

15-27 Following are selected transactions of the Thorn Corporation for the years 19X1 and 19X2. The company closes its books on December 31.

19X1

Jan. 1 Issued $150,000 of 7%, 10-year convertible bonds at 98. Interest is payable on January 1 and July 1. The conversion feature permits the holder of each $1,000 bond to convert it into 15 shares of $60 par value Thorn Corporation common stock.

Mar. 14 Purchased, as a temporary investment, 2,400 shares of Stonewood, Inc. common stock at a total cost of $47,520.

July 1 Paid semiannual interest and recorded semiannual discount amortization (straight-line method) on convertible bonds.

1 Purchased, as a long-term investment, thirty $1,000, 9% Batt Company bonds at 103. The bonds pay interest on July 1 and January 1 and mature in 10 years.

Dec. 20   Stonewood, Inc. declared a cash dividend of $0.60 per common share plus a 10% stock dividend, payable on January 12 to stockholders of record on December 30. (Thorn Corporation records dividend income when dividends are received.)

     31   Recorded accrued interest payable and semiannual discount amortization on convertible bonds and accrued interest receivable and semiannual premium amortization on Batt Company bonds. (Thorn Corporation does not use reversing entries.)

19X2

Jan. 1   Paid semiannual interest on convertible bonds and received semiannual interest on Batt Company bonds.

      2   $15,000 of convertible bonds were converted to common stock.

     13   Received cash and stock dividends from Stonewood, Inc. (declared on December 20, 19X1).

Feb. 11   Sold all Stonewood, Inc. stock for $52,800.

REQUIRED
Record the above transactions in general journal form.

15-28 The following transactions relate to certain bonds acquired by Handel Corporation as a long-term investment.

19X2

Mar. 1   Purchased $600,000 (face value) of Damon, Inc. 20-year, 8% bonds dated January 1, 19X2, directly from the issuing company for $609,520 plus accrued interest. Interest is paid January 1 and July 1.

July 1   Received semiannual interest on Damon, Inc. bonds and amortized the related bond premium.

Dec. 31   Accrued interest receivable on Damon, Inc. bonds and amortized the related bond premium. (Handel Corporation does not use reversing entries.)

19X4

Jan. 2   Received semiannual interest on Damon, Inc. bonds.

May   1   Sold the Damon, Inc. bonds at 101 plus accrued interest. A selling commission of $500 was deducted from the proceeds. Amortized bond premium to date of sale.

REQUIRED
Record the above transactions in general journal form.

15-29 On January 2, 19X1, Keller Corporation purchased, as a long-term investment, 6,000 shares of Navee Company common stock at a cost of $13 per share, including commissions and taxes. On December 31, 19X1, Navee Company announced a net income of $120,000 for the year and a dividend of $1.10 per share, payable January 20, 19X2, to stockholders of record on January 10, 19X2. Keller Corporation received its dividend on January 21, 19X2.

REQUIRED
(a) Assume the stock acquired by Keller Corporation represents 12% of the voting stock of Navee Company. Prepare all journal entries appropriate for

this investment (and the dividend), beginning with the purchase on January 2, 19X1, and ending with the receipt of the dividend on January 21, 19X2. (Keller Corporation does not recognize dividend income when the dividends are declared.)

(b) Assume the stock acquired by Keller Corporation represents 30% of the voting stock of Navee Company. Prepare all journal entries appropriate for this investment (and the dividend), beginning with the purchase on January 2, 19X1, and ending with the receipt of the dividend on January 21, 19X2.

ALTERNATE PROBLEMS

15-24A On January 1, 19X6, Rival, Inc. sold at 105 a $400,000 issue of 8% bonds that mature in 20 years. Bond interest is payable on June 30 and December 31. Rival's accounting year ends on December 31.

REQUIRED

(a) Show all entries pertaining to the bonds for the year 19X6.
(b) Present the entries necessary to record properly the retirement of half of the bonds at 105 plus accrued interest on April 1, 19X9.

15-25A Vendo, Inc., which closes its books on December 31, is authorized to issue $300,000 of 9%, 15-year bonds dated March 1, 1980, with interest payments on March 1 and September 1.

REQUIRED

Present general journal entries to record the following events, assuming the bonds were (a) sold at 96 on March 1, 1980; (b) sold at 102 plus accrued interest on July 1, 1980.

(1) The bond issue.
(2) Payment of the first semiannual period's interest and amortization on that date of any related bond premium or discount (straight-line method).
(3) Accrual of bond interest expense and any related bond premium or discount amortization at December 31, 1980 (compute to the nearest dollar).
(4) Retirement of $200,000 of the bonds at 101 on March 1, 1990.

15-27A Following are selected transactions of the Cable Corporation for the years 19X7 and 19X8. The company closes its books on December 31.

19X7

Jan.   1   Issued $200,000 of 8%, 15-year bonds payable at 97. Interest is payable on January 1 and July 1.

May 19   Purchased, as a long-term investment, 3,000 shares of Monroe, Inc. common stock at a total cost of $54,000. Monroe, Inc. has several hundred thousand shares of stock outstanding.

July   1   Paid semiannual interest and recorded semiannual discount amortization (straight-line method) on bonds.

Sept. 1   Purchased, as a temporary investment, twenty $1,000, $7\frac{1}{2}$% Rand Company bonds at 102 plus accrued interest. The bonds pay interest on June 1 and December 1.

Dec. 2 Received semiannual interest on Rand Company bonds.

18 Monroe, Inc. declared a cash dividend of $0.50 per common share plus a 15% stock dividend, payable on January 10 to stockholders of record on December 30. (Cable Corporation records dividend income when dividends are received.)

31 Recorded accrued interest payable and semiannual discount amortization on bonds payable and accrued interest receivable on Rand Company bonds. (Cable Corporation does not use reversing entries.)

19X8

Jan. 1 Paid semiannual interest on bonds payable.

2 $20,000 of bonds payable were retired at 99.

11 Received cash and stock dividends from Monroe, Inc. (declared on December 18, 19X7).

Feb. 1 Sold Rand Company bonds at 101 plus accrued interest.

REQUIRED
Record the above transactions in general journal form.

15–28A The following transactions relate to certain bonds acquired by Arcan Corporation as a long-term investment.

19X2

Feb. 1 Purchased $500,000 (face value) of Knox, Inc. 20-year, 9% bonds dated January 1, 19X2, directly from the issuing company for $485,660 plus accrued interest. Interest is paid January 1 and July 1.

July 1 Received semiannual interest on Knox, Inc. bonds and amortized the related bond discount.

Dec. 31 Accrued interest receivable on Knox, Inc. bonds and amortized the related bond discount. (Arcan Corporation does not use reversing entries.)

19X4

Jan. 2 Received semiannual interest on Knox, Inc. bonds.

May 1 Sold the Knox, Inc. bonds at 99 plus accrued interest. A selling commission of $600 was deducted from the proceeds. Amortized bond discount to date of sale.

REQUIRED
Record the above transactions in general journal form.

BUSINESS DECISION PROBLEM

In reviewing the preliminary data for the 19X3 financial statements of Street Company, Anna Lizer, controller, is surprised at the large amount of dividend income— $35,910. She knows the company has only one common stock investment—a long-term investment in the stock of Clad Corporation. She asks you to review the transactions affecting the account and determine what should be the proper dividend income for 19X3.

The Dividend Income account shows the following entries for 19X3:

Jan.	18	Cash dividend	$ 7,875
	18	Stock dividend	7,980
Dec.	31	Income earned	11,550
	31	Dividend declared	2,835
	31	Dividend accrued	5,670
		Total	$35,910

You know it is the policy of Street Company to record dividend income when the dividends are received. You discover the following additional information about the common stock investment in Clad Corporation:

(1) Street Company purchased 5,250 shares of Clad Corporation, as a long-term investment, in 19X0 for $84,000. These shares represent 15% of the outstanding, voting shares of Clad Corporation.

(2) On December 31, 19X2, Clad Corporation announced a cash dividend of $1.50 per share and an 8% stock dividend, payable January 17, 19X3, to stockholders of record on January 10, 19X3. Street Company received these dividends on January 18, 19X3. The market value of a share of Clad Corporation's common stock on January 18, 19X3 was $19.

(3) On December 31, 19X3, Clad Corporation announced a net income for the year of $77,000. The Street Company bookkeeper used the equity method to record 15% of this amount as income for Street Company, crediting $11,550 to the Dividend Income account.

(4) Also on December 31, 19X3, Clad Corporation announced a $0.50 per share cash dividend, payable January 17, 19X4, to stockholders of record on January 10, 19X4. The president expressed regret that, because of a cash flow problem, the corporation was not able to declare its regular $1.50 per share dividend. The president indicated the corporation would have the cash flow problem straightened out by the end of January, at which time it fully intended to declare a special cash dividend of $1.00 per share. Based on this announcement, the Street Company bookkeeper debited Dividends Receivable for the dividend of $0.50 per share (on 5,670 shares). In addition, the bookkeeper accrued the special dividend of $1.00 per share (debiting Dividends Receivable). These amounts were credited to Dividend Income.

REQUIRED

Compute the proper amount of 19X3 dividend income for Street Company. Also, indicate the correct treatment for any items currently in the Dividend Income account that do not belong there.

PRESENT VALUES AND EFFECTIVE INTEREST AMORTIZATION

This appendix expands on the ideas in Chapter 15 related to the amortization of bond premium and discount. In our examples of Chapter 15, the amounts of bond premium and discount amortized were equal, or "straight-line," amounts for each accounting period. Here we illustrate a somewhat more sophisticated approach called the "effective interest," "compound interest," or "scientific" method of calculating the periodic amount of bond premium or discount amortization. To give some background to the subject of effective interest amortization, we introduce briefly the concept of present value and the techniques of bond valuation.

PRESENT VALUES

The Concept of Present Value

Would you rather receive a dollar now or a dollar one year from now? Most persons would answer, "a dollar now." Intuition tells us that a dollar now is more valuable than receiving the same amount sometime in the future. There are sound reasons for choosing the earlier dollar, the most obvious of which concerns risk. Because the future is always uncertain, an event may occur that would prevent us from receiving the dollar at the later date. To avoid this risk, we choose the earlier date.

A second reason for choosing the earlier date is that the dollar received now could be invested; one year from now we could have not only the dollar, but also the interest income for the period. The risk and interest factors, therefore, enable us to generalize that (1) the right to receive an amount of money now—its **present value**—is normally worth more than the right to receive the same amount later—its future value; (2) the longer one must wait to receive an amount, the less attractive the receipt is; and (3) the difference in the present value of an amount and its future value is a function of interest (or more specifically, principal × interest rate × time period). The more risk associated with any situation, the higher the appropriate interest rate.

The next illustration supports these generalizations. What amount could we accept now that would be as valuable as receiving $100 one year from now if the appropriate interest rate is 10%? We recognize intuitively that a 10% interest rate indicates that we should accept less than $100, or more specifically, approximately $91. This estimate is based on the realization that the $100 to be received in the future must equal the present value (100%) plus 10% interest on the present value. Thus, in our example, the $100 future receipt must be 1.10 times the present value. Dividing ($100/1.10), we obtain a present value of $90.90. In other words, under the given conditions we would do as well to accept $90.90 now as to wait one year and receive $100. To confirm the equality of a $90.90 receipt now to a $100 receipt one year later, we may calculate the future value of $90.90 at 10% for one year as follows:

$$\$90.90 \times 1.10 \times 1 \text{ year} = \$100 \text{ (rounded)}$$

Thus, the present value of a future receipt can be computed by discounting (deducting an interest factor) the future receipt back to the present at an appropriate interest rate. We present this schematically below.

Present value, $90.90	⟵	Discounted for one year at 10%	⟵	Future value, $100

If either the time period or the interest rate were increased, the resulting present value would decrease. If more than one time period is involved, compound interest computations are appropriate.

Use of Present Value Tables

Because present value tables, such as Table I on page 989, are widely available, it is not necessary for us to know, or to present here, the various formulas for interest computations. Table I can be used to compute the present value amounts in the illustrations and problem materials that follow. Simply stated, for many combinations of time periods and interest rates, present value tables provide a multiplier that when applied to the dollar amount of a future receipt determines its present value.

Present value tables are used as follows. First, determine the number of interest compounding periods involved (three years compounded annually is three periods, three years compounded semiannually is six periods, three years compounded quarterly is 12 periods, and so on). The number of periods covered in the table is indicated in the extreme left-hand column.

Next, determine the interest rate per compounding period. Note that interest rates are usually quoted on a *per year* basis. Therefore, only in the case of annual compoundings will the quoted interest rate be the interest rate per compounding period. In other cases, the rate per compounding period is the rate per year divided by the number of compounding periods in a year. For example, an interest rate of 10% per year would be 10% for one compounding period if compounded annually, 5% for two compounding periods if compounded semiannually, and $2\frac{1}{2}\%$ for four compounding periods if compounded quarterly.

To apply the table to any given situation, locate the factor that is to the right of the appropriate number of compounding periods and beneath the appropriate interest rate per compounding period. Then multiply this factor by the number of dollars involved.

Note the logical progressions among multipliers in Table I. All values are less than 1.0 because the present value will always be smaller than the future amount if the interest rate is greater than zero. Also, as the interest rate increases (moving from left to right in the table) or the number of periods increases (moving from top to bottom), the multipliers become smaller.

EXAMPLE 1   Compute the present value of $100 one year hence, at 10% interest compounded annually.

> Number of periods (one year, annually) = 1
> Rate per period (10%/1) = 10%
> Multiplier = 0.909
> Present value = $100.00 × 0.909 = $90.90
> (Note that this agrees with our earlier illustration.)

EXAMPLE 2   Compute the present value of $116.99 two years hence, at 8% compounded semiannually.

> Number of periods (two years, semiannually) = 4
> Rate per period (8%/2) = 4%
> Multiplier = 0.855
> Present value = $116.99 × 0.855 = $100 (rounded)

The Annuity Form of Cash Flows

Using present value tables, we can compute the present value of any single future receipt or series of future receipts. One pattern of cash receipts that appears often, however, is subject to a more convenient treatment. This pattern, known as the **annuity form,** can be described as *equal amounts equally spaced over a time period.*

For example, $100 is to be received at the end of each of the next three years as an annuity. As shown below, the present value of this annuity can be computed from Table I by computing the present value of each of the three individual receipts and summing them (assuming interest to be 5% annually).

Future Receipts (annuity)				PV Multiplier (Table I)		Present Value
Yr. 1	Yr. 2	Yr. 3				
$100			×	0.952	=	$ 95.20
	$100		×	0.907	=	90.70
		$100	×	0.864	=	86.40
				Total present value		$272.30

Table II (page 990) provides a single multiplier for computing the present value of a series of future cash receipts that are in the annuity form. Referring to Table II in the "3 periods" row and under the 5% column, we see that the multiplier is 2.723. Applied to the amount of the annuity, $100, it results in a present value of $272.30. Of course, this is the same as the present value derived from the several multipliers of Table I. For annuities of 5, 10, or 20 years, the computations avoided by using annuity tables are considerable.

Bond Valuations

In Chapter 15 we explained that (1) the essence of a bond investment is lending money; (2) the amount received by the lender consists of a series (usually semi-annual) of interest income amounts and a single lump sum repayment of the bond principal; and (3) bonds are sold at premiums or discounts as a means of adjusting their effective interest rates to the prevailing market rate at the time they are issued.

Because of the role of interest in bond investments, the selling price (or valuation) of a bond that is necessary to yield a specific rate can be determined as follows:

(1) Use Table I to compute the present value of the future principal repayment at the desired (or effective) rate of interest.

(2) Use Table II to compute the present value of the future series of interest receipts at the desired (or effective) rate of interest.

(3) Add the present values obtained in (1) and (2).

We illustrate in Exhibit A-1 the valuation of a $100,000 issue of 8%, 4-year bonds paying interest semiannually and sold on the date of issue to yield 8%.

We use the 4% column in both tables because the interest rate is 8% compounded semiannually (8%/2 = 4% per compounding period), and we use the eight periods hence line, because there are eight semiannual periods in four years. The multiplier from Table I is applied to the $100,000 because the principal repayment is a single sum. Because the eight semiannual interest receipts are in the annuity form, we use the multiplier from Table II to compute their present value. Note that the computation in Exhibit A-1 confirms the observation that the price of 8% bonds sold to yield 8% should be face (or par) value.

EXHIBIT A-1
Valuation of a Bond Issue
Using Present Value Tables

Future Cash Receipts	Multiplier (Table I)	Multiplier (Table II)	Present Values
Principal repayment, $100,000 (a single amount received eight semiannual periods hence)	0.731		$ 73,100
Interest receipts, $4,000 at end of each of eight semiannual interest periods		6.733	26,900 (rounded)
Total present value (or issue price) of bond			$100,000

EFFECTIVE INTEREST AMORTIZATION

Most bonds sell at more or less than their face value, and therefore accounting for them involves amortizing bond premium or bond discount. For the remainder of this illustration, we show (1) how the $100,000 bond issue used earlier would be valued if it were sold to yield either 6% or 10% compounded semiannually, and (2) how the bond discount and premium amounts would be determined under the effective interest method of amortization.

We calculate the amount of discount and premium in our illustration as follows:

	Bonds Sold at Discount (to Yield 10%)		Bonds Sold at Premium (to Yield 6%)	
	Present Value Multiplier	Present Value	Present Value Multiplier	Present Value
Principal receipt of $100,000 (eight semiannual periods hence, factors from Table I)	0.677	$67,700	0.789	$ 78,900
Interest receipts of $4,000 each (a series of eight in annuity form, factors from Table II)	6.463	25,852	7.020	28,080
Selling price of bond issues		$93,552		$106,980
Amount of bond discount or premium		$ 6,448		$ 6,980

These results show that an investor wishing to earn 10%, compounded semiannually, must discount the bonds by $6,448 (that is, pay only $93,552 for them). An investor paying as much as a $6,980 premium for the bonds would still earn 6%, compounded semiannually, on the investment.

As we explained in Chapter 15, the book value of bonds consists of their face value plus any unamortized premium or less any unamortized discount. Thus, at the time of issuance, the book value of the bonds is equal to their selling price. To calculate the periodic amount of amortization using the effective interest method:

(1) Determine the period's interest expense by multiplying the bonds' book value at the beginning of the period involved by the desired (or effective) interest rate.

(2) Determine the period's amortization by comparing the period's interest expense [step (1) above] to the amount of interest actually paid. If the interest expense is greater than the amount of interest paid, the difference is the discount amortization; if the expense is less than the interest paid, the difference is the premium amortization.

Face value of bonds	$100,000
Less: Discount	6,448
Book value of bonds at beginning of period	$ 93,552
Multiply by the interest rate per interest period (10%/2 = 5%)	× 0.05
Interest expense for first period (rounded)	$ 4,678
Actual interest paid ($100,000 × 0.08 × $\frac{6}{12}$)	4,000
First period's discount amortization	$ 678

Exhibits A–2 and A–3 summarize the calculations, related account balances, and the general progressions involved in the other periods of our illustration. Using the effective interest amortization method changes only the periodic amount of discount or premium amortization. All reasoning and accounting techniques used in the illustrations in Chapter 15 are equally applicable to any method of determining the amount of bond discount or premium amortization.

The effective interest method of amortization is often justified as being more precise than the straight-line method. This contention probably rests on the fact that, by incorporating a changing amount of total interest expense, the effective interest method results in a uniform rate of interest throughout the life of the bonds. Obviously, this increased precision is offset by the added complexity and the fact that the difference between the two methods would often be considered immaterial.

EXHIBIT A–2
Bonds Sold at a Discount
Periodic Interest Expense, Amortization, and Book Value of Bonds

Year	Interest Period	(A) Interest Paid (4% of face value)	(B) Interest Expense (5% of bond book value)	(C) Periodic Amortization (B − A)	(D) Balance of Unamortized Discount (D − C)	(E) Book Value of Bonds, End of Period ($100,000 − D)
(at issue)					$6,448	$ 93,552
1	1	$4,000	$4,678	$678	5,770	94,230
	2	4,000	4,712	712	5,058	94,942
2	3	4,000	4,747	747	4,311	95,689
	4	4,000	4,784	784	3,527	96,473
3	5	4,000	4,824	824	2,703	97,297
	6	4,000	4,865	865	1,838	98,162
4	7	4,000	4,908	908	930	99,070
	8	4,000	4,930*	930	0	100,000

*Adjusted for cumulative rounding error of $24.

EXHIBIT A-3
Bonds Sold at a Premium
Periodic Interest Expense, Amortization, and Book Value of Bonds

Year	Interest Period	(A) Interest Paid (4% of face value)	(B) Interest Expense (3% of bond book value)	(C) Periodic Amortization (A − B)	(D) Balance of Unamortized Premium (D − C)	(E) Book Value of Bonds, End of Period ($100,000 + D)
	(at issue)				$6,980	$106,980
1	1	$4,000	$3,209	$791	6,189	106,189
	2	4,000	3,186	814	5,375	105,375
2	3	4,000	3,161	839	4,536	104,536
	4	4,000	3,136	864	3,672	103,672
3	5	4,000	3,110	890	2,782	102,782
	6	4,000	3,083	917	1,865	101,865
4	7	4,000	3,056	944	921	100,921
	8	4,000	3,079*	921	0	100,000

PROBLEMS

Note: Use Tables I and II (pages 989 and 990, respectively) to solve the following problems.

A-1 Use Tables I and II to compute the present value of each of the following:
  (a) $70,000 10 years hence if the annual interest rate is:
    (1) 8% compounded annually.
    (2) 8% compounded semiannually.
    (3) 8% compounded quarterly.
  (b) $300 to be received at the end of each year for the next seven years if money is worth 12% per year compounded annually.
  (c) $75 to be received at the end of each six months for the next eight years if the interest rate is 10% per year compounded semiannually.
  (d) A $500,000 inheritance 20 years hence if money is worth 10% per year compounded annually.
  (e) $600 to be received each half-year for the next nine years plus a single sum of $10,000 at the end of nine years if the interest rate is 8% per year compounded semiannually.

A-2 Using Table II, calculate the present value of a five-year, $2,000 annuity if the interest rate is 6% per year compounded annually. Verify your answer by using Table I. Briefly explain how these tables are related.

A-3 You have an opportunity to purchase a bond to be issued by a local hospital. The bond has a face value of $5,000, will pay 6% interest per year in semiannual payments, and will mature in five years. How much should you pay for the bond if you want to earn 8% interest per year compounded semiannually on your investment?

A-4 Tempco, Inc. plans to issue $100,000 of 8% bonds that will pay interest semiannually and mature in five years. Assume that the effective interest rate is 10% per year compounded semiannually.

(a) Compute the selling price of the bonds.

(b) Construct a table similar to Exhibit A-2 for the first two years of the bonds' life.

(c) Present journal entries to properly amortize the bond premium or discount for the first two semiannual interest periods, using the effective interest method.

A-5 Complete the requirements of Problem A-4 if the effective interest rate is 6% per year compounded semiannually. For requirement (b), construct a table similar to Exhibit A-3.

A-6 A $20,000 four-year, 6% bond issue (with interest paid semiannually) is being sold at a time when the effective interest rate is 8% per year compounded semiannually.

(a) Compute the selling price of the bonds.

(b) Prepare a schedule similar to Exhibit A-2 for the four years of the bonds' life.

(c) Compute the amount of bond premium or discount to be amortized each year (1) under the straight-line method and (2) under the effective interest method.

(d) Compare the differences in reported income *each year* under the two methods in (c). Do you consider these differences material? Why?

(e) What arguments might one advance for (or against) each of the approaches to bond premium and discount amortization in (c)?

A-7 Dunn Corporation plans to issue $5,000,000 of 20-year, 10% bonds that pay interest semiannually. Assume that the effective interest rate is 8% per year compounded semiannually.

(a) Compute the issue price of the bonds.

(b) Prepare a schedule similar to Exhibit A-3 for the first three years of the bonds' life.

(c) Present journal entries to record the sale of the bonds on their issue date and the payments of interest and semiannual amortization of bond premium or discount for the first year.

(d) What would be the gain or loss if one-fifth of the bonds were retired for $1,025,000 on the interest date in the middle of the third year of the bonds' life?

(e) How would the remaining bonds be presented on the balance sheet at the end of the third year of the bonds' life?

A-8 Complete the requirements of Problem A-7 if the effective interest rate is 12% per year compounded semiannually. For requirement (b), prepare a schedule similar to Exhibit A-2.

A-9 In managing your investment portfolio, you have a policy of rejecting new investment opportunities if they yield less than an 8% effective annual return.

On January 1, 19X0, you have an opportunity to invest in either or both of the following:

(1) $10,000 face value bonds of the Bolton Corporation at 105. The bonds have a nominal interest rate of 9%.

(2) $10,000 face value bonds of the Cordite Corporation at 95. The bonds have a nominal interest rate of 7%.

Both investments pay interest semiannually on June 30 and December 31, and both mature in five years (December 31, 19X4).

REQUIRED

Decide whether either or both of these investments qualify for your portfolio. Support your answer with calculations.

16
Accounting Principles; Accounting for Inflation

In Chapter 1 we touched briefly on the role of generally accepted accounting principles as "the rules" by which financial accounting statements are prepared. The phrase "generally accepted accounting principles" encompasses a wide spectrum of accounting guidelines, ranging from basic concepts and standards to detailed methods and procedures.[1] There are principles covering every aspect of financial accounting and reporting. We have already discussed many of the methods and procedures within the domain of generally accepted accounting principles, such as inventory pricing methods and depreciation methods. In this chapter we shall focus on the most fundamental and pervasive principles of accounting, an understanding of which is indispensable to anyone who must use financial accounting data. We shall also consider the topics of interperiod income tax allocation and accounting for inflation.

HISTORICAL DEVELOPMENT

In contrast to the physical sciences, no immutable or natural laws, such as the law of gravity, exist in accounting. The closest approximation to a law in accounting is probably the use of arithmetic functions and logic. Because there is no basic natural accounting law, accounting principles have been developed on the basis of their *usefulness*. Consequently, the growth of accounting is more closely related to experience and practice than to the foundation provided by ultimate law. As such, accounting principles tend to evolve rather than be discovered, to be flexible rather than precise, and to be subject to relative evaluation rather than being ultimate or final.

Conventional accounting comprises a relatively recent body of knowledge. Although the origin of double-entry bookkeeping has been traced back to the fourteenth century, most important accounting developments have occurred in the last century.

[1]A comprehensive statement of accounting principles and concepts was published in 1970 by the AICPA: *Statements of the Accounting Principles Board, No. 4*, "Basic Concepts and Accounting Principles Underlying Financial Statements of Business Enterprises," American Institute of Certified Public Accountants, New York, 1970.

If we think of accounting as an information system, its recent and rapid development is largely explained by the economic history of the last eight to ten decades. During this time, (1) the development of giant industrial firms, (2) the existence of large stockholders' groups, (3) the pronounced separation of ownership and management of large corporate firms, (4) the rapid growth of industrial and economic activity, and (5) the expansion of government regulation of industry were all factors that helped create the large groups of interested parties who require a constant stream of reliable financial information concerning the economic entities they own, manage, or regulate. To be meaningful, this information must be prepared according to some agreed-on standards and procedures.

Accounting principles—very much like common law—originate from problem situations such as changes in the law, tax regulations, new business organizational arrangements, or new financing or ownership techniques. In response to the effect such problems have on financial reports, certain techniques or procedures will be tried. Through comparative use and analysis, one or more of the original techniques will be found most suitable, become widely used, and then be considered a generally accepted accounting principle. Organizations such as the Financial Accounting Standards Board (FASB), the American Institute of Certified Public Accountants (AICPA), the Securities and Exchange Commission (SEC), the Internal Revenue Service, and the American Accounting Association— and the literature each publishes—are instrumental in the development of most accounting principles.

The general acceptance of accounting principles is not determined by formal voting by or survey of practicing accountants. Rather, these principles are established by a more or less common awareness of their widespread use. References in authoritative accounting literature are probably the most substantive evidence of general acceptance of a particular accounting principle.

In particular, pronouncements by the FASB are probably the most direct evidence of whether or not there is general acceptance of a specific accounting principle. Organized in 1973, the FASB issued more than 29 statements dealing with generally accepted accounting principles during its first six years. Before the creation of the FASB, pronouncements by the AICPA, many of which are still in effect, represented the most authoritative indicators of general acceptance.

During the two decades ending in 1960, the AICPA issued approximately 50 *Accounting Research Bulletins* and *Accounting Terminology Bulletins*. These bulletins dealt with a variety of problems and, although they lacked formal legal status, they had considerable influence on generally accepted practice. In 1960, the AICPA established an 18-member Accounting Principles Board (APB) to issue authoritative "opinions" on problems related to generally accepted accounting principles. Many of the 31 opinions issued during its existence were preceded by considerable research, wide circulation of "exposure drafts," and partial revisions based on the resulting feedback. These opinions increased in importance in 1964 when the AICPA required that any departure from an opinion be disclosed in a footnote to the financial statements or in the accompanying auditor's report. When the FASB succeeded the APB in 1973, this requirement was extended to cover pronouncements issued by the FASB.

BASIC PRINCIPLES

The accounting principles we consider in this section are among the most important ideas in accounting theory. Although the treatment here is less than exhaustive, it should provide sufficient background for further studies of accounting. The discussion of each principle begins with a brief description.

Accounting Entity

Each business entity should be accounted for separately.

An accounting entity consists of the *people, assets,* and *activities* devoted to a specific economic purpose. Our Cole Clinic example from the early chapters provides some good examples. The clinic's basic objective is to provide medical services for Dr. Cole's patients. Its activities are all those activities associated with the medical practice. The persons of the entity are Dr. Cole, his nurse, his receptionist, and any other assistants he might employ. The entity's assets include all assets used directly or indirectly for treating patients, such as medical instruments, waiting room furniture, and medical supplies. Only those liabilities specifically related to Dr. Cole's work should be reflected in the accounting records of the medical practice—for example, accounts payable for medical supplies.

If the entity concept is properly followed, Dr. Cole's other property and economic activities should not be reflected in the financial records of the medical practice. For example, his residence, his investments in securities, his wife's personal automobile, and any other business ventures should not be included. To include the costs, expenses, and revenues of these activities in the accounting records of the medical practice would certainly impair the value of these records in reporting on the financial status and the operating results of the clinic. The usefulness of the entity concept is quite obvious here. If Dr. Cole owns other businesses, such as rental properties, a separate and complete set of self-balancing accounting records and financial reports should be kept for each distinct accounting entity.

The entity concept does not negate the legal fact that in proprietorships and partnerships an all-inclusive legal liability exists. In other words, business assets are available to personal creditors, and business creditors may have legal access to both business and personal assets in these noncorporate business organizations.

Accounting Period

Accounting reports are related to specific time periods—typically, one year.

The operations of most businesses are virtually continuous except for some changes associated with cyclical time periods, seasons, or dates. Thus, any division of the total life of a business into segments based on annual time periods is somewhat artificial. In spite of this artificiality, the idea of accounting periods is quite useful. Many taxes are assessed on an annual basis. By convention, comprehensive reports to stockholders are made annually. In addition, many other noneconomic factors tend to cause the year to be considered a natural division of time.

For special purposes, accounting reports may be tied to other time periods. For instance, many companies prepare *interim* financial reports for time spans of less than one year, such as quarterly (three months) or even monthly periods. To compare data for periods of more than one year, many firms prepare five- or ten-year summaries, which are usually statistical and tabular abstracts of related financial statements.

The combined effect of the entity concept and the concept of periodicity can be seen in the following grid, which uses Dr. Cole's situation as an example:

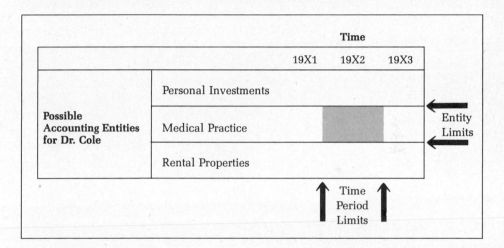

The box in the center of the grid isolates Dr. Cole's medical practice for the year 19X2. Proper accounting requires that both the entity and the time period be identified in financial reports.

As useful as it is, the idea of artificially "cutting off" the business at the end of a certain time period presents many problems. Transactions occurring and consummated entirely within one accounting period present few problems. Many transactions bridge two or more periods, however, and their total effect on the entity must often be properly allocated among these periods. Problems of *periodicity* are closely related to the concept of "matching revenue and expense" and are more fully developed later in the chapter.

Materiality

Accounting transactions so small or insignificant that they do not affect one's actions will be recorded as is most expedient.

Sound accounting procedures require effort and cost money. When the amounts involved are too small to have a significant effect on the overall picture, the application of theoretically correct accounting procedures is hardly worth its cost. For example, accounting theory asserts that assets acquired and used over several accounting periods should first be recorded as assets, with systematic amounts of depreciation expense then recognized in each of the periods in which the assets are used (directly or indirectly) to earn revenues. The principle of materiality, however, permits the costs of such items as small tools, pencil sharpeners, and waste paper baskets to be expensed when acquired because they are "immaterial" in amount. Many firms set dollar limits, such as $25 or $100, below which the costs of all items are expensed.

The concept of materiality is relative—what is immaterial for General Motors Corporation may be quite material for smaller companies. Also, the nature of the transaction should be considered. A difference of $1,000 in depreciation expense might be considered immaterial, but the same discrepancy in cash could be termed material.

The materiality of an item in a financial statement is usually judged in comparison to a related amount. For example, to determine the effect of the inclusion or omission of an income statement item, one would express the item as a percentage of net income; a current asset item might be expressed as a percentage of total current assets, and so on. Accounting literature is not precise about what quantitative proportions should be deemed material. Specific instances can be found in which 5 to 15% of related amounts are considered material, but this matter is at best subject to judgment. Always remember, however, that although a given series of transactions might *each* be considered immaterial in amount, their aggregate effect could be quite material in certain circumstances.

Conservatism

Accounting measurements take place in a context of significant uncertainties, and possible errors in measurement should tend toward understatement rather than overstatement of net assets and income.

Accounting determinations are often based on estimates of future events and are therefore subject to a range of interpretations that may be optimistic or pessimistic. In the early 1900s many abuses were perpetrated on financial statement users by overly optimistic measurements of assets and estimates of income. Consequently, it became reassuring for the investor to know that the "most conservative" accounting procedures were being used. In some instances, banks would write down handsome multistory home office buildings and show them on the balance sheet at a nominal value of $1. The intention was to make obvious the understatement of assets as evidence of conservative accounting and financial strength.

More recent thinking in this area has recognized that intentional understatement of net assets and income can be as misleading as overly optimistic accounting treatments. For example, stockholders might erroneously choose to sell their stock in a company that grossly understates its income through overly conservative accounting procedures. Also, a conservative treatment in one accounting period may cause the reported income for many other periods to be overstated. This is true of the banks referred to above. A building written down to $1 is, in a sense, "overdepreciated" and therefore both assets and income are understated for that period. Then, during the next 30 to 50 years as the banks use these buildings, their income will be overstated because the related building depreciation expense was omitted from the income statements of those periods.

Today, conservatism is the accountant's reaction to situations in which significant uncertainties exist about the outcome of transactions still in progress. In contrast to the earlier intentional understatements of net assets and income, conservative accounting procedures are now followed in circumstances in which the accountant is unsure of the proper measure to use. The preference is that any possible errors in measuring net assets and income should be in the direction of understatement rather than overstatement. From the range of possible accounting determinations to be applied in these cases, the one that results in the lowest current statement of net assets and income should be used.

Consistency   **Unless otherwise disclosed, accounting reports are to be prepared on a basis consistent with the preceding period.**

In many instances, more than one method of applying a generally accepted accounting principle is possible. In other words, two firms may have identical operating situations and each might choose a different—but equally acceptable—accounting method and thus report different amounts for the same types of transactions.

Changes in accounting procedures that lead to different reported values may affect the amount of reported income. Under certain circumstances, a firm could, by design, increase or decrease its reported earnings simply by changing from one generally accepted accounting principle to another that yields different values. It is this situation that justifies the consistency principle. Financial statement users should know when and to what extent reported earnings result in some part from changes in accounting techniques. In Chapter 14 we discussed the manner in which the effects of changes in accounting principles are to be reported.

Full Disclosure   **All facts necessary to make financial statements not misleading must be disclosed.**

Often facts or conditions exist that, although not specifically part of the financial statement data for the period reported, have considerable influence on the financial status of the firm. Such conditions may pertain to the period covered by the statements or to the period immediately afterward. To properly inform the readers, the firm should make them aware of this additional information. Certain provisions of leases, significant amounts of purchases commitments, and notice of pending lawsuits or settlements are examples of items that should be disclosed in footnotes to the financial statements. Likewise, if the company issues a large amount of securities or has a casualty loss after the balance sheet date, this information and any other definite factors that may significantly affect the operations of the firm should be imparted to the reader, even though the situation arose subsequent to the balance sheet date. Firms are responsible for disclosing such events that occur between the balance sheet date and the date of their report. If a report is submitted to the SEC as part of a registration statement for the sale of securities, the period extends to the effective date of registration.

A company should also disclose a summary of the accounting principles it follows in preparing its financial statements. This disclosure requirement recognizes that different firms may use different accounting procedures for similar transactions and that therefore the usefulness of the financial statements is enhanced if the users are aware of the accounting procedures being used. Items disclosed in a summary of accounting principles would include, among others, depreciation methods, inventory pricing methods, methods of accounting for intangibles, and consolidation procedures.

Objectivity

Whenever possible, accounting entries must be based on objectively determined evidence.

The concept of objectivity requires that accounting data be bias-free and verifiable. Objectivity is desirable so that users of accounting reports feel that the data they rely on are not subject to the capricious whim of either management or the accountant who prepares or audits the statements. Consequently, whenever possible, accounting determinations are based on actual invoices, documents, bank statements, and physical counts of items involved.

Not all accounting determinations can be totally objective. Periodic depreciation and the assumptions made as to the eventual collectibility of credit sales are examples of relatively subjective factors routinely incorporated into accounting reports. Any group of accountants required to determine independently the depreciation expense for a given period on an item of special-purpose equipment would probably come up with a range of suggested amounts. One might expect the range to be in some proportion to the degree of subjectivity involved.

Obviously, variations in accounting measurements lead to variations in reported income. Thus, the more subjective accounting records become, the greater variety there may be in reported income. Because highly subjective determinations are not readily verifiable, a user of subjectively derived accounting reports is unable to know where in the possible range of reportable income figures this particular statement falls. An even greater disadvantage is that the user has no way of knowing what motives might have governed the individual preparing the statements. Was he or she trying to be "fair" or was there an attempt to minimize or maximize reported income? In a real situation there is no reliable source of answers to this question. For this reason, accountants, and particularly independent auditors, look for objective evidence to support the accounting data in financial reports.

Going Concern

In the absence of evidence to the contrary, a business is assumed to have an indefinite life.

With few exceptions, business organizations have no anticipated termination date. Most firms continue to operate profitably for indefinite periods and are, in fact, *going concerns*. For those firms that do not succeed, there are usually indications of impending termination for some time before operations actually cease.

The going concern assumption has important implications for accounting procedures. It allows one to defer costs—such as ending inventories, prepaid expenses, and undepreciated asset balances—that are to be charged against the revenues of future periods. Furthermore, the going concern assumption relates to the use of cost-based accounting measures rather than market-based liquidation values. Firms that expect to continue in profitable operations do not ordinarily sell their operating assets; therefore, potential liquidation prices for the assets at the end of an accounting period may not be especially relevant. In this sense, the going concern assumption helps justify the use of historical cost as the primary basis for accounting entries.

The Measuring Unit

The unit of measure in accounting shall be the base money unit of the most relevant currency.

Although other descriptive information is often relevant, money is the common measure for the recording of accounting transactions. By expressing all assets and equities in terms of money, the accountant creates a common denominator that permits addition and subtraction of all forms of assets and equities and makes possible the preparation of financial statements. Expressing all statement items in money terms also permits the ready comparison of (1) the various elements included in the financial statements of a firm, (2) different sets of statements for the same firm, and (3) the statements of two or more firms. This principle also assumes the unit of measure is stable; that is, changes in its general purchasing power are not considered sufficiently important to require adjustments to the basic financial statements.

Historical Cost Measurement

Accounting measures are primarily based on historical costs.

The dollar amounts in account balances represent the accounting measures of the items about which information is being collected. Possible sources of these measures are opinions of management, professional appraisals, various market prices, and historical costs. Accountants have experimented with all of these sources at various times, but with few exceptions, they have relied on historical cost whenever it is available. Most practicing accountants feel that sources other than historical cost are so subjective that their use should be seriously limited.

We can describe *historical cost* as the money equivalent of the object given up (and/or those obligations assumed) in an exchange transaction. Most accountants probably agree that no asset has a single ultimate value and that for the millions of exchanges that take place daily the exchange price is probably the best indicator of the value of an item at the time of the transaction.

Historical costs tend to be highly objective because under classical assumptions they are derived in the marketplace by informed, rational, and independent parties. Also, the details of the original transaction can easily be verified by consulting the documents that are customarily executed at the time of exchange (deeds, bills of sale, checks, and mortgages). An advantage of historical cost measurement that is often overlooked is that the data are a natural by-product of the exchange transaction itself and are therefore available at little additional cost or effort. Relative objectivity is probably the primary justification for historical cost-based accounting measures, but their natural availability at negligible cost is also an important factor—especially when the historical cost method is compared with more expensive sources of values such as professional appraisals.

Matching Expenses with Revenues

To the extent feasible, all expenses related to given revenues are matched with and deducted from those revenues for the determination of periodic income.

The income statement is, in a general sense, an index of an entity's economic yield for a given accounting period. Consider the following computation:

Revenues	$100,000	Dollar measure of product or service
Related expenses	80,000	Dollar measure of resources consumed in providing product or service
Net income	$ 20,000	Wealth created, or economic yield

For this computation to be meaningful and valid, the revenues and expenses must be related. In other words, only expenses incurred in generating periodic revenues should be deducted from those revenues to derive the amount of periodic yield. To include either unrelated revenues or expenses or to omit either related revenues or expenses impairs, dollar for dollar, the significance of the income computation. The proper matching of revenues and expenses is accomplished primarily through the accrual accounting techniques illustrated throughout the text.

Revenue Recognition at Point of Sale

With limited exceptions, revenue is recognized at the point of sale.

At first, this principle may seem obvious. Modern business operations are often so complicated and so extended, however, that practical questions arise concerning the point at which revenue should be recognized. With the exceptions discussed later in this section, generally accepted accounting principles require the recognition of revenues in the accounting period in which the sale is deemed to have occurred. Moreover, the "matching principle" (explained above) dictates that expenses related to those revenues must be matched with them in that period. Thus, operating together, the combined effect of the two principles is to require the recognition of revenues, related expenses, and therefore *income* in the period of sale.

For services, the sale is deemed to occur when the service is performed. When merchandise is involved, it is probably most useful to think of the sale as taking place when title to the goods transfers from seller to buyer. In many situations this will coincide with the delivery of the merchandise. If it ever becomes important to determine whether or not a sale has occurred, it will be a matter of law set forth in the Uniform Commercial Code.[2]

[2]*The Uniform Commercial Code* is a codification of many statutes and common law related to commerce. It has been widely adopted to replace often widely varying state laws.

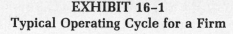

EXHIBIT 16–1
Typical Operating Cycle for a Firm

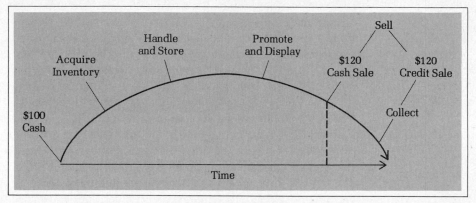

To understand the logic of and the exceptions to the principle of recognizing revenues at point of sale, we must consider some underlying factors. For most firms, some sort of cash-to-cash operating cycle exists; this is diagramed in Exhibit 16–1.

In reality, most firms are engaged in many partially overlapping operating cycles represented by this diagram:

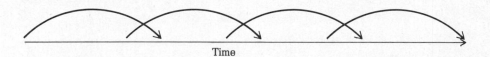

For our purposes, it is sufficient to consider the isolated cycle. As shown in Exhibit 16–1, the firm starts with $100 cash and then uses the cash to acquire, handle, store, promote, display, and finally sell the inventory. In a cash sale, inventory is immediately converted to $120 cash. If the sale is made on credit terms, the collection process must be accomplished. The $20 difference between the cash at the cycle's beginning and at its end, reduced by any applicable noncash expenses, is the income generated by the operating cycle.

Throughout the cycle, the firm's efforts are toward the eventual sale of the goods and collection of the sales price. From a purely theoretical view, accountants would like to be able to recognize some part of the income for each phase of the cycle. Because all allocation methods would be arbitrary and based on estimates, however, the income is not recognized until the point of sale. At the point of sale, one knows (1) the basic cost, (2) the fact that a sale has occurred, (3) the selling price, and (4) that the seller either has received cash or has an enforceable claim against the customer. Prior to the point of sale, some of these items may be unknown. Hence, the sale is reasonably considered "the critical event" in the operating cycle.

**Other Bases
for Revenue
Recognition**

COLLECTION BASES For selected exceptions, times other than the point of sale are used to recognize revenue. Methods that delay recognition until cash is collected are known as **collection basis methods.** These methods usually relate to installment credit sales. A very conservative method, known as the **cost recovery basis,** considers all cash collections a return of costs until all costs are recovered; the remaining collections are considered to be all gross profit.

A more widely used version of the collection basis is known as the **installment basis.** The installment basis takes its name from the popular sales term for purchases of moderate to large dollar amounts. In effect, the installment method treats each dollar received as part return of cost and part gross profit. The specific proportion of each is determined by the relationship between the cost and the sales prices of the merchandise involved. For example, assume that on October 1, 19X7, a refrigerator costing $450 is sold for $600 with installment terms consisting of a 20% down payment and the balance due in 24 equal payments of $20 on the last day of each month. Under the installment basis, because the cost was 75% of the selling price ($450/$600), each dollar collected will be considered 75% return of costs and 25% gross profit. The resulting gross profit during the three years would be recognized as follows:

	19X7 Down Payment	19X7 Three $20 Payments	19X8 Twelve $20 Payments	19X9 Nine $20 Payments	Totals
Total received (100%)	$120	$60	$240	$180	$600
Considered return of cost (75%)	90	45	180	135	450
Considered gross profit (25%)	30	15	60	45	150

The installment basis of revenue recognition should be used when firms have no reasonable basis for estimating the extent of collectibility of the installment receivables. Companies that are able to reasonably predict and make accruals for future losses should not employ the installment basis. Instead, they should recognize revenue at point of sale and match with it an appropriate estimate of uncollectible accounts. These companies may, however, still elect to use the installment basis for income tax purposes, for which it may be advantageous to delay gross profit recognition until the time cash is collected.

PERCENTAGE OF COMPLETION Some operations, such as the construction of roads, dams, and large office buildings, take a long time and therefore cover several accounting periods. In such situations, the point-of-sale recognition basis does not work very well, because the earnings from several years of construction work may be reported as the income of only the period in which the project was completed and sold. Consequently, another scheme of revenue recognition known as **percentage of completion (POC)** is used.

The POC basis simply allocates the estimated total gross profit on a contract among the several accounting periods involved, in proportion to the estimated percentage of the contract completed each period. This reliance on estimated gross profit figures may be justified in part because large, long-term contracts are usually based on detailed engineering plans and specific, highly binding contracts among financially secure parties. Most often, estimates of the percentage of contract completion are tied to the proportion of total costs that have been incurred.

For example, assume that a dam was to be constructed during no more than a two-year period beginning July 1, 19X1. The contract price was $3 million, with estimated total costs of $2.4 million and thus an estimated gross profit of $600,000. If the total cost incurred in 19X1 was $720,000 (that is, 30% of the estimated total), then $180,000 (or 30% of the estimated total gross profit) would be recognized in 19X1. Similarly, if another 50% of the total estimated costs were incurred in 19X2, then 50% of the estimated total gross profit (or $300,000) would be recognized in 19X2. Under the POC basis, the gross profit would be reflected among the three calendar years as follows:

| | (Dollars in Thousands) | | | |
	19X1	19X2	19X3	Total
Cost incurred	$720	$1,200	$480	$2,400
Percent of total costs	30%	50%	20%	100%
Gross profit to be recognized	$180	$ 300	$120	$ 600

In long-term construction, it is quite apparent that the POC basis of revenue recognition more reasonably reflects reported income as an indicator of productive effort than would the point-of-sale basis.

INTERPERIOD INCOME TAX ALLOCATION

Generally accepted accounting principles provide guidelines for the preparation of financial accounting statements. When businesses prepare their income tax returns—whether federal, state, or local—they are guided by the procedures and rulings of the taxing agencies. In any given year, there may be timing differences that cause the accounting income before taxes computed on the books (pretax accounting income) to differ from taxable income computed on the tax return.

Timing Differences

When **timing differences** exist, revenue and expense items that affect pretax accounting income in one period enter into the calculation of taxable income in a different period. Eventually, however, the total amount of revenue or expense reported in both sets of records over a period of time will be the same. Timing differences arise because tax laws either (1) require certain revenues and expenses to be recognized in different periods than do generally accepted accounting principles or (2) permit businesses to use a different method of accounting for revenues or expenses on the tax return than is used in determining pretax accounting income. In the latter case, businesses normally select an accounting method for tax purposes that will minimize their current tax liability.

A typical example of a timing difference concerns depreciation methods. A company may use an accelerated depreciation method in the tax return and straight-line depreciation in arriving at accounting income. As another example, a firm making installment credit sales may recognize revenue at the point of sale in determining accounting income but use the installment basis of revenue recognition for tax purposes.

Whenever timing differences cause pretax accounting income to differ from taxable income, the income tax expense to be included in the income statement should be based on the revenue and expense amounts reported in the income statement (that is, the tax expense should be based on the pretax accounting income). To do otherwise leads to the presentation of distorted information in the income statement.

The process of apportioning income tax expense to the income statement over the time periods affected by timing differences is known as **interperiod income tax allocation.** To illustrate this process and the distortions that result if it is not employed, assume the following data: On January 1, 19X1, the Carey Company paid $1,000 for a fixed asset with a useful life of four years and no expected salvage value. Carey Company uses straight-line depreciation on its books, but selects the sum-of-the-years'-digits method for tax purposes. This represents the only timing difference between information collected in the accounts and the tax return. In each of the years 19X1 through 19X4, the company generates an "income before depreciation and taxes" amount of $1,000. We shall assume an income tax rate of 50%.

Carey Company's taxable income and income tax payable to the Internal Revenue Service for the years 19X1 through 19X4 is as follows:

	19X1	19X2	19X3	19X4
Income before depreciation and taxes	$1,000	$1,000	$1,000	$1,000
Depreciation (sum of the years' digits)	400	300	200	100
Taxable income	$ 600	$ 700	$ 800	$ 900
Income tax liability (50% of taxable income)	$ 300	$ 350	$ 400	$ 450

The pretax accounting income for each of the four years differs from the taxable income because of the depreciation timing difference.

	19X1	19X2	19X3	19X4
Income before depreciation and taxes	$1,000	$1,000	$1,000	$1,000
Depreciation (straight line)	250	250	250	250
Pretax accounting income	$ 750	$ 750	$ 750	$ 750

The reporting of taxes in the income statement if income tax allocation is not followed (that is, income tax expense is equal to the actual tax liability for the year) is shown in Part A of the following schedule. Part B shows the effect on income tax expense and net income if tax allocation is used.

	19X1	19X2	19X3	19X4
A. *Without Income Tax Allocation*				
Pretax Accounting Income	$750	$750	$750	$750
Income Tax Expense	300	350	400	450
Net Income	$450	$400	$350	$300

B. *With Income Tax Allocation*

Pretax Accounting Income	$750	$750	$750	$750
Income Tax Expense	375	375	375	375
Net Income	$375	$375	$375	$375

Accountants consider the presentation in A distorted because there is not a normal relationship (in this example, 50%) portrayed between pretax accounting income and income tax expense. Based on the amounts reported in the four years, the percentage relationship is 40%, 46.7%, 53.3%, and 60%, respectively. A related distortion occurs in the net income figure, which, in this illustration, decreases throughout the four-year period even though pretax accounting income is constant during that time. The reason, of course, is the timing difference, with income tax expense in Part A based on taxable income and not on pretax accounting income.

In Part B the income tax expense is allocated to each year according to the pretax accounting income. This income tax allocation procedure produces a normal annual relationship between pretax accounting income and income tax expense. Also, net income moves in harmony with pretax accounting income. Because, in this example, pretax accounting income remains constant from one year to the next, net income, under tax allocation procedures, also remains constant.

Deferred Tax Accounts

Under income tax allocation, the annual charge to income tax expense is not equal to the income tax liability for the period. **Deferred tax** accounts are needed to balance the analysis. The journal entries recording income tax expense for Carey Company for 19X1 through 19X4 illustrate this point.

19X1	Income Tax Expense	375	
	Income Tax Payable		300
	Deferred Tax Credits		75

To record income tax for 19X1.

19X2	Income Tax Expense	375	
	Income Tax Payable		350
	Deferred Tax Credits		25

To record income tax for 19X2.

19X3	Income Tax Expense	375	
	Deferred Tax Credits	25	
	Income Tax Payable		400

To record income tax for 19X3.

19X4	Income Tax Expense	375	
	Deferred Tax Credits	75	
	Income Tax Payable		450

To record income tax for 19X4.

The balance in the Deferred Tax Credits account represents the tax effect of timing differences. For example, the $75 balance at the end of 19X1 is equal to the tax rate, 50%, times the timing difference in 19X1 of $150. The balance in the account is deferred for allocation to income tax expense (as a reduction of the expense) in the future. Once the timing differences have completely worked themselves out, the Deferred Tax Credits account will have a zero balance. This occurs at the end of 19X4 for the Carey Company, as shown in the following T account.

Deferred Tax Credits

19X3	25	19X1	75
19X4	75	19X2	25

The balance in the Deferred Tax Credits account should be classified in the balance sheet as a liability. The amounts disclosed are frequently quite large; it is not unusual for the deferred tax credits reported by major corporations to run into millions of dollars.

Some timing differences will first cause pretax accounting income to be less than taxable income. Initially, then, the income tax payable will exceed the charge to income tax expense, and a Deferred Tax Charges account will be debited to balance the analysis. This account balance reflects the amount of tax payments that will be allocated to income tax expense (as an increase in the expense) in the future. As with the Deferred Tax Credits account, the Deferred Tax Charges account will have a zero balance after the timing differences have completely worked themselves out. Deferred tax charges should be classified in the balance sheet as an asset.

ACCOUNTING FOR INFLATION

Inflation has an impact on virtually every aspect of economic affairs, including investment decisions, pricing policies, marketing strategies, and salary and wage negotiations. Persons making economic decisions utilize financial data prepared by accountants. Conventional financial statements, however, contain no explicit adjustments for the impact of inflation on the financial data. The usefulness of financial statements would likely increase if they contained supplementary information about the effects of inflation and changing prices on the enterprise.

Exactly what type of supplementary information to report during inflationary periods is an unresolved issue for accountants. Two approaches have been proposed: (1) adjust conventional financial data for changes in the general purchasing power of the dollar, and (2) incorporate current value measurements of the goods and services used or held by an enterprise. We shall now examine these two approaches.

General Purchasing Power Adjustments

The general purchasing power of the dollar is a measure of its ability to buy goods and services. **Price-level changes** are changes in the prevailing exchange ratio between money and goods or services. Whenever there is a rise in the general level of prices for goods and services, the general purchasing power of the dollar

TRIPLE-DIGIT INFLATION

In 1974 and 1979, the rate of inflation in the United States reached the 10% to 13% range. Top government policymakers and ordinary citizens were concerned about the possible economic and social consequences of these double-digit inflation rates. These rates were modest, however, compared with those experienced in Argentina in the late 1970s. Argentina's inflation rate of 170% in 1978 and approximately 150% in 1979 gave it the distinction of having the highest inflation rates in the world at that time!

In the face of such extreme inflation, every facet of an Argentine's economic life was geared to devising stratagems to protect the value of his or her money. The economy, in many respects, became one dominated by speculation rather than production. Here are some examples of financial activity within Argentina's triple-digit inflation economy:

Individual investors and corporate treasurers were constantly alert to changing interest rates on short-term bank deposits, moving spare pesos (Argentina's unit of currency) in and out of such deposits in response to interest rate changes. To be ready to shift funds quickly, 75% of Argentina's bank savers bought certificates of deposit with terms of 30 days or less. Because bank interest rates were uncontrolled and banks were free to change them at any time, some interest rates reached a level of 140% per year. One bank, for example, examined its loan demand daily; if additional funds were needed, it merely increased its interest rate on savings. If other banks did not react by raising their rates, increased funds began to flow in within a few days.

Sophisticated financial maneuvers continually turned money over to take advantage of any differences between (1) the rate of inflation, and (2) the rate of change in the conversion ratio between the dollar and the peso. When the rate of inflation was higher than the dollar's rise against the peso, for example, speculators used a maneuver known as the "reverse bicycle" to generate gains. This procedure consisted of (1) borrowing dollars, (2) using the dollars to buy a peso bond with the principal and interest indexed to the inflation rate (the amounts of principal and interest were increased at a rate equal to the inflation rate), (3) liquidating the bond after holding it a month or so, and (4) using the proceeds (with some left over) to repay the loan. In addition to the "reverse bicycle," other financial maneuvers had such names as "bicycle" and "tricycle"—all named because the continual turnover of money required to make them work was likened to a pedaling action.

Stock investment activity increased dramatically, causing the stock market to become quite volatile. Prices of some stocks would double or triple (or more) in a short time, evidencing the speculative nature of the investments. At the extreme, some stocks jumped 1,500% in one speculative burst of activity in mid-1979.

Many retailers were relatively less concerned about making sales and more interested in the impact of inflation on the values of their real estate and merchandise inventory. Most retailing in Argentina is done through boutiques and corner food stores. Often the owners bought these stores as real-estate investments to hedge against the impact of inflation. As long as their property values increased, sales were of lesser importance. This phenomenon led to some merchandise being greatly overpriced (and also not selling), such as knit sport shirts priced at $140 each and cotton pajamas priced at $90 each.

Argentina's economy was surviving its triple-digit inflation in the late 1970s, although how long it could continue to do so was also a matter of speculation. The government instituted a program to gradually reduce inflation over several years, hoping to bring it under control without creating massive unemployment. Should the program succeed, interest rates of 140%, "reverse bicycles," stock price jumps of 1,500%, and knit sport shirts priced at $140 will be relegated to the lore of Argentina's financial history.

SOURCE: Everett G. Martin, "Anyone in Argentina Can Give You Lessons On Beating Inflation," *The Wall Street Journal*, July 16, 1979.

declines; this is **inflation**. In contrast, **deflation** is an increase in the dollar's general purchasing power as the general level of prices declines. Because inflation has been the prevailing price-level movement of the last few decades, our discussion is in that context. If a significant period of deflation occurred, most of the problems we consider here would occur in a reversed form.

PRICE INDEXES   Price-level changes are measured through price indexes. A **price index** represents a series of measurements, stated as percentages, indicating the relationship between (a) the weighted average price of a sample of goods and services at various points in time and (b) the weighted average price of a similar sample of goods and services at a common, or base, date.

For example, assume we wish to construct a price index for a single commodity that was priced at $1.60 in December, 19X2, $2.00 in December, 19X3, and $3.00 in December, 19X4. If we select December, 19X3 as our base date, our price index will express the price of this commodity in December of 19X2, 19X3, and 19X4 as a percentage of its price in December, 19X3. The 19X2 price is 80% ($1.60/$2.00) of the 19X3 price, while the 19X4 price is 150% ($3.00/$2.00) of the 19X3 price. The percentage relationship on the base date is, of course, always 100%. The price index for each date is as follows (the percent sign is understood but usually not shown with index numbers):

December 19X2	80
December 19X3	100
December 19X4	150

Some prominent examples of price indexes are the Consumer Price Index and the Gross National Product Implicit Price Deflator. The FASB recommends that the Consumer Price Index be used for any general purchasing power adjustments.[3] The more frequent calculation of the Consumer Price Index (monthly) is one advantage it has over the GNP Implicit Price Deflator (calculated quarterly).

CONVERSION FACTORS   Index numbers permit amounts stated in terms of dollars of general purchasing power at any particular time to be restated in terms of dollars of different purchasing power at another time. The procedure is to multiply the amount to be restated by the following conversion factor:

$$\frac{\text{Index You Are Converting TO}}{\text{Index You Are Converting FROM}}$$

For example, suppose we acquired a parcel of land for $5,000 in December, 19X3, when the general price index was 100. Suppose also that the general price index for various times was as follows:

December 19X2	80
December 19X3	100
December 19X4	150
Average for 19X4	125

---

[3]*Statement of Financial Accounting Standards No. 33, Financial Reporting and Changing Prices,* Financial Accounting Standards Board, Stamford, Conn., 1979.

We may restate the cost of land in terms of the December, 19X4 dollar by multiplying the $5,000 by the conversion factor 150/100 (December, 19X4 index/ December, 19X3 index). The resulting measure is $7,500, the cost of the land stated in dollars of December, 19X4 general purchasing power. The conversion process works in the other direction as well. The cost of the land in terms of the December, 19X2 dollar is $5,000 × 80/100 = $4,000. The amounts $5,000, $7,500, and $4,000 each represent the cost of the land, but the unit of measure in which the cost is expressed is different in each case. Usually, amounts stated in "old" dollars will be converted to current dollars because of the latter's greater relevance to the overall economic situation.

Events that occur fairly evenly throughout the year, such as sales, are assumed to be originally stated in dollars of the average purchasing power for the year. Consider a firm with sales of $50,000 for 19X4. These sales are assumed to have been made at the average price index for 19X4. The calculation $50,000 × 150/125 = $60,000 represents the conversion of these sales into dollars of December, 19X4 general purchasing power.

ADJUSTMENT PROCEDURES Basically, general purchasing power adjustments cause all items in the financial statements to be stated in dollars with a common purchasing power content. Conversion factors are used to make the adjustments. Our illustrations will state the converted data in terms of the dollar's purchasing power at the latest balance sheet date.

Balance sheet conversion. Before a balance sheet may be converted, one must separate **monetary assets and liabilities** from nonmonetary items. Monetary assets consist of cash and other assets, such as receivables, that represent the right to receive a fixed number of dollars in the future, regardless of price-level changes. Monetary liabilities are obligations to disburse a fixed number of dollars in the future, regardless of price-level changes. Most liabilities are monetary.

By their nature, monetary items in a balance sheet are already stated in dollars of current purchasing power at the balance sheet date and therefore do not require any further adjustment. All other balance sheet accounts comprise the **nonmonetary items.** Nonmonetary items are adjusted by conversion factors.

Holding monetary items during a period of rising prices creates inflation gains and losses on these items. For example, suppose you hold $1,000 cash during a period when the general price level increases from 100 to 150. Obviously, at the end of the period your $1,000 will buy fewer goods and services than it would at the beginning of the period. This decrease in your ability to buy goods and services as a result of inflation is an *inflation loss on cash*. The amount of the loss is $500, calculated by multiplying the percentage increase in prices, 50%, by the $1,000 cash you held.

Next, assume you also had a note payable of $800 outstanding during the time the general price index increased from 100 to 150. As a result of inflation, you owe dollars whose general purchasing power at the end of the period is less than it was at the beginning of the period. The decrease in the general purchasing power of the dollars with which you will settle the liability represents an *inflation gain on the note payable.* The amount of the gain is $400 (50% × $800). Inflation gains and losses on monetary items are included in statements adjusted for price-level changes.

To illustrate a simple balance sheet conversion, we assume Abbott Company organized on January 1, 19X4, when the general price index was 100. Its opening balance sheet was as follows:

Abbott Company
Balance Sheet
January 1, 19X4

Assets		Owners' Equity	
Cash	$ 5,000	Common Stock	$75,000
Inventory	30,000		
Land	40,000		
Total Assets	$75,000	Total Owners' Equity	$75,000

Assume no further transactions occurred during 19X4, but the general price index increased to 150. Abbott Company's balance sheet at the end of 19X4, in conventional terms, would still be the same as shown above. The price-level adjusted balance sheet at December 31, 19X4, would be as follows (the conversion computations are shown in parentheses):

Abbott Company
General Purchasing Power Balance Sheet
December 31, 19X4

Assets		
Cash	$ 5,000	(Monetary asset, no adjustment needed)
Inventory	45,000	($30,000 × 150/100)
Land	60,000	($40,000 × 150/100)
Total Assets	$110,000	
Owners' Equity		
Common Stock	$112,500	($75,000 × 150/100)
Deficit	(2,500)	(Inflation loss on cash, 50% × $5,000)
Total Owners' Equity	$110,000	

Income statement conversion. We shall use the following income statement and related data of the Hardy Company as the basis for a simple conversion of an income statement into a price-level adjusted income statement.

Hardy Company
Income Statement
For the Year 19X4

Sales	$60,000	(Sales made uniformly throughout the year)
Cost of Goods Sold	$30,000	(Goods purchased when price index was 100)
Depreciation Expense	5,000	(Related asset bought when price index was 80)
Other Expenses	7,000	(Expenses incurred uniformly throughout the year)
Total Expenses	$42,000	
Net Income	$18,000	

The average price index for the year was 125, and the price index at year-end was 150. Hardy Company's price-level adjusted income statement appears below (the conversion computations are shown in parentheses):

Hardy Company
General Purchasing Power Income Statement
For the Year 19X4

Sales	$72,000	($60,000 × 150/125)
Cost of Goods Sold	$45,000	($30,000 × 150/100)
Depreciation Expense	9,375	($5,000 × 150/80)
Other Expenses	8,400	($7,000 × 150/125)
Total Expenses	$62,775	
Net Income	$ 9,225	

Of course, any inflation gains or losses on monetary items held by Hardy Company would also be included in Hardy Company's general purchasing power income statement.

ADVANTAGES OF ADJUSTED DATA Generally accepted accounting principles use the dollar as a measuring unit and assume it is stable (that is, that there are no significant price-level changes); therefore, all dollars are considered economically equal. Quite obviously there has been inflation in a single year that strains the stable dollar assumption and certainly some multiyear periods that invalidate it. Some of the benefits of making adjustments for changes in the general purchasing power of the dollar are (1) better comparisons of financial data through time, (2) improved additivity of financial data, and (3) increased disclosure of information through calculation of inflation gains and losses on monetary items.

Comparability of data through time. Assume that Company A's sales revenues are as indicated for the three years 19X2–19X4 and that the average price-level indexes are as shown.

	Average Price-level Index	Unadjusted Sales
19X2	75	$1,000,000
19X3	90	1,170,000
19X4	125	1,380,000

Further assume that the price-level index at the end of 19X4 is 150.

The unadjusted sales figures indicate a healthy increase in sales. However, if we convert the dollars stated in the average price-level index for 19X2, 19X3, and 19X4 to the dollar as of the end of 19X4 (the latest balance sheet date), we discover a significant need for price-level adjustment.

	Average Price-level Index	Unadjusted Sales	Conversion Factor	Restated Sales
19X2	75	$1,000,000	150/75	$2,000,000
19X3	90	1,170,000	150/90	1,950,000
19X4	125	1,380,000	150/125	1,656,000

Adjusting the data to a common dollar indicates that sales activity has decreased rather than increased. One can easily imagine the erroneous operating decisions that could result from data distortions of this type.

Additivity of financial data. The basic mathematical law of additivity asserts that only like units can be added or subtracted. Supporters of general price-level adjustments claim that the addition and subtraction of dollars of different purchasing power violates the law of additivity. Suppose Company A (from above) purchased a building in 19X1 for $5,400,000 when the price-level index was 60, and the building is being depreciated $270,000 per year. Company A's other expenses for 19X4, totaling $900,000, were incurred and paid uniformly throughout the year. The conventional income statement for 19X4 and the data restated in terms of the 19X4 year-end dollar appear as follows:

	Historical		Conversion Factor	Restated	
Sales		$1,380,000	150/125		$1,656,000
Depreciation Expense	$270,000		150/60	$ 675,000	
Other Expenses	900,000		150/125	1,080,000	
Total Expenses		1,170,000			1,755,000
Net Income (Loss)		$ 210,000			$ (99,000)

In the conventional, historical cost income statement, depreciation expense, expressed in 19X1 dollars, is added to other expenses, expressed in average 19X4 dollars, and then subtracted from sales, also expressed in average 19X4 dollars. In the restated income statement, all items are stated in dollars of a common general purchasing power. The restated amounts for 19X4 are decidedly different from the unadjusted amounts. The board of directors of Company A may have declared a dividend for 19X4 based on the net earnings calculated in the historical income statement. The restated numbers show that the dividend is not supported by 19X4 earnings.

The problem of nonadditivity also affects the balance sheet. Company A, for example, purchased a building in 19X1. Other assets held at the end of 19X4 were acquired at other points in time, some in 19X4 and others in other years. Yet the dollar measures of these resources, expressed in dollars of varying purchasing power, are added together in the balance sheet. If general price-level restatements were applied, the dollar measures would all be converted to a common dollar.

Inflation gains and losses on monetary items. There is no counterpart to inflation gains and losses on monetary items in conventional financial statements. Only through general price-level adjustments are these gains and losses computed and reported. Because they indicate how well management has managed monetary items during periods of inflation or deflation, their disclosure should increase the usefulness of the income statement as a performance report.

Current Value Accounting

The current value approach receiving the most attention from accountants is **replacement cost** accounting. The replacement cost of an asset is the current cost of acquiring a similar asset. Under a system of replacement cost accounting, current operating income is determined by subtracting from revenue the replacement cost of assets used in the earning process. Assets are reported in the balance sheet at their replacement costs. Changes in the replacement cost of an asset are recorded in the period the change in value occurs. Holding gains and holding losses are therefore reflected in the accounts.

We present a simple example to illustrate the basic concepts of a replacement cost system. Assume Bilmark, Inc. started business on January 1, 19X1, by issuing $100,000 of common stock and acquiring the following assets:

Cash	$10,000
Inventory (7,500 units @ $10)	75,000
Land	15,000

During the year, Bilmark, Inc. sold 5,000 inventory units at $16 each and incurred cash operating expenses of $18,000. Bilmark's historical cost income statement for 19X1 would be as follows:

Bilmark, Inc.
Income Statement
For the Year 19X1

Sales	$80,000	(5,000 units @ $16)
Cost of Goods Sold	$50,000	(5,000 units @ $10)
Operating Expenses	18,000	
Total Expenses	$68,000	
Net Income	$12,000	

Further, assume that before any inventory was sold in 19X1 its replacement cost increased to $11 per unit and remained there until the end of the year. Also assume the replacement cost of land increased to $19,000 by year-end. We will now illustrate the various components of a replacement cost system—current operating income, realized holding gains and losses, unrealized holding gains and losses—and the change in the content of the balance sheet.

CURRENT OPERATING INCOME Current operating income shows earnings after first providing for the replacement of assets used in operations. Expenses are measured at their replacement costs. Current operating income, therefore, indicates the profitability of operations at the level of operating costs the company currently faces. It also represents the maximum dividend the company could pay out and still maintain its present level of operations. Bilmark's current operating income is $7,000, as follows:

Sales	$80,000	
Cost of Goods Sold	$55,000	(5,000 units @ $11)
Operating Expenses	18,000	
Total Expenses	$73,000	
Current Operating Income	$ 7,000	

REALIZED HOLDING GAINS AND LOSSES A holding gain refers to an increase, and a holding loss refers to a decrease, in the replacement cost of an asset while it is held by a company. When the asset is sold or used in operations (and its cost is therefore charged to expense), the holding gain or loss is realized. A realized holding gain (or loss) is measured as the difference between the replacement cost expense amount and the historical cost expense amount. Realized holding gains less realized holding losses plus current operating income will equal the historical cost net income amount. Bilmark, Inc. realized a $5,000 holding gain on inventory in 19X1, computed as the difference between the replacement cost of goods sold ($55,000) and the historical cost of goods sold ($50,000).

UNREALIZED HOLDING GAINS AND LOSSES　Increases in the replacement costs of assets still on hand at year-end are identified as unrealized holding gains. Assets on hand at year-end whose replacement costs have fallen below their acquisition costs create unrealized holding losses. Bilmark, Inc. has unrealized holding gains on its 2,500 units of ending inventory and its land. The replacement cost of inventory increased by $1.00 per unit, and land increased in value from $15,000 to $19,000.

Unrealized Holding Gains:	Inventory	$2,500
	Land	4,000
	Total	$6,500

　　A characteristic of a replacement cost system is the separation of holding gains and losses from current operating income. Financial statement readers may use holding gains and losses to evaluate management's effectiveness in timing its acquisition of assets. One of many unresolved questions in replacement cost accounting is how best to report holding gains and losses (for example, as part of net income or in a new and separate statement). Accountants agree, however, that such gains and losses are items that affect owners' equity.

BALANCE SHEET CONTENT　A comparison of Bilmark, Inc.'s assets at December 31, 19X1, under replacement cost accounting and under historical cost accounting follows:

Assets	Replacement Cost	Historical Cost
Cash	$ 72,000	$ 72,000
Inventory	27,500	25,000
Land	19,000	15,000
Total Assets	$118,500	$112,000

The $6,500 difference between the asset totals represents Bilmark's unrealized holding gains at December 31, 19X1. Under replacement cost accounting, Bilmark's assets increased $18,500 during 19X1 ($118,500 minus $100,000). The owners' equity also increased $18,500 ($7,000 current operating income plus $5,000 realized holding gain plus $6,500 unrealized holding gains).

　　Proponents of replacement cost accounting contend that the use of replacement costs would introduce more economic reality into financial reports during inflationary periods than would general purchasing power adjustments. On the other hand, the determination of replacement costs would also introduce more subjectivity into the accounting measurement process. Replacement cost accounting is in its early stages of development in the United States, and many theoretical and measurement issues must be considered before the approach can be fully evaluated.

AUTHORITATIVE POSITIONS   Both the Securities and Exchange Commission (SEC) and the Financial Accounting Standards Board (FASB) are concerned about the impact of inflation on financial statements.

Securities and Exchange Commission. In 1976, a significant development occurred in financial reporting when the SEC adopted rules requiring approximately 1,000 large, publicly held companies to disclose certain replacement cost data in a note to their financial statements. The companies were required to disclose the replacement cost of (1) inventories, (2) productive capacity, (3) cost of goods sold, and (4) depreciation, depletion, and amortization. These data, of course, do not constitute a complete replacement cost system, but the SEC rules have caused companies to gain experience in compiling and reporting some replacement cost data.

Financial Accounting Standards Board. In 1979, the FASB issued a standard dealing with financial reporting in an inflationary environment.[4] The standard applies to publicly held companies with more than $1 billion in assets or more than $125 million in inventories and gross property, plant, and equipment. These companies must disclose selected information to supplement their basic, historical cost financial statements. Income from continuing operations, computed using both general purchasing power adjustment procedures and replacement cost procedures, must be disclosed. Reporting both of these income amounts provides a basis for the FASB to assess their usefulness. Other data to be disclosed include (1) the inflation gain or loss on net monetary items, (2) the replacement cost amounts at year-end of inventory and property, plant, and equipment, (3) increases or decreases for the year in replacement cost amounts of inventory and property, plant, and equipment, net of the effect of general inflation, and (4) a five-year summary of selected data accompanied by disclosure of the Consumer Price Index for each year in the summary.[5] In response to these disclosures now required by the FASB, SEC withdrew its replacement cost disclosure requirements.

[4]*Ibid.*

[5]The five-year summary contains three items—(1) income from continuing operations, (2) income per common share from continuing operations, and (3) net assets at year-end—which are computed using general purchasing power adjustments and replacement cost procedures. The summary also contains (1) net sales and other operating revenues, (2) increases or decreases in replacement cost amounts of inventory and property, plant, and equipment, net of general inflation, (3) inflation gain or loss on net monetary items, (4) cash dividends declared per common share, and (5) market price per common share at year-end.

KEY POINTS TO REMEMBER

(1) Each of the following is an important basic accounting principle:

accounting entity	objectivity
accounting period	going concern
materiality	measuring unit
conservatism	historical cost
consistency	matching expenses with revenues
full disclosure	point-of-sale revenue recognition

(2) The installment basis of revenue recognition treats each dollar received as part return of cost and part gross profit.

(3) The percentage-of-completion basis recognizes gross profit in proportion to the amount of the total contract completed in each period.

(4) Interperiod income tax allocation is a process of apportioning income tax expense to the income statement based on the pretax accounting income. It is used when there are timing differences between pretax accounting income and taxable income.

(5) Two possible responses to inflation are (a) to adjust financial statements for changes in the general purchasing power of the dollar, and (b) to move to a system of current value accounting.

(6) General purchasing power adjustments cause financial data to be stated in dollars of constant purchasing power.

(7) Replacement cost accounting reflects operating expenses at their replacement costs and shows replacement costs in the balance sheet.

QUESTIONS

16-1 How would you go about proving to someone that a particular accounting technique is or is not a generally accepted accounting procedure?

16-2 Discuss the origin of accounting principles.

16-3 Present, in one sentence of your own words, a description of each of the following accounting principles:

accounting entity	objectivity
accounting period	going concern
materiality	measuring unit
conservatism	historical cost
consistency	matching expenses with revenues
full disclosure	point-of-sale revenue recognition

16-4 Why do accounting principles emphasize the use of historical cost as a basis for measuring assets?

16-5 How do accountants justify using the point of sale for revenue recognition when revenue recognition at some earlier point has so much theoretical appeal?

16-6 Explain the procedures and justification for using the following bases of revenue recognition: (a) the installment basis; (b) the percentage-of-completion basis.

16-7 What are timing differences between pretax accounting income and taxable income? Give an example of a timing difference.

16-8 What is meant by interperiod income tax allocation? Why do accountants employ interperiod income tax allocation?

16-9 What does the balance in the Deferred Tax Credits account reflect? Where should this account be classified in the financial statements?

16-10 How does interperiod income tax allocation differ from tax allocation within a period discussed in Chapter 14?

16-11 Identify and briefly explain two proposed approaches to improving financial data during inflationary periods.

16-12 Explain how price-level indexes can be used to convert the dollars of one year to those of another year.

16-13 Define inflation. What difficulty does inflation cause for financial accounting?

16-14 Define monetary assets and monetary liabilities. Give examples of each.

16-15 Alt Company makes sales uniformly during a year. Last year's sales were $120,000, and the current year's sales were $153,000. The average general price index last year was 150 and this year 170. At the current year-end it is 200. Restate the sales for the two years in terms of the current year-end dollar.

16-16 How is current operating income computed in a replacement cost accounting system? What is the significance of the current operating income amount?

EXERCISES

16-17 Indicate the basic principle or principles of accounting that underlie each of the following independent situations.
  (a) Dr. Belamin is a practicing radiologist. Over the years she has accumulated a personal investment portfolio of securities. Virtually all of the securities have been purchased from her earnings as a radiologist. The investment portfolio is not reflected in the accounting records of her medical practice.
  (b) A company purchases a stapler for use by the office secretary. The stapler cost $10 and has an estimated useful life of 10 years. The purchase is debited to the Office Supplies Expense account.
  (c) A company sells a product that has a 2-year warranty covering parts and

labor. In the same period that sales are recorded, an estimate is made of future warranty costs and debited to the Product Warranty Expense account.

(d) A company pays $10,000 for equipment that has an estimated useful life of 12 years and no salvage value. The amount is debited to the Equipment account and will be depreciated over a 12-year period.

(e) A company purchased a parcel of land several years ago for $35,000. The land is estimated to have a current market value of $55,000. The land account balance is not increased, but remains at $35,000.

16–18 For each of the following independent situations, determine how much revenue should be reported in the current period and how much should be deferred to a future period. If either the installment method or percentage-of-completion method is applicable, determine the appropriate gross profit amounts rather than revenue amounts.

(a) Purchased merchandise for $24,000 that will be sold the first day of the next period for $32,000.

(b) Took an order for merchandise that is to be acquired for $3,800 and sold for $4,700 during the next period.

(c) Sold during this period $4,000 of service contracts for which it is estimated that 70% of the required service costs will be incurred in future periods.

(d) Sold $60,000 of undeveloped real estate lots on installment terms. Of the $60,000, 10% was collected during this period. No reasonable estimate of the collectibility of the remaining balances is possible. The cost of the property sold is $40,000.

(e) Accomplished approximately 35% of the work on an order of machinery that will be completed during the first month of the next period and sold for $70,000. Total estimated cost for the machinery when completed is $49,000.

16–19 On October 1, 19X2, Rascher Appliance Company sold a combination refrigerator–freezer for $900 on terms of 10% down on the date of purchase, with 27 equal monthly payments beginning November 1, 19X2. The appliance cost $540. Compute the amount of gross profit to be shown in each calendar year involved using the following revenue recognition methods:

(a) The cost recovery method.
(b) The installment method.
(c) The point-of-sale method.

16–20 The bottom portion of Kornell, Inc. income statements for 19X1 and 19X2 were as follows:

	19X2	19X1
Income before Taxes	$36,000	$28,000
Income Tax Expense	15,000	17,000
Net Income	$21,000	$11,000

In 19X1 Kornell, Inc. received an advance payment of $6,000, which was subject to income tax in 19X1, but not reported in accounting income until 19X2. The income tax rate is 50%. Kornell, Inc. did not employ interperiod income tax allocation.

(a) Identify the distortions in Kornell's income statements that arise from the failure to use interperiod income tax allocation.

(b) Redo the bottom portion of Kornell's income statements, using interperiod income tax allocation.

16-21 The Branden Company purchased a parcel of land for $45,000 several years ago when the general price index was 90. The year-end index for each of the four most recent years has been:

19X1	108
19X2	120
19X3	126
19X4	135

Compute the restated amount for land that would appear in a general purchasing power balance sheet at December 31, (a) 19X1; (b) 19X2; (c) 19X3; (d) 19X4. Balance sheet data are to be stated in terms of the general purchasing power of the dollar as of the balance sheet date.

16-22 Lemon, Inc. organized on January 1 of the current year by issuing common stock in exchange for $2,000 cash and land valued at $2,000. Its balance sheet at this point was:

Cash	$2,000	Common Stock	$4,000
Land	2,000		
	$4,000		

The company engaged in no further transaction during the year. The general price index was 100 on January 1 and 120 on December 31. Prepare the general purchasing power balance sheet at December 31, stated in terms of the December 31 dollar.

16-23 On January 2, 19X5, the Stream Company purchased 3,000 inventory items at $50 each. On January 4 the purchase price increased to $54 per unit. During 19X5, Stream Company sold 2,500 of these items. If Stream Company followed replacement cost accounting procedures, what would be the amount of (a) the cost of goods sold expense in 19X5, (b) the realized holding gain on inventory in 19X5, and (c) the unrealized holding gain on inventory at December 31, 19X5?

PROBLEMS

16-24 Below are listed certain unrelated accounting situations and (where applicable) the accounting treatment, in journal entry form, that has been followed in the records of the firms involved.

(1) Because of a local bankruptcy, machinery obviously worth $30,000 was acquired at a "bargain" purchase price of $22,000. Accounting treatment:

Machinery	22,000	
Cash		22,000

(2) Tom Balke, a consultant operating a sole proprietorship, withdrew $4,000 from the business and purchased securities as a gift to his wife. Accounting treatment:

Investments	4,000	
Cash		4,000

(3) The Ready State Bank, by action of the board of directors, wrote down the value of its home office building to a nominal amount of $100. The objective was to bolster its customers' confidence in the financial strength of the bank by obviously understating bank assets. Accounting treatment:

Retained Earnings	774,900	
Buildings		774,900

(4) For many years, McCarthy Company has capitalized and depreciated all asset acquisitions in excess of $100. This year the company has decided that henceforth acquisitions of less than $300 are to be immediately expensed.

(5) The fiscal year of Sullivan, Inc. ends on June 30. It is now July 10, and financial statements for the year just ended are being prepared. During the July 4 holiday weekend, a fire destroyed most of the inventories of the company. Because there is some question whether the company had violated local fire regulations, it has not been determined whether the loss is covered by insurance. This possible loss is reflected in the financial statements for the year just ended. Accounting treatment:

Fire Loss	95,000	
Merchandise Inventory		95,000

(6) Nash Company received a binding offer of $70,000 for a parcel of land it owns and for which it paid $47,000 two years ago. The indicated gain was recorded in the accounts. Accounting treatment:

Land	23,000	
Income from Increase in Value of Land		23,000

(7) Because of an increase in the general level of prices, Sentry, Inc. determined that there was approximately a $3,500 understatement in the recorded depreciation expense of its store building and decided to reflect this in its accounts. Accounting treatment:

Depreciation Expense	3,500	
Accumulated Depreciation		3,500

REQUIRED
(a) In each of the given situations, indicate which generally accepted accounting principles are applicable and whether they have been used appropriately.
(b) If you decide the accounting treatment is not generally accepted, discuss the effect of the departure on the balance sheet and the income statement.

16-25 On December 1, 19X7, Woodstock Company initiated a policy of permitting customers to buy goods on an installment basis. Sales of $60,000 were made during December on an installment basis. Terms were 15% down on the date of purchase, with 24 equal monthly payments beginning January 2, 19X8. The cost of the goods sold on the installment basis was $33,000. Woodstock Company elects to use the installment basis to report the gross profit from these sales on its income tax return. On its books the company recognizes the revenue and related cost of goods sold at the time the sale is made.

REQUIRED
(a) Assuming all installment collections are made as scheduled, how much gross profit from these December installment sales will Woodstock Company report on its income tax return for (1) 19X7, (2) 19X8, and (3) 19X9?
(b) Assuming all installment collections are made as scheduled, how much gross profit from these December installment sales will Woodstock Company report on its books for (1) 19X7, (2) 19X8, and (3) 19X9?
(c) Assume the only timing difference between the books and the income tax return for 19X7 is the reporting of the gross profit on the December installment sales. If Woodstock Company has a pretax accounting income of $400,000 for 19X7, what is the amount of its 19X7 taxable income?
(d) Assume the 19X7 income tax rate is 40%. What balance will Woodstock Company show in its Deferred Tax Credits account at December 31, 19X7?

16-26 On November 1, 19X2, Seabilt, Inc. signed a contract to build a large sea-going oil tanker. Completion and sale of the ship were scheduled for October, 19X4. The total contract price for the ship was $8,000,000 and the total estimated cost was $5,000,000. The contract specified the following cash payments by the buyer:

$500,000 on signing the contract;
$3,500,000 when the ship is considered one-half completed;
$3,200,000 when the ship is completed;
$800,000 ninety days after completion.

It was agreed that the degree of completion would be considered equal to the proportion of estimated total cost incurred by the builder. Seabilt accounts for operations on a calendar-year basis. Costs for the ship were incurred and paid as follows:

November and December, 19X2	$ 600,000
The year 19X3	3,000,000
The year 19X4	1,400,000

The ship was finished and the sale was consummated October 20, 19X4.

REQUIRED
(a) Calculate the gross profit (or loss) that would be reported each year if a cash basis of accounting (cash receipts less cash disbursements) were used.
(b) Calculate the gross profit that would be reported each year on an accrual

basis of accounting using: (1) the point-of-sale method of revenue recognition; (2) the percentage-of-completion method of revenue recognition.

(c) Comment on the relative usefulness of these approaches to periodic income determination.

16-27 Robin Company acquired a new machine on January 1, 19X1, at a cost of $9,600. It estimated the new machine will have a useful life of four years and a salvage value of $600. Straight-line depreciation is used in the accounts, while double declining-balance depreciation is selected for tax purposes. This is the only difference between pretax accounting income and taxable income. Robin Company had "income before depreciation and taxes" of $16,000 in 19X1, $24,000 in 19X2, $20,000 in 19X3, and $30,000 in 19X4. Assume the income tax rate is 50%.

REQUIRED

(a) Prepare a schedule deriving taxable income and the income tax liability for the years 19X1 through 19X4.

(b) Prepare a schedule deriving pretax accounting income for the years 19X1 through 19X4.

(c) Prepare journal entries to record (1) income taxes for the years 19X1 through 19X4, using interperiod income tax allocation, and (2) the payment of taxes. Assume Robin Company pays its tax liability in full in the year following its recognition in the accounts.

16-28 Halet Company reported the following conventional income statement for 19X3:

Halet Company
Income Statement
For the Year 19X3

Sales		$400,000
Cost of Goods Sold		230,000
Gross Profit on Sales		$170,000
Operating Expenses:		
Depreciation Expense—Equipment	$ 8,000	
Patent Amortization Expense	6,000	
Selling Expenses	30,000	
Administrative Expenses	50,000	
Income Taxes	36,000	
Total Operating Expenses		130,000
Net Income		$ 40,000

Additional Data:

(1) Sales, selling expenses, and administrative expenses have taken place evenly throughout the year, and income taxes have accrued ratably throughout the year.

(2) The goods sold were acquired when the general price index was 150.

(3) The equipment being depreciated was purchased when the general price index was 100.

(4) Halet Company acquired a patent for $60,000 at a general price index of 120. The patent is being written off over 10 years.

(5) The general price index averaged 160 for the year 19X3 and was 180 at December 31, 19X3.

REQUIRED

Prepare a general purchasing power income statement for 19X3, stated in terms of the dollar at December 31, 19X3. Ignore the calculation of any inflation gain or loss on monetary items.

16-29 Appearing below is a list of accounts, their year-end balances, and the assumed general price-level index on the date each account was established.

	Balance	Assumed Price-level Index
Cash	$ 70,000	125
Notes Receivable	10,000	120
Buildings	300,000	75
Supplies on Hand	15,000	90
Patent (less amortization of $50,000)	40,000	80
Term Mortgage Payable	150,000	100

REQUIRED

Assume the current price-level index is 135.

(a) For each item, compute the amount that would appear in a general purchasing power balance sheet stated in dollars of current purchasing power.

(b) Identify each monetary item. Assume the balance of each monetary item has not changed since it was established by the company. Compute the inflation gain or loss on each monetary item.

(c) Comment on the effect that omission of general price level adjustments tends to have on the balance sheet; the income statement.

16-30 Assume you have just started a summer internship in the controller's office of Donahue, Inc., a large merchandising firm. The controller, Mr. Kapabil, wants you, as your first project, to familiarize him with developments in the area of inflation accounting. He knows that accountants have been experimenting with adjusting data for general price-level changes and compiling data under replacement cost accounting procedures. For your first meeting with him, he asks you to be prepared to discuss the following items:

(1) What is the basic difference between adjusting financial data for general price-level changes and employing replacement cost accounting procedures?

(2) What are the benefits of adjusting financial data for general price-level changes?

(3) What is an inflation gain or loss on monetary items? Will the fact that Donahue, Inc. has large inventory balances adversely affect the calculation of its inflation gain or loss on monetary items?

(4) What are the benefits of employing replacement cost accounting procedures?

(5) Are there any significant disadvantages associated with replacement cost accounting?

(6) What is the difference between a realized holding gain and an unrealized holding gain?

(7) How does current operating income under replacement cost accounting differ from net income under historical cost accounting?

(8) What does the current operating income amount under replacement cost accounting disclose?

REQUIRED

In preparation for your meeting with Mr. Kapabil, write out brief answers to each of the above items.

ALTERNATE PROBLEMS

16-25A The following events relate to the sale of a machine by Tanner Equipment Company in April, 19X1.

March   Tanner received a sales order accompanied by a $680 deposit from the customer, as is usual when special devices are custom-ordered for the machine. The machine was acquired on account from a local supplier at a cost of $5,200. Purchase terms required net cash payment in May.

April   The machine modification was completed and it was sold for a total price of $6,800 (including the deposit) on terms that required the customer to pay an additional $3,400 at the time of sale and the balance before the end of the following month.

May   Tanner paid its supplier for the machine. The customer made the final payment on the machine.

REQUIRED

(a) Calculate the amount of gross profit (or loss) that would be reported each month if a cash basis accounting treatment (cash receipts less cash disbursements) were used.

(b) Prepare journal entries to properly reflect the accrual accounting treatment of these transactions (*Hint*: For the first March transaction, credit the liability account Customer Deposit.) What is the reported gross profit for each month? Assume a perpetual inventory method.

(c) Comment briefly on the usefulness of each method in (a) and (b) to a manager concerned with evaluating the effect of these transactions on the firm's operations.

16-26A On December 1, 19X1, Spaceco, Inc. signed a contract to build a space station shuttle. Completion and sale of the shuttle were scheduled for November 19X3. The total contract price for the shuttle was $10,000,000, and total estimated cost was $8,000,000. The contract specified the following cash payments by the buyer:

> $1,000,000 upon signing the contract;
> $4,000,000 when the shuttle is considered one-half completed;
> $4,000,000 when the shuttle is completed;
> $1,000,000 ninety days after completion.

It was agreed that the degree of completion would be considered equal to the proportion of estimated total cost incurred by the builder. Spaceco accounts for operations on a calendar-year basis. Costs for the shuttle were incurred and paid as follows:

December 19X1	$ 940,000
The year 19X2	4,800,000
The year 19X3	2,260,000

The shuttle was finished and the sale was consummated November 8, 19X3.

REQUIRED
(a) Calculate the gross profit (or loss) that would be reported each year if a cash basis of accounting (cash receipts less cash disbursements) were used.
(b) Calculate the gross profit that would be reported each year on an accrual basis of accounting using: (1) the point-of-sale method of revenue recognition; (2) the percentage-of-completion method of revenue recognition.
(c) Comment on the relative usefulness of these approaches to periodic income determination.

16-27A On January 2, 19X5, Corcoran, Inc. leased a parcel of land it owned to a tenant for three years, 19X5, 19X6, and 19X7, for $500 per month. Corcoran, Inc. collected the entire $18,000 rent on January 2, 19X5. The $18,000 was subject to tax in 19X5. This is the only difference between pretax accounting income and taxable income. Corcoran, Inc. had "income before rent revenue and taxes" of $30,000 in 19X5, $34,000 in 19X6, and $40,000 in 19X7. Assume the income tax rate is 50%.

REQUIRED
(a) Prepare a schedule deriving taxable income and the income tax liability for the years 19X5 through 19X7.
(b) Prepare a schedule deriving pretax accounting income for the years 19X5 through 19X7.
(c) Prepare journal entries to record (1) income taxes for the years 19X5 through 19X7, using interperiod income tax allocation, and (2) the payment of taxes. Assume Corcoran, Inc. pays its tax liability in full in the year after its recognition in the accounts.

16-28A York, Inc. reported the following conventional income statement for 19X2:

York, Inc.
Income Statement
For the Year 19X2

Sales		$250,000
Cost of Goods Sold		140,000
Gross Profit on Sales		$110,000
Operating Expenses:		
Depreciation Expense—Equipment	$10,000	
Depreciation Expense—Building	30,000	
Selling Expenses	24,000	
Administrative Expenses	16,000	
Income Taxes	14,000	94,000
Net Income		$ 16,000

Additional Data:
(1) Sales, selling expenses, and administrative expenses have taken place evenly throughout the year, and income taxes have accrued ratably throughout the year.
(2) The goods sold were acquired at a general price index of 120.
(3) Equipment depreciation of $4,000 relates to equipment purchased when the general price index was 80. The rest of the equipment was purchased when the index was 88.
(4) The building was constructed at a time when the general price index was 66.
(5) The general price index averaged 110 for the year 19X2 and was 132 at December 31, 19X2.

REQUIRED
Prepare a general purchasing power income statement for 19X2, stated in terms of the dollar at December 31, 19X2. Ignore the calculation of any inflation gain or loss on monetary items.

BUSINESS DECISION PROBLEM

Fliteway Company started operations at the beginning of 19X1. Its primary asset is a helicopter, which is used in the following ways:
(1) For carrying passengers between a major air terminal and a downtown heliport. As a new business promotion, the company sold booklets of one-way tickets. Each booklet contained 10 tickets and was priced at $200. Three hundred of these booklets were sold. During 19X1, purchasers of the booklets used 1,800 of the tickets.
(2) For passenger charter flights. A deposit of 30% of the charter fee is required when a charter flight is booked. On December 31, 19X1, the company had deposits of $7,500 for scheduled charter flights. The company received a total of $26,000 for charter flights flown during 19X1.

(3) For construction material and equipment transportation. Building contractors may rent the helicopter for $130 an hour for use in moving material and equipment to and from construction sites. Contractors used the helicopter a total of 180 hours during 19X1. Of this total, 20 hours occurred in December, for which the company has not yet received payment.

(4) For "Save A Life" efforts during holidays. The state rents the helicopter for $80 an hour on holiday weekends to carry a medical team to accident locations. The state used the helicopter 60 hours in 19X1. The company has not yet collected for 12 hours of use in December.

The bookkeeper for Fliteway Company has prepared the following schedule of revenue for 19X1:

One-way ticket booklets (300 @ $200)	$ 60,000
Charter flights made	26,000
Deposits on charter flights scheduled	7,500
Contractors (160 hours @ $130)	20,800
"Save A Life" program (48 hours @ $80)	3,840
Total Revenue	$118,140

The president of Fliteway Company has asked you to evaluate whether the bookkeeper has correctly determined the 19X1 revenue in accordance with generally accepted accounting principles.

REQUIRED

Has the bookkeeper correctly determined the 19X1 revenue? If not, prepare a revised 19X1 revenue schedule. Give reasons for any changes you make from the bookkeeper's schedule.

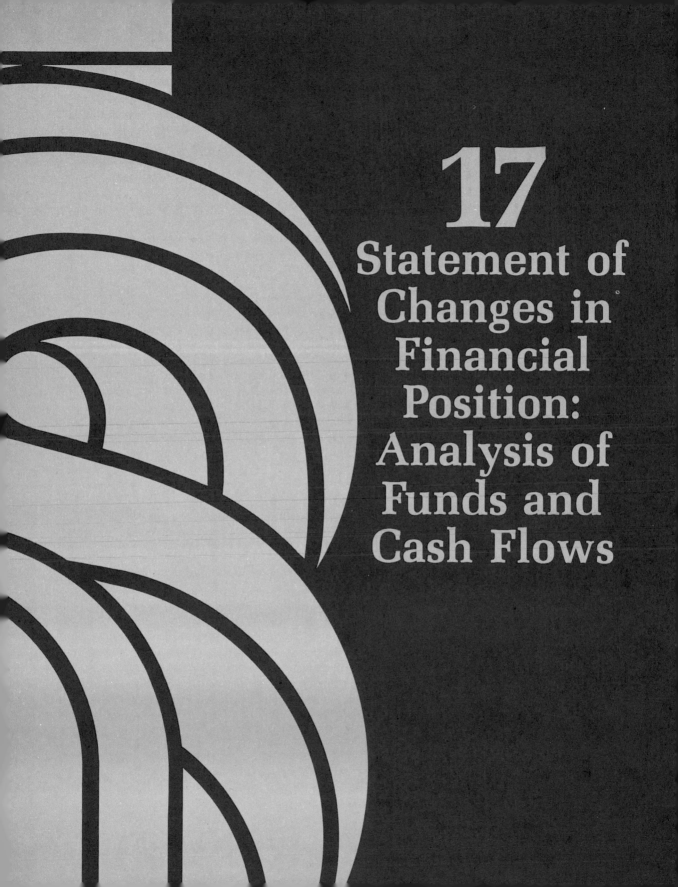

17
Statement of Changes in Financial Position: Analysis of Funds and Cash Flows

As part of its continuing effort to facilitate financial analysis by external users of information, the Accounting Principles Board, in its Opinion No. 19,[1] classified the **Statement of Changes in Financial Position** as a basic financial statement to be included in the accounting reports of business enterprises along with the other customary statements. This statement provides information that is unavailable in the balance sheet and the income statement (or that is provided only indirectly) about the flow of funds and changes in financial position during the period. Because the statement of changes in financial position focuses on the sources and uses of funds, it often is referred to as a *funds statement.*

We begin our discussion with the concept of funds flow and then move through the necessary steps to prepare the statement of changes in financial position. Finally, we describe an approach to cash flow analysis and the preparation of cash flow statements.

DEFINITION OF FUNDS

To most people, the term "funds" denotes cash. Business executives and financial analysts, however, prefer to think of the net circulating capital of a business as the firm's "funds." Therefore, the most common definition of funds is **working capital**—*current assets less current liabilities.*

Consider the logic of this definition. A company acquires inventory on credit, converts it into receivables, then into cash, pays its short-term creditors, and then repeats the cycle over and over again. This process itself, for profitable companies, generates additional working capital. Working capital is also injected into the system by other means, among the most important of which are sales of noncurrent assets, long-term borrowing, and sales of equity securities. On the other hand, working capital is continually being depleted by such activities as purchases of noncurrent assets, repayment of long-term debt, and payment of dividends. The effect of all these activities can be seen in the diagram at the top of page 587.

---

[1]*Opinions of the Accounting Principles Board, No. 19,* "Reporting Changes in Financial Position," American Institute of Certified Public Accountants, New York, 1971.

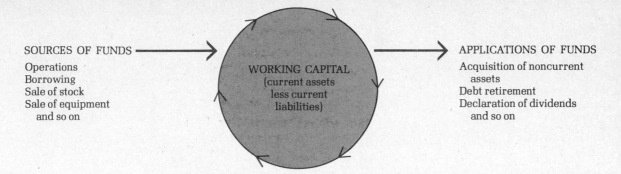

SOURCES OF FUNDS

Operations
Borrowing
Sale of stock
Sale of equipment
  and so on

WORKING CAPITAL
(current assets
less current
liabilities)

APPLICATIONS OF FUNDS

Acquisition of noncurrent
  assets
Debt retirement
Declaration of dividends
  and so on

Because circulating capital is the lifeblood of an enterprise, financial analysts are vitally interested in it when examining a particular firm. Even a profitable company can be anemic with respect to working capital, and a poor working capital position can lead to financial and operating difficulties. The liquid, or net current, resources of a firm are of great importance to its operations, and this broader concept of funds provides a most useful perspective.

USEFULNESS OF STATEMENT OF CHANGES IN FINANCIAL POSITION

The statement of changes in financial position discloses all important changes in financial position during an accounting period; it details the sources and uses of funds. Working capital increases when funds provided by various activities exceed the funds used. Working capital decreases when funds used exceed funds provided.

Knowing the sources of a company's working capital and the ways that capital is used, an analyst can tell a great deal about the strengths and weaknesses of the firm and about the policies of its management. One advantage of the statement of changes in financial position is that it summarizes the major asset acquisitions and the financing activities of the firm during the accounting period. Hence, over time, the analyst can observe management's spending and borrowing habits. In addition, one may discover in the statement of changes in financial position: (1) clues to the firm's ability to pay dividends and its subsequent dividend policy, and (2) whether there may be a need for future financing. Finally, analysts have found the information on these statements extremely useful when comparing companies.

THE EFFECT OF TRANSACTIONS ON WORKING CAPITAL

When preparing a statement of changes in financial position, one should keep in mind the effect of various transactions on working capital. Let us use a simple example, therefore, to illustrate how transactions may be analyzed. Exhibit 17-1 presents the XYZ Company's balance sheet at the end of Year 2 and Year 1. Exhibit 17–2 is the company's income statement for Year 2.

EXHIBIT 17–1

XYZ Company
Balance Sheets

	Dec. 31, Year 2	Dec. 31, Year 1
Assets		
Cash	$ 16,000	$ 5,000
Accounts Receivable	10,000	15,000
Inventory	30,000	30,000
Plant Assets	55,000	55,000
Accumulated Depreciation	(10,000)	(5,000)
Total Assets	$101,000	$100,000
Liabilities and Stockholders' Equity		
Accounts Payable	$ 20,000	$ 25,000
Dividends Payable	3,000	—
Common Stock	50,000	50,000
Retained Earnings	28,000	25,000
Total Liabilities and Stockholders' Equity	$101,000	$100,000

EXHIBIT 17–2

XYZ Company
Income Statement
For the Year Ended December 31, Year 2

Sales	$35,000	
Cost of Goods Sold	20,000	(1)
Gross Profit	$15,000	
Operating Expenses and Income Taxes (excluding depreciation)	4,000	(2)
	$11,000	
Depreciation Expense	5,000	(3)
Net Income	$ 6,000	

Now, suppose that XYZ Company engaged in the following transactions during Year 2:

(1) Sold $20,000 inventory for $35,000 on account.
(2) Paid $4,000 operating expenses and income taxes in cash.
(3) Recorded $5,000 annual depreciation.
(4) Collected $40,000 of accounts receivable.
(5) Replenished the inventory by purchasing $20,000 merchandise on account.
(6) Paid $25,000 on accounts payable.
(7) Declared dividends of $3,000, to be paid in Year 3.

In Exhibit 17–2, we have keyed the income statement with the relevant transaction numbers.

THE INCREASED EMPHASIS ON FUNDS FLOW

It is always interesting to speculate on the reasons for the appearance of new developments at the time they do, on why they did not appear earlier or postpone their appearance until later. For years a long struggle has been going on to develop the accrual basis of accounting, and the struggle still goes on. In essence the accrual basis itself developed and is developing in an effort to overcome the shortcomings of cash movements as indicators of the results of operations. And yet the newer emphasis on "funds flows" and "cash flows" seems to run counter to the movement to perfect an accrual accounting. Three factors, among others, account for the crosscurrents. The first of these is the lack of uniformity in accounting procedures, especially in the treatment of the "non-fund" transactions. For example, investment analysts appear initially to have developed "cash flow" analysis in response to the wide divergence of procedures within specific industries. As the range of acceptable accounting procedures becomes narrowed, this factor will lose its importance. The second factor is the tendency in times of stress to throw off more sophisticated concepts and revert to more primitive ones. The stress involved is that created by the combined effect of inflation and high taxes; the sophisticated concept is that of accrual accounting; the more primitive one is, of course, the elemental idea of a cash movement. As the problems created for accounting by inflation and high taxes are solved, this second factor should become much less powerful.

The third factor is the extent to which accounting has identified itself with the measurement of corporate net profit, to the virtual exclusion of other aspects of business activity. As a result, the only report on operating activities that is published in the majority of cases is the report of net income. To the extent that "funds statements" give additional information on what went on in the accounting entity during the period, they supply a welcome expansion of the information supplied to readers of published financial reports. Current developments therefore should lead to a permanent improvement in reporting practices.

From preface (by Maurice Moonitz) to Perry Mason, "Cash Flow" Analysis and The Funds Statement, pp. xi-xii, copyright American Institute of Certified Public Accountants, New York, 1961.

Let us see what change has occurred in the working capital, or "funds," of the XYZ Company during Year 2. We calculate this change as follows:

	Dec. 31, Year 2	Dec. 31, Year 1	Increase (Decrease)
Current Assets:			
Cash	$16,000	$ 5,000	$11,000
Accounts Receivable	10,000	15,000	(5,000)
Inventory	30,000	30,000	—
Total Current Assets	$56,000	$50,000	$ 6,000
Current Liabilities:			
Accounts Payable	$20,000	$25,000	($ 5,000)
Dividends Payable	3,000	—	3,000
Total Current Liabilities	$23,000	$25,000	($ 2,000)
Working Capital	$33,000	$25,000	$ 8,000

The $8,000 increase in working capital results from a $6,000 increase in current assets and a $2,000 decrease in current liabilities. Working capital is a "net" concept—current assets less current liabilities. Thus, it is increased by increases in current assets and by decreases in current liabilities; conversely, it is decreased by decreases in current assets and by increases in current liabilities.

One way of analyzing the factors that account for the increase of $8,000 in working capital is to consider the effect of each of the period's transactions on the balance sheet of the XYZ Company:

Transaction and Effect on Balance Sheet			Effect on Working Capital
(1) Sold $20,000 inventory for $35,000 on account.			
Accounts Receivable	35,000		$35,000 increase
Retained Earnings (revenue)		35,000	
Retained Earnings (expense)	20,000		
Inventory		20,000	($20,000) decrease

Note that this transaction resulted in an increase of $35,000 in one current asset (accounts receivable) and a decrease of $20,000 in another (inventory). The net result was an increase in working capital of $15,000. Because revenue and expense accounts are summarized and closed to retained earnings, their impact in a balance sheet is reflected in the retained earnings account.

(2) Paid $4,000 in cash for operating expenses and income taxes.			
Retained Earnings (expense)	4,000		
Cash		4,000	($ 4,000) decrease

Here, the decrease in a current asset (cash) resulted in a decrease in working capital.

(3) Recorded $5,000 annual depreciation.

| Retained Earnings (expense) | 5,000 | | None |
| Accumulated Depreciation | | 5,000 | |

No current assets or current liabilities were involved in this entry; therefore, there was no effect on working capital.

(4) Collected $40,000 of accounts receivable.

| Cash | 40,000 | | None |
| Accounts Receivable | | 40,000 | |

This entry increased one current asset and decreased another by the same amount; the amount of working capital was not changed.

(5) Replenished the inventory by purchasing $20,000 merchandise on account.

| Inventory | 20,000 | | None |
| Accounts Payable | | 20,000 | |

Here, both current assets and current liabilities were increased by the same amount, with no resulting effect on working capital.

(6) Paid $25,000 on accounts payable.

| Accounts Payable | 25,000 | | None |
| Cash | | 25,000 | |

Because both a current asset and a current liability were equally reduced, there was no effect on working capital.

(7) Declared dividends of $3,000.

| Retained Earnings | 3,000 | | |
| Dividends Payable | | 3,000 | ($ 3,000) decrease |

Here, the increase in a current liability resulted in a decrease in working capital.

| Change in Working Capital in Year 2 | | | $ 8,000 increase |

Obviously, for most businesses, analyzing all the year's transactions to account for the net change in working capital during the year would be a tedious job. We can make several important observations about the foregoing procedure, however, to develop a more efficient approach to the preparation of a statement of changes in financial position.

(1) Transactions involving only current assets and liabilities can be ignored, because there is no net effect on funds. Such transactions as collections on account, purchases of merchandise, and payments on account do not change working capital. Transactions (4), (5), and (6) are examples of such activities.

(2) Transactions involving both current and noncurrent accounts do have an effect on funds. These may be divided into two groups:

(a) Routine operating transactions recording the sale of goods, reduction of inventories, and most reflections of expense affect one or more current accounts and also (ultimately) the Retained Earnings account. These transactions are already summarized in the net income figure, so there is no need to analyze them. Examples are transactions (1) and (2) in the foregoing illustration. One merely observes that funds were "provided by operations," using the net income figure. As explained below, however, some adjustments are almost always necessary.

(b) Nonroutine transactions such as purchase or sale of plant assets, long-term borrowing or repayment, sale or repurchase of stock, and declaration of dividends affect one or more current accounts but are not included in the net income figure. These transactions must be analyzed separately. An example is transaction (7).

(3) Transactions involving only noncurrent accounts have no effect on funds. Recording depreciation, as in transaction (3), affects only the Accumulated Depreciation and Retained Earnings accounts on the balance sheet and has no effect on funds. Therefore, *if the net income figure is used to summarize "working capital provided by operations," the depreciation must be added back to net income* to arrive at the correct amount of working capital provided by routine transactions described in 2(a) above. We can see the rationale for this treatment of depreciation expense by looking at Exhibit 17–2. Transactions (1) and (2) provide a net increase in working capital from operations of $11,000. If we start with the net income figure of $6,000, we must add to it the $5,000 depreciation expense to obtain the $11,000 funds provided by operations.

In fact, any write-offs or amortization of noncurrent items deducted on the income statement must be added back to net income to arrive at the amount of funds provided by operations. Other examples of such write-offs include amortization of patents, leaseholds, goodwill, and bond discount. An item such as amortization of bond premium *would be deducted from the net income figure* on the statement of changes in financial position.

The above observations apply only to analysis of transactions affecting working capital. In addition, certain transactions resulting in significant financial changes that may involve only noncurrent accounts, but that do not affect working capital, are to be reported on the statement of changes in financial position, according to Accounting Principles Board *Opinion No. 19*. These include transactions involving issuance of securities for long-term assets, conversion of long-term debt or preferred stock into common stock, and donations of long-term assets. They are best analyzed individually in preparing a statement of changes in financial position, and we shall discuss them later in this chapter.

Exhibit 17–3 shows a statement of changes in financial position for the XYZ Company for Year 2.

EXHIBIT 17–3

XYZ Company
Statement of Changes in Financial Position
For the Year Ended December 31, Year 2

Sources of Working Capital
Operations:

Net Income	$ 6,000	
Add Expenses Not Decreasing Working Capital:		
Depreciation	5,000	
Total Sources of Working Capital		$11,000

Uses of Working Capital

Declaration of Dividends		3,000
Increase in Working Capital		$ 8,000

Changes in Working Capital Components
Increases (Decreases) in Current Assets:

Cash	$11,000	
Accounts Receivable	(5,000)	
Increase in Current Assets		$ 6,000
Increases (Decreases) in Current Liabilities:		
Accounts Payable	($ 5,000)	
Dividends Payable	3,000	
Decrease in Current Liabilities		(2,000)
Increase in Working Capital		$ 8,000

FORM OF STATEMENT OF
CHANGES IN FINANCIAL POSITION

The statement of changes in financial position should be headed with the name of the company and the title of the statement. Because it is a statement of flows, it should, like the income statement, show the period being covered. The first part of the statement, which presents the events causing the change in funds, has two major sections, **Sources of Working Capital** (or Sources of Funds) and **Uses of Working Capital** (or Uses of Funds). The difference between the totals of these two sections is the net change in working capital during the period. The first item in the statement, working capital provided by operations, is usually presented by starting with net income and adding (or deducting) items included in net income that had no effect on working capital. In Exhibit 17–3, working capital from operations is the only source of funds for the year.

The second part of the statement, labeled **Changes in Working Capital Components,** details the changes in the various current asset and liability accounts for the period. Note that the working capital change detailed in this part equals the working capital change analyzed in the first part of the statement.

The Accounting Principles Board indicated that the statement of changes in financial position should report separately the effects of any extraordinary items and should also clearly disclose the proceeds (reduced by any related expenses that consume working capital) from sales of long-term assets outside the normal course of business. The statement thus separates the effects of extraordinary, unusual, or nonrecurring items, net of taxes, from the resources provided by normal operations.

Financial analysts often focus their attention on a company's reported earnings per share. Because companies may follow different accounting policies, particularly in the manner of writing off assets, some analysts find reported earnings-per-share figures unsatisfactory for making comparisons between companies. Instead of relying entirely on earnings per share, they may also calculate **funds flow per share.** In doing this, they simply replace the earnings figure by the amount of funds provided by operations. Because depreciation, amortization, and other asset write-offs are not reflected in such funds, many analysts feel that the funds flow per share is a useful supplement to the earnings figure as a measure of comparison among companies.

The APB disapproved of accountants reporting per-share figures that are based on funds flow or cash flow. The board evidently feared that some readers would use the data as a substitute for earnings data. Indeed, such practice could prove deceptive because, over time, the most reliable indicator of a firm's performance is generally its earnings. Nevertheless, analysts will probably continue to make their own per-share computations of funds flow.

WORKSHEET ILLUSTRATION OF FUNDS FLOW ANALYSIS

Let us now analyze the activities of the XYZ Company for Year 3, using a worksheet to aid in preparing a statement of changes in financial position. Consider the comparative condensed balance sheets for Years 2 and 3 in Exhibit 17-4 and the income statement for Year 3 in Exhibit 17-5. Assume that during the year the following transactions took place, in addition to routine transactions:

(1) At the end of the year, the company sold plant assets having a book value of $4,000 ($7,000 cost − $3,000 accumulated depreciation) for $4,000 cash.

(2) New plant assets were purchased at the end of the year for $8,000.

(3) Additional common stock was sold at par value, $10,000.

(4) Dividends of $4,000 were declared, to be paid in Year 4.

EXHIBIT 17-4

XYZ Company
Balance Sheets

	Dec. 31, Year 3	Dec. 31, Year 2
Assets		
Cash	$ 21,000	$ 16,000
Accounts Receivable	19,000	10,000
Inventory	35,000	30,000
Plant Assets	56,000	55,000
Accumulated Depreciation	(12,000)	(10,000)
Total Assets	$119,000	$101,000
Liabilities and Stockholders' Equity		
Accounts Payable	$ 22,000	$ 20,000
Dividends Payable	4,000	3,000
Common Stock	60,000	50,000
Retained Earnings	33,000	28,000
Total Liabilities and Stockholders' Equity	$119,000	$101,000

EXHIBIT 17-5

XYZ Company
Income Statement
For the Year Ended December 31, Year 3

Sales	$50,000
Cost of Goods Sold	30,000
Gross Profit	$20,000
Operating Expenses and Income Taxes (excluding depreciation)	6,000
	$14,000 ← Funds provided
Depreciation Expense	5,000 by operations
Net Income	$ 9,000

We proceed by the following steps to construct the statement of changes in financial position.

STEP 1 First, using balance sheet figures, calculate the change in working capital for the period. A detailed calculation of the working capital change for XYZ Company during Year 3 follows.

	Dec. 31, Year 3	Dec. 31, Year 2	Increase (Decrease)
Current Assets:			
Cash	$21,000	$16,000	$ 5,000
Accounts Receivable	19,000	10,000	9,000
Inventory	35,000	30,000	5,000
Total Current Assets	$75,000	$56,000	$19,000
Current Liabilities:			
Accounts Payable	$22,000	$20,000	$ 2,000
Dividends Payable	4,000	3,000	1,000
Total Current Liabilities	$26,000	$23,000	$ 3,000
Working Capital	$49,000	$33,000	$16,000

The $16,000 net increase in working capital is the amount to be accounted for.

STEP 2 Prepare a worksheet to analyze the changes in the noncurrent accounts and identify the sources and uses of working capital for the period. Exhibit 17–6 shows the worksheet for XYZ Company, which is prepared in the following manner.

Heading and Form. The worksheet heading includes the name of the company, an identification of the statement the worksheet deals with, and the time period covered by the analysis.

The worksheet form illustrated in Exhibit 17–6 has a description column and four money columns. There is a debit and credit column for each of the two headings "Changes in Noncurrent Accounts" and "Analyzing Entries."

Changes in Noncurrent Accounts. The content of the worksheet focuses on the company's noncurrent accounts.

(1) The first information entered is a listing of the noncurrent accounts in the description column. For each noncurrent account the debit or credit change in the account balance for the period is entered in the appropriate column under the heading "Changes in Noncurrent Accounts." Plant Assets for XYZ Company increased from $55,000 at December 31, Year 2, to $56,000 at December 31, Year 3, so the $1,000 increase is entered in the debit column. Accumulated Depreciation increased from $10,000 to $12,000—the $2,000 increase is entered in the credit column. The changes in Common Stock and Retained Earnings are handled the same way.

(2) At this point, the first two columns are totaled. The difference between the column totals equals the working capital change calculated in Step 1. The working capital change is entered on the worksheet—an increase in the debit column, a decrease in the credit column—and then the two columns are totaled to show their equality. Exhibit 17–6 shows the $16,000 working capital increase for XYZ Company in the debit column.

EXHIBIT 17-6

XYZ Company Worksheet for Statement of Changes in Financial Position For the Year Ended December 31, Year 3				
	Changes in Noncurrent Accounts		Analyzing Entries	
Description	Debit	Credit	Debit	Credit
Plant Assets	1,000		(d) 8,000	(c) 7,000
Accumulated Depreciation		2,000	(c) 3,000	(b) 5,000
Common Stock		10,000		(e) 10,000
Retained Earnings		5,000	(f) 4,000	(a) 9,000
	1,000	17,000		
Increase in Working Capital	16,000			
	17,000	17,000		
Sources of Working Capital				
Net Income			(a) 9,000	
Add: Depreciation			(b) 5,000	
Sale of Plant Assets			(c) 4,000	
Sale of Common Stock			(e) 10,000	
Uses of Working Capital				
Purchase of Plant Assets				(d) 8,000
Declaration of Dividends				(f) 4,000
			43,000	43,000

(3) After the first two amount columns are totaled and double-ruled, the phrase "sources of working capital" is written in the description column. Several lines are skipped to allow for all possible sources of funds, and the phrase "uses of working capital" is written in the same column.

As noted earlier, only transactions involving *both* current and noncurrent accounts have a net effect on working capital. As a result, *the change in working capital for a period will equal the net change in the noncurrent accounts.* The first two amount columns demonstrate this equality. Because there are fewer transactions affecting noncurrent accounts than current accounts, it is efficient to review the changes in noncurrent accounts to determine the sources and uses of funds. The worksheet is set up to do such an analysis.

Analyzing Entries. Review the noncurrent accounts and reconstruct the entries, in summary form, to explain the changes that occurred during the period. If the transaction affected working capital, we enter the appropriate amount in the lower portion of the worksheet as either a source or use of working capital. A debit entry in the lower portion reflects an increase in working capital; a credit entry means a decrease in working capital. When all the changes in noncurrent accounts have been explained, our analysis is complete. The analyzing entries in Exhibit 17–6 are explained below.

(a)   Because the first item on the statement of changes in financial position is funds provided by operations, we begin by reviewing income statement data for their impact on noncurrent accounts and working capital. Entry (a) on the worksheet shows the increase in Retained Earnings from the $9,000 net income, with the offsetting debit as a source of funds from net income.

(b)   Depreciation expense does not affect working capital. Entry (b) credits Accumulated Depreciation for the $5,000 of depreciation and debits $5,000 under sources of working capital as an addition to net income, because depreciation expense must be added to net income to derive funds provided by operations (identified by the arrow as $14,000 on the income statement in Exhibit 17–5).

(c)   The sale of plant assets increased working capital by $4,000, decreased Accumulated Depreciation by $3,000, and decreased Plant Assets by $7,000. Entry (c) reflects these effects.

(d)   Entry (d) reconstructs the analysis for the purchase of plant assets. The entry debits Plant Assets for $8,000 and credits $8,000 as a use of working capital for the purchase of plant assets.

(e)   The sale of common stock provided $10,000 of working capital and increased the common stock account balance. Entry (e) debits $10,000 as a source of working capital from the sale of common stock and credits $10,000 to Common Stock.

(f)   The declaration of the $4,000 dividend is reconstructed in entry (f). This transaction reduced working capital and retained earnings—the entry debits Retained Earnings and credits uses of working capital for a declaration of dividends. Also in Year 3, the $3,000 dividend declared in Year 2 was paid, but the payment did not affect working capital. It reduced both a current liability and a current asset (dividends payable and cash) by $3,000, with no net effect on funds. The dividend payment affects only current accounts and, thus, is not analyzed on the worksheet.

At this point, for each noncurrent account, the debit or credit balance of the analyzing entries equals the change shown in the first two columns. Thus, our analysis is complete. We total and double-rule the last two columns to complete the worksheet. The analyzing entries are for worksheet purposes only and are not recorded in the accounts.

STEP 3   Prepare the statement of changes in financial position. We find information for the sources and uses of working capital in the lower portion of the worksheet. The schedule prepared in Step 1, if detailed enough, gives us the necessary data for entering the changes in working capital components. The changes in working capital components may also be derived from the comparative balance sheets. The completed statement of changes in financial position for the XYZ Company for Year 3 is shown in Exhibit 17–7.

The form of the statement of changes in financial position in Exhibit 17–7 is typical of those seen in financial reports. If there is a net loss for the period, it appears in the same position as Net Income when depreciation and other adjustments added result in an increase in working capital. If depreciation and other adjustments are less than the net loss, however, then funds have been *applied to* operations, and the amounts should be shown with the Uses of Working Capital section.

EXHIBIT 17–7

XYZ Company
Statement of Changes in Financial Position
For the Year Ended December 31, Year 3

Sources of Working Capital		
Operations:		
Net Income	$9,000	
Add Expenses Not Decreasing Working Capital:		
Depreciation	5,000	
Total from Operations		$14,000
Sale of Plant Assets		4,000
Sale of Common Stock		10,000
Total Sources of Working Capital		$28,000
Uses of Working Capital		
Purchase of Plant Assets	$8,000	
Declaration of Dividends	4,000	
Total Uses of Working Capital		12,000
Increase in Working Capital		$16,000
Changes in Working Capital Components		
Increases (Decreases) in Current Assets:		
Cash	$5,000	
Accounts Receivable	9,000	
Inventory	5,000	
Increase in Current Assets		$19,000
Increases (Decreases) in Current Liabilities:		
Accounts Payable	$2,000	
Dividends Payable	1,000	
Increase in Current Liabilities		3,000
Increase in Working Capital		$16,000

SIGNIFICANT CHANGES NOT AFFECTING FUNDS

We stated earlier that the Accounting Principles Board *Opinion No. 19* broadened the concept of the funds statement to include all important aspects of a firm's financing and investing activities, regardless of whether cash or other elements of working capital are actually affected. This ruling enables significant financial developments to be shown that otherwise might not be emphasized in any accounting report. The special types of transactions mentioned in *Opinion No. 19* include the issuance of securities for noncurrent assets and the conversion of long-term debt or preferred stock to common stock. Transactions involving donated assets would also be included. Transactions involving stock dividends and stock split-ups are not to be reported, according to the opinion.

These special types of transactions are presented in the statement of changes in financial position as both a source *and* use of working capital. Suppose that a corporation acquired land having a fair market value of $80,000 by issuing 800 shares of $100 par value common stock. This transaction would be reported in the statement of changes in financial position as follows:

Sources of Working Capital
Issuance of common stock for land $80,000

Uses of Working Capital
Purchase of land by issuance of common stock $80,000

The analysis of this transaction in the worksheet for a statement of changes in financial position requires *two* analyzing entries. The first entry—debiting Land, $80,000 and crediting Common Stock, $80,000—reflects the impact of the transaction on the noncurrent accounts. The second entry debits $80,000 under the sources of working capital as "issuance of common stock for land" and credits $80,000 under the uses of working capital as "purchase of land by issuance of common stock." Thus, the second entry shows the transaction as both a source and a use of working capital.

The foregoing example illustrates the approach taken to present certain significant transactions that have no effect on working capital. The approach is consistent with the view that this type of transaction is both a financing and an investing transaction, although the presentation supports somewhat of a "fiction" that an inflow and an outflow have occurred. Note, however, that because these transactions do not affect working capital, the amounts shown in Sources of Working Capital and Uses of Working Capital offset each other. Thus, the difference between Total Sources of Working Capital and Total Uses of Working Capital may still be brought into agreement with the change in working capital for the period.

COMPREHENSIVE ILLUSTRATION

The procedures described above can be followed regardless of the size or complexity of a business firm's operations. We now present a more comprehensive exercise to illustrate the techniques for preparing a somewhat more complex statement of changes in financial position.

The comparative balance sheets and income statement for the Superior Corporation are presented in Exhibits 17–8 and 17–9 (pages 602–603), respectively. During Year 2, the following transactions occurred, in addition to routine transactions:

(1) Equipment costing $6,000 with $4,000 accumulated depreciation was abandoned.

(2) The investment in M Company stock, which originally cost $10,000, was sold for $30,000. This was the only security investment Superior Corporation had ever owned, and the sale was considered an extraordinary event. Taxes increased by $5,000 as a result of the gain on the sale.

(3) Equipment costing $5,000 was purchased.

(4) Early in the year, a patent with a fair value of $30,000 was acquired by issuing 250 shares of common stock.

(5) Bonds payable of $20,000 were retired at par value.

(6) Dividends of $10,000 were declared.

The first step is to determine the change in working capital. The calculation is shown here in abbreviated form, without listing the current items in detail:

	Dec. 31, Year 2	Dec. 31, Year 1	Increase (Decrease)
Current Assets	$179,000	$170,000	$ 9,000
Current Liabilities	59,000	80,000	(21,000)
Working Capital	$120,000	$ 90,000	$30,000

The increase of $30,000 in working capital is the amount to be accounted for.

The next step is to prepare a worksheet for the statement of changes in financial position. Exhibit 17–10 (page 604) shows the worksheet for Superior Corporation. The analyzing entries are explained below.

(a) *Opinion No. 19* states that the effects of extraordinary items should be reported separately from the effects of normal items. Because Superior Corporation has an extraordinary item, our starting point for determining funds provided by operations is the "income before extraordinary item" of $29,000. Entry (a) debits this income amount under sources of working capital and credits Retained Earnings for the same amount.

(b), (c), and **(d)** Three expenses deducted in determining the $29,000 income before extraordinary item had no impact on working capital. Therefore, they must

EXHIBIT 17–8

Superior Corporation
Balance Sheets

Assets	Dec. 31, Year 2	Dec. 31, Year 1	Increase (Decrease)
Current Assets			
Cash	$ 22,000	$ 20,000	$ 2,000
Accounts Receivable (net)	55,000	60,000	(5,000)
Inventory	90,000	80,000	10,000
Prepaid Expenses	12,000	10,000	2,000
Total Current Assets	$179,000	$170,000	$ 9,000
Investments			
Investment in M Company Stock	$ —	$ 10,000	($10,000)
Long-term Assets			
Plant and Equipment	$165,000	$166,000	($ 1,000)
Accumulated Depreciation	(38,000)	(34,000)	(4,000)
Patents (net)	29,000	—	29,000
Total Long-term Assets	$156,000	$132,000	$24,000
Total Assets	$335,000	$312,000	$23,000
Liabilities and Stockholders' Equity			
Current Liabilities			
Accounts Payable	$ 30,000	$ 40,000	($10,000)
Dividends Payable	10,000	8,000	2,000
Accrued Liabilities	19,000	32,000	(13,000)
Total Current Liabilities	$ 59,000	$ 80,000	($21,000)
Long-term Debt			
Bonds Payable	$ 50,000	$ 70,000	($20,000)
Stockholders' Equity			
Common Stock ($100 par value)	$125,000	$100,000	$25,000
Paid-in Capital in Excess of Par Value	5,000	—	5,000
Retained Earnings	96,000	62,000	34,000
Total Stockholders' Equity	$226,000	$162,000	$64,000
Total Liabilities and Stockholders' Equity	$335,000	$312,000	$23,000

be added to the $29,000 to derive the effect on working capital of ordinary operations. This is done in entries (b), (c), and (d).

Entry (b) analyzes the depreciation expense by debiting $8,000 under sources of working capital as an addition to the income before extraordinary item and crediting $8,000 to Accumulated Depreciation.

EXHIBIT 17–9

Superior Corporation
Income Statement
For the Year Ended December 31, Year 2

Sales		$360,000
Cost of Goods Sold		240,000
Gross Profit		$120,000
Operating Expenses and Income Taxes		
(excluding depreciation, amortization, and loss)	$80,000	
Depreciation Expense	8,000	
Patent Amortization Expense	1,000	
Loss on Disposal of Equipment	2,000	91,000
Income before Extraordinary Item		$ 29,000
Extraordinary Item:		
Gain on Sale of M Company Stock	$20,000	
Less: Income Taxes	5,000	15,000
Net Income		$ 44,000

Patent amortization expense is analyzed in a similar fashion in entry (c), with a debit of $1,000 under sources of working capital as an addition to the income amount and a credit of $1,000 to Patents (net).

Entry (d) reflects the effect of the abandonment of equipment with a book value of $2,000. The abandonment caused a $2,000 loss, but did not affect working capital. Entry (d) debits $2,000 under sources of working capital as an addition to the income before extraordinary item, debits $4,000 to Accumulated Depreciation, and credits $6,000 to Plant and Equipment.

Depreciation expense, patent amortization expense, and the loss on disposal of equipment total $11,000. Adding these expenses to the $29,000 income before extraordinary item gives us $40,000 of working capital provided by ordinary operations.

(e) Given the surrounding circumstances, the sale of M Company stock by Superior Corporation was considered extraordinary. The transaction increased working capital by a net amount of $25,000 (cash proceeds from the sale were $30,000, but income taxes on the gain amounted to $5,000). The transaction also eliminated the $10,000 balance in the investment account and increased net income by $15,000. Entry (e) summarizes this transaction with a $25,000 debit as a source of working capital from the sale of M Company stock and credits of $10,000 to Investment in M Company Stock and $15,000 to Retained Earnings.

(f) Entry (f) analyzes the purchase of equipment costing $5,000. The purchase increased equipment and decreased working capital. Plant and Equipment is debited for $5,000 and a use of working capital for the purchase of equipment is credited for $5,000.

EXHIBIT 17–10

Superior Corporation
Worksheet for Statement of Changes in Financial Position
For the Year Ended December 31, Year 2

Description	Changes in Noncurrent Accounts Debit	Changes in Noncurrent Accounts Credit	Analyzing Entries Debit		Analyzing Entries Credit	
Investment in M Company Stock		10,000			(e)	10,000
Plant and Equipment		1,000	(f)	5,000	(d)	6,000
Accumulated Depreciation		4,000	(d)	4,000	(b)	8,000
Patents (net)	29,000		(g)	30,000	(c)	1,000
Bonds Payable	20,000		(i)	20,000		
Common Stock		25,000			(g)	25,000
Paid-in Capital in Excess of Par Value		5,000			(g)	5,000
Retained Earnings		34,000	(j)	10,000	(a)	29,000
					(e)	15,000
	49,000	79,000				
Increase in Working Capital	30,000					
	79,000	79,000				
Sources of Working Capital						
Income before Extraordinary Item			(a)	29,000		
Add: Depreciation			(b)	8,000		
Amortization			(c)	1,000		
Loss on Disposal of Equipment			(d)	2,000		
Extraordinary Item: Sale of M Company Stock			(e)	25,000		
Issuance of Common Stock for Patent			(h)	30,000		
Uses of Working Capital						
Purchase of Equipment					(f)	5,000
Purchase of Patent by Issuing Common Stock					(h)	30,000
Retirement of Bonds Payable					(i)	20,000
Declaration of Dividends					(j)	10,000
				164,000		164,000

(g) and (h)   The acquisition of a patent by issuing common stock is one of the significant transactions affecting financial position that must be reported in the funds statement even though it does not affect working capital. As explained earlier, this situation requires two analyzing entries on the worksheet.

Entry (g) reconstructs the effect of the transaction on the noncurrent accounts. The entry debits $30,000 to Patents (net) and credits $25,000 to Common Stock and $5,000 to Paid-in Capital in Excess of Par Value.

Entry (h) reflects $30,000 as both a source and a use of working capital. Issuance of Common Stock for Patent is debited under sources of working capital and Purchases of Patent by Issuing Common Stock is credited for $30,000 under uses of working capital.

(i) The retirement of bonds payable utilized $20,000 of working capital. Entry (i) shows the effect of the transaction by debiting Bonds Payable for $20,000 and crediting $20,000 as a use of working capital for the retirement of bonds payable.

(j) The effect of the dividends declaration is portrayed in entry (j). Retained Earnings is debited for $10,000 and Declaration of Dividends under uses of working capital is credited for $10,000.

Once the worksheet is completed, the final step is to prepare the statement of changes in financial position for Superior Corporation. The statement is shown in Exhibit 17–11 (page 606). The worksheet provides the information on the sources and uses of working capital. The detail of the changes in working capital components is obtained from the comparative balance sheets shown in Exhibit 17–8.

CASH FLOW STATEMENTS

When preparing financial statements for external users, some firms may elect to prepare the statement of changes in financial position showing the sources and uses of cash rather than working capital. The requirements of *Opinion No. 19* still apply, however. Such statements, which should also be titled "statement of changes in financial position," should include any significant financing and investing activities, even though cash was not directly affected. Because the focus is on cash rather than on working capital, the title "statement of changes in financial position—cash basis" may be appropriate. These statements are often referred to as **cash flow statements,** the term we shall use here for ease of discussion.

The management of cash flows is a critical function in the operation of a business enterprise. Cash flow statements may be prepared and used internally as part of the process of planning and controlling cash movements. Internal cash flow statements need not adhere to the guidelines of *Opinion No. 19,* but they may be similar in format nonetheless. Cash budgets are also important to the management of cash flows. We discuss cash budgets in Chapter 26. Our focus here, however, is on cash flow statements prepared for users external to the business.

The cash flow statement has two major sections, one reporting the sources of cash and the other showing the uses of cash. No separate section reports changes in working capital components, because changes in most elements of working capital other than cash are disclosed as adjustments necessary to derive cash provided by operations.

EXHIBIT 17-11

Superior Corporation
Statement of Changes in Financial Position
For the Year Ended December 31, Year 2

Sources of Working Capital

Operations:

Income before Extraordinary Item	$29,000	
Add Expenses Not Decreasing Working Capital:		
Depreciation	8,000	
Amortization	1,000	
Loss on Disposal of Equipment	2,000	
Total from Operations		$40,000
Extraordinary Item: Sale of M Company Stock (net of taxes)		25,000
Issuance of Common Stock for Patent		30,000
Total Sources of Working Capital		$95,000

Uses of Working Capital

Purchase of Equipment	$ 5,000	
Purchase of Patent by Issuing Common Stock	30,000	
Retirement of Bonds Payable	20,000	
Declaration of Dividends	10,000	
Total Uses of Working Capital		65,000
Increase in Working Capital		$30,000

Changes in Working Capital Components

Increases (Decreases) in Current Assets:

Cash	$ 2,000	
Accounts Receivable	(5,000)	
Inventory	10,000	
Prepaid Expenses	2,000	
Increase in Current Assets		$ 9,000
Increases (Decreases) in Current Liabilities:		
Accounts Payable	($10,000)	
Dividends Payable	2,000	
Accrued Liabilities	(13,000)	
Decrease in Current Liabilities		(21,000)
Increase in Working Capital		$30,000

Cash Flow from Operations

Cash provided by operations constitutes one of the sources of cash. It is determined by converting the net income amount (calculated on an accrual basis) to net income on a cash basis. Net income on a cash basis considers only cash receipts as revenue and subtracts from cash receipts only cash outlays for merchandise and expenses.

To better understand the process of converting a net income number from an accrual amount to a cash basis amount, let us first consider the procedures for converting individual revenues and expenses from an accrual to a cash basis. These procedures are diagramed below.

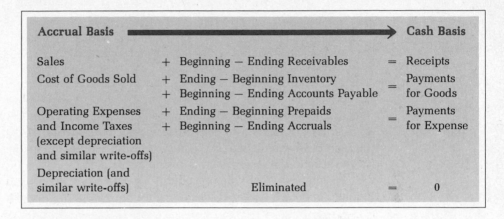

Accrual Basis	⟶		Cash Basis
Sales	+ Beginning — Ending Receivables	=	Receipts
Cost of Goods Sold	+ Ending — Beginning Inventory + Beginning — Ending Accounts Payable	=	Payments for Goods
Operating Expenses and Income Taxes (except depreciation and similar write-offs)	+ Ending — Beginning Prepaids + Beginning — Ending Accruals	=	Payments for Expense
Depreciation (and similar write-offs)	Eliminated	=	0

The adjustments diagramed here fall into two categories:

Changes in noncurrent accounts. Some expenses, such as depreciation, affect only noncurrent balance sheet accounts and have no effect on cash. These expenses do not appear in a cash basis income statement and, therefore, must be eliminated when converting an accrual basis income statement to a cash basis income statement. The above diagram shows the elimination of these items.

Changes in working capital accounts. When we focus on cash, we must also consider how changes in working capital accounts affect cash flows from operations. As the above diagram shows, we adjust the appropriate revenues and expenses on the accrual income statement for changes in accounts receivable, inventories, prepaid expenses, accounts payable, and accrued liabilities to obtain the cash basis amounts. For example, if there were sales of $10,000 for a period and accounts receivable increased from $3,000 to $4,000 during the same period, we conclude that the cash collections for the period were $9,000.

Individual revenues and expenses on a cash basis are not shown in the cash flow statement. Instead, cash provided by operations is presented by starting with the accrual net income figure and adjusting that number to a cash basis amount. The adjustments are derived from the two categories we established above to adjust individual revenues and expenses to cash basis amounts. The adjustments for expenses affecting only noncurrent accounts are handled in the same way that they were in deriving working capital from operations. Depreciation expense, for example, is added to the accrual net income amount. The other category of adjustments—the changes in various components of working capital—is handled as shown in the following schedule:

Working Capital Item	Change in Working Capital: Adjustment of Accrual Basis Net Income to Convert to Cash Basis Net Income	
	Add	Deduct
Accounts Receivable	Decrease	Increase
Inventory	Decrease	Increase
Prepaid Expenses	Decrease	Increase
Accounts Payable	Increase	Decrease
Accrued Liabilities	Increase	Decrease

For example, we would add a decrease in accounts receivable during the period to accrual net income to convert to a cash basis figure. If accounts receivable increased, we would deduct the increase from accrual net income. The remainder of the schedule is interpreted in a similar fashion.

In summary, then, the procedures for converting an accrual basis net income amount to a cash basis net income figure may be portrayed as follows:

> Accrual Basis Net Income
> + Depreciation and Similar Write-offs
> + or − Changes in Accounts Receivable, Inventory, Prepaid Expenses, Accounts Payable, and Accrued Liabilities
> = Cash Basis Net Income

Illustration of Cash Flow Analysis

To demonstrate the preparation of a cash flow statement, we shall again use the statements of XYZ Company from Exhibits 17–4 and 17–5. For convenience they are repeated in Exhibit 17–12.

We also repeat the nonroutine transactions that took place in Year 3.

(1) Plant assets with a cost of $7,000 and accumulated depreciation of $3,000 were sold for $4,000 cash.

(2) New plant assets were purchased for $8,000 cash.

(3) Common stock was sold at par value for $10,000 cash.

(4) Dividends of $4,000 were declared, to be paid in Year 4. Dividends of $3,000 declared in Year 2 were paid.

Remember that our general approach in determining the sources and uses of working capital was to review the changes in all noncurrent accounts to identify the events affecting working capital. When dealing with a cash flow statement, our general approach will be to review all balance sheet accounts (except cash) to identify the events affecting cash flows. Although a worksheet may be used to aid in the preparation of a cash flow statement, it is not really necessary in such a reasonably simple situation as that of XYZ Company. The approach we describe below does not require a worksheet.

EXHIBIT 17-12

XYZ Company
Balance Sheets

Assets	Dec. 31, Year 3	Dec. 31, Year 2	Liabilities and Stockholders' Equity	Dec. 31, Year 3	Dec. 31, Year 2
Cash	$ 21,000	$ 16,000	Accounts Payable	$ 22,000	$ 20,000
Accounts Receivable	19,000	10,000	Dividends Payable	4,000	3,000
Inventory	35,000	30,000	Common Stock	60,000	50,000
Plant Assets	56,000	55,000	Retained Earnings	33,000	28,000
Accumulated Depreciation	(12,000)	(10,000)	Total Liabilities and		
Total Assets	$119,000	$101,000	Stockholders' Equity	$119,000	$101,000

XYZ Company
Income Statement
For the Year Ended December 31, Year 3

Sales		$50,000
Cost of Goods Sold		30,000
Gross Profit		$20,000
Operating Expenses and Income Taxes (excluding depreciation)	$6,000	
Depreciation Expense	5,000	11,000
Net Income		$ 9,000

STEP 1   Determine the net increase or decrease in cash during the year by comparing the cash balances on the comparative balance sheets. In the case of XYZ Company, a $5,000 increase is the amount to be accounted for; this figure appears on the bottom of the cash flow statement in Exhibit 17-13 (page 610).

STEP 2   Determine the cash provided from operations. This step involves identifying the adjustments made to convert net income from an accrual amount to a cash basis figure. For XYZ Company, these adjustments are as follows:

(1) Depreciation expense for the year was $5,000. This amount is added to the accrual income amount, because depreciation is a noncash expense.

(2) Accounts receivable increased $9,000 during the year. The increase is deducted from the accrual income amount in the cash flow statement. This adjustment represents, in essence, the conversion of sales revenue to a cash receipts amount; cash collections of accounts receivable were $9,000 less than sales revenue on the accrual basis.

EXHIBIT 17–13

XYZ Company
Statement of Changes in Financial Position—Cash Basis
For the Year Ended December 31, Year 3

Sources of Cash

Operations:

Net Income	$9,000	
Add (Deduct) Items to Convert Net Income to Cash Basis:		
Depreciation	5,000	
Accounts Receivable Increase	(9,000)	
Inventory Increase	(5,000)	
Accounts Payable Increase	2,000	
Total from Operations		$ 2,000
Sale of Plant Assets		4,000
Sale of Common Stock		10,000
Total Sources of Cash		$16,000

Uses of Cash

Purchase of Plant Assets	$8,000	
Payment of Dividends	3,000	
Total Uses of Cash		11,000
Net Increase in Cash		$ 5,000

(3) Inventory increased $5,000 during the year. The increase is deducted from the accrual income amount. This adjustment, in combination with the accounts payable adjustment explained in (4), represents the conversion of cost of goods sold under accrual accounting to a "cash payments for goods purchased" amount.

(4) Accounts payable increased $2,000 during the year. The increase is added to the accrual income amount. This adjustment is made because cash payments in settlement of accounts payable were $2,000 less than goods purchased during the current period.

Applying these adjustments to the $9,000 accrual net income gives cash provided by operations (that is, cash basis income) of $2,000. These adjustments are shown in Exhibit 17–13.

STEP 3   Analyze the changes in all balance sheet accounts that have not been analyzed in Step 2 to determine the events affecting cash flows. For any event that does affect cash flow, classify it properly as either a source or a use of cash. The analysis for XYZ Company consists of the following items:

(1) Plant assets increased $1,000 during the year. Two events caused this change. The sale of plant assets (cost of $7,000 and accumulated depreciation of $3,000) for $4,000 cash was a source of cash. The purchase of plant assets for $8,000 was a use of cash.

(2) Accumulated depreciation increased $2,000. Two events that we have already considered—depreciation expense of $5,000 and the sale of assets with accumulated depreciation of $3,000—explain this change.

(3) Dividends payable increased $1,000. Two events also explain this change. Dividends of $3,000 were paid—a use of cash. The declaration of dividends of $4,000 did not affect cash flows during this period.

(4) Common stock increased $10,000, as a result of the sale of additional stock. This event was a source of cash.

(5) Retained earnings increased $5,000 as a result of net income of $9,000 and a $4,000 dividend declaration. Net income appears in the cash flow statement as the starting point for cash provided by operations. A dividend declaration, as noted above, does not affect cash flows.

STEP 4 Complete the cash flow statement and make sure that the difference between total sources of cash and uses of cash is equal to the change in cash balances calculated in Step 1. As a result of the foregoing analysis, the cash flow statement for XYZ Company would appear as shown in Exhibit 17–13.

KEY POINTS TO REMEMBER

Statement of Changes in Financial Position

(1) *Funds,* or *working capital,* is defined as current assets less current liabilities.

(2) The statement of changes in financial position explains the net increase or decrease in funds during the period.

(3) In preparing a statement of changes in financial position, one must review all changes in noncurrent assets, noncurrent liabilities, and owners' equity for effects on working capital.

(4) A worksheet may be used to aid in the preparation of a statement of changes in financial position.

(5) Write-offs of noncurrent items (such as depreciation and amortization) do not affect funds. If any of these items are reflected in the net income (or income before extraordinary items) figure, they must be added back to determine funds provided by operations.

(6) Changes in noncurrent balance sheet accounts that do not affect funds, but that result from major financing or investing transactions, should be shown on the statement of changes in financial position.

Cash Flow Statement

(1) The cash flow statement explains the net increase or decrease in cash during the period.

(2) In preparing cash flow statements, one must review all changes in balance sheet accounts other than Cash for cash flow effects.

    (a) To determine cash from operations, one must adjust the accrual income figure to convert it to a cash basis amount.

    (b) Other cash inflows and outflows can be determined by analyzing all changes in balance sheet accounts other than those accounted for in (a).

(3) Changes in noncurrent balance sheet accounts that do not affect cash, but that result from major financing or investing transactions, should be shown on the cash flow statement.

QUESTIONS

17-1 Define the term "funds" as used by business executives and financial analysts.

17-2 What is the difference between a statement of changes in financial position portraying working capital flow and a cash flow statement?

17-3 What information is shown by the statement of changes in financial position (working capital flow) that is not readily available from the balance sheet and income statement?

17-4 What are the major *sources* of a firm's working capital? What are the major *uses* of working capital?

17-5 In determining working capital provided by operations, why must depreciation be added back to net income? Give examples of other income statement items that would be added to net income in deriving working capital provided by operations.

17-6 Home Company sold for $14,000 cash long-term investments originally costing $6,000. Income taxes on the extraordinary gain were $2,000. Describe how this event would be handled in a statement of changes in financial position (working capital flow).

17-7 For each of the following transactions, state whether working capital would be increased, decreased, or remain unaffected. Where appropriate, give the amount of the change.

    (a) Paid a current note payable in cash, $1,000.

    (b) Sold 500 shares of $30 par value common stock at $40 a share.

    (c) Declared a cash dividend of $15,000.

    (d) Sold plant assets for $14,000; the assets had an original cost of $30,000 and accumulated depreciation of $12,000.

    (e) Sold short-term marketable securities, having a carrying value of $7,000, for $9,000.

    (f) Paid the dividend in (c).

    (g) Purchased inventory on account, $20,000.

    (h) Purchased plant assets for $46,000.

    (i) Sold bonds payable with a $100,000 face value at 102.

17-8 Foley Company acquired a $300,000 building by issuing $300,000 worth of bonds payable. Describe how this transaction will be reported in the statement of changes in financial position (working capital flow).

17-9 Because of unforeseen circumstances, Kidd Company abandoned a piece of equipment that was not fully depreciated. The asset had cost $7,000, and $6,200 of depreciation had accumulated at the time of abandonment. What effect did this abandonment have on the working capital of Kidd Company?

17-10 When a worksheet is prepared for the statement of changes in financial position (working capital flow), all changes in noncurrent balance sheet accounts are analyzed. Why?

17-11 If a business had a net loss for the year, under what circumstances could the statement of changes in financial position show working capital provided by operations?

17-12 During the year, Statford Company had $900 amortization of bond premium. Explain how this item would be handled in calculating working capital provided by operations.

17-13 A company declared but did not pay a $6,000 cash dividend and a 10% stock dividend during the current year. Describe how these two items will be treated when a statement of changes in financial position (working capital flow) for the year is prepared.

17-14 A merchandising company is preparing a cash flow statement. Net income for the year is $50,000. Accounts receivable total $14,000 at the beginning of the year and $19,000 at the end of the year. Explain how the change in accounts receivable for the year would be presented on the cash flow statement.

17-15 A merchandising firm is preparing a cash flow statement. Net income for the year is $37,000. Its beginning inventory was $16,000 and its ending inventory was $12,000. Accounts payable were $7,000 at the beginning of the year and $8,000 at the end of the year. Explain how the changes in inventory and accounts payable for the year would be presented on the cash flow statement.

17-16 On December 20 of the current year, Doran Company declared a $10,000 cash dividend to be paid January 15 of the following year. How would the treatment of this declaration in a statement of changes in financial position differ from its treatment in a cash flow statement? Assume that both are prepared for the current year.

EXERCISES

17-17 The income statement of the Cliver Company for this year shows net income of $75,000. The following information is available:
(1) Uncollectible accounts expense for year, $6,000.
(2) Depreciation expense for year, $11,000.
(3) Patent amortization expense for year, $4,000.
(4) Sales on account for year, $92,000.
(5) Purchases of merchandise on account for year, $60,000.
Calculate the amount of working capital provided from operations for this year's statement of changes in financial position.

17-18 The following information was obtained from the Spartan Company's comparative balance sheets.

	Dec. 31, 19X1	Dec. 31, 19X0
Cash	$14,000	$11,000
Accounts Receivable	30,000	28,000
Inventory	50,000	35,000
Prepaid Expenses	3,000	2,000
Plant Assets (net of accumulated depreciation)	97,000	84,000
Accounts Payable	35,000	25,000
Accrued Liabilities	12,000	8,000
Common Stock	80,000	80,000
Retained Earnings	67,000	47,000

Calculate the change in working capital for the year 19X1.

17-19 Refer to the balance sheet information in Exercise 17-18. Suppose you knew, by looking at the income statement, that depreciation on plant assets for 19X1 was $9,000 and that no assets had been sold during the year. How much working capital has been applied to the purchase of plant assets during the year?

17-20 Refer to the balance sheet information in Exercise 17-18 and assume that you know the following:

Net income per income statement	$30,000
Dividends declared and paid	10,000
Cost of plant assets purchased	?
Depreciation on plant assets	9,000

Prepare a statement of changes in financial position (working capital flow) for 19X1.

17-21 The Hahn Company had the following income statement for the current year:

Sales	$200,000
Cost of Goods Sold	120,000
Gross Profit	$ 80,000
Operating Expenses	56,000
Net Income	$ 24,000

Hahn Company owns no plant assets. Additional information follows.

	End of Year	Beginning of Year
Accounts Receivable	$14,000	$18,000
Inventory	20,000	15,000
Accrued Liabilities	5,000	10,000
Accounts Payable	11,000	9,000

Using the above information, calculate the cash provided from operations that would appear in a cash flow statement.

17-22 Refer to the information in Exercise 17-21. Calculate the following amounts for the current year:
(a) Cash collected from customers.
(b) Cash payments for goods purchased.
(c) Cash payments for operating expenses.

PROBLEMS

17-23 Comparative balance sheets at December 31 of 19X0 and 19X1 for the Lowe Company are shown below.

Lowe Company
Balance Sheets

	Dec. 31, 19X1	Dec. 31, 19X0
Assets		
Cash	$ 10,000	$16,000
Accounts Receivable (net)	17,000	9,000
Inventory	46,000	37,000
Prepaid Expenses	5,000	3,000
Plant Assets	90,000	70,000
Accumulated Depreciation	(50,000)	(46,000)
Total Assets	$118,000	$89,000
Liabilities and Stockholders' Equity		
Accounts Payable	$ 22,000	$ 8,000
Common Stock	60,000	54,000
Retained Earnings	36,000	27,000
Total Liabilities and Stockholders' Equity	$118,000	$89,000

Net income per income statement for 19X1 was $19,000. There were no extraordinary items. Dividends of $10,000 were declared and paid during 19X1. Plant assets were purchased for cash, and later in the year additional common stock was issued for cash.

REQUIRED
(a) Calculate the change in working capital during 19X1.
(b) Prepare a worksheet for a statement of changes in financial position for 19X1.
(c) Prepare a statement of changes in financial position (working capital flow) for 19X1.

17-24 The Retained Earnings account of the Hokin Company for this year reveals the following:

Beginning Balance		$34,000
Add: Net Income		21,000
		$55,000
Less: Stock Dividend	$ 8,000	
Cash Dividend	12,000	20,000
Ending Balance		$35,000

Comparative balance sheets at December 31 of last year and this year are presented below.

Hokin Company
Balance Sheets

	Dec. 31, This Year	Dec. 31, Last Year
Assets		
Cash	$ 14,000	$ 12,000
Accounts Receivable (net)	40,000	31,000
Inventory	78,000	80,000
Prepaid Expenses	4,000	3,000
Plant Assets	206,000	190,000
Accumulated Depreciation	(20,000)	(16,000)
Goodwill (less amortization)	28,000	30,000
Total Assets	$350,000	$330,000
Liabilities and Stockholders' Equity		
Accounts Payable	$ 40,000	$ 38,000
Accrued Liabilities	10,000	16,000
Bonds Payable	125,000	110,000
Common Stock	140,000	132,000
Retained Earnings	35,000	34,000
Total Liabilities and Stockholders' Equity	$350,000	$330,000

One of the transactions during the year was the sale for $6,000 of old equipment that had cost $13,000 and had $7,000 accumulated depreciation. Amortization of goodwill amounting to $2,000 was included as an expense on the income statement. There were no extraordinary items. The dividends were declared and paid this year.

REQUIRED
(a) Calculate the change in working capital during this year.
(b) Prepare a worksheet for a statement of changes in financial position for this year.
(c) Prepare a statement of changes in financial position (working capital flow) for this year.

17-25 The Linder Company's comparative balance sheets at December 31 of this year and last year are shown below, together with this year's income statement and retained earnings statement.

Linder Company
Balance Sheets

	Dec. 31, This Year	Dec. 31, Last Year
Assets		
Cash	$ 30,000	$ 13,000
Accounts Receivable (net)	52,000	45,000
Inventories	74,000	63,000
Prepaid Expenses	12,000	11,000
Long-term Investments	—	15,000
Land	168,000	130,000
Buildings	225,000	200,000
Accumulated Depreciation—Buildings	(37,000)	(30,000)
Equipment	220,000	225,000
Accumulated Depreciation—Equipment	(60,000)	(45,000)
Patents (less amortization)	15,000	18,000
Total Assets	$699,000	$645,000
Liabilities and Stockholders' Equity		
Accounts Payable	$ 42,000	$ 45,000
Notes Payable (short-term)	15,000	60,000
Accrued Liabilities	12,000	14,500
Bonds Payable	150,000	150,000
Premium on Bonds Payable	7,000	7,500
Common Stock ($100 par value)	375,000	300,000
Paid-in Capital in Excess of Par Value	18,000	15,000
Retained Earnings	80,000	53,000
Total Liabilities and Stockholders' Equity	$699,000	$645,000

Linder Company
Retained Earnings Statement
For the Current Year

Beginning Balance	$ 53,000
Add: Net Income	87,000
	$140,000
Less: Cash Dividend	60,000
Ending Balance	$ 80,000

Linder Company
Income Statement
For the Current Year

Sales		$900,000
Cost of Goods Sold		600,000
Gross Profit		$300,000
Operating Expenses and Taxes	$179,500	
Depreciation Expense	25,000	
Patent Amortization Expense	3,000	
Interest Expense	8,000	
Loss on Retirement of Equipment	2,000	217,500
Income before Extraordinary Item		$ 82,500
Extraordinary Item:		
Gain on Sale of Long-term Investments	$ 6,000	
Less: Income Taxes	1,500	4,500
Net Income		$ 87,000

During the year the following transactions occurred:

(1) Land was purchased for $38,000.

(2) Long-term investments, costing $15,000, were sold for $21,000. The circumstances associated with this sale qualified it as an extraordinary event for Linder Company. The gain on the sale caused taxes to increase $1,500.

(3) An expenditure of $25,000 was made for buildings.

(4) Equipment that cost $5,000 and had $3,000 accumulated depreciation was abandoned.

(5) Interest expense on the income statement consisted of $8,500 paid less amortization of $500 bond premium.

(6) 750 shares of common stock were sold at $104 per share.

(7) Dividends of $60,000 were declared and paid.

REQUIRED

(a) Calculate the change in working capital during this year.

(b) Prepare a worksheet for a statement of changes in financial position for this year.

(c) Prepare a statement of changes in financial position (working capital flow) for this year.

17-26 Refer to the data given for the Lowe Company in Problem 17-23.

REQUIRED

Prepare a statement of changes in financial position—cash basis (cash flow statement) for 19X1 for the Lowe Company.

17-27 Refer to the data given for the Hokin Company in Problem 17-24 and the income statement of the Hokin Company shown below.

Hokin Company
Income Statement
For the Current Year

Sales		$188,000
Cost of Goods Sold		100,000
Gross Profit		$ 88,000
Depreciation Expense	$11,000	
Goodwill Amortization Expense	2,000	
Other Operating Expenses and Taxes	54,000	67,000
Net Income		$ 21,000

REQUIRED

Prepare a statement of changes in financial position—cash basis (cash flow statement) for the current year for the Hokin Company.

17-28 The members of the board of directors of Dorn Corporation were quite impressed with the firm's performance during the past year. They were particularly pleased that the firm doubled its net income with only a 50% increase in sales volume, as shown by the company's income statements.

Dorn Corporation
Income Statements

	This Year	Last Year
Sales	$2,700,000	$1,800,000
Cost of Goods Sold	1,800,000	1,200,000
Gross Profit	$ 900,000	$ 600,000
Operating Expenses	660,000	480,000
	$ 240,000	$ 120,000
Income Taxes	120,000	60,000
Net Income	$ 120,000	$ 60,000

The board members were somewhat dismayed by the company's financial position, however. Not only did working capital decline from the previous year, but the ratio of current assets to current liabilities had dropped below 200%. Comparative balance sheets are shown on page 620.

Dorn Corporation
Balance Sheets

	Dec. 31, This Year	Dec. 31, Last Year
Assets		
Cash	$ 180,000	$ 430,000
Receivables	360,000	180,000
Inventory	1,260,000	840,000
Prepaid Expenses	60,000	50,000
Total Current Assets	$1,860,000	$1,500,000
Land	240,000	120,000
Plant and Equipment	1,140,000	720,000
Accumulated Depreciation	(300,000)	(240,000)
Total Assets	$2,940,000	$2,100,000
Liabilities and Stockholders' Equity		
Accounts Payable	$ 580,000	$ 250,000
Accrued Liabilities	300,000	230,000
Income Taxes Payable	120,000	60,000
Total Current Liabilities	$1,000,000	$ 540,000
8% Mortgage Note Payable	200,000	—
Common Stock ($50 par value)	1,320,000	1,200,000
Retained Earnings	420,000	360,000
Total Liabilities and Stockholders' Equity	$2,940,000	$2,100,000

The board's chairman has asked you to prepare an analysis of the changes in financial position, showing what has happened to the firm's working capital during the year. In your investigation, you learn that the following events occurred during the year:

(1) The firm acquired a $120,000 land site by issuing 2,400 shares of common stock at par value.
(2) Dividends were declared and paid (before the issuance of the new shares above) at $2.50 per share.
(3) Equipment that had cost $80,000 was sold for its book value of $40,000.
(4) The firm acquired $500,000 of new equipment by paying $300,000 and giving an 8% mortgage note of $200,000.

REQUIRED
(a) Prepare a worksheet for a statement of changes in financial position for this year.
(b) Prepare a statement of changes in financial position (working capital flow) for this year.
(c) Write a brief discussion of the major points to be brought to the attention of the board of directors.

ALTERNATE PROBLEMS

17–23A Comparative balance sheets at December 31 of 19X0 and 19X1 for the Polk Company are shown below.

Polk Company
Balance Sheets

	Dec. 31, 19X1	Dec. 31, 19X0
Assets		
Cash	$ 7,000	$ 5,000
Accounts Receivable (net)	16,000	11,000
Inventory	30,000	22,000
Prepaid Expenses	2,000	4,000
Plant Assets	80,000	65,000
Accumulated Depreciation	(28,000)	(20,000)
Total Assets	$107,000	$87,000
Liabilities and Stockholders' Equity		
Accounts Payable	$ 10,000	$13,000
Bonds Payable	15,000	—
Common Stock	60,000	60,000
Retained Earnings	22,000	14,000
Total Liabilities and Stockholders' Equity	$107,000	$87,000

Net income per income statement for 19X1 was $12,000. There were no extraordinary items. Dividends of $4,000 were declared and paid during 19X1. Plant assets were purchased for cash, and later in the year, bonds payable were sold for cash.

REQUIRED

(a) Calculate the change in working capital during 19X1.

(b) Prepare a worksheet for a statement of changes in financial position for 19X1.

(c) Prepare a statement of changes in financial position (working capital flow) for 19X1.

17–24A The Retained Earnings account of the Cedar Company for this year reveals the following:

Beginning Balance		$55,000
Add: Net Income		41,000
		$96,000
Less: Stock Dividend	$10,000	
Cash Dividend	20,000	30,000
Ending Balance		$66,000

Comparative balance sheets at December 31 of last year and this year are presented below.

Cedar Company
Balance Sheets

	Dec. 31, This Year	Dec. 31, Last Year
Assets		
Cash	$ 9,000	$ 12,000
Accounts Receivable (net)	41,000	37,000
Inventory	60,000	52,000
Prepaid Expenses	4,000	5,000
Plant Assets	250,000	216,000
Accumulated Depreciation	(33,000)	(25,000)
Total Assets	$331,000	$297,000
Liabilities and Stockholders' Equity		
Accounts Payable	$ 32,000	$ 24,000
Accrued Liabilities	10,000	6,000
Bonds Payable	80,000	80,000
Discount on Bonds Payable	(7,000)	(8,000)
Common Stock	150,000	140,000
Retained Earnings	66,000	55,000
Total Liabilities and Stockholders' Equity	$331,000	$297,000

During the year, Cedar Company sold for $11,000 old equipment that had cost $20,000 and had $9,000 accumulated depreciation. Amortization of bond discount amounting to $1,000 was included in interest expense on the income statement. There were no extraordinary items. The dividends were declared and paid this year.

REQUIRED
(a) Calculate the change in working capital during this year.
(b) Prepare a worksheet for a statement of changes in financial position for this year.
(c) Prepare a statement of changes in financial position (working capital flow) for this year.

17-25A The Wildbrook Company's comparative balance sheets at December 31 of this year and last year, together with this year's income statement and retained earnings statement, are shown on pages 623 and 624.

Wildbrook Company
Balance Sheets

	Dec. 31, This Year	Dec. 31, Last Year
Assets		
Cash	$ 23,000	$ 11,000
Accounts Receivable (net)	26,000	27,000
Inventories	51,000	45,000
Prepaid Expenses	6,000	4,000
Long-term Investments	—	10,000
Land	120,000	85,000
Plant and Equipment	300,000	265,000
Accumulated Depreciation	(105,000)	(92,000)
Patents (less amortization)	17,000	20,000
Total Assets	$438,000	$375,000
Liabilities and Stockholders' Equity		
Accounts Payable	$ 16,000	$ 19,000
Notes Payable (short-term)	16,000	28,000
Dividends Payable	47,000	32,000
Accrued Liabilities	6,000	4,000
Bonds Payable	50,000	50,000
Premium on Bonds Payable	5,400	6,000
Common Stock ($100 par value)	205,000	160,000
Paid-in Capital in Excess of Par Value	18,600	15,000
Retained Earnings	74,000	61,000
Total Liabilities and Stockholders' Equity	$438,000	$375,000

Wildbrook Company
Income Statement
For the Current Year

Sales		$650,000
Cost of Goods Sold		430,000
Gross Profit		$220,000
Operating Expenses and Taxes	$132,400	
Depreciation Expense	21,000	
Patent Amortization Expense	3,000	
Interest Expense	7,600	
Loss on Retirement of Equipment	2,000	166,000
Income before Extraordinary Item		$ 54,000
Extraordinary Item:		
Gain on Sale of Long-term Investments	$ 8,000	
Less: Income Taxes	2,000	6,000
Net Income		$ 60,000

Wildbrook Company
Retained Earnings Statement
For the Current Year

Beginning Balance	$ 61,000
Add: Net Income	60,000
	$121,000
Less: Cash Dividend	47,000
Ending Balance	$ 74,000

During the year the following transactions occurred:
(1) Land was purchased for $35,000.
(2) Long-term investments, costing $10,000, were sold for $18,000. The circumstances associated with this sale qualified it as an extraordinary event for Wildbrook Company. The gain on the sale caused taxes to increase $2,000.
(3) An expenditure of $45,000 was made for buildings.
(4) Equipment that cost $10,000 and had $8,000 accumulated depreciation was abandoned.
(5) Interest expense on the income statement consisted of $8,200 paid less amortization of $600 bond premium.
(6) 450 shares of common stock were sold at $108 per share.
(7) Dividends of $47,000 were declared.

REQUIRED
(a) Calculate the change in working capital during this year.
(b) Prepare a worksheet for a statement of changes in financial position for this year.
(c) Prepare a statement of changes in financial position (working capital flow) for this year.

17-26A Refer to the data given for the Polk Company in Problem 17-23A.

REQUIRED
Prepare a statement of changes in financial position—cash basis (cash flow statement) for 19X1 for the Polk Company.

17-27A Refer to the data given for the Cedar Company in Problem 17-24A and the income statement of the Cedar Company shown below.

Cedar Company
Income Statement
For the Current Year

Sales		$301,000
Cost of Goods Sold		180,000
Gross Profit		$121,000
Depreciation Expense	$17,000	
Other Operating Expenses and Taxes	56,000	
Interest Expense	7,000	80,000
Net Income		$ 41,000

REQUIRED

Prepare a statement of changes in financial position—cash basis (cash flow statement) for the current year for the Cedar Company.

BUSINESS DECISION PROBLEM

A. Powers, president of Powers, Inc., has hired you as a consultant. He believes his bookkeeper has made an error in this year's financial statements. The income statement shows that Powers operated at a loss, but the president believes the year must have been profitable. In support of this belief, Powers points out that both cash and working capital are much higher this year than last year. These changes were accomplished without selling any long-term assets or issuing any bonds or common stock. Further, during the current year the company declared and paid a $7,000 cash dividend.

This year's income statement and comparative balance sheets at December 31 of this year and last year are shown below.

Powers, Inc.
Income Statement
For the Current Year

Sales		$245,000
Cost of Goods Sold		110,000
Gross Profit		$135,000
Operating Expenses and Taxes	$112,000	
Depreciation Expense	24,000	
Patent Amortization Expense	5,000	141,000
Net Loss		($ 6,000)

Powers, Inc.
Balance Sheets

Assets	Dec. 31, This Year	Dec. 31, Last Year
Cash	$ 22,000	$ 12,000
Accounts Receivable	63,000	40,000
Inventory	58,000	60,000
Land	70,000	70,000
Plant and Equipment	300,000	300,000
Accumulated Depreciation	(100,000)	(76,000)
Patents (net)	37,000	42,000
Total Assets	$450,000	$448,000

Liabilities and Stockholders' Equity

Accounts Payable	$ 70,000	$ 53,000
Accrued Liabilities	13,000	15,000
Common Stock	340,000	340,000
Retained Earnings	27,000	40,000
Total Liabilities and Stockholders' Equity	$450,000	$448,000

REQUIRED

(a) Prepare a statement of changes in financial position (working capital flow) for the current year.

(b) Prepare a statement of changes in financial position—cash basis (cash flow statement) for the current year.

(c) Did the bookkeeper make an error? Explain.

18
Analysis and Interpretation of Financial Statements

Many individuals and groups are interested in the data appearing in a firm's financial statements, including managers, owners, prospective investors, creditors, labor unions, governmental agencies, and the general public. For the most part, these parties are interested in the profitability and financial strength of the firm in question, although such other factors as size, growth, and the firm's efforts to meet its social responsibilities may also be of interest. Managers, owners, and prospective investors may seek answers to the following questions: How do profits compare with those of previous years? How do profits compare with other firms in the industry? Creditors may ask: Will our debt be repaid on time? Will the interest payments be met? Unions may ask: How can we show that the firm can support a particular wage increase? Regulatory agencies may ask: What rate of return should the firm be permitted? Is the firm enjoying windfall profits? These are the kinds of questions that can be answered by interpreting the data in financial reports.

Various techniques are used to analyze and interpret the data appearing in financial statements. In the following pages, we shall concentrate on some widely used methods of evaluation. In many cases, management may profitably use these techniques to plan and control its own operations, but in this discussion our viewpoint will be primarily that of an outsider.

SOURCES OF INFORMATION

Except for closely held companies, business firms publish financial statements at least annually, and most large companies also issue them quarterly. Normally, annual statements are attested to by certified public accountants, and the careful analyst will read the accountant's opinion to determine the reliability of the given data. Companies listed on the stock exchanges submit annual statements to the Securities and Exchange Commission. These statements, which are available to any interested parties, are generally more useful than annual reports because they furnish a greater amount of detail. Even more detail can be found in prospectuses submitted to the SEC by certain companies issuing large amounts of new securities.

For data not provided by the financial statements, a trained analyst has a number of sources: personal interviews with company management, contacts with research organizations, trade association data, and subscriptions to financial services that periodically publish analytical data for many firms. The analyst also can obtain useful information from financial newspapers such as the *Wall Street Journal* and *Barron's* and from magazines devoted to financial and economic reporting, such as *Business Week* and *Forbes*. Data on industry norms, average ratios, and other relationships are available from such agencies as Dun & Bradstreet and Robert Morris and Associates. It is often useful to compare the performance of a particular firm with that of the industry. Both Dun & Bradstreet and Robert Morris and Associates compile industry statistics for a wide variety of manufacturers, wholesalers, and retailers. A useful feature of the Dun & Bradstreet statistics is that they report not only median performance, but the performance of firms in the upper quartile and the lower quartile of the industry. An important feature of the statistics of Robert Morris and Associates is the reporting of statistics by size of organization.

ANALYTICAL TECHNIQUES

Absolute dollar amounts of profits, sales, assets, and other key data are not very meaningful when studied individually. For example, knowing that a company reports annual earnings of $1 million is of little value unless these earnings can be related to other data. One million dollars in profit might represent excellent performance for a company with less than $10 million in invested capital. On the other hand, such earnings would be meager for a firm that has several hundred million dollars in invested capital. Thus, the most significant information to be derived in analysis concerns the relationships between two or more variables, such as the relation of earnings to assets, earnings to sales, and earnings to stockholders' investment. To describe these relationships clearly and to make comparisons easy, the analyst states these relationships in terms of ratios and percentages.

For example, the relationship of $15,000 in earnings to $150,000 in sales might be expressed as a 10% ($15,000/$150,000) rate of earnings on sales. To describe the relationship between sales of $150,000 and inventory of $20,000, a ratio or a percentage might be used: $150,000/$20,000 may be expressed as 7.5, 7.5:1, or 750%.

Often, selected items in successive financial statements are compared, with changes expressed as percentages. For example, if a firm's earnings increased from $40,000 last year to $48,000 this year, the $8,000 increase related to the base year is expressed as a 20% increase ($8,000/$40,000). To express a dollar increase or decrease as a percentage, however, the base year amount must be a positive figure. If, for example, a firm had a net loss of $4,000 in one year and earnings of $20,000 in the next, the $24,000 increase cannot be expressed as a percentage. Similarly, if a firm showed no marketable securities in last year's balance sheet but showed $15,000 of such securities in this year's statement, the $15,000 increase cannot be expressed as a percentage.

When evaluating a firm's financial statements for two or more years, analysts often use a method called **horizontal analysis**. This type of analysis is useful in detecting improvement or deterioration in a firm's performance and in spotting trends. The term **vertical analysis** is often used to describe the study of a single year's financial statements.

Horizontal Analysis

COMPARATIVE FINANCIAL STATEMENTS The most commonly encountered form of horizontal analysis is that of **comparative financial statements** for two or more years, with dollar and percentage changes shown for important items and classification totals. Dollar increases and decreases are divided by the earliest year's data to obtain percentage changes. The 19X4 and 19X5 financial statements of Able Company, a manufacturer of electronic components and accessories, are shown in Exhibits 18–1, 18–2, and 18–3. We shall use the data in these statements throughout this chapter to illustrate various analytical techniques.

When examining financial statements, the analyst will focus immediate attention on significant items only. Large percentage changes frequently occur in items whose dollar amounts may not be significant compared with other items on the statements. For example, although a large percentage change in the Able Company balance sheet occurred in Prepaid Expenses, the analyst would take scant notice of this item in an initial examination of changes. Instead, attention would be directed first to changes in totals—assets, current assets, long-term assets, current liabilities, and so on. Next, changes in significant individual items, such as receivables and inventory, would be examined. These changes may be related to certain changes in income statement items to see whether or not they are favorable.

For example, observe that the total assets increased 17.4% (Exhibit 18–1), while sales increased 29.7% (Exhibit 18–2). Thus, a fairly large percentage increase in sales was supported by a much smaller rate of increase in assets. Furthermore, the 20.6% increase in inventory was also considerably less than the increase in sales. These results reflect quite favorably on the firm's performance. In addition, the 29.7% increase in sales was accompanied by an increase in accounts receivable of only 18.5%; on the surface, it appears that the sales growth was not associated with a relaxation in credit policy.

Looking at the income statement, we can see that the 38.9% gross profit increase outstripped the rate of increase in sales, indicating a higher mark-up rate in the latest year. Net income, however, increased only 21.8%; we are therefore alerted to the fact that expenses must have grown disproportionately. This can be discerned in the 44.7% increase and the 52.4% increase in selling and administrative expenses, respectively.

From this limited analysis of comparative financial statements, an analyst would conclude that operating performance for the latest year appeared to be favorable. Further analysis, however, using some of the techniques described later in the chapter, might cause the analyst to modify that opinion. One reservation emerging from the foregoing analysis is that operating expenses, particularly administrative expenses, have increased at a fairly high rate. Since many selling expenses, such as sales salaries, commissions, and advertising, are expected to

EXHIBIT 18–1

Able Company
Comparative Balance Sheets
(Thousands of Dollars)

	Dec. 31, 19X5	Dec. 31, 19X4	Increase (Decrease)	Percent Change
Assets				
Current Assets:				
Cash	$ 5,500	$ 4,200	$ 1,300	30.9
Marketable Securities	1,500	2,400	(900)	(37.5)
Accounts Receivable (less allowance for uncollectible accounts of $2,400 in 19X5 and $2,000 in 19X4)	61,600	52,000	9,600	18.5
Inventories (lower of cost [first-in, first-out] or market)	76,000	63,000	13,000	20.6
Prepaid Expenses	900	600	300	50.0
Total Current Assets	$145,500	$122,200	$23,300	19.1
Long-term Assets:				
Property, Plant and Equipment (net of Accumulated depreciation)	$ 45,000	$ 40,000	$ 5,000	12.5
Investments	1,800	1,600	200	12.5
Total Long-term Assets	$ 46,800	$ 41,600	$ 5,200	12.5
Total Assets	$192,300	$163,800	$28,500	17.4
Liabilities and Stockholders' Equity				
Liabilities				
Current Liabilities:				
Notes Payable	$ 5,700	$ 3,000	$ 2,700	90.0
Accounts Payable	22,000	24,100	(2,100)	(8.7)
Accrued Liabilities	30,000	27,300	2,700	9.9
Total Current Liabilities	$ 57,700	$ 54,400	$ 3,300	6.1
Long-term Liabilities:				
$8\frac{1}{2}\%$ Debenture Bonds Payable	$ 25,000	$ 20,000	$ 5,000	25.0
Total Liabilities	$ 82,700	$ 74,400	$ 8,300	11.2
Stockholders' Equity				
7% Preferred Stock, $100 Par Value	$ 8,000	$ 8,000	$ —	—
Common Stock, $5 Par Value	20,000	14,000	6,000	42.9
Paid-in Capital in Excess of Par Value	7,500	5,500	2,000	36.4
Retained Earnings	74,100	61,900	12,200	19.7
Total Stockholders' Equity	$109,600	$ 89,400	$20,200	22.6
Total Liabilities and Stockholders' Equity	$192,300	$163,800	$28,500	17.4

EXHIBIT 18-2

Able Company
Comparative Income Statements
(Thousands of Dollars)

	Year Ended Dec. 31, 19X5	Year Ended Dec. 31, 19X4	Increase (Decrease)	Percent Change
Net Sales	$415,000	$320,000	$95,000	29.7
Cost of Goods Sold	290,000	230,000	60,000	26.1
Gross Profit	$125,000	$ 90,000	$35,000	38.9
Operating Expenses:				
Selling Expenses	$ 39,500	$ 27,300	$12,200	44.7
Administrative Expenses	50,440	33,100	17,340	52.4
Total Operating Expenses	$ 89,940	$ 60,400	$29,540	48.9
Operating Income	$ 35,060	$ 29,600	$ 5,460	18.4
Interest Expense	2,200	1,900	300	15.8
Net Income before Income Taxes	$ 32,860	$ 27,700	$ 5,160	18.6
Income Taxes	14,100	12,300	1,800	14.6
Net Income for Year	$ 18,760	$ 15,400	$ 3,360	21.8
Earnings per Share	$5.35	$5.30		
Dividends per Share	1.50	.90		

EXHIBIT 18-3

Able Company
Comparative Retained Earnings Statements
(Thousands of Dollars)

	Year Ended Dec. 31, 19X5	Year Ended Dec. 31, 19X4	Increase (Decrease)	Percent Change
Retained Earnings, Jan. 1	$61,900	$49,580	$12,320	24.8
Net Income for Year	18,760	15,400	3,360	21.8
Total	$80,660	$64,980	$15,680	24.1
Dividends:				
On Preferred Stock	$ 560	$ 560	$ —	—
On Common Stock	6,000	2,520	3,480	138.0
Total	$ 6,560	$ 3,080	$ 3,480	114.0
Retained Earnings, Dec. 31	$74,100	$61,900	$12,200	19.7

rise somewhat proportionately with sales but administrative expenses are not, an investigation of the reasons for the large increase in the latter expense might be indicated.

TREND ANALYSIS To observe percentage changes over time in selected data, it is often helpful to compute **trend percentages.** Most companies provide summaries of data for the past five or ten years in their annual reports. Such information enables the analyst to look at changes over a longer period of time than two years. For example, suppose you were interested in sales and earnings trends for Able Company for the past five years. The dollar data, taken from the company's published annual report in the fifth year (19X5) of the period, are shown below:

Able Company
Annual Performance (Millions of Dollars)

	Year 1	Year 2	Year 3	Year 4	Year 5
Sales	$202.0	$175.0	$243.0	$320.0	$415.0
Net Earnings	10.9	10.3	13.5	15.4	18.8

Although we can perceive a fairly healthy growth pattern for this company by inspecting the above data, we can determine the pattern of change from year to year more precisely by calculating trend percentages. To do this, we select a base year and then divide the data for each of the other years by the base year data. The resultant figures are actually indexes that show changes occurring throughout the period. If we choose Year 1 as the base year, all data for Years 2 through 5 will be related to Year 1, which is represented as 100%.

To create the following table, we divided each year's sales, from Year 2 through Year 5, by $202, the Year 1 sales in millions of dollars. Similarly, the net earnings for Years 2 through 5 were divided by $10.9, the Year 1 net earnings in millions of dollars.

Annual Performance (Percentage of Base Year)

	Year 1	Year 2	Year 3	Year 4	Year 5
Sales	100%	87%	120%	158%	205%
Net Earnings	100	94	124	141	172

The trend percentages reveal that the growth in earnings outstripped the growth in sales for Years 2 and 3, then fell below the sales growth in the last two years. We have already seen, in our analysis of comparative statements, that a disproportionate increase in operating expenses emerged in 19X5 (Year 5). We might therefore further analyze the 19X4 data to determine if net income was affected for the same reason or if the reduced growth rate was caused by other factors.

Some care must be exercised in interpreting trend percentages. Remember that all index percentages are related to the *base year.* Thus, the change between the Year 2 sales index (87%) and the Year 3 sales index (120%) represents a 33%

increase in terms of the *base year* dollars. To express the increase as a percentage of Year 2 dollars, we would divide the 33% increase by the Year 2 sales index, 87%, to obtain an increase of 38%. One must also be careful to select a base year that is representative. For example, consider the following sales and earnings data during the identical period for a competing company (which we shall call the Baker Company):

Baker Company
Annual Performance

	Year 1	Year 2	Year 3	Year 4	Year 5
Sales (millions of dollars)	$192.3	$204.4	$225.0	$299.0	$414.6
(Percentage of base year)	100%	106%	117%	155%	216%
Net Earnings (millions of dollars)	$ 1.9	$ 3.0	$ 4.0	$ 6.5	$ 10.0
(Percentage of base year)	100%	158%	210%	342%	526%

Note that the pattern of sales growth for Baker Company is not too dissimilar to that of Able Company. The net earnings growth, however, when judged from trend percentages, appears to be almost twice as good as that of Able Company. Using an unrepresentative base year for Baker Company, when earnings were depressed, makes the earnings trend misleading. In Year 1, Baker Company earned less than 1% of sales ($1.9/$192.3). But in the later years of the period, the more normal relationship between earnings and sales prevailed, and earnings were roughly 2 to $2\frac{1}{2}$% of sales. The earnings/sales relationship for Able Company was relatively normal in Year 1.

Other data that the analyst may wish to relate to sales and earnings over a period of years are such items as total assets, plant investment, and expenditures for research and development.

EFFECT OF INFLATION   As we saw in Chapter 16, financial information reported on a historical cost basis during a period of inflation does not portray economic reality. Not only may the true financial position and operating performance of a given year be distorted, but comparisons made for a firm over time and with other firms may be deceptive. In the foregoing analysis, for example, sales and net earnings growth for firms such as Able Company would be considerably less if the data were adjusted for the effects of inflation. Many other relationships, unless adjusted for inflation, would likewise be distorted. When income statement items, such as sales, are related to balance sheet items, distortion may occur because the sales figure is expressed in dollars of fairly current vintage (current prices are used), while inventories (especially LIFO inventories) and plant and equipment include dollar amounts of earlier price levels.

The financial analyst should therefore attempt to determine the effect of inflation on the data being examined. We have already mentioned the standard of the FASB to require that certain operating data of large public firms, reflecting adjustments for inflation, be reported in supplementary form; we have also mentioned that the SEC requires disclosure of replacement cost for certain data of large public firms.

Recently, some firms have voluntarily reported the effect of inflation on some of their operating data. In its 1978 annual report, General Motors presented trend percentages for sales and earnings during a six-year period, showing both unadjusted and adjusted data. (See the boxed insert below.)

INFLATION-ADJUSTED TREND PERCENTAGES FOR GENERAL MOTORS

In its 1978 annual report, General Motors presented, as a part of its letter to stockholders,[1] six-year trend percentages for sales and earnings, showing both unadjusted figures and the same figures adjusted for inflation using the Consumer Price Index. The data are shown in the table below:

General Price-level Adjustment for Inflation
(Millions of Dollars Except Per Share Amounts)

	1978	1977	1976	1975	1974	Base Year 1973
Sales, as reported	$63,221.1	$54,961.3	$47,181.0	$35,724.9	$31,549.5	$35,798.3
Percent Increase (Decrease) over 1973	77%	54%	32%	—	(12%)	—
Sales in constant dollars*	43,086.2	40,305.0	36,831.6	29,497.4	28,430.9	35,798.3
Percent Increase (Decrease) over 1973	20%	13%	3%	(18%)	(21%)	—
Net income, as reported	3,508.0	3,337.5	2,902.8	1,253.1	950.1	2,398.1
Percent Increase (Decrease) over 1973	46%	39%	21%	(48%)	(60%)	—
Net income in constant dollars*	2,390.8	2,447.5	2,266.1	1,034.7	856.2	2,398.1
Percent Increase (Decrease) over 1973	—	2%	(6%)	(57%)	(64%)	—
Profit margin, as reported	5.5%	6.1%	6.2%	3.5%	3.0%	6.7%
Earnings per share—($ per share)						
As reported	12.24	11.62	10.08	4.32	3.27	8.34
Constant dollars*	8.34	8.51	7.86	3.56	2.95	8.34

*Adjustment to constant dollar basis has been determined by applying the Consumer Price Index to the data for 1974 through 1978 with 1973 as the base year.

Notice that, when adjusted for general price-level changes, the 77% increase in sales over the 1973 base year figure becomes an increase of only 20%. Even more startling is the revelation that there was no increase whatever in net income during the period. Furthermore, there was an actual erosion of GM's profit margin (rate of return on sales) from 6.7% in 1973 to 5.5% in 1978. This decrease was attributed to higher raw material costs and higher wage rates.

[1] General Motors *Annual Report*, 1978, p. 18.

Vertical Analysis

The relative importance of various items in financial statements can be highlighted by showing them as percentages of a key figure or total. Calculation of such percentages is particularly useful in presenting income statement data. For example, the items on the income statement are usually shown as a percentage of the sales figure, as illustrated in Exhibit 18–4 for the 19X5 income statement of Able Company.

COMMON-SIZE STATEMENTS   When percentages of a key figure on a financial statement are shown alone, without the corresponding dollar figures, the resulting statements are called **common-size** statements. Common-size income statements for Able Company are compared with those of Baker Company in Exhibit 18–5.

We see from Exhibit 18–5 that Baker Company has a smaller gross profit margin percentage than does Able Company. The disparity might be due either to lower sales prices or to higher production costs for Baker Company. Selling and administrative expenses as a percentage of sales were fairly comparable, except that, combined, they were a higher percentage of the sales dollar for Able Company than for Baker Company in 19X5. The interest expense as a percentage of sales in 19X4 was somewhat higher for Baker Company than for Able Company; however, note that in 19X5 this percentage for Baker Company was twice that for Able Company. Considering Baker Company's very low rate of net income to net sales (2.2% in 19X5), the interest percentage is significant. Yet Able Company's higher rate of return on sales (about double that of Baker Company) is due mainly to Able's better gross profit margin.

EXHIBIT 18–4

Able Company
Income Statement
For the Year Ended December 31, 19X5

Net Sales	$415,000	100.0%
Cost of Goods Sold	290,000	69.9
Gross Profit	$125,000	30.1%
Operating Expenses:		
Selling Expenses	$ 39,500	9.5%
Administrative Expenses	50,440	12.2
Total Operating Expenses	$ 89,940	21.7%
Operating Income	$ 35,060	8.4%
Interest Expense	2,200	.5
Net Income before Income Taxes	$ 32,860	7.9%
Income Taxes	14,100	3.4
Net Income for Year	$ 18,760	4.5%

We may also employ common-size percentages to analyze balance sheet data, although less successfully than with income statement data. For example, if for a period of several years we state current assets and fixed assets as a percentage of total assets, we can determine whether a company is becoming more or less liquid. By determining the percentage that each current asset bears to the total current assets, we may observe any changes in these ingredients of working capital.

The best balance sheet use of common-size statements is probably with the sources of capital (equities). The proportions of the total capital supplied by short-term creditors, long-term creditors, preferred stockholders, and common stockholders of Able Company are shown below for 19X5:

	Amount (Millions of Dollars)	Common-Size Percentage
Current debt	$ 57.7	30%
Long-term debt	25.0	13
Preferred stock equity	8.0	4
Common stock equity	101.6	53
	$192.3	100%

A glance at the percentages shown reveals that 53% of Able Company's capital is supplied by the common shareholders and 47% by preferred stockholders and creditors. We shall discover shortly that such percentages are useful in appraising the financial structure of a firm.

EXHIBIT 18–5

	Able and Baker Companies Common-Size Income Statements (Percentage of Net Sales)			
	Able Company		Baker Company	
	Year Ended Dec. 31, 19X5	Year Ended Dec. 31, 19X4	Year Ended Dec. 31, 19X5	Year Ended Dec. 31, 19X4
Net Sales	100.0%	100.0%	100.0%	100.0%
Cost of Goods Sold	69.9	71.9	73.8	74.9
Gross Profit	30.1%	28.1%	26.2%	25.1%
Operating Expenses:				
Selling Expenses	9.5	8.5	8.6	8.2
Administrative Expenses	12.2	10.4	12.3	11.4
Total Operating Expenses	21.7%	18.9%	20.9%	19.6%
Operating Income	8.4%	9.2%	5.3%	5.5%
Interest Expense	.5	.6	1.0	.8
Net Income before Income Taxes	7.9%	8.6%	4.3%	4.7%
Income Taxes	3.4	3.8	2.1	2.3
Net Income for Year	4.5%	4.8%	2.2%	2.4%

ANALYSIS OF OPERATING PERFORMANCE

In evaluating the operating performance of a firm, the analyst invariably uses **rate of return** analysis. This analysis, which deals with the firm's profitability, relates either the operating income or the net income to some base, such as the average total assets, average stockholders' equity, or the year's sales. The resultant percentage can be compared with similar rates for the firm in past years or to other firms. The most important relationships are:

(1) Return on assets.
(2) Return on common stockholders' equity.
(3) Return on sales.

**Return
on Assets**

The rate of return on the total assets available to a firm is probably one of the most useful measures of the firm's profitability and efficiency. It is calculated by dividing the year's operating income (income before deducting interest and income tax expense) by the average total assets employed during the year:

$$\text{Rate of Return on Assets} = \frac{\text{Operating Income}}{\text{Average Total Assets}}$$

Because the return for a year is being earned on assets employed throughout the year, and assets may vary during that time, it is useful to compute the return on the *average* amount of assets. The approximate average may be obtained by summing the beginning and ending asset totals and dividing by two.

If the percentage is to be a true index of productivity and accomplishment, it should not be influenced by the manner in which the company is financed. Therefore, we use income before interest charges as a measure of the dollar return in the numerator. As a result, we may compare the return for a company having a relatively high proportion of debt with that of a company using mostly owners' equity to finance its assets.

For example, assume that Company X and Company Y each have $500,000 in average total assets and that each has income of $70,000 before interest expense and taxes. Suppose that Company X has no interest-bearing debt but Company Y has $200,000 of 10% bonds payable outstanding. The bottom portions of the income statements of the two companies (rearranged to highlight the effect of interest and taxes) are shown in Exhibit 18-6 (we assume a 40% effective income tax rate).

Company X and Company Y are earning the same percentage return, 14%, on their assets ($70,000 income before interest and taxes divided by $500,000 average total assets). Company Y, however, is financed partially by bonds. Thus, its interest expense of $20,000 less a 40% tax benefit of $8,000 makes its final net income $12,000 less than that of Company X. This difference is due solely to the manner in which the two companies are financed and is unrelated to their *operational accomplishment*. We can see why the return on assets is normally mea-

EXHIBIT 18-6

Partial Income Statements		
	Company X	**Company Y**
Operating Income (Income before Interest Expense and Income Taxes)	$70,000	$70,000
Interest Expense (10% of $200,000)	—	20,000
	$70,000	$50,000
Income Taxes (40%)	28,000	20,000
Net Income for Year	$42,000	$30,000

sured before interest and income taxes. As will be pointed out later, however, the judicious use of debt in financing may be beneficial to the owners of a business.

The return on assets, sometimes called the **productivity ratio,** is useful for comparing similar companies operating in the same industry. It also aids management in gauging the effectiveness of its asset utilization. When this ratio is considered together with such relationships as return on stockholders' equity and return on sales (explained below), much insight can be gained about the operating performance of a firm.

The return on assets of Able Company for 19X5 and 19X4 is calculated below:

		19X5	19X4
Operating Income		$ 35,060	$ 29,600
Total Assets:			
Beginning of Year	(a)	$163,800	$142,500
End of Year	(b)	192,300	163,800
Average [(a + b)/2]		178,050	153,150
Rate of Return on Average Assets		19.7%	19.3%

Return on Common Stockholders' Equity

The rate of return to the common shareholders is calculated using net income less preferred stock dividend requirements. This ratio measures the ultimate profitability of the investment to the common stockholders. Although it can be figured either before or after taxes, it is commonly done after taxes as follows:

$$\text{Rate of Return on Common Stockholders' Equity} = \frac{\text{Net Income} - \text{Preferred Dividend Requirements}}{\text{Average Common Stockholders' Equity}}$$

Again, we emphasize that the return is earned on the stockholders' equity remaining invested *throughout* the year. Because this amount varies during the year, we commonly approximate the average investment by summing the beginning and ending balances and dividing by two.

The rate of return for Able Company in 19X5 and 19X4 is calculated below:

		19X5	19X4
Net Income		$ 18,760	$15,400
Less: Preferred Dividend Requirements (7% of $8,000)		560	560
Common Stock Earnings		$ 18,200	$14,840
Common Stockholders' Equity:			
Beginning of Year	(a)	$ 81,400	$63,500
End of Year	(b)	101,600	81,400
Average [(a + b)/2]		$ 91,500	$72,450
Rate of Return on Common Stockholders' Equity		19.9%	20.5%

Able Company's rate of return for both years was better than the median rate of return for the electronic accessories industry, which was about 16% in 19X5.

Return on Sales   Another important measure of operating performance is the rate of return on the net sales of a firm. In practice, the most commonly used version of this ratio is **net income to net sales.** When component percentages, or common-size percentages, are available with the income statement, return on sales equals the net income percentage and is calculated as follows:

$$\text{Return on Sales} = \frac{\text{Net Income}}{\text{Net Sales}}$$

The calculations for Able Company are given below:

	19X5	19X4
Net Income	$ 18,760	$ 15,400
Net Sales	415,000	320,000
Return on Sales	4.5%	4.8%

The median ratio for 19X5 for the electronic components and accessories industry was about 5.7%. Thus, Able Company's rate of return was slightly below average.

Net income to net sales percentages are indexes of performance to be used solely when studying similar companies in the same industry or when comparing different periods for the same company. The rate of return on sales varies widely from industry to industry. Some firms may operate in an industry characterized by low profit margins and high turnover of their principal assets. (The ratio of net sales to average total assets is called *asset turnover.*) For example, most meat processing companies and supermarkets seldom have a net income to net sales ratio exceeding 2%. They have huge sales volumes, however, and turn over their assets (especially inventory) many, many times. In contrast, a company manufacturing and selling fine grand pianos might be expected to have an extremely high ratio of net income to net sales. Because production capabilities of making pianos are inherently limited, turnover of assets would be very low. As a general rule, firms that deal in relatively slow-moving products involving fairly long production periods require higher profit margins in order to earn a respectable rate of return on assets and on the owners' investment.

USING THE NET INCOME FIGURE

When analyzing the operating performance of a company, intelligent analysts make their own evaluations of the reported net income of a firm. Above all, they are interested in the prospects for future income. They therefore analyze, as far as they are able, the factors influencing the net income figure. If possible, they wish to determine which segments of the business contribute the most to net income and what the future prospects are for such segments. In this respect, the analysts' inquiries frequently lead them to sources of information other than the financial statements. An analyst can usually determine from the statements themselves, however, (1) how representative the net income figure is and (2) whether or not it was arrived at by conservative accounting principles.

To determine whether the net income is representative of the earning capability of the firm, the analyst scrutinizes the income statement. Often, any unusual and/or nonrecurring items that have been included in the determination of net income are eliminated for analytical purposes. Such items as gains and losses on sales of fixed assets or securities, casualty losses, and the like, are either omitted or apportioned to a number of years' income calculations.

The analyst should also examine such factors as inventory pricing techniques and depreciation methods (and rates) to determine their effect on net income. Company policies for investment tax credits (whether included in income immediately or deferred to future periods) and for recording of fringe benefit costs (such as pension costs) must also be reviewed. The analyst wants to know whether the company's net income falls in the low, or conservative, end of the spectrum of possible amounts or whether it is on the high side. Once this is determined, it is possible to proceed to a more informed evaluation of a company's operating performance, stock values, growth potential, and so on.

Earnings per Share

Because stock market prices are quoted on a per-share basis, it is useful to calculate a firm's earnings on the same basis. *Earnings per share* for common stock are usually given prominence in reports because both analysts and investors consider the relationship of prices and earnings to be quite important. An independent public accountant computing earnings per share for *reporting* purposes should follow procedures described in Accounting Principles Board *Opinion No. 15*, "Earnings Per Share," published by the AICPA. These procedures are discussed in Chapter 14.

Analysts may use the earnings-per-share figures that are available in annual reports—if they find such computations meaningful—or they may make their own computations. We shall compute earnings per share by dividing common stock earnings (net income less any preferred dividend requirements) by the average number of shares outstanding during the year, as follows:[2]

[2]Analysts usually use the number of shares outstanding at the close of the year to make this calculation. However, a more meaningful figure would be the average number of shares outstanding during the year. The AICPA's Accounting Principles Board suggested the use of a weighted average that takes into account the periods of time during which various amounts of stock were outstanding.

$$\text{Earnings per Share} = \frac{\text{Net Income} - \text{Preferred Dividend Requirements}}{\text{Average Number of Common Shares Outstanding}}$$

The following calculations are made for Able Company:

		19X5	19X4
Net Income		$18,760	$15,400
Less: Preferred Dividend Requirements (7% of $8,000)		560	560
Common Stock Earnings		$18,200	$14,840
Common Shares Outstanding:			
Beginning of Year	(a)	2,800	2,800
End of Year	(b)	4,000	2,800
Average [(a + b)/2]		3,400	2,800
Earnings per Share		$5.35	$5.30

Able Company's earnings per share increased only slightly in 19X5 because a large number of additional shares were issued during the year.

Price–Earnings Ratio

When the market price of a share of stock is divided by the earnings per share, the resulting ratio is called the **price–earnings ratio.** For many analysts and investors, this ratio is an important tool in assessing stock values. For example, after evaluating the strong and weak points of several companies in an industry, the analyst may compare price–earnings ratios to judge which is a "best buy."

When determining the price–earnings ratio, it is customary to use the latest market price and to use the common stock earnings for the last four quarters of a company's operations. In our calculation for Able Company, we will use the 19X5 common stock earnings and the market price at the end of that year, $37\frac{1}{2}$:

$$\text{Price–Earnings Ratio} = \frac{\text{Market Price per Common Share}}{\text{Common Stock Earnings per Share}} = \frac{\$37.50}{\$\ 5.35} = 7.0$$

In other words, the market price of a share of Able Company common stock was 7 times the amount that share earned for the year. By itself, this multiplier is not particularly meaningful, although price–earnings ratios well below ten often indicate a depressed market price. A prospective investor might compare this ratio with that of Baker Company or with the average for the (electronic accessories) industry. Coupled with a fair evaluation of the strengths and weaknesses of several investment prospects and some knowledge of the industry itself, the price–earnings ratio might help the investor decide whether the stock was overvalued in the market or an attractive investment.

Yield and Dividend Payout

The expectations of investors vary a great deal with personal economic circumstances and with the overall economic outlook. Some investors are more interested in price appreciation of a stock investment than present income in the form of dividends; in the future, when shares are disposed of, only part of the gains may be taxed under the capital gains provision of the income tax laws, while dividends are almost fully taxable. Other investors are more concerned with dividends than price appreciation. Such investors desire a high *yield,* or dividend rate of return, on their investments. Yield is normally calculated by dividing the current annual dividends per share by the current price of the stock. In the case of Able Company, we use the 19X5 dividends and the year-end price per share to calculate yield, as follows:

$$\text{Dividend Yield} = \frac{\text{Common Dividends per Share}}{\text{Market Price per Share}} = \frac{\$\ 1.50}{\$37.50} = 4\%$$

Investors who emphasize the yield on their investments may also be interested in the **dividend payout ratio** of a firm, which is the percentage of the common stock earnings paid out in dividends. The payout ratio indicates whether a firm has a conservative or a liberal dividend policy and may also indicate whether the firm is attempting to conserve funds for internal financing of growth. For Able Company, we calculate the payout ratio for 19X5 as follows:

$$\text{Dividend Payout Ratio} = \frac{\text{Common Dividends per Share}}{\text{Common Earnings per Share}} = \frac{\$1.50}{\$5.35} = 28\%$$

Both the yield and the dividend payout ratio for the common shares of Able Company were relatively low in 19X5. The firm had embarked on an expansion program and was attempting to conserve funds to finance acquisitions internally.

Low payout ratios can have a depressing effect on the market price of a stock, and reducing the payout ratio sometimes may have a dramatic effect on the stock price. In 1978, for example, General Motors reduced its payout ratio by cutting its year-end dividend, and within two weeks the common stock price skidded down 10%.

Payout ratios for typical, seasoned industrial corporations vary between 40% and 60%. Many corporations, however, may need funds for internal financing of growth and thus will pay out little or nothing in dividends. At the other extreme, some companies, principally utility companies, may pay out as much as 80% or 90% of their earnings. Utilities have less need of retaining funds for growth because the bulk of their financing is through long-term debt. It is said that they "trade on the equity" to a large extent. We discuss this idea in greater detail in the next section.

TRADING ON THE EQUITY

The expression *trading on the equity* designates the use of borrowed funds, particularly long-term debt, in the capital structure of a firm. Trading *profitably* on the equity means that the borrowed funds generate a higher rate of return than the rate that must be paid for the use of the funds. The excess, of course, accrues to the benefit of the common shareholders in that it magnifies, or increases, their earnings. To illustrate, let us return to the example given in Exhibit 18–6. In this case, both Companies X and Y have assets of $500,000. Company X has its entire capital in common stockholders' equity, while Company Y has $200,000 in 10%, long-term debt and $300,000 in common stockholders' equity. Both firms have $70,000 operating income (income before interest and taxes). For the sake of clarity, we repeat the net income calculation below, together with percentages earned on assets and on stockholders' equity.

	Company X	Company Y
Operating Income	$70,000	$70,000
Interest expense (10% of $200,000)	—	20,000
	$70,000	$50,000
Income taxes (40%)	28,000	20,000
Net income for year	$42,000	$30,000
Return on assets:		
For both companies: $70,000/$500,000 =	14%	14%
Return on stockholders' equity:		
For Company X: $42,000/$500,000 =	8.4%	
For Company Y: $30,000/$300,000 =		10%

Note that Company Y achieved a higher return on its stockholders' investment than did Company X. We can account for this additional 1.6% on stockholders' equity as follows:

14% earned on $200,000 borrowed	$28,000
10% interest paid for use of funds	20,000
Trading on equity gain before income tax	$ 8,000
Less 40% income tax	3,200
Trading on equity gain after taxes	$ 4,800
$4,800 gain ÷ $300,000 stockholders' equity =	1.6%

The fact that Company Y was able to earn 14% on its assets (including the $200,000 borrowed) and pay only 10% on the money borrowed permitted it to gain $8,000 before income taxes. The gain became $4,800 after deducting 40% for taxes. The after tax gain of $4,800 is a 1.6% return on the stockholders' equity of $300,000. Magnifying gains for the shareholders in this manner is sometimes referred to as the use of **leverage.**

Leverage in the capital structure must be used judiciously because some risk is involved. Leverage can also magnify losses. Suppose that the income before interest and income taxes had been only $30,000, representing a 6% return on the assets of $500,000. The after tax return for Company Y would be only $6,000 ($30,000 − [$20,000 interest + $4,000 taxes]). The return on stockholders' equity would then be only 2% ($6,000/$300,000) compared with a return of 3.6% for Company X ($30,000 − $12,000 taxes = $18,000; $18,000/$500,000 = 3.6%).

In general, companies with stable earnings can afford more debt in their capital structure than those with fluctuating earnings. Because of their stable earnings, utility companies may have as much as 70% of their financial structure in debt, while most industrial companies rarely have more than 50% debt financing.

ANALYSIS OF FINANCIAL STRENGTH

The ultimate source of any company's financial strength is its earning power. For this reason, we have stressed the operating performance and earning power of the business firm in our discussion thus far. However, certain other relationships that give the analyst insight into the financial strength of a company can be perceived in financial statements. The first of these relationships concerns the company's financial structure and its fixed charges. The second relates to the company's working capital position.

Equity Ratio   A good way to observe the manner in which a company is financed is to calculate the **equity ratio,** which is the common stockholders' equity divided by the company's total assets.

$$\text{Equity Ratio} = \frac{\text{Common Stockholders' Equity}}{\text{Total Assets}}$$

We commonly use year-end balances for the elements in this ratio rather than averages because we are interested mainly in the capital structure at a particular point in time. The calculations for Able Company are as follows:

	19X5	19X4
Common Stockholders' Equity	$101,600	$ 81,400
Total Assets	$192,300	$163,800
Equity Ratio	53.0%	49.7%

The equity ratio is readily available if one has already calculated common-size percentages from the balance sheet, as we did earlier in the chapter (page 637). At the close of 19X5, 53% of Able Company's capital was being provided by common shareholders and 47% by debtors and preferred shareholders. Because the analyst is interested mainly in whether the company may be trading on the equity too heavily, the equity ratio gives a clue to the extent of the firm's borrowing in relation to its assets.

When we attempt to analyze a firm's leverage, there is sometimes a question about how to handle any preferred stock outstanding. Remember that the dividends on ordinary preferred stock are not a fixed charge, such as bond interest, but a contingent charge (contingent on declaration by the firm's board of directors). Despite this fact, when examining a company's long-term position, most analysts treat regular preferred stock as debt. They evidently feel that preferred dividends should be treated as a fixed charge, because ordinarily such dividends must be paid in order for distributions to be made to the common shareholders. Usually, preferred stock is included with stockholders' equity *for analytical purposes* only when the preferred stock is convertible into common and is likely to be converted in the near future.

Although no explicit rules of thumb or standards exist for equity ratios, the analyst may have a general idea of what a company's financial structure should be. Should a company's equity ratio fall outside the subjective range of percentages the analyst has in mind, it will be investigated further.

Bond Interest Coverage

A further step an analyst may take to evaluate the size of a company's debt is to observe the relationship of interest charges to earnings. For example, a company may have an extremely low equity ratio, indicating heavy borrowing. However, if its earnings are sufficient, even in poor years, to meet the interest charges on the debt several times over, the analyst may regard the situation quite favorably. As we have seen, heavy leverage coupled with safety is desirable.

Analysts, particularly long-term creditors, almost always calculate the **bond interest coverage,** sometimes called **times interest earned.** This ratio is determined by dividing the operating income (income before bond interest and income taxes) by the annual bond interest:

$$\text{Bond Interest Coverage} = \frac{\text{Operating Income}}{\text{Annual Bond Interest}}$$

The computations for Able Company are as follows:

	19X5	19X4
Operating Income	$35,060	$29,600
Annual Bond Interest (8½% of Bonds Payable)	$ 2,125	$ 1,700
Times Interest Earned	16.5	17.4

In other words, Able Company's income available to meet interest charges was approximately 17 times the amount of its interest expense. Obviously, Able Company has an exceptionally good margin of safety. Generally speaking, a company that earns its interest several times before taxes in its poorest year is regarded as a satisfactory risk by long-term creditors.

Preferred Dividend Coverage

Quite naturally, preferred stockholders would like to know what assurance there is that dividends will continue to be paid. They may therefore wish to calculate their **dividend coverage.** To compute the number of times preferred dividends are earned, we combine the annual bond interest and preferred dividend requirements and divide operating income (income before interest and income taxes) by the combined amount:

$$\text{Preferred Dividend Coverage} = \frac{\text{Operating Income}}{\text{Annual Bond Interest} + \text{Preferred Dividend Requirements}}$$

The calculations for Able Company show ample protection for the preferred dividends:

	19X5	19X4
Operating Income	$35,060	$29,600
Annual Bond Interest	$ 2,125	$ 1,700
Preferred Dividend Requirements	560	560
	$ 2,685	$ 2,260
Times Preferred Dividends Earned	13.1	13.1

The preferred dividend requirement was combined with the bond interest in the calculations because bond interest is a prior charge against earnings—that is, it must be paid before any preferred dividends can be distributed.[3] Sometimes an inexperienced analyst will calculate the preferred dividend coverage by dividing net income after income taxes by the dividend requirement. If we did this for the Able Company in 19X5, the result would be a coverage of 33.5 times ($18,760/$560). This is obviously an absurd result, since the bond interest coverage is only 16.5 times. Inasmuch as bond interest is a prior charge, the protection for dividends on a junior security such as preferred stock cannot be better than the protection for the bond interest.

Analysis of Working Capital Position

The analysis of a company's working capital position is sometimes called *short-term credit analysis*, because it emphasizes factors of particular importance to short-term creditors, who are principally interested in the company's ability to repay its current obligations on time. Long-term creditors and investors, however, should also be concerned about a company's current position. Shortages of working capital can sometimes force a company into disadvantageous borrowing at inopportune times and unfavorable interest rates, and can also affect its ability to pay interest and dividends. Many long-term debt contracts contain provisions that require the borrowing firm to maintain an adequate current position.

A firm's **working capital** is the difference between its current assets and current liabilities. For Able Company in 19X5, working capital (in thousands of dollars) was $87,800 (current assets of $145,500 minus current liabilities of $57,700).

We can best judge the adequacy of a firm's working capital in relation to its sales and to the ratio between current assets and current debt. Compare the following sets of 19X5 data for Able Company and Baker Company.

[3]Because bond interest is tax deductible and preferred dividends are not, some analysts place the dividends on the same basis as the interest by dividing them by (1 − tax rate). Thus, with a 40% tax rate, the dividends would be converted to $933. We have chosen to ignore this technicality in our discussion.

| | (Thousands of Dollars) | |
	Able	Baker
Current Assets	$145,500	$139,549
Current Liabilities	57,700	90,136
Working Capital	$ 87,800	$ 49,413
Sales	$415,000	$414,644

In this example, the ratio of sales to working capital (called **working capital turnover**) is 4.7 for Able ($415,000/$87,800) and 8.4 for Baker ($414,644/$49,413). One might wonder about this disparity. How much working capital should there be to support a given amount of sales? One way of determining which of the two companies has a better defensive position is to calculate the current ratio.

CURRENT RATIO   The current ratio is simply the current assets divided by the current liabilities:

$$\text{Current Ratio} = \frac{\text{Current Assets}}{\text{Current Liabilities}}$$

This ratio is a measure of a firm's ability to meet its current obligations on time and to have funds readily available for current operations. As shown by the calculations below, Able Company improved its position in 19X5 and has a current ratio of 252%.

	19X5	19X4
Current Assets	$145,500	$122,200
Current Liabilities	$ 57,700	$ 54,400
Current Ratio	2.52	2.25

This represents a better current position than that of Baker Company, which had a ratio of only 155% ($139,549/$90,136). There is evidence that Baker Company's working capital may be too small to support its volume of sales.

For many years, some short-term creditors have relied on a rule of thumb that the current ratio for industrial companies should exceed 200%. This fairly arbitrary guideline probably developed from the premise that, because inventories frequently amount to as much as one-half of current assets, the remaining, more liquid current assets should at least equal the current debt. It is not a completely reliable rule, since many companies have operated successfully with lower current ratios. Nonetheless, the 200% rule can be used as a general guide. When there is a low current ratio, the analyst should attempt to determine whether or not the situation is temporary. It is also useful to find out if the company has access to a line of credit so that refinancing can be accomplished easily in the event of difficulty.

QUICK RATIO   Sometimes analysts calculate the ratio between the liquid, or "quick," current assets and the current liabilities. The **quick current assets** are cash, marketable securities, and receivables. The main item omitted is, of course, the inventory. Prepaid items are also omitted, but they are usually not material in amount. The quick ratio may give a better picture than the current ratio of a company's ability to meet current debts and to take advantage of discounts offered by creditors. When taken together with the current ratio, it gives the analyst an idea of the influence of the inventory figure in the company's working capital position. For example, a company might have an acceptable current ratio, but if its quick ratio falls much below 100%, the analyst might become uneasy about the size of the inventory and then be prompted to analyze the inventory position more carefully. Again, the 100% rule of thumb for the quick ratio is an arbitrary standard and is used only as a reference point to alert the analyst to the need for further scrutiny.

We calculate the quick ratio for Able Company as follows:

$$\text{Quick Ratio} = \frac{\text{Cash} + \text{Marketable Securities} + \text{Receivables}}{\text{Current Liabilities}}$$

	19X5	19X4
Cash, Marketable Securities, and Receivables	$68,600	$58,600
Current Liabilities	$57,700	$54,400
Quick Ratio	1.19	1.08

INVENTORY TURNOVER   An analyst concerned about a company's inventory position may wish to compute the company's average inventory turnover. This figure indicates whether the inventory is disproportionate to the amount of sales. Excessive inventories not only tie up company funds and increase storage costs but may also lead to subsequent losses if the goods become outdated or unsalable. The computation is made in various ways, but it always involves dividing some measure of sales volume by a measure of the typical inventory level. Most accountants use cost of goods sold as a measure of sales volume and the average inventory for the year as a measure of the typical inventory level, as follows:

$$\text{Inventory Turnover} = \frac{\text{Cost of Goods Sold}}{\text{Average Inventory}}$$

Using this measure for Able Company gives the following results:

		19X5	19X4
Cost of Goods Sold		$290,000	$230,000
Beginning Inventory	(a)	$ 63,000	$ 48,000
Ending Inventory	(b)	76,000	63,000
Average Inventory [(a + b)/2]		$ 69,500	$ 55,500
Inventory Turnover		4.17	4.14

The major reason for using cost of goods sold in the calculation is that the inventory measure in the denominator is a *cost* figure; it is therefore reasonable to use a cost figure in the numerator. Many credit agencies and analysts in the business world commonly use the sales amount instead of cost of goods sold to calculate inventory turnover, however. Calculated in this manner, Able Company's turnover is 5.97 times in 19X5, better than the 5.72 median turnover for the industry reported by a credit agency for 19X5. Analysts who want to compare a firm's inventory turnover with industry averages computed in this manner should use the sales figure in the calculations.

Usually, the average inventory is obtained by adding the year's beginning and ending inventories and dividing by two. Since inventories taken at the beginning and end of the year are likely to be lower in some cases than the typical inventory, an unrealistically high turnover ratio may result. If monthly inventory figures are available, a 12-month average should be used. Furthermore, one should be careful in calculating inventory turnover ratios for companies that use last-in, first-out inventory measurement methods. In calculating inventory turnover, company management may wish to restate the inventories at current prices using price indexes or other available data. Outside analysts may not be in a position to make such adjustments and may have to make some subjective allowance for overstatement of turnover.

A low inventory turnover can, of course, result from an overextended inventory position or from inadequate sales volume. For this reason, appraisal of inventory turnover should be accompanied by scrutiny of the quick ratio and analysis of trends in both inventory and sales to find out what has occurred. Inventory turnover figures vary considerably from industry to industry, and analysts frequently compare a firm's experience with industry averages.

AVERAGE COLLECTION PERIOD   A widely used method of measuring the average quality of the trade receivables of a firm is to calculate the **average collection period.** This calculation, sometimes called **day's sales outstanding,** is made as follows:

$$\text{Average Collection Period} = \frac{\text{Trade Accounts Receivable}}{\text{Year's Sales}} \times 365$$

Note that the above equation results from first calculating the average day's sales (sales/365) and then dividing this figure into the balance of accounts receivable to discover how many average days' sales are uncollected. In the computation, the numerator should be the end-of-year receivables before deducting the allowance for uncollectible accounts, and only credit sales should be in the denominator. In the following calculations, we assume that all of Able Company's sales were credit sales.

	19X5	19X4
End-of-Year Receivables (before allowance for Uncollectible Accounts) (a)	$ 64,000	$ 54,000
Net Credit Sales (b)	415,000	320,000
Average Collection Period [(a/b) × 365]	56 days	62 days

Analysts calculate average collection period to discover how large a portion of the trade accounts are slow or overdue. The median collection period for the electronic accessories industry in 19X5 was 58 days; therefore, Able Company's receivables appear to be reasonable in size. A rough rule of thumb sometimes used by credit agencies is that the average collection period should not exceed $1\frac{1}{3}$ times the net credit period. Thus, the average collection period of a firm selling on 30-day net terms should probably not exceed 40 days.

LIMITATIONS OF FINANCIAL ANALYSIS

The ratios, percentages, and other relationships we have described in this chapter are merely the result of analytical techniques. Often, their value is only to isolate areas requiring further investigation. Moreover, they must be interpreted with due consideration given to general economic conditions, conditions of the industry in which the companies operate, and the position of individual companies within the industry.

One should also be aware of the inherent limitations of financial statement data. Problems of comparability are frequently encountered for a number of reasons. Companies otherwise similar may employ different accounting methods, which can cause problems in comparing certain key relationships. For instance, one might expect the inventory turnover to be different for a company using LIFO than for one using FIFO in inventory costing. The effect of inflation may distort certain computations, especially those resulting from horizontal analysis. As an example, trend percentages calculated from unadjusted data may be deceptive. Sometimes, gains over time in sales, earnings, and other key figures disappear when the underlying data are adjusted to remove distortion caused by changes in price levels.

One must be quite careful even when comparing companies in a particular industry. Such factors as size, diversity of product, and mode of operations can make the firms completely dissimilar. For example, companies such as Oscar Mayer and Company and Hormel might be compared without special difficulty because both are meat processors fairly similar in size and mode of operations. However, certain problems would be encountered in comparing either of these companies with Armour and Company, whose operations are much more diverse and many times the size of Oscar Mayer or Hormel.

KEY POINTS TO REMEMBER

The important ratios covered in this chapter are summarized below:

Analysis of Operating Performance

$$\text{Rate of Return on Assets} = \frac{\text{Operating Income}}{\text{Average Total Assets}}$$

$$\text{Rate of Return on Common Stockholders' Equity} = \frac{\text{Net Income} - \text{Preferred Dividend Requirements}}{\text{Average Common Stockholders' Equity}}$$

$$\text{Rate of Return on Sales} = \frac{\text{Net Income}}{\text{Net Sales}}$$

$$\text{Price--Earnings Ratio} = \frac{\text{Market Price per Common Share}}{\text{Common Stock Earnings per Share}}$$

$$\text{Dividend Yield} = \frac{\text{Common Dividends per Share}}{\text{Market Price per Share}}$$

$$\text{Dividend Payout Ratio} = \frac{\text{Common Dividends per Share}}{\text{Common Stock Earnings per Share}}$$

Analysis of Financial Strength

$$\text{Equity Ratio} = \frac{\text{Common Stockholders' Equity}}{\text{Total Assets}}$$

$$\text{Bond Interest Coverage} = \frac{\text{Operating Income}}{\text{Annual Bond Interest}}$$

$$\text{Preferred Dividend Coverage} = \frac{\text{Operating Income}}{\text{Annual Bond Interest} + \text{Preferred Dividend Requirements}}$$

$$\text{Current Ratio} = \frac{\text{Current Assets}}{\text{Current Liabilities}}$$

$$\text{Quick Ratio} = \frac{\text{Cash} + \text{Marketable Securities} + \text{Receivables}}{\text{Current Liabilities}}$$

$$\text{Inventory Turnover} = \frac{\text{Cost of Goods Sold}}{\text{Average Inventory}}$$

$$\text{Average Collection Period} = \frac{\text{Trade Accounts Receivable}}{\text{Year's Sales}} \times 365$$

QUESTIONS

18-1 What are trend percentages, and how are they calculated? What pitfalls must an analyst avoid when preparing trend percentages?

18-2 Distinguish between horizontal analysis and vertical analysis of financial statements.

18-3 The following data are taken from the income statements of the Vickers Company. Using Year 1 as the base year, calculate trend percentages.

	Year 1	Year 2	Year 3	Year 4
Sales	$600,000	$660,000	$690,000	$720,000
Earnings	30,000	35,000	36,000	39,000

18-4 You know that Aker Company had net income of $1 million and that Brown Company had net income of $5 million during the past year. Both companies manufacture electrical components for the building trade. What additional information would you need to compare the profitability of the two companies? Discuss your answer.

18-5 Under what circumstances can return on sales be used to appraise the profitability of a company? Can this ratio be used to compare the profitability of companies from different industries? Explain.

18-6 What is the purpose of calculating the rate of return on assets? Give reasons why the income measure used in this calculation does not include a deduction for interest or for income taxes.

18-7 What does the rate of return on common stockholders' equity measure? Why would the income measure in this ratio be calculated *after* interest expense and income taxes?

18-8 What are common-size percentages, and how are they used?

18-9 Spectra, Inc. earned $4.50 per share of common stock in the current year and paid dividends of $2 per share. The most recent market price of the common stock is $42.75 per share. Calculate (a) the price–earnings ratio, (b) the dividend yield, and (c) the dividend payout ratio.

18-10 Explain, by giving an example, what is meant by trading on the equity.

18-11 Why is it dangerous for a company with unstable earnings to trade heavily on the equity?

18-12 Discuss the significance of the equity ratio, and explain how it is computed.

18-13 What is the usefulness of determining bond interest coverage, and how is it calculated?

18-14 List three important ratios for evaluating the current position of a firm, and state how they are used.

18-15 What is meant by the yield on a common stock investment? Give an example of a computation determining yield.

18-16 Utility companies usually have a high "payout" ratio compared with industrial companies. What is meant by a payout ratio? Why would utility companies find it possible to continue high payout ratios?

EXERCISES

Note: In the following exercises, inventory turnover is to be calculated using Cost of Goods Sold in the numerator.

18-17 Consider the following income statement data from the Republic Company for this year and last year:

	This Year	Last Year
Sales	$720,000	$540,000
Cost of Goods Sold	504,000	351,000
Selling Expenses	108,000	97,200
General Expenses	64,800	54,000
Income Taxes	15,000	12,000

(a) Prepare a comparative income statement, showing increases and decreases in dollars and in percentages.
(b) Prepare common-size income statements for each year.
(c) Comment briefly on the changes between the two years.

18-18 Columbia Company has a current ratio of 275% (2.75 to 1) on December 31 of the current year. On that date its current assets were as follows:

Cash		$ 75,000
Accounts Receivable	$180,000	
Less: Allowance for Uncollectible Accounts	10,000	170,000
Merchandise Inventory		235,000
Prepaid Expenses		15,000
		$495,000

(a) What was the firm's working capital on December 31?
(b) What was the quick ratio on December 31?
(c) If the company paid a current note payable of $20,000 immediately after December 31, what effect would the transaction have on the current ratio? on working capital?

18-19 Columbia Company, whose current assets are shown in Exercise 18-18, had net sales of $1,200,000 during the current year. The beginning inventory for the year was $205,000. Cost of goods sold for the year amounted to $880,000.
(a) What was the average collection period for receivables?
(b) What was the average inventory turnover for the year?

18-20 From the following data taken from the 19/8 annual report of Dow Jones & Company, Inc., publishers of the *Wall Street Journal* and *Barron's*, calculate the working capital and the current ratio.

Current Assets	$93,699,000

Current Liabilities:	
Current Maturities of Long-term Debt	$ 3,843,000
Accounts Payable	10,598,000
Accrued Wages, Royalties, etc.	11,012,000
Accrued Taxes	14,258,000
Profit Sharing and Retirement Contributions Payable	4,653,000
Other Payables	4,585,000
Unexpired Subscriptions	46,150,000
Total Current Liabilities	$95,099,000

Is there anything unusual about this information that would suggest a modification of the normal way in which the working capital and the current ratio are calculated?

18-21 The Weston Corporation pays a quarterly dividend of $1.25 per share of common stock. Its earnings after taxes during the past four quarters of operation were $680,000. The company has 50,000 shares of $100 par value common stock and 20,000 shares of $50 par value, 8% preferred stock outstanding. The current market price of the common shares is $120.
(a) Calculate the earnings per share for the common stock.
(b) Calculate the price–earnings ratio for the common stock.
(c) What is the current dividend yield on the common stock?

18-22 The Dayton Company has total assets of $1,000,000. It earns, on the average, $100,000 before income taxes. At the present time there is no long-term debt outstanding. The company wishes to acquire an additional $200,000 in funds on which it plans to earn 12% before income taxes. It can borrow the money at 9% or issue additional common stock. The effective tax rate is 40%. There are now 10,000 shares of common stock outstanding. Calculate the earnings per share expected (a) if the additional funds are borrowed and (b) if an additional 2,000 shares are sold.

18-23 The following information is available for the Drexel Company:

	Dec. 31, This Year	Dec. 31, Last Year
Total Assets	$1,600,000	$1,500,000
Current Liabilities	$ 200,000	$ 160,000
Bonds Payable (10% Interest Rate)	500,000	500,000
Common Stock ($100 Par Value)	750,000	750,000
Retained Earnings	150,000	90,000
	$1,600,000	$1,500,000

For the latest year, net sales amounted to $2,850,000, and net income after income taxes was $114,000. The income tax rate was 40%. Calculate the following for *this* year:
(a) Return on assets.   (b) Return on common stockholders' equity.
(c) Return on sales.   (d) Bond interest coverage.
(e) Equity ratio.

PROBLEMS

Note: Unless otherwise indicated, inventory turnover is to be calculated using Cost of Goods Sold in the numerator in the following problems.

18–24 Net sales, net income, and total asset figures for Kormica Plastics, Inc. for five consecutive years are given below.

	Annual Amounts (Thousands of Dollars)				
	Year 5	Year 4	Year 3	Year 2	Year 1
Net Sales	$91,200	$85,300	$81,500	$72,600	$64,800
Net Income	4,740	4,180	3,800	2,610	2,590
Total Assets	52,500	49,100	47,500	44,900	41,500

REQUIRED
(a) Calculate trend percentages, using Year 1 as the base year.
(b) Calculate the return on sales for each year. (Rates above 3.4% are considered good for plastics and synthetics companies; rates above 6% are considered very good.)
(c) Comment on the results of your analysis.

18–25 Selected information for the Bayfield Company, taken from the current year's and last year's financial statements, follows.

	This Year	Last Year
Net Sales	$960,000	$840,000
Cost of Goods Sold	624,000	588,000
Bond Interest Expense	10,000	8,000
Income Taxes	21,000	18,000
Net Income (after income taxes)	36,000	30,000
Accounts Receivable, Dec. 31 (before allowance for uncollectible accounts)	108,000	96,000
Inventory, Dec. 31	104,000	88,000
Common Stockholders' Equity	400,000	370,000
Total Assets	620,000	580,000

REQUIRED
Calculate the following for *this* year:
(a) Return on assets.
(b) Return on sales.
(c) Return on common stockholders' equity.
(d) Average collection period.
(e) Inventory turnover.
(f) Bond interest coverage.

18–26 Consider the following financial statements for the Banning Company for the past two years.

During the year just ended, management obtained additional bond financing to enlarge its productive facilities. The company faced higher costs during the year for such things as fuel, materials, and freight. Because temporary government price controls were in effect, though, a planned price increase on products was delayed several months.

As a holder of both common and preferred stock, you are interested in analyzing the financial statements for the past two years.

Banning Company
Balance Sheets
(Thousands of Dollars)

	Dec. 31, This Year	Dec. 31, Last Year
Assets:		
Cash	$ 10,000	$ 7,000
Accounts Receivable (net)	30,000	26,000
Inventories	60,000	40,000
Prepaid Expenses	8,000	7,200
Plant and Other Assets (net)	260,000	219,800
	$368,000	$300,000
Liabilities and Stockholders' Equity:		
Current Liabilities	$ 42,000	$ 37,000
Bonds Payable (8%)	100,000	75,000
7% Preferred Stock, $50 Par Value	50,000	50,000
Common Stock, $10 Par Value	150,000	120,000
Retained Earnings	26,000	18,000
	$368,000	$300,000

Banning Company
Income Statements
(Thousands of Dollars)

	This Year	Last Year
Sales	$450,000	$390,000
Cost of Goods Sold	320,000	270,000
Gross Profit	$130,000	$120,000
Operating Expenses	100,000	88,000
Operating Income	$ 30,000	$ 32,000
Bond Interest Expense	8,000	6,000
Income before Income Taxes	$ 22,000	$ 26,000
Income Tax Expense	9,000	12,000
Net Income	$ 13,000	$ 14,000

REQUIRED

(a) Calculate the following for each year: current ratio, quick ratio, inventory turnover (inventory was $36 million two years ago), equity ratio, times interest earned, times preferred dividend earned, return on assets (total assets were $296 million two years ago), return on common stockholders' equity (the common stock equity was $132 million two years ago).

(b) Calculate common-size percentages for each year's income statement.

(c) Calculate the apparent amount of common dividends per share paid during the year just ended.

(d) Comment on the results of your analysis.

18-27 You own both preferred and common stock of the Zip–Kote Corporation, a manufacturer of paints and varnishes, and you are analyzing the firm's performance for the most recent year. The following data were taken from the firm's latest annual report.

	Dec. 31, This Year	Dec. 31, Last Year
Total Assets	$3,200,000	$2,800,000
Current Liabilities	$ 350,000	$ 300,000
Bonds Payable (10% Interest Rate)	800,000	800,000
9% Preferred Stock, $100 Par Value	250,000	250,000
Common Stock, $50 Par Value	1,500,000	1,200,000
Retained Earnings	300,000	250,000
Total Liabilities and Stockholders' Equity	$3,200,000	$2,800,000

For the latest year, net sales amounted to $7,500,000, and net income after income taxes was $360,000. The income tax rate was 40%.

REQUIRED

(a) Calculate the following for *this* year:
  (1) Return on sales.
  (2) Return on assets.
  (3) Return on common stockholders' equity.
  (4) Equity ratio.
  (5) Bond interest coverage.
  (6) Preferred dividend coverage.

(b) Your review of trade association statistics and information provided by credit agencies reveals the following data on industry norms:

	Median	Upper Quartile
Return on Sales	3.5%	5.7%
Return on Assets	15.6%	20.5%
Return on Stockholders' Equity	11.2%	20.5%
Equity Ratio	50.0%	62.0%

Comment on the performance of Zip–Kote Corporation, compared with industry performance.

18-28 Following are the 19X8 financial statements for Delaware Company, with almost all dollar amounts missing.

Delaware Company
Balance Sheet
December 31, 19X8

Cash	$?	Current Liabilities	$?
Accounts Receivable (net of		8% Bonds Payable	?
allowance for uncollectible		Common Stock	?
accounts)	?	Retained Earnings	$ 28,000
Inventory	?		
Equipment (net)	?		
		Total Liabilities	
		and Stockholders'	
Total Assets	$180,000	Equity	$180,000

Delaware Company
Income Statement
For the Year 19X8

Net Sales	$?
Cost of Goods Sold	?
Gross Profit	?
Operating Expenses	?
Operating Income	?
Interest Expense (Bonds)	?
Income before Income Taxes	?
Income Taxes (40%)	?
Net Income	$18,000

The following information about Delaware Company's 19X8 financial statements is available:

(1) Quick ratio, 1.5:1.
(2) Inventory turnover (inventory at beginning of 19X8 was $61,000), 4 times.
(3) Return on sales, 5%.
(4) Average collection period, 51.71 days. Allowance balance is $1,000.
(5) Gross profit rate, 30%.
(6) Return on assets (total assets at beginning of 19X8 were $140,000), 20%.
(7) Equity ratio, 60%.
(8) The Interest Expense relates to the Bonds Payable that were outstanding all year.

REQUIRED
Compute the missing amounts, and complete the financial statements of Delaware Company. *Hint:* Complete the income statement first.

18-29 Ohio Instruments, Inc. is a manufacturer of various medical and dental instruments. Financial statement data for the firm are given below.

	(Thousands of Dollars)
This Year:	
Net Sales	$200,000
Net Income (after income taxes)	9,000
Dividends	4,000
Interest Expense	2,000
Income Taxes	7,800

Ohio Instruments, Inc.
Balance Sheets
(Thousands of Dollars)

	Dec. 31, This Year	Dec. 31, Last Year
Assets		
Cash	$ 3,200	$ 3,000
Accounts Receivable (net of allowance of $1,300 last year and $1,200 this year)	26,800	27,700
Inventory	55,000	32,000
Total Current Assets	$ 85,000	$62,700
Plant Assets (net)	32,500	28,300
Other Assets	2,500	1,000
Total Assets	$120,000	$92,000
Liabilities and Stockholders' Equity		
Notes Payable—Banks	$ 6,000	$ 5,000
Accounts Payable	17,500	12,000
Taxes Payable	2,800	2,000
Accrued Liabilities	8,700	9,000
Total Current Liabilities	$ 35,000	$28,000
Long-term Debt	20,000	14,000
Total Liabilities	$ 55,000	$42,000
Common Stock ($100 Par Value)	$ 41,000	$31,000
Retained Earnings	24,000	19,000
Total Stockholders' Equity	$ 65,000	$50,000
Total Liabilities and Stockholders' Equity	$120,000	$92,000

REQUIRED

(a) Using the given data, calculate items (1) through (8), for *this* year. Compare the performance of Ohio Instruments, Inc. with industry averages (given below), and comment on its operations.

	Median Ratios for Manufacturers of Medical and Dental Instruments
(1) Current ratio.	3.03
(2) Quick ratio.	1.2 times
(3) Average collection period.	59 days
(4) Net sales to ending inventory.	4.9 times
(5) Equity ratio.	52.0%
(6) Return on assets.	18.6%
(7) Return on stockholders' equity.	10.9%
(8) Return on sales.	4.2%

(b) Calculate the dividends paid per share of common stock. (Use average number of shares outstanding during the year.) What was the payout ratio?

(c) If the most recent price per share of common stock is $150, what is (1) the price–earnings ratio? (2) the dividend yield?

ALTERNATE PROBLEMS

Note: Unless otherwise indicated, inventory turnover is to be calculated using Cost of Goods Sold in the numerator in the following problems.

18–24A Net sales, net income, and total asset figures for Cortland Steel Corporation for five consecutive years are given below.

	Annual Amounts (Thousands of Dollars)				
	Year 5	Year 4	Year 3	Year 2	Year 1
Net Sales	$82,500	$73,400	$61,200	$51,700	$45,900
Net Income	5,820	4,150	3,860	3,180	2,720
Total Assets	61,500	58,000	56,000	54,000	52,000

REQUIRED

(a) Calculate trend percentages, using Year 1 as the base year.

(b) Calculate the return on sales for each year. (Rates above 3.2% are considered good for steelworking and rolling mill companies; rates above 4.3% are considered very good.)

(c) Comment on the results of your analysis.

18–25A Selected information for the Canadian Company, taken from the current year's and last year's financial statements, follows.

	This Year	Last Year
Net Sales	$1,000,000	$800,000
Cost of Goods Sold	600,000	320,000
Bond Interest Expense	20,000	10,000
Income Taxes	30,000	18,000
Net Income (after income taxes)	40,000	28,000

	This Year	Last Year
Accounts Receivable, Dec. 31 (before allowance for uncollectible accounts)	180,000	150,000
Inventory, Dec. 31	90,000	70,000
Common Stockholders' Equity	430,000	370,000
Total Assets	950,000	850,000

REQUIRED

Calculate the following for *this* year:

(a) Return on assets.

(b) Return on sales.

(c) Return on common stockholders' equity.

(d) Average collection period.

(e) Inventory turnover.

(f) Bond interest coverage.

18–26A Consider the following financial statements for the Cornwall Company for the past two years.

During the year just ended, management obtained additional bond financing to enable it to add to its productive facilities. The company faced higher costs during the year for such things as fuel, materials, and freight. Because temporary government price controls were in effect, though, a planned price increase on products was delayed several months.

As a holder of both common and preferred stock, you are interested in analyzing the financial statements for the past two years.

Cornwall Company
Balance Sheets
(Thousands of Dollars)

	Dec. 31, This Year	Dec. 31, Last Year
Assets:		
Cash	$ 18,200	$ 14,600
Accounts Receivable (net)	30,000	24,000
Inventories	48,000	36,000
Prepaid Expenses	1,800	1,400
Plant and Other Assets (net)	150,000	120,000
	$248,000	$196,000
Liabilities and Stockholders' Equity:		
Current Liabilities	$ 40,000	$ 27,000
Bonds Payable (9%)	60,000	30,000
6% Preferred Stock, $50 Par Value	10,000	10,000
Common Stock, $10 Par Value	100,000	100,000
Retained Earnings	38,000	29,000
	$248,000	$196,000

Cornwall Company
Income Statements
(Thousands of Dollars)

	This Year	Last Year
Sales	$360,000	$275,000
Cost of Goods Sold	252,000	178,750
Gross Profit	$108,000	$ 96,250
Operating Expenses	74,800	69,450
Operating Income	$ 33,200	$ 26,800
Interest Expense (on Bonds)	5,400	2,700
Income before Income Taxes	$ 27,800	$ 24,100
Income Tax Expense	13,900	12,050
Net Income	$ 13,900	$ 12,050

REQUIRED
(a) Calculate the following for each year: current ratio, quick ratio, inventory
    turnover (inventory was $20 million two years ago), equity ratio, times
    interest earned, times preferred dividends earned, return on assets (total
    assets were $164 million two years ago), return on common stockholders'
    equity (the common stock equity was $110 million two years ago).
(b) Calculate common-size percentages for each year's income statement.
(c) Calculate the apparent amount of common dividends per share paid dur-
    ing the year just ended.
(d) Comment on the results of your analysis.

18–28A Following are the 19X8 financial statements for Price Company, with almost
       all dollar amounts missing:

Price Company
Balance Sheet
December 31, 19X8

Cash	$?		Current Liabilities	$?
Accounts Receivable (net of			8% Bonds Payable	?
allowance for uncollectible			Common Stock	?
accounts)	?		Retained Earnings	40,000
Inventory	?			
Equipment (net)	?			
			Total Liabilities	
			and Stockholders'	
Total Assets	$150,000		Equity	$150,000

Price Company
Income Statement
For the Year 19X8

Net Sales	$?
Cost of Goods Sold	?
Gross Profit	?
Operating Expenses	?
Operating Income	?
Interest Expense (on Bonds)	?
Income before Income Taxes	?
Income Taxes (40%)	?
Net Income	$15,000

The following information about Price Company's 19X8 financial statements is available:
(1) Quick ratio, 1.6:1.
(2) Inventory turnover (inventory at beginning of 19X8 was $40,000), 3.5 times.
(3) Return on sales, 6%.
(4) Average collection period, 17.52 days. Allowance balance is $2,000.
(5) Gross profit rate, 30%.
(6) Return on assets (total assets at beginning of 19X8 were $130,000), 20%.
(7) Equity ratio, 70%.
(8) Interest Expense relates to the Bonds Payable that were outstanding all year.

REQUIRED
Compute the missing amounts, and complete the financial statements of Price Company. *Hint:* Complete the income statement first.

BUSINESS DECISION PROBLEM

Middleton, Inc., a wholesaler of electrical supplies, has been in business four years. The company has had modest profits and has experienced few operating difficulties until this year. The president, George Olson, has come to the First United Bank, where you are a loan officer, to discuss his company's working capital problems. Olson explains that expanding his firm has created difficulties in meeting obligations when they come due, and the firm has been unable to take cash discounts offered by manufacturers for timely payment. He would like to borrow $40,000 from First United. At your request, Olson submits the following financial data for the past two years.

	This Year	Last Year
Net Sales	$520,000	$400,000
Net Income (after income taxes)	12,400	7,200
Dividends	3,000	1,500
Interest Expense	6,000	5,800
Income Taxes	4,200	2,400
Total Assets Two Years Ago		253,000
Total Stockholders' Equity Two Years Ago		110,400

Middleton, Inc.
Balance Sheets

	Dec. 31, This Year	Dec. 31, Last Year
Assets		
Cash	$ 16,300	$ 18,100
Accounts Receivable (net of allowance of $4,000 last year and $6,000 this year)	114,500	72,000
Inventory	112,200	80,000
Prepaid Expenses	2,200	1,900
Total Current Assets	$245,200	$172,000
Plant Assets (net)	120,000	125,000
Total Assets	$365,200	$297,000
Liabilities and Stockholders' Equity		
Notes Payable—Banks	$ 24,500	$ 15,000
Accounts Payable	88,300	66,800
Taxes Payable	4,200	2,400
Accrued Liabilities	5,000	1,200
Total Current Liabilities	$122,000	$ 85,400
7% Mortgage Payable	69,400	72,000
Total Liabilities	$191,400	$157,400
Common Stock	$150,000	$125,000
Retained Earnings	23,800	14,600
Total Stockholders' Equity	$173,800	$139,600
Total Liabilities and Stockholders' Equity	$365,200	$297,000

You decide to calculate the following items for both years from the given data and compare them with typical ratios for an electrical supplies wholesaler provided by a commercial credit firm:

	Typical Ratios for Electrical Supplies Wholesalers
(a) Current ratio	2.27
(b) Quick ratio	1.1
(c) Average collection period	43 days
(d) Net sales to ending inventory	7.2 times
(e) Equity ratio	48%
(f) Return on assets	9.1%
(g) Return on stockholders' equity	4.8%
(h) Return on sales	1.8%

REQUIRED

Based upon your analysis, decide whether and under what circumstances you would grant Mr. Olson's request for a loan. Explain the reasons for your decision.

19
Consolidated
Financial Statements

Much of the growth of large modern corporations is the result of a steady pattern of acquisition and combination of existing firms. Corporations may acquire the resources of other firms or control over them for such economic reasons as product diversification, market penetration, control of costs through large-scale operations, assurance of raw material supplies, and tax savings. Other motives for business combinations may be a desire for large size, a desire for power, or a desire to enhance the operating record of the acquiring company.

Although business firms may be combined in a variety of ways, the terms used to describe the various types of combinations have become somewhat blurred in modern business journalism. The term *merger*, for example, is often used to describe almost any type of business combination. Technically, however, a merger takes place when one company acquires the assets of another and the latter dissolves. The acquiring firm pays the owners of the purchased firm cash or securities and continues to operate with the resources of the acquired firm. A **consolidation** occurs when existing firms exchange their properties for the securities of a new firm and the old firms dissolve. Neither of these two types of business combinations generally creates any new accounting problems.

One of the most common ways that a business pursues the objectives of a combination is to acquire a controlling interest in the voting shares of one or more other companies. The affiliated companies continue to operate as separate legal entities. Practically all of the corporations listed on the organized stock exchanges own all or a majority of the voting stock of other companies. This type of relationship calls for a special type of financial statements, called **consolidated financial statements,** which we shall describe in this chapter.

PARENT–SUBSIDIARY RELATIONSHIP

When a corporation controls the policies and operations of other corporations through ownership of their stock, financial statements of the combined group are commonly presented in published reports. The purpose of such consolidated statements is to portray the financial position and operating results of affiliated companies as a single economic unit. The company holding all or a majority of the stock of the others is the **parent** company, while the wholly owned or majority-held companies are called **subsidiaries.** It is important to observe that the individual companies of a group are *legal entities,* each of which has separate financial statements. When the financial data of these legal entities are combined, the resulting statements reveal a picture of the group as an *economic entity,* as shown in the diagram on page 670.

TAKEOVERS

In modern business journalism, the term "takeover" is as commonplace as "merger" or "acquisition." The term is apt, because many current business combinations occur in an atmosphere of hostility; acrimony and lawsuits abound. As the decade of the 1970s comes to a close, predatory firms are attempting to acquire well-run companies with growth opportunities, undervalued assets, and balance sheets beefed up by increasing earnings. Although these attractions are readily discerned by potential buyers, they make the target firms especially reluctant to accept offers. Such companies don't need outside capital.[1]

Despite the lawsuits and acrimony, takeovers have recently accelerated. In the first six months of 1978, 37 mergers or acquisitions involving more than $100 million were announced, compared with 20 in the first half of 1977 and only 14 in all of 1975. Almost all of the offers have been for prices clearly in excess of the underlying book values of the firms involved.

Back in the 1950s, firms sometimes acquired other companies at bargain prices with the idea of resuscitating them. Often such companies had several years' operating losses. The acquiring firm would "buy" the operating losses because they could be offset against its own profits for a number of past years and several years in the future for income tax purposes. The income tax laws have since been amended to require that acquisitions be for a "business purpose," and, accordingly, acquisitions made primarily to obtain a loss-carryover have been effectively eliminated. Today's mergers, for the most part, emphasize quality.

No one has written more eloquently on the subject of corporate expansion and acquisition than Arthur Stone Dewing in his monumental work on the financial policy of corporations. Dewing cites four motives for corporate acquisitions: ambition, creative impulse, profits, and speculation.[2] He might have added another motive: survival. Thus, as the world's oil reserves dwindle, huge oil firms such as Exxon, Shell, and Gulf are acquiring coal mines and diversifying into other forms of energy. Similarly, a short time after the Civil Aeronautics Board relaxed its regulation of air fares and route allocations, a number of prospective airline combinations surfaced: Pan Am with National, Continental with Western, and North Central with Southern. For obvious reasons, the large tobacco companies are diversifying into many other lines of business.

One of the disquieting aspects of business combinations is that small enterprises often merely become pawns for human ambition in the game of business achievement, and large firms become even larger. One financial writer recently observed that Exxon's assets ($38 billion) and Shell's sales ($39 billion) are each about equal to the entire Italian national budget.

[1]*Wall Street Journal,* September 6, 1978.
[2]Dewing, Arthur Stone, *The Financial Policy of Corporations,* New York: The Ronald Press Company, 1953, pp. 812–13.

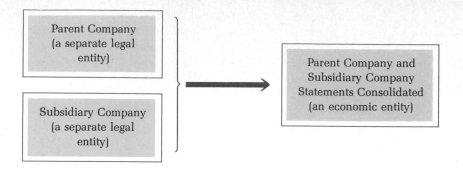

Consolidated financial statements convey a picture of the total resources controlled by a parent company and the aggregate results of operations for the group, that are difficult to perceive when viewing only a series of separate reports of the individual companies. Consolidated statements are particularly valuable to the management and stockholders of the parent company. In addition, creditors, government agencies, and the general public can be kept informed of the magnitude and scope of an economic enterprise through consolidated statements.

Except in unusual circumstances, most companies prepare consolidated statements when more than 50% of the subsidiary's stock is held by the controlling company. With this kind of control, the parent can usually direct the policies and activities of the subsidiary. On the other hand, the accounts of some subsidiaries may be excluded from consolidated statements even though they are wholly or majority owned. For example, subsidiaries engaged in activities completely unrelated to those of the parent and other affiliates are normally excluded from consolidated statements. For example, Sears, Roebuck and Company does not include its insurance firm, Allstate, in its consolidated statements, because the economic operations of an insurance company (and its accounts) are not compatible with the reporting of the merchandising and manufacturing companies presented in the consolidated statements. For similar reasons, Ford, General Motors, and FMC Corporation exclude the accounts of their wholly owned finance and insurance companies when they prepare consolidated financial statements.

Sometimes wholly-owned or majority-held subsidiaries are located in foreign countries that restrict the parent's control of assets and operations; when the restrictions are severe, the accounts of the subsidiaries may be excluded from the consolidated statements.

Whenever the accounts of a subsidiary firm are not included in the consolidated statements, the parent company's investment is shown in the consolidated balance sheet as "Investment in Unconsolidated Subsidiary."[1] The investment is accounted for under the equity method. This method of accounting, discussed in Chapter 15, will be reviewed in this chapter.

---

[1]Often firms report condensed financial statements of unconsolidated subsidiaries in footnotes to the consolidated balance sheet.

ACQUISITION OF SUBSIDIARIES

A corporation may obtain a subsidiary either by establishing a new firm and holding more than half of its voting stock or by acquiring more than half of the voting stock of an existing firm. Both methods have been extensively used. When an existing firm is acquired, however, the method of acquisition may play an important role in the manner of accounting for the subsidiary.

One of the most common methods of acquiring an existing firm is to give up cash, other assets, notes, or debt securities. Generally, this is called a "purchase" of a subsidiary, and the **purchase** method of reporting is used in consolidated financial statements. We will discuss this method of acquisition first in this chapter. Another method, called "pooling of interests" involves exchanging stock of the acquiring company for substantially all of the shares of another firm. We will discuss the **pooling** method of accounting and reporting later in the chapter.

CONSOLIDATED BALANCE SHEETS AT ACQUISITION DATE

Creating a Subsidiary Company

Let us assume that, on January 1, 19XX, P Company established a new, wholly owned subsidiary, S Company, for the purpose of marketing P Company's products. P Company acquired all of the common stock of S Company for $100,000 cash. To record this transaction, P Company debits Investment in S Company and credits Cash for $100,000. In its records, S Company debits Cash and credits Common Stock for $100,000. Condensed balance sheets before and after the creation of the subsidiary are given in Exhibit 19-1.

EXHIBIT 19-1

Before Creating S Company		After Creating S Company			
P Company **Balance Sheet** **January 1, 19XX**		**P Company** **Balance Sheet** **January 1, 19XX**		**S Company** **Balance Sheet** **January 1, 19XX**	
Cash and Other Assets	$750,000	Cash and Other Assets	$650,000	Cash	$100,000
		Investment in S Company	100,000		
	$750,000		$750,000		$100,000
Liabilities	$200,000	Liabilities	$200,000	Liabilities	$ –0–
Common Stock	400,000	Common Stock	400,000	Common Stock	100,000
Retained Earnings	150,000	Retained Earnings	150,000	Retained Earnings	–0–
	$750,000		$750,000		$100,000

Reciprocal Items

EXHIBIT 19-2

P and S Companies
Consolidated Balance Sheet Worksheet
January 1, 19XX

	P	S	Eliminations Debit	Eliminations Credit	Consolidated Balance Sheet
Cash and Other Assets	650,000	100,000			750,000
Investment in S	100,000	—		100,000	—
	750,000	100,000			750,000
Liabilities	200,000	—			200,000
Common Stock					
P Company	400,000				400,000
S Company		100,000	100,000		—
Retained Earnings					
P Company	150,000				150,000
	750,000	100,000	100,000	100,000	750,000

Notice that the only change in P Company's balance sheet is a shift of $100,000 from Cash and Other Assets to Investment in S Company. The latter represents the 100% ownership of S Company common stock, giving P Company control over the resources of S Company ($100,000 cash). Thus the $100,000 Investment in S Company on P Company's balance sheet and the $100,000 owners' equity (Common Stock) on the subsidiary's balance sheet can be viewed as reciprocal items. If we are to combine (consolidate) the accounts on the balance sheets of the two companies at January 1, the reciprocal items must be eliminated. Otherwise there would be a "double-counting" of assets and owners' equity. The eliminating entry to be made in a consolidated worksheet debits Common Stock (S Company) for $100,000 and credits Investment in S Company for $100,000. The worksheet showing how the balance sheets are consolidated is given in Exhibit 19-2. Note that, after eliminating the reciprocal elements, the consolidated balance sheet (the right-hand column in Exhibit 19-2) is identical with that of P Company before the creation of the subsidiary. This is logical, because P Company commands no more resources than it did formerly. Also, observe that the stockholders' equity on the consolidated balance sheet is that of the parent company. The stockholders' equity on a consolidated balance sheet is that of *outside* shareholders; *the intercompany equity existing on the balance sheets is always eliminated.*

Acquisition of an Existing Firm

The general concept of consolidating affiliated companies is always the same, whether a subsidiary is created or an existing firm is acquired. Intercompany items, such as intercompany owners' equity, are eliminated so that the consoli-

EXHIBIT 19-3

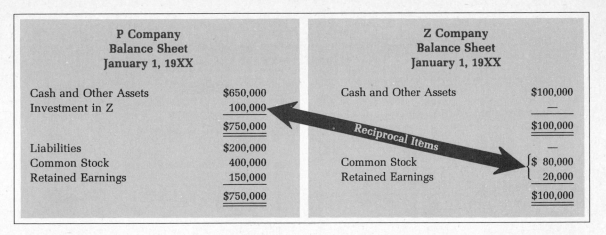

P Company Balance Sheet January 1, 19XX		Z Company Balance Sheet January 1, 19XX	
Cash and Other Assets	$650,000	Cash and Other Assets	$100,000
Investment in Z	100,000		—
	$750,000		$100,000
Liabilities	$200,000		—
Common Stock	400,000	Common Stock	$ 80,000
Retained Earnings	150,000	Retained Earnings	20,000
	$750,000		$100,000

dated statements show the interests of outsiders. (Later we will discuss the elimination of other intercompany items.)

Suppose that P Company, instead of creating a new firm, purchased 100% of the common stock of an existing firm, Z Company, for $100,000. In this case, we assume that Z Company *already has* $100,000 in Cash and Other Assets, and that it has no liabilities. The only difference from our previous example of a created subsidiary is that Z Company's $100,000 of stockholders' equity is composed of $80,000 of Common Stock and $20,000 of Retained Earnings.

The entry on P Company's books to record the acquisition is a debit to Investment in Z Company for $100,000 and a credit to Cash for $100,000. No entry is made in the records of Z Company, because payment is made to current shareholders of Z Company. Therefore, the balance sheets of the two companies *immediately after the acquisition* are as shown in Exhibit 19-3.

A comparison of the balance sheets in Exhibit 19-3 with the balance sheets after acquisition in Exhibit 19-1 reveals that the only significant difference is that the owners' equity of Z Company consists of $80,000 Common Stock and $20,000 Retained Earnings rather than $100,000 Common Stock. Thus, in this case, the reciprocal items are the $100,000 Investment in Z Company on P Company's balance sheet and the Common Stock and Retained Earnings ($80,000 + $20,000) on Z Company's balance sheet. To avoid double-counting of assets and owners' equity, these items must be eliminated when preparing a worksheet to consolidate the accounts of the two firms. The worksheet entry debits Common Stock (Z Company) for $80,000, debits Retained Earnings (Z Company) for $20,000, and credits Investment in Z Company for $100,000. The worksheet to prepare the consolidated balance sheet is shown in Exhibit 19-4 (page 674).

EXHIBIT 19-4

P and Z Companies
Consolidated Balance Sheet Worksheet
January 1, 19XX

	P	Z	Eliminations Debit	Eliminations Credit	Consolidated Balance Sheet
Cash and Other Assets	650,000	100,000			750,000
Investment in Z	100,000	—		100,000	—
	750,000	100,000			750,000
Liabilities	200,000	—			200,000
Common Stock					
P Company	400,000				400,000
Z Company		80,000	80,000		
Retained Earnings					
P Company	150,000				150,000
Z Company		20,000	20,000		
	750,000	100,000	100,000	100,000	750,000

CONSOLIDATED BALANCE SHEETS AFTER ACQUISITION DATE

In accounting periods following a parent–subsidiary affiliation, the parent company ordinarily accounts for its asset, Investment in Subsidiary, by the **equity** method. Under this method, the parent company periodically reflects on its own records its share (100% in our example) of the subsidiary's earnings by debiting the Investment in Subsidiary account and crediting Income from Investment in Subsidiary. The latter item eventually increases the Retained Earnings of the parent company. (If the subsidiary has a loss, the entry would be a debit to Loss from Investment in Subsidiary and a credit to Investment in Subsidiary, the debit eventually reducing the parent's Retained Earnings.) Whenever the subsidiary pays dividends, the parent company debits Cash and credits the Investment in Subsidiary account for the amount received.

To illustrate, let us return to the example (Exhibit 19-1), in which P Company created a subsidiary, S Company, by purchasing 100% of S Company's stock for $100,000 cash. We shall assume that, during the year following acquisition, P Company earned $40,000 *before* taking up earnings from S Company and paid no dividends. We shall also assume that S Company earned $20,000, paying $10,000 in dividends.

To record its share of S Company's earnings and to record the dividends received, P Company makes the following entries *in its own records*:

Investment in S Company	20,000	
Income from Investment in S (Retained Earnings)		20,000

To record 100% of S Company earnings for the current year.

Cash	10,000	
Investment in S Company		10,000

To record dividends received from S Company.

The balance sheets of P Company and S Company at December 31, 19XX are given in Exhibit 19–5.

Let us review the changes that have occurred in these two balance sheets since the date of acquisition. P Company's Cash and Other Assets have increased by $50,000. This increase consists of P Company's own net income of $40,000, plus $10,000 in dividends received from S Company. (For simplicity, we have assumed that all of P Company's net income increased Cash and Other Assets, with liabilities remaining unchanged.) The Investment in S Company has increased by $10,000 ($20,000 of S Company earnings, less $10,000 dividends received). P Company's Retained Earnings has increased by $60,000 ($40,000 of its own net income, plus $20,000 S Company net income).

For S Company, Cash and Other Assets has increased $15,000, along with a $5,000 increase in liabilities. Thus, *net* assets have increased $10,000. The corresponding increase of $10,000 in Retained Earnings resulted from net income of $20,000 less $10,000 dividends declared and paid. Exhibit 19–6 (page 676) shows a worksheet to prepare a consolidated balance sheet at December 31, 19XX.

EXHIBIT 19–5

P Company Balance Sheet December 31, 19XX		S Company Balance Sheet December 31, 19XX	
Cash and Other Assets	$700,000	Cash and Other Assets	$115,000
Investment in S	110,000		—
	$810,000		$115,000
Liabilities	$200,000	Liabilities	$ 5,000
Common Stock	400,000	Common Stock	100,000
Retained Earnings	210,000	Retained Earnings	10,000
	$810,000		$115,000

EXHIBIT 19–6

P and S Companies
Consolidated Balance Sheet Worksheet
December 31, 19XX

	P	S	Eliminations Debit	Eliminations Credit	Consolidated Balance Sheet
Cash and Other Assets	700,000	115,000			815,000
Investment in S	110,000	—		110,000	—
	810,000	115,000			815,000
Liabilities	200,000	5,000			205,000
Common Stock					
P Company	400,000				400,000
S Company		100,000	100,000		—
Retained Earnings					
P Company	210,000				210,000
S Company		10,000	10,000		—
	810,000	115,000	110,000	110,000	815,000

Whenever consolidated statements are prepared after the acquisition date, the worksheet entries eliminate the intercompany equity existing *at the date of the consolidated statements.* Since P Company has a 100% interest in S Company, its interest includes all of the Common Stock and Retained Earnings of S Company. Therefore, the eliminating entry on the worksheet debits Common Stock (S Company) for $100,000, debits Retained Earnings (S Company) for $10,000, and credits Investment in S Company for $110,000.

A formal consolidated balance sheet is given in Exhibit 19–7. Note that the Cash and Other Assets of both firms have been combined, as well as the liabilities. The intercompany equity (100% of S Company stockholders' equity) has been eliminated; therefore, the stockholders' equity is that of the parent company.

EXHIBIT 19–7

P and S Companies
Consolidated Balance Sheet
December 31, 19XX

Cash and Other Assets	$815,000	Liabilities	$205,000
		Common Stock	400,000
		Retained Earnings	210,000
	$815,000		$815,000

MAJORITY-HELD SUBSIDIARIES

When a firm owns more than half but less than a 100% interest in another firm, the parent company's interest is called a **majority interest.** The interest of the other (outside) stockholders of the subsidiary company is called the **minority interest.** In preparing a consolidated balance sheet for a parent company and a majority-held subsidiary, the assets and liabilities of the affiliated companies are combined in the usual way in order to give a picture of the total resources and liabilities of the affiliated companies. The parent company's equity in the subsidiary at the date of the consolidated statements is eliminated as before, but in this case, the equity represents less than 100% of the subsidiary's common stock and retained earnings. The amount of the subsidiary's common stock and retained earnings not eliminated represents the minority interest in the subsidiary and will appear on the consolidated balance sheet.

For example, assume that P Company purchased 80% of the voting stock of Q Company on January 1, 19XX, for $160,000. After the acquisition, the separate balance sheets of the two firms appeared as shown in Exhibit 19–8.

Note that Q Company's owners' equity in this example is $200,000, consisting of $150,000 of Common Stock and $50,000 Retained Earnings. The equity acquired by P Company is therefore $160,000 (80% of $200,000), which is the amount P Company paid to acquire its interest. This intercompany equity at the date of preparing consolidated statements is eliminated. The remaining 20% minority interest, however, must be shown in the consolidated balance sheet. In other words, the minority, or outside, shareholders have a $40,000 interest in the stockholders' equity of Q Company (20% of $200,000). The worksheet entry to eliminate the intercompany equity and to reflect the minority interest debits Common Stock (Q Company) for $150,000, debits Retained Earnings (Q Company) for

EXHIBIT 19–8

P and Q Companies
Balance Sheets
January 1, 19XX

	P	Q
Cash and Other Assets	$590,000	$220,000
Investment in Q	160,000	—
	$750,000	$220,000
Liabilities	$200,000	$ 20,000
Common Stock	400,000	150,000
Retained Earnings	150,000	50,000
	$750,000	$220,000

EXHIBIT 19-9

P and Q Companies
Consolidated Balance Sheet Worksheet
January 1, 19XX

	P	Q	Eliminations Debit	Credit	Consolidated Balance Sheet
Cash and Other Assets	590,000	220,000			810,000
Investment in Q	160,000	—		160,000	—
	750,000	220,000			810,000
Liabilities	200,000	20,000			220,000
Minorcity Interest				40,000	40,000
Common Stock					
P Company	400,000				400,000
Q Company		150,000	150,000		
Retained Earnings					
P Company	150,000				150,000
Q Company		50,000	50,000		
	750,000	220,000	200,000	200,000	810,000

$50,000, credits Investment in Q Company for $160,000, and credits Minority Interest for $40,000. The worksheet to prepare the consolidated balance sheet is given in Exhibit 19-9.

A formal consolidated balance sheet for the two companies, prepared from the right-hand column of the worksheet, is given in Exhibit 19-10. Note that the total consolidated stockholders' equity of $590,000 consists of the parent com-

EXHIBIT 19-10

P and Q Companies
Consolidated Balance Sheet
January 1, 19XX

Cash and Other Assets	$810,000	Liabilities		$220,000
		Stockholders' Equity:		
		Minority Interest	$ 40,000	
		Common Stock	400,000	
		Retained Earnings	150,000	590,000
	$810,000			$810,000

pany's common stock and retained earnings (totaling $550,000) and the $40,000 minority interest. Thus the interests of outside shareholders (the parent firm's shareholders and minority shareholders in the subsidiary) are portrayed in the consolidated balance sheet. Sometimes, in formal consolidated balance sheets, the minority interest amount is shown between the liabilities and the stockholders' equity. Most financial analysts, however, consider the minority interest a part of stockholders' equity, and it is probably a better practice to classify it with the stockholders' equity.

DIFFERENCES BETWEEN ACQUISITION COST AND BOOK VALUE

So far in our examples, we have assumed that the amount paid by the parent company to acquire a particular interest in a subsidiary was exactly equal to the book value of the interest acquired. In the real world this rarely happens. In fact, the parent firm almost always pays more for its interest than is shown by the book values on the subsidiary's balance sheet. This occurs for one of two reasons, or a combination of them. The first reason is that the recorded values of the subsidiary's assets are often understated in terms of current, fair-market values. Anyone familiar with the inflation of recent years will recognize that this situation is common. The second reason is that the parent firm may be willing to pay an additional amount for an unrecorded asset of the subsidiary—goodwill—if the subsidiary's earning power or its potential earning power is higher than normal for similar firms.

Suppose that P Company acquires a 100% interest in the voting stock of Y Company for $125,000 when Y Company has the balance sheet depicted in Exhibit 19–11. Obviously, in this illustration, P Company is paying $125,000 for a 100% interest in a firm that has a net book value of $100,000. Assume that, during negotiations for the purchase, it was determined that Y Company's plant and equipment were undervalued by $15,000 and that its potential for future superior earnings was valued at an additional $10,000.

EXHIBIT 19–11

P Company Balance Sheet January 1, 19XX		Y Company Balance Sheet January 1, 19XX	
Cash and Other Assets	$XXX,XXX	Current Assets	$ 40,000
Investment in Y	125,000	Plant and Equipment	60,000
	$XXX,XXX		$100,000
Liabilities	$XXX,XXX	Liabilities	$ —
Common Stock	XXX,XXX	Common Stock	80,000
Retained Earnings	XXX,XXX	Retained Earnings	20,000
	$XXX,XXX		$100,000

In preparing a consolidated balance sheet, a worksheet entry would be made to eliminate the intercompany equity and to reflect the additional asset values established by the acquisition. The entry would include the following debits: Common Stock (Y Company), $80,000; Retained Earnings (Y Company), $20,000; Plant and Equipment, $15,000; and Goodwill from Consolidation, $10,000. A credit of $125,000 would be made to Investment in Y Company. Thus, in preparing a consolidated balance sheet, the intercompany equity in the recorded book values of the subsidiary is eliminated, and an additional amount of assets, $25,000, is reflected in the consolidated balance sheet. The Goodwill from Consolidation[2] appears as an intangible asset on the consolidated balance sheet. In the consolidated statements of subsequent years, the amount paid in excess of the equity acquired in a subsidiary is amortized over the life of the assets to which the amount has been assigned. In the case of goodwill, the period cannot exceed 40 years.

One rarely encounters a situation in which the parent company pays less than the equity acquired for a particular interest in a subsidiary company. (See the boxed insert on page 669.) If this situation occurs, an analogous treatment is used to prepare a consolidated balance sheet. If the difference is attributed to an overvaluation of subsidiary assets, the eliminating entry on the worksheet shows credits to such assets. On the other hand, if the difference is attributed to a poor earnings record of the subsidiary company, an account called "Excess of Book Value of Investment in Subsidiary over Cost of Equity Acquired" is credited. In a consolidated balance sheet, such an amount is probably best subtracted from the total of the consolidated assets.

CONSOLIDATED INCOME STATEMENT

So far we have dealt only with consolidated balance sheets. Now we shall look at the problem of consolidating the income statements of affiliated firms. If we wish to show the scope of operations of affiliated companies as an entity, it is logical that we combine the revenues, cost of goods sold, and expenses of the several companies. In preparing a consolidated income statement, however, we should present only the results of transactions with firms and individuals *outside* the entity. Any intercompany transactions, such as intercompany sales and purchases, should be eliminated. Likewise, revenue and expense amounts representing services rendered by one firm to an affiliated firm should be eliminated. Otherwise, the consolidated income statement would give a distorted picture of the extent of the group's operations.

For example, if a single company has two divisions, one manufacturing products and another marketing them, the transfer of products from the manufacturing division to the marketing division would not be regarded as sales transactions.

---

[2]Often this is called "Excess of Cost over Book Value of Investment in Subsidiary." Many accountants and financial analysts, however, prefer to call it "Goodwill from Consolidation."

EXHIBIT 19-12

P Company Income Statement For the Year 19XX		S Company Income Statement For the Year 19XX	
Sales	$500,000	Sales (including $30,000 sold to P Company)	$200,000
Cost of Goods Sold (including $30,000 of purchases from S Company)	300,000	Cost of Goods Sold	140,000
Gross Profit	$200,000	Gross Profit	$ 60,000
Operating Expenses (including income taxes)	160,000	Operating Expenses (including income taxes)	40,000
Net Income	$ 40,000	Net Income	$ 20,000

Only sales by the marketing division would be reflected in the firm's income statement. The same situation exists when two separate firms make up one consolidated entity.

To illustrate the procedures for preparing a consolidated income statement, we use the separate income statements of P Company and its 75%-held subsidiary, S Company, shown in Exhibit 19-12. For simplicity, we assume that P Company has not yet reflected its 75% share of S Company's net income in its own income statement.[3]

We have indicated in the income statements that $30,000 of S Company's sales were to P Company. Assume that P Company, in turn, sold all of this merchandise to outsiders. In preparing a consolidated income statement, we must therefore eliminate $30,000 from the sales reported by S Company and the purchases (in cost of goods sold) reported by P Company. The worksheet to prepare a consolidated income statement for the two firms is given in Exhibit 19-13 (page 682).

In Exhibit 19-13, the $30,000 in S Company's sales and the reciprocal amount in P Company's cost of goods sold have been completely eliminated, so that only sales to outsiders are reflected in the consolidated income statement. Notice that, from the standpoint of the entity, this elimination has no effect on consolidated net income, because the same amount is excluded from both sales and cost of goods sold. It does, however, avoid distorting the sales volume and costs of the group. Of the total $60,000 aggregate net income of the two firms, the minority interest of $5,000 (25% of S Company net income) is deducted, so that the consolidated net income of the affiliated firms is reported as $55,000. Thus, the $55,000

---

[3]If P Company had already included its share of S Company's earnings in its own income statement, this amount would have to be eliminated to avoid double-counting, because the revenues and expenses of the two firms are to be consolidated.

EXHIBIT 19-13

P and S Companies
Consolidated Income Statement Worksheet
For the Year Ended December 31, 19XX

	P	S	Eliminations Debit	Credit	Consolidated Income Statement
Sales	500,000	200,000	30,000		670,000
Cost of Goods Sold	300,000	140,000		30,000	410,000
Gross Profit	200,000	60,000			260,000
Expenses (including income taxes)	160,000	40,000			200,000
Net Income	40,000	20,000			60,000
Minority Interest in Net Income of S (25% of $20,000)					(5,000)
Consolidated Net Income					55,000

EXHIBIT 19-14

P and S Companies
Consolidated Income Statement
For the Year Ended December 31, 19XX

Sales	$670,000
Cost of Goods Sold	410,000
Gross Profit	$260,000
Expenses (including income taxes)	200,000
Net Income before Minority Interest	$ 60,000
Less: Minority Interest in Net Income of S Company	5,000
Consolidated Net Income	$ 55,000

consolidated net income consists of $40,000 (the parent's net income from its own operations) plus $15,000 (the parent's 75% interest in the subsidiary net income of $20,000). The consolidated net income statement, shown in Exhibit 19-14, is prepared directly from the last column of the worksheet.

EXHIBIT 19-15

P and S Companies
Consolidated Retained Earnings Statement
For the Year Ended December 31, 19XX

Consolidated Retained Earnings, January 1	$260,000
Add: Consolidated Net Income for the Year	55,000
	$315,000
Less: Dividends Declared (by P Company)	25,000
Consolidated Retained Earnings, December 31	$290,000

CONSOLIDATED RETAINED EARNINGS STATEMENT

Preparation of a consolidated retained earnings statement for affiliated firms is a relatively simple task, and worksheets are rarely required. Using our previous example, assume that the January 1, 19XX balance of consolidated retained earnings for P and S Companies amounted to $260,000, and that P Company declared cash dividends of $25,000 during the year 19XX. The consolidated retained earnings statement for the two companies for the year is given in Exhibit 19-15.

Observe that the consolidated retained earnings balance is increased by consolidated net income, which consisted of P Company's earnings plus its 75% share of S Company's earnings ($40,000 + $15,000 = $55,000). Remember that P Company will make an entry *on its books* to accrue the $15,000 income from S Company, by increasing the Investment in S Company account. Only dividends declared by the parent company will appear in the consolidated retained earnings statement. As we pointed out earlier, dividends received by the parent company from the subsidiary are credited to the Investment in Subsidiary account. Dividends paid by the subsidiary to the minority shareholders reduce the minority interest in the consolidated balance sheet.

OTHER INTERCOMPANY ACCOUNTS

Because affiliated companies often engage in a wide variety of intercompany transactions, treating the resulting amounts in consolidated statements can be fairly complex. For example, there may be intercompany loans, intercompany bond and preferred stockholdings, or plant and equipment transfers. Because this chapter is intended only as an introduction to the subject of consolidated statements, we discuss here only some of the most commonly encountered relationships: intercompany receivables and payables and intercompany profit in assets.

Intercompany Receivables and Payables

In our example of the preparation of a consolidated income statement (Exhibit 19-13), S Company, a 75%-held subsidiary, sold merchandise to P Company for $30,000 during the year. Suppose that, at the end of the year, P Company still owed $15,000 to S Company for some of the merchandise. P Company would therefore have an account payable to S Company for $15,000 in its balance sheet at the end of the year, while S Company would show a receivable from P Company for the same amount. The consolidated balance sheet should show receivables and payables with *outsiders;* otherwise both total receivables and payables of the consolidated entity will be overstated. Therefore, the reciprocal receivable and payable of $15,000 must be eliminated in preparing the consolidated balance sheet, as shown in the following partial worksheet:

	P	S	Eliminations Debit	Eliminations Credit	Consolidated Balance Sheet
Assets					
Accounts Receivable	80,000	60,000		15,000	125,000
⋮					
Liabilities					
Accounts Payable	45,000	40,000	15,000		70,000
⋮					

Unrealized Intercompany Profit in Assets

In the above example, when S Company sold P Company $30,000 worth of merchandise, we assumed that P Company in turn sold all of it to outside parties. As far as the entity is concerned, a profit was *realized* on *all* of the merchandise. If the merchandise had cost S Company $22,000, and P Company eventually sold all of it to outsiders for $36,000, the entity would have made a profit of $14,000 on the merchandise. Remember that the only elimination necessary to avoid double-counting was to exclude $30,000 from S Company sales and $30,000 from P Company's cost of goods sold.

Suppose, however, that P Company sold only part of the merchandise to outsiders and still had $10,000 worth of the merchandise in its inventory at year end. Also assume that S Company's cost for the remaining $10,000 worth of merchandise had been $8,000. In this situation, the $2,000 of S Company profit residing in the inventory of P Company is *unrealized* from the standpoint of the entity. In a consolidated balance sheet, the $2,000 would be eliminated from P Company's inventory amount and from the retained earnings of S Company. This elimination would be made in addition to the elimination of $30,000 from S Company's sales and P Company's cost of goods sold, which we explained in our illustration of preparing the consolidated income statement.

In addition to merchandise, a firm may sell an affiliate such assets as securities, plant, and equipment. Following our general rule, any intercompany profit residing in the assets of the entity must be eliminated in preparing consolidated financial statements; only profits earned in dealing with outsiders can be reflected in consolidated net income and in consolidated retained earnings statements.

The technical procedures for handling the detailed adjustments for such items in preparing consolidated financial statements are somewhat complex; they are explored in detail in advanced accounting courses.

CONSOLIDATED STATEMENTS—POOLING METHOD

So far in our discussion, we have assumed that an acquiring company *purchased* a controlling interest in the shares of another firm by issuing cash, other assets, or debt. Thus a purchase and sale transaction occurred, and we used the **purchase method** to prepare consolidated statements in all of the foregoing examples. On the other hand, when the acquiring company obtains substantially all (90% or more) of a subsidiary company's shares by *issuing its own shares*, a "pooling of interests" is said to have occurred.[4] Basically, two sets of interests have "united," rather than a purchase and sale transaction taking place.

In this case, to record the parent's investment in the subsidiary and prepare consolidated financial statements, the **pooling method** is used. Under this method, the parent company records its investment at its share of the book value of the subsidiary's net assets, ignoring any current fair value of these assets. To prepare a consolidated balance sheet, the recorded book values of the affiliated firms are simply combined. Thus, this method avoids any revaluation of the subsidiary's assets or establishing the value of any goodwill in the combination.

Assume that P Company acquired all of the common stock of S Company by issuing its own stock to the shareholders of S Company and that before the acquisition, the two companies had the balance sheets shown in Exhibit 19–16 (page 686). To effect the acquisition, P Company issued 1,500 shares of its own $100 par value common stock for the 2,000 shares of S Company stock. No matter what the market price of P Company's stock happens to be,[5] the investment is recorded at the *net asset* value of S Company, as follows:

Investment in S Company Stock	240,000	
Common Stock		150,000
Paid-in Capital from Pooling of Interests		90,000

To record the issuance of 1,500 shares of
stock in the acquisition of 2,000 shares of
S Company stock.

Observe that the amount debited to P Company's investment account is equal to the recorded net asset value of S Company ($265,000 − $25,000 = $240,000). Common Stock is credited with the par value of P Company stock issued in the exchange, while the $90,000 difference is credited to Paid-in Capital from Pooling

---

[4]The criteria for determining whether a pooling has occurred are set forth in *Opinions of the Accounting Principles Board, No. 16*, "Business Combinations," American Institute of Certified Public Accountants, New York, 1970, p. 297.

[5]The market value of each firm's stock would play an important part in determining the number of P Company's shares to be exchanged for the subsidiary's shares. Once the negotiations are completed, the market value of shares plays no role whatsoever in the recording of the parent's investment or in the preparation of consolidated statements.

EXHIBIT 19-16

P and S Companies
Balance Sheets
January 1, 19XX

	P	S
Assets	$500,000	$265,000
Liabilities	$ 50,000	$ 25,000
Common Stock ($100 Par Value)	350,000	200,000
Retained Earnings	100,000	40,000
	$500,000	$265,000

of Interests. The latter amount is the equivalent of the $40,000 in retained earnings of S Company, which will be taken up into consolidated retained earnings, and $50,000 in paid-in capital in excess of par value ($200,000 par value of S Company stock minus $150,000 par value of P Company stock).

The worksheet to prepare a consolidated balance sheet immediately after the acquisition would appear as shown in Exhibit 19-17. The formal consolidated balance sheet for the affiliated companies would appear as shown in Exhibit 19-18.

EXHIBIT 19-17

P and S Companies
Consolidated Balance Sheet Worksheet
January 1, 19XX

	P	S	Eliminations Debit	Eliminations Credit	Consolidated Balance Sheet
Other Assets	500,000	265,000			765,000
Investment in S	240,000	—		240,000	—
	740,000	265,000			765,000
Liabilities	50,000	25,000			75,000
Common Stock					
P Company	500,000				500,000
S Company		200,000	200,000		
Paid-in Capital from Pooling	90,000		40,000		50,000
Retained Earnings					
P Company	100,000				100,000
S Company		40,000			40,000
	740,000	265,000	240,000	240,000	765,000

EXHIBIT 19–18

P and S Companies
Consolidated Balance Sheet
January 1, 19XX

Assets	$765,000
Liabilities	$ 75,000
Common Stock	500,000
Paid-in Capital from Pooling of Interests	50,000
Retained Earnings	140,000
	$765,000

Consolidated statements for periods after the acquisition are prepared in the same manner as those we have already discussed for a purchase type of acquisition, using the equity method of carrying the investment in the subsidiary.

POOLING AND PURCHASE METHODS COMPARED

We can see from Exhibits 19–17 and 19–18 that the pooling method does not result in an increase in total assets for the entity, because the acquiring firm's investment is stated at the book value of the subsidiary's net assets. In contrast, the purchase method of consolidation almost invariably results in an upward valuation of subsidiary assets or the emergence of goodwill. The implication here is that reported earnings in future periods will be higher under the pooling method, because the method avoids the amortization of higher asset values or goodwill against revenues.

Another facet of the pooling method is that the retained earnings of both the parent and the subsidiary company are combined, whereas under the purchase method, the parent's share of the subsidiary's retained earnings at the date of acquisition is eliminated in preparing a consolidated balance sheet. A corollary point is that, under the pooling method, the subsidiary's net income for *the entire year* can be combined with the parent's net income, regardless of the acquisition date during the year. Under the purchase method, only subsidiary earnings since the date of acquisition can be combined.

Combination by pooling has been widely used since the mid-1960s, because this method enables companies to show an immediate (often synthetic) improvement in their earnings records *purely as a result of the combination* rather than through improved operations. For some time, combining firms were allowed wide latitude in selecting methods of recording and consolidation, regardless of the nature of the exchange, with the result that the pooling method was selected for most combinations. In 1970, however, the Accounting Principles Board issued *Opinion No. 16*, "Business Combinations," which curtailed certain of the abuses by specifying more restrictive criteria that combining firms must meet in order to use the pooling method of accounting.

UNCONSOLIDATED COMPANIES

When a corporation has a long-term stock investment in another company whose accounts are not included in the consolidated statements, the parent's method of carrying the investment as an asset obviously has an effect on the financial statements. *Opinion No. 18* of the Accounting Principles Board[6] prescribes the appropriate accounting for such situations. We have already described the accounting treatment for long-term investments in Chapter 15, so we shall merely summarize the main points here:

(1) When the investment in such stock exceeds 50% of the total, the equity method is required, since the investing company has a controlling interest and can dictate the investee's operating and financial policies. The investing company therefore will currently take up as income its share of investee's net income instead of waiting for a dividend distribution.

(2) When the investment is 50% or less but at least 20%, the investing company can normally exercise significant influence over the investee's operating and financial policies. Therefore, the equity method is generally also appropriate here.

(3) When the investment is less than 20%, the cost method should be used, and the investing company should include in its income only dividends received from the investee.

USEFULNESS OF CONSOLIDATED STATEMENTS

Consolidated statements are designed to present an integrated report of an economic unit comprising a number of business enterprises related through stock ownership. In fact, there is no other way to depict, fairly concisely, the extent of resources and scope of operations of many companies subject to common control.

The statements do have certain limitations, however. The status or performance of weak constituents in a group can be "masked" through consolidation with successful units. Rates of return, ratios, and trend percentages calculated from consolidated statements may sometimes prove deceptive because they are really composite calculations. Shareholders and creditors of controlled companies

---

[6]*Opinions of the Accounting Principles Board, No. 18*, "The Equity Method of Accounting for Investments in Common Stock," American Institute of Certified Public Accountants, New York, 1971, p. 355.

who are interested in their legal rights and prerogatives should look to the separate financial statements of the relevant constituent companies.

In recent years, supplemental disclosures have improved the quality of consolidated statements, particularly those of entities with diversified lines of business, commonly called conglomerates. Both the Financial Accounting Standards Board[7] and the Securities and Exchange Commission have stipulated requirements for the disclosure, by business segments of certain firms, of information regarding revenue, income from operations, and identifiable assets.

DEMONSTRATION PROBLEM FOR REVIEW

The Montana Company purchased 75% of the common stock of the Utah Company on January 1, 19XX, for $180,000. On that date, the stockholders' equity of Utah Company consisted of $200,000 of common stock and $40,000 in retained earnings. Separate balance sheets of the two firms at December 31, 19XX, are given below:

Montana and Utah Companies
Balance Sheets
December 31, 19XX

Assets	Montana	Utah
Investment in Utah	$195,000	—
Other Assets	305,000	$300,000
	$500,000	$300,000
Liabilities and Stockholders' Equity		
Liabilities	$100,000	$ 40,000
Common Stock	300,000	200,000
Retained Earnings	100,000	60,000
	$500,000	$300,000

Neither firm declared or paid dividends during the year. At the end of the year, Utah Company owed $7,000 to Montana Company for a loan made during the year.

REQUIRED
Prepare a consolidated balance sheet worksheet at December 31, 19XX.

---

[7]*Statements of Financial Accounting Standards, No. 14*, "Financial Reporting for Segments of a Business Enterprise," Financial Accounting Standards Board, Stamford, Conn. 1976.

SOLUTION TO DEMONSTRATION PROBLEM

Montana and Utah Companies
Consolidated Balance Sheet Worksheet
December 31, 19XX

	Montana	Utah	Eliminations Debit	Eliminations Credit	Consolidated Balance Sheet
Investment in Utah	195,000	—		(a) 195,000	—
Other Assets	305,000	300,000		(b) 7,000	598,000
	500,000	300,000			598,000
Liabilities	100,000	40,000	(b) 7,000		133,000
Minority Interest				(a) 65,000	65,000
Common Stock:					
Montana Company	300,000				300,000
Utah Company		200,000	(a) 200,000		
Retained Earnings:					
Montana Company	100,000				100,000
Utah Company		60,000	(a) 60,000		
	500,000	300,000	267,000	267,000	598,000

Notice that Utah Company had earnings of $20,000 during the year, because its retained earnings increased from $40,000 to $60,000, and no dividends were declared. At December 31, Montana Company's investment of $195,000 consisted of the $180,000 originally paid plus $15,000, its 75% share of Utah Company's earnings. At December 31, the minority interest is 25% of the total stockholders' equity of Utah Company (25% of $260,000 = $65,000).

KEY POINTS TO REMEMBER

(1) When a corporation acquires another company's stock by exchanging assets, notes, or debt securities, the acquisition is regarded as a purchase. If less than 90% of the other company's stock is acquired, the acquisition is regarded as a purchase, regardless of the media of exchange. If, however, the acquiring company issues its own shares and obtains 90% or more of the other firm's shares, the transaction is regarded as a pooling, or uniting, of interests.

(2) In a purchase type of combination, the acquiring company initially records its investment at cost. Any cost in excess of the book value of the acquired firm's net assets is allocated among specific assets where possible; any unallocated amount is regarded as goodwill. The latter must be amortized over a period of years.

(3) In a pooling type of combination, the parent firm records its investment in accordance with the book value of the acquired firm's net assets. Cost (as measured by the market value of shares exchanged) is ignored. The acquired

firm's retained earnings at acquisition date are added to those of the acquiring company. Earnings of both companies for the period when the acquisition occurred are likewise combined.

(4) When a parent company carries its investment in a subsidiary under the equity method, as illustrated in this chapter, the accounting procedure is as follows:

(a) The parent periodically debits Investment in Subsidiary and credits Income from Subsidiary for its share of subsidiary earnings. Dividends received from the subsidiary are debited to Cash and credited to Investment in Subsidiary.

(b) When a consolidated balance sheet is prepared, the parent's equity in the subsidiary existing at the *time of statement preparation* is eliminated.

(5) When investments in shares of other companies whose accounts are not included in consolidated statements equal 20% or more of such firms' voting shares, the equity method is appropriate; if less than 20%, the investment in shares of other companies should be carried at acquisition cost. In the latter case, subsidiary income is reflected by the parent company only when dividends are received from a subsidiary.

QUESTIONS

19–1 What is the difference between a merger and a consolidation? How do these business combinations differ from a parent–subsidiary relationship?

19–2 Contrast the corporate "takeovers" of the late 1970s with those of the 1950s.

19–3 What is the purpose of consolidated financial statements?

19–4 Under what conditions may the accounts of wholly-owned or majority-owned subsidiaries be excluded from consolidated financial statements?

19–5 FMC Corporation, in a recent annual report, showed in its consolidated financial statements an amount under *Investments* that included a 100% interest in FMC Finance Corporation and a 50% interest in Ketchikan Pulp Corporation and its subsidiaries. The latter investment represents a 50–50 joint venture with Louisiana–Pacific Corporation. Why weren't the accounts of these firms consolidated with the accounts of FMC and its other subsidiaries? On what accounting basis are the investments in these unconsolidated subsidiaries carried?

19–6 What is the difference between a *purchase* acquisition and a *pooling of interests?*

19–7 P Company purchased all of the common stock of S Company for $200,000 when S Company had $150,000 of common stock and $50,000 of retained earnings. If a consolidated balance sheet were prepared immediately after the acquisition, what amounts would be eliminated in preparing it?

19–8 Suppose, in Question 19-7, that P Company had acquired only 75% of S Company's common stock, paying $150,000. If a consolidated balance sheet were prepared immediately after the acquisition, what amounts would be eliminated in preparing this statement? What amount of minority interest would appear in the consolidated balance sheet?

19-9 Explain the entries to be made in a parent company's records under the *equity* method of accounting to (a) reflect its share of the subsidiary's net income for the period, and (b) record the receipt of dividends from the subsidiary.

19-10 P Company purchased 80% of the common stock of S Company on January 1 of the current year for $200,000. During the year, S Company had $50,000 of net income and paid $20,000 in cash dividends. What amount will appear in P Company's balance sheet as Investment in S Company at the end of the year?

19-11 Able Company purchased an interest in Baker Company for $150,000 at a time when Baker Company had $100,000 of common stock and $40,000 of retained earnings.
   (a) If Able Company had acquired a 100% interest in Baker Company, what amount of Goodwill from Consolidation would appear on the consolidated balance sheet? (Assume that Baker's assets are fairly valued.)
   (b) If Able had acquired only a 90% interest in Baker Company, what amount of Goodwill from Consolidation would appear?

19-12 Puritan Company purchased an 80% interest in Reese Company at the start of the current year. Puritan Company had $500,000 net income for the current year before reflecting its share of Reese Company's net income. If Reese Company had net income of $50,000 for the year, what is the consolidated net income for the year?

19-13 Arden Company, which owns 75% of Brent Company, sold merchandise during the year to Brent Company for $25,000. The merchandise had cost Arden Company $20,000. If Brent Company in turn sold all of the merchandise to outsiders for $30,000, what eliminating entry related to these transactions would be made in preparing a consolidated income statement for the year?

19-14 Suppose, in Question 19-13, that Brent Company still owed Arden Company $12,000 for the merchandise acquired during the year. What eliminating entry would be made for this item in preparing a consolidated balance sheet at the end of the year?

19-15 What rules govern the choice between the cost and equity methods of carrying an investment in another company whose accounts are not to be consolidated with those of the parent company?

19-16 What are the inherent limitations of consolidated financial statements?

EXERCISES

19-17 Eagle Company purchased all of the common shares of Hawk Company for $280,000 cash at the beginning of the current year. On this date the stockholders' equity of Eagle Company consisted of $600,000 in common stock and $150,000 in retained earnings, while Hawk Company had $240,000 in common stock and $40,000 in retained earnings.

(a) Give the worksheet eliminating entry to prepare a consolidated balance sheet on the acquisition date.

(b) What amount of total stockholders' equity will appear on the consolidated balance sheet?

19-18 Parker Company purchased 75% of the common stock of Rowe Company for $210,000 in cash and notes when the stockholders' equity of Rowe Company consisted of $200,000 in common stock and $80,000 in retained earnings. At the date of acquisition, the stockholders' equity of Parker Company consisted of $700,000 in common stock and $120,000 in retained earnings. Show how the stockholders' equity would appear in a consolidated balance sheet prepared at the date of acquisition.

19-19 Ames Company purchased all of the common shares of Boone Company for $500,000 cash and notes at the beginning of the current year. Balance sheets of the two firms immediately after the acquisition were as follows:

	Ames	Boone
Current Assets	$1,000,000	$150,000
Investment in Boone Company	500,000	—
Plant and Equipment	4,500,000	350,000
	$6,000,000	$500,000
Liabilities	$1,200,000	$ 60,000
Common Stock	4,000,000	400,000
Retained Earnings	800,000	40,000
	$6,000,000	$500,000

During the negotiations for the purchase, Ames Company determined that the appraised value of Boone's plant and equipment was $375,000. Furthermore, Ames concluded that an additional $35,000 asked for by Boone's shareholders was warranted because Boone's earning power was somewhat better than the industry average. Give the worksheet eliminating entry to prepare a consolidated balance sheet on the acquisition date.

19-20 Able Company purchased an 80% interest in Baker Company for $480,000 cash at the beginning of the current year. During the year, Baker Company earned $80,000 net income and declared and paid half its earnings in dividends. Able Company carries its investment in Baker Company on the equity method. What is the carrying value of Able Company's account "Investment in Baker Company" at the close of the year?

19-21 Ontario Company has an 80% interest in Toronto Company. During the current year, Toronto Company sold merchandise costing $60,000 to the Ontario Company for $80,000. In preparing a consolidated income statement for the period, what worksheet eliminating entry should be made, assuming that Ontario Company sold all of the merchandise to outsiders?

19-22 On January 1, 19XX, the Edson Company purchased for $150,000 cash a 90% stock interest in Martin Company, which then had $100,000 of common stock outstanding and retained earnings of $40,000. On December 31, 19XX, after Edson had taken up its share of Martin's earnings, the balance sheets of the two companies were as follows:

	Edson	Martin
Investment in Martin	$168,000	—
Other Assets	132,000	$180,000
	$300,000	$180,000
Liabilities	$ 30,000	$ 20,000
Common Stock	200,000	100,000
Retained Earnings	70,000	60,000
	$300,000	$180,000

Martin Company did not declare or pay dividends during the year. In a consolidated balance sheet prepared on December 31, 19XX:

(a) What would be the amount of common stock?

(b) What would be the amount of consolidated retained earnings?

(c) What would be the amount of the minority interest?

19-23 Green Company entered into a pooling arrangement with Brown Company whereby Green acquired all of Brown's 3,000 shares of $50 par value common stock by issuing 1,200 shares of its own $100 par value common stock. At this time, Green's stock was selling for $175 a share. Before the combination, the two companies had the following balance sheets:

	Green	Brown
Net Assets	$600,000	$180,000
Common Stock	$480,000	$150,000
Retained Earnings	120,000	30,000
	$600,000	$180,000

(a) Give the entry on Green Company's records to record the issuance of its stock to acquire Brown's stock.

(b) What would be the consolidated retained earnings in a consolidated balance sheet prepared immediately after the pooling?

PROBLEMS

19-24 The Dallas Company purchased all of the common stock of the Denton Company for cash on January 1, 19XX, after which the separate balance sheets of the two corporations appeared as follows:

Dallas and Denton Companies
Balance Sheets
January 1, 19XX

Assets	Dallas	Denton
Investment in Denton	$ 280,000	—
Other Assets	720,000	$300,000
Total Assets	$1,000,000	$300,000

Liabilities and Stockholders' Equity

Liabilities	$ 500,000	$ 60,000
Common Stock	400,000	200,000
Retained Earnings	100,000	40,000
Total Liabilities and Stockholders' Equity	$1,000,000	$300,000

During the negotiations for the purchase of Denton Company's stock, Dallas Company determined that the appraised value of "Other Assets" of Denton Company amounted to $325,000.

REQUIRED

(a) Give the worksheet entry to eliminate the intercompany equity relationship and to reflect the appraised value of Denton Company's assets.

(b) What amount of total assets should appear on a consolidated balance sheet prepared at January 1?

(c) What amount of total stockholders' equity should appear on a consolidated balance sheet prepared at January 1?

19-25 On January 1, 19XX, Nebraska Company purchased all of the common stock of Omaha Company for $180,000 cash. The stockholders' equity of Omaha Company consisted of $150,000 in common stock and $30,000 in retained earnings. On December 31, 19XX, the separate balance sheets of the two firms were as follows:

Nebraska and Omaha Companies
Balance Sheets
December 31, 19XX

	Nebraska	Omaha
Assets		
Cash	$ 40,000	$ 20,000
Accounts Receivable	60,000	25,000
Investment in Omaha	200,000	—
Other Assets	450,000	170,000
Total Assets	$750,000	$215,000
Liabilities and Stockholders' Equity		
Accounts Payable	$ 30,000	$ 15,000
Common Stock	600,000	150,000
Retained Earnings	120,000	50,000
Total Liabilities and Stockholders' Equity	$750,000	$215,000

During the year, Omaha Company had net income of $30,000. At December 31, Omaha owed Nebraska $5,000 on account for merchandise.

REQUIRED

(a) What amount of dividends did Omaha Company declare and pay during the year?

(b) Give the journal entries made during the year by Nebraska Company affecting the account Investment in Omaha Company.

(c) What amount of total assets would appear in a consolidated balance sheet prepared on December 31, 19XX?

19-26 On January 1, 19XX, Palomar Company purchased 80% of the common stock of Sims Company for $280,000 cash, after which the separate balance sheets of the two firms were as follows:

Palomar and Sims Companies
Balance Sheets
January 1, 19XX

	Palomar	Sims
Assets		
Investment in Sims	$280,000	—
Other Assets	620,000	$260,000
Total Assets	$900,000	$260,000
Liabilities and Stockholders' Equity		
Liabilities	$ 90,000	$ 10,000
Common Stock	650,000	200,000
Retained Earnings	160,000	50,000
Total Liabilities and Stockholders' Equity	$900,000	$260,000

REQUIRED

Prepare a consolidated balance sheet worksheet at January 1, 19XX. Assume that any amount paid by Palomar Company in excess of the equity acquired in the net assets of Sims Company is attributable to goodwill.

19-27 Alpha Company owns 80% of the common stock of Beta Company. The income statements of the two companies for the current year are shown below. In its income statement, Alpha Company has not recorded its share of Beta Company's net income.

Alpha and Beta Companies
Income Statements
For the Current Year

	Alpha	Beta
Sales	$450,000	$280,000
Cost of Goods Sold	360,000	210,000
Gross Profit	$ 90,000	$ 70,000
Expenses (including income taxes)	42,000	38,000
Net Income	$ 48,000	$ 32,000

During the year, Alpha Company sold Beta Company merchandise for $50,000, which had cost Alpha $35,000. Beta Company sold all of this merchandise to outsiders.

REQUIRED

Prepare a consolidated income statement worksheet for the current year.

19-28 On October 1, 19XX, Ames Company entered into a pooling type of combination with Crypton Company, in which Ames obtained all of Crypton's 20,000 shares of $25 par value common stock by issuing 4,000 shares of its own $100 par value common stock. At this time, Ames Company's stock was selling at $160 a share. Before the pooling, the two companies had the following balance sheets:

Ames and Crypton Companies
Balance Sheets
October 1, 19XX

	Ames	Crypton
Assets		
Total Assets	$1,200,000	$650,000
Liabilities and Stockholders' Equity		
Liabilities	$ 120,000	$ 80,000
Common Stock	900,000	500,000
Retained Earnings	180,000	70,000
Total Liabilities and Stockholders' Equity	$1,200,000	$650,000

REQUIRED
(a) Give the entry on Ames Company's records to record the acquisition of Crypton Company's common stock.
(b) Prepare a consolidated balance sheet worksheet at October 1, 19XX.
(c) If a consolidated income statement were prepared for the first nine months of the year, what would be the consolidated net income for the period, assuming that Ames's earnings per share were $8 and Crypton's earnings per share were $2.75? (Both are calculated before pooling.)

19-29 On January 1, 19XX, Ohio Company acquired an interest in Kent Company for $340,000, consisting of $200,000 cash and $140,000 in notes payable. The following information is available about the two companies at December 31, 19XX:

	Ohio	Kent	Consolidated
Assets			
Cash	$ 50,000	$ 25,000	$ 75,000
Accounts Receivable	80,000	60,000	120,000
Merchandise Inventory	120,000	80,000	200,000
Investment in Kent (at equity)	380,000		
Other Assets	360,000	285,000	645,000
Excess of Cost over Equity Acquired in Kent			20,000
Total Assets	$990,000	$450,000	$1,060,000
Liabilities and Stockholders' Equity			
Accounts Payable	$ 80,000	$ 40,000	$ 100,000
Notes Payable	130,000	50,000	180,000
Common Stock	600,000	300,000	600,000
Retained Earnings	180,000	60,000	180,000
Total Liabilities and Stockholders' Equity	$990,000	$450,000	$1,060,000

REQUIRED

(a) Is the acquisition of Kent Company by Ohio Company being treated as a purchase or a pooling of interests? Explain.

(b) What ownership percentage of Kent Company did Ohio Company acquire?

(c) How much of Kent Company's retained earnings are included in the consolidated retained earnings? Kent paid no dividends in 19XX.

(d) What were Kent Company's earnings for the year?

(e) What were the amounts of intercompany receivables and payables at December 31?

ALTERNATE PROBLEMS

19-24A The Barton Company purchased 80% of the voting stock of the Hunt Company on January 1, 19XX, after which the separate balance sheets of the two companies appeared as follows:

Barton and Hunt Companies
Balance Sheets
January 1, 19XX

	Barton	Hunt
Assets		
Investment in Hunt	$240,000	—
Other Assets	460,000	$400,000
Total Assets	$700,000	$400,000
Liabilities and Stockholders' Equity		
Liabilities	$160,000	$120,000
Common Stock	400,000	200,000
Retained Earnings	140,000	80,000
Total Liabilities and Stockholders' Equity	$700,000	$400,000

In purchasing Hunt Company's shares, Barton Company determined that any excess of the amount paid over the equity acquired in Hunt is attributed entirely to the superior earnings potential of that company.

REQUIRED

(a) Give the worksheet entry to eliminate the intercompany equity relationship and to reflect the goodwill.

(b) What amount of total assets should appear on a consolidated balance sheet prepared at January 1?

(c) What amount of total stockholders' equity should appear on a consolidated balance sheet prepared at January 1?

19-25A On January 1, 19XX, Royal Company purchased all of the common stock of Porter Company for $260,000 cash. The stockholders' equity of Porter Company consisted of $200,000 of common stock and $60,000 of retained earnings. On December 31, 19XX, the separate balance sheets of the two firms were as follows:

Royal and Porter Companies
Balance Sheets
December 31, 19XX

	Royal	Porter
Assets		
Cash	$ 60,000	$ 70,000
Accounts Receivable	80,000	50,000
Investment in Porter	300,000	—
Other Assets	500,000	205,000
Total Assets	$940,000	$325,000
Liabilities and Stockholders' Equity		
Accounts Payable	$ 50,000	$ 25,000
Common Stock	600,000	200,000
Retained Earnings	290,000	100,000
Total Liabilities and Stockholders' Equity	$940,000	$325,000

During the year, Porter Company had net income of $56,000. At December 31, Porter owed Royal $8,000 on account for merchandise.

REQUIRED
(a) What amount of dividends did Porter Company declare and pay during the year?
(b) Give the journal entries made during the year by Royal Company affecting the account Investment in Porter Company.
(c) What amount of total assets would appear in a consolidated balance sheet prepared on December 31, 19XX?

19-26A On January 1, 19XX, Burns, Inc. purchased 70% of the voting stock of Vine, Inc. for $500,000. At that date, Vine had $500,000 in common stock outstanding and $150,000 in retained earnings. On December 31, 19XX, the separate balance sheets of the two companies were as follows:

Burns, Inc. and Vine, Inc.
Balance Sheets
December 31, 19XX

	Burns	Vine
Assets		
Investment in Vine	$ 514,000	—
Other Assets	986,000	$800,000
Total Assets	$1,500,000	$800,000
Liabilities and Stockholders' Equity		
Liabilities	$ 200,000	$130,000
Common Stock	1,000,000	500,000
Retained Earnings	300,000	170,000
Total Liabilities and Stockholders' Equity	$1,500,000	$800,000

During the year, Vine, Inc. paid $20,000 in dividends.

REQUIRED

Prepare a consolidated balance sheet worksheet at December 31, 19XX. Assume that any amount paid by Burns in excess of the equity acquired in Vine is attributable to goodwill.

19–27A Seneca Company purchased a 90% interest in York Company on January 1, 19XX. The income statements for the two companies for the year 19XX are given below. Seneca Company has not yet taken up its share of York Company's net income for the year.

Seneca and York Companies
Income Statements
For the Year Ended December 31, 19XX

	Seneca	York
Sales	$900,000	$600,000
Cost of Goods Sold	600,000	400,000
Gross Profit	$300,000	$200,000
Operating Expenses (including taxes)	230,000	150,000
Net Income	$ 70,000	$ 50,000

York Company did not pay any dividends during the year. Seneca sold merchandise costing $50,000 to York for $80,000, all of which York sold to outsiders during the year.

REQUIRED

Prepare a consolidated income statement worksheet for the year ending December 31, 19XX.

19–28A On September 30, 19XX, Western Company entered into a pooling type of combination with Lambert Company in which Western obtained all of Lambert's 10,000 shares of $25 par value common stock by issuing 2,000 shares of its own $100 par value common stock. At this time, Western's stock was selling at $200 per share. Before the pooling, the two companies had the following balance sheets:

Western and Lambert Companies
Balance Sheets
September 30, 19XX

	Western	Lambert
Assets		
Total Assets	$850,000	$325,000
Liabilities and Stockholders' Equity		
Liabilities	$100,000	$ 25,000
Common Stock	600,000	250,000
Retained Earnings	150,000	50,000
Total Liabilities and Stockholders' Equity	$850,000	$325,000

REQUIRED

(a) Give the entry on Western Company's books to record the acquisition of Lambert's stock.

(b) Prepare a consolidated balance sheet worksheet at September 30, 19XX.

(c) If a consolidated income statement were prepared for the first nine months of the year, what would be the consolidated net income for the period, assuming that Western's earnings were $50,000 and Lambert's earnings were $25,000?

BUSINESS DECISION PROBLEM

The ABC Corporation is a manufacturing company whose principal product is microwave ovens. It has an 80% interest in a subsidiary company, Scrub–All Company, which makes automatic dishwashers. It also has a 100% interest in a finance subsidiary, ABC Finance Corporation, created by ABC Corporation to finance sales of its products to customers. The parent company's only other investment is a 10% interest in the common stock of Apex Company, which manufactures chrome parts for both microwave ovens and dishwashers. A condensed consolidated balance sheet for the entity for the current year is given below.

ABC Corporation and Subsidiaries
Consolidated Balance Sheet
December 31, 19XX

Assets		
Current Assets		$29,400,000
Investment in Stock of ABC Finance		
Corporation (100%) at underlying equity		15,200,000
Investment in Stock of Apex Company (10%)		
at cost		5,400,000
Other Assets		32,500,000
Excess of Cost over Equity Acquired in		
Net Assets of Scrub–All Company		1,500,000
Total Assets		$84,000,000
Liabilities and Stockholders' Equity		
Current Liabilities		$14,500,000
Long-term Liabilities		28,000,000
Stockholders' Equity:		
Minority Interest	$ 3,500,000	
Common Stock	25,000,000	
Retained Earnings	13,000,000	41,500,000
Total Liabilities and Stockholders' Equity		$84,000,000

The balance sheet given above, along with other financial statements, was furnished to shareholders before their annual meeting, and all shareholders were invited to submit questions to be answered at the meeting. As chief financial officer of the ABC Corporation, you have been appointed to respond to the questions at the meeting.

REQUIRED

Answer the following questions selected from among those submitted:

(a) Why are investments in Apex Company and ABC Finance Corporation shown on the balance sheet, while the investment in Scrub–All Company is omitted?

(b) What is meant by the carrying value "underlying equity" for the investment in ABC Finance Corporation?

(c) Why is the investment in Apex Company shown at cost, while the investment in ABC Finance Corporation is shown at underlying equity?

(d) Explain the meaning of the asset "Excess of Cost over Equity Acquired in Net Assets of Scrub–All Company."

(e) What is meant by "minority interest" and to what company is this account related?

20
Accounting for Business Segments: Departments and Branches

W hen a business enterprise is composed of subdivisions or segments, as most firms are, management analysis, planning, and control logically should conform to such segments. Accounting and reporting procedures, therefore, should be designed to permit management to measure the performance of each segment. In this chapter we examine the problems of accounting for business segments and analyzing their performance.

TYPES OF SEGMENTATION

A business may be subdivided in many ways. Segments of an enterprise may be classified in terms of (1) organizational units (departments, divisions, branches, subsidiaries, or other accounting or legal entities) or (2) areas of economic activity (industries, product lines, markets, or geographical areas). Often, organizational units are established to comprise the operation of a particular area of economic activity.

Many firms have found with experience that large or complex operations are directed most easily when segmented according to organizational unit. We have already discussed the accounting processes dealing with subsidiary companies in Chapter 19. In this chapter we shall deal primarily with the accounting and reporting processes for departments and branches. (Accounting for divisions is similar to departmental accounting.)

EXTERNAL REPORTING OF SEGMENT OPERATIONS

Until about 1970, accounting and reporting for business segments were done largely to benefit management, and reports to outsiders were confined to the business as a whole. Indeed, many companies have been reluctant to reveal detailed data on business segments for a number of reasons, including competitive harm, technical difficulties of allocating common costs among segments, and lack of investor need for such information.

Beginning in the mid-1960s, a number of professional organizations, including the Financial Executives Research Foundation, the Financial Analysts Federation, and the National Association of Accountants, initiated studies to determine the desirability and possible methods of reporting information on business segments in external financial reports. Later, the Accounting Principles Board of the AICPA, along with other organizations, encouraged companies to report segmental data. In 1969, the Securities and Exchange Commission issued rules for reporting on segments in registration statements, which it extended in 1970 to certain annual reports.

The Financial Accounting Standards Board issued *Statement No. 14* in 1976, and later several amending statements, requiring that certain annual financial statements of publicly owned companies disclose segmental data on the enterprise's operations in different industries, foreign operations and export sales, and major customers.[1] In general, it is management's prerogative to classify the various segments and the basis on which the firm's operations will be reported.

INTERNAL REPORTING OF SEGMENT OPERATIONS

Financial reports for such organizational segments as divisions, departments, and branches may consist of both operating (income) statements and balance sheets; when the organizational unit is not a legal entity, however, balance sheets are usually not relevant. In any event, emphasis is naturally placed on the measurement of operating performance, and some form of income or operating statement is most useful to management when making decisions about the operation of the segment. Such a statement may answer the following questions:

(1) What amount is each segment contributing to the firm's profits?

(2) Should the segment be expanded or discontinued?

(3) Are expenses reasonable, or are they out of line with budget estimates?

(4) Are any corrective actions or controls indicated?

(5) Are prices and sales policies realistic?

(6) Where should the greatest promotional effort be exerted?

Normally, when a segment such as a department or a division generates revenue, it becomes a **profit center.** The accounting system is usually designed to provide both revenue and expense data for the segment, and its manager's success is gauged by the segment's contribution to the firm's operating results. Some firms have departments that do not generate revenue but are departmentalized because of their importance as functional entities. Thus, a firm may have a central

---

[1]*Statement of Financial Accounting Standards No. 14,* "Financial Reporting for Segments of a Business Enterprise," Financial Accounting Standards Board, Stamford, Conn., 1976.

purchasing department, a maintenance department, and other "support" departments. Often such segments are designated **cost** or **expense centers.** Managers of such departments have responsibility for cost rather than profit. Their performance is measured by their ability to keep operations within budgeted amounts established by higher management.

An important aspect of any approach to measuring performance is that costs may be classified as *controllable* or *not controllable.* Department or division managers should be held accountable only for costs in areas over which they can exercise control—usually costs that are directly incurred by their departments. On the other hand, as we shall discuss later, some common costs of the total enterprise, which are not controllable at the segment level, are frequently assigned, or allocated, to the various departments or other segments. If budgets are used to measure a manager's performance, it is a good idea to identify costs considered to be within the manager's discretion and to segregate, in reports, those over which he or she has no control.

In the following sections of this chapter we shall emphasize departmentalized operations in which the departments are profit centers. Although we use a medium-sized departmentalized firm in our illustration, the concepts can be generalized to other types of segments and to firms of different sizes.

DEPARTMENTAL OPERATIONS

Departmentalization is a common and logical type of segmentation for many firms. In manufacturing and merchandising firms, departments are generally classified by product sold. The very term "department store" signifies a type of merchandising by product. Common segments of a department store are housewares, appliances, furniture, linens, men's clothing, and women's clothing. Food stores are also commonly departmentalized by products such as meat, produce, groceries, delicatessen, and so forth. Sometimes departments are also classified by type of customer. For example, firms selling such products as floor coverings, lighting fixtures, and heating and air conditioning units may separate commercial sales operations from residential sales activity.

The methods of accounting and reporting for departmental operating activity depend on the performance measures used and the degree of analysis desired by management. For some firms, operating data may be desired only to the extent of identifying gross profit by department. In others, management may wish to determine a net income figure for each department. Still others may adopt an intermediate performance measure, such as gross profit less only those expenses directly incurred by the department. We shall examine the means of developing these various performance measures.

Departmental Gross Profit   The main reason for analyzing gross profit by department is that it permits management to review pricing policies and supplier costs. Comparisons can be made among departments to determine areas with high gross profit margins and in which areas major promotional efforts should be made. Comparisons can also be made with gross profit margins achieved in other periods, or with average percentage statistics for other firms selling the same lines. (These statistics may be obtained from trade association publications and credit agencies.) Often, very low gross profit margins signal a need to investigate purchasing policies or to revise prices.

To obtain gross profit figures by department, a firm will customarily keep separate departmental accounts for sales, purchases, and inventory, and for discounts, returns, and allowances related to sales and purchases transactions. Transportation costs on purchases must also be segregated. Because firms frequently receive incoming shipments for a number of departments, it is often easier to analyze freight costs by department at the end of the accounting period than as individual freight bills being received and recorded throughout the accounting period.

When a firm maintains journals or other books of original entry, special columns must be provided for purchases, sales, and discounts by department. Large firms with many departments usually have sophisticated accounting systems, often computerized, which dispense with journals. Under such systems, a code is assigned to each department; input data are identified by department code; and when the transactions are processed, the data are classified and tabulated by department.

Exhibit 20-1 (page 708) is a departmental income statement for Decorator Lighting Company, which accumulates gross profit data by department. This firm, segmented into two departments—residential and commercial—sells lighting fixtures in a large retail outlet for retail residential customers and for individual builders who purchase fixtures for single-home construction. In addition, the company sells in a market that supplies lighting fixtures for large-scale contractors engaged in the construction of office buildings, motels, and other commercial installations.

Departmental Net Income

Ordinarily, it is not difficult to maintain an accounting system in which departmental reporting is carried only to the point of measuring gross profit. A firm that desires a more refined measure of operating performance, however, is faced with the problem of assigning operating expenses to the departments. If a measure of departmental net income is desired, it is necessary to trace *all* expenses to departments.

Some expenses may be readily identified with the operation of particular departments, while others cannot. To identify expenses with departments, it is helpful to classify them into the following two general categories:

Direct expenses: Those operating expenses traceable to and incurred for the benefit of a single department and thus ordinarily controllable by the department.

EXHIBIT 20-1

Decorator Lighting Company
Income Statement
For the Year Ended December 31, 19XX

	Residential Dept.	Commercial Dept.	Total
Sales	$330,000	$220,000	$550,000
Less: Sales Returns and Allowances	(4,000)	(5,500)	(9,500)
Sales Discounts	(6,000)	(4,500)	(10,500)
Net Sales	$320,000	$210,000	$530,000
Cost of Goods Sold:			
Inventory, Jan. 1	$ 88,000	$ 42,000	$130,000
Purchases	194,000	144,000	338,000
Less: Purchases Returns	(4,500)	(2,000)	(6,500)
Purchases Discounts	(3,500)	(3,000)	(6,500)
Transportation In	6,000	4,000	10,000
Merchandise Available for Sale	$280,000	$185,000	$465,000
Less: Inventory, Dec. 31	72,000	38,000	110,000
Cost of Goods Sold	$208,000	$147,000	$355,000
Gross Profit on Sales	$112,000	$ 63,000	$175,000
Operating Expenses:			
Selling Expenses			$ 70,000
Administrative Expenses			60,000
Total Operating Expenses			$130,000
Income before Income Taxes			$ 45,000
Income Tax Expense			15,100
Net Income			$ 29,900
Ratio of Gross Profit to Net Sales	35%	30%	

Indirect expenses: Those operating expenses incurred primarily for the benefit of the entire firm and thus neither traceable to nor controllable by a specific department.

For example, payroll expense related to personnel who work exclusively in one department is a *direct expense* of that department. Payroll expense related to administrative personnel whose work benefits all departments is an *indirect expense* of the operating departments. A firm usually has many indirect or common expenses, incurred for the benefit of more than one department. Some examples are heat, light, maintenance, depreciation, and other occupancy expenses, office salaries, executive salaries, and a variety of other administrative expenses. These expenses must be fairly apportioned to the operating departments if the measure of departmental net income is to be meaningful. Because it is difficult and cumbersome to attempt any apportionment of common expenses at the time they are incurred, they are usually analyzed and allocated to departments at the end of the accounting period.

Assume that the $130,000 operating expenses for Decorator Lighting Company in Exhibit 20-1 consisted of the following:

Sales Salaries Expense	$ 45,000
Advertising Expense	15,000
Delivery Expense	10,000
Insurance Expense (on merchandise)	6,000
Occupancy Expense	16,000
Uncollectible Accounts Expense	3,000
Office Salaries Expense	20,000
Other Administrative Expense	15,000
	$130,000

In preparing a departmental income statement, Decorator Lighting might analyze these expenses and the income tax expense of $15,100 as follows:

Sales Salaries Expense. The sales force for the residential department is separate from that of the commercial department. Therefore, the sales salaries for each department can be directly determined from payroll records, which show $25,000 for the residential department and $20,000 for the commercial department.

Advertising Expense. Of the company's $15,000 advertising expense, $7,000 was spent on newspaper and television advertising of residential lighting products, $3,000 on producing illustrated brochures with price lists for commercial customers, and $5,000 on general newspaper advertising directed at both markets. The latter amount was allocated on the basis of relative sales. ($330,000/$550,000 = 60% residential; $220,000/$550,000 = 40% commercial.)

	Residential	Commercial	Total
Direct Advertising	$ 7,000	$3,000	$10,000
Indirect Advertising	3,000	2,000	5,000
	$10,000	$5,000	$15,000

Delivery Expense. Products are delivered to all commercial customers via Ace Trucking Service at a cost of $2,000. All residential deliveries are made with the company's own truck or via United Delivery Service and total $8,000. Thus, departmental delivery costs can be determined directly.

Insurance Expense *(on merchandise).* The cost of insurance is based on the average inventories of the two departments:

Residential ($88,000 + $72,000)/2 = $ 80,000   80/120 × $6,000 = $4,000
Commercial ($42,000 + $38,000)/2 = $ 40,000   40/120 × $6,000 =   2,000
                                                          $120,000 $6,000

Occupancy Expense. Rent, maintenance, and utility expenses are included in this item, which is allocated on the basis of square feet of floor space used by each department. Of the total floor space, $\frac{5}{8}$ is occupied by the residential department and $\frac{3}{8}$ by the commercial department. Of the $16,000 total cost, $10,000 is apportioned to the residential department and $6,000 to the commercial department.

Uncollectible Accounts Expense. The firm maintains a separate customers' ledger for each department and determines its expense from uncollectible accounts by aging the accounts. Estimated uncollectible accounts totaled $1,600 for residential customers and $1,400 for commercial customers. (If the provision had been based on a percentage of sales, the uncollectible accounts expense would be apportioned according to the relative sales of the two departments.)

Office Salaries and Other Administrative Expense. Often, salaries of office personnel and other administrative expenses are allocated to departments on the basis of the relative sales of each department. Because a good share of this cost is related to billings, collections, customer inquiries, and correspondence, using relative sales as a basis for apportionment is not as arbitrary as it may appear. The alternative is to attempt an analysis of time spent by office employees on the affairs of each department and to estimate administrative supplies used, correspondence, and other office expenses by department. Such analysis is liable to be costly and time-consuming, and it may not provide much additional accuracy. Decorator Lighting uses relative sales as a basis here, as it does for indirect advertising (shown earlier), apportioning 60% of the expenses to the residential department and 40% to the commercial department:

	Residential 60%	Commercial 40%	Total
Office Salaries Expense	$12,000	$ 8,000	$20,000
Other Administrative Expense	9,000	6,000	15,000
	$21,000	$14,000	$35,000

Income Tax Expense. Because Decorator Lighting Company is a corporation, it must pay federal income taxes at the appropriate rates on various portions of its taxable income. Here we assume that the total tax on $45,000 income (see Exhibit 20–1) is $15,100. If the departmental figures are extended to after-tax net income, as shown in Exhibit 20–2, the only realistic way to apportion the tax expense is on the basis of income before taxes. Thus, $32,400/$45,000 × $15,100 = $10,872 tax expense for the residential department, and $12,600/$45,000 × $15,100 = $4,228 tax expense for the commercial department. Some accountants believe that, because departments are not taxable entities, allocation of tax expense among them does not result in meaningful performance measures; they would extend the departmental figures only to net income before taxes.

A summary of the operating expenses and income tax expense, giving the direct expenses and allocated indirect expenses of each department, is shown below.

	Residential Dept.			Commercial Dept.		
	Direct	Indirect	Total	Direct	Indirect	Total
Sales Salaries Expense	$25,000		$25,000	$20,000		$20,000
Advertising Expense	7,000	$ 3,000	10,000	3,000	$ 2,000	5,000
Delivery Expense	8,000		8,000	2,000		2,000
Insurance Expense (on merchandise)	4,000		4,000	2,000		2,000
Occupancy Expense		10,000	10,000		6,000	6,000
Uncollectible Accounts Expense	1,600		1,600	1,400		1,400
Office Salaries Expense		12,000	12,000		8,000	8,000
Other Administrative Expense		9,000	9,000		6,000	6,000
	$45,600	$34,000	$79,600	$28,400	$22,000	$50,400
Income Tax Expense		$10,872			$ 4,228	
			$15,100	$130,000		

This departmental expense distribution was used to prepare the income statement for Decorator Lighting Company shown in Exhibit 20–2 (page 712), which extends the departmental operating results through net income after taxes.

Departmental Contribution to Indirect Expenses

Operating statements that extend departmental results to net income measures are often criticized on the grounds that the indirect or common expenses are not controllable at the departmental level and therefore should not be assigned to departments when measuring performance. A further criticism is that the bases for assignment of indirect expenses are frequently arbitrary; when allocation of such expenses is not equitable, the performance measure becomes clouded, and management may reach improper conclusions about departmental operations.

Some accountants favor an intermediate type of performance measure as a means of appraising departmental operating results. The **departmental contribution to indirect expenses** is obtained by deducting the direct departmental expenses from departmental gross profit. The resulting amount is a measure of the

EXHIBIT 20-2

Decorator Lighting Company
Income Statement
For the Year Ended December 31, 19XX

	Residential Dept.	Commercial Dept.	Total
Net Sales	$320,000	$210,000	$530,000
Cost of Goods Sold	208,000	147,000	355,000
Gross Profit on Sales	$112,000	$ 63,000	$175,000
Operating Expenses:			
Sales Salaries Expense	$ 25,000	$ 20,000	$ 45,000
Advertising Expense	10,000	5,000	15,000
Delivery Expense	8,000	2,000	10,000
Insurance Expense (on merchandise)	4,000	2,000	6,000
Occupancy Expense	10,000	6,000	16,000
Uncollectible Accounts Expense	1,600	1,400	3,000
Office Salaries Expense	12,000	8,000	20,000
Other Administrative Expense	9,000	6,000	15,000
Total Operating Expenses	$ 79,600	$ 50,400	$130,000
Income before Income Taxes	$ 32,400	$ 12,600	$ 45,000
Income Tax Expense	10,872	4,228	15,100
Net Income	$ 21,528	$ 8,372	$ 29,900

department's contribution to the firm's pool of common or indirect expenses incurred for the benefit of all operating units. Using this measure eliminates the need for allocating the indirect expenses. Although this approach emphasizes direct expenses, it should not be assumed that all aspects of direct expenses are controllable at the departmental level. Higher management may direct that a certain amount of, say, advertising expense be incurred by a department. The advertising expense is properly described as direct and no allocation is required, but to say it is fully controllable at the departmental level would be incorrect. This is one example of the subtle aspects of departmental performance measurement.

A departmental operating statement showing departmental contributions appears in Exhibit 20-3. Direct expenses are segregated from indirect expenses according to the summary of operating expenses appearing on page 711.

ANALYSIS OF DEPARTMENTAL PERFORMANCE

To monitor the performance of a firm's departments or other operating segments, managers continually review the operating data, looking at sales trends, gross profit percentages, operating expenses as percentages of sales, and such final performance measures as net income and contribution to indirect expenses. This

EXHIBIT 20–3

Decorator Lighting Company
Income Statement Showing
Departmental Contributions to Indirect Expenses
For the Year Ended December 31, 19XX

	Residential Dept.	Commercial Dept.	Total
Net Sales	$320,000	$210,000	$530,000
Cost of Goods Sold	208,000	147,000	355,000
Gross Profit on Sales	$112,000	$ 63,000	$175,000
Direct Operating Expenses:			
Sales Salaries Expense	$ 25,000	$ 20,000	$ 45,000
Advertising Expense	7,000	3,000	10,000
Delivery Expense	8,000	2,000	10,000
Insurance Expense (on merchandise)	4,000	2,000	6,000
Uncollectible Accounts Expense	1,600	1,400	3,000
Total Direct Expenses	$ 45,600	$ 28,400	$ 74,000
Contribution to Indirect Expenses	$ 66,400	$ 34,600	$101,000
Indirect Operating Expenses:			
Advertising Expense			$ 5,000
Occupancy Expense			16,000
Office Salaries Expense			20,000
Other Administrative Expense			15,000
Total Indirect Expenses			$ 56,000
Income before Income Taxes			$ 45,000
Income Tax Expense			15,100
Net Income			$ 29,900

analysis may prompt management to change pricing policies, select different suppliers, attempt a different product mix within a department, redirect promotional efforts, or even discontinue a department.

To illustrate some of these aspects of departmental analysis, let us consider the following condensed operating statement of a departmentalized merchandising firm:

	Total	Department 3	Other Departments
Sales	$500,000	$100,000	$400,000
Cost of Goods Sold	335,000	75,000	260,000
Gross Profit	$165,000	$ 25,000	$140,000
Direct Expenses	$ 78,000	$ 18,000	$ 60,000
Indirect Expenses	52,000	12,000	40,000
Total Expenses	$130,000	$ 30,000	$100,000
Net Income (Loss)	$ 35,000	($ 5,000)	$ 40,000

Because we are emphasizing the operations of Department 3, we have combined the data for other departments. Note that Department 3 showed a net loss of $5,000 for the period and that the gross profit percentage for this department is only 25% ($25,000/$100,000) compared with an average of 35% ($140,000/$400,000) for other departments. If this percentage has dropped from previous years for Department 3 or is well below industry averages, the reason should be ascertained. For example, pricing policy and product acquisition costs might be reviewed to see if changes are indicated. Perhaps certain low mark-up items sold by Department 3 should be deemphasized and stronger promotional effort made for other products.

Suppose management's strategy were to increase Department 3 sales prices by an average of 10%, through an increase in promotional outlays of $2,500, with the expectation that volume (in units of product) would remain unchanged. If

MEASUREMENT AND CONTROL
OF DIVISIONAL PERFORMANCE

To measure divisional performance by means of a profit figure arrived at after deducting items which are neither controllable at divisional level nor directly related to divisional activity is to use a measure which is arbitrary to the extent that the allocations are arbitrary. It is not independent of conditions outside the division, and may lead divisions into courses of action detrimental to the company. It could, moreover, mislead head office executives into thinking that a division was making a loss or a very small profit, and that therefore it should be liquidated. This could happen even though the facts were that, while the division was failing to make an adequate contribution to the head office expenses and profit, it was making *some* contribution, sufficient perhaps to keep it operating in the hope of eventual recovery.

Most company executives are aware of these arguments against expense allocations but are not always convinced by them. The counterargument most commonly used is that divisions must be made aware that there are nondivisional costs to be covered out of their earnings before the company as a whole can show a profit. Unless this awareness is sharpened by showing the central expense allocations on the divisional profit statements each month, the division may, in pricing policies and other marketing decisions, plan to contribute less than its due share of the company's net income. Moreover, it is argued, if the division were an independent company it would have a top administration of its own.

These counterarguments are not convincing. It is true that some methods of overhead allocation (e.g., allocations based on divisional sales) create possibilities for a division to diminish its contribution to the company's over-all profitability while increasing its own apparent net profit. But such aberrations result simply from the fact of allocation itself. Apart from such allocation practices, *so long as corporate (i.e., nondivisional) expenses are independent of divisional activity,* whatever policies maximize divisional net profits will also maximize divisional contributions to corporate profits before the allocation of corporate expenses. In the general case, in other words, corporate net profits will not suffer if corporate fixed expenses are left unallocated.

SOURCE: David Solomons, *Divisional Performance: Measurement and Control,* Financial Executives Research Foundation, Inc., New York, 1965. Reprinted by permission.

management's expectations proved correct, the price change would bring sales to $110,000, gross profit to $35,000, and the gross profit percentage to almost 32% ($35,000/$110,000). Instead of a net loss of $5,000, the department would show a net income of $2,500, because there would be a $7,500 improvement ($10,000 sales increase less $2,500 additional promotion expense) in operating results.

On the other hand, suppose that management decided not to alter prices, but expected that a $2,500 additional outlay for promotion would increase volume of products sold by 10%. Would the outlay improve results? This action would also result in $110,000 sales revenue, but cost of goods sold would increase 10%, to $82,500. Gross profit would increase only $2,500, to $27,500. Because the additional promotion cost equals this increase, the same net loss of $5,000 would result. Clearly, if competitive conditions do not permit price increases, any additional promotional costs would have to be less than increases in gross profit that result from the increased volume of products sold.

Suppose that management is considering the elimination of Department 3. How would this affect the firm's net income? The departmental contribution approach gives us a clue. Department 3 has a contribution to indirect expenses of $7,000 (gross profit of $25,000 less direct expenses of $18,000). This amount would be lost if Department 3 were eliminated, reducing the net income of the firm to $28,000. We assume here that the $18,000 direct expenses of Department 3 would all be eliminated or "saved," but that the $12,000 indirect costs would now have to be apportioned to the remaining departments, because these are common expenses of operating the entire firm and are normally inescapable. (In the real world, a firm sometimes experiences a reduction in common expenses when the scope of its operations is reduced.)

If the firm can substitute a new department for Department 3 or expand other departments and in either case generate more than $7,000 contribution to indirect expenses, then perhaps Department 3 might well be discontinued. Another possibility would be to rent this department's space to outsiders at a net return higher than $7,000.

Sometimes one department's operations complement, or contribute to, the success of others. In that case, discontinuing a department may reduce sales in other areas. For example, a food store that discontinues its delicatessen or bakery department, or a hardware store that drops its garden center, may suffer a general loss in patronage. Therefore, management may have to weigh many factors.

This discussion is only a brief introduction to cost and revenue analysis. A more extensive treatment is given to this subject, and to segment contribution analysis, in Chapter 25.

BRANCH SEGMENTS

Many business firms expand by opening new outlets, or **branches,** at different locations. The development of suburban shopping centers has provided the impetus for branch marketing of goods and services by many firms, especially retail stores, banks, and savings and loan companies. Both wholesale and retail merchandising companies have expanded their marketing territories through widespread branch operations.

Typically, the various branches offer the same goods or services and follow a fairly standardized mode of operation. A manager appointed for each branch normally is responsible for the profitability of the outlet. From a managerial point of view, each branch is regarded as an accounting entity, even though branches are usually segments of a single legal entity—a corporation, partnership, or sole proprietorship—whatever the firm may be. The principal outlet, from which the firm's activities are normally directed, is often referred to as the **home office.**

Generally, merchandising policies, advertising, and promotion are directed or heavily influenced by the home office. Although branches may be given some latitude in acquiring merchandise, often a major portion of goods is purchased centrally.

The accounting system for branch operations should be designed to furnish management with complete and timely information to measure branch profitability. The size and complexity of branch operations, geographic location, and degree of autonomy, among other things, may influence the type of accounting system adopted. Most systems, however, are variations of two basic schemes: centralized accounting by the home office and decentralized accounting by the branch.

Centralized Branch Records

Under a **centralized** accounting system, the home office maintains most of the records needed to account for branch operations. Thus, separate asset, liability, revenue, and expense records for each branch are maintained at the home office. Typically, cash is transferred to the branch to establish a working fund for small disbursements. This fund is ordinarily kept on an imprest basis (like a petty cash fund) and replenished regularly by the home office on the basis of expense vouchers or summaries submitted by the branch. A branch that collects any amounts in its operations is often required to deposit such amounts in a home office bank account and transmit deposit slips and lists of the remittances to the home office for recording. The branch also transmits all other documents such as copies of sales invoices and credit memos to the home office for recording. The data needed to record branch transactions may be transmitted by a telecommunication or similar device, with the documents being forwarded at periodic intervals. In some cases, the documents may be filed at the branch, with periodic audits by either home office auditors or independent accountants.

Decentralized Branch Records

Under a **decentralized** accounting system, each branch ordinarily maintains a comprehensive set of accounting records for its operations and prepares periodic financial statements to be forwarded to the home office. Normally, the forms of the records and statements are standardized for all branches, so that they may be conveniently analyzed by the home office and integrated into the financial reports of the organization as a whole. Emphasis is often placed on the operating, or income statement, accounts. For example, the branch may keep accounts for current assets such as cash, accounts receivable, and inventory, but the home office may retain the accounts for equipment, fixtures, and accumulated depreciation.

In place of owners' equity accounts, the branch will have an account called **Home Office,** the balance of which represents amounts of advances or assets received from the home office plus accumulated branch earnings not transferred back to the home office. A reciprocal account called **Branch Office** is maintained in the ledger of the home office. When both accounts are posted and up to date, the dollar balances should be identical.

In looking at the branch as an accounting entity, the Home Office account may be viewed either as a capital account or as a liability. Likewise, the Branch Office balance on the books of the home office may be viewed either as an investment amount or as a receivable. Actually, the classification of these accounts is not especially important; the branch is only an accounting segment, and when its accounts are combined with those of the home office, the balances are offset against each other and neither of the accounts appears in the combined financial statements.

Illustration of Decentralized Accounting

Assume that on May 1 of the current year the Foto–Art Company, retailer of photographic equipment, opened a branch called the Western Branch in another city, leasing the store facilities and fixtures. The home office transferred $20,000 in cash and $40,000 in merchandise to the branch to begin operations. To record the transfer establishing the branch, the following entries would be made on the two sets of records:

Home Office Records			Western Branch Records		
Western Branch	60,000		Cash	20,000	
Cash		20,000	Shipments from Home Office	40,000	
Shipments to Western Branch		40,000	Home Office		60,000

This entry establishes the investment in the branch (or receivable from the branch) for the amount of cash and merchandise advanced to the new outlet. The amount shown in Western Branch's reciprocal account, $60,000, is the same as the amount of capital received from the home office.

Generally, when merchandise is shipped from the home office to the branch, it should be differentiated from branch acquisitions purchased from outsiders. Therefore, an account **Shipments to Branch** is credited on the home office records, and an account **Shipments from Home Office** is debited on the branch records whenever the home office transfers merchandise to the branch. On the home office records, the credit balance in the Shipments to Branch account can be considered an offset, or contra account, to the Purchases account. On the branch records, the Shipments from Home Office debit balance can be considered a purchases amount. When the branch closes its books, it closes the Shipments from Home Office account to the Income Summary account. Likewise, the home office closes the Shipments to Branch balance to its own Income Summary account.

The transactions occurring in May, including the transfer of assets establishing the branch, are shown in summary form:

Summary of May Transactions	Home Office Records		Western Branch Records		
(1) Home office opened Western Branch, transferring $20,000 cash and $40,000 merchandise.	Western Branch Cash Shipments to Western Branch	60,000	20,000 40,000	Cash Shipments from Home Office Home Office	20,000 40,000	60,000
(2) Purchased $15,000 merchandise from outsiders.				Purchases Accounts Payable	15,000	15,000
(3) Sold merchandise on account for $30,000.				Accounts Receivable Sales	30,000	30,000
(4) Incurred $5,000 selling expense and $3,000 general expense; of the total, $2,000 was on account.				Selling Expense General Expense Cash Accounts Payable	5,000 3,000	6,000 2,000
(5) Collected $24,000 on account from customers.				Cash Accounts Receivable	24,000	24,000
(6) Paid $12,000 to creditors on account.				Accounts Payable Cash	12,000	12,000
(7) Sent $10,000 cash to home office.	Cash Western Branch	10,000	10,000	Home Office Cash	10,000	10,000
(8) Home office general expense attributed to Western Branch was $1,000.	Western Branch General Expense	1,000	1,000	General Expense Home Office	1,000	1,000

After the foregoing entries have been posted to the Western Branch's ledger, the trial balance for the branch would appear as shown on page 719.

The Western Branch next records any necessary end-of-period adjustments in the usual fashion. For the sake of brevity, we assume that no adjustments are required except to record the ending inventory, estimated at $37,000. (This entry is shown together with the closing entries beginning on page 720.)

**Foto–Art Company
Western Branch
Trial Balance
May 31, 19XX**

	Debit	Credit
Cash	$16,000	
Accounts Receivable	6,000	
Home Office		$51,000
Accounts Payable		5,000
Sales		30,000
Purchases	15,000	
Shipments from Home Office	40,000	
Selling Expense	5,000	
General Expense	4,000	
	$86,000	$86,000

**Branch
Financial
Statements**

After the branch has recorded any necessary adjusting entries, financial statements can be prepared. Exhibits 20–4 and 20–5 show the May income statement and balance sheet at May 31 for the Western Branch. Note in the balance sheet that the net income for the period is added to the balance of the Home Office account. Actually, the branch's net income would be closed to the Home Office account at the end of the accounting period, as shown later in the closing entries.

EXHIBIT 20–4

**Foto–Art Company
Western Branch
Income Statement
For the Month of May, 19XX**

Sales		$30,000
Cost of Goods Sold:		
Beginning Inventory	—	
Purchases	$15,000	
Shipments from Home Office	40,000	
Goods Available for Sale	$55,000	
Less: Ending Inventory	37,000	
Cost of Goods Sold		18,000
Gross Profit on Sales		$12,000
Operating Expenses:		
Selling Expense	$ 5,000	
General Expense	4,000	
Total Operating Expenses		9,000
Net Income		$ 3,000

EXHIBIT 20–5

Foto–Art Company
Western Branch
Balance Sheet
May 31, 19XX

Assets		Liabilities and Home Office Equity		
Cash	$16,000	Accounts Payable		$ 5,000
Accounts Receivable	6,000	Home Office	$51,000	
Inventory	37,000	Net Income	3,000	54,000
	$59,000			$59,000

Combined Financial Statements

At the end of the accounting period, when the various branches submit their financial statements (or alternatively, adjusted trial balances) to the home office, the data can be combined into a single set of statements for the whole enterprise. The worksheets on the following page provide a convenient vehicle for compiling and integrating the data for the company. In the illustration, the data for home office operations are assumed. Note that the reciprocal amounts of $40,000 representing shipments from the home office to the branch are eliminated and the accounts do not appear in the combined income statement. Likewise, the home office and branch office accounts, with a $54,000 balance, are eliminated when the combined balance sheet is prepared.

End-of-Period Procedures

We mentioned earlier that adjusting entries, if needed, would be recorded on the branch office records before financial statements are prepared. In our example, the only adjustment required is to record the ending inventory. The following adjusting entry is made:

May 31	Inventory	37,000	
	Income Summary		37,000
	To record the ending inventory.		

After financial statements are prepared, the following closing entries are recorded by the branch:

May 31	Sales	30,000	
	Income Summary		30,000
	To close the Sales account to the Income Summary account.		
31	Income Summary	55,000	
	Purchases		15,000
	Shipments from Home Office		40,000
	To close the Purchases and Shipments from Home Office accounts.		

EXHIBIT 20-6

Foto-Art Company
Income Statement Worksheet
Home Office and Western Branch
For the Month of May, 19XX

	Home Office	Western Branch	Eliminations	Combined Income Statement
Sales	$65,000	$30,000		$ 95,000
Cost of Goods Sold:				
Inventory, May 1	$38,000	—		$ 38,000
Purchases	70,000	$15,000		85,000
Shipments to Branch	(40,000)		$40,000	
Shipments from Home Office		40,000	(40,000)	
Goods Available for Sale	$68,000	$55,000		$123,000
Less: Inventory, May 31	28,000	37,000		65,000
Cost of Goods Sold	$40,000	$18,000		$ 58,000
Gross Profit on Sales	$25,000	$12,000		$ 37,000
Operating Expenses:				
Selling Expense	$ 9,000	$ 5,000		$ 14,000
General Expense	7,000	4,000		11,000
Total Operating Expenses	$16,000	$ 9,000		$ 25,000
Net Income	$ 9,000	$ 3,000		$ 12,000

Foto-Art Company
Balance Sheet Worksheet
Home Office and Western Branch
May 31, 19XX

	Home Office	Western Branch	Eliminations	Combined Balance Sheet
Assets				
Cash	$ 20,000	$16,000		$ 36,000
Accounts Receivable	36,000	6,000		42,000
Inventory	28,000	37,000		65,000
Western Branch	54,000		($54,000)	
Fixed Assets, Net of Accumulated Depreciation	80,000			80,000
Total Assets	$218,000	$59,000	($54,000)	$223,000
Liabilities and Stockholders' Equity				
Accounts Payable	$ 18,000	$ 5,000		$ 23,000
Accrued Liabilities	2,000			2,000
Home Office		54,000	($54,000)	
Common Stock	150,000			150,000
Retained Earnings	48,000			48,000
Total Liabilities and Stockholders' Equity	$218,000	$59,000	($54,000)	$223,000

31	Income Summary	9,000	
	Selling Expense		5,000
	General Expense		4,000

To close the operating expense accounts.

| 31 | Income Summary | 3,000 | |
| | Home Office | | 3,000 |

To close the Income Summary to the
Home Office account.

On May 31, the home office will make a corollary entry to the last entry shown above, to reflect the branch net income:

| May 31 | Western Branch | 3,000 | |
| | Net Income—Western Branch | | 3,000 |

To reflect net income of Western Branch.

In closing its records, the home office will close the account Net Income—Western Branch to its Income Summary account.

KEY POINTS TO REMEMBER

(1) Business segments may consist of organizational units (departments, branches, divisions, or subsidiaries) or areas of economic activity (industries, product lines, or markets). Accounting and reporting by segment are indispensable to management and are becoming more important to investors, creditors, and other outsiders.

(2) A segment may be (a) a profit center (generating both revenues and expenses), where the manager is responsible for the profitability of the segment, or (b) a cost (or expense) center, where the manager is responsible for staying within budgeted amounts of expense.

(3) Expenses incurred by, or for the benefit of, a segment are often called direct expenses; common expenses incurred for more than one segment are called indirect expenses. The latter expenses are often allocated to segments on some appropriate basis.

(4) Reporting for departments of a firm may be extended to one of three operating measures: gross profit, contribution to indirect expenses, or net income. When a net income measure is used, both direct and allocated indirect expenses are deducted from gross profit. When a contribution approach is used, only direct expenses are deducted from departmental gross profit.

(5) A firm with branches may operate under centralized accounting at the home office, with all operating data forwarded by branches for processing, or decentralized accounting, under which the branch keeps a complete set of records and reports periodically to the home office.

(6) Under decentralized branch accounting, the home office charges a Branch Office account with assets transferred to the branch. This account is similar to an investment or receivable account. The branch credits a reciprocal Home Office account, which is similar to an owners' equity account or a payable account. The branch closes its net income to this account. Periodically, the branch transfers amounts back to the home office, reducing the balances of the Branch Office and Home Office accounts.

QUESTIONS

20-1 How may business firms be segmented by (a) organizational units and (b) economic activity?

20-2 What is the source and nature of current requirements for reporting segmental data to parties outside the firm?

20-3 Distinguish between a *profit center* and a *cost (or expense) center.*

20-4 Distinguish between *direct expenses* and *indirect* or *common expenses.* Which are more likely to be controllable at the department level?

20-5 When a firm wishes to measure gross profit by department, what basic modifications are needed in the chart of accounts and records of original entry?

20-6 Suggest an allocation basis for each of the following common expenses of a departmentalized firm that uses a net income measure to determine the profitability of departments.
(a) Janitorial expense.
(b) Firm manager's salary.
(c) Utilities (heat, light, and air conditioning).
(d) Sales salaries.
(e) Uncollectible accounts.
(f) Property taxes.

20-7 What is meant by departmental contribution to indirect expenses? What advantages does this measure have over net income in measuring departmental performance?

20-8 Department H of a discount store shows a contribution to indirect expenses of $13,000 and a net loss of $8,000 (before taxes). The firm believes that discontinuance of Department H will not affect sales, gross profit, or direct expenses of other departments. If total indirect expenses remain unchanged, what effect will discontinuance of Department H have on the net income (before taxes) of the firm?

20-9 Department X of a firm has a gross profit of $80,000, representing 40% of net departmental sales. Direct departmental expenses are $60,000. Management believes that an increase of $7,000 in advertising coupled with a 5% average increase in sales prices will permit the physical volume of products sold to remain the same next period but improve the department's contribution to indirect expenses. If management's expectations are correct, what will be the effect on this contribution?

20-10 Department Y of a firm has a gross profit of $60,000, representing 40% of net departmental sales. Management believes that an increase of $15,000 in advertising will increase volume of product sold by 20%. Other direct departmental expenses are $40,000. What effect will this decision have on Department Y's contribution to indirect expenses?

20-11 Explain the major recordkeeping differences between centralized and decentralized branch accounting.

20-12 When branch accounting is decentralized, what is the nature of the Branch Office account on the home office books? What is the nature of the Home Office account on the branch books?

20-13 At the beginning of the year, the home office transferred $60,000 cash and $20,000 in supplies to establish a branch. During the period the branch earned $8,000. At the close of the period, the branch transferred $5,000 cash to the home office. When financial statements are prepared for the firm, what amount should be eliminated in the Branch Office and Home Office accounts?

20-14 What is the nature of the account Shipments to Branch on the home office books? What is the nature of the account Shipments from Home Office on the branch books? What disposition is made of these accounts at the close of the accounting period?

20-15 After the ending inventory was recorded and all revenues and expense accounts closed, the records of the Kaytown branch of Regional Shoe Stores, Inc. included the following account balances: Home Office, $42,500 (credit) and Income Summary, $14,200 (credit). Present journal entries to complete the closing of the branch books and any related entries in the home office records.

EXERCISES

20-16 Selected data for the Landon Company, which operates three departments, are given below.

	Dept. A	Dept. B	Dept. C
Inventory	$ 50,000	$ 90,000	$40,000
Equipment (average cost)	150,000	90,000	60,000
Payroll	270,000	240,000	90,000
Square feet of floor space	18,000	9,000	3,000

During the year, the company's common expenses included the following:

Depreciation on equipment	$18,000
Real estate taxes	12,000
Personal property taxes (on inventory and equipment)	7,200
Personnel department expenses	15,000

Using the most causally related bases, prepare a schedule allocating the common expenses to the three departments.

20-17 The Barbour Corporation has four departments, all of which appear to be profitable except Department 4. Operating data for the current year are as follows:

	Total	Depts. 1–3	Dept. 4
Sales	$800,000	$680,000	$120,000
Cost of Goods Sold	535,000	442,000	93,000
Gross Profit	$265,000	$238,000	$ 27,000
Direct Expenses	$130,000	$108,000	$ 17,000
Indirect Expenses	105,000	97,000	13,000
Total Expenses	$235,000	$205,000	$ 30,000
Net Income (Loss)	$ 30,000	$ 33,000	($ 3,000)

(a) Calculate the gross profit percentage for Departments 1–3 combined and for Department 4.

(b) Assuming that the operating data for next year will be the same as for the current year, what effect would elimination of Department 4 have on total firm net income? (Ignore the effect of income taxes.)

20–18 Operating results for Department B of the Bassock Company during the current year are as follows:

Sales	$180,000
Cost of Goods Sold	126,000
Gross Profit on Sales	$ 54,000
Direct Expenses	40,000
Indirect Expenses	22,000
Total Expenses	$ 62,000
Net Loss	($ 8,000)

If Department B could maintain the same physical volume of product sold, while raising selling prices an average of 15% and making an additional advertising expenditure of $15,000, what would be the effect on the department's net results (net income or net loss)? (Ignore income taxes in your calculations.)

20–19 Suppose that Department B in Exercise 20–18 could increase physical volume of product sold by 10% if it spent an additional $6,000 on advertising while leaving selling prices unchanged. What effect would this have on the department's net results (net income or net loss)? (Ignore income taxes in your calculations.)

20–20 Southtown Branch of Walker Tax Service, which has decentralized accounting records, was opened on July 1 of the current year and had the following transactions in July:

July 1 The home office transferred $5,000 cash and $12,000 in equipment to the branch.

15 The branch collected $4,000 in fees for services.

20 The branch paid $6,500 in operating expenses.

30 The home office allocated $1,800 of home office general expense to the branch.

31 The branch collected $6,000 in fees for services and sent $4,000 cash to the home office.

31 The branch recorded depreciation on equipment, $200. (Debit Operating Expenses.)

31   The branch closed its revenue and expense accounts, debiting Fee Revenue $10,000, crediting Operating Expenses $8,500, and crediting Income Summary $1,500.

31   The branch reported its net income of $1,500 to the home office.

Journalize the foregoing entries on the branch books and on the home office books.

20-21 Western Branch had a beginning balance of $28,000 in its Home Office account. During the current month, Western received $32,000 in merchandise shipments from the home office. At the close of the month, the home office informed the branch that its share of home office general expense was $3,800. After closing its records, Western Branch determined its net income to be $12,400. The branch then sent $8,000 cash to the home office.

(a) Give the entry to be made by the branch on receiving the $32,000 in merchandise from the home office.

(b) What amount would be in the Home Office account after all entries were made for the current month?

PROBLEMS

20-22 Beautifloor, Inc. retails floor coverings through two departments, Carpeting and Hard Covering (tile and linoleum). Operating information for the current year appears below.

	Carpeting Dept.	Hard Covering Dept.
Inventory, January 1	$ 25,000	$ 8,000
Inventory, December 31	20,000	12,000
Net Sales	320,000	200,000
Purchases	202,000	159,000
Purchases Returns	4,000	2,000
Purchases Discounts	2,000	1,000
Transportation In	7,000	4,000
Direct Departmental Expenses	48,000	21,000

Indirect operating expenses of the firm were $40,000.

REQUIRED

(a) Prepare a departmental income statement showing departmental contribution to indirect expenses and net income of the firm. Assume an overall effective income tax rate of 30%.

(b) Calculate the gross profit percentage for each department.

(c) If the indirect expenses were allocated 70% to the Carpeting Department and 30% to the Hard Covering Department, what would be the net income of each department after taxes?

20-23 The following information was obtained from the ledger of Baxter Candies, Inc. at the end of the current year:

Baxter Candies, Inc.
Trial Balance
December 31, 19XX

	Debit	Credit
Cash	$ 14,000	
Accounts Receivable (net)	52,000	
Inventory, December 31	60,000	
Equipment and Fixtures (net)	180,000	
Accounts Payable		$ 36,000
Common Stock		150,000
Retained Earnings		60,000
Sales—Department X		280,000
Sales—Department Y		120,000
Cost of Goods Sold—Department X	140,000	
Cost of Goods Sold—Department Y	72,000	
Sales Salaries Expense	64,000	
Advertising Expense	14,000	
Insurance Expense (on merchandise)	8,000	
Uncollectible Accounts Expense	3,000	
Occupancy Expense	12,000	
Office and Other Administrative Expense	27,000	
	$646,000	$646,000

The firm analyzes its operating expenses at the end of each period in order to prepare an income statement that will exhibit net income by department. From payroll records, advertising copy, and other records, the following tabulation was obtained:

	Direct Expense Dept. X	Direct Expense Dept. Y	Indirect Expense	Allocation Basis for Indirect Expense
Sales Salaries Expense	$49,000	$15,000		
Advertising Expense	6,000	2,000	$ 6,000	Relative sales
Insurance Expense	5,000	3,000		
Uncollectible Accounts Expense	2,000	1,000		
Occupancy Expense			12,000	Floor space
Office and Other Administrative Expense	4,000	3,000	20,000	6 to 4 ratio (X to Y)

Department X occupies 10,000 square feet of floor space and Department Y, 5,000 square feet. Indirect expenses should be allocated to departments as indicated above.

REQUIRED

Prepare a departmental income statement showing net income by department. Assume an overall effective income tax rate of 35%.

20-24 Mallory's is a retail store with eight departments including a garden department, which has been operating at a loss. The following condensed income statement gives the latest year's operating results.

	Garden Department	All Other Departments
Sales	$140,000	$600,000
Cost of Goods Sold	84,000	400,000
Gross Profit	$ 56,000	$200,000
Direct Expenses	$ 45,000	$ 70,000
Indirect Expenses	20,000	80,000
Total Expenses	$ 65,000	$150,000
Net Income (Loss)	($ 9,000)	$ 50,000

REQUIRED

(a) Calculate the gross profit percentage for the garden department and for the other departments as a group.

(b) Suppose that if the garden department were discontinued, the space occupied could be rented to an outside firm for $6,000 per year, and the common (indirect) expenses of the firm would be reduced by $3,000. What effect would this action have on the firm's net income? (Ignore income taxes in your calculations.)

(c) It is estimated that if an additional $3,000 were spent on advertising, prices in the garden center could be raised an average of 5% without a change in physical volume of products sold. What effect would this have on operating results of the garden department? (Again, ignore income taxes in your calculations.)

20-25 Certain operating information is shown below for the Carbondale Department Store:

	Dept. A	Dept. B	All Other Departments
Sales	$180,000	$240,000	$500,000
Direct Expenses	30,000	46,000	160,000
Indirect Expenses	30,000	35,000	65,000
Gross Profit Percentage	30%	40%	50%

The managers are disappointed with the operating results of Department A. They do not believe that competition will permit raising prices; however, they believe that spending $6,000 more for promoting this department's products will increase the physical volume of products sold by 20%.

An alternative is to discontinue Department A and use the space to expand Department B. It is believed that Department B's physical volume of products sold can thus be increased 37.5%. Special sales personnel are needed, however, and Department B's direct expenses would increase by $20,000. Neither alternative would appreciably affect the total indirect departmental expense.

REQUIRED

(a) Calculate the contribution now being made to indirect expenses by Department A, by Department B, and by the combination of other departments.

(b) Which of the two alternatives should management choose: increase promotional outlays for Department A, or discontinue Department A and expand Department B? Support your answer with calculations.

20-26 Davis, Inc., which operates a large music store in Madison, Wisconsin, made arrangements in May of the current year to open a branch in Green Bay.

Recordkeeping for the branch will be decentralized. A summary of the branch's transactions for May is given below.

May 1 The Madison store transferred $15,000 cash and $25,000 in merchandise to the Green Bay branch.
     3 Purchased $24,000 in merchandise on account from various dealers.
    10 Paid $6,000 on accounts payable.
    15 Sales to date: cash, $8,000; on account, $14,000.
    18 Collections on account from customers were $4,500.
    20 Selling expenses for the branch were $3,000 and general expenses were $2,000; of the total, $1,800 was on account and the remainder paid in cash.
    25 Sent $10,000 cash to Madison store.
    30 Sales during the last half of the month: cash, $6,000; on account, $12,000.

REQUIRED

(a) Journalize the May transactions on the books of the Green Bay branch.
(b) Make the necessary adjusting and closing entries on the Green Bay branch records, assuming that the May 31 inventory is $28,000.
(c) Journalize the May transactions requiring entries on the books of the Madison home office, including the entry to record the net income of the branch.
(d) State the balance that will appear in the Home Office account in the Green Bay branch's ledger on May 31.

20-27 The reciprocal accounts of the home office and branch operations of Value Paint Stores as they appear near the end of the accounting year are shown below.

Branch Account
(Home Office records)

Date	Explanation	Debit	Credit	Balance
11/30	Balance			78,200
12/5	Merchandise shipped	15,400		93,600
12/28	Equipment sent	500		94,100

Home Office
(Branch records)

Date	Explanation	Debit	Credit	Balance
11/30	Balance			78,200
12/5	Merchandise received		14,500	92,700
12/31	Net income		8,400	101,100
12/31	Cash remitted	6,000		94,100

REQUIRED

(a) Review the above accounts in terms of any needed updating and the appropriateness of their ending balances. If you discover any apparent bookkeeping errors, assume that the home office records are correct. Prepare any needed adjustments in journal entry form.

(b) Prepare a brief analysis leading to what you consider to be the correct end-of-year balances for these accounts.

(c) What eliminating entry would be appropriate on a worksheet used to prepare combined balance sheets for the home office and the branch?

ALTERNATE PROBLEMS

20-22A Stammond, Inc., a retail store, has two departments, Appliances and Furniture. Operating information for the current year appears below.

	Appliance Dept.	Furniture Dept.
Inventory, January 1	$ 60,000	$ 45,000
Inventory, December 31	37,800	24,000
Net Sales	560,000	380,000
Purchases	320,000	240,000
Purchases Discounts	4,000	3,000
Transportation In	9,000	8,000
Direct Departmental Expenses	99,800	41,000

Indirect operating expenses of the firm were $90,000.

REQUIRED

(a) Prepare a departmental income statement showing departmental contribution to indirect expenses and net income of the firm. Assume an overall effective income tax rate of 40%.

(b) Calculate the gross profit percentage for each department.

(c) If the indirect expenses were allocated 60% to the Appliance Department and 40% to the Furniture Department, what would be the net income of each department after taxes?

20-23A The following information was obtained from the ledger of Patton, Inc. at the end of the current year:

Patton, Inc.
Trial Balance
December 31, 19XX

	Debit	Credit
Cash	$ 18,000	
Accounts Receivable (net)	70,000	
Inventory, December 31	45,000	
Equipment and Fixtures (net)	97,000	
Accounts Payable		$ 34,000
Common Stock		120,000
Retained Earnings		30,000
Sales—Department A		360,000
Sales—Department B		140,000
Cost of Goods Sold—Department A	216,000	
Cost of Goods Sold—Department B	70,000	

Sales Salaries Expense	74,000	
Advertising Expense	31,000	
Insurance Expense (on merchandise)	10,000	
Uncollectible Accounts Expense	3,000	
Occupancy Expense	16,000	
Office and Other Administrative Expense	34,000	
	$684,000	$684,000

Analysis of operating expenses at the end of each period enables the firm to prepare a departmental income statement. Analysis of payroll records, advertising copy, and other documents permitted the preparation of the following tabulation:

	Direct Expense Dept. A	Dept. B	Indirect Expense	Allocation Basis for Indirect Expenses
Sales Salaries Expense	$48,000	$20,000	$ 6,000	Equally
Advertising Expense	15,000	6,000	10,000	Relative sales
Insurance Expense	8,000	2,000		
Occupancy Expense			16,000	Floor space
Uncollectible Accounts Expense	2,000	1,000		
Office and Other Administrative Expense	17,000	9,000	8,000	3 to 1 ratio (A to B)

Department A occupies 5,000 square feet of floor space, while Department B has 3,000 square feet. Indirect expenses should be allocated to departments as indicated above.

REQUIRED
Prepare a departmental income statement showing net income by department. Assume an overall effective income tax rate of 30%.

20–24A The management of Richmond's Department Store is concerned about the operation of its sporting goods department, which has not been very successful. The following condensed income statement gives the latest year's results:

	Sporting Goods Department	All Other Departments
Sales	$340,000	$1,700,000
Cost of Goods Sold	255,000	1,105,000
Gross Profit	$ 85,000	$ 595,000
Direct Expenses	$ 46,000	$ 237,000
Indirect Expenses	32,000	171,000
Total Expenses	$ 78,000	$ 408,000
Net Income	$ 7,000	$ 187,000

REQUIRED
(a) Calculate the gross profit percentage for the Sporting Goods department and for the other departments as a group.
(b) Calculate the percentage return of net income on sales for the Sporting Goods department and for the other departments as a group, ignoring the effect of income taxes.

(c) It is estimated that if an additional $10,000 are spent on promotion of sporting goods, average prices can be raised 5% without affecting physical volume of goods sold. What effect would this have on the operating results of the Sporting Goods department? (Ignore the effect of income taxes.)

(d) Alternatively, it is estimated that physical volume of goods sold can be increased 6% if an additional $6,000 are spent on promotion of sporting goods and prices are not increased. Assuming that operating expenses remain the same, what effect would this have on the operating results of the Sporting Goods department? (Ignore the effect of income taxes.)

20-26A Lorn's, Inc. operates a store selling men's shoes, hosiery, and other men's furnishings in Chicago. The firm opened a branch in Rockford, Illinois, on June 1 of the current year. A summary of the branch's June transactions is given below:

June 1   The home office in Chicago transferred $20,000 cash and $70,000 merchandise to the Rockford branch.

12   Purchased $14,000 merchandise on account from various dealers.

15   Sales to date: cash, $11,000; on account, $9,000.

19   Collected $4,000 on account from customers.

21   Paid $10,000 on accounts payable.

25   Selling expenses for the branch were $13,200 and general expenses were $2,100; of the total, $3,800 was on account and the remainder paid in cash.

26   The home office informed the Rockford branch that $2,000 home office general expense was being allocated to the branch.

30   Sales during the last half of the month: cash, $14,000; on account, $18,000.

REQUIRED

(a) Journalize the June transactions on the books of the Rockford branch.

(b) Make the necessary adjusting and closing entries on the Rockford branch records, assuming that the June 30 inventory is $55,000.

(c) Journalize the June transactions requiring entries on the books of the Chicago home office, including the entry to record the net income of the branch.

(d) Prepare an analysis of the balance that will appear in the Home Office account in the Rockford branch's ledger on June 30.

20-27A The reciprocal accounts of the home office and branch operations of Volume Paint Stores as they appear near the end of the accounting year follow.

Branch Account
(Home Office records)

Date	Explanation	Debit	Credit	Balance
11/30	Balance			56,400
12/5	Merchandise shipped	22,300		78,700
12/28	Equipment sent	3,700		82,400

Home Office
(Branch records)

Date	Explanation	Debit	Credit	Balance
11/30	Balance			56,400
12/5	Merchandise received		23,200	79,600
12/31	Net income		6,800	86,400
12/31	Cash remitted	3,000		82,400

REQUIRED

(a) Review the above accounts in terms of any needed updating and the appropriateness of their ending balances. If you discover any apparent bookkeeping errors, assume that the home office records are correct. Prepare any needed adjustments in journal entry form.

(b) Prepare a brief analysis leading to what you consider to be the correct end-of-year balances for these accounts.

(c) What eliminating entry would be appropriate on a worksheet used to prepare combined balance sheets for the home office and the branch?

BUSINESS DECISION PROBLEM

Ross Automotive, Inc. is a franchised distributor for the Excel line of automobile tires and batteries. Tom Tabor and Bob Benson currently are managing the firm as part of an agreement providing that they may buy the business five years from now from the firm's founder and only stockholder, Fred Folder. During this period, Tom and Bob draw moderate salaries and share a bonus fund defined as 40% of net income before bonuses and income taxes. Division of the bonus fund between Tom and Bob is based on the ratio of net dollar sales of tires and batteries, recognizing that Tom "runs the tire business" and Bob "runs the battery business."

The following statement summarizes the operating year just ended on which the bonus computation is to be based.

Net Sales:		
Tires	$630,000	
Batteries	270,000	$900,000
Cost of Goods Sold:		
Tires	$480,000	
Batteries	160,000	$640,000
Gross Profit		$260,000
Operating Expenses:		
Installation Labor	42,000	
Sales Salaries	39,000	
Sales Commissions	27,000	
Advertising	18,000	
Building Occupancy	20,000	
Administration	64,000	210,000
Net Income before Bonuses and Income Taxes		$ 50,000

(a) Using the above data, compute the agreed-on bonus for Tom and Bob.

(b) After seeing the results of your computations in (a) above, Bob questions the equity of the planned bonus distribution. While admitting that tires account for a majority of total revenues, he suspects that the sales figures do not reflect the real generation of profit by the tire and the battery segments of the business. Because of Bob's concern, you agree to prepare a "departmental" operating statement showing, by product line, sales, cost of goods sold, gross profit, total direct expenses, contribution to indirect expenses, allocation of indirect expenses, and net income before bonuses and income taxes. (Round all final amounts to the nearest dollar.)

After studying the records and consulting the various personnel involved, you determine the following regarding this year's expenses:

Installation labor represents four tire mounters, each earning $8,000 per year, and one battery installer earning $10,000 per year.

Sales salaries represent three tire and one battery salespersons, each earning a base salary of $500 per month. A fifth person, who serves as sales manager, earns $15,000 per year. It is agreed that two-thirds of her salary should be allocated to tire operations because tire customers often require extra credit approval procedures.

Sales commission rates are 1% on all sales for the sales manager and 2% on sales for each of the tire and battery salespersons.

Advertising expense involves separate tire ads costing $10,000 and battery ads costing $2,000. Ads featuring both tires and batteries cost $6,000, which is to be allocated on the basis of relative dollar sales volumes.

Building occupancy expense is allocated on the basis of the total square footage of space used for each function:

	Tires	Batteries
Storage and Installation Space	50,000	20,000
Sales Areas	15,000	5,000
Administration	5,000	5,000

Administrative expense includes Tom's and Bob's salaries of $20,000 each. The balance represents general administrative expenses, which are to be allocated on the basis of relative cost of goods sold in that this would represent some measure of the amount of goods handled during the period.

(c) Calculate the bonus division based on: (1) relative contributions of each product line to indirect expenses and (2) relative net incomes before bonuses and income taxes. Also, briefly justify what you consider to be the most equitable basis for dividing the bonus between Tom and Bob.

(d) After seeing your presentation in (b) above, Tom admits that differences in contribution and profit rates result mostly from the very competitive nature of the tire business. To improve the situation, Tom suggests two plans: (1) a direct mail advertising campaign costing $7,500 estimated to increase tire sales by 10%; and (2) a television ad series stressing the quality of Excel tires, which would cost $25,000 and permit a 5% sales price increase on tires while maintaining the same unit volume of sales. Except for sales commission, changes in operating expenses would be negligible. Calculate the relative attractiveness of each of these plans and recommend one.

21
Accounting for Manufacturing Operations

> **Inventing is a combination of brains and materials.**
> **The more brains you use, the less materials you need.**
>
> CHARLES F. KETTERING

So far, our discussion of accounting systems and procedures has related mainly to merchandising firms and firms selling services. Another important segment of industry comprises manufacturing firms.

Although the accounting principles and techniques described earlier are applicable to manufacturing firms, accounting for manufacturing operations tends to be more complex because additional activities are involved in producing a product than in simply purchasing a product for resale as in a merchandising firm. Because specific purchase prices are known, the cost of goods purchased for resale is relatively easy to determine. In manufacturing operations, however, the costs of all inputs must be accumulated and allocated to calculate the cost of the units produced. In addition, manufacturers must account for the buying, selling, and administrative activities that are common to other types of firms. These and other accounting problems related to manufacturing operations are considered in this and the two following chapters.

Manufacturing operations vary widely in complexity. The approach we have taken in this chapter to account for manufacturing activities represents the adaptation of a general accounting system to a relatively simple manufacturing operation using the periodic inventory method. No specific product costing system is involved. The two primary cost accounting systems, referred to as "job order costing" and "process costing," are considered in Chapters 22 and 23.

KEY CONCEPTS IN MANUFACTURING ACCOUNTING

Cost of Goods Manufactured

The primary difference between merchandising and manufacturing firms is that merchandising firms *buy* finished products to sell while manufacturers *make* the products they sell. This is apparent in the following comparative illustration of cost of goods sold for each:

Merchandising Firm		Manufacturing Firm	
Beginning Merchandise Inventory	$100	Beginning Finished Goods Inventory	$100
Add: Net Cost of Merchandise Purchases	400	Add: Cost of Goods Manufactured	400
Goods Available for Sale	$500	Goods Available for Sale	$500
Less: Ending Merchandise Inventory	200	Less: Ending Finished Goods Inventory	200
Cost of Goods Sold	$300	Cost of Goods Sold	$300

736

Note on the manufacturing firm's statement that Cost of Goods Manufactured corresponds to Net Cost of Merchandise Purchases on the merchandising firm's statement. In both cases, these amounts represent costs of finished goods ready for

FACTORIES IN SPACE

In spite of its remoteness, temperature extremes, and lack of oxygen, outer space may be the location for factories of the future.* The attraction of outer space for manufacturing activities stems primarily from the virtual absence of gravity and atmosphere. In the microgravity of space, weights would be reduced to a thousandth or even a millionth of what we experience on earth. Large quantities of materials could be lifted or moved with minuscule applications of force. Most important, manipulations of raw materials would be possible in the near zero gravity of space that are not possible on earth.

Space is a natural, almost perfect vacuum chamber. Atmospheric pressure 200 miles up is only ten billionths of that at sea level. With no atmosphere, there would be no wind, rain, or snow; nor would there be any rust or natural corrosion of building materials. Even more important for all chemically oriented production processes is the molecular purity provided by the vast natural vacuum chamber of space.

The revolutionary microintegrated circuits that are the heart of all new computers are made from silicon crystals. A single crystal the size of a child's fingernail can perform the computational function of 5,000 transistors or store 16,000 bits of randomly accessed data. The effectiveness of crystals is closely associated with their "smoothness," or internal uniformity. "Grown" in laboratories on earth, gravity causes these crystals to form unevenly, severely reducing the quality and yield of acceptably uniform crystals. Produced in a gravity-free space factory, such crystals would be of great uniformity and have vastly increased capacities for electronic microprocessing devices.

In space it will be possible to chemically isolate pure or near pure batches of our bodies' own cells, cell components, hormones, and enzymes. On earth, attempts to isolate or synthesize these materials are severely hampered by gravity, which causes convection currents within fluids and gaseous mixtures and results in impure or unpredictable mixes. Produced in space factories free of gravity, the purity and precision of these mixtures would be enhanced far beyond that currently possible on earth.

The utility of metals can be increased by isolating pure forms of a specific metal with a desired characteristic or by optimally combining two or more metals with desired properties. In molten states, heavier metals tend to settle and lighter metals tend to float, resulting in impurities or nonuniform alloys. In addition, at the required high temperatures, containers have a tendency to break down and contaminate the materials being processed. The microgravity environment of space-based metallurgical processes offers such possibilities as near pure metals; uniform mixes of metals into near perfect alloys; the uniform dispersion of gaseous bubbles throughout a metal to create a lightweight, super strong "foam" metal; the even dispersion of graphite lubricants in metals to create self-lubricating metal alloys, which would greatly extend the life of machine bearings; and the elimination of potentially contaminating containers through electromagnetic suspension of metals being processed (they would simply float in air).

By earthbound standards, space factories may be quite costly, and no doubt environmental hazards are yet to be discovered and dealt with. The accounting problems related to these exotic assets, processes, and products—product costing, depreciation and amortization periods, and income recognition patterns—provide a fascinating challenge to those who will someday account for factories in space . . . today's accounting students.

*For a fascinating description of these prospects, see "Industry's New Frontier in Space," Fortune, January 29, 1979, p. 77, and "Space Will Be the Next Big Construction Site," Fortune, February 26, 1979, p. 63.

resale. The merchandising firm bought its goods in their finished state and does not have the problem of determining their cost. The manufacturing firm, however, must account for the costs of acquiring and converting raw materials into finished products.

Product and Period Costs

Product costs are all costs necessary to bring a manufactured product to the point of completion. Thus, all the costs of factory materials and labor, as well as such other factory costs as utilities, depreciation, insurance, and repairs are accumulated and incorporated into the total cost of the products manufactured.

Earlier, when accounting for service and merchandising organizations, amounts for such items as wages, salaries, depreciation, and utilities were shown as expense and deducted from revenue. In manufacturing accounting, however, all such "expenses" for the factory are "capitalized" (treated as an asset) and become the cost of goods manufactured. Such costs represent additions to an inventory of finished goods (an asset) and are not deducted from revenues as cost of goods sold until the period in which the related products are sold to customers.

Period costs are those costs charged to expense in the period incurred. The benefits associated with such costs are considered to expire in that time period rather than being related to whatever product may have been produced in that period. Traditionally, nonfactory administrative expenses and selling expenses are considered period costs and are therefore expensed each period as they are incurred. Distinguishing between product and period costs is not always easy. Many functions in a manufacturing firm—such as higher level administrative salaries, personnel departments, and plant security departments—may benefit both factory and nonfactory activities. The costs of such functions are often allocated partly as product cost and partly as period cost, using allocation techniques similar to those illustrated in Chapter 20.

Based on the above concepts, income statements for manufacturing firms have the following form:

Sales		$500
Cost of Goods Sold (all factory costs)		300
Gross Profit on Sales		$200
Operating Expenses:		
Nonfactory Administrative Expenses	$50	
Selling Expenses	70	120
Net Income		$ 80

Multiple Inventory Accounts

Most manufacturing operations are continuous, so that at any point in time units of product are at various stages of completion. Consequently, at least three inventory accounts are usually maintained, as follows:

(1) The *Raw Materials Inventory* account reflects all factory materials that have been acquired but not yet placed into production. Various subunits such as

bearings or other parts may be included. (Even though these items may be finished products for the supplying firm, they are raw materials for the using firm.) Raw materials are carried at their net delivered cost.

(2) The *Work in Process Inventory* account reflects all factory costs associated with units of product that are begun but not completed at the date for which the firm's financial statements are prepared.

(3) The *Finished Goods Inventory* account reflects all factory costs associated with the units of product completely manufactured but not yet sold.

All three inventory accounts represent current assets. Accounting for changes in these accounts and their use in the financial statements are explained later in the chapter.

Manufacturing Cost Categories

Factory costs are usually accounted for in the following three categories:

(1) *Raw Materials* (often called *direct materials*) include all of the important raw materials or parts that will physically make up the product. Examples are steel sheets, electric motors, chemicals, and paint. (Small amounts of such incidental items as glue, lubricants, and polishing compounds are often accounted for as *factory supplies* and included under Factory Overhead.)

(2) *Direct Labor* includes the primary costs of employing workers who apply their skills directly to the manufacture of the product. Material cutters, assemblers, and painters are examples of such workers. (Costs of employing other workers who work indirectly on the product, such as supervisors, inspectors, material handlers, and machinery maintenance personnel, are considered *indirect labor* costs and included under Factory Overhead.)

(3) *Factory Overhead* (sometimes called *manufacturing overhead* or *factory burden*) includes *all* other factory costs not included in Raw Materials or Direct Labor. Factory Overhead may include:

Factory supplies used
Indirect factory labor
Insurance on factory
   building and equipment
Taxes on factory building
   and equipment
Repairs and maintenance on
   factory building and
   equipment

Factory utilities (heat,
   light, power)
Depreciation on factory
   building and equipment
Small tools consumed
Factory payroll taxes and
   other fringe benefits

As noted earlier, factory overhead specifically excludes nonfactory administrative expenses and selling expenses.

ASPECTS OF FINANCIAL STATEMENTS
UNIQUE TO MANUFACTURING ACCOUNTING

The aspects of financial statements unique to manufacturing accounting are concentrated in the income statement. These are explained and related to an illustrative manufacturing situation in the following sections.

Calculating Cost of Goods Manufactured

Stated simply, the cost of goods manufactured for an operating period is the sum of all costs necessary to bring the manufactured products to the point of completion. Specifically, it is the costs associated with (amounts are assumed):

Beginning Work in Process Inventory		$ 40,000
Add: Raw Materials (placed into production)	$200,000	
Direct Labor	300,000	
Factory Overhead	100,000	600,000
Total Manufacturing Costs		$640,000
Deduct: Ending Work in Process Inventory		20,000
Cost of Goods Manufactured		$620,000

Notice that the $620,000 Cost of Goods Manufactured represents the total manufacturing cost for the period, $640,000, adjusted for the change in work in process inventories. In other words, the cost of goods manufactured during this period is the cost of partially completed products carried forward from last period ($40,000) plus the total manufacturing cost of this period ($600,000) less the cost of partially completed products this period ($20,000) to be carried forward and completed in the next period. Remember that ending inventories of one period become the beginning inventories of the subsequent period.

Calculating Cost of Goods Sold and Net Income

As indicated earlier, computing the cost of goods sold for a manufacturer differs only in terminology from the computation for a merchandising firm. The inventory is more explicitly termed Finished Goods, and Cost of Goods Manufactured rather than Purchases is added to Finished Goods. Cost of Goods Sold is calculated as:

Beginning Finished Goods Inventory	$ 80,000
Add: Cost of Goods Manufactured	620,000
Total Finished Goods Available	$700,000
Less: Ending Finished Goods Inventory	100,000
Cost of Goods Sold	$600,000

Note that the $600,000 cost of goods sold figure is the cost of goods manufactured ($620,000) adjusted for the $20,000 change (increase, in this case) in Finished Goods Inventory. Quite logically, if during the period Finished Goods Inventory increases by $20,000 (from $80,000 to $100,000), then we must have sold $20,000 less than we manufactured. Also note that the cost of goods sold includes only factory costs; no nonfactory administrative expenses or selling expenses are involved. Instead, the cost of goods sold is deducted from sales revenues to generate a gross profit on sales from which nonfactory administrative expenses and selling expenses are deducted to determine the net income (or loss) for the period.

In Exhibit 21-1, we have used a typical plant layout (schematic floor plan) to illustrate the relationships that exist between manufacturing activities and the important aspects of accounting reports for manufacturers. All amounts are assumed. The balance sheet is not included because multiple inventories (raw materials, work in process, and finished goods) are the only important items distinguishing a balance sheet for a manufacturer.

On the left side of Exhibit 21-1 are listed, in their natural order, the various steps in the manufacturing process, starting with the acquisition of raw materials, through the manufacture and sale of finished goods, to the computation of net income for the period. The steps are keyed with circled numbers to the various activity areas of a hypothetical factory, which is diagramed in the center of Exhibit 21-1. The arrows associate these activity areas with the related amounts reflected in the cost of goods manufactured statement and the income statement.

Exhibit 21-1 indicates the sequence of manufacturing activities and the parallels that exist between the activity centers of a factory and the accounting reports for a manufacturing operation. Also highlighted is the separation of product costs (the accumulation of raw materials, direct labor, and factory overhead) from period costs (nonfactory administrative and selling expenses).

Exhibit 21-2 presents a formal version of the cost of goods manufactured statement and an income statement for a typical manufacturing firm. All amounts are assumed. Note that these statements correlate with those summarized in Exhibit 21-1 and reflect the generalizations made earlier regarding the accumulation of cost of raw materials, direct labor, and factory overhead as the cost of goods manufactured. In turn, the cost of goods manufactured is added to finished goods to determine the cost of goods sold and gross profit on sales. Finally, nonfactory administrative expenses and selling expenses are deducted to derive net income.

The cost of goods manufactured statement presents the several cost categories in the general order in which they are incurred. In a sense, the first costs incurred are the costs carried forward from the preceding period as beginning work in process. Next, raw materials used is determined (the beginning inventory plus the net delivered cost of raw materials purchased, less the ending raw materials inventory). The cost of direct labor follows, usually shown as a single figure. Factory overhead is then added as a list of all factory costs other than raw materials and direct labor. If the list of overhead costs is extensive, only the total factory overhead may be shown with reference made to a supporting schedule of factory overhead costs. Beginning work in process, raw materials used, direct labor, and factory overhead are added to determine total manufacturing costs. Finally, the ending work in process is deducted to derive cost of goods manufactured.

On the income statement of a manufacturing firm, the cost of goods sold is determined in much the same manner as for a merchandising concern—except that cost of goods manufactured, rather than merchandise purchases, represents

EXHIBIT 21–1
Relationships among Manufacturing Activities, Factory Layout, and Accounting Reports

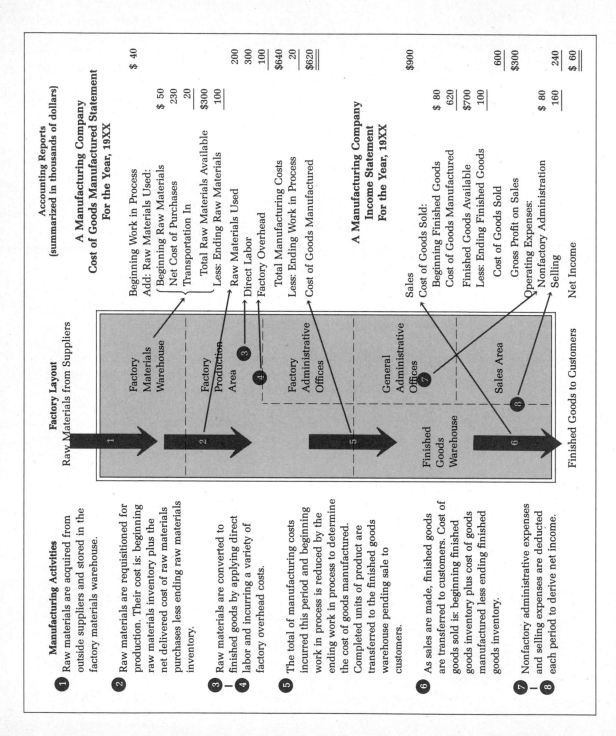

EXHIBIT 21-2

A Manufacturing Company
Cost of Goods Manufactured Statement
For the Year Ended December 31, 19XX

Beginning Work in Process Inventory		$ 40,000
Raw Materials:		
Beginning Raw Materials Inventory	$ 50,000	
Net Cost of Raw Materials Purchased	230,000	
Transportation on Raw Materials Purchased	20,000	
Cost of Raw Materials Available	$300,000	
Less: Ending Raw Materials Inventory	100,000	
Raw Materials Used		200,000
Direct Labor		300,000
Factory Overhead:		
Depreciation	$ 10,000	
Utilities	19,000	
Insurance	5,000	
Property Taxes	20,000	
Indirect Labor	30,000	
Factory Supplies Used	7,000	
Other Factory Overhead	9,000	
Total Factory Overhead		100,000
Total Manufacturing Cost		$640,000
Less: Ending Work in Process Inventory		20,000
Cost of Goods Manufactured		$620,000

A Manufacturing Company
Income Statement
For the Year Ended December 31, 19XX

Net Sales		$900,000
Cost of Goods Sold:		
Beginning Finished Goods Inventory	$ 80,000	
Cost of Goods Manufactured	620,000	
Goods Available for Sale	$700,000	
Less: Ending Finished Goods Inventory	100,000	
Cost of Goods Sold		600,000
Gross Profit on Sales		$300,000
Operating Expenses:		
Administrative Expenses	$ 80,000	
Selling Expenses	160,000	240,000
Net Income		$ 60,000
Earnings per Share of Capital Stock		$3

the addition to finished goods inventory. Gross profit on sales must be sufficient to absorb both nonfactory administrative expenses and selling expenses if there is to be any net income.

SPECIAL ACCOUNTS FOR MANUFACTURING

Many accounts appearing in the ledger of a manufacturing firm, such as Cash, Accounts Receivable, and Sales, are similar to those of service and merchandising firms. The unique aspects of manufacturing, however, have led to the use of several special accounts. Important among these are the Raw Materials Inventory, Raw Materials Purchases, Work in Process Inventory, Finished Goods Inventory, Factory Plant and Equipment, and Manufacturing Summary accounts. As explained later in this chapter, the Manufacturing Summary account is used to summarize the cost of goods manufactured during the end-of-period closing procedures (in much the same way as the Income Summary account is used to summarize periodic income for most firms).

Accounts Related to Raw Materials

When the periodic inventory method assumed in this chapter is used, accounting for the acquisition and use of raw materials is recorded in the four accounts appearing below. In each account an assumed normal balance amount and a brief description of the activities recorded are given.

Raw Materials Inventory	Transportation In
50,000 (The cost of unused raw materials as determined by a periodic physical inventory count)	20,000 (The specific amounts paid to have raw materials transported to the factory)

Raw Materials Purchases	Raw Materials Returns and Allowances
240,000 (The purchase price of raw materials acquired throughout this period)	10,000 (The cost of raw materials returned to suppliers and of any related cost adjustments)

Entries in the Raw Materials Inventory account are made only at the end of the period when a new ending physical inventory count is made. During the period, no entries are made to reflect the requisition of raw materials into production. Determining the ending raw materials inventory involves counting all units on hand, identifying an appropriate cost price per unit (perhaps from a recent purchase invoice or supply catalog), multiplying quantity by price, and combining all items for a total inventory figure.

The other three accounts are used throughout the period to record (1) purchasing raw materials, (2) related returns and adjustments, and (3) the costs of transporting raw materials purchases to the factory. In all cases, offsetting debits and credits are typically made to Accounts Payable or Cash. At the end of the accounting period, the balances of all purchases-related accounts are used to calculate the cost of goods manufactured and are adjusted through or closed to the Manufacturing Summary account as illustrated later in this chapter.

Work in Process Inventory Account

The Work in Process Inventory account reflects the costs of products that have been begun but are not completed at the end of the accounting period. All or some part of raw materials may have been added, but some portions of direct labor and factory overhead are yet to be applied. In a general accounting system using periodic inventory procedures, the amount of work in process is estimated at the end of the period, usually by a production supervisor or someone else familiar with the manufacturing process. An illustrative calculation using assumed amounts appears below.

Estimated Cost of Work in Process Inventory

	Estimated Cost per Finished Unit of Product	Average Proportion Applied	
Raw Materials:			
Material A (wood)	$2	100%	$ 2
Material B (paint)	4	25	1
Direct Labor	8	50	4
Factory Overhead	6	50	3
			$10
Number of Units in Ending Inventory		×	2,000
Estimated Cost of Ending Work in Process Inventory			$20,000

Estimating the ending work in process inventory typically involves: (1) estimating the amount of each manufacturing cost element associated with a finished unit of product, (2) multiplying each cost by an appropriate estimate of the average proportion applied, (3) summing the estimated costs for the various factors, and (4) multiplying by the number of units in the ending inventory. Once determined, the new work in process figure becomes the recorded amount of work in process for the end of the current period and the beginning of the subsequent period. Both the beginning and ending balances of Work in Process are used to calculate the cost of goods manufactured for the period. Adjusting for the increase or decrease in work in process inventory is illustrated later in the chapter.

Finished Goods Inventory

The balance in the Finished Goods Inventory account represents the recorded cost of finished products awaiting sale to customers. Using periodic inventory procedures, the ending finished goods inventory is determined by: (1) estimating the average cost per finished unit of product for each manufacturing cost element, (2) making a physical count of the unsold finished units of product on hand, (3) multiplying the units by the estimated total cost per unit, and (4) aggregating the total finished goods inventory cost. An illustrative calculation using assumed amounts follows.

Valuation of Finished Goods Inventory

	Raw Materials A	Raw Materials B	Direct Labor	Factory Overhead	Total Unit Cost	Units on Hand	Total Cost of Inventory
Product:							
101	$3	$—	$ 4	$3	$10	2,500	$ 25,000
102	4	2	8	6	20	3,000	60,000
103	3	1	12	9	25	600	15,000
Totals						6,100	$100,000

Notice that different amounts of each manufacturing cost may be applied to various products. Entries to the Finished Goods Inventory account occur only at the end of the accounting period when a new balance is determined. Both the beginning and ending balances of Finished Goods are involved in computing the cost of goods sold for the period. Adjusting entries for the change in Finished Goods Inventory are illustrated later in the chapter.

Plant and Equipment Accounts

Depending on their nature, manufacturing activities may involve extensive investments in factory buildings and production equipment. In a real sense, these assets are gradually consumed and their utility is transformed into the cost of producing the firm's products. Therefore, depreciation on plant and equipment is an important element of factory overhead. Periodic computations of depreciation are similar to those illustrated for long-term assets in Chapter 10. Should a firm rent or lease rather than own its productive facilities, such rental payments would be accounted for as factory overhead. When the investment in productive facilities is extensive and varied, a control account titled Plant and Equipment is often used with a subsidiary ledger to reflect the detailed balances for each specific building and type of equipment.

Manufacturing Summary Account

Manufacturing firms use both a Manufacturing Summary account and an Income Summary account. The Manufacturing Summary account, as its name implies, summarizes the total manufacturing costs for the period and determines the cost of goods manufactured. As is true for the Income Summary account, entries are made only during the closing procedures, and the account itself is closed at that time. Stated simply, the balance of the Manufacturing Summary account will equal the cost of goods manufactured for the period when: (1) all accounts for factory costs are closed to the Manufacturing Summary account, and (2) the Raw Materials Inventory and Work in Process Inventory accounts are adjusted through the Manufacturing Summary account (beginning balances entered as debits and ending balances entered as credits). The Manufacturing Summary and Income Summary accounts are illustrated in Exhibit 21–3 in T-account form, using the data from Exhibit 21–1 (individual entries are portrayed to emphasize cost flows).

Notice that before closing, the balances of these accounts agree with the related statement totals in Exhibit 21–1: Cost of goods manufactured is $620,000 and net income is $60,000. The balance of the Manufacturing Summary account comprises a series of entries reflecting: (1) debits for the manufacturing costs carried forward to this period as beginning raw materials and work in process inventories, and the other manufacturing costs incurred during this period, such as raw materials purchases, transportation in, direct labor, and factory overhead,

EXHIBIT 21–3

Manufacturing Summary

19XX				19XX			
Dec. 31	Work in Process Inventory (Beginning)	40,000		Dec. 31	Work in Process Inventory (Ending)	20,000	
31	Raw Materials Inventory (Beginning)	50,000		31	Raw Materials Inventory (Ending)	100,000	
31	Purchases of Raw Materials (net)	230,000		31	(To close to Income Summary)	620,000	
31	Transportation In	20,000					
31	Direct Labor	300,000					
31	Factory Overhead (total)	100,000					
		740,000				740,000	

Income Summary

19XX				19XX			
Dec. 31	Finished Goods Inventory (Beginning)	80,000		Dec. 31	Sales	900,000	
31	Cost of Goods Manufactured	620,000		31	Finished Goods Inventory (Ending)	100,000	
31	General Administrative Expenses (total)	80,000					
31	Selling Expenses (total)	160,000					
31	(To close to Retained Earnings)	60,000					
		1,000,000				1,000,000	

and (2) credits representing the ending raw materials and work in process inventories. In effect, we are deducting these amounts (because they are carried forward as costs of the subsequent manufacturing period). Had Raw Materials Returns and Allowances been involved in this illustration, the debit for purchases would have been for the gross amount of purchases and an additional credit would appear in the Manufacturing Summary account for Raw Materials Returns and Allowances. In turn, the Manufacturing Summary account is closed to the Income Summary, becoming an important factor in determining net income for the period.

Notice that the finished goods inventory is not part of the cost of goods manufactured. Rather, the beginning and ending finished goods inventory amounts appear, respectively, as a debit and a credit in the Income Summary account. This procedure properly adjusts the cost of goods manufactured for the change in finished goods so that the cost of goods sold can be determined. Use of both the Manufacturing Summary account and the Income Summary account is illustrated in the comprehensive example of manufacturing accounting appearing later in this chapter.

END-OF-PERIOD PROCEDURES
FOR A MANUFACTURING FIRM

Most end-of-period procedures for manufacturing firms are similar to those presented for other types of firms in Chapters 4 and 5. In the remainder of this chapter we present a comprehensive illustration of these procedures for a manufacturing firm, including preparation and use of the worksheet to adjust the general ledger accounts, preparation of financial statements from data on the worksheet, and procedures for closing the temporary accounts at year-end. The illustration is designed to highlight the unique aspects of manufacturing accounting.

Worksheet for a Manufacturing Firm

Remember from Chapter 4 that using a worksheet facilitates adjusting the general ledger accounts and preparing financial statements because

(1) It makes apparent in one location the balance of all general ledger account balances.

(2) It makes apparent the effects of any adjustment.

(3) It provides for grouping all adjusted account balances involved in preparing each financial statement.

(4) It provides evidence of the arithmetical accuracy of the computed net income.

Worksheets for manufacturing firms differ from those presented in Chapters 4 and 5 only in that an additional set of columns is provided for the accounts that make up the cost of goods manufactured statement, and, of course, that three, rather than one, inventory accounts are involved. Other basic aspects of the worksheet are similar for all firms:

(1) The unadjusted trial balance is transcribed from the general ledger to the first set of money columns.

(2) Appropriate adjustments are formulated in the second set of money columns.

(3) Unadjusted account balances and related adjustments are combined to derive adjusted balances for all accounts, which are then extended to the appropriate set of columns representing each major financial statement.

(4) Each set of statement columns is balanced in turn, to check the arithmetical accuracy of the worksheet.

Exhibit 21–4 presents the worksheet for Bass Manufacturing, Inc. for an accounting year ending on December 31, 19XX. Remember that in preparing monthly or quarterly financial statements, adjustments on the worksheets are not recorded and posted to the general ledger. When annual statements are prepared, however, both adjusting entries and closing entries are recorded in the general journal and posted to the general ledger. The adjusting entries for our end-of-year illustration are as follows (explanations are provided only for those adjustments unique to manufacturing accounting). The adjustments on the worksheet are keyed to the parenthetical numbers of general journal entries below.

(1)	Manufacturing Summary*	10,000	
	Manufacturing Summary*	6,000	
	Raw Materials Inventory		10,000
	Work in Process Inventory		6,000

To transfer beginning inventories of raw materials and work in process to the Manufacturing Summary account.

(2)	Raw Materials Inventory	18,000	
	Work in Process Inventory	8,000	
	Manufacturing Summary*		18,000
	Manufacturing Summary*		8,000

To record ending inventories of raw materials and work in process.

(3)	Income Summary	20,000	
	Finished Goods Inventory		20,000

To transfer beginning inventory of finished goods to the Income Summary account.

(4)	Finished Goods Inventory	26,000	
	Income Summary		26,000

To record the ending finished goods inventory.

*These entries would often be combined, but are shown separately for clarity.

EXHIBIT 21-4

Bass Manufacturing, Inc.
Manufacturing Worksheet
For the Year Ended December 31, 19XX

Account Titles	Trial Balance Debit	Trial Balance Credit	Adjustments Debit	Adjustments Credit	Cost of Goods Manufactured Debit	Cost of Goods Manufactured Credit	Income Statement Debit	Income Statement Credit	Balance Sheet Debit	Balance Sheet Credit
Cash	13,000								13,000	
Accounts Receivable	45,000								45,000	
Allowance for Uncollectible Accounts		1,000		[9] 9,000						10,000
Raw Materials Inventory	10,000		[2] 18,000	[1] 10,000					18,000	
Work in Process Inventory	6,000		[2] 8,000	[1] 6,000					8,000	
Finished Goods Inventory	20,000		[4] 26,000	[3] 20,000					26,000	
Factory Supplies on Hand	2,000		[10] 2,000						4,000	
Office Supplies on Hand	1,000		[11] 1,000						2,000	
Prepaid Insurance	4,000			[5] 3,000					1,000	
Machinery and Equipment	90,000								90,000	
Accumulated Depreciation—Machinery and Equipment		20,000		[7] 6,000						26,000
Accounts Payable		7,000								7,000
Long-term Notes Payable—9%		40,000								40,000
Common Stock—$10 Par Value		50,000								50,000
Retained Earnings		20,000								20,000
Dividends Declared	4,000								4,000	
Sales		450,000						450,000		
Raw Materials Purchases	120,000				120,000					
Raw Materials—Returns		6,000				6,000				
Transportation In	2,000				2,000					
Direct Labor	77,000		[6] 4,000		81,000					
Indirect Labor	43,000		[6] 3,000		46,000					
Utilities	20,000				16,000		4,000			
Repairs and Maintenance	10,000				8,000		2,000			

EXHIBIT 21-4 (continued)

Account Titles	Trial Balance Debit	Trial Balance Credit	Adjustments Debit	Adjustments Credit	Cost of Goods Manufactured Debit	Cost of Goods Manufactured Credit	Income Statement Debit	Income Statement Credit	Balance Sheet Debit	Balance Sheet Credit
Rental on Plant Facilities	30,000				24,000		6,000			
Rental on Furniture and Fixtures	10,000				8,000		2,000			
Factory Supplies Used	15,000			(10) 2,000	13,000					
Administrative Salaries	25,000				15,000		10,000			
Office Salaries	15,000		(6) 1,000				16,000			
Office Supplies Used	4,000			(11) 1,000			3,000			
Sales Salaries	16,000		(6) 2,000				18,000			
Advertising Expense	9,000						9,000			
Interest Expense	3,000		(8) 1,000				4,000			
	594,000	594,000								
Manufacturing Summary			(1) 10,000 (1) 6,000	(2) 18,000 (2) 8,000	10,000 6,000	18,000 8,000				
Income Summary			(4) 20,000	(3) 26,000			20,000	26,000		
Insurance			(5) 3,000		2,000		1,000			
Wages Payable				(6) 10,000						10,000
Depreciation—Machinery and Equipment			(7) 6,000		6,000					
Interest Payable				(8) 1,000						1,000
Uncollectible Accounts Expense			(9) 9,000				9,000			
Income Tax Expense			(12) 17,000				17,000			
Income Tax Payable				(12) 17,000						17,000
			137,000	137,000	357,000	32,000				
Cost of Goods Manufactured						325,000	325,000			
					357,000	357,000	446,000	476,000	211,000	181,000
Net Income							30,000			30,000
							476,000	476,000	211,000	211,000

Notice the effect of these adjusting entries. Amounts of beginning inventories are debited to the related summary accounts, and amounts of ending inventories are credited to the related summary accounts. Because both cost of goods manufactured and cost of goods sold are normally debit balances, these entries in effect add the beginning inventories and subtract the ending inventories, resulting in a proper adjustment whether the inventories increase or decrease during the period. Also, of course, the inventory accounts are updated to reflect their new balances.

Because the remaining adjustments parallel those of other firms, only the adjustment data are presented.

(5) Unexpired insurance, $1,000.
(6) Unpaid wages and salaries at year-end (by category): direct labor, $4,000; indirect labor, $3,000; office salaries, $1,000; and sales salaries, $2,000.
(7) Depreciation on machinery and equipment, $6,000.
(8) Accrued interest payable at year-end, $1,000.
(9) Uncollectible accounts expense is estimated at 2% of sales.
(10) Factory supplies on hand, $4,000.
(11) Office supplies on hand, $2,000.
(12) Estimated income taxes, $17,000.

Once the adjustments have been entered on the worksheet, the adjusted balance of each account is extended to the appropriate set of money columns. Notice that both the debit and credit amounts for each related inventory adjustment are extended to the cost of goods manufactured columns and the income statement columns. This worksheet technique places both the beginning and ending inventory figures (rather than only the net change) in each set of columns, thereby facilitating the necessary computations.

Allocation of Costs and Expenses

As mentioned earlier, the sharing of responsibilities or facilities by personnel in production, selling, and nonfactory administration often requires that the totals of certain expenses be allocated on some such rational basis as square feet of space used or number of persons involved. Our illustration assumes the following allocations:

Expense:	Total	Factory	Nonfactory Administration	Selling
Utilities	$ 20,000	$16,000	$ 2,000	$ 2,000
Repairs and Maintenance	10,000	8,000	1,000	1,000
Rental—Plant Facilities	30,000	24,000	3,000	3,000
Rental—Furniture and Fixtures	10,000	8,000	1,000	1,000
Administrative Salaries	25,000	15,000	8,000	2,000
Office Salaries	16,000	—	8,000	8,000
Insurance	3,000	2,000	—	1,000
	$114,000	$73,000	$23,000	$18,000

These allocations are reflected on the worksheet by extending the appropriate amounts to each set of columns. For example, $16,000 of the total utilities expense of $20,000 would be extended to the cost of goods manufactured columns and the other $4,000 to the income statement column. When preparing the income statement, the further division of the $4,000 between nonfactory administration and selling should be reflected.

After all other relevant amounts are extended, the cost of goods manufactured columns are added; the amount needed to balance them (a credit of $325,000) is the cost of goods manufactured figure for this period. The $325,000 credit needed to balance the cost of goods manufactured columns is then extended as a debit to the income statement columns. When these columns are added, the $30,000 debit needed to balance them represents net income for the period. The $30,000 is then extended as a credit to balance the balance sheet columns. When operating losses occur, the *credit* needed to balance the income statement columns is extended as a debit to balance the balance sheet columns. This completes the worksheet.

Preparation of Financial Statements

Properly completed, the worksheet contains all the data necessary to prepare the cost of goods manufactured statement, the income statement, the retained earnings statement, and the balance sheet. Exhibit 21–5 (appearing on pages 755 through 758) presents those statements for Bass Manufacturing, Inc. as they would be prepared from the data on the worksheet in Exhibit 21–4. Observe that the key income statement figures—cost of goods manufactured and net income—agree with the amounts needed to balance the related worksheet columns.

Closing Entries

The worksheet also provides all the data necessary to prepare closing entries for the temporary accounts at the end of the year. First, using a compound entry, the Manufacturing Summary account is debited for the total of all temporary accounts appearing in its debit column on the worksheet, and each of those accounts is credited for its respective balance. Then the Manufacturing Summary account is credited for the total of all temporary accounts appearing in its credit column of the worksheet and each of those is debited for its respective balance. After these entries are made, the balance of the Manufacturing Summary account is equal to the cost of goods manufactured, or $325,000. Entries are then made to close the Manufacturing Summary account, revenues, and expenses to the Income Summary account, which in turn is closed to Retained Earnings. Closing procedures are completed when the Dividends Declared account is closed to Retained Earnings. Following are the closing entries for Bass Manufacturing, Inc.:

Manufacturing Summary	341,000	
Raw Materials Purchases		120,000
Transportation In		2,000
Direct Labor		81,000
Indirect Labor		46,000
Utilities		16,000
Repairs and Maintenance		8,000
Rent on Plant Facilities		24,000

Rent on Furniture and Fixtures	8,000	
Factory Supplies Used	13,000	
Administrative Salaries	15,000	
Insurance	2,000	
Depreciation on Machinery and Equipment	6,000	

To close the temporary manufacturing accounts having debit balances to the Manufacturing Summary account.

Raw Materials Returns and Allowances	6,000	
Manufacturing Summary		6,000

To close the temporary manufacturing accounts having credit balances to the Manufacturing Summary account.

Income Summary	426,000	
Utilities		4,000
Repair and Maintenance		2,000
Rent on Plant Facilities		6,000
Rent on Furniture and Fixtures		2,000
Administrative Salaries		10,000
Office Salaries		16,000
Office Supplies Used		3,000
Sales Salaries		18,000
Advertising		9,000
Interest Expense		4,000
Insurance		1,000
Uncollectible Accounts Expense		9,000
Income Tax Expense		17,000
Manufacturing Summary		325,000

To close all expense accounts and the Manufacturing Summary account to the Income Summary account.

Sales	450,000	
Income Summary		450,000

To close Sales to the Income Summary account.

Income Summary	30,000	
Retained Earnings		30,000

To close the Income Summary account to Retained Earnings.

Retained Earnings	4,000	
Dividends Declared		4,000

To close the Dividends Declared account to Retained Earnings.

After the closing entries are recorded and posted, the general ledger reflects only the balances of those assets, liabilities, and owners' equity accounts that will be carried forward as beginning balances for the subsequent year.

PROBLEMS OF VALUING MANUFACTURING INVENTORIES

Because inventories frequently constitute a significant portion of the firm's total assets, their proper valuation is an important aspect of manufacturing accounting. A proper determination of periodic income depends on proper inventory valuation. Inventory errors affect reported income in corresponding amounts. Further,

EXHIBIT 21-5
Financial Statements of Bass Manufacturing, Inc.

Bass Manufacturing, Inc.
Cost of Goods Manufactured Statement
For the Year Ended December 31, 19XX

Beginning Work in Process Inventory		$ 6,000
Raw Materials Used:		
Beginning Raw Materials Inventory	$ 10,000	
Raw Materials Purchased (net)	114,000	
Transportation on Raw Materials	2,000	
Cost of Raw Materials Available	$126,000	
Less: Ending Raw Materials Inventory	18,000	
Cost of Raw Materials Used		108,000
Direct Labor		81,000
Factory Overhead:		
Indirect Labor	$ 46,000	
Utilities	16,000	
Repairs and Maintenance	8,000	
Rent on Plant Facilities	24,000	
Rent on Furniture and Fixtures	8,000	
Factory Supplies Used	13,000	
Administrative Salaries	15,000	
Insurance	2,000	
Depreciation on Machinery and Equipment	6,000	
Total Factory Overhead		138,000
Total Manufacturing Cost		$333,000
Less: Ending Work in Process Inventory		8,000
Cost of Goods Manufactured		$325,000

EXHIBIT 21–5 (continued)
Financial Statements of Bass Manufacturing, Inc.

Bass Manufacturing, Inc.
Income Statement
For the Year Ended December 31, 19XX

Net Sales			$450,000
Cost of Goods Sold:			
Beginning Finished Goods Inventory		$ 20,000	
Cost of Goods Manufactured		325,000	
Goods Available for Sale		$345,000	
Less: Ending Finished Goods Inventory		26,000	
Cost of Goods Sold			319,000
Gross Profit on Sales			$131,000
Operating Expenses:			
Nonfactory Administration:			
Utilities	$ 2,000		
Repairs and Maintenance	1,000		
Rent on Plant Facilities	3,000		
Rent on Furniture and Fixtures	1,000		
Administrative Salaries	8,000		
Office Salaries	8,000		
Uncollectible Accounts	9,000		
Total Nonfactory Administration		$ 32,000	
Selling:			
Utilities	$ 2,000		
Repairs and Maintenance	1,000		
Rent on Plant Facilities	3,000		
Rent on Furniture and Fixtures	1,000		
Administrative Salaries	2,000		
Office Salaries	8,000		
Insurance	1,000		
Office Supplies	3,000		
Sales Salaries	18,000		
Advertising	9,000		
Total Selling Expenses		48,000	
Total Operating Expenses			80,000
Income from Operations			$ 51,000
Less: Interest Expense			4,000
Income before Income Taxes			$ 47,000
Income Taxes			17,000
Net Income			$ 30,000
Earnings Per Share of Capital Stock			$6

EXHIBIT 21–5 (continued)
Financial Statements of Bass Manufacturing, Inc.

Bass Manufacturing, Inc.
Balance Sheet
At December 31, 19XX

Assets

Current Assets:		
Cash		$ 13,000
Accounts Receivable	$45,000	
Less: Allowance for Uncollectible Accounts	10,000	35,000
Inventories:		
Raw Materials	$18,000	
Work in Process	8,000	
Finished Goods	26,000	52,000
Prepaid Expenses:		
Factory Supplies on Hand	$ 4,000	
Office Supplies on Hand	2,000	
Prepaid Insurance	1,000	7,000
Total Current Assets		$107,000
Long-term Assets:		
Machinery and Equipment	$90,000	
Less: Accumulated Depreciation	26,000	64,000
Total Assets		$171,000

Liabilities and Stockholders' Equity

Current Liabilities:		
Accounts Payable		$ 7,000
Wages Payable		10,000
Interest Payable		1,000
Income Taxes Payable		17,000
Total Current Liabilities		$ 35,000
Long-term Notes Payable (9%, due 5 years hence)		40,000
Total Liabilities		$ 75,000
Stockholders' Equity:		
Common Stock, $10 Par Value, Authorized and Issued 5,000 Shares	$50,000	
Retained Earnings	46,000	96,000
Total Liabilities and Stockholders' Equity		$171,000

EXHIBIT 21–5 (continued)
Financial Statements of Bass Manufacturing, Inc.

Bass Manufacturing, Inc.	
Retained Earnings Statement	
For the Year Ended December 31, 19XX	
Retained Earnings, Beginning of Year	$20,000
Add: Net Income for Year	30,000
	$50,000
Less: Dividends Declared	4,000
Retained Earnings, End of Year	$46,000

unit cost values derived from inventory valuations often play a central role in production contract negotiations, product pricing decisions, and management's overall efforts to control production costs. Thus, an effective manufacturing operation depends on reliable accounting for product costs.

Valuing the materials inventory presents no unusual problems. Routine procedures are used to determine the physical quantity of each item on hand at the end of the period. Purchase prices, paid to or offered by suppliers, are typically available for pricing each item of the materials inventory. Thoroughness and accuracy in counting, pricing, and aggregating the total value of the inventory are essential.

By definition, valuing ending work in process inventories involves estimating the degree of completion of the specific units of product. In its simplest form, ending work in process inventory may consist of a single batch of products at a uniform stage of completion. In "assembly-line" operations, the ending work in process inventory may be a group of products at varying stages of completion, ranging from those units barely started to those nearing completion. When multiple products are involved, many combinations of partially finished products are possible. A meaningful determination of work in process inventory demands informed and consistent estimation of the degree of completion of work in process.

Knowledge of product design specifications and cost data relating to various production inputs are necessary to determine both work in process and finished goods inventories. The cost of raw materials and direct labor can often be related *directly* to each unit of product and is reasonably estimated as some normal or average quantity of materials or direct labor multiplied by some normal or average cost or rate for each factor. Factory overhead, however, can only be related *indirectly* to units of product. The appropriate amounts per unit of product for such costs as factory supervision, depreciation, utilities, and property taxes are not readily apparent. Most firms therefore assume that the amount of factory overhead to be applied to products is in proportion to some other known and important production variable such as direct labor hours or direct labor costs. A *factory overhead rate* is determined by dividing the total overhead cost by the total of the base used to apply overhead. For example, the cost of goods manufactured statement for Bass Manufacturing, Inc. (Exhibit 21–5) shows total direct labor costs of $81,000 and total factory overhead of $138,000. Thus, this firm might compute its factory overhead rate as:

$$\text{Factory Overhead Rate} = \frac{\text{Total Factory Overhead}}{\text{Total Direct Labor Cost}} = \frac{\$138,000}{\$\ 81,000} = 170\% \text{ of Direct Labor Cost}$$

From this factory overhead rate, an ending work in process inventory that involved—say, $5,000 of direct labor—would be assigned $8,500 (1.7 × $5,000) of factory overhead. The same approach would be used for valuing ending finished goods.

In manufacturing accounting, a general accounting system using the periodic inventory method may be satisfactory for small, stable, single-product firms. The limitations of this approach become critical, however, in more complex, multi-product manufacturing operations. When periodic inventory procedures are used, the amounts determined for raw materials used and cost of goods sold are really residual, or "plug," figures and offer little opportunity for management control. Also, periodic inventory procedures provide for income determination only at the end of the period when new ending inventories are taken, while management may need reliable current product cost data on a day-to-day basis. Because multiple products may involve widely varying types and amounts of materials, production techniques, and a variety of production routines in a series of departments, the complexities resulting from multiple products justify a more sophisticated approach to accounting for product costs. These realizations underlie the development of cost accounting systems using perpetual inventories. Cost accounting systems are discussed in Chapters 22 and 23.

KEY POINTS TO REMEMBER

(1) Product costs comprise all costs necessary to bring the manufactured product to the point of completion.

(2) Manufacturers have three inventory accounts—Raw Materials, Work in Process, and Finished Goods.

(3) Manufacturing costs are accounted for in three categories: (1) raw materials, (2) direct labor, and (3) factory overhead (all manufacturing costs other than raw materials and direct labor).

(4) In manufacturing accounting, all product costs—raw materials, direct labor, and factory overhead—are capitalized; that is, they become the cost of goods manufactured and represent additions to the asset finished goods inventory.

(5) Cost of goods manufactured equals the total of all manufacturing costs adjusted for the change in work in process inventory.

(6) Cost of goods sold equals cost of goods manufactured adjusted for the change in finished goods inventory.

(7) Neither cost of goods manufactured nor cost of goods sold includes nonfactory administrative expenses or selling expenses.

(8) Worksheets for manufacturing firms have an additional set of columns for the cost of goods manufactured.

(9) Closing procedures for manufacturers incorporate a Manufacturing Summary account into which are closed all temporary accounts related to the cost of goods manufactured. In turn, the Manufacturing Summary account is closed to the Income Summary account.

QUESTIONS

21-1 In what two important ways is accounting for a manufacturing firm more complex than accounting for a merchandising firm?

21-2 How are "product costs" accounted for differently from "period costs"? Give examples of each.

21-3 What is the basic format for the income statement of a manufacturing firm?

21-4 Name the three inventory accounts maintained by manufacturing firms and briefly describe the nature of each.

21-5 Name and briefly describe the three major categories used to account for manufacturing costs.

21-6 List six examples of factory overhead costs.

21-7 In what way are total manufacturing costs different from cost of goods manufactured?

21-8 If total manufacturing costs are $340,000 and beginning and ending work in process inventories are $20,000 and $10,000, respectively, what is the amount of cost of goods manufactured?

21-9 If beginning and ending finished goods inventories are $40,000 and $50,000, respectively, what is the cost of goods manufactured if the cost of goods sold is $300,000?

21-10 Identify and briefly describe the normal balance and typical entries in the four accounts usually maintained for the purchase and use of raw materials.

21-11 What information is necessary to estimate the ending work in process inventory? The ending finished goods inventory?

21-12 Briefly describe the nature and timing of the entries one would expect to see in the Manufacturing Summary account.

21-13 Briefly outline what might be considered the format of a worksheet for a manufacturing company. What four steps are followed to prepare such a worksheet?

21-14 "Preparation of a worksheet does not specifically affect the general ledger." Do you agree or disagree with this statement? Why?

21-15 Briefly explain the year-end closing procedures for a manufacturing firm.

21-16 In what important way is the assignment of factory overhead to the work in process and finished goods inventories different from the assignment of raw materials and direct labor costs? Briefly explain the approach that is widely used to assign factory overhead.

EXERCISES

21-17 The following account balances are available from the ledger of Davis Manufacturing Company:

	Beginning of Year	End of Year
Raw Materials Inventory	$20,000	$ 5,000
Work in Process Inventory	30,000	20,000
Finished Goods Inventory	40,000	35,000
Direct Labor		80,000
Raw Materials Purchases (net)		60,000
Indirect Labor		30,000
Depreciation—Factory		8,000
Factory Supplies Used		5,000
Repairs and Maintenance—Factory		7,000
Nonfactory Administration (total)		20,000
Selling Expenses (total)		15,000

Prepare a cost of goods manufactured statement for the current year.

21-18 Davis Manufacturing Company (see Exercise 21–17) sold 14,000 units of product for $20 each during the current year. Five thousand shares of capital stock are outstanding at year-end. Prepare an income statement for the year.

21-19 For each of the following unrelated columns of data, compute the cost of goods manufactured and the cost of goods sold.

	A	B	C
Selling Expense	$190	$ 320	$ 220
Factory Insurance	90	70	130
Nonfactory Administration	85	150	100
Ending Finished Goods	410	1,100	1,200
Factory Taxes	120	90	80
Raw Materials (beginning)	180	310	110
Direct Labor	900	700	2,300
Factory Maintenance	70	110	200
Raw Materials Purchased	400	620	440
Beginning Finished Goods	270	1,400	1,200
Increase (Decrease) in Work in Process	50	0	(230)
Factory Utilities	80	320	700
Factory Depreciation	200	900	600
Indirect Labor	320	200	1,200
Factory Supplies Used	140	180	360
Raw Materials (ending)	90	220	70

21-20 During the current year, Colfax Factories, Inc. recorded the following costs and expenses:

Raw Materials Used	$ 40,000
Direct Labor	100,000
Factory Supplies Used	20,000
Indirect Labor	30,000
Sales Commissions	15,000
Factory Supervision	25,000
Nonfactory Administration	10,000
Other Factory Overhead	5,000

Assume that Colfax assigns factory overhead on the basis of direct labor costs.
(a) Compute the factory overhead rate to be used.
(b) Indicate the total valuation that should be placed on the ending work in process inventory that has been assigned $4,000 of raw materials cost and $10,000 of direct labor cost.

21-21 Excello Manufacturing Company's accounting department has estimated that each completed unit of its product involves an average of 4 pounds of raw materials costing $2 per pound and 5 hours of direct labor costing $6 per hour. Factory overhead is assigned on the basis of total direct labor cost incurred. For the current year these were $72,000 and $120,000, respectively.
(a) Assuming that the ending finished goods inventory comprises 4,000 units, determine its proper accounting valuation.
(b) Assuming that the ending work in process inventory involves 800 units to which all raw materials have been added but for which only 60% of the direct labor has been applied, determine its proper accounting valuation.

21-22 The only product of May Manufacturers, Inc. is produced in a continuous process. At the end of the current year, the ending inventories of work in process and finished goods were as follows:

	Estimated Amounts Applied Per Unit		
	Raw Materials	Direct Labor	Total Units
Work in Process	$ 8	$10	2,000
Finished Goods	10	20	6,000

Assuming that factory overhead is assigned at the rate of 80% of direct labor cost, compute the cost of the ending work in process and finished goods inventories.

21-23 Using the following summarized data, prepare the compound entries (similar to those illustrated in the chapter) to adjust for related ending inventories and to close the temporary manufacturing accounts at year-end to the Manufacturing Summary and, in turn, to close the Manufacturing Summary to the Income Summary account.

	Beginning of Year	End of Year
Raw Materials Inventory	$8,000	$ 9,000
Work in Process Inventory	3,000	7,000
Raw Materials Purchases (net)		70,000
Direct Labor		90,000
Factory Overhead (total)		60,000
Nonfactory Administration (total)		25,000
Selling Expenses (total)		12,000

21-24 Following are the Cost of Goods Manufactured columns from a worksheet at the end of the current year for Ross Manufacturing, Inc. For simplicity, data are summarized and in amounts of not more than three digits.

	Cost of Goods Manufactured	
	Debit	Credit
Raw Materials Purchases	80	
Returns and Allowances—Raw Materials		5
Direct Labor	50	
Transportation In—Purchases	10	
Indirect Labor	20	
Factory Supervision	10	
Factory Utilities	8	
Factory Supplies Used	6	
Depreciation on Equipment	12	
Depreciation on Factory Building	16	
Other Factory Overhead	30	
Manufacturing Summary:		
Raw Materials Inventory	7	12
Work in Process Inventory	11	3
	260	20
Cost of Goods Manufactured		240
	260	260

Using these data, prepare a cost of goods manufactured statement for the current year.

PROBLEMS

21-25 Appearing below in alphabetical order are selected account balances taken from the completed year-end worksheet of the Excello Manufacturing Company:

Administrative Salaries*	$10,000	Raw Materials, Dec. 31	$ 6,000
Advertising and Promotion	12,000	Work in Process, Dec. 31	8,000
Depreciation—Machinery	7,000	Finished Goods, Dec. 31	13,000
Depreciation—Office Equipment*	5,000	Maintenance—Machinery	3,000
Depreciation—Sales Fixtures	4,000	Other Factory Overhead	9,000
Direct Labor	65,000	Other Selling Expenses	5,000
Factory Supervision	6,000	Raw Materials Purchases	30,000
Factory Supplies Used	6,000	Rent—Factory	4,000
Indirect Labor	5,000	Rent—Nonfactory Area*	15,000
Inventories:		Returns—Purchases	1,000
Raw Materials, Jan. 1	2,000	Sales	220,000
Work in Process, Jan. 1	3,000	Sales Salaries	10,000
Finished Goods, Jan. 1	18,000	Transportation In	4,000

*These amounts are to be allocated 40% to nonfactory administration and 60% to the sales department.

REQUIRED

Using the above data, prepare a cost of goods manufactured statement and an income statement for the current year (disregard income tax and earnings per share considerations).

21–26 The following journal entries were made to adjust the inventory amounts and to close the temporary manufacturing accounts of Brooks Factory, Inc. at year-end:

Manufacturing Summary	16,000	
Manufacturing Summary	9,000	
Raw Materials Inventory (beginning)		16,000
Work in Process (beginning)		9,000

To transfer beginning inventories of raw materials and work in process to the Manufacturing Summary account.

Raw Materials Inventory (ending)	24,000	
Work in Process (ending)	5,000	
Manufacturing Summary		24,000
Manufacturing Summary		5,000

To record the ending inventories of raw materials and work in process.

Manufacturing Summary	455,000	
Direct Labor		120,000
Indirect Labor		80,000
Transportation In		8,000
Depreciation—Factory		20,000
Depreciation—Equipment		15,000
Repairs and Maintenance—Factory		12,000
Factory Supplies Used		6,000
Other Factory Overhead		34,000
Raw Materials Purchases		160,000

To close temporary manufacturing accounts
having debit balances to Manufacturing
Summary account.

Returns and Allowances—Raw Materials	6,000	
Manufacturing Summary		6,000

To close temporary manufacturing accounts
having credit balances to the
Manufacturing Summary account.

REQUIRED
Using the above information, prepare a cost of goods manufactured statement
for the current year.

21-27 The data below relate to three independent production periods of Wade Manufacturing Company. Missing data are indicated by question marks.

	A	B	C
Raw Materials:			
Beginning Inventory	$ 20	$ 70	$ 40
Purchases	?	300	210
Ending Inventory	30	40	?
Total Used	150	?	190
Direct Labor	300	420	370
Factory Overhead:			
Factory Supplies Used	40	?	50
Indirect Labor	70	60	140
Other	?	80	160
Total Factory Overhead	230	210	?
Work in Process Inventories:			
Beginning	?	30	110
Ending	20	?	40
Finished Goods Inventories:			
Beginning	?	160	30
Ending	140	40	140
Cost of Goods Manufactured	720	?	?
Cost of Goods Sold	670	900	?

REQUIRED
Using the above data, calculate the cost of goods manufactured and cost of
goods sold. (It is suggested that you list in order the items appearing on the cost
of goods manufactured statement and the cost of goods sold computation, fill in
the known data, and from those calculate the missing amounts.)

21-28 The following data relate to estimating the ending work in process and finished
goods inventories of the Goode Manufacturing Company.

	Estimated Cost of Completed Unit of Product	Estimated Proportions Applied to Work in Process
Raw Materials:		
A	4 lb. @ $3/lb.	100%
B	1 lb. @ $8/lb.	50%
Direct Labor:		
Cutting	0.5 hr. @ $8/hr.	80%
Assembly	2 hr. @ $6/hr.	40%

For the manufacturing period, total direct labor was $120,000 and total factory overhead was $90,000. Factory overhead is assigned to products on the basis of this ratio.

REQUIRED
Using the above data, calculate the cost of (a) an ending finished goods inventory of 700 units, (b) an ending work in process inventory of 400 units.

21–29 The following balances appear in the cost of goods manufactured and the income statement columns of a worksheet prepared at December 31 for the current year's operations of the Bayside Corporation.

	Cost of Goods Manufactured		Income Statement	
	Debit	Credit	Debit	Credit
Sales				200,000
Raw Materials Purchases (net)	50,000			
Transportation In	2,000			
Direct Labor	58,000			
Indirect Labor	15,000			
Utilities	900			
Repairs and Maintenance	1,600			
Depreciation—Machinery	1,500			
Insurance	1,900			
Property Taxes	2,100			
Selling Expenses			23,000	
Administrative Expenses			17,000	
Income Tax Expense			4,400	
Manufacturing Summary:				
Raw Materials Inventory	14,000	11,000		
Work in Process Inventory	8,000	10,000		
Income Summary:				
Finished Goods Inventory	———	———	22,000	16,000
	155,000	21,000		
Cost of Goods Manufactured	———	134,000	134,000	———
	155,000	155,000	200,400	216,000
Net Income			15,600	———
			216,000	216,000

REQUIRED

(a) Prepare a cost of goods manufactured statement and an income statement for the Bayside Corporation. Assume that 4,000 shares of capital stock are outstanding at year-end.

(b) Prepare entries to adjust the inventories and to close the temporary manufacturing accounts, the Manufacturing Summary account, the revenue and expense accounts, and the Income Summary account.

21-30 Two inventors, organized as Ace, Inc., consult you regarding a planned new product. They have fairly good estimates of the cost of materials, labor, overhead, and other expenses involved but need to know how much they should charge for each unit in order to earn a before-tax profit in the first year that is equal to 10% of their estimated total long-term investment of $300,000.

A review of their plans indicates that each unit of the new product would require:

> *Raw Materials:*
> 2 lb. of a material costing $3 per pound
>
> *Direct Labor:*
> 1.5 hr. of a metal former's time at $4 per hour
> 0.5 hr. of an assembler's time at $6 per hour

Major items of production overhead would be $36,000 annual rent on a factory building, and $24,000 on machinery. Other production overhead is estimated at 100% of total direct labor costs. Nonfactory administrative expenses and selling expense are estimated to be 20% and 30%, respectively, of total sales revenues.

The consensus is that during the first year 9,000 units of product should be produced for selling and another 1,000 units for the next year's beginning inventory. Also, an extra 2,000 pounds of materials will be purchased as beginning inventory for the next year. Because of the nature of the manufacturing process, all units started must be completed, so work in process inventories would be negligible.

REQUIRED

(a) Incorporate the above data into a projected cost of goods manufactured statement and compute the unit production cost.

(b) Prepare a projected income statement (filling in the sales amount as the last item) that would provide for the target amount of profit.

(c) Rounded to the nearest dollar, what unit sales price should the inventors charge for the new product?

21-31 The trial balance for the Delbert Manufacturing Corporation at the end of the current year follows:

	Debit	Credit
Cash	$ 8,000	
Accounts Receivable	44,500	
Allowance for Uncollectible Accounts		$ 1,000
Raw Materials Inventory, January 1	28,000	
Work in Process Inventory, January 1	12,000	
Finished Goods Inventory, January 1	15,000	
Factory Machinery	140,000	
Accumulated Depreciation—Machinery		33,000
Factory Buildings	125,000	
Accumulated Depreciation—Factory Buildings		12,000
Land	20,000	
Accounts Payable		27,000
Long-term Notes Payable—8%		40,000
Common Stock—$200 Par (all outstanding)		200,000
Retained Earnings		30,000
Sales		300,000
Raw Materials Purchases	72,000	
Purchase Returns		4,000
Direct Labor	90,000	
Indirect Labor	22,000	
Utilities	3,500	
Repairs and Maintenance	2,800	
Property Taxes	3,200	
Selling Expenses (control account)	36,000	
Nonfactory Administrative Expenses (control account)	25,000	
	$647,000	$647,000

The following information is available for adjusting the accounts:
(1) Inventories at December 31 are: raw materials, $24,500; work in process, $14,000; and finished goods, $12,000.
(2) Accrued wages and salaries at December 31 are: direct labor, $1,200; indirect labor, $300; and selling salaries, $2,000.
(3) Annual amounts of depreciation to be recorded are: factory buildings, $5,000; machinery, $7,000.
(4) Accrued utilities payable at December 31 are: $300.
(5) Uncollectible accounts expense is: $\frac{1}{2}$% of sales. (Debit this expense to the control account for selling expenses.)
(6) Assume an income tax rate of 30% of income before taxes.

REQUIRED
(a) Prepare a manufacturing worksheet for the year. Assume that the utilities and property taxes apply entirely to manufacturing activities.
(b) Prepare a cost of goods manufactured statement and an income statement.
(c) Prepare a balance sheet.
(d) Prepare closing entries (similar to those illustrated in this chapter).

21-32 The trial balance of the Wilson Company at December 31 of the current year is given below, together with most of the worksheet adjustments. (Preparation of adjusting entries for inventories is part of the problem solution.)

	Trial Balance Debit	Trial Balance Credit	Adjustments Debit	Adjustments Credit
Cash	6,500			
Raw Materials Inventory, Jan. 1	10,500		(2) ?	(1) ?
Work in Process Inventory, Jan. 1	8,200		(2) ?	(1) ?
Finished Goods Inventory, Jan. 1	12,300		(4) ?	(3) ?
Prepaid Insurance	800			(5) 400
Factory Machinery	65,000			
Accumulated Depreciation— Factory Machinery		14,700		(6) 5,000
Unamortized Cost of Patents	12,000			(7) 900
Accounts Payable		17,000		
Common Stock—$100 Par Value		50,000		
Retained Earnings		13,300		
Dividends Declared	10,000			
Sales		182,000		
Raw Materials Purchases (net)	43,000			
Direct Labor	52,000		(8) 1,200	
Indirect Labor	18,000		(8) 300	
Utilities	2,600			
Repairs and Maintenance—Factory	1,100			
Rent—Buildings	5,000			
Sales Salaries Expense	14,000			
Advertising Expense	4,000			
Nonfactory Administrative Expense	12,000			
	277,000	277,000		
Manufacturing Summary			(1) ?	(2) ?
			(1) ?	(2) ?
Income Summary			(3) ?	(4) ?
Insurance—Factory			(5) 400	
Depreciation—Machinery			(6) 5,000	
Amortization of Patents			(7) 900	
Wages Payable				(8) 1,500
Income Tax Expense			(9) 5,500	
Income Tax Payable				(9) 5,500
			?	?

Additional information:
(1) Of the total rent on buildings, $4,500 is for the factory; the remainder is nonfactory administrative expense.
(2) Of the total utilities paid, $2,000 is for the factory; the remainder is nonfactory administrative expense.

(3) December 31 inventories are: raw materials, $12,000; work in process, $7,000; and finished goods, $11,000.

(4) Patent amortization applies to factory operations.

REQUIRED

(a) Complete the manufacturing worksheet.

(b) Prepare a cost of goods manufactured statement and an income statement.

(c) Prepare closing entries similar to those illustrated in this chapter.

ALTERNATE PROBLEMS

21-25A Selected account balances taken from the completed year-end worksheet of the Exuma Manufacturing Company are presented below in alphabetical order.

Administrative Salaries*	$18,000	Raw Materials, Dec. 31	$ 16,000
Advertising and Promotion	22,000	Work in Process, Dec. 31	11,000
Depreciation—Machinery	12,000	Finished Goods, Dec. 31	15,000
Depreciation—Office Equipment*	10,000	Maintenance—Machinery	10,000
Depreciation—Sales Fixtures	7,000	Other Factory Overhead	6,000
Direct Labor	90,000	Other Selling Expenses	7,000
Factory Supervision	8,000	Raw Materials Purchases	60,000
Factory Supplies Used	5,000	Rent—Factory	14,000
Indirect Labor	11,000	Rent—Nonfactory Area*	12,000
Inventories:		Returns—Purchases	2,000
Raw Materials, Jan. 1	5,000	Sales	300,000
Work in Process, Jan. 1	7,000	Sales Salaries	14,000
Finished Goods, Jan. 1	30,000	Transportation In	3,000

*These amounts are to be allocated 50% to Nonfactory Administration and 50% to the sales department.

REQUIRED

Using the above data, prepare a cost of goods manufactured statement and an income statement for the current year (disregard considerations of income tax and earnings per share).

21-28A The following data relate to estimating the ending work in process and finished goods inventories of the Grand Manufacturing Company.

	Estimated Cost of Completed Unit of Product	Estimated Proportions Applied to Work in Process
Raw Materials:		
A	2 lb. @ $6/lb.	100%
B	2 lb. @ $5/lb.	60%
Direct Labor:		
Cutting	2.5 hr. @ $6/hr.	50%
Assembly	2 hr. @ $5/hr.	25%

For the manufacturing period, total direct labor was $240,000 and total factory overhead was $384,000. Factory overhead is assigned to products on the basis of this ratio.

REQUIRED
Using the above data, calculate the cost of (a) an ending finished goods inventory of 900 units. (b) an ending work in process inventory of 600 units.

21-29A The following balances appear in the Cost of Goods Manufactured and the Income Statement columns of a worksheet prepared at December 31 for the current year's operations of the Blandel Corporation.

	Cost of Goods Manufactured		Income Statement	
	Debit	Credit	Debit	Credit
Sales				280,000
Raw Materials Purchases (net)	80,000			
Transportation In	5,000			
Direct Labor	50,000			
Indirect Labor	22,000			
Utilities	3,000			
Repairs and Maintenance	4,000			
Depreciation—Machinery	1,500			
Insurance	1,000			
Property Taxes	2,500			
Selling Expenses			18,000	
Administrative Expenses			12,000	
Income Tax Expense			30,000	
Manufacturing Summary:				
Raw Materials Inventory	9,000	13,000		
Work in Process Inventory	6,000	4,000		
Income Summary:				
Finished Goods Inventory			28,000	15,000
	184,000	17,000		
Cost of Goods Manufactured		167,000	167,000	
	184,000	184,000	255,000	295,000
Net Income			40,000	
			295,000	295,000

REQUIRED
(a) Prepare a cost of goods manufactured statement and an income statement for the Blandel Corporation. Assume that 10,000 shares of capital stock are outstanding at year-end.
(b) Prepare general journal entries to adjust the inventories and to close the temporary manufacturing accounts, the Manufacturing Summary account, the revenue and expense accounts, and the Income Summary account.

21–30A You are consulted by Novelties, Inc., a group of investors planning a new product. They have fairly good estimates of the cost of materials, labor, overhead, and other expenses involved but need to know how much they should charge for each unit of the new product in order to earn a before-tax profit in the first year that is equal to 10% of their estimated total long-term investment of $400,000.

A review of their plans indicates that each unit of the new product would require:

Raw Materials:
  3 lb. of a material costing $4 per pound

Direct Labor:
  2.5 hr. of a die cutter's time at $6 per hour
  2.0 hr. of an assembler's time at $5 per hour

Major items of production overhead would be $30,000 annual rent on a factory building, and $10,000 on machinery. Other production overhead is estimated at 60% of total direct labor costs. Nonfactory administrative expenses and selling expense are estimated to be 10% and 20%, respectively, of total sales revenues.

The consensus is that during the first year 4,000 units of product should be produced for selling and another 1,000 units for the next year's beginning inventory. Also, an extra 5,000 pounds of materials will be purchased as beginning inventory for the next year. Because of the nature of the manufacturing process, all units started must be completed, so work in process inventories would be negligible.

REQUIRED
(a) Incorporate the above data into a projected cost of goods manufactured statement and compute the unit production cost.
(b) Prepare a projected income statement (filling in the sales amount as the last item) that would provide for the target amount of profit.
(c) Rounded to the nearest dollar, what unit sales price should the investors charge for the new product?

21–31A The trial balance for the Dollton Boatbuilders Corporation at the end of the current year is given below:

	Debit	Credit
Cash	$ 12,000	
Accounts Receivable	40,000	
Allowance for Uncollectible Accounts		$ 2,000
Raw Materials Inventory, January 1	18,000	
Work in Process Inventory, January 1	9,000	
Finished Goods Inventory, January 1	22,000	

	Debit	Credit
Factory Machinery	153,000	
Accumulated Depreciation—Machinery		41,000
Factory Buildings	205,000	
Accumulated Depreciation—Factory Buildings		30,000
Land	30,000	
Accounts Payable		27,000
Long-term Notes Payable—9%		60,000
Common Stock—$50 Par (all outstanding)		100,000
Retained Earnings		150,000
Sales		410,000
Raw Materials Purchases	124,000	
Purchase Returns—Raw Materials		2,000
Direct Labor	80,000	
Indirect Labor	30,000	
Utilities	8,000	
Repairs and Maintenance	4,000	
Property Taxes	7,000	
Selling Expenses (control account)	48,000	
Nonfactory Administrative Expenses (control account)	32,000	
	$822,000	$822,000

The following information is available for adjusting the accounts:

(1) Inventories at December 31 are: raw materials, $10,000; work in process, $18,000; and finished goods, $12,000.

(2) Accrued wages and salaries at December 31 are: direct labor, $1,700; indirect labor, $300; and selling salaries, $1,000.

(3) Annual amounts of depreciation to be recorded are: factory buildings, $6,000; machinery, $8,000.

(4) Accrued utilities payable at December 31 are: $500.

(5) Uncollectible accounts expense is: 1% of sales, (Debit this expense to the control account for selling expenses.)

(6) Assume an income tax rate of 40% of income before taxes.

REQUIRED

(a) Prepare a manufacturing worksheet for the year. Assume that the utilities and property taxes apply entirely to manufacturing activities.

(b) Prepare a cost of goods manufactured statement and an income statement.

(c) Prepare a balance sheet.

(d) Prepare closing entries (similar to those illustrated in this chapter).

21-32A The trial balance of the Woodson Company at December 31 of the current year is given below, together with most of the worksheet adjustments. (Preparation of adjusting entries for inventories is part of the problem solution.)

	Trial Balance Debit	Trial Balance Credit	Adjustments Debit		Adjustments Credit	
Cash	4,000					
Raw Materials Inventory, Jan. 1	9,300		(2)	?	(1)	?
Work in Process Inventory, Jan. 1	11,000		(2)	?	(1)	?
Finished Goods Inventory, Jan. 1	17,400		(4)	?	(3)	?
Prepaid Insurance	1,800				(5)	900
Factory Machinery	98,000					
Accumulated Depreciation—Factory Machinery		8,400			(6)	4,000
Unamortized Cost of Patents	17,500				(7)	1,000
Accounts Payable		22,000				
Common Stock, $200 Par Value		40,000				
Retained Earnings		30,000				
Dividends Declared	6,000					
Sales		340,000				
Raw Materials Purchases (net)	90,000					
Direct Labor	85,000		(8)	2,000		
Indirect Labor	32,000		(8)	700		
Utilities	4,500					
Repairs and Maintenance—Factory	1,900					
Rent—Buildings	8,000					
Sales Salaries Expense	25,000					
Advertising Expense	9,000					
Nonfactory Administrative Expense	20,000					
	440,400	440,400				
Manufacturing Summary			(1)	?	(2)	?
			(1)	?	(2)	?
Income Summary			(3)	?	(4)	?
Insurance—Factory			(5)	900		
Depreciation—Machinery			(6)	4,000		
Amortization of Patents			(7)	1,000		
Wages Payable					(8)	2,700
Income Tax Expense			(9)	22,000		
Income Tax Payable					(9)	22,000
				?		?

Additional information:
(1) Of the total rent on buildings, $6,000 is for the factory; the remainder is nonfactory administrative expense.
(2) Of the utilities paid, $3,000 is for the factory; the remainder is nonfactory administrative expense.
(3) December 31 inventories are: raw materials, $14,000; work in process, $6,000; and finished goods, $12,000.
(4) Patent amortization applies to factory operations.

REQUIRED

(a) Complete the manufacturing worksheet.

(b) Prepare a cost of goods manufactured statement and an income statement.

(c) Prepare closing entries similar to those illustrated in this chapter.

BUSINESS DECISION PROBLEM

Robert Brown, an engineer, has approached you for some accounting advice. In their spare time during the past year, Brown and his college-aged son, Greg, have been manufacturing a small weed-trimming sickle in a rented building near their home. Greg, who has had one accounting course in college, is responsible for keeping the books.

Brown is obviously pleased about the results of their first year's operations as he hands you the following "Income Report" prepared by Greg. He asks you to look things over before they leave on a well-deserved vacation to the Bahamas, after which they plan to expand their business significantly.

Income Report

Sales (9,200 units at $15.95 each)		$146,740
Expenses of producing 10,000 units:		
Raw materials:		
Pre-casted blades at $3 each	$ 33,000	
Pre-turned handles at $2 each	21,000	
Labor costs of hired assembler	13,000	
Labor costs of hired painter	12,000	
Rent on building	6,000	
Rent on machinery	3,000	
Utilities	2,000	
Other production costs	4,000	
Advertising	12,000	
Sales commissions	20,000	
Delivery of products to customers	4,000	
Total expenses	$130,000	
Less: Ending inventory of 800 units at average production costs of $13 (or $130,000/10,000 units)	10,400	
Cost of sales		119,600
Net Income		$ 27,140

After you examine the income report, Mr. Brown, in response to your questions, assures you that (1) there has been no theft or spoilage of materials, (2) no partially completed units are involved, (3) he and his son have averaged about 30 hours each per week in the business, and (4) he is in approximately the 40% income tax bracket (before considering the sickle venture).

REQUIRED

(a) Review the report to identify any apparent discrepancy in the cost of raw materials used.

(b) Recalculate the cost of goods manufactured, the average cost per unit produced, and the net income for the year, including a provision for estimated income taxes on the earnings.

(c) What factors should Mr. Brown consider regarding the profitability of his venture as a basis for deciding to expand it significantly?

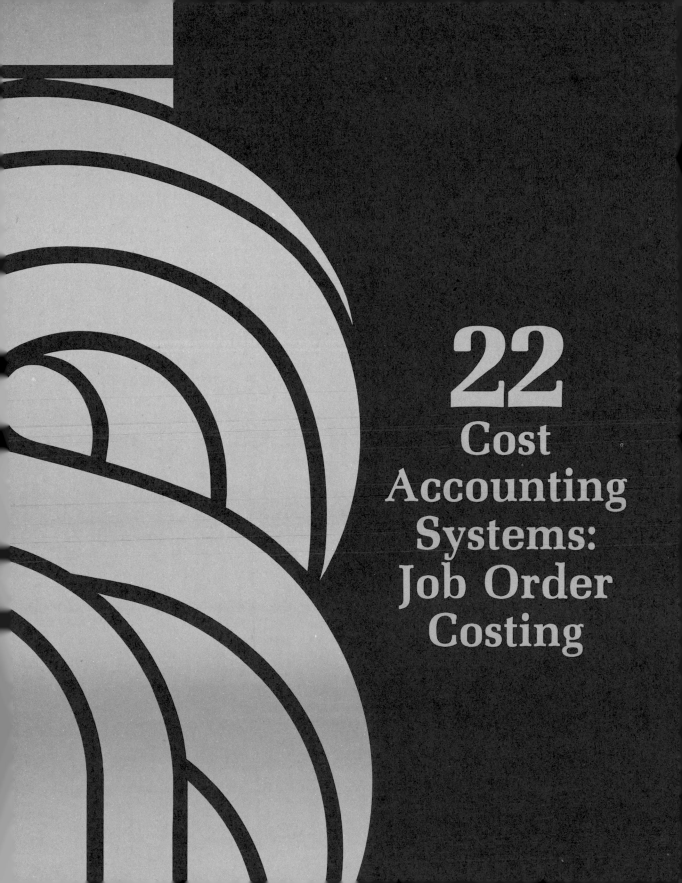

22
Cost Accounting Systems: Job Order Costing

So soon as we begin to count the cost, the cost begins.

HENRY DAVID THOREAU

I n Chapter 21 we introduced the concepts of multiple manufacturing inventories, cost of goods manufactured, and financial statements for a manufacturing concern. We used an approach that adapted a general accounting system to a relatively simple manufacturing operation using periodic inventory procedures. We cited the significant limitations of that approach as a primary justification for the development of specialized cost accounting systems and the use of perpetual inventories to provide more meaningful cost data. In this and the following chapter we introduce important aspects of cost accounting and illustrate two of the more important types of cost accounting systems for manufacturing firms.

LIMITATIONS OF COST DETERMINATIONS

Perhaps the first consideration in studying cost accounting should be a review of the inherent limitations of most cost determinations. Misconceptions prevail that accounting cost figures are minutely exact and that for any asset, product, or unit of activity, a precise amount can be properly described as *the* cost. Although an exhaustive consideration of these issues is beyond the scope of this chapter, a review of several examples should provide a realistic perspective.

Determining cost consists basically of accumulating the total costs incurred in doing something and then allocating these costs among the various units of accomplishment during a given period. Any unit of activity, service rendered, or product manufactured may be involved. Accounting procedures for both the accumulation and the allocation of costs may necessarily involve somewhat arbitrary choices. Often no single cost measurement or allocation scheme is demonstrably better than any other. Therefore, the accountant must choose, rationally but nonetheless arbitrarily, from among a group of equally defensible approaches to cost measurement and allocation. Following are several examples, the first two of which you have become aware of in chapters already studied.

Assumed cost flows. The purchase prices of raw materials often vary throughout the year. Assigning costs to cost of goods sold and ending inventories may involve arbitrarily assuming a cost flow such as FIFO, LIFO, or some form of average cost.

Depreciation estimates. The service potential of long-lived assets contributes to many operating periods. No method exists of charging to a given period what might be considered the precise amount of the asset's cost. Instead, periodic depreciation expense is based on tentative estimates of useful life and salvage value as well as an often arbitrary choice between straight-line and one of several accelerated depreciation methods.

Allocated joint costs. Joint costs are costs that are common to two or more products or manufacturing processes. Costs of raw materials, supervisors' salaries, and service department costs are often joint costs. In a lumbering mill operation, for example, there is no single precise way to allocate the cost of a whole log to the several wood products that result: prime clear boards used for furniture, rough construction-grade boards, the bark that is sold as mulching to landscapers, and the sawdust that becomes paper. Joint product costs are often allocated arbitrarily on the basis of the relative sales value, weights, or volumes of each joint product. In Chapter 23 we illustrate accepted allocation techniques for joint products and service departments.

Realistically then, what we might think of loosely as *the* cost of something is actually what happens to be *a* recorded cost of that thing, often determined by our choices from among a series of perhaps equally valid available assumptions.

Another aspect of the limitations of cost determination is that the concept of cost has many variations, and different versions may be most useful for different purposes. Ordinarily, cost systems are designed to provide "full average cost," or the total of all costs divided by all output. For example, if costs of $100,000 are incurred in producing 80,000 units of product, the average unit cost is $1.25 ($100,000 ÷ 80,000). Suppose that in evaluating the opportunity to accept an additional overseas order for 10,000 units, our production engineers advise that producing the additional 10,000 units would raise total costs to $108,000. In its decision to accept or reject the offer, management could think of a new full average unit cost of $1.20 ($108,000 ÷ 90,000 units) or the incremental unit cost of $0.80 (the $8,000 increase in cost divided by the 10,000 unit increase in production). If the contemplated selling price is $1.00 per unit, using the $1.20 average cost results in a loss of $0.20 per unit, whereas using the incremental unit cost of $0.80 results in a profit of $0.20 per unit. Neither of these resulting costs is wrong, nor the other right. Rather, depending on certain management decision situations, either one may be defended as most appropriate. This and other instances of management's use of "different cost for different purposes" are illustrated in subsequent chapters.

The important thing to realize here is that, as necessary and useful as cost data are, they are complex and have inherent limitations. Users of cost data must be aware of the specific assumptions made, the costing procedures used, and the proper application of the variations of cost data that they may need.

THE NATURE AND ADVANTAGES
OF COST ACCOUNTING SYSTEMS

Any orderly method of developing cost information constitutes cost accounting. Typically, some amount of cost is accumulated and related to some unit of activity or accomplishment. Some examples are accumulating the costs of cutting or forming materials, assembling parts, and the painting and finishing that might result in a finished unit of product such as a lawnmower, a piece of furniture, a computer, or a custom-designed executive jet aircraft. Although a cost system could be a special analysis maintained independently of a firm's formal accounting records, most comprehensive cost systems are integrated into the general ledger accounts of the firm.

We shall illustrate cost accounting systems in the context of a manufacturing situation involving unit product costs. Remember, however, that reliable "cost-per-unit-of-accomplishment" data are vital to decision makers in all economic endeavors. For example, a municipality may need to know the cost per ton of snow removal or of solid waste collection; a hospital, the cost of providing various surgical or diagnostic services; a railroad, the cost per ton-mile of hauling freight; and an insurance company, the cost of providing various combinations of home-owner protection to specific groups of policyholders. Many of the costing concepts and techniques used in manufacturing costing systems are applicable to non-manufacturing situations.

Use of Perpetual Inventories

The inherent weaknesses of using periodic inventory procedures for manufacturing operations were discussed in Chapter 21. Cost of raw materials used and cost of goods sold tend to be residual (or "plug") figures, relatively current cost data are available only at end-of-period intervals, and many significant departmental cost details are not readily apparent. For these reasons, cost accounting systems incorporate perpetual inventory procedures. That is, additions to and deductions from all inventory accounts, raw materials, work in process, and finished goods are recorded as they occur. The more current cost information and greater cost controls provided justify the additional bookkeeping costs of perpetually maintaining the inventory accounts. Even when perpetual inventory records are maintained, these records are customarily verified by physical inventory at least once a year. Necessary adjustments for errors and unrecorded inventory shrinkages can then be made. The flow of product costs (raw materials, direct labor, and factory overhead) through the various perpetual inventory accounts of a simple cost accounting system is readily apparent in both the simplified and more comprehensive illustrations appearing in this chapter.

Timely Product Costing

A cost accounting system for a manufacturing concern would be inadequate if it did not provide for the timely determination of product costs. To begin with, product costs are needed to arrive at inventory amounts for work in process and for finished goods; these amounts are required in the preparation of financial statements. Obviously, to properly determine income, one must have some method of identifying costs with the products sold and the products that remain on hand in a finished or unfinished state.

Efficiency and profitability provide equally compelling reasons for knowing product costs. Management uses engineering studies and cost analysis to establish standards and budgets for efficient performance. Only by knowing product costs can management compare actual costs with established norms and take remedial action when necessary.

Management also needs product cost data to establish price lists and to submit bids on special orders for its products. Although many factors, including marketing and legal constraints, may affect pricing decisions, unit product costs are often an important determinant. Furthermore, once prices are established, knowledge of costs enables management to determine profit margins. It can then intelligently direct its efforts to the promotion of its more profitable items. We should mention, however, that whenever management utilizes cost figures, it should consider the possibility that some costs may be out of date. Because cost figures are historical, they may not always be currently relevant. When used for pricing purposes, costs should be updated as much as possible.

To identify costs with a product or a group of products, a manufacturer must trace factory costs—raw materials, direct labor, and factory overhead—to lots or batches of product. Tracing raw materials and labor costs to products is fairly routine. To account for the raw materials used, a firm may keep track of the costs of materials requisitioned for production of readily identifiable groups of products. Labor costs can similarly be accounted for by time-keeping methods or by identifying the product with the payroll costs of personnel in those operations or departments that produce the product. It is not as simple, however, to trace the cost of factory overhead to a product or to groups of products. Obviously, a firm cannot directly determine the amount of depreciation, utilities expense, supervisory salaries, and so on that should be identified with different products or groups of products. Consequently, an estimation procedure using a predetermined overhead rate is employed to assign overhead costs throughout the production period.

Use of Predetermined Overhead Rates

Many of the concepts and procedures underlying the use of **predetermined overhead rates** are extensive and complex. In this chapter, we give only a basic treatment, sufficient to convey a general understanding of the use of these rates in product costing.

Before the beginning of an accounting period, management normally prepares budgets; it will translate sales forecasts into production budgets, which in turn permit estimates of plant utilization and activity. Such activity can be measured in a number of different ways—direct labor hours, direct labor costs, machine hours, and so on. Using historical data and projected activity levels, the total factory overhead to be incurred can be estimated. The overhead rate is computed by dividing the estimated total factory overhead by the selected measure of activity. Calculations of predetermined overhead rates are usually based on year-long production periods.

Assume that the number of direct labor hours used is the most appropriate measure of activity for applying overhead in a given situation. If the projected

THE LAW OF COSTS

Cost determination ... is a difficult and intricate accounting undertaking. The total costs of any operation have only a limited utility because totals cannot be readily correlated with the multiple products or services that are produced and sold. Hence costs, to mean anything, must be differentiated and such differentiation is always difficult. Thus, two facts emerge which merit attention at the outset: (1) Costs are not simple and can be obtained only by the painstaking analytical process called cost accounting; and (2) unless authentic specific costs are obtained, the management of the entity concerned is navigating by guesswork and, figuratively speaking, is more or less at sea.

In physics there is a well known "law of the conservation of mass" which holds that matter cannot be created or destroyed. Thus, in any closed system, subject to no external forces, the mass remains constant irrespective of its changes in form. In the case of costs incurred by a given entity (in a sense, a closed system), a somewhat similar law applies, namely, that all costs incurred must be borne, sooner or later, by someone. They cannot be escaped.

Three things can happen to the costs from the standpoint of the incurring entity. One possibility is that certain costs, as such, will be directly reimbursed or otherwise recovered. A second possibility is that the costs will be relayed or passed on to the buyer of the products or services, plus a profit margin if the selling prices more than cover the costs. A third possibility is that the costs will have to be absorbed for the simple reason that the selling prices commanded by the products or services fall short of the cost of delivering them—hence a loss is sustained. This inexorable law dramatizes the importance of doing everything possible to identify all costs and to learn everything pertinent about their behavior and ultimate disposition.

An interesting sidelight, in this context, is how do rapidly mounting pollution-abatement costs fit in? The answer is that social pressure is forcing these previously unaccounted "external diseconomies" or "external costs" to be borne internally. In terms of the law of costs, what is happening is that the boundaries of the closed cost systems are being extended to take in more territory. This significant trend obviously makes cost accountability just that much more imperative.

Example

A good illustration of cost determination is found in the familiar mileage reimbursement transaction. If you allow someone to drive your car 100 miles, you could do it on a gratis basis; or you could just have him pay for the fuel he consumed (say 100 miles $\times$ 3¢ per mile = $3.00); or, if the intent is to recover full costs, you'll charge from ten to fourteen cents per mile depending on your particular car and the quality of the road. Only in this way would you be fully repaid for not only the car's "rolling" costs (mainly fuel, tires and lubrication) but also for its prorata "standing" costs (depreciation, insurance, license and major maintenance).

If your cost-accounting prospect understands this, he has passed an important test. He is beginning to grasp the real why of cost accounting. He will then readily appreciate that the full-time cost accountant deals continuously with hundreds or even thousands of diverse cost situations somewhat akin in their nature to this one-vehicle illustration.

SOURCE: Dixon Fagerberg, Jr., "The Selling of Cost Accounting," *Management Accounting*, June 1974, pp. 23–24. © 1974 by the National Association of Accountants. Reprinted by permission.

number of direct labor hours is 100,000 and the estimated total factory overhead is $150,000, the overhead rate may be calculated

$$\text{Overhead Rate} = \frac{\text{Estimated Overhead}}{\text{Estimated Direct Labor Hours}}$$

$$= \frac{\$150,000}{100,000 \text{ hours}}$$

$$= \$1.50 \text{ per direct labor hour}$$

If, during the accounting period, a particular group or lot of products requires 50 direct labor hours of production time, $75 of overhead (50 × $1.50) will be charged to this group of products.

Before selecting the basis for applying overhead to products, one should carefully analyze the relationship between overhead incurred and various alternative measures of activity. Probably the most common bases are those related to direct labor hours or to direct labor cost. In some situations, where there is a high degree of equipment use relative to manual labor, machine-hours may be a more appropriate base.

By using a predetermined overhead rate, management can estimate the overhead costs of any job at any stage of completion, computing "costs to date" both for control purposes and for inventory costing. This method also eliminates wide fluctuations in unit costs that might result if actual recorded overhead costs were assigned to products during short interim periods when production departed markedly from average levels. For example, assume that normal production is 100,000 direct labor hours per year and that production fluctuates seasonally throughout the year. Suppose also that a large share of actual factory overhead cost is spread fairly evenly throughout the months of the year. (Such costs as depreciation, maintenance, power and light, and supervisory costs would remain fairly constant from month to month.) If, in a particular month, production fell far below the monthly average of 8,333 direct labor hours (100,000 direct labor hours ÷ 12 months), and *actual* factory overhead costs were assigned to units of product, unit costs would increase abruptly because the factory overhead would be assigned to fewer units of product than usual. Similarly, in months of increased production, unit costs would decrease.

Exhibit 22–1 illustrates the differences that can exist between assigned overhead costs based on actual monthly overhead rates and those based on one annual overhead rate. The estimated annual rate in this example is $1.50 per direct labor hour ($150,000 ÷ 100,000 direct labor hours). The actual monthly rates vary from $3.10 in February to only $1.10 in July, with only the months of April, September, and October even approaching the annual average of $1.50 per direct labor hour. Using actual rates, if it is assumed that a particular unit of product typically requires three direct labor hours, a unit produced in July when production activity was highest would be assigned overhead costs of $3.30 (3 × $1.10). In

EXHIBIT 22-1
Comparison of Actual Monthly
and Estimated Annual Overhead Rates

	Factory Overhead Costs Incurred Each Month*	Direct Labor Hours Worked Each Month	Overhead Rates Based on Actual Monthly Costs	Estimated Annual Overhead Rate	Range in Actual Overhead Rate Per Direct Labor Hour
January	$ 9,900	4,000	$2.48	$1.50	
February	9,300	3,000	3.10	1.50	$3.10 (highest)
March	10,500	5,000	2.10	1.50	
April	12,300	8,000	1.54	1.50	**
May	14,100	11,000	1.28	1.50	
June	14,700	12,000	1.23	1.50	
July	16,500	15,000	1.10	1.50	$1.10 (lowest)
August	15,300	13,000	1.18	1.50	
September	13,500	10,000	1.35	1.50	**
October	12,300	8,000	1.54	1.50	**
November	11,100	6,000	1.85	1.50	
December	10,500	5,000	2.10	1.50	
Annual Amounts	$150,000	100,000	—	$1.50	

*Assumed to be $7,500 each month plus $0.60 per direct labor hour.
**These are the only months in which actual monthly rates approach the annual rate.

contrast, a unit that happened to be produced in February when production activity was lowest would be assigned overhead costs of $9.30 (3 × $3.10). The $6.00 difference is hardly defensible, especially when, as is often the case, the two units of product may be virtually indistinguishable physically. Clearly, it would be unrealistic to base product costs on allocations of actual monthly overhead amounts. The use of a predetermined overhead rate employing a yearly average produces more meaningful unit cost figures.

Accounting for the accumulation of actual factory overhead and the application of a predetermined overhead rate involves special accounting procedures. These are introduced in the following section on flow of product costs and are explained further in the comprehensive illustration of job order costing appearing later in this chapter.

Flow of Product Costs

To introduce the basic ideas of cost accounting systems, we present a simplified illustration in the next few pages. The final part of this chapter supplements this illustration with a more detailed example incorporating a widely used technique for assigning costs to manufactured products. The beginning illustration involves a first phase of accumulating product costs and a second phase of tracing these costs as they sequentially become (1) work in process, during manufacturing operations; (2) finished goods, when completed; and (3) cost of goods sold, when sold.

As you follow the illustration, keep in mind that the cumulative debit amounts of all product costs are going to be capitalized (treated as assets) and will eventually become debits to a finished goods inventory account.

ACCUMULATING PRODUCT COSTS   The basic relationships in this illustration underlie all cost accounting systems, although in practice there are several variations of the account titles used here. For simplicity in presenting these basic concepts, we assume there is no beginning inventory and use convenient money amounts in all entries. Each entry is explained and its effect keyed to related accounts shown here in T-account form.

Acquisition of Materials:

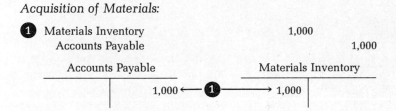

The perpetual inventory procedures for purchasing merchandise explained in Chapter 9 are used to derive the amount of this entry. Because all factory materials are being accounted for, both raw materials and factory supplies are included in this transaction.

Recording Factory Payroll:

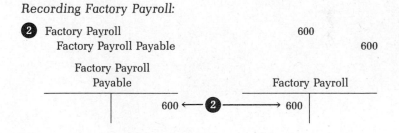

As illustrated here, the total factory payroll includes both direct and indirect labor. Later, these two items will be handled separately. Data for this entry would come from a detailed analysis of factory payroll records.

Recording Other Factory Costs as Overhead:

3 Factory Overhead	1,000	
Accumulated Depreciation		400
Utilities Payable		300
Prepaid Insurance		200
Property Tax Payable		100

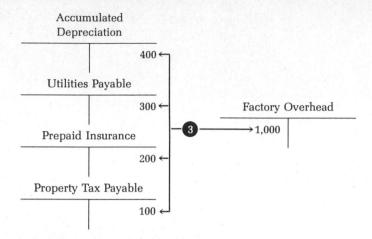

Realistically, factory overhead would include many more items than are shown here. We chose these particular items to illustrate depreciation, accruals, and the write-off of prepaid items.

At this point, all product costs have been accumulated into debit balances in the Materials Inventory, Factory Payroll, and Factory Overhead accounts. We are now ready to trace these costs through to Finished Goods and Cost of Goods Sold.

TRACING PRODUCT COSTS   In this phase of our illustration we show how the product costs accumulated earlier as debit balances in the accounts are transferred sequentially through Work in Process and Finished Goods to the Cost of Goods Sold account. Descriptions, journal entries, and explanations for each step are keyed to the cost flow diagram in Exhibit 22–2 (page 788). As you read the material, trace each entry in the cost flow diagram.

Recording Requisitions of Raw Materials and Factory Supplies:

❹ Work in Process	600	
Factory Overhead	200	
Materials Inventory		800

This entry reflects the requisition of all materials to be used in production by the various parties. Raw materials (or direct materials) are charged directly to the Work in Process account. Costs of factory supplies (or indirect materials) become part of factory overhead. We assume here, as is often the case in practice, that the Materials Inventory account is the control account for both raw materials and factory supplies. Note that the portion of materials not used in this accounting period is indicated by the balance in the Materials Inventory account.

Recording Distribution of Factory Payroll:

❺ Work in Process	500	
Factory Overhead	100	
Factory Payroll		600

Work in Process is debited for the $500 of direct labor, and Factory Overhead is debited for the $100 of indirect labor. Observe that the total factory payroll is distributed, leaving a zero balance in the Factory Payroll account. The division of total factory payroll into direct and indirect labor is based on a detailed analysis of the job description, wage rates, and hours worked of each employee.

Recording Application of Factory Overhead:

6	Work in Process	1,200	
	Factory Overhead		1,200

This entry adds the third and final category of factory costs to work in process. Note that the amount of this entry is *not* equal to the $1,300 of actual factory overhead incurred at this time. As explained earlier, most firms do *not* apply the actual amount of overhead incurred each period to the goods manufactured during that period. Instead, overhead is applied at average rates that reflect estimates of total annual production volume and total overhead costs for the year.

Recording Completed Production:

7	Finished Goods	2,000	
	Work in Process		2,000

This entry reflects the assignment of costs to completed production and the transfer of those costs from Work in Process to Finished Goods. As explained later, the amount of this entry is derived from production records, the details of which will vary with the particular product costing system used by the firm. The balance remaining in the Work in Process account represents the costs assigned to the ending work-in-process inventory.

Recording Cost of Goods Sold:

8	Cost of Goods Sold	1,400	
	Finished Goods		1,400

This entry transfers the cost of finished products sold to the Cost of Goods Sold account. The balance remaining in the Finished Goods account reflects costs assigned to the ending inventory of finished goods.

Exhibit 22–2 (page 788) diagrams the results of the foregoing entries as the various product costs move through the manufacturing accounts:

Entries (1) through (3) accumulate factory costs into three accounts, Materials Inventory, Factory Payroll, and Factory Overhead.

Entry (4) reflects the requisition of both raw materials and factory supplies.

Entry (5) distributes the total factory payroll, including direct and indirect labor. At this point, debits in the Factory Overhead account reflect the actual factory overhead incurred.

EXHIBIT 22–2
Tracing Product Costs
Through a Cost Accounting System

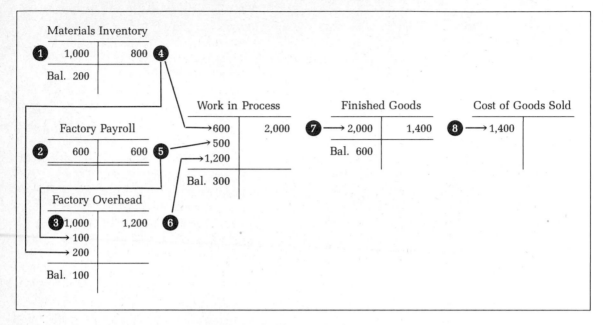

Entry (6) applies factory overhead in an amount based on predetermined estimates of total annual overhead costs and production levels. The $100 balance in the Factory Overhead account represents an amount of actual overhead incurred but not yet applied to work in process, the nature and disposition of which are explained later in the chapter. After entry (6), the Work in Process account has been charged for all three categories of product costs: raw materials, direct labor, and estimated factory overhead.

Entry (7) transfers to Finished Goods the costs assigned to completed production. The $300 remaining in the Work in Process account consists of the costs assigned to the goods that are only partially completed at this point.

Entry (8) transfers to Cost of Goods Sold the costs of the finished goods sold. The balance in the Finished Goods account represents the costs assigned to the goods that are finished but not yet sold.

So far, we have presented the important aspects of cost accounting systems including the use of perpetual inventory procedures, the provision of timely product costs, the use of predetermined overhead rates, and an illustration of the flow of product costs through a cost accounting system. We now turn to an illustration of a widely used cost accounting system known as job order cost accounting.

JOB ORDER COST SYSTEMS

There are two basic types of cost accounting systems: job order cost accounting and process cost accounting. **Job order cost accounting** (sometimes called **job lot** or **specific order** costing) is appropriate when production is characterized by a discontinuous series of products or jobs undertaken either to fill specific orders from customers or for a general stock of products from which future orders will be filled. This type of costing is widely used in construction, printing, and machine shop operations. Often the products or batches of products vary in their material components and manner of production. In contrast, **process cost accounting** lends itself most readily to the production of a large volume of undifferentiated products, manufactured in a "continuous flow" operation, such as distillation of fuels or the manufacture of paint, chemicals, wire, and similar items. Essentially the same ingredients and operations are involved during each period of manufacture.

A major purpose of either system is to allocate manufacturing costs to products to determine unit costs. In a job order system, costs are identified with specific jobs to determine the cost of products manufactured. In a process system, costs are identified with production processes and averaged over the products made during the period. The system we shall illustrate here is that of job order costing; the basic concepts of process costing are presented in Chapter 23.

Exhibits 22–3 through 22–7 show some of the important accounting forms used in job order costing as they might appear during use. In a job order cost system, each of the three inventory accounts—Materials Inventory, Work in Process, and Finished Goods—will have a subsidiary ledger in which unit costs are accounted for. **Materials ledger cards** (Exhibit 22–3) for each type of material or factory supply used make up the subsidiary record for the Materials Inventory account; these show quantities received, issued and on hand, unit costs, and total amounts. **Materials requisition forms** (Exhibit 22–4) are used for the initial recording of the issuances of raw materials to various jobs or of factory supplies for general factory use. **Time tickets** (Exhibit 22–5) are used for the initial recording of the amount of time spent and the individual employee labor cost incurred for each individual job or as a part of factory overhead. **Job cost sheets** serve as the subsidiary records for the Work in Process account. As shown in Exhibit 22–6, the sheets indicate, for each job in process, the costs of raw materials, direct labor, and applied overhead identified with the job. When a job is completed, the total cost is divided by the number of units in the lot to obtain a unit cost. Also at this time, the job's cost sheet is removed from the Work in Process ledger and an entry is made in the **Finished Goods ledger,** which is the subsidiary record for Finished Goods. The cards in this ledger (Exhibit 22–7) are identified by the stock number and name of the product and show quantities, unit costs, and total costs of the various lots of product awaiting sale. We shall now turn to the comprehensive illustration of job order costing, which will show how these forms are used.

EXHIBIT 22-3
Materials Ledger Card

Materials Ledger Card

Stock No. __32__

Description __1/8 Steel Wire__   Reorder Quantity __4,000 ft.__

Supplier __Steel Supply Corp.__   Minimum Quantity __1,000 ft.__

	Received				Issued				Balance		
Date	Rec'g. Report No.	Units	Price	Total Price	Mat'l. Req'n. No.	Units	Price	Total Price	Units	Price	Total Price
19XX											
8/1	320	4,000	0.20	800.00					4,000	0.20	800.00
8/5					567	700	0.20	140.00	3,300	0.20	660.00
8/9	332	4,000	0.21	840.00					{ 3,300	0.20	660.00 }
									{ 4,000	0.21	840.00 }

EXHIBIT 22-4
Materials Requisition Form

Materials Requisition

Date ____8/5____   Job. No. ____372____   Requisition No. ____567____

Item	Quantity		Unit Price	Amount
	Authorized	Issued		
Stock No. 32 (1/8" wire)	700 ft.	700 ft.	0.20	$140
Total				$140

Authorized by: _J. E. K._   Issued by: _J. A. P._   Received by: _F. W. C._

EXHIBIT 22–5
Time Ticket

Time Ticket						
Employee Name _James L. Kitt_				Employee No. ___42___		
Skill Specification _Wire Former_				Payroll Period Ending _8/16/XX_		

Time Started	Time Stopped	Total Time	Hourly Labor Rate	Department	Job No.	Total Cost
8:00	12:00	4.0	$4.00	A	372	$16.00
1:00	2:00	1.0	4.00	A	372	4.00
Totals		5.0				$20.00
Approved by _R.h.J._						

EXHIBIT 22–6
Job Cost Sheet

Job Cost Sheet					
Customer _Ace Fabricators, Inc._			Job No. ___372___		
Product _Bracket-H3_			Date Promised _9/1/XX_		
Quantity _200_			Dates: Started _8/1_ Completed _8/20_		

Raw Materials		Direct Labor		Cost Summary	
Mat'l. Req'n. No.	Amount	Payroll Summary Dated	Dept.	Amount	
				Raw Materials	700.00
567	140.00	8/2	A	70.00	
573	180.00	8/9	A	240.00	Direct Labor	600.00
591	200.00	8/16	B	190.00	
603	180.00	8/23	B	100.00	Factory Overhead (applied at):
					150% of direct labor cost	900.00
				Total Cost	2,200.00
Totals	700.00			600.00	Units Finished 200 Unit Cost 11.00

EXHIBIT 22–7
Finished Goods Ledger Card

Finished Goods Ledger Card										
Stock No. __H3__										
Item __Bracket-H3__								Minimum Quantity __50__		
Manufactured			Sales			Balance				
Job No.	Quantity	Total Cost	Invoice No.	Quantity	Total Cost	Date	Quantity	Unit Cost	Total Cost	
372	200	2,200.00				8/20	200	11.00	2,200.00	
			123	100	1,100.00	8/25	100	11.00	1,100.00	

To illustrate job order cost accounting, we make the following three assumptions:

(1) Conroy Company uses raw materials A and B to produce two products, Y and Z.

(2) The company also uses raw material C, which is classified as factory supplies because it is employed in all parts of the factory and is not incorporated directly into products Y and Z.

(3) A predetermined overhead rate based on direct labor hours is used to assign factory overhead to products.

Accounting for Materials

When raw materials or factory supplies are received, a materials clerk records the amounts in the materials ledger as additions to the balances on the appropriate ledger cards. At the end of the accounting period, the total purchases for the period are posted from the voucher register or invoice register to Materials Inventory. After this has been done, the amount added to the control account equals the sum of the amounts added to the materials ledger cards during the period.

When raw materials (A and B, in this case) are requisitioned for specific orders or jobs, the materials clerk records the reductions (credits) on the appropriate materials ledger cards. Cost clerks then enter these amounts in the materials section of the job cost sheets for the specific jobs in which the material is being used. Amounts on requisitions representing factory supplies for general factory use (material C) will be handled by the materials clerk in the same fashion as amounts for raw materials. The amounts, however, will be charged to the Factory Overhead account, because they cannot be identified feasibly with particular jobs.

For example, assume the following:

(1) The Conroy Company purchased $2,500 of material A, $1,500 of material B, and $500 of material C during its first month of operation.

(2) $1,000 of material A was requisitioned for Job 1 and $500 of material B was requisitioned for Job 2. $200 of material C was requisitioned for general factory use.

The effect of these transactions is shown in Exhibit 22-8. Notice that in each subsidiary ledger there are *matching* postings (debits for debits and credits for credits) totaling each entry to the related general ledger control account.

Accounting for Labor

To identify labor costs with specific jobs, *time tickets* are used to accumulate the hours spent on various jobs by each employee. Hourly wage rates can then be used to compute the labor costs for the various jobs. Periodically, these records are sorted and the direct labor amounts posted to the job cost sheets.

Although a number of accounts can be used to record payroll costs, we use our simplified illustration to show how direct and indirect labor costs can be recorded in the accounts. To continue our example, we assume the following:

(3) Total direct labor hours used and charges incurred during the period:
Job 1—200 hours, $800 total direct labor.
Job 2—100 hours, $400 total direct labor.

(4) Indirect labor payroll for the period, $500.

The effect of these transactions is shown in Exhibit 22-9, where we use the Work in Process account, its subsidiary ledger (the job cost sheets), the Factory Overhead account, and the Factory Payroll account. Note that we do not show the debit entry in the Factory Payroll account that would be part of the entry to record accrual of the liability for factory payroll.

Accounting for Overhead

We have demonstrated in Exhibits 22-8 and 22-9 the manner in which factory supplies used and indirect labor cost for the period are introduced into the accounts. In our example, the cost of the factory supplies amounted to $200 and the indirect labor cost was $500. Other overhead costs are charged to the Factory Overhead account as they are incurred or by way of adjusting entries at the end of the accounting period. For instance, assume that in addition to the factory supplies used and indirect labor costs, the following overhead costs were incurred during the period: utilities, $50; repairs, $60; depreciation, $80; insurance, $40. The entries to record these items are given below in summary general journal form:

(5)	Factory Overhead—Utilities	50	
	Factory Overhead—Repairs	60	
	Factory Overhead—Depreciation	80	
	Factory Overhead—Insurance	40	
	Cash (or Accounts Payable)		110
	Accumulated Depreciation		80
	Prepaid Insurance		40

EXHIBIT 22-8
Entries for Purchase and Requisition of Raw Materials and Factory Supplies

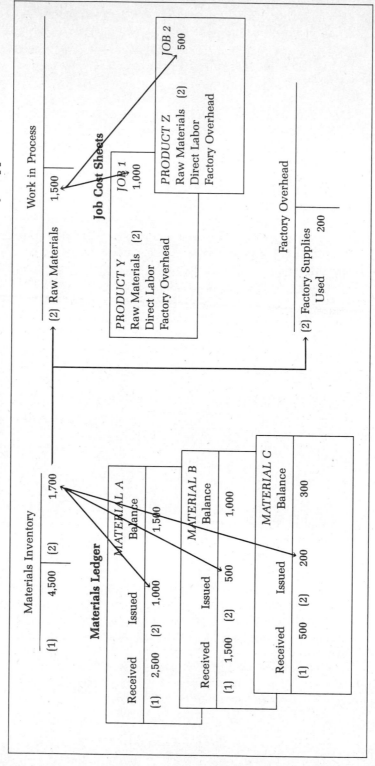

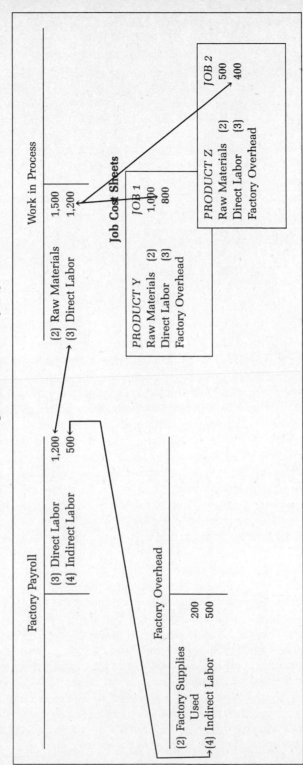

EXHIBIT 22-9
Entries for Assignment of Factory Payroll

The debits in entry (5) are shown as they would appear in the Factory Overhead account (see Exhibit 22–10). The other accounts credited in the entry (Cash, Accumulated Depreciation, and Prepaid Insurance) are omitted from the exhibit, because they are only indirectly involved in the example.

As explained earlier, actual overhead is not identified directly with specific jobs. Instead, through the use of a predetermined overhead rate, the Work in Process account is charged with estimated overhead absorbed. We assume that the Conroy Company has determined that overhead should be charged to jobs on the basis of direct labor hours. Through its forecasting and budgeting process it has determined an overhead rate of $3 per direct labor hour. Because Job 1 accumulated 200 hours, $600 of overhead cost would be applied to this job, while Job 2, requiring 100 hours, would absorb $300 of overhead cost. In general journal form, the entry to charge the Work in Process account with estimated overhead would be:

(6)	Work in Process	900	
	Factory Overhead		900
	(Job 1, $600; Job 2, $300)		

Exhibit 22–10 shows how the overhead items would be reflected in the accounts.

After overhead cost has been entered on the job cost sheets, all elements of cost to date—raw materials, direct labor, and overhead—can be totaled. This sum represents the cost of the job from its inception to its present stage of completion. In our example, we see that $2,400 ($1,000 + $800 + $600) has been expended on Job 1 by the end of the accounting period. Frequently, management may compare the calculated cost for a job not yet completed with the cost of similar jobs in the past. Knowing such costs enables management to take any necessary steps to control costs. In addition, accumulating cost by jobs permits an evaluation of the work-in-process inventory.

In Exhibit 22–10, the $900 overhead cost applied to jobs was credited to the Factory Overhead account. Some accountants prefer to credit a separate account, Applied Overhead, but this is merely a bookkeeping nicety and not essential to our conceptual discussion.

Note that the amount of overhead applied to jobs during the period is $30 less than the actual overhead incurred ($930). In fact, it would be unusual in any month for the amount applied to equal the actual overhead cost. There are several reasons for this. First, estimates of the total overhead cost for the year and the activity in labor hours were used to calculate the overhead rate. Second, production activity normally fluctuates from month to month. Finally, the actual pattern of incurring overhead cost may also vary from month to month. Therefore, one can expect either debit or credit balances monthly in the Factory Overhead account. When there is a debit balance in the account, the amount is called **underapplied** (or **underabsorbed**) overhead. A credit balance would be **overapplied** (or **overabsorbed**) overhead. When interim statements are prepared, the balance in the Factory Overhead account can be shown on the balance sheet as a deferred debit or a deferred credit. If a balance exists at the end of the accounting

EXHIBIT 22-10

Entries for Assignment of Factory Overhead

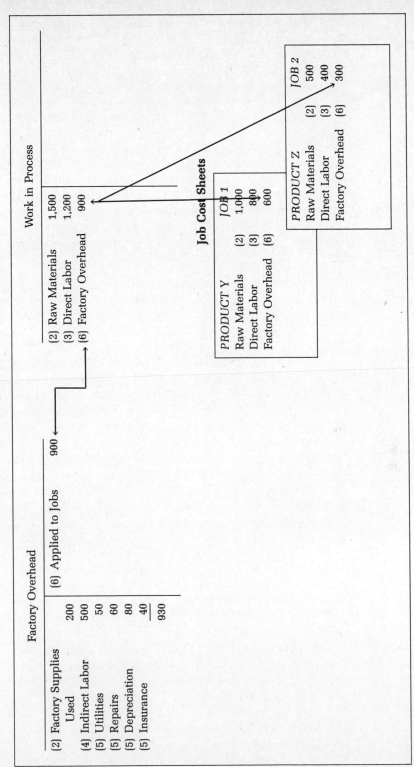

year, it is usually closed to the Cost of Goods Sold account. For example, if the Factory Overhead account had a $30 debit balance at the end of the year, the following entry might be made:

Cost of Goods Sold	30
Factory Overhead	30

To close the Factory Overhead account.

Actually, any residual balance in the overhead account at the end of any period pertains to unfinished goods, finished goods, and goods that have been sold. If desired, one could analyze the labor hours (or other overhead application base) involved in each of these categories and then apportion the residual amount in the overhead account to each category on the basis of relative labor hours. Such procedure is justified, however, only when the residual balance is a material amount.

Accounting for Finished Goods

When job orders are completed, the unit cost of items is obtained by dividing the total accumulated cost by the number of units produced. The job sheets can then be removed from the Work in Process ledger and filed. At the same time, entries are made in the Finished Goods ledger, showing quantities, unit cost, and total cost of the items entered. At the end of the period, an entry is also made crediting Work in Process and debiting Finished Goods for the total cost of the jobs completed during the period. When units of product are sold, the appropriate cost of the units is removed from the finished goods ledger cards for those items; at the end of the accounting period, an entry is made in the general ledger crediting Finished Goods and debiting Cost of Goods Sold.

To illustrate the entries made in accounting for finished goods, assume that Job 1, costing $2,400, was completed during the period, resulting in 1,000 units of product Y, and that 400 units of product Y were sold for $4 each. Job 2 was still in process at the end of the period. The entries to record the transfer of the units of product Y to finished goods and to reflect the sale of 400 units are:

(7)	Finished Goods	2,400	
	Work in Process		2,400

Job 1 completed, producing 1,000 units of product Y at $2.40 per unit.

(8)	Cost of Goods Sold	960	
	Finished Goods		960

Cost of 400 units of product Y at $2.40 each.

(9)	Accounts Receivable	1,600	
	Sales		1,600

Sold 400 units of product Y at $4 per unit.

After transactions (7) through (9) are entered, the relevant accounts and subsidiary records would appear as shown in Exhibit 22–11. Note three points: There is an obvious parallel between the physical flow of goods and the related accounting entries; the various subsidiary ledgers contain a detailed analysis of the aggregate amounts appearing as balances in their related general ledger control accounts; and the sale of finished goods involves entries at both the selling price and the related amount of cost.

EXHIBIT 22–11
Entries for Completion and Sale of Product

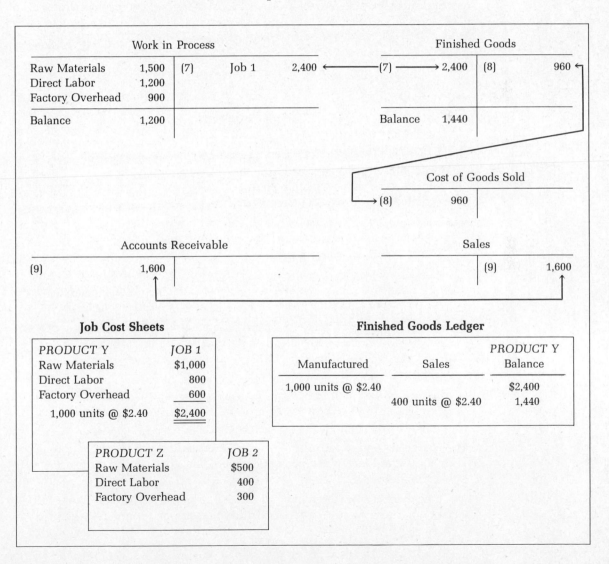

COST ACCOUNTING SYSTEMS
AND FINANCIAL STATEMENTS

When perpetual inventory procedures are used in cost accounting systems, the ending balances of all three inventory accounts will reflect the period's routine transactions that increase and decrease inventories. These ending balances require adjustment only if a discrepancy becomes apparent from taking a year-end physical inventory. Note also that the cost of goods sold figure has been accumulated throughout the year in a general ledger account and can be placed directly on the income statement. Detailed information is available in the related accounts for preparing analyses of cost of goods manufactured and cost of goods sold. The format of financial statements for firms using cost accounting systems is similar to that illustrated in Chapter 21.

KEY POINTS TO REMEMBER

(1) The basic concept of cost accounting is the accumulation and allocation of cost to some unit of activity or accomplishment.

(2) Virtually all cost data are based on assumptions about—and relatively arbitrary choices among—equally defensible accounting procedures. Users of cost data should be aware of both the variations inherent in cost data and any resulting limitations to the data used.

(3) Cost accounting systems provide timely unit product costs through the use of perpetual inventory procedures and predetermined factory overhead rates.

(4) Predetermined overhead rates are computed by estimating the coming year's total factory overhead cost and dividing it by an estimate of some unit of activity (such as direct labor hours, direct labor costs, or factory machine hours).

(5) A cost accounting system is basically a method of accumulating the costs of raw materials, direct labor, and factory overhead and allocating them sequentially to work in process, finished goods, and cost of goods sold.

(6) Job order costing lends itself to the production of a discontinuous series of jobs or products that may vary in their component materials and mode of manufacture. Process costing is most useful when undifferentiated products are made in a continuous flow operation.

(7) Detailed inventory records and requisitions must differentiate between raw materials and factory supplies and accumulate the cost of raw materials by job number.

(8) Detailed payroll records and time tickets must differentiate among direct labor, indirect labor, and nonfactory labor costs and accumulate direct labor costs by job number.

(9) When all related postings are complete, the raw materials ledger cards, job order cost sheets, and finished goods ledger should present a detailed analysis of the balances in the Raw Materials, Work in Process, and Finished Goods accounts, respectively.

(10) Under- or overapplied overhead is expected at the end of interim accounting periods and is shown as deferred debits or credits on interim balance sheets. If the amount is immaterial, it is closed to Cost of Goods Sold at year-end; if material, it may be allocated among the Work in Process, Finished Goods, and Cost of Goods Sold accounts.

QUESTIONS

22-1 What are the two primary objectives of cost accounting systems?

22-2 What are the limitations of most accounting cost determinations?

22-3 In a manufacturing operation, what important advantages do perpetual inventory procedures have over periodic inventory procedures?

22-4 Identify several important uses of unit product costs. Why might management need unit product costs before the end of the operating year?

22-5 What is a predetermined factory overhead rate, and how, in general, is it determined?

22-6 Briefly justify the use of a predetermined annual factory overhead rate as opposed to actual monthly factory overhead.

22-7 A manufacturing company employs an overhead rate of 150% of direct labor cost. The job cost sheet for Job 301 shows that $4,000 in raw materials has been used on the job and that $6,000 in direct labor has been incurred. If 1,000 units of product have been produced on Job 301, what was the unit cost of the product?

22-8 Briefly explain the sequential flow of product costs through a cost accounting system.

22-9 For what types of manufacturing activities are job order costing systems most appropriate? For what types are process costing systems most appropriate?

22-10 What type of records would be used or maintained for the following manufacturing activities?
(a) Determining the amount of a specific material that is on hand.
(b) Issuing raw materials for production.
(c) Assigning the direct labor cost for a particular worker.
(d) Accumulating the cost of a particular product or batch of products.
(e) Determining the amounts and cost of completed products on hand.

22-11 Explain the general format and give examples of the data that would appear on (a) a materials ledger card, (b) a job cost sheet, and (c) a finished goods ledger card.

22-12 Briefly explain (a) the concept of a control account and a subsidiary ledger, (b) the three inventory accounts in a manufacturing cost system that are often control accounts, (c) the name of the subsidiary ledger record for each account in

(b) above, and (d) how one would determine that a control account and subsidiary ledger are in agreement.

22–13 For what reason could it be said that the sale of a manufactured product is recorded at two different amounts?

22–14 The Ajax Company records both actual overhead and applied overhead in a single Factory Overhead account. At the end of January, the account has a credit balance. Has overhead been underapplied or overapplied during January? What is the significance of this balance, and how should it be treated in the January financial statements?

22–15 Outline the disposition of an amount of underapplied overhead, assuming it exists either at the end of an interim accounting period or at the end of the accounting year. In the latter case, how would materiality affect the treatment?

22–16 Astro Manufacturing Company applies factory overhead at the rate of 150% of direct labor cost. During the current period, Astro incurred $70,000 of direct labor costs and $102,000 of factory overhead costs. What is the amount of over- or underapplied factory overhead? What disposition should be made of the balance in Factory Overhead?

EXERCISES

22–17 Selected data for the Fabrication Department of the Randolph Manufacturing Company are presented below:

Estimated factory overhead cost for the year	$120,000
Estimated direct labor cost for the year (at $6 per hour)	96,000
Actual factory overhead cost for January	10,000
Actual direct labor cost for January (1,300 hours)	8,060

Assuming that direct labor cost is the basis for applying factory overhead:
(a) Calculate the predetermined overhead rate.
(b) Present a journal entry to apply factory overhead for January.
(c) By what amount is factory overhead over- or underapplied in January?
(d) How would the amount in (c) be reflected in January's financial statements?

22–18 Using the data in Exercise 22–17, but assuming that the basis for applying factory overhead is direct labor *hours*, complete requirements (a) through (d).

22–19 During the coming accounting year, Boatman, Inc. anticipates the following costs, expenses, and operating data:

Raw Materials (8,000 pounds)	$12,000
Direct Labor (@ $6 per hour)	24,000
Factory Supplies Used	2,000
Indirect Labor	4,000
Sales Commissions	9,000
Factory Administration	2,000
Nonfactory Administration	3,000
Other Factory Overhead*	10,000

*Provides for operating 36,000 machine hours.

     (a) Calculate the predetermined overhead rate for the coming year for each of the following application bases: (1) direct labor hours, (2) direct labor costs, and (3) machine hours.

     (b) For each case in (a), what would be the proper application of factory overhead to Job No. 63, to which 6 direct labor hours, $40 of direct labor cost, and 70 machine hours have been charged?

22-20 Master Factories, Inc. applies factory overhead on the basis of 80% of direct labor cost. An analysis of the related accounts and job order cost sheets indicates that during the year total factory overhead incurred was $100,000 and that at year-end Work in Process, Finished Goods, and Cost of Goods Sold included $6,000, $30,000, and $84,000, respectively, of direct labor charges.

     (a) Determine the amount of over- or underapplied overhead at year-end.

     (b) Present a journal entry to close the factory overhead account at year-end assuming: (1) the amount was not considered material, and (2) the amount was considered material.

22-21 Assuming a routine manufacturing activity, present journal entries (account titles only) for each of the following transactions:

     (a) Purchased raw materials on account.

     (b) Recorded factory payroll earned but not paid.

     (c) Requisitioned both raw materials and factory supplies.

     (d) Assigned direct and indirect factory payroll costs.

     (e) Recorded factory depreciation, property tax expense, and insurance expense.

     (f) Applied factory overhead to production.

     (g) Completed monthly production.

     (h) Sold finished goods.

22-22 Following is a cost flow diagram similar to Exhibit 22-2 in which all or part of typical manufacturing transactions (or account entries) are indicated by parenthetical letters on the debit or credit side of each account.

Materials Inventory	
(a)	(c)

Factory Payroll		Work in Process		Finished Goods		Cost of Goods Sold	
(b)	(d)	(c) (d) (f)	(g)	(g)	(h)	(h)	

Factory Overhead	
(c) (d) (e)	(f)

For each parenthetical letter, indicate the apparent transaction or procedure that has taken place by presenting a general journal entry (disregard amounts).

22–23 For each of the typical manufacturing transactions or activities indicated by the parenthetical letter in the cost flow diagram in Exercise 22–22, briefly identify the detailed forms, records, or documents (if any) that would probably underlie each journal entry.

22–24 Following are summary data from the Job Cost Sheets of Morse Company:

Job No.	Started	Finished	Shipped	Balance May 1	May Production Costs Added
1	4/10	4/20	5/9	$2,400	
2	4/18	4/30	5/20	1,800	
3	4/24	5/10	5/25	900	$2,000
4	4/28	5/20	6/3	1,200	1,700
5	5/15	6/10	6/20		800
6	5/22	6/18	6/28		1,300

Using the above data, compute (a) the finished goods inventory at May 1 and on May 31, (b) the work-in-process inventory at May 1 and May 31, and (c) the cost of goods sold for May.

22–25 Before the completed production for the month of June is recorded, the work in process amount for Ball Company appears as follows:

Work in Process

Balance June 1	4,000	
Raw Materials	12,000	
Direct Labor	8,000	
Factory Overhead	6,000	

Assume that completed production for June is represented by Jobs 107, 108, and 109 with total costs of $7,000, $10,000, and $8,000, respectively.
(a) Determine the cost of unfinished jobs at June 30 and prepare a journal entry recording completed production.
(b) Using general journal entries, record the sale on account of Job 107 for $11,000.

22–26 A manufacturing company has the following account in its cost records:

Work in Process

Raw Materials	24,000	(To Finished Goods)	47,500
Direct Labor	16,000		
Factory Overhead	12,000		

The company applies overhead to production at a predetermined rate based on *direct labor cost*. Assume that the company uses a job order cost system and that Job 110, the only job in process at the end of the period, has been charged with raw materials of $1,000. Complete the following cost sheet for Job 110.

Cost Sheet—Job 110 (in process)

Raw Materials	$_____
Direct Labor	_____
Factory Overhead	_____
Total Cost	$_____

PROBLEMS

Note: In all problems, assume perpetual inventory procedures, a single factory overhead account, first-in, first-out costing for inventories, and that the Materials Inventory account serves as the control account for both raw (direct) materials and factory supplies.

22-27 Bar Manufacturing, Inc. expects the following costs and expenses during the coming year.

Raw Materials	$16,000
Direct Labor (@ $4 per hour)	60,000
Sales Commissions	12,000
Factory Supervision	13,000
Indirect Labor	30,000
Factory Depreciation*	10,000
Factory Taxes*	5,000
Factory Insurance*	4,000
Factory Supplies Used	12,000
Factory Utilities*	6,000

*The factory building contains a sales showroom that occupies about 20% of the floor space involved.

REQUIRED
(a) Compute a predetermined factory overhead rate, assuming an application is to be made on the basis of direct labor hours.
(b) Present a journal entry to apply factory overhead during an interim period when 1,800 direct labor hours were worked.
(c) What amount of overhead would be assigned to Job 466, to which $24 in direct labor had been charged?

22-28 Selected ledger accounts of the Cornell Company are shown on page 806 for the month of February (the second month of its accounting year).

Materials Inventory		
Feb. 1 Bal.	6,000	February Credits 22,000
February Debits	20,000	

Factory Overhead		
February Debits 27,000	Feb. 1 Bal.	2,000
	February Credits	24,000

Work in Process		
Feb. 1 Bal.	4,000	February Credits 68,000
February Debits:		
Raw Materials	18,000	
Direct Labor	30,000	
Overhead	24,000	

Factory Payroll Payable		
February Debits 38,000	Feb. 1 Bal.	9,000
	February Credits	35,000

Finished Goods		
Feb. 1. Bal.	15,000	February Credits 75,000
February Debits	68,000	

REQUIRED

(a) What amount of factory supplies was requisitioned for production during February?

(b) How much *indirect labor* cost was apparently *incurred* during February?

(c) If the factory overhead rate is based on direct labor cost, what rate is in use?

(d) Was factory overhead for the month of February under- or overapplied, and by what amount?

(e) Was factory overhead for the first two months of the year under- or overapplied, and by what amount?

(f) What is the cost of production completed in February?

(g) What is the cost of goods sold for February?

22-29 Harn Manufacturing had the following inventories at the end of its last fiscal year:

Materials Inventory	$8,000
Work in Process	2,000
Finished Goods	7,000

During the first month of the current year, the following transactions occurred:

(1) Purchased materials on account, $17,000.

(2) Factory payroll incurred, $30,000.

(3) Requisitioned raw materials of $16,000 and factory supplies of $6,500.

(4) Assigned total factory payroll, of which $5,000 was considered indirect labor.

(5) Other factory overhead incurred, $12,000. (Credit Accounts Payable.)

(6) Applied factory overhead on the basis of 80% of direct labor costs.

(7) Determined completed production to be $55,000.

(8) Determined cost of goods sold to be $50,000.

REQUIRED

(a) Prepare general journal entries to record the above transactions.
(b) If the above transactions were for a full year's operations and the over- or underapplied overhead was considered material, present a journal entry to close the overhead account to the appropriate accounts using an allocation in proportion to the ending balances in those accounts. Round computations to the nearest dollar.

22-30 At the beginning of the current year, the Suma Company estimated that it would incur $30,000 of factory overhead cost during the year, using 10,000 direct labor hours to produce the desired volume of goods. On January 1 of the current year, beginning inventories of Materials, Work in Process, and Finished Goods were $7,500, $-0-, and $12,000, respectively.

REQUIRED

Prepare general journal entries to record the following transactions for the current year:

(a) Purchased materials on account for $12,000.
(b) Of the total dollar value of materials used, $8,000 represented raw materials and $2,500 were factory supplies used.
(c) Total factory labor amounted to $40,000 (10,000 hours at $4 an hour).
(d) Of the factory labor, 80% was direct and 20% indirect.
(e) Factory overhead, based on direct labor hours, was assigned to work in process.
(f) Actual factory overhead other than those items already recorded amounted to $13,000. (Credit Accounts Payable.)
(g) Ending inventories of Work in Process and Finished Goods were $8,000 and $16,000, respectively. (Make separate entries.)
(h) The balance in Factory Overhead was closed to Cost of Goods Sold.

22-31 Following are certain operating data for Ghee Manufacturing Company during its first month of the current year's operations.

	Materials Inventory	Work in Process	Finished Goods
Beginning Inventory	$6,000	$2,000	$27,000
Ending Inventory	2,000	4,000	3,000

Total sales were $200,000, on which the company earned a 40% gross profit. Ghee uses a predetermined factory overhead rate of 120% of direct labor costs. Factory overhead applied was $36,000. Exclusive of factory supplies used, total factory overhead incurred was $28,000 and was overapplied by $2,000.

REQUIRED

Compute the following items. It is suggested that you set up the T accounts involved in the manufacturing cost flows as shown in Exhibit 22-2, fill in the known amounts, and then use the normal relationships among the various accounts to compute the unknown amounts.

(a) Cost of goods sold.
(b) Cost of goods manufactured.

(c) Direct labor incurred.
(d) Raw materials used.
(e) Factory supplies used.
(f) Total materials purchased.

22-32 Following is a summary of the job order cost sheets related to the production of Bohn Manufacturing, Inc. during the first month of the current operating year. The same overhead rate has been used for all jobs.

Job No.	Raw Materials	Direct Labor	Factory Overhead
109	$ 400	$ 280	$210
110	570	360	270
111	1,100	1,300	975
112	900	720	540
113	500	480	360

Job 109 was in process at the end of the preceding year, at which time it had incurred $240 of direct labor charges and total charges of $620. Job 113 is the current month's ending work in process.

REQUIRED
(a) What is the apparent factory overhead rate?
(b) What is the total of raw materials requisitioned in the current month?
(c) What is the total direct labor incurred in the current month?
(d) If factory overhead is underapplied by $240 at the end of the current month, what is the total factory overhead incurred during the month?
(e) If finished goods inventory decreased during the month by $500, what is the cost of goods sold for the month?

22-33 Summarized data for the first month's operation of Fred's Welding Foundry are presented below. A job order cost system is used.
(1) Materials purchased on account, $22,000.
(2) Amounts of materials requisitioned and foundry labor used:

Job No.	Materials	Foundry Labor
1	$1,400	$ 800
2	2,300	1,700
3	1,000	700
4	4,000	1,400
5	1,500	900
6	500	300
As foundry supplies	2,000	
As indirect labor		1,100

(3) Foundry overhead is applied at the rate of 200% of direct labor cost.
(4) Miscellaneous foundry overhead incurred:

Prepaid foundry insurance written off	$ 400
Property taxes on foundry building accrued	800
Foundry utilities payable accrued	1,700
Depreciation on foundry equipment	2,500
Other costs incurred on account	3,500

(5) Ending work in process consisted of Jobs 4 and 6.

(6) Jobs 1 and 3 and one-half of Job 2 were sold on account for $5,500, $4,500, and $4,800, respectively.

REQUIRED

(a) Open general ledger T accounts for Materials Inventory, Foundry Payroll, Foundry Overhead, Work in Process, Finished Goods, and Cost of Goods Sold. Also set up subsidiary T accounts to serve as job cost sheets for each job.

(b) Prepare general journal entries to record the summarized transactions for the month, and post the entries appropriate to any accounts listed in (a) above. Key each entry to the related parenthetical letter in the problem data.

(c) Determine the balances of any accounts necessary and prepare schedules of jobs in ending work in process and jobs in ending finished goods to confirm that there is agreement with the related control accounts.

22-34 During June, its first month of operations, Karl Manufacturing Company completed the transactions listed below. Karl uses a simple job order costing system. Materials requisitions and the factory payroll summary are analyzed on the 15th and the last day of each month, and charges for raw materials and direct labor are entered directly on specific job order cost sheets. Factory overhead at the rate of 140% of direct labor costs is recorded on individual job cost sheets at the time a job is completed and at month-end for any job then in process. At month-end, entries are made to the general ledger accounts summarizing materials requisitions, distribution of factory payroll costs, and the application of factory overhead for the month. All other general ledger entries are made as they occur.

(1) Purchased materials on account, $28,000.

(2) Paid miscellaneous factory overhead costs, $7,400.

(3) Paid the semimonthly factory payroll, $22,000.

(4) An analysis of materials requisitions and the factory payroll summary for June 1–15 indicates the following distribution of costs:

Job No.	Materials Requisitioned	Factory Labor
1	$4,400	$ 8,000
2	2,100	3,600
3	900	2,400
Factory supplies used	1,700	
Indirect labor		8,000
	$9,100	$22,000

(5) Jobs 1 and 2 were completed on June 15 and transferred to Finished Goods on the next day. (Enter the appropriate factory overhead amounts on the job cost sheets, mark them completed, and make a general journal entry transferring the appropriate amount of cost to the Finished Goods account.)
(6) Paid miscellaneous factory overhead costs, $5,200.
(7) Job 1 was sold on account for $41,000 (and its cost of sales recognized in the general ledger).
(8) Paid the semimonthly factory payroll, $21,600.
(9) An analysis of materials requisitions and factory payroll summary for June 16–30 indicates the following distribution of costs:

Job No.	Materials Requisitioned	Factory Labor
3	$ 5,200	$ 3,800
4	4,100	7,400
5	1,700	2,800
6	600	900
Factory supplies used	1,400	
Indirect labor		6,700
	$13,000	$21,600

(10) Jobs 3 and 4 were completed on June 30 and transferred to Finished Goods on the same day. [See instruction (5), above.]
(11) Job 3 was sold on account for $34,000 (and its cost of sales recognized in the general ledger).
(12) Recorded the following additional factory overhead:

Depreciation on factory building	$ 5,500
Depreciation on factory equipment	3,400
Expiration of factory insurance	900
Accrual of factory taxes payable	1,500
	$11,300

(13) Monthly entries are recorded in the general ledger for the costs of all materials used.
(14) Monthly entries are recorded in the general ledger for the distribution of factory payroll costs.
(15) Factory overhead is recorded on the job cost sheets for jobs in ending work in process and in the general ledger for all factory overhead applied during the month.

REQUIRED
(a) Set up the following general ledger T accounts: Materials Inventory, Factory Payroll Summary, Factory Overhead, Work in Process, Finished Goods, Cost of Goods Sold, and Sales.
(b) Set up subsidiary ledger T accounts for each of Jobs 1 through 6. These are to serve as job cost sheets.

(c) Noting the accounting procedures described in the first paragraph of the problem, do the following:

    (1) Record general ledger journal entries for all transactions. Note that general ledger entries are *not* required in transactions (4) and (9). Post only those portions of these entries affecting the general ledger accounts set up in requirement (a), above.

    (2) Enter the applicable amounts directly on the appropriate job cost sheets for transactions (4), (5), (9), (10), and (15). Note parenthetically the nature of each amount entered.

(d) Present a brief analysis showing that the general ledger accounts for Work in Process and for Finished Goods agree with the related job cost sheets.

(e) Explain in one sentence each what is represented by the balance of each general ledger account established in (a).

ALTERNATE PROBLEMS

22-27A Arrow Manufacturing, Inc. expects the following costs and expenses during the coming year:

Raw Materials	$21,000
Direct Labor (@ $4 per hour)	72,000
Sales Commissions	12,000
Factory Supervision	8,000
Indirect Labor	4,800
Factory Depreciation*	9,000
Factory Taxes*	4,000
Factory Insurance*	2,000
Factory Supplies Used	7,000
Factory Utilities*	3,000

*The factory building contains a sales showroom that occupies about 30% of the floor space involved.

REQUIRED

(a) Compute a predetermined factory overhead rate assuming an application is to be made on the basis of direct labor hours.

(b) Present a journal entry to apply factory overhead during an interim period when 1,400 direct labor hours were worked.

(c) What amount of overhead would be assigned to Job 325, to which $26 in direct labor had been charged?

22-29A Boom Manufacturing had the following inventories at the end of its last fiscal year:

Materials Inventory	$4,000
Work in Process	2,000
Finished Goods	7,000

During the first month of the current year, these transactions occurred:
(1) Purchased materials on account, $19,000.
(2) Factory payroll incurred, $33,000.
(3) Requisitioned total materials of $17,000, of which $4,000 was considered factory supplies.
(4) Assigned total factory payroll, of which $6,000 was considered indirect labor.
(5) Other factory overhead incurred, $11,000. (Credit Accounts Payable.)
(6) Applied factory overhead on the basis of 80% of direct labor costs.
(7) Determined ending work in process to be $7,600.
(8) Determined ending finished goods to be $14,400.

REQUIRED
(a) Prepare general journal entries to record the above transactions.
(b) If the above transactions were for a full year's operations and the over- or underapplied overhead was considered material, present a journal entry to close the overhead account to the appropriate accounts using an allocation in proportion to the ending balances in those accounts. Round computations to the nearest dollar.

22-30A At the beginning of the current year, the Star Company estimated that it would incur $25,000 of factory overhead cost during the year, using 10,000 direct labor hours to produce the desired volume of goods. On January 1 of the current year, beginning inventories of Materials, Work in Process, and Finished Goods were $9,000, $-0-, and $16,000, respectively.

REQUIRED
Prepare general journal entries to record the following transactions for the current year:
(a) Purchased materials on account for $22,000.
(b) Of the total dollar value of materials used, $19,000 represented raw materials and $5,000 were factory supplies used.
(c) Total factory labor amounted to $60,000 (12,000 hours at $5 an hour).
(d) Of the factory labor, 75% was direct and 25% indirect.
(e) Factory overhead, based on direct labor hours, was assigned to Work in Process.
(f) Actual factory overhead other than those items already recorded amounted to $4,000. (Credit Accounts Payable.)
(g) Ending inventories of Work in Process and Finished Goods were $9,500 and $22,000, respectively. (Make separate entries.)
(h) The balance in Factory Overhead was closed to Cost of Goods Sold.

22-32A Following is a summary of the job order cost sheets related to the production of Moss Manufacturing, Inc. during the first month of the current operating year. The same overhead rate has been used for all jobs.

Job No.	Raw Materials	Direct Labor	Factory Overhead
109	$ 380	$ 420	$273
110	660	280	182
111	1,700	1,400	910
112	1,100	880	572
113	420	320	208

Job 109 was in process at the end of the preceding year, at which time it had incurred $120 of direct labor charges and total charges of $384. Job 113 is the current month's ending work in process.

REQUIRED
(a) What is the apparent factory overhead rate?
(b) What is the total of raw materials requisitioned in the current month?
(c) What is the total direct labor incurred in the current month?
(d) If factory overhead is overapplied by $370 at the end of the current month, what is the total factory overhead incurred during the month?
(e) If finished goods inventory increased during the month by $520, what is the cost of goods sold for the month?

22-33A Summarized data for the first month's operation of John's Casting Foundry are presented below. A job order cost system is used.
(1) Materials purchased on account, $30,000.
(2) Amounts of materials requisitioned and foundry labor used:

Job No.	Materials	Foundry Labor
1	$1,600	$1,200
2	1,800	2,000
3	1,200	3,000
4	5,000	4,400
5	2,500	2,800
6	1,500	600
As foundry supplies	4,000	
As indirect labor		6,000

(3) Foundry overhead is applied at the rate of 150% of direct labor cost.
(4) Miscellaneous foundry overhead incurred:

Prepaid foundry insurance written off	$ 600
Property taxes on foundry building accrued	1,300
Foundry utilities payable accrued	1,500
Depreciation on foundry equipment	3,000
Other costs incurred on account	5,600

(5) Ending work in process consisted of Jobs 4 and 6.
(6) Jobs 1 and 3 and one-half of Job 2 were sold on account for $7,500, $11,000, and $6,000, respectively.

REQUIRED
(a) Open general ledger T accounts for Materials Inventory, Foundry Payroll, Foundry Overhead, Work in Process, Finished Goods, and Cost of Goods Sold. Also set up subsidiary T accounts to serve as job cost sheets for each job.
(b) Prepare general journal entries to record the summarized transactions for the month, and post the entries appropriate to any accounts listed in (a) above. Key each entry to the related parenthetical letter in the problem data.

(c) Determine the balances of any accounts necessary and prepare schedules of jobs in ending work in process and jobs in ending finished goods to confirm that there is agreement with the related control accounts.

BUSINESS DECISION PROBLEM

Lux Manufacturing Company is planning to make and sell a newly designed fuel director valve for use in small aircraft manufactured by other companies. If made with traditional materials, the valve would require the following raw materials and labor:

Materials:	A—5 pounds @ $2 each
	B—6 pounds @ $3 each
	C—4 pounds @ $6 each
Labor:	Casting—3 hours @ $4 per hour
	Finishing—3 hours @ $5 per hour
	Assembling—2 hours @ $6 per hour

Overhead costs in these departments should be $9 per direct labor hour.

Management is also considering using a new synthetic material, D, perfected in space technology activities. Making the body of the valve out of material D would alter the cost and manufacturing procedures as follows: Eight pounds of D, costing $5 per pound, would replace both materials A and B. Casting and finishing labor time would be reduced by 50%. However, each valve would require 4 hours of machining labor costing $10 per hour and performed on a highly specialized, partially automated machine. Factory overhead in the machining department is based on machine hours at the rate of $5 per machine hour.

Lux's marketing department advises management that the valve made of traditional materials would sell for 50% over the company's cost and that aircraft manufacturers will be willing to pay an additional 20% for the valve made of the new lightweight "space" material.

REQUIRED
Based on the relative gross profit per unit, present an analysis showing the relative advantage of the manufacturing alternative you recommend.

23
Cost Accounting Systems: Process Costing

For which of you, desiring to build a tower, does not
first sit down and count the cost . . . ?

LUKE 14:28

This chapter explains and illustrates the concepts and procedures typical of a process costing system that involves more than one processing department. The concluding sections deal with the related concerns of accounting for the costs of service departments, joint products, and by-products.

In Chapter 22, we explained that a process cost system is appropriate in accounting for costs in the production of a large volume of relatively homogeneous products manufactured in a "continuous flow" operation. Producers of fuel, chemicals, cement, paint, and similar goods find this system useful.

In job order costing, where production is discontinuous or where materials and operations performed vary with products, costs must be identified with the specific job or order being produced before unit costs can be determined. In contrast, costs in a process system are identified with a **cost center** (a processing or production department) *during a period of time*—usually a month. A separate work-in-process account is kept for each processing or production department, and monthly costs are accumulated in these accounts. At the end of each month, costs are summarized for each cost center in a **cost of production report.** This report provides the unit cost information that can be used to determine costs of goods transferred from process to process and finally into the finished goods inventory. Thus, whereas a job order system has one work-in-process account supported by a number of job order cost sheets, a process system has several work-in-process accounts, each supported by a monthly cost of production report. The following diagram illustrates process cost flows for a liquid product, the production of which involves only two successive processes, mixing and bottling. To simplify the illustration, we have assumed that there is no incomplete production in process at the beginning or end of the period.

Note the following in the diagram (the various costs would be accumulated as debit balances in the Materials Inventory, Factory Payroll, and Factory Overhead accounts in much the same manner as illustrated in Chapter 22):

(1) Except that there is more than one work-in-process account, process cost flows are parallel to those illustrated earlier for job order costing systems.

(2) Each work-in-process department may incur varying amounts of raw material, direct labor, and factory overhead costs.

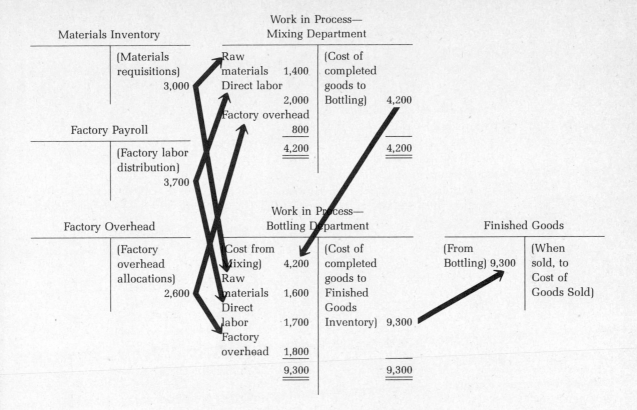

(3) In sequential processes, the costs of prior departments are transferred to and become part of the total cost incurred by the subsequent department.

(4) Upon completion in the final process, the cumulative cost of completed production is transferred to Finished Goods Inventory and, upon sale, becomes Cost of Goods Sold.

Let us now examine how to account for these costs.

DETERMINING UNIT COSTS

In order to trace the cost of products transferred from one processing department to another and eventually into finished goods, we must calculate unit costs. When unit costs are calculated on a monthly basis, a firm can compare its current costs with those of prior periods and thus determine when cost control measures are needed.

Unit cost determination is basically an averaging process. For example, assume that during January of the current year, the mixing department incurred

$1,400 of raw materials cost, $2,000 of direct labor cost, and $800 of overhead cost in processing 800 gallons of product. The unit cost for each gallon would be:

$$\frac{\text{Total Costs for January}}{\text{Total Work Accomplished}} = \frac{\$4,200}{800 \text{ gallons}} = \$5.25 \text{ per gallon}$$

Equivalent Units

In the above computation, we assumed that the 800 gallons were begun and completed during the month. Suppose, however, that unfinished units were in process at the beginning and end of the period. Assume that, of the 800 gallons handled during January, 200 were 25% complete in December and 100 were 50% complete at the end of January. Clearly, it would be incorrect to figure the January unit cost by treating all 800 gallons as if they had been started and finished in January. Instead, we should convert the processing done on 800 gallons into a

FOCUSING YOUR COST INFORMATION

In extremely simple situations economic effectiveness can sometimes be determined by ordinary counting or measuring. How many feet of ditch are dug by a man in a day? How many tons of hay per day are baled by a field crew? However, when larger organizations—business, governmental, institutional—are the accountable units, then dollars enter the picture and formal systematic monetarized cost-keeping becomes mandatory.

To be an effective tool, such costing must be sharply focused. It must get down to "unit" costs or "costs per." Examples are cost per gallon, cost per kilowatt hour, rent and utility costs per square foot of floor space, administrative cost per employee or per dollar of sales. The list could go on and on. Without "costs per," your information is superficial. The mere compiling of total costs, such as depicted in the usual income statement, falls far short of attaining the specific cost knowledge required to obtain genuine operating economy. While some may have better economic intuition than others, it is nevertheless true that no matter how good a guesser one is, he is going to get off course without the map-and-compass of pinpointed unit costing. . . .

After "costs per," there is no more important information than the aggregate cost of the individual products (or product groups) or services (or service groups) that you are selling. Suppose you make two products, say picnic tables and garbage cans, and your total profit for the year is such-and-such. Query: How much was earned or lost on the tables, how much on the cans? It is surprising how many entities don't really know. They can be making or losing more money than they think on one or the other. But if they were armed with reliable costs, they could eliminate or cut back the losing or less profitable items and push the more profitable ones. That way they would be helping not only themselves but also the general economy.

It is remarkable how often, when an expert manager is called in to turn a sick operation around, the first thing he seeks is the source of the losses so he can eliminate the losers. That done, he can proceed to push the winners.

SOURCE: Dixon Fagerberg, Jr., "The Selling of Cost Accounting," *Management Accounting*, June 1974, pp. 23–24. © 1974 by the National Association of Accountants. Reprinted by permission.

smaller number of **equivalent units** of completed product. For example, 100 gallons half completed during the period is equivalent to 50 gallons begun and completed; 200 gallons three-fourths completed is equivalent to 150 gallons begun and completed, and so on. In our example, we would calculate the equivalent units of work for January as follows:

	Total Units Involved (gallons)		Proportion Completed This Month		Equivalent Units
From beginning inventory	200	×	75%	=	150
Begun and finished in January	500	×	100%	=	500
Begun but not finished in January	100	×	50%	=	50
	800				700

If we can assume that materials, labor, and overhead were added gradually throughout processing, the correct unit cost for January would be:

$$\frac{\text{Total Costs for January}}{\text{Equivalent Units Processed}} = \frac{\$4,200}{700 \text{ gallons}} = \$6 \text{ per gallon}$$

Unit cost calculations may be complicated by the fact that in many manufacturing operations materials are added at a different rate or at a different time than are labor and overhead (which together are called *conversion costs*). For example, materials may be added at the beginning of the process, while conversion costs are added evenly throughout the process. When this is true, the number of equivalent units used to calculate the unit cost of materials in a batch of product will be different from the number used to compute the unit cost of conversion.

Exhibit 23-1 graphically presents the revised computation of equivalent units when all materials are added initially and conversion costs are incurred evenly throughout the process. Because all materials for beginning work in process were added during the previous period (when these units were started), no equivalent units for materials are shown this period for this batch. But any unit of product begun this period would have all materials added at the start of this period, so both the 500 units begun and completed and the 100 units only begun (ending work in process) are assigned full equivalent units for materials. For conversion costs, (1) the 200 units in beginning work in process represent only 75% of 200 (150) equivalent units because only the final 75% of processing was done this period; (2) each of the 500 units of product both begun and completed this period equals one equivalent unit because all conversion was accomplished this period; and (3) the 100 units in ending work in process equal only 50 (50% of 100) equivalent units because only one-half of their processing was accomplished this period. Under these assumptions, the number of equivalent units completed for the period is not the same for materials as for conversion costs. Consequently, the computations of cost per equivalent unit require separate calculations for the two cost components, which are then totaled. In our illustration, these are:

EXHIBIT 23-1
Graphic Illustration of Equivalent Units
(Raw Materials Added Initially; Conversion Incurred Evenly Throughout Period)

Product "Batches"	Proportion of Work Accomplished this Period					Equivalent Units	
	(Start) 0%	25%	50%	75%	(Finish) 100%	Materials	Conversion
Beginning work in process (200 units, 25% completed)							
Raw Materials						–0–	
Conversion							150
Those begun and finished this period (500 units)							
Raw Materials						500	
Conversion							500
Ending work in process (100 units, 50% completed)							
Raw Materials						100	
Conversion							50
						600	700

$$\frac{\text{Raw Materials Cost}}{\text{Equivalent Units}} = \frac{\$1,400}{600} = \quad \$2.333 \text{ for materials}$$

$$\frac{\text{Conversion Costs}}{\text{Equivalent Units}} = \frac{\$2,000 + \$800}{700} = \quad \$4.000 \text{ for conversion}$$

Total cost for a whole unit processed this period $6.333

Note again that equivalent unit costs are average costs for a specific period and are derived by dividing the total costs for the period by the related amount of work accomplished during that period.

COST FLOWS ILLUSTRATED

For an example of the operation of a process cost system, assume that the Kleeno Company produces an industrial cleaner called Kleeno, which it markets in one-gallon bottles. There are two processing departments: the Mixing Department and the Bottling Department. In the Mixing Department, various ingredients are added at the start of the process and conversion costs are incurred evenly throughout processing. In the Bottling Department, where the cleaner is bottled, labeled, and placed in cartons, both raw materials and conversion costs are assumed to occur evenly throughout the process. The company uses a predetermined overhead rate of 50% of direct labor costs in both departments. On June 1, there were 6,000 gallons in the Mixing Department, one-third complete with respect to conversion costs; the cost of this inventory was $8,400. There was no inventory in the Bottling Department on June 1.

Materials

On June 1, the firm had a balance of $15,000 in the Materials Inventory account, and during June it purchased $20,000 worth of materials on account. A summary entry for June purchases would be:

Materials Inventory	20,000	
Accounts Payable		20,000

To record June materials purchased.

The raw materials requisitioned during June for each processing department and the factory supplies for general factory use are shown in the following summary entry:

Work in Process—Mixing Department	26,000	
Work in Process—Bottling Department	2,100	
Factory Overhead	3,000	
Materials Inventory		31,100

To record materials and supplies used in June.

Labor

The factory payroll for June indicated that direct labor costs were: Mixing Department, $28,000; Bottling Department, $8,400. Indirect labor costs of supervisors amounted to $7,000. A summary entry to distribute these costs would be as follows:

Work in Process—Mixing Department	28,000	
Work in Process—Bottling Department	8,400	
Factory Overhead	7,000	
Factory Payroll		43,400

To distribute payroll for June.

In recording the payroll, the accountant would have made an earlier debit to the Factory Payroll account for the $43,400 and credited various liabilities for amounts withheld and net wages. We shall ignore this entry here to keep our illustration simple.

Factory Overhead

So far, we have charged $3,000 of factory supplies and $7,000 of indirect labor to the Factory Overhead account. Assume that other overhead costs (maintenance, power, depreciation, and so on) total $8,300. In recording these amounts, we would credit various accounts such as Accumulated Depreciation, Accounts Payable, and Prepaid Expenses. For simplicity, we credit Other Accounts in our summary entry:

Factory Overhead	8,300	
Other Accounts		8,300

To record various factory expenses.

The Kleeno Company allocates factory overhead to each department at a rate of 50% of direct labor costs. (As explained in Chapter 22, a firm would obtain this rate at the beginning of the year by estimating factory overhead and direct labor costs.) The entry to charge the Mixing and Bottling Departments with factory overhead would be:

Work in Process—Mixing Department		
(50% of $28,000)	14,000	
Work in Process—Bottling Department		
(50% of $8,400)	4,200	
Factory Overhead		18,200

To charge estimated overhead to processing departments.

Actual costs charged to the Factory Overhead account total $18,300, while the foregoing entry allocated only $18,200 to the processing departments, resulting in $100 of underapplied overhead. Recall that accumulated amounts of under- or overapplied overhead can be carried as deferred balance sheet charges or credits until the end of the year and then either closed to Cost of Goods Sold or allocated among the inventories and Cost of Goods Sold (see Chapter 22, page 796). At this point, the two work-in-process accounts would contain the following amounts as debit entries:

	Mixing Department	Bottling Department
Beginning Balance	$ 8,400	$ –0–
Raw Materials	26,000	2,100
Direct Labor	28,000	8,400
Factory Overhead	14,000	4,200
	$76,400	$14,700

In accounting for the operations of each department, the total amounts of these charges must be accounted for either as the costs attached to goods transferred out or as the cost of ending work-in-process inventory.

EXHIBIT 23-2
Kleeno Company
June Production Report
(gallons)

	Mixing Department	Bottling Department
In process, June 1 (percent processed)	6,000 ($33\frac{1}{3}\%$)	-0-
Started (or transferred in) during June	26,000	24,000*
Total gallons involved	32,000	24,000
Transferred out during June	24,000	20,000
In process, June 30 (percent processed)	8,000 (75%)	4,000 (25%)

*Although all units literally start in the initial department, it is common to say that units transferred into a subsequent department are "started" in that department that period.

COST OF GOODS TRANSFERRED OUT AND INVENTORIES

Now that we have explained how raw materials, labor, and overhead costs are charged to the work-in-process accounts for each processing department, let us see how costs are determined for goods transferred out and goods remaining uncompleted.[1] Exhibit 23-2 shows the June production report for the two processing departments. Several key observations should be noted regarding the production report:

(1) All unit figures are in whole gallons rather than equivalent units.

(2) The beginning work in process (6,000) plus units started (26,000) constitute the total number of units to be accounted for (32,000). They are accounted for as units transferred out (24,000) plus units in ending work in process (8,000), totaling 32,000 gallons.

(3) Units started (26,000) reduced by units in ending work-in-process inventory (8,000) constitute units both started and completed (18,000) in that period.

(4) As the arrow indicates, the number of units transferred out of the Mixing Department (24,000) is equal to the number of units transferred into the Bottling Department (24,000).

We shall now examine how costs are allocated to the various units, beginning with the Mixing Department.

---

[1]Calculations can be performed on either the first-in, first-out (FIFO) or weighted average basis. We will illustrate the FIFO basis in this chapter.

Mixing Department

Remember that in the Mixing Department, raw materials are added at the start of the mixing process, but conversion costs are incurred evenly throughout the process. Therefore, as indicated earlier, separate calculations of equivalent units and cost per equivalent unit are necessary for raw materials and conversion costs. For the Mixing Department these are:

	Total Units Involved	Conversion Completed This Month	Equivalent Units Raw Materials (added initially)	Conversion (added throughout)
Transferred Out:				
From June 1 inventory	6,000	$\frac{2}{3}$	–0–	4,000
Started and completed	18,000	1	18,000	18,000
Total transferred out	24,000			
June 30 Inventory	8,000	$\frac{3}{4}$	8,000	6,000
Total units involved	32,000			
Total equivalent units			26,000	28,000
Related costs:				
Raw materials			$26,000	
Direct labor and overhead				$42,000
Equivalent Unit Costs:				
Raw materials ($26,000/26,000)			$1.00	
Conversion ($42,000/28,000)				$1.50

In allocating costs to various units of product, there are three batches of Kleeno to be considered: (1) units completed from the June 1 inventory, (2) units begun and completed in June, and (3) units begun but not completed in June. The cost of the first two batches, which were completed during June, would be transferred to the Bottling Department during June, while the cost of the third batch would be assigned to the Mixing Department's inventory. The cost allocation is shown in the Mixing Department's June cost of production report, Exhibit 23–3.

The composition of costs for the three batches of product handled by the Mixing Department can be explained as follows:

(1) *Beginning inventory.* The 6,000 gallons in the beginning inventory had all the raw materials needed and one-third of the required work added last month, for a total cost, in May, of $8,400. In June, the remaining work (two-thirds) was done to complete the units. Because the conversion cost of a full unit is $1.50, we multiply by the equivalent units (4,000 gallons) to obtain the $6,000 cost to complete this batch. Thus, this batch cost $14,400, or $2.40 per unit.

(2) *Started and completed in June.* During June, all required raw materials and work were applied to the 18,000 gallons started and completed. The materials

EXHIBIT 23-3
Kleeno Company
Mixing Department
Cost of Production Report for June

			Current Equivalent Units	Unit Cost
Costs to Be Accounted for:				
Beginning work in process		$ 8,400		
Raw materials		26,000	26,000	$1.00
Conversion costs:				
Direct labor	$28,000			
Factory overhead	14,000	42,000	28,000	1.50
Total costs to account for		$76,400		

Total Units Involved	Allocation of Costs	Total Cost		Unit Cost
6,000	Beginning Inventory (33⅓% processed):			
	Cost from previous month	$ 8,400		
	Raw materials (all added last month)	–0–		
	Conversion (6,000 × 66⅔% × $1.50)	6,000	$14,400	$2.40
18,000	Units Started and Completed:			
	Raw materials (18,000 × $1.00)	$18,000		
	Conversion (18,000 × $1.50)	27,000	45,000	2.50
24,000	Total Units Transferred Out		$59,400	2.475*
8,000	Ending Inventory (75% processed):			
	Raw materials (8,000 × $1.00)	$ 8,000		
	Conversion (8,000 × 75% × $1.50)	9,000	17,000	
32,000	Totals Accounted for		$76,400	

*To avoid carrying forward multiple unit cost figures (some at $2.40 and some at $2.50), all units completed in a period are carried forward at a combined average unit cost figure ($2.475).

added this month at $1.00 per gallon and a full unit of conversion cost of $1.50, are applied to each of the 18,000 units, resulting in a cost of $45,000, or $2.50 per unit. The total cost of the 24,000 gallons in the two batches transferred to the Bottling Department amounts to $59,400, and the average cost of the two batches is $2.475 per gallon ($59,400/24,000).

(3) *Ending inventory.* The 8,000 units begun but not completed in June contain all required raw materials but only three-fourths of the needed work. Therefore, the per-unit raw materials cost of $1.00 is multiplied by 8,000 gallons to obtain the $8,000 materials cost; however, the $1.50 conversion cost is multiplied by the equivalent units of work performed (8,000 × $\frac{3}{4}$ = 6,000) to obtain the $9,000 conversion cost.

Notice that the Cost of Production Report fully accounts for the 32,000 units of product involved and the total costs of $76,400 charged to the Mixing Department in June.

The entry to transfer the work completed in the Mixing Department during June is:

Work in Process—Bottling Department	59,400	
Work in Process—Mixing Department		59,400

To transfer cost of completed work
from Mixing to Bottling.

The Work in Process account for the Mixing Department would now appear as follows:

Work in Process—Mixing

June 1 (beginning balance)	8,400	Transferred to Bottling	
Raw Materials	26,000	Department	59,400
Direct Labor	28,000		
Factory Overhead	14,000		
June 30 (ending balance)	17,000		

Note that all costs charged to this account have been accounted for as either transferred out or remaining as ending inventory.

Bottling Department

Because there was no beginning inventory in this department, the units handled during June consisted only of the 24,000 gallons received from the Mixing Department; these units cost $2.475 per gallon, for a total cost of $59,400. We assume that the cost of the added raw materials, labor, and overhead are incurred evenly throughout the bottling process. These costs, totaling $14,700, cannot be averaged over the units handled, because not all of the 24,000 units were completed. Therefore, we must convert the work performed into equivalent units and obtain an equivalent unit cost, as follows:

	Total Units Handled		Conversion Completed This Month		Equivalent Units
Transferred out (all units started and completed in June)	20,000	×	1	=	20,000
June 30 inventory	4,000	×	$\frac{1}{4}$	=	1,000
	24,000				21,000

Total added costs
  (Raw Materials $2,100 + Labor $8,400 + Overhead $4,200) $14,700

Equivalent unit cost per gallon ($14,700/21,000) $ 0.70

EXHIBIT 23–4
Kleeno Company
Bottling Department
Cost of Production Report for June

Costs to Be Accounted for:			Current Equivalent Units	Unit Cost
Beginning work in process		$ –0–		
Transferred from Mixing Department		59,400		
Raw materials	$2,100			
Direct labor	8,400			
Factory overhead	4,200	14,700	21,000	$0.70
Total cost to account for		$74,100		

Total Units Involved	Allocation of Costs	Total Cost		Unit Cost
20,000	Units Started and Completed:			
	Mixing Department costs (20,000 × $2.475)	$49,500		
	Raw materials and conversion (20,000 × $.70)	14,000	$63,500	$3.175
4,000	Ending Inventory (25% processed):			
	Mixing Department costs (4,000 × $2.475)	$ 9,900		
	Raw materials and conversion			
	(4,000 × 25% × $.70)	700	10,600	
24,000	Totals Accounted for		$74,100	

The cost allocation for the two batches handled is shown in the Bottling Department's June cost of production report, Exhibit 23–4. The composition of costs for the two batches processed by the Bottling Department can be explained as follows:

(1) *Started and completed in June.* Each of the 20,000 units started and completed during June has a full unit measure of added raw materials, labor, and overhead cost. This cost of $0.70 per unit incurred in the Bottling Department can simply be added to the $2.475 per-gallon cost of the Mixing Department to obtain the completed unit cost of $3.175 per gallon. Multiplying this amount by 20,000 gallons, we obtain $63,500 as the cost of the goods transferred to the finished goods inventory.

(2) *Ending inventory.* The 4,000 units begun but not completed in June contain a full unit measure of the Mixing Department cost ($2.475 per gallon), but are only one-fourth complete with respect to all costs of bottling. Therefore, the Mixing Department unit cost of $2.475 is multiplied by 4,000 gallons to obtain the $9,900 total cost from the previous department; however, the $0.70 equivalent unit cost of bottling is multiplied by 1,000 gallons (4,000 × ¼) to obtain the $700 total bottling cost in the ending inventory.

Observe that the cost allocations in the cost of production report are reflected in the journal entry transferring the cost of completed units ($63,500) to Finished Goods Inventory and as the ending balance of Work in Process—Bottling ($10,600).

The entry to transfer the cost of completed work in the Bottling Department during June is:

Finished Goods	63,500	
Work in Process—Bottling Department		63,500
To transfer cost of completed work		
to Finished Goods.		

The Work in Process account for the Bottling Department would now appear as follows:

Work in Process—Bottling

June 1 (beginning balance)	-0-	Transferred to	
Transferred in from		Finished Goods	63,500
Mixing Department	59,400		
Raw Materials	2,100		
Direct Labor	8,400		
Factory Overhead	4,200		
June 30 (ending balance)	10,600		

Again, note that all costs accumulated to this point have been accounted for.

Finished Goods and Cost of Goods Sold

In further tracing the cost flows for a process cost system, we find that the entries made are similar to those made in a job order cost system. We shall assume that during June the Kleeno Company sold goods costing $45,000 for $60,000. In summary form, the entries to reflect the sales would be:

Accounts Receivable	60,000	
Sales		60,000
To record June sales.		
Cost of Goods Sold	45,000	
Finished Goods		45,000
To record cost of goods sold in June.		

An Overview of Process Costing

As you review the Kleeno Company example, note these basic patterns and relationships in process costing.

(1) Product costs are accumulated in three pools: raw materials, direct labor, and factory overhead; the latter two are often termed conversion costs.

(2) Physical units to be accounted for consist of any beginning work in process and any units started (or transferred in). Physical units are accounted for by transferring them out or having them as ending work in process.

(3) All cost factors, including any beginning inventory costs, are combined as work in process and constitute an amount of cost to be accounted for.

(4) Through the use of equivalent unit computations, the production accomplished this period is measured in whole units and divided into the related total cost amounts to determine this period's equivalent unit cost.

(5) By using equivalent unit costs for the current period, costs are assigned to units transferred out and ending work in process, the total of which should equal the cost to be accounted for in (3) above.

ACCOUNTING FOR SERVICE DEPARTMENTS

Most factories are so large and so complex that there is naturally a high degree of organizational specialization in their operations. Production is usually accomplished in a series of specialized departments, which may include such finely focused departments as cutting, preshaping, dressing (grinding), subassembly, final assembly, painting, and packaging. In addition to these production departments, there is typically a series of highly specialized *service* departments, which may engage in activities related to purchasing, materials handling, personnel, warehousing, inspection, power, maintenance, and even factory dispensaries and cafeterias. Whereas production departments perform direct work on products, service departments provide production departments with support services that contribute indirectly to the completion of products.

Service Departments as Cost Centers

Service departments are often viewed by management as cost centers. As such, the costs of each service department are accumulated so that management can identify the total cost of providing such services as repairs, building maintenance, and factory power. Also, unit costs for each service (such as maintenance cost per square foot of floor space) can be derived for comparison with other operating periods and/or other sources of the service such as outside contractors. A well-designed accounting system should account for service departments as cost centers.

Service Department Costs as Product Costs

Although service departments do not perform actual work on specific products, they do provide essential services to the production departments. Thus, service department costs are appropriately considered among those costs incurred by the related production departments and should be included in final product costs.

This section explains how service costs are accumulated and assigned to individual products.

Because, by their nature, service departments do not use raw materials or direct labor, their costs are part of factory overhead. Because these departments do not perform direct work on a product, however, overhead rates, in the strict sense, are not computed for them. Instead, service department costs are usually assigned to various production departments according to an allocation base that reflects the approximate benefits received by each production department. In other words, service department costs become part of product costs by being allocated among several production departments, using the allocation base considered most appropriate for each, and becoming part of each production department's overhead to be applied to work in process.

The diagram of T accounts (with typical titles and amounts) in Exhibit 23–5 illustrates how service department costs: (1) are accumulated on a cost center basis, (2) are allocated to one or more production departments, and (3) become part of the product costs when factory overhead is applied for each production department. To simplify this illustration, the amounts assumed result in no over- or underapplied overhead.

Note how the $4,000 is accumulated as the total cost for the Maintenance Department, then $1,000 and $3,000 are allocated to the Mixing and Bottling departments, respectively. The allocated service department costs are in turn included in the total of $18,000 and $12,000 of overhead applied from the respective production departments. Similar observations can be made for the Power Department.

Method of Cost Allocation

Costs are allocated among various departments on a base that logically reflects the proportion of the service or activity that benefits each department. Some examples of costs that are often allocated as well as bases that might be used for their allocation are listed below.

Service Cost	Possible Allocation Base
Personnel Salaries	Number of employees in each department
Building Depreciation	Square feet of floor space used
Power	Machine hours used
Building Maintenance	Square feet of floor space used
Machine Maintenance	Machine hours used
Heat and Light	Cubic feet of building space used

Of course, whenever the concern for cost control justifies it, elaborate devices and schemes may be devised for measuring service benefits. Some examples are departmental electric meters, vouchers or tickets reflecting actual hours of services requested and used, and elaborate weighting techniques in which requests for rush or peak hour services are assigned higher costs than requests that can be honored at the convenience of the service department.

To allocate a particular cost, the total cost is simply divided among a series of departments in proportion to departmental shares of the appropriate base activity.

EXHIBIT 23-5
Allocation of Service Department Costs
to Production Departments' Overhead Accounts

Maintenance Department
(a service department)

(Various costs either identifiable with or allocated to this service department)		Allocated to:	
		Mixing	1,000
	4,000	Bottling	3,000
	4,000		4,000

Power Department
(a service department)

(Various costs either identifiable with or allocated to this service department)		Allocated to:	
		Mixing	4,000
	6,000	Bottling	2,000
	6,000		6,000

Factory Overhead—Mixing

(Various overhead costs either identifiable with or allocated to this production department)		Applied to Work in Process	
	13,000		18,000
Allocations from:			
Maintenance Department	1,000		
Power Department	4,000		
	18,000		18,000

Factory Overhead—Bottling

(Various overhead costs either identifiable with or allocated to this production department)		Applied to Work in Process	
	7,000		12,000
Allocations from:			
Maintenance Department	3,000		
Power Department	2,000		
	12,000		12,000

Work in Process—Mixing

Raw Materials	XX	
Direct Labor	XX	
Factory Overhead	18,000	

Work in Process—Bottling

Raw Materials	XX	
Direct Labor	XX	
Factory Overhead	12,000	

For example, suppose that $8,000 of personnel department cost is to be allocated between a mixing department with 15 employees and a bottling department with 25 employees and that the number of production employees is to be the allocation base. The two distinct steps involved and illustrative calculations are:

$$(1) \quad \frac{\text{Total Cost to be Allocated}}{\text{Total Allocation Base}} = \text{Allocation Rate}$$

$$\frac{\$8,000}{40 \text{ employees}} = \$200 \text{ per employee}$$

$$(2) \quad \frac{\text{Allocation}}{\text{Rate}} \times \frac{\text{Amount of Allocation Base}}{\text{Related to Department}} = \frac{\text{Specific Amount}}{\text{Allocated}}$$

$$\$200 \times 15 \text{ employees} = \$3{,}000 \text{ (for mixing)}$$

$$\$200 \times 25 \text{ employees} = \$5{,}000 \text{ (for bottling)}$$

It is often useful to check allocations and verify that the sum of allocated amounts equals the total amount to be allocated.

Exhibit 23-6 is an illustration of the type of worksheet often used to accumulate and allocate factory overhead in a multidepartment factory operation that includes service departments. Note that:

(1) Three categories of costs are involved:
  (a) Those directly identifiable with departments.
  (b) Those requiring allocations to departments.
  (c) Service department costs allocated to production departments.
(2) A total overhead amount is first accumulated for each service department and each production department.
(3) After service department costs are allocated, the total overhead is assigned to the production departments only.
(4) The final amounts assigned to each production department are the amounts used to calculate departmental overhead rates. (See the footnotes to Exhibit 23–6.)

The amounts and proportions in Exhibit 23–6 have been chosen for simplicity of presentation. Also, the variety of costs shown is unrealistically simple in order to stress the basic concepts.

An obvious question is: Why are service department costs not allocated to other service departments? More sophisticated allocation techniques may involve allocations of some service department costs to other service departments and even mutual assignment of all of one or more service departments' costs to all other service departments. In many instances, these refinements do not result in materially different allocations; such detailed discussions are beyond our present objectives.

JOINT PRODUCTS

Often, the processing of raw materials results in two or more products of significant commercial value. Such products derived from a common input are properly termed **joint products,** and the related cost of the raw materials is a **joint cost.** An obvious example of a raw material whose processing results in joint products is crude oil, from which a wide variety of fuels, solvents, lubricants, and residual petrochemical pitches are derived. Cattle, from which the meat packer obtains many cuts and grades of meat, hides, and other products, are another example.

EXHIBIT 23–6
Overhead Distribution Worksheet
For 19XX

	Totals	Service Departments Building Maintenance	Machine Repairs	Production Departments Mixing	Bottling	Accounting Record or Allocation Base
Directly Identifiable with Departments:						
Indirect labor	$ 85,000	$ 8,000	$20,000	$38,500	$18,500	Factory payroll analysis
Factory supplies used	24,000	3,000	2,000	9,000	10,000	Requisition forms
Allocated to Departments:						
Building depreciation	6,000	600	1,200	3,000	1,200	Square feet of floor space
Personal property taxes	4,000	400	800	1,500	1,300	Assessed value of equipment used
Total Manufacturing Overhead	$119,000	$12,000	$24,000	$52,000	$31,000	
Allocation of Service Departments:						
Building maintenance (assumed as $\frac{2}{3}$ for mixing and $\frac{1}{3}$ for bottling):		($12,000)		8,000	4,000	Square feet of factory area used
Machinery repairs (assumed as $\frac{1}{6}$ for mixing and $\frac{5}{6}$ for bottling):			($24,000)	4,000	20,000	Machine hours
Totals	$119,000			$64,000*	$55,000**	

*Assuming a factory overhead allocation base of 20,000 machine hours, the overhead rate for the Mixing Department would be $3.20 per machine hour (or $64,000 ÷ 20,000 machine hours).
**Assuming a factory overhead allocation base of $110,000 direct labor dollars, the overhead rate for the Bottling Department would be $0.50 per direct labor dollar (or $55,000 ÷ $110,000 of direct labor costs).

There is no way to allocate a joint cost among joint products in such a way that management may make decisions on whether or not to continue production or what price to charge for a joint product. To decide to produce one joint product is to decide to produce all related joint products, even if some are to be discarded. Hence, to make informed decisions about joint products, management must compare the total revenues generated by all joint products with their total production cost.

The primary reason for allocating a joint cost among two or more products is to be able to price the ending inventories of joint products in order to determine periodic income. Probably the most popular method of allocating joint costs for inventory pricing purposes is the **relative sales value** method. Like the cost allocations explained earlier, this approach is an exercise in arithmetic proportions. Here, the total joint cost is allocated to the several joint products in the proportions that their individual sales values bear to the total sales value of all joint products at the split-off point (where physical separation is possible). For example, assume that 50,000 55-gallon barrels of crude oil costing $1,200,000 will be processed into 800,000 gallons of fuel selling for $0.75 a gallon, 400,000 gallons of lubricants selling for $2 a gallon, and 1,000,000 gallons of petrochemical residues selling for $0.20 per gallon. The following calculations illustrate how this joint cost would be allocated using the relative sales value approach.

Joint Products	Quantity (Gallons) Produced	Unit Sales Value	Product Sales Value	Proportion of Total Sales Value
Fuel	800,000	$0.75	$ 600,000	6/16
Lubricants	400,000	2.00	800,000	8/16
Residues	1,000,000	0.20	200,000	2/16
Total sales value			$1,600,000	16/16

Allocations of total and per-unit joint costs would be:

	Proportion of Materials Cost	Allocated Cost	Quantity Produced	Cost Per Unit
Fuel	6/16 × $1,200,000	$ 450,000 ÷	800,000 =	$0.5625 per gallon
Lubricants	8/16 × $1,200,000	600,000 ÷	400,000 =	$1.50 per gallon
Residues	2/16 × $1,200,000	150,000 ÷	1,000,000 =	$0.15 per gallon
		$1,200,000		

Note that the relative sales value approach results in assigned unit costs that are the same percentage of the selling price for each product. In our illustration the cost per unit equals 75% of the sales value per unit.

BY-PRODUCTS

By-products are products that have relatively little sales value compared with the other products derived from a process. By-products are considered incidental to the manufacture of the more important products. For example, the sawdust or shavings generated in a lumber planing mill or in the cutting department in a furniture factory is a by-product.

The appropriate accounting procedure for by-products is to assign them an amount of cost equal to their sales value less any disposal costs. This net amount is charged to an inventory account for the by-product and credited to the work-in-process account to which the original materials were charged. For example, consider a furniture factory in which walnut boards are processed through a cutting and shaping department. In processing $40,000 worth of lumber, 800 bushels of sawdust and shavings are generated, which, after treatment costing $80, can be sold for $1.00 per bushel. The following accounts illustrate the amounts and entries involved:

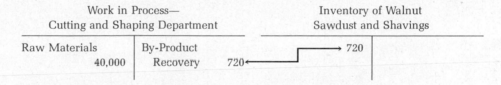

	Work in Process— Cutting and Shaping Department		Inventory of Walnut Sawdust and Shavings
Raw Materials 40,000	By-Product Recovery 720	720 →	→ 720

The net effect of this procedure is to reduce the costs of the main products by the net amount recovered from by-products.

DEMONSTRATION PROBLEM FOR REVIEW

Sheen, Inc. produces a liquid furniture polish in two sequential processes organized as the Mixing Department and the Bottling Department. Raw materials are added initially in the Mixing Department; all other costs in both departments are considered to be incurred evenly throughout the processes. Following are cost data for the month of May:

	Mixing Department	Bottling Department
Beginning work in process inventory	$ 588	(none)
May's operating costs:		
Raw materials	2,400	$ 650
Direct labor	3,500	2,600
Factory overhead	1,400	1,950
	$7,888	$5,200

Beginning work in process consisted of 800 gallons, 50% processed; 8,000 gallons were started in the Mixing Department. Ending work-in-process inventories were 2,000 gallons (30% processed) for the Mixing Department and 400 gallons (25% processed) for the Bottling Department.

REQUIRED
(a) Prepare a production report for May reflecting the activities of both departments.
(b) For each department: (1) calculate the equivalent units accomplished and the equivalent unit costs for May, (2) prepare a cost of production report for May, and (3) prepare journal entries to record the transfer of completed units.

SOLUTION TO DEMONSTRATION PROBLEM

(a)
Sheen, Inc.
May Production Report
(gallons)

	Mixing Department		Bottling Department	
In process, May 1 (percent processed)	800	(50%)	(none)	
Started (transferred in) during May	8,000		6,800	
Total gallons involved	8,800		6,800	
Transferred out during May	6,800		6,400	
In process, May 31 (percent processed)	2,000	(30%)	400	(25%)

(b) (1) (Mixing Department)

	Total Units Involved	Conversion Completed This Month	Equivalent Units Materials (added initially)	Equivalent Units Conversion (added throughout)
Transferred Out:				
From May 1 inventory	800	50%	–0–	400
Started and completed	6,000	100%	6,000	6,000
Total transferred out	6,800			
May 31 Inventory	2,000	30%	2,000	600
Total units involved	8,800			
Total equivalent units			8,000	7,000
Total related costs:				
Raw materials			$2,400	
Direct labor and overhead				$4,900
Equivalent Unit Costs:				
Raw materials ($2,400/8,000)			$0.30	
Conversion ($4,900/7,000)				$0.70

(2) (Mixing Department)

Sheen, Inc.
Mixing Department
Cost of Production Report for May

			Current	Equivalent
			Units	Unit Cost
Costs to Be Accounted for:				
Beginning work in process		$ 588		
Raw materials		2,400	8,000	$0.30
Conversion costs:				
Direct labor	$3,500			
Factory overhead	1,400	4,900	7,000	0.70
Total cost to account for		$7,888		

Total Units Involved	Allocation of Costs	Total Cost		Unit Cost
800	Beginning Inventory (50% processed):			
	Cost from previous month	$ 588		
	Raw materials (all added last month)	–0–		
	Conversion (800 × 50% × $0.70)	280	$ 868	$1.085
6,000	Units Started and Completed:			
	Raw materials (6,000 × $0.30)	$1,800		
	Conversion (6,000 × $0.70)	4,200	6,000	1.00
6,800	Total Units Transferred Out		$6,868	1.01
2,000	Ending Inventory (30% processed):			
	Raw materials (2,000 × $0.30)	$ 600		
	Conversion (2,000 × 30% × $0.70)	420	1,020	
8,800	Totals Accounted for		$7,888	

(3) (Mixing Department)

Work in Process—Bottling	6,868	
Work in Process—Mixing		6,868

To record completion of 6,800 units at a
cost of $1.01 per unit and their transfer to
the Bottling Department.

(b) (1) (Bottling Department)

	Total Units Involved	Conversion Completed This Month	Equivalent Units (all costs added evenly)
Transferred out (all units started and completed in May)	6,400	100%	6,400
May 31 inventory	400	25%	100
Total units involved	6,800		
Total equivalent units			6,500
Total related costs (raw materials, $650; direct labor, $2,600; overhead, $1,950)			$5,200
Equivalent unit cost ($5,200/6,500)			$ 0.80

(2) (Bottling Department)

Sheen, Inc.
Bottling Department
Cost of Production Report for May

			Current Equivalent Units	Unit Cost
Costs to Be Accounted for:				
Beginning work in process		$ –0–		
Transferred from Mixing Department		6,868		
Raw materials	$ 650			
Direct labor	2,600			
Factory overhead	1,950	5,200	6,500	$0.80
Total cost to account for		$12,068		

Total Units Involved	Allocation of Costs	Total Cost	Unit Cost
6,400	Units Started and Completed:		
	Mixing Department costs		
	(6,400 × $1.01)	$6,464	
	Raw materials and conversion		
	(6,400 × $0.80)	5,120	$11,584	$1.81
400	Ending Inventory (25% processed):		
	Mixing Department costs		
	(400 × $1.01)	$ 404	
	Raw materials and conversion		
	(400 × 25% × $0.80)	80	484
6,800	Totals Accounted for	$12,068	

(3) (Bottling Department)

Finished Goods Inventory	11,584	
Work in Process—Bottling		11,584

To record completion of 6,400 units at a
cost of $1.81 per unit and their transfer to
the Finished Goods Inventory.

KEY POINTS TO REMEMBER

(1) Process cost accounting results in averaging the total process costs for a time
period over the related amount of production accomplished during that
period.

(2) When there is ending work-in-process inventory, the measurement of work
accomplished in a period requires that partially completed units be converted to a smaller number of equivalent units.

(3) When materials are added and conversion accomplished at different rates (or
unevenly), equivalent units must be computed separately for each cost factor.

(4) The flows of manufacturing costs and related journal entries are similar for
process and job order cost systems.

(5) The total of all costs in beginning inventories and all costs charged to work in
process must be accounted for as cost of ending work in process plus cost of
goods transferred out.

(6) In assigning manufacturing costs, it is helpful to think of three batches of
products: units transferred out from beginning work-in-process inventories,
units both begun and completed this period, and units remaining in ending
work-in-process inventories.

(7) The total cost to be accounted for in a department includes any cost associated with units transferred in from another department.

(8) Service department costs are overhead costs that are allocated to production
departments and eventually assigned to products as part of the production
departments' overhead.

(9) Joint products are products of significant value originating from a common
raw material or process. Joint product costs are allocated among joint products primarily for purposes of inventory costing.

(10) By-products have relatively insignificant sales value and are valued at their
net recoverable amount, which is removed from the related work-in-process
account and charged to an appropriate inventory account.

QUESTIONS

23-1 What are the important differences between job order and process cost systems? Give two examples of industries that would probably use each system.

23-2 In what way are all manufacturing costs for a series of processing departments accumulated as finished goods inventory?

23-3 Why do unit cost computations in a manufacturing process require the use of equivalent unit computations?

23-4 What is meant by the expression that process cost accounting is basically an averaging computation?

23-5 What is meant by the term "equivalent unit"?

23-6 Why is it sometimes necessary to have separate equivalent unit computations for raw materials and for conversion costs?

23-7 Describe the three "batches" of products that are typically involved in a period's production under the FIFO approach to inventory accounting. In what special situation would there be only two "batches"?

23-8 What is meant by the expression that in each department's work-in-process account all charges must be accounted for either as being transferred out or as ending work-in-process inventory?

23-9 How can the finished products of one department be the raw materials for another department? Give an example.

23-10 Contrast service departments with production departments. Give three examples of service departments.

23-11 Why might service departments be treated as cost centers?

23-12 Explain what is meant by each of the following statements:
(a) Service departments do not work directly on products.
(b) Service department costs are factory overhead costs.
(c) Overhead rates are not used for service departments.
(d) In spite of (c), service department costs become part of product costs.

23-13 What criterion is used in choosing a base for allocating a cost to several departments?

23-14 How is an "allocation rate" calculated? How is the specific amount to be allocated to a department calculated?

23-15 Briefly describe the general format, data, and calculations that would appear on an overhead distribution worksheet for a company with a number of production and service departments.

23-16 Define joint products, and give two examples of industries that have joint products because of the nature of their raw materials.

23-17 If allocated joint costs are irrelevant for management decisions, what is the justification for allocating joint costs among joint products?

23-18 Define by-products, and briefly describe accepted procedures in accounting for them.

EXERCISES

23-19 Waco Company makes a powdered rug shampoo concentrate in two sequential departments, Compounding and Drying. The only raw materials involved are added initially in the Compounding Department. All other costs are added evenly throughout each process. In the Compounding Department, beginning work in process was 2,000 pounds (50% processed), 8,000 pounds were started in process, 7,000 pounds transferred out, and ending work in process was 40% processed. In the Drying Department, there was no beginning work in process, 6,200 pounds were transferred out, and the ending work in process was 75% processed. Prepare a production report for the current month, and calculate the relevant amounts of equivalent units for each department.

23-20 The Dilution Department performs one of a series of processes in which a fluid chemical coating concentrate is mixed with a thinner after which it is considered a finished product. Records indicate that the Dilution Department has been charged with $21,500 of raw materials and $5,000 of direct labor costs. The factory overhead rate is 150% of direct labor costs. Beginning work in process was $6,200, and ending work in process totaled $2,700. One-half of this period's completed product is sold on account at a price equal to 140% of its cost. Prepare journal entries to record: (1) the various costs charged to the Dilution Department this period, (2) transfer of this period's completed product, and (3) sale of one-half of this period's production.

23-21 Following are selected operating data for the Blending Department for the month of April. Tinting and packaging operations are carried out subsequently in other departments.

Beginning inventory	6,000 units, 50% complete
Units both begun and completed	20,000 units
Ending inventory	8,000 units, 75% complete

Calculate the equivalent units accomplished, assuming that
(a) all raw materials are added and conversion accomplished evenly throughout the process;
(b) all raw materials are added initially and conversion is incurred evenly throughout.

23-22 In its first month's operation, Department No. 1 incurred charges for raw materials (3,000 units) of $15,000, direct labor of $4,800, and factory overhead of $2,400. At the end of the month, 2,200 units had been completed and transferred out and those remaining were completed with respect to raw materials but only 25% complete with respect to conversion. Assuming materials are added initially and conversion occurs evenly, compute:
(a) The equivalent units for raw materials and conversion.
(b) The equivalent unit costs for raw materials, direct labor, and factory overhead.
(c) The total cost to be assigned to the units transferred out.
(d) The total cost to be assigned to the ending inventory. Prove that your solutions to (c) and (d) account for the total cost involved.

23-23 Following is the work-in-process account (and certain annotations) for the first of four departments in which Arrow, Inc. makes its only product.

Work in Process—Department 1

Beg. Bal. (400 units,		Transferred to Department 2:	
75% complete)	2,800	Beginning Inventory	
Raw Materials		(400 units)	——— (a)
(4,000 units @ $3)	12,000	Current Period's	
Direct Labor	13,200	Production (3,000 units)	——— (b)
Factory Overhead	4,950		
Ending Bal. [(c) ———			
units, 20% complete]	(d) ———		

Assuming that raw materials are added initially and conversion is incurred evenly throughout, compute the amounts necessary to fill in the four blanks above.

23-24 Following are the charges (and certain annotations) appearing in the work-in-process account for the final processing department of the Bonn Company for the month of April.

Beginning inventory (600 units, 50% complete)	$ 3,500
Transferred in from preceding department (4,000 units)	14,000
Direct labor for current period	7,000
Factory overhead applied in current period	10,500

Assuming that conversion costs are incurred evenly throughout and that all units (except 1,000 units, 20% complete) were completed and transferred to finished goods, compute the unit costs for:
(a) Goods transferred out from April's beginning inventory.
(b) Goods transferred out from current production.
(c) Ending work-in-process inventory.

23-25 Presented below are certain operating data for the four departments that make up Barton Manufacturing Company.

	Departments			
	Service		Production	
	1	2	1	2
Total overhead costs either identifiable with or allocated to each department	$9,000	$15,000	$24,000	$63,000
Square feet of factory floor space			20,000	40,000
Number of factory workers			20	80
Planned direct labor hours for the year			40,000	90,000

Allocate to the two production departments the costs of Service Departments 1 and 2 using as a base, factory floor space and number of workers, respectively.

What would be the apparent overhead rate for each production department if planned direct labor hours were the overhead application base?

23-26 Marston, Inc. produces joint products A, B, and C from a common raw material, a batch of which costs $120,000. At the point at which each product first becomes separable, the following quantities and unit sales prices are available.

Product	Quantity (lb.)	Selling Price/Pound
A	12,000	$10.00
B	10,000	6.00
C	40,000	0.50

Using the relative sales value approach, calculate the amount of joint cost to be assigned to a pound of each product.

PROBLEMS

Note: The firms in all of the following problems use the first-in, first-out method (as illustrated in the chapter) to compute equivalent units and costing inventories.

23-27 Cosmic Fabrics, Inc. manufactures quality placemats in three consecutive processing departments: Cutting, Printing, and Packaging. The following information was taken from unit production reports for the month of May:

	Units in Beginning Inventory	Percent Complete	Units Started in May	Units in Ending Inventory	Percent Complete
Cutting Department	2,000	50	14,000	4,000	25
Printing Department	3,000	$33\frac{1}{3}$	?	5,000	60
Packaging Department	2,000	25	?	3,000	50

Raw materials are added at the start of the process in the Cutting Department, but are added evenly throughout processing in the Packaging Department. No raw materials are used in the Printing Department. Conversion costs are incurred evenly in all processing departments.

REQUIRED
(a) Calculate the number of units started or transferred in during May in the Printing and Packaging Departments.
(b) Calculate the equivalent units of work relating to (1) materials and (2) conversion costs in each department.

23-28 Photochem, Inc. produces a film developer in two sequential processes designated Phase I and Phase II. Photochem was shut down for the month of June, when all employees took their annual vacations. Production was begun on July 1. The following operating data are applicable to July:

	Phase I	Phase II
Units started in process	24,000	
Units transferred in from Phase I		20,000
Units in ending work in process		
(on the average, 40% processed)	4,000	5,000
Cost charged to departments:		
Raw materials	$19,200	$16,000
Direct labor	7,000	10,000
Factory overhead	6,200	14,800

Assume all manufacturing costs are incurred evenly throughout each process and that three-fourths of July's production was sold on account at a price equal to 160% of its cost.

REQUIRED
(a) Briefly explain the status at July 31 of the units started in process during July.
(b) For each department, calculate the equivalent units of production and the equivalent units cost for July.
(c) Prepare journal entries to record the completion and transfer of products from each department and the sale of three-fourths of July's production.

23-29 The Grande Restaurant operates a plant to produce its own steak sauce, called Xtacy Sauce, which is marketed regionally. The sauce is produced in two processes, blending and bottling. In the Blending Department, all materials are added at the start of the process, while labor and overhead are incurred evenly throughout the process. An incomplete account for Work in Process—Blending Department follows:

Work in Process—Blending Department

Jan. 1 Inventory (2,000		Transferred to Bottling	
gallons, 75% processed)	5,500	Department (10,000 gallons)	———
January charges:			
Materials (12,000 gallons)	18,000		
Direct Labor	10,000		
Factory Overhead	6,800		
Jan. 31 Inventory			
(——— gallons, 50% processed)	———		

REQUIRED
Calculate the following amounts:
(a) Number of units in the January 31 inventory.
(b) Equivalent units for calculating unit materials cost and unit conversion cost.
(c) Unit conversion cost for January.
(d) Cost of the units transferred to the Bottling Department.
(e) Cost of the incomplete units in the January 31 inventory.

23-30 The Gordon Company makes a food seasoning powder, processing it through a Compounding Department and a Packaging Department. In the Packaging

Department, processing costs of material, labor, and overhead are incurred evenly throughout the process. Costs charged to the Packaging Department in August were:

Inventory, Aug. 1 (6,000 units, 50% complete)	$ 18,600
Transferred from Compounding (30,000 units)	63,000
Material	8,700
Labor	33,800
Overhead	16,900
	$141,000

At August 31, there were 8,000 units in process, 25% completed.

REQUIRED
Calculate the following for the Packaging Department:
(a) Equivalent units for determining unit processing cost during August.
(b) Equivalent unit processing cost.
(c) Total cost of units transferred to finished goods.
(d) Inventory cost at August 31.

23–31 Custer Laboratories, Inc. produces one of its products in two successive departments. All raw material is added at the beginning of the process in Department 1; no raw material is used in Department 2. Conversion costs are incurred evenly in both departments. At January 1, inventories were as follows:

Raw Materials	$6,000
Work in Process—Department 1 (2,000 units, 40% complete)	4,040
Work in Process—Department 2	–0–
Finished Goods Inventory (2,000 units @ $6.00)	12,000

During January, the following transactions occurred:
(1) Raw materials costing $16,000 were purchased on account.
(2) 16,000 units of raw material at $0.75 per unit were placed into process in Department 1.
(3) Total payroll costs were distributed—$30,800 of direct labor to Department 1, $14,000 of direct labor to Department 2, and $11,000 of indirect labor to Factory Overhead.
(4) Other actual factory overhead costs were $13,000. (Credit "Other Accounts.")
(5) Overhead was allocated (applied) to the two processing departments, $15,400 to Department 1 and $7,600 to Department 2.
(6) 13,000 completed units were transferred from Department 1 to Department 2. The 5,000 remaining units in Department 1 were 20% completed with respect to conversion costs.
(7) 9,000 completed units were transferred from Department 2 to the Finished Goods Inventory. The remaining 4,000 units in Department 2 were 75% completed with respect to conversion costs.
(8) 6,000 units were sold on account at $9 per unit. The company uses first-in, first-out for inventory costing.

REQUIRED
(a) Record the January transactions in general journal form.
(b) State the balances remaining in the accounts for Raw Materials, in each work-in-process account, and in Finished Goods.

23-32 The Revbon Company produces a cosmetic product in three consecutive processes. The costs of Department 2 for the month of May were as follows:

Cost from Department 1		$55,200
Costs added in Department 2:		
Raw materials	$6,300	
Direct labor	9,000	
Overhead	3,600	18,900

Department 2 had no inventory on May 1. During May, units handled were as follows:

Units received from Department 1	23,000
Units transferred to Department 3	18,000
Units in process, May 31	5,000

Of the units in process on May 31, one-half were 80% complete and one-half 40% complete. Both materials and conversion costs occur evenly throughout the process in Department 2.

REQUIRED
Prepare the cost of production report of Department 2 for the month of May.

23-33 Following are selected operating data for the production and service departments of Robbin Company for the current operating period.

	Departments			
	Service		Production	
	1	**2**	**1**	**2**
Overhead Costs (identified by department)				
Factory supplies used	$ 4,000	$ 6,700	$21,200	$ 43,000
Indirect labor	8,100	12,000	27,000	120,000
Square feet of building floor space used	3,000	4,500	7,500	15,000
Assessed value of equipment used	$10,000	$30,000	$60,000	$100,000
Cubic yards of factory space used			80,000	120,000
Machine hours			16,000	64,000
Direct labor costs			$40,000	$80,000

Building depreciation of $16,000 is to be allocated on the basis of square feet of floor space. Personal property taxes of $6,000 are to be allocated on the basis of assessed values of equipment used. Service Departments 1 and 2 are to be allocated to production departments on the basis of cubic yards of factory space and machine hours, respectively.

REQUIRED
(a) Prepare an overhead distribution worksheet similar to Exhibit 23–6.
(b) Compute the factory overhead rates for Production Departments 1 and 2 using machine hours and direct labor cost, respectively, for allocation bases.

23–34 James Company produces joint products A and B and a by-product B-1 from a common raw material and manufacturing process involving sequential processing departments for blending and for distilling, after which the three products become separable and are considered finished goods.

Because of the nature of the operation, there are no beginning or ending work-in-process inventories. For the current period, charges to Work in Process—Distilling were:

Transferred in from blending	$84,200
Direct labor	20,500
Factory overhead	26,900

REQUIRED
Assuming that the following quantities and sales prices are available when the products become separable, (a) allocate the joint costs to each joint product on the basis of relative sales value; (b) prepare journal entries to record the current period's product completion in and transfer from the distilling department to finished goods.

Product	Quantity (lb.)	Unit Price
A	8,000	$ 5.50
B	12,000	13.00
B-1	2,000	1.00*

*Special freight charges of $400 are incurred in selling product B-1 for this price.

ALTERNATE PROBLEMS

23–28A Poston, Inc. produces a shoe polish in two sequential processes designated Phase I and Phase II. Poston was shut down for the month of August, when all employees took their annual vacations. Production was begun on September 1. The following operating data are applicable to September:

	Phase I	Phase II
Units started in process	18,000	
Units transferred in from Phase I		16,000
Units in ending work in process (on the average, 25% processed)	2,000	4,000
Cost charged to departments:		
Raw materials	$ 5,250	$12,000
Direct labor	24,750	21,000
Factory overhead	11,250	8,600

Assume all manufacturing costs are incurred evenly throughout each process and that three-fourths of September production was sold on account at a price equal to 140% of its cost.

REQUIRED

(a) Briefly explain the status at September 30 of the units started in process during September.

(b) For each department, calculate the equivalent units of production and the equivalent units cost for September.

(c) Prepare journal entries to record the completion and transfer of products from each department and the sale of three-fourths of September production.

23–29A The Dobbs Restaurant operates a plant to produce its own regionally marketed salad dressing, called Dobbs Sauce. The sauce is produced in two processes, blending and bottling. In the Blending Department, all raw materials are added at the start of the process, while labor and overhead are incurred evenly throughout the process. An incomplete account for Work in Process—Blending Department follows.

Work in Process—Blending Department

Jan. 1 Inventory (3,000		Transferred to Bottling	
gallons, $\frac{1}{3}$ complete)	8,700	Department (10,000 gallons)	_____
January charges:			
Materials (8,000 gallons)	19,200		
Labor	6,000		
Overhead	6,740		
January 31 Inventory			
(_____ gallons, $\frac{4}{5}$ complete)	_____		

REQUIRED

Calculate the following amounts:

(a) Number of units in the January 31 inventory.

(b) Equivalent units for calculating unit materials cost and unit conversion cost.

(c) Unit conversion cost for January.

(d) Cost of the units transferred to the Bottling Department.

(e) Cost of the incomplete units in the January 31 inventory.

23–30A The Grand Company makes a scouring powder, processing it through a Compounding Department and a Packaging Department. In the Packaging Department, processing costs of raw material, labor, and overhead are incurred evenly throughout the process. Costs charged to the Packaging Department in October were:

Inventory, Oct. 1 (4,000 units, 25% complete)	$ 3,900
Transferred from Compounding (38,000 units)	32,300
Material	5,300
Labor	7,000
Overhead	4,800
	$53,300

At October 31, there were 6,000 units in process, 50% completed.

REQUIRED

Calculate the following for the Packaging Department:

(a) Equivalent units for determining unit processing cost during October.

(b) Equivalent unit processing cost.

(c) Total cost of units transferred to finished goods.

(d) Inventory cost at October 31.

23-31A Cotter Laboratories, Inc. produces one of its products in two successive departments. All raw material is added at the beginning of the process in Department 1; no raw material is used in Department 2. Conversion costs are incurred evenly in both departments. At August 1, inventories were as follows:

Raw Materials	$ 5,000
Work in Process—Department 1 (6,000 units, 25% complete)	4,350
Work in Process—Department 2	None
Finished Goods Inventory (4,000 units @ $3.30)	13,200

During August, the following transactions occurred:

(1) Materials costing $15,000 were purchased on account.

(2) 16,000 units of raw material at $0.75 per unit were placed into process in Department 1.

(3) Total payroll costs were distributed—$23,400 of direct labor to Department 1, $14,960 of direct labor to Department 2, and $6,700 of indirect labor to Factory Overhead.

(4) Other actual factory overhead costs were $9,700. (Credit "Other Accounts.")

(5) Overhead was allocated (applied) to the two processing departments at a rate of 25% of direct labor cost.

(6) 20,000 completed units were transferred from Department 1 to Department 2. The 2,000 remaining units in Department 1 were 50% completed with respect to conversion costs.

(7) 15,000 completed units were transferred from Department 2 to the Finished Goods Inventory. The remaining 5,000 units in Department 2 were 40% completed with respect to conversion costs.

(8) 9,000 units were sold on account at $7 per unit. The company uses first-in, first-out for inventory costing.

REQUIRED

(a) Record the August transactions in general journal form.

(b) State the balances remaining in the accounts for Raw Materials, in each work-in-process account, and in Finished Goods.

23-32A The Beau-T Company produces a dandruff shampoo in three consecutive processes. The costs of Department 2 for the month of June were as follows:

Cost from Department 1		$14,400
Costs added in Department 2:		
Materials	$ 4,920	
Labor	12,800	
Overhead	3,700	$21,420

Department 2 had no inventory on June 1. During June, units handled were as follows:

Units received from Department 1	12,000
Units transferred to Department 3	8,000
Units in process, June 30	4,000

Of the units in process on June 30, one-half were 75% complete, one-fourth 50% complete, and one-fourth 20% complete. Both materials and conversion costs occur evenly throughout the process in Department 2.

REQUIRED
Prepare the cost of production report of Department 2 for the month of June.

BUSINESS DECISION PROBLEM

Coffer's, Inc. makes a new "space-age" adhesive in a single process that blends and bottles the product, which currently sells for $8.00 a gallon. Market demand for the product seems good, but management is not satisfied with what it considers to be a low profit margin on the product and has sought your advice.

Because of its concern, management has allocated a fund of $15,000 for some program of product promotion or cost reduction or both. Members of the firm's controller's office and marketing staff have identified three possible plans.

Plan A   Devote all funds to product promotion that will allow all costs and the sales volume to remain the same, but will permit a $1.00 per gallon sales price increase.

Plan B   Spend $10,000 on product promotion and $5,000 on cost reduction techniques. This will maintain sales volume, permit a price increase of $0.50 per gallon, and reduce direct labor costs by 20% on each gallon.

Plan C   Devote all funds to cost reduction efforts. Sales volume and price will not change. For each gallon produced, however, raw materials cost will be reduced 5%, direct labor cost reduced 30%, and factory overhead reduced 15%.

The controller's office also provides you with operating data for a typical period as follows (all materials are added initially, conversion occurs evenly throughout the process):

	Costs
Beginning work in process, 4,000 gallons (25% processed)	$ 18,000
Units started in process, 20,000 gallons	
Ending work in process, 8,000 gallons (75% processed)	
Cost charged to the department:	
Raw materials	70,000
Direct labor	56,700
Factory overhead	27,300
	$172,000

Using the data from this representative production period, analyze the apparent relative benefits to be derived from each plan and make a recommendation supported by relevant calculations.

24

Cost–Volume–Profit
Relationships

> **Economy is in itself a source of great revenue.**
>
> SENECA (4 B.C.?–A.D. 65)

Most of this text has been devoted to financial accounting, which deals primarily with historical data. As we have seen, the main purpose of financial accounting is to provide reports on the economic unit in the aggregate or on major segments of the unit. Because a firm's financial reports are used by outsiders as well as by management, the information included must be accumulated and reported in accordance with generally accepted accounting principles. Because outsiders depend on such reports to measure the success of a firm and its management, a high degree of objectivity and standardization must be employed in their preparation.

Managerial accounting, on the other hand, concerns the development and analysis of data for the purpose of *internal planning* and *decision making*. Both historical and estimated data may be used, and, although managerial accounting draws on many concepts from economics, engineering, cost accounting, and finance, there are no rigid approaches or constraints in its application. Any concept, approach, or method that yields satisfactory and beneficial data for management needs in current operations or in planning future operations may be used. Probably the most basic technique used by management in its internal planning and decision making is **cost behavior analysis.**

Costs are monetary expressions of the sacrifices made by a firm in attempting to generate revenues sufficient for profitable operations. Costs are usually incurred before revenues are received and are generally subject to greater managerial control than revenues. Because of their significant influence on potential profit, management is extremely interested in how costs that may be expected from various operating alternatives compare with one another and with past costs.

COST BEHAVIOR ANALYSIS

Cost behavior analysis is most often defined as *the study of the ways in which specific costs respond to changes in the volume of business activity.* In other words, as the volume of business activity changes, does a total cost factor increase or decrease, does it change proportionately, or does it not respond at all? Costs may also change in response to other factors, of course. An increase in total property taxes may be due to an increased assessment rate, and an increase in total wage expense may be the result of higher wage rates. Presumably, neither of these increases is related to changes in the volume of business activity.

Cost behavior analysis is one of the most important elements in the planning, control, and decision making of business firms. In manufacturing firms, it is particularly useful for planning production levels, budgeting factory costs, estimating costs for particular orders, and directing promotional effort. It can also be used for such purposes as evaluating the relative profitability of products and determining a company's break-even activity level.

Although cost behavior analysis is most commonly applied to manufacturing costs, it can be just as useful in service businesses. Whenever management is concerned about what costs are likely to be for a particular operation, the analyses presented here are appropriate in one form or another.

The Activity Base

For meaningful analysis, costs must be related to some measure of business activity. In a factory operation, available measures include units of product, direct labor hours, machine hours, and percent of capacity (although the latter must first be expressed in terms of time or amount of product). The cost analyst must consider the way the analysis will be used and then select the most relevant and useful activity base to which costs can be related. For example, if management wishes to use the analysis for control purposes and to establish responsibility for costs, the analyst should select measures that are meaningful to those responsible for incurring costs. One may, of course, use several bases, depending on the objectives of the analysis.

Cost-Volume Graphs

One of the most useful tools for relating cost changes to volume changes is the cost–volume graph. As shown in Exhibit 24–1, costs in dollars are measured along the vertical axis of the graph, and some measure of business volume is presented along the horizontal axis. With costs in thousands of dollars and volume in thousands of units of production, for example, point A in Exhibit 24–1 shows that production of 30,000 units has an associated cost of $20,000, and point B represents a cost of $30,000 for 50,000 units.

The value of cost–volume graphs lies in the fact that when available cost–volume data are plotted on the same graph, other cost–volume relationships may be estimated by fitting a line to the known points. This is illustrated in Exhibit 24–2, where for simplicity we have used three known data points. (In reality, a graph plotted with so few points could not be expected to be very reliable.) The known data represented by the solid points in the graph in Exhibit 24–2 (page 854) are:

Volume (units)	Cost (dollars)
10,000	10,000
20,000	15,000
40,000	25,000

By connecting the known data points with a straight line, we may impute the costs associated with any other production volume. For example, the open points indicate that for volumes of 5,000, 35,000, and 50,000 units, the related costs would be

EXHIBIT 24–1
Graphical Presentation
of Cost–Volume Relationships

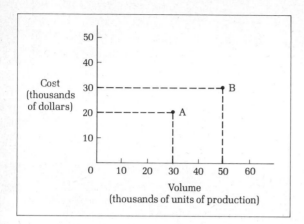

EXHIBIT 24–2
Estimation of Cost–Volume Relationships
from Known Data

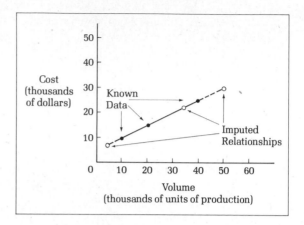

$7,500, $22,500, and $30,000, respectively. Some important limitations to the validity of cost–volume relationships imputed in this manner will be discussed later in the chapter.

Classifications of Cost Behavior Patterns

For purposes of analyzing their behavior patterns, factory costs are usually classified as *variable, fixed,* or *semivariable.* The classification of factory costs into these distinct groups is seldom a simple matter, however. Costs frequently behave in an erratic and inconsistent manner, and the cost analyst must be quite circumspect in analyzing their behavior.

Despite the difficulties of classification, the study of approximate cost behavior patterns can be extremely helpful in planning and analyzing operations. Let us examine the ways in which cost–volume graphs vary among the three cost classifications.

Variable costs are those costs that change proportionately with changes in the volume of activity. Raw (or direct) materials cost, for example, usually behaves in this manner. Direct labor cost can also often be classified as variable.

Exhibit 24–3 is a typical variable cost graph. As illustrated here, a purely variable cost pattern will always pass through the origin, because zero cost is associated with zero volume. Also, because variable costs respond in direct proportion to changes in volume, a variable cost line will always slope upward to the right. The steepness of the slope will depend on the amount of cost associated with each unit of volume; the greater the unit cost the steeper the slope. (Remember that the slopes of two graphs can be compared visually only when the axis scales are identical. The best way to see this is to draw a few graphs with the same data and different scales or with the same scales and different data.)

EXHIBIT 24-3
Variable Cost Pattern

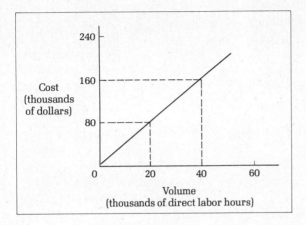

EXHIBIT 24-4
Fixed Cost Pattern

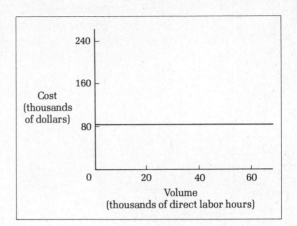

FIXED AND "MOVING" EXPENSES

We come now to the important problem of analyzing moving expenses, those that depend so directly on sales that they vary, or should vary, with every change in sales. How much they vary is what we wish to determine. We can be sure of only one thing in advance, namely that some of them will vary more, in proportion to a given change in sales, than others. It is also obvious that moving expenses, like fixed expenses, will jump to new levels if the fluctuation in sales is large enough to induce a change in the structure of the business. We shall assume that this does not take place. When it does, a fresh study of the problem is usually required.

This definition of moving expense may seem obvious and clear. That it is not so experience attests. In at least one large business that attempted to classify moving and fixed expenses there was an unbelievable amount of confusion. There were two or three conflicting theories abroad in the institution as to how one recognized a moving expense. One theory was that any expense intimately connected with the sales end of the business was per se a moving expense, and its adherents applied it meticulously. In one branch of this institution, to take a small but picturesque illustration, it was customary to serve tea to customers once a week or once a month. . . . Attendance had no relation to changes in sales; the cost of the tea did not vary at all. Nevertheless, this infinitesimal expense was carefully segregated and applied to selling expense, which of course was classified as a moving expense.

The correct and the only correct definition of a moving expense is that it moves with sales. The situation is vaguely reminiscent of the Renaissance battles over the Copernican theory, which stated that the earth moves, and of the heresy trial of Galileo. It will be recalled that Galileo left the trial, after his recantation, muttering to himself, "Nevertheless it moves." The same goes for a moving expense.

SOURCE: Horace C. Levinson, *Chance, Luck and Statistics*. © 1939, 1963 by Dover Publications, Inc. Reprinted by permission.

In Exhibit 24–3, where volume is measured in direct labor hours, the total variable dollar cost is twice as great at 40,000 hours as at 20,000 hours, as should be expected.

Fixed costs (sometimes called nonvariable costs) are those that are usually related to a time period and remain unchanged when the volume of activity changes. Examples are depreciation on buildings and property taxes.

By definition, fixed costs do not respond to changes in volume and are therefore represented by horizontal lines on a cost–volume graph. Exhibit 24–4 illustrates a situation in which fixed costs are $80,000 regardless of the volume level considered.

Semivariable costs are sometimes called **mixed costs** because they can be described analytically as having both fixed and variable components. A semivariable cost is one that increases or decreases linearly with changes in activity, but is also some positive amount at zero activity, as shown in Exhibit 24–5. Changes in total semivariable costs are therefore not proportional to changes in operating volume.

As an example of a semivariable cost, consider a firm's utility expense. Even if the firm were to shut down production for one period, it would be required to pay a minimum amount for utilities. When production resumed, the cost of heat, light, and power would increase as production increased. Total production costs, in fact, are virtually always semivariable.

For purposes of cost analysis, it is often helpful to divide a semivariable cost into its fixed and variable components. This can be accomplished by any one of several approaches that vary in their degree of sophistication. One simple method entails plotting on a graph the amount of cost experienced at several levels of volume. If cost behavior in actual situations were perfectly correlated, the observations (points) would form a straight line. More realistically, we would expect only a discernible pattern as shown in Exhibit 24–6.

EXHIBIT 24–5
Semivariable Cost Pattern

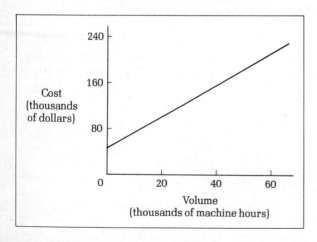

EXHIBIT 24–6
Analysis of Semivariable Cost

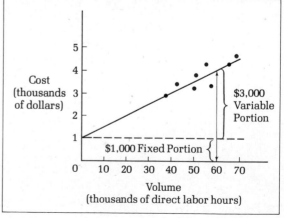

The line in Exhibit 24–6 has been subjectively determined to give a good approximation to the pattern of data points. Extending this line to the vertical axis indicates a $1,000 fixed portion. If we subtract this $1,000 fixed cost from the total $4,000 cost at 60,000 direct labor hours, we find that $3,000 is the total variable portion. Thus, the rate of variation is $3,000/60,000, or $0.05, per direct labor hour. Hence, we could describe this semivariable cost as $1,000 plus $0.05 per direct labor hour.

This approach can be made somewhat more rigorous by fitting the line to the cost observation pattern (data points) by the method of least squares. That technique is beyond the scope of this text but is illustrated in most introductory statistics texts.

When there are too few cost observations available to plot a graph or when the analyst wishes to avoid fitting lines to data, the **high–low** method is sometimes used to approximate the position and slope of the cost line. This relatively simple method consists of comparing costs at the highest and lowest levels of activity for which representative cost data are available. The variable cost per activity unit (here, per direct labor hour) is determined by dividing the difference in costs at these two levels by the difference in activity. The fixed element of cost is then isolated by multiplying the variable cost per unit by either the top or bottom level of activity and then subtracting the resulting product from the total cost at the activity level selected. For example, assume that the lowest and highest levels of activity were 40,000 and 60,000 direct labor hours, respectively, and that total costs were as shown below for these two levels.

	Level of Activity	Total Cost
High	60,000 direct labor hours	$4,200
Low	40,000 direct labor hours	3,000
(Difference)	20,000 (increase)	$1,200 (increase)

Because an increase of 20,000 direct labor hours causes a $1,200 increase in total cost (and only the variable portion of the cost could increase), the variable portion of the total semivariable cost must be $1,200 divided by 20,000 direct labor hours, or $0.06 per direct labor hour. Subtracting the total variable portion from the total semivariable cost at each activity level, we derive the fixed portion of total cost as follows:

	Low	High
	Volume Levels	
Total semivariable cost	$3,000	$4,200
Less variable portions:		
$0.06 × 40,000 direct labor hours	2,400	
$0.06 × 60,000 direct labor hours		3,600
Fixed portion of total cost	$ 600	$ 600

Thus the high–low analysis tells us that for any volume level there is $600 of fixed cost plus a variable portion of $0.06 per direct labor hour, which can be formulated as

$$\text{Total Cost} = \$600 + (\$0.06 \times \text{Direct Labor Hours})$$

In other words, we can now easily compute the total cost for varying numbers of direct labor hours. Obviously, if either the high or low value used in this method is far from representative of the actual cost behavior, the resulting cost formula will be inexact.

The semivariable cost pattern is of special significance because it best represents the pattern of total cost for the firm. This relationship is developed further in a later section of this chapter.

Relevant Range   The foregoing illustrations of cost behavior are oversimplified because they portray linear cost behavior over the entire range of possible activity. Actually, plotting costs against volume may not always produce a single straight line. For example, certain costs may increase abruptly at intervals in a "step" pattern; others may exhibit a curvilinear pattern when plotted over a wide range of activity. Examples of these cost patterns are shown graphically in Exhibit 24–7.

It is clear from the graphs that an assumption of linear costs over the entire scale on either axis in these two cases would lead to some degree of error. The significance of this error is often mitigated by the fact that many of the firm's decisions involve relatively small changes in volume around some midrange amount, here indicated by the vertical lines. Thus the actual pattern of costs at extremely low or high volume levels is not relevant to the firm's decisions. All that is necessary is that the cost pattern be reasonably linear within the relevant range of volume.

EXHIBIT 24–7
Illustration of Relevant Ranges

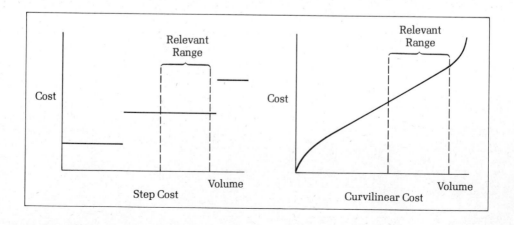

Although the relevant ranges for many cost factors can only be approximated, it is often necessary to consider these ranges for the practical application of cost behavior analysis. Throughout this chapter, unless specifically qualified, references to fixed cost assume that a relevant range has been determined.

Total Versus Per-Unit Costs

Thus far our discussion has been concerned with behavior patterns of total costs. It is also important, however, to compare per-unit cost and total cost patterns so that the differences become apparent and there is less inclination to confuse the two.

Consider the following cost–volume data for activity levels of 0 to 1,000 units.

Activity Volume (units)	Variable Cost ($1/unit)		Fixed Cost ($1,000/period)		Semivariable Cost ($500 + $0.50/unit)	
	Total	Per Unit	Total	Per Unit	Total	Per Unit
0	$ 0	—	$1,000	—	$ 500	—
200	200	$1	1,000	$5	600	$3
500	500	1	1,000	2	750	1.50
1,000	1,000	1	1,000	1	1,000	1

Note that a constant cost per unit causes a variable total cost pattern; in fact, it is necessary if total cost is to vary in proportion to volume (and thus agree with our definition of variable costs). With a fixed cost, the cost per unit decreases proportionately with an increase in volume because the same total amount is spread over larger amounts of production as volume increases. Finally, the reason for the semivariable per-unit pattern is that although the variable portion per unit remains constant, the fixed portion decreases proportionately as volume increases, and the net result is a less-than-proportionate decrease. These patterns are summarized in Exhibit 24–8.

Another important observation here is that total fixed costs and per-unit variable costs can be thought of as *stable* costs, because they remain constant as volume is changed. Per-unit fixed costs and total variable costs are *unstable* in that they are valid at only *one* volume level. In the following section, we show how the stable forms of cost expressions—*total* fixed cost and *per-unit* variable cost—are incorporated in a general formula for total cost that is valid over a wide range of operating volumes.

EXHIBIT 24–8
Patterns of Total and Per-Unit Costs
as Volume Increases

Cost Category	Total Costs	Per-Unit Costs
Variable	Increase proportionately	Remain constant
Fixed	Remain constant	Decrease proportionately
Semivariable	Increase less than proportionately	Decrease less than proportionately

Planning
Total Costs

Budgeting for a business firm, which is treated in detail in Chapter 26, usually consists of a financial plan that reflects anticipated or planned amounts of such items as revenues, costs, cash balances, and net income. Underlying most aspects of budgeting is some assumed volume of activity or sales, as well as an analysis of the total cost to be incurred for that level of operation. Obviously, then, cost behavior analysis is a vital aspect of most budgets.

FIXED PLANS   A relatively simple approach to estimating total cost is the **fixed** or **static plan.** Here an attempt is made to determine what costs should be at a given level of activity, such as normal capacity. Fixed plans list costs and the amounts to be anticipated at some specific level of operation. One of the major defects of fixed plans is that actual levels of activity and planned levels of activity are seldom the same. For this reason, with fixed plans actual cost at one level of volume must often be compared to planned costs at another level of volume. This tends to make the comparison less meaningful, if not erroneous, because any variable cost elements involved will reflect the actual—not the planned—activity levels.

FLEXIBLE PLANS   The recognized limits of fixed plans have led to the development of flexible plans. **Flexible plans** are based on a formula for total costs like that used earlier (page 858) to describe total semivariable cost: total cost = fixed cost + (variable cost per unit × volume). This parallel is explained as follows.

During any operating period, virtually all firms incur costs that fit each of the three cost behavior patterns—variable, semivariable, and fixed. Quite logically, the pattern representing a firm's total cost is the sum of all three patterns. As shown in the following diagram, when all three patterns are added by "stacking" them on a single graph, the result is a semivariable cost pattern.

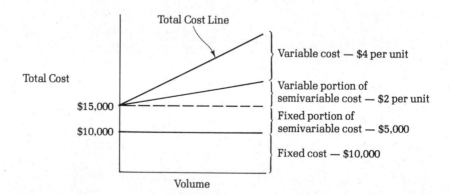

We have assumed that total fixed cost is $10,000, semivariable cost has a fixed portion of $5,000 and a variable portion of $2 per unit, and that variable costs are $4 per unit. When all cost factors are "stacked" on one graph, the top line is the total cost line and indicates a semivariable pattern. By combining the stable expressions of each cost pattern (*total* for fixed cost and *per unit* amounts for variable cost), we can state a general formula for total cost that will be applicable to a wide range of operating volumes.

$$\text{Total Cost} = \text{Total Fixed Cost} + \left(\begin{array}{l} \text{Variable} \\ \text{Cost} \quad \times \text{Volume} \\ \text{per Unit} \end{array} \right)$$

In our example

$$\text{Total Cost} = \$15{,}000 + (\$6 \times \text{Volume})$$

Thus, at zero volume, total cost is $15,000, or the total of all fixed cost. At 5,000 units of volume, total cost is $45,000, or $15,000 + ($6 × 5,000). At 10,000 units of volume, total cost is $75,000, or $15,000 + ($6 × 10,000). Notice that when volume is doubled from 5,000 to 10,000 units, total cost responds, but less than proportionately—thus reflecting our definition of total semivariable cost.

By using a flexible plan, a firm can forecast costs at different levels of activity. In Exhibit 24–9, each type of cost behavior pattern is considered in the flexible plan formula. For simplicity, only a single item is shown for raw materials and for direct labor, only three items make up overhead, and selling and administrative costs are shown as a single amount. The dollar amounts have been chosen for ease of manipulation, and the 10,000-unit activity level is incorporated for illustrative purposes.

EXHIBIT 24–9
Cost Factors in a Flexible Plan Formula
for Total Cost at 10,000 Units of Volume

Type of Cost	Total Cost	=	Total Fixed Cost	+	Variable Cost per Unit	×	Volume
Raw Materials (variable)	$20,000	=			($2.00	×	10,000 units)
Direct Labor (variable)	25,000	=			(2.50	×	10,000 units)
Factory Overhead:							
Factory Supplies (variable)	10,000	=			(1.00	×	10,000 units)
Property Taxes (fixed)	4,000	=	$ 4,000				
Maintenance (semivariable)	7,000	=	5,000	+	(.20	×	10,000 units)
Selling and Administrative							
Expense (semivariable)	9,000	=	6,000	+	(.30	×	10,000 units)
Total Cost	$75,000	=	$15,000	+	($6.00	×	10,000 units)
Aggregate Flexible Plan Formula:	Total Cost	=	$15,000	+	($6.00	×	10,000 units)

We see from Exhibit 24–9 that combining the various cost factors into the aggregate flexible plan formula permits us to determine expected costs not only at the 10,000-unit level but also at other levels simply by inserting the appropriate volume figure in the final formula. For example, total planned cost at 8,000 units is $15,000 + ($6 \times 8,000) = $63,000; at 12,000 units it is $15,000 + ($6 \times 12,000) = $87,000.

A word of caution is appropriate here. Because flexible planning relies so heavily on cost behavior analysis, all the limitations of the latter (assumed linearity, relevant ranges, and so on) apply. Also, we repeat, analyzing many costs into fixed and variable components is often quite complex and inexact in actual situations. All these limitations to some degree affect the potential contribution of managerial accounting. In many cases, the analytical approach presented here will be the best available.

COST–VOLUME–PROFIT ANALYSIS

Cost analysis is so basic to the management process that entire books have been devoted to the subject. In our discussion, we shall survey some basic applications related to cost–volume–profit relationships and profit planning.

For purposes of illustration, the following data for Spencer Company will be used throughout the next several sections.

Spencer Company
Condensed Income Statement

Sales (10,000 units @ $20)		$200,000
Costs:		
Variable Cost (10,000 units @ $12)	$120,000	
Total Fixed Cost	60,000	
Total Cost		180,000
Net Income		$ 20,000

This information assumes that any semivariable costs have been divided into their fixed and variable portions and combined with the purely fixed and purely variable cost elements. We shall now examine some of the ways in which this information is used.

Break-even Analysis

Management frequently finds it useful to know the level of revenue or number of units of sales at which there is no net income or loss. The level at which total revenue equals total cost is called the **break-even point.** Sometimes it is expressed in terms of percent of capacity, but more frequently it is given in dollars or in units of sales. Let us calculate the break-even point, using the condensed income statement data for Spencer Company.

EXHIBIT 24–10
Break-even Chart

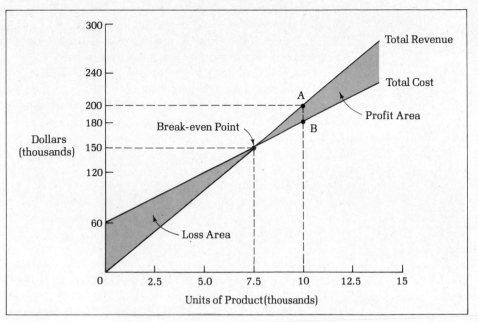

THE BREAK-EVEN CHART   For the break-even chart we use the same basic graph employed earlier to explain and portray cost behavior patterns. In this case, however, the vertical axis measures both total revenue and total cost. Let us demonstrate the construction of a break-even chart with the Spencer Company data.

As before, volume is measured along the horizontal axis. For the Spencer Company the activity base is units of product, and for convenience we choose the scale shown in Exhibit 24–10. Total revenue and total cost are measured in thousands of dollars along the vertical axis. Let us first determine the total revenue line.

With zero revenue for zero sales, we know that the graph of total revenue must always pass through the origin; this gives us one point on the line. In general, then, we may draw the total revenue line by connecting the origin with any other point that represents total revenue for some volume amount. For example, for Spencer Company, total revenue for 10,000 units is $200,000, which gives us point A, and to construct the total revenue line we simply connect point A and the origin and extend the line to the right.

We now construct the total cost line in the manner discussed previously. With fixed cost of $60,000, the total cost line must intersect the dollar axis at $60,000. We could locate another point by calculating the total cost at some volume as $60,000 plus the number of units times the variable cost per unit. For Spencer Company, however, we are given total cost of $180,000 for 10,000 units, and from this can plot point B. We are now able to draw the total cost line for Spencer Company as shown in Exhibit 24–10.

Extending the dashed lines as indicated from the point of intersection of the two graphed lines to the two axes, we find the break-even point (where total revenue equals total cost) for Spencer Company to be 7,500 units of production or $150,000 of total sales revenue. Note that all points lying below the break-even point indicate a loss, while points above the break-even level represent profit. The profit and loss areas are indicated by the shaded areas on our graph. The amount of profit or loss at any volume level is determined by measuring the vertical distance between the total cost and total revenue lines. Clearly, a profit is indicated when the total revenue line is above the total cost line, and a loss is indicated when the reverse is true.

ASSUMPTIONS IN BREAK-EVEN ANALYSIS   In our construction of a break-even chart, we assumed linear relationships over a wide range of activity. This method implies that total fixed cost and variable cost per unit are constant over the entire range and that selling price per unit remains the same regardless of the sales volume. It also implies that when more than one product is involved, as sales volume varies, each product's percent of the total sales (*sales mix*) remains the same.

Break-even charts represent a type of *static analysis*, because they are drawn with the assumption that certain existing relationships among sales prices, costs, and volume remain the same and that sales mix is unvarying. Although this limits their usefulness to some degree, break-even charts are a convenient reference framework for measuring the way in which an expected change in certain factors will affect a company's profit and loss picture. For example, changes in selling prices or variable costs will result in changes in the *slope* of both the total revenue line and the total cost line, while changes in fixed cost result in vertical shifts of the total cost line.

BREAK-EVEN FORMULAS   By definition, the break-even point is the volume level at which total revenue equals total cost (and thus profit is zero). To calculate the break-even point, we restate this basic equality as an equation in either of the following forms:

$$\text{Total Revenue} = \text{Total Cost}$$

$$\frac{\text{Unit}}{\text{Sales Price}} \times \text{Volume} = \frac{\text{Total}}{\text{Fixed Cost}} + \left(\frac{\text{Variable Cost}}{\text{per Unit}} \times \text{Volume} \right)$$

Using the data for Spencer Company and letting X be the unknown volume, TFC, total fixed cost, and VCU, variable cost per unit, we have:

$$\text{Break-even Sales} = \text{TFC} + (\text{VCU} \times \text{Volume})$$

$$\$20(X) = \$60,000 + \$12(X)$$

$$\$8(X) = \$60,000$$

$$X = 7,500 \text{ units}$$

Multiplying 7,500 units by the sales price of $20 yields break-even sales revenue of $150,000. Of course, the answers derived by formula should, and do, agree with the graphic solutions.

CONTRIBUTION MARGIN **Contribution margin** is defined as revenue minus variable costs. The significance of either total or per-unit contribution margin is that it is the amount available to first absorb fixed costs and then possibly provide net income. Thus, at the break-even point, total contribution margin equals total fixed cost.

Using the data for Spencer Company, we see that:

(1) Contribution margin per unit (CMU) equals $8 (the unit sales price of $20 less unit variable cost of $12).

(2) Total contribution margin at 7,500 units equals $60,000 ($8 × 7,500 units), which is exactly the amount of fixed costs and therefore the break-even point.

(3) At 10,000 units, $80,000 of total contribution margin is generated. This fully absorbs the fixed costs of $60,000 and also provides $20,000 of net income (see the original data on page 862).

Two fairly common analyses related to contribution margin are widely used to compute break-even points. The first is:

$$\text{Break-even Sales (in units)} = \frac{\text{Total Fixed Cost}}{\text{Unit Contribution Margin}}$$

$$= \frac{\$60,000}{\$8}$$

$$= 7,500 \text{ units}$$

The second method involves the concept of **contribution margin ratio,** which is defined as

$$\frac{\text{Unit Sales Price} - \text{Unit Variable Cost}}{\text{Unit Sales Price}}$$

For Spencer Company, this would be ($20 − $12)/$20, or 0.4. Intuitively, the contribution margin ratio is simply the fractional expression of that portion of the sales price that is contribution margin. It is used as follows:

$$\text{Break-even Sales (in dollars)} = \frac{\text{Total Fixed Cost}}{\text{Contribution Margin Ratio}}$$

$$= \frac{\$60,000}{0.4}$$

$$= \$150,000$$

This alternate solution can be verified by dividing by the unit sales price:

$$\$150,000/\$20 = 7,500 \text{ units}$$

which is indeed the break-even volume. And, of course, any break-even computation may be verified by preparing a related income statement that should show
net income to be zero.

**Planning
Net Income**

A business firm may wish to estimate the effect on net income of contemplated
changes in selling prices or costs, or it may wish to determine the increase in sales
volume needed to arrive at a desired net income. When a firm has made a careful
study of cost behavior, the analytical framework we have just discussed becomes
quite helpful in planning net income. Both the formula and the contribution margin approaches to break-even analysis can be slightly modified to determine target amounts of sales revenue designed to provide planned amounts of net income.
The essence of the modification is to convert from break-even sales to desired
sales and to add the amount of net income to the other amounts that total revenues must cover. For example, suppose Spencer Company wants to estimate
the sales volume required to earn $24,000 net income before taxes. We proceed
as follows:

$$\begin{array}{c} \text{Desired Sales} \\ \text{(in units)} \end{array} = \begin{array}{c} \text{Total} \\ \text{Fixed Cost} \end{array} + \begin{array}{c} \text{Total} \\ \text{Variable Cost} \end{array} + \begin{array}{c} \text{Target Net Income} \\ \text{before Taxes} \end{array}$$

$$\$20(X) = \$60,000 \quad + \$12(X) \quad + \$24,000$$

$$\$8(X) = \$84,000$$

$$X = 10,500 \text{ units}$$

A brief income computation verifies the analysis.

Sales (10,500 units @ $20)		$210,000
Variable Cost (10,500 units @ $12)	$126,000	
Total Fixed Cost	60,000	
Total Cost		186,000
Net Income before Taxes		$ 24,000

The contribution approaches provide the same results. First we have

$$\begin{array}{c} \text{Desired Volume} \\ \text{(in units)} \end{array} = \frac{\text{Total Fixed Cost + Target Net Income before Taxes}}{\text{Unit Contribution Margin}}$$

$$= \frac{\$60,000 + \$24,000}{\$8}$$

$$= 10,500 \text{ units}$$

Alternatively, we may use

$$\begin{aligned}\text{Desired Volume}\atop\text{(in dollars)}\end{aligned} = \frac{\text{Total Fixed Cost} + \text{Target Net Income before Taxes}}{\text{Contribution Margin Ratio}}$$

$$= \frac{\$60,000 + \$24,000}{0.4}$$

$$= \$210,000$$

The two formulas simply express the same volume in different ways, because $\$210,000/\$20 = 10,500$ units.

Sometimes it may be desirable to express the target net income as a percentage of sales rather than as a dollar amount. This is easily incorporated in a net income planning formula. Assuming we want a profit of 20% of sales, we proceed as follows:

$$\begin{aligned}\text{Desired Sales}\atop\text{(in units)}\end{aligned} = \begin{aligned}\text{Total}\atop\text{Fixed Cost}\end{aligned} + \begin{aligned}\text{Total}\atop\text{Variable Cost}\end{aligned} + \begin{aligned}\text{Target Net Income}\atop\text{before Taxes}\end{aligned}$$

$$\$20(X) = \$60,000 \quad\quad + \$12(X) \quad\quad + 0.20[\$20(X)]$$

$$\$20(X) = \$60,000 \quad\quad + \$12(X) \quad\quad + \$4(X)$$

$$\$4(X) = \$60,000$$

$$X = 15,000 \text{ units}$$

In this situation, desired sales would be 15,000 units, or $300,000, of which the desired 20% profit would be $60,000.

Effect of Income Taxes

Suppose that the management of Spencer Company wishes to determine the sales level needed to produce a desired net income *after income taxes*. Assume that the target net income after taxes is $14,000 and the income tax rate is 30%. The only adjustment required in the equations is to divide the after-tax net income by the factor $(1 - 0.30)$, that is, by 1.0 minus the tax rate. This converts the net income amount in the equation to a before-tax figure.

$$\text{Desired Sales (in dollars)} = \frac{\$60,000 + \$14,000/(1 - 0.30)}{0.40}$$

$$= \frac{\$60,000 + \$14,000/0.70}{0.40}$$

$$= \frac{\$80,000}{0.40} = \$200,000$$

Break-even Analysis and Multiple Products

As indicated earlier, one of the assumptions necessary in break-even analysis is that only one product is involved or that the product mix (the ratio of each product to the total number of products sold) is constant. Break-even sales can be computed for a mix of two or more products by calculating the *weighted average contribution margin.* Assume that a company sells products A and B at the unit sales prices and variable costs indicated below, it has $60,000 total fixed costs, and its product mix is two units of A for each unit of B.

	A	B
Unit selling price	$12	$5
Unit variable costs	6	2
Unit contribution margin	$ 6	$3

With two units of A providing $6 each and one unit of B providing $3, the total contribution margin generated by each group of three product units is $15. Because three units of product are involved, the weighted average unit contribution margin is $15/3, or $5. Our break-even calculation is:

$$\text{Break-even Volume} = \frac{\text{Total Fixed Cost}}{\text{Weighted Average Unit Contribution Margin}}$$

$$= \frac{\$60,000}{\$5}$$

$$= 12,000 \text{ units}$$

This calculation can be verified by noting that if the product mix is two units of A to one unit of B and a total of 12,000 units are sold, then the total contribution margin generated is exactly equal to the total fixed cost, as shown below.

Product	Product Mix	Volume Sold	Unit Contribution Margin	Total Contribution Margin
A	2/3	8,000	$6	$48,000
B	1/3	4,000	3	12,000
		12,000		$60,000

The concepts explained here could be applied to any product mix or number of products.

A PERSPECTIVE ON COST ANALYSIS

Managing costs is a prevailing concern of management. The concepts introduced in this chapter underlie most efforts to analyze and project cost in a variety of decision situations. In actual applications, because projections of future costs are subject to many complicating factors, for most companies they are *estimates* of *probable* costs rather than precise determinations. Properly used, with full recognition of their limitations, cost behavior analyses can be highly useful to management.

KEY POINTS TO REMEMBER

(1) Unlike financial accounting, managerial accounting is not limited to historical cost data, nor is it constrained by generally accepted accounting principles; its only criterion is usefulness to management.

(2) Behavior of total cost in response to volume changes can be divided into three basic categories within a relevant range:
Variable—responds proportionately, with zero cost at zero volume.
Fixed—constant.
Semivariable—responds, but less than proportionately, owing to a fixed component.

(3) Total cost for most firms is best represented by the semivariable cost pattern.

(4) Semivariable costs may be divided into fixed and variable subelements using either graphic plottings or the "high-low" method.

(5) It is often feasible to assume linearity of cost because it is approximately true within the range of volume relevant to the analysis.

(6) Per-unit costs behave as follows when volume is increased:
Variable—remains constant.
Fixed—decreases proportionately.
Semivariable—decreases less than proportionately.

(7) A general formula for planning total cost is:

Total Cost = Total Fixed Cost + (Variable Cost per Unit × Volume)

(8) The break-even point (revenues equal costs) can be derived by graph, formulas, or contribution margin analysis.

(9) Contribution margin is defined as revenues minus variable costs.

(10) Break-even and contribution margin formulas can be restated to provide estimates of target sales for planning net income.

(11) Break-even computations involving multiple products incorporate the concept of a weighted average contribution margin.

QUESTIONS

24-1 In what important ways do the objectives and constraints of financial and managerial accounting differ?

24-2 Define the terms "cost behavior" and "relevant range."

24-3 Identify some common activity bases in terms of which the volume of a manufacturing operation might be stated. What general criterion might be used in choosing a base?

24-4 Name, define, and plot on a graph the three most widely recognized cost behavior patterns. Plot activity horizontally and cost vertically.

24–5 Explain: (a) how a semivariable cost can be thought of as "partly fixed and partly variable," and (b) why total cost for a firm is best represented by the semivariable cost pattern.

24–6 Briefly describe two techniques for dividing a semivariable cost into its fixed and variable subelements.

24–7 "Actual costs often behave in a nonlinear fashion. Therefore, assumptions of linearity invalidate most cost behavior analysis." Do you agree or disagree with this statement? Briefly defend your position.

24–8 Describe how per-unit proportions of the three basic cost patterns respond to volume increases.

24–9 Present a formula for planning total costs, and explain how semivariable costs are incorporated into the formula.

24–10 Define and briefly explain three approaches to break-even analysis.

24–11 The Crusty Donut Shop has fixed costs per month of $630. Variable costs are 30% of sales. What amount of monthly sales will allow the shop to break even?

24–12 The Jiffy Car Wash has fixed costs per month of $3,000. Variable costs are 40% of sales. The average amount collected per car serviced during the past year has been $4. How many cars must be serviced per month to break even?

24–13 You have drawn a graphic portrayal of cost–volume–profit relationships for a company on a break-even chart, after being informed of certain assumptions. Explain how the lines on the chart would change (a) if fixed costs increased over the entire range of activity, (b) if selling prices per unit decreased, and (c) if variable costs per unit increased.

24–14 Define "contribution margin." Is it best expressed as a total amount or as a per-unit amount? In what way is the term descriptive of the concept?

24–15 Explain the approach to break-even analysis that is used for a mix of two or more products.

24–16 Explain how break-even formulas can be extended to provide income-planning analyses.

24–17 In planning net income, how can an after-tax amount of net income be incorporated into the planning formula?

EXERCISES

24–18 Set up a cost–volume graph similar to those presented in the chapter with proportional scales from 0 to 20,000 (in 2,000-unit increments) for cost and volume. Plot each of the following groups of cost data using different marks for each group. After completing the graph, indicate the type of cost behavior exhibited by each group.

Volume (applicable to each group)	Group A Costs	Group B Costs	Group C Costs
1,000	$ 3,700	$ 900	$3,000
3,000	5,100	2,700	3,000
5,000	6,500	4,500	3,000
10,000	10,000	9,000	3,000

24-19 Apply the high-low method of cost analysis to the three cost data groups in Exercise 24-18. What cost behavior patterns are apparent? How would each be expressed as a cost formula?

24-20 The highest and lowest levels of activity for the Coster Company were 30,000 direct labor hours and 20,000 direct labor hours, respectively. If maintenance cost was $76,000 at the 30,000-hour level and $56,000 at the 20,000-hour level, what cost might be expected at an operating level of 25,000 direct labor hours?

24-21 During the past year Wexon, Inc. has operated within the relevant range of its fixed costs. Monthly production volume during the year has ranged from 14,000 to 20,000 units of product and corresponding average manufacturing costs have ranged from $1.85 to $2.00 per unit. Determine the total cost behavior pattern that Wexon, Inc. is experiencing.

24-22 Following are selected data related to the major cost categories experienced by Rolston Company at varying levels of operating volumes.

	Total Cost	Total Cost	Per-Unit Cost	Total Cost	Per-Unit Cost
Operating volume (units)	3,000	4,000	4,000	5,000	5,000
Direct labor (variable)	$1,800	$2,400	————	————	————
Factory supervision (semivariable)	2,800	3,600	————	————	————
Factory depreciation (fixed)	2,000	2,000	————	————	————

Assuming that all operating volumes are within the relevant range, calculate the appropriate costs in each column where blanks appear.

24-23 The Newmann Company has analyzed its overhead costs and derived a generalized formula for their behavior: $18,000 + $4 per direct labor hour employed. The company expects to utilize 60,000 direct labor hours during the next accounting period. What overhead rate per direct labor hour should be applied to jobs worked during the period?

24-24 Following are the amounts of various cost categories Donovan Factories experiences in producing and selling its only product.

Raw materials	$4 per unit of product
Direct labor	$6 per direct labor hour*
Factory overhead	$8,000 plus $4 per direct labor hour
Selling	$10,000 plus $1 per unit of product
Administrative	$6,000 plus $0.20 per unit of product

*Each unit of product requires one-half direct labor hour.

Combine the various cost factors into a general total cost formula for Donovan Factories, and use the formula to determine the total cost for producing and selling 12,000 units.

24-25 Set up a break-even chart similar to Exhibit 24-10 with proportional scales from 0 to $72,000 (in $6,000 increments) on the vertical axis and from 0 to 12,000 units of production (in increments of 2,000 units) on the horizontal axis. Then prepare a break-even chart for Omarr Company, assuming that total fixed costs are $18,000 and that unit selling price and unit variable cost for the company's one product are $6 and $4, respectively.

24-26 Compute the break-even point expressed in units of production for each of the following independent situations. Then confirm each of your answers using contribution margin ratio analysis.

	Unit Selling Price	Unit Variable Cost	Total Fixed Cost
(a)	$12	$9	$24,000
(b)	15	9	54,000
(c)	10	6	30,000

24-27 In each of the three situations presented in Exercise 24–26, what would be the desired sales volume to earn the following related amounts of net income before income taxes? (a) $4,200; (b) $12,000; and (c) equal to 20% of sales revenues.

24-28 The Sunn Company sells a single product for $14 per unit. Variable costs are $6 per unit and fixed costs are $4 per unit at an operating level of 10,000 units.
(a) What is the Sunn Company's break-even point in units?
(b) How many units must be sold to earn $42,000 before income taxes?
(c) How many units must be sold to earn $42,000 after income taxes, if the tax rate is 40%?

24-29 Dawn Company has $76,000 total fixed costs, sells products A and B with a product mix of three units of A to two of B, and has selling prices and variable costs that result in contribution margins per unit of $5 and $2 for products A and B, respectively. Compute the break-even point.

24-30 The Astro Corporation made a net profit last year of $150,000 after income tax. Its fixed costs were $450,000. The selling price per unit of its product was $80, of which $20 was a contribution to fixed cost and net income. The income tax rate was 40%.
(a) How many units of product were sold last year?
(b) What was the break-even point in units?
(c) The company wishes to increase its net income after taxes by 20% this year. If selling prices and the income tax rate remain unchanged, how many units must be sold?

PROBLEMS

24-31 A graph depicting cost–volume relationships for the Bolivar Company is shown below.

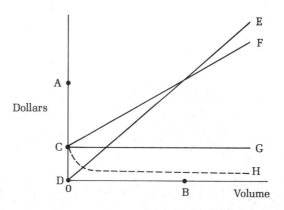

REQUIRED

For each of the following items, choose a labeled point or line on the graph that *best* represents the behavior of each item as operating volume is increased. Answers may be the same for more than one part. Answer each item independently.

(a) total sales revenues   (b) total cost for the firm
(c) variable cost per unit (d) total variable cost
(e) total fixed cost   (f) fixed cost per unit
(g) total semivariable cost (h) break-even point

24-32 Selected operating data for the Boston Company in four independent situations are shown below.

	A	B	C	D
Sales	$90,000	$_____	$_____	$80,000
Variable Expense	$_____	$16,000	$_____	$_____
Fixed Expense	$_____	$14,000	$15,000	$51,000
Net Income (Loss)	$15,000	$10,000	$ 9,000	($15,000)
Units Sold	15,000	_____		
Unit Contribution Margin	$3.00	$2.00		
Contribution Margin Ratio			0.40	_____

REQUIRED

Determine the amounts to fill in the blanks for each independent situation. (Show your calculations.)

24-33 During a recent six-month period, Tasco, Inc.'s monthly volume of production and its total monthly maintenance expenses were as follows.

	Units Produced	Maintenance Expense
Mar.	42,000	$35,200
Apr.	30,000	28,000
May	60,000	46,000
June	55,000	43,000
July	70,000	52,000
Aug.	50,000	40,000

REQUIRED

Assume all volumes are in the relevant range.

(a) Explain why the data indicate that the maintenance expense is neither a fixed nor a variable expense.
(b) Construct a graph similar to that in Exhibit 24–6 and plot the above cost observations.
(c) Fit a line (by sight) to the cost observation dots, and estimate the cost formula.
(d) Confirm your answer in (c) by means of a high–low analysis.

24-34 Rumford Manufacturing produces a single product requiring the following raw materials and direct labor inputs:

Description	Cost per Unit of Input	Required per Unit of Product
Material A	$ 4/lb.	12 oz.
Material B	2/lb.	8 oz.
Material C	10/gal.	0.2 gal.
Cutting labor	6/hr.	1/4 hr.
Shaping labor	8/hr.	1/2 hr.
Finishing labor	4/hr.	3/4 hr.

Factory overhead consists of factory supplies, $0.40 per unit of product; indirect labor, $6,000 per year plus $0.80 per unit of product; factory maintenance, $12,000 per year plus $0.50 per unit of product; factory depreciation, $8,000 per year; and annual factory property taxes, $16,000. Selling and administrative expense include the salaries of a sales manager earning $20,000 per year, an office manager earning $10,000 per year, two salespersons each of whom is paid a base salary of $7,000 per year and a commission of $3 per unit sold. Advertising and promotion of the product are done through a year-round media package program costing $1,000 per week.

REQUIRED
(a) Analyze all cost and expense factors in a manner permitting the determination of a general formula (based on units of production) for total cost.
(b) Assuming a relevant range of from 10,000 to 30,000 units, what would be the estimated unit cost for producing and selling 10,000 units? 20,000 units? Explain the variation in unit cost at the two levels of production.
(c) If 15,000 units were produced and sold in a year, what selling price would result in a net income of $30,000 before income taxes?

24-35 The Francis Company has accumulated total factory overhead costs for two levels of activity (within the relevant range) as follows:

	Low	High
Activity (direct labor hours)	30,000	50,000
Total Factory Overhead Cost	$63,000	$77,000

The total overhead costs include variable, fixed, and semivariable (mixed) costs. The company knows that at 50,000 direct labor hours the total cost breakdown is as follows:

Variable Costs	$20,000
Fixed Costs	30,000
Semivariable Costs	27,000

The company wishes to separate the semivariable costs into fixed and variable categories.

REQUIRED
(a) Using the high–low method of cost analysis, determine the variable portion of the semivariable costs per direct labor hour. Also determine the *total* fixed cost component of the semivariable cost.
(b) What should the total planned overhead cost be at a level of 40,000 direct labor hours?

24-36 Following are total cost data for Ames Manufacturing Company, a firm that has a normal capacity per period of 20,000 units of product, which sell for $15 each. For the foreseeable future, sales volume should continue to equal normal capacity of production.

Raw Materials	$ 80,000
Direct Labor	40,000
Variable Overhead	10,000
Fixed Overhead (Note 1)	50,000
Selling Expense (Note 2)	25,000
Administrative Expense (fixed)	20,000
	$225,000

Note 1: Beyond normal capacity, fixed overhead costs increase $3,000 for each 1,000 units *or fraction thereof* until a maximum capacity of 23,000 units is reached.

Note 2: Selling expenses are a 5% sales commission plus shipping costs of $0.50 per unit.

REQUIRED
(a) Using the information available, prepare a flexible plan formula to estimate Ames' total costs at various production volumes up to normal capacity.
(b) Prove your answer in (a) against the total cost figure at 20,000 units as shown.
(c) Calculate the planned total cost at 16,000 units, and explain why total cost did not decrease in proportion to the reduced volume.
(d) If Ames were operating at normal capacity and accepted an order for 500 more units, what would it have to charge for the order to make a profit of $5 per unit on the new sale?

24-37 Donna, Inc. sells a single product for $40 per unit, of which $15 is contribution margin. Total fixed costs are $35,000 and net income before income taxes is $13,000.

REQUIRED
Determine the following (show key computations):
(a) The present sales volume in dollars.
(b) The break-even point in units.
(c) The sales volume necessary to earn a profit of $19,000 before taxes.
(d) The sales volume necessary to earn a before-tax income equal to 20% of sales revenue.
(e) The sales volume necessary to earn an after-tax income of $28,000 if the tax rate is 30%.

24-38 The controller of the Aris Company is preparing data for a conference concerning certain *independent* aspects of its operations.

REQUIRED
Prepare answers to the following questions for the controller.
(a) Total fixed costs are $420,000 and a unit of product is sold for a price that is $3.50 in excess of its unit variable cost. What is break-even unit sales volume?

(b) 50,000 units of product each having a unit variable cost of $8 are to be sold at a price that will enable the product to absorb $220,000 of fixed costs. What is the minimum unit sales price that can be charged to break even?

(c) Net income before taxes of $60,000 is desired after covering $300,000 of fixed costs. What is the minimum contribution margin ratio that must be maintained if total sales revenues are to be $1,440,000?

(d) Net income before taxes is 10% of sales revenues, the contribution margin is 40%, and the break-even dollar sales volume is $150,000. What is the amount of total revenue?

(e) Total fixed costs are $150,000, variable cost per unit is $4, unit sales price is $16. What dollar sales volume is necessary to generate a profit of $18,000 after paying income taxes of 40%?

24-39 The Shalon Company has recently leased facilities for the manufacture of a new product. Based on studies made by its accounting personnel, the following data are available:

Estimated Annual Sales: 30,000 units

Estimated Costs	Amount	Unit Cost
Material	$ 75,000	$2.50
Direct Labor	60,000	2.00
Overhead	36,000	1.20
Administrative Expense	24,000	0.80
	$195,000	$6.50

Selling expenses are expected to be 10% of sales and the selling price is $10 per unit. (**Note:** Ignore income taxes in this problem.)

REQUIRED
(a) Compute a break-even point expressed in dollars and in units. Assume that overhead and administrative expenses are fixed but that other costs are fully variable.

(b) What would the total profit be if 25,000 units were sold?

(c) How many units must be sold in order to make a profit of 10% of sales?

24-40 Slater Company manufactures and sells three products as indicated below.

	Economy	Standard	Deluxe
Unit sales	10,000	6,000	4,000
Unit sales price	$12	$20	$30
Unit variable cost	$ 8	$14	$19

REQUIRED
Assume that total fixed costs are $87,000.

(a) Compute the net income based on the sales volumes shown above.

(b) Compute the break-even point expressed as total dollars of revenue and as specific unit sales volume for each product.

(c) Prove your break-even calculation by computing the total contribution margin related to your answer in (b).

ALTERNATE PROBLEMS

24-32A Selected operating data for the Hust Company in four independent situations are shown below.

	A	B	C	D
Sales	$80,000	$_____	$_____	$70,000
Variable Expense	$_____	$12,000	$_____	$_____
Fixed Expense	$_____	$14,000	$30,000	$30,000
Net Income (Loss)	$10,000	$ 4,000	$12,000	($ 2,000)
Units Sold	7,000	_____		
Unit Contribution Margin	$5.00	$2.25		
Contribution Margin Ratio			0.70	_____

REQUIRED

Determine the amounts to fill in the blanks for each independent situation. (Show your calculations.)

24-33A During the past operating year, Nashco, Inc.'s monthly volume of production and its total monthly maintenance expenses were as follows:

	Units Produced	Maintenance Expense		Units Produced	Maintenance Expense
Jan.	60	$11,200	July	62	$11,400
Feb.	72	12,700	Aug.	77	13,300
Mar.	78	13,400	Sept.	64	11,700
Apr.	65	11,600	Oct.	80	13,600
May	70	12,500	Nov.	76	13,200
June	75	13,200	Dec.	78	13,400

REQUIRED

Assume all volumes are in the relevant range.

(a) Explain why the data indicate that the maintenance expense is neither a fixed nor a variable expense.

(b) Construct a graph similar to that in Exhibit 24–6 and plot the above cost observations.

(c) Fit a line (by sight) to the cost observation dots, and estimate the cost formula.

(d) Confirm your answer in (c) by means of a high–low analysis.

24-34A Random Manufacturing produces a single product requiring the following raw materials and direct labor inputs:

Description	Cost per Unit of Input	Required per Unit of Product
Material A	$ 6/lb.	24 oz.
Material B	3/lb.	12 oz.
Material C	8/gal.	0.5 gal.
Cutting labor	8/hr.	3/4 hr.
Shaping labor	10/hr.	1/4 hr.
Finishing labor	4/hr.	1/2 hr.

Factory overhead consists of factory supplies, $1.25 per unit of product; indirect labor, $8,000 per year plus $1.20 per unit of product; factory maintenance, $15,000 per year plus $0.80 per unit of product; factory depreciation, $10,000 per year; and annual factory property taxes, $20,000. Selling and administrative expense includes the salaries of a sales manager earning $15,000 per year, an office manager earning $12,000 per year, two salespersons each of whom is paid a base salary of $8,000 per year and a commission of $4 per unit sold. Advertising and promotion of the product are done through a year-round media package program costing $500 per week.

REQUIRED
(a) Analyze all cost and expense factors in a manner permitting the determination of a general formula (based on units of production) for total cost.
(b) Assuming a relevant range of from 30,000 to 40,000 units, what would be the estimated unit cost for producing and selling 30,000 units? 40,000 units? Explain the variation in unit cost at the two levels of production.
(c) If 35,000 units were produced and sold in a year, what selling price would result in a net income of $50,000 before income taxes?

24–35A The Casper Company has accumulated total factory overhead costs for two levels of activity (within the relevant range) as follows:

	Low	High
Activity (direct labor hours)	30,000	50,000
Total Factory Overhead Cost	$52,000	$74,000

The total overhead costs include variable, fixed, and semivariable (mixed) costs. The company knows that at 50,000 direct labor hours the total cost breakdown is as follows:

Variable Costs	$40,000
Fixed Costs	15,000
Semivariable Costs	19,000

The company wishes to separate the semivariable costs into fixed and variable categories.

REQUIRED
(a) Using the high–low method of cost analysis, determine the variable portion of the semivariable costs per direct labor hour. Also determine the *total* fixed cost component of the semivariable cost.
(b) What should the total planned overhead cost be at a level of 40,000 direct labor hours?

24–37A Drake, Inc. sells a single product for $90 per unit, of which $30 is contribution margin. Total fixed costs are $81,000 and net income before income taxes is $15,000.

REQUIRED
Determine the following (show key computations):
(a) The present sales volume in dollars.
(b) The break-even point in units.

(c) The sales volume necessary to earn a profit of $21,000 before taxes.

(d) The sales volume necessary to earn a before-tax income equal to 20% of sales revenue.

(e) The sales volume necessary to earn an after-tax income of $36,000 if the tax rate is 40%.

24-38A The controller of the Boyd Company is preparing data for a conference concerning certain *independent* aspects of its operations.

REQUIRED

Prepare answers to the following questions for the controller.

(a) Total fixed costs are $178,500 and a unit of product is sold for a price that is $4.25 in excess of its unit variable cost. What is break-even unit sales volume?

(b) 35,000 units of product each having a unit variable cost of $8 are to be sold at a price that will enable the product to absorb $175,000 of fixed costs. What is the minimum unit sales price that can be charged to break even?

(c) Net income before taxes of $60,000 is desired after covering $180,000 of fixed costs. What is the minimum contribution margin ratio that must be maintained if total sales revenues are to be $600,000?

(d) Net income before taxes is 20% of sales revenues, the contribution margin ratio is 50%, and the break-even dollar sales volume is $84,000. What is the amount of total revenues?

(e) Total fixed costs are $160,000, variable cost per unit is $18, unit sales price is $30. What dollar sales volume is necessary to generate a profit of $14,000 after paying income taxes of 30%?

24-40A Spence Company manufactures and sells three products as indicated below.

	Race	Shaft	Bearing
Unit Sales	20,000	30,000	50,000
Unit Sales Price	$6.00	$14.00	$2.00
Unit Variable Cost	$2.50	$ 9.00	$1.00

REQUIRED

Assume that total fixed costs are $67,500.

(a) Compute the net income based on the sales volumes shown above.

(b) Compute the break-even point expressed as total dollars of revenue and as specific unit sales volume for each product.

(c) Prove your break-even calculation by computing the total contribution margin related to your answer in (b).

BUSINESS DECISION PROBLEM

Following are total cost data for Porter Manufacturing Company, a firm that has a normal capacity per period of 8,000 units of product that sell for $20 each. For the foreseeable future, sales volume should continue to equal normal capacity of production.

Raw Materials	$ 48,000
Direct Labor	32,000
Variable Overhead	16,000
Fixed Overhead (Note 1)	24,000
Selling Expense (Note 2)	20,000
Administrative Expense (fixed)	6,000
	$146,000

Note 1: Beyond normal capacity, fixed overhead costs increase $800 for each 500 units *or fraction thereof* until a maximum capacity of 11,000 units is reached.
Note 2: Selling expenses consist of a 10% sales commission and shipping costs of $0.50 per unit. Porter has a policy of paying only one-half of the regular sales commission rate on any sale amounting to 500 or more units.

Porter's sales manager has received an order for 1,200 units from a large discount chain at a special price of $18 each, F.O.B. factory. The controller's office has furnished the following additional cost data related to the special order:
(1) Changes in the product's construction will reduce raw materials $2.00 per unit.
(2) Special processing will add 25% to the per-unit direct labor costs.
(3) Variable overhead will continue at the same proportion of direct labor costs.
(4) Other costs should not be affected.

REQUIRED
(a) Present an analysis supporting a decision to accept or reject the special order. Assume Porter's regular sales will not be affected by this special order.
(b) What is the lowest unit sales price Porter could receive and still make a before-tax profit of $1,800 on the special order?

25
Special
Analyses
for
Management

Management is a powerfully evocative term. To workers it suggests some distant and impersonal "they" who, driven instinctively toward higher profits and wage restraints, must be tamed by union muscle and government discipline; to executives it means action planned to effectuate certain results that translate ultimately into a bottom-line figure; to academicians management is that fascinating amalgam of art and science which tantalizingly invites endless and varied speculations.

DR. CLARENCE C. WALTON
PRESIDENT, THE CATHOLIC UNIVERSITY OF AMERICA

One of the most important justifications for a well-developed accounting system is its role as a continuing source of operational information for management. A high correlation exists between the quality of information available to management and the overall success of the operating decisions based on that information. In this chapter we consider briefly the management decision-making process and some cost concepts that are used often in managerial analyses. The ways in which accounting information is used in such analyses are then illustrated in a series of examples.

MANAGEMENT AND THE DECISION-MAKING PROCESS

There are many definitions of "management." In the broad sense, anyone who directs the activities of others is a manager. For a typical manufacturing firm, this includes shop supervisors, department heads, the plant supervisor, division managers, and the company president. A large, complex firm would have many management levels in addition to these.

The specific nature of a manager's activities varies with the level of management. As depicted in Exhibit 25–1, top management is responsible for establishing long-range goals and policies, including major financial arrangements, expansion into foreign operations, and possible mergers with other firms. Middle-level management may deal with the strategies and tactics related to the automation of a department, the establishment of new product lines, and perhaps the direction of the merchandising emphases among various products. Such matters as daily production quotas, compliance with planned costs, and other fairly detailed day-to-day operating concerns are the responsibility of lower-level management. To varying degrees, therefore, all levels of management are involved in decision making.

Decision making requires that a choice be made among alternatives, although the decision-making process as a whole covers a much more comprehensive spectrum of activities. There is probably no finer analogy of the business decision process than the play of a well-organized football team. Virtually all the

EXHIBIT 25-1

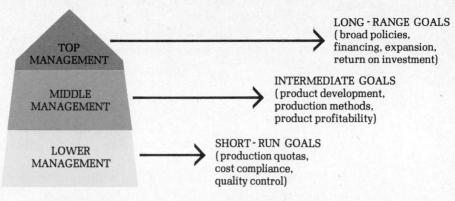

LONG-RANGE GOALS
(broad policies,
financing, expansion,
return on investment)

INTERMEDIATE GOALS
(product development,
production methods,
product profitability)

SHORT-RUN GOALS
(production quotas,
cost compliance,
quality control)

THE FIRM'S
MANAGEMENT HIERARCHY

elements of decision making are present in football—the awareness of the objectives and goals that lead to winning; the balancing of such short-run goals as first downs with the long-run goals of winning games and conference championships; the presence of organization, strategy, and tactics in a "hostile" environment where inaction and poor performance result in losses; the development of plays with the hope of achieving particular results; the moment of commitment in the huddle, immediately followed by the period of execution; and finally, the informal evaluation of performance on the field followed by a formal evaluation as game films are analyzed.

Of course, not all decision making is so well organized and patterned nor, possibly, so scientific. To some degree, good managers rely on what may be called intuition but is more accurately recognized as the subtle insights gained through previous related experiences. Also, many decision situations contain qualitative factors, the effects of which are not easily quantifiable or subject to scientific analysis. Some examples of common qualitative considerations are the possible reactions of competitors, employees, regulatory agencies, and consumer groups. Most decision situations, however, do involve quantifiable factors and thus lend themselves to numerical analysis.

Phases of Decision Making

Decision making may be divided roughly into a planning phase, an execution phase, and an evaluation phase incorporating some form of adaptive or remedial feedback. The following diagram illustrates the sequential nature of the elements of most decision processes.

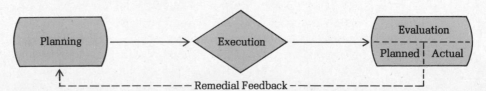

The **planning phase** begins with the identification of a goal. *Goal identification* is the specification of objectives to be sought or accomplished. One of the most common business goals is the long-run optimization of net income. Other goals include target rates of growth in sales revenues or total assets and target shares in various markets. Still other goals, having to do with such objectives as leadership in product research, innovation, and quality, are difficult to measure. Probably the most widely recognized goal is a specified return on assets. In Chapter 18 we described one measure of this return as the ratio of income before interest and taxes to assets employed to earn that income. The calculation of return on assets can be modified in a number of ways, depending on the preferences of management. One variation is to use after-tax income to calculate the ratio.

The next steps in planning are to identify feasible alternative courses of action for achieving the desired goals and to estimate their qualitative and quantitative effects on the specified goals. Accounting plays an important role here because the quantifiable aspects of analysis rely heavily on accounting data.

Because all planning involves the future, it must be done with less than perfect information and therefore implies an element of uncertainty. Advanced treatments of decision theory weigh the value of additional information that reduces the uncertainty of decision situations against the cost of obtaining the information. Also, recognition of the uncertainties of decision analyses has led to the use of probabilistic determinations of the results to be expected from various courses of action. These subjects, however, are beyond the scope of this text.

The **execution phase** begins with the actual moment of "decision"—the commitment of management to a specific plan of action. Because of the complexity of modern industry, in which an individual corporation may manufacture tens of thousands of products and sell them in worldwide markets, plans may be so elaborate that lead times of several years are often necessary. Poor planning, or the absence of planning, may lead to operating crises that carry significant penalties for the firm in terms of extra costs, lost opportunities, and—in extreme cases—bankruptcy.

Once a decision has been made, the plan is implemented. Implementation usually involves the acquisition and commitment of materials, labor skills, and long-lived assets such as machinery and buildings. Management is kept informed through periodic accounting reports on the acquisition and use of these facilities during the execution phase.

In the **evaluation phase,** steps are taken to *control* the outcome of a specific plan of action. Virtually every important aspect of business—costs, product quality, inventory levels, and sales revenues—must be reasonably well controlled if a firm is to operate successfully. Measuring performance is an essential element of control; to exercise control, management must be able to compare current operations with desired operations and take remedial action when significant unfavorable variations exist. Accounting data and reports play a key role in informing management about performance in various areas during the evaluation phase of decision making. The discussions of budgeting and standard costs presented in Chapter 26 provide examples of how accounting contributes to management control.

Decision processes do not, of course, fall into three neatly divided phases. The sheer multiplicity of goals and related options for their implementation often generate quite complex decision environments. Changes in competition, technology, and customer demand must be taken into consideration. Furthermore, most management teams are engaged in all decision-making phases at any given time. They may be planning decisions in one area, executing them in a second, and evaluating them in a third.

MANAGEMENT ANALYSES AND REPORTS

Management analyses and reports are any schedules, computations, or reports requested by management as an aid in carrying out its duties. They take many forms, including comprehensive summaries of past operating data, elaborate projections of future operating data, and highly specific analyses of how certain operating procedures have affected or may affect particular cost or revenue factors. Generally speaking, top managers need broad, highly summarized reports, and lower-level managers require more specialized reports containing greater detail. Management reports often relate to specific departments or operations and reflect particular operating responsibilities.

Exhibit 25–2 illustrates the sequential incorporation of accounting cost data into the performance reports prepared for successively higher echelons of management. Such a system of reports tends to assure a continuity of cost accountability from the lowest operating units to the highest levels of management. The preparation and use of performance reports is developed further in Chapter 26.

Remember that these reports are intended for management's use and are not totally constrained by generally accepted accounting principles. Although much of the financial data that appear on published financial statements may also be used, management reports may contain any sort of estimate of costs, revenues, or values deemed relevant to the analysis. The quality of management analyses and reports depends on their timeliness, clarity, conciseness, and relevance to the problem being investigated to a greater extent than what might be termed their dollar-and-cents accuracy. Any type of data that is useful to management may be included in management reports.

COST CONCEPTS

Because of the great variety of managerial problems and the flexibility allowable in management reports and analyses, many important cost concepts and terms are in general use. After reviewing the cost categories discussed in earlier chapters, we will discuss some others that are frequently encountered. These categories, of course, are not always mutually exclusive—some costs fall into more than one category.

EXHIBIT 25-2

Performance Report—Vice President of Production
For the Month of August, 19XX

	Budgeted Cost	Actual Cost	Over (Under)
Administration	$ 14,700	$ 19,100	$ 4,400
Machining	122,300	120,000	(2,300)
Fabricating	118,600	122,300	3,700
Assembly	118,400	118,600	200
	$374,000	$380,000	$ 6,000

Performance Report—Manager of Machining Operations
For the Month of August, 19XX

	Budgeted Cost	Actual Cost	Over (Under)
Lathe Department	$ 56,200	$ 51,000	$(5,200)
Drilling Department	40,200	39,000	(1,200)
Finishing Department	25,900	30,000	4,100
	$122,300	$120,000	$(2,300)

Performance Report—Supervisor of Drilling Department
For the Month of August, 19XX

	Budgeted Cost	Actual Cost	Over (Under)
Raw Materials	$16,000	$15,800	$(200)
Direct Labor	18,000	16,700	(1,300)
Factory Overhead: (listed in detail)	6,200	6,500	300
	$40,200	$39,000	$(1,200)

First let us quickly review some terms. **Product costs** are the costs of producing a product and are capitalized as inventory until the product is sold. **Period**

costs are identified with and recognized as expenses of the period in which they are incurred. Whereas **direct costs** can be readily identified with a product, department, or activity, **indirect costs** are *not* readily identified with products or activities and are usually allocated by some arbitrary formula to various products and activities. **Variable costs** respond proportionately to changes in production volume, while **fixed costs** remain constant as volume changes. **Semivariable costs** respond to volume changes, but less than proportionately. **Joint costs** are costs common to two or more products or activities.

Some other important cost concepts and associated terminology are discussed below.

Historical cost is the money or other valuable consideration paid (and/or the cash equivalent of any obligations assumed) to acquire goods or services. This is often termed "actual" cost. With some exceptions, financial accounting records are based on historical costs adjusted for depreciation where applicable. While historical costs are appropriate for reporting net income and financial position under generally accepted accounting principles, they may not be the best basis for, nor even relevant to, certain management analyses and reports.

Replacement cost is the current cash equivalent necessary to duplicate a particular asset. Replacement costs typically are more relevant than historical costs to managerial decisions. For example, in setting the selling price for a refrigerator that had cost $200 to acquire but would cost $400 to replace, an appliance store manager would probably rely more on replacement cost than on historical cost. While replacement costs are quite relevant to management decisions, the replacement cost of many unique assets can only be estimated.

Out-of-pocket costs require expenditures in the current period. Wages and utilities expenses are examples of out-of-pocket costs. Current depreciation on equipment purchased in earlier periods may be a cost of some activity, but it is not an out-of-pocket cost because no current funds are spent.

Sunk costs are costs incurred in the past that cannot be recovered. For example, if materials were purchased for a particular project but remain unused and cannot be returned, any portion of their acquisition cost that cannot be recovered is properly termed a sunk cost.

Avoidable costs are costs that can be avoided, and **unavoidable costs** are costs that cannot be avoided, in following a specific course of action. For example, if we were considering closing down a regional warehouse, many operating expenses such as utilities would probably be avoidable. Other operating costs, however, such as depreciation and property taxes would be unavoidable, unless of course, we not only closed the warehouse but also sold it. If the warehouse were sold, both the depreciation and taxes would properly be considered avoidable costs.

Opportunity costs are those measurable sacrifices associated with forgoing some alternative. For example, the decision to attend college for a particular term may necessitate forgoing the opportunity to earn income. Thus, one opportunity cost of attending college would be the wage income that could have been earned. Determining opportunity costs involves many "what if" questions and as such is often quite difficult. Although omitted from financial statements, opportunity costs are often relevant to management decisions.

Marginal cost is the cost associated with completing one more unit of production or activity. Although the concept of marginal cost is very useful in theoretical economics, unfortunately, marginal cost is not easily determined in many real world situations. In recognition of this impracticality, the closely related concept of incremental or differential cost is frequently used in decision-making situations.

Incremental or differential costs are the increases or decreases in various costs that result from pursuing one course of action rather than another. One cannot assume that variable costs are always differential and that fixed costs are never differential, although this is often the case. For example, if a decision concerns whether to use one truck for ten trips or five trucks for two trips to haul ten loads of materials, the cost of truck fuel is a variable cost but is not a differential cost. If a special permit is required for each truck used, the difference in the cost of permits is a differential cost. Many costs that are fixed within the relevant range become incremental or differential costs for decisions concerning activity beyond the relevant range.

DIFFERENTIAL ANALYSIS

One of the most useful tools for decision making, **differential analysis** is based on the widely accepted decision rule that *only those aspects of a choice that will differ among alternatives are relevant to a decision*. A major step in differential analysis is the identification of differential costs, which we have just discussed, and any differential revenues among the alternatives. The differences in such key variables as revenues and costs often determine the attractiveness of each alternative.

For example, when you are deciding which theater to attend, the admission price is irrelevant (has no effect) if each theater charges the same price. However, if the taxi fare is $4 to one and $3 to the other, then the differential cost of $1 is relevant to (has an effect on) the choice. The decision process may be streamlined by concentrating only on those factors that are different; this is the basis of differential analysis. For example, suppose a firm has a choice of using certain facilities to produce and sell either product A or product B. The decision is to be in favor of the product promising the most net income based on the following estimated operating data:

| | Alternatives | |
	Product A	Product B
Units that can be sold	12,000	18,000
Unit selling price	$ 8	$ 6
Manufacturing costs:		
Variable (per unit)	$ 3	$ 2
Fixed (total)	$32,000	$32,000
Selling and administrative expenses:		
Variable (per unit)	$ 1	$ 1
Fixed (total)	$ 6,000	$ 6,000

One way of comparing the alternatives is to prepare conventional income statements for each. In this example, comparative income statements would appear as follows:

	Alternatives		
	Product A	Product B	Difference
Revenues			
(12,000 units @ $8)	$96,000		
(18,000 units @ $6)		$108,000	$12,000
Cost of goods sold (manufacturing costs):			
Variable (12,000 @ $3 unit)	$36,000		
(18,000 @ $2 unit)		$ 36,000	-0-
Fixed (total)	32,000	32,000	-0-
Selling and administrative expenses:			
Variable (@ $1 per unit)	12,000	18,000	$ 6,000
Fixed (total)	6,000	6,000	-0-
Total expenses	$86,000	$ 92,000	$ 6,000
Net income	$10,000	$ 16,000	$ 6,000

This analysis shows a $6,000 increase in net income associated with alternative B as a result of a $12,000 increase in total revenues that is partially offset by a $6,000 increase in variable selling and administrative expense.

Differential analysis of the same situation might be presented as illustrated below, where consideration is limited to those revenue and expense factors that differ if product B is produced rather than product A.

Differential revenues:	
Revenues forgone on first 12,000 units, ($8 − $6) × 12,000	($24,000)
Additional revenues from increased sales volume, $6 × 6,000 units	36,000
Net additional revenues	$12,000
Differential costs:	
Increase in variable selling and administrative expense, 6,000 units at $1	6,000
Net differential income in favor of product B	$ 6,000

Quite clearly, the differential approach shows the same net advantage for alternative B as the income statements, but does so much more concisely. This is why management so often uses differential analysis in decision making. The format of differential analysis computations can vary, of course, but incremental revenues and costs must be properly calculated. In the situation illustrated here, some analysts would identify the revenues forgone by selecting alternative B instead of alternative A as an opportunity cost and list it with differential costs. The net result, however, would be the same.

Intuition might at first suggest that favorable alternatives are those having the greatest revenues, increased revenues, smallest costs, or decreased costs. These generalizations are not always true. Even decreased revenues can lead to increased profit if related costs are sufficiently reduced at the same time. On the other hand, even though revenues may hold constant or increase, if related costs increase sufficiently, the differential income may be negative.

Differential analysis is useful in a variety of fairly common decision situations. In the following sections of this chapter we shall illustrate a number of them, such as whether to (1) accept an order at a special price, (2) make or buy needed items, (3) discontinue an unprofitable department, (4) sell or process further, and (5) emphasize production of one product or another.

ILLUSTRATIONS OF DECISION ANALYSIS

The Special Order

Frequently, business firms are approached by purchasers who wish a price concession on special orders. The prospective purchaser may suggest a price or ask for a bid. Sometimes the order may be for a particularly large quantity, permitting certain cost reductions for the manufacturer. Often the buyer may request the firm to produce a special version of a product to be identified with the buyer's private brand. As long as there are no overriding qualitative considerations, management should evaluate such propositions fully and be receptive to their profit potential.

Assume that Company A makes a nationally advertised automobile accessory, which it sells to distributors at a price of $16. A discount firm has asked the company to supply 2,000 units of the accessory for $14 per unit. The accessory would carry the brand name of the discount firm. If Company A were to accept the order, a special machine attachment would be needed to differentiate the product and imprint the private brand. This attachment would cost $1,500 and would be discarded after the order was processed. Also assume that Company A has unused production capacity, and thus no change in fixed cost is anticipated. The following unit cost data are available for the regular production of the item:

Raw material	$ 5
Direct labor	4
Variable overhead	2
Fixed overhead (allocated)	3
Total cost per accessory	$14

At first glance, it appears that the proposition would be unprofitable because the unit cost figure shown here is $14, the same as the buyer's offered price, and an additional cost of $1,500 will have to be incurred to process the order. However, the fixed overhead of $3 included in the $14 total unit cost is not relevant to the decision, because Company A's total fixed costs will be incurred whether the special order is accepted or not. Therefore, it should not be considered in the decision. The following differential cost and revenue analysis reveals that the special order should be accepted:

Increase in revenue (2,000 units × $14)		$28,000
Increase in costs:		
Raw material	$ 5 per unit	
Direct labor	4 per unit	
Variable overhead	2 per unit	
	$11 × 2,000 units	$22,000
Cost of special attachment		1,500
Total differential cost		23,500
Net advantage in accepting special order		$ 4,500

We see from the foregoing analysis that the differential costs of accepting the order consist of the variable production costs and the additional cost of the attachment needed to differentiate the product. Actually, if it accepted any price higher than $11.75 (total differential costs of $23,500 ÷ 2,000), the company would earn a profit on the order.

Note that excess production capacity is significant to the special order decision. In the absence of sufficient excess capacity, the additional production would probably cause additional amounts of "fixed costs" to be incurred. Also observe

STARTING FROM SCRATCH

There is another aspect of a corporation in which constant change demands constant creative reassessment: its own internal arrangements for producing what it needs with what it has got. Departmental structures, routine meetings, standard documents and procedures have a way of taking on a life of their own. They may have been right for the intake of raw material and distribution of factories and marketing practices, and range and balance of products which existed when they were set up; but all these may change, and yet the organization, the meetings, the standard returns of facts and figures may well remain unchanged and become more and more of a drag on the work. There is a good game called "Starting from Scratch" in which management asks itself how it would organize its current production given its current resources *and nothing else.* You have to produce so much a week, and here are your factories and your capital. Organize them. The results can be illuminating, even if they only make people face truths which they had been concealing from themselves. One big British chain store has an attitude of looking at all their internal organization and asking, "Why should we keep it?" It is a more creative question than, "Why should we change it?"

There is a story that the Royal Artillery were giving a demonstration to some visiting Europeans on Salisbury Plain in the 1950s. The visitors were most impressed with the speed and precision of the light artillery crew, but one of them asked what was the duty of the man who stood at attention throughout the whole demonstration.

"He's number six," the adjutant explained.

"I too can count. But why is he there?"

"That's his job. Number six stands at attention throughout."

"But why then do you not have five?"

No one knew. It took a great deal of research through old training manuals, but finally they discovered his duty.

He was the one who held the horses.

SOURCE: *Management and Machiavelli* by Antony Jay. Copyright © 1967 by Antony Jay. Reprinted by permission of Holt, Rinehart and Winston, Publishers and Hodder & Stoughton, Ltd.

that although the $1,500 special attachment in this example is a fixed cost (because it does not respond to volume over the 2,000 unit range), it is relevant to this decision.

Specific qualitative factors to be considered here include ascertaining: (1) that the special price does not constitute unfair price discrimination prohibited under the Robinson–Patman Act, (2) that regular sales at regular prices are not to be unfavorably affected by the sales of the chain store, and (3) that the long-run price structure for the product is not adversely affected by the special order. Significant concern in any of these areas might be a basis for rejecting the special order despite the potential of $4,500 profit.

Make or Buy?

Many manufacturing situations require the assembly of large numbers of specially designed subparts or subassemblies. Usually, the manufacturer must choose between making these components and buying them from outside suppliers. In each situation, management should evaluate the relative costs of the two choices. Because making a component requires using some portion of the firm's manufacturing capacity, the natural presumption is that no more attractive use of that capacity is available.

To illustrate the make-or-buy decision, we shall assume that a company has been making 10,000 units of a necessary component at the following costs:

Raw materials	$ 9,000
Direct labor	12,000
Variable factory overhead	5,000
Fixed factory overhead	24,000
Total costs	$50,000
Cost per unit ($50,000/10,000)	$5

Investigations by the purchasing department indicate that a comparable component can be purchased in sufficient quantities at a unit price of $4.50, with an indicated savings of $0.50 per unit. At first glance, the opportunity to purchase seems most attractive. The analysis of differential costs, however, shows quite the contrary.

An analysis of operations indicates that purchase of the component will enable the firm to avoid only 80% of the variable overhead and 75% of the fixed overhead associated with producing the component. A differential analysis follows:

	Make Part	Buy Part	Differential if Part is Bought*
Cost of 10,000 units:			
Raw materials	$ 9,000		($ 9,000)
Direct labor	12,000		(12,000)
Variable factory overhead	5,000	$ 1,000	(4,000)
Fixed factory overhead	24,000	6,000	(18,000)
Purchase price of components		45,000	45,000
	$50,000	$52,000	$ 2,000

*Parentheses indicate decrease.

Another approach to this analysis confirms the more comprehensive one above.

Cost to purchase component (10,000 × $4.50)		$45,000
Less costs avoided by purchasing:		
Raw materials	$ 9,000	
Direct labor	12,000	
Variable factory overhead	4,000	
Fixed factory overhead	18,000	43,000
Increase in acquisition cost by purchasing		$ 2,000

These analyses assume that the manufacturing capacity released by the decision to purchase would not be used. However, should there be an opportunity to use this capacity in a way that would generate more than $2,000 of contribution margin, then the opportunity to purchase the components would become attractive. Also to be considered in this situation are such qualitative factors as any important effects on employee relations and the probability of the levels of quality and supply remaining acceptable.

Dropping Unprofitable Segments

The operations of most firms are carried out within organizational segments divided along product lines, departments, branches, or sales territories. A well-designed accounting system will attempt to identify the performance of each segment of the firm so that management can make informed decisions concerning its operations. The basic question is often whether or not to discontinue unprofitable segments of a business.

EXHIBIT 25-3

Zeta Company
Condensed Income Statement
For the Year Ended June 30, 19XX
(Thousands of Dollars)

		Departments		
	Totals	A	B	C
Sales	$1,400	$700	$400	$300
Cost of Goods Sold:				
Variable Costs	$ 600	$300	$125	$175
Fixed Costs	400	200	150	50
Total Cost of Goods Sold	$1,000	$500	$275	$225
Gross Profit on Sales	$ 400	$200	$125	$ 75
Operating Expenses:				
Variable Expenses	$ 130	$ 40	$ 20	$ 70
Fixed Expenses	170	80	60	30
Total Operating Expenses	$ 300	$120	$ 80	$100
Net Income (Loss)	$ 100	$ 80	$ 45	($ 25)

Assume that the condensed income statement of Exhibit 25-3 reflects last year's operations of Zeta Company, which is made up of Departments A, B, and C. It might seem at first that the firm's total income could be raised to $125,000 by discontinuing Department C and avoiding the $25,000 operating loss shown for that segment of the company. The following differential analysis, however, indicates that the firm's overall income would be decreased, rather than increased, by discontinuing Department C:

Decrease in revenues		$300,000
Decrease in costs and expenses:		
Variable cost of goods sold	$175,000	
Variable operating expenses	70,000	245,000
Decrease in total contribution margin (and net income) from discontinuing Department C		$ 55,000

Thus we see that even though Department C reports a $25,000 annual loss, it does generate a contribution margin of $55,000 toward the absorption of fixed costs and expenses. Consequently, discontinuing Department C would not increase the firm's income to $125,000 but would decrease it to $45,000. The $80,000 difference represents fixed costs that have been allocated to Department C, which presumably the company would not avoid.

In order to highlight the central issue, this illustration did not introduce several other factors that management must often consider in decisions of this type. Among these are: (1) the potential termination of employees and consequent effects on the morale of all employees; (2) the possible effects on patronage (for example, customers of Departments A and B may go to other firms for all their purchases if Department C's products are no longer available from the same source); and (3) the question of whether the capacity currently used in Department C could be used in other ways to generate contribution margin for the firm.

Sell or Process Further?

Most firms experience production situations that offer the possibility of either selling products at one point in the production sequence or processing them further and selling them at a higher price. Examples are finished versus unfinished furniture, regular or high-test gasoline, and unassembled kits versus assembled units of product. These process-further decision situations present another opportunity to apply differential analysis.

Assume that Company B makes and sells 50,000 unfinished telephone stands with the following operating figures per unit:

Current sales price		$12.00
Costs:		
Raw materials	$4.00	
Direct labor	2.00	
Variable overhead	1.50	
Fixed overhead*	1.00	8.50
Gross profit per unit		$ 3.50

*Applied at 50% of direct labor costs (total fixed overhead is $60,000).

The company now has excess productive capacity, which it expects will remain available in the foreseeable future. Consequently, management believes that part of this excess capacity could be used to paint and decorate the telephone stands and sell them at $15 per unit in the finished furniture market. A study carried out by the company's production department indicates that the additional processing will add $1.30 to the raw materials costs and $0.80 to the direct labor costs of each unit and that variable overhead will continue to be incurred at 75% of direct labor costs.

This decision situation gives us an opportunity to illustrate how failure to properly consider cost behavior factors can lead to an erroneous decision. The following analysis, using average total unit costs, indicates that the telephone stand should not be processed further—an erroneous decision, as we shall see.

New sales price per unit		$15.00
Costs:		
Raw materials ($4 + $1.30)	$5.30	
Direct labor ($2 + $0.80)	2.80	
Variable overhead (75% of direct labor costs)	2.10	
Fixed overhead (applied at 50% of direct labor costs)	1.40	
Total costs		11.60
Gross margin if processed further		$ 3.40

Because this analysis shows that the prospective gross margin after processing further would be $0.10 smaller than at the earlier stages, the decision to process further would be rejected.

There are two defects in the foregoing analysis. First, it includes amounts of costs that are common to both alternatives. The manufacturing costs to bring the product to the original point of sale (as unfinished furniture) are the same for either choice and are therefore irrelevant. Second, the fixed factory overhead is erroneously treated in the analysis as though it will increase in proportion to direct labor costs. With excess capacity, fixed overhead should not increase and therefore it is not a relevant cost factor. In other words, the analysis is unnecessarily complicated and contains a cost analysis error.

In contrast, the strict differential analysis shown below supports the proposal to process further.

	Per Unit	Totals for 50,000 Units
Differential revenues ($15 − $12)	$3.00	$150,000
Differential costs:		
Raw materials	$1.30	$ 65,000
Direct labor	0.80	40,000
Variable overhead	0.60	30,000
Fixed overhead	0	0
Total differential costs	2.70	$135,000
Excess of differential revenue over differential costs	$0.30	$ 15,000

Both the per-unit and total differential analyses indicate the advantage of processing further.

Product Emphasis

Because most firms produce several products, management must continually examine operating data and decide which combination of products offers the greatest total long-run profit potential. The decisions related to product emphasis are seldom as simple as determining the most profitable product and confining production to that one product. Typically, management is faced with such operational constraints as limited demand for the most profitable products, the competitive necessity of offering a line of products with a variety of qualities and capacities, and, in seeking better utilization of existing capacity, the need to produce other products even though they are less profitable.

In product emphasis analysis, an important and widely accepted generalization is that *the firm's income is optimized when it maximizes the contribution margin earned per unit of constraining resource.* The concept of constraining resource stems from the realization that as a firm increases its volume, some resource is eventually exhausted and thus "constrains," or limits, the continued expansion of the firm. Which resources are constraining will depend on the firm, the operating conditions, and even the products under consideration. Typical examples are key raw materials, labor skills, machine capacities, and factory floor space or storage space. Simply stated, management has optimized the firm's product mix when it maximizes the contribution earned on each unit of the particular resource that limits increased production.

To illustrate product emphasis decisions, assume that Beta Company produces products X, Y, and Z, and factory machine capacity is its constraining resource. Beta Company has been operating at 90% of capacity, and management wants to decide to which product to devote the unused capacity. The following data represent Beta Company's current operations:

	Products		
	X	Y	Z
Per-unit data:			
Sales price	$20	$22	$6
Variable costs	8	16	2
Contribution margin	$12	$ 6	$4
Fixed costs*	6	2	1
Net income	$ 6	$ 4	$3

*Allocated on basis of machine hours at $1.00 per hour.

Intuition might suggest that the extra capacity should be devoted either to product Y, which has the highest sales price, or to product X, which has the highest per-unit contribution margin and net income. As we shall demonstrate, however, an analysis of the *contribution margin of each product per unit of constraining factor* reveals that product Z should receive the added capacity.

Note that fixed costs are allocated among products on the basis of machine hours, which in our example are the constraining resource. Furthermore, the unit allocations of fixed costs, above, indicate that product X requires three times as many machine hours as product Y and six times as many as product Z. The contribution per unit of machine capacity for each product is:

	Products		
	X	Y	Z
Contribution margin per unit	$12	$6	$4
Units of machine capacity required (as indicated by the allocation of fixed costs)	6	2	1
Contribution margin per unit of machine capacity (the constraining resource)	$ 2	$3	$4

Use of the remaining capacity will generate a greater contribution margin if devoted to product Z. As this simple example illustrates, in deciding product emphasis management should use contribution per unit of constraining resource, rather than the relative sales prices, unit contribution margins, or even unit profit of various products.

Acquisition of Long-term Assets

Because of the large amount of funds and the long-term commitments that may be involved, management decisions related to the acquisition of long-lived assets are often complex. These capital budgeting decisions will be considered in Chapter 27.

VARIABLE COSTING

In the earlier chapter on manufacturing, all factory costs—raw (or direct) materials, direct labor, and factory overhead—were considered product costs. As such, these costs were capitalized as inventory during the production period and recognized as expense (cost of goods sold) only when the related merchandise was sold. This method of attaching all factory cost to the product is often descriptively termed **full** or **absorption costing.**

In contrast, some firms use **variable costing** to determine the cost of their manufactured product.[1] Under variable costing, only variable manufacturing costs are capitalized as inventory. Any fixed manufacturing costs are treated as period costs and expensed in the period incurred. Exhibit 25-4 (page 898) contrasts the two approaches to costing. We see that the only difference between absorption and variable costing is that fixed factory overhead is capitalized under absorption costing and expensed under variable costing.

In general, variable costing (carrying only variable costs in the inventory accounts listed under the current assets of the balance sheet) is considered a departure from orthodox financial accounting. The AICPA has insisted that published financial reports attested to by CPAs be prepared on an absorption costing basis. It believes that all factory costs should be attributed to products and that inventories of work in process and finished goods should contain their allocable

---

[1]Variable costing is widely referred to as "direct costing." The latter is a misnomer, however, in that it is not *direct* costs—but *variable* costs—that are capitalized under "direct" costing. This distinction is readily apparent in Exhibit 25-4.

EXHIBIT 25-4
**Comparison of Absorption
and Variable Costing**

Typical Manufacturing Cost (or Expense)	Typical Behavior Pattern	Absorption Costing Product Cost	Absorption Costing Period Cost	Variable Costing Product Cost	Variable Costing Period Cost
Direct Cost:					
Raw Materials	Variable	X		X	
Labor	Variable	X		X	
Indirect Cost:					
Factory Overhead	Variable	X		X	
Factory Overhead	Fixed	X			X
Other Cost:					
Nonfactory Administration	(may vary)		X		X
Selling	(may vary)		X		X

share of factory costs, both fixed and variable. Likewise, the Internal Revenue Service has generally insisted on the use of absorption costing in determining net income for tax purposes.

Although variable costing should not be used to prepare financial statements for external use, management may find variable costing statements useful for analytical purposes. A principal benefit is that variable costing usually causes net income figures to move in the same direction as sales. With absorption costing, net income may increase in periods when production volume outstrips sales and decrease when the company outsells production and thus reduces inventory levels. Because management's thinking is more compatible with the idea that sales and net income should vary directly with each other, variable costing statements may be preferable for managerial purposes.

A comparison of condensed, partial income statements for the Excel Company for four periods, using both absorption costing and variable costing, is presented in Exhibit 25-5 to demonstrate the effects just discussed. For this simple illustration, we have assumed that a single item is sold for $5 per unit, that variable product costs are $1 per unit, and that fixed product costs are $300 per period. Sales and production figures, in units, are given for the four periods:

	Period 1	Period 2	Period 3	Period 4	Total
Sales (in units)	100	100	100	100	400
Production (in units)	100	150	50	100	400

The Excel Company normally produces and sells 100 units per period. Note, however, that in Period 2 the company produced an additional 50 units for inventory that are sold in Period 3 together with the 50 units produced in Period 3.

EXHIBIT 25-5

The Excel Company
Partial Income Statements

Absorption Costing

	Period 1	Period 2	Period 3	Period 4
Sales (100 units @ $5)	$500	$500	$500	$500
Cost of Goods Sold:				
Beginning Inventory	0	0	$150	0
Cost of Goods Manufactured	$400	$450	350	$400
Available for Sale	$400	$450	$500	$400
Ending Inventory	0	150	0	0
Cost of Goods Sold	400	300	500	400
Gross Profit	$100	$200	$ 0	$100

Variable Costing

	Period 1	Period 2	Period 3	Period 4
Sales (100 units @ $5)	$500	$500	$500	$500
Cost of Goods Sold:				
Beginning Inventory	0	0	$ 50	0
Variable Cost of Goods Manufactured	$100	$150	50	$100
	$100	$150	$100	$100
Ending Inventory	0	50	0	0
Variable Cost of Sales	100	100	100	100
Contribution Margin	$400	$400	$400	$400
Fixed Costs	300	300	300	300
Gross Profit	$100	$100	$100	$100

In the absorption costing statement shown in the top half of Exhibit 25-5, fixed product costs of $300 per period and variable product costs of $1 per unit produced are included in the cost of goods manufactured. The $150 inventory shown at the end of Period 2 consists of $50 variable costs (50 units $\times$ $1) and $100 fixed costs. (Because one-third of the units produced remain in inventory, one-third of the $300 fixed costs is assigned to the inventory.)

In the variable costing statement shown in the lower half of Exhibit 25-5, only variable product costs at $1 per unit produced are included in the cost of goods manufactured. Likewise, the inventory at the end of Period 2 consists only of $1 variable product cost times the 50 units in the inventory. The $300 fixed costs are deducted from contribution margin each period.

A total of $400 gross profit is reported for the four periods under both methods. However, the variable costing method shows the same gross profit figures each period, which are correlated with the constant sales volume over the four periods. On the other hand, under the absorption costing method, gross profit moves up and down with production. The reason, of course, is that the fixed costs are added to the inventory when production outstrips sales and released when the company sells its entire inventory. Sometimes management can become quite perturbed with results from absorption costing statements—especially when profits do not improve despite an appreciable increase in sales volume. The controller of the company, however, can always prepare income statements under both approaches and explain their differences, provided that the proper analysis has been made to segregate variable and fixed costs.

To highlight the effect of variable costing on inventories and income in the foregoing illustration, we considered only manufacturing (or product) costs. When detailed income statements are prepared under the variable costing method, fixed and variable costs of all types, including selling and administrative costs, must be properly segregated. An example of a more detailed income statement prepared in accordance with the variable costing concept is shown in Exhibit 25–6.

The term **manufacturing margin,** which appears in Exhibit 25–6, is sometimes used to describe the difference between revenue and variable cost of goods sold. Then contribution margin is obtained by deducting variable selling and administrative expenses from the manufacturing margin, and finally, all types of

EXHIBIT 25–6

Conroy Company
Variable Costing Income Statement
For the Year Ended December 31, 19XX

Sales (20,000 units @ $5)		$100,000
Variable Cost of Goods Sold:		
Beginning Inventory (12,000 units @ $3)	$36,000	
Cost of Goods Manufactured (18,000 units @ $3)	54,000	
Goods Available for Sale	$90,000	
Ending Inventory (10,000 units @ $3)	30,000	60,000
Manufacturing Margin		$ 40,000
Variable Selling and Administrative Expense:		
Variable Selling Expense	$ 8,000	
Variable Administrative Expense	4,000	12,000
Contribution Margin		$ 28,000
Deduct: Fixed Costs and Expenses:		
Fixed Manufacturing Cost	$12,000	
Fixed Selling Expense	5,000	
Fixed Administrative Expense	3,000	20,000
Net Income		$ 8,000

fixed costs—manufacturing, selling, and administrative—are deducted to arrive at net income.

We may make the following generalizations about the differences in reported income under absorption and variable costing:

(1) When sales are balanced to production (with inventories unchanged), both costing systems result in the same reported income. See Periods 1 and 4 in Exhibit 25-5.

(2) When production exceeds sales (inventory increases), absorption costing reports the higher income. See Period 2 in Exhibit 25-5.

(3) When sales exceed production (inventory decreases), variable costing reports the higher income. See Period 3 in Exhibit 25-5.

(4) The difference in reported income is equal to the fixed overhead per unit of inventory multiplied by the change in inventory units. See Periods 2 and 3 in Exhibit 25-5.

(5) Over the long run, both costing systems will report the same income, because in the long run, production and sales for most firms must be balanced.

The advantages and disadvantages most often associated with the use of variable costing originate in the fact that under variable costing no fixed overhead costs are assigned to inventory carrying values. They can be summarized as follows:

Advantages of variable costing:

(1) Management may have a more general awareness of cost behavior factors in the firm's operations and be more prone to use this information in short-term decision situations in which contribution margin analysis is most appropriate.

(2) Reported net income tends to follow sales volume. (This may not be true under absorption costing.)

(3) Cost–volume–profit relationships are more easily discerned from variable costing income statements than from conventional absorption costing statements.

Disadvantages of variable costing:

(1) It is often difficult to classify a number of cost factors into their fixed and variable components as required with this method, and results are only tentative.

(2) Accounting measures derived under variable costing are not in accord with generally accepted accounting principles, nor are they acceptable for reporting purposes under the Internal Revenue Code.

(3) Inventories (and therefore working capital and owners' equity) tend to be understated.

(4) Carrying inventories at only their variable costs may lead to long-run pricing decisions that provide for recovery of variable cost only rather than total cost and thus does not produce net income in the long run.

KEY POINTS TO REMEMBER

(1) Decision making, which is essentially choosing among alternatives, usually comprises three phases: planning, execution, and evaluation.

(2) Managerial analyses and reports may contain not only the traditional accounting data found in financial statements but also other data useful to management such as replacement costs and opportunity costs.

(3) The general concept of cost can be used with the following specific meanings:

product cost	semivariable cost	sunk cost
period cost	fixed cost	avoidable cost
direct cost	historical cost	marginal cost
indirect cost	replacement cost	differential cost
variable cost	out-of-pocket cost	opportunity cost

(4) Differential analysis is the study of those amounts that are expected to differ among alternatives.

(5) In a decision situation, differential analysis is favorable whenever revenues increase more than costs increase or decrease less than costs decrease.

(6) Differential analysis may be applied in the following decision situations:

Whether to accept orders at special prices.
Whether to make or buy needed components.
Whether to drop or continue unprofitable segments.
Whether to sell or process further.
Which products to emphasize.

(7) Variable costing differs from absorption costing in that it does not assign fixed overhead as a product cost, but expenses it in the period incurred.

QUESTIONS

25–1 In what key ways do management reports differ from financial statements?

25–2 Define *goal identification*. Identify four fairly common examples of general managerial goals or objectives.

25–3 Briefly explain each of the following terms as they relate to decision making, and indicate how accounting methods can be employed in each.
(a) Planning phase.
(b) Execution phase.
(c) Evaluation phase.

25–4 Briefly define:
(a) Historical cost.   (b) Replacement cost.
(c) Out-of-pocket cost.   (d) Sunk cost.
(e) Avoidable cost.   (f) Marginal cost.
(g) Differential cost.   (h) Opportunity cost.

25-5 "The higher the level of management receiving reports, the more detailed the reports should be." Comment.

25-6 Although separate phases of decision making are identifiable, management will usually be involved in all phases at the same time. Explain.

25-7 List several common aspects of decision making that are often not subject to quantification.

25-8 Explain what is meant by the term *differential analysis*.

25-9 Explain how differential analysis can be applied to decisions in each of the following areas:
(a) Special orders.
(b) Making or buying product components.
(c) Dropping unprofitable segments of the firm.
(d) Selling or processing further.
(e) Product emphasis.

25-10 Operating at 80% of capacity, Acme Company produces and sells for $20 each 16,000 units of its only product. Per-unit costs are: raw materials, $4; direct labor, $6; variable factory overhead, $1.50; and fixed factory overhead, $3. A special order is received for 1,000 units. Based on this information, what price should Acme charge in order to make a gross profit of $1,500 on the special order?

25-11 Frame-it Company produces unassembled picture frames at average per-unit costs of: raw materials, $X; direct labor, $Y; and factory overhead, $Z. The company can assemble the frames at a unit cost of $0.80 and raise the selling price from $4.95 to $5.95. Could you advise management whether or not to assemble the frames without knowing the specific amounts of manufacturing costs? How? What is the apparent advantage or disadvantage of assembling the frames?

25-12 Explain the concept of *constraining resource*, and present a general rule to use in optimizing product mixes.

25-13 "In differential analysis, one can generally count on variable cost being relevant and fixed cost not being relevant." Comment.

25-14 If both approaches to a decision lead to the same conclusion, why might differential analysis be considered superior to a comprehensive analysis that reflects all revenues and costs?

25-15 What is variable costing? List its advantages and disadvantages.

25-16 What generalizations can be made about the difference in reported income between variable and absorption costing?

25-17 Assume the data in Exercise 25-10 (disregarding the special order opportunity) represents the first year's operations of Acme Company, except that fixed and variable selling and administrative expenses per unit produced are $1.50 and $0.50, respectively, and 14,000 of the 16,000 units produced were sold. What would be the difference in reported income for the year determined under absorption costing and under variable costing?

EXERCISES

25-18 Describe the type of cost data or information represented by each of the cost amounts identified below by a letter in parentheses. In some instances, more than one description may be appropriate.

Bass Company needs a certain production task performed on one of its products. The operation can be accomplished by a machine that was purchased earlier for $100,000 (a) and used for a period of time but is now idle and stored. Although it has been "depreciated down" to $60,000 (b) on the books, it can be sold now for only $2,000 (c). To be used, the machine will need to be cleaned and adjusted, which would cost $1,000 (d). For $4,000 (e) per year, Bass could have another firm perform the operation in question and rent its own machine to a competitor for $3,000 (f) per year. If the machine is sold before the next personal property assessment date, the company would not have to pay $600 (g) in personal property taxes.

25-19 In each of four independent cases, the amount of differential revenue or differential cost is as follows (parenthesis indicate decreases):

	(1)	(2)	(3)	(4)
Increases (decreases) in:				
Revenues	$15,000	$-0-	?	?
Costs	?	?	($9,000)	$-0-

For each case, determine the missing amount that would be necessary to create a situation in which differential revenues and costs would be:
(a) $7,000 favorable.
(b) $6,000 unfavorable.
Be sure to indicate whether your answer reflects increases or decreases.

25-20 The Stabus Company sells a single product for $15 per unit. At an operating level of 8,000 units, variable costs are $6 per unit and fixed costs $5 per unit.

The Stabus Company has been offered a price of $7 per unit on a special order of 2,000 units by Sabin Discount Stores, which would use its own trade name on the item. If Stabus Company accepts the order, raw materials cost will be $1.50 less per unit than for regular production. However, special stamping equipment costing $3,500 would be needed just to process the order; it would then be discarded.

Assuming that volume remains within the relevant range, prepare an analysis of differential revenues and costs to determine whether Stabus Company should accept the special order.

25-21 Bell Company regularly sells its only product for $80 per unit and has a 25% profit on each sale. It accepted a special order for a number of units, the production of which would absorb part of its unused capacity. The special order sales price was 50% of the normal price, but the profit margin was only 20% of the regular dollar profit. What, apparently, is: (a) Bell's profit per unit on the special order? (b) Bell's total variable cost per unit? and (c) Bell's average fixed cost per unit on regular sales?

25-22 Albin Company now incurs a total cost of $67,500 in producing 9,000 units of a component needed in the assembly of its major product. The component can be purchased from an outside supplier for $6 per unit. A related cost study indicates that the total cost of the component includes fixed costs equal to 50% of the variable costs involved.

(a) Should Albin buy the component if no other opportunity exists to utilize the released capacity? Present your answer in the form of differential analysis.

(b) What would be your answer to (a) if the released capacity could be used in a project that would generate $10,000 of contribution margin?

25-23 Scott Manufacturing Company produces a line of electric household food mixers consisting of a deluxe model, a custom model, and an economy model. Last year's sales of the deluxe models incurred a net loss of $10,000; sales were $200,000, cost of goods sold $160,000, and operating expenses $50,000. Because of the indicated loss of $10,000, management is considering discontinuing the deluxe model. A cost study indicates that 20% of the cost of goods sold and 40% of operating expenses are fixed and that elimination of the deluxe model would have no material effect on the total fixed cost incurred. Prepare a differential analysis of the effects of dropping the deluxe model, and recommend whether or not it should be dropped. What related qualitative factors should be considered?

25-24 Morrow Machine Company makes a partially completed assembly unit that it sells for $25 per unit. Normally, 40,000 units are sold each year. Variable unit cost data on the assembly are as follows:

Raw Materials	$7
Direct Labor	$8
Variable Overhead	$4

The company is now using only 80% of its normal capacity; it could fully use its normal capacity by processing the assembly further and selling it for $30 per unit. If the company does this, materials and labor costs will each increase by $1.50 per unit and variable overhead will go up by $0.75 per unit. Fixed costs will increase from the present level of $160,000 to $190,000.

Prepare an analysis showing whether or not the company should process the assemblies further and sell them for $30.

25-25 Following is an analysis of selected data for each of the two products Trojan Company produces.

	Product A	Product B
Per-unit data:		
Sales prices	$40	$28
Production costs:		
Variable	12	7
Fixed	9	6
Selling and administrative expenses:		
Variable	8	5
Fixed	6	6
Net Income	5	4

In Trojan's operation, machine capacity is the company's constraining resource, and machine hours are the bases for allocating fixed production costs. Assuming that all production can be sold at a normal price, prepare an analysis showing which of the two products should be produced with any unused productive capacity that Trojan might have.

25-26 Douglas Company sells its product for $22 per unit. Manufacturing costs per unit are: variable cost, $8; fixed cost at normal operating level of 12,000 units, $4. Variable selling costs are $5 per unit sold. Fixed selling costs and administrative costs (all fixed) total $20,000. Douglas Company had no beginning inventory in 19X1. During 19X1, the company produced 12,000 units and sold 9,000. Would net income before taxes for Douglas Company in 19X1 be higher if calculated on a variable costing basis or if calculated using absorption costing? Indicate reported income using each method.

25-27 During its first year, Raley, Inc.'s operations were such that it showed a $4-per-unit profit under absorption costing but would have reported a total profit $4,000 less under variable costing. If production exceeded sales by 500 units and an average contribution margin of $66\frac{2}{3}\%$ was maintained, what is the apparent: (a) fixed cost per unit? (b) variable cost per unit? (c) sales price per unit? and (d) unit sales volume if total profit under absorption costing was $30,000?

PROBLEMS

25-28 Following are total cost data for Powell Manufacturing Company, a firm that has a normal capacity per period of 8,000 units of product that sell for $25 each. For the foreseeable future, sales volume should continue to equal normal capacity.

Raw Materials	$ 40,000
Direct Labor	28,000
Variable Overhead	21,000
Fixed Overhead (Note 1)	18,000
Selling Expense (Note 2)	14,000
Administrative Expense (fixed)	7,000
	$128,000

Note 1: Beyond normal capacity, fixed overhead costs increase $800 for each 500 units *or fraction thereof* until a maximum capacity of 10,000 units is reached.

Note 2: Selling expenses consist of a regular 6% sales commission and shipping costs of $0.25 per unit. Powell has a policy of paying only three-fourths of the regular sales commission rate on sales totaling 501 to 1,000 units and only two-thirds the regular commission on sales totaling 1,000 units or more.

Powell's sales manager has received an order for 1,200 units from a large discount chain at a special price of $15 each, F.O.B. factory. The controller's office has furnished the following additional cost data related to the special order:

(1) Changes in the product's design will reduce raw materials $0.60 per unit.
(2) Special processing will add 20% to the per-unit direct labor costs.
(3) Variable overhead will continue at the same proportion of direct labor costs.
(4) Other costs should not be affected.

REQUIRED
(a) Present an analysis supporting a decision to accept or reject the special order.
(b) What is the lowest price Powell could receive and still make a $600 profit before income taxes on the special order?
(c) What general qualitative factors should Powell consider?

25-29 Sportship, Inc. currently makes the nylon convertible top for its main product, a fiberglass boat designed especially for water skiing. The cost of producing the 1,200 tops needed each year are:

Nylon fabric	$48,000
Aluminum tubing	18,600
Frame fittings	4,200
Direct labor	30,000
Variable overhead	5,400
Fixed overhead	30,000

Kerns Company, a specialty fabricator of synthetic materials, has offered to make the needed tops of comparable quality at a price of $90 each, F.O.B. shipping point. Sportship would have to furnish its own trademark insignia at a unit cost of $3.50. Transportation in would be $6 per unit to be paid by Sportship, Inc.

Sportship's chief accountant prepared a cost analysis, which showed that only 20% of what is considered fixed overhead could be avoided if the tops were purchased. The tops have been made in a remote section of Sportship's factory building, using equipment for which no alternate use is apparent in the foreseeable future.

REQUIRED
(a) Prepare a differential analysis showing whether or not you would recommend that the convertible tops be purchased from Kerns Company.
(b) Assuming that the production capacity released by purchasing the tops could be devoted to a subcontracting job for another company that netted a contribution margin of $6,000, what is the maximum purchase price that Sportship, Inc. could pay for the tops?
(c) Identify two important qualitative considerations that Sportship, Inc. might well consider in deciding whether to purchase the needed tops.

25-30 Based on the following analysis of last year's operations of Custer, Inc., a financial vice-president of the company believes that the firm's total net income could be increased by $20,000 if the Soft Goods Division were to be discontinued. (Amounts are given in thousands of dollars.)

	Totals	All Other Divisions	Soft Goods Division
Sales	$2,500	$1,900	$600
Cost of Goods Sold:			
Variable	(850)	(600)	(250)
Fixed	(450)	(320)	(130)
Gross Profit	$1,200	$ 980	$220
Operating Expenses:			
Variable	(630)	(450)	(180)
Fixed	(280)	(220)	(60)
Net Income (Loss)	$ 290	$ 310	($ 20)

REQUIRED

Provide answers for each of the following *independent* situations:

(a) Assuming that fixed costs and expenses would not be affected by discontinuing the Soft Goods Division, prepare an analysis showing why you agree or disagree with the vice-president.

(b) Assuming that discontinuance of the Soft Goods Division will enable the company to avoid 20% of the fixed portion of cost of goods sold and 25% of the fixed operating expenses allocated to the Soft Goods Division, calculate the resulting effect on net income.

(c) Assume that in addition to the cost avoidance in (b) above, the production capacity released by discontinuance of the Soft Goods Division can be used to produce 6,000 units of a new product that would have a variable cost per unit of $9 and would require additional fixed costs totaling $18,000. At what unit price must the new product be sold if the company is to increase total net income of the firm by $30,000?

25-31 Review the operating data for Powell Manufacturing Company presented in Problem 25-28. *Disregard the special order opportunity.*

Powell is considering whether to improve its profit by continuing to produce 8,000 units of product but processing each unit further and selling it at a higher price. In addition to the information presented in Problem 25-28, consider the following:

(1) Raw materials cost would increase by $2.00 a unit.

(2) Direct labor would increase 40%.

(3) Variable overhead should continue as the same proportion of direct labor costs.

(4) The further processing will require an amount of additional fixed factory capacity equal to that required for making an additional 1,500 units of product.

REQUIRED

Assuming all orders are for fewer than 500 units each:

(a) Determine the effect on Powell's profit of processing further and raising the unit selling price to $30.

(b) What is the smallest increase in per-unit selling price that Powell could accept and still decide to process further?

25-32 Blendo, Inc. manufactures a deluxe model and a standard model of a household food blender. Because of limited demand, for several years production has been at 80% of estimated capacity, which is thought to be limited by the number of machine hours available. At present levels of operations, a profit analysis for each product line shows the following:

Per-Unit Data	Deluxe		Standard	
Sales price		$180		$70
Production costs:				
Raw materials	$79		$10	
Direct labor	30		20	
Variable factory overhead	12		8	
Fixed factory overhead*	20	$141	8	$46
Variable operating expenses		15		10
Fixed operating expenses		6		4
Total costs		$162		$60
Operating income		$ 18		$10

*Assigned on the basis of machine hours at normal capacity.

Management wants to utilize the company's present excess capacity by increasing production.

REQUIRED
(a) What general decision guideline is applicable in this situation?
(b) Assuming that sufficient units of either product can be sold at existing prices to fully use existing capacity and that fixed costs will not be affected, prepare an analysis showing which product line should be emphasized if net income for the firm is the decision basis.

25-33 The Superior Company makes a product with total unit manufacturing costs of $8, of which $5 is variable. No units were on hand at the beginning of 19X0. During 19X0 and 19X1, the only product manufactured was sold for $12 per unit and there were no changes in the cost structure. The company uses the first-in, first-out inventory method. Production and sales for 19X0 and 19X1 were:

	Units Manufactured	Units Sold
19X0	120,000	90,000
19X1	120,000	130,000

REQUIRED
(a) Prepare gross profit computations for 19X0 and 19X1 using absorption costing.
(b) Prepare gross profit computations for 19X0 and 19X1 using variable costing.
(c) Explain how your answers illustrate the related generalizations presented in the chapter regarding the differences between reported income (or gross profit) under absorption and variable costing.

25–34 Summarized data for the first year's operations of Standard Factories, Inc. are as follows:

Sales (75,000 units)	$6,000,000
Production costs (80,000 units):	
Raw materials	1,760,000
Direct labor	1,440,000
Factory overhead:	
Variable	1,080,000
Fixed	640,000
Selling and administrative costs and expenses:	
Variable	336,000
Fixed	480,000

REQUIRED

(a) Prepare an income statement based on full absorption costing.
(b) Prepare an income statement based on variable costing.
(c) Assume you have to make a relatively quick decision on whether to accept a special one-time order for 1,000 units at a price of $60 per unit. Which income statement presents the most relevant data? Based solely on this data, what would be the apparent profit or loss on the special order?
(d) Suppose the ending inventory were destroyed by fire. Which income statement would you use as a basis for filing an insurance claim for the fire loss? Why?

ALTERNATE PROBLEMS

25–28A Following is total cost data for Amos Manufacturing Company, a firm that has a normal capacity per period of 20,000 units of product, which sell for $20 each. For the foreseeable future, regular sales volume should continue to equal normal capacity.

Raw Materials	$100,000
Direct Labor	80,000
Variable Overhead	50,000
Fixed Overhead (Note 1)	44,000
Selling Expense (Note 2)	60,000
Administrative Expense (fixed)	20,000
	$354,000

Note 1: Beyond normal capacity, fixed overhead costs increase $3,000 for each 1,000 units *or fraction thereof* until a maximum capacity of 24,000 units is reached.

Note 2: Selling expenses consist of a 10% sales commission and shipping costs of $1 per unit. Amos has a policy of paying only one-half of the regular sales commission rate on any sale amounting to $2,000 or more.

Amos' sales manager has received a special order for 2,500 units from a large discount chain at a special price of $16 each, F.O.B. factory. The controller's office has furnished the following additional cost data related to the special order:

(1) Changes in the product's design will reduce raw materials $1.50 per unit.
(2) Special processing will add 10% to the per-unit direct labor costs.
(3) Variable overhead will continue at the same proportion of direct labor costs.
(4) Other costs should not be affected.

REQUIRED

(a) Present an analysis supporting a decision to accept or reject the special order.
(b) What is the lowest price Amos could receive and still make a profit of $5,000 before income taxes on the special order?
(c) What general qualitative factors should Amos consider?

25-29A Nautaline, Inc. currently makes the nylon mooring cover for its main product, a fiberglass boat designed for tournament bass fishing. The cost of producing the 2,000 covers needed each year are:

Nylon fabric	$40,000
Wood battens	8,000
Brass fittings	4,000
Direct labor	16,000
Variable overhead	12,000
Fixed overhead	20,000

Classic Company, a specialty fabricator of synthetic materials, has offered to make the needed covers of comparable quality at a price of $39 each, F.O.B. shipping point. Nautaline would have to furnish its own trademark insignia at a unit cost of $2.50. Transportation in would be $2 per unit to be paid by Nautaline, Inc.

Nautaline's chief accountant prepared a cost analysis, which showed that only 30% of what is considered fixed overhead could be avoided if the covers were purchased. The covers have been made in a remote section of Nautaline's factory building, using equipment for which no alternate use is apparent in the foreseeable future.

REQUIRED

(a) Prepare a differential analysis showing whether or not you would recommend that the mooring covers be purchased from Classic Company.
(b) Assuming that the production capacity released by purchasing the covers could be devoted to a subcontracting job for another company that netted a contribution margin of $5,000, what is the maximum purchase price that Nautaline could pay for the covers?
(c) Identify two important qualitative considerations that Nautaline, Inc. might well consider in deciding whether to purchase the needed covers.

25-30A Based on the following analysis of last year's operations of Stanlon, Inc., a financial vice-president of the company believes that the firm's total net income could be increased by $20,000 if the Soft Goods Division were to be discontinued. (Amounts are given in thousands of dollars.)

	Totals	All Other Divisions	Soft Goods Division
Sales	$3,500	$2,800	$700
Cost of Goods Sold:			
Variable	(1,420)	(1,100)	(320)
Fixed	(940)	(800)	(140)
Gross Profit	$1,140	$ 900	$240
Operating Expenses:			
Variable	(510)	(330)	(180)
Fixed	(370)	(290)	(80)
Net Income (Loss)	$ 260	$ 280	($ 20)

REQUIRED

Provide answers for each of the following *independent* situations:

(a) Assuming that fixed costs and expenses would not be affected by discontinuing the Soft Goods Division, prepare an analysis showing why you agree or disagree with the vice-president.

(b) Assuming that discontinuance of the Soft Goods Division will enable the company to avoid 30% of the fixed portion of cost of goods sold and 40% of the fixed operating expenses allocated to the Soft Goods Division, calculate the resulting effect on net income.

(c) Assume that in addition to the cost avoidance in (b) above, the production capacity released by discontinuance of the Soft Goods Division can be used to produce 6,000 units of a new product that would have a variable cost per unit of $15 and require additional fixed costs totaling $15,000. At what unit price must the new product be sold if the company is to increase the firm's total net income by $45,000?

25-31A Review the operating data for Amos Manufacturing Company presented in Problem 25-28A. *Disregard the special order opportunity.*

Amos is considering whether to improve its profit by continuing to produce 20,000 units of product but processing each unit further and selling it at a higher price. In addition to the information presented in Problem 25-28A, consider the following:

(1) Raw materials cost should increase by $1.80 a unit.

(2) Direct labor should increase 20%.

(3) Variable overhead should continue as the same proportion of direct labor costs.

(4) Further processing would require additional fixed factory capacity equal to that required for making an additional 1,500 units of product.

REQUIRED

Assuming all sales orders are for $2,000 or less:

(a) Determine the effect on Amos' profit of processing further and raising the unit selling price to $25.00.

(b) What is the smallest per-unit selling price that Amos could accept and still make an incremental profit of $30,000?

25–32A Roan, Inc. manufactures both automatic and manual models of residential water softeners. Because of limited demand, for several years production has been at 90% of estimated capacity, which is thought to be limited by the number of machine hours available. At present levels of operations, a profit analysis for each product line shows the following:

Per-Unit Data		Automatic		Manual
Sales price		$340		$180
Production costs:				
Raw materials	$60		$35	
Direct labor	50		30	
Variable factory overhead	30		15	
Fixed factory overhead*	60	$200	30	$110
Variable operating expenses		40		10
Fixed operating expenses		70		40
Total costs		$310		$160
Operating income		$ 30		$ 20

*Assigned on the basis of machine hours at normal capacity.

Management wants to utilize the company's present excess capacity by increasing production.

REQUIRED
(a) What general decision guideline is applicable in this situation?
(b) Assuming that sufficient units of either product can be sold at existing prices to fully use existing capacity and that fixed costs will not be affected, prepare an analysis showing which product line should be emphasized if net income for the firm is the decision basis.

25–33A The Boman Company produces a product with total unit manufacturing costs of $15, of which $8 is variable cost. No units were on hand at the beginning of 19X0. During 19X0 and 19X1, the only product manufactured was sold for $20 per unit and there were no changes in the cost structure. The company uses the first-in, first-out inventory method. Production and sales for 19X0 and 19X1 were:

	Units Manufactured	Units Sold
19X0	80,000	70,000
19X1	80,000	60,000

REQUIRED
(a) Prepare gross profit computations for 19X0 and 19X1 using absorption costing.
(b) Prepare gross profit computations for 19X0 and 19X1 using variable costing.
(c) Explain how your answers illustrate the related generalizations presented in the chapter regarding the differences between reported income (or gross profit) under absorption and variable costing.

BUSINESS DECISION PROBLEM

Medallion, Inc. manufactures an automatic model and a manual model of a household dehumidifier. Because of limited demand, for several years production has been at 80% of estimated capacity, which is thought to be limited by the number of machine hours available. At present levels of operations, a profit analysis for each product line shows the following:

Per-Unit Data	Automatic		Manual	
Sales price		$250		$90
Production costs:				
Raw materials	$50		$13	
Direct labor	30		15	
Variable factory overhead	45		10	
Fixed factory overhead*	30	$155	12	$50
Variable operating expenses		35		12
Fixed operating expenses		20		8
Total costs		$210		$70
Operating income		$ 40		$20

*Assigned on the basis of machine hours at normal capacity.

Management wants to utilize the company's present excess capacity by increasing production.

REQUIRED

Present answers for the following questions in each *independent* situation:

(a) Assuming that sufficient units of either product can be sold at existing prices to fully utilize existing capacity and that fixed costs will not be affected:

(1) To which product should the excess capacity be devoted if the decision basis is maximization of sales revenue?

(2) What would be your answer to (1) if the decision were based on contribution margin per unit of product?

(3) Prepare an analysis showing which product line should be emphasized if net income for the firm is the decision basis.

(4) What general decision guideline is applicable in this situation?

(b) Suppose the excess capacity represents 10,000 machine hours, which can be used to make 4,000 automatic units or 10,000 manual units or any proportionate combination. The only market available for these extra units is a foreign market in which the sales prices must be reduced by 20% and in which no more than 6,000 units of either model can be sold. All costs will remain the same except that the selling commission of 10% of the regular selling prices (included in variable operating expenses) will be avoided. Prepare an analysis showing which product should be emphasized and the effect on the firm's net income.

(c) Assume that the excess capacity can be used as indicated in (b) above and that the firm's market research department believes that the production available from using the excess capacity exclusively on either model can be sold in the domestic market at regular prices if a promotion campaign costing $150,000 is undertaken for the automatic model or $200,000 for the manual model. Prepare an analysis indicating for which product the campaign should be undertaken.

26
Standard Costs and Budgeting

> Dispatch is the soul of business; and nothing contributes more to dispatch than method. Lay down a method for everything, and stick to it inviolably, as far as unexpected incidents may allow.
>
> LORD CHESTERFIELD
> (LETTER TO HIS SON, FEBRUARY 5, 1750)

In our discussion of job order and process costing, we demonstrated that accounting provides management with the "actual" costs of a firm's activities and products. In Chapter 25 we showed that, if it is to carry out its functions of planning, control, decision making, and performance measurement, *management must not only know actual costs but must also have some reasonable idea of what costs should be.* To plan operations, costs must be planned, and to exercise cost control, actual costs must be compared with planned costs. To measure performance and make rational decisions, management must know whether given amounts of costs are favorable (actual less than planned) or unfavorable (actual greater than planned). The need to plan costs and to know what costs should be has led to the development of standard costs and budgeting.

The processes of determining standard costs and developing budgets are similar in that they both involve planning what costs and cost-related aspects of operations ought to be. **Standard product costs** are derived through a detailed determination of what quantities should be used and what prices should be paid for production inputs—raw materials, direct labor, and factory overhead. **Budgeting** uses standard costs to formulate a comprehensive financial plan for a wide array of operational activities such as sales, production, operating expenses, and cash flows. In standard costing and in the broader area of budgeting, the major objective is to compare planned and actual costs in order to identify differences, or variances, and take appropriate corrective action. In this chapter, we illustrate the determination and use of standard costs and conclude with a discussion of budgeting procedures.

STANDARD COSTS

Standard costs are those amounts that analysis has shown *should* be incurred for raw materials, direct labor, and factory overhead. Standard costs are developed prior to the operating periods to which they apply and remain in effect until circumstances require their revision. Routine comparison of actual costs with standard costs permits management to operate on the principle of **management by exception.** This means that management concentrates its efforts on those aspects of operations that are out of line with standards, therefore causing unfavorable variances.

Standard costs may be used more or less informally in periodic management reports devoted to cost control. It is well accepted, however, that they are most effective when they and their related variances are recorded in the general ledger accounts. The integrated use of standard costs is referred to as *standard cost accounting*. Products are costed at standard unit amounts, and any differences above or below standard costs are recorded in specific accounts as unfavorable and favorable variances, respectively.

DETERMINATION OF STANDARD COSTS

Establishing standard costs can be a complex task. For example, determining standards for materials costs requires many important decisions concerning optimum types, combinations, qualities, quantities, and prices for all materials. The process of deriving standard labor costs often involves time-and-motion studies and choices among various combinations of labor skills and machine operations. Determining standard overhead costs requires an analysis of plant layout, equipment capacities, specific production techniques, and cost behavior patterns. People from a number of areas—accounting, production, product engineering, purchasing, personnel, management, and even labor unions may all contribute to the development of cost standards.

Most companies establish cost standards on the basis of some reasonably attainable (rather than theoretically perfect) level of efficiency. If the determined standards are too seldom or too easily attainable, they tend to lose their motivating force and cease to be a standard of performance against which actual performance can be meaningfully measured. Standards should be updated from time to time whenever significant changes occur in prices, materials used, production technology, labor rates or contracts, or product design. In the final analysis, the variances determined with the aid of standard costs can be meaningful only if the standards used represent a potentially attainable level of efficiency under current operating conditions.

Ordinarily, a manufacturing firm establishes standard costs for each of its products. Each standard cost consists of a standard raw materials cost, a standard direct labor cost, and a standard factory overhead cost.

Raw Materials Standards

The standard cost of raw materials used to make a finished unit is the product of two factors: **standard usage** and **standard price.** Usually, to determine the quantities of raw materials that should be used to make a unit of product, product engineers and other production personnel first determine the quality needed, production runs, normal spoilage, and other factors. Standard prices are often calculated by purchasing department and accounting personnel after specifications, price quotations from suppliers, possible discounts, and related factors have been considered.

To begin our illustration, assume that the Abbott Manufacturing Company makes only product A, a very simple product that requires one type of raw material, X. If the standard usage is two pounds of X to make one unit of A, and the standard price of X is determined to be $1 a pound, the standard materials cost for a unit of product is $2.

Direct Labor Standards

The standard cost of direct labor used to make a finished unit is also the product of two factors: **standard time** and **standard rate.** Using time-and-motion studies or other analyses of labor operations, job analysts and other production personnel set the standard time to be allotted to each operation. Union representatives may also have considerable influence in setting time standards. Standard rates are usually set by contracts negotiated between management and labor unions. If, for Abbott Manufacturing Company, the standard direct labor time to make a unit of product A was set at 1 hour and the standard labor rate was $6 per hour, the standard cost for direct labor would be $6 per unit of product.

Factory Overhead Standards

Many of the difficulties of accounting for factory overhead were discussed in earlier chapters. The inherent complexities of overhead costs—their variety, their indirect association with production, and the presence of both fixed and variable cost elements—require a different approach to determining standards for factory overhead.

Typically, some form of flexible budgeting is used to estimate the amount of factory overhead costs that should be expected at or near the anticipated level of production that would be considered normal capacity for the firm. Standard rates for factory overhead are determined by dividing the total amount of standard overhead by the units of normal production capacity. Production capacity is usually expressed in direct labor hours, direct labor costs, or perhaps machine hours. Often, a separate rate is calculated for **fixed overhead** and for **variable overhead**. A columnar flexible budget for the only production department of the Abbott Manufacturing Company appears below. The budget indicates that factory overhead is applied on the basis of direct labor hours and that 10,000 direct labor hours per month is considered normal capacity. The standard amounts of factory overhead at various levels of operation are shown.

Abbott Manufacturing Company
Flexible Factory Overhead Cost Budget
For the Month of June 19XX

	Production Levels			
Percent of Normal Capacity	80%	90%	100%	110%
Standard Direct Labor Hours	8,000	9,000	10,000	11,000
Budgeted Factory Overhead:				
Variable costs:				
Factory supplies used	$ 800	$ 900	$ 1,000	$ 1,100
Indirect labor	1,600	1,800	2,000	2,200
Power	2,400	2,700	3,000	3,300
Other	3,200	3,600	4,000	4,400
Total variable overhead	$ 8,000	$ 9,000	$10,000	$11,000
Fixed costs:				
Supervisory salaries	$12,000	$12,000	$12,000	$12,000
Depreciation	8,000	8,000	8,000	8,000
Other	10,000	10,000	10,000	10,000
Total fixed overhead	$30,000	$30,000	$30,000	$30,000
Total Budgeted Factory Overhead	$38,000	$39,000	$40,000	$41,000

Note that factory overhead is separated into total variable and total fixed cost elements, that variable overhead increases proportionately as production levels increase, and that fixed overhead does not respond to changes in production levels. At Abbott Manufacturing Company's normal capacity of 10,000 direct labor hours, the budget indicates a standard variable overhead rate of $1 per direct labor hour ($10,000 ÷ 10,000 direct labor hours) and a standard fixed factory overhead rate of $3 per direct labor hour ($30,000 ÷ 10,000 direct labor hours).

The columnar approach to flexible budgeting shown above provides standard cost amounts only for the operating levels indicated at the head of each column. Thus, some form of interpolation would be required to determine the standard factory overhead cost at, say, 93% or 97% of normal capacity. This problem is easily solved by restating the factory overhead cost budget as a cost formula, as was illustrated in Chapter 24.

$$\begin{matrix} \text{Total} \\ \text{Factory} \\ \text{Overhead} \end{matrix} = \begin{matrix} \text{Total} \\ \text{Fixed} \\ \text{Overhead} \end{matrix} + \left(\begin{matrix} \text{Variable} \\ \text{Overhead} \\ \text{Per Unit} \end{matrix} \times \begin{matrix} \text{Production} \\ \text{Volume} \end{matrix} \right)$$

$$\$40,000 = \$30,000 + \left(\$1 \times \begin{matrix} 10,000 \text{ direct} \\ \text{labor hours} \end{matrix} \right)$$

By incorporating the appropriate number of direct labor hours, the cost formula can provide the standard factory overhead cost amount for any number of direct labor hours. This formula version of the flexible budget is used throughout our illustration of determining standard factory overhead costs.

Total Standard Costs

Most firms prepare for each product a standard cost card that summarizes the standard cost for raw materials, direct labor, and factory overhead. Based on the preceding concepts, Abbott Manufacturing Company's standard cost summary for product A would appear as follows:

Abbott Manufacturing Company Standard Cost Summary—Product A		
Raw materials (2 pounds @ $1 per pound)		$ 2
Direct labor (1 hour @ $6 per hour)		6
Factory overhead (applied on basis of direct labor hours):		
Variable (1 hour @ rate of $1 per direct labor hour)	$1	
Fixed (1 hour @ rate of $3 per direct labor hour)	3	4
Total standard cost per unit of product A		$12

Thus, under normal conditions and operating at normal capacity, product A should be produced for a total cost of $12 per unit. We use these standard costs in our illustration of cost variance determination.

Cost Variances   Even in well-managed companies in which cost standards are carefully established and currently maintained, actual costs often differ from standard costs.
Differences may result from either short, isolated lapses or longer-term general
fluctuations in efficiency, or perhaps from a change in production methods that
makes previous standards inapplicable. Once variances occur, they should be
analyzed for indications of their cause so that appropriate action may be taken.

Suppose that during the month of June, Abbott Manufacturing Company produced 9,800 units of product A, for which it incurred the following actual costs
(assume there are no work-in-process inventories):

Raw Materials (20,600 pounds @ $1.05 per pound)		$ 21,630
Direct Labor (9,700 hours @ $6.10 per hour)		59,170
Factory Overhead:		
Variable	$ 8,700	
Fixed	30,000	38,700
Total actual production costs incurred in June		$119,500

In Exhibit 26–1 the actual costs are compared with standard costs for 9,800 units of
product, and the differences, or variances, for each cost category are calculated.
The standard costs are the unit standard costs from our standard cost summary for
product A multiplied by the actual quantity of 9,800 units produced in June. Note
that there are both favorable and unfavorable variances and that the overall net
variance of $1,900 is unfavorable. For management to initiate remedial action, the
variance for each manufacturing cost element must be analyzed to determine the
underlying causal factors related to prices paid, quantities used, and productive
capacity utilized. The following paragraphs present these analyses and the related
journal entries (in summary form) for recording the variances.

EXHIBIT 26–1
Comparison of Actual and Standard Costs of Product A
For the Month of June 19XX

	Actual Costs (9,800 units)	Standard Costs (9,800 units)	Variances Favorable	Variances Unfavorable
Raw Materials	$ 21,630	$ 19,600		$2,030
Direct Labor	59,170	58,800		370
Factory Overhead:				
Variable	8,700	9,800	$1,100	
Fixed	30,000	29,400		600
	$119,500	$117,600	$1,100	$3,000
Net total variance (unfavorable)			$1,900	

Raw Materials Variances

Variances for raw materials stem primarily from paying more or less than the standard price for raw materials and from using more or less than the standard quantity of raw materials. Abbott Manufacturing Company's raw materials variances for the month of June are computed and recorded as follows:

Price Variance = **Price Differential** × **Actual Quantity**
($1.05 − $1.00)   ×   20,600 pounds   = $1,030 *Unfavorable*

Usage Variance = **Usage Differential** × **Standard Price**
(20,600 − 19,600) × $1   =   1,000 *Unfavorable*

Total Variance $2,030 *Unfavorable*

The total raw materials variance is the sum of two unfavorable factors: an unfavorable price variance of $1,030 caused by paying $0.05 per pound above the standard price for 20,600 pounds of materials and a $1,000 unfavorable usage variance resulting from using 1,000 pounds more than the standard amount of materials at a standard cost of $1 per pound. Notice that the total $2,030 variance accounts for the difference between total actual and total standard materials costs as indicated in Exhibit 26-1. These variances would call for a consultation with the purchasing department and the production supervisors. The unfavorable price variance may have been caused by a lapse on the part of purchasing personnel. On the other hand, it may have resulted from improper substitution of more expensive materials than those specified, or simply from an increase in supplier prices. The excess usage might be traced to poor handling by inexperienced workers, inattention to specifications, or even theft.

The journal entry to record costs and variances follows.

Work in Process (standard price and		
quantities)	19,600	
Raw Materials Usage Variance	1,000	
Raw Materials Price Variance	1,030	
Raw Materials Inventory (actual price		
and quantities)		21,630

To record raw materials used in June
and related cost variances.

Note that the journal entry debits Work in Process for standard costs, records the two unfavorable variances as debits (analogous to losses or expenses), and records the actual costs of raw materials requisitioned during the month of June.[1]

---

[1]In our illustration, we recognize and record the raw materials price variance at the time materials are started into production. Some firms prefer to recognize and record the price variance when material purchases are recorded.

Direct Labor Variances

Variances for direct labor result from paying more or less than the standard wage rates for direct labor and from using more or less than the standard amount of direct labor hours. Abbott Manufacturing Company's direct labor variances are computed and recorded as shown below. Note that the basic calculations are the same as for raw materials, but the term *rate* is used instead of *price* and the term *efficiency* instead of *usage*.

Rate Variance   = **Rate Differential**   × **Actual Hours**
  ($6.10 − $6.00)   ×   9,700   = $970 *Unfavorable*

Efficiency Variance = **Efficiency Differential** × **Standard Rate**
  (9,800 − 9,700)   × $6   = 600 *Favorable*

Total Variance $370 *Unfavorable*

The $970 unfavorable direct labor rate variance results from paying $0.10 per hour above standard for 9,700 direct labor hours actually worked. The $600 favorable direct labor efficiency variance is a result of producing June's output in 100 direct labor hours less than the standard allowed, where each hour has a standard rate of $6. Again, the total unfavorable variance of $370 fully explains the difference between total actual and total standard direct labor costs as indicated in Exhibit 26–1.

The favorable direct labor efficiency variance might be credited to the production supervisor, who presumably oversees the production teams. The unfavorable labor rate variance could have resulted from assigning more highly paid employees than specified, paying overtime, or paying increased labor rates because of recently negotiated wage contracts.

The journal entry to record costs and variances follows.

Work in Process (standard rate and hours)	58,800	
Direct Labor Rate Variance	970	
Direct Labor Efficiency Variance		600
Factory Payroll Payable (actual costs)		59,170

To record direct labor costs and related cost variances.

The journal entry shown charges Work in Process with standard direct labor costs, records the unfavorable labor rate variance as a debit and the favorable labor efficiency variance as a credit (analogous to a gain), and records the liability for direct labor at the amount owed, which is determined by actual hours worked and actual rates paid.

Factory Overhead Variances

Variances for factory overhead are often identified with two major sources. Incurring more or less total overhead costs than the amount budgeted for the level of production achieved results in a *controllable* variance. Operating a production level above or below the normal capacity results in a *volume* variance.[2] The total factory overhead variance is the sum of these two variances or the difference between total actual factory overhead and the total factory overhead applied at standard rates to the actual units produced. Abbott Manufacturing Company's total factory overhead variance for the month of June is (see original data on page 920):

Total overhead applied at standard rates	
(9,800 units produced × $4 standard overhead rate)	$39,200
Actual factory overhead ($8,700 variable + $30,000 fixed)	38,700
Total overhead variance (favorable)	$ 500

Because the actual overhead is less than the standard amount of overhead, the $500 difference is a favorable variance. Computation of the factory overhead variances and the journal entry to record them are as follows:

Controllable Variance:

Budgeted overhead for actual production attained		
($30,000 fixed + 9,800 × $1 variable)	$39,800	
Actual overhead	38,700	
Controllable variance		$1,100 *Favorable*

Volume Variance:

Normal capacity in direct labor hours	10,000 hours	
Standard direct labor hours for actual production		
(9,800 units × 1 hour)	9,800 hours	
Production capacity not used	200 hours	
Standard fixed overhead rate	× $3	
Volume variance		600 *Unfavorable*

Total Overhead Variance $ 500 *Favorable*

The journal entry to record costs and variances follows.

Work in Process (at standard overhead		
rates)	39,200	
Overhead Volume Variance	600	
Controllable Overhead Variance		1,100
Factory Overhead (actual overhead costs)		38,700

To record standard factory overhead and related variances.

CONTROLLABLE OVERHEAD VARIANCE   The $1,100 favorable controllable overhead variance is a measure of how well the actual factory overhead costs

[2]Appendix B to this chapter presents an alternate three-variance analysis for factory overhead that isolates variances for spending, efficiency, and volume.

have been kept within the limits set by the budget. Controllable overhead variances typically originate with variable overhead costs; fixed overhead costs tend to be routinely estimated and relatively stable. A small portion of Abbott's favorable controllable variance, $100, resulted from the 9,800 units being produced in only 9,700 hours. This "savings" of 100 hours multiplied by the $1 standard variable overhead rate is the overhead cost avoided by producing 9,800 units of product in 100 hours less than the overhead budget allows. The remaining $1,000 of favorable controllable variance results from spending less than the budget allows for various overhead items. Abbott's overhead budget indicates that total overhead for June should be $39,700 ($30,000 fixed overhead plus $1 variable overhead for each of the 9,700 direct labor hours actually worked). Because actual overhead incurred was only $38,700, the $1,000 difference represents a savings of overhead costs. A detailed analysis of actual and budgeted overhead costs would indicate to what extent each overhead cost (such as factory supplies and indirect labor) contributed to the favorable variance. Department supervisors are usually responsible for controllable overhead variances.

OVERHEAD VOLUME VARIANCE   The overhead volume variance reflects the costs associated with using factory facilities at more or less than normal capacity. Volume variances are measured by the differences between normal capacity and the standard hours allowed for *actual units produced* times the fixed overhead rate. With Abbott's monthly capacity of 10,000 direct labor hours and only 9,800 hours being allowed for June's production of 9,800 units of product, 200 hours of capacity were not utilized.[3] Each of these hours has an implied cost equal to the fixed overhead rate of $3 per direct labor hour, resulting in a total unfavorable overhead volume variance of $600 ($3 × 200). When utilization exceeds normal capacity, the favorable overhead volume variance represents the amount of fixed overhead "saved" by employing the factory facilities beyond normal capacity.

Note that variable overhead costs play no role in volume variances. Because variable overhead costs respond to the level of production, failure to produce means that related variable costs are not incurred and therefore cannot contribute to volume variances. In contrast, fixed overhead does not respond (within the relevant range) to changes in production levels. Failure to produce does not avoid any portion of fixed overhead. Nor does producing beyond normal capacity increase fixed overhead (within the relevant range). Therefore, only fixed factory overhead potentially leads to volume variances.

Volume variances can be caused by anything that leads to use of the factory facilities at more or less than normal capacity. Common examples of such factors are idle time because of machine breakdowns, uneven job scheduling, and insufficient sales orders to justify production at normal capacity. Production supervisors can often correct volume variances caused by machine breakdowns and

[3]Although in our example only 9,700 hours were worked, 100 of these hours were avoided by better-than-standard production efficiency (the favorable controllable overhead variance). The other 200 hours, therefore, represent an appropriate measure of plant underutilization.

uneven scheduling. When the cause is insufficient sales, it is general management's responsibility to increase sales through product advertising and sales promotion and to seek other ways to more fully utilize factory facilities.

The summary journal entry for overhead costs (page 923) charges Work in Process with the standard overhead for the actual production attained, records each of the overhead variances in an appropriately titled variance account, and credits Factory Overhead for the actual overhead costs incurred.

STANDARD COSTS IN FINANCIAL STATEMENTS

When the standard costs and related variances for direct materials, direct labor, and factory overhead are recorded as illustrated here, the Work in Process account is debited for each in amounts representing standard quantities and standard prices. All variances, whether favorable or unfavorable, are carried in separate accounts with appropriate titles. To record completed production for Abbott Manufacturing Company for the month of June, the following entry would be made:

Finished Goods (at standard cost)	117,600	
Work in Process (at standard cost)		117,600

To record completion of June's production
of 9,800 units at a standard unit cost of $12.

As each month's production is sold, the related amounts of standard costs are transferred from Finished Goods to Cost of Goods Sold.

The reporting of standard costs and related variances is usually limited to financial reports intended for management's use only. The following partial income statement illustrates how variances are often reported on interim financial statements for internal use (the amount of sales is assumed).

Abbott Manufacturing Company
Income Statement
For the Month Ended June 30, 19XX

Sales	$166,600
Cost of Goods Sold—at Standard Cost	117,600
Gross Profit—at Standard Cost	$ 49,000
Less: Net Unfavorable Cost Variance	1,900
Gross Profit	$ 47,100

The total net variance could be broken down into subvariances or possibly detailed in a schedule of variances accompanying the financial statements.

At the end of the operating year it is fairly common practice to close the variance accounts by transferring their balances to Cost of Goods Sold. In effect, this converts the Cost of Goods Sold account from standard costs to actual costs. If large variances exist at year-end and there is evidence that the standards may have been inapplicable, there is some justification for allocating all or part of the variances to Work in Process, Finished Goods, and Cost of Goods Sold.

BUDGETING

For the typical business entity, a **budget** is a formalized plan setting forth *management's intended actions and their anticipated effects on key business variables* such as sales, production, expenses, and cash flows. Formulated in quantitative terms, budgets rely heavily on accounting concepts and procedures. In fact, a comprehensive budgeting effort enables us to prepare projected financial statements for the budget period. Thus, in a sense, budgeting is the act of accounting now for the activities of future operating periods.

ADVANTAGES OF BUDGETING

A Plan for Accomplishing Objectives

Budgeting requires the formulation of a thorough plan of operations for the budget period. Indeed, the budgeting process is often referred to as "profit planning." In constructing the budget, management must obtain and analyze data relating to such aspects of future operations as the prices, quantities, types, and availability of production inputs, the anticipated demand for finished goods, and the availability of sources of financing. Consideration must be given to the coordination required among operating departments, outside suppliers, creditors, and other parties involved in the operations of the business. The budget must be in harmony with the long-run goals of the company as well as with short-run objectives such as target amounts of costs and income. There is significant truth in the observation that, even if they were destroyed as soon as they were completed, budgets would be justified in terms of the communication and coordination that occur during their preparation.

Without planning, most complex ventures are prone to develop crises. Without coordination, a "fine" wheelbarrow can be produced at "reasonable" costs and sold in "impressive" quantities at "competitive" prices and still result in an unbearable operating loss. Only when a comprehensively prepared budget shows that planned activities can be expected to lead to an acceptable net income has management done what it can to plan successful operations. In a real sense, then, budgeting provides management with a view of the future that serves as an early warning system for those contemplated actions that might lead to unacceptable results.

MANAGEMENT CONSULTING
AND THE CPA FIRM

In a sense, the management staff of every firm provides in-house consultation to those ultimately making the decisions that govern the life and fortunes of that firm. However, the rapid growth in recent decades of management consulting as a profession indicates that decision makers have turned to consultants outside their firms for advice and information with increasing frequency. This increasing reliance on outsiders is often associated with: (a) the exploding complexity of modern, heavily regulated, internationally-based, technologically-paced business, (b) the need for highly specialized skills not present—and often difficult to justify on a standing basis—in the firm's management team, and (c) the relative independence and objectivity provided by outside consultants when difficult, career-threatening decisions must be made. Although most people readily identify the CPA firm with the annual financial audit and some income tax advice, probably few are aware of the extensive role the CPA plays in management consulting.

The CPA firm's entry into management consulting no doubt was founded on its familiarity with the client-firm's operations stemming from annual audits, its broadly based skills and insights derived from dealing with a wide array of clients, and the management letter it often prepared as a significant aspect of the annual audit. CPA firms began supplementing their staffs with experts specializing in many technical fields. Eventually all major CPA firms had identifiable management advisory service (MAS) departments, and MAS fees were a substantial portion of total billings. They now provide advice in such diverse fields as strategic planning, executive recruiting, actuarial studies, psychological testing, opinion polls, governmental regulation, and computer technology.

The extent to which the CPA firm has penetrated the MAS market is impressive by any standard. One source indicates that the MAS departments in CPA firms are now growing at twice the rate of their audit staffs; that a CPA firm is among the top three management consulting firms, each of which has annual MAS billings approaching $120 million; and that six of the top ten management consulting firms are CPA firms with total MAS billings of $443 million, or 54 percent of the total MAS billings for the group.[1]

Following the recent relaxation of prohibitions on advertising by CPAs, a major CPA firm placed in a nationally circulated business magazine a two-page ad headlined, "The bottom line lets you see where you've been. Your accountants should help you see where you're going." The ad concludes, "The way we look at it, the bottom line isn't where an accountant's usefulness to a client ends. In some ways, it's only the beginning."[2] Perhaps this freedom to promote management advisory services will lead to even higher levels of MAS activity by CPA firms.

The MAS horizon is not without clouds, however. Critics, including U.S. congressional committees, have raised the question of "audit independence" if one department of a CPA firm advises "how to run" a company and another department in that same CPA firm later audits "how well" the company is being run. To date, CPA firms have apparently defended themselves successfully against these charges.[3] However, the Securities and Exchange Commission recently issued criteria for judging the acceptability of various MAS categories for CPA firms.[4] In all probability, many important aspects of this issue are yet to be settled.

The MAS phenomenon highlights just how varied are the skills to be mastered, challenges to be met, problems to be solved, and the career paths to be followed by those studying what we simplistically term accounting. Indeed, debits and credits have come a long way!

[1]"The New Shape of Management Consulting," *Business Week*, May 21, 1979.
[2]*Business Week*, May 21, 1979.
[3]Representative is: Stanley R. Klion, "MAS Practice: Are the Critics Justified?," *The Journal of Accountancy*, June 1978, p. 72.
[4]Accounting Series Release No. 264, Securities and Exchange Commission, June 14, 1979.

**Control
of Operations**

Because it is a highly detailed statement of intended operating results, a budget provides management with a wide array of target conditions with which actual results can be compared to test whether remedial action is necessary. Reasonably frequent comparisons of budgeted and actual operating data are sound operating procedures. This, of course, provides a natural base for the application of "management by exception" principles.

**A Basis of
Performance
Measurement**

A firm is successful because its key personnel do their jobs efficiently, reliably, and with general adherence to plans. For all major aspects of a firm's operation, a well-developed budget sets forth criteria for a high level of performance. Therefore, *properly used,* a budget can be a significant motivational force because managers at various levels know that their actual performance will be evaluated by comparison with a desired level of performance.

BUDGET PREPARATION

Even though specific budgeting procedures vary widely among firms, all business enterprises engaged in a comprehensive budgeting effort must consider certain elements of budget preparation. These are the budget committee, the budget period, and the master budget.

**The Budget
Committee**

A firm's budget committee generally consists of representatives from all major areas of the firm, such as sales, production, and finance, and is headed by the firm's controller. The committee is responsible for coordinating the preparation of the budget, initiating budget procedures, collecting and integrating data from various organizational units, supervising the review and modification of original estimates, and directing the implementation of the budget. When all departments participate in formulating the budget, it is more likely to be accepted as a reasonable standard of performance. In the absence of such participation, the budget's potential for motivation is often lost because it is viewed as an unreasonable goal imposed by outsiders who do not fully understand the department's operations.

**The Budget
Period**

The time period covered by a budget varies according to the nature of the specific activity involved. Cash budgets may cover a week or a month, production budgets a month or a calendar quarter, general operating budgets a calendar quarter or year, and budgets for acquisition of long-lived assets (often termed capital expenditures budgets) may cover several years. Generally speaking, the longer the budget period, the more likely it is that the budget will be reviewed and subsequently revised to consider the latest information available. In one interesting refinement in period-by-period budgeting, termed **continuous budgeting,** the coming year is dealt with in terms of quarterly periods. At any given time, the firm has four sequential quarterly budgets, and as each quarter expires, it adds a new quarterly budget. With this system, regardless of the time of the year, the current budget always covers the current calendar quarter plus the next three quarters. Continuous budgeting can also be carried out in monthly periods.

The Master Budget

A **master budget** is a comprehensive planning document that integrates all the detailed budgets for the various specialized activities of the firm. As indicated earlier, if sufficiently comprehensive, a master budget contains the data necessary to formulate projected (sometimes called pro forma) financial statements for the budget period.

The details of a master budget vary according to whether the firm's operations are manufacturing, merchandising, or service oriented. In this chapter we will illustrate budgeting for a small manufacturing operation, Moore Company. The key components of Moore Company's master budget are:

Sales budget
Production budget
Raw materials budget   Provide a basis for
Direct labor budget   projected income statement
Factory overhead budget
Operating expense budget

Capital expenditures budget   Provide a basis for
Cash budget   projected balance sheet

The major steps in preparing the master budget are as follows (assuming the prior development of long-run goals and plans):

(1) Prepare sales forecast.

(2) Determine production volume.

(3) Estimate manufacturing costs and operating expenses.

(4) Determine cash flows and other financial effects.

(5) Formulate projected financial statements.

Estimating sales volume is usually the initial step in constructing a master budget. Once sales are forecast, production volume can be set to provide for the desired changes, if any, in finished goods inventories. When production volume is known, reliable estimates can be made for raw materials, direct labor, factory overhead, and operating expenses. When standard costs are available, they should, of course, be incorporated. With estimates of these costs and expenses, cash flows and the related effects on other accounts can be projected. Then, with proper consideration for capital expenditures and related financing, projected financial statements can be prepared. Aspects of the detailed budgets may indicate unacceptable situations such as excessive costs, exceeded capacities, or cash shortages for which revisions would have to be made. Of course, early identification of potential operating crises is a key advantage of budgeting.

ILLUSTRATIONS OF BUDGETS

We shall illustrate the preparation of a relatively simple master budget for Moore Company. Budgeted financial statements are not illustrated because they would be virtually identical with the financial statements studied earlier throughout the text. The amounts used, unless correlated with other aspects of the illustration, are chosen for convenience.

Sales Budget

Because estimated sales volume influences items appearing in several other budgets, the sales budget is prepared first. The anticipated unit sales volume is based on a sales forecast that reflects prior periods' sales, expected general economic conditions, related market research, and specific industry trends. Reasonably reliable sales forecasts are important because their determination affects such variables as the quantities to be produced, operating expenses, and cash requirements. Overestimating sales volume can lead to large unwanted inventories, which in turn result in extra storage costs and possibly sales price reductions in an effort to liquidate the excess inventory. Underestimating sales can lead to loss of sales revenues and perhaps lasting customer ill-will stemming from unfilled orders.

The estimated unit sales volume of each product is multiplied by planned unit prices to derive an estimate of total sales revenues. The calculations may be classified by sales territory or salesperson or both. A sales budget is illustrated in Exhibit 26–2. To use the sales budget to full advantage, data on actual sales should be classified in the same manner as budgeted sales so that comparisons may be made between budgeted and actual sales on the basis of sales area or salesperson.

EXHIBIT 26–2
Moore Company
Sales Budget
For the Quarter Ended June 30, 19XX

	Estimated Unit Sales Volume	Unit Selling Price	Total Sales
Product A: East Area	40,000	$10	$ 400,000
West Area	28,000	10	280,000
Total product A	68,000	10	$ 680,000
Product B: East Area	20,000	$13	$ 260,000
West Area	11,000	13	143,000
Total product B	31,000	13	$ 403,000
Total sales revenues			$1,083,000

EXHIBIT 26-3
Moore Company
Production Budget (in Units)
For the Quarter Ended June 30, 19XX

	Products	
	A	B
Estimated units to be sold	68,000	31,000
Desired ending inventories	12,000	4,000
Amounts to be available	80,000	35,000
Less beginning inventories	10,000	5,000
Total production to be scheduled	70,000	30,000

Production Budget

The production budget reflects the quantity of each product to be produced during the budget period. Scheduled production should specifically provide for anticipated sales and desired ending inventories and, of course, take into consideration the beginning inventories of each product. Assume Moore Company wants to increase its inventory of product A and decrease its inventory of product B by 20%. Moore's production budget appears in Exhibit 26-3. It is hoped that the scheduled production will approach full utilization of plant capacity. If not, management should investigate ways to make use of the excess capacity. Note that the desired change in inventory of each product is accomplished by scheduling the appropriate production volumes.

Raw Materials Budget

The quantities of raw materials to be acquired to meet scheduled production and desired ending inventory requirements are presented in the raw materials budget. Any beginning inventories of raw materials must be considered in estimating acquisitions for the budget period. The quantities to be acquired are multiplied by the anticipated unit cost prices to calculate the total dollar amounts of raw materials purchases. In the raw materials budget illustrated in Exhibit 26-4 (page 932), it is assumed that Moore Company uses only two raw materials, X and Y, in producing products A and B. Even though the quarterly totals of raw materials purchases may be coordinated well with quarterly production requirements, the day-to-day management of inventories should be such that there are neither excess inventories nor items out of stock.

Direct Labor Budget

The direct labor budget presents the number of direct labor hours necessary for the production volume planned for the budget period. These hours are multiplied by the applicable hourly labor rates to determine the total dollar amounts of direct labor costs to be budgeted. In the direct labor budget for Moore Company (Exhibit 26-5), we have assumed that both products A and B require manufacturing work in two production departments, Machining and Finishing, as follows:

	Machining Department	Finishing Department
Product A	0.5 hours	0.3 hours
Product B	1.0 hours	0.4 hours

EXHIBIT 26-4
Moore Company
Raw Materials Budget
For the Quarter Ended June 30, 19XX

| | Units of Raw Materials | |
	X	Y
Production requirements:		
Product A (2 units per finished product)	140,000	60,000
Product B (1 unit per finished product)	70,000	30,000
Total units required for production	210,000	90,000
Desired ending inventories	30,000	20,000
Total units to be available	240,000	110,000
Less beginning inventories	40,000	30,000
Total units to be purchased	200,000	80,000
Unit purchase prices	$0.60	$0.80
Total raw materials purchases	$120,000	$64,000

Factory Overhead Budget

Recall from earlier chapters that factory overhead comprises all factory costs that are not raw materials or direct labor. Examples of factory overhead are factory supplies, indirect labor and factory supervisory salaries, utilities, depreciation, maintenance, taxes, and insurance. Because of the variety of cost factors, factory overhead includes both fixed and variable cost elements.

Factory overhead can be budgeted using a fixed budget that specifies the amounts of overhead costs that should be incurred *at a specific* production volume, usually normal capacity. A major problem, however, is that actual production volume seldom turns out to be the budgeted production volume. Under a fixed budget, management is thus faced with comparing actual costs at one production volume with planned costs at a different volume. For many cost factors,

EXHIBIT 26-5
Moore Company
Direct Labor Budget
For the Quarter Ended June 30, 19XX

	Machining Department	Finishing Department
Direct labor hours required for production:		
Product A: (70,000 units × 0.5 hours)	35,000	
(70,000 units × 0.3 hours)		21,000
Product B: (30,000 units × 1.0 hours)	30,000	
(30,000 units × 0.4 hours)		12,000
Total direct labor hours	65,000	33,000
Hourly rate for direct labor	$5.00	$6.00
Total direct labor costs	$325,000	$198,000

such variations between actual and budgeted costs would not be meaningful. To avoid this problem, factory overhead should be budgeted using a flexible budgeting approach.

A flexible factory overhead budget for the machining department of Moore Company is shown in Exhibit 26–6. Note that the budget separates variable and fixed overhead cost elements and presents budgeted factory overhead costs for three different volumes of direct labor hours. Flexible budgets may take the columnar form as shown in Exhibit 26–6 or may be stated as a general total cost formula as developed in Chapter 24 and used in the standard costs section of this chapter. For the machining department of Moore Company for the quarter ending June 30, the overhead formula would be (assuming a planned operating volume of 65,000 direct labor hours):

$$\begin{array}{ccc} \text{Total} & \text{Total} & \left(\begin{array}{cc} \text{Variable} & \text{Production} \\ \text{Factory} = \text{Fixed} + \text{Overhead} \times \text{Volume} \\ \text{Overhead} & \text{Overhead} & \text{Per Unit} \end{array}\right) \end{array}$$

$$\$169,000 = \$104,000 + \left(\quad \$1 \quad \times \begin{array}{c} 65,000 \text{ direct} \\ \text{labor hours} \end{array}\right)$$

Notice that the formula agrees with the related column in Exhibit 26–6.

EXHIBIT 26–6
Moore Company
Factory Overhead Budget—Machining Department
For the Quarter Ended June 30, 19XX

	Variable Cost per Direct Labor Hour	Overhead Costs at		
		60,000 Direct Labor Hours	65,000 Direct Labor Hours	70,000 Direct Labor Hours
Variable costs:				
Factory supplies	$0.30	$ 18,000	$ 19,500	$ 21,000
Indirect labor	0.40	24,000	26,000	28,000
Utilities	0.20	12,000	13,000	14,000
Maintenance	0.10	6,000	6,500	7,000
Total variable overhead	$1.00	$ 60,000	$ 65,000	$ 70,000
Fixed costs:				
Supervisory salaries		$ 30,000	$ 30,000	$ 30,000
Depreciation on equipment		15,000	15,000	15,000
Utilities		20,000	20,000	20,000
Maintenance		12,000	12,000	12,000
Property taxes and insurance		27,000	27,000	27,000
Total fixed overhead		$104,000	$104,000	$104,000
Total factory overhead		$164,000	$169,000	$174,000

A flexible factory overhead budget should be prepared for each production department. Departmental budgets are flexible to permit them to be adjusted for purposes of control and performance evaluation, and for changing levels of production volume. The various departmental factory overhead budgets provide information to support the total factory overhead budget included in the master budget. A particular level of production volume is usually selected for the master budget, so that a total factory overhead cost may be estimated for use in preparing the cash budget and projected financial statements. In our example, the production volume selected is derived from the direct labor budget (indicating 65,000 direct labor hours for the machining department), as shown in Exhibit 26–5.

Operating Expense Budgets

Operating expenses are composed of selling and general administrative expenses and are often budgeted using the flexible budget approach just illustrated for factory overhead. One key difference is that certain variable selling and administrative expenses, such as sales commissions, may vary with *sales volume* rather than production volume. As was true for factory overhead, for purposes of departmental cost control and performance measurement, various supplementary schedules would be prepared to relate specific portions of total selling and administrative expenses to specific departments or cost centers.

Budgeted Income Statement

With the information available from the budgets discussed above, a budgeted income statement can be prepared. Material amounts of other income or expense and estimated income taxes would be incorporated. The budgeted income statement may be supported by a schedule or statement of cost of goods sold.

The projected net income shown would be reviewed for its adequacy in relation to total sales revenues and perhaps the related amount of assets employed. If the ratio of income to sales or assets is smaller than desired, management should review each component of the master budget for possible ways to increase projected net income.

Capital Expenditures Budget

Expenditures for plant and equipment are among the most important transactions of many firms. Chapter 27 considers some approaches to choosing among capital outlay proposals. Because of the large amounts involved and the relatively long lives of capital assets, such expenditures should be well planned. Even companies that are not growing must eventually replace their equipment. For expanding companies—especially those subject to high technological obsolescence—the budgeting of capital expenditures can be most challenging.

In its simplest form, a capital expenditures budget is a list of types of equipment and the amounts budgeted for their acquisition in each of a series of future operating periods, as illustrated in Exhibit 26–7. Capital outlay decisions may have significant effects on aspects of other budgets, such as production capacities in production budgets, depreciation expense in factory overhead and operating expense budgets, and related cash expenditures in the cash budget. For example, the $50,000 to be spent in the quarter ending June 30 appears as an April cash disbursement in the cash budget for Moore Company shown in Exhibit 26–8.

Cash Budget

The cash budget portrays the projected flows of cash during the budget period. Cash receipts are shown in terms of their sources and cash disbursements in

EXHIBIT 26-7
Moore Company
Capital Expenditure Budget
For the Year Ended December 31, 19XX

Expenditures	March 31	June 30	September 30	December 31
Machinery	$7,000	$10,000		$40,000
Delivery equipment		8,000	8,000	
Conveyor system			40,000	6,000
Computer		32,000		
Totals	$7,000	$50,000	$48,000	$46,000

terms of their uses. The difference between these two flows determines the net periodic change in cash balances.

Because of the characteristic time lags between many routine transactions and their related effects on cash, the proper budgeting of cash often requires that certain data contained in other budgets be analyzed to determine their impact on cash flows. Sales precede collections from customers, purchases precede payments on account, depreciation usually does not represent current cash outlays, and, of course, several types of prepayments may call for cash outlays before the related expenses are recognized in the accounts. Generally speaking, the shorter the budget period, the more significant may be the differences between cash flows and related aspects of the firm's operations.

For an example of one important aspect of cash budgeting, assume that Moore Company has analyzed the collection of its total credit sales in any month as follows:

(1) 30% is collected in the month of sale and receives a 2% cash discount. (The cash received is thus 30% of the credit sales $\times$ 0.98.)

(2) 50% is collected in the month following sale and no discounts are involved.

(3) 18% is collected in the second month following sale. The remaining 2% of accounts become uncollectible accounts and are written off.

Assuming estimated monthly credit sales of $350,000 in February, $340,000 in March, and $370,000 in April, Moore Company's cash receipts from credit customers for the month of April could be budgeted in the following manner:

		Collections Received During		
	Monthly Credit Sales	February	March	April
February:	$350,000 $\times$ (30% $\times$ 0.98)	$102,900		
	350,000 $\times$ 50%		$175,000	
	350,000 $\times$ 18%			$ 63,000
March:	$340,000 $\times$ (30% $\times$ 0.98)		99,960	
	340,000 $\times$ 50%			170,000
April:	$370,000 $\times$ (30% $\times$ 0.98)			108,780
				$341,780

EXHIBIT 26–8
Moore Company—Cash Budget
For the Quarter Ended June 30, 19XX

	April	May	June
Cash receipts:			
Cash sales	$ 18,000	$ 15,000	$ 17,500
Collections from customers	341,780	350,000	358,000
Sale of investments	8,000	—	—
Short-term borrowing	40,000	—	—
Other sources	3,220	6,000	6,500
Total cash receipts	$411,000	$371,000	$382,000
Cash disbursements:			
Manufacturing costs	$280,000	$290,000	$285,000
Operating expenses	60,000	61,000	58,000
Capital expenditures	50,000	—	—
Income taxes	—	—	30,000
Dividends	15,000	—	—
Other disbursements	4,000	9,000	19,000
Total cash disbursements	$409,000	$360,000	$392,000
Net cash provided (applied)	$ 2,000	$ 11,000	($ 10,000)
Beginning cash balance	20,000	22,000	33,000
Ending cash balance	$ 22,000	$ 33,000	$ 23,000

Moore Company's cash budget for the quarter ended June 30, 19XX, shown in Exhibit 26–8, reflects some of the more common examples of cash receipts and disbursements.[4] Note how virtually every other element of the master budget has had some effect on the cash budget.

Cash is an asset particularly crucial to the operation of a business. When a firm runs short of cash, operating crises can occur within a few days. Without sufficient cash balances, payrolls cannot be met, cash discounts are not available, credit obligations may not be met on a timely basis, and the volume of operations may be generally curtailed. Eventually the firm's credit standing suffers and further credit may be available only on less desirable terms. Although having too little cash carries the greatest potential penalties, excessively large cash balances represent unused resources. Excess cash should be placed in short-term income-producing investments or used for such strategic purposes as debt retirement.

[4]The cash budget is an internal document that management uses to plan operations. Its format may differ from a cash flow statement, which reports actual cash flows for a past period to external users. The latter statement, discussed in Chapter 17, is subject to the guidelines set forth in *Opinions of the Accounting Principles Board No. 19*, "Reporting Changes in Financial Position," American Institute of Certified Public Accountants, New York, 1971.

Budgeted Balance Sheet

The budgeted balance sheet presents the balances anticipated for the various balance sheet items at the end of the budget period. Assuming all other budgeting procedures have been properly coordinated, the budgeted balance sheet is extremely useful in reviewing the firm's projected financial position. Management is then able to identify potential financial problems—for example, by assessing the adequacy of the projected current ratio and equity ratio—and can revise plans or take other corrective actions if necessary.

PERFORMANCE REPORTS

The use of budgets for cost control and the evaluation of performance entails the preparation of periodic performance reports. Such reports compare budgeted and actual data and show any existing variances. To facilitate their preparation, authority and responsibility for the incurrence of each cost element should be clearly defined within the firm's organizational structure. In addition, the accounting system should be sufficiently detailed and coordinated to provide necessary data for reports designed for the particular use of individuals or cost centers having primary responsibility for specific costs. This detail is often maintained in subsidiary records or generated through other analyses.

Exhibit 26-9 illustrates a quarterly performance report related to Moore Company's factory overhead for the Machining Department. Note that it has been assumed that actual production was 60,000 direct labor hours rather than the 65,000 originally estimated, and that the budgeted amount for the corresponding volume level from the flexible budget in Exhibit 26-6 is compared with the actual costs.

Budget variances in the performance report identify aspects of the business that should be reviewed. As shown in Exhibit 26-9 (page 938), variances related to individual items may require investigation even though the overall variance is immaterial. There may be justifiable reasons for any variance, including the possibility that certain conditions have developed that make the present budget an invalid performance standard. In any event, investigation of the causes of variances should be beneficial to the firm, to control and evaluate current operations and to assist the budget committee in future budget preparations.

KEY POINTS TO REMEMBER

(1) The total net variance for each manufacturing cost element (raw materials, direct labor, and factory overhead) is the difference between total actual costs and total standard costs.

(2) For the following variances, you should be able to compute the amount, label it favorable or unfavorable, explain its basic implications, and indicate the managerial position typically held responsible for the variance.

raw materials price	direct labor efficiency
raw materials usage	controllable factory overhead
direct labor rate	factory overhead volume

EXHIBIT 26–9
Moore Company
Machining Department
Performance Report—Factory Overhead
For the Quarter Ended June 30, 19XX

	Budgeted at Actual Hours	Actual Overhead Costs	Variances Over (Under) Budget	Percent of Budget
Variable costs:				
Factory supplies	$ 18,000	$ 18,400	$400	2.2%
Indirect labor	24,000	23,280	(720)	(3.0)
Utilities	12,000	12,100	100	0.8
Maintenance	6,000	5,920	(80)	(1.3)
Total variable overhead	$ 60,000	$ 59,700	($300)	(0.5)
Fixed costs:				
Supervisory salaries	$ 30,000	$ 30,000		
Depreciation on equipment	15,000	15,000		
Utilities	20,000	20,000		
Maintenance	12,000	12,420	$420	3.5
Property taxes and insurance	27,000	26,700	(300)	(1.1)
Total fixed overhead	$104,000	$104,120	$120	0.1
Total factory overhead	$164,000	$163,820	($180)	(0.1)

(3) When standard costs are incorporated into the general ledger, inventories are carried at standard costs, with unfavorable variances recorded as debits and favorable variances recorded as credits.

(4) A comprehensive budget provides management with a plan for accomplishing objectives and a basis for controlling operations and measuring performance.

(5) You should know the basic format for and the key data appearing in each of the following budgets:

sales budget	factory overhead budget
production budget	capital expenditures budget
raw materials budget	cash budget
direct labor budget	

(6) Flexible budgeting allows management to vary the budget to amounts that can be appropriately compared with costs incurred at actual operating volumes attained.

(7) A performance report compares budgeted and actual amounts and shows any variances between the two amounts.

QUESTIONS

26-1 What is the difference between standard costs and budgets?

26-2 What types of skills would be required of a group responsible for establishing standard costs in a manufacturing concern?

26-3 "Standard costs can be set too high or too low for motivational purposes." Comment.

26-4 If Summa Company used 4,200 pounds of raw materials costing $3.50 per pound for a batch of products that should have taken 4,000 pounds costing $4 per pound, what are the raw materials variances?

26-5 Name and briefly describe two variances included in the total factory overhead variance.

26-6 What is the justification for analyzing the total variance related to, say, raw materials?

26-7 "Total actual cost exactly equals total standard cost, so everything must be okay." Comment.

26-8 If actual factory overhead is $31,000, budgeted overhead for the production level attained is $29,800, the fixed factory overhead rate is $4 per direct labor hour, and actual production is 300 direct labor hours beyond normal capacity, what are the factory overhead variances?

26-9 Who in the firm might be considered typically responsible for each of the following variances?
(a) Raw materials price and usage variances.
(b) Direct labor rate and efficiency variances.
(c) Factory overhead controllable and volume variances.

26-10 Briefly explain how standard cost variances are reported on financial statements.

26-11 List and briefly explain three advantages of budgeting.

26-12 What is meant by continuous budgeting?

26-13 Define *master budget.*

26-14 List, in the order in which they would be prepared, the various budgets that might make up a master budget for a small manufacturing company.

26-15 Why is the sales budget prepared first for most firms?

26-16 If beginning finished goods inventory is 5,000 units, anticipated sales volume is 32,000 units, and the desired ending finished goods inventory is 7,500 units, what number of units should be produced?

26-17 Three pounds of material X (costing $6 per pound) and 4 pounds of material Y (costing $3 per pound) are required to make one unit of product Z. If management plans to increase the inventory of material X by 500 pounds and reduce the inventory of material Y by 800 pounds during a period when 2,000 units of product Z are to be produced, what are the budgeted purchases costs of material X and material Y?

26-18 What is the total cost formula used in flexible budgeting?

26-19 What defect in fixed budgets is avoided by the use of flexible budgets?

26-20 What basic information would you expect to see on a performance report?

26-21 Why are projected financial statements often prepared as part of a comprehensive budgeting process?

EXERCISES

26-22 Appearing below are actual and standard cost data for raw materials and direct labor related to the production of 2,000 units of a product.

	Actual Costs	Standard Costs
Raw materials	2,800 units @ $5.10	3,000 units @ $5
Direct labor	6,300 hours @ $6.30	6,000 hours @ $6

Determine the following variances:
(a) Raw materials price.
(b) Raw materials usage.
(c) Direct labor rate.
(d) Direct labor efficiency.

26-23 Beerman Company considers 6,000 direct labor hours or 3,000 units of product its normal monthly capacity and has standard variable and fixed factory overhead rates of $2 and $4, respectively, for each direct labor hour. During the current month, $35,600 of factory overhead was incurred in working 5,600 direct labor hours to produce 2,700 units of product. Determine the following variances for factory overhead, and indicate whether each is favorable or unfavorable:
(a) Controllable
(b) Volume

26-24 From the following data, determine the actual costs incurred for raw materials, direct labor, and factory overhead.

	Standard Costs	Variances Over (Under) Budget
Raw Materials:	$44,000	
Price variance		$1,300
Usage variance		(2,100)
Direct Labor:	28,000	
Rate variance		700
Efficiency variance		1,100
Factory overhead:	76,000	
Controllable variance		(1,900)
Volume variance		(2,100)

26-25 For producing and selling 2,500 units of its only product for the month ended April 30, 19XX, Mono Company's records reflect the following selected data.

	Standard Unit Costs	Actual Unit Costs
Raw materials	$ 4.40	$ 4.50
Direct labor	12.00	11.60
Factory overhead	9.00	8.80

Assuming that the product sells for $38.00 per unit and that Mono Company uses standard costs in its general ledger accounts, prepare a partial summary income statement (through gross profit) showing how any existing total net variances would be presented.

26-26 For each independent situation below, determine the missing amounts indicated by the question marks.

Number of Units	A	B	C	D
In beginning inventory	8,000	?	9,000	?
Produced	17,000	22,000	?	47,000
Available	?	?	38,000	68,000
Sold	19,000	31,000	?	?
In ending inventory	?	3,000	12,000	15,000

26-27 Nantucket Company is preparing its comprehensive budget for the month of July. Using the given estimates, determine the amounts required in each part below. (Note that estimates may be related to more than one part.)

(a) What should total sales revenues be if territories A and B are estimating 4,000 and 8,000 units, respectively, and the unit selling price is $32.50?

(b) If the beginning finished goods inventory is estimated at 2,200 units and the desired ending inventory is 4,500 units, how many units should be produced?

(c) What dollar amount of raw materials should be purchased at $3 per pound if each unit of product requires 4 pounds and beginning and ending direct materials inventories are to be 7,000 and 4,500 pounds, respectively?

(d) How much direct labor cost should be incurred if each unit produced requires 2.5 hours at an hourly rate of $6?

(e) How much factory overhead should be incurred if there is fixed factory overhead of $34,000 and variable factory overhead of $3.20 per direct labor hour?

(f) How much operating expense should be incurred if fixed and variable operating expenses are $22,000 and $1.80 per unit sold, respectively?

26-28 Appearing below are summary data from a performance report for the Maze Company for the month of June in which 9,600 units were produced. The budget reflects the company's normal capacity of 10,000 units.

	Budget (10,000 units)	Actual Costs (9,600 units)	Variances Over (Under) Budget
Raw materials	$ 35,000	$ 34,400	($600)
Direct labor	70,000	69,700	(300)
Factory overhead: variable	24,000	24,200	200
fixed	18,000	18,100	100
Total	$147,000	$146,400	($600)

(a) What is the general implication of the performance report? Why might the significance of the report be questioned?

(b) Revise the performance report using the concept of flexible budgeting, and comment on the general implication of the revised report.

26-29 Bell Company sells on terms of 2/10, net 30 and has had gross credit sales for the months of May and June of $80,000 and $70,000, respectively. Analysis of Bell's operations indicates that customers' payments on account are patterned as follows (all percentages are of total monthly credit sales):

	Receiving Discount	Beyond Discount Period	Totals
In month of sale	50%	15%	65%
In month following sale	20%	10%	30%
Uncollectible accounts, returns, allowances			5%
			100%

Determine the estimated cash to be collected on customers' accounts in the month of June.

PROBLEMS

26-30 The following summary data relate to the operations of Marston Company for the month of April, in which 19,000 finished units were produced.

	Standard Unit Costs	Total Actual Costs
Raw materials:		
Standard: 4 pounds @ $1.50 per pound	$ 6.00	
Actual: 78,000 pounds @ $1.40 per pound		$109,200
Direct labor:		
Standard: 3 hours @ $8 per hour	24.00	
Actual: 56,500 hours @ $8.20 per hour		463,300
Factory overhead:		
Standard: Variable of $1 per direct labor hour and $120,000 fixed for normal monthly capacity of 60,000 direct labor hours	9.00	
Actual		180,000
Total	$39.00	$752,500

REQUIRED
Determine the following variances and indicate whether each is favorable or unfavorable.
(a) Raw materials price variance and usage variance.
(b) Direct labor rate variance and efficiency variance.
(c) Factory overhead controllable variance and volume variance.

26-31 A summary of Jason Company's manufacturing variance report for the month of May appears on page 943.

	Total Standard Cost (4,800 units)	Total Actual Cost (4,800 units)	Variances (favorable)
Raw materials	$19,200	$ 20,460	$1,260
Direct labor	48,000	51,000	3,000
Factory Overhead:			
Variable	4,800	4,500	(300)
Fixed	24,000	25,000	1,000
	$96,000	$100,960	$4,960

Standard raw materials cost per unit of product is 2 pounds at $2 each, and standard direct labor cost is 2 hours at $5 per hour. The total actual raw materials cost represents 9,300 pounds purchased at $2.20 each; total actual direct labor cost represents 10,000 hours at $5.10 each. Standard variable and fixed factory overhead are $0.50 and $2.50, respectively, per direct labor hour (based on a normal capacity of 10,000 direct labor hours or 5,000 units of product).

REQUIRED
(a) Calculate variances for raw materials price and usage, direct labor rate and efficiency, and controllable factory overhead and overhead volume.
(b) Prepare single compound entries in general journal form (as illustrated in the chapter) to record standard costs, actual costs, and related variances for raw materials, direct labor, and factory overhead.
(c) Prepare journal entries to record the completion of all units, their transfer to Finished Goods, and the subsequent sale of 4,400 units on account at $32 each (assume no beginning finished goods inventory).
(d) Prepare a partial income statement (through cost of goods sold), showing gross profit based on standard costs, the incorporation of variances, and gross profit based on actual costs.

26-32 Romax Company manufactures a single product and uses a standard costing system. The nature of its product dictates that raw materials be used as purchased and no ending work-in-process inventories occur. Per-unit standard product costs are: raw materials, $6 (2 pounds); direct labor, $4 (one-half hour); variable factory overhead, $2 (based on direct labor hours); and fixed overhead, $5 (based on a normal monthly capacity of 8,000 direct labor hours).

Romax accounts for all inventories at standard cost and records each variance in a separate account. The following data relate to the month of May, when 15,000 finished units were produced.

REQUIRED
(a) Assuming that 31,000 pounds of raw materials were purchased on account at $3.10 a pound and used in May's production, present a single compound journal entry to record actual costs, standard costs, and any raw materials variances.
(b) Assuming that 7,800 direct labor hours were worked at an average hourly rate of $7.80, present a single compound journal entry to record actual costs, standard costs, and any direct labor variances.
(c) Assuming that total factory overhead incurred was $112,800, present a single

compound journal entry to record actual and standard factory overhead costs and any factory overhead variances.

(d) Set up T accounts for Work in Process, Finished Goods, and Cost of Goods Sold. Enter the amounts for (a), (b), and (c), above. Assuming that no beginning inventories exist, all production was completed, and all but 500 units were sold, present journal entries to (1) record production completed and (2) record costs of goods sold at standard costs. Post these entries.

26-33 Babbock, Inc. sells on terms of 5% discount for "cash and carry" or 2/10, net 30 and estimates its total gross sales for the second calendar quarter of next year as follows: April, $120,000; May, $80,000; and June, $110,000. An analysis of operations indicates the following customer collection patterns:

	Portions of Total Sales
In month of sale:	
Cash at time of sale	15%
On account, during discount period	25%
On account, after discount period	10%
In month following sale:	
On account, during discount period	20%
On account, after discount period	10%
In second month following sale:	
On account, after discount period	15%
Average portion uncollectible	5%
	100%

REQUIRED

Prepare an estimate of the cash to be collected from customers during the month of June.

26-34 During the first calendar quarter of 19X1, Promo Enterprises, Inc. is planning to manufacture and introduce a new product in two areas. Market research indicates that sales will be 8,000 units in the urban region at a unit price of $30 and 4,000 units in the rural region at $32 each. Since the sales manager expects the product to catch on, he has asked that production be sufficient to generate a 3,000-unit ending inventory. The production manager has furnished the following estimates related to manufacturing costs and operating expenses.

	Variable (per unit)	Fixed (total)
Manufacturing Costs:		
Raw materials:		
A (3 pounds @ $3 each)	$9	—
B (4 pounds @ $1.50 each)	6	—
Direct labor (one-half hour per unit)	4	—
Factory overhead:		
Depreciation	—	$ 5,000
Factory supplies	0.30	4,000
Supervisory salaries	—	7,500
Other	0.40	18,000

Operating Expenses:
Selling:

Advertising	—	5,000
Sales salaries and commissions	0.25*	6,000
Other	0.50*	4,000
Administrative:		
Office salaries	—	1,600
Supplies	0.10	500
Other	0.04	800

*Varies with number of units sold.

REQUIRED
(a) Assuming that the desired ending inventories of materials A and B are 5,000 and 10,000 units, respectively, and that work-in-process inventories are immaterial, prepare budgets for the calendar quarter in which the new products will be introduced for each of the following operating factors:
(1) Total sales revenues.
(2) Production (in units).
(3) Raw materials purchases cost.
(4) Direct labor costs.
(5) Factory overhead costs.
(6) Operating expenses.
(b) Using data generated in (a), prepare a projected income statement for the calendar quarter. Assume an overall effective income tax rate of 40%.

26-35 Clay, Inc. is a wholesaler for its only product, a deluxe wireless electric drill, which sells for $30 each and costs Clay $20 each. At December 1, 19X1, Clay's management requested a cash budget for the month of December, and the following selected account balances at November 30 were gathered by the accounting department.

Cash	$ 50,000
Marketable Securities (at cost)	60,000
Accounts Receivable (all trade)	780,000
Inventories (12,000 units)	240,000
Operating Expenses Payable	44,000
Accounts Payable (all merchandise)	352,000
Note Payable	75,000

Actual sales for October and November were 30,000 and 40,000 units, respectively. Projected unit sales for December and January are 60,000 and 30,000, respectively. Experience indicates that 50% of sales should be collected in the month of sale, 30% in the month following sale, and the balance in the second month following sale. Uncollectibles, returns, and allowances are negligible.

Purchases are planned to provide for ending inventories equal to 20% of next month's unit sales volume; approximately 60% are paid for in the month of purchase and the balance in the following month.

Monthly operating expenses are budgeted at $4 per unit sold plus a fixed amount of $80,000 including depreciation of $20,000. Except for depreciation,

80% of operating expenses are paid in the month incurred and the balance in the following month.

Special year-end transactions anticipated include:

(a) Declaration of a $15,000 cash dividend to be paid two weeks after the date of record of December 20.

(b) Sale of one-half of the marketable securities held on November 30; a gain of $6,000 is anticipated.

(c) Payment of $16,000 monthly installment (includes interest) on the note payable.

(d) Trade-in of an old computer originally costing $400,000 and now having accumulated depreciation of $340,000 at a gain of $80,000 on a new computer costing $700,000. Sufficient cash is to be paid at the time of trade so that only 50% of the total price will have to be financed.

(e) Clay's treasurer has a policy of maintaining a minimum cash balance of $50,000 at month-end and has a standing arrangement with the bank to borrow any amount necessary up to a limit of $100,000.

REQUIRED

Prepare a cash budget for Clay, Inc. for the month of December 19X1. It is suggested that you begin your solution by scheduling collections from customers, payments on account for merchandise, and payments for operating expenses. Pattern your solution after Exhibit 26–8 on page 936.

26–36 The Polishing Department of the Maxim Manufacturing Company operated during April 19X1 with the following factory overhead cost budget based on 5,000 hours of monthly productive capacity.

Maxim Manufacturing Company
Factory Overhead Budget—Polishing Department
For the Month of April 19X1

Variable costs:		
Factory supplies	$ 40,000	
Indirect labor	160,000	
Utilities	85,000	
Patent royalties on secret process	122,500	
Total variable overhead		$407,500
Fixed costs:		
Supervisory salaries	$ 30,000	
Depreciation on factory equipment	24,000	
Factory taxes	5,000	
Factory insurance	2,000	
Utilities	12,000	
Total fixed overhead		73,000
Total factory overhead		$480,500

The Polishing Department was operated for 4,500 hours during April and incurred the following factory overhead costs:

Factory supplies	$ 38,200
Indirect labor	141,700
Utilities (usage factor)	82,000
Utilities (base factor)	13,500
Patent royalties	109,300
Supervisory salaries	32,000
Depreciation on factory equipment	24,000
Factory taxes	5,000
Factory insurance	2,000
Total factory overhead incurred	$447,700

REQUIRED

Using a flexible budgeting approach, prepare a factory overhead cost performance report for the Polishing Department for the month of April 19X1. Pattern your solution after Exhibit 26–9 on page 938.

ALTERNATE PROBLEMS

26–30A The following summary data relate to the operations of Hooper Company for the month of April in which 4,600 finished units were produced.

	Standard Unit Costs	Total Actual Costs
Raw materials:		
Standard: 3 pounds @ $2.00 per pound	$ 6.00	
Actual: 14,000 pounds @ $2.10 per pound		$ 29,400
Direct labor:		
Standard: 1.5 hours @ $6 per hour	9.00	
Actual: 7,200 hours @ $5.80 per hour		41,760
Factory overhead:		
Standard: Variable of $4 per direct labor hour and $75,000 fixed for normal monthly capacity of 7,500 direct labor hours	21.00	
Actual		105,000
Total	$36.00	$176,160

REQUIRED

Determine the following variances and indicate whether each is favorable or unfavorable.

(a) Raw materials price variance and usage variance.

(b) Direct labor rate variance and efficiency variance.

(c) Factory overhead controllable variance and volume variance.

26–31A A summary of James Company's manufacturing variance report for the month of June appears on page 948.

	Total Standard Cost (9,700 units)	Total Actual Cost (9,700 units)	Variances (favorable)
Raw materials	$ 34,920	$ 34,500	$ (420)
Direct labor	93,120	98,770	5,650
Factory Overhead:			
Variable	23,280	22,680	(600)
Fixed	58,200	60,000	1,800
	$209,520	$215,950	$6,430

Standard raw materials cost per unit of product is 3 pounds at $1.20 each and standard direct labor cost is 1.2 hours at $8 per hour. Total actual raw materials cost represents 30,000 pounds purchased at $1.15 each; total direct labor cost represents 11,900 hours at $8.30 each. Variable and fixed factory overhead are $2.00 and $5.00, respectively, per direct labor hour (based on a normal capacity of 12,000 direct labor hours or 10,000 units of product).

REQUIRED

(a) Calculate variances for raw materials price and usage, direct labor rate and efficiency, and controllable factory overhead and overhead volume.

(b) Prepare single compound entries in general journal form (as illustrated in the chapter) to record standard costs, actual costs, and related variances for raw materials, direct labor, and factory overhead.

(c) Prepare journal entries to record the completion of all units, their transfer to Finished Goods, and the subsequent sale of 8,700 units on account at $30 each (assume no beginning finished goods inventory).

(d) Prepare a partial income statement (through cost of goods sold) showing gross profit based on standard costs, the incorporation of variances, and gross profit based on actual costs.

26-32A Brandon Company manufactures a single product and uses a standard costing system. The nature of its product dictates that raw materials be used as purchased and there are no ending work-in-process inventories. Per-unit standard product costs are: raw materials, $4 (one pound); direct labor, $20 (2.5 hours); variable factory overhead, $5 (based on direct labor hours); and fixed overhead, $15 (based on a normal monthly capacity of 15,000 direct labor hours or 6,000 units of product).

Brandon Company accounts for all inventories at standard cost and records each variance in a separate account. The following data relate to the month of June, when 5,800 finished units were produced.

REQUIRED

(a) Assuming that 6,200 pounds of raw materials were purchased on account at $3.80 a pound and used in June's production, present a single compound journal entry to record actual costs, standard costs, and any raw materials variances.

(b) Assuming that 15,000 direct labor hours were worked at an average hourly rate of $8.10, present a single compound journal entry to record actual costs, standard costs, and any direct labor variances.

(c) Assuming that total factory overhead incurred was $119,500, present a

single compound journal entry to record actual and standard factory overhead costs and any factory overhead variances.

(d) Set up T accounts for Work in Process, Finished Goods, and Cost of Goods
Sold. Enter the amounts for (a), (b), and (c). Assuming that no beginning
inventories exist, all production was completed, and all but 900 units were
sold, present journal entries to (1) record production completed and (2)
record cost of goods sold at standard costs. Post these entries.

26–34A During the first calendar quarter of 19X1, Runn Enterprises, Inc. is planning
to manufacture a new product and introduce it in two areas. Market research
indicates that sales will be 6,000 units in the urban region at a unit price of
$27, and 9,000 units in the rural region at $22 each. Since the sales manager
expects the product to catch on, he has asked that production be sufficient to
generate a 4,000-unit ending inventory. The production manager has furnished the following estimates related to manufacturing costs and operating expenses.

	Variable (per unit)	Fixed (total)
Manufacturing Costs:		
Raw materials:		
A (2 pounds @ $1.20 each)	$2.40	—
B (5 pounds @ $0.80 each)	4.00	—
Direct labor (two hours per unit)	12.00	—
Factory overhead:		
Depreciation	—	$5,000
Factory supplies	0.20	3,000
Supervisory salaries	—	6,100
Other	0.50	3,000
Operating Expenses:		
Selling:		
Advertising	—	4,000
Sales salaries and commissions	$1.00*	5,000
Other	0.20*	3,000
Administrative:		
Office salaries	—	2,100
Supplies	0.10	1,000
Other	0.20	1,200

*Varies with number of units sold.

REQUIRED

(a) Assuming that the desired ending inventories of materials A and B are
7,000 and 15,000 units, respectively, and that work-in-process inventories
are immaterial, prepare budgets for the calendar quarter in which the
new products will be introduced for each of the following operating
factors:
(1) Total sales revenues.
(2) Production (in units).
(3) Raw materials purchases cost.
(4) Direct labor costs.
(5) Factory overhead costs.
(6) Operating expenses.

(b) Using data generated in (a), prepare a projected income statement for the calendar quarter. Assume an overall effective income tax rate of 30%.

26-35A Klass, Inc. is a wholesaler for its only product, a deluxe wireless rechargeable electric shaver, which sells for $20 each and costs Klass $12 each. At June 1, 19X1, Klass' management requested a cash budget for the month of June, and the following selected account balances at May 31 were gathered by the accounting department.

Cash	$ 16,000
Marketable Securities (at cost)	40,000
Accounts Receivable (all trade)	580,000
Inventories (12,000 units)	144,000
Operating Expenses Payable	86,000
Accounts Payable (all merchandise)	169,200
Note Payable	60,000

Actual sales for April and May were 20,000 and 50,000 units, respectively. Projected unit sales for June and July are 40,000 and 30,000, respectively. Historical experience indicates that 50% of sales should be collected in the month of sale, 30% in the month following sale, and the balance in the second month following sale. Uncollectibles, returns, and allowances are negligible.

Purchases are planned to provide for ending inventories equal to 30% of next month's sales volume; approximately 70% are paid for in the month of purchase and the balance in the following month.

Monthly operating expenses are budgeted at $3 per unit sold plus a fixed amount of $80,000 including depreciation of $15,000. Except for depreciation, 60% of operating expenses are paid in the month incurred and the balance in the following month.

Special transactions anticipated in June include:

(a) Declaration of a $15,000 cash dividend to be paid two weeks after the date of record of June 20.

(b) Sale of all but $5,000 of the marketable securities held on May 31; a gain of $8,000 is anticipated.

(c) Payment of $32,000 installment (includes interest) on the note payable.

(d) Trade-in of an old company plane originally costing $80,000 and now having accumulated depreciation of $60,000 at a gain of $30,000 on a new plane costing $400,000. Sufficient cash is to be paid at the time of trade so that only 50% of the total purchase price will have to be financed.

(e) Klass' treasurer has a policy of maintaining a minimum cash balance of $10,000 at month-end and has a standing arrangement with the bank to borrow any amount necessary up to a limit of $50,000.

REQUIRED
Prepare a cash budget for Klass, Inc. for the month of June 19X1. It is suggested that you begin your solution by scheduling collections from customers, payments on account for merchandise, and payments for operating expenses. Pattern your solution after Exhibit 26-8 on page 936.

BUSINESS DECISION PROBLEM

Bonanza, Inc. has just hired Tommy Ledger as its new controller. Tommy, although he has had "little formal accounting training," professes to be highly experienced and to have learned accounting "the hard way" in the field. At the end of his first month's work, Tommy prepared the following cost variance report.

Bonanza, Inc.
Cost Variance Analysis
For the Month of June 19XX

	Total Actual Cost	Total Budgeted Cost	Variances (favorable)
Raw materials	$ 27,360	$ 32,000	$ (4,640)
Direct labor	50,730	60,000	(9,270)
Factory overhead	51,300	60,000	(8,700)
	$129,390	$152,000	$(22,610)

In his presentation to accompany the report at Bonanza's end-of-the-month management meeting, Tommy indicated that things were going "fantastically." "As the figures indicate," he said, "the firm is beating its budget in all cost categories." Tom's good news made everyone at the meeting happy and furthered Tom's acceptance as a member of the management team.

After the management meeting, Carl Burns, Bonanza's general manager, called you as an independent consultant and asked that you review Tom's report. Carl's concern stemmed from the fact that Bonanza has never operated as favorably as Tom's report seems to imply, and Carl knows of no explanation for the apparent significant improvement.

While reviewing Tom's report, you are provided the following cost and operating data for the month of June: Bonanza has a monthly normal capacity of 10,000 direct labor hours or 4,000 units of product. Standard costs per unit for its only product are: raw materials, 4 pounds at $2 each; direct labor, 2.5 hours at $6 each; and variable and fixed overhead rates per direct labor hour of $2 and $4, respectively. During June, Bonanza produced 3,400 units of product using 15,200 pounds of raw materials costing $1.80 each, 8,900 direct labor hours at an average rate of $5.70 each, and incurred $51,300 of total factory overhead costs.

After reviewing Bonanza's cost data for June, you call Tom and tell him that his cost report contains one of the classical errors in budgeting and explain how he can remedy it. In response to your suggestion, Tom revises his report as follows:

	Total Actual Cost	Total Budgeted Cost	Variances (favorable)
Raw materials	$ 27,360	$ 27,200	$160
Direct labor	50,730	51,000	(270)
Factory overhead	51,300	51,000	300
	$129,390	$129,200	$190

Tom's revised report is accompanied by remarks expressing regret at the oversight in the original report, but reassuring management that in view of the small variances in the revised report, the company has met its budget in all cost categories and has no basis for concern.

In your role as consultant:

(a) Verify that Tom's actual cost figures are apparently correct.
(b) Explain how the proportions of Tom's original variances bring into question the validity of the budgeted cost figures.
(c) Identify and explain the "classical" budgeting error that Tom apparently incorporated into his original cost report.
(d) Verify the apparent correctness of Tom's revised budget figures.
(e) Explain why, even though substantially correct, Tom's revised report figures could be considered deficient.
(f) Further analyze Tom's revised variances, isolating underlying potential causal factors. In what ways do your analyses indicate to management bases for concern? Briefly, suggest a remedial approach that management might take regarding any apparent problem area.

THREE-VARIANCE ANALYSIS FOR FACTORY OVERHEAD

Chapter 26 illustrates the analysis of total factory overhead variance into a controllable variance and a volume variance. A refinement to this approach involves dividing the total factory overhead variance into three variances: (1) a *spending* variance, (2) an *efficiency* variance, and (3) a *volume* variance. Because volume variances are the same under either approach, the only difference is that the controllable variance is further divided into a spending variance and an efficiency variance. Of course, the total overhead variance is the same, regardless of the number of variances determined. For convenience, the overhead data for Abbott Manufacturing Company from the illustration in the chapter (see Exhibit 26–1) are repeated here.

	Actual Costs (9,800 units)	Standard Costs (9,800 units)	Variances (favorable)
Factory Overhead:			
Variable	$ 8,700	$ 9,800	$1,100
Fixed	30,000	29,400	(600)
Totals	$38,700	$39,200	$ 500

Also remember that, at its normal capacity of 10,000 direct labor hours, Abbott's standard factory overhead rates per direct labor hour are $1 variable and $3 fixed and that 9,700 direct labor hours were used to produce 9,800 units of product.

The three overhead variances for Abbott Manufacturing Company for the month of June are calculated as follows.

Spending Variance

Budgeted overhead for the actual hours worked		
($30,000 fixed + 9,700 × $1 variable)	$39,700	
Actual overhead	38,700	
Spending variance		$1,000 *Favorable*

Efficiency Variance

Budgeted overhead for actual production attained		
($30,000 fixed + 9,800 × $1 variable)	$39,800	
Budgeted overhead for actual hours worked		
($30,000 fixed + 9,700 units × $1 variable)	$39,700	
Efficiency variance		100 *Favorable*

Volume Variance

Normal capacity in direct labor hours	10,000 hours	
Standard direct labor hours for actual production		
(9,800 units × 1 hour)	9,800 hours	
Production capacity not used	200 hours	
Standard fixed overhead rate	× $3	
Volume variance		600 *Unfavorable*

Total Overhead Variance $ 500 *Favorable*

The journal entry to record costs and variances follows.

Work in Process (at standard rates)	39,200	
Overhead Volume Variance	600	
Overhead Efficiency Variance		100
Overhead Spending Variance		1,000
Factory Overhead (actual overhead costs)		38,700

To record standard factory overhead and related variances.

Overhead Spending Variance

The overhead spending variance reflects how much more (unfavorable) or less (favorable) was spent on factory overhead than the budget would allow for the *actual hours worked*. Abbott's overhead budget indicates that overhead costs should be $30,000 plus $1 for each hour actually worked. Therefore, the budget would allow a total of $39,700 for the 9,700 direct labor hours worked in June. Because total actual overhead incurred was only $38,700, the $1,000 difference is a favorable overhead spending variance. Thus, according to overhead standards, the company has avoided $1,000 of overhead costs.

A review of detailed spending records would show how the $1,000 savings accumulated from savings in the many types of costs making up factory overhead, such as factory supplies, indirect labor, factory utilities, and factory repairs. Although there may be exceptions, control of spending for factory overhead is usually the responsibility of the production department supervisors. As a general rule, the variable portions of overhead costs account for most of the spending variance. Fixed costs, however, can also vary from the budgeted amount because of price changes occurring after the budget has been prepared and put into use. For example, supervisor's salaries are normally classified as fixed costs; if they are increased after the budget has been prepared, actual fixed costs will vary from those budgeted.

Overhead Efficiency Variance

The overhead efficiency variance shows how much overhead cost was either added or saved by operating above or below the standard level of labor efficiency. In June, Abbott's employees worked 9,700 direct labor hours but produced 9,800 units of product, for which the overhead standards would have allowed 9,800 hours. Thus June's operations may be said to have resulted in a savings of 100 direct labor hours, each of which avoided the standard variable overhead rate of $1, giving a total favorable efficiency variance of $100. Note that fixed factory overhead does not enter into the efficiency variance, for as a fixed cost, no part of it would be avoided by operating fewer hours nor would any extra amount of fixed overhead be incurred (within the relevant range) by operating more than the normal number of hours for a given amount of production. In other words, a difference in direct labor hours would affect only the total variable overhead; fixed overhead would remain constant, at least within the relevant range. Since it is so closely tied to the efficiency of production, the overhead efficiency variance is usually the responsibility of the production supervisor.

Overhead Volume Variance

The computation and analyses for overhead volume variances are the same for either the two- or the three-variance approach to factory overhead variances; therefore, they are not repeated here. (See page 923 for this material.)

The journal entry for overhead costs (page 923) charges Work in Process with the standard overhead for the actual production attained, records each of the three variances in an appropriately titled variance account, and credits Factory Overhead for the actual overhead costs incurred.

Determining three variances for factory overhead is often justified because of the clear separation of what would be the controllable variance into a spending element and an efficiency element. This distinction is even more significant when one realizes that a controllable variance might approach zero simply because a very unfavorable spending variance is being virtually offset by a very favorable efficiency variance (or vice versa). This potential for offsetting favorable and unfavorable cost elements could "hide" important operating data from management.

PROBLEMS

B-1 Using the following data, calculate overhead spending, efficiency, and volume variances for each independent situation:

	A	B	C
Total actual overhead	$53,000	$41,500	$173,400
Normal capacity (in direct labor hours)	5,000	8,000	20,000
Standard overhead rates:			
Variable (per direct labor hour)	$2.50	$1.50	$6.00
Fixed (per direct labor hour)	$8.00	$3.75	$2.50
Actual direct labor hours worked	4,700	8,200	19,900
Standard direct labor hours allowed for			
actual production	4,500	7,800	20,300

B-2 Zayre Company uses a standard cost system, has a monthly normal production capacity of 20,000 direct labor hours or 5,000 units of product, and has standard variable and fixed overhead rates per direct labor hour of $2.50 and $4, respectively. During July, Zayre incurred $128,200 of total overhead, working 19,600 direct labor hours to produce 4,800 units of product.

REQUIRED

(a) Compute overhead variances for spending, efficiency, and volume.

(b) Briefly explain the meaning of each variance in terms of operating and budgeting variables.

B-3 Using the data in Problem 26–30 (page 942), compute overhead variances for spending, efficiency, and volume.

B-4 Using the data in Problem 26–31 (page 943), compute overhead variances for spending, efficiency, and volume.

B-5 Using the data in Problem 26–30A (page 947), compute overhead variances for spending, efficiency, and volume.

B-6 Using the data in Problem 26–31A (page 948), compute overhead variances for spending, efficiency, and volume.

B-7 Acme, Inc. uses a standard cost system, has a monthly normal production capacity of 5,000 direct labor hours or 2,500 units of product, and has standard variable and fixed overhead rates per direct labor hour of $6 and $12, respectively. During May, Acme incurred $90,600 of total overhead costs, working 4,700 direct labor hours to produce 2,550 units of product.

REQUIRED

(a) Compute a controllable overhead variance and an overhead volume variance. Briefly describe the operating implications of the variances.

(b) Compute overhead variances for spending, efficiency, and volume. Briefly describe the operating implications of the variances.

(c) In what significant way does this situation justify a three-variance analysis of factory overhead?

27
Capital Budgeting

Time is money . . . and very good money to those who reckon
interest by it.

CHARLES DICKENS

U sing accounting data in planning long-term investments in plant and equipment is known as **capital budgeting.** The term reflects the fact that for most firms the total costs of all attractive investment opportunities exceed the available investment capital. Thus, management must ration, or budget, investment capital among competing investment proposals. In deciding which new long-term assets are to be acquired, one of management's important tasks is to seek those investments that promise to optimize return on the funds employed.

Capital budgeting is most valuable for organizations in which managers are responsible for the long-run profitability of their area of concern and are therefore encouraged to develop new products and more efficient production processes. Firms often place the responsibility for capital budgeting decisions with their most capable employees because such decisions determine how large sums of money are to be invested and commit the firm for extended periods into the future, during which many important factors can only be estimated. Furthermore, investment decision errors are often difficult and costly to remedy or abandon.

Managers as well as accountants should be familiar with the special analytical techniques used to evaluate the relative attractiveness of alternative uses of available capital. In this chapter we shall first discuss the nature and procedures of capital budgeting, how required investment earning rates are determined, the time value of money, and the effect of income taxes on capital expenditure decisions. We shall conclude by illustrating three approaches to capital expenditure analysis: the *net present value method, payback analysis,* and the *average rate of return.*

ELEMENTS OF CAPITAL BUDGETING

Many firms have a capital budgeting calendar calling for consideration of capital expenditure proposals at regular intervals—say, every six months or a year. Proposals are usually examined with respect to (1) compliance with capital budget policies and procedures; (2) aspects of operational urgency, such as the need to replace critical equipment; (3) established criteria for minimum return on capital investments; and (4) consistency with the firm's operating policies and long-run goals. Proposals calling for relatively small cash outlays may require the approval

INNOVATION, PRODUCTIVITY, AND INCOME

Society produces needed goods and services primarily by taking advantage of investment opportunities that promise to return more money than they cost to finance. Innovation, productivity, and reported income play central roles in our society's long-term collective industrial effort, but such phenomena cannot be directly or precisely measured. Recently, observers have expressed concern regarding the apparent long-term trends in these important variables for U.S. industry.

Innovation relates to the development of new materials, production processes, and products. Our real income or standard of living is closely related to a relatively high level of technological innovation. But recent measures of U.S. innovative efforts indicate significant declines from the standards that gave acceptance to such terms as "Yankee know-how" and "Yankee ingenuity."

Research and development expenditures, as a proportion of the gross national product, have fallen to only three-fourths of what they were in the mid-1960s. Exploratory costs in the oil industry, for instance, have declined almost exactly in proportion to corresponding costs for the gross national product. Between 1957 and 1967, exploratory costs per barrel of oil produced fell 25 percent. In 1954 the United States imported only 14 percent of its oil, but by 1974 this figure had risen to 40 percent. Over roughly the same period, the profits to be gained from foreign oil doubled, while those from domestic sources remained almost static. In another instance, over the past two decades, the proportion of marketed U.S.-developed inventions has fallen from more than four in five to only slightly over one in two. Throughout the 1970s, one-third of all U.S. patents have been granted to citizens of foreign countries.

Productivity has followed innovation. Recent statistics indicate that the annual growth in U.S. productivity has fallen from about 3.5 percent during the 1960s to a little over 2.0 percent in the 1970s. Among the top ten modern industrial nations, the United States ranks last.

Among the causes for declining productivity are a 500 percent increase in energy costs in five years, reduced expenditures for research and development, a substitution of social goals (environmental pollution, worker safety) for technological and economic goals, and a general air of political and economic instability that tends to increase the perceived risk of every investment opportunity.

Although its specific role is widely debated, reported income is a basic factor in investment decisions. Mobile capital logically tends to flow away from activities reporting relatively low income rates toward those associated with relatively high income rates. When the methods used to report income are faulty, the soundness of related investment decisions is reduced to a corresponding degree. Although accounting reports always contain some degree of error in estimations and timing, some economists feel that recent events have combined to cause significant and prevailing overstatements of reported income. These errors stem from accountants' reliance on historical cost and their failure to adjust accounts for inflation.

Specifically, income is often overstated when historical costs, rather than current higher replacement costs, are used as the basis for depreciation and costing of sales. Compounding these overstatements is the fact that income taxes paid and dividends declared are often based on income figures that have not been adjusted for current value depreciation or inflation. In 1978, when record corporate profits were reported, it has been estimated that (1) fully one-third of reported profits were illusionary, stemming from understatement of depreciation expense and "phantom" price level gains on inventory; (2) an extra 17 billion dollars in taxes was paid on this illusory portion of reported income; (3) although dividends paid out were only 42 percent of reported income, they were an unacceptable 65 percent of adjusted income; and (4) the real or adjusted amount of earnings retained for growth was only 40 percent of the unadjusted amounts stated in annual reports.

Accountants have already recognized these problems. The real challenge will be to formulate solutions that do not themselves create other problems.

of lower management only, whereas more comprehensive proposals will be subject to approval at higher management levels, perhaps including the board of directors. These comprehensive proposals and the decisions based on them profoundly affect a firm's long-run success.

Once approved, capital expenditures should be monitored to make certain that amounts and purposes are consistent with the original proposal. At appropriate intervals, the actual rates of return earned on important expenditures should be compared with the rates projected for them. Knowing that these reviews will occur encourages those responsible to formulate thorough and realistic proposals, and often provides an incentive for improving overall capital budgeting procedures.

CAPITAL EXPENDITURE ANALYSIS

The scope of capital expenditures can vary widely, ranging from the routine replacement of production equipment to the construction of entire factory complexes. Whatever their size, most production projects have three recognizable stages:

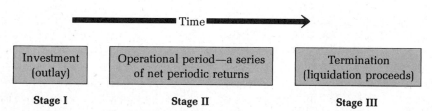

Investment (Stage I) consists of the net cash outlay for a project or an asset. Net periodic returns during the life of the project (Stage II) may result from either an excess of periodic revenues over related expenses or a periodic saving in some expense. Finally, because most efficient firms replace capital equipment before it becomes worthless, the termination of a project (Stage III) often results in some amount of liquidation proceeds.

The attractiveness of a particular investment is determined in large part by the quantitative relationship between the investment in Stage I and the receipts expected in Stages II and III. This relationship is usually expressed as a ratio known as the **rate of return:**

$$\text{Rate of Return} = \frac{\text{Returns}}{\text{Investment}}$$

All other things being equal, the greater the expected rate of return, the more attractive the investment opportunity. Proposed investments can be ranked according to their expected rates of return, and capital outlays can be allocated among those investments considered the most attractive. Capital expenditure analysis, then, in its simplest terms, consists of judging the adequacy or attractiveness of income-producing or cost-saving opportunities in relation to required investments. The results of this analysis are among the most important input data in capital budgeting decisions.

Three questions of considerable concern in capital budgeting are:

(1) How does one determine an acceptable rate of return for a given project?

(2) How can one meaningfully compare investments made now with returns to be received in the future?

(3) In what terms should investments and returns be measured?

These challenging problems are considered in the following sections of this chapter.

REQUIRED RATES OF RETURN

In determining an acceptable rate of return for a given project, one must consider not only the required capital outlay, but the costs associated with the acquisition of that capital. Whether funds are borrowed or provided by the firm's stockholders, the parties providing them expect to be reasonably compensated for their use. When the money is borrowed (usually through a bond issue), the interest paid by the firm is obviously a cost of using the funds. When stockholder funds are used, an assumption is made that some combination of dividend payments and growth in the value of the capital stock will compensate stockholders for furnishing the investment capital. The cost to the firm of acquiring the funds used in capital investment projects—typically expressed as an annual percentage rate—is called the **cost of capital.**

Determining the actual cost of capital for a firm may require complex calculations, and even well-informed authorities in finance disagree about certain aspects of these calculations. Many firms use an approach that distinguishes among the various sources of financing.

A firm may acquire capital by issuing preferred or common stock, by using retained earnings, by borrowing, or by some combination of these. Consequently, the overall cost of capital for a given project may reflect the cost rates of the several sources of funds in proportion to the amounts obtained from each source. This has led to the concept of the **weighted average cost of capital,** which can be illustrated as follows.

Assume that a particular company had acquired capital through all four sources, in the proportions indicated below and with the cost percentages as shown.

Source of Capital	Proportion of Total	Capital Cost Percentage	Weighted Cost Percentage
Debt	40%	8%	3.2%
Preferred stock	10	9	0.9
Common stock	20	12	2.4
Retained earnings	30	12	3.6
Weighted average cost of capital			10.1%

Multiplying the proportion of each capital source by its cost percentage provides weighted cost factors whose sum is the weighted average cost of capital. This percentage (in this case 10.1%) can then be used as a basis of comparison to determine the attractiveness of proposed investments.

Logically, in order for a capital investment to be considered favorably by a firm, its expected rate of return must be *at least as great* as the cost of capital. Thus, *the cost of capital represents a minimum required rate of return.* In other words, a firm whose cost of capital is 10% will ordinarily be interested in investing only in those assets or projects whose expected rate of return is greater than 10%. An investment whose return is less than the cost of capital would be economically detrimental, although firms will sometimes disregard their cost of capital if qualitative considerations override the quantitative aspects of the decision. Qualitative considerations include the desire to maintain an image, the desire to maintain research leadership in the field, and the need to maintain full employment of the work force during a business slowdown.

Some firms consider only those investments whose rate of return is at least a certain number of percentage points higher than the cost of capital. This **buffer margin** acts as a safety factory in recognition of the fact that because all proposals rely heavily on estimates of costs and future returns, the estimated rate of return may be in error. Of course, even proposals whose expected rate of return is higher than the **cutoff rate** (cost of capital plus buffer margin) may be rejected if other investment opportunities offer still higher returns.

THE TIME VALUE OF MONEY

We have seen that in determining the desirability of a proposed capital investment, management compares the amount of investment required at the beginning of a project with its expected returns, typically a series of returns extending several years or more into the future. This comparison, which is so important in capital outlay decisions, cannot be made properly using the absolute amounts of the future returns because *money has a time value.* As discussed in Appendix A to Chapter 15, the time value of money originates in the realization that the right to receive an amount of money today is worth more than the right to receive the same amount at some future date, because a present receipt can be invested to earn interest over the intervening time interval. Thus, if 10% annual interest can be obtained on investments, $100 received today is equal in value to $110 to be received one year from now. Today's $100 has a **future value** of $110 one year from now; conversely, the **present value** of a receipt of $110 expected one year from today is $100. Appendix A (page 538) contains a more detailed presentation of the concept of present values and techniques for their determination. Students not familiar with these two underlying aspects of capital budgeting should review these materials.

Obviously, the difference between present and future values is a function of principal amounts, interest rates, and time periods. The greater the principal amount, interest rate, or time period involved, the greater the amount by which a future value is reduced, or *discounted,* in deriving its present value. For example, the following table shows just how significant the time value of money can be at various interest rates and time periods.

Present Value of $100 Discounted for Years and Interest Rates Shown (rounded to nearest dollar)

Years Discounted	Interest Rates		
	5%	10%	20%
1	$95	$91	$83
2	91	83	69
3	86	75	58
4	82	68	48
5	78	62	40
10	61	39	16
20	38	15	3
30	23	6	—
40	14	2	—
50	9	1	—

As the table indicates, $100 five years from now has a present value of $78, $62, or only $40 if the applicable interest rates are 5%, 10%, and 15%, respectively. Note also that the greater the time period or the interest rate, the greater the difference between the future value of $100 and its current value. Comparing a current investment with its future returns without discounting the returns to their present value would result in a substantive overstatement of the economic significance of the returns. Obviously, then, it is important to recognize the time value of money in capital budgeting procedures.

We should also recognize that techniques for discounting future cash flows to their present values are applicable to both cash receipts and cash outlays. In other words, the current value of the *right to receive*—or the current value of the *obligation to pay*—a sum in the future is its present value computed at an appropriate interest rate. Intuitively, of course, we maximize our economic position by arranging to receive amounts as early as possible and postponing amounts to be paid as long as possible. The intrinsic role of these generalizations is apparent in the illustrations of capital budgeting appearing later in the chapter.

USING PRESENT VALUE TABLES

Although discount formulas are easily understood in theory, the associated calculations can be tedious. Present value tables are widely available and simplify our work considerably. Tables I and II on pages 989 and 990 give the present values of $1 for a number of rates and time periods. The amounts in these tables are called **present value factors,** or **discount factors,** because one can convert any given cash flow to its present value by multiplying the amount of the cash flow by the appropriate factor.

SINGLE SUM FLOWS   Table I gives present value factors for amounts to be received in a single sum at the end of a specified number of time periods. We use Table I when we wish to determine the present value of sporadic cash flows—when the returns expected on an investment, or the expenditures it requires, are unequal amounts or are expected at irregular intervals during the life of the investment or at the end of its life. An excerpt from Table I is presented in Exhibit 27-1.

To illustrate the use of Table I, assume that an investment project promises a return of $2,000 at the end of two years and another $1,000 at the end of five years. Suppose 10% is the desired rate of return. The factor given in the 10% column of the table for two periods from now is 0.826; the factor for five periods from now is 0.621. The total present value of the combined flows is $2,273, calculated as follows:

Future Receipts		PV Factor	Present Value
2 years from now	$2,000	0.826	$1,652
5 years from now	1,000	0.621	621
			$2,273

EXHIBIT 27-1
Present Value of $1 Received
in the Future
(Excerpted from Table I)

Periods Hence	Rate per Compounding Period						
	2%	3%	4%	5%	6%	8%	10%
1	0.980	0.971	0.962	0.952	0.943	0.926	0.909
2	0.961	0.943	0.925	0.907	0.890	0.857	0.826
3	0.942	0.915	0.889	0.864	0.840	0.794	0.751
4	0.924	0.888	0.855	0.823	0.792	0.735	0.683
5	0.906	0.863	0.822	0.784	0.747	0.681	0.621
10	0.821	0.744	0.676	0.614	0.558	0.463	0.386
20	0.673	0.554	0.456	0.377	0.312	0.215	0.149
30	0.552	0.412	0.308	0.231	0.174	0.099	0.057

ANNUITY FLOWS We can compute the present value of any end-of-period cash flows using Table I. If cash flows are the same each period over a number of periods, however, they are in the form of an annuity, and using an annuity table is more convenient. Generally, annuity tables are merely cumulative versions of single sum tables. Table II, for example, is an annuity table based on present value factors from Table I. Exhibit 27–2 is excerpted from Table II.

If a project is expected to have cash inflows of $1,000 at the end of each of the next three periods and 6% is the desired interest rate, we need only multiply $1,000 by the factor for three periods at 6% (2.673) to obtain the present value, $2,673. Alternatively, using Table I, we could multiply $1,000 successively by the first three factors in the 6% column (0.943, 0.890, and 0.840) and then sum the products. The advantage of Table II is that a single present value factor is provided for two or more equal periodic amounts occurring evenly throughout a series of periods. When analyzing investments involving extended series of equal cash flows, the savings in computational effort can be significant.

Tables I and II both assume that all cash flows occur at the end of the periods shown. This assumption is somewhat simplistic, because cash receipts or cost savings from most industrial investments occur in a steady stream throughout the operating period. Nevertheless, such tables are usually used in the business world, principally because of their availability and ease of use. Obviously, these tables understate present values of flows that are gradual throughout the period, because the present values of cash flows early in the period are greater than those of similar inflows or outlays at the end of the period. The difference in the factors, however, is normally not material.

EXHIBIT 27–2
Present Value of $1 Annuity Received
at the End of Each Period
(Excerpted from Table II)

Periods Hence	Rate per Compounding Period						
	2%	3%	4%	5%	6%	8%	10%
1	0.980	0.971	0.962	0.952	0.943	0.926	0.909
2	1.942	1.914	1.886	1.859	1.833	1.783	1.736
3	2.884	2.829	2.775	2.723	2.673	2.577	2.487
4	3.808	3.717	3.630	3.546	3.465	3.312	3.170
5	4.714	4.580	4.452	4.330	4.212	3.993	3.791
10	8.983	8.530	8.111	7.722	7.360	6.710	6.145
20	16.351	14.878	13.590	12.462	11.470	9.818	8.514
30	22.397	19.600	17.292	15.373	13.765	11.258	9.427

MEASUREMENT OF INVESTMENTS AND RETURNS

When present value analysis is used to make investment decisions, investments and returns must be stated in the form of *cash* flows. This is necessary because present value determinations are basically interest calculations, and only money amounts—cash flows—are properly used in interest calculations. Furthermore, only **incremental cash flows** that will occur if the project is accepted should be considered in the analysis. Often, accounting data used to make decisions are not in the form of cash because accrual methods are used for accounts receivable, accounts payable, and accrued revenues or expenses. Such data must be restated in terms of their cash amounts.

For example, an important feature of accrual accounting is that the cost of an asset should be apportioned over its life through depreciation accounting. When present value analysis is used, any cash involved in the cost of an asset is considered a cash outlay at the time the asset is paid for. In measuring future returns related to the asset, depreciation as an accounting expense is irrelevant because it does not represent a cash outlay. As we shall see, however, depreciation affects periodic income tax payments, and because tax payments are cash outlays, depreciation provisions indirectly affect cash flows by reducing tax payments.

Likewise, earnings from projects should not be influenced by the accrual process. The timing of collections is important, however, because the essence of present value analysis is that cash received can be reinvested. If accruals at the beginning and end of periods are roughly the same or are not material in amount, they are often ignored in restating accounting data in the form of cash flows.

After-Tax Cash Flows

Income taxes, both federal and state, are important to investment decisions; for many large companies, the combined federal and state income tax rate may exceed 50%. The general effect of income taxes is to reduce the economic significance of all taxable receipts and deductible outlays. For example, assuming a 40% tax rate, a $40,000 before-tax gain would increase taxable income by $40,000 and income taxes by $16,000 (40% $\times$ $40,000), resulting in a $24,000 after-tax gain. A $15,000 before-tax expense would reduce taxable income by $15,000 and income taxes by $6,000 (40% of $15,000), resulting in a $9,000 after-tax expense. Because income tax rates can be substantial, management has a continuing responsibility to minimize the firm's income tax. After-tax cash flows are more relevant than before-tax cash flows because they represent the amounts available to retire debt, finance expansions, or pay dividends. For these reasons, it is imperative to formulate investment decision analyses in terms of after-tax cash flows.

Illustration of After-Tax Cash Flows

Thinking in terms of after-tax cash flows represents a significant departure from the concern for accrual-based accounting for revenues and expenses that dominates much of your earlier study of accounting. Exhibit 27–3 is designed to build on the familiar traditional income statement illustrating (1) the conversion of after-tax income to after-tax cash flows, (2) the confirmation of that amount as actual cash flows, and (3) the determination of the individual after-tax cash flow

EXHIBIT 27-3
Illustration of Determining After-Tax Cash Flows

		(A) Traditional Income Statement	(B) Income Statement Cash Inflows (Outflows)	(C) Individual After-Tax Cash Inflow (Outflow) Effects
Cash revenues (Sales)		$100,000	$100,000	$60,000
Cash expenses	$60,000		(60,000)	(36,000)
Depreciation	20,000			8,000
Total expense		80,000		
Before-tax net income		$ 20,000		
Income tax at 40%		8,000	(8,000)	
After-tax income		$ 12,000		
Add back depreciation		20,000		
After tax cash flows		$ 32,000	$ 32,000	$32,000

effects of receiving revenues, incurring cash expenses, and recording depreciation. An understanding of Exhibit 27-3 should provide a basis for studying the more comprehensive illustrations of capital budgeting later in the chapter.

The area in Exhibit 27-3 set off in color is recognized as the traditional income statement, showing revenues minus expenses and income taxes, resulting in an after-tax income of $12,000. For simplicity, revenues and cash expenses are assumed to involve no significant accruals. Ordinarily, after-tax net income does not represent after-tax cash flows. This is, of course, because depreciation expense—a noncash expense—has been deducted to derive taxable income. As indicated in Column A of Exhibit 27-3, converting the $12,000 of after-tax income to after-tax cash flows requires adding back the depreciation of $20,000, resulting in $32,000 of after-tax cash flows.[1] It is this amount to which present value computations are properly applied.

Column B of Exhibit 27-3 confirms the determination in Column A of $32,000 as the amount of after-tax cash flows. This is accomplished by simply listing the amounts in Column A that constitute cash inflows (revenues of $100,000) and cash outflows (cash expenses of $60,000 and income tax payments of $8,000). Depreciation is excluded because it does not represent a cash payment.

Column C in Exhibit 27-3 illustrates determination of the individual amounts of after-tax cash flows for each item on the income statement. This approach will be used in the comprehensive illustrations of capital budgeting appearing later in the chapter. Amounts in Column C are determined as follows (again, a 40% income tax rate is assumed):

[1]If present, other amounts of noncash expenses such as amortization of intangible assets and discount on bonds would also have to be added back.

Receipt of $100,000 cash revenues. Receipt of $100,000 cash revenues would, by itself, increase taxable income by $100,000, adding $40,000 ($100,000 × 40%) to income taxes. The $60,000 after-tax cash inflow is the difference between the $100,000 cash revenue received and the related $40,000 increase in income taxes (a cash outflow).

Payment of $60,000 in cash expenses. Paying $60,000 in cash expenses represents a deductible cash outflow that reduces taxable income by $60,000 and thus reduces income taxes by $24,000 ($60,000 × 40%). The $36,000 net cash outflow is the difference between the $60,000 actually paid out for expenses and the $24,000 of income tax payments avoided by virtue of their tax deductibility.

Notice that *avoiding a cash outflow* has the same effect on net cash flows as a cash inflow. In other words, total net cash inflows can be increased by adding to cash inflows or by avoiding cash outflows.

Recording $20,000 of depreciation expense. Although depreciation expense is tax deductible, there is no related cash expenditure during the period. Therefore, the after-tax cash flow effect of a depreciation deduction is simply the related amount of income taxes avoided. The $20,000 deduction reduces taxable income $20,000 and income taxes $8,000 ($20,000 × 40%). Again, because it represents avoidance of an outflow, the after-tax cash flow effect of the depreciation deduction is that of a cash inflow. Depreciation expense and similar noncash expense deductions are often referred to as "tax shields" because they shield an equal amount of income from whatever income tax rate is applicable.

Combining the after-tax cash flow effect of each individual amount shown in Column C again confirms that net cash inflows total $32,000. It will be helpful to realize that the after-tax cash flow effect of cash receipts and cash expenses is derived by multiplying the before-tax amounts by (1 − the tax rate). In contrast, the after-tax cash flow effect of depreciation deductions is derived by multiplying the before-tax amounts by the tax rate. In our example:

$$\text{Cash revenues } \$100,000 \times (1 - 0.4) = \$60,000$$
$$\text{Cash expenses } \$\ 60,000 \times (1 - 0.4) = (36,000)$$
$$\text{Depreciation expense } \$20,000 \times 0.4 = \underline{\quad 8,000}$$
$$\text{Net cash flows} \qquad\qquad \underline{\underline{\$32,000}}$$

SUMMARY OF CONCERNS
UNDERLYING CAPITAL BUDGETING

(1) The typical investment pattern involves a present investment of funds resulting in anticipated returns, often extending years into the future.

(2) The basic question in capital budgeting is whether investments made now are justified by related future returns.

(3) Because money has a time value and returns often occur years in the future, returns must be discounted to their present values to be properly compared with investments made now.

(4) To properly use discounting (interest) calculations, amounts in capital budgeting analyses must be stated in terms of cash flows.

(5) Because income tax rates are substantial, capital budgeting analyses should be formulated in terms of after-tax cash flows.

Up to this point in the chapter, a number of important aspects of capital budgeting have been presented to provide a background for the review of several approaches to capital expenditure analysis. These background materials have been formulated to focus on the analytical concept known as **net present value.** It is generally conceded that the net present value approach is conceptually and analytically superior to the other two approaches that will be illustrated and commented upon, *cash payback* and *average rate of return.*

NET PRESENT VALUE ANALYSIS

The basic considerations of net present value analysis are shown schematically in Exhibit 27–4.

Referring to the items in the diagram, we can explain the basic steps in the net present value approach as follows:

(1) Determine in terms of incremental after-tax cash flows the amount of the investment outlay required.

(2) Estimate in terms of incremental after-tax cash flows the amounts and timing of future operating receipts or cost savings.

EXHIBIT 27–4
Schematic Diagram of Net Present Value Analysis

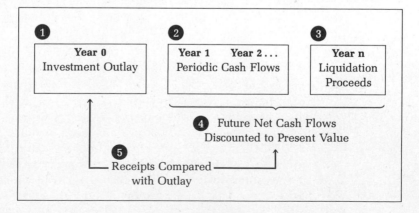

(3) Estimate any incremental after-tax liquidation proceeds to be received upon termination of the project.

(4) Discount all future cash flows to their present value at an appropriate interest rate, usually the minimum desired rate of return on capital.

(5) Subtract the investment outlay from the total present value of future cash flows to determine *net* present value. If net present value is zero or positive (returns equal or exceed investment), then the project has a rate of return equal to or exceeding the minimum desired rate and should be accepted. Negative net present values indicate that the project's return is less than desired and the project should be rejected.

To illustrate net present value analysis, assume that, with a minimum desired return of 10%, management is considering the purchase of a machine costing $12,000 that will save $6,000 annually in cash operating expenses, will have a useful life of three years, will be depreciated by $3,500 per year, and will be sold for $2,000 cash at the end of the third year. Also, assume that all income and gains are taxed at 60%.

Exhibit 27-5 presents a net present value analysis of the machine as an investment project. Note how the format follows the schematic analysis presented in Exhibit 27-4: Future returns are stated in terms of after-tax cash flows; then, through the use of Tables I and II, the present values of future cash flows are determined and compared with the investment. The computations shown in Exhibit 27-5 are explained below.

Annual cash expense savings. Cash savings or expense reductions have the same operating effects as cash revenues, income, or gains. Of course, they also have the same tax consequence (that of increasing income taxes). In our example, saving $6,000 in expenses each year raises taxable income by $6,000, which leads to a $3,600 ($6,000 × 60%) increase in taxes. Thus, the annual after-tax cash flow is $2,400—the $6,000 savings less the $3,600 tax increase. Because $2,400 is saved each year for three years, it can be treated as an annuity. Its present value factor of 2.487 is taken from Table II on the line for three periods and the column for 10% (the minimum return desired). The analysis shows that, with desired return at 10% and income taxes at 60%, saving $6,000 annually for the next three years is equivalent to receiving $5,969 *now*.

Annual depreciation tax shield. Recording depreciation does not in itself, of course, involve cash flows. When long-lived assets are purchased and used in business, however, depreciation may be deducted in the calculation of taxable income. Therefore, the right to deduct depreciation has a cash flow *effect* in that related amounts of income tax payments are avoided. The taxes avoided are equal to the depreciation deduction multiplied by the applicable tax rate. In our illustration, the annual $3,500 depreciation deduction and the 60% tax rate result in an annual tax shield of $2,100 ($3,500 × 60%). Because they cause cash tax

EXHIBIT 27–5
Illustration of Net Present Value Analysis—After-Tax Cash Flows
(Rounded to Nearest Dollar)

Analysis of After-Tax Cash Flows		Present Value Factors at 10% (Table I or II)	Total Present Value	Projected After-Tax Cash Flows			
				Year 0	Year 1	Year 2	Year 3
ANNUAL CASH EXPENSE SAVINGS							
Annual cash expense saving	$6,000						
Less income tax @ 60%	3,600						
After-tax expense savings	$2,400	(II) 2.487	$ 5,969		$2,400	$2,400	$2,400
ANNUAL DEPRECIATION TAX SHIELD							
Annual depreciation deduction	$3,500						
Applicable income tax rate	0.60						
Annual tax shield provided	$2,100	(II) 2.487	5,223		2,100	2,100	2,100
LIQUIDATION PROCEEDS							
Sales price of machine	$2,000						
Net book value (original cost of $12,000 less accumulated depreciation of $10,500)	1,500						
Gain on sale	$ 500						
Income tax on gain @ 60%	$ 300						
After-tax proceeds of sale:							
Sales price	$2,000						
Less tax on gain	300						
	$1,700	(I) 0.751	1,277				1,700
Total present value of future cash flows			$12,469				
Investment required in machine			(12,000)	($12,000)*			
Net positive present value			$ 469				

*Outflow.

payments to be avoided, tax shields have the same effect as cash *inflows*. Being of equal amounts equally spaced in time, like the annual savings in expense, the tax shield in our example can also be treated as an annuity. Its present value, calculated with the same present value factor of 2.487 from Table II, is $5,223.

When the present values of the tax shields provided by the same total depreciation deduction under the straight-line method are compared with those under an accelerated depreciation plan such as the sum-of-the-years'-digits, an interesting aspect of tax planning is revealed. The straight-line depreciation deduction in Exhibit 27–5 is $3,500 per year for three years, for a total of $10,500, which results in a tax shield with a total present value of $5,223. The present value of the tax shield provided by the same total depreciation deduction taken under the sum-of-the-years'-digits method (where the fractional denominator is $3 + 2 + 1 = 6$) is computed as follows:

Year	Yearly Fraction of $10,500	Depreciation Deduction	Tax Shield at 60%	Present Value Factor (Table I)	Total Present Value
1	$\frac{3}{6}$	$ 5,250	$3,150	0.909	$2,863
2	$\frac{2}{6}$	3,500	2,100	0.826	1,735
3	$\frac{1}{6}$	1,750	1,050	0.751	789
		$10,500			$5,387

Therefore, in our illustration, taking the same total $10,500 depreciation deduction under the sum-of-the-years'-digits would increase the present value of the total tax shield from $5,223 to $5,387, an increase of $164. The significance of this simple example of tax planning is obvious. In terms of present value analysis, the effect of choosing the depreciation method in the real world could well be measured in thousands or millions of dollars.

Liquidation proceeds. One variable that contributes to the relative attractiveness of an investment in capital equipment is the amount that can be realized when the asset is liquidated. Liquidation proceeds on very long-lived assets are sometimes disregarded because their occurrence is so far in the future that the amounts are difficult to predict, and their present values tend to be small. Where useful lives are short, however, liquidation proceeds may be a deciding factor in the analysis. In our illustration, the machine originally costing $12,000 is depreciated over three years to a book value of $1,500 and then sold for $2,000 cash. The resulting $500 gain increases income taxes by $300, which, deducted from the sales price of $2,000, produces a net after-tax cash flow of $1,700. Because this is a single sum to be received at the end of year 3, its present value of $1,277 is derived by multiplying the $1,700 by the factor 0.751 from Table I (three periods hence at 10%).

Required investment. Proper consideration of the required investment involves neither an income tax nor a present value calculation. The $12,000 investment itself is not tax deductible; the related depreciation deductions are, and of course these are incorporated earlier into our analysis. Since the investment expenditure is immediate, there is no deferral and therefore no discounting for present value required. Thus, $12,000 represents the after-tax present value of the required investment outflow.

Decision rule. With its savings of cash expense, depreciation tax shield, and liquidation proceeds, the $12,000 investment results in future cash flows with a total present value of $12,469 and therefore has a net present value of $469. This indicates that the return on the capital invested, adjusted for the time value of money, is in excess of the 10% return rate sought and that the investment is acceptable.

Another interpretation of our analysis would be that as much as $12,469 could be paid for the machine and still retain the desired rate of return of 10%. Paying more than $12,469 for the machine would result in a return of less than 10%.

Excess Present Value Index

Alternative capital expenditure proposals may be compared in terms of their **excess present value index.** This index is defined as the ratio

$$\text{Excess Present Value Index} = \frac{\text{Total Present Value of Net Future Cash Flows}}{\text{Initial Cash Investment}}$$

For the investment presented in Exhibit 27–5, the excess present value index would be:

$$\frac{\$12,469}{12,000} = 1.0391$$

The higher the ratio of return to investment, the more attractive is the proposal. Although the excess present value index may be a convenient measure for ranking various proposals, note that it does not reflect the amount of the investment. Two proposals, requiring initial cash investments of $5,000 and $5,000,000, respectively, could have identical excess present value indexes but could hardly be considered equal investment opportunities.

NET PRESENT VALUE ANALYSIS AND TASK-ORIENTED DECISIONS

A slightly different decision rule for net present value analysis can be appropriate when decisions involve choosing among alternative means of accomplishing some task. Suppose management is considering the acquisition of parts needed in the production process. All feasible alternatives from purchasing to producing the parts will, of course, result in costs to the firm. Therefore, the decision rule is to seek the alternative that, in terms of future after-tax cash flows, *has the least total present value* (because we are now dealing with outflows). This should assure that the firm incurs the least economic sacrifice in accomplishing the task.

Exhibit 27–6 (page 974) illustrates net present value analysis applied to a task-oriented decision. Assume that the firm needs certain parts during the next three years and can either:

EXHIBIT 27-6

Net Present Value Analysis in Decision to Acquire Parts
(Amounts Rounded to Nearest Dollar)

Analysis of After-Tax Cash Flows		Present Value Factor at 8% (Tables I or II)	Total Present Value*	Projected After-Tax Cash Flows			
				Year 0	Year 1	Year 2	Year 3
PURCHASE OF PARTS:							
Required cash deposit	$10,000	(I) 1.000	($10,000)	($10,000)			
Annual purchase price of parts	$17,000						
Less income tax savings @ 60%	10,200						
After-tax price of parts	$ 6,800	(II) 2.577	(17,524)		($6,800)	($6,800)	($ 6,800)
Return of deposit at end of third year	$10,000	(I) 0.794	7,940				10,000
Total present value of purchasing parts			($19,584)				
PRODUCTION OF PARTS:							
Purchase price of machine	$30,000	(I) 1.000	($30,000)	(30,000)			
Depreciation of machine:							
Annual depreciation deduction	$ 9,000						
Applicable income tax rate	0.60						
Annual tax shield provided	$ 5,400	(II) 2.577	13,916		5,400	5,400	5,400
Annual net cash operating expenses	$ 4,000						
Less income tax savings @ 60%	2,400						
After-tax annual cash operating expense	$ 1,600	(II) 2.577	(4,123)		(1,600)	(1,600)	(1,600)
Liquidation proceeds:							
Net book value of machine (original cost $30,000 less accumulated depreciation of $27,000)	$ 3,000						
Cash sales proceeds	1,000						
Net loss on liquidation	$ 2,000						
Income tax benefit, @ 60%	$ 1,200						
Net cash flow ($1,000 sale price and $1,200 tax benefit)	$ 2,200	(I) 0.794	1,747				2,200
Total present value of producing parts			($18,460)				
DIFFERENCE (in favor of production)			$ 1,124				

*Amounts in parentheses represent outflows.

(1) Enter a three-year contract to purchase the needed parts, making an immediate required $10,000 cash contract assurance deposit to the supplier, which will be returned at the end of the contract, and paying a net delivered purchase price of $17,000 each year, or

(2) Produce the needed parts by buying, for $30,000 cash, a machine that will incur $4,000 of cash operating expenses each year, be depreciated $9,000 each year, and be sold at the end of the third year for $1,000 cash.

An income tax rate of 60% is applicable, and an 8% return is desired.

Exhibit 27-6 is structured like Exhibit 27-5 in that it shows the determination of after-tax cash flows, the appropriate present value factors from Tables I and II, and the resulting net present values of each aspect of acquiring the parts either by purchase or production. Because the $18,460 net present value of the cash flows related to producing the parts is smaller by $1,124 than those of purchasing the parts, the firm is better off producing the parts. This quantitative type of analysis assumes, of course, that all qualitative aspects such as product quality and reliability of supply are reasonably comparable.

Elements of the analysis in Exhibit 27-6 are explained as follows:

Required cash deposit. Deposits of this nature do not involve tax-deductible expenditures or taxable receipts because no deductible expense or taxable income is recorded. Note, however, that giving up use of the $10,000 in funds for three years does "cost" the firm, in terms of present value, $2,060 (or the $10,000 present value of the deposit less its $7,940 present value when returned). Also, note that omission of this subtle factor in the analysis would have erroneously influenced the decision in favor of purchasing the needed parts.

Annual purchase price of parts. The $17,000 annual purchase price of the parts is tax deductible in that it becomes part of the total costs and expenses of operating the business. Because the after-tax amounts of $6,800 are equal and evenly spaced over time (the annuity form), present value Table II is appropriate (8% column, 3 periods). The resulting total present value is $17,524.

Purchase price of machine. The $30,000 purchase of equipment is not in itself a tax-deductible transaction because no expense has been incurred. It is the related *use of the equipment* in the operation of the business that allows a series of periodic depreciation deductions to be made on the related tax returns. Thus, no adjustment to after-tax dollars is required. Because the payment is made immediately, the present value is equal to the amount of payment, $30,000.

Annual depreciation expense. Each year's depreciation deduction of $9,000 provides a tax shield equal to 60% of the deduction, or $5,400. Because these amounts are in the annuity form, Table II is applicable, resulting in a total present value for the inflows of $13,916.

Annual cash operating expenses. These are quite clearly cash outflows involving deductible expenses and requiring adjustment to after-tax amounts. Again, because the periodic cash flows are equal each year (the annuity form), present value Table II is appropriate, resulting in a total present value of $4,123.

Liquidation at a loss. This liquidation at a loss involves two sources of cash inflows—the $1,000 cash sales proceeds and the $1,200 tax payments avoided by virtue of the deductibility of the $2,000 loss incurred. The combined $2,200 cash flow effect occurs three years in the future as a single sum. Present value Table I is appropriate, indicating a present value of $1,747.

Again, for task-oriented decisions, the rule is to seek the alternative requiring the least investment in terms of present values.

CASH PAYBACK ANALYSIS

Cash payback analysis is a form of capital expenditure analysis that, for reasons explained below, is considered by many to be less sophisticated than net present value analysis. The **cash payback period** is *the time in years that it will take the net future after-tax cash inflows to equal the original investment.*

Assume for purposes of illustration that a firm is considering purchasing either machine A or machine B, for which the following data are given:

Machine	Investment Required	Estimated Annual Savings in After-Tax Cash Expenses	Useful Life
A	$10,000	$2,500	8 years
B	15,000	5,000	3 years

Cash payback is computed using the formula

$$\frac{\text{Original Investment}}{\text{Annual Net Cash Inflows}} = \text{Cash Payback in Years}$$

Thus, for the two machines, we obtain:

(A) $\dfrac{\$10,000}{\$2,500}$ = 4-year cash payback

(B) $\dfrac{\$15,000}{\$5,000}$ = 3-year cash payback

This analysis shows that machine A will pay back its required investment in four years, while machine B will take only three years. Because the decision rule in cash payback analysis is that *the shorter the payback period the better,* machine B would be considered the better investment.

Concern for the payback of investments is quite natural because the shorter a project's payback period, the more quickly the funds invested in that project are returned and available for other investments. In very high-risk investments, the payback period provides an indication of how soon a firm would be "bailed out" of an investment should it prove unattractive.

The primary limitation to cash payback analysis is that the *relative profitability of various investments is not specifically considered.* Note, for example, that in the foregoing illustration machine B has the best (shorter) cash payback period. However, its useful life, which is ignored in cash payback analysis, indicates that machine B will stop generating cash inflows just at the time payback is completed. Consequently there will be no opportunity for profit to be generated. In contrast, although machine A has the longer payback period, it will generate future cash inflows for four years beyond its payback and thus promises to be profitable.

Regardless of its failure to consider profitability, cash payback analysis is widely used in industry, probably because of its relative simplicity. It can be useful in conjunction with other analyses or as a preliminary screening device for investment projects under consideration.

AVERAGE RATE OF RETURN

Still another approach to capital outlay analysis, **average rate of return** relies heavily on accounting determinations of net income. This measure is calculated according to the formula

$$\text{Average Rate of Return} = \frac{\text{Expected Average Annual Net Income}}{\text{Average Investment}}$$

Note that here the variables are not after-tax cash flows but the traditional accounting net income (with depreciation deducted) and accounting measurements for assets (based primarily on historical costs).

In the earlier illustration, machine A required an initial investment of $10,000, provided $2,500 annual cash inflows from operations, and had a useful life of eight years. Assuming no salvage value, annual straight-line depreciation on machine A would be $10,000/8, or $1,250, so that average annual net income would be $1,250 (the operating cash inflows of $2,500 less depreciation of $1,250).

A simple way to calculate average investment is to add the beginning and ending investments and divide by 2. In our illustration, machine A has no salvage value, so the ending investment is zero, and average investment is therefore ($10,000 + $0)/2 = $5,000.

The average rate of return on machine A is:

$$\frac{\$1,250}{\$5,000} = 25\%$$

The decision rule for average rate of return analyses is: *the higher the return, the more attractive the investment.*

As an approach to capital expenditure analysis, the average rate of return is often defended as being most easily understood by management personnel who are accustomed to thinking in accounting terms and concepts. It has two major limitations, however. First, the calculations rely heavily on accounting computations of net income, depreciation, and asset measures, and are thus subject to the same arbitrary choices with regard to such factors as straight-line versus accelerated depreciation and historical cost valuations versus current valuations. Second, average rate of return calculations do not consider the time value of money. Future cash flows are treated the same as current cash flows. Our discussion of net present value analysis amply illustrates the often substantial differences between future values and related current values discounted by even moderate interest rates.

As an example of how deceptive the average annual income figures used in average rate of return computations can be, consider three investment proposals that each require a $40,000 initial investment and promise the annual cash inflows shown in Exhibit 27-7. Note that cash flows are concentrated in year 1 in proposal A, are uniform in proposal B, and are concentrated in year 5 for proposal C. Because average rate of return calculations fail to consider the timing of cash flows from operations, these three proposals would be designated as having identical average rates of return of 10% and therefore would be considered equally attractive when analyzed in this manner. Such an implication is hardly defensible in view of the substantial differences in the relative net present values of the operating cash flows. In our illustration, the difference between the present values of A and C is $12,960, an amount equal to 41% of C's present value.

CAPITAL BUDGETING—A PERSPECTIVE

Because it incorporates aspects of such fields as economics, finance, business management, and accounting, the subject of capital budgeting is too complex to treat comprehensively in an introductory accounting book. The goal of this chapter has been simply to provide some insight into problem-solving techniques in capital budgeting by stating decision rules in their simplest form, showing the relevance of present value concepts and after-tax cash flows, and creating an awareness of the potentials and limitations of several widely used approaches to capital expenditure analysis. The illustrations have been formulated to highlight key relationships, and operational realism has been considered secondary. The rudiments presented here should serve as a basis for further study and an understanding of related subject areas.

KEY POINTS TO REMEMBER

(1) Capital budgeting is the planning of long-lived asset investments; capital expenditure analysis is basically the examination of how well prospective future returns justify related present investments.

EXHIBIT 27-7
Present Value Comparison of Equal Annual Average Incomes

	Proposals		
	A	B	C
Annual net cash inflows			
Year 1	$46,000	$10,000	$ 1,000
2	1,000	10,000	1,000
3	1,000	10,000	1,000
4	1,000	10,000	1,000
5	1,000	10,000	46,000
Aggregate net cash inflows	$50,000	$50,000	$50,000
Average annual net cash inflows	$10,000	$10,000	$10,000
Deduct depreciation ($40,000/5)	8,000	8,000	8,000
Average annual net income	$ 2,000	$ 2,000	$ 2,000
Average rate of return on investment			
$2,000/($40,000/2)	10%	10%	10%
Present value of net cash inflows at 10%:			
(A) One year hence, $45,000 ($\times$ 0.909)	$40,905		
5-year annuity of $1,000 ($\times$ 3.791)	3,791		
	$44,696		
(B) 5-year annuity of $10,000 ($\times$ 3.791)		$37,910	
(C) 5-year annuity of $1,000 ($\times$ 3.791)			$ 3,791
5-years hence, $45,000 ($\times$ 0.621)			27,945
			$31,736

(2) Cost of capital is a measure of the firm's cost for investment capital and usually represents the minimum acceptable return for investment opportunities.

(3) The time-value-of-money concept recognizes that the farther into the future cash flows occur, the less economic worth they have now. Present value tables enable us to conveniently convert future cash flows to their present values at appropriate interest rates.

(4) After-tax cash flows probably represent the most relevant measure of the prospective returns of proposed investments.

(5) Cash flows from revenues and expenses are converted to after-tax amounts by multiplying them by the factor $(1 - r)$, where r is the income tax rate. Depreciation deductions are converted to their after-tax cash flow effect by multiplying the deduction by the applicable income tax rate.

(6) Net present value analysis compares the present value of net future cash flow returns to the investment. Projects having zero or positive net present values are acceptable.

(7) When evaluating task-oriented decision alternatives, the comparable alternative with the lowest net present value is most attractive.

(8) Cash payback analysis measures the time in years necessary for the net future after-tax cash flows to equal the original investment. When this type of analysis is used, the shorter the payback period, the more attractive the investment.

(9) Average rate of return analysis compares the annual average net income to the average investment. The higher this ratio, the more attractive the investment.

(10) Cash payback analysis fails to consider the relative profitability of alternative projects. Average rate of return analysis fails to consider the time value of money.

QUESTIONS

27-1 What is the nature of capital budgeting?

27-2 List three reasons why capital budgeting decisions are often important.

27-3 What are the three stages typical of most investments?

27-4 Briefly describe the concept of "weighted average cost of capital."

27-5 In what sense does the cost of capital limit a firm's investment considerations?

27-6 Briefly describe the concept of the time value of money.

27-7 In which percent columns and periods hence lines in Table I would you expect to find the smallest conversion factors? Why?

27-8 In which percent columns and periods hence lines in Table II would you expect to find the largest conversion factors? Why?

27-9 Where in Table II will you find the factor equal to the sum of the factors for periods 1, 2, and 3 at 5% in Table I? Explain their equivalence.

27-10 Explain how before-tax cash operating expenses and depreciation deductions are converted to after-tax amounts.

27-11 What amounts are compared in net present value analysis? State the related decision rule.

27-12 Briefly explain how sum-of-the-years'-digits depreciation might be of greater benefit to a firm than straight-line depreciation even though the total depreciation is the same.

27-13 What is the decision rule when net present value analysis is used in task-oriented decisions?

27-14 Define cash payback, state the related decision rule, and specify an important limitation of this analysis.

27-15 Define average rate of return, state the related decision rule, and specify an important limitation to this analysis.

27-16 You have the right to receive $10,000 at the end of each of the next 3 years and consider money worth 12%. Using Table II, compute the present value involved. Illustrate how Table I can be used to confirm your answer.

27-17 A company plans to accumulate 60% of its needed investment capital by issuing bonds having a capital cost percentage of 10%, and the balance is to be raised by issuing stock having a capital cost percentage of 8%. What would be the weighted average cost of capital for the total amount of capital?

27-18 A rich uncle has offered you the opportunity to stipulate which of two ways your inheritance will be specified: (a) $400,000 one year after his death, or (b) $100,000 on his death and $110,000 each year at the end of the first, second, and third year following his death. If money is worth 12%, what is the relative advantage of the most attractive alternative?

27-19 You can settle a debt with either a single payment now of $50,000 or with payments of $16,000 at the end of each of the next 4 years. If money is worth 10%, what is the relative advantage of your most attractive alternative? If money is worth 12%, would your answer change? Why?

EXERCISES

27-20 (a) Assuming money is worth 10%, compute the present value of:
   (1) $2,500 to be received 10 years from today.
   (2) The right to inherit $1,000,000 40 years from now.
   (3) The right to receive $400 at the end of each of the next 6 years.
   (4) The obligation to pay out $900 at the end of each of the next 15 years.
   (5) The right to receive $3,000 at the end of the 13th, 14th, and 15th year from today.
   (b) Confirm your answer to (a)–(5) by using Table II and subtracting the present value of a 12-year annuity from a 15-year annuity (isolating the three relevant years).

27-21 For each of the following independent situations, compute the after-tax income and convert it to an amount of after-tax cash flows that could be properly incorporated into net present value analyses.

	A	B	C
Cash revenues received	$80,000	$200,000	$150,000
Cash expenses paid	50,000	120,000	140,000
Depreciation expense	10,000	30,000	20,000
Income tax rate	30%	40%	60%

27-22 Using the data in Exercise 27–21, (a) calculate (as shown in Column C of Exhibit 27–3) the individual after-tax cash flow effect of each relevant item in each independent situation, and (b) confirm the fact that the sum of the individual after-tax cash flows in each situation equals the after-tax income converted to after-tax cash flows.

27-23 Master, Inc. plans to finance its expansion by raising the needed investment capital from the following sources in the proportions and with the respective capital cost percentages indicated.

Source	Proportion	Capital Cost Percentage
Bonds	40%	12%
Preferred stock	10	6
Common stock	30	8
Retained earnings	20	10
	100%	

Calculate the weighted average cost of capital.

27-24 Using the following data and rounding to the nearest dollar, compute the cash payback, average rate of return, net present value, and excess present value index.

Investment, $10,000
Expected annual cash savings, $4,000
Depreciation: straight-line, 5 years, no salvage value
Applicable income tax rate, 30%
Minimum desired rate of return, 15%

27-25 Assuming a desired return of 10% annually, use the appropriate present value table to make informed decisions in each of the following unrelated situations.
(a) You are to inherit $2,000,000 in 20 years. What is the smallest amount that you would sell your inheritance for now? (Assume no taxes are applicable.)
(b) Your firm can accomplish a task by either of two methods, which require the following after-tax cash outlays:

	Method A	Method B
Outlays at end of:		
Year 1	$ -0-	$ 1,000
Year 2	8,000	5,000
Year 3	4,000	6,000
Totals	$12,000	$12,000

Which alternative is most attractive? By how much?
(c) How much should you be willing to pay for an investment that will provide after-tax cash income of $6,000 at the end of each of the next 10 years and in addition at the end of the 10th year provide a nontaxable refund of $4,000 of your original investment?

27-26 A machine costing $30,000 will be depreciated over its four-year useful life, assuming no salvage value. If a 30% income tax rate is applicable and an 8% annual return is desired, compute the total present value of the tax shields that would be provided by straight-line depreciation and by sum-of-the-years'-digits depreciation.

27-27 Your company can accomplish a certain necessary production task by following one of the three alternatives shown below with their related cash outflows.

		Cash Expenses Incurred at End of				
Alternative	Year 0	Year 1	Year 2	Year 3	Year 4	Year 5
A	$1,000	$1,000	$1,000	$1,000	$1,000	$1,000
B	$3,000	—	—	800	1,000	2,000
C	$2,000	—	—	—	—	4,000

If income taxes are 40% and a 15% return is desired, which alternative is most attractive and by how much?

27-28 A special-purpose machine costing $20,000 will save Custom Company $4,000 per year in cash operating expenses for the next 10 years. Straight-line depreciation with zero salvage value will be used, and the minimum desired rate of return is 12%. Assuming an income tax rate of 30% and rounding amounts to the nearest dollar, compute:
(a) Cash payback period.
(b) Average rate of return.
(c) Net present value.

PROBLEMS

27-29 At a cost of $15,000, Brown Company can acquire a special machine that will afford annual savings of $5,000 in cash operating expenses. No salvage value is expected at the end of its five-year useful life. Assume an income tax rate of 30% and a 12% after-tax minimum desired rate of return.

REQUIRED
Assuming straight-line depreciation and rounding amounts to the nearest dollar, calculate:
(a) The cash payback period.
(b) The average rate of return.
(c) The net present value and the excess present value index.

27-30 Abarr Company is contemplating purchasing for $27,000 cash a machine that should save $15,000 in cash operating expenses each year. Straight-line depreciation will be used, and although it is estimated that the machine can be sold for only $2,000 at the end of its three-year useful life, the Internal Revenue Service has insisted on an estimated salvage value of $3,000. At the end of the second year, a motor in the machine will be overhauled at a cash cost of $3,000 (fully deductible in year 2).

REQUIRED
Assuming an income tax rate of 40% and a desired annual return of 15%, compute the net present value of this investment and its excess present value index (round amounts to the nearest dollar).

27-31 Major Company has just been awarded a three-year contract to manufacture a subcomponent for a missile system being produced for the Air Force. At one point in their production, the subcomponents must pass a very special inspection process. To accomplish these tests, Major can either (1) subcontract the tests to another company at a net cash cost of $20,000 for each year of the contract or (2) purchase for $21,000 a testing machine that will incur annually $10,000 of cash operating expenses. The testing machine would require a major alignment costing $4,000 cash at the end of the second year; even though it probably can be sold as scrap at the end of the contract for $2,000 cash, the machine will be depreciated on a straight-line basis assuming no salvage value.

REQUIRED
Using net present value analysis, determine whether Major Company should subcontract the tests or acquire and use the machine. Assume that the alignment cost is fully tax deductible in year 2, that a tax rate of 40% is applicable, and that an annual return of 12% is desired.

27–32 You have an opportunity to invest in a concession at a world exposition. In order to more fully exploit the building and exhibits that are to be built, the venture is expected to cover a five-year period consisting of a preliminary year, the two years of formal exposition, and a two-year period of reduced operation catering primarily to tourists.

The terms of the concession agreement specify that:
(1) At inception, a $10,000 deposit is paid to Global Expo, Inc., the promoting organization. This amount is returned in full at the end of the 5 years if the operator maintains the concession in order and keeps it open during scheduled hours.
(2) Certain fixtures are required to be installed. They will cost the operator $90,000, be depreciated on the straight-line method, and become the property of Global Expo, Inc. at the end of the 5 years.

After careful investigation and consultation with local experts, you conclude that the following schedule should reflect the operating income of the concession (amounts in thousands of dollars):

	Year 1	Year 2	Year 3	Year 4	Year 5
Sales (all cash)	$220	$790	$900	$380	$130
Total operating expenses (all cash except depreciation on fixtures)	200	710	790	340	120
Projected net income	$ 20	$ 80	$110	$ 40	$ 10

REQUIRED
Assuming an income tax rate of 40% and that term (1) is complied with, how much would you be willing to pay in cash at the beginning of the 5 years for this investment opportunity if you desire an annual return of 15%? (Round amounts to nearest dollar.)

27–33 For a certain contract, Indio, Inc. needs 10,000 bearings in each of the next five years. The bearings can be produced on a machine that Indio is now evaluating using net present value analysis with a minimum desired return of 12% per year. Indio has a combined income tax rate of 40% on all income, gains, and losses.

Listed below are six factors related to the purchase and use of this machine.

(a) The machine will be purchased for $45,000 cash.

(b) Sum-of-the-years'-digits depreciation will be taken on the machine during its five-year useful life. Salvage value is assumed to be zero. (Note: For this part you will need a set of answers for each year's depreciation deduction.)

(c) Cash operating expenses of the machine will be $6,000 for each of the five years.

(d) (i) A spare parts inventory costing $5,000 cash must be acquired immediately and maintained at this level throughout the production period of the machine.

(ii) At completion of the contract, the spare parts inventory of $5,000 can be returned to the supplier for a full cash refund.

(e) At the end of the second year the machine will require a major overhaul that will cost $8,000 and be fully expensed for tax purposes.

(f) At the end of 5 years the machine will be sold for $4,000 cash.

REQUIRED

For each of the six items, fill in the following form, showing calculations wherever necessary. [Calculations will usually be limited to part (1).] *Do not* combine the effect of two or more factors. Note that you are not asked to compute present values. Read the entire problem before starting.

(1) ATCFE _____

Calculate the amount of the *after-tax cash flow* effect of each factor. *Place parentheses* around amounts having the effect of cash outflows.

(2) Year(s) _____

Indicate the timing of the cash flow effect. Use 0 to indicate immediately and 1, 2, 3, 4, or 5 for each year(s) you believe involved.

(3) PV Factor _____

Choose from the present value Tables I or II and put the PV multiple you would apply (if any) to convert the related amount(s). Place 1.0 in this space if no present value conversion is necessary.

ALTERNATE PROBLEMS

27-29A At a cost of $32,000, Davis Company can acquire a special machine that will afford annual savings of $10,000 in cash operating expenses. No salvage value is expected at the end of its eight-year useful life. Assume an income tax rate of 40% and a 20% minimum desired rate of return.

REQUIRED

Assuming straight-line depreciation and rounding amounts to the nearest dollar, calculate:

(a) The cash payback period.

(b) The average rate of return.

(c) The net present value.

27–30A Omicron Company is contemplating purchasing for $18,000 cash a machine that should save $12,000 in cash operating expenses each year. Straight-line depreciation will be used, and although it is estimated that the machine can be sold for only $1,000 at the end of its three-year useful life, the Internal Revenue Service has insisted on an estimated salvage value of $3,000. At the end of the second year, a motor in the machine will be overhauled at a cash cost of $3,000 (fully deductible in year 2).

REQUIRED

Assuming an income tax rate of 30% and a desired annual return of 20%, compute the net present value of this investment and its excess present value index. (Round amounts to the nearest dollar.)

27–31A Conrad Company has just been awarded a three-year contract to manufacture a subcomponent for a computer system being produced for a food-processing plant. At one point in their production, the subcomponents must pass a very special inspection process. To accomplish these tests, Conrad can either (1) subcontract the tests to another company at a net cash cost of $12,000 for each year of the contract or (2) purchase for $16,500 a testing machine that will incur annually $6,000 of cash operating expenses. The testing machine would require a major alignment costing $3,000 cash at the end of the second year, and even though it probably can be sold as scrap at the end of the contract for $4,000 cash, the machine will be depreciated on a straight-line basis assuming no salvage value.

REQUIRED

Using net present value analysis, determine whether Conrad Company should subcontract the tests or acquire and use the machine. Assume that the alignment cost is fully tax deductible in year 2, that a tax rate of 40% is applicable, and that an annual return of 12% is desired.

27–32A You have an opportunity to invest in a concession at a world exposition. In order to more fully exploit the building and exhibits that are to be built, the venture is expected to cover a five-year period consisting of a preliminary year, the two years of formal exposition, and a two-year period of reduced operation catering primarily to tourists.

The terms of the concession agreement specify that:

(1) At inception, a $12,000 deposit is paid to Exposition, Inc., the promoting organization. This amount is returned in full at the end of the 5 years if the operator maintains the concession in order and keeps it open during scheduled hours.

(2) Certain fixtures are required to be installed. They will cost the operator $65,000, be depreciated on the straight-line method, and become the property of Exposition, Inc. at the end of the 5 years.

After careful investigation and consultation with local experts, you conclude that the following schedule should reflect the operating income of the concession (amounts in thousands of dollars):

	Year 1	Year 2	Year 3	Year 4	Year 5
Sales (all cash)	$200	$740	$950	$330	$160
Total operating expenses (all cash except depreciation on fixtures)	170	650	820	280	140
Projected net income	$ 30	$ 90	$130	$ 50	$ 20

REQUIRED

Assuming an income tax rate of 30% and that term (1) is complied with, how much would you be willing to pay in cash at the beginning of the 5 years for this investment opportunity if you desired an annual return of 12%? (Round amounts to nearest dollar.)

BUSINESS DECISION PROBLEM

Karen Corporation, a small limited-venture investment firm, has recently identified an investment opportunity involving a five-year franchise for acquiring and operating a route of well-placed vending machines. Karen's treasurer, however, after preparing the investment analysis appearing below, has recommended to Karen's investment committee that the investment be rejected. Ms. Jackson, chairperson of the investment committee, finds it difficult to accept the treasurer's analysis because she "feels intuitively" that the investment should be attractive. For this reason, she has retained you as an independent consultant to review the treasurer's analysis and recommendation. You are provided with the following data and summary of the treasurer's analysis:

Required investment: $200,000 cash for a group of vending machines to be depreciated on a straight-line basis, five-year useful life, with a zero salvage value.

Projected cash revenues and expenses:

Year	Cash Revenues	Cash Expenses
1	$200,000	$ 90,000
2	180,000	80,000
3	130,000	50,000
4	100,000	40,000
5	90,000	40,000
	$700,000	$300,000

Source of capital: Karen plans to raise 60% of the needed capital by issuing bonds, 30% by issuing stock, and the balance from retained earnings. For these sources, the capital cost percentages are 8%, 12%, and 16%, respectively. Karen has a policy of seeking a return equal to the weighted average cost of capital plus five percentage points as a "buffer margin" for the uncertainties involved.

Income taxes: Karen assumes an overall income tax rate of 30%.

Treasurer's analysis:

Average cost of capital (8% + 12% + 16%) ÷ 3 = 12%

Total cash revenues		$700,000
Total cash expenses	$300,000	
Total depreciation	200,000	
Total expenses		500,000
Project net income over 5 years		$200,000
Average annual income ($200,000 ÷ 5)		$ 40,000
Present value factor of 5-year annuity at 12%		× 3.605
Present value of future returns		$144,200
Required investment		200,000
Negative net present value		$ 55,800

Recommendation: Reject investment because of insufficient net present value.

REQUIRED

As a consultant, you are retained to accomplish the following:

(a) Review the treasurer's analysis, identifying any questionable aspects and briefly commenting on the apparent effect of each such item on the treasurer's analysis.

(b) Prepare your own analysis of the investment, including a calculation of the proper cost of capital and discount rates, a net present value analysis of the project, and a brief recommendation to Ms. Jackson regarding the investment.

(c) Because of her concern for the uncertainties of the vending machine business, Ms. Jackson also has asked you to provide analyses supporting whether or not your recommendation would change:

(1) If estimates of projected cash revenues were reduced by 10%, or

(2) If the "buffer margin" were doubled.

PRESENT VALUE TABLES

TABLE I
Present Value of $1.00
Received in the Future

Periods Hence	Rate per Compounding Period									
	2%	3%	4%	5%	6%	8%	10%	12%	15%	20%
1	0.980	0.971	0.962	0.952	0.943	0.926	0.909	0.893	0.870	0.833
2	0.961	0.943	0.925	0.907	0.890	0.857	0.826	0.797	0.756	0.694
3	0.942	0.915	0.889	0.864	0.840	0.794	0.751	0.712	0.658	0.579
4	0.924	0.889	0.855	0.823	0.792	0.735	0.683	0.636	0.572	0.482
5	0.906	0.863	0.822	0.784	0.747	0.681	0.621	0.567	0.497	0.402
6	0.888	0.838	0.790	0.746	0.705	0.630	0.564	0.507	0.432	0.335
7	0.871	0.813	0.760	0.711	0.665	0.583	0.513	0.452	0.376	0.279
8	0.854	0.789	0.731	0.677	0.627	0.540	0.467	0.404	0.327	0.233
9	0.837	0.766	0.703	0.645	0.592	0.500	0.424	0.361	0.284	0.194
10	0.821	0.744	0.676	0.614	0.558	0.463	0.386	0.322	0.247	0.162
11	0.804	0.722	0.650	0.585	0.527	0.429	0.350	0.287	0.215	0.135
12	0.789	0.701	0.625	0.557	0.497	0.397	0.319	0.257	0.187	0.112
13	0.773	0.681	0.601	0.530	0.469	0.368	0.290	0.229	0.163	0.093
14	0.758	0.661	0.577	0.505	0.442	0.340	0.263	0.205	0.141	0.078
15	0.743	0.642	0.555	0.481	0.417	0.315	0.239	0.183	0.123	0.065
16	0.728	0.623	0.534	0.458	0.394	0.292	0.218	0.163	0.107	0.054
17	0.714	0.605	0.513	0.436	0.371	0.270	0.198	0.146	0.093	0.045
18	0.700	0.587	0.494	0.416	0.350	0.250	0.180	0.130	0.081	0.038
19	0.686	0.570	0.475	0.396	0.331	0.232	0.164	0.116	0.070	0.031
20	0.673	0.554	0.456	0.377	0.312	0.215	0.149	0.104	0.061	0.026
30	0.552	0.412	0.308	0.231	0.174	0.099	0.057	0.033	0.015	0.004
40	0.453	0.307	0.208	0.142	0.097	0.046	0.022	0.011	0.004	0.001
50	0.372	0.228	0.141	0.087	0.054	0.021	0.009	0.003	0.001	—

TABLE II
Present Value of $1.00 Annuity
Received at End of Each Period

Periods Hence	\multicolumn{10}{c}{Rate per Compounding Period}									
	2%	3%	4%	5%	6%	8%	10%	12%	15%	20%
1	0.980	0.971	0.962	0.952	0.943	0.926	0.909	0.893	0.870	0.833
2	1.942	1.914	1.886	1.859	1.833	1.783	1.736	1.690	1.626	1.528
3	2.884	2.829	2.775	2.723	2.673	2.577	2.487	2.402	2.283	2.106
4	3.808	3.717	3.630	3.546	3.465	3.312	3.170	3.037	2.855	2.589
5	4.714	4.580	4.452	4.330	4.212	3.993	3.791	3.605	3.352	2.991
6	5.601	5.417	5.242	5.076	4.917	4.623	4.355	4.111	3.784	3.326
7	6.472	6.230	6.002	5.786	5.582	5.206	4.868	4.564	4.160	3.605
8	7.326	7.020	6.733	6.463	6.210	5.747	5.335	4.968	4.487	3.837
9	8.162	7.786	7.435	7.108	6.802	6.247	5.760	5.328	4.772	4.031
10	8.983	8.530	8.111	7.722	7.360	6.710	6.145	5.650	5.019	4.192
11	9.787	9.253	8.761	8.306	7.887	7.139	6.495	5.988	5.234	4.327
12	10.575	9.954	9.385	8.863	8.384	7.536	6.814	6.194	5.421	4.439
13	11.348	10.635	9.986	9.394	8.853	7.904	7.103	6.424	5.583	4.533
14	12.106	11.296	10.563	9.899	9.295	8.244	7.367	6.628	5.724	4.611
15	12.849	11.938	11.118	10.380	9.712	8.560	7.606	6.811	5.847	4.675
16	13.578	12.561	11.652	10.838	10.106	8.851	7.824	6.974	5.954	4.730
17	14.292	13.166	12.166	11.274	10.477	9.122	8.022	7.120	6.047	4.775
18	14.992	13.754	12.659	11.690	10.828	9.372	8.201	7.250	6.128	4.812
19	15.679	14.324	13.134	12.085	11.158	9.604	8.365	7.366	6.198	4.844
20	16.351	14.878	13.590	12.462	11.470	9.818	8.514	7.469	6.259	4.870
30	22.397	19.600	17.292	15.373	13.765	11.258	9.427	8.055	6.566	4.979
40	27.356	23.115	19.793	17.159	15.046	11.925	9.779	8.244	6.642	4.997
50	31.424	25.730	21.482	18.256	15.762	12.234	9.915	8.304	6.661	4.999

28
Income Taxes and Their Effect on Business Decisions

This is as strange a maze
as e'er men trod.
WILLIAM SHAKESPEARE

Except for a brief period during the Civil War, the United States had no federal income tax until 1913, when ratification of the Sixteenth Amendment settled the question of its constitutionality. The tax was originally intended strictly as a revenue-producing measure, and the first tax rates ranged from 1% on taxable income over $3,000 ($4,000 for a married couple) to 7% on taxable income in excess of $500,000. Since then, federal taxation has changed in both purpose and magnitude. No longer simply a source of revenue, it is also an instrument of economic and social policy. Through its taxing powers, the government can attempt to bring about a more equitable distribution of income, stimulate economic growth, combat inflation and unemployment, and finance projects it determines to be in the national interest.

The federal income tax system is administered by the Internal Revenue Service, an agency of the Treasury Department. The numerous revenue acts passed since 1913 were first codified in 1939 and then recodified as the Internal Revenue Code of 1954. Regulations interpreting the code have been published from time to time by the IRS, but the ultimate interpretive authority lies with the federal court system, which adjudicates conflicts between the IRS and taxpayers.

The IRS has verified that the collection rate of federal income taxes is well over 90%. Such success is surely impressive, especially considering that the system depends on a high degree of voluntary compliance with quite complex tax laws and regulations. While it is true that certain taxes are withheld at the source, and that employers, financial institutions, and other agencies are required to report on individuals' earnings, the system relies to a great extent on taxpayers assessing and reporting their own obligations.

As tax rates have increased and regulations have become more complex, a large proportion of the nation's taxpayers have turned to accountants, attorneys, and others for assistance in preparing their tax returns. Professional help may also be sought in arranging business and personal affairs in such a way that tax liability is minimized. Few business decisions are made without first considering which possible alternatives judged consistent with the business objective will have the most desirable tax effect. Indeed, when large amounts of money are involved, this factor is so important that many accountants and attorneys confine their practices to such special areas as estate planning, pension plans, wage and stock option plans, and reorganizations and mergers.

Whether they call on professionals for assistance or not, taxpayers will generally benefit from a basic understanding of the structure of the tax system and the options it provides.

CLASSIFICATION OF TAXPAYERS

For purposes of federal income taxation, there are four main classes of taxpayers: individuals, corporations, estates, and trusts. Here we shall deal with individuals and corporations, leaving estates and trusts to a more advanced course.

Although they are business entities, sole proprietorships and partnerships are not taxable entities. Instead, the owners of such firms must include their shares of business income along with income from other sources in their respective individual tax returns. The allocable shares of their business income are taxed directly to them whether or not they have withdrawn such amounts. In conjunction with this

TWO VIEWS OF THE INCOME TAX LAW

In my own case the words of such an act as the Income Tax, for example, merely dance before my eyes in a meaningless procession; cross-reference to cross-reference, exception upon exception—couched in abstract terms that offer no handle to seize hold of—leave in my mind only a confused sense of some vitally important, but successfully concealed, purport, which it is my duty to extract, but which is within my power, if at all, only after the most inordinate expenditure of time. I know that these monsters are the result of fabulous industry and ingenuity, plugging up this hole and casting out that net, against all possible evasion; yet at times I cannot help recalling the saying of William James about certain passages of Hegel; that they were no doubt written with a passion of rationality; but that one cannot help wondering whether to the reader they have any significance save that the words are strung together with syntactical correctness.

Judge Learned Hand

There is a constant cry and a natural desire for a "simple" income tax law. America can have a simple income tax law anytime it wants it. It would not be especially difficult to draft. . . . The trouble is you wouldn't want that law. You wouldn't stand for it. Americans would not tolerate any "simple" income tax law. Why? The reason is simple. Any "simple" income tax law would take a "meat axe" approach. It would be outrageously discriminatory. It would be grossly inequitable and unfair to a lot of people.

Laurens Williams

SOURCE: (for Williams quotation): Laurens Williams, "Your Future Federal Taxes," 9 The Tax Executive 113, 124-5 (1957). Published with permission of Tax Executives Institute, Inc.

requirement, each partnership must file an *information return* showing the results of the firm's operations and the respective shares of net income accorded to each partner.

Corporations, on the other hand, are taxable entities and are taxed directly on their earnings. When these earnings are distributed, the shareholders receiving them must include amounts received as dividend income on their individual returns. Although this practice has led to the allegation that corporate earnings are subject to "double taxation," it is generally conceded that the bulk of corporate taxes are passed on to the consumer in the long run.

Under Subchapter S of the Internal Revenue Code, certain corporations generally are not taxed but pass income and losses through to their owners somewhat like partnerships. Firms meeting the criteria listed there are referred to as *Subchapter S Corporations*.

Because of the many technical differences in the tax computations for individuals and corporations, we will consider them separately. Thus, we first discuss the more salient features of individual income tax and then briefly cover some important aspects of corporate income tax. In reading this discussion, keep in mind that the provisions of the tax laws relating to tax rates, exemption amounts, various prescribed limits, and other details often change over time.

INDIVIDUAL TAX FORMAT

Generally, individuals who are citizens of the United States are taxed on all income from whatever source, unless it is specifically excluded by law. Thus, the gross income to be reported in an individual's tax return consists of total income and gains *less exclusions*. To convert this amount to **taxable income,** however, various deductions and exemptions are permitted. These must be enumerated in the individual's return (Form 1040) or in supporting schedules for which additional forms may be provided.

Although the manner in which this information is detailed in the return varies from time to time, there is a basic, logical format to the computation of taxable income. This format, illustrated in Exhibit 28–1, describes the classifications used in the tax laws and is a useful frame of reference in compiling the information needed to prepare an individual's tax return.

After the tax is computed by applying the appropriate rates to taxable income, certain credits against the tax may be allowed. We discuss these later in the chapter.

Gross Income   As mentioned above, gross income is defined as income from all sources, less allowable exclusions. Some of the most common types of gross income are: wages, salaries, bonuses, fees, tips, interest, dividends, profits or shares of profits from businesses, pensions, annuities, rents, royalties, prizes, and taxable gains on sale of property or securities. The list also includes income from gambling and even illegal income, such as that from theft or embezzlement. (Racketeers and other

EXHIBIT 28–1
Format for Determining
Taxable Income—Individuals

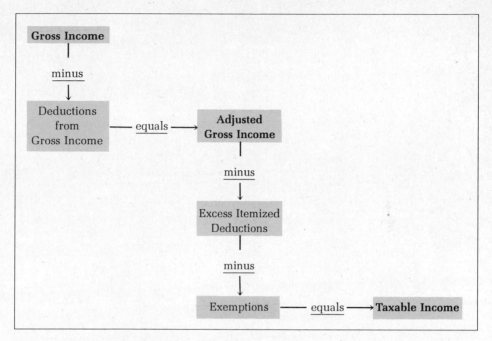

criminals have often been more easily apprehended through income tax investigations than through regular criminal investigation.)

Special rules and procedures are applicable to certain of these sources of gross income in determining the portion to be included. For example, gains that qualify as capital gains are accorded special treatment. Because of the importance of this subject, we shall treat it separately later in this chapter.

Some of the items excluded by law from gross income are: interest on certain state and municipal bonds; social security payments; gifts, bequests, and inheritances; workmen's compensation for sickness or injury; state unemployment benefits; certain disability benefits; life insurance proceeds received at the death of the insured; and scholarships not requiring services from degree candidates. The exclusions also exempt amounts of pensions and annuities that are a return of capital invested in them and the first $100 in dividend income ($200 for a married couple filing jointly, except that neither spouse may take part of the other's $100 exclusion).

The exclusions dealing with interest on state and municipal bonds and with gifts, bequests, and inheritances are important in tax planning for some taxpayers. For example, persons in high tax rate brackets often purchase state and municipal bonds to escape federal income tax on the interest. This particular exclusion will be explained more fully later, in the discussion of tax shelters.

Deductions from Gross Income

Individual taxpayers are generally permitted two types of deductions: deductions from gross income to arrive at "adjusted gross income" and deductions from adjusted gross income in proceeding with the tax calculation. The first type can be broadly characterized as most business expenses and expenses incurred in the production of rents and royalties, while the second can be generally described as allowable deductions that are more personal in nature.

The calculation of **adjusted gross income** is important in the taxation of individuals because the amount of certain personal deductions may be affected by it. Generally, the purpose of determining adjusted gross income is to provide a more equitable base for certain other calculations than that provided by a gross income measure. Thus, a person who generates a large amount of gross income by incurring large amounts of business expenses or other related costs of producing such income is provided a base for determining personal deductions that is fairly comparable to the income of a wage-earner or salaried taxpayer who does not have such business expenses.

Deductions permitted the individual taxpayer in arriving at adjusted gross income are as follows (remember these are subject to change):

(1) *Trade and business deductions.* These are the ordinary and necessary expenses attributable to a trade or business carried on by the taxpayer, provided such activity does not consist of performance of services as an employee. Generally, these expenses are offset against business revenue and the net amount is included in adjusted gross income.

(2) *Employee deductions.* For the most part, an employee may deduct travel and related expenses incurred in connection with employment (but not commuting costs) and the unreimbursed portion of employment expenses connected with employment where the employer has a reimbursement plan. An outside salesperson can deduct all unreimbursed costs attributable to the employer's business. Employees may also deduct moving costs necessitated by job transfers.

(3) *Losses from sales or exchanges of property.* When business or investment property is sold or exchanged, generally losses are deductible in arriving at adjusted gross income. However, losses on the sale or exchange of "personal-use" property are not deductible.

(4) *Excess of long-term capital gains over short-term capital losses.* A taxpayer who has an excess of long-term capital gains over short-term losses (as explained later in this chapter) may deduct 60% of this excess in calculating adjusted gross income.

(5) *Net operating loss deduction.* Generally, when a business has an operating loss in a particular year, that amount, which is of no tax benefit for that year, may be carried back to the three preceding years and forward to the next seven years to reduce the tax liability for those years. After certain adjustments, the loss is carried back to the earliest year of the period first, then successively to each succeeding period, if unused. A taxpayer may elect to forego the carryback and only carry the loss forward seven years.

(6) *Other deductions.* Certain other deductions, relating to rents, royalties, pensions, profit-sharing, and bond purchase plans of self-employed individuals are allowed.

Deductions from Adjusted Gross Income

An individual taxpayer may deduct from adjusted gross income certain itemized personal expenses specified by the tax law, or may, in lieu of itemizing expenses, take advantage of a standard deduction called the **zero bracket amount.** The zero bracket amount is incorporated in the tax rate tables and schedules. In 1979, this amount was $3,400 for married taxpayers filing a joint return and $2,300 for single taxpayers or those qualifying as head of a household. A taxpayer not itemizing personal expenses automatically receives the benefit of the zero bracket amount when using the tax tables or schedules. On the other hand, a single taxpayer having $10,000 in itemized deductions would deduct only $7,700 (called "excess itemized deductions") in calculating taxable income. The taxpayer would automatically receive the benefit of the remaining $2,300 by using the tax schedules.

Personal expenses that may be itemized and deducted from adjusted gross income are classified as follows:

(1) *Medical expenses.* With certain limitations, a taxpayer may deduct medical and dental expenses for self and dependents not compensated for by insurance or otherwise. One-half of any health insurance premiums paid each year may be deducted, up to $150. The remainder of such premiums paid are added to other medical expenses, and the total is deductible to the extent that it exceeds 3% of adjusted gross income. Medicine and drug costs are includible only to the extent that they exceed 1% of adjusted gross income.

For example, a taxpayer with an adjusted gross income of $20,000 has the following medical expenses: health insurance premiums, $400; medicine and drugs, $320; and other medical expenses of $500 not compensated for by insurance. The deduction is calculated as follows:

One-half of insurance premiums, $200, but limited to $150			$150
Balance of insurance premiums		$250	
Other medical expense		500	
Medicine and drugs	$320		
Less 1% of $20,000 adjusted gross income	200	120	
		$870	
Less 3% of $20,000 adjusted gross income		600	270
Medical deduction			$420

(2) *Taxes.* State and local income taxes, real estate taxes, personal property taxes, and sales taxes are deductible. Federal taxes do not qualify as itemized deductions, nor do flat fees paid for most types of licenses (auto, driver's, pet, etc.). Variable auto license fees required by some states may be deductible. State and local gasoline taxes are no longer deductible.

(3) *Interest.* With certain minor exceptions, interest paid on any form of personal indebtedness is deductible in computing tax liability.

(4) *Charitable contributions.* The amount of gifts made to religious, scientific, educational, and other charitable organizations can be deducted but may not exceed 50% of adjusted gross income. Certain other limitations may also apply, as in the case of noncash contributions and gifts to foundations. Gifts to individuals or labor unions, and donations to organizations whose major activity is to influence legislation are not deductible.

(5) *Casualty losses.* To the extent that they exceed $100 each, certain casualty and theft losses are deductible unless compensated for by insurance. Casualty losses must be sudden and unexpected, however; uninsured losses from fire, accident, windstorm, and so forth qualify as deductions. Certain "gradual" events leading to a loss (such as termite damage and dutch elm disease) may disqualify a loss deduction.

(6) *Miscellaneous deductions.* Permissible deductions in this category include certain expenses that are often related to a taxpayer's income or to his or her profession but are not deductible in arriving at adjusted gross income. Some of the most important are the following:

Professional dues	Cost of business entertainment
Subscriptions to professional publications	Gambling losses (but only to the extent of gains, which are includible in gross income)
Union dues	
Cost of job-related work clothing, small tools, and safety equipment	Employment agency fees
Safe-deposit box rental (to store securities)	Educational expenses related to *present position,* incurred to improve or maintain skills or to meet employers' requirements
Fees paid for income-tax assistance	

Personal Exemptions

In arriving at taxable income, the individual taxpayer is permitted (at the present time) to deduct $1,000 for each *personal exemption* he or she may legally claim. Married taxpayers filing jointly are allowed an exemption each, plus one for each dependent. Additional exemptions are granted taxpayers who are (1) 65 or over or (2) blind.

To qualify a taxpayer for a dependency exemption under the tax laws, a person must (1) be closely related to the taxpayer or have lived in the household for the entire year as a member of the family; (2) have less than $1,000 income (this test is ignored for taxpayer's children under 19 years of age or who are full-time students); (3) have received more than half of his or her support from the taxpayer; (4) if married, not be filing a joint return with a spouse.

Both the amount of the exemption and the qualifications for a dependent have been altered from time to time.

DETERMINING TAX LIABILITY

Once taxable income has been computed, the tax liability is found by applying the appropriate tax rate to taxable income. Individual taxpayers who elect not to itemize their personal deductions may, in certain instances, use simplified tax tables that incorporate both the zero bracket amount (in lieu of itemized deductions) and the number of claimed exemptions. If deductions are itemized, or if either the tax table income or number of exemptions claimed exceeds those shown in the tables, the taxpayer must use tax schedules. Schedules are provided for (1) single taxpayers, (2) married taxpayers filing a joint return, (3) married taxpayers filing separately, and (4) unmarried taxpayers who qualify as "heads of households." Exhibit 28–2 (page 1000) uses 1979 rates to illustrate the first two of these schedules.

Probably the most striking feature of the tax rate schedules is that the rates are sharply *progressive* with respect to income—they increase quickly with income increments. Another significant feature is that single taxpayers generally are subject to a higher tax liability than married persons with comparable income who file joint returns. This disparity, ironically, resulted from an attempt by Congress in 1948 to put certain groups of taxpayers on a more equitable footing. Before that time, married taxpayers in community property states (those in which income earned by either spouse is by law allocated equally between them) could file separate tax returns and pay less tax than a couple with comparable income who did not have community property status. To achieve equity, Congress amended the law to permit "income splitting" in all states, a feature now incorporated in the joint return tax schedule. In the process, more of the tax burden was shifted to single taxpayers.

Unmarried taxpayers who qualify as heads of households determine their tax liability from tables or schedules (not shown) whose rates fall between those of single taxpayers and married taxpayers filing jointly. Generally, the qualifications can be met by unmarried taxpayers who pay more than one-half the cost of maintaining a home in which a parent resides, if that parent qualifies the taxpayer for a dependency exemption. A taxpayer who pays more than half the cost of maintaining his or her *own* home where a relative resides for whom a dependency exemption may be claimed or where unmarried children, adopted stepchildren, foster children, or grandchildren reside may also qualify as head of household.

EFFECTIVE AND MARGINAL TAX RATES

Often, when persons identify their "income tax bracket" by a tax rate, they are referring to the percentage rate appearing in the tax schedule beside the bracket in which their taxable income falls. For example, a single taxpayer with $30,000 taxable income might indicate that he or she is in "the 44% tax bracket." While this **marginal,** or incremental, rate is an important tax consideration, it does not represent the portion of taxable income that is to be relinquished to the government, since it applies only to the excess over $28,800. This person's tax liability, computed from the schedule in Exhibit 28–2, would actually be slightly less than 27% of taxable income:

EXHIBIT 28-2
Tax Rate Schedules

Single Individuals					
Taxable Income				Tax	On Excess
Over	Not Over	Pay	+	Rate	Over
. . .	$ 2,300	. . .		. . .	. . .
$ 2,300	3,400	. . .		14%	$ 2,300
3,400	4,400	$ 154		16%	3,400
4,400	6,500	314		18%	4,400
6,500	8,500	692		19%	6,500
8,500	10,800	1,072		21%	8,500
10,800	12,900	1,555		24%	10,800
12,900	15,000	2,059		26%	12,900
15,000	18,200	2,605		30%	15,000
18,200	23,500	3,565		34%	18,200
23,500	28,800	5,367		39%	23,500
28,800	34,100	7,434		44%	28,800
34,100	41,500	9,766		49%	34,100
41,500	55,300	13,392		55%	41,500
55,300	81,800	20,982		63%	55,300
81,800	108,300	37,677		68%	81,800
108,300	. . .	55,697		70%	108,300

Married Individuals Filing Joint Returns and Surviving Spouses					
Taxable Income				Tax	On Excess
Over	Not Over	Pay	+	Rate	Over
. . .	$ 3,400	. . .		. . .	. . .
$ 3,400	5,500	. . .		14%	$ 3,400
5,500	7,600	$ 294		16%	5,500
7,600	11,900	630		18%	7,600
11,900	16,000	1,404		21%	11,900
16,000	20,200	2,265		24%	16,000
20,200	24,600	3,273		28%	20,200
24,600	29,900	4,505		32%	24,600
29,900	35,200	6,201		37%	29,900
35,200	45,800	8,162		43%	35,200
45,800	60,000	12,720		49%	45,800
60,000	85,600	19,678		54%	60,000
85,600	109,400	33,502		59%	85,600
109,400	162,400	47,544		64%	109,400
162,400	215,400	81,464		68%	162,400
215,400	. . .	117,504		70%	215,400

Tax on $28,800	$7,434
44% of excess over $28,800	528
Tax liability	$7,962
Effective tax rate ($7,962/$30,000)	26.54%

Thus, the **effective tax rate** in this situation is 26.54%, the tax liability divided by taxable income. This rate conveys the impact of the tax "bite" more accurately than the marginal rate.

Nonetheless, the marginal tax rate is extremely important in one's tax thinking; it is especially useful in tax planning. For example, a single taxpayer who has an opportunity, by expending some additional time and effort, to augment personal income should probably think in terms of the marginal rate of tax. Given a taxable income of $30,000, an additional $1,000 will be taxed at the 44% rate, leaving the taxpayer only $560. He or she may well feel that this additional amount does not justify relinquishing leisure time. The additional effect of any state and local income taxes should also be considered.

Although the tax rates go as high as 70%, the maximum rate applied to "personal service taxable income" is 50%. Such income consists of wages, salaries, and similar types of compensation. Through a rather complex formula, the portion of personal service income included in taxable income (after all deductions) is extracted. The remaining portion of taxable income is taxed at the rates applicable before the extraction.

CAPITAL GAINS AND LOSSES

One means of responding to the effect of high tax rates, as many taxpayers have discovered, is to have a good part of income subject to preferential tax treatment. One of the most prominent tax preferences is the special treatment of certain gains on the sale or exchange of a "capital asset" as defined in the tax law.

Although determining whether an asset qualifies as a **capital asset** can be difficult, such assets generally consist of any of the taxpayer's property except receivables, inventories, real and depreciable business property, certain governmental obligations, and rights to literary and other artistic works. Under certain conditions, however, business real estate and depreciable assets may be treated as capital assets when gains from sales of such assets exceed losses.

CLASSIFICATION BY HOLDING PERIOD When capital assets are sold or exchanged, the gains or losses are classified as **long-term** if the assets have been held more than one year and **short-term** if the holding period is one year or less. This classification is significant in determining the effect of such gains and losses on the tax liability. To meet various tests of the law, we combine the gains and losses in a certain fashion:

(1) Long-term gains and losses are "netted" to obtain *net long-term capital gain or loss.*

(2) Short-term gains and losses are "netted" to obtain *net short-term capital gain or loss.*

The amounts obtained in these two steps must be analyzed to determine their effect on adjusted gross income.

NET GAINS   When net long-term capital gains exceed net short-term capital losses, the difference is called **net capital gain,** and 60% of this amount is deducted in determining adjusted gross income. (If the taxpayer does not have a net short-term loss, then 60% of any net long-term gain is deducted.) The following examples, each having the same net gain from capital asset transactions, illustrate how the amount of any net capital gain is determined:

	Mr. Smith	Ms. Greene	Ms. Jones	Mr. Brown
Net long-term gain (loss)	$4,000	$3,000	$2,000	($4,000)
Net short-term gain (loss)	(1,000)	–0–	1,000	7,000
Net gain	$3,000	$3,000	$3,000	$3,000
Deductible in computing adjusted gross income	$1,800	$1,800	$1,200	$ –0–

Mr. Smith has a net capital gain of $3,000, the excess of the $4,000 net long-term gain over the $1,000 net short-term loss. Ms. Greene also has a net capital gain of $3,000, the excess of the $3,000 net long-term gain over "zero" amount of net short-term loss. Both of these taxpayers can deduct 60% of the net capital gain, or $1,800, in computing adjusted gross income. Ms. Jones has $2,000 net capital gain, the excess of the $2,000 net long-term gain over "zero" amount of net short term loss. Her deduction will therefore be $1,200. Her net short-term gain of $1,000 is fully taxable. Mr. Brown does not have a net capital gain because he did not have a net long-term gain. His $4,000 net long-term loss is offset against his $7,000 short-term gain and the $3,000 excess short-term gain is fully taxable.

Taxpayers who have a "net capital gain" are therefore taxed on such gains at only 40% of their marginal tax rate. Thus, if Ms. Jones in the foregoing example were in the 55% marginal tax rate bracket, she would pay only $440, or 22% of her $2,000 net long-term capital gain. Since the highest marginal tax rate is 70% for any taxpayer, the maximum marginal tax on net long-term gains is 28%.

NET LOSSES   If the net amount from capital asset transactions is a loss, individuals and other noncorporate taxpayers are entitled, with certain restrictions, to offset the loss against ordinary income up to $3,000 in any year. In determining the amount that may be offset, short-term losses are considered first, on a dollar-for-dollar basis, and then long-term losses are considered on a "2 for 1" basis. Thus, $2 of net long-term loss will offset only $1 of ordinary gross income. The amount of losses that are not offset is called the **net capital loss** and may be carried forward indefinitely and used to offset capital gains or $3,000 ordinary income of each year. In carrying forward, the losses retain their long- or short-term character.

Suppose that a taxpayer had a net short-term loss of $2,300 and a net long-term loss of $1,800 this year. To obtain the $3,000 capital loss deduction against ordinary income this year, the $2,300 net short-term loss would be used first, and then, to yield the remaining $700 portion of the deduction, $1,400 of the net long-term loss would have to be used. The remaining $400 can be carried forward to be used in succeeding years. Although this carryforward must be used on a 2 for 1 basis when offset against ordinary income, it can nevertheless be used in full if offset against long-term gains in the future.

INCOME AVERAGING

Individual taxpayers who have annual incomes that vary a great deal may wish to exercise an "income averaging" option permitted by the tax law. This option is especially useful to a taxpayer with an unusually large amount of income in a particular year, because it permits a lower rate of taxation on a certain amount of the increased income. The averaging process thus places the taxpayer on a more equitable footing with others who have the same aggregate income spread evenly over the same period.

In the averaging procedure a formula is employed that uses the average taxable income of the previous four years as a base with which to measure the current year's level of income. Although space does not permit a complete discussion of the process, it may be useful to point out that a taxpayer will receive no advantage from the averaging method unless the current year's taxable income is at least $3,000 more than 120% of the average of the prior four years' taxable income. In addition, the taxpayer generally must be self-supporting (that is, not someone else's dependent) during the base period to qualify for income averaging. This facet of the law often prevents recent college graduates from using the averaging option in their first few years of full-time employment.

CREDITS AGAINST THE TAX

Once the income tax has been calculated, certain credits may be applied to reduce the amount owed. Some of the principal credits are the earned income credit, credit for dependent care, and political contributions.

EARNED INCOME CREDIT Certain low income individuals are allowed a refundable credit against the tax equal to 10% of the first $5,000 of earned income, up to a maximum of $500. The credit is reduced $1.25 for every $10 of adjusted gross income (or earned income, if greater) above $6,000, phasing out completely at $10,000. The taxpayer must meet eligibility requirements defined in the law, however. Eligible employees may elect to have advance payments of the earned income credit added to their paychecks each pay period.

DEPENDENT CARE CREDIT   A tax credit is available for taxpayers who maintain a household and incur expenses in caring for a child under age 15 for whom the taxpayer may claim a dependency exemption or an incapacitated dependent or spouse, if the expenses were incurred to permit the taxpayer to be gainfully employed. The amount of the credit is 20% of the employment-related expenses up to a maximum of $2,000 for one qualifying individual and $4,000 for two or more qualifying individuals.

POLITICAL CONTRIBUTIONS CREDIT   Fifty percent of political contributions may be applied as a credit against the tax up to a maximum of $50 ($100 in the case of a joint return).

OTHER CREDITS   Credits against the tax are also available for part of the cost of energy-conserving items. Fifteen percent of the first $2,000 of qualifying expenditures for home insulation is allowed. Similarly, 30% of the first $2,000 and 20% of the next $8,000 of expenditures for solar energy and similar equipment may be taken as a credit.

WITHHOLDING AND ESTIMATED TAX

Ordinarily, tax returns must be filed within $3\frac{1}{2}$ months of the close of the individual's taxable year. Because most taxpayers are on a calendar year basis, they must file their returns by April 15 following the end of the taxable year. During the taxable year, the employers of wage-earners and salaried employees will have withheld tax payments based on the employees' estimated earnings and the number of withholding allowances claimed. Taxpayers who have income not subject to withholding (beyond a certain amount) must estimate income for the current year and file a Declaration of Estimated Tax. The estimated tax, less the amounts expected to be withheld, is paid in four installments. Therefore, when the tax return is filed, the amounts paid through the withholding or declaration process are offset as credits against the total tax liability. Certain other credits that may also be taken are specified in the tax law.

BASIS OF DETERMINING TAXABLE INCOME

Most individuals' taxable income is determined on a **cash basis.** Taxable earnings from various sources are includible in gross income when received, and deductions are recognized when the allowable related expenditures are paid. The cash basis of taxation has wide appeal because it is fairly simple and requires perhaps the least amount of attention to recordkeeping.

Even a taxpayer on the cash basis should be aware of certain exceptions provided by the law. Although certain income may not be directly paid to the taxpayer, the law may consider it to be a *constructive receipt* if it comes under the effective control of the taxpayer. Thus, interest on savings accounts credited to the taxpayer constitutes taxable income whether or not it is withdrawn. Likewise, any checks received that represent taxable income are taxable whether or not they are cashed before the close of the taxable year.

Generally, payments made during the taxable year are deductible in determining the year's taxable income if they meet the criteria for deductions. However, expenditures representing prepayments for a period of time must usually be allocated to the periods involved. For example, the cost of long-term assets must be allocated to the periods of use through depreciation accounting. Likewise, prepayments of insurance, rent, and similar items must be allocated to the years involved rather than deducted totally in the year of payment. Some prepayments, however, are permitted as deductions in the year of payment. Under certain circumstances, real estate taxes may be paid a year in advance and a deduction taken; also, in certain cases, prepaid interest has been allowed as a deduction when the prepayment period was not extremely long.

Cash basis taxpayers, particularly those in certain service types of business, sometimes can arrange their pattern of billings and disbursements near year-end in such a way that tax liability is minimized. For example, the expectation that tax rates will be reduced next year would suggest that billings should be delayed to postpone revenue recognition, but that expenditures qualifying as deductions should be made this year.

The **accrual basis** of accounting must be used, for the most part, by trading or manufacturing firms, because inventories are a factor in determining their income. Revenue must be recognized when sales are made, and inventories must be considered in determining the cost of products sold. Although some prepayments and accruals may be ignored, the method followed must be consistent and provide a reasonable income determination. Thus, it is less likely that the taxable income of an accrual basis taxpayer will be substantially affected by altering the pattern of receipts or expenditures.

INDIVIDUAL RETURN ILLUSTRATION

To illustrate some of the more common elements of an individual income tax computation, we present an example of a fairly typical situation in Exhibit 28–3. This example shows the relevant tax data for the joint return of John and Mary Travis. Although some of this information would be shown in separate schedules and more detail would be revealed, we have condensed the data into a single schedule to conserve space.

John and Mary Travis are both under 65 years of age and have three children who qualify as dependency exemptions. John operates a tax service. He files a Declaration of Estimated Tax each year and pays the estimated tax quarterly.

EXHIBIT 28–3
John and Mary Travis
Joint Federal Income Tax Return Information
19XX

Net income from Travis Tax Service:				
Fees collected		$46,000		
Ordinary and necessary expenses		18,000	$28,000	
Salary (of wife)			5,600	
Interest on savings accounts			1,400	
	Husband	**Wife**		
Dividend income	$800	$ 50		
Less exclusion: $100 maximum				
for each spouse	100	50		
	700	–0–	700	
Excess of net long-term capital gains over net				
short-term capital losses		$3,000		
Long-term capital gain deduction (60%)		1,800	1,200	
ADJUSTED GROSS INCOME			$36,900	
Deductions from adjusted gross income:				
Medical expense (One-half of $400				
health insurance premiums, but limited to $150)		$ 150		
Taxes:				
Real estate tax on home	$1,600			
State income tax	1,530			
State sales tax	320	3,450		
Interest on home mortgage		1,500		
Charitable contributions		850		
Miscellaneous (professional dues, nurse's				
uniforms, etc.)		200		
Total itemized deductions		$6,150		
Less zero bracket amount		3,400		
Excess itemized deductions			2,750	
			$34,150	
Less exemptions: 5 × $1,000			5,000	
TAXABLE INCOME			$29,150	
Tax: $4,505 + 32% of $4,550			$ 5,961	
Less credit against tax:				
Political contributions $240 × 50% = $120,				
limited to $100			100	
			$5,861	
Less prepayments:				
Tax withheld from salary		$ 680		
Estimated taxes paid quarterly		4,430		
Total tax withheld or prepaid			5,110	
Balance of tax due with return			$ 751	

Mary works part-time as a nurse and has tax withheld from her salary. During the year, John sold at a $4,000 gain some securities he had held over a year and also realized a loss of $1,000 on securities held for less than a year. The Travis family's medical expenses were not significant during the year. Other data in Exhibit 28–3 are self-explanatory.

CORPORATE INCOME TAXES

The corporation is a taxable entity, separate and apart from its shareholders, and must file an annual tax return whether or not it owes any tax. Certain corporations, such as banks, insurance companies, and cooperatives, are subject to special tax provisions. Tax regulations for even those corporations that are not specially treated can be quite complex. Our discussion will be limited to a few of the major distinguishing features of corporate taxation.

Corporate Tax Rates

The following schedule gives the current rates applied to the taxable income of corporations:

If taxable income is		Amount plus	Tax is % of	Excess over
Over	But not over			
–0–	$ 25,000	–0–	17	–0–
$ 25,000	50,000	$ 4,250	20	$ 25,000
$ 50,000	75,000	9,250	30	50,000
$ 75,000	100,000	16,750	40	75,000
$100,000	—	26,750	46	100,000

According to the above schedule, a corporation with taxable income of $60,000 would compute its tax as follows:

$$\$9,250 + 30\% \text{ of } \$10,000 = \$12,250$$

The effective tax rate in this example is 20.4% ($12,250/$60,000).

In computing the tax liability for corporate taxable income over $100,000, the following short-cut calculation can be used: (46% of taxable income) − $19,250. (The $19,250 figure is the amount obtained by multiplying the percentage difference between 46% and the tax rate for each taxable income bracket times $25,000 and summing the amounts obtained.)

Corporate taxpayers must pay estimated tax in quarterly installments, just like individuals. Their final returns, however, are due within $2\frac{1}{2}$ months of the close of their calendar or fiscal years.

Corporate Tax Base

The tax base for corporations is taxable income: gross income minus all allowable deductions. There is no "adjusted gross income" for corporations. Corporation deductions can be classified as ordinary or special deductions. Ordinary deductions are the usual expenses (with certain exceptions) of doing business and producing revenue. The most prominent special deduction is a credit for 85% of dividends received from other domestic corporations (100% if such other corporations are affiliates).

The deduction for dividends received is intended to reduce the effect of "triple" taxation. If this deduction did not exist, the distributing corporation, receiving corporation, and shareholders of the receiving corporation (if they subsequently received the dividends) would all have to pay tax on the earnings.

The net operating loss deduction, which also applies to individuals, permits business losses of a particular year to be offset against the income of other years in calculating the ultimate tax liability for those years. Briefly, if there is an operating loss in a particular year, it can be offset against the income of three preceding years, beginning with the earliest. If unused losses remain, they can be carried forward successively to the next seven years and used to compute taxable income. The corporation may elect to forego the carryback and only carry the loss forward seven years.

When a corporation's capital losses exceed its capital gains, such losses are not offset against ordinary gross income. They are carried back three years and forward five years and offset against capital gains in those years in the manner just described for a net operating loss. When a corporate capital loss is carried back or forward, it is treated as a short-term capital loss regardless of the holding period. Although the excess of long-term capital gains over short-term capital losses is fully includible in gross income, with no provision for a 60% deduction (as in the case of individual taxpayers), this amount is taxed at a maximum rate of 28%.

Charitable contributions of corporations are limited to 5% of taxable income, computed before considering the contributions and the special deduction for dividends received. Any contributions in excess of the limitation can be carried forward and qualify for deduction during the five succeeding years.

Corporate Tax Illustration

An example of the effect of the foregoing items on the corporate tax computation is illustrated in Exhibit 28–4. In this example we use the following data from the company's income statement:

Gross profit on sales	$200,000
Dividends from unaffiliated domestic corporations	20,000
Gain on sale of capital asset (long term)	10,000
	$230,000
Business expenses, including charitable contributions of $10,000	150,000
Reported income before taxes	$ 80,000

The firm also had an unused net capital loss carryforward of $3,000 from preceding years.

EXHIBIT 28-4
Corporate Tax Computation

Gross profit		$200,000
Dividends from domestic corporations		20,000
Gain on sale of capital asset	$10,000	
Less: Net capital loss carryforward	3,000	7,000
		$227,000
Less: Business expenses, less charitable contributions, $10,000		140,000
		$ 87,000
Charitable contributions, limited to 5% of $87,000		4,350
		$ 82,650
Dividends received deduction, 85% of $20,000		17,000
Taxable income		$ 65,650
Less: Excess of long-term gain over short-term loss, to be taxed at 28%		7,000
Taxable at regular rates		$ 58,650
Regular tax ($9,250 + 30% × $8,650)		$ 11,845
Alternative tax on excess of long-term gain over short-term loss, 28% of $7,000		1,960
Total tax liability		$ 13,805

TAX AVOIDANCE AND BUSINESS DECISIONS

Taxpayers who deliberately misstate their taxable income, whether by omitting income or claiming fraudulently contrived deductions, are practicing **tax evasion.** This, of course, is illegal, and the penalties for such a practice can be severe. However, taxpayers are perfectly within their rights to practice **tax avoidance**—to arrange their business affairs in such a way that their tax liability is minimized.

Timing of Transactions

Many methods of minimizing taxes center on the timing of transactions. As we have already noted, deferring sales of certain property so that the holding period is over one year may qualify any resulting gain for preferential treatment under capital gain provisions of the tax laws. In certain other sales of property, a taxpayer might sell on an installment basis rather than for a lump sum payment. If the initial year's receipt does not exceed 30% of the selling price, the taxpayer may be able to spread any gain over the life of the contract and thereby reduce taxes.

Timing (and perhaps a degree of clairvoyance) is also an important factor when a taxpayer's principal residence is sold at a gain. Under a long-standing provision of the IRS Code, the gain will not be taxable if an amount at least as great as the selling price[1] is invested in a new residence during the period beginning 18 months before the sale and ending 18 months[2] after the sale. The basis of the new residence is reduced by the gain not recognized; thus, the tax is deferred. Another Code provision, however, grants a once-in-a-lifetime exclusion of $100,000[3] of gain on the sale of a residence for taxpayers who are at least 55 years old and have used the property as their principal residence for three of the five preceding years. Because this exclusion can be used only on one sale transaction, the taxpayer must decide when to use it. If a taxpayer sells his residence at a gain of less than $100,000, he must speculate on the possibility of a larger gain being realized on a future residence.

Earlier we mentioned the possibility that cash basis taxpayers may take steps to affect their pattern of receipts and expenditures. For example, some taxpayers can arrange to concentrate their personal deductions in a particular year. In the following year, if their itemized deductions are below the zero bracket amount (because of the shifting process), they can take advantage of the zero bracket amount.

These are just a few of many possible examples in which the timing of transactions can alter the impact of income taxes. Because they often deal with the disposition of property, it is wise to investigate thoroughly the tax consequences of any contemplated property sales and the possible forms the sale may take.

Tax Shelters

As they become more affluent, some taxpayers look for **tax shelters**—investments that, by their nature, create either tax-exempt income or a probable deductible tax loss. They may, for example, invest in state or municipal securities, the interest on which is exempt from federal income tax. Interest rates on these securities are typically lower than on interest-taxable securities of the same quality because of the tax shelter feature. Their attractiveness, therefore, depends on the marginal tax rate of the taxpayer. Suppose a taxpayer in a 30% marginal tax rate bracket had $20,000 to invest, with a choice between $6\frac{1}{2}\%$ municipal bonds and 9% industrial bonds (interest taxable) of equal merit. The municipal bonds would provide $1,300 tax-free income, while the industrial bonds would provide only $1,260 after-tax income ($1,800 − $540 tax). As the marginal tax rate increases, the investment in municipal bonds becomes more attractive. On the other hand, a taxpayer in the 26% tax bracket would find the 9% bonds more attractive.

A number of tax shelters permit the taxpayer a tax-free cash inflow on an investment and also a loss for tax purposes. Many involve groups of taxpayers, typically in limited partnerships, who make a joint investment in such ventures as apartment complexes and oil properties. Revenues from rents and royalties exceed out-of-pocket (cash) operating costs, so there is a distributable amount of

---

[1]Selling price here means "adjusted selling price" as defined by the Internal Revenue Code (selling price less expenses of fix-up and sale).

[2]If the residence is to be constructed, the period is 24 months.

[3]$50,000 for married taxpayers filing separately.

cash for investors; however, because of large write-offs (particularly through accelerated depreciation), there is a tax loss allocable to the investors. Suppose, for example, that an investment of $20,000 resulted in a cash inflow of $1,500 and a $1,000 operating loss allocation for a particular taxpayer. If the investor is in the 40% marginal tax bracket, the tax-free distribution of $1,500 is the equivalent of $2,500 in ordinary taxable income [$1,500/(1 − 0.40)]. Add the $1,000 loss allocation, because it can be offset against other income, and you have a $3,500 return before taxes, or a before-tax return of $17\frac{1}{2}$%. The after-tax return is $1,500 + $400 = $1,900, or a $9\frac{1}{2}$% return. Taxpayers involved in these sheltering activities must carefully examine the "at risk" provisions of the tax laws that may limit the amount of loss deduction.

Forms of Business Organization

Most large businesses are operated as corporations in order to have wider access to capital, to limit liability, or to enjoy other advantages of incorporation explained in Chapter 13. For smaller businesses, with perhaps a single owner or a few owners, the form of ownership may well be influenced by tax considerations.

Let us examine some of the general factors to be considered in determining the relative tax effects. First, all income of single proprietorships and partnerships is taxable to the owners as earned, whether or not it is distributed. Second, while corporations must pay a tax on earnings, they may deduct reasonable salaries paid to owners. Furthermore, corporations may pay out only a portion of the earnings as dividends (as long as accumulations are not deemed unreasonable). Other relevant factors are the amount of the business earnings and the amount of the owners' other income.

For example, consider the comparative tax effects of the corporate and sole proprietorship forms of organization for a married individual whose business is expected to generate $40,000 net income annually. Half of this amount will be withdrawn each year (as a salary, if the corporate form is used). The owner's other income, less all deductions and exemptions, will be about $8,000 annually. A comparison of the total tax effect of the two forms of organization is shown in Exhibit 28–5 (page 1012).

The example assumes that no dividends would be distributed by the corporation. This policy might require justification if questioned by the IRS. Generally, the IRS may impose a penalty on unreasonable retention of earnings unless a genuine business purpose can be shown. Of course, the owner will be taxed on the $16,600 earnings retained ($20,000 − $3,400 tax) if they should be distributed either currently or in the future. If they are distributed currently, the total income from salary, dividends, and other sources would be $44,600 ($28,000 + $16,600), on which the tax would be $12,204.[4] Adding the $3,400 corporate tax to this amount results in $15,604. Thus the apparent advantage of the corporate form shown in Exhibit 28–5 would be lost. On the other hand, suppose that dividend distributions can be postponed indefinitely or for a fairly long period of time. Then the owner may find the corporate form of organization advantageous. This is especially true if, through earnings retention and growth, the corporate stock

---

[4]We have ignored the dividend exclusion of $100 in this computation.

EXHIBIT 28–5
Comparative Tax Results
in Two Forms of Organization

		Corporation	Sole Proprietorship
Income from business		$40,000	$40,000
Less: Owner's salary		20,000	—
Taxable business income		$20,000	$40,000
Corporate tax on $20,000 at 17%		$ 3,400	
Salary	$20,000		
Other income less deductions and exemptions	8,000		8,000
	$28,000		$48,000
Tax on $28,000 ($4,505 + 32% of $3,400)		5,593	
Tax on $48,000 ($12,720 + 49% of $2,200)			$13,798
Total tax		$ 8,993	$13,798

increases in value; at a future date the owner may exercise the option of selling all or part of the shares and receive preferential capital gains treatment on any gains.

Obviously, no general rule or formula can be given for determining the form of organization that is most beneficial for tax purposes. The type of analysis we have illustrated may be modified in response to changes in the levels of business income, other income, reasonableness of salary levels, dividend policy, and other factors. The addition of owners and increases in the size and scope of the business may be influential. Finally, depending on the nature of the ownership, small corporations can sometimes elect to be taxed as partnerships.

Other Business Decisions

In earlier chapters we discussed some of the major areas in which a choice of acceptable accounting alternatives influences tax liability. One of these was the choice of depreciation methods. In particular, we examined the effects of *accelerated depreciation* methods, which generally enable a business to postpone taxes and thereby enjoy the use over a period of time of funds otherwise unavailable in that period. We also pointed out how firms that use the LIFO method of inventory pricing can reduce the effect of taxes during a period of rising prices.

Another area relates to asset acquisitions, where certain tax credits may be allowed. From time to time, Congress has enacted legislation permitting a percentage of the cost of certain newly acquired assets to be offset as a credit to the tax liability in the year of acquisition. If such credits are available to a firm, they should be considered when decisions are made about the cost of assets and the timing of their purchase.

Although these examples are among the most prominent of many situations in which choices or alternatives affect tax liability, many others might be mentioned. To be emphasized, however, is the fact that the tax consequences of choices and the possible forms of business transactions must be *explored in advance*. Once decisions have been implemented with regard to the form of business organization, financing methods, asset acquisitions, and even accounting methods, it is often difficult, and in some cases infeasible, to change the tax consequences by remedial action.

KEY POINTS TO REMEMBER

(1) The four main classes of taxpayers are individuals, corporations, estates, and trusts. Firms operating as sole proprietorships and partnerships are not taxable entities.

(2) The tax format for individual taxpayers is:

	Gross Income	(All income, minus exclusions)
minus	Deductions from Gross Income	(Business expenses and expenses incurred in the production of income)
equals	Adjusted Gross Income	
minus	Excess Itemized Deductions	(Deductible personal expenses or, in lieu of these, a zero bracket amount incorporated in the tax tables)
minus	Personal Exemptions	($1,000 each for taxpayer, spouse, and each dependent)
equals	Taxable Income	

(3) The *effective* tax rate is the tax liability divided by taxable income. The *marginal* tax rate, the rate applicable to additional increments of income, is important in determining the tax effect of proposed transactions.

(4) Gains and losses on sales or exchanges of capital assets are *long-term* if the assets have been held over one year and *short-term* if the assets have been held one year or less.

    (a) Long-term gains and losses are "netted" to obtain net long-term gain or loss, and short-term gains and losses are "netted" to obtain net short-term gain or loss.

    (b) The excess of any net long-term gains over net short-term losses is called *net capital gain;* 60% of this amount is deducted in computing adjusted gross income of individuals.

    (c) Net losses from capital asset transactions can be offset against ordinary income up to $3,000 in any year by noncorporate taxpayers. Any unused amount, called the "net capital loss," can be carried forward to future years to be offset against capital gains or $3,000 ordinary income of each year. Long-term losses are used up at the rate of $1 for each $1 of capital gains, but at the rate of $2 for each $1 of ordinary income.

(5) The tax format for corporations is:

	Gross Income	(All business revenue, gains, dividends, etc.)
minus	Regular Deductions	(Business expenses, with exceptions, such as a limitation on charitable contributions)
minus	Special Deductions	(85% of dividends received from domestic corporations; 100% of affiliate dividends)
equals	Taxable Income	

(6) Net capital gains of corporations cannot be reduced by the 60% deduction available to individuals. Such gains, however, are taxed at a maximum rate of 28%. Net capital losses cannot be offset against ordinary income, but they may be carried back three years and forward five years to be offset against capital gains of those years.

QUESTIONS

28-1 In addition to raising revenue, what other purposes are served by the federal income tax?

28-2 Name the four major classes of taxpaying entities for federal income tax purposes.

28-3 How is the net income from sole proprietorships and partnerships taxed? Must either of these business entities file a federal income tax return?

28-4 Describe the general format used to determine an individual's taxable income.

28-5 Of the following items, identify those that can be *excluded* from gross income: (1) interest on savings accounts, (2) interest on municipal bonds, (3) social security payments (benefits), (4) gambling gains, (5) bonuses, (6) life insurance proceeds paid at death of insured, (7) royalties, (8) scholarship of a degree candidate, not requiring services.

28-6 Give a broad description of the deductions allowable in computing an individual's adjusted gross income, and name two examples.

28-7 Why is the concept of adjusted gross income important in the calculation of an individual's taxable income?

28-8 Sue Mills, who operates a real estate agency as a sole proprietorship, had the following expenditures for the current year:
   (1) Interest on office building mortgage.
   (2) Interest on home mortgage.
   (3) Property taxes on home.
   (4) Expenses of automobile used solely in business.
   (5) License on business automobile.
   (6) License on personal automobile.
   (7) State gasoline tax—business automobile.
   (8) State gasoline tax—personal automobile.
   (9) Dues to realty association.
   (10) Church contributions by Mills family.
   (11) Loss on sale of office building.
   (12) $800 net short-term capital loss on personal investments.
   (13) Uninsured termite damage to home.

For each of these items, indicate whether it is (a) deductible in obtaining adjusted gross income, (b) deductible from adjusted gross income, or (c) nondeductible.

28-9 What is meant by a personal exemption?

28-10 What are the criteria for determining whether a person qualifies as a dependent of a taxpayer?

28-11 June Stern, who is single, has adjusted gross income of $16,000 this year. Personal expenses qualifying as itemized deductions amount to $1,800. Calculate her tax, using the appropriate schedule in Exhibit 28-2 (page 1000).

28-12 Michael Yee, a single taxpayer, expects to have taxable income of $24,000 this year. (a) What is his *marginal* rate of tax? (b) Explain how Yee might use his marginal tax rate in tax planning. (c) What is the *effective* rate of tax? Use the appropriate schedule in Exhibit 28-2 (page 1000).

28-13 An individual taxpayer had a net long-term capital gain of $8,000 and a net short-term capital loss of $2,000 for the current year. What amount resulting from such gains and losses will be included in adjusted gross income?

28-14 During the current year, an individual taxpayer had a net short-term capital loss of $500 and a net long-term capital loss of $6,000. (a) How much of these losses can be offset against ordinary income of this year? (b) How much can be carried forward to next year? (c) If the taxpayer has no capital gains or losses next year, what amount can be deducted from next year's ordinary income?

28-15 What is meant by a *constructive receipt*?

28-16 What is the "dividends received" deduction for corporations, and how is it employed in calculating corporate income tax?

28-17 Differentiate between *tax evasion* and *tax avoidance*.

28-18 What is a *tax shelter*? Give an example.

28-19 What tax factors might be considered by the owner or owners of a small business in choosing the form of business organization?

28-20 A 58-year-old taxpayer plans to sell his residence at a gain of $45,000 and build a new residence within a year. What income tax decision will be required of this taxpayer?

EXERCISES

28-21 Calculate the adjusted gross income for the joint return of George and Linda Wilson from the following data:

Share of partnership net income	$28,000
Interest on municipal bonds	3,000
Dividend income—George	400
Dividend income—Linda	60
Lottery prize	300
Gift from relative	1,500
Long-term capital gain on sale of securities	2,000

28-22 The joint return of Ralph and Joan Fisher shows that they have two dependents and that their adjusted gross income is $28,000. Using the relevant data from the items shown below, calculate their taxable income.

Real estate taxes	$1,600	Gambling losses (gambling	
Charitable contributions	·500	gains of $600 included	
Contribution to relative	200	in gross income)	$1,200
Union dues	120	Health insurance premiums	260
State income taxes	1,720	Surgical costs not reimbursed	
Interest on home mortgage	850	by insurance	900
State sales tax	80	Medicine and drugs	150
State gasoline tax	90	Automobile licenses	32

28-23 Using the appropriate schedule in Exhibit 28-2 (page 1000), calculate the amount of tax due from Barbara Owens, a single taxpayer who has given you the following information:

Gross income	$21,000.00
Deductions to determine adjusted gross income	1,600.00
Allowable itemized personal expenses	2,400.00
Tax withheld from salary	2,428.50
Payments of estimated tax	600.00

28-24 Fred Adams expects his taxable income, after all deductions (less the $2,300 zero bracket amount) and one exemption, to be approximately $24,000 this year. He is 27, unmarried, and resides in a state where the state income tax is 10% on income over $15,000. He has an opportunity to work on weekends and earn an additional $3,000 per year. How much of this additional amount would he be able to keep, after taxes? Use the appropriate schedule in Exhibit 28-2 (page 1000).

28-25 The following are the capital gains and losses for four separate taxpayers identified as A, B, C, and D. For each taxpayer, indicate the amount to be included in gross income, if any, and the amount deductible from gross income, if any, to determine adjusted gross income.

	A	B	C	D
Long-term capital gains	$2,200	$1,000	$ 500	$3,500
Long-term capital losses	200	3,000	2,500	500
Short-term capital gains	100	–0–	3,500	500
Short-term capital losses	500	500	–0–	200

28-26 The Underhill Corporation had net income of $80,000 before taxes during the current year. In arriving at this amount, the corporation included $10,000 in dividends from nonaffiliated domestic corporations and a $20,000 long-term gain on the sale of property. Calculate the corporation's federal income tax for the year, using the rate schedule given on page 1007.

PROBLEMS

28-27 Alan and Rachel Meyer have three school-age children and are filing a joint income tax return. Mr. Meyer, whose salary is $22,000 as an accountant for the Ajax Corporation, operates a tax service in his spare time. During the current year, he had $4,800 in gross income and $1,800 business expenses in his tax service. He received $400 in dividends from his investments and $500 interest on municipal bonds. Mrs. Meyer had $90 in dividend income on stocks owned by her. In addition, Mr. Meyer sold for $90 per share 100 shares of stock purchased five years ago for $50 per share. Income taxes withheld from Meyer's salary for the year amounted to $2,750, and his payments of estimated tax were $360. Personal expenses of the Meyer family for the year included the following:

Mortgage payments (of which $1,500 was interest)	$3,600
Real estate taxes	1,600
State income taxes	1,200
State sales taxes	180
Charitable contributions	320
Health insurance premiums	340
Other medical and dental expenses	800
Accidental damage to personal automobile (total damage, $450; Meyer paid $200 of this because of $200 deductible insurance provision)	200
License fees for auto, pets, etc.	50

REQUIRED
Calculate the amount of tax due (or overpayment) to be shown on the joint income tax return of Mr. and Mrs. Meyer for the current year. Use the appropriate schedule in Exhibit 28-2 (page 1000).

28-28 The following items relate to the federal income taxes of individuals who itemize their deductions in computing their tax. The items are not related to one another and are to be considered independently.
  (1) Fee paid employment agency for obtaining employment.
  (2) Payment of repair bill of $100 for damage to pleasure automobile from skid on icy road (not compensated for by insurance).
  (3) Labor union dues.
  (4) Contribution to "Empty Stocking Fund" formed by neighbors for children of a needy family.
  (5) State income tax paid.
  (6) Federal cigarette tax.
  (7) State gasoline tax for pleasure car.
  (8) State fishing license.
  (9) Damage to lawn due to usual August dry spell.
  (10) Fee paid by unemployed student to take the CPA examination.
  (11) Fee paid to Smith & Brown, investment consultants, for advice on personal portfolio of securities.

(12) Cost of cleaning uniform paid by train conductor.
(13) Fair market value of furniture given to the Salvation Army.
(14) Entertainment expense of an outside salesman, not reimbursed.
(15) Life insurance premiums paid.
(16) Trade and business expenses of sole proprietorship.
(17) Net short-term loss of $1,200 on sale of securities.

REQUIRED

For each of the above items, indicate whether it is (a) not deductible, (b) deductible in determining adjusted gross income, or (c) deductible from adjusted gross income.

28-29 Thomas and Karen Klein are married and are both under 65 years of age. They have one child, Tim, who is 18 years old and a full-time student at a university; they contribute over half of his support. Tim earned $1,500 from part-time work during the year.

Karen Klein operates a retail dress shop. Her records are kept on the accrual basis; however, all sales are for cash. The following information is available for the year's operations:

Cash receipts	$46,200
Merchandise inventory, January 1	10,200
Merchandise purchases	32,000
Rent	2,800
Utilities and supplies	180
Salaries of part-time help	3,900
Insurance	120
Merchandise inventory, December 31	12,200

Thomas Klein's salary as a purchasing agent for a local firm was $26,000, and income tax withheld was $5,800. Quarterly payments of estimated tax totaled $1,200. The following information for the year was compiled from Klein's checkbook and other sources:

Dividends received:		
Dow Chemical (Thomas)		$ 800
Shell Oil (Thomas)		400
Alcoa (Karen)		85
Interest Income:		
Savings account		500
City of Houston bonds		200
Real estate tax on home		1,700
State sales tax		120
Drugs and medicines		524
Medical expense (other than drugs and health insurance)		920
State income tax paid		630
Contribution to United Fund		200
Accountant's services (preparing last year's income tax return)		150
Auto license on personal car		50
Safety deposit box rental		20
Subscriptions—professional journals		80

Country club dues	500
Winnings at horse races	120
Interest expense on mortgage	1,100
Health insurance premiums	450

During the year, Thomas had the following corporate stock sales:

Security	Holding Period	Cost	Proceeds
Dow Chemical	five years	$1,850	$3,350
American Motors	three months	3,000	2,000
Datatron	eight months	450	650

REQUIRED

Compute the amount of tax due (or any overpayment) to be reported in filing the Kleins' joint income tax return. Use the appropriate schedule in Exhibit 28-2 (page 1000).

28-30 The following information for the current year is taken from the records of the Nu-Art Corporation:

Sales	$200,000
Interest earned on Boeing bonds	5,000
Dividends received on Exxon stock	10,000
Dividends received on Atikokan stock (a Canadian company)	4,000
Cost of goods sold	130,000
Selling and administrative expenses (excluding contributions)	31,000
Contributions (United Fund, etc.)	2,000
Long-term capital gain on sale of property	8,000

In addition, the corporation had a net capital loss carryforward of $2,000 from prior years, and a $1,000 contribution deduction carryforward.

REQUIRED

Prepare a schedule showing the computation of Nu-Art Corporation's total income tax liability for the year, using the rate schedule given on page 1007.

28-31 Keith Jackson, who is married and has one dependent, plans to open a business that is expected to have a net income of $50,000 annually before taxes. He is trying to decide whether, for tax purposes, the business should be operated as a corporation (shares to be owned by his wife and himself) or as a sole proprietorship. Jackson has income from securities amounting to $10,000 per year, and he estimates that his itemized deductions will be about $8,000 each year.

   Jackson would expect to take an annual salary of $25,000 if the business were a corporation, and have one-half of the corporate income after taxes paid in dividends. On the other hand, he would expect to withdraw $30,000 each year if the business were operated as a sole proprietorship.

REQUIRED

Prepare an analysis showing the expected tax results of the two types of business organization in this situation. You will need to use both the corporate rate schedule given in the chapter (page 1007) and the appropriate schedule in Exhibit 28-2 (page 1000).

ALTERNATE PROBLEMS

28-27A Leon and Alice Bailey, who have two young children, are filing a joint federal income tax return. Mr. Bailey's salary as credit manager for the Syncro Company is $32,000, from which $4,800 was withheld for federal income tax. Mrs. Bailey works part-time as an interior decorator; her gross receipts for the year were $3,600 and her business expenses were $600. The couple paid $500 estimated tax during the year. Mr. Bailey's dividend income during the year amounted to $480; his wife's dividend income was $120. Mrs. Bailey also received a small bequest of $800 from a relative who died during the year. During the year, Mr. Bailey had a long-term capital gain of $2,600 and a short-term loss of $600 from the sale of securities.

The family's personal expenses for the year included the following:

Contributions to United Fund and house of worship	$ 500
Health insurance premiums	360
Storm damage to trees (not insured)	240
State fishing and hunting licenses	36
Medical and dental expense (not paid by insurance)	920
State sales taxes	210
Real estate taxes	2,000
Interest on home mortgage	1,600
State income tax paid	2,800

REQUIRED
Calculate the amount of tax due (or overpayment) to be shown in the Baileys' joint income tax return for the current year. Use the appropriate schedule in Exhibit 28-2 (page 1007).

28-28A The following items relate to the federal income taxes of individuals who itemize their deductions in computing their tax. The items are not related to one another and are to be considered independently.
(1) Purchase of Christmas seals (stamps) from tuberculosis association.
(2) Travel expenses (overnight) of science teacher attending scientific convention.
(3) Federal excise tax on jewelry purchase.
(4) Dog license.
(5) Tuition for Dale Carnegie course taken by insurance salesperson to improve selling skills.
(6) Loss of elm trees due to Dutch elm disease.
(7) Cost of spike shoes bought by professional baseball player.
(8) Cost of piano and ballet lessons for daughter.
(9) Cost of repairing water pipes that burst during unusually severe freeze.
(10) Costs of traveling in search of employment.
(11) Net short-term capital loss of $500.
(12) Wagering losses of $300 (gains of $600 included in gross income).
(13) Accountant's fee for preparing income tax return.
(14) Cost of professional magazine subscriptions paid by university professor.
(15) Car pool expenses driving to and from work in excess of amounts received from passengers.

REQUIRED

For each of the above items, indicate whether it is (a) not deductible, (b) deductible in determining adjusted gross income, or (c) deductible from adjusted gross income.

28-29A Jay Ritter and his wife, Katie, are both under 65 years of age and have two children. Jay furnished over half the support for his mother-in-law, who lives with them. Her total income consists of $800 interest on a savings account. Katie has no outside employment. Jay owns an office building from which rentals for the year totaled $14,000. During the year, he made the following expenditures related to the building:

Heat	$ 820
Janitor service	2,700
Depreciation	2,400
Interest on mortgage	1,600
Real estate taxes	2,100
Insurance premiums on 3-year policy (paid January 1)	540

Jay's salary as sales manager for an insurance firm was $36,000, from which $6,500 was withheld for federal income taxes during the year. He also paid $500 in estimated tax during the year. The following information for the year was compiled from his checkbook and other sources:

Dividends received:	
FMC Stock (Jay)	$1,500
Illinois Power Co. (Katie)	250
Interest income:	
Savings account	600
City of Casper Bonds	450
Real estate tax on home	1,500
State sales tax	140
Drugs and medicines	520
Medical expense (other than drugs and health insurance)	2,160
State income tax paid	3,200
Contribution to United Fund	400
Accountant's services (preparing last year's income tax return)	80
Dues to athletic club	600
Auto license on personal car	40
Safety deposit box rentals	30
Subscriptions—professional journals	70
Lottery winnings	250
Interest expense on mortgage	1,400
Health insurance premiums	320

During the year Jay sold the following corporate stock:

Security	Holding Period	Cost	Proceeds
FMC	two years	$3,000	$4,200
Dow-Jones, Inc.	nine months	1,200	800
American Tobacco Co.	three months	400	600

REQUIRED

Compute the amount of tax due (or any overpayment) to be reported in filing the Ritters' joint income tax return. Use the appropriate schedule in Exhibit 28–2 (page 1000).

28–30A The following information for the current year is taken from the records of the Plateau Company:

Sales	$3,200,000
Cost of goods sold	1,900,000
Interest expense	18,000
Selling and administrative expenses (excluding contributions)	920,000
Dividends received from wholly-owned affiliate	10,000
Dividends received from Burlington Industries	20,000
Long-term gain on sale of assets	12,000
Charitable contributions	25,000

In addition, the corporation had a *net capital loss carryforward* of $4,000.

REQUIRED

Prepare a schedule showing the computation of the total income tax liability for the year for the Plateau Company, using the rate schedule given on page 1007.

BUSINESS DECISION PROBLEM

At the beginning of the current year, Jennifer Cortland received a $50,000 bequest from a relative. She asks your advice about the income tax treatment of the bequest and also about several possible investment opportunities. Her alternatives are to invest the $50,000 in a partnership owned by two acquaintances, or to purchase either 9% high-grade industrial bonds or 6% tax-exempt municipal bonds.

Jennifer's share of the partnership net income would be 20%. Partnership net income is expected to average $20,000 annually for the next several years. Jennifer tells you that if she invests in the partnership, she expects to withdraw only one-half of her share of net income annually.

Jennifer is unmarried and under 65 years of age. Her annual salary is $42,000, and she estimates that her itemized deductions will amount to $8,300 for the year.

REQUIRED

(a) How is the $50,000 bequest handled for income tax purposes?
(b) Which of the three investment alternatives should Jennifer choose? (Ignore the problem of risk in determining the best alternative.) Give calculations showing after-tax income to support your choice.

Appendixes

EXAMPLES OF FINANCIAL STATEMENTS
OF MAJOR CORPORATIONS

On the following pages are actual financial statements of two major corporations:

American Motors Corporation
FMC Corporation

Notes to the financial statements and the accountants' report are included with the statements for American Motors Corporation. Although several items in the footnotes relate to matters not dealt with in an introductory accounting course, they are included to illustrate the comprehensive nature of a complete set of financial statements and accompanying footnotes. For FMC Corporation, only the main bodies of the financial statements are reprinted here; notes to the statements and the accountants' report have been omitted.

ACCOUNTANTS' REPORT

To the Board of Directors and Stockholders
American Motors Corporation
Southfield, Michigan

Detroit, Michigan
November 9, 1978

We have examined the accompanying consolidated balance sheets of American Motors Corporation and consolidated subsidiaries as of September 30, 1978 and 1977, and the related statements of net earnings, additional paid-in capital, earnings retained for use in the business, and changes in financial position for the years then ended. Our examinations were made in accordance with generally accepted auditing standards, and accordingly included such tests of the accounting records and such other auditing procedures as we considered necessary in the circumstances.

In our opinion, the consolidated financial statements referred to above present fairly the financial position of American Motors Corporation and consolidated subsidiaries at September 30, 1978 and 1977, and the results of their operations and changes in their financial position for the years then ended, in conformity with generally accepted accounting principles applied on a consistent basis.

Touche Ross & Co.

Certified Public Accountants

CONSOLIDATED STATEMENT OF NET EARNINGS
American Motors Corporation and Consolidated Subsidiaries

	(Dollars in Thousands) Year Ended September 30	
	1978	1977
REVENUES		
Net sales	$2,585,428	$2,236,896
Other income (Note K)	21,866	16,565
	$2,607,294	$2,253,461
COSTS AND EXPENSES		
Cost of products sold, other than items below	$2,198,542	$1,921,358
Selling, advertising and administrative expenses	241,313	211,944
Amortization of tools and dies	39,709	40,254
Depreciation and amortization of plant and equipment	23,766	20,892
Cost of pensions (Note 1)	41,456	35,431
Interest	22,318	17,346
	$2,567,104	$2,247,225
EARNINGS BEFORE TAXES ON INCOME AND EXTRAORDINARY CREDITS	$ 40,190	$ 6,236
Taxes on income (Note H)	16,100	3,170
EARNINGS BEFORE EXTRAORDINARY CREDITS	$ 24,090	$ 3,066
Extraordinary credits (Note H)	12,600	5,200
NET EARNINGS	$ 36,690	$ 8,266
Per share (Note M)		
Earnings per share of Capital Stock and Capital Stock equivalents		
Earnings before extraordinary credits	$ .80	$ .10
Extraordinary credits	.41	.17
Net earnings	$ 1.21	$ .27
Earnings per share on a fully diluted basis		
Earnings before extraordinary credits	$ .75	$ .10
Extraordinary credits	.41	.17
Net earnings	$ 1.16	$ .27

See notes to financial statements.

CONSOLIDATED BALANCE SHEETS
American Motors Corporation and Consolidated Subsidiaries

	(Dollars in Thousands)	
	Sept. 30, 1978	Sept. 30, 1977
ASSETS		
CURRENT ASSETS		
Cash and marketable securities, at cost	$ 75,058	$ 60,189
Accounts receivable (Note B)	198,581	177,969
Accounts receivable from affiliated companies (Note D)	41,292	38,970
Inventories	340,155	328,532
Prepaid expenses	13,549	12,363
TOTAL CURRENT ASSETS	$668,635	$618,023
INVESTMENTS AND OTHER ASSETS		
Investments in and advances to unconsolidated subsidiaries (Notes D and N)	$ 78,342	$ 78,185
Miscellaneous advances and investments (Note C)	13,967	8,003
TOTAL INVESTMENTS AND OTHER ASSETS	$ 92,309	$ 86,188
PROPERTY, PLANT AND EQUIPMENT (Note D)		
Land	$ 7,921	$ 7,932
Buildings and improvements	147,969	140,881
Machinery and equipment, including tools and dies	337,833	344,650
	$493,723	$493,463
Less accumulated depreciation	272,113	252,197
TOTAL PROPERTY, PLANT AND EQUIPMENT	$221,610	$241,266
GOODWILL ARISING FROM ACQUISITIONS	11,517	11,866
	$994,071	$957,343
LIABILITIES AND STOCKHOLDERS' EQUITY		
CURRENT LIABILITIES		
Short-term bank borrowings (Note D)	$ 69,425	$ 57,550
Current maturities of long-term debt (Note E)	4,404	25,973
Accounts payable	332,469	350,573
Accrued expenses	106,356	79,994
Taxes on income (Note H)	4,038	1,032
TOTAL CURRENT LIABILITIES	$516,692	$515,122
LONG-TERM LIABILITIES (Note E)		
Long-term debt	$ 78,916	$ 86,272
Other liabilities	40,583	35,108
TOTAL LONG-TERM LIABILITIES	$119,499	$121,380
STOCKHOLDERS' EQUITY (Notes D, E, F and G)		
Capital stock	$ 50,313	$ 50,168
Additional paid-in capital	130,884	130,680
Earnings retained for use in the business	176,683	139,993
TOTAL STOCKHOLDERS' EQUITY	$357,880	$320,841
	$994,071	$957,343

See notes to financial statements.

CONSOLIDATED STATEMENT OF CHANGES IN FINANCIAL POSITION
American Motors Corporation and Consolidated Subsidiaries

	(Dollars in Thousands) Year Ended September 30	
	1978	1977
SOURCES OF WORKING CAPITAL		
From operations		
Earnings before extraordinary credits	$ 24,090	$ 3,066
Depreciation and amortization of plant, equipment, tools and dies	63,475	61,146
Amortization of goodwill and debt discount,		
and other noncash charges	13,141	15,761
FROM OPERATIONS	$100,706	$ 79,973
Extraordinary credits (Note H)...............................	12,600	5,200
Repayment of advances by unconsolidated subsidiaries and		
current maturities of long-term receivables...................	3,342	32,808
Sale of plant and other sources	762	23,550
	$117,410	$141,531
APPLICATIONS OF WORKING CAPITAL		
Net additions to property, plant and equipment	$ 41,233	$ 46,631
Current maturities of long-term debt (Note E)	7,906	26,040
Investments in and advances to unconsolidated subsidiaries	16,014	21,826
Other applications	3,215	3,906
	$ 68,368	$ 98,403
NET INCREASE IN WORKING CAPITAL	$ 49,042	$ 43,128
WORKING CAPITAL AT BEGINNING OF THE YEAR	102,901	59,773
WORKING CAPITAL AT END OF THE YEAR	$151,943	$102,901
CHANGES IN COMPONENTS OF WORKING CAPITAL		
Cash and marketable securities	$ 14,869	$ (31,111)
Accounts receivable	22,934	57,923
Inventories	11,623	(11,690)
Prepaid expenses	1,186	5,567
Short-term bank borrowings.................................	(11,875)	5,520
Current maturities of long-term debt.........................	21,569	(4,430)
Accounts payable..	18,104	(624)
Accrued expenses	(26,362)	19,184
Taxes on income	(3,006)	2,789
NET INCREASE IN WORKING CAPITAL	$ 49,042	$ 43,128

CONSOLIDATED STATEMENT OF ADDITIONAL PAID-IN CAPITAL

	(Dollars in Thousands) Year Ended September 30	
	1978	1977
Balance at beginning of the year	$130,680	$129,987
From issuance of Capital Stock upon acquisition of subsidiaries and		
exercise of stock options (86,949 shares in 1978		
and 305,383 shares in 1977)...............................	204	693
Balance at end of the year....................................	$130,884	$130,680

CONSOLIDATED STATEMENT OF EARNINGS RETAINED FOR USE IN THE BUSINESS

	(Dollars in Thousands) Year Ended September 30	
	1978	1977
Balance at beginning of the year	$139,993	$131,727
Net earnings for the year	36,690	8,266
Balance at end of the year....................................	$176,683	$139,993

See notes to financial statements.

NOTES TO FINANCIAL STATEMENTS

Years ended September 30, 1978 and 1977

NOTE A—SUMMARY OF ACCOUNTING POLICIES

The following is a summary of significant accounting policies followed in the preparation of the financial statements. The policies conform to generally accepted accounting principles and have been consistently applied.

PRINCIPLES OF CONSOLIDATION

The consolidated financial statements include the accounts of the Company and its United States and Canadian subsidiaries (except those engaged in leasing, financing, retail selling and realty activities). Intercompany accounts and transactions have been eliminated. The investments in unconsolidated subsidiaries and 20% or more owned affiliates are stated at equity in net assets of such companies.

INVENTORY VALUATION

Inventories are stated at the lower of cost (first-in, first-out method) or market.

DEPRECIATION AND AMORTIZATION

Property, plant and equipment is stated at cost and depreciated over the estimated useful lives of the assets. The declining balance method is used for approximately 65% of the total depreciable assets and the straight line method for the remainder. Deferred tool and die costs are amortized ratably over the estimated production of the models to which such tools and dies relate.

GOODWILL ARISING FROM ACQUISITIONS

The unallocated excess of cost of investments in consolidated subsidiaries over equities in net assets acquired prior to 1971 is not being amortized because, in the opinion of management, there has been no diminution of value. Amounts arising subsequent thereto are amortized over periods not exceeding forty years.

AMORTIZATION OF DEBT EXPENSE

Debt discount and related issuance expenses are amortized over the life of the related debt.

WARRANTY AND ADVERTISING

Estimated costs related to all product warranties are provided for at time of sale. Advertising and sales promotion expenditures, in general, are charged to operations as incurred.

PENSION PLAN COSTS

Total pension cost for the year includes current service costs and the amortization of past service costs over periods ranging up to forty years. The general policy is to fund pension costs as they are charged to operations.

AUDIT COMMITTEE

The Company has an Audit Committee consisting of outside members of the Board of Directors. The Committee meets regularly to review with management and Touche Ross & Co. the Company's accounting policies and internal and external audit plans and results.

NOTE B—ACCOUNTS RECEIVABLE

Accounts receivable are stated net of an allowance for doubtful accounts of $600,000 in 1978 and 1977.

NOTE C—MISCELLANEOUS ADVANCES AND INVESTMENTS

Miscellaneous advances and investments are stated net of an allowance for possible future losses of $1,202,000 in 1978 and $2,909,000 in 1977.

NOTE D—SHORT-TERM BANK BORROWINGS

American Motors Corporation has $25,625,000 outstanding at September 30, 1978, pursuant to three revolving credit agreements. In 1978, the weighted average interest rate, which varies for each of the borrowings, was 8.7%. In connection with these borrowings and the $21,500,000 term loan (Note E), capital stock of certain subsidiaries, intercompany receivables and a mortgage on a manufacturing facility (with a net carrying value of approximately $98,300,000) have been provided as collateral. A mortgage on another manufacturing facility (with a net carrying value of approximately $7,600,000) provides additional collateral to the lenders under two of these credit agreements. The agreements contain covenants principally relating to levels of working capital, consolidated debt and guarantees, net worth and the prohibition of cash dividends.

AM General Corporation, a wholly owned subsidiary, has $42,400,000 outstanding at September 30, 1978, under a revolving credit agreement providing for maximum borrowings of $51,630,000. A commitment fee of 1/2 of 1% is paid on the undrawn portion of the credit. During 1978, the weighted average interest rate was 9.4%. AM General has pledged certain assets as security and has agreed to maintain specified levels of working capital and net worth. American Motors Corporation has guaranteed this borrowing.

These credit agreements expire January 31, 1979, and management expects the outstanding credits will be renewed.

NOTES TO FINANCIAL STATEMENTS

Other miscellaneous short-term borrowings at September 30, 1978 were $1,400,000.

NOTE E—LONG-TERM LIABILITIES

(Dollars in Thousands)

	1978	1977
Long-term Debt, net of current maturities Term-loan	$20,000	$25,000
6% Convertible Subordinated Debentures, less unamortized discount, based on imputed interest rate of 8-1/2% ($3,246 in 1978 and $3,733 in 1977)	28,464	30,077
9% Bonds, less unamortized discount of $442 in 1978 and $505 in 1977	22,558	22,995
6% Convertible Bonds	5,805	5,805
Miscellaneous notes and mortgages	2,089	2,395
	$78,916	$86,272

TERM LOAN
The term loan provides for a $1,500,000 payment in May, 1979 with the balance to be repaid in eight semiannual installments beginning in November 1979. In 1978, the weighted average interest rate was 9.6%. The term loan is collateralized as set forth in Note D.

6% CONVERTIBLE SUBORDINATED DEBENTURES
The 6% Convertible Subordinated

Debentures require repayments of $2,100,000 annually on October 1, 1978 to 1987, with a final repayment of $12,810,000 on October 1, 1988. These debentures are presently convertible into Capital Stock at $11.48 per share. At September 30, 1978, 2,945,121 shares of Capital Stock are reserved for possible conversion of the Debentures. Warrants which had been issued in connection with the Debentures expired on October 2, 1978.

9% BONDS
The 9% Bonds require annual repayments of $500,000 in 1979, $1,000,000 in 1980 to 1982, $2,000,000 in 1983 to 1985, $3,000,000 in 1986 to 1988 and final repayment of $5,000,000 in 1989.

6% CONVERTIBLE BONDS
At September 30, 1978, 774,000 shares of Capital Stock were reserved for possible conversion of the Bonds at a conversion price of $7.50 per share. The Bonds require repayments of $1,305,000 on April 1, 1991, and $4,500,000 on April 1, 1992.

AGGREGATE MATURITIES
The aggregate annual maturities of long-term debt for the five years ending September 30, 1983 are as follows: $4,404,000, $8,398,000, $8,387,000, $8,357,000 and $9,272,000.

OTHER LONG-TERM LIABILITIES
Other liabilities include extended product warranty, capitalized leases, deferred income taxes and long-term obligations assumed in connection with acquisitions.

NOTE F—CAPITAL STOCK
Authorized at September 30, 1978, are 50,000,000 shares of Capital Stock, $1.66-2/3 par value. The

issued and outstanding shares at September 30, 1978 and 1977, are as follows:

	1978	1977
Issued shares	30,391,216	30,304,267
In treasury	203,233	203,233
Outstanding shares	30,187,983	30,101,034

NOTE G—STOCK OPTIONS
At September 30, 1978, 655,000 shares of Capital Stock are reserved for issuance to key employees under stock option plans.

A summary of the transactions for the year ended September 30, 1978, with respect to the stock option plans follows:

	SHARES
Options outstanding at October 1, 1977	498,605
Options granted at prices ranging from $4.13 to $6.63	147,500
	646,105
Less options terminated	115,990
Less options exercised at $3.94 per share	2,000
Options outstanding at September 30, 1978, at prices ranging from $3.94 to $8.69 per share	528,115

Options for 254,515 shares granted prior to October 1, 1977, are exercisable at September 30, 1978.

The option prices for options outstanding at September 30, 1978, are not less than market value on the date of grant. With respect to options granted under the 1972 Stock Option Plan, the Plan provides for cash payment to the optionee at exercise date of a credit factor adjustment which is an amount measured by the difference between the value of the shares at the date of grant and the then market value, but not to exceed

90% of the value on date of grant. Further, under this Plan, at exercise, an equal number of options may be surrendered in exchange for cash measured by the difference between the value at date of grant reduced by the credit factor adjustment and the market value. Amounts which may be paid in cash are recorded annually as compensation expense.

NOTE H—TAXES ON INCOME

Taxes on income for the year ended September 30, 1978, include United States income taxes of $12,600,000 and foreign and other income taxes of $3,500,000. The factors resulting in an effective tax rate of less than 48% include permanent differences between earnings before taxes and income reported on the United States income tax return, as well as investment tax and other credits of $980,000 and foreign tax credits of $1,255,000.

The United States income tax return for 1978 will reflect a tax liability of $2,900,000 after giving effect to timing differences in the recognition of expenses for financial statements and the tax return, a $7,968,000 tax benefit of a net operating loss carryforward and a foreign tax credit carryforward of $4,632,000. The utilization of the net operating loss and foreign tax credit carryforward is recognized as an extraordinary credit.

Taxes on income for the year ended September 30, 1977, include a charge representing United States income taxes of $5,200,000 and a provision for foreign and other income taxes of $1,300,000, reduced by $3,330,000 representing principally a change in prior years estimated income taxes.

The United States income tax return for 1977 reflected a tax loss after giving recognition to certain deductions which had been reported in prior year financial statements. The reduction of income taxes resulting from the utilization of such prior years accounting deductions was shown as an extraordinary credit.

At September 30, 1978, approximately $22,500,000 of investment tax credit and foreign tax credit carryforward, expiring at varying dates through 1985, is available to offset future tax liabilities. In addition, a foreign consolidated subsidiary has a tax loss carryforward of approximately $8,000,000. The financial statements at September 30, 1978, do not reflect possible future tax benefits of approximately $7,400,000 relating to established warranty and other reserves which are not deductible for tax purposes until payments are made. Such future tax benefits will be recognized when they are realizable.

United States income taxes have not been provided on approximately $11,000,000 of earnings permanently reinvested in foreign subsidiaries.

NOTE I—PENSION PLANS

The principal pension plans of the Company and its subsidiaries are trusteed plans and cover substantially all employees. The actuarial value of vested benefits determined annually for all plans exceeded the total of the fund assets and the Company's recorded liabilities by approximately $225,000,000.

NOTE J—COMMITMENTS AND CONTINGENT LIABILITIES

American Motors Corporation has commitments and guarantees approximating $68,000,000 incurred in the ordinary course of business for tooling, equipment, financing of export sales and borrowing of an unconsolidated subsidiary. Additionally, $4,700,000 of interest-bearing deposits are maintained with respect to commitments under certain contracts.

Rental commitments under noncancelable operating leases include manufacturing facilities and equipment, warehouses and one-third of the office space in a commercial office facility owned by American Motors Realty Corporation, an unconsolidated subsidiary. Rental commitments for operating leases are as follows:

1979	$ 7,800,000
1980	7,200,000
1981	6,100,000
1982	5,000,000
1983	4,500,000
1984–1996	26,900,000
Total	$57,500,000

In addition, the present value of capitalized lease commitments aggregates approximately $8,800,000 and annual rental payments average $1,300,000 in each of the next five years.

As would be expected in the ordinary course of business, there are various legal actions and claims pending against American Motors Corporation and its subsidiaries. In the opinion of management, the ultimate liability, if any, with respect to these matters will not be material.

The Company plans a $27,500,000 expansion of the Jeep manufacturing facility at Toledo, Ohio, and anticipates such expansion will be completely financed by additional long-term borrowings.

NOTE K—OTHER INCOME

Other income includes interest on

NOTES TO FINANCIAL STATEMENTS

marketable securities and customer notes, royalties and commissions, and, in 1977, gain on the sale of a plant. Other income also includes the equity in net earnings of unconsolidated subsidiaries and 20% or more owned affiliates, other than retail automotive outlets, of $657,000 in 1978 and $497,000 in 1977. The expenses incurred with respect to retail outlets are classified as selling expenses.

NOTE L—RESEARCH AND DEVELOPMENT COSTS

During 1978 and 1977, $48,400,000 and $43,300,000, respectively, was expensed for Company-sponsored research and development activities.

NOTE M—EARNINGS PER SHARE

The computation of earnings per share in 1978 is based upon the average shares of Capital Stock outstanding and Capital Stock equivalents attributable to stock options and shares contingently issuable in connection with acquisitions.

The computation of fully diluted earnings per share in 1978 is based upon the average shares and equivalents mentioned above together with the average shares issuable upon conversion of the Convertible Debentures and Bonds.

The computation of earnings per share in 1977 is based upon the average shares of Capital Stock outstanding.

NOTE N—AMERICAN MOTORS REALTY CORPORATION

American Motors Realty Corporation, a wholly owned unconsolidated subsidiary, is engaged in the ownership and leasing of automobile dealership facilities to the Company's franchised dealers and in the ownership and operation of a commercial office facility. Summarized financial information for American Motors Realty Corporation for the years ended September 30, 1978 and 1977, is as follows:

	(Dollars in Thousands)	
	1978	1977
Operations		
Revenues	$14,261	$ 12,058
Net loss	$ 1,138	$ 281
Balance sheet		
Assets		
Cash and other assets	$ 7,624	$ 7,101
Properties, net	90,971	93,232
	$98,595	$100,333
Liabilities and Stockholder's Equity		
Accounts payable and accrued expenses	$ 9,098	$ 8,794
Mortgages and notes payable	51,549	50,924
Notes payable to parent	22,738	24,267
Stockholder's equity	15,210	16,348
	$98,595	$100,333

NOTE O—OPERATIONS BY SEGMENT

American Motors Corporation operates principally in two segments: General Automotive and Special Government Vehicles. Operations in the General Automotive segment involve the manufacture, assembly and sale of passenger cars and utility and recreational vehicles and their related parts and accessories in the United States, Canada and other foreign countries. Operations in the Special Government Vehicles segment primarily involve the assembly and sale of specialized vehicles, including tactical trucks, postal service vehicles and transit buses principally to agencies of the United States and foreign governments and various metropolitan transit authorities. The Company also operates three subsidiary companies engaged in the manufacture and sale of plastic injection moldings and the assembly and sale of lawn and garden tractors. These subsidiaries are shown as Other Operations.

Net sales by business segment relates to unaffiliated customers. Transfers between business segments were not material. Export sales, primarily to Asia, Africa and Latin America, were $264,114,000. Sales to domestic government agencies, principally by the Special Government Vehicles segment, were $270,630,000.

Operating profit consists of revenue less operating expenses. In computing operating profit, none of the following items have been added or deducted: general corporate expenses, interest expense (net), equity in earnings of unconsolidated subsidiaries and income taxes.

Depreciation and amortization for the General Automotive and the Special Government Vehicles segments, was $59,562,200, and $2,644,000, respectively; capital expenditures were $38,900,000 and $741,000, respectively.

Identifiable assets are those assets that are used in the operations of each segment. Corporate assets are principally cash, marketable securities and investments in unconsolidated subsidiaries.

Foreign operations provided less than 10% of consolidated net sales and employed less than 10% of consolidated assets and, therefore, have not been segregated.

NOTE P—REPLACEMENT COST INFORMATION

In compliance with regulations of the Securities and Exchange Commission, the Company will include certain estimated replacement cost information for inventories, productive capacity, cost of sales and depreciation and amortization in its Form 10-K report to be filed with the Commission.

NOTE Q—RECLASSIFICATIONS

The 1977 financial statements have been reclassified to conform with the 1978 financial statements.

Year ended September 30, 1978 (Dollars in Thousands)	General Automotive	Special Government Vehicles	Other Operations	Consolidated
Net sales	$2,165,171	$348,353	$71,904	$2,585,428
Operating profit (loss)	$ 63,880	$ (2,186)	$ 5,415	$ 67,109
Equity in earnings of unconsolidated subsidiaries				657
General corporate expenses				(9,952)
Interest expense, net				(17,624)
Earnings (loss) before taxes on income and extraordinary credits	$ 44,220	$ (9,590)	$ 5,560	$ 40,190
Identifiable assets	$ 608,534	$206,245	$46,440	$ 861,219
Corporate assets				132,852
Total assets at September 30, 1978				$ 994,071

NOTE R—QUARTERLY FINANCIAL DATA (UNAUDITED)

(Dollars in Thousands Except Per Share)

	First Quarter		Second Quarter		Third Quarter		Fourth Quarter		Total	
	1978	1977	1978	1977	1978	1977	1978	1977	1978	1977
Revenues	$563,088	$563,360	$644,416	$539,024	$708,128	$582,933	$691,662	$568,144	$2,607,294	$2,253,461
Earnings before taxes on income and extraordinary credits	2,223	1,179	3,767	2,506	7,122	2,013	27,078	538	40,190	6,236
Taxes on income	900		2,100		4,010	400	9,090	2,770	16,100	3,170
Earnings (loss) before extraordinary credits	1,323	1,179	1,667	2,506	3,112	1,613	17,988	(2,232)	24,090	3,066
Extraordinary credits	600		1,000		3,010		7,990	5,200	12,600	5,200
Net earnings	1,923	1,179	2,667	2,506	6,122	1,613	25,978	2,968	36,690	8,266
Per share (Note M)										
Primary										
Earnings (loss) before extraordinary credits	$ .04	$ .04	$ .06	$ .08	$ .10	$ .06	$ .60	$ (.08)	$ .80	$ .10
Net earnings	.06	.04	.09	.08	.20	.06	.86	.09	1.21	.27
Fully diluted										
Earnings (loss) before extraordinary credits	.04	.04	.06	.08	.10	.06	.55	(.08)	.75	.10
Net earnings	.06	.04	.09	.08	.20	.06	.81	.09	1.16	.27

The second quarter of 1977 includes a gain on the sale of a plant.

Taxes on income were provided based on the estimated annual effective rate determined at the end of each quarter.

The extraordinary tax credit in 1978 represents the reduction of income taxes resulting from utilization of net operating loss carryforward and foreign tax credit carryforward and, in 1977, utilization of prior year accountig deductions for income tax purposes.

FMC Corporation's consolidated statement of income

(Dollars in thousands except per share data)	Year ended December 31 1978	1977
Revenue		
Sales	$2,912,766	$2,292,215
Equity in net earnings of affiliated companies	7,129	6,989
Other income	31,559	32,432
Total revenue	2,951,454	2,331,636
Costs and expenses		
Cost of sales	2,286,759	1,752,494
Selling, general and administrative expenses	338,358	278,748
Research and development	66,056	54,241
Interest expense	51,015	42,334
Total costs and expenses	2,742,188	2,127,817
Income before income taxes	209,266	203,819
Provision for income taxes (Note 8)	68,357	76,705
Income from continuing operations	140,909	127,114
Loss from discontinued operations (Note 15)	—	6,469
Net income	$ 140,909	$ 120,645
Earnings per common share		
Primary (Note 1)		
Income from continuing operations	$4.22	$3.80
Loss from discontinued operations	—	$ .20
Net income	$4.22	$3.60
Assuming full dilution (Note 1)		
Income from continuing operations	$3.87	$3.51
Net income	$3.87	$3.33

FMC Corporation's consolidated statement of retained earnings

(Dollars in thousands except per share data)	Year ended December 31 1978	1977
Consolidated retained earnings		
Retained earnings at beginning of year	$743,228	$661,985
Net income	140,909	120,645
Cash dividends:		
Common stock—$1.25 per share in 1978 and		
$1.10 per share in 1977	(40,074)	(35,215)
Preferred stock—$2.25 per share	(4,186)	(4,187)
Retained earnings at end of year	$839,877	$743,228

See principal accounting policies and other notes to consolidated financial statements.

FMC Corporation and Consolidated Subsidiaries

FMC Corporation's consolidated balance sheet

(Dollars in thousands, except per share data)	December 31 1978	1977
Assets		
Current assets		
Cash	$ 11,582	$ 9,208
Marketable securities	206,512	308,442
Notes and accounts receivable, less allowance for doubtful accounts (1978, $18,179; 1977, $11,544)	427,352	351,293
Inventories (Notes 3 and 4)	459,429	425,549
Other receivables, prepayments and future tax benefits	82,932	96,316
Total current assets	1,187,807	1,190,808
Investments (Notes 5 and 6)	81,228	63,867
Property, plant and equipment		
Land and improvements	98,920	91,779
Buildings	249,685	231,454
Machinery and equipment	1,154,128	1,038,629
Construction in progress	87,201	51,975
Total property, plant and equipment	1,589,934	1,413,837
Less accumulated depreciation	670,467	586,589
Net property, plant and equipment	919,467	827,248
Patents and deferred charges	19,965	21,072
Intangibles of companies acquired	40,361	38,538
Total assets	$2,248,828	$2,141,533
Liabilities and stockholders' equity		
Current liabilities		
Short-term debt	$ 48,165	$ 38,149
Accounts payable, trade and other	391,388	387,900
Accrued and other liabilities	180,769	174,611
Current portion of long-term debt (Note 7)	2,456	859
Income taxes payable (Note 8)	58,095	60,357
Total current liabilities	680,873	661,876
Long-term debt, less current portion (Note 7)	447,864	466,831
Deferred taxes (Note 8)	65,075	50,486
Minority interests in subsidiaries	5,866	10,592
Stockholders' equity (Notes 7, 9 and 10)		
Preferred stock, no par value, authorized 5,000,000 shares; issued 1,860,545 shares in 1978 and 1,860,575 shares in 1977, $2.25 cumulative convertible; preference value $93,027	11,628	11,629
Common stock, $5 par value, authorized 60,000,000 shares, issued 32,310,270 shares in 1978 and 32,303,793 shares in 1977	161,551	161,519
Capital in excess of par value of capital stock	40,727	40,521
Retained earnings	839,877	743,228
Treasury stock, common, at cost, 242,103 shares in 1978 and 269,538 shares in 1977	(4,633)	(5,149)
Total stockholders' equity	1,049,150	951,748
Total liabilities and stockholders' equity	$2,248,828	$2,141,533

Commitments and contingent liabilities (Notes 7, 11, 14 and 16)
See principal accounting policies and other notes to consolidated financial statements.

FMC Corporation and Consolidated Subsidiaries

FMC Corporation's consolidated changes in financial position

(Dollars in thousands)	1978	1977
Source of working capital		
Income from continuing operations	$140,909	$127,114
Items not affecting working capital:		
Provision for depreciation	97,228	77,986
Provision for deferred Federal income tax regarding non-current assets	14,589	8,178
Equity in earnings of affiliated companies in excess of dividends received	(6,340)	(5,525)
Unrealized translation loss on long-term debt	—	7,536
Working capital provided from continuing operations	246,386	215,289
Loss from discontinued operations	—	(6,469)
Items not affecting working capital:		
Loss on disposal of non-current assets	—	9,267
Provision for depreciation	—	1,198
Deferred Federal income tax charge regarding non-current assets	—	82
Working capital provided from discontinued operations	—	4,078
Total working capital provided from operations	246,386	219,367
Disposal of property, plant and equipment	5,821	5,128
Proceeds from long-term financing	27,725	29,270
Sale of investment in affiliate	—	31,593
Decrease in investment due to acquisition of controlling interest in affiliates	—	20,534
Decrease in patents and deferred charges	2,592	3,191
Total	282,524	309,083
Application of working capital		
Additions to property, plant and equipment	191,817	171,135
Non-current assets of companies acquired:		
Property, plant and equipment	3,451	54,680
Other, net	1,507	5,239
Dividends paid to stockholders	44,260	39,402
Reduction of long-term debt	46,732	29,431
Increase (decrease) in other investments	11,021	(5,363)
Other, net	5,734	3,210
Total	304,522	297,734
Increase (decrease) in working capital	$ (21,998)	$ 11,349
Changes in working capital		
Cash and marketable securities	$ (99,556)	$ 14,225
Trade receivables	76,059	55,015
Inventories	33,880	38,752
Other current assets	(13,384)	19,209
Increase (decrease) in current assets	(3,001)	127,201
Short-term debt	10,016	28,544
Accounts payable and accruals	9,646	85,312
Current portion of long-term debt	1,597	321
Income taxes payable	(2,262)	1,675
Increase in current liabilities	18,997	115,852
	$ (21,998)	$ 11,349

See principal accounting policies and other notes to consolidated financial statements.
FMC Corporation and Consolidated Subsidiaries

GLOSSARY

Chapter numbers following the description of each term indicate where elaborations upon the term may be found.

Absorption Costing A product costing method in which all manufacturing costs are treated as product costs. (Ch. 25)

Accelerated Depreciation Any depreciation method under which the amounts of depreciation expense taken in the earlier years of an asset's life are larger than those amounts taken later. (Ch. 10)

Account A record of the additions, deductions, and balances of individual assets, liabilities, owners' equity, revenues, and expenses. The basic component of a formal accounting system. (Ch. 2)

Accounting The process of recording, classifying, reporting, and interpreting the financial data of an organization. (Ch. 1)

Accounting Cycle Steps in the processing of business transactions during the accounting year: (1) analyzing transactions, (2) recording in journals, (3) posting to general ledger, (4) adjusting the accounts, (5) preparing financial statements, and (6) closing temporary accounts. (Ch. 3)

Accounting Entity Those people, assets, and activities devoted to a specific economic purpose and for which a separate accounting should be made. (Chs. 1, 16)

Accounting Equation An expression of the equivalency in dollar amounts of assets and equities in double entry bookkeeping; often stated as: Assets = Liabilities + Owners' Equity. (Ch. 1)

Accounting Period That time period, typically one year, to which accounting reports are related. (Ch. 16)

Accounting Principles See Generally Accepted Accounting Principles.

Accrual Basis The accounting basis whereby revenues are recognized in the period earned whether actually received or not and expenses are recognized and matched with the related revenues of the period whether actually paid or not. (Ch. 1)

Accrue To accumulate or increase; also to recognize such accumulation or increases, usually during the adjustment step of the accounting cycle. (Ch. 3)

Accumulated Depreciation A contra account to the related asset account reflecting the cumulative amounts recorded as depreciation for a specific asset or group of assets. (Chs. 1, 2)

Adjusted Gross Income An income tax term denoting the amount obtained by subtracting from gross income certain business expenses and expenses incurred in producing rents and royalties. (Ch. 28)

Adjusting Entries Those entries resulting from an attempt to reflect in the accounts various changes that may be appropriate although no source document is normally available; usually made to align recorded costs or revenues with the accounting period or to reflect unrecorded revenues and costs. (Ch. 3)

After-Tax Cash Flow The net amount of any receipt or expenditure after incorporating the effects of income taxes. (Ch. 27)

AICPA The American Institute of Certified Public Accountants, the national professional organization of CPAs in the United States. (Ch. 1)

Allowance for Uncollectible Accounts A contra asset account with a normal credit balance shown on the balance sheet as a deduction from accounts receivable to reflect the expected realizable amount of accounts receivable. (Ch. 8)

Allowance Method An accounting procedure whereby in the period in which credit sales occur, the related amount of uncollectible accounts expense is estimated and recorded in the contra asset account Allowance for Uncollectible Accounts. (Ch. 8)

Amortization The periodic writing off or charging to expense of some amount of cost (usually associated with intangible assets). (Ch. 10)

APB The Accounting Principles Board of the AICPA, a committee of the AICPA responsible for formulating accounting principles until it was replaced in 1973 by the FASB. (Ch. 1)

Appropriation of Retained Earnings Segregation or restriction of a portion of retained earnings that reduces the amount that would otherwise be available for dividends. No transfer of funds is necessarily involved, and the aggregate amount of retained earnings remains unchanged. (Ch. 14)

Articles of Co-Partnership The formal written agreement among partners setting forth important aspects of the partnership such as name, nature, duration, and location of the business, capital contributions, duties, and profit and loss ratios. (Ch. 12)

Articles of Incorporation A document prepared by persons organizing a corporation in the United States that sets forth the structure and purposes of the corporation and specifics regarding stock to be issued. (Ch. 13)

Assets Those economic resources of an entity that can usefully be expressed in monetary terms; some examples are cash, accounts receivable, inventories, and plant and equipment. (Ch. 1)

Automated Data Processing The use of mechanical-electronic machines to process data. (Ch. 6)

Average Age of Receivables Trade accounts receivable divided by year's sales multiplied by 365. (Ch. 18)

Average Rate of Return A method of capital outlay analysis that focuses on the ratio of expected average annual net income to the related average investment. (Ch. 27)

Avoidable Costs Costs that may be avoided by following some course of action. (Ch. 25)

Balance Sheet A financial report showing the financial position of an entity in terms of assets, liabilities, and owners' equity at a specific date. (Ch. 1)

Bank Reconciliation A procedure or analysis explaining the various items such as deposits in transit, checks outstanding, bank charges, and errors that lead to differences between the balance shown on a bank statement and the related cash account in the general ledger. (Ch. 7)

Betterments Extraordinary repairs to an asset resulting in increased capacity and/or extended useful life. (Ch. 10)

Bond A form of interest-bearing note payable, usually issued by the borrower for relatively long periods to a group of lenders. Bonds may incorporate a wide variety of special provisions relating to security for the debt involved, methods of paying the periodic interest payments, and maturity and retirement provisions. (Ch. 15)

Bond Discount Excess of the face value of a bond over its issue price. Bond discount arises when the coupon rate of the bond is below the market rate of interest for that type of bond. (Ch. 15)

Bond Interest Coverage Income before interest expense and income taxes divided by bond interest. Sometimes called *times interest earned*. (Ch. 18)

Bond Premium The excess of the issue price of a bond over its face value. Bond premium arises when the coupon interest rate of the bond is greater than the market rate for that type of bond. (Ch. 15)

Bond Sinking Fund A fund accumulated through required periodic contributions (and investment income thereon) to be used for the retirement of a specific bond issue. (Ch. 15)

Book Value Per Share The dollar amount of net assets represented by one share of stock; computed by dividing the amount of stockholders' equity associated with a class of stock by the outstanding number of shares of that class of stock. (Ch. 13)

Breakeven Point That level of business volume at which total revenue equals total costs. (Ch. 24)

Budgeting A process of formal financial planning. (Ch. 26)

By-products Those products having relatively little sales value compared with other products derived from a process. An example would be the wood shavings generated in a shaping department of a furniture factory. (Ch. 23)

Calendar Year Firms are said to be on a calendar year when their accounting year ends on December 31. (Ch. 3)

Capital Budgeting Planning long-term investments in plant and equipment. (Ch. 27)

Capital Gains and Losses Gains and losses from the sale or exchange of certain assets qualifying as "capital assets." Specific tax treatment of capital gains and losses depends on the length of time for which the assets were held ("short term" for one year or less, "long term" otherwise) and the net result of combining long- and short-term gains and losses. (Ch. 28)

Capital Lease A lease that transfers to the lessee substantially all of the benefits and risks related to ownership of the property. The lessee records the leased property as an asset and establishes a liability for the lease obligation. (Ch. 10)

Capital Ratios The quantitative relationship among the balances of partners' capital accounts. This is often a factor reflected in the distribution of partnership profits and may be calculated using either beginning or average balances. (Ch. 12)

Cash Basis The accounting basis in which revenues are recognized only when money is received and expenses are recognized when money is paid. (Chs. 1, 17)

Cash Discount An amount, often 1 or 2 percent of the purchase price, that a buyer may deduct for paying within the discount period. (Ch. 5)

Cash Flow Statement Also called Statement of Changes in Financial Position—Cash Basis. A statement of changes in financial position that shows the sources and uses of cash rather than net working capital. (Ch. 17)

Cash Flow *See* After-Tax Cash Flow.

Cash Over and Short An account

in which are recorded the amounts by which actual daily cash collections differ from the amounts recorded as being collected. (Ch. 7)

Cash Payback Period   A method of capital outlay analysis that considers the time in years that it will take the related net future cash inflows to equal the original investment. (Ch. 27)

Chart of Accounts   A listing of the account titles and numbers of all accounts found in the general ledger. (Ch. 3)

Check Register   A special journal used in place of a cash disbursements journal when the voucher system of controlling expenditures is used, for recording all checks written in payment of vouchers. (Ch. 7)

Closing Procedures   The final step in the accounting cycle in which the balances in all temporary accounts are transferred to the owners' capital account, leaving the temporary accounts with zero balances. (Ch. 3)

Collection Bases   Bases for those infrequently used procedures in which revenue recognition is delayed until related amounts of cash are collected. The cost recovery basis and the installment basis are examples. (Ch. 16)

Common-Size Statements   A form of financial statement analysis in which only the relative percentages of financial statement items, rather than their customary dollar amounts, are shown. (Ch. 18)

Common Stock   Basic ownership class of corporate capital stock, carrying the right to vote, share in earnings, participate in future stock issues, and share in any liquidation proceeds after prior claims have been settled. (Ch. 13)

Comparative Financial Statements   A form of horizontal financial analysis involving comparison of two or more periods' statements with dollar and percentage changes shown. (Ch. 18)

Compound Journal Entry   An entry containing more than one debit and/or credit entry. (Ch. 3)

Conservatism   An accounting principle dictating that judgmental determinations in accounting should tend toward understatement rather than overstatement of assets and income. (Ch. 16)

Consistency   An accounting principle dictating that, unless otherwise disclosed, accounting reports are to be prepared on a basis consistent with the preceding period. (Ch. 16)

Consolidated Statements   Financial statements prepared with intercompany (reciprocal) accounts eliminated in order to portray the financial position and operating results of two or more affiliated companies as a single economic entity. (Ch. 19)

Consolidation   A union of firms such that the existing firms exchange their properties for the securities of a new firm and the old firms dissolve. (Ch. 19)

Consumer Price Index   A price-level index of consumer goods and services published monthly by the Bureau of Labor Statistics of the Department of Labor. (Ch. 16)

Contingent Liability   A potential obligation, the eventual occurrence of which usually depends on some future event beyond the control of the firm. Contingent liabilities may originate with lawsuits, credit guarantees, and contested income tax assessments. (Ch. 11)

Contribution Margin   The excess of revenue over variable costs; thus, the amount contributed toward the absorption of fixed cost and eventually the generation of profit. (Ch. 24)

Contribution Margin Ratio   That portion of the sales price that is contribution margin. (Ch. 24)

Control Account   A general ledger account, the balance of which reflects the aggregate balances of many related subsidiary accounts. Most firms maintain such records for credit customers and for creditors. (Ch. 6)

Controller   Usually the highest ranking accounting officer in a firm. (Ch. 1)

Convertible Bond   A bond incorporating the right of the bondholder to convert the bond to capital stock under prescribed terms. (Ch. 15)

Corporation   A legal entity created by the granting of a charter from an appropriate governmental authority and owned by stockholders who have limited liability for corporate debt. (Ch. 13)

Cost Behavior Analysis   Study of the ways in which specific costs respond to changes in the volume of business activity. (Ch. 24)

Cost Center   Sometimes called expense centers. A division of a business with which specific costs can be identified. (Ch. 20)

Cost Method   A method of accounting by a parent company for investments in subsidiary companies in which the parent company maintains the investment in subsidiary account at its cost, not recognizing periodically its share of subsidiary income or loss. *See also* Equity Method. (Ch. 19)

Cost of Capital   *See* Weighted Average Cost of Capital.

Cost of Goods Manufactured   *See* Manufacturing Costs.

Cost of Production Report   A periodic summary of the costs associated with a processing cost center and the calculation of per unit costs for work in process and finished units transferred out. (Ch. 23)

CPA   Certified Public Accountant, a professional accountant who has passed the Uniform CPA Examination, satisfied other requirements regarding education, professional experience, and character, and been licensed to practice public accounting by a state, district, or territory. (Ch. 1)

Credit (Entry) An entry on the right-hand side (or in the credit column) of any account. (Ch. 2)

Credit Memorandum A form used by a seller to notify a customer of a reduction in the amount considered owed by the customer. (Ch. 5)

Current Assets Those assets that will either be used up or converted to cash within the normal operating cycle of the business or one year, whichever is longer. (Ch. 5)

Current Liabilities All obligations that will require within the coming year or the operating cycle, whichever is longer, (1) the use of existing current assets or (2) the creation of other current liabilities. (Ch. 11)

Current Ratio Current assets divided by current liabilities. (Ch. 18)

Current Value The market or economic value of some item at a point in time. (Ch. 16)

Current Value Accounting An approach to accounting based on some version of current economic values (such as replacement costs), in contrast to historical costs. Typically, some form of realized or unrealized holding gains and losses are recognized. (Ch. 16)

Data Processing System The various recording, storing, and printing machines and related records that make up a firm's information processing system. (Ch. 6)

Debit (Entry) An entry on the left-hand side (or in the debit column) of any account. (Ch. 2)

Debit Memorandum A form issued by a customer requesting some adjustment in the amount owed to the vendor. (Ch. 5)

Declaration of Estimated Tax Income tax procedures requiring taxpayers with minimum amounts of income not subject to income tax withholding to submit quarterly estimates and payments of related income taxes owed. (Ch. 28)

Deferred Tax Accounts Accounts used in interperiod income tax allocation procedure, in which are recorded differences between the amounts of income taxes actually paid and amounts recognized in the accounts. Excess payments are Deferred Tax Charges; an excess of amounts recognized over taxes paid are Deferred Tax Credits. (Ch. 16)

Deficit A negative (or debit) balance in the retained earnings account of a corporation. (Ch. 14)

Departmental Contribution The excess of departmental gross profit over direct departmental expenses; contributed to the absorption of the firm's pool of common or indirect costs. (Ch. 20)

Depletion Accounting Determination of the estimated average unit cost of natural resources acquired or developed, such as mineral deposits and timber, and recognition of periodic depletion expense in proportion to the fraction of the total resources available that is extracted and sold each operating period. (Ch. 10)

Depreciation The decline in economic potential of limited-life assets originating from wear, deterioration, and obsolescence. (Ch. 10)

Depreciation Expense That portion of the original utility and cost of a tangible constructed asset that is recognized as having expired and thus becomes an expense. (Chs. 1, 10)

Differential Analysis A concept of limiting consideration in a decision situation to only those factors that will differ among alternatives. (Ch. 25)

Differential Costs Those costs that will differ between two courses of action. (Ch. 25)

Direct Expenses (Costs) Those costs that can be readily identi-fied with a particular department or activity. (Ch. 20)

Direct Labor All labor of workers applying their skills directly to the manufacture of products. The labor of workers indirectly supporting the manufacturing process is accounted for as indirect labor, part of factory overhead. (Ch. 21)

Direct (or Raw) Materials All important raw materials or parts physically making up the product. Incidental amounts of materials are accounted for as indirect materials, a part of factory overhead. (Ch. 21)

Direct Write-Off Method An accounting procedure in which uncollectible accounts are charged to expense in the period they are determined to be uncollectible. (Ch. 8)

Discontinued Operations Those operating segments of a company that have been sold, abandoned, or disposed of during the operating period. Related operating income (or loss) and related gains or losses on disposal are to be reported separately on the income statement. (Ch. 14)

Discount Period The number of days beyond the related sales invoice date during which payment entitles the buyer to deduct any cash discount offered (often 1 or 2%). (Ch. 5)

Discounts Lost An account reflecting the amount of cash discounts available but not taken. *See* Net Price Method of Recording Purchases. (Ch. 6)

Dividend A distribution to stockholders of a corporation usually in cash, sometimes in the stock of the corporation and known as a stock dividend, and much less frequently in property and known as a dividend in kind. (Ch. 13)

Dividend Payout Ratio Common stock dividends divided by common stock earnings. (Ch. 18)

Double Declining-Balance Depreciation Method A depreciation method that allocates depreciation expense to each year in an accelerated pattern by applying a constant percentage to the declining net book value of the asset. A constant percentage equal to twice the straight-line rate is currently allowed by the IRS for new depreciable assets. (Ch. 10)

Double Entry Accounting System A method of accounting that recognizes the duality of a transaction (source and disposition) such that any change in one account also causes a change in another account. For example, the receipt of cash would result in an increase in the cash account but would also require the recognition of an increase in liability, owners' equity, or revenue account or a decrease in an expense account or in some other asset account. (Ch. 2)

Earnings Per Share Net income less any preferred dividend requirements divided by the number of common shares outstanding. (Chs. 14, 18)

Effective Interest Amortization A method of allocating bond premium or discount to various periods that results in a constant effective rate of interest and varying periodic amortization allocations. (Ch. 15, App. A)

Effective Tax Rate The amount of tax liability divided by related taxable income. (Ch. 28)

Equity Method A method of accounting by parent companies for investments in subsidiaries in which the parent's share of subsidiary income or loss is periodically recorded in the parent company's accounts. *See also* Cost Method. (Ch. 19)

Equity Ratio Stockholders' equity divided by total assets. (Ch. 18)

Equivalent Units The smaller number of full measures of work accomplished that is the equivalent of a larger number of par-

tially accomplished work units. For example, 1,000 units 60% processed is equivalent to 600 units fully processed. (Ch. 23)

Excess Present Value Index Ratio of the total present value of net future cash flows to the related cash investment. (Ch. 27)

Expenses Expired costs incurred by a firm in the process of earning revenue. (Ch. 1)

Factory Overhead All manufacturing costs not considered direct materials or direct labor, including indirect materials, indirect labor, and factory depreciation, taxes, and insurance. (Ch. 22)

FASB The Financial Accounting Standards Board of the American Institute of CPAs, a nongovernmental group organized in 1973 to replace the Accounting Principles Board and to promulgate authoritative rules for the general practice of financial accounting. (Ch. 1)

Federal Unemployment Taxes (FUTA) A federal tax levied against employers to help finance administration of the various unemployment compensation programs operated by the states. (Ch. 11)

FICA Federal Insurance Contribution Act under which the income of an individual is taxed to support a national social security program providing retirement income, medical care, and death benefits. Employers pay a matching amount of tax on their eligible employees. (Ch. 11)

FIFO (First-In, First-Out) Inventory Pricing A valuation method that assumes that the oldest (earliest purchased) goods on hand are sold first, resulting in an ending inventory priced at the most recent acquisition prices. (Ch. 9)

Financial Accounting Those accounting activities leading pri-

marily to publishable, general purpose financial statements such as the income statement, statement of financial position, and statement of changes in financial position. (Ch. 1)

Finished Goods Units of product for which production has been completed. (Ch. 21)

Finished Goods Ledger A record of the amounts acquired, sold, and on hand, and the related costs of a specific finished product. In aggregate, finished goods ledger cards serve as a perpetual inventory record of finished goods and as a subsidiary ledger for the Finished Goods account. (Ch. 22)

Fiscal Year Firms are said to be on a fiscal year when their accounting year ends on a date other than December 31. (Ch. 3)

Fixed Assets Sometimes called long-term assets, long-lived assets, or plant and equipment. May include land, building, fixtures, and equipment. (Chs. 5, 10)

Fixed Costs Those costs whose total remains constant within the relevant range even though the volume of activity may vary. (Ch. 24)

Flexible Budget A financial plan formulated so that the operating volume assumed can be varied to agree with actual volume of activities attained. (Chs. 24, 26)

F.O.B. ("Free on Board") Term used in conjunction with the terms factory, shipping point, or destination to indicate the point in the delivery of merchandise at which the purchaser begins to bear freight costs. (Ch. 5)

Full Disclosure An accounting principle stipulating that all facts necessary to make financial statements not misleading must be disclosed. (Ch. 16)

Funds Defined most narrowly as cash; more widely considered to be the amount of net working capital or current assets less current liabilities. (Ch. 17)

General Journal A record of original entry in which are recorded all transactions not recorded in the special journals maintained by the business. (Ch. 6)

General Ledger A grouping or binding of the accounts in which the activities of an entity are recorded. (Ch. 2)

Generally Accepted Accounting Principles A group of standards or guides to action in preparing financial accounting reports. Their content and usefulness have evolved over many decades. (Chs. 1, 16)

Going Concern An accounting principle dictating that, in the absence of evidence to the contrary, a business is assumed to have an indefinite life. (Chs. 1, 16)

Goodwill That value that derives from the ability of a firm to earn more than a normal rate of return on its physical assets. Goodwill is recognized in the accounts only when it is acquired through specific purchase and payment (as opposed to gradual development). (Ch. 10)

Governmental Accounting A subdivision of accounting practice relating primarily to accounting for federal, state, or local governmental units. (Ch. 1)

Gross Profit The excess of sales price over the net delivered cost of the product sold (sometimes called gross margin). (Ch. 5)

Gross Profit Inventory Method A procedure for estimating the cost of ending inventories by multiplying the representative cost of goods sold percentage times sales and deducting that amount from goods available for sale. (Ch. 9)

Hardware A term used to describe the computer and its associated equipment. (Ch. 6)

Historical Cost The money equivalent of the object given up (and/or those obligations assumed) in an exchange transaction. (Chs. 1, 10, 16)

Horizontal Analysis See Trend Analysis.

Income Averaging A tax regulation provision allowing those having relatively large amounts of taxable income in one year to, in effect, average that income over several years in order to reduce the progressive effects of the tax rates. (Ch. 28)

Income Statement A financial report showing the results of an entity's operations in terms of revenues, expenses, and net income for a period of time. (Ch. 1)

Income Summary Account An account used only during the closing procedures and to which all temporary revenue and expense accounts are closed. At this point, the balance in the Income Summary account summarizes the firm's net income for the period. In turn, the Income Summary account is closed to the owners' capital account. (Ch. 4)

Incremental Cost See Differential Expenses.

Indirect Expenses (Costs) Those costs (expenses) that are not readily identified with a particular department and are often allocated among departments on some rational basis. (Ch. 20)

Individual Earnings Record A detailed record maintained by an employer for each employee showing gross earnings, overtime premiums, all withholdings, payroll tax data, and net earnings paid, by calendar quarter. (Ch. 11)

Information System The coordinated efforts to record, organize, and present analyses and reports related to specific areas of activity and concern. (Ch. 1)

Installment Accounts Those accounts receivable or payable for which payments or collections are routinely scheduled over extended periods such as 24 or 36 months. (Ch. 8)

Intangible Assets A term applied by convention to a group of long-term assets that generally do not have physical existence, including patents, copyrights, franchises, trademarks, and goodwill. (Ch. 10)

Interactive Processing A type of processing in which master file information in an electronic data processing system is available at random, and transactions may be processed in any order. (Ch. 6)

Interim Financial Statements Financial statements prepared at dates other than the closing of the firm's accounting year. Most monthly and quarterly financial statements are interim statements. (Ch. 4)

Internal Auditing A continuing appraisal of a firm's operations accomplished by the firm's own internal audit staff to determine whether management's financial and operating policies are being properly implemented. (Ch. 1)

Internal Control A plan of organization and all of the coordinate methods and measures adopted within a business to safeguard its assets, check the accuracy and reliability of its accounting data, promote operating efficiency, and encourage adherence to prescribed managerial policies. (Ch. 7)

Internal Revenue Code The codification of numerous revenue acts passed by Congress since 1913. Interpretation and application of the Code is supplemented by extensive Internal Revenue Code Regulations. (Ch. 28)

Interperiod Income Tax Allocation Apportionment of income tax expense to the income statement over the time periods affected by timing differences between the recognition of revenue and expense on accounting statements and on related income tax returns. (Ch. 16)

Inventory Turnover Cost of goods sold divided by average inventory. (Ch. 18)

Investment Credit An income tax provision allowing taxpayers to deduct from what would otherwise be their tax liability in the year of acquisition certain portions of the cost of newly acquired assets. (Ch. 28)

Investments A category on the balance sheet where assets consisting of securities of other companies, sinking funds, and other long-term holdings are reported. Temporary investments in marketable securities are properly shown as current assets. (Ch. 15)

Invoice A document used in business transactions that sets forth the precise terms regarding date, customer, vendor, quantities, prices, and freight and credit terms of a transaction. (Ch. 5)

Invoice Register A special journal, sometimes called a purchase journal, in which all acquisitions on account are chronologically recorded. (Ch. 6)

IRS The Internal Revenue Service of the federal government, primarily responsible for applying the current tax codes and regulations and collection of income taxes for the federal government. (Ch. 28)

Job Cost Sheets A record of the specific manufacturing costs applied to a given job. When fully recorded, job cost sheets serve as a subsidiary ledger to the Work in Process account. (Ch. 22)

Job Order Cost Accounting A method of cost accounting, sometimes called job lot or specific order costing, in which manufacturing costs are assigned to specific jobs or batches of specialized products. (Ch. 22)

Joint Costs Those costs common to two or more products or activities. (Ch. 23)

Joint Products Two or more products having significant value and derived from common inputs such as materials or processing. (Ch. 23)

Journals Tabular records in which business transactions are analyzed in terms of debits and credits and recorded in chronological order before being posted to the general ledger accounts. (Ch. 3)

Lease A contract between the lessor (owner) and lessee (tenant) for the rental of property. (Ch. 10)

Leasehold Improvements Those expenditures made by the lessee to alter or improve leased property. Such improvements typically revert to the lessor upon termination of the lease. (Ch. 10)

Liabilities Present obligations resulting from past transactions that require the firm to pay money, provide goods, or perform services in the future. (Ch. 11)

LIFO (Last-In, First-Out) Inventory Pricing A valuation method that assumes that the most recently purchased goods are sold first, resulting in an ending inventory priced at the earliest related acquisition prices experienced. (Ch. 9)

Long-term Assets Relatively long-lived assets employed in operating the firm. Some examples are land, buildings, and equipment. Sometimes called fixed assets or plant and equipment. (Chs. 5, 10)

Long-term Liabilities Debt obligations of the firm not due within the current operating cycle of the firm or one year, whichever is longer. Examples are mortgage notes payable and bonds payable. (Ch. 15)

Lower of Cost or Market Rule An accounting procedure providing for inventories to be carried at their acquisition price or their replacement price at the balance sheet date, whichever is lower. (Ch. 9)

Management by Exception The practice of focusing the manager's attention on those aspects of operations that deviate from planned or expected results. (Ch. 26)

Managerial Accounting Those accounting procedures carried out by an organization's accounting staff primarily to furnish its management with accounting analyses and reports needed for decision making. (Chs. 1, 25)

Manufacturing Costs Those costs, comprising raw materials, direct labor, and factory overhead, necessary to bring the product to the point of completion. Selling and nonfactory administrative costs are specifically excluded. (Ch. 21)

Manufacturing Margin The excess of revenues over variable manufacturing costs; an amount often presented on variable costing income statements. (Ch. 25)

Manufacturing Summary Account An account (used only during closing procedures) to which all temporary manufacturing costs and expenses are closed, resulting in a balance equal to the cost of goods manufactured. In turn, the Manufacturing Summary account is closed to the Income Summary account. (Ch. 21)

Marginal Cost The cost associated with completing one more unit of production or activity. (Ch. 25)

Marginal Tax Rate The tax rate applicable to additional increments of taxable income, especially relevant to considering the after-tax consequence of proposed transactions. (Ch. 28)

Mark-up Percentage The amount of gross profit expressed as a percentage of sales. (Ch. 5)

Master Budget A comprehensive plan comprising all operating budgets related to sales, production, operating expenses, and finance. May include pro forma financial statements for the budgeting period. (Ch. 26)

Matching Expenses with Revenues

An accounting principle requiring that, to the extent feasible, all expenses related to given revenues be deducted from those revenues for the determination of periodic income. (Ch. 16)

Materiality The concept that accounting transactions so small or insignificant as to not affect one's actions may be recorded as is most expedient. (Ch. 16)

Measuring Unit The unit of measure in an accounting transaction, typically the base money unit of the most relevant currency. (Chs. 1, 16)

Merchandise Inventory An asset account in which is recorded the purchase price of merchandise held for resale. Sometimes simply termed inventory. (Ch. 5)

Merchandising The business activity of buying and selling goods already made, in contrast to a manufacturer or a service-oriented business. (Ch. 5)

Merger A union of firms in which one company acquires the assets of another and the latter company dissolves. (Ch. 19)

Minicomputer A small computer designed for small- and medium-scale processing that can be operated by personnel with a minimum of training. (Ch. 6)

Minority Interest That portion of capital stock in a subsidiary corporation not owned by the controlling (parent) company. (Ch. 19)

Monetary Items Those assets and liabilities representing money or a claim for a fixed number of dollars in the future regardless of changes in price levels. Examples are cash, receivables, investments in notes and bonds, and most liabilities. (Ch. 16)

Multiple-step Income Statement An income statement in which one or more intermediate amounts (such as gross profit on sales) are derived before the ordinary, continuing income is reported. (Ch. 14)

Net Income The excess of revenues earned over related expenses incurred, usually portrayed by the final figure on the income statement. (Ch. 1)

Net Present Value Analysis A method of capital outlay analysis that compares a required investment amount with the present value of resulting net future cash flows discounted at the minimum desired rate of return. (Ch. 27)

Net Price Method of Recording Purchases An accounting procedure whereby purchases are recorded at amounts that anticipate the taking of any cash discounts available. When discounts are not taken, the amounts paid in excess of the recorded purchase price are charged to the account Discounts Lost. (Ch. 6)

Normal Balance The debit or credit balance of an account corresponding to the side of the account on which increases are recorded (debits for assets and expenses; credits for liabilities, owners' equity, and revenues). (Ch. 2)

Notes Receivable Discounted An account usually shown on the balance sheet as a contra account to Notes Receivable; used to record the amount of notes discounted (sold) to others with recourse and disclosing the contingent liability stemming from the possibility that the original maker of the note will default and the firm will become liable for payment of the note. (Ch. 8)

Objectivity An accounting principle requiring that, whenever possible, accounting entries be based on objective (verifiable) evidence. (Chs. 1, 16)

Opportunity Cost Those measurable sacrifices associated with forgoing some alternative. (Ch. 25)

Organization Costs Expenditures incurred in launching a business

(usually a corporation); may include attorney's fees, various registration fees paid to state governments, and other start-up costs. (Ch. 10)

Out-of-Pocket Costs Costs requiring expenditures in the current period. (Ch. 25)

Overapplied Overhead The excess of overhead applied to production over the amount of overhead incurred. Such amounts are shown on interim balance sheets as deferred credits but are closed to cost of goods sold on year-end financial statements. (Ch. 22)

Overhead Rate The amount of overhead costs for some period divided by the amount of some measure of production activity such as direct labor hours. May be calculated on an actual cost incurred basis or on an estimated or predetermined basis. (Ch. 22)

Owners' Equity The interest or claim of an entity's owners in the entity's assets; equal to the excess of assets over liabilities. (Ch. 1)

Par Value An amount specified in the corporate charter for each share of stock and imprinted on the face of each stock certificate. Usually determines the legal capital of the corporation. (Ch. 13)

Parent Company A company holding all or a majority of the stock of another company, which is called a subsidiary. (Ch. 19)

Partnership A voluntary association of two or more persons for the purpose of conducting a business for a profit. (Ch. 12)

Percentage of Completion A method of revenue recognition that allocates the estimated gross profit on a long-term project among the several accounting periods involved, in proportion to the estimated percentage of the contract completed each period. (Ch. 16)

Performance Reports Documents

portraying, for a given operating unit, planned amounts of cost, actual costs incurred, and any related variances. (Ch. 26)

Period Costs (Expenses) Those costs (expenses) associated with the time period in which they are incurred (rather than with the product being produced). (Ch. 21)

Periodic Inventory Method A method of accounting for inventories in which no record is made in the inventory account for the purchase or sale of merchandise at the time of such transactions. (Ch. 5)

Perpetual Inventory Method A method of accounting for inventories in which both purchases and sales of merchandise are reflected in the inventory account at the time such transactions occur. (Chs. 5, 9)

Personal Exemptions A prescribed amount that a taxpayer may deduct for himself or herself and each qualified dependent in computing taxable income. Additional exemptions are allowed for taxpayers who are 65 years of age or older and/or blind. (Ch. 28)

Petty Cash Fund A special, relatively small cash fund established for making minor cash disbursements in the operation of a business. (Ch. 7)

Plant Assets See Long-term Assets.

Plant (or Equipment) Ledger A subsidiary ledger for long-lived assets, containing detailed data for each material asset, including description, acquisition date, location, cost, depreciation, and disposition. (Ch. 10)

Pooling of Interests Uniting of ownership interests of two or more companies through the exchange of 90% or more of the firms' voting stocks. (Ch. 19)

Post-Closing Trial Balance A listing of account titles and each of their balances after closing entries have been recorded and posted; all temporary accounts should have zero balances. (Ch. 4)

Posting The formal transcribing of amounts from the journals to the ledger(s) used in an accounting system. (Ch. 3)

Posting References A series of abbreviations used in the posting step of the accounting cycle to indicate to where or from where some entry was posted; account numbers and one- or two-letter abbreviations of journal titles are typically used. (Ch. 3)

Predetermined Overhead Rates Estimated overhead rates determined in advance for applying overhead to production during an operating period (usually one year). The rate is calculated by dividing total estmated overhead costs by the estimated amount of the activity (such as direct labor hours) used to assign factory overhead. See Factory Overhead. (Ch. 22)

Preemptive Right The right of a stockholder to maintain his or her proportionate ownership in a corporation by having the right to purchase an appropriate share of any new stock issue. (Ch. 13)

Preferred Stock A class of corporate capital stock typically receiving priority over common stock in the matter of dividend payments and distribution of assets should the corporation be liquidated. (Ch. 13)

Present Value The estimated current worth of amounts to be received (or paid) in the future from which appropriate amounts of discount (or interest) have been deducted. (Ch. 15, App. A, Ch. 27)

Present Value Factors Sometimes called discount factors. Multipliers found in present value tables formulated to show the present value of one dollar (or a one dollar annuity) discounted at various interest rates and for various time periods. (Ch. 15, App. A, Ch. 27)

Price-Earnings Ratio The market price of a share of stock divided by the related earnings per share. (Ch. 18)

Price Index A series of measurements, stated as percentages, indicating the relationship between the weighted average price of a sample of goods and services at various points in time and the weighted average price of a similar sample of goods and services at a common, or base, date. (Ch. 16)

Price Level Conversions Restatement of amounts stated in dollars of a particular price level to an amount appropriate for the price levels at another time. (Ch. 16)

Process Cost Accounting A method of assigning costs to relatively homogeneous products in an often continuous, high-volume operation. (Ch. 23)

Product Costs Those costs properly associated with the product being produced (as opposed to the time period in which the costs were incurred). Product costs become period costs (expenses) when the related products are sold. (Ch. 21)

Production Report A report (usually for a department) showing the beginning inventory of units, units started, units finished and transferred out, and any ending inventory of units. (Ch. 23)

Productivity Ratio See Return on Assets.

Profit Center A division of a business with which both costs and revenues, and thus profit, can be identified. (Ch. 20)

Promissory Note A written promise to pay a certain sum of money on demand or at a determinable future time. (Ch. 8)

Proprietorship A form of business organization in which one person owns the business; sometimes termed sole proprietorship. (Ch. 1)

Purchase Order A document completed by the purchasing firm setting forth the quantities, descriptions, prices, and vendor for merchandise to be purchased. (Ch. 5)

Purchase Requisition   A form used within a firm to initiate the procedures leading to the purchase of needed items. (Ch. 5)

Purchases   The title of the account in which is recorded the acquisition price of merchandise held for resale by companies using the periodic inventory method. (Ch. 5)

Purchasing Power   The ability to purchase goods or services. The purchasing power of money decreases when price levels increase in that it takes more money to purchase a given amount of goods or services. (Ch. 16)

Raw Materials   All factory materials acquired but not yet placed in production. (Often a synonym for direct materials.) (Ch. 21)

Raw Materials Ledger Card   A record of the amounts received, issued, and on hand and related costs of a specific raw material item. In aggregate, raw materials ledger cards serve as a perpetual inventory record and as a subsidiary ledger for the Raw Materials account. (Ch. 22)

Real Time Processing   Updating computer records at the time transactions occur. (Ch. 6)

Receivable   An amount due from a customer, employee, or other party, usually further described as an account receivable or note receivable and representing an asset of the business. (Ch. 7)

Receiving Report   A document used within a firm to formally record the quantities and descriptions of merchandise received. (Ch. 5)

Records of Original Entry   Usually, the various journals incorporated in the firm's accounting system. *See also* Journals. (Ch. 3)

Relevant Range   That range of changes in the volume of activity within which the assumptions made regarding cost behavior patterns are valid. (Ch. 24)

Replacement Costs   The current cash equivalent necessary to duplicate some asset. (Ch. 16)

Retail Inventory Estimation Method   A procedure for estimating ending inventories by (1) maintaining detailed records of all goods acquired and on hand at both retail and cost prices (and any changes in these), (2) calculating a cost-to-retail percentage, (3) estimating ending inventory at retail prices by subtracting sales from the retail price of merchandise available for sale, and (4) reducing the estimated inventory at retail to cost by applying the cost-to-retail percentage. (Ch. 9)

Return on Assets   Income before interest expense and income tax divided by average total assets. (Ch. 18)

Return on Sales   Net income divided by net sales. (Ch. 18)

Return on Stockholders' Equity   Net income less preferred dividends divided by average common stockholders' equity. (Ch. 18)

Revenue   The amount of cash received or claims established against customers stemming from the provision of goods or services by the firm. (Ch. 1)

Revenue Recognition at Point of Sale   An accounting principle requiring that, with few exceptions, revenues be recognized at the point of sale. (Ch. 16)

Reversing Entries   A bookkeeping technique whereby adjusting entries involving subsequent receipts or payments are literally reversed on the first day of the following accounting period. The net result of this procedure is to permit the routine recording of subsequent related receipts and payments without having to recognize the portions that were ac-

crued at an earlier date. (Ch. 4)

Running Balance Account   An account form having columns for debit entries, credit entries, and for the account balance. Sometimes called the "three-column" account form. (Ch. 1)

Sales   The title of the account in which revenues from the sale of goods held for resale are recorded for merchandising and manufacturing companies. (Ch. 5)

Sales Returns and Allowances   A contra account to Sales in which is recorded the selling price of merchandise returned by customers and/or the amounts of sales price adjustments allowed customers. (Ch. 5)

SEC   Securities and Exchange Commission, the federal agency that regulates the sale and exchange of most securities. (Ch. 1)

Segmentation of a Business   The division of a business into subunits along organizational lines such as departments, divisions, branches, or subsidiaries or according to areas of economic activity such as industries, product lives, markets, or geographic areas. (Ch. 20)

Semivariable Costs   Those costs, sometimes called mixed costs, the total of which responds, but less than proportionately, to changes in the volume of activity. (Ch. 24)

Sequential Processing   A type of processing in which transaction data must be organized in a particular order, and all master files must be read. (Ch. 6)

Service Departments   Those departments or cost centers that provide special support activities to various production departments. Examples are purchasing, personnel, and maintenance departments. (Ch. 23)

Shared Costs   Those costs whose benefit is shared by two or more departments. (Ch. 20)

Single-step Income Statement An income statement in which the ordinary, continuing income of the business is derived in one step by subtracting total expenses from total revenues. (Ch. 14)

Sinking Fund Cash and other assets accumulated and segregated for some specific purpose such as retiring debt. (Ch. 15)

Software A term used to describe the programs, written procedures, and other documentation associated with use of computers. (Ch. 6)

Source Document Any written document evidencing a business transaction, such as a bank check or deposit slip, sales invoice, or cash register tape. (Ch. 3)

Special Journals Those journals, or records of original entry other than the general journal, that are designed for recording specific types of transactions such as cash receipts, sales, purchases, and cash disbursements. (Ch. 6)

Specific Identification Inventory Pricing A method involving the physical identification of goods actually sold and goods remaining on hand and pricing the latter at the actual prices paid for them. (Ch. 9)

Standard Costs Those costs, usually expressed on a per-unit basis, that under ideal operating conditions should be incurred for direct materials, direct labor, and factory overhead. (Ch. 26)

Standard Deduction A prescribed amount that may be deducted from adjusted gross income by a taxpayer in lieu of itemizing his or her deductible personal expenses. (Ch. 28)

State Unemployment Tax A payroll tax levied on employers by states to finance state unemployment compensation programs. (Ch. 11)

Stated Value A nominal amount that may be assigned to each share of no par stock and accounted for much as if it were par

value. (Ch. 13)

Statement of Changes in Financial Position A statement showing for a period of time the resources provided and resources applied and thus explaining the change in funds during the period for the firm. (Ch. 17)

Statement of Financial Position An alternate title for a balance sheet, a financial statement showing an entity's financial position in terms of assets, liabilities, and owners' equity at a specific date. (Ch. 1)

Statement of Owners' Equity A financial statement reflecting the beginning balance, additions to, deductions from, and the ending balance of owners' equity for a specified time period. (Ch. 1)

Stock Dividends Additional shares of its own stock issued by a corporation to its present stockholders in proportion to their present ownership interests. (Ch. 14)

Stock Split Additional shares of its own stock issued by a corporation to its present stockholders in proportion to their current ownership interests without changing the balances in the related stockholders' equity accounts. A stock split increases the number of shares outstanding and reduces the per-share market value of the stock. (Ch. 14)

Straight-Line Depreciation Method Allocates uniform amounts of depreciation expense to each full period of an asset's useful life. (Ch. 10)

Subchapter S Corporations Those corporations qualifying for income tax treatment as partnerships. (Ch. 28)

Subsidiary Company See Parent Company.

Subsidiary Ledger A group of accounts, not part of the general ledger, that explain or reflect the detail (such as individual customer balances) underlying the

balance in a related control account (such as Accounts Receivable) in the general ledger. (Ch. 6)

Sum-of-the-Years'-Digits Depreciation Method An accelerated depreciation method that allocates depreciation expense to each year in a fractional proportion, the denominator of which is the sum of the years' digits in the useful life of the asset. (Ch. 10)

Sunk Costs Past costs that cannot be recovered. (Ch. 25)

T Account An abbreviated form of the formal account; use is usually limited to illustrations of accounting techniques. (Ch. 2)

Tax Allocation within a Period The apportionment of total income taxes among the various sources of income or loss shown on an income statement. (Ch. 14)

Tax Avoidance Arrangement of business affairs in such a way as to minimize the impact of income taxes; in contrast to tax evasion, tax avoidance is legal and considered an aspect of sound management. (Ch. 28)

Tax Credit (or Income Tax Credit) An amount that may be deducted directly from what would otherwise be the tax liability disregarding the tax credit. (Ch. 28)

Tax Evasion A deliberate misstatement of factors determining taxable income. Tax evasion is illegal and subjects the taxpayer to legal prosecution. *See also* Tax Avoidance. (Ch. 28)

Tax Shelter An investment that by its nature or by qualifying for special tax treatment creates either tax-exempt income or anticipated deductible tax losses (which shelter other income from income taxation). (Ch. 28)

Taxable Income Gross income less deductions from gross income, itemized personal expenses (or a standard deduction), and personal exemptions. (Ch. 28)

Time Value of Money An expression of the ability of money to earn interest, the total potential for which is a function of the principal amount, the applicable interest rate, and the time period involved. (Ch. 11, App. A, Ch. 27)

Trade Discounts The differences between suggested retail prices and those prices at which wholesale purchasers are able to buy merchandise. (Ch. 5)

Trade Receivables and Payables Those assets and liabilities arising from the ordinary open account transactions between a business and its regular trade customers or suppliers. (Ch. 8)

Trading on the Equity The use of borrowed funds to generate a return in excess of the interest rate that must be paid for the funds. (Ch. 18)

Transaction Any event or activity of the firm leading to entries in two or more accounts. (Ch. 1)

Transportation In An account for recording the freight charges on merchandise purchased and held for resale. (Ch. 5)

Transportation Out An account for recording the freight charges incurred in the delivery of merchandise sold to customers. (Ch. 5)

Treasury Stock Shares of outstanding stock that have been reacquired by the issuing corporation for purposes other than retiring the stock. Treasury stock is recorded at cost and the account is shown on the balance sheet as a deduction from total stockholders' equity. (Ch. 13)

Trend Analysis An approach to financial statement analysis involving comparison of the same item over two or more years. Often trend percentages are calculated by choosing a base year and stating the amounts of subsequent years as a percentage of that base year. (Ch. 18)

Trial Balance A listing of the account titles in the general ledger, their respective debit or credit balances, and the totals of all accounts having debit balances and all accounts having credit balances. (Ch. 2)

Unadjusted Trial Balance A trial balance of the general ledger accounts taken before the adjusting step of the accounting cycle. (Ch. 4)

Uncollectible Accounts Those receivables, sometimes called doubtful accounts, the collection of which is not expected to occur in the normal course of credit transactions. (Ch. 8)

Uncollectible Accounts Expense The expense stemming from the inability of a business to collect an amount previously recorded as a receivable. Sometimes called bad debts expense. Normally classified as a selling or administrative expense. (Ch. 8)

Underapplied Overhead The excess of actual overhead costs incurred over the amounts applied to production. On interim balance sheets such amounts appear as deferred charges but are closed to cost of goods sold on year-end statements. (Ch. 22)

Units of Production Depreciation Method A depreciation method that allocates depreciation expense to each operating period in proportion to the amount of the asset's expected total production capacity used each period. (Ch. 10)

Variable Costing A product costing method in which only variable manufacturing costs are associated with the product; fixed manufacturing costs are treated as period costs in the period incurred. (Ch. 25)

Variable Costs Those costs the to-

tal of which responds proportionately to changes in volume of activity. (Ch. 25)

Variances Differences, which may be favorable or unfavorable, between standard costs and actual costs. Variances are usually isolated for price and usage factors for raw materials and rate and efficacy factors for direct labor. For factory overhead, variances may be isolated for factors related to spending, efficiency, and volume. (Ch. 26, App. B)

Vertical Analysis An approach to financial statement analysis highlighting the quantitative relationship between amounts in the same financial statement. (Ch. 18)

Voucher Register A special journal or record of original entry (in lieu of a purchases journal) for recording in numerical order all vouchers supporting the disbursement of funds. (Ch. 7)

Voucher System A system for controlling expenditures requiring the preparation and approval of individual voucher forms for each expenditure contemplated. (Ch. 7)

Weighted Average Cost of Capital Expressed as a percentage, the cost to the firm of acquiring investment capital, weighted to reflect the specific cost rates associated with and proportions used from specific sources such as equity securities, debt, and internally generated funds. (Ch. 27)

Weighted Average Inventory Pricing A method that spreads the total dollar cost of all goods available for sale equally among all units. (Ch. 9)

Withdrawals (Owners') The amounts that proprietors or partners choose to withdraw, usually in cash and for personal objectives, from the assets of the firm. (Ch. 1)

Working Capital The excess of

current assets over current liabilities. (Chs. 5, 17, 18)

Work in Process Units of product that have been begun but not completed. (Ch. 21)

Worksheet An informal accounting document used in adjusting the accounts in which the unadjusted trial balance is copied from the general ledger, adjustments are formulated and recorded on the worksheet, and adjusted balances for each account calculated and extended to specific columns. Financial statements can be prepared from a completed worksheet. (Ch. 4)

CHECKLIST OF KEY FIGURES

7–26 (a) Adjusted balance, $9,279

7–27 (b) Vouchers payable credit in voucher register, $5,890; Cash credit in check register, $4,087.50

7–28 Vouchers payable credit in voucher register, $2,095; Cash credit in check register, $985

7–22A No key figure

7–24A (a) Adjusted balance, $10,365.28

7–25A No key figure

7–26A (a) Adjusted balance, $6,861

7–27A (b) Vouchers payable credit in voucher register, $6,045; Cash credit in check register, $3,985

Business Decision Problem (Chapter 7)
(a) $1,169.50 discrepancy

8–25 (a) Total Uncollectible Accounts Expense, $7,200; (b) Total Uncollectible Accounts Expense, $10,300

8–26 (b) Net accounts receivable, $42,730

8–27 (b) Net accounts receivable, $91,140

8–28 (b)(1) 9.28%

8–29 (b) Interest expense adjustment, $75

8–30 Interest expense adjustment on Dec. 31, $70

8–31 No key figure

8–26A (b) Net accounts receivable, $80,850

8–27A (b) Net accounts receivable, $70,770

8–28A Interest income adjustment on Dec. 31, $10

8–29A (b) Interest income adjustment, $7

8–30A Interest income adjustment on Dec. 31, $40

Business Decision Problem (Chapter 8)
Projected gross profit on sales, $212,333

9–28 (a) LIFO, $32,000; weighted average, $36,400

9–29 (a) $176,000

9–30 (b) Weighted average

9–31 (a)(1) $58,400

9–32 (a) Cost-to-retail percentage, 66%

9–33 (a) $36,000

9–34 (b) Inventory loss, $70

9–28A (a) FIFO, $12,400; Weighted average, $11,400

9–29A (a) $84,000

9–31A (a)(2) $20,900

9–32A (a) Cost-to-retail percentage, 75%

9–34A (b) Inventory loss, $47

Business Decision Problem (Chapter 9)
No key figure

10–26 Building, $2,030,000

10–27 (b) Year 2, $7,200; (c) Year 2, $6,750

10–28 No key figure

10–29 (b) $20,000

10–30 No key figure

10–31 (e) Depreciation expense, $2,250

10–26A Building, $1,663,500

10–27A (b) 19X3, $19,825; (c) 19X3, $16,800; (d) 19X3, $18,300

10–28A No key figure

10–29A (c) $8,100

10–31A 19X1 depreciation, Ford truck, $2,412

Business Decision Problem (Chapter 10)
(b) Year 1: Straight-line, $66,500; SYD, $106,400; DDB, $150,000

11–23 (a) $4,950

11–24 (a) Payroll payable, $68,400

11–25 Sales tax liability, $2,646

11–26 (a) Payroll payable, $38,180

11–27 (a) Net earnings total, $137,218; (b)(2) Payroll tax expense, $14,768

11–23A (b) $3,175

11–24A (a) Payroll payable, $50,000

11–25A Excise tax liability, $7,200

11–26A (a) Payroll payable, $20,180

11–27A (a) Net earnings total, $116,630; (b)(2) Payroll tax expense, $10,286

Business Decision Problem (Chapter 11)
No key figure

12–23 (a)(2) Hunt, $5,000; Mellon, $3,000

12–24 (a)(3) MacNeil, $6,000; Trevino, $9,000; Hawk, $3,000

12–25 (c) Credit to Boone, Capital, $14,000; (d) Credit to Boone, Capital, $16,000

12–26 No key figure

12–27 (b) Gill, $9,000; Capp, $6,000

12–28 Total capital, Dec. 31, 19X2, $50,000

12–29 (a) Cash distributed: Fox, $10,000; Glenn, $20,000; Hale, $37,000

12–30 No key figure

12–24A (a)(4) Field, $12,120; Mahoney, $13,560; Sack, $16,320

12–25A No key figure

12–26A No key figure

12–28A Total capital, Dec. 31, 19X6, $78,000

12–29A (b) Cash distributed: Duran, $20,500; Fitch, $14,500

Business Decision Problem (Chapter 12)
No key figure

13–23 (b) Total stockholders' equity, $659,000

13–24 (a) Preferred dividends, $21,000; common dividends, $63,000; (d) Preferred dividends, $12,000; common dividends, $72,000

13–25 (c) Total stockholders' equity, $1,522,000

13–26 (a) Preferred stock, $53; common stock, $17

13–27 (b) $25 per share

13–28 (c) Total stockholders' equity, $1,383,400

13–29 No key figure

13–23A (b) Total stockholders' equity, $1,192,000

13–24A (a) Preferred dividends, $35,000; common dividends, $105,000

13-25A (c) Total stockholders' equity, $1,387,750
13-28A (c) Total stockholders' equity, $1,405,300
Business Decision Problem (Chapter 13)
  (a) Total assets, $247,400

14-24 (a) Net income, $48,000
14-25 (b) Retained earnings, Dec. 31, 19X2, $257,000
14-26 (a) $4.05
14-27 (b) Retained earnings, Dec. 31, 19XX, $448,200
14-28 (b) $127,400
14-29 (c) Total stockholders' equity, $1,457,100
14-24A (a) Net income, $70,000
14-25A (b) Retained earnings, Dec. 31, 19X9, $216,400
14-26A (b) $6.95
14-27A (b) Retained earnings, Dec. 31, 19XX, $408,250
Business Decision Problem (Chapter 14)
  (2) 19X7, $52.75; 19X8, $45.00

15-24 (a) Semiannual discount amortization, $1,200
15-25 (a)(4) Loss on bond retirement, $5,500
15-26 No key figure
15-27 19X1 semiannual convertible bond discount amortization, $150; Feb. 11, 19X2 gain on sale of investments, $5,280
15-28 May 1, 19X4 loss on sale of investments, $2,980
15-29 (a) Dividend income, $6,600
15-24A (b) Loss on bond retirement, $1,625
15-25A (b)(4) Loss on bond retirement, $636
15-27A Jan. 2, 19X8 loss on bond retirement, $360
15-28A May 1, 19X4 gain on sale of investments, $7,120
Business Decision Problem (Chapter 15)
  No key figure

A-1 (a)(1) $32,410; (c) $812.85; (e) $12,535.40
A-2 $8,424
A-3 $4,596.65
A-4 (a) $92,288
A-5 (a) $108,520
A-6 (a) $18,659.80
A-7 (a) $5,988,250; (d) Gain on bond retirement, $161,308
A-8 (a) $4,246,500; (d) Loss on bond retirement, $170,300
A-9 No key figure

16-24 No key figure
16-25 (a)(1) $4,050; (c) $377,050
16-26 (b)(2) 19X3, $1,800,000
16-27 (a) 19X4 income tax liability, $14,700; (b) 19X4 pretax accounting income, $27,750
16-28 Net income, $20,100
16-29 No key figure
16-30 No key figure
16-25A (a) March, $680; April, $3,400; May, $2,480 loss
16-26A (a) 19X3, $1,740,000; (b)(2) 19X3, $565,000

16-27A (a) 19X7 income tax liability, $20,000; (b) 19X7 pretax accounting income, $46,000
16-28A Net income, $5,600
Business Decision Problem (Chapter 16)
  19X1 revenue, $90,200

17-23 (c) Total sources of working capital, $29,000
17-24 (c) Working capital provided from operations, $34,000
17-25 (c) Working capital provided from operations, $112,000; total sources of working capital, $209,500
17-26 Total sources of cash, $24,000
17-27 Cash provided from operations, $22,000
17-28 (b) Total sources of working capital, $580,000
17-23A (c) Total sources of working capital, $35,000
17-24A (c) Working capital provided from operations, $59,000
17-25A (c) Working capital provided from operations, $79,400; total sources of working capital, $144,000
17-26A Total sources of cash, $21,000
17-27A Cash provided from operations, $60,000
Business Decision Problem (Chapter 17)
  (a) Total sources of working capital, $23,000; (b) Total sources of cash, $17,000

18-24 (a) Year 5: net sales, 140.7%; net income, 183.0%; total assets, 126.5%
18-25 (a) Return on assets, 11.1%
18-26 (b) Net income this year, 2.9%
18-27 (a) Return on assets, 22.67%
18-28 Gross profit, $108,000; inventory, $65,000
18-29 (b) Dividends paid per share, $11.11
18-24A (a) Year 5: net sales, 179.7%; net income, 214%; total assets, 118.3%
18-25A (a) Return on assets, 10%
18-26A (b) Net income this year, 3.9%
18-28A Gross profit, $75,000; inventory, $60,000
Business Decision Problem (Chapter 18)
  This year: (a) 2.01; (c) 84.6 days; (g) 7.91%

19-24 (b) Total consolidated assets, $1,060,000
19-25 (c) Total consolidated assets, $760,000
19-26 Total consolidated assets, $960,000
19-27 Consolidated net income, $73,600
19-28 (b) Total consolidated assets, $1,850,000
19-29 No key figure
19-24A (b) Total consolidated assets, $876,000
19-25A (c) Total consolidated assets, $957,000
19-26A Total consolidated assets, $1,831,000
19-27A Consolidated net income, $115,000
19-28A (b) Total consolidated assets, $1,175,000
Business Decision Problem (Chapter 19)
  No key figure

20-22   (a) Contribution to indirect expenses: Carpeting, $64,000; Hard Covering, $23,000

20-23   Net income: Dept. X, $32,370; Dept. Y, $6,630

20-24   (b) Reduction in net income, $2,000

20-25   (a) Contribution to indirect expenses: Dept. A, $24,000; Dept. B, $50,000; all others, $90,000

20-26   (d) $44,000

20-27   (b) Corrected end-of-year balance, $80,600

20-22A   (a) Contribution to indirect expenses: Appliances, $113,000; Furniture, $73,000

20-23A   Net income: Dept. A, $19,460; Dept. B, $12,740

20-24A   (c) Increase in net income, $7,000

20-26A   (d) Balance, $97,700

20-27A   (b) Corrected end-of-year balance, $60,200

Business Decision Problem (Chapter 20)

    (a) Bonuses: Tom, $14,000; Bob, $6,000; (b) contribution to indirect expenses; Tires, $51,100; Batteries, $63,900

21-25   Cost of goods manufactured, $129,000; net income, $25,000

21-26   Cost of goods manufactured, $445,000

21-27   Period (A): purchases, $160; other factory overhead, $120

21-28   (a) $33,600; (b) $12,000

21-29   (a) Cost of goods manufactured, $134,000; net income, $15,600

21-30   (a) Cost of goods manufactured, $300,000; (b) target sales, $600,000; (c) $67

21-31   (a) Cost of goods manufactured, $204,800; net income, $19,390

21-32   (a) Cost of goods manufactured, $128,100; net income, $16,000

21-25A   Cost of goods manufactured, $202,000; net *loss*, $7,000

21-28A   (a) $78,300; (b) $26,400

21-29A   (a) Cost of goods manufactured, $167,000; net income, $40,000

21-30A   (a) Cost of goods manufactured, $300,000; target sales, $400,000

21-31A   (a) Cost of goods manufactured, $266,500; net income, $29,040

21-32A   (a) Cost of goods manufactured, $226,800; net income, $28,300

Business Decision Problem (Chapter 21)

    (a) Materials inventory discrepancies exist; (b) cost of goods manufactured, $90,000

22-27   (a) $5 per direct labor hour

22-28   (a) $4,000; (d) $3,000 underapplied, (g) $75,000

22-29   (b) Underapplied overhead allocated to cost of goods sold, $2,500

22-30   (h) Overapplied overhead, $500

22-31   (a) Cost of goods sold, $120,000; (d) raw materials used, $38,000

22-32   (a) 75% of direct labor costs; (c) $2,900

22-33   (c) Ending work in process, $9,600; ending finished goods, $7,900

22-34   (d) Ending work in process, $11,180; ending finished goods, $32,600

22-27A   (a) $1.80 per direct labor hour

22-29A   (b) Overapplied overhead closed to cost of goods sold, $413

22-30A   (h) Underapplied overhead, $1,500

22-32A   (a) 65% of direct labor costs; (c) $3,180

22-33A   (c) Ending work in process, $19,000; ending finished goods, $12,900

Business Decision Problem (Chapter 22)

    Advantage (greater profit per unit sold) of using new material, $17.40

23-27   (a) Units transferred in: Printing, 12,000; Packaging, 10,000

23-28   (b) Phase I, 21,600 equivalent units at cost of $1.50; Phase II, 17,000 equivalent units at cost of $2.40

23-29   (b) Equivalent units: materials, 12,000; conversion costs, 10,500; (d) $31,100

23-30   (a) 27,000 equivalent units; (c) $119,800

23-31   (a) Equivalent unit costs: Dept. 1, materials, $0.75; conversion, $3.50; Dept. 2, (all costs) $1.80; (b) ending balances: raw materials, $10,000; work in process: Dept. 1, $7,250, Dept. 2, $22,320; finished goods, $30,150

23-32   Cost of units transferred out, $59,400; ending work in process, $14,700

23-33   (b) Overhead rates for production: Dept. 1, $4 per maching hour; Dept. 2, 250% of direct labor costs

23-34   Joint cost allocated to Product A, $28,600; Product B, $101,400

23-28A   (b) Phase I, 16,500 equivalent units at a cost of $2.50; Phase II, 13,000 equivalent units at a cost of $3.20

23-29A   (b) Equivalent units: materials, 8,000; conversion, 9,800; (d) $37,200

23-30A   (a) 38,000 equivalent units; (c) $46,850

23-31A   (a) Equivalent unit costs: Dept. 1, materials, $0.75, conversion, $1.50; Dept. 2 (all costs), $1.10; (b) ending balances: raw materials, $8,000; work in process, Dept. 1, $3,000; Dept. 2, $12,850; finished goods, $32,300

23-32A   Cost of units transferred out, $26,400; ending work in process, $9,420

Business Decision Problem (Chapter 23)

    Net benefit of: Plan A, $1,000; Plan B, $1,640; Plan C, $3,880

24-31   (a) Line DE: (e) line CG; (h) either point A or point B

24-32   For A: variable expense, $45,000; fixed expense, $30,000

24-33   (d) Total cost is $10,000 fixed cost plus $0.60 per unit variable cost

24-34   (a) Formula: total cost equals total fixed cost of $138,000 plus $19.20 per unit produced

24-35   (a) Variable portion, $0.40 per direct labor hour; fixed cost is $4,000

24-36   (a) Formula: total cost equals fixed cost of $70,000 plus $7.75 per unit variable cost

24-37   (a) $128,000; (c) $3,600 units

24-38   (a) 120,000 units; (c) 25%; (e) $240,000

24-39   (a) Break-even in units, 13,333.3; (c) 17,143 units

24-40   (a) $33,000; (b) break-even unit volumes: 7,250 of Economy; 4,350 of Standard; 2,900 of Deluxe

24-32A For A: variable expenses, $45,000; Fixed expenses, $25,000

24-33A (d) Total cost: $4,000 total fixed cost plus $120 per unit variable cost

24-34A Formula: total cost is $122,000 fixed cost plus $33 variable cost per unit

24-35A (a) Variable cost portion, $0.30 per direct labor hour; fixed cost portion, $4,000

24-37A (a) $288,000; (c) 3,400 units

24-38A (a) 42,000 units; (c) 40%; (e) $450,000

24-40A (a) $202,500; (b) break-even unit volumes: Race, 5,000; Shaft, 7,500; Bearing, 12,500

Business Decision Problem (Chapter 24)
(a) Profit on new order, $4,320; (b) lowest per unit price, $15.79 (rounded)

25-28   (a) Profit on order, $780; (b) $14.84 (rounded)

25-29   (a) Net disadvantage of buying, $7,200; (b) $89

25-30   (a) Net income would decrease by Soft Goods Dept.'s contribution margin of $170,000; (c) $38.50 per unit

25-31   (a) $400 loss; (b) $5.05 (rounded) per unit

25-32   (b) Emphasize Standard model; it generates $4.40 more contribution margin per unit of capacity

25-33   (a) Gross profit: (19X0), $360,000; (19X1), $520,000; (b) Gross profit: (19X0), $270,000; (19X1), $550,000

25-34   (a) Net income, $571,500; (b) net income, $531,500

25-28A (a) Incremental profit per unit, $0.95; (b) $17.11

25-29A (a) Disadvantage to buying, $1,000; (b) $41

25-30A (a) Net income would decrease by Soft Goods Dept.'s contribution margin of $200,000; (c) $46 per unit

25-31A (a) Profit increase, $22,000; (b) $5.44 (rounded) per unit

25-32A (b) Emphasize Manual model; it generates $10 more contribution margin per unit of capacity

25-33A (a) Gross profit: (19X0), $350,000; (19X1),

$300,000; (b) Gross profit: (19X0) $280,000; (19X1) $160,000

Business Decision Problem (Chapter 25)
(a)(3) Relative contribution margin per unit of machine capacity: Automatic, $36; Manual, $40

26-30   (a) Materials variances: price, $7,800 (favorable); usage, $3,000 (unfavorable); (c) overhead variances: controllable, $3,000 (unfavorable); volume, $6,000 (unfavorable)

26-31   (a) Materials variances: price, $1,860 (unfavorable); usage, $600 (favorable); overhead variances: controllable, $300 (favorable); volume, $1,000 (unfavorable); (d) gross profit based on actual costs, $47,840

26-32   (a) Materials variances: price, $3,100 (unfavorable); usage, $3,000 (unfavorable); (c) overhead variances: controllable, $2,800 (unfavorable); volume, $5,000 (unfavorable)

26-33   June collections from customers, $95,305

26-34   (a)(1) $368,000; (a)(2) 15,000 units; (a)(3) $255,000; (a)(4) $60,000; (a)(5) $45,000; (a)(6) $29,000; (b) net income, $45,000

26-35   Collections from customers, $1,440,000; amount necessary to borrow, $34,000

26-36   Total budgeted overhead at 4,500 hours, $439,750

26-30A (a) Materials variances: price, $1,400 (unfavorable); usage, $400 (unfavorable); (c) overhead variances: controllable, $2,400 (unfavorable); volume, $6,000 (unfavorable)

26-31A (a) Materials variances: price, $1,500 (favorable); usage, $1,080 (unfavorable); overhead variances: controllable, $600 (favorable); volume, $1,800 (unfavorable); (d) gross profit based on actual costs, $66,650

26-32A (a) Materials variances: price, $1,240 (favorable); usage, $1,600 (unfavorable); overhead variances: controllable, $500 (unfavorable); volume, $3,000 (unfavorable)

26-34A (a)(1) $360,000; (a)(2) 19,000 units; (a)(3) $142,000; (a)(4) $228,000; (a)(5) $30,400; (a)(6) $40,000; (b) net income, $14,000

26-35A Collections from customers, $780,000; amount necessary to borrow, $30,000

Business Decision Problem (Chapter 26)
(a) Actual cost amounts are correct; (c) original budget based on normal capacity rather than actual output; (e) total budgeted overhead is actually total overhead applied, variances are net total variances with significant offsetting favorable and unfavorable subvariances; (f) material variances: price, $3,040 (favorable); usage, $3,200 (unfavorable); direct labor variances: rate, $2,670 (favorable); efficiency, $2,400 (unfavorable);

1056

CHECKLIST OF KEY FIGURES

overhead variances: controllable, $5,700 (favorable); volume, $6,000 (unfavorable)

B-1 Situation A variances: spending, $1,250 (unfavorable); efficiency, $500 (unfavorable); volume, $4,000 (unfavorable)

B-2 (a) Overhead variances: spending, $800 (favorable); efficiency, $1,000 (unfavorable); volume, $3,200 (unfavorable)

B-3 Overhead variances: spending, $3,500 (unfavorable); efficiency, $500 (favorable); volume, $6,000 (unfavorable)

B-4 Overhead variances: spending, $500 (favorable); efficiency, $200 (unfavorable); volume, $1,000 (unfavorable)

B-5 Overhead variances: spending, $1,200 (unfavorable); efficiency, $1,200 (unfavorable); volume, $6,000 (unfavorable)

B-6 Overhead variances: spending, $1,120 (favorable); efficiency, $520 (unfavorable); volume, $1,800 (unfavorable)

B-7 (a) Overhead variances: controllable, $-0-; volume, $1,200 (favorable); (b) Overhead variances: spending, $2,400 (unfavorable); efficiency, $2,400 (favorable); volume, $1,200 (favorable)

27-29 (a) 3.41 years; (b) 18.67%; (c) $862, excess present value index, 1.0575

27-30 Net present value, $1,071, excess present value index, 1.03967

27-31 Net advantage of subcontracting test, $921
27-32 Net present value of future cash flows, $72,190
27-33 (a) ATCFE ($45,000), Year 0, PV factor, 1.0; (c) ATCFE ($3,600), Year 1-5, PV factor, 3.605; (f) ATCFE $2,400, Year 5, PV factor, .567
27-29A (a) 4.21 years; (b) 22.5%; (c) negative net present value, $2,839
27-30A Net present value, $2,318; excess present value index, 1.129
27-31A Difference in favor of subcontracting tests, $2,295
27-32A Net present value of future cash flows, $140,623
Business Decision Problem (Chapter 27)
(b) Weighted average cost of capital, 10% plus buffer of 5% = 15% discount rate; net present value of future cash flows, $38,413

28-27 Tax liability, $3,241.08
28-28 No key figure
28-29 Tax liability, $7,419.78
28-30 Tax liability, $10,000
28-31 Total tax, corporate form, $13,433.25
28-27A Tax liability, $5,642.92
28-28A No key figure
28-29A Tax liability, $7,459
28-30A Tax liability, $141,690
Business Decision Problem (Chapter 28)
(b) After-tax income, partnership investment, $26,833

INDEX